American Casebook Series
Hornbook Series and Basic Legal Texts
Nutshell Series

of

WEST PUBLISHING COMPANY
P.O. Box 3526
St. Paul, Minnesota 55165
January, 1983

ACCOUNTING

Fiflis and Kripke's Teaching Materials on Accounting for Business Lawyers, 2nd Ed., 684 pages, 1977 (Casebook)

ADMINISTRATIVE LAW

Davis' Cases, Text and Problems on Administrative Law, 6th Ed., 683 pages, 1977 (Casebook)

Davis' Basic Text on Administrative Law, 3rd Ed., 617 pages, 1972 (Text)

Davis' Police Discretion, 176 pages, 1975 (Text)

Gellhorn and Boyer's Administrative Law and Process in a Nutshell, 2nd Ed., 445 pages, 1981 (Text)

Mashaw and Merrill's Introduction to the American Public Law System, 1095 pages, 1975, with 1980 Supplement (Casebook)

Robinson, Gellhorn and Bruff's The Administrative Process, 2nd Ed., 959 pages, 1980, with 1983 Supplement (Casebook)

ADMIRALTY

Healy and Sharpe's Cases and Materials on Admiralty, 875 pages, 1974 (Casebook)

AGENCY—PARTNERSHIP

Fessler's Alternatives to Incorporation for Persons in Quest of Profit, 258 pages, 1980 (Casebook)

Henn's Cases and Materials on Agency, Partnership and Other Unincorporated Business Enterprises, 396 pages, 1972 (Casebook)

AGENCY—PARTNERSHIP—Continued

Reuschlein and Gregory's Hornbook on the Law of Agency and Partnership, 625 pages, 1979, with 1981 pocket part (Text)

Seavey's Hornbook on Agency, 329 pages, 1964 (Text)

Seavey and Hall's Cases on Agency, 431 pages, 1956 (Casebook)

Seavey, Reuschlein and Hall's Cases on Agency and Partnership, 599 pages, 1962 (Casebook)

Selected Corporation and Partnership Statutes and Forms, 556 pages, 1982

Steffen and Kerr's Cases and Materials on Agency-Partnership, 4th Ed., 859 pages, 1980 (Casebook)

Steffen's Agency-Partnership in a Nutshell, 364 pages, 1977 (Text)

AMERICAN INDIAN LAW

Canby's American Indian Law in a Nutshell, 288 pages, 1981 (Text)

Getches, Rosenfelt and Wilkinson's Cases on Federal Indian Law, 660 pages, 1979, with 1983 Supplement (Casebook)

ANTITRUST LAW

Gellhorn's Antitrust Law and Economics in a Nutshell, 2nd Ed., 425 pages, 1981 (Text)

Gifford and Raskind's Cases and Materials on Antitrust, approximately 732 pages, 1983 (Casebook)

Oppenheim, Weston and McCarthy's Cases and Comments on Federal Antitrust Laws, 4th Ed., 1168 pages, 1981 (Casebook)

LAW SCHOOL PUBLICATIONS—Continued

ANTITRUST LAW—Continued

Posner and Easterbrook's Cases and Economic Notes on Antitrust, 2nd Ed., 1077 pages, 1981, with 1982–83 Supplement (Casebook)

Sullivan's Hornbook of the Law of Antitrust, 886 pages, 1977 (Text)

See also Regulated Industries, Trade Regulation

BANKING LAW

See Regulated Industries

BUSINESS PLANNING

Epstein and Scheinfeld's Teaching Materials on Business Reorganization Under the Bankruptcy Code, 216 pages, 1980 (Casebook)

Painter's Problems and Materials in Business Planning, 791 pages, 1975, with 1982 Supplement (Casebook)

Selected Securities and Business Planning Statutes, Rules and Forms, 485 pages, 1982

CIVIL PROCEDURE

Casad's Res Judicata in a Nutshell, 310 pages, 1976 (text)

Cound, Friedenthal and Miller's Cases and Materials on Civil Procedure, 3rd Ed., 1147 pages, 1980 with 1982 Supplement (Casebook)

Cound, Friedenthal and Miller's Cases on Pleading, Joinder and Discovery, 643 pages, 1968 (Casebook)

Ehrenzweig, Louisell and Hazard's Jurisdiction in a Nutshell, 4th Ed., 232 pages, 1980 (Text)

Federal Rules of Civil-Appellate-Criminal Procedure—West Law School Edition, 383 pages, 1982

Hodges, Jones and Elliott's Cases and Materials on Texas Trial and Appellate Procedure, 2nd Ed., 745 pages, 1974 (Casebook)

Hodges, Jones and Elliott's Cases and Materials on the Judicial Process Prior to Trial in Texas, 2nd Ed., 871 pages, 1977 (Casebook)

Kane's Civil Procedure in a Nutshell, 271 pages, 1979 (Text)

Karlen's Procedure Before Trial in a Nutshell, 258 pages, 1972 (Text)

Karlen and Joiner's Cases and Materials on Trials and Appeals, 536 pages, 1971 (Casebook)

Karlen, Meisenholder, Stevens and Vestal's Cases on Civil Procedure, 923 pages, 1975 (Casebook)

Koffler and Reppy's Hornbook on Common Law Pleading, 663 pages, 1969 (Text)

CIVIL PROCEDURE—Continued

McBaine's Cases on Introduction to Civil Procedure, 399 pages, 1950 (Casebook)

McCoid's Cases on Civil Procedure, 823 pages, 1974 (Casebook)

Park's Computer-Aided Exercises on Civil Procedure, 118 pages, 1976 (Coursebook)

Shipman's Hornbook on Common-Law Pleading, 3rd Ed., 644 pages, 1923 (Text)

Siegel's Hornbook on New York Practice, 1011 pages, 1978 with 1981–82 Pocket Part (Text)

See also Federal Jurisdiction and Procedure

CIVIL RIGHTS

Abernathy's Cases and Materials on Civil Rights, 660 pages, 1980 (Casebook)

Cohen's Cases on the Law of Deprivation of Liberty: A Study in Social Control, 755 pages, 1980 (Casebook)

Lockhart, Kamisar and Choper's Cases on Constitutional Rights and Liberties, 5th Ed., 1298 pages plus Appendix, 1981, with 1982 Supplement (Casebook)—reprint from Lockhart, et al. Cases on Constitutional Law, 5th Ed., 1980

Vieira's Civil Rights in a Nutshell, 279 pages, 1978 (Text)

COMMERCIAL LAW

Bailey's Secured Transactions in a Nutshell, 2nd Ed., 391 pages, 1981 (Text)

Epstein and Martin's Basic Uniform Commercial Code Teaching Materials, 2nd Ed., approximately 600 pages, 1983 (Casebook)

Henson's Hornbook on Secured Transactions Under the U.C.C., 2nd Ed., 504 pages, 1979 with 1979 P.P. (Text)

Murray's Commercial Law, Problems and Materials, 366 pages, 1975 (Coursebook)

Nordstrom and Clovis' Problems and Materials on Commercial Paper, 458 pages, 1972 (Casebook)

Nordstrom and Lattin's Problems and Materials on Sales and Secured Transactions, 809 pages, 1968 (Casebook)

Nordstrom, Murray and Clovis' Problems and Materials on Sales, 515 pages, 1982 (Casebook)

Nordstrom's Hornbook on Sales, 600 pages, 1970 (Text)

Selected Commercial Statutes, 1367 pages, 1981

Speidel, Summers and White's Teaching Materials on Commercial and Consumer Law, 3rd Ed., 1490 pages, 1981 (Casebook)

LAW SCHOOL PUBLICATIONS—Continued

COMMERCIAL LAW—Continued

Stockton's Sales in a Nutshell, 2nd Ed., 370 pages, 1981 (Text)

Stone's Uniform Commercial Code in a Nutshell, 507 pages, 1975 (Text)

Uniform Commercial Code, Official Text with Comments, 994 pages, 1978

UCC Article 8, 1977 Amendments, 249 pages, 1978

UCC Article 9, Reprint from 1962 Code, 128 pages, 1976

UCC Article 9, 1972 Amendments, 304 pages, 1978

Weber and Speidel's Commercial Paper in a Nutshell, 3rd Ed., 404 pages, 1982 (Text)

White and Summers' Hornbook on the Uniform Commercial Code, 2nd Ed., 1250 pages, 1980 (Text)

COMMUNITY PROPERTY

Huie's Texas Cases and Materials on Marital Property Rights, 681 pages, 1966 (Casebook)

Mennell's Community Property in a Nutshell, 447 pages, 1982 (Text)

Verrall's Cases and Materials on California Community Property, 3rd Ed., 547 pages, 1977 (Casebook)

COMPARATIVE LAW

Barton, Gibbs, Li and Merryman's Law in Radically Different Cultures, approximately 1048 pages, 1983 (Casebook)

Glendon, Gordon, and Osakwe's Comparative Legal Traditions in a Nutshell, 402 pages, 1982 (Text)

Langbein's Comparative Criminal Procedure: Germany, 172 pages, 1977 (Casebook)

CONFLICT OF LAWS

Cramton, Currie and Kay's Cases-Comments-Questions on Conflict of Laws, 3rd Ed., 1026 pages, 1981 (Casebook)

Scoles and Hay's Hornbook on Conflict of Laws, 1085 pages, 1982 (Text)

Scoles and Weintraub's Cases and Materials on Conflict of Laws, 2nd Ed., 966 pages, 1972, with 1978 Supplement (Casebook)

Siegel's Conflicts in a Nutshell, 469 pages, 1982 (Text)

CONSTITUTIONAL LAW

Engdahl's Constitutional Power in a Nutshell: Federal and State, 411 pages, 1974 (Text)

Lockhart, Kamisar and Choper's Cases-Comments-Questions on Constitutional Law, 5th Ed., 1705 pages plus Appendix, 1980, with 1982 Supplement (Casebook)

CONSTITUTIONAL LAW—Continued

Lockhart, Kamisar and Choper's Cases-Comments-Questions on the American Constitution, 5th Ed., 1185 pages plus Appendix, 1981, with 1982 Supplement (Casebook)—reprint from Lockhart, et al. Cases on Constitutional Law, 5th Ed., 1980

Manning's The Law of Church-State Relations in a Nutshell, 305 pages, 1981 (Text)

Miller's Presidential Power in a Nutshell, 328 pages, 1977 (Text)

Nowak, Rotunda and Young's Hornbook on Constitutional Law, 2nd Ed., approximately 1000 pages, 1983 (Text)

Rotunda's Modern Constitutional Law: Cases and Notes, 1034 pages, 1981, with 1982 Supplement (Casebook)

Williams' Constitutional Analysis in a Nutshell, 388 pages, 1979 (Text)

See also Civil Rights

CONSUMER LAW

Epstein and Nickles' Consumer Law in a Nutshell, 2nd Ed., 418 pages, 1981 (Text)

McCall's Consumer Protection, Cases, Notes and Materials, 594 pages, 1977, with 1977 Statutory Supplement (Casebook)

Schrag's Cases and Materials on Consumer Protection, 2nd Ed., 197 pages, 1973 (Casebook)—reprint from Cooper, et al. Cases on Law and Poverty, 2nd Ed., 1973

Selected Commercial Statutes, 1367 pages, 1981

Spanogle and Rohner's Cases and Materials on Consumer Law, 693 pages, 1979, with 1982 Supplement (Casebook)

See also Commercial Law

CONTRACTS

Calamari & Perillo's Cases and Problems on Contracts, 1061 pages, 1978 (Casebook)

Calamari and Perillo's Hornbook on Contracts, 2nd Ed., 878 pages, 1977 (Text)

Corbin's Text on Contracts, One Volume Student Edition, 1224 pages, 1952 (Text)

Fessler and Loiseaux's Cases and Materials on Contracts, 837 pages, 1982 (Casebook)

Freedman's Cases and Materials on Contracts, 658 pages, 1973 (Casebook)

Friedman's Contract Remedies in a Nutshell, 323 pages, 1981 (Text)

Fuller and Eisenberg's Cases on Basic Contract Law, 4th Ed., 1203 pages, 1981 (Casebook)

CONTRACTS—Continued

Jackson and Bollinger's Cases on Contract Law in Modern Society, 2nd Ed., 1329 pages, 1980 (Casebook)

Keyes' Government Contracts in a Nutshell, 423 pages, 1979 (Text)

Reitz's Cases on Contracts as Basic Commercial Law, 763 pages, 1975 (Casebook)

Schaber and Rohwer's Contracts in a Nutshell, 307 pages, 1975 (Text)

Simpson's Hornbook on Contracts, 2nd Ed., 510 pages, 1965 (Text)

COPYRIGHT

Nimmer's Cases and Materials on Copyright and Other Aspects of Law Pertaining to Literary, Musical and Artistic Works, Illustrated, 2nd Ed., 1023 pages, 1979 (Casebook)

See also Patent Law

CORPORATIONS

Hamilton's Cases on Corporations—Including Partnerships and Limited Partnerships, 2nd Ed., 1108 pages, 1981, with 1981 Statutory Supplement (Casebook)

Hamilton's Law of Corporations in a Nutshell, 379 pages, 1980 (Text)

Henn's Cases on Corporations, 1279 pages, 1974, with 1980 Supplement (Casebook)

Henn's Hornbook on Corporations, 3rd Ed., approximately 1170 pages, 1983 (Text)

Jennings and Buxbaum's Cases and Materials on Corporations, 5th Ed., 1180 pages, 1979 (Casebook)

Selected Corporation and Partnership Statutes, Regulations and Forms, 556 pages, 1982

Solomon, Stevenson and Schwartz' Materials and Problems on the Law and Policies on Corporations, 1172 pages, 1982 (Casebook)

CORRECTIONS

Krantz's Cases and Materials on the Law of Corrections and Prisoners' Rights, 2nd Ed., 735 pages, 1981, with 1982 Supplement (Casebook)

Krantz's Law of Corrections and Prisoners' Rights in a Nutshell, 353 pages, 1976 (Text)

Model Rules and Regulations on Prisoners' Rights and Responsibilities, 212 pages, 1973

Popper's Post-Conviction Remedies in a Nutshell, 360 pages, 1978 (Text)

Robbins' Cases and Materials on Post Conviction Remedies, 506 pages, 1982 (Casebook)

CORRECTIONS—Continued

Rubin's Law of Criminal Corrections, 2nd Ed., 873 pages, 1973, with 1978 Supplement (Text)

CREDITOR'S RIGHTS

Epstein's Debtor-Creditor Law in a Nutshell, 2nd Ed., 324 pages, 1980 (Text)

Epstein and Landers' Debtors and Creditors: Cases and Materials, 2nd Ed., 689 pages, 1982 (Casebook)

Epstein and Sheinfeld's Teaching Materials on Business Reorganization Under the Bankruptcy Code, 216 pages, 1980 (Casebook)

Riesenfeld's Cases and Materials on Creditors' Remedies and Debtors' Protection, 3rd Ed., 810 pages, 1979 with 1979 Statutory Supplement and 1981 Case Supplement (Casebook)

Selected Bankruptcy Statutes, 351 pages, 1979

CRIMINAL LAW AND CRIMINAL PROCEDURE

Cohen and Gobert's Problems in Criminal Law, 297 pages, 1976 (Problem book)

Davis' Police Discretion, 176 pages, 1975 (Text)

Dix and Sharlot's Cases and Materials on Criminal Law, 2nd Ed., 771 pages, 1979 (Casebook)

Federal Rules of Civil-Appellate-Criminal Procedure—West Law School Edition, 383 pages, 1982

Grano's Problems in Criminal Procedure, 2nd Ed., 176 pages, 1981 (Problem book)

Heymann and Kenety's The Murder Trial of Wilbur Jackson: A Homicide in the Family, 340 pages, 1975 (Case Study)

Israel and LaFave's Criminal Procedure in a Nutshell, 3rd Ed., 438 pages, 1980 (Text)

Johnson's Cases, Materials and Text on Substantive Criminal Law in its Procedural Context, 2nd Ed., 956 pages, 1980 (Casebook)

Kamisar, LaFave and Israel's Cases, Comments and Questions on Modern Criminal Procedure, 5th ed., 1635 pages plus Appendix, 1980 with 1982 Supplement (Casebook)

Kamisar, LaFave and Israel's Cases, Comments and Questions on Basic Criminal Procedure, 5th Ed., 869 pages, 1980 with 1982 Supplement (Casebook)—reprint from Kamisar, et al. Modern Criminal Procedure, 5th ed., 1980

LaFave's Modern Criminal Law: Cases, Comments and Questions, 789 pages, 1978 (Casebook)

LaFave and Scott's Hornbook on Criminal Law, 763 pages, 1972 (Text)

CRIMINAL LAW AND CRIMINAL PROCEDURE—Continued

Langbein's Comparative Criminal Procedure: Germany, 172 pages, 1977 (Casebook)

Loewy's Criminal Law in a Nutshell, 302 pages, 1975 (Text)

Saltzburg's American Criminal Procedure, Cases and Commentary, 1253 pages, 1980 with 1982 Supplement (Casebook)

Saltzburg's Introduction to American Criminal Procedure, 702 pages, 1980 with 1982 Supplement (Casebook)—reprint from Saltzburg's American Criminal Procedure, 1980

Uviller's The Processes of Criminal Justice: Investigation and Adjudication, 2nd Ed., 1384 pages, 1979 with 1979 Statutory Supplement and 1980 Update (Casebook)

Uviller's The Processes of Criminal Justice: Adjudication, 2nd Ed., 730 pages, 1979. Soft-cover reprint from Uviller's The Processes of Criminal Justice: Investigation and Adjudication, 2nd Ed. (Casebook)

Uviller's The Processes of Criminal Justice: Investigation, 2nd Ed., 655 pages, 1979. Soft-cover reprint from Uviller's The Processes of Criminal Justice: Investigation and Adjudication, 2nd Ed. (Casebook)

Vorenberg's Cases on Criminal Law and Procedure, 2nd Ed., 1088 pages, 1981 (Casebook)

See also Corrections, Juvenile Justice

DECEDENTS ESTATES

See Trusts and Estates

DOMESTIC RELATIONS

Clark's Cases and Problems on Domestic Relations, 3rd Ed., 1153 pages, 1980 (Casebook)

Clark's Hornbook on Domestic Relations, 754 pages, 1968 (Text)

Krause's Cases and Materials on Family Law, 1132 pages, 1976, with 1978 Supplement (Casebook)

Krause's Family Law in a Nutshell, 400 pages, 1977 (Text)

EDUCATION LAW

Morris' The Constitution and American Education, 2nd Ed., 992 pages, 1980 (Casebook)

EMPLOYMENT DISCRIMINATION

Cooper, Rabb and Rubin's Fair Employment Litigation: Text and Materials for Student and Practitioner, 590 pages, 1975 (Coursebook)

EMPLOYMENT DISCRIMINATION—Continued

Player's Cases and Materials on Employment Discrimination Law, 878 pages, 1980 with 1982 Supplement (Casebook)

Player's Federal Law of Employment Discrimination in a Nutshell, 2nd Ed., 402 pages, 1981 (Text)

Sovern's Cases and Materials on Racial Discrimination in Employment, 2nd Ed., 167 pages, 1973 (Casebook)—reprint from Cooper et al. Cases on Law and Poverty, 2nd Ed., 1973

See also Women and the Law

ENERGY AND NATURAL RESOURCES LAW

Rodgers' Cases and Materials on Energy and Natural Resources Law, 995 pages, 1979 (Casebook)

Selected Environmental Law Statutes, 768 pages, 1983

Tomain's Energy Law in a Nutshell, 338 pages, 1981 (Text)

See also Environmental Law, Oil and Gas, Water Law

ENVIRONMENTAL LAW

Currie's Cases and Materials on Pollution, 715 pages, 1975 (Casebook)

Federal Environmental Law, 1600 pages, 1974 (Text)

Findley and Farber's Cases and Materials on Environmental Law, 738 pages, 1981 (Casebook)

Findley and Farber's Environmental Law in a Nutshell, approximately 332 pages, 1983 (Text)

Hanks, Tarlock and Hanks' Cases on Environmental Law and Policy, 1242 pages, 1974, with 1976 Supplement (Casebook)

Rodgers' Hornbook on Environmental Law, 956 pages, 1977 (Text)

Selected Environmental Law Statutes, 768 pages, 1983

See also Energy and Natural Resources Law, Water Law

EQUITY

See Remedies

ESTATES

See Trusts and Estates

ESTATE PLANNING

Casner and Stein's Estate Planning under the Tax Reform Act of 1976, 2nd Ed., 456 pages, 1978 (Coursebook)

Kurtz' Cases, Materials and Problems on Family Estate Planning, 853 pages, 1983 (Casebook)

LAW SCHOOL PUBLICATIONS—Continued

ESTATE PLANNING—Continued

Lynn's Introduction to Estate Planning, in a Nutshell, 2nd Ed., 378 pages, 1978 (Text)

See also Taxation

EVIDENCE

Broun and Meisenholder's Problems in Evidence, 2nd Ed., 304 pages, 1981 (Problem book)

Cleary and Strong's Cases, Materials and Problems on Evidence, 3rd Ed., 1143 pages, 1981 (Casebook)

Federal Rules of Evidence for United States Courts and Magistrates, 325 pages, 1979

Graham's Federal Rules of Evidence in a Nutshell, 429 pages, 1981 (Text)

Kimball's Programmed Materials on Problems in Evidence, 380 pages, 1978 (Problem book)

Lempert and Saltzburg's A Modern Approach to Evidence: Text, Problems, Transcripts and Cases, 2nd Ed., 1296 pages, 1983 (Casebook)

Lilly's Introduction to the Law of Evidence, 486 pages, 1978 (Text)

McCormick, Elliott and Sutton's Cases and Materials on Evidence, 5th Ed., 1212 pages, 1981 (Casebook)

McCormick's Hornbook on Evidence, 2nd Ed., 938 pages, 1972, with 1978 pocket part (Text)

Rothstein's Evidence, State and Federal Rules in a Nutshell, 2nd Ed., 514 pages, 1981 (Text)

Saltzburg's Evidence Supplement: Rules, Statutes, Commentary, 245 pages, 1980 (Casebook Supplement)

FEDERAL JURISDICTION AND PROCEDURE

Currie's Cases and Materials on Federal Courts, 3rd Ed., 1042 pages, 1982 (Casebook)

Currie's Federal Jurisdiction in a Nutshell, 2nd Ed., 258 pages, 1981 (Text)

Federal Rules of Civil-Appellate-Criminal Procedure—West Law School Edition, 383 pages, 1982

Forrester and Moye's Cases and Materials on Federal Jurisdiction and Procedure, 3rd Ed., 917 pages, 1977 with 1981 Supplement (Casebook)

Merrill and Vetri's Problems on Federal Courts and Civil Procedure, 460 pages, 1974 (Problem book)

Redish's Cases, Comments and Questions on Federal Courts, approximately 905 pages, 1983 (Casebook)

Wright's Hornbook on Federal Courts, 4th Ed., approximately 816 pages, 1983 (Text)

FUTURE INTERESTS

See Trusts and Estates

HOUSING AND URBAN DEVELOPMENT

Berger's Cases and Materials on Housing, 2nd Ed., 254 pages, 1973 (Casebook)—reprint from Cooper et al. Cases on Law and Poverty, 2nd Ed., 1973

See also Land Use

INDIAN LAW

See American Indian Law

INSURANCE

Dobbyn's Insurance Law in a Nutshell, 281 pages, 1981 (Text)

Keeton's Cases on Basic Insurance Law, 2nd Ed., 1086 pages, 1977

Keeton's Basic Text on Insurance Law, 712 pages, 1971 (Text)

Keeton's Case Supplement to Keeton's Basic Text on Insurance Law, 334 pages, 1978 (Casebook)

Keeton's Programmed Problems in Insurance Law, 243 pages, 1972 (Text Supplement)

York and Whelan's Cases, Materials and Problems on Insurance Law, 715 pages, 1982 (Casebook)

INTERNATIONAL LAW

Henkin, Pugh, Schachter and Smit's Cases and Materials on International Law, 2nd Ed., 1152 pages, 1980, with Documents Supplement (Casebook)

Jackson's Legal Problems of International Economic Relations, 1097 pages, 1977, with Documents Supplement (Casebook)

Kirgis' International Organizations in Their Legal Setting, 1016 pages, 1977, with 1981 Supplement (Casebook)

Weston, Falk and D'Amato's International Law and World Order—A Problem Oriented Coursebook, 1195 pages, 1980, with Documents Supplement (Casebook)

Wilson's International Business Transactions in a Nutshell, 393 pages, 1981 (Text)

INTRODUCTION TO LAW

Dobbyn's So You Want to go to Law School, Revised First Edition, 206 pages, 1976 (Text)

Hegland's Law School: Survival and Beyond in a Nutshell, approximately 300 pages, 1983 (Text)

Kinyon's Introduction to Law Study and Law Examinations in a Nutshell, 389 pages, 1971 (Text)

See also Legal Method and Legal System

JUDICIAL ADMINISTRATION

Carrington, Meador and Rosenberg's Justice on Appeal, 263 pages, 1976 (Casebook)

Leflar's Appellate Judicial Opinions, 343 pages, 1974 (Text)

Nelson's Cases and Materials on Judicial Administration and the Administration of Justice, 1032 pages, 1974 (Casebook)

JURISPRUDENCE

Christie's Text and Readings on Jurisprudence—The Philosophy of Law, 1056 pages, 1973 (Casebook)

JUVENILE JUSTICE

Fox's Cases and Materials on Modern Juvenile Justice, 2nd Ed., 960 pages, 1981 (Casebook)

Fox's Juvenile Courts in a Nutshell, 2nd Ed., 275 pages, 1977 (Text)

LABOR LAW

Gorman's Basic Text on Labor Law—Unionization and Collective Bargaining, 914 pages, 1976 (Text)

Leslie's Labor Law in a Nutshell, 403 pages, 1979 (Text)

Nolan's Labor Arbitration Law and Practice in a Nutshell, 358 pages, 1979 (Text)

Oberer, Hanslowe and Andersen's Cases and Materials on Labor Law—Collective Bargaining in a Free Society, 2nd Ed., 1168 pages, 1979, with 1979 Statutory Supplement and 1982 Case Supplement (Casebook)

See also Employment Discrimination, Social Legislation

LAND FINANCE

See Real Estate Transactions

LAND USE

Hagman's Cases on Public Planning and Control of Urban and Land Development, 2nd Ed., 1301 pages, 1980 (Casebook)

Hagman's Hornbook on Urban Planning and Land Development Control Law, 706 pages, 1971 (Text)

Wright and Gitelman's Cases and Materials on Land Use, 3rd Ed., 1300 pages, 1982 (Casebook)

Wright and Webber's Land Use in a Nutshell, 316 pages, 1978 (Text)

See also Housing and Urban Development

LAW AND ECONOMICS

Manne's The Economics of Legal Relationships—Readings in the Theory of Property Rights, 660 pages, 1975 (Text)

LAW AND ECONOMICS—Continued

See also Antitrust, Regulated Industries

LAW AND MEDICINE—PSYCHIATRY

Cohen's Cases and Materials on the Law of Deprivation of Liberty: A Study in Social Control, 755 pages, 1980 (Casebook)

King's The Law of Medical Malpractice in a Nutshell, 340 pages, 1977 (Text)

Shapiro and Spece's Problems, Cases and Materials on Bioethics and Law, 892 pages, 1981 (Casebook)

Sharpe, Fiscina and Head's Cases on Law and Medicine, 882 pages, 1978 (Casebook)

LEGAL CLINICS

See Office Practice

LEGAL HISTORY

Presser and Zainaldin's Cases on Law and American History, 855 pages, 1980 (Casebook)

See also Legal Method and Legal System

LEGAL METHOD AND LEGAL SYSTEM

Aldisert's Readings, Materials and Cases in the Judicial Process, 948 pages, 1976 (Casebook)

Bodenheimer, Oakley and Love's Readings and Cases on an Introduction to the Anglo-American Legal System, 161 pages, 1980 (Casebook)

Davies and Lawry's Institutions and Methods of the Law—Introductory Teaching Materials, 547 pages, 1982 (Casebook)

Dvorkin, Himmelstein and Lesnick's Becoming a Lawyer: A Humanistic Perspective on Legal Education and Professionalism, 211 pages, 1981 (Text)

Fryer and Orentlicher's Cases and Materials on Legal Method and Legal System, 1043 pages, 1967 (Casebook)

Greenberg's Judicial Process and Social Change, 666 pages, 1977 (Coursebook)

Kempin's Historical Introduction to Anglo-American Law in a Nutshell, 2nd Ed., 280 pages, 1973 (Text)

Kimball's Historical Introduction to the Legal System, 610 pages, 1966 (Casebook)

Mashaw and Merrill's Introduction to the American Public Law System, 1095 pages, 1975, with 1980 Supplement (Casebook)

Murphy's Cases and Materials on Introduction to Law—Legal Process and Procedure, 772 pages, 1977 (Casebook)

Reynolds' Judicial Process in a Nutshell, 292 pages, 1980 (Text)

See also Legal Research and Writing

LAW SCHOOL PUBLICATIONS—Continued

LEGAL PROFESSION

Aronson's Problems in Professional Responsibility, 280 pages, 1978 (Problem book)

Aronson and Weckstein's Professional Responsibility in a Nutshell, 399 pages, 1980 (Text)

Mellinkoff's The Conscience of a Lawyer, 304 pages, 1973 (Text)

Mellinkoff's Lawyers and the System of Justice, 983 pages, 1976 (Casebook)

Pirsig and Kirwin's Cases and Materials on Professional Responsibility, 3rd Ed., 667 pages, 1976, with 1981 Supplement (Casebook)

Smith's Preventing Legal Malpractice, 142 pages, 1981 (Text)

LEGAL RESEARCH AND WRITING

Cohen's Legal Research in a Nutshell, 3rd Ed., 415 pages, 1978 (Text)

Dickerson's Materials on Legal Drafting, 425 pages, 1981 (Casebook)

Felsenfeld and Siegel's Writing Contracts in Plain English, 290 pages, 1981 (Text)

Gopen's Writing From a Legal Perspective, 225 pages, 1981 (Text)

How to Find the Law With Special Chapters on Legal Writing, 7th Ed., 542 pages, 1976. Problem book available (Coursebook)

Mellinkoff's Legal Writing—Sense and Nonsense, 242 pages, 1982 (Text)

Rombauer's Legal Problem Solving—Analysis, Research and Writing, 4th Ed., approximately 350 pages, 1983 (Coursebook)

Squires and Rombauer's Legal Writing in a Nutshell, 294 pages, 1982 (Text)

Statsky's Legal Research, Writing and Analysis, 2nd Ed., 167 pages, 1982 (Coursebook)

Statsky's Legislative Analysis: How to Use Statutes and Regulations, 216 pages, 1975 (Text)

Statsky and Wernet's Case Analysis and Fundamentals of Legal Writing, 576 pages, 1977 (Text)

Teply's Programmed Materials on Legal Research and Citation, 334 pages, 1982. Student Library Exercises available (Coursebook)

Weihofen's Legal Writing Style, 2nd Ed., 332 pages, 1980 (Text)

LEGISLATION

Davies' Legislative Law and Process in a Nutshell, 279 pages, 1975 (Text)

Nutting and Dickerson's Cases and Materials on Legislation, 5th Ed., 744 pages, 1978 (Casebook)

Statsky's Legislative Analysis: How to Use Statutes and Regulations, 216 pages, 1975 (Text)

LOCAL GOVERNMENT

McCarthy's Local Government Law in a Nutshell, 386 pages, 1975 (Text)

Michelman and Sandalow's Cases-Comments-Questions on Government in Urban Areas, 1216 pages, 1970, with 1972 Supplement (Casebook)

Reynolds' Hornbook on Local Government Law, 860 pages, 1982 (Text)

Stason and Kauper's Cases and Materials on Municipal Corporations, 3rd Ed., 692 pages, 1959 (Casebook)

Valente's Cases and Materials on Local Government Law, 2nd Ed., 980 pages, 1980 with 1982 Supplement (Casebook)

MASS COMMUNICATION LAW

Gillmor and Barron's Cases and Comment on Mass Communication Law, 3rd Ed., 1008 pages, 1979 (Casebook)

Ginsburg's Regulation of Broadcasting: Law and Policy Towards Radio, Television and Cable Communications, 741 pages, 1979 (Casebook)

Zuckman and Gayne's Mass Communications Law in a Nutshell, 2nd Ed., 473 pages, 1983 (Text)

MILITARY LAW

Shanor and Terrell's Military Law in a Nutshell, 378 pages, 1980 (Text)

MORTGAGES

See Real Estate Transactions

NATURAL RESOURCES LAW

See Energy and Natural Resources Law, Environmental Law, Oil and Gas, Water Law

OFFICE PRACTICE

Binder and Price's Legal Interviewing and Counseling: A Client-Centered Approach, 232 pages, 1977 (Text)

Edwards and White's Problems, Readings and Materials on the Lawyer as a Negotiator, 484 pages, 1977 (Casebook)

Hegland's Trial and Practice Skills in a Nutshell, 346 pages, 1978 (Text)

Shaffer's Legal Interviewing and Counseling in a Nutshell, 353 pages, 1976 (Text)

Strong and Clark's Law Office Management, 424 pages, 1974 (Casebook)

Williams' Legal Negotiation and Settlement, 207 pages, 1983 (Coursebook)

OIL AND GAS

Hemingway's Hornbook on Oil and Gas, 2nd Ed., approximately 535 pages, 1983 (Text)

OIL AND GAS—Continued

Huie, Woodward and Smith's Cases and Materials on Oil and Gas, 2nd Ed., 955 pages, 1972 (Casebook)

Lowe's Oil and Gas Law in a Nutshell, approximately 365 pages, 1983 (Text)

See also Energy and Natural Resources Law

PARTNERSHIP

See Agency—Partnership

PATENT LAW

Choate and Francis' Cases and Materials on Patent Law, 2nd Ed., 1110 pages, 1981 (Casebook)

See also Copyright

POVERTY LAW

Brudno's Poverty, Inequality, and the Law: Cases-Commentary-Analysis, 934 pages, 1976 (Casebook)

Cooper, Dodyk, Berger, Paulsen, Schrag and Sovern's Cases and Materials on Law and Poverty, 2nd Ed., 1208 pages, 1973 (Casebook)

LaFrance, Schroeder, Bennett and Boyd's Hornbook on Law of the Poor, 558 pages, 1973 (Text)

See also Social Legislation

PRODUCTS LIABILITY

Noel and Phillips' Cases on Products Liability, 2nd Ed., 821 pages, 1982 (Casebook)

Noel and Phillips' Products Liability in a Nutshell, 2nd Ed., 341 pages, 1981 (Text)

PROPERTY

Aigler, Smith and Tefft's Cases on Property, 2 volumes, 1339 pages, 1960 (Casebook)

Bernhardt's Real Property in a Nutshell, 2nd Ed., 448 pages, 1981 (Text)

Boyer's Survey of the Law of Property, 766 pages, 1981 (Text)

Browder, Cunningham, Julin and Smith's Cases on Basic Property Law, 3rd Ed., 1447 pages, 1979 (Casebook)

Burby's Hornbook on Real Property, 3rd Ed., 490 pages, 1965 (Text)

Burke's Personal Property in a Nutshell, approximately 318 pages, 1983 (Text)

Chused's A Modern Approach to Property: Cases-Notes-Materials, 1069 pages, 1978 with 1980 Supplement (Casebook)

Cohen's Materials for a Basic Course in Property, 526 pages, 1978 (Casebook)

Donahue, Kauper and Martin's Cases on Property, 2nd Ed., approximately 1350 pages, 1983 (Casebook)

PROPERTY—Continued

Hill's Landlord and Tenant Law in a Nutshell, 319 pages, 1979 (Text)

Moynihan's Introduction to Real Property, 254 pages, 1962 (Text)

Phipps' Titles in a Nutshell, 277 pages, 1968 (Text)

Uniform Land Transactions Act, Uniform Simplification of Land Transfers Act, Uniform Condominium Act, 1977 Official Text with Comments, 462 pages, 1978

See also Housing and Urban Development, Real Estate Transactions, Land Use

REAL ESTATE TRANSACTIONS

Bruce's Real Estate Finance in a Nutshell, 292 pages, 1979 (Text)

Maxwell, Riesenfeld, Hetland and Warren's Cases on California Security Transactions in Land, 2nd Ed., 584 pages, 1975 (Casebook)

Nelson and Whitman's Cases on Real Estate Transfer, Finance and Development, 2nd Ed., 1114 pages, 1981 (Casebook)

Osborne's Cases and Materials on Secured Transactions, 559 pages, 1967 (Casebook)

Osborne, Nelson and Whitman's Hornbook on Real Estate Finance Law, 3rd Ed., 885 pages, 1979 (Text)

REGULATED INDUSTRIES

Gellhorn and Pierce's Regulated Industries in a Nutshell, 394 pages, 1982 (Text)

Morgan's Cases and Materials on Economic Regulation of Business, 830 pages, 1976, with 1978 Supplement (Casebook)

Pozen's Financial Institutions: Cases, Materials and Problems on Investment Management, 844 pages, 1978 (Casebook)

White's Teaching Materials on Banking Law, 1058 pages, 1976, with 1980 Case and Statutory Supplement (Casebook)

See also Mass Communication Law

REMEDIES

Dobbs' Hornbook on Remedies, 1067 pages, 1973 (Text)

Dobbs' Problems in Remedies, 137 pages, 1974 (Problem book)

Dobbyn's Injunctions in a Nutshell, 264 pages, 1974 (Text)

Friedman's Contract Remedies in a Nutshell, 323 pages, 1981 (Text)

LAW SCHOOL PUBLICATIONS—Continued

REMEDIES—Continued

Leavell, Love and Nelson's Cases and Materials on Equitable Remedies and Restitution, 3rd Ed., 704 pages, 1980 (Casebook)

McCormick's Hornbook on Damages, 811 pages, 1935 (Text)

O'Connell's Remedies in a Nutshell, 364 pages, 1977 (Text)

York and Bauman's Cases and Materials on Remedies, 3rd Ed., 1250 pages, 1979 (Casebook)

REVIEW MATERIALS

Ballantine's Problems

Black Letter Series

Smith's Review Series

West's Review Covering Multistate Subjects

SECURITIES REGULATION

Ratner's Securities Regulation: Materials for a Basic Course, 2nd Ed., 1050 pages, 1980 with 1982 Supplement (Casebook)

Ratner's Securities Regulation in a Nutshell, 300 pages, 1978 (Text)

Selected Securities and Business Planning Statutes, Rules and Forms, 485 pages, 1982

SOCIAL LEGISLATION

Brudno's Income Redistribution Theories and Programs: Cases-Commentary-Analyses, 480 pages, 1977 (Casebook)—reprint from Brudno's Poverty, Inequality and the Law, 1976

LaFrance's Welfare Law: Structure and Entitlement in a Nutshell, 455 pages, 1979 (Text)

Malone, Plant and Little's Cases on Workers' Compensation and Employment Rights, 2nd Ed., 951 pages, 1980 (Casebook)

See also Poverty Law

TAXATION

Chommie's Hornbook on Federal Income Taxation, 2nd Ed., 1051 pages, 1973 (Text)

Dodge's Federal Taxation of Estates, Trusts and Gifts: Principles and Planning, 771 pages, 1981 with 1982 Supplement (Casebook)

Garbis and Struntz' Cases and Materials on Tax Procedure and Tax Fraud, 829 pages, 1982 (Casebook)

Gunn's Cases and Materials on Federal Income Taxation of Individuals, 785 pages, 1981 (Casebook)

Hellerstein and Hellerstein's Cases on State and Local Taxation, 4th Ed., 1041 pages, 1978 with 1982 Supplement (Casebook)

TAXATION—Continued

Kahn's Handbook on Basic Corporate Taxation, 3rd Ed., Student Ed., 614 pages, 1981 with 1982 Supplement (Text)

Kahn and Gann's Corporate Taxation and Taxation of Partnerships and Partners, 1107 pages, 1979, with 1981 Supplement (Casebook)

Kragen and McNulty's Cases and Materials on Federal Income Taxation, Vol. I: Taxation of Individuals, 3rd Ed., 1283 pages, 1979 with 1982 Supplement (Casebook)

Kragen and McNulty's Cases and Materials on Federal Income Taxation, Vol. II: Taxation of Corporations, Shareholders, Partnerships and Partners, 3rd Ed., 989 pages, 1981 with 1982 Supplement (Casebook)

Kramer and McCord's Problems for Federal Estate and Gift Taxes, 206 pages, 1976 (Problem book)

Lowndes, Kramer and McCord's Hornbook on Federal Estate and Gift Taxes, 3rd Ed., 1099 pages, 1974 (Text)

McCord's 1976 Estate and Gift Tax Reform-Analysis, Explanation and Commentary, 377 pages, 1977 (Text)

McNulty's Federal Estate and Gift Taxation in a Nutshell, 3rd Ed., approximately 500 pages, 1983 (Text)

McNulty's Federal Income Taxation of Individuals in a Nutshell, 3rd Ed., approximately 425 pages, 1983 (Text)

Posin's Hornbook on Federal Income Taxation of Individuals, approximately 425 pages, 1983 (Text)

Rice's Problems and Materials in Federal Estate and Gift Taxation, 3rd Ed., 474 pages, 1978 (Casebook)

Rice and Solomon's Problems and Materials in Federal Income Taxation, 3rd Ed., 670 pages, 1979 (Casebook)

Rose and Raskind's Advanced Federal Income Taxation: Corporate Transactions—Cases, Materials and Problems, 955 pages, 1978 (Casebook)

Selected Federal Taxation Statutes and Regulations, 1218 pages, 1982

Soboloff and Weidenbruch's Federal Income Taxation of Corporations and Stockholders in a Nutshell, 362 pages, 1981 (Text)

TORTS

Christie's Cases and Materials on the Law of Torts, approximately 1250 pages, 1983 (Casebook)

Green, Pedrick, Rahl, Thode, Hawkins, Smith and Treece's Cases and Materials on Torts, 2nd Ed., 1360 pages, 1977 (Casebook)

LAW SCHOOL PUBLICATIONS—Continued

TORTS—Continued

Green, Pedrick, Rahl, Thode, Hawkins, Smith, and Treece's Advanced Torts: Injuries to Business, Political and Family Interests, 2nd Ed., 544 pages, 1977 (Casebook)—reprint from Green, et al. Cases and Materials on Torts, 2nd Ed., 1977

Keeton's Computer-Aided and Workbook Exercises on Tort Law, 164 pages, 1976 (Coursebook)

Keeton, Keeton, Sargentich and Steiner's Cases and Materials on Torts, and Accident Law, approximately 1344 pages, 1983 (Casebook)

Kionka's Torts in a Nutshell: Injuries to Persons and Property, 434 pages, 1977 (Text)

Malone's Torts in a Nutshell: Injuries to Family, Social and Trade Relations, 358 pages, 1979 (Text)

Prosser's Hornbook on Torts, 4th Ed., 1208 pages, 1971 (Text)

Shapo's Cases on Tort and Compensation Law, 1244 pages, 1976 (Casebook)

See also Products Liability

TRADE REGULATION

McManis' Unfair Trade Practices in a Nutshell, 444 pages, 1982 (Text)

Oppenheim, Weston, Maggs and Schechter's Cases and Materials on Unfair Trade Practices and Consumer Protection, 4th Ed., approximately 1000 pages, 1983 (Casebook)

See also Antitrust, Regulated Industries

TRIAL AND APPELLATE ADVOCACY

Appellate Advocacy, Handbook of, 249 pages, 1980 (Text)

Bergman's Trial Advocacy in a Nutshell, 402 pages, 1979 (Text)

Goldberg's The First Trial (Where Do I Sit?) (What Do I Say?) in a Nutshell, 396 pages, 1982 (Text)

Hegland's Trial and Practice Skills in a Nutshell, 346 pages, 1978 (Text)

Jeans' Handbook on Trial Advocacy, Student Ed., 473 pages, 1975 (Text)

McElhaney's Effective Litigation, 457 pages, 1974 (Casebook)

Nolan's Cases and Materials on Trial Practice, 518 pages, 1981 (Casebook)

Parnell and Shellhaas' Cases, Exercises and Problems for Trial Advocacy, 171 pages, 1982 (Coursebook)

TRUSTS AND ESTATES

Atkinson's Hornbook on Wills, 2nd Ed., 975 pages, 1953 (Text)

TRUST AND ESTATES—Continued

Averill's Uniform Probate Code in a Nutshell, 425 pages, 1978 (Text)

Bogert's Hornbook on Trusts, 5th Ed., 726 pages, 1973 (Text)

Clark, Lusky and Murphy's Cases and Materials on Gratuitous Transfers, 2nd Ed., 1102 pages, 1977 (Casebook)

Gulliver's Cases and Materials on Future Interests, 624 pages, 1959 (Casebook)

Gulliver's Introduction to the Law of Future Interests, 87 pages, 1959 (Casebook)—reprint from Gulliver's Cases and Materials on Future Interests, 1959

Halbach (Editor)—Death, Taxes, and Family Property: Essays and American Assembly Report, 189 pages, 1977 (Text)

McGovern's Cases and Materials on Wills, Trusts and Future Interests: An Introduction to Estate Planning, 750 pages, 1983 (Casebook)

Mennell's Cases and Materials on California Decedent's Estates, 566 pages, 1973 (Casebook)

Mennell's Wills and Trusts in a Nutshell, 392 pages, 1979 (Text)

Powell's The Law of Future Interests in California, 91 pages, 1980 (Text)

Simes' Hornbook on Future Interests, 2nd Ed., 355 pages, 1966 (Text)

Turrentine's Cases and Text on Wills and Administration, 2nd Ed., 483 pages, 1962 (Casebook)

Uniform Probate Code, 5th Ed., Official Text With Comments, 384 pages, 1977

Waggoner's Future Interests in a Nutshell, 361 pages, 1981 (Text)

WATER LAW

Trelease's Cases and Materials on Water Law, 3rd Ed., 833 pages, 1979 (Casebook)

See also Energy and Natural Resources Law, Environmental Law

WILLS

See Trusts and Estates

WOMEN AND THE LAW

Kay's Text, Cases and Materials on Sex-Based Discrimination, 2nd Ed., 1045 pages, 1981 (Casebook)

Thomas' Sex Discrimination in a Nutshell, 399 pages, 1982 (Text)

See also Employment Discrimination

WORKMEN'S COMPENSATION

See Social Legislation

XII

LAW IN
RADICALLY
DIFFERENT CULTURES

By

JOHN H. BARTON
Stanford Law School

JAMES LOWELL GIBBS, JR.
Department of Anthropology
Stanford University

VICTOR HAO LI
East-West Center
Honolulu, Hawaii

JOHN HENRY MERRYMAN
Stanford Law School

AMERICAN CASEBOOK SERIES

ST. PAUL, MINN.
WEST PUBLISHING CO.
1983

COPYRIGHT © 1983 By WEST PUBLISHING CO.
50 West Kellogg Boulevard
P.O. Box 3526
St. Paul, Minnesota 55165

Printed in the United States of America

Library of Congress Cataloging in Publication Data

Main entry under title:

Law in radically different cultures.

  (American casebook series)
  Includes index.
  1. Law—United States. 2. Law—Botswana. 3. Law—China. 4. Law—Egypt.
  5. Comparative law. I. Barton, John H. II. Series.
K583.L38 1983   340'.2   82-24802
                    342

   ISBN 0-314-70396-6

B., G., L. & M.Law in Rad. Dif Cultures ACB

PREFACE AND ACKNOWLEDGMENTS

Most comparative law teaching and scholarship is, for good historical and practical reasons, fragmented. The focus is on the law of one jurisdiction (China, USSR) or a small number (France and Germany, perhaps also Italy and Latin America). Most comparative law courses in American universities deal with the continental Western European law, since this is an area with which we have important trade, cultural and military relationships, and because it represents a contrasting legal tradition within Western culture. The range of comparison here is quite narrow: the societies and legal systems in Western Europe (including Britain, Ireland and Scandinavia) and all of North and South America, with only minor exceptions, closely resemble each other.

The questions we have chosen to address in this book are: what do legal systems look like in radically different cultures? Is it possible to identify legal constants running through such societies? What kinds of social differences are correlated with significant differences in legal systems?

We have identified the following categories of radically different cultures: 1) Western (as above). 2) Eastern. Here we think of China and Japan as the most prominent examples. 3) Religious. Hindu, Muslim, and Jewish societies fall into this category. 4) Traditional. Here the variety of examples is enormous: tribal systems in Africa, traditional systems among the Indian populations of Mexico, Guatemala, and other parts of Latin America, and many others. In some cases it will be difficult to distinguish a traditional from a religious society. Still, we keep returning to the pre-industrial society as revealing an important variable. 5) Soviet. This is a more debatable category. The Soviet Union and its satellites may constitute a distinctive group of societies, but there is a persuasive argument that they are not radically different from other Western societies. 6) International. The society of nations clearly is radically different from those in the previous categories. The difficulty is one of parallelism: problems that make sense in terms of the first five categories do not translate easily into international equivalents. This is important because we use problems as a principal substantive device in the course.

We decided to include the first four kinds of societies in the above list and to focus on a specific jurisdiction within each of these four. This gives us the opportunity to learn more about the relations between the law and the society and about the way law is currently evolving. Given the wide variations that exist within the cultures (e.g. between the U.S.S.R. and the U.S.A. or between Japan and the P.R.C.), any such choice risks a certain loss in representativeness. However, the gain in concreteness when we deal with a specific jurisdiction more than offsets any such loss. The four examples we have chosen are Botswana, California, the People's Republic of China (P.R.C.) and Egypt.

We also decided to use a problem method. This reflects our concern with the "law in action," as opposed to straightforward doctrinal analysis. It also offers an opportunity to consider how and why issues that are considered legal in one culture may be treated by bureaucratic or religious institutions in another.

We have chosen four common social problems: (1) someone with property, who holds office and has social status, dies: who gets the property, the office, and the status? (2) a crime is committed: what process does the society use to identify and deal with the criminal? (3) promises are made and relied on but not kept: how does the society deal with "breach of contract"? (4) at a time when there is world-wide concern for population control, in what ways does a society's legal system affect family size? Each of these problems is examined within each of our four cultures. The sixteen problem/culture units make up the bulk of the book. They are preceded by a brief introductory note on law and by introductions to each of the four cultures.

Although we include a good deal of specially prepared text to summarize information and help direct the student, most of the material is intended to help the student think about the problems and arrive at her or his own syntheses and conclusions. Such a book contemplates a different kind of student preparation for class and a different kind of conduct in class from that familiar to much undergraduate instruction, although law students and teachers will recognize the pattern. The student is expected to study and think about the material in advance of the class for which it is assigned and the class itself is a forum for discussion of that material in which the students do most of the talking in response to questions and hints from the teacher. The questions we have distributed throughout the book are there to help students prepare for class and to provide beginning points for classroom discussion.

Primary responsibility for the preparation of materials was divided among the four authors along two dimensions: Professor Barton took responsibility for preparation of the introductory and problem materials dealing with Egypt, Professor Gibbs likewise for Botswana, Professor Li for the People's Republic of China, and Professor Merryman for California/USA. Problem one was drafted and the materials edited by Professor Merryman, Problem two by Professor Gibbs, Problem three by Professor Li, and Prob-

PREFACE AND ACKNOWLEDGMENTS

lem four by Professor Barton. In addition, we repeatedly read and criticized each other's work. We were greatly assisted by and extend our sincere appreciation to the following former students, who were the authors of first drafts of the problems indicated:

PROBLEM I (Inheritance)

Traditional	Marie L. Roehm and Sandra L. Willis
Eastern	Joan M. Travostino
Islam	Rikki L. Quintana

PROBLEM II (Embezzlement)

Traditional	Lynda Ann McNeive
Eastern	Scott I. Canel
Islam	David B. Temin

PROBLEM II (Contract)

Traditional	Lawrence J. Harding
Eastern	Eve Maria Fitzsimmons and Kenneth G. Whyburn
Islam	Mary G. Swift

PROBLEM IV (Population Control)

Eastern	Samuel L. Torres
Islam	Jeffrey N. Newland

During the early phases of this project, Victor Miramontes prepared additional background materials on Egypt, and Rikki L. Quintana, Joan M. Travostino and Sandra L. Willis served as research assistants. The Norman Fund for Innovation in Legal Studies supported many of the exceptional costs of preparing thesis materials.

In a later phase, the National Endowment for the Humanities supported field research in Botswana and Egypt, under Grant EH 20081-81-0239. Kenneth R. Barrett, Lawrence S. Molton, Leylâ Neyzi, Andrew K. Powell, and Rosalind Z. Wiggins assisted in the final manuscript preparation. Many other students helped in and out of class. And Mary Peabody typed, assembled, and organized innumerable editions of the materials and cheerfully and with good humor made all the arrangements that had to be made.

The National Endowment for the Humanities Grant enabled Professor Barton to carry out a short period of data collection in Egypt and Professor Gibbs to undertake a similar short period of research in Botswana. Space precludes listing the names of the many individuals who provided assistance in the field research. However, we wish to acknowledge that many Egyptian officials and private citizens answered Professor Barton's questions and kindly provided assistance in other ways. In Botswana many officials of the Government of Botswana (in Gaborone and elsewhere); of the University of Botswana and Swaziland; and of the American Embassy, U.S. International Cooperation Agency, and Peace Corps were generous in providing Professor Gibbs with information, suggestions, and comments. Dr. Q. N. Parsons and Mr. Alec Campbell prepared careful critiques of earlier versions of the Botswana sections of the manuscript. Both officials and private citizens were gracious in offering Dr. Gibbs home hospitality.

The authors are grateful to various publishers and international organizations for generously providing many documents for this book. They wish to acknowledge permission to reproduce the following copyrighted material.

Academic Press, Inc. (London) Ltd., for John Comaroff, Talking Politics: Oratory and Authority in a Tswana Chiefdom," in *Political Language and Oratory in Traditional Societies*, ed., Maurice Bloch, 1975.

Academica for W. J. O. Jeppe, *Local Government in Southern Africa*, ed. by W. B. Vosloo, D. A. Kotze, and J. J. O. Jeppe, 1974.

African Law Studies for Simon Roberts, "Tradition and Change at Mochudi: Competing Jurisdictions in Botswana," *African Law Studies* 17, 1979.

George Allen & Unwin (Publishers) Ltd. for S. Nasr, *Ideals and Realities of Islam*, 1966.

The American Council of Learned Studies for Benjamin Schwartz, "On Attitudes Toward Law in China," in M. Katz, editor, *Government Under Law and the Individual*, 1957.

The American Law Institute and the National Conference of Commissioners on Uniform State Laws, with permission of the Permanent Editorial Board for the Uniform Commercial Code, for Official Comment Number 6 to Section 2-615 and Official Comments Numbers 2 and 3 to Section 2-715 from the *1978 Official Text, The Uniform Commercial Code*, 1982.

American Sociological Association for Stewart Macaulay, "Non-Contractual Relations in Business: A Preliminary Study," *American Sociological Review*, Volume 28, 1963.

The W. H. Anderson Company for Wesley Gilmer, Jr., *Cochran's Law Lexicon* (Gilmer's Revision 1973).

Association for Asian Studies, Inc., for G. William Skinner, "Marketing and Social Structure in Rural China," *Journal of Asian Studies*, XXIV, No. 1, 1964, and XXIV, No. 3, 1965.

The Association of Social Anthropologists for John Comaroff and Simon Roberts, "The Invocation of Norms in Dispute Settlement: The Tswana Case," ed. by Ian Hammett, *Social Anthropology and Law*, 1977.

Athlone Press, University of London, for James N. D. Anderson, *Law Reform in the Muslim World*, 1976, by permission of the Humanities Press Inc., Atlantic Highlands, N.J.; and Sybille Van der Sprenkel, *Legal Institutions in Manchu China*, 1962.

Basic Books, Inc., Publishers, for Marvin B. Sussman, Judith N. Cates, and David J. Smith with collaboration of Lososka K. Clausen, *The Family and Inheritance*, 1970, by Russell Sage Foundation.

Bobbs-Merrill Co., Inc., for Jerome Hall, *Theft, Law and Society*, 1952.

The Botswana Society, Botswana Notes and Records, for Justice Akinola Aguda, *Legal Development in Botswana from 1885 to 1966*, 1973; for M. D. Crone, "Aspects of the 1971 Census of Botswana," volume 4, 1972; Ron H. Paul, *A Review of Botswana: A Short Political History, by Anthony Sillery.* Volume 7, 1975; Simon Roberts, "Kgatla Law and Social Change," 2, 1970; Anthony Sillery, "Comments on Two Articles," 8, 1976; B. C. Thema, "The Changing Pattern of Tswana Social and Family Relations," volume 4, 1972; and J. M. Walker, "Bamalete Contract Law," 1, 1968.

University of Botswana, for World Population Year Conference Report, 1974.

University of British Columbia Press, for Maurice Freedman, "The Family in China, Past and Present," *Pacific Affairs*, volume 34, 1962.

British Institute of International and Comparative Law, for J. N. D. Anderson, "Recent Reforms in the Islamic Law of Inheritance," *Int'l & Comp. Law Quarterly*, vol. 14, 1965.

Butterworth & Co. for Simon Roberts, "Botswana," in *Judicial and Legal Systems in Africa*, ed. by Anthony N. Allott, 1970.

University of California Press, for Anthony N. Allott, "The Future of African Law," in *African Law*, Kuper & Kuper, eds., 1965.

Cambridge University Press, for Noel Coulson, *Succession in the Muslim Family*, 1971.

The Carolina Population Center, University of North Carolina at Chapel Hill, for Haifa Shanawany, "Stages in the Development of a Population Control Society, ed. by A. R. Omran, 1973; Abdel R. Omran, "Prospects for Accelerating the Transition in Egypt," in *Egypt: Population Problems and Prospects*, ed. by Abdel R. Omran, 1973.

The Centre for Islamic Legal Studies Journal for D. Hall and

PREFACE AND ACKNOWLEDGMENTS

Abubakar Abbas, "Comparative Survey of the Islamic Law and the Common Law Relating to the Sale of Goods."

The University of Chicago Law Review, for Sheldon J. Plager, "The Spouse's Nonbarrable Share: A Solution in Search of a Problem," Vol. 33, 1966.

The University of Chicago Press, for Noel Coulson, *Conflicts and Tensions in Islamic Jurisprudence*, 1969; John Comaroff and Simon Roberts, *Rules and Processes: The Cultural Logic of Dispute in an African Context*, 1981.

University of Chicago Press for William L. Parish and Martin K. Whyte, *Village and Family in Contemporary China*, 1978.

Centre d'etudes et de documentation economique for anonymous French-language excerpt, author unknown.

William Clifford, *Introduction to African Criminology*, 1974.

Columbia Human Rights Law Review, for Maitre El-Kharboutly and Aziza Hussein, "Law and the Status of Women in the Arab Republic of Egypt," No. 8, 1976.

Columbia Journal of Transnational Law, for Nicholas Kourides, Note, "The Influence of Islamic Law on Contemporary Middle Eastern Legal Systems," 384, 1970.

Columbia University Press, for William A. Hance, *Population, Migration, and Urbanization in Africa*, 1970; and R. K. Som, "Some Demographic Indicators for Africa," in *Population of Tropical Africa*, ed. by J. C. Caldwell and C. Okonjo, 1968.

John Comaroff, "Tswana Transformation 1953-1975," in *Ethnographic Survey of Africa, Southern Africa*, Part III, 1976 reprint.

"Comparative Evidence from Egypt and Morocco," 11 *Government and Opposition* 426, 1976.

Crown Publishers, Inc., for Norman Dacey, *How To Avoid Probate*, The National Estate Planning Council, 1965.

The Daily News, Gaborone, Botswana, various articles.

East-West Population Institute, for Chi-hsien Tuan, translator of *Guangdong Province Planned Birth Ordinance*, excerpts by Pichao Chen.

Egyptian Gazette, "Farmers Accept Birth Control," Feb. 2, 1981.

Faber and Faber Limited, for Isaac Schapera, *Married Life in an African Tribe*, 1941.

Family Planning Perspectives, for Frederick S. Jaffe and Deborah Oakley, "Observations on Birth Planning in China, 1977," 1978; Henshaw, Forest, Sullivan and Tietze, "Abortion Services in the United States, 1979 and 1980," Volume 14, Number 1, 1982.

PREFACE AND ACKNOWLEDGMENTS

Fiani & Partners, Cairo, for "Law 43 of 1974 on Arab and Foreign Capital Investment and Free Zones," *Egypt Investment Directory*, 1980/1981.

Foreign Languages Press, for Mao Tse-Tung, "The Bankruptcy of the Idealist Conception of History," from *Selected Works of Mao Tse-Tung*, Volume IV, 1967.

Foundation Press, for Thomas L. Shaffer, *The Planning and Drafting of Wills and Trusts*, 1979.

Lawrence P. Frank, for *Khama and Jonathan: A Study of Authority and Leadership in Southern Africa*, 1975.

Geographical Magazine, London, for Gerald Blake, "Land of One-Third of All Arabs," volume 16, 1974.

Government and Opposition, *A Journal of Comparative Politics*, for John Waterbury, "Corruption, Political Stability and Development."

Gulf Publishing Company, for Bar Association of San Francisco, Probate Committee. *How to Live—How to Die—With California Probate*, 1970.

Robert Hale, Limited, for Eric Robin, *White Queen in Africa*, 1967.

Harper & Row, Publishers, Inc., for Victor H. Li, "Human Rights in the Chinese Context," in Ross Terrill, editor, *The China Difference*, 1979.

Harvard International Law Journal, for Thomas Huang, "Reflections on Law and Economy in the People's Republic of China," vol. 14, 1973.

Harvard Law Review Association, for Note, "Legal Analysis and Population Control: The Problem of Coercion," vol. 84, 1971.

Holmes and Meier Publishers, Inc., for Anthony N. Allott, "Evidence in African Customary Law," in *Readings in African Law*, Volume 1, ed. by E. Cotran and N. N. Rubin.

Holt, Rinehart & Winston, for Hani Fakhouri, *Kafr El-Elow: An Egyptian Village in Transition*, 1972.

Hong Kong University Press, for M. J. Meijer, *Marriage Law and Policy in the Chinese People's Republic*, 1971.

Hoover Institute Publications, for Farhat J. Ziadeh, *Lawyers, the Rule of Law and Liberalism in Modern Egypt*, 1968.

Indian Institute of Islamic Studies, for Harold Barclay, "Study of an Egyptian Village Community," III, *Studies in Islam*, 1966.

The Indian Law Institute, for Tahir Mahmood, *Family Law Reform in the Muslim World*, 1972.

PREFACE AND ACKNOWLEDGMENTS

Indiana University Press, for Iliya Harik, *The Political Mobilization of Peasants: A Study of an Egyptian Community*, 1974.

Institute of International Relations, Taiwan, for "Draft Decision (by the Central Committee of the Communist Party, July 1978) Concerning Some Problems in Speeding Up the Development Industry," (Part 2) *Issues and Studies*, Vol. 15, 1979.

International Planned Parenthood Federation, *Africa Link*, for Rebecca J. Cook, "Abortion Law in Commonwealth Africa," volume 3, No. 2, 1975; John C. Kabagambe, "Demographic Trends and Family Planning in Africa," July 1979; F. Olu Okediji, "Socio-Legal Consideration and Family Planning Programmes in Africa," 1975; Dr. F. T. Sai and others, "Rapporteur's Report From International Planned Parenthood Federation Regional Conference on Family Welfare and Development," in *Africa Link*, 1976, vol. 3, no. 4.

Ithaca Press, for Enid Hill, *Makhama! Studies in the Egyptian Legal System, Courts and Crimes, Law and Society*, 1979.

The Johns Hopkins University Press, for Haines, *Africa Today*, excerpts, 1955.

Journal of Administration Overseas, for William Tordoff, "Local Administration in Botswana—Part I," 1973, by permission of the Controller of Her Majesty's Stationery Office.

Journal of International Law and Economics, for Peter Feuerle, "Economic Arbitration in Egypt: The Influence of a Soviet Legal Institution," 61, 1972.

Librairie Philosophique J. Vrin, for Louis Gardet, *La Cite Musulmane; Vie Social et Politique*, 1976.

Librairie de la Societe, for Abd-el-Razzab Ah-El Sanhoury, *Le Droit Musulman comme Element de Refonte du Code Civil Egyptien, Introduction A L'Etude Du Droit Compare, Recueil, D'Etudes en L'Honneur d'Edouard Lambert*, 1938.

Librairie Generale de Droit et de Jurisprudence, for Magdi Khalil Sobhy, *Le Dirigisme Economique et Les Contrats, Etude De Droit Compare*, 1967.

The London School of Economics and Political Science, for Maurice Freedman, *Lineage Organization in Southeastern China*, 1958.

Los Angeles Times, for Victor H. Li, "China's Trial: Schizophrenia at the Bar," February 2, 1982.

Louisiana Law Review, for George Pugh, "Administration of Criminal Justice in France: An Introductory Analysis," 23 *Louisiana Law Review* 1, 1962.

Luzac & Company, for Abdur Rahim, *The Principles of Muhammadan Jurisprudence*, 1911.

PREFACE AND ACKNOWLEDGMENTS

Martinus Nijhoff Publishers, for Dietrich Loeber, "Comparing Chinese Enterprise Administration and Settlement of Contract Disputes with Soviet Practices," 1 *Review of Socialist Law*, 1975, and John Henry Merryman, "The Convergence (and Divergence) of the Civil Law and the Common Law," in M. Cappelletti, editor, *New Perspectives for a Common Law of Europe*, 1978.

Max Planck Institut, Germany, for John Henry Merryman, "Judicial Responsibility in the United States," 41 *Rabels Zeitschrift*, 1977.

The Middle East Institute, for Bruce M. Borthwick, *Religion and Politics in Israel and Egypt;* and Henry Cattan, "The Law of Waqf," in *Law in the Middle East*, ed. by M. Khadduri and M. Liebesny, 203, 1955.

Middle East Executive Reports, Ltd., for Ann Elizabeth Mayer, *Islamic Law and Banking in the Middle East Today*, October 1979.

The MIT Press, for C. K. Yang, *A Chinese Village in Early Communist Tradition*, 1959.

Mmogi wa Dikgang, for Eric Lekhutile, "Serowe Village Scene."

New England Journal of Medicine, for Carl Djerassi, *The Politics of Contraception*, vol. 303, 1980.

State University of New York Press, for Herbert Liebesny, *The Law of the Near and Middle East*, 1975.

New York University School of Law, for Edmond N. Cahn, "An Outline of Three Great Systems," in *Social Meanings of Legal Concepts*, 1948.

Oceana Publications, for Roy D. Weinberg, *Family Planning and the Law*, 1979.

Oliver and Boyd, for Isaac Schapera, "An Anthropologist's Approach to Population Growth: Studies in the Bechuanaland Protectorate," in *The Numbers of Man and Amimals*, ed. by J. B. Cragg and N. W. Pirie, 1955.

Oxford University Press, for Allan Osborne, "Rural Development in Botswana: A Qualitative View" in the *Journal of Southern African Studies*, volume 2, 1976.

Q. N. Parsons, *The Evolution of Modern Botswana: Historical Revisions in the Evolution of Modern Botswana*, ed. by Louis Picard and Philip Morgan.

Penguin Books Ltd., for *THE KORAN*, N. J. Dawood, translator, fourth edition, 1974.

Population Council, for Bernard Berelson, "An Evaluation of the Effects of Population Control Programs," in *Studies in Family Planning* 5, no. 1 (January 1974); and Pi-chao Chen with the collaboration of Ann Elizabeth Miller, "Lessons from the Chinese experience: China's planned birth program and its transferability," in *Studies in Family Planning* 6, no. 18 (October 1975).

The Population Crisis Committee, for "Balancing Population and Food," Population and Family Planning in the People's Republic of China, 1971.

Population Information Program, Johns Hopkins University, for Pi-chao Chen and Adrienne Kols, "Population and Birth Planning in the People's Republic of China," *Population Reports*, Series J. No. 25, 1982.

Presses Universitaires de France, for Mahmood M. Mostafa, *L'Evolution de la Procedure Penale en Egypt*, 1973.

Princeton University Press, for Abraham L. Udovitch, *Partnership and Profit in Medieval Islam*, 1970; Charles F. Westoff and Norman B. Ryder, *The Contraceptive Revolution*, 1977.

Princeton University Press for Charles F. Westoff and Norman B. Ryder, *The Contraceptive Revolution*, 1977.

The Punjab Religious Book Society, All Pakistan Legal Decisions, for Syed Ameer Ali, *Mohammedan Law*, volume 2.

Random House, Inc., for Robert Bolt, *A Man For All Seasons* 1962; Edgar Snow, *The Other Side of the River*, 1962.

Routledge & Kegan Paul Limited, for Octagon Books, for Hamed Ammar, *Growing Up in an Egyptian Village: Silwa, Province of Aswan*, 1954, and Isaac Schapera, "Oral Sorcery among the Natives of Bechuanaland," in Essays presented by C. G. Seliman, ed. by E. E. Evans Pritchard, et al. 1934.

Royal Anthropological Institute, for John Comaroff, "Rules and Rulers: Political Processes in a Tswana Chiefdom," 1978, *Man*, Vol. 13, No. 1, 1978.

School of Oriental and African Studies (University of London), for Simon Roberts, *Botswana I: Tswana Family Law, Restatement of African Law*, 1972; G. William Skinner, "Vegetable Supply and Marketing in Chinese Cities," *China Quarterly*, 1978.

Harold K. Schneider, A map from *The Africans: An Ethnological Account*, 1981.

T. Paul Schultz, "Fertility Patterns and Their Determinants In The Arab Middle East," in *Economic Development and Population Growth in the Middle East*, 1972.

Onalenna Doo Selolwane, *Poems: Abortion and The Beginning*, 1980–81.

M. E. Sharpe, Inc., for Husan Chi-wen, "Criticism of 'On Socialist Democracy and the Legal System,'" *Chinese Law and Government*, Volume 10, No. 3, 1977, and "Constitution of the People's Republic of China" (1978), in *Chinese Law and Government*, Vol. 11, 1978; "The Case of Li I-che," Vol. 10, 1977.

Social Science Research Council, for Victor H. Li, "The Drive to Legalization," in Anne Thurston and Jason Parker, editors, *Humanistic and Social Science Research in China*, 1980.

PREFACE AND ACKNOWLEDGMENTS

Stanford University Press, for John Henry Merryman, *The Civil Law Tradition: An Introduction to the Legal Systems of Western Europe and Latin America*, 1969.

James Stepanik, "Supply Planning in China," in *China Business Review.*

Betsy Stephens, Family Planning Follow-up Study Paper No. 5, 1977, National Institute for Research in Development and African Studies, University of Botswana, Documentation Unit.

Supreme Council for Population and Family Planning, Egypt, for Excerpt from "National Strategy Framework of Population, Human Resource Development, and the Family Planning Program," December 1980.

Union Research Institute, Hong Kong, for *Documents of Chinese Communist Party Central Committee, September 1956–April 1969*, Volume I, 1971.

Wadsworth Publishing Company, Van Nostrand Reinbold Co., Division of Litton Educational Publishing Company, for Erwin O. Smigel, *Public Attitudes Toward Stealing as Related to the Size of the Victim Organization*, 1970.

University of Washington Press, for David Buxbaum, *Chinese Family Law and Social Change in Historical and Comparative Perspective;* Myron Cohen, "Family Partition as Contractual Process in Taiwan: A Case Study from South Taiwan"; in David Buxbaum, editor, *Chinese Family Law and Social Change in Historical and Comparative Perspective*, 1978; Shuzo Shiga, "Family Property and the Law of Inheritance in Traditional China," in David Buxbaum, editor, *Chinese Family Law and Social Change in Historical and Comparative Perspective*, 1978.

Washington Law Review Association, University of Washington, for John N. Hazard, *Soviet Socialism and Embezzlement*, No. 26, 1951.

West Publishing Company, for Lawrence M. Friedman, "The Law of Succession in Social Perspective," in Edward C. Halbach, *Death, Taxes and Family Property*, 1977 and Paul G. Haskell, "Restraints Upon the Disinheritance of Family Members," in Edward C. Halbach, *Death, Taxes and Family Property*, 1977; William F. Hatcher, "The English System: Simplified Probate in a Similar Context," in Edward C. Halbach, *Death, Taxes and Family Property*, 1977.

Westview Press, for Gordon Bennett, *Huadong: The Story of a Chinese People's Commune*, 1978; and Victor H. Li, *Law Without Lawyers: A Comparative View of Law in China and the United States*, 1978, Stanford Alumni Association and Westview Press.

John Wiley & Sons, Inc., for Clinard & Abbott, *Crime in Developing Countries*, 1973.

PREFACE AND ACKNOWLEDGMENTS

University of Wisconsin, for Lawrence M. Friedman, "The Law and the Living, the Law of the Dead: Property, Succession and Society," in the *Wisconsin Law Review*, 1966 and Gerald D. Robin, "The Corporate and Judicial Disposition of Employee Thieves," in the *Wisconsin Law Review*, 967.

Witwatersrand University Press, for Isaac Schapera, "The Work of Tribal Courts in the Bechuanaland Protectorate," *African Studies* 2, 1943.

Yale University Press, for Hoyt Alverson, *Mind in the Heart of Darkness*, 1978.

The maps of Botswana were prepared by Willem Terluin of Word Graphics of Stanford University. Word Graphics also prepared the photographic prints for the chapters on Botswana and the newspaper facsimiles of the *Botswana Daily News*. Copies of *Daily News* were made available by courtesy of the Library of the Hoover Institution, Stanford University. The Botswana photographs (except those incorporated in newspaper articles) are by James Lowell Gibbs, Jr.

We deeply appreciate the assistance of all. Without their help, we would not have been able to complete this work.

JOHN H. BARTON
JAMES LOWELL GIBBS, JR.
VICTOR HAO LI
JOHN HENRY MERRYMAN

March, 1983

SUMMARY OF CONTENTS

SUMMARY OF CONTENTS

PART V: POPULATION PLANNING

TABLE OF CONTENTS

TABLE OF CONTENTS

TABLE OF CONTENTS

TABLE OF CONTENTS

TABLE OF CONTENTS

TABLE OF CONTENTS

PART V: POPULATION PLANNING

TABLE OF CONTENTS

*

LAW IN
RADICALLY
DIFFERENT CULTURES

*

Part I

BACKGROUND

Chapter 1

INTRODUCTORY NOTE ON LAW

There is no end to definitions and to disputes about the nature of law. While we do not intend to get involved in all that here, it is important to adopt a working conception of law—a framework for comparison. The following excerpt identifies a number of variables that are useful in comparing legal systems within the West and that should be no less effective when comparing legal systems in radically different cultures.

John Henry Merryman, "The Convergence (and Divergence) of the Civil Law and the Common Law", in Mauro Cappelletti (ed.), New Perspectives for a Common Law of Europe. Boston: Sijthoff Publishing Co., 1978, pp. 222–227.

. . . Legal rules are what most people think of as law, and a good deal of the work of comparative lawyers is devoted to the description and evaluation of such rules. Much of the concern about divergence of legal systems is phrased in terms of rules, and much of the effort toward unification of law is rule-oriented. But there is a very important sense in which a focus on rules is superficial and misleading: superficial because rules literally lie on the surface of legal systems whose true dimensions are found elsewhere; misleading because we are led to assume that if rules are made to resemble each other something significant by way of *rapprochement* has been accomplished. . . .

. . . To speak of the convergence of legal systems implies that there are significant differences between them. A focus on rules limits the attention to only one kind of difference and equates "legal system" with "legal rules." A more adequate definition of a legal system, however, would include a number of additional components: legal extension, legal penetration, legal culture, legal structures, legal actors, and legal processes. These are highly interrelated concepts, and each of them is further related to the form and content of the rules of law in the system. Like other social systems, the legal system has boundaries, and its components are interrelated by an internal logic. Legal extension and legal penetration help to define the boundaries of the legal system; the legal culture is its internal logic; legal structures, actors and processes describe its component parts

1

and the way they function. These unfamiliar concepts require explanation.

In every society, much is left to custom and tradition, to religion, to informal negotiation and settlement, to social convention and peer influence, but the precise location of the boundaries between such non-legal matters and those of legal concern—the *extension* of the legal system—is unlikely to be always and precisely the same. The range of variation becomes particularly significant if we identify law with the official legal system, manned and operated by the state. The degree to which that system seeks to penetrate and control social life is often quite different from the extent to which it actually does so. For example, large numbers of Guatemalans, Brazilians, Ethiopians, and Congolese live much of their lives relatively free of any substantial contact with the official legal system, which actually applies with most force to an urban oligarchy and rapidly loses its power as one moves down the socio-economic scale and away from the major cities. In a substantial number of such nations the paper legal system will look much like that of France or Spain or Italy, or of England or the United States. But if one looks at the actual role of law in the lives of important elements of the population—the *penetration* of the legal system—the resemblance is only superficial. Thus along two dimensions, the aspects of social life that the law proposes to affect and the extent to which it actually does so, the scale of divergence of legal extension and legal penetration between societies can be, and often is, substantial. Both the social reach and the social grasp of the law are important variables.

By legal *culture* is meant those historically conditioned, deeply rooted attitudes about the nature of law and about the proper structure and operation of a legal system that are at large in the society. Law is, among other things, an expression of the culture; ideas about law are part of the intellectual history of a people. Such ideas are very powerful; they limit and direct thinking about law, and in this way they profoundly affect the composition and operation of the legal system. A prominent example is found in the quite different prevailing views of the role of judges in the Civil Law and Common Law, but there are many others: the effects of the separate existence of courts of law and of equity during the formative period of the Common Law; the conflict in pre-Revoluntionary France between the King and the provincial *parlements*; the role of the civil jury in the Common Law; the resistance to Roman law influences in England during the formative period of the Common Law; the list is endless. Differences in modern legal systems can often be explained only by reference to such historical-cultural influences, which have great contemporary power.

Courts, legislatures, administrative agencies, law schools and bar associations are all familiar examples of legal *structures*. They are the composite units that do the work of the system, and their composition and attributes vary widely among legal systems; one can, for example, contrast the German system of a plurality of federal Supreme Courts and the unified Supreme Court of the United States. Legal *actors* refers to the professional roles played by participants in the system: advocates, notaries, police, judges, administrative officials, legal scholars, etc. Here again there are substantial areas of divergence: consider the Civil Law notary and instructing judge, who have no counterparts in the Common Law. Legal processes refers to legislative and administrative action, judicial proceedings, the private ordering of legal relations, and legal education. Here the range of divergence is illustrated by contrasting criminal proceedings in English and Italian courts, or legal education in, say, Belgium and New Zealand.

Each of these aspects of the legal system is a potential dimension of convergence and divergence. Each is, in a very important way, more fundamental than rules of law to a discussion of the *rapprochement* of the Civil Law and Common Law. The point can be illustrated by a metaphor: let the complex of legal structures, actors, and processes be thought of as the machinery of the law—as the law machine. Certain kinds of rules, the kind Professor Hart calls "primary rules of obligation," are commonly the focus of rule-centered legal study. A typical civil code is made up primarily of such rules, which can be thought of as statements of demand on the law machine. An example of such a rule is Article 1382 of the Code Napoléon, to the effect that one who injures another is liable for compensation. Thus, if X unjustifiably injures Y (the "if" part of the rule), it should follow that Y will be compensated (the "then" part of the rule).

However, the result does not necessarily follow. Some legal work must be done in order to bring it about. The law machine must be set into operation, in this case by Y bringing the appropriate action against X in the appropriate French court. Eventually, if the machine functions properly, an official judgment will be issued to the effect that X owes Y a certain amount of money as compensation. If X does not pay, Y can make a further demand on the law machine to have X's property seized and sold in order to satisfy the judgment. Again, if the machine functions properly (and if X has property within the court's jurisdiction that can be seized and sold for this purpose), Y may be paid.

It is important that the society have appropriate primary rules of obligation, appropriate in the sense that they are directed toward controlling undesirable social behavior and encouraging people to do what is socially beneficial. The determination of what kinds of conduct to encourage and what kinds to discourage is a very complicated and often controversial matter. But, fascinating as such questions are, they are not truly *legal* questions. They are, instead, primarily social, economic and political questions. For example, the question whether, as a matter of legislative policy, there should be a rule requiring X to compensate Y if X damages Y's property is only incidentally a legal question. The same is true of most other primary rules of law.

What is "legal" about a primary legal rule is that it assumes, or calls into play, the law machine. It is the law machine that does the legal work for the society, that consumes the resources, that determines how and to what extent the precept stated in the primary rule shall be translated into social consequences. The primary legal rule is basically a statement of a desired social outcome. The law machine is the mechanism for bringing it about. When we study primary legal rules we are studying what society asks. The mere request will of course affect social behavior to some extent (although we know very little about the nature and intensity of that effect). But if we are really interested in knowing something about the legal system in any society we quickly have to expand our vision to include the law machine—the complex of legal structures, actors and processes. We will not get very far in that effort by studying merely the rules of law.

There clearly are important interrelationships in any society between the extension and penetration of the law, the legal culture, the law machine, and the rules of law. Still, it takes little empirical investigation to establish that the legal rules in two societies can look very much alike without insuring that other dimensions of the legal order are equivalent to each other. It may be that similar primary rules exercise (or symbolize) a deeper converging influence, but it is equally possible that the same words have totally dissimilar functional meanings in the two systems. . . .

NOTE

As we proceed in this course, try to keep these variables in mind. What do the materials suggest are the significant differences among the four legal systems in legal extension; in legal penetration; in legal culture; in legal institutions, actors and processes; in primary legal rules? Should other variables be added to the list in order to provide an adequate framework for comparison of the legal systems in radically different cultures?

Chapter 2

INTRODUCTORY NOTE ON WESTERN CULTURE AND WESTERN LAW

Western culture is too familiar to teacher and student alike to require (or to permit) brief description, and none will be attempted here. It is the dominant culture in Europe, the USSR, the Anglo-American world, and Latin America. As everyone knows, legal systems within this culture area vary a good deal from one to another, and "comparative law" courses in which legal systems within the West are compared with each other are commonly taught in the law schools. In this course, however, we treat the West as a single culture area which includes the European civil law and the Anglo-American common law as well as the socialist law of the USSR and Cuba and the capitalist law of the U.S.A. and, for example, Argentina. The point is amplified in the following excerpt.

John Henry Merryman, The Civil Law Tradition: An Introduction to the Legal Systems of Western Europe and Latin America, Stanford, California: Stanford University Press, 1969, pp. 1–5.

National legal systems are frequently classified into groups or families. Thus the legal systems of England, New Zealand, California, and New York are called "common law" systems, and there are good reasons to group them together in this way. But it is inaccurate to suggest that they have identical legal institutions, processes, and rules. On the contrary, there is great diversity among them, not only in their substantive rules of law, but also in their institutions and processes.

Similarly, France, Germany, Italy, and Switzerland have their own legal systems, as do Argentina, Brazil, and Chile. It is true that they are all frequently spoken of as "civil law" nations, and we will try in this book to explain why it makes sense to group them together in this way. But it is important to recognize that there are great differences between the operating legal systems in these countries. They have quite different legal rules, legal procedures, and legal institutions. Even in Eastern Europe, despite the strong forces tending to produce uniformity within the Soviet sphere of influence, a similar, if less pronounced, diversity exists. Although these nations are commonly lumped together as "socialist law" nations, there is a great deal of variation among them, even in fundamental matters. . . . Such differences in legal systems are reflections of the fact that for several centuries the world has been divided up into individual states, under intellectual conditions that have emphasized the importance of state sovereignty and encouraged a nationalistic emphasis on national characteristics and traditions. In this sense, there is no such thing as

5

the civil law system, *the* common law system, or *the* socialist law system. Rather, there are many different legal systems within each of these three groups or families of legal systems. But the fact that different legal systems are grouped together under such a rubric as "civil law," for example, indicates that they have something in common, something that distinguishes them from legal systems classified as "common law" or "socialist law." . . .

Of the great variety of living legal traditions, the three mentioned above are of particular interest because they are in force in powerful, technologically advanced nations and because they have been exported, with greater or less effect, to other parts of the world. Of the three, the civil law tradition is both the oldest and the most widely distributed. The traditional date of its origin is 450 B.C., the supposed date of publication of the XII Tables in Rome. It is today the dominant legal tradition in most of Western Europe, all of Central and South America, many parts of Asia and Africa, and even a few enclaves in the common law world (Louisiana, Quebec, and Puerto Rico). It was, until recently, the dominant legal tradition in most of the countries of Eastern Europe (including the Soviet Union), which have since become socialist law countries. . . .

The date commonly used to mark the beginning of the common law tradition is A.D. 1066, when the Normans defeated the defending natives at Hastings and conquered England. If we accept that date, the common law tradition is slightly over 900 years old. It is sobering to recall that when the *Corpus Juris Civilis* of Justinian was published in Constantinople in A.D. 533, the civil law tradition, of which it is an important part, was already older than the common law is today. As a result of the remarkable expansion and development of the British Empire during the age of colonialism and empire, however, the common law was very widely distributed. It is today the legal tradition in force in Great Britain, Ireland, the United States, Canada, Australia, and New Zealand, and has had substantial influence on the law of many nations in Asia and Africa.

The socialist law tradition is generally said to have originated at the time of the October Revolution. Before that event, the dominant legal tradition in the Russian Empire was the civil law. One intention of the Soviet revolutionaries was to abolish the burgeois civil law system and substitute a new socialist legal order. The actual effect of their reform was to impose certain principles of socialist ideology on existing civil law systems and on the civil law tradition. Under the influence of the Soviet Union and Marxist thought, similar legal changes have taken place in those states of Eastern Europe (and in other countries, such as Cuba) that were parts of the civil law tradition before they became socialist states. The result is a young, vigorous legal tradition that still displays its essentially hybrid nature.

The socialist attitude is that all law is an instrument of economic and social policy, and that the common law and civil law traditions basically reflect a capitalistic, bourgeois, imperialist, exploitative society, economy, and government. Socialists see our legal system as incorporating and perpetuating a set of goals and ideals that they regard as socially and economically unjust. At the same time, the common law appears to a Soviet lawyer to be unsystematic and undeveloped, in comparison with carefully drawn Soviet legislation that builds on the civil law tradition of system and of order. Finally, to a socialist lawyer, both the civil law and common law traditions are subject to criticism because they embody but do not clearly state their ideologies. Such a lawyer sees our legal systems as devices by which bourgeois ideals are concealed in ostensibly neutral legal forms, which are then used to exploit the proletariat.

The fact that these three legal traditions are all of European origin should give us pause. There are, of course, many other legal traditions in today's world, and new ones are forming. The dominance of the three traditions of which we have spoken is the direct result of Western European imperialism in earlier centuries and Soviet imperialism in this century (just as the dominance of Roman law in an earlier age was a product of Roman imperialism). . . .

NOTE

We assume that Western law is an integral expression or part of Western culture and that it differs from law outside the West. Stated another way, our basic assumption is that some important differences in legal systems (as we have defined them) are related to cultural differences. One of our purposes in this course is, accordingly, to learn what is Western about Western law. (It may surprise you to know that this is a relatively novel inquiry; little work appears to have been done on the topic.) Here are a few preliminary speculations:

Western Law, Modern Law, Legal Evolution, and Legal Development. We must first deal with a complication that is caused by evolutionary theories of law. Such theories treat traditional legal systems as earlier stages in legal development, which one can expect to be followed by emergence into modern systems that look like contemporary common law, civil law, or socialist law systems. While it is comforting to think in this way that one's own legal system is advanced and others are backward or primitive, an alternative possibility is that they are merely different. Although they will change over time, there is no assurance that the outcome will resemble what we now think of as modern legal systems in the West. Still, there may be a tendency toward parallel movements in societies, and thus in legal systems. Maine's hypothesis of a movement of "progressive societies" from "status to contract" (Sir Henry Sumner Maine, Ancient Law, London: John Murray, 1897, 16th ed., p. 170) has some validity (particularly with respect to family law and the law of property) in Western capitalist societies and in colonial areas under their dominance. There is, however, no convincing evidence that a similar evolution would take place in a non-Western system insulated against Western influence. It may be sounder to assume that different cultures may evolve in different directions and that the notion of a uniform evolutionary direction of the sort implied by the use of such terms as "modern" or "developed" is an unproved assumption.

Progress. The idea of progress receives significant expression in Western law. "Progress," "development," "modernization," and "law reform" are interrelated concepts that were at one time peculiar to Western culture, although they have been widely exported in the last century and a half. The idea of progress refers to the notion that society is somehow moving toward a better state of earthly affairs or, in the alternative, that the possibility of continuous improvement in the social condition is there if we only think clearly and manage things properly. We are so habituated in one or the other form of this attitude that we seldom question it. It is worth recalling, however, that the progressive credo is a belief—a faith ultimately not subject to empirical verification. In earlier times it appears to have been much less widely held. Bury (John Bury, The Idea of Progress, London: Macmillan, 1920) places its origins in the 17th century, with Jean Bodin and Francis Bacon. By the time of Voltaire and the Age of Reason it had become embedded in Western thought. Indeed, the Age of Reason is itself a peculiarly progress-permeated notion. Reason was not a modern invention, but in the medieval world its principal function was to demonstrate the truth of revealed knowledge, to justify the state of man and society. What was new about the Age of Reason was its faith in reason as an agent of progress.

During the 19th century an evolutionary view of progress became dominant, in part as a reaction to the unfulfilled optimism of the French Revolution, fueled by the thought of Hegel, Marx and Darwin. Carl Becker * has summarized the difference: ". . . whereas the eighteenth century held that man can by taking thought add a cubit to his stature, the nineteenth century held that a cubit was to be added to his stature whether he took thought or not." In the current century, at least in the U.S., there has been a strong return to the 18th century view: "can-do," "progress is our most important product," planning, social engineering and all that. It is this confidence in progress that underlies much Western (and particularly American) legal thought: a curious mixture of belief in the inevitability of social betterment and in the special ability of lawyers to hasten and direct the process.

This attitude receives its most characteristic expression in law reform. "Tinkering," "following" and "leading" sum up three kinds of law reform. Tinkering accepts the existing system, seeks to keep it operating, and makes occasional adjustments to improve its efficiency—e.g. by providing more judges when the judicial backlog seems unmanageable. "Following" refers to the sort of law reform intended to adjust the legal system to social change—to the rise of a credit economy, for example. "Leading" law reform, on the contrary, uses law to change society. Most people, when they think of law reform, refer to some mixture of all three kinds, but for many the emphasis has been on leading law reform. Law, properly employed, is for them an instrument of development, not merely a response to it. Such a view of law reform obviously derives support from the idea of progress; one must envision the possibility of achieving a better society in order to propose specific measures for attaining it—to lead the way to progress through law reform.

* Carl Becker, "Progress," 12 Encyclopedia of the Social Sciences 495, 1934.

Optimism of this kind is a necessary premise of much of the work of legislatures, executives, administrative agencies and courts. The amount of "leading" law reform activity in the West in the past two centuries is enormous. An early example is the Constitution of the United States, a law reform that had extraordinary influence, establishing a style of constitution-making later emulated in many parts of the world. The constitutions of Latin American nations that achieved independence in the 19th century, and that frequently used the U. S. Constitution as a model, are further early examples. The post-revolutionary legislation in France, culminating in the great French codes; the law reform movement in England in the early 19th century; the establishment of the Italian state in the mid-19th century and the adoption of the Italian codes; the unification of Germany under Bismarck, and the adoption of the German codes; the institutionalization of law reform in the United States by the establishment of law revision commissions in New York, California, and other states; the similar establishment of the Law Commission in England; all these are specific examples of significant law reform activity. If one adds to this the staggering increase in the total volume of reformist legislation emanating from international, national, state and local legislative bodies, and includes the body of administrative legislation and of "law-making" judicial activity, the total begins to look impressive. It is plausible to characterize Western societies as engaged in continuous, extensive, some might say hyperactive law reform.

Legalism. Legalism is the belief (and practice) that law should be the principal organizing framework of government and society. Legalism in this sense is the rough equivalent of "the rule of law," of "the principle of legality," of what the Germans call the Rechtstaat, of "due process of law." From this point of view the United States is notoriously legalistic, as commentators have never tired of pointing out since early in the 19th century; there is a tendency, which may be irreversible, to make an increasing range of governmental and social processes conform to a legal model. Although the United States is generally considered an extreme case of legalism, other Western legal systems certainly share this characteristic. A contrast is often struck with Chinese law, with a specific reference to the historical debate between the Confucionists and the Legalists. In a quite different but related sense legalism can refer to the disposition among members of a society to use law as a way of resolving disputes. Here again we are told that the West is legalistic (i.e. litigious) while other cultures, such as those of China, Japan and Korea, are much less inclined toward litigation.

Secularism. Although there have been important religious influences on Western law (particularly Christian and Jewish), it has been characterized since the Reformation by the ideal, if not always the practice, of secularism: a separation of the law from religious doctrine and religious institutions. Canon law, once a powerful and vital force, is no longer a source of law; it has diminished to a status like that of the internal regulations of a labor union or the by-laws of a corporation. In other legal cultures, however, religion and law are much more closely related to each other. This is obviously so of Islamic law, Hindu law, Buddhist law, Jewish law, and is also true of a number of other traditional legal cultures.

One form the secular-religious law distinction can take concerns the relative importance of purportedly immutable principles or of a body of revealed law not subject to human variation. The potential impact of strict immutability on law-making and on the interpretation of laws is of course substantial. In a thoroughly secular legal system law can be changed by mortals and interpretation can be governed by utilitarian or other temporal considerations. Even in secular Western systems, however, some appetite for a set of fundamental, immutable principles continues to exist, whether residing in a constitution or in general principles of law somehow found to govern the activity of the legal system. Still, the distinction between mutable and immutable laws has some importance when we compare Western with Islamic law.

Sovereignty and Statism. The modern state is a Western invention, and the classical system of international law, in which the subjects are sovereign states, is also Western. The ideas of the state and of sovereignty also have an internal face. All persons within the state are subject to the law of that state. A related proposition is that the state and the individual are the only sources of law. This attitude reached a climax with the French revolution, one of whose objectives was to abolish the law-making and law administering powers of guilds, corporations, local autonomies of various kinds, and other so-called "intermediate associations." Another objective was to deprive the Church of law-making power (compare secularism). From a very messy late feudal society in which law-making and law-administering were distributed among a wide variety of persons and agencies at a wide variety of levels and locations within and outside the state, the legal universe was simplified into one occupied by only two actors: the individual and the state. In the French legal system after the revolution those ideas received direct expression in a legal system that made no provision for corporations or other "intermediate associations" (such as labor unions, foundations, etc.), an extreme posture that was soon relaxed to permit their legal existence and to give legal effect to their "legal acts." One way to perceive the French revolutionary reform is as a rather drastic attempt to introduce a "common law" for all Frenchmen, a development that had occurred more gradually in England over a much longer period of time.

Rights, Duties, and Individualism. The idea is that Western law is peculiarly imbued with a concern for the *rights* of *individuals*. By "rights" is meant not only constitutionally protected rights of free speech, due process of law, and the like, but also ordinary "subjective rights" of the sort that grow out of property, contract and tort. By contrast, it is suggested that in other legal systems—particularly those in Asia—the emphasis is on duties. The legal apparatus exists to ensure that the individual's *duties* are understood and performed. Thus in traditional Chinese law, it is said, there was little or no provision for civil lawsuits. The legal apparatus existed as a means of expressing and enforcing the will of the Emperor. Private law, in other words, is much more highly developed in the West than in some other cultures, where all, or most, law is public law.

In socialist nations, particularly in the Soviet Union, where it is a fundamental principle that none of the means of production, including land, may be privately owned, the legal system is less concerned with the recognition and enforcement of private rights than in bourgeois systems. Still, there is substantial private litigation in Soviet courts, and the Soviet constitution speaks at length about individual rights.   In other socialist nations in East Europe, where the prohibition against private ownership of the means of production is less rigorous (there is even a constitutional guarantee of the right to own land in Yugoslavia, for example) the applicability of this generalization about rights, duties, and individualism needs less qualification than it might require in the Soviet Union itself.

The Western emphasis on the protection and enforcement of private rights, when contrasted with the relative absence of such an emphasis in other cultures, suggests a possible relation to individualism and to assumptions about equality.   Thus it has been suggested that in certain obviously superior cultures, such as the ancient Greek and the traditional Chinese, it was easy to take the view that Greeks and Chinese were clearly superior to other people. The notion of equality of human beings and of the worth of the individual would naturally be rejected, if it arose.   According to this view of matters, the notion of individual rights appeared in Roman law in part becaue the Romans were aware of the relative superiority of Greek culture.   As cultural inferiors, it was in their interest to develop the notion of individual rights and of equality.   Nietsche expressed similar ideas.

In the Western tradition, the emphasis is strongly on individuals as the bearers of legal rights and duties.   This emphasis reached a crescendo at the time of the American and French revolutions, and as a consequence groups still today can be made the bearers of such rights and duties in Western law only by treating them as though they are individuals.   For this purpose we speak of a corporation as a "legal person."   As a legal person, the corporation can enter contracts, own property and commit torts.   A corporation can also commit some, but not all, crimes.   Can you understand why?

Logically Formal Rationality.   Max Weber identified a style of a legal thought that he called "logically formal rationality" as uniquely Western.   It is described in the following excerpt:

Max Rheinstein, Introduction, in Max Weber on Law in Economy and Society. Cambridge: Harvard University Press, 1954, p. xlviii.

In the field of law the two basic activities are those of creating law and of finding the law once created. With respect to both, Weber establishes two methodological categories: they can be irrational or rational. Also, law making and law finding can proceed rationally or irrationally either with respect to formal or to substantive criteria.

Law makers and law finders proceed in a formally irrational manner in so far as they are guided by means which are beyond the control of reason, such as an oracle, a prophetic revelation, or an ordeal.

Irrationality of the substantive kind exists in so far as law makers or law finders fail to be guided by general norms and proceed either in pure arbitrariness or jump to their conclusions in a completely casuistic manner upon the basis of emotional evaluations of every single case. This ideal type which has no counterpart in reality is approximated by the tyrant as well as the khadi, i.e, the Moslem judge who sits in the market place and, at least seemingly, renders his decisions without any reference to rules or norms but in what appears to be a completely free evaluation of the particular merits of every single case. The type would also be approximated by that kind of wise man who, ably applying the Solomonic hunch, would seem to represent the ideal of the German school of free law or of the American realists.

Rational on the other hand are the activities of law makers and law finders in so far as they are guided by rational considerations, which, in turn, can again be of the substantive or the formal kind.

Substantively rational are law makers or finders in so far as they consciously follow (more or less) clearly conceived and articulated general principles of some kind. These principles may be those of a religion, or a system of ethical thought, or of a notion of *raison d'état*, or power policy planfully formulated and conceived. Substantively rational, for instance, is Mohammedan law in so far as its "makers and finders have been trying to implement the religious thought and commands of the Prophet; substantively rational is Soviet law is so far as it is conceived as a means to bring about, to preserve, and to elaborate the social system of the Communist ideology; substantively rational, too, is any law which a conqueror imposes upon a subject population as a means of maintaining and strengthening his rule, or the law by means of which a ruling nation tries to "elevate" the population of a backward territory to its own, "higher" level of civilization.

Finally, the methods of law making and law finding may be rational not in a substantive but in a formal way. Formally rational is a law in so far as significance in both substantive law and procedure is ascribed exclusively to operative facts which are determined not from case to case but in a generically determined manner. Again, such formal rationality may be of two different kinds. Those facts which are to be significant in the determination of legal relationships, especially of rights and duties, may be of a purely extrinsic character: a contract is binding or not depending on whether or not it has been reduced to writing, or whether a seal has been employed, or whether certain formulary words have been used; whether or not a defendant has been validly summoned depends on whether or not certain visible or audible acts have been performed under exact observance of clearly prescribed formalities such as oral communication of the summons before a certain number of witnesses, or personal delivery of a formulary writing by a certain public official, and so on. Whether or not an interest in a piece of land has been effectively conveyed depends upon whether or not a clod of earth or some other symbol of the land or a formalized instrument in writing has been delivered in a particular manner, for instance on the very land itself, or before a judge, or in the presence of witnesses, and so on.

Lastly, law making and law finding can be logically rational in so far as they proceed upon the basis of generic rules which neither are determined by any religious, ethical, political, or other system of ideology, nor regard as relevant the observance of formalized acts observable by the senses, but are formulated by the use of generic concepts of an abstract character. In Weber's own words, law making and law finding are formally rational in the logical manner in so far as "the legally relevant facts are determined in a process of logical interpretation of meaning and as fixed legal concepts are thus created and applied in the form of strictly abstract rules." The way in which the term "logically formal rationality" is applied later on makes it clear that by it Weber means exactly that method of legal thought which in modern jurisprudence has become known as "jurisprudence of concepts" or "conceptual jurisprudence (*Begriffsjurisprudenz*)," and which has been so ardently attacked by the New Jurisprudence of Free Law and Jurisprudence of Interests in Germany, by Gény and Lambert in France, and by Sociological Jurists and Realists in America.

To Weber this kind of legal thought appears as a peculiar product of Western civilization and one which cannot be found in other legal systems, especially those of the Orient. . . .

NOTE

One potential difficulty with Weber's ideas is his tendency to equate "Western" with "Capitalist." Weber was, however, familiar with Marx and was himself the author of an important work on capitalism: The Protestant Ethic and The Spirit of Capitalism. The appropriate distinctions were known to him, although one occasionally gets the impression in reading his examples and arguments that he has bourgeois capitalist legal systems in mind when describing categories of legal thought typical of the West. As it happens, however, socialist lawyers in the West habitually employ patterns of legal thought indistinguishable from those identified by Weber as "logically formal rationality," so the distinction has no great importance.

Weber's "logically formal rationality," is a style of legal reasoning. To understand it, we need to look at all the varieties he described. Here is the list:

1. Formally irrational. e.g., oracle, ordeal, flipping a coin.

2. Substantively irrational. Determination not based on principle. e.g., so-called "qadi justice."

3. Substantively rational. Decision consciously executing policy principle. e.g., banning DES in beef because of health hazard.

4. Formally rational. Decision employing principle abstracted from (although at some level probably justifiable by) policy.

  a. "Extrinsic" (a better word would be "formalistic," but this creates confusion with "formal") e.g., requirements of form for certain legal acts (that a contract or a will must be in writing).

  b. Logical. Decision based on systematic concepts and principles that are part of a coherent set of legal propositions. In short, conceptual legal reasoning. It is possible, indeed probable, that the results obtained in concrete cases by employing substantively rational methods will often differ from those reached using formally rational methods. Thus a legally correct (i.e. formally rational) result in a case may appear to be socially undesirable (i.e., it may seem to be substantively irrational).

As the text states, there has been a reaction against the extremes of conceptualism in Western law. Still, it is impossible to think at all without concepts; it is the extreme to which conceptualism was taken in 19th century German legal thought that was remarkable. In the U.S. since the end of the 19th century two important counter-influences have been sociological jurisprudence (a form of substantively rational reasoning of which Roscoe Pound was the leading figure) and legal realism (a devastating attack on conceptualism by a group of scholars, inspired in part by Holmes, including among others Thurman Arnold, Carl Llewellyn, Leon Green and J. W. Bingham of Stanford).

Progress, legalism, secularism, sovereignty, individualism and logically formal rationality probably are not exclusive attributes of Western law. Some, perhaps all, of them may occur in the legal systems of other cultures, and it is possible that what is truly Western about Western law is the peculiar combination of these attributes—the cultural profile of our law—when compared with law in other cultures. Whether that is so, and whether there are other fundamental attributes of legal systems, Western or other, to add to this list, are questions we should know a good deal more about at the end of this course.

Despite a few legal relics of its Spanish history (principally community property), California falls within the Anglo-American Common Law component of the Western legal tradition, as do all the states except Louisiana and Puerto Rico. California was chosen because we treat Western law as the bench mark against which the others are to be compared. For this purpose it is important that the Western example be as familiar to us, and to the students in the course, as possible. That justifies the choice of the United States, but our federal structure makes it necessary to turn to state law on most questions. Since we had to choose a state, California seemed a reasonable choice for a course prepared and, at least initially, taught in a California university. That consideration aside, California is sufficiently representative of American society to be a reasonable choice and sufficiently large and complex to be interesting.

Here are some basic facts about California. It is the third largest state (after Alaska and Texas), with an area of 158,693 square miles, and has the largest population of all the states—23,773,000 in 1980—roughly 10% of the population of the United States. Over 92% of the population live in metropolitan areas (though California is agriculturally the most productive of all the states). The per capita personal income in 1980 was $10,856 (the national figure was $9,458) and the gross state product per capita was $13,100 (the gross national product per capita was $11,350).

As of 1981, California had 335 trial and 14 appellate courts whose benches were occupied by 1026 trial and 66 appellate judges. (These figures do not include the federal district courts and judges in California). As of 1981 there were 76,000 lawyers in the state. This works out to approximately one trial judge for every 71,000 and one lawyer for every 312 persons (or about 1.4 trial judges and 320 lawyers per 100,000 population).

SUGGESTED READING

Bury, John, The Idea of Progress, London: Macmillan, 1920.

Carlyle, Robert W., and Carlyle, A. J., A History of Medieval Political Theory in the West, New York: Barnes & Noble, 1903–1906.

Cohen, Jerome Alan, Chinese Mediation on the Eve of Modernization, 54 Calif.L.Rev. 1201, 1966.

Coulson, N. J., Islamic Law, in J. Duncan M. Derrett, An Introduction to Legal Systems 54, 1968.

David, René and Brierly, John E. C., Major Legal Systems in the World Today, London: Sweet & Maxwell, 1978.

Ehrmann, Henry W., Comparative Legal Cultures, Englewood Cliffs, New Jersey: Prentis Hall, 1976.

Hahm, Pyong-Choon, The Korean Political Tradition and Law, Seoul, Korea: Hollym, 1976.

Stein, Peter and Shand, John, Legal Values in Western Society, Edinburgh: Edinburgh University Press, 1974.

Maine, Henry Sumner, Ancient Law, London: John Murray (16th ed.), 1897.

McAleavy, H., Chinese Law, in J. Duncan M. Derrett, An Introduction to Legal Systems 105, 1968.

Merryman, John Henry, The Civil Law Tradition, Stanford: Stanford University Press, 1969.

Merryman, John Henry, Comparative Law and Social Change: On the Origins, Style, Decline and Revival of the Law and Development Movement, 25 American Journal of Comparative Law 457, 1977.

Shklar, Judith N., Legalism, Cambridge: Harvard University Press, 1964.

Weber, Max, Max Weber on Law in Economy and Society (Max Rheinstein, ed.) (2d Ed.), Cambridge: Harvard University Press, 1954.

Chapter 3

INTRODUCTORY NOTE ON EGYPT
AND EGYPTIAN LAW

There are three great religious law traditions, Hinduism, Islam, and Judaism; of these, we have chosen Islam. Within Islam, Egypt has long been a cultural center and has also been particularly prominent in the tradition's intellectual response to the Western challenge. But Egypt also represents an effort to adapt continental European ("civil") law to the needs of a developing nation. Moreover, Egypt is quite unlike our other developing nations. Although it faces social pressures like the others—a population of about 40 million, with a per capita income of about $480 (1979), still 55% rural (1980) but with great rural-urban migration—its response is quite different. Its government tends to rely upon bureaucracy rather than legal, political, or ideological motivations. At the same time, in spite of a great deal of corruption, the bureaucracy follows elaborate legal rules. And, most important, the nation has focused great resources on education.

Egypt is a narrow crowded ribbon of people concentrated along the Nile. For most of the last two millenia, it has been ruled from abroad: by the Roman empire, by various Islamic empires, by the Ottoman empire, and by the British government. Only with the Naguib/Nasser revolution of 1952 did it gain real independence—but at a major cost to the legal and political institutions that had been evolving during the 19th and 20th centuries. Each of these phases has brought its own law; this introductory note will provide brief background on three of the phases: the Islamic phase, the 19th and 20th century reform and modernization phase, and the contemporary post-revolutionary phase.

A. ISLAM AND ISLAMIC LAW

NOTE

Muhammed was a merchant in Mecca, a trading city in what is now Saudi Arabia. During his thirties, he became interested in virtuous living and meditated extensively. Around the age of forty, following visions during these meditations, he became a prophet and called first his wife and friends and later a broader community to monotheism. There were Christian and Jewish communities in the Arab region, but the Arab communities generally practiced a somewhat superstitious, polytheistic paganism—it is to these last communities that Muhammed primarily directed his mission.

Muhammed's preaching divided the city and led to his persecution. About ten years after his first public preaching, he led a group of his followers to Medina, a city more friendly to his views. (This trip in 622, the Hejira, is the beginning of the Islamic calendar [1]). There, Muhammed played a role

---

1. Thus, A.H. 0 = AD 622. Comparison of later dates, however, is complicated by the fact that the Islamic calendar uses a 354/355 day year, with an elaborate leap year system.

16

in settling disputes between Jews and Arabs, and the new religious community provided a framework for "political" leadership as well as "religious" leadership, as the community of believers, the *umma*, began to replace previous tribal organizing principles. Reflecting a combination of factors, religious, economic, and tribal, the new community organized a series of raids against Mecca, leading by 630 to the occupation of Mecca itself. Many other regions submitted voluntarily.

On Muhammed's death in 632, there was debate whether there should be another leader or whether the community should instead emphasize the need for each individual to obey God. Most chose the former alternative and Abu-Bakr, another merchant who had been Muhammed's close friend and lieutenant, became the first Caliph, or leader. The new leadership supported the spread of Muhammed's message, both by sending out preachers and by more military means. By 644, most of the fertile crescent, Egypt, and Iran had been conquered. Little more than a century later, Islamic power extended from Spain and Morocco in the West to Afghanistan and Pakistan in the East.

The spread of Islam was not as straightforward as is commonly assumed in the West. Within 25 years of Muhammed's death, there was a division within the *umma* over the choice of Caliph; those who favored Ali, the Prophet's first cousin and son-in-law, separated and became one of the two major branches of Islam, the *Shiite* branch, which is still practiced in Iran and certain areas of the southern Arabian peninsula. The more orthodox branch, the *Sunni* branch, is followed in most of the remainder of the Muslim world, including Egypt. And Islam was itself conquered several times, most notably by the Turks from Central Asia, who established what evolved into the Ottoman empire, centered in Istanbul.

The invasions and the frequent leadership struggles produced a world in which the behavior of the leaders frequently deviated far from the strict norms of Islam. But Islam remained through the catastrophes and produced one of the major intellectual and cultural flowerings of history. Poetry and the arts flourished. Islamic scholars translated the philosophical works of ancient Greece, commented on them, and preserved them to give to the West during the Crusades. Astronomy, medicine, and mathematics were advanced far beyond anything in the Western world. From era to era, the focus of this culture moved over different parts of the Islamic world; but starting around the year 1000, Egypt was one of the leading centers, possessing the Al Azhar university and major libraries.

The religion itself is a call to reform and to behavior far above the standards that had prevailed among the Arab tribes. There is a strong emphasis on individual responsibility before God, who is absolutely one and absolutely transcendent. He is merciful and expects his followers to be merciful. He is also just and expects his followers to keep his law. The Quran, the sayings of the Prophet, placed in a collected form shortly after Muhammed's death, emphasizes the last judgment, the delights of the saved and the sufferings of the damned.

There is some variation in detail, but the central demands placed upon the believer are simple to define, if not to execute. The "five pillars" are to profess the faith ("There is no God but God, and Muhammed is his prophet,") to pray at the specified times and in the specified ways, to fast during the month of Ramadan, to give alms to the poor, and to make the pilgrimage to Mecca. Some authors would add the duties to abstain from wine and to participate in the spread of the faith as through the *jihad*, the holy war. But many would also emphasize sincerity, loyalty, and gratefulness to one's neighbors and the care of the poor and unfortunate. The Quran is filled with pleadings to remedy the injustices of society. And for many Muslim individuals, piety appears to be the central personal theme. Sufiism, an Islamic tradition emphasizing mysticism and personal religious experience, has long had great popular appeal in Egypt.

There are many themes in the associated philosophy and culture; three deserve special emphasis. The first is the strong sense of individual moral responsibility—so strong that, as will be seen, an individual's oath constituted a major form of legal proof. Perhaps as a natural result of this strong sense of responsibility and of the feelings between people facing the responsibility together, there is a fierce sense of human equality. There is no priesthood and practically no hierarchy—the *ulema* (or Ayatollah in Iran) does have respect, particularly in rural regions, but ideally gains it from his wisdom rather than from any formal authority. The closely related sense of equality, which extends to women only as a limited improvement on previous Arab practice, is almost certainly one of the factors explaining Islam's current missionary success. Second, there is a sense of the arbitrariness of the will of God. The world—and the law—are as they are because God chose arbitrarily to make them that way. Although there was a philosophical school that argued in Graeco-Christian fashion that God could do only what was reasonable, this was only a small heterodox position. The orthodox position, clearly related to a sense of God's utter transcendence, is that law, as revealed through the Prophet, is arbitrary. It is thus man's task to follow this law and not to impose his own human analysis, picking among, rationalizing, and modifying God's commands. Third, since God is so great, the world is practically unreal in comparison. Thus, at least in some areas, it does not matter so much if earthly realities do not measure up to the divine ideal. For example, God does not ask the impossible and it is better that a political government pass a frankly pagan law than that the divine law be contaminated by pagan additions.

The law which was believed revealed was the *sharia*. This revelation includes a wide variety of religious, moral, and social principles, along with principles that a Westerner would recognize as legal. All were part of the *sharia*. The law applied to the *umma*, the community of believers. Other religious communities were tolerated in the areas conquered by Islam and permitted to apply their own laws to govern their internal relations. Thus, the fundamental jurisdictional principle was not territorial, as in contemporary Western law, but personal.

Seyyed Nasr, Ideals and Realities of Islam, New York: Frederick A. Praeger, 1966, pp. 93–94, 96.

The *Shari'ah* is the Divine Law by virtue of accepting which a person becomes a Muslim. Only he who accepts the injunctions of the *Shari'ah* as binding upon him is a Muslim although he may not be able to realize all of its teachings or follow all of its commands in life. The *Shari'ah* is the ideal pattern for the individual's life and the Law which binds the Muslim people into a single community. It is the embodiment of the Divine Will in terms of specific teachings whose acceptance and application guarantees man a harmonious life in this world and felicity in the hereafter. . . .

The *Shari'ah* is Divine Law, in the sense that it is the concrete embodiment of the Divine Will according to which man should live in both his private and social life. In every religion the Divine Will manifests itself in one way or other and the moral and spiritual injunctions of each religion are of Divine origin. But in Islam the embodiment of the Divine Will is not a set only of general teachings but of concrete ones. Not only is man told to be charitable, humble or just, but how to be so in particular instances of life. The *Shari'ah* contains the injunctions of the Divine Will as applied to every situation in life. It is the Law according to which God wants a Muslim to live. It is therefore the guide of human action and encompasses every facet of human life. By living according to the *Shari'ah* man places his whole existence in God's "hand". The *Shari'ah* by considering every aspect of human action thus sanctifies the whole of life and gives a religious significance to what may appear as the most mundane of activities. . . .

Such a Law is the blue print of the ideal human life. It is a transcendent law which is at the same time applied in human society, but never fully realized because of the imperfections of all that is human. The *Shari'ah* corresponds to a reality that transcends time and history.

NOTE

The *sharia* judges were the *qadis* who decided individual cases, and were also responsible for many functions that are today considered executive. For example, the *qadi* would enforce judgments, supervise the execution of wills, and exercise police powers in his district.

The traditional sources of this law were the Quran itself, together with the *sunna* or the custom of the early Islamic community by which the reliability of individual *hadith* (sayings of the Prophet) were judged, the *ijma* or the consensus of the Islamic community, and *qiyas* and *ijtihad* or, respectively, analogies and personal reasoning from the first three sources. The intellectual guardianship and authoritative statement of the law were the responsibility of the juristic schools, not of the state or the *qadi*. Thus, not only was there no legislation; neither was there a doctrine of stare decisis or common-law type of law making. Interpretation and statement of principles were the tasks of the *ulema*, or upright scholars, of the society, and of the *mufti*, or legal advisors to the *qadi*. The doctors of Al Azhar still issue *fatwas* or opinions on controversial points of law. There were four major juristic schools (summarized on Chart I) that evolved during the first centuries of Islam. By about the third century of the Islamic era, the door of *ijtihad* (personal reasoning) was closed, permitting no further change in the law. The only flexibility left then was to

CHART I.   THE SCHOOLS OF ISLAMIC JURISPRUDENCE

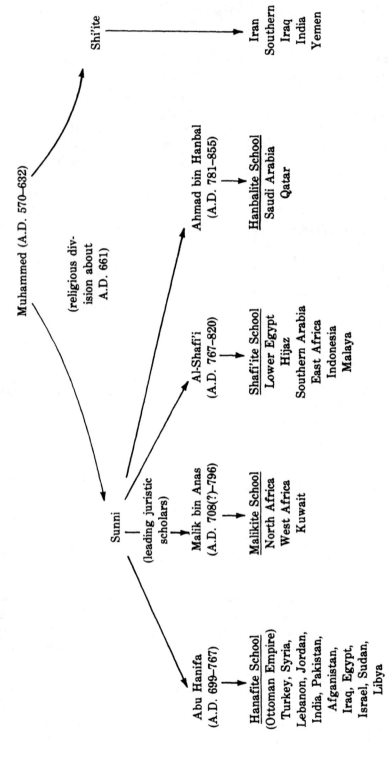

For sources, see Hassan, Afchar, "The Muslim Conception of Law," International Encyclopedia of Comparative Law, Vol. II, Chapter 1, pp. 90–96, J. C. B. Mohr, Tubingen, 1975.

[C5741]

reject the law or to pick and choose among the doctrines of the existing schools.

Since the law was God's law and could not be changed and since moral and legal principles were so intertwined, the role of the state was very different from that in the contemporary West. The state had in effect no significant legislative authority. To the contrary, its responsibility, as suggested by the task of the first Caliphs, was to uphold and help enforce and spread the *sharia*. It was through this responsibility that the state gained its legitimacy. (Some of the more religious rules of the *sharia* were enforcible only in conscience rather than through the community, however.)

The inflexibility of such a law was sensed early on and led, even in traditional Islamic law, to escape devices. From a theoretical viewpoint, the most important of these was the doctrine of *siyasa*—a doctrine that the government in fact seeks the public interest (for the ruler has some knowledge of God's purpose for the society), that this pursuit of the public interest may necessitate deviation from the *sharia*, and that obedience is due the ruler even if he deviates. This doctrine legitimated the rule of the foreign conquerers of Islam. It also permitted some division between the civil authority and the Caliphate. At the procedural level, the corresponding discretion and flexibility were reflected in the creation of *mazalim* or political ruler's courts that could avoid the limitations of the *sharia* courts and often became, in direct contradiction to the *sharia*, a means of appeal from the *qadi*'s decision. There was an obvious tension between the political reality and the *sharia* ideal of government. For the philosophical reasons specified above and perhaps also because the society lacked a sense of progress, this tension was not thought to be troublesome. This fact is itself an important aspect of Islamic law.

B. EGYPT IN TRANSITION

NOTE

The pattern of political power in Egypt was never simple. After the Ottoman Turks conquered Egypt in 1516, they imposed a pasha or viceroy as a local governor and supported this governor with a corps of Janissaries (who also had the task of controlling over-ambitious governors). Real political power was held, however, by the Mameluke Beys, a body of military slaves and mercenaries who had previously held power in Egypt, perpetuating themselves by recruiting successors. These Beys became the effective provincial governors in Egypt, and the Turkish viceroy was their pawn. Although the Caliphate was in Istanbul, effective religious authority (to the extent it is reasonable to speak of such authority in Islam) probably rested with the *ulema* of Al Azhar and the villages.

Napoleon conquered this world in 1798, posing as the protector of Islam against the Beys:

Panayiotis Vatikiotis, (quoting an Arabic source) The Modern History of Egypt, New York: Frederick A. Praeger, 1969, p. 38.

"O *Shaykhs, qadis, imams* . . . and officers of the town, tell your nation that the French are friends of true Muslims, and proof of this is that they went to Rome and destroyed the Papal See which had always urged the Christians to fight Islam; then went to Malta and expelled from it the Knights of Malta who claimed that God required them to fight the Muslims. Thus, the French at all times were sincere friends of the Ottoman Sultan and enemies of his enemies. The Mamelukes refused to obey the Sultan, and obeyed him only as a means to satisfy their greed. Blessed are those Egyptians who agree with us . . . ."

NOTE

Although it was driven out three years later by an Anglo-Turkish expedition, the short period of French control proved enormously important for the future of Egypt. Napoleon created a General Council which was later disbanded, but was the precursor of a Parliament. (There is an Islamic tradition that a ruler has a duty to consult with the *ulema*, but this tradition had not led to the creation of any standing institutions in Egypt.) Napoleon also created an Institute of Egypt—also disbanded for a period—that introduced French scholarly techniques and scientific knowledge. Perhaps most important, he introduced a printing press (with the nerve to obtain Arabic type from the Vatican!). Not only was Egypt's intellectual system shaken; its new reformers would look to France.

Out of the political and military confusion that followed the Anglo-Turkish defeat of France there arose the first of Egypt's modernizers, Muhammed Ali, an Albanian officer who came to Egypt with the Turkish expeditionary force. During his rule from 1805 to 1848, he took over large quantities of land, keeping some for his own account and giving some to his assistants as a sort of fiefdom. He built a modern Army and the supporting industry to provide armaments, uniforms, and ships. He sent Egyptians abroad for education and introduced a state school system to supplement the Azhar system of religious education. What apparently paid for all this was the cultivation of cotton introduced by 1820 and operated as a monopoly by Ali himself.

After a few relatively ineffective rulers in mid-century, the pace of development became faster under Ali's grandson, Ismail, who ruled from 1863–79. The costs of development, however, together with Ismail's enormous expenditures to gain favors from Istanbul, outstripped Egypt's capability. Ismail went into debt to the Europeans and had to accept the creation of a cabinet and the inclusion of European ministers in it. This discredited his regime domestically, producing opposition both from the Army and from the reconstituted Assembly. The Army intervened (the Orabi mutiny) and in 1882 the British also intervened. They supplanted Turkey as the outside controlling power, but ruled much more firmly.

During this era, Egypt moved, not entirely of its own accord, towards adoption of a Western style legal system (a process to be examined in more detail in Problem III). Part of the motivation was to regularize legal relations with Westerners. The consuls of the various Western nations asserted jurisdiction over disputes affecting their own nationals. This was perhaps less degrading than its analogues in China, for under *sharia* principles jurisdiction followed the religion of the person rather than the national status of the territory. Nevertheless, it was considered a breakthrough for Egypt when

Nubar Pasha, one of Ismail's advisors, succeeded in replacing these consular jurisdictions by "Mixed Tribunals," courts which included both European and Egyptian judges and applied a European-derived code. There were also intellectual reasons for change. Quadra Pasha, a graduate of a language school that Ismail had founded, translated the French legal code into Arabic, and developed a European-style codification of the *sharia*. (Later on he also translated the statutes of the Mixed Tribunals, which had originally been written in French.) All that remained was the final promulgation of a European-style code and the creation of European-style courts for domestic controversies—both done the year after the British took over Egypt. The *qadi* courts were left with jurisdiction over only certain family and inheritance law matters. Both Mixed Tribunals and *qadi* courts remained in existence until after World War II, when their jurisdiction was transferred to the regular national courts.

In spite of the fact that Western law was imposed, the bar that evolved around this law quickly grew to gain more prestige than that associated with the *sharia*. The first modern law school was founded in 1858, and the bar for the new court system naturally became a major intellectual bridge between Europe and the traditional Islamic culture. Legal scholars looked particularly to Paris—often receiving advanced degrees there. In the process, they transmitted many Western ideas of government and democracy to the society.

Islam itself was beginning to face up to the Western challenge. The intellectual initiator was Jamal al-Din al-Afghani (1858–97) who had been involved in political intrigue through much of the Mid East and Europe, and who taught at Al Azhar between 1871 and 1879. He emphasized both the rational-scientific reform of Islam and the liberation of Islamic nations from European control through Ottoman leadership. Afghani's student, Shaykh Muhammed Abduh (1849–1905) was probably the most influential of these early reformers. Abduh was the son of a Delta farmer; his early training was entirely religious. Although in exile in Paris and Beirut during some earlier periods, he was a judge in the new national courts from 1889 and Grand Mufti from 1899 to 1905. He sought to reform Al Azhar itself, improved the training of *qadis*, and helped found a system of private modern Muslim schools for children. His theological publications called, at least implicitly, for a new *ijtihad* in which the intellectual foundations of the *sharia* would be entirely rethought in line with modern concerns.

The Islamic reformers and the new lawyer class played an important role in the next phase of Egyptian politics—a phase which endured until the 1952 revolution. The two groups formed a natural alliance to seek a modern independent political democracy, in opposition to the British, the King, and the more conservative Islamic elements. The high point of their efforts—and a suggestion of the problems they faced—was perhaps the formal independence of 1922 and the Constitution of 1923. Saad Zaghlul (1857–60(?)–1927), a member of the Afghani-Abduh group at Al Azhar and a former student at the French law school in Cairo, formed the *Wafd* (delegation) party, initially a group which would be a delegation representing Egyptian interests at the Paris Peace Conference following World War I. The British objected, Zaghlul was arrested, riots broke out, eventually the British let the *Wafd* delegation go to Paris but appointed a new Egyptian government of *Wafd* opponents. In

1922, the British then issued a unilateral declaration that Egypt was independent and sovereign, but reserved certain crucial points that were unacceptable to the *Wafd*. The British-sponsored government appointed a committee, also unacceptable to the *Wafd*, to draft a new Constitution. Even that constitution was changed from above before promulgation. When the *Wafd* won the election in 1923 and Zaghlul took power, he compromised on many of the issues on which he had earlier been intransigent. Then the British Governor General of the Sudan was assassinated the following year, and the British military forced out Zaghlul.

It went on like this until 1952. The liberal democratic effort failed, broken, depending on whom one believes, by the parochialism of the parties or by the divide-and-conquer tactics of the British.

These events, together with the profound philosophical difficulties of modernizing Islam, brought their own reaction—the evolution of a more fundamental Islamic view. Rashid Rida (d. 1935) argued that Islam should return to its sources—from which it had deviated, he suggested, as early as the year 37 of the Hejira. A Pakh Islamic scholar of international reputation, Muhammed Iqbal, criticized Europe in 1930 for its lack of spiritual values. The return to Islam reached a more political level with the spread of the Muslim Brotherhood and of Young Egypt during the 1930's. Both societies emphasized individual morality, Islamic and Egyptian nationalism, and the rejection of European ideas. The former evolved into a terrorist movement; the latter into a political party.

This movement toward independence and re-Islamization affected the law as well. In 1937, agreement was reached to terminate the Mixed Courts after a transition period that would end in 1949. Abd al-Razzaq al Sanhuri, a leading jurist, organized the redrafting of the Civil Code to combine Islamic concepts with the Code's Western concepts. This effort, begun in the 1930's, came to fruition in 1949. But even at the 1933 fiftieth anniversary celebration of the original Western codes, the *ulemas* boycotted the ceremony.

C. THE REVOLUTION AND ITS AFTERMATH

Raymond Baker, Egypt's Uncertain Revolution Under Nasser and Sadat, Cambridge: Harvard University Press, 1978, pp. 7–11.

Disillusioned with the performance of the constitutional regime, large numbers of Egyptians by the mid-thirties had begun to look for alternative forms of political organization. Of the variety of non-liberal political movements, the Moslem Brotherhood elicited the most impressive response. A true mass movement founded by the charismatic Hassan el-Banna in 1928, the brotherhood looked, in el-Banna's words, to the "Islamizing" of Egypt as the means of redemption from the "slow annihilation and profound and complete corruption" occasioned by the British colonial presence. While the movement activists accepted the basic premises of modernization, they lashed out both against the British and against the Egyptians who cooperated with them and slavishly imitated Western ways. The brotherhood's analysis of imperialism was a sophisticated one. It distinguished between "external imperialism," the naked force of the occupying power, and "domestic imperialism," those Egyptian groups and individuals who served the occupiers consciously or unconsciously and profited from their presence. The brotherhood was particularly sensitive to the dangers imperialism posed to the Moslem community's cultural identity. Egyptians were warned against this "cultural imperialism, which entered the minds of the people with its teachings and thoughts" and which tried "to dominate the social situation in the country." Hassan el-Banna described the destruction wrought by such domination:

> Young men were lost, and the educated were in a state of doubt and confusion . . . I saw that the social life of the beloved Egyptian nation was oscillating between her dear and precious Islamism which she had inherited, defended, lived with and become accustomed to, and made powerful during thirteen centuries, and this severe Western invasion which is armed and equipped with all the destructive and degenerative influences of money, wealth, prestige, ostentation, material enjoyment, power, and means of propaganda.

This onslaught of the West was deadly and effective, the brothers argued; it produced "dejection and moral defeat: a dead pacifism, lowly humiliation and acceptance of the status quo." Throwing off all loyalties to the established order, the brotherhood exuded a spirit of revolution. By 1948 the society could claim, without exaggeration, to speak for a million Egyptians. This astounding success was an indicator of the bankruptcy of the regular political groups and the constitutional order itself.

Already weakened by a corrupt and inefficient ruling class, Egypt's constitutional order had been shaken by an array of unfavorable historical circumstances in the forties. Britain leaned heavily on Egypt in World War II and did not hesitate to claim its wartime rights—and more—under the 1936 agreement. While fighting was under way in North Africa, the Egyptian King Farouk in 1942 moved to form a government headed by a minister suspected of pro-Axis sympathies. An alarmed British ambassador instructed the commander of British troops in Egypt to surround Farouk's palace. Farouk was ordered to install a Wafdist government under Nahas Pasha, who was viewed as more amenable to British influence. The king yielded to this British show of force, and the leader of the nationalist Wafd came to power under the protection of British guns! The prestige of both the crown and the Wafd was seriously undermined by this incident.

Political life in the forties was marked by the meaningless circulation of Wafdist and minority governments, all of which were incapable of instituting reform or securing the evacuation of the British. The Palestine War of 1948 might have diverted attention from

Egypt's domestic ills and even restored King Farouk's sagging popular esteem, but rapid Egyptian defeat crushed those possibilities. In 1950 the Wafd led by Nahas Pasha won a last victory at the polls. Temporarily buoyed by an artificial boom in cotton prices brought on by the Korean War, the new government was soon weakened by charges of widespread official corruption, involving the Nahas family itself. In the last stages before the Revolution of 1952 the instances of imprisonments, violent strikes and demonstrations, killings and assassinations, and plots and purges increased sharply.

In 1951, in an effort to strengthen his position, Wafdist head of government Nahas inaugurated a struggle against the British by unilaterally abrogating the 1936 Anglo-Egyptian treaty, which provided the legal basis for British presence in Egypt. A program of sabotage and guerrilla attacks against the British base in the Suez Canal Zone was begun, with the Wafdist government relying on the Moslem Brotherhood and left-wing groups to carry out the attacks. The struggle threatened to end in stalemate. The Egyptians did not possess the means to defeat the British army of eighty thousand, although they could make maintenance of the British base in the Canal Zone difficult and costly. The British government was unwilling to reoccupy Egypt proper in order to secure its position; it chose instead to respond with limited guerrila counterattacks.

One such attack had far-reaching effects. On January 25, 1952, the British announced their intention of expelling from the Canal Zone all units of Egyptian police suspected of aiding the guerrillas. Heavily armed British troops and tanks surrounded the Egyptian police headquarters in Ismailia and demanded surrender. On orders from Cairo, the Egyptian police refused to submit. The British opened fire. Before they were compelled to surrender, the Egyptians had lost forty-one men, with seventy-two wounded, to only three deaths for the British. In Cairo the incident was regarded as a massacre. Reaction was explosive and aimed as much against the government for its inept handling of the incident as against the British. A large section of central Cairo was looted and burned by angry crowds and about a dozen lives were lost before the Egyptian army restored order.

Farouk dismissed Nahas, head of the Wafd government, the next day and thereby initiated a period of crisis from which the ancien régime never recovered. In the next five months no one proved capable of forming a strong government.

Egypt in Revolution. Subjective signs that Egypt was approaching a revolutionary moment in its history were seen in the late forties and early fifties in the growing appeal of radical thought and movements of the left and right. The perceived relevance of the several varieties of Marxism that took root in Egypt derived from Marxism's acceptance of aspects of the Western achievement while at the same time it called for revolt against it. Marxism sounded the call for industrialization, but for an industrialization cleansed by social revolution of the Western capitalist contagion. It provided a persuasive demonology to explain the disruptions and disorientations experienced in the colonial situation. And Marxism gave expression to the instinctive anarchist feeling of a society that had been profoundly dislocated in its fundamental socioeconomic structures.

Marxism was not the only ideology that served to canalize the sense of social disintegration born during the colonial confrontation and its aftermath. The history of revolutionary politics in Egypt often reveals congeries of conspirators who had held Islamic fundamentalist as well as Marxist views. There have even been individuals who fluctuated between the two ideologies. This apparent anomaly disappears when it is realized that in Egypt the evocative power of "Islamic" theoretical formulations was used by the brotherhood to appeal to the same discontented groups that might have been attracted to Marxism. The Moslem Brotherhood assuaged the trauma of the disintegrating colonial situation with the promise of a "conservative transition," modernization cleansed by Islam of racist, individualistic, corrupt capitalism as well as of atheistic, tyrannical, and materialist communism.

The call for revolution from both the left and the right was increasingly heard as the bankruptcy of Egypt's liberal age became apparent. From the wide array of contenders for the nationalist mantle, it was a movement of military conspirators—the Free Officers led by Gamal Abdul Nasser—that ultimately destroyed the monarchy and eliminated the colonial presence. It was from their coup d'état of July 1952 that the instruments were forged to make possible a real break with the colonial past. And it was Nasser who led the Egyptian people at Suez in 1956, when the colonial legacy was at last repudiated.

How did the military conspirators orient themselves and demarcate the arena for their decisive social action? How did they understand the "logic of their situation"? Through their words and behavior the Free Officers expressly defined this realm of their social action, and they have thereby left a concrete record for its reconstruction here. But the significance of that reconstruction is not limited to Egypt. For the recognition and destruction of a colonial situation in Egypt by the Free Officers was understood by them to be related to the larger historical process of decolonization. Egypt's revolution was seen as partaking of that "repossession of the world" and that "call for its remaking" which has marked the modern era.

The Free Officers saw themselves as vindicators of the promise of Egypt's nationalist movement. That claim was challenged, by the Moslem Brothers among others. Yet through their efforts to destroy Egypt's colonial dependency the military conspirators did give new meaning to a history that for the mass of Egyptians had become meaningless. By seizing power and using it to destroy the material and cultural structures of colonial domination, they placed the revolutionary transformation of Egypt and the redefinition of its role in global politics on the historical agenda. The coup d'état moved toward revolution. The process of building an authentic political community was at last begun. Egypt's revolutionaries aimed to transform their society, and that transformation was itself part of the global drama of decolonization and national renaissance.

NOTE

The initial coup d'etat placed Muhammad Naguib in power in July 1952, Gamal Abdul Nasser forced out Naguib in 1954; on his death in 1970, he was succeeded by Anwar Sadat, another Free Officer. Hosni Mubarak replaced Sadat upon the latter's assassination in 1981.

The Free Officers group's point of cohesion was Egyptian nationalism; its greatest political asset was that it was Egyptian. Its most effective political tool has understandably been foreign policy. In 1956, Nasser negotiated the withdrawal of British forces. After the breakdown of negotiations for finance for the Aswan dam, he nationalized the Suez Canal later the same year. This led to a first Mid-East war in which an Anglo-Israeli invasion force was turned back, not by the force of Egyptian arms, but by the force of U.S.-Soviet diplomacy. A later war with Israel in 1967 and intervention in the Yemen Civil War between 1962 and 1967 were disastrous for Egypt, but the nation did well enough in the 1973 war with Israel that it gained the internal confidence for the negotiation process now underway. During the 1952–81 period, the society shifted its alignment from the U.S. to the Soviet Union and back again and sought several abortive unions with other Arab nations. This was in part a rather subtle policy responding to needs to maintain national unity, to protect the status of the military without letting it become too powerful, and to encourage the flow of economic assistance.

On the domestic side, however, the regime has done much less well, appearing to lack any coherent philosophy except that of remaining in power. The regime has systematically sought to neutralize every possible competitive power center. Following an assassination attempt against Nasser in 1954, the Muslim Brotherhood was suppressed. A number of the leading corporations were nationalized and put under the control of managers placed in impossible administrative positions. Political party structures have been regularly reformed, and thus kept weak. There is a constitution, and the elaborate structures adapted from French administrative law are generally respected; but the system is designed to give the military leadership effective control.

The result is that decisions, at least under Sadat, have been made by a form of court politics: bureaucratic factions attempting to gain the President's ear and the President's effort to respond to those pressures in a way that both maintains his power and satisfies his overall goals for the evolution of the society. This process is discussed in the following excerpts:

Raymond Baker, Egypt's Uncertain Revolution Under Nasser and Sadat, Cambridge: Harvard University Press, 1978, pp. 161–164.

President Sadat (like Nasser before him) has spoken repeatedly of the sovereignty of the law and his aim to create a "state of institutions." But a close look at Egypt's major civilian institutions (the presidency, the parliament, the press, and the Arab Socialist Union) reveals that the undoubted liberalization during the Sadat years has not been grounded in such a state.

The Presidency. Egypt's president is constitutionally a strong one who appoints vice presidents, a prime minister, his cabinet, and the governors of Egypt's twenty-four governorates or provinces. He is popularly elected after nomination by the parliament. Sadat has been elected twice in unopposed elections, with the people asked to vote yes or no on his candidacy. In addition to a veto power, the president has emergency powers to issue binding decrees when the parliament, by a two-thirds majority, delegates such authority.

In practice, virtually all important decisions in domestic and foreign affairs are made by the president and his staff. Furthermore, constitutional myths notwithstanding, the power of the president rests ultimately on his support in the military.

The Parliament. It is true that the parliament, the unicameral People's Assembly, has played a larger role in the Sadat years than before. Particularly important has been the assembly's investigatory role. As controversial as its hearings on sequestration abuses have been its reports on Egypt's land reclamation program. An assembly subcommittee issued a report published in *al-Akhbar*, which concluded that despite the millions of pounds spent, one-fourth of the lands reclaimed from the Western Desert (in the so-called New Valley) were once again reverting to desert sand. The committee revealed that a drastic reduction of the irrigation budget for the area was responsible. In 1974 the assembly expanded its land-reclamation activities, sending specialists to all major land-reclamation areas. Spectacular press headlines resulted: in spite of the increased water from the High Dam, not one feddan had actually been added to Egypt's total agricultural land area. A closer look at the findings reveals that, under the pressure of Egypt's alarming population growth, agricultural land was being used for housing and commercial purposes. In addition, the investigating committee regaled the reading public with reports on corruption: *al-Akhbar* blamed the former centers of power; *al-Iqtisad* drew attention to planning and administrative deficiencies.

The acerbity of parliamentary discussion and debate even of extremely sensitive issues has at times been surprising. Roughly ten months before the October War *al-Ahram* reported the comment of one Assembly member that "people have heard so much about preparation for the battle that they are fed up with slogans uttered here and there without result." The member went on to complain "about

the problem of the youth who are in a state of anxiety over the lack
of clarity in our basic problem, the liberation of our territory."
Among other signs of the increased vitality of the parliament under
Sadat is the fact that government ministers who report to the assembly at times have been subjected to harsh questioning and outspoken
attacks on their performance.

Despite these gains, it is still true that the parliament has no role
in major policy decisions. John Waterbury of the American Universities Field Staff in Cairo, a close and reliable observer of the Egyptian
scene, has summarized the method of the parliament's deliberations:

> The normal pattern . . . has been to tear a given policy to
> pieces in committee . . ., to give ample newspaper . . .
> coverage to the findings, and then to have the Assembly as a
> whole approve the policy with marginal modifications.

In the fall of 1976 the legalization of a limited version of a multiparty
system for the elections to the assembly held promise of making
Egypt's parliament a more significant political forum. (That important development will be analyzed shortly as part of a review of the
role of the Arab Socialist Union.) So far in crucial policy areas, however, the assembly has been largely irrelevant.

The Press. Alarmed by the riots of January 1977 and the defiant
coverage of those events by the leftist press, Anwar es-Sadat moved
to sharply circumscribe journalistic freedom. The press of the Sadat
era became if anything even more conformist than during Nasser's
years.

The initial liveliness of the press in the seventies obscured the fact
that discussion of sensitive issues took place within fairly well defined boundaries. The Egyptian press since 1960 has been owned by
Egypt's unique political party. Every journalist today has to be a
member of the ASU, and all discussion in the press is to take place
within the context of the "basic documents of the revolution": in
practice, this has meant that the role of the press has been largely
explanation and advocacy of government positions. Granted, Sadat
has officially abolished censorship and it was possible, at least until
January 1977, to identify with ease competing positions on as important an issue as the meaning of Nasser's legacy. Nevertheless,
Sadat has set limits to the national dialogue on Egypt's recent past:
on numerous occasions the president has stated categorically that he
shared responsibility for every decision made in Egypt since the July
revolution. By clearly identifying himself with the past, Sadat has
set boundaries for the critical review of Nasser's legacy. Also instructive about the actual degree of autonomy of the press is the fate
of M. H. Haikal, the most powerful journalist in Egypt during the
Nasser era. When Haikal persisted in criticizing Sadat's American
connection and in describing the result of the October War as "no

victory, no defeat," Sadat in early 1974 removed him from the editorship of *al-Ahram*.

The ASU. There remains the Arab Socialist Union, Egypt's sole political party during the Nasser era and the first years of Sadat's rule. At first Sadat showed no real interest in reviving the ASU after the failure of the "political solution" under Nasser. The subsequent attempt to use the ASU as one base for the coup attempt against him in 1971 did not endear the ASU to Sadat. The new president looked instead toward establishment of a market economy to develop Egypt. The ASU was thereby deprived of what was to have been its major role—that is, to constitute the driving force for Egypt's economic modernization. When Sadat's statement of evaluation and guidelines for the future of the ASU was published on August 9, 1974, it was clear that the organization, at least for the time being, was to play no major role in Sadat's Egypt. Ihsan Abdul Kudus, the journalist closest to Sadat, wrote in *al-Ahram*:

> In reality the ASU is an official organization, like any other governmental unit, and it could have been called the Ministry for Political and Popular Affairs.

In the fall of 1974 Sadat revealed his real thinking about the ASU for the first time: he raised the issue of moving away from a one-party system. A parliamentary committee was appointed to consider the question of a return to multiparty politics in Egypt. During the first days of public debate, urban middle-class elements (represented by the professionals and intellectuals of Cairo and Alexandria) called for expanded political liberties and a restoration of party competition. Their voices were overwhelmed by the opposition of the members of Egypt's official "popular" organizations representing farmers, workers, women, and students. They rejected the political license of a multiparty system that would undermine the gains of the revolution. Sadat concluded from the debates that Egypt was not ready for a democratization of its political structure, and the issue was put aside for fifteen months.

In January 1976 Sadat reopened the debate. A new and more powerful commission was ordered by the president to consider once again the question of parties. This time Sadat identified himself with a moderate position between the advocates of continued one-party rule and those who called for the formation of additional parties. He warned of the dangers of excessive political fragmentation and took sharp exception to any possibility of the military being drawn into active political participation in any parties formed. But Sadat did argue that Egypt would benefit from a more active political life. He suggested that political "groupings" around right, left, and center platforms be formed within the ASU and allowed to compete in the fall elections to the People's Assembly.

NOTE

Such a political arrangement was promulgated in 1977, with new political parties permitted. Subsequently, the ASU was abolished and the new parties became more independent; Arthur Banks, Political Handbook of the World, New York: McGraw-Hill, 1981, p. 167.

Raymond Baker, Egypt's Uncertain Revolution Under Nasser and Sadat, Cambridge: Harvard University Press, 1978, p. 13.

(1) Egypt's revolutionary rulers as yet have been unable to generate the institutions, systems, and relations which they themselves see as essential to the social reconstruction of their country.

(2) There have been many causes for the failures of Nasser and Sadat, but most critical has been the absence among the Free Officers of organization and of ideology.

(3) This lack of institutionalization and ideology has hampered a coherent, self-generated approach to the problems Egypt has faced since 1952. Basic decisions on the character of Egypt's new political-economic order, and correlative regional and international alignments, were too long delayed. Despite the domestic roots of their core motivations, Egypt's new rulers allowed their regime to be defined to an excessive degree by the responses made to external crisis stimuli and to the counter-responses of the environment. The Free Officers have been unable to devise and carry out the basic public policies demanded by their own vision of change.

(4) In Egypt a political-economic order has taken form that is characterized by sharply limited competence for the tasks of modernization. It is an order without secure social moorings, an order in which political power is both personalized and bureaucratized. The essential question of the relation of the market mechanism to political authority in regulating society has not been resolved. Ironically, such a system of social organization itself erects new and formidable barriers to the task set by the Free Officers for themselves and their people: the revolutionary transformation of Egypt.

Panayiotis Vatikiotis, Some Political Consequences of the 1952 Revolution in Egypt, in Political and Social Change in Modern Egypt, New York: Oxford University Press (P. Holt ed.) 1968, pp. 368–369, 372–373.

While it is easy for soldiers to seize power, it is not easy for them to govern effectively under conditions of induced massive change. The centralization of power in Egypt is not a surprising phenomenon; it has a long history that needs no elaboration here. The accession to power of a radical officer group, which aimed at the establishment of a new revolutionary order, tended to increase the centralization of both political and economic power. The formulation of an all-embracing revolutionary policy for the modernization of Egyptian society was thus incompatible with notions of diffused power.

*   *   *

If the efforts of the military régime to organize popular support for their revolution proved difficult, the question of a new political apparatus for the control of government was more crucial once the old *élite* had been destroyed.

*   *   *

In the absence of wide participation by the citizens in the conduct of public affairs, at the local, provincial, or national level, a new state apparatus became necessary. Unwilling to risk their newly acquired power, the Free Officers had to consolidate their gains. Anxious to impose a new order of revolutionary achievement as outlined in their proclamations between 1952 and 1956, the military junta sought at first to recruit the cadres of their new power structure from their most obvious ally: the armed forces.

President 'Abd al-Nāṣir has consistently reminded the armed forces that they constitute the vanguard and base of the revolution in Egypt. They have been in effect the major source of his active support, as well as his hungriest clients for power. Quickly army officers were first given watch-dog duties over civilian administrative organizations. Soon thereafter they acquired permanent bureaucratic functions. When in 1957 the nationalization of foreign commercial interests and capital began seriously, culminating in the July 1961 "socialist" measures, military personnel found themselves in key positions, responsible for the planning of economic and social policy. Diplomatic posts, provincial governorships, and all conceivable appointments in the higher echelons of state administrative services were opened to them.

*   *   *

The mass exodus of foreigners, long resident in Egypt, from 1956 to date represented a minor drain of human resources trained in certain tasks essential to the maintenance of a modern state, especially in the fields of trade, commerce, industry, and ancillary services ranging from insurance and the liberal professions to skilled crafts. The military could not provide adequate replacements for all these categories. The need to recruit native civilians from a variety of social strata into top technical and administrative state posts became urgent. Economic planners, development engineers, statisticians, and experts in a wide range of technical fields were brought into the various national organizations, many of which were directly controlled by the government, while others enjoyed quasi-independent status, to cope with the emergence of the state as the largest single *entrepreneur* and social services agency in Egypt.

The expansion of the public sector economy—its almost total control of the national economy—was organized into such bodies as planning commissions, economic councils, various boards dealing with trade and public services. Both military officers and civilian technologists were appointed to head many of these agencies. The expropriation of foreign and native capitalists, the nationalization of commercial enterprises, public utilities, the Suez Canal, and the socialist laws of 1961-2 made it impossible for the new *élite* to remain confined to the military institution. Its expansion to embrace an ever-wider civilian element became necessary.

A new state technocracy came into existence which was not a consulting one, but an integral part of the state bureaucracy. It did not belong to a fully formed professional community; it had no corporate ethos with all the independent attributes that this implies. Its members simply became state employees: a state technocracy, that is, which, when bureaucratized because the state required its skills and services, did not constitute a separate *élite* with serious political potential. Even though the economic and social interests of this new technocracy seem to converge with those of the ruling military *élite*, it cannot, so far, act as a check upon the power of the modernizing leader, because it has no alternative to state employment. Moreover, it cannot find refuge, or room to manoeuvre, in a civilian political force. . . .

NOTE

The economy has done only moderately well under the Revolutionary Government. Industrialization has been occurring—industry contributed 35% of the national output in 1979 as compared with 21% in 1950. Over the period from 1960 to 1979, the GDP grew at almost 6% per year in real terms, reaching about $17 billion in current dollars in 1979. This growth, however, has been especially rapid during the later part of the period. Earlier, the economy stayed only slightly ahead of population growth.

On the other hand, even early on the regime did relatively well in delivering social services. Between 1960 and 1979, the crude death rate fell from 19 per thousand to 12 per thousand. Over the 1949-74 period, the number of students in primary schools increased by more than a factor of 3; that in secondary schools by more than a factor of 20. Even with the growing population, these numbers are impressive. So also are the number of students going on to the universities. Although rote training tends to be emphasized, even at the university level, there have been major efforts to improve the university system and Al Azhar has been reformed to include contemporary scientific and technical topics in its curriculum.

The political transition from Nasser to Sadat was extremely important. Sadat survived a strong challenge the year after he took power and proved willing to run heavy risks as exemplified by his visit to Jerusalem in 1977 and his provision of a haven for the dying Shah of Iran.

His basic economic policy of *infitah* or openness, although criticized from the left, appears to have been extremely popular. This policy is one of opening up economic activity to private enterprise. On the domestic side, it has encouraged the growth of small scale enterprise in areas like furniture and textiles, mainly for domestic use. Many of the cooperatives and accoutrements of Socialism from the Nasser days are either gone or mere empty shells. And on the international side, *infitah* has involved a major turn from a Soviet orientation toward a Western orientation. Sadat expelled Soviet military advisers as early as 1972, and his Camp David gamble paid off heavily for the economy: it has produced some Western foreign investment, the ability to obtain oil from the area of the Sinai returned by Israel, and a position as one of the world's largest recipients of U.S. foreign assistance. Moreover, Sadat benefitted from Nasser's educational policies: Egypt is one of the Mid-East's leading sources of expatriate labor—about one-tenth of the work force is employed abroad, at skill levels ranging from the unskilled to the professional jurist. The resulting inflow of capital, which in large part bypasses the government, is of great help to the economy.

These foreign remittances have been especially important to the rural regions which are beginning to change rapidly. Enough villagers are becoming educated that the *ulema* at the local mosque is no longer alone in possessing the authority that comes from education. Judges assigned to the rural regions say that the case load there has increased rapidly in the latter part of the 1970s, although it has not been possible to confirm this point in the official Ministry of Justice figures (which were available up to 1978 for this publication). The rural picture is clearly very different from that portrayed by Tewfik el Hakim in the late 1930s (and often said to be accurate at least into the 60s) of villagers mistrusting all outside authority and particularly all legal authority.

In spite of the real popularity of *infitah* at all levels, not just among the wealthy, the regime is not clearly stable. The rate of economic progress is slow, even in the areas receiving foreign assistance. The nation is having to import a large portion of its food. Housing construction is using up some of the best existing farmland at about the same rate that desert reclamation is producing new farmland. Infant mortality is very high. Cairo's public services fell behind with the inflow of refugees from the Suez area during the 1967 war and have never caught up. The problems are shown by riots in the poorer neighborhoods of Cairo in 1977 and again in the spring of 1981.

The current, and very important, religious revival may also be a source of political instability. The revival is evidenced by increased attendance at religious services and by an increase in the number of university women wearing veils (probably on their own initiatives). Although the revival transcends any specific religious movement, it has led both to demands for law reform in the Islamic pattern and to the rise of new militant movements. Sadat cited the risks associated with these movements in early September 1981 to support his arrest of a large number of Muslim and Coptic (Christian) religious leaders and his assumption of direct authority over the mosques. Moreover, it is alleged that those responsible for his assassination (only a month later) were acting from religious motives.

D. THE CURRENT LEGAL SYSTEM

The *qadi* courts were abolished in 1956, and the current judicial system, shown in Chart II, is modeled very closely on the French pattern. This system involves two concepts that might be unfamiliar to an American reader. First, there are separate court systems, one to deal with normal private controversies and one for administrative issues. The regular court system includes several forms of primary tribunals, courts of appeal, and the Cour de Cassation or court of cassation. On the administrative side, there are several levels of administrative courts under the general title of the Conseil d'Etat. This adapted French system is already complex; its evolution in a heavily bureaucratic system is predictably even more formal and complex. The entire judicial pattern is further complicated in Egypt by the addition of special courts such as a Constitutional court and several security-offense oriented courts, one, the Court of Ethics, deriving from a quite controversial 1980 law.

The second continental adaptation is the *Ministère public* or *parquet* (French terms) or *niyaba* (Arabic term). This is a bureaucratically-organized group of judges, which works for the government and has many prosecutorial-style responsibilities. It also, however, has, at least ideally, the traditions and tenure patterns to ensure a judge's sense of obligation and independence. And it is given many judicial responsibilities—to follow up citizen complaints and prosecute if appropriate, to supervise and control police investigations, and to represent the interests of minors affected by litigation. To all indications, the *niyaba* is trusted by the people while the police are not.

The education of the bar follows an essentially Western pattern. *Sharia* law is taught, naturally with greater emphasis at Al Azhar, for its application to inheritance issues, alongside topics like Commercial Law, Labor and Social Security Law, and International Organizations and International Arab Relations. The institutions are huge—the University of Cairo Law School, one of about 12 in the nation, has a student body of over 12,000, out of 135,000 in the entire university. Since library facilities are poor, and there are very few texts, many of which are themselves inadequate, the classroom itself has to be the basic place for learning, something very difficult in the predictable large classes. Law is an undergraduate discipline as in Europe. And examinations severely reduce the number of students moving up from level to level.

In spite of the clear acceptance of French traditions by the bar, there is currently some pressure to return to Islamic sources. This is a result of the global Islamic revival. Leaders throughout the Mid-East are understandably fearful that the revolutionary fundamentalism in power in Iran will spread, even though that fundamentalism is deriving from a Shi'ite tradition rather than a Sunni tradition.

Sensing the potential ferment, parliament has commissioned studies of draft reforms of existing codes to make the codes more Islamic. The Constitution was amended in 1980 to make "the principles of Islamic law the principal source of legislation," rather than "a principal source" and several courts, relying on this amendment, have struck down contracts (one involving Al Azhar itself) with interest provisions, on the grounds that these provisions violate Islamic law and are therefore unconstitutional. Reforms in the criminal area, however, would arouse much more significant opposition among the legal community, and it is much less likely that these will proceed.

CHART II. THE EGYPTIAN COURT SYSTEM

SUPREME CONSTITUTIONAL COURT

Jurisdiction over Constitutional questions, interpretations upon request of Minister of Justice, and conflicts of jurisdiction

CONSEIL D'ETAT
(Administrative Court)

SECTION FOR LEGAL ADVICE AND LEGISLATION
Provides legal opinions to different government branches

JUDICIAL SECTION

SUPREME ADMINISTRATIVE COURT

COURT OF ADMINISTRATIVE JUDICATURE

ADMINISTRATIVE COURTS
Jurisdiction, at various levels, over government employment and contract issues, tax questions, and requests for annulment of administrative decisions

COUR DE CASSATION
(5 Judges, located in Cairo)
Hears "appeals" from regular courts.

COURTS OF APPEALS
(3 Judges each in 7 courts around the nation)
Appellate jurisdiction and initial felony jurisdiction

PRIMARY TRIBUNALS
(3 Judges in each court, one court in each governerate)
Appeals from summary tribunals and has initial civil jurisdiction if more than £500 (about $750) at issue

SUMMARY TRIBUNALS
(1 Judge each, 1 court in each district)
Initial jurisdiction in remaining cases

COURT OF ETHICS
Established in 1980 for the protection of ethics against immorality

STATE SECURITY COURTS
Includes High Courts and summary tribunals, with military participation.

Data derived from: Ahmed Khafagy, (Vice-President of the Court of Cassation), An Outline on the Egyptian Judicial System (Typescript 1980).

SUGGESTED READING

Egypt

Hamed Ammar, Growing Up in an Egyptian Village: Silwa, Province of Aswan, London: Routledge & Paul, 1954.

Gabriel Baer, Studies in the Social History of Modern Egypt, Chicago: University of Chicago Press, 1969.

Raymond Baker, Egypt's Uncertain Revolution Under Nasser and Sadat, Cambridge: Harvard University Press, 1978.

Peter Holt, Political and Social Change in Modern Egypt, New York: Oxford University Press, 1970.

James Mayfield, Rural Politics in Nasser's Egypt: A Quest for Legitimacy, Austin: University of Texas Press, 1971.

Social Problems, Vol. 28, 1981, No. 4, Special Issue on Development Processes and Problems, General Trends and the Egyptian Case.

Panayiotis Vatikiotis, The Modern History of Egypt, New York: Praeger Publishers, 1969.

Panayiotis Vatikiotis, Some Political Consequences of the 1952 Revolution in Egypt, in Political and Social Change in Modern Egypt, P. Holt, ed., New York: Oxford University Press, 1968.

Islam

Arthur Arberry, ed., Religion in the Middle East; Three Religions in Concord and Conflict (Vol. II, Islam), Cambridge: Cambridge University Press, 1969.

Louis Gardet, La Cite Musulmane: Vie Social et politique, Paris: Librairie Philosophique J. Vrin, 4th ed., 1976.

Sir Hamilton Gibb, Modern Trends in Islam, Chicago: University of Chicago Press, 1947.

Marshall Hodgson, The Venture of Islam: Conscience and History in a World Civilization (3 vols.), Chicago: University of Chicago Press, 1974.

Peter Holt, ed., The Cambridge History of Islam (2 vols.), Cambridge: Cambridge University Press, 1970.

Malcolm Kerr, Islamic Reform, Berkeley: University of California Press, 1966.

Ralph Linton, The Tree of Culture, New York: Alfred Knopf, 1955.

Seyyed Nasr, Ideals and Realities of Islam, New York: Frederick A. Praeger, 1966.

G. Von Grunebaum, Islam; Essays in the Nature and Growth of a Cultural Tradition, The American Anthropological Association, Memoir No. 81, 1955.

John Williams, ed., Themes of Islamic Civilization, Berkeley: University of California Press, 1971.

Law

James Anderson, Islamic Law in the Modern World, New York: New York University Press, 1959.

Jasper Brinton, The Mixed Court of Egypt, New Haven: Yale University, rev. ed. 1969.

Noel Coulson, A History of Islamic Law, Edinburgh: Edinburgh University Press, 1964.

Noel Coulson, Conflicts and Tensions in Islamic Jurisprudence, Chicago: University of Chicago Press, 1969.

T. El Hakim, The Maze of Justice, 1947. (This is a novel, written in the 1930's by a member of the *niyaba* stationed in the countryside.)

David Forte, Islamic Law: The Impact of Joseph Schacht, 1 Loyola of Los Angeles International and Comparative Law Annual 1, 1978.

Enid Hill, Mahkama! Studies in the Egyptian Legal System: Courts and Crimes, Law and Society, London: Ithica Press, 1979.

Majid Khadduri and Herbert Liebesny, eds., Law in the Middle East, Washington: Middle East Institute, 1955.

Herbert Liebesny, The Law of the Near and Middle East, Albany: State University of New York Press, 1975.

J. O'Kane, Islam in the New Egyptian Constitution: Some Discussions in al-Ahram, Middle East Journal, Vol. 26, 1972, p. 137; the text of the Constitution is available in Middle East Journal, Vol. 26, 1972, p. 55.

J. Robert, L'Égypte Moderne et ses Constitutions, Rev. du Droit Public et de la Sci. Polit. en France et a L'Étranger, Vol. 81, 1965, p. 856.

Joseph Schacht, An Introduction to Islamic Law, Oxford: Clarendon Press, 1964.

G. Tixier, L'Union des Républiques, Arabes et la Constitution Egyptienne du 11 September 1971, Rev. du Droit Public et de la Sci. Polit. en France et a L'Étranger, Vol. 88, 1972, p. 1129.

Farhat Ziadeh, Lawyers, The Rule of Law and Liberalism in Modern Egypt, Stanford, California: Hoover Institutions Publications, 1968.

Chapter 4

INTRODUCTORY NOTE ON BOTSWANA AND TSWANA LAW *

A. LAW OF BOTSWANA AS ROOTED IN TRADITIONAL LAW

NOTE

The law of the contemporary nation of Botswana has many sources, including current statutory law, received Roman-Dutch and common law, and traditional or "customary" law. However, because traditional law is still important in the day-to-day lives of many of the citizens of Botswana and as a source of law applied in the courts, we have chosen Botswana as exemplary of traditional law even though customary law is but one component of current law in Botswana.

Traditional or customary law is characteristic of "traditional" societies, those societies which most legal scholars label collectively "pre-industrial." **
Modern Botswana cannot be labeled a traditional society because it is a society in transition. It has a rapidly growing industrial and urbanizing compo-

* This chapter has benefited from the comments of students who have used it in previous versions. But it has gained most of all from careful critiques by Q. N. Parsons and Alec Campbell, to whom I am most grateful. But, of course responsibility for the final result is mine. Space did not allow inclusion of all the variations in ethnography of Tswana peoples or nuances in the history of the development of scholarly understanding of Botswana that, as long-time specialists in Tswana studies, they brought to my attention.

** The typology of societies used here is that of the sociologist, Gerhard Lenski. (Human Societies: A Microlevel Introduction to Sociology, New York: McGraw Hill, 1970.) It is similar to schemes used by many anthropologists, particularly that of Walter Goldschmidt. (Man's Way: A Preface to the Understanding of Human Society. New York: Holt, Rinehart and Winston, 1959.) In using Lenski's scheme which places societies on a continuum from "traditional" to "indus-

trial," I wish to acknowledge certain problems that arise if the terminology is taken too literally and to disclaim some assumptions that the typology may seem to imply. I recognize that all societies, even industrial ones, have traditions and, therefore, a traditional component. Similarly, I recognize that all contemporary societies are equally "modern" simply because they exist in the here and now. Most important of all, by using this typology I do not mean to imply an inevitable evolutionary movement from one type or stage to another or that all societies eventually must become "industrial." Finally, I would note that, although Lenski's scheme classifies societies in terms of their material base, rather than their cultural superstructure, it suggests that different aspects of each type's cultural superstructure (i.e., law and socio-political organization) are related in patterned ways. It is this characteristic of the typology that makes it so useful for this casebook.

40

nent and more and more people derive income from urban-industrial employment both inside the country and outside. However, Botswana does have proportionately a larger population component that is traditional in social organization and outlook than the other three nations we are studying. The "modern" segment of the population, although it comprises the elite and is growing, is not numerically dominant.

1. Traditional Society

Can we speak of *the* pre-industrial society? In reality, the "pre-industrial society" is not a unilithic kind of society, but includes several sub-types which differ in significant ways that we will mention below.

a. Types of Traditional Societies

First, we review the types of pre-industrial societies, characterizing them in terms of subsistence modes (i.e., the basic way of obtaining the necessities of life) and listing them in terms of increasing socio-technical complexity. There are "foraging" societies, that is, hunting and gathering or fishing societies; simple and advanced herding societies; simple and advanced horticultural societies; and simple and advanced agrarian societies. Foraging societies subsist primarily by hunting, gathering, fishing, or some combination of those. Herding societies subsist primarily from the animal products of their herds. Both foragers and herders are nomadic, but advanced herders differ from simple ones in using horses or camels for transport. Horticultural and agricultural societies base their subsistence on plants. Simple horticulturalists lack the plow as well as metallurgy including iron tools and weapons. Advanced horticulturalists have metallurgy and, before the period of European exploration, lacked the plow and (except in Sub-Saharan Africa) iron tools and weapons. Agrarian societies are distinguished from horticultural ones by having the plow, and advanced agrarian societies are distinguished from simple ones by having iron tools and weapons.

The "higher" * the societal type, the greater the capacity to mobilize energy and the more complex the forms of social organization. Thus, correlated with differences in mode of subsistence (and co-varying societal type) are factors such as differences in: the size of groups, the permanence of their settlements, the extent of division of labor, organizational complexity, and amount of leisure time available to their members.

b. Overall Features of Pre-industrial Societies

Let us look at what all pre-industrial societies as a group share, when contrasted with industrial societies. Communities are smaller in pre-industrial societies, although they increase in size as one moves through the set of societal types. Because the communities are smaller they are characterized by face-to-face or primary relationships rather than secondary ones. The most important basis for relationships is kinship; hence these societies often are referred to as "kin-dominated." Even in advanced agrarian societies kinship groupings such as lineages and clans remain important as the group around

* "Higher" is used in the sense of socio-technical complexity, not in the sense of evolutionary stage.

which many activities are organized and as a structural building block in some levels of political organization.

Kinship is but one of a series of overlapping links that bind persons who live in communities characterized by primary relationships. Thus, individuals are bound by economic, political, and religious ties, etc. as well as those of kinship. These overlapping ties sometimes are referred to as "multiplex" ties.

A sharp division of labor by sex typifies pre-industrial societies. In fact, role allocation on the basis of ascriptive criteria in general is found in such societies. (Ascriptive criteria are those which are biologically given.) Therefore, many roles are allocated on the basis of sex, kinship, noble birth, age, and—sometimes—birth order. Conversely, role allocation by achievement (i.e., individual effort) is less important in pre-industrial societies than in industrial ones—at least than in the ideology of industrial societies.

Except in agrarian societies, there is relatively little specialization of labor in pre-industrial societies and, for this and other reasons, norms tend to be more widely shared than in the more heterogeneous industrial societies. But, societal stereotypes notwithstanding, there is no uniformity of belief in norms or of adherence to them.

c. Differences Among Pre-industrial Societies

The differences that separate types of pre-industrial societies are as important as their similarities. As noted above, populations are more sedentary and settlements larger and more permanent in the societies with greater socio-technical complexity. While equality of status is a dominant dimension in foraging societies inequality of status is important in the "higher" societal types. Thus, agrarian societies are most likely to be stratified, to have social classes—including a hereditary nobility—or castes. In the more complex pre-industrial societies, including advanced horticultural ones, political power and its correlate, legal authority, are likely to be in the hands of an elite group. Because communities are larger in these societies, a more complex political organization is needed. "Constitutional" principles go beyond kinship and territoriality to include various kinds of clientship and patronage. Legal structures, like the related political ones, are likely to exist in several layers,—dominated by persons of higher rank. Law differs in its substantive content in these more complex societies (e.g., there is more focus on property) and, procedurally, it is more complex.

In the world of actual societies, as opposed to the scholar's world of societal types, particular societies may not fit exactly into a typology. The indigenous society of the dominant people of Botswana, the Tswana, as it existed in, say, the 17th century generally has been classified as "advanced horticultural." * And the introduction of the plow in the 19th century changes its classification to an advanced agricultural (or agrarian) society. Without a doubt contemporary Tswana society is an in-between type, best classified as "indus-

* Historians of southern Africa observe that where various Tswana groups are placed in such a typology obviously has changed over time. A second point to be made is that the stock keeping aspect of Tswana subsistence has a strong influence on Tswana settlement patterns and social organization. However, the Lenski typology is not finely calibrated enough to distinguish agrarian societies with a major stock keeping emphasis from those without.

trial-agrarian." This type is no less real than the "as-if-pure" types Lenski has chosen to isolate for his typology and is fairly frequent in the empirical world. Contemporary Botswana is a fast-changing society in which the urban/industrial sector is growing apace. Its legal system also is changing—although not as fast—and it shows many of the same, complex, "in between" qualities as the society.

2. Traditional Law

a. *Sources of Traditional Law*

Traditional law can be defined as law based on "tradition," a body of unwritten doctrine that generally is accepted as being rather permanent. As such, traditional law does not differ absolutely from the other three kinds of law we are studying in these materials, which we are characterizing in a "rough and ready" way as: Western, Eastern and religious.

A traditional legal system differs from the other three types of legal systems relatively rather than absolutely. Except for the absence of written precedents it shares virtually all of the sources of law of the other kinds of systems. What is unique about traditional law is the proportionate weighting of the various sources of law. More than, say, Western law, traditional law is rooted in custom and, to some extent, morality and religion rather than formal written precedent or—normally—legislation. However, traditional law is not identical with custom, for only some customs are treated as laws, that is subject to the sanctions that are imposed by the legal process. Compared to religious law, traditional law is less rooted in religious tenets but, again, more in custom. Like all law, traditional law is rooted also in values and cultural postulates, albeit values and postulates that are not codified in books and documents.

b. *Other Features of Traditional Law*

Because of its significant roots in local custom, traditional law, like traditional religion, is highly indigenous and localized, although, sometimes as a culture has spread beyond its original borders its law has diffused, too. In being localized traditional law contrasts with Western law which is more imperialistic—as, incidentally, is Islam and Islamic law. So there are virtually as many varieties of traditional law as there are traditional cultures.

In most traditional legal systems, there is less focus on the rights of the individual and more on those of the group than in Western law. Many observers have labeled this feature "collective responsibility." Those rights which do exist generally inhere as much in kinship status as in citizenship defined by residence in a particular area.

Procedurally, traditional law is less formal and technical than Western law and, in many societies, it does not sharply distinguish between civil and criminal law. In some societies traditional law does not involve third party arbitration—the imposition of a solution by a third party—but mediation, in which the third party attempts to arrange a mutually acceptable solution which is voluntarily assented to by the parties. In still other traditional societies dispute settlement does not involve a third party at all, but direct interaction of the two parties themselves. These materials do not include a society where either direct party settlement or mediation are the most formal type of dispute settlement.

Derived from the fact that traditional law is not sharply separated from other social institutions, where there is third party settlement of disputes, the person who does the adjudicating usually is not a distant specialist, but a person who is linked to the litigants by other roles: as neighbor, kinsperson, or tribal political authority. The adjudicator, because of the multiple links to one or both of the litigants is in a position, sometimes, to attempt informal settlement of a dispute before turning to adjudication.

Using Weber's terminology (see chapter 2), traditional law can be characterized as "formally irrational," in that it often makes use of procedures that are believed to involve the intervention of the supernatural, such as ordeals. There is also "substantive irrationality" in that criteria other than general rules may be used as the basis for deciding cases. Although these attributes are defined as "irrational" from the perspective of Western law and social science, they are anything but that from the perspective of those who are the clients of such a system.

From the inside out, from what the anthropologist calls the "emic" perspective, what Weber sees as the "irrationality" of traditional legal systems is rational. Because they stress reconciliation and resolution over what Weber calls "rationality," traditional legal systems seem to individual litigants to be particularly responsive to their needs.

Substantively, traditional law varies from society to society. Thus, the law of property is more elaborated among sedentary horticulturalists and agrarian peoples than among nomadic hunters and gatherers or pastoralists. And arson is more heavily sanctioned legally in societies with closely packed thatch-roofed houses than it was among the traditional igloo-dwelling Eastern Eskimo. Substantive law varies with mode of subsistence and with values, but this is no less so for other kinds of law than traditional law. The area in which traditional law is substantively most unique is in the development of the law of persons.

As we noted at the beginning of Section A, traditional law (or "customary" law as it is styled in Botswana) is only one component of law in Botswana. This pre-industrial law has persisted because some (not all) aspects of pre-industrial (i.e., traditional) social organization have also continued there. Among these is the chieftancy, which we will examine later. Technically speaking, one could even argue that the non-statutory component of Botswana law is no longer "traditional" because the written legal studies of 20th century anthropoligists, most of which are excerpted in these materials, are used as sources of written precedent in some Botswana courts! But, hewing to our relativistic perspective, it nonetheless is true that the traditional component of social organization and law is writ larger in Botswana than in the other three societies we are examining. So, Botswana provides our example of a—relatively—traditional legal system.

QUESTIONS

As you read through this casebook keep this basic set of questions in mind:

1. What features are characteristic of all legal systems whether in industrial or pre-industrial societies?

2. What is the effect on a legal system of the absence of a substantial body of written precedent?

3. Conventional wisdom suggests that law in pre-industrial societies generally is less "advanced" than that of industrial societies. But are there ways in which law in pre-industrial societies is more advanced?

4. We think of "custom as King" in traditional societies. But to what extent is custom a source of law in industrialized societies too? How is custom taken account of in the legal processes of those societies?

5. In pre-industrial societies, where customary law is inadequate for modern conditions, how is it augmented with other kinds of law? With what consequences—both positive and negative?

B.   BOTSWANA: A NATION WITH A UNIQUE GEO-GRAPHICAL AND SOCIAL HABITAT

1.   Overview

NOTE

Botswana is a landlocked nation located in southern Africa, bordering the Republic of South Africa to the southeast and south, Namibia (South West Africa) to the west and north, Zambia to the north, and Zimbabwe (formerly Rhodesia) to the northeast and east. (See maps on pp. 46 and 47). It is about the size of France, larger than California and somewhat smaller than Texas. Before achieving independence in 1966 Botswana was a British protectorate known as Bechuanaland.

Much of Botswana's territory lies in one of Africa's major deserts, the Kalahari, which comprises most of the western part of the country. So, although she has about 220,000 square miles of territory, Botswana has a population of only about 940,000, making her one of the least densely populated African nations. Not surprisingly, the major factor influencing the distribution of Botswana's population within its borders and shaping its development is the scarcity of water.

Because of the distribution of water and the unreliability of rainfall, Botswana's dominant people, the Tswana, have depended more on stock-raising than on agriculture for their basic subsistence, and the export of beef is a source of income for the country. The eastern part of the country has a greater rainfall and is relatively well watered for at least part of the year. Even before the days of the Protectorate which was established in 1885, it was

NATIONS OF AFRICA (1979)

1. GAMBIA
2. GUINEA-BISSAU
3. SIERRA LEONE
4. LIBERIA
5. TOGO
6. BENIN
7. EQUATORIAL GUINEA
8. LESOTHO
9. SWAZILAND
10. MALAWI
11. BURUNDI
12. RWANDA
13. DJIBOUTI

From: Harold K. Schneider, The Africans: An Ethnological Account. Englewood Cliffs, N.J.: Prentice-Hall, 1981, p. 6.   [C6079]

the area of greatest concentration of population and the pathway for Europeans trekking from South Africa to Rhodesia in search of agricultural and mineral wealth. (Botswana itself early foretold promise of mineral wealth but, fortunately for her history, this only recently has been confirmed.) Even today the rail line linking South Africa and Zimbabwe passes through populated eastern Botswana.

REPUBLIC OF BOTSWANA
(Showing Main Towns, Roads, Railroad and Main Natural Features)

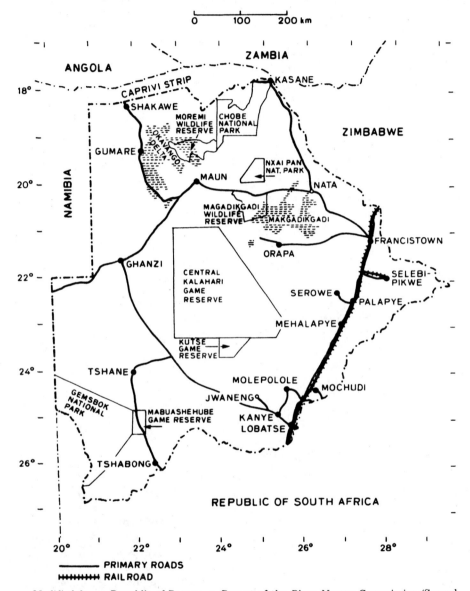

Modified from: Republic of Botswana, Report of the *Place Names Commission* (Second List of Names and Recommended Spellings.) Government Printer. Gaborone, Botswana, July 1981.   [C6083]

A related point to be noted is that from early on an aspect of Botswana's cultural habitat has been the necessity of contending with Europeans and European-dominated neighboring territories. Only two of the four states or territories bordering Botswana, Zambia, and Zimbabwe are independent black states.

Historically, the initial danger from encroaching white Europeans was that the territory would be colonized. After Britain granted protectorate status, it was that as British power vis-a-vis the Boers of South Africa waxed and waned, Bechuanaland might be incorporated into South Africa or Rhodesia with British acquiescence or even connivance.* Even now, how to become logistically and economically less interdependent with the Republic of South Africa is a concern in many quarters in Botswana as it is for many of the countries in southern Africa.

Before Europeans contended with Africans for the territory that is now Botswana, various African groups themselves competed for it. Anthropologists believe that in Late Stone Age times, southern Africa was occupied by hunting and gathering peoples who occupy some of the more remote, less populated areas of Botswana. In fact, there is "evidence for the continuity of settlement of groups [in the Kalahari] today going back 40,000 years or more."** But some three thousand years ago, a group of people speaking a language that was the precursor of the great Bantu sub-family of languages so widely spoken in southern Africa began to move south and east from their homeland in the Cameroons at the eastern edge of West Africa. By 400–500 A.D. the descendants of the original emigrants were moving into what is now Botswana, their proto-Bantu language having differentiated into many distinct, but closely-related Bantu languages. Having acquired agriculture, the culturally more advanced Bantu emigrants began to amalgamate with the hunting, gathering and herding Khoisan peoples, in most instances displacing their culture, which survived in forms such as the Khoisan clicks of the Bantu Nguni languages. In other instances, the Khoisan cultures survived more intact, as in the case of the Bushmen who were pushed further and further into the less well-watered remote areas.

The indigenous foraging and herding peoples of Botswana and nearby regions are referred to collectively as Khoisan. This is a composite term constructed by Isaac Schapera. It is derived from *San* and *Khoi*, the terms given to themselves by hunter-gatherers and herders respectively at the Cape, in South Africa. But, within Botswana most hunter-gatherers in fact speak a *Khoi*-related language. Thus, it is simplest to speak of Khoisan hunter-gatherers and Khoisan herders. In much of the literature on Botswana these peoples are referred to as San, or Sarwa—a term which implies client-like (virtually serf-like) status.

---

* The fact that Botswana was not only South Africa's hostage, which is so frequently asserted, but Rhodesia's as well, is documented and lucidly expressed in Q. N. Parsons, The Evolution of Modern Botswana: Historical Revisions, in The Evolution of Modern Botswana, edited by Louis Picard and Philip Morgan (in press).

** John E. Yellen, "Archaelogical Excavations in Western Ngamiland," in 3 Botswana Notes and Records 276, (1971), cited in Q. N. Parsons, The Evolution of Modern Botswana: Historical Revisions, in The Evolution of Modern Botswana, edited by Louis Picard and Philip Morgan (in press).

REPUBLIC OF BOTSWANA (Showing Kalahari Desert, and Major Tribal Territories)

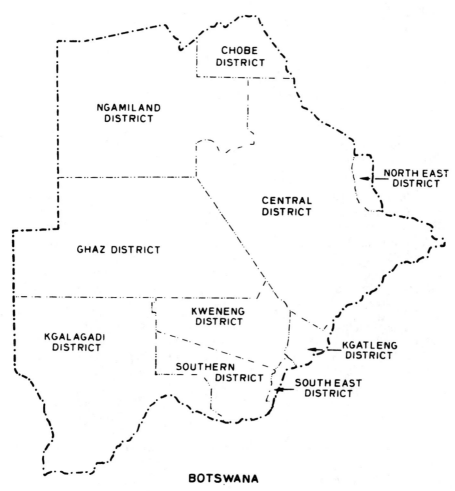

BOTSWANA

SHOWING DISTRICTS
MODIFIED AFTER MAP OF THE REPUBLIC OF BOTSWANA
PREPARED AND DISTRIBUTED BY THE DEPARTMENT OF
SURVEYS AND LANDS. GABORONE, BOTSWANA. 1980.

—·—·— INTERNATIONAL BOUNDARIES
—·—·— DISTRICT BOUNDARIES

[C6084]

The Bantu speakers who entered southern Africa many centuries ago are black Africans and by far the largest of the population groups of southern Africa, including Botswana. They are usually classed in four major divisions: Nguni, Tsonga, Sotho, and Venda (Schapera 1956).* The Sotho are further subdivided into the Southern Sotho, the Tswana or Western Sotho, and the Northern or Transvaal Sotho.

The Tswana (or Western Sotho) are the dominant ethnic group in Botswana; indeed, the country is named for them. In reading about Botswana it is helpful to be familiar with various terminological usages derived from Bantu linguistic forms which build on the root -tswana by attaching prefixes of varying meaning. Thus, the country is Botswana, its people collectively are Batswana (Ba is the plural prefix attached to the stem ntu which means a person in Zulu), their language (an official language in Botswana along with English) is Setswana and a Tswana individual is a Motswana. Setswana also means Tswana custom and culture.

Following this kind of usage each of the constituent Tswana peoples (formerly referred to as "tribes") sometimes are referred to using the Ba- prefix along with the tribal designation, e.g., Bangwato, Balete, etc. There are many different Tswana peoples but the major groups are the: Ngwato, Kgatla, Ngwaketse, Kwena, Tawana, Rolong (also called Tshidi), Tlokwa, and Lete or Malete. As noted above they sometimes are referred to as Bangwato, Bakgatla, etc.

Although the Batswana are the dominant people of Botswana there are other indigenous African peoples who are citizens. Depending on how one counts heavily "Tswanacized" peoples the proportion of non-Tswana can reach as high as 55%. These other ethnic groups include peoples such as the Kalanga, Tswapong, Subiya, Yei, Mbukushu, and Khoisan. It is a fallacy to think of Botswana as a mono-ethnic although it is often characterized that way, largely because Setswana is so widely spoken in Botswana. Parsons comments tellingly:

Q. N. Parsons, The Evolution of Modern Botswana; Historical Revisions in the Evolution of Modern Botswana, edited by Louis Picard and Philip Morgan (in press), pp. 2–4. Footnotes omitted.

The name Botswana—and its colonial version of Bechuanaland (i.e. be- or ba-Tswana-land)—have led many observers into the false assumption that Botswana is a mono-ethnic state. But Botswana is only a mono-ethnic state in as far as a Tswana minority has successfully imposed its culture on a majority population of extremely diverse ethnic origins. Such success has been considerable because of the continuing legitimacy of the Tswana states, which expanded over the area of Botswana in the precolonial and early colonial periods, as colonial "tribal reserves" and post-independence districts. But other ethnic identities have by no means disappeared.

* Isaac Schapera, Government and Politics in Tribal Societies, London: Watts, 1956, p. 7.

Only the south-east of the Republic of Botswana can approach the claim of being wholly Tswana in ethnic composition. This is the area from which Tswana dynasties—derived from neighbouring parts of South Africa—spread their dominion over the rest of Botswana. However, even here there is a significant non-Tswana population. . . .

Every region outside the south-east has only a minority of "true" Tswana by ancestry—though by modern linguistic convention all citizens of Botswana are commonly referred to as *Batswana*. . . .

Botswana, then, has as many "tribes" as other African countries and a diversity between ethnic identities—between cultivators and hunter-gatherers—that can scarcely be matched elsewhere in the world. Yet one hears, with one exception, little of "tribalism" in Botswana politics. The exception is the periodic demand by educated Kalanga for regional cultural-linguistic rights. What is remarkable in Botswana is how much, up till now, the legitimacy of Tswana-dom has been accepted and even supported by non-Tswana groups. The first political party to adopt the word Botswana rather than Bechuanaland into its title, the Botswana Independence Party, was founded by and receives its main support from non-Tswana in the north-west.

. . . Botswana is "mono-ethnic" only in so far as Tswana culture has achieved national legitimacy. That legitimacy is considerable at present, but has been and may be challenged as social conditions change.

NOTE

Tswana peoples are found in even larger numbers in South Africa than in Botswana. The total population of Botswana is 936,600.* There is a Tswana population of 1,700,000 in the Republic of South Africa (including the population in Bophutaswana, claimed by South Africa to be an independent nation). The Tswana of Botswana, therefore, are far outnumbered by the Tswana of the Republic.

How have the Tswana become so dominant in their region of southern Africa? To understand the answer to this question, it is important to know something of Tswana social and political organization, the topic to which we now turn.

2. A Socio-Cultural Sketch of Contemporary Tswana Society

NOTE

The following exerpt provides a pithy, thematic overview of current Tswana society and culture.

* Preliminary population figure from the 1981 census.

Hoyt Alverson, Mind in the Heart of Darkness: Value and Self Identity Among the Tswana of Southern Africa. New Haven and London: Yale University Press, 1978, pp. 10–12, 14–15. Headings inserted by the editor are in brackets.

[*Distribution of the Tswana Peoples.*] . . . Today the Tswana peoples are found throughout Botswana, the western Transvaal, and northeastern Cape Province. Small enclaves are also found in southwestern Zimbabwe (Rhodesia), Namibia (South-West Africa), and the northwestern Orange Free State. Throughout this vast region the Tswana coexist with other Bantu-speaking peoples. There is some variation in dialect and other components of culture but in the main the Tswana are culturally "homogeneous." Tswana political units are based on a putative kinship principle which serves to divide the society into discrete groups. Most of these groups constitute chiefdoms, where centralized authority resides in a single ruler or chief, his council, and his kin or others whose loyalty and allegiance is given directly to him. In modern times the underpinnings of these groupings have been profoundly altered by the existence of nation states and colonial regimes. Hence the concept of chiefdom and the distinctions based on it are more and more confined to "memory culture": ceremony, oral history, and anthropologists' observations.*

Today there are over two million people who call themselves "Tswana," or agree that such a label applies to them. One-third live in Botswana, the other two-thirds in the Republic of South Africa. In "pre-contact" times these numbers were much smaller.

[*Agriculture, Water, and Habitat.*] Traditionally the Tswana were a self-subsistent agricultural and pastoral people. Since aboriginal times they have practiced hoe agriculture with rotating fallow. During the nineteenth century they adopted plow agriculture, using their own oxen as draft power. Food production was, and in Botswana still is, mixed and eclectic. Agricultural practice is limited more by resource availability than by "inertia" or lack of ideas.

Water was and still is the single most important variable in determining the scope, scale, and mix of various food-production strategies. The climate in this "platteland," or upland savanna, is rather uniform, except for rainfall. The westernmost Tswana area, the Namibia-Botswana border, is desert, with 250 millimeters of rain or less per annum. Agriculture there is confined to animal husbandry and kitchen gardens where ground water is available. As one moves east, the desert continues for some five hundred linear kilometers and gradually gives way to mixed scrub, associated with greater mean annual rainfall. In the area about one hundred kilometers west of the modern rail line through Botswana, the desert ends and veld or savanna commences. Here the rainfall varies from around five hun-

---

* Later sections of this chapter trace out modifications in governmental structures in Botswana that have eliminated chiefdoms as official territorial units and altered the role of chief.

dred millimeters to about eight hundred millimeters per annum in the central Transvaal.

The rain falls in a single season, November through March. Arable agriculture is pretty much confined to this period. Since frost is light even in the dead of winter, it is only the lack of water that prevents year-round agriculture. The principal indigenous crops grown are sorghum, millet, and, since contact with the Europeans, maize. These are supplemented by varieties of melons and squashes, in addition to wild berries and tubers.

[*Animal Husbandry and Hunting.*] Animal husbandry is valued equally with arable agriculture by the Tswana, although its nutritional importance is much less. Goats, sheep, cattle, and pigs are kept, as well as chickens. Dogs and, since contact, donkeys, mules, and horses are nonfood animals used in a variety of ways. Roughly speaking, livestock represent in Tswana culture what the "investment portfolio" represents in ours. One keeps stock for a variety of goals, long- and short-term, some practical, others symbolic or expressive. In all cases animals are a central measure of one's worth, self-esteem, and peace of mind. Animals were not traditionally grown for sale, in the sense we think of in our own beef-hungry society of universal salability. Hunting is important to all Tswana, and every Tswana loves a guinea fowl or rabbit in the pot, even if today it is hunted by running it down in a pickup truck. In pre-contact times hunting of large game was a collective, "age-set" endeavor and was done with spears, axes, and clubs. Today systematic hunting is not typical of the Tswana, except in some Kalahari communities where arable agriculture is not possible because of a shortage of water.

[*Diet.*] The Tswana, both today and aboriginally, derive a very high proportion of their total caloric and protein intake from a beer called *bojalwa*—a light, chalky beverage made from sorghum or millet, a culture of bacteria, and now malt. While diet is varied and fairly rich in protein by African standards, improper nourishment (or even what by our criteria counts as malnutrition) is an important factor in the epidemiology of disease.

[*Residence Patterns.*] Both traditionally and today, many of the Tswana maintain a complex pattern of residence. Typically each Tswana has three residences, although only one is officially "home." Each Tswana lives, first, in a home village. Villages are "nucleated" settlements composed of wards or sections that are, ideally, territorial groupings of kin by descent and marriage. Villages can vary in population from a few hundred to several thousand. The modern "tribal capitals" of Serowe, Mochudi, Molepolole, Kanye, and Ramoutswa range from ten thousand to twenty thousand inhabitants. It is in a village that the Tswana usually maintains a permanent residence and here he lives when he is not working on the agricultural lands, which are in some instances many kilometers from the

SEROWE FROM "KHAMA HILL," 1981. A portion of Serowe from "Khama Hill," where Sir Seretse Khama, Botswana's first president, and some of his chiefly forebears are buried. This view shows only a small portion of one of the wards. Serowe has a population estimated as high as 30,000 persons. Like most Tswana towns, it spreads over a considerable area. Each family's "compound" normally is demarcated by a low wall of sticks of hard, weathered wood or a living fence of thick shrubs. These family homesite boundaries are clearly visible in the photograph.

village. At the "lands" he often maintains a second residence, whose quality, size, and elaborateness reflect the amount of time he chooses to live there. Generally he will live there during the rainy season, when plowing, planting, and harvesting are taking place. Cattle are kept (at least for a good part of the year) at a third location, called the "cattle posts." Here the accommodations are rudimentary, and those staying there are typically adolescents or others whose labor is cheap. These are ideally areas with a rich natural grass cover and a water supply, though when cattle are moved it is most often in search of water.

A RENDERING BY THE TSWANA ARTIST, E. B. LEKHUTILE, OF A SEROWE SCENE

[C6085]

[*The Household and Sex Roles.*] The household usually contains a core of a husband and his wife or wives, children, perhaps the parents of the husband or wife and the children of certain sons, and typically (in older days) daughters whose "bride wealth" had not been received. The division of labor by sex and age is less rigid—that is to say, less mutually exclusive—now than in times past, though sex constitutes by our standards a very rigid, vertical, caste-like cleavage affecting every aspect of human relations. Men and women see each other as members of different "groupings" and in many social activities one's sex may be a more important criterion for association than ties such as marriage and kinship.

Men have had and still do have enormous power over the disposition of a wife's labor. Generally men dominate women psychologically. Women were in past times, with few exceptions, legal minors dependent on some man or men. There is no real folk conception of an illegitimate inequality between men and women. The relations between the sexes are seen as based on a *proper* inequality (like the relationships between adults and minors in our own society).

[*Kinship.*] Tswana society puts great emphasis on kinship as the basis on which the political, juridical, economic, and religious aspects of society are organized. Sedimented in the terminology of the kinship system are the most important principles for recruitment to social roles: sex, age of one individual relative to that of another (senior versus junior), and lineage membership. These are the three main criteria that determine entitlement to most of the other roles an individual will ocupy in his lifetime—roles which are "elaborations" of these basic entitlements. Most important in the history of the Tswana peoples has been the founding of autonomous chiefdoms based upon the breaking up of royal lineages, often under the leadership of dissident members or heirs to statuses or chattels. Tswana chiefdoms (there are fifty distinct ones named by the Tswana) are in fact political communities.

[*The Supernatural.*] What we call the *supernatural* or sacred is a very important part of daily life for almost all Tswana. The distinction between the known and the unknown or the sacred and the profane (that is to say, what we verify or falsify versus what we accept on faith) has no analogy in Tswana society. The world is the world; life is life; and people living or dead are people somewhere carrying out their human work. The Tswana speak of the "created order." This includes stones and witches alike. God is autonomous but *definitely a part of creation as much a creator.* Evil is committed by incarnate and nonincarnate agencies, all of which are part of the *natural* or "created" order. God is very much alive for believers, present but hardly active for most, and maybe dead for a sizable minority. Less than half the Tswana I met in Botswana professed any religion, in the sense of affiliation with a church or other organized body of believers.

The belief that there exist animate and intelligent nonanimal beings, who may be benign or malevolent, is nearly universal, from the ministries of the national government to the most remote rural villages. These are the kind of living forms we call ghosts, spirits, witches and so forth. In addition to these nonanimal living forms there exist *certain modes of human intending* which cause effects directly, *independent* of any overt action of those intending. For example, sorcery can affect the victim's life and welfare. Even envy and jealousy can bring about illness in those who are its objects. *Motives*, or modes of intending, *can pollute or cleanse the world just as do the "spirits."*

The Tswana believe in what we call rational explanation. In their system of knowing there is the unknown but there are few "myster-

BUILDINGS ADJOINING THE *KGOTLA* AT MOCHUDI. The *kgotla* at Mochudi is surrounded by many fine examples of traditional Tswana "town houses," and by some newer house forms, some of which now are used for non-residential purposes. In Mochudi, courtyard entrances and the corners of walls enclosing compounds are decorated with handsome stylistic patterns in grey and black (cf. Campbell). These town dwellings generally—but not always—are more elaborate than those found at "the lands." (Alec Campbell, *The Guide to Botswana* (Third edition). Johannesburg and Gaborone: Winchester Press, 1980, p. 371.)

ies." The unknown remains unknown because of inadequate methods and too little time to use even these. The world is orderly and that is why knowledge is orderly. As far as I can tell, there is nothing for the Tswana that is inherently irreducible to a rational system of belief.

QUESTION

As you read the rest of this chapter, consider the following question:

To what extent did (and does) Botswana's indigenous culture—especially the legal system—enable her people to remain culturally intact and viable through the period of the Bantu diaspora, European missionization and exploration, the Protectorate and, now, independence?

3. An Overview of Botswana's Government

NOTE

The following excerpt describes the government and legal system of the nation-state of Botswana. It serves as a matrix within which the one third of Batswana who are citizens of Botswana carry out the life ways Alverson describes in the ethnographic sketch you have just read.

Alec Campbell, The Guide to Botswana. Johannesburg and Gaborone: Winchester Press, 1980, pp. 385–395. Heading and other material inserted by editor is in brackets.

Central Government. Since the Constitution was drawn up and signed before Independence in 1966 there has been no change in the form of Government. . . . Botswana is one of [very few] countries in Africa with a multi-party democracy.* The National Assembly, as Parliament is called, consists of the President, who is elected by the Assembly, 32 constituency members, four specially elected members, the Attorney-General (with no voting power) and the Speaker. The latter may be elected from members of the Assembly or from others but since its inception, through four Parliaments, a non-member has been elected. Presently three political parties have members: . . . .**

The National Assembly's function is based on the Westminster pattern with Government and Opposition, its role being that of a democratically-elected multi-party parliament. . . . The Assembly makes all laws for governance of the country and these, with any amendments, must pass through four stages in the House. . . .

* One is Botswana's neighbor, Zimbabwe.

** The parties are: the Democratic Party which has 29 elected and four specially elected members, the Botswana National Front two and the Botswana Peoples' Party one. A fourth political party, the Botswana Independence Party, lost its only seat at the last election.

There is also the normal Cabinet system, with the President as Chairman, and members being the 11 Ministers, four Assistant Ministers, and the Attorney-General. There is no Prime Minister and the Vice-President acts as Leader of the House.

* * *

An intriguing feature of the "parliamentary process" in Botswana is the existence of a House of Chiefs, Tribal Authorities consisting of Chiefs of the eight main tribes and five Sub-Chiefs whose tribes were traditionally resident on State Land. Constitutionally, Parliament is unicameral but the House of Chiefs exists separately in its own constitutional right. Its function is to consider matters referred by Government or the National Assembly and meetings are conducted in parliamentary fashion with a Question Time, debates on proposed Bills and votes on motions.

Constitutionally, any new or amended legislation concerning Chieftainship, Land Tenure, Customary Law and Courts, and amendments to the Constitution must, after First Reading in the National Assembly, be referred to the House of Chiefs, which has 30 days for comments and recommendations. Its report is tabled in the Assembly but not debated and the latter may choose to be influenced by it or not. This procedure is not formal; the House of Chiefs' report is in the hands of Assembly Members before the Second Reading and may influence the debate which can lead to the House proposing an amendment to its own Bill in Committee Stage.

The House of Chiefs, therefore, is able to influence certain legislation but does not carry the force of law and the Assembly is not obliged to act upon its recommendations.

Administration. Botswana is divided into nine District Council and four Town Council areas. District Council areas each involve one or more of the original Tribal Areas and some freehold or State land.

. . .

The country is divided into 32 constituencies each of which elects one member to the National Assembly. These constituencies are subdivided into about 180 polling districts each of which separately elects a Councillor to its local Council.

. . . The President appoints his Ministers from those elected to the National Assembly in a general election, and from specially elected Members of the Assembly selected by it from a list provided by the President. . . . These Ministers form the Cabinet which has the executive responsibility of the elected Government. . . .

Each Ministry is staffed by government officers who are permanent civil servants. The senior officer is the Permanent Secretary who is directly responsible to the Minister of his Ministry. . . . Each Ministry includes a Division of Government or a number of Government Departments . . . [and] this system is known as the Central Government. . . .

Two departments do not, in fact, fall directly into any Ministry—the Attorney-General's Chambers and the Department of Audit. In addition, there are two commissions; the Judicial Service Commission which appoints and controls the Registrar of the High Court and the Magistracy, and the Public Service Commission responsible for discipline and examinations in the Public Service.

[*Local Government.*] Alongside the Central Government is Local Government. Separate elections are held for Local Government when District and Town Councillors are elected. Each Council elects its own Chairman and various committees, and is responsible to the Minister of Local Government and Lands. These Councils also have their own permanent staff, including a Council Secretary, Treasurer, Education Secretary, etc.

District Councils have important responsibilities in the provision of primary education, rural health facilities, welfare services, village water supplies and rural roads.

*   *   *

Much of the traditional power of the Chiefs has gone. They form the House of Chiefs . . . [and] still control the customary courts which work alongside the Magistrates' Courts. . . .

Land is divided into three categories—Tribal Land, State Land and Freehold Land. Traditionally the Chiefs had the power to allocate the use of all tribal land. Recently, however, Land Boards have been set up in each tribal area in terms of the Tribal Land Act . . . which are responsible for the allocation of Tribal Land involving more than 75 per cent of the country. State Land, which includes about 18 per cent of the country, is administered directly by Central Government. . . .

The Law. The Rule of Law is the foundation on which the Democratic State of Botswana is built. Botswana can state that since its inception in 1966 the Constitution has remained unchanged save for minor amendments on procedural matters. . . . [The structure of the executive branch and the legislature, established by the Constitution, and already described, are reviewed again in the deleted segment as is the process of enacting bills in the Parliament.]

The Constitution also contains a code of human rights which is enforceable by the High Court.

The system of justice can be divided: on one hand is the Botswana Court of Appeal, the High Court and Subordinate Courts (Magistrates' Courts), and on the other the Customary Courts. Generally the former deal with "formal" law, that is, the combination of Statutory Law, Case Law and the Common Law of the country known as Roman-Dutch Law; * while the latter deal with the complex of laws

* More exactly, this should be styled "Cape Colonial Law," see section D1 below.

which are the particular inheritance of the Tswana. Recently Customary Courts have been dealing more and more with Statute Law.

Subordinate and Customary Courts are located throughout the country and have limited jurisdiction. Criminal matters are governed by the Criminal Procedure and Evidence Act and the Penal Code. Customary Courts are governed by the Customary Courts Act which is under the administration of the Ministry of Local Government and Lands. There is a Customary Courts Commissioner whose duties include the review of all cases involving a prison sentence of more than six months or a fine exceeding P200.

The Subordinate Courts were formerly presided over by District Administrators, but increasingly their place is being taken by professional lawyers. The High Court consists of the Chief Justice, appointed by the President, and such number, if any, of puisne judges as may be prescribed from time to time. Higher still is the Botswana Court of Appeal. There is a normal system of appeal from lower to higher Courts and cases can be taken on appeal from Customary Courts to Subordinate Courts and so to the High Court.

The Chiefs have always held their own tribal or customary courts (*dikgotla*). They appointed village and ward courts, normally presided over by their relatives. Until 1891, and the establishment of the formal court system, these courts dealt with all criminal and civil matters. After this date certain cases were tried only by formal courts and appeal existed from the customary courts to them. In 1943 the Native Courts Proclamation made provision for the recognition, constitution, powers and jurisdiction of these courts although they still remained under the administration of the Chiefs.* In 1966 the Customary Court Act and, in 1971 under it, the Customary Court Procedure Rules were promulgated making the courts much more formal and providing for paid court presidents, many of whom are commoners. Today, the two systems of Courts work well together in providing the country with its necessary administration of justice.**

4. An Historical Flashback: The Centrality of the Tswana Chieftaincy

NOTE

We have seen that two issues faced by Botswana are the scarcity of water and the danger of South African domination. Two other issues, implicit in the Campbell excerpt, are (1) how successfully to democratize governance— to shift from the autocratic (in the non-pejorative sense) rule of chiefs; and

* Many of these changes were anticipated in the Native Tribunals Proclamation of 1934.

** The nature of the imposed statutory court system and its interaction with the indigenous customary legal system are traced in more detail in sections D and E below.

(2) how more fully to integrate the dual legal system. Keep them in mind as you move through the Tswana materials in this book.

Alverson's sketch on pages 52–58 stressed the fact that autonomous chiefdoms have been important in Tswana history although chieftaincy is now somewhat less important than it used to be. In spite of this, as Campbell's profile of Botswana government reveals of the way in which the legislature and its procedures are structured, attention is paid to chiefs. Why has the chieftainship been such a central institution in Tswana society and Tswana culture? To answer this question, let's flash back to the end of the great Bantu migration, to the period between 1500 and 1800.

A feature of the Tswana state that contributed to its adaptiveness during its period of Tswana expansion is that it is absorptive. Citizenship in a Tswana chiefdom was acquired not only by birth (parentage) and/or by being born in a particular place (territoriality). It could be acquired by pledging allegiance to a chief. Thus, the head of a small tribe or a ward within a large town might take his patrilineal kinsmen and others linked to him by various ties and leave his chief to attach himself and his followers to another chief who was more powerful, wealthier, or wiser in dispensing justice. The emigrant and his group would begin life in their new chiefdom with low status, but in time, through loyal service and ties of marriage, gradually would be absorbed. And many such in-migrants were not even Tswana.

Being absorptive meant that Tswana chiefdoms could become populous and being populous increased the polity's ability to contend against other expanding groups. The ability to absorb *and* to *manage* expanding heterogeneous populations was due to the fact that the Tswana state/chiefdom was constitutionally complex. Its "constitution" involved a sophisticated combination or organizational principles including allegiance, rank, age, territoriality, and bureaucratic delegation of authority and responsibility in a hierarchical chain of command. Kinship was not a *sine qua non* for membership in a chiefdom but it was an important principle for eligibility for most offices. In addition, cross-cousin marriage as a kinship institution was used to create or consolidate political power, and, thus, was an important integrative device in the Tswana state. Thus, rank, age-set ties, marriage links, residence, all cross-cut potentially divisive ties of kinship and origin to weave together a heterogeneous population. And a stratified hierarchy of chiefs and affiliated bureaucrats at each level organized and managed that population.

The effectiveness of such a political structure further increased its attractiveness to potential immigrants and to indigenous non-horticulturalists who were encountered, for "nothing succeeds like success." Thus, the foreign origin of many of a Tswana chief's subjects, paradoxically, enhanced the power of the chief and his kin group because these subjects, from the beginning were in a condition of special dependence on the chief.* They were less free to act with others against the Chief or his kin group.

As the absorptive state developed and refined its political structure over time the chief became—and remained—the kingpin—literally—of Tswana culture.**

* Cf. Isaac Schapera, Government and Politics in Tribal Societies, London: Watts, 1956, p. 124.

** Scholars of Southern Africa disagree as to whether these precolonial rulers should be styled "chiefs," "kings," or

By 1800 the outlines of the Tswana states had developed and crystallized. *Why* did they develop in the preceding three hundred or so years? The best answer is that being absorptive was to be adaptive during that period of the close of the Bantu diaspora. It also has been suggested that the Tswana state became more powerful at this time because its stronger patrilineal organization made it more effective against hunting and gathering groups like the Bushmen and its stock keeping increased its absorptive potential by making it possible to make clients of "foreigners" hired as herders. Other sources of growth and power for the state during this time, it has been suggested, were access to iron and control of access to European traders.*

An amalgamation into larger chiefdoms at the end of the 18th century left the Tswana in a strong position. And a good thing that was, because the indigenous Tswana states were about to face a double onslaught—what commonly is referred to as the "Zulu wars" and the bursting onto the scene of a sustained European presence. The Zulu wars and their impact on the indigenous Tswana states are summarized by Alverson:

Hoyt Alverson, Mind in the Heart of Darkness: Value and Self-Identity among the Tswana of Southern Africa. New Haven: Yale University Press, 1978, pp. 18–19.

Two events provided the foundation of platteland ** history. First there were the violent interethnic wars waged by the Zulu chief Shaka and his successors. Spawned by combinations of population pressures, technological innovations, and megalomania, these wars affected virtually all of southern Africa. The second event was the migratory expansion of the Afrikaners from the coastal regions of Cape Province and from Natal to the interior platteland.*** Both of these events took place during the brief period between 1823 and about 1840.

The indigenous upheavals begun by Shaka in the second decade of the nineteenth century are known in Zulu as *mfecane* and in Sotho or Tswana as *difaqane*, which means in both languages "the time of great troubles." The origin of this spread of conquest societies was Zululand, where the Zulu under Shaka developed a new form of military organization based on the same economic surplus as in the older societies. Shaka's exploits occasioned the appearance of similar organizations among other Nguni-speaking groups, such as the Swazi and Ndebele (Matebele). In 1823 this latter group, under Mzilikazi, one

"princes." Since "king" implies no one sovereign above him, the Setswana term *kgosi* (glossed as "king" or "chief") perhaps is best translated as "king" when referring to those rulers in the precolonial situation who were fully independent of other rulers. "Paramount chief" fits the later situation after these rulers came under the authority of a colonial power.

* Martin Legassick, "The Sotho-Tswana Peoples before 1800," in African Societies in Southern Africa, edited by Leonard Thompson. New York: Praeger Publishers, 1969.

** platteland = the high veld, a high, central plateau area of South Africa, which extends into Botswana.

*** The impact on Botswana of the Boer expansion is noted in an excerpt on pp. 65–66.

of Shaka's client lieutenants, penetrated deeply into the platteland occupied by the Sotho and Tswana. This invasion of the Sotho-Tswana world by the Matebele led to profound population movements, including the migrations of the Sotho into the hills of modern Lesotho and of the Tswana into the western Transvaal and modern Botswana. These movements precipitated many changes in the structure of the older societies. Continuous warfare and a search for territorial security added to the extent of these social changes. As more and more groups began to gain their own economic surplus by means of predatory warfare and fewer and fewer by their own indigenous agriculture, total agricultural production in the region declined dramatically. Reduced total production necessitated increased interethnic predation as a means of gaining a livelihood. Thus the necessity either of waging war or of defending oneself against invaders became a cardinal consideration in the organization of society.

One of the most important social changes among both the Nguni and the Sotho-Tswana was the adaptation of the age-regiments to largely military purposes . . . what were once fraternities of men united by common age, yet divided by varied kinship ties, became private armies. In the days before the *difaqane* the age-sets had competed with the lineages in the exercise of power. Now they became a power unto themselves under the direct command of the chief or, significantly, under that of his appointed deputies. By means of the age-based regiments, different communities were organized into larger and larger units whose sole raison d'être was armed combat.

The use of leaders who were not necessarily relatives of the chief yet were appointed by him to command the age-regiment activities created new opportunities for rebellion and division within these societies. No longer were the age-grades hedged in by kinship restrictions and the power held by royalty. With each appointed bureaucrat having a standing army at his disposal, the temptations and opportunities of rebellion and revolution were greatly increased. This opportunity is illustrated by the appearance of various renegade groups that hived off from what had up till then been unitary societies.

NOTE

The process Alverson describes is not qualitatively distinct from that of amalgamation, for fission and fusion are opposite sides of the same coin, after all. The important fact to note is that the indigenous Tswana states were dynamic and utilized political processes to adapt to changing circumstances. Throughout, the role of chiefs remained important, even when some of their appointees gained relative power vis-a-vis the chief.

The Tswana absorptive state was resilient in the face of the Zulu wars. Was it as resilient in the face of the simultaneous onslaught, that of a sustained European presence?

5. The History of the Tswana 1800–1953: Sustained European Contact

The following excerpt was written by I. Schapera whose work was excerpted briefly earlier in this chapter. Schapera is an anthropologist, South African by birth, who carried out the best known modern fieldwork among the Tswana. This field work was done between 1929 and 1950, much of it centering on Tswana traditional law. Schapera, who is Professor (Emeritus) of the London School of Economics and Political Science, wrote the excerpt during the time of the Protectorate, before Botswana gained its independence. His account was selected because it is so succinct, even though it is Eurocentric.

Isaac Schapera, The Tswana (Ethnographic Survey of Africa, Southern Africa Part III). London: International African Institute, 1953 (1976 reprint), pp. 15–16. Footnote deleted.

The impact of Western civilization coincided with the beginning of the 19th century. In 1801 the Tlhaping, the southernmost tribe, were reached by a small party of explorers from the Cape, and in 1816 the first Christian mission to the Tswana was established among them. During the next 30 years most of the other tribes, except those in the far north, were visited sporadically by traders, hunters, and explorers, and mission stations were also established among the Rolong (1822), Hurutshe (1836), Mmanaana-Kgatla (1843), and Kwena (1846). Livingstone's discovery of Lake Ngami (1849) opened up the road to the north, with its great wealth of ivory and other hunting spoils, and the number of European visitors rapidly increased.

Meanwhile, in 1837, the Boer Voortrekkers from the Cape had settled in the Transvaal, after defeating and expelling the Tebele. By 1852, when their independence was formally recognized by the British authorities, there were already some 20,000 of them in the country, organized into several small states which subsequently amalgamated to form the South African Republic. They established small townships and farmed the surrounding land; they also claimed all the local Natives as their subjects, and exacted forced labour from them. Their policy ultimately caused several tribes to move across the ill-defined border into the present Protectorate (1852–69). Among these were the Mmanaana-Kgatla, Malete, Tlôkwa, Kgafêla-Kgatla, and two groups of Hurutshe. Some afterwards returned to the Transvaal, but those named above have been in the Protectorate ever since.

The Boers also resented the increasing contacts of the western tribes with Englishmen, especially missionaries, whom they accused of hostile propaganda and of supplying firearms to the chiefs. They accordingly tried on several occasions to extend their boundary farther west, especially after 1868, when diamonds were discovered at Kimberley. These attempts led to armed conflict with such tribes as the Kwena, Rolong, and Tlhaping. The outcome was that in 1884 the British ultimately responded to Native appeals, and proclaimed a Protectorate over the country south of the Molopo and west of the Republic. Friction with the Boers persisted, and in March, 1885, the Protectorate was extended to include the tribes farther north. In September the southern half of the Protectorate became a Crown Colony, known as British Bechuanaland, which 10 years later was annexed to the Cape. It was intended at the same time (1895) to transfer the administration of the Protectorate (north of the Molopo) to the British South Africa Company, organized by Cecil Rhodes in 1889. The chiefs of the Ngwato, Kwena, and Ngwaketse went to England to protest, and it was ultimately agreed that, in return for certain land and other concessions on their part, their tribes would remain directly under the Crown.*

By the end of the 19th century, the whole territory of the Tswana had been partitioned among the Cape Colony in the south, Great Britain in the north, and the South African Republic in the east. Native locations or reserves were set aside for them in the Transvaal (1884 onwards), British Bechuanaland (1889), and the Protectorate (1899 onwards), but much of the land formerly held by the tribes, especially in the Transvaal, was already owned and occupied by Europeans. The powers of the chiefs had everywhere been curtailed, and their people made to pay annual taxes to the European Governments. There were also mission stations, schools, and resident traders in every important tribe; European clothing and utensils had been widely adopted; and men from all over the territory were going out periodically to work on the mines and in other European areas. These influences were all intensified during the present century, especially after the Cape Colony and the Transvaal were incorporated into the Union of South Africa (1910). Both here and in the Protectorate the system of tribal administration was also reformed, economic and educational developments were promoted, and health services introduced. As a result, the tribal life of the Tswana now differs markedly, in some respects, from the pattern described by the first European visitors 150 years ago.**

NOTE

The Schapera excerpt is an abbreviated, bare-bones account. Two dimensions should be underscored. First is the role of prominent Tswana chiefs in

* Q.N. Parsons (personal communication, 1981) makes an interesting observation on the 19th century Tswana chiefs' ability to operate and to deal with bureaucracies: "The chiefs developed their own bureaucracy c. 1900 by appointing educated relatives and/or talented commoners to a secretariat to write letters of state [and] record *kgotla* judgments. The first bureaucrats pre-1900 were foreign secretaries acting as royal secretaries in negotiations with white traders, prospectors, and foreign powers." (Cf. Quentin Neil Parsons, "Khama III, The Bamangwato and the British, with Special Reference to 1895–1923," Edinburgh University Ph.D. dissertation, 1973).

** Hoyt Alverson's Mind in the Heart of Darkness: Value and Self Identity among the Tswana of Southern Africa, (New Haven: Yale University Press 1978, pp. 16–43) contains a longer social and historical overview which focuses on a wider geographical area, more explicitly on politico-economic issues and is less Euro-centric in orientation.

securing protectorate status for their territory. This shows great assertiveness and political skill on their part. It suggests that they were quite comfortable dealing with Queen Victoria's bureaucracy.

Second is that the first phase of rural (tribal) government under Protectorate was one of "parallel rule." "It showed the maximum regard for the customary authority of the Chiefs, and it restricted intervention to such measures as were necessary to satisfy the more simple requirements of local rule such as the collection of tax and the preservation of order." * This system followed two precedents from outside Africa, American Indian reservations in North America and protected princedoms in India.** This phase lasted until 1934 and was followed by a phase of "indirect rule." "It operated with the emphasis on 'indirect' compared to other British African dependencies." "The policy of replacing native authorities by systems of representative local government such as were implemented in the British dependencies in West Africa [was] not applied to [the] Bechuanaland Protectorate under British rule." ***

British intentions were not entirely liberal, but this form of governance had at least two advantages for the Tswana. It kept indigenous political institutions, including the legal system, intact, and it reduced the number of resident European administrators.

6. History of the Botswana Tswana 1953–1975: Achieving Independence

NOTE

The following excerpt was written by another South African anthropologist, John Comaroff. Comaroff has done recent fieldwork among the Tswana, both in Botswana and in South Africa. Separately and together with his collaborator, Simon Roberts, he has published extensively on Tswana law, social organization, and political organization. Comaroff, who is Associate Professor of Anthropology at the University of Chicago, wrote this excerpt to update the volume from which the previous excerpt (by Schapera) was abstracted. This piece provides an historical review of the changes in governance structures, including the development of political parties, that led up to and resulted from independence. Also among these changes is deliberate reduction in the authority of chiefs.

John Comaroff, "Tswana Transformations 1953–1975," in The Tswana, by Isaac Schapera, (Ethnographic Survey of Africa, Southern Africa Part III). London: International African Insti-

* Lord Hailey, An African Survey (Revised 1956). London: Oxford University Press, 1957, p. 272.

** Q.N. Parsons, personal communication, 1981.

*** W.J.O. Jeppe, "Local Government in Southern Africa," edited by W.B. Vosloo, D. A. Kotze, and W.J.O. Jeppe. Pretoria and Capetown: Academica, 1974, p. 138.

tute, 1953 (1976 reprint), pp. 69–70. Emphasis supplied. Footnotes
omitted. Material inserted by editor in brackets.

It is primarily in the latter years of the period under review that
the most significant developments occurred in Botswana: the earlier
phase, 1953–1965, culminated in the winding down of the colonial administration and preparations for independence. During this phase,
there was little manifest change in either the system of local government or national policy . . . .

The emergent post-colonial political system, however, involved a
fundamental redistribution of authority. This system was founded
upon the Westminster model . . . . [The structure of this system
of government, including the role of the House of Chiefs, is described
in the Campbell excerpt in section B3.]

It was not only at the national level that the role of traditional
authorities was redelimited. By the time Botswana became an independent republic, a Local Government Committee (1963) had already
recommended substantial changes in administrative organization.
The legislation which followed was construed by many Tswana as an
attack on the chiefship and the traditional order; in reply, the ruling
Botswana Democratic Party asserted their commitment to the creation of a modern development-orientated regime in which patterns of
the past were respected but not uncritically retained.

Essentially, the new system of local government is based upon
three major laws. The *first*, the *Chieftainship Law, 1965*, regulates
the recognition, suspension or removal of chiefs and their representatives, deputy chiefs and headmen. While the designation of chiefs
remains an indigenous prerogative, the president maintains final
sanction over the outcomes of local level political processes. . . .

The *second*, the *Local Government (District Councils) Law,
1965*, established district councils elected by popular vote along party
political lines. Control over matters of local policy passed to the
council and its sub-committees, with administrative and financial
functions being managed by a modernized bureaucracy. Council
chairmen are elected by council members; and, although most of the
early ones were chiefs, few now are.

The transfer of control away from traditional authorities, who had
enjoyed greater autonomy than their counterparts in most other British territories, was justified in a White Paper (No. 21 of 1964):
" . . . it cannot be expected that the chief, however enlightened
and hard-working, will win popular support and active cooperation in
carrying out policies which are ultimately not of his own and his people's making. . . . Local government therefore should not depend
on the chiefs." Consistent with this policy, many important resources were also removed from chiefly hands. Thus the distribution
of land became the exclusive function of Land Boards created by the
Tribal Land Act, 1968. This *third* Act formalized the procedure for

the allocation, registration and arbitration of land claims, and set up the necessary clerical and administrative machinery. . . . The Land Board itself is ultimately controlled by the District Council and the Ministry of Local Government and Lands, each of which designates two of its members. The chief is an *ex officio* board member and has the right to appoint another. Initially, chairmen were usually chiefs; but, since 1974–5, the Ministry has begun to select others.

Similarly, other legislation has transferred the potentially valuable rights over stray cattle from the chief to the district administration. The latter now manages the collection of most local finance (local tax, court fines, license fees, etc.) as well as its distribution in the form of salaries, funds for development, welfare, education and so on. Moreover, the maintenance of order has become the task of the Botswana police and council-paid local policemen. The control of force is no longer the domain of office-holders and their regiments.

Finally, the district administration has assumed direct responsibility for supervising local development through its District Development Committee (D.D.C.). Ideally, each village should have a Village Development Committee (V.D.C.) to organize new projects with the (council) Assistant Community Development Officer. . . . The achievements of the V.D.C.s have not been noteworthy to date. They have often been opposed vigorously by chiefs, without whose aid their success is inevitably limited. In the past, public projects were a chiefly concern; indeed, the success of office-holders depended partly upon material innovation. Many Tswana suggest that the modern chief is essentially a civil servant. His "subjects" are represented in parliament and district council by elected representatives, and his effective power is a function of personal factors rather than of his formal authority. The only aspect of the office which is relatively unaltered is the judicial one.*

NOTE

The Comaroff excerpt elides much of the political history of Botswana between 1953 and 1975. Again, that history involves a prominent role for a man who is thought of by his people as a chief. The first President of Botswana, Sir Seretse Khama, was heir to the Chieftaincy among the Ngwato, the largest of the Tswana tribes. In 1949, in a series of events detailed in Chapter 9, he was denied access to the chieftaincy basically because of his marriage to an English woman without prior permission of his tribe. Ultimately, in 1956, he was allowed to participate in Protectorate political affairs as a private citizen. Before independence he founded the Botswana Democratic party which won the first parliamentary elections and named him his country's first

* For a comprehensive historical review and commentary on local government in Botswana, focusing particularly on the post-independence period, see W.J.O. Jeppe, "Local Government in Bot-swana" in Local Government in Southern Africa, edited by W.B. Vosloo, D.A. Kotze, and W.J.O. Jeppe. Pretoria and Capetown: Academica, 1974, pp. 134–162.

President. He died in 1980. It can be argued that the successes of Botswana's development-oriented government are due largely to Sir Seretse's
prestige, charisma, and political acumen as a person of chiefly stock—not to
mention his excellent education.

7.   A Note on the Persistence of Chiefly Power

NOTE

The chieftaincy was the central Tswana cultural institution in the 18th century. But it is less so today. Recall Alverson's suggestion that "the concept
of the chiefdom and the distinctions based on it are more and more confined
to 'memory culture': ceremony, oral history, and anthropologists' observations." And Comaroff chronicled the government's detachment of chiefs
from authority. Q. N. Parsons (personal communication 1981) observes that
the "chieftaincy" is not just one man. The analytical focus, he argues, should
be on the *dikgosana*, "royal headmen" as a group: "Individual chiefs wax and
wane . . . but the overall . . . institution of rule by *dikgosana* keeps
on going—despite or probably because of factional competition among and
absorption of non-royal prominent commoners by marital alliance and patronage over land-allocation, etc. A chief never rules without his uncles and
more besides."

Examination of mid-twentieth century settlement patterns provides an intriguing insight into why, in spite of all this, the chieftaincy remains important
to Tswana and the Tswana view of proper social existence. The "natural" or
typical settlement pattern for a culture focused as much on stock-keeping as
the Tswana would be dispersed settlement in small hamlets, a pattern commonly found among East African pastoralists. Such a pattern is particularly
likely where the availability of water is problematical. The Tswana are unusual as stock-persons in that they have their primary residence in towns and
villages, as Alverson notes. Why?

**John Comaroff, "Tswana Transformations 1953–1975," in the
Tswana, by Isaac Schapera, (Ethnographic Survey of Africa,
Southern Africa Part III). London: International African Insti-
tute, 1953 (1976 reprint) p. 71. Footnotes deleted.**

. . . given rainfall patterns and the contingencies of dry land
crop cultivation and stock management, it would be in the material
interests of tribesmen to live scattered alongside their agricultural
holdings rather than in compact settlements. The need to move out
from village to fields immeasurably complicates the organization of
production. Indeed, among the Barolong, the chiefdom with the
highest rates of arable production in Botswana, the population *does*
live permanently scattered. Concentrated settlement has been resisted there expressly because this would decrease outputs. In other
words, the general residence pattern occurs *in spite of* ecological and
material considerations. [The reasons for the general residence pattern . . .] lie in the fact that the chiefship is village based.

It is in the interests of the chief that tribesmen be domiciled in the capital, since his political control is most effectively exercised when they are concentrated. As a result, office-holders endeavour to exert pressure upon their subjects to return to the village whenever possible. Similarly, it is generally the concern of headmen, and others who wish to gain influence, that people should not scatter permanently. For, while Tswana may move between two or more loci of activity, the major public political arena is firmly established at the centre.

The political factor was particularly persuasive in the past, then, because village concentration was actively encouraged by those who controlled such key resources as land, stock and the devolution of political offices.

NOTE

And, today, district councils are still headquartered in the chiefs' former capitals.*

Although in some of his writings Comaroff suggests that changing government policies concerning the chieftaincy will have significant effects on other aspects of indigenous Tswana life, these changes have been less drastic than one would predict—so far. Chiefs' official roles have been truncated, but they manage, in many cases, to remain powerful figures:

John Comaroff, "Tswana Transformations 1953–1975," in the Tswana, by Isaac Schapera, (Ethnographic Survey of Africa, Southern Africa Part III). London: International African Institute, 1953 (1976 reprint), p. 72. Footnotes deleted.

Their loss of constituted authority does not necessarily mean that chiefs and headmen no longer have *any* access to power. But the extent to which they exercise influence depends largely upon personal skills. By exploiting the respect which some of the population retain for the office, a perceptive traditional leader may extend his legitimacy. Moreover, a number of residual politico-economic resources may remain at his disposal. For example, a recent essay has shown that an able office-holder may manipulate his intercalary position between the administration and his people in order to recruit support for himself from both sources. Membership of the District Council, the Land Board, perhaps the V.D.C.,** and other bodies may enable the active local authority to have a considerable effect upon public affairs. In addition, their former hegemony over economic resources has left some chiefs and headmen in control of considerable personal wealth in land, cash and other capital holdings (boreholes, agricultural machinery, transport facilities, etc.). These assets may

* When chieftaincy, the core Tswana cultural institution falters, people disperse. Adam Kuper, citing Pauw, has analyzed an instance where this has occurred in a Tswana chiefdom in South Africa. (cf. Adam Kuper, "The Social Structure of the Sotho-Speaking Peoples of Southern Africa," in Africa, vol. 45, 1975.

** Village District Council.

be employed for both economic and political purposes; their scarcity guarantees high returns, in terms of both cash and patronage, from loans and the extension of usufruct. By virtue of their activities in this sphere, a chief or headman may expand his informal control. As this suggests, the *de facto* power of modern office-holders is highly variable, and is achieved in spite of severe limitations upon authority. Of course, such variability existed in the past as well, but for rather different reasons.

The circumstances which have transformed the chiefship have also created opportunities for the emergence of other powerful individuals. Hence wealthy commoners (merchants, successful farmers, agricultural entrepreneurs) and recruits to the cadres of government (M.P.s, party leaders, district councillors, government employees) may figure prominently in the affairs of their local communities. Again, their influence is not uniform; unfortunately, however, the political role of "new men," in rural Botswana is not yet systematically documented.

NOTE

Thus, in most areas, even though the logistics of stock keeping would seem to mandate otherwise, settlement patterns still reflect the importance of the chiefs' capitals as, politically, where the action is.

QUESTIONS

1. Traditional Tswana society seemed to be one in which most important roles were allocated on the basis of ascriptive criteria (sex, noble birth, age, birth order, and kinship). How pervasive was this ascriptivity? Do you see any hints in the materials that there was any scope for non-ascriptive (i.e., achievement-related) criteria in role allocation? Put another way, is there any evidence that ascription and achievement are competing modes in Tswana society? Later, in the chapter on political succession, look for evidence that *legitimated* ascriptive status may be a function of personal achievement.

2. Tswana chiefs played an important role in persuading the British to establish a Protectorate over what is now Botswana. Why do you think the chiefs were able successfully to "negotiate the bureaucracy" of British government and corporate and missionary organizations?

3. If chieftaincy is such a central institution for the Tswana, why hasn't Tswana society disintegrated in the face of the chieftaincy's weakening?

4. To think about now and answer after reading later chapters on the Tswana:

   (a) This section has presented traditional Tswana sociocultural institutions as functioning to adapt the Tswana to their past geographical and social environments. How adaptive are they in their current environment? Do Tswana legal institutions increase the degree of adaptivity or detract from it?

(b) What has been and is the role of law in upholding the role and centrality of cultural institutions which the Tswana value highly such as the chieftaincy, the keeping of cattle, and the assumed superiority of men over women?

(c) Did the political effects of preferential cousin marriage have any impact on the ability of Tswana political authorities to deal with other indigenous peoples? What about their ability to deal with Europeans?

(d) Are there consequences of patterned cousin marriage other than political ones? As you read the chapter on inheritance in Botswana consider the effects on inheritance.

5. To think about as you read the next section of this chapter:

(a) Have chiefs had more access to imposed (received) Western law than other Tswana? Have they used such access as a means to preserve their individual power?

(b) The persistence of power in the hands of chiefs suggests the persistence of some of the values and structural principles (e.g. importance of rank) that underlie the chieftaincy. Does it also suggest inequality before the law? In traditional law? In imposed law? If so, what tensions does this create in the modern, multi-party state?

C. TSWANA LAW

NOTE

Tswana indigenous law was traditional, but it was also African law. What characterizes African law as opposed to traditional law in general?

1. African Traditional Law

NOTE

African traditional law is largely unwritten and, therefore, its sources lie mainly in custom and tradition. But it also has roots in ethics, morality, a society's understanding of everyday processes of human behavior and—in some societies—new customs in the form of edicts from chiefs and/or councils, i.e., what we, in the West, like to call "legislation."

Traditional law in Africa is localized, again like traditional law in general, but it is more localized since there are more separate languages and cultures in Africa than in any other continental area. Collective responsibility, another common feature of traditional law is widespread in Africa. But rights do not inhere solely in groups and certainly not in the law as an abstract entity. Because most African societies focus strongly on personal status and role relationships, rights are felt to inhere in statuses and role relationships—in a position like "father," or "wife" or "chief" and their respective role expectations.

Most African societies are horticultural and, hence, quite sedentary. Edgerton links this sedentism to a concern about the expression of overt conflict because sedentary peoples, unlike nomadic ones, cannot easily move and leave conflict behind.* Therefore, the argument goes, settled populations have a preference for the indirect expression of aggression. A consequence for African law is that a significant category of offenses is witchcraft, sorcery, and other anti-social acts that express aggression indirectly. In the primary relationships that categorize small to medium scale African villages and towns, or wards of indigenous cities, Africans are sensitive to psychological pressures and, thus, to the potential activation of witchcraft or sorcery. Put more broadly, in Africa, the sanctions on which the legal process depends lean not only on the physical force that is a kingpin of standard scholarly definitions of law, but equally on reciprocity (more precisely, *denial* of reciprocity) and psychological pressures.

The supernatural impinges on the law in another way as well, in the use of oaths and ordeals as a way of obtaining or assessing evidence or assessing guilt. This pattern is widespread in Africa.

Like traditional law everywhere, law in Africa tends to be less institutionally discrete, less separated out as an institution. Therefore, it lacks the specialists that characterize Western law, attorneys, and relatively much of the procedural elaboration of law in the West. On the total continuum of the range of legal systems of non-literate societies, however, African law is quite institutionalized and formalized.

2. Tswana Traditional Law

a. The Chieftaincy

NOTE

By now it probably is clear that the Tswana traditional legal system was organized around the chieftaincy and—when he conducted himself properly—the incumbent chief. This is because of the centripetal force of the chieftaincy in Tswana life.

b. The Kgotla

NOTE

To understand the second distinctive feature of the Tswana legal system one must know something of the spatial arrangement of Tswana towns.

Isaac Schapera, A Handbook of Tswana Law and Custom, London: Oxford University Press, 1955, second edition, pp. 8–9.

The smaller villages consist as a rule of a single hamlet or cluster of homesteads. Each hamlet is normally, but not necessarily, arranged on a circular plan, with the component homesteads distributed in a ring and facing inwards towards a central open space. Within this central space are found one or more cattle-kraals, and, close to

* cf. Robert Edgerton, The Individual in Cultural Adaptation: A Study of Four East African Peoples, Berkeley: University of California Press, 1971.

each, a booth-like or crescentic windbreak of stout poles, where the men of the hamlet meet to discuss their affairs. This meeting-place (*kgotla*) is the dominant feature of each hamlet and plays an extremely important part in the public life of its people. The bigger villages are made up of several or many such hamlets (according to the size of the village), clearly separated from one another by lanes or roads of varying width. The inhabitants of each hamlet belong to a distinct social and administrative unit of the tribe, generally a ward, and always have their own *kgotla* where they meet to discuss their affairs. The *kgotla* of the Chief's hamlet, situated in the centre of the tribal capital, is the seat of the tribal administration. Here the Chief administers justice, receives reports, and interviews people, and here are held many of the tribal gatherings and ceremonies. The great cattle-kraal adjoining it is also a place of political and ritual importance. Here secret meetings of the Chief's advisers and headmen are held, and here also the Chief is generally buried when he dies.

NOTE

One meaning of the term *kgotla*, then, is a central meeting place where important administrative/political, ritual, and ceremonial events take place. The place and the term are closely associated with the political/administrative units, its political head, and the people who comprise it by pledging allegiance to him. *Kgotla* is also used to refer to the ward as a territorial and administrative unit. "We are one kgotla," people say. The two meanings of the term reinforce the identification of the people of a territorial/administrative unit with that unit, and with its head.

c.　The Lekgotla—An Assembly

NOTE

A cognate term, to *kgotla* is *lekgotla*, which refers to an assembly, a group of men gathered at the *kgotla* for a particular purpose. The court is only one such assembly. Again, Isaac Schapera provides a clear explanation. Keep in mind that he is writing about the colonial period, primarily the 1930's and 1940's:

Isaac Schapera, Government and Politics in Tribal Societies, London: Watts, 1956, pp. 43–44.*

. . . among Sotho, and especially Tswana, almost all matters of public concern are discussed finally at a popular assembly (commonly termed *pitsô*), which ordinary tribesmen are also expected to attend. Such assemblies, summoned by the chief whenever he thinks fit, are in some tribes held very often, at times almost weekly, except when the people are busy at their fields. They usually meet in the council-

---

* A fuller treatment of these assemblies appears in Isaac Schapera, A Handbook of Tswana Law and Custom, London: Oxford University Press, 1955, 2d ed., pp. 80–83.

place (*kgotla*) adjoining the chief's residence. Normally only the men present in the capital are summoned, perhaps merely to be told of some forthcoming ceremony, to receive instructions about public labour, or to listen to other formal announcements; and if necessary the message is communicated to outlying settlements through their local rulers. But on important occasions, as when new laws are proposed or other big decisions have to be made, the whole tribe is convened; if the matter is at all critical (such as a serious internal dispute or threatened invasion), attendance may even be compulsory. A crucial meeting of this kind is sometimes held in the open veld some distance from the capital, and the men all come to it armed and ready for trouble; it is then usually also preceded or followed by a collective drive for game.

The people sit in a big semi-circle facing the chief and his senior relatives; other leading men are in front, but otherwise there is no special arrangement. The chief, who presides, briefly explains the purpose of the meeting. If it is a matter requiring discussion, some of his advisers then give a lead by stating the views that they may have reached with him beforehand in private. They are usually but not necessarily followed by other important men, after which anybody else who wishes may speak or ask questions. The chief finally sums up what has been said and announces his decision. The assembly itself, it is important to note, seldom raises topics for discussion; it merely deliberates upon the issues presented to it, and thus enables him to ascertain public opinion. The meeting normally lasts for only part of the day, but if the matter is sufficiently weighty or controversial to attract many speakers it may be spread over two days or more. It is in any event continued until a decision has been reached. There is no special system of voting, the speeches made and the general mood being sufficient to indicate the trend of opinion; but occasionally, as among the Kgatla, if the discussion reveals marked disagreement the chief may ask the men to group themselves according to their views, and the relative strength of the different parties is then clearly seen.

NOTE

Meeting in full tribal assembly for decision-making or decision ratification is unusual in sub-Saharan Africa. The tribal *lekgotla* is a distinctive feature of the Tswana legal system. New law may be made and old law reinforced by the adult men of the tribe acting in concert in a *lekgotla*. (Readers are cautioned that in some later excerpts in these materials writers on the Tswana use the term *kgotla* when they are referring not to the meeting place but to *lekgotla*, the group of men assembled there.)

d. Hierarchical Arrangement of Courts

NOTE

The structure of Tswana traditional legal system is hierarchical in that there are a series of courts of progressively greater jurisdiction, with that of initial jurisdiction being the local court. Recall that Tswana towns are divided into wards, headed by an hereditary official, the "ward-head" and his court is the local court, the court of initial jurisdiction. He makes decisions with the aid of his senior brothers, paternal uncles, and a few other wise men. They are "assessors" who remind him of the law and help him recall precedent. Assessors as junior co-judges are found in customary courts at all levels.

Cases from the ward-head's court may be appealed to the court of the village head. In his court he is assisted by the heads of the various wards. In most Tswana chiefdoms the next—and highest—level of traditional court is that of the tribe's chief, the chief's court located in the chief's headquarters' town, the tribal capital.

In some tribes, notably the Kgatla, there is an administrative division intermediate between the village and the chiefdom called the "section." In those tribal areas cases may be appealed from the village head's court, to that of the section head, who is the head of the senior ward in the section chief's court. Obviously, the nature of the hierarchy of administrative divisions and appellate sequence for cases is similar to that in the West.

There were other bodies apart from the regular courts which helped ameliorate disputes. Before a case was taken to the ward court an attempt was made to settle it in the court of the family group, which, evidently, was a kind of "moot." In more traditional times there were also regimental courts that dealt with offenses pertaining to the initiation "schools" and regimental matters.

I have described the structure of Tswana traditional courts as they existed before significant continual European influence. That structure can be diagrammed as shown on page 78.

e. Unique Features of Tswana Traditional Law

NOTE

The Tswana legal system is unique among traditional Sub-Saharan legal systems in the elaboration of its tribal assembly (*lekgotla*) and focus on this form of legislative activity. Also relatively unique in Sub-Saharan legal systems is the fact that it makes no recourse to oaths or ordeals, and the fact it honors executory contracts.

QUESTION

1. What are the functions of the tribal-wide *lekgotla*? What is its impact vis-a-vis the chieftaincy?

HIERARCHY OF TSWANA CUSTOMARY COURTS
IN THE MID–COLONIAL PERIOD (c. 1930)

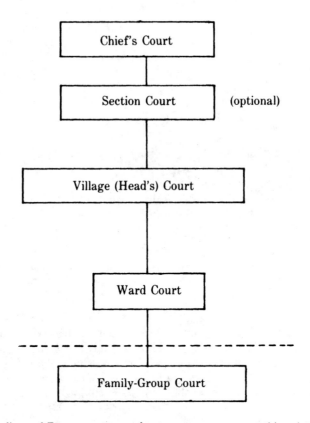

The proceedings of Tswana courts need not concern us more at this point except to observe that they do not involve a consistent distinction between "civil" and "criminal" law. The proceedings are described in Chapter 15.

[C6080]

D. THE INTRUSION OF EUROPEAN LAW IN BOTSWANA

NOTE

Since the late 19th century Tswana law has coexisted side-by-side with European law. Let us trace the history of European law in Botswana for it has resulted in a dual system of law in which customary or traditional law coexists with imposed or "received" law. Amalgamating the two kinds of legal systems is a process currently underway in Botswana and in most recently-independent African nations as well. The history of imposed law we will trace is that summarized in very condensed form in the Campbell excerpt in Section B3.

1. Early Post-Protectorate Judicial Developments and Court Structure

NOTE

We begin our historical review by recalling that an important date in the late 19th century history of Botswana was 1895, when Britain declared Bechuanaland to be a British Protectorate. There were several grounds for that action. One that was stated prominently at the time was that the peoples of the area (including British subjects) were being protected from the incursions of the still-expanding Afrikaners. But, a second interpretation chosen by most recent writers on the subject says that Britain took over Bechuanaland for strategic reasons. Alverson notes that the establishment of German protectorates in Southwest Africa and Tanganyika, combined with the possibility of German alliances with the Boer republic of Transvaal and its mini-protectorates of Stellaland and Goshen, created the possibility of a German "coast-to-coast colonial presence in Africa (which . . . would [have] effectively block[ed] Britain's access to the interior and the fabled wealth it contained." * Establishment of the Bechuanaland Protectorate ended that possibility.

Britain's Foreign Jurisdiction Act (1890) was the legal basis for British judicial involvement in the Protectorate:

Anthony Sillery, Comments on Two Articles in 8 Botswana Notes and Records, 1976, p. 294.**

The principle of Foreign Jurisdiction was originally a device whereby British subjects could be tried and their cases adjudicated by a British Court under British law in a foreign country. Later it became the legal basis for the assumption and management of British protectorates, including the Bechuanaland Protectorate. A protectorate was a territory which the protecting Power undertook to defend from external aggression without the responsibility for internal administration. A British Protectorate, unlike a colony, was not British soil, its people were not British subjects, and the local ruler's powers as to domestic issues were unimpaired.

In the course of time Foreign Jurisdiction was so interpreted and extended as to confer upon the Crown complete jurisdiction over the indigenous people of protectorates as well as over British subjects. As a result, a protectorate for practical purposes became the same as a colony. But the old protectorate concept died hard and was still alive in the last decade of the 19th century.

* Hoyt Alverson, Mind in the Heart of Darkness, New Haven: Yale University Press, 1978, p. 25. Cf. also, Ron H. Paul, Bechuanaland Revisited: A Review of Botswana: A Short Political History by Anthony Sillery. In Botswana Notes and Records, Volume 7, 1975, p. 208.

** The Sillery article comments on an article by the Chief Justice of the Botswana High Court (see later excerpt) and one other article.

NOTE

In 1846 the Governor of the Cape Colony was appointed High Commissioner for the areas adjacent or contiguous to the eastern and northeastern frontiers of the Colony and, in that capacity, "the supreme authority in South Africa for the supervision of fringe areas inhabited mainly or wholly by black Africans." * But it was not until 1891 that a formal administration was created, although the Protectorate had been declared in 1885. Jeppe describes the Order-in-Council which established that administration and the nature of the administration:

W.J.O. Jeppe, "Local Government in Botswana," in Local Government in Southern Africa, edited by W.B. Vosloo, D.A. Kotze, and W.J.O. Jeppe. Pretoria and Capetown: Academica, 1974, p. 134.

In terms of the Order-in-Council of May 1891 the British High Commissioner (stationed in Cape Town at the time) was given authority to appoint administrative and judicial staff in the protectorate. In June 1891 a proclamation was accordingly passed which provided for the appointment of a resident commissioner, with assistant commissioners serving under him. The assistant commissioners, stationed in the districts of the protectorate, were given jurisdiction as resident magistrates but the jurisdiction of their courts was limited to exclude all cases in which Africans were concerned, unless such cases were in the interest of good order or the prevention of violence. Provision was also made for the appointment of chiefs to exercise jurisdiction over tribesmen under tribal law and custom.

With the exceptions of serious criminal matters and litigation between tribesmen and foreigners, the tribal chiefs were thus left undisturbed in their application of tribal law in the tribal courts.

The only important limitation of the authority of the chiefs was the provision that the right to occupation or ownership of land was subject to approval by the British High Commissioner.

NOTE

An earlier section revealed that the Protectorate arrangements left local level political and legal institutions largely in their traditional form, in the hands of ruling oligarchies. This duality was partly at the expressed insistence of prominent Tswana chiefs. But note that, under the Protectorate arrangements, not only the High Commissioner but the "Resident" Commissioner resided outside of Bechuanaland in South Africa **. That the

---

* Anthony Sillery, Botswana: A Short Political History, London: Methuen and Co., Ltd., 1974, p. 53. (Cf. also: Justice Akinola Aguda, "Legal Development in Botswana from 1885 to 1966" in 5 Botswana Notes and Records, 1973, p. 54.)

** The High Commissioner resided first in Capetown and, later, in Pretoria. The Resident Commissioner resided in Mafeking, also in South Africa, which was the capital of Bechuanaland, even though it did not lie within Bechuanaland's boundaries. (Richard P. Stevens, Historical Dictionary of The Republic of Botswana. Metuchen, New Jersey: The Scarecrow Press, Inc., 1975, pp. 67–68, 94, 123.)

persons who served as magistrates were not legally trained,* but colonial officers who added on this judicial role also is worth noting. Finally, note that the courts of the administrators-cum-magistrates existed primarily for Europeans residing in the Protectorate, not for Africans. Aguda comments pointedly on the penultimate point:

Justice Akinola Aguda, "Legal Development in Botswana from 1885 to 1966," in 5 Botswana Notes and Records, 1973, p. 54.

It was quite clear . . . that it was not the intention of Her Majesty's Government to create an independent judiciary for this Protectorate even though England at that time could boast, and justifiably so, of having enjoyed the full benefits of an independent judiciary for at least three or four centuries. Indeed, it was never contemplated that professional lawyers would be appointed to the judicial positions. What was anticipated, and which in fact happened, was that administrative officers who were directly or indirectly responsible to the High Commissioner and who took instructions directly or indirectly from him, would discharge judicial functions merely as part of their normal duties.

NOTE

The absence of an independent, trained judiciary during the Protectorate period has had consequences which plague the legal system of Botswana even today, for there still are very few Batswana with legal training and, consequently, senior levels of the judiciary still are almost entirely expatriate. In the private sector there is a very small bar in Botswana. As of March 1980, there were 19 attorneys in private practice. Of these, 13 were resident in Botswana; 2 in South Africa, 3 in Zambia, and 1 in Zimbabwe.**   Only 3 of this group were Batswana.

The 1891 Order in Council that established the Bechuanaland administration and European courts was a bit ambiguous as to what European law was to be applied and as of what exact date it was to be applied. Was it to be English common law, including that body of law known as Equity or, given the geographical location of Bechuanaland and the fact that its senior administrator was a High Commissioner who resided in the South African capital of Pretoria, was it to be the Roman-Dutch law of South Africa? This issue has continued to beset Botswana's legal system down through the years. Thus, the decision in a contemporary case may turn on whether the appropriate precedent is South African or from (English) common law.

I. G. Brewer, "Sources of the Criminal Law of Botswana," 18 Journal of African Law, 1974, pp. 25–26. Footnotes omitted. Emphasis supplied.

. . . It was recognised by the authorities that there were doubts as to the precise meaning of the reception clause in the 1891

---

* The use of lay magistrates was common practice throughout the British empire.

** "List of Attorneys," Consular Section, American Embassy, Gaborone, Botswana, March 1980.

Proclamation * and in 1909 a Proclamation was issued the purpose of which was, in the words of the preamble to the Proclamation, to "remove such doubts". This Proclamation repealed section 19 of the 1891 Proclamation ** and provided that:

> ". . . the laws in force in the Colony of the Cape of Good Hope on 10th day of June, 1891 shall *mutatis mutandis* and so far as not inapplicable be the laws in force and to be observed in the said Protectorate. . . ."

. . .

Having seen that the unwritten general criminal law in force in Botswana after 1891 was the unwritten substantive criminal law in force in the Colony of the Cape of Good Hope on June 10th, 1891, the question arises as to the nature of that law. The whole body of law was generally called Roman-Dutch law, and indeed in a later proclamation it was expressly referred to as "Roman-Dutch common law" but the use of this expression was entirely inappropriate. There is no doubt that in the early days the common law in force in the Cape Colony was the Roman-Dutch common law. This was the system of law applied in the province of Holland during the Dutch Republic and which was brought to South Africa in 1652 by the early European settlers. However, after the Cape was ceded to Britain in 1814 the law, including the criminal law, was influenced and substantially modified by English law. The use of the expression "Roman-Dutch law" therefore tells only part of the story and it would be more appropriate to refer to the common law in force in Botswana as *Cape Colonial Law*.

NOTE

I. G. Brewer is correct in concluding that the imposed law of Botswana should be referred to as "Cape Colonial" law. But this term has not taken hold in the literature and, most commonly, the received law of Botswana still is referred to as "Roman Dutch" law.

Akinola Aguda is a Nigerian who served as Chief Justice of the High Court of Botswana after independence. Some of his writing was excerpted earlier in this section. In the same article he has commented on the consequences for the statutory law of Botswana of receiving Cape Colonial Law as imposed law:

Justice Akinola Aguda, "Legal Development in Botswana from 1885 to 1966," in Botswana Notes and Records, 5, 1973, p. 57. Footnotes omitted.

In the first place, the so-called Roman-Dutch Law is now neither Roman nor Dutch. Secondly, that system of law as at 1891 is, in the

---

* Legislation in the Protectorate took the form of proclamations (edicts) issued by the High Commissioner.

** Section 19 of the 1891 Proclamation provided that ". . . the law to be administered shall, as nearly as the circumstances of the country will permit, be the law for the time being in force in the colony of the Cape of Good Hope . . ." (Brewer, p. 24).

eyes of modern jurists, primitive, and it is that law that is regarded as the common law, not that law as subsequently developed in other countries. No doubt it has since been developed by South Africa but in the eyes of modern jurists it must, clearly, be regarded as a primitive system of law in 1891; and there were no professional judges in this country to develop it. The result of this is that the courts of this country had, and still have, to consult South African writers, whose opinions are based on that law as subsequently developed by their courts or the courts of other countries. Thirdly, neither in this country nor in any other civilized countries in the world, is learning in 19th century Dutch regarded as worthwhile academic pursuits . . . and Roman law has similarly ceased to be regarded as a subject for worthwhile pursuit and has made its honourable exit out of law courses in most of the Law Faculties of the more renowned universities in Europe and North America. Therefore, neither lawyers practising in this country nor the Judges have any real chance of searching for what a particular principle of law was under the Roman-Dutch Law as at 1891, except through interpretations. The only saving grace in this situation is that quite fortunately, until very recently, most of the judges who were subsequently called upon to carry out judicial duties in this country were all persons who were brought up under the English common law as applied elsewhere and therefore naturally made efforts to develop the common law of this country along the lines of the law with which they were familiar.* Still certain other archaic aspects of the Roman-Dutch law system have had to be corrected by legislation.

NOTE

The Cape colonial legacy which Mr. Justice Aguda details continues to influence the legal system in Botswana, most notably in the heavy use of South African precedents, the use of South African lawyers as counsel, and the appointment of South African jurists to the Botswana appellate bench, although this pattern is changing. The changes will be described in the concluding section.

From the beginning, the received law included the much-discussed "repugnancy clause." This held that customary law was to be applied only so far as it was "not incompatible with the due exercise of Her Majesty's power and jurisdiction or repugnant to morality, humanity, or natural justice or injurious to the welfare of the Africans." ** Even in the Customary Law Act of 1969, in force today, customary law is defined as: ". . . the customary law of [any] tribe or community so far as it is not incompatible with the provisions of any written law or contrary to morality, humanity, or natural justice." †

---

* Cf. Section E below.

** African Courts Proclamation, 1961, cited in I. G. Brewer, "Sources of the

Criminal Law of Botswana." 18 Journal of African Law, 1974, p. 34.

† Laws of Botswana, Cap. 14.02.

QUESTIONS

1. What were the factors that led to the establishment of a dual court system?

2. What two distinct strands of Western law comprised the "received" law of Botswana?

3. Why is "Cape Colonial" a better term for this received common law than "Roman-Dutch?"

4. What does the repugnancy clause suggest about the ethnocentrism of Western colonial rulers in then Bechuanaland?

2. Later Judicial Developments and Court Structure Under the Protectorate

a.   Customary Courts

NOTE

At the beginning of the Protectorate there were virtually no modifications made in the authority and operation of the traditional customary courts. But, gradually the scope and operation of the traditional courts was limited in various ways, as shown in the chart of Customary Courts (p. 86). Simon Roberts summarizes some of the ways in which that was done:

Simon Roberts, "The Survival of the Traditional Tswana Courts in the National Legal System of Botswana," 16 Journal of African Law, 1972, pp. 105–107. Some footnotes omitted; others renumbered.

The simple dual system of laws and courts which was . . . established could not continue indefinitely, and the width of jurisdiction enjoyed by the traditional authorities was gradually eroded. Early on the powers of the Chiefs to try cases of murder and disputes involving non-Africans were withdrawn and their decisions in other matters were made subject to appeal to the magistrates' courts. And in the years 1926 and 1927 respectively, legislation limiting the powers of the traditional courts over witchcraft and marriages celebrated under the Marriage Proclamation was passed. But no steps were taken to prescribe the membership of different traditional courts or to define their jurisdiction in general terms, and in practice they continued to settle disputes coming before them according to the customary procedures with very little encouragement or interference on the part of the administration.

It was only with the enactment of the Native Tribunals Proclamation in 1934, under which individual dispute settlement agencies were expressly recognised and incorporated in the formal court system of the Protectorate, that a general attempt was made to modify the traditional dispute settlement procedures.[1] This Proclamation, which was similar to those enacted in East and Central Africa at that time, established two classes of Native Tribunals, Senior and Junior, within which existing agencies might be recognised. The jurisdiction of any tribunal so recognised was to be confined to "natives" and to be exercised in civil and criminal matters "in accordance with native law and custom." Procedural rules made under the Proclamation included the requirement that the proceedings of any recognised tribunal should be recorded in writing.

The categories of tribunal established by the Proclamation corresponded closely to the higher-level agencies existing under customary law, as Senior Tribunals were to be presided over by a Chief or his appointed representative,[2] and Junior Tribunals by a headman. No provision was made for the recognition of dispute settlement agencies below the level of headman, but agencies which were not recognised were permitted to function informally as tribunals of arbitration.
. . .

Whatever the original intention behind the Proclamation of 1934, only a very small number of the traditional Tswana dispute settlement agencies eligible for recognition were ever absorbed into the formal courts system. The Chief's Court of each of the seven Tswana tribes occupying defined tribal territories at the time the Proclamation was brought into force was immediately recognised as a Senior Tribunal, as were the courts of a number of Chief's representatives situation in more important villages outside the tribal capitals, but recognition was extended to relatively few courts at ward level. . . .*

The very limited recognition given to traditional dispute settlement agencies at ward level is not difficult to explain. To have recognised ward courts more lavishly in 1934 would simply have

1. The administration's interference with the powers of the Chiefs was fiercely resisted at every stage. Notable among the earlier disputes was Regent Isang Pilane's struggle with the administration over the right to grant divorces to Africans married under the Marriage Proclamation (the history of this dispute can be found in Botswana National Archives, File J. 647). Later, when the 1934 Proclamations were introduced, Regent Tshekedi Khama of the Ngwato and Chief Bathoen II of the Ngwaketse contested their validity in the courts. [Citation omitted.]

2. Even before the period of the Protectorate some Chiefs were in the habit of appointing official representatives to act in administrative and judicial capacities over members of the tribe and subject peoples living in outlying settlements. The habit seems to have originated among the Ngwato: . . . .

* While senior tribunals by and large were chief's courts and courts of Chief's representatives, junior tribunals were more varied. They were courts of headmen which might be courts of principal wards in tribal capital courts of the traditional ruler of a non-Tswana group (Simon Roberts, "The Survival of the Traditional Tswana Courts in the National Legal System of Botswana," 16 Journal of African Law, 1972, p. 107.)

imposed intolerable burdens of administration and supervision. Particularly important was the fact that all recognised courts were required to maintain a written record of their proceedings; there were insufficient clerks available even for the very limited number of tribunals actually recognised. Another consideration which must have deterred the administration from granting recognition more widely was that in many instances the traditional ward organisation was already breaking down in 1934, and wards were in some cases no longer neatly defined on a geographical basis.

THE CUSTOMARY COURT STRUCTURE (as it was found when the Protectorate was established and as it was modified in 1934)

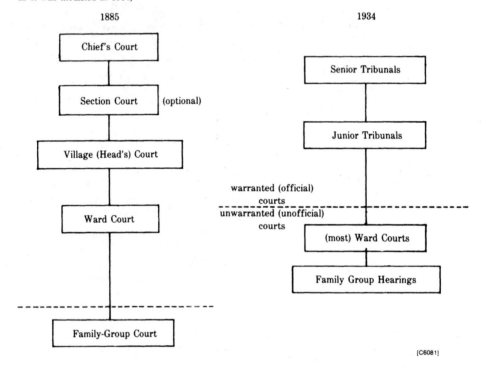

NOTE

Although most ward courts and courts below that level did not have official standing and, thus, were "unwarranted," they continued to serve an important function, acting more or less as they had before the Proclamation was issued. These courts, for most Batswana, acted as the court of first instance. Schapera describes the situation in 1943:

Isaac Schapera, "The Work of the Tribal Courts in the Bechuana-land Protectorate," 2 African Studies, 1943, p. 29.

. . . Almost all litigation is still heard first in the ward courts. Sometimes a case ends there, the court's verdict being accepted as final by the parties concerned. Generally, however, the court in effect merely holds a preparatory examination, and then sends the case, with its finding, to a higher tribunal; or else an appeal is lodged against its decision. This corresponds to the practice before the Proclamation was issued.

NOTE

The other changes wrought by the Proclamation of 1934 and another similar Proclamation of 1935 were to remove a variety of offenses from the purview of the customary courts, to affirm the right of appeal to the statutory (largely European) courts, and to make procedural changes that required that the members of the sitting court be specified and that procedural rules be formalized. The punishments available to the customary courts also were changed.

The changes set in place by the 1934 Proclamation were modified and revised in the Native Courts Proclamation issued in 1943. "This was itself replaced in 1961 by the African Courts Proclamation, later known as the Customary Courts Proclamation (1968), which followed the pattern of previous Proclamations by curtailing the powers of customary courts through limiting the offenses that could be dealt with and the punishments that could be awarded." *

The 1943 changes in particular, like the changes in 1934, were not welcomed wholeheartedly by chiefs. Contention over the role of the courts was a political struggle, a duel as to who would have power over the lives of the Motswana man in the ward, so to speak. Such contention continues today. Roberts provides some of the flavor of this tug-of-war:

Simon Roberts, "Tradition and Change at Mochudi: Competing Jurisdictions in Botswana," African Law Studies, 1979, number 17, p. 48. Footnote omitted.

. . . governmental interference with the traditional laws gave rise to a continuing battle with the administration. It is not possible to trace this history in any detail here, but I shall mention family law as one area in which the policies initially formulated gave rise to early difficulties. Even before the Protectorate was declared Tswana tribesmen had been married in accordance with Christian rites by various missionaries, and the rulers made no objection to this. But with the enactment of a Marriage Proclamation, and the assumption of powers by magistrates to grant matrimonial relief, the rulers felt that their authority over their subjects was being interfered with: *they* should be responsible, they argued, for policing the Christian marriages of their subjects and where necessary granting matrimonial relief. For several years, the Kgatla chief flouted government authority by divorcing Kgatla tribesmen married according to Christian rites. Of course, in the long run the Chiefs did not win this particular battle; but they did succeed in making it very difficult for their

* I. G. Brewer, "Sources of the Criminal Law of Botswana," 18 Journal of African Law (1974), p. 33.

tribesmen to marry in accordance with the national law (e.g., by demanding a high "fee" for the necessary certificate stating that the parties concerned were not married to other people by customary law); and they manipulated Tswana law in such a way that the relief available on marital breakdown appeared more favorable than that allowed in the national courts.

QUESTIONS

1. What kinds of offenses were removed from the purview of customary courts under the legislation of the 1920's and 1930's? Why?

2. Is it surprising that Tswana chiefs would use their position in the customary court structure to maintain their strategic power position in Tswana society?

3. What kinds of punishments do you think the colonial administration would remove from traditional authorities?

b. Statutory Courts

NOTE

The 1930's was a time when there were changes in the system of statutory courts, as well as in the customary courts, as shown in the chart of statutory courts (p. 89).

Although a High Court had been empowered by the Order-in-Council of 1891, it was not actually established until 1939. The terms of the establishing proclamation continued the policy of very limited access for black Africans and routinized the practice which had been established earlier of using "native assessors" when cases came before it which involved customary law:

Justice Akinola Aguda, "Legal Development in Botswana from 1885 to 1966," 5 Botswana Notes and Records, 1973, p. 55. Footnotes omitted.

. . . The newly established High Court was created as a Superior Court of Record and given unlimited jurisdiction in criminal and civil cases. In general, all the jurisdiction, power and authority vested in the Supreme Court of South Africa were also given to the High Court. However, the proclamation said that:

> no civil cause or action to which natives only are parties and no civil cause or action to which either party is a European and in which the amount claimed or the value of the subject-matter in dispute does not exceed five hundred pounds shall be instituted in or removed into the High Court save with the leave of the Judge upon application made to him in Chambers.

In other words, the High Court was created primarily for Europeans in an African country. The natives of this country were precluded from access to the High Court of their country only because they were natives, except when the Judge gave them leave. The High

Court was made a Court of Appeal and Review to all other courts inferior to it. A Judge of the High Court was empowered to ask for the assistance of not more than two administrative officers in criminal as well as in civil cases: likewise, he may call to his assistance one or more Native assessors.

THE STATUTORY COURT STRUCTURE (as it was created by the 1891 Order-in-Council and as it was modified in 1939)

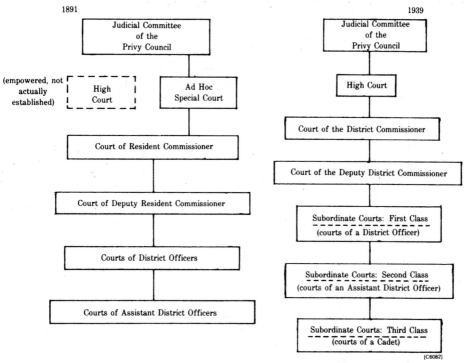

NOTE

At the same time that the High Court was actually established the existing courts of Protectorate administrative officers were replaced by three grades of "subordinate" courts. (See the chart above).

Justice Akinola Aguda, "Legal Development in Botswana from 1885 to 1966," 5 Botswana Notes and Records, 1973, pp. 55–56. Footnotes omitted. Editor's insertion in brackets.

[The grades of subordinate courts were:] (1) Courts of a District Officer, to be called Subordinate Courts of the First Class; (2) courts of an Assistant District Officer, to be called Subordinate Courts of the Second Class; and (3) Courts of a Cadet, to be called Subordinate Courts of the Third Class. The territorial limits in the jurisdiction of these courts were co-extensive with the limits of the administrative jurisdiction of the officers concerned, whilst their substantive jurisdictions were limited to claims where either party is a European and, in any event, subject to maximum claims at £500, £200 and £10 redictions were limited to claims where either party is a European and, in any event, subject to maximum claims at £500, £200 and £10 respectively. In other words, these courts were created mainly for cases involving Europeans; and this fact was further emphasized by a subsequent amendment which, very curiously, gave a clerk of the court power not to issue a writ if in his opinion the suit is one suitable to be heard in a Native Court.

NOTE

A further change in the system of statutory courts was brought about in 1954. Until then, appeal from the High Court of the, then, Bechuanaland Protectorate was to the Judicial Committee of the Privy Council in London. In that year an Order-in-Council established a single, joint Court of Appeal for the three High Commission Territories of Basutoland, Bechuanaland, and Swaziland. That format continued until independence when a separate Court of Appeal for Botswana was established by the new nation's constitution.

NOTE

A word of summary is in order. From the granting of the Protectorate until the coming of Independence, Botswana had a dual legal system. For the most part, customary courts applied customary law to the majority of the population, Batswana and other black Africans who see their lives as governed by the custom and culture of one of the Tswana peoples (less and less frequently referred to as "tribes"). The limitations placed on this court system by the colonial power were relatively minor. They involved restricting the power to handle cases that involved violence or in other ways threatened the stability of the political order (e.g., not paying taxes), and matters where an African had taken an action that might be construed as indicating willingness to have his or her life governed by the imposed Cape Colonial common law (e.g., marrying under statutory law or making a will).

The statutory courts, on the other hand, applied Cape Colonial common law to a minority of the population, Europeans, (including "Europeans" of African birth) other expatriates, and Batswana whose education and/or profession or occupation caused their lives not to be governed by customary law, but to be oriented in some significant respects to Cape Colonial law. For historical reasons outlined in earlier portions of this section, a great deal of the legislative (via proclamations) and judicial (via appellate precedents) input of the dual courts system was from South Africa. Thus, it took on something of the flavor of a culturally and racially separatist judicial system. How to overcome this would be the legacy handed to the nation as she moved from being the Bechuanaland Protectorate to becoming the democratic state of Botswana.

QUESTION

1. In what ways was the supremacy of received law expressed in the pre-independence legal system of Botswana?

THE HIGH COURT, LOBATSE. The chambers of the High Court of Botswana, a building which, prior to its present use, served as the site for the meetings of the first Legislative Council of the, then, Protectorate of Bechuanaland.

3. Post-Independence Judicial Developments

NOTE

The structure of the contemporary, post-independence legal system of Botswana is described in the excerpt by Alec Campbell in section B3 above. You will find it helpful to re-read that excerpt at this point. In diagrammatic form the structure of Botswana's legal system looks as follows:

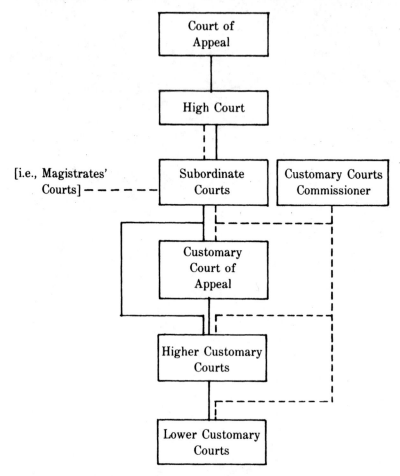

Modified from: Simon Roberts, "Botswana," in Judicial and Legal Systems in Africa, edited by Anthony N. Allott. London: Butterworth's, 1970, p. 312.   [C6086]

NOTE

The changes in Botswana's legal system that followed in the years shortly after independence are reflected in the description of that legal system in the Campbell excerpt (B3). The most notable changes include: the establishment of the position of Attorney General and of the Judicial Service Commission which recommends to the President the appointment of justices and magistrates for the various levels of the statutory court system; and the trans-

GABORONE CHIEF MAGISTRATE, MR. G.L. PATEL, 1981

formation of subordinate courts to magistrates' courts, presided over by four levels of magistrates, Chief Magistrates, Senior Magistrates, and Group I and Group II Magistrates.

NOTE

In reviewing the structure and operation of Botswana's legal system, the essential question is: how can a dual legal system be brought into harmony with the stated, fervently felt ideals of a society which is non-racial and democratic?

By and large, the duality which characterized the legal system at the time of independence continues. First, there is an asymmetry in the legal system. It is structured so that the appellate process is from customary courts to statutory courts, notwithstanding that customary courts now apply some statutory law. Second, while the customary courts continue to be used by Batswana who are traditional-oriented, the statutory courts are used by Batswana whose day-to-day lives are more heavily influenced by the Western mode, and by Botswana citizens of European background and expatriates. But there are many exceptions. Any citizen can and does use the court system where he or she feels that particular circumstances make it to his or her advantage to do so. Speaking to this issue, Simon Roberts describes the situation among the Kgatla, one of the major Tswana peoples:

Simon Roberts, "Tradition and Change at Mochudi: Competing Jurisdictions in Botswana," African Law Studies, 1979, number 17, pp. 46–47.

Apart from this limited original jurisdiction in the magistrate, the respective areas of competence of the national courts and the Kgatla courts are clear-cut when looked at from the angle of the lawyer, because the Customary Law (Application and Ascertainment) Act, 1969, provides quite elaborate rules specifying when national law or customary law should apply. But we should not make the mistake of imagining that Kgatla tribesmen see these two systems of law with their respective agencies in the same light. For tribesmen, the two agencies represent *choices* that they seek to manipulate in developing their strategies in litigation; and the jurisdiction of the magistrate to hear disputes founded in customary law may provide an important bargaining counter.

Nonetheless, a false picture would be presented if it were suggested that the magistrate's court and the Chief's court represent rival agencies, each more or less equally successful in attracting business. Despite the fact that the threat of resort to the magistrate is a frequent ingredient of litigation strategies, the magistrate's court does an insignificant amount of business compared with the Chief's court: in several of the years over the last decade the magistrate heard less than a dozen civil cases.

CUSTOMARY COURT IN SESSION IN THE SEROWE *KGOTLA*, 1981. Mr. P. Martin, Senior Subordinate Tribal Authority hears a case on August 3, 1981 in customary court in Serowe. Mr. Martin is the person on the far left of the picture wearing the white knit cap. Uniformed members of the Police Force who served as prosecutors are at the table in the center of the photograph. The traditional wall which surrounds the *kgotla* is in the middle background. In the far background are some of the buildings housing the administration offices of the Central District Administration. It is common to hold customary court hearings outdoors in the (southern hemisphere) winter, so that participants and spectators can benefit from the warmth of the sun.

NOTE

Beginning in 1969 the Government of Botswana has attempted to integrate the two court systems, with an eye to preserving somewhat the rich tradition of the customary law while extending what are perceived as the benefits of received statutory law. The Customary Law and Ascertainment Act of 1969 is the major instrument for furthering that judicial integration. One effect of this legislation is to extend the jurisdiction of the (national, statutory) courts to try cases in which the litigants seek the application of customary law. In fact, the general premise of the Act is that all of the courts of Botswana, in the exercise of their original jurisdiction, will apply customary law where, by virtue of the Act or any other statute, it is "properly applied," and where it is not properly applied they will apply the common (i.e., Cape Colonial) law. The High Court and the Subordinate Courts may hear cases involving tribesmen and may apply customary law in the exercise of their original jurisdiction,—not just in an appellate capacity vis-a-vis customary courts. Because of this, the legislation contains statutory guidelines as to when customary law is to be applied and, if so, which tribal group's customary law is applicable.

In the same vein, customary courts may now apply general common (i.e. Cape Colonial) law in some areas. for example, in exercising their criminal jurisdiction the customary courts are to be guided by the statutory Penal Code enacted in 1964. But note that areas excluded from the customary courts' purview are still wide:

Simon Roberts, "Botswana," in Judicial and Legal Systems in Africa, edited by A.N. Allott. Second edition. London: Butterworth's, 1970, pp. 268–269. From section A5, Customary Courts of First Instance.

3 Jurisdiction—original—*a Civil*. A Customary Court may exercise civil jurisdiction over causes and matters justiciable under any law administered by the Court (see paras. 8 and 9, post) * where all the parties are tribesmen, or the defendant consents in writing to the jurisdiction of the Court, and the defendant is ordinarily resident within the area of jurisdiction of the Court, or the cause of action arose wholly therein.

In exercising this jurisdiction no Court may try a case in which the claim or value of the matter in dispute exceeds the maximum amount set out in its warrant.

In the absence of an express provision conferring jurisdiction, the following matters are excluded from the jurisdiction of a Customary Court:

　　i any cause or proceeding whereby divorce or declaration of nullity of marriage or an order for judicial separation is sought;

　　ii any cause or proceeding arising in connection with a testamentary disposition of property;

* Law to be administered.

iii any cause or proceeding arising in connection with the administration of a deceased's estate to which any law of the Territory applies;

iv any cause or proceeding arising under the law relating to insolvency;

v any cause or proceeding involving matters or relationships to which customary law is inapplicable.

b Criminal. A Customary Court may exercise criminal jurisdiction in connection with criminal charges and matters in which the accused is a tribesman or consents in writing to the jurisdiction of the Court, and the charge relates to the commission of an offence committed either wholly or partly within the jurisdiction of the Court.

In the exercise of this jurisdiction no Court may impose a fine or other punishment in excess of the maximum set out in its warrant.

In the absence of an express provision conferring jurisdiction, cases in which the accused is charged with any of the following offences are excluded from the jurisdiction of a Customary Court:

i treason, riot or any offence involving the security or safety of the State;

ii an offence in consequence of which death is alleged to have occurred;

iii bigamy;

iv any offence under Chapter X (Corruption and the Abuse of Office) or Chapter XI (Offences Relating to the Administration of Justice) of the Penal Code;

v bribery, perjury or subornation of perjury or conspiring to defeat the course of justice;

vi an offence concerning counterfeit currency;

vii robbery, where the person accused is of or above the age of twenty-one years;

viii extortion by means of threats or by abuse of authority;

ix an offence against insolvency law or company law;

x rape;

xi contravention of prohibitions relating to precious stones, gold and other precious metals;

xii such other offences as may be prescribed.

4 Jurisdiction—appellate—Nil.

8 General law. A Customary Court may administer:

i the provisions of any written law which the Court is expressly authorised to administer by any written law [A.C.P., s. 12 (*b*), as repealed and replaced by Law 57/1968];

ii the provisions of any law which the Court is authorised to administer by Order of the President, published in the *Gazette*.

In the exercise of their jurisdiction the Customary Courts "may be guided by the provisions of the Penal Code". Prior to 1968, the Customary Courts only had jurisdiction to administer customary criminal law. It is now intended that the Penal Code should ultimately entirely replace customary criminal law, and the Customary Courts are being encouraged, as an intermediate step, to exercise their criminal jurisdiction as far as possible in conformity with the Code.

9 Customary law. The Customary Courts administer customary law in all circumstances not covered by para. 8, ante. For these purposes customary law means "in relation to any particular tribe or tribal community, the customary law of that tribe or tribal community so far as it is not incompatible with the provisions of any written law or contrary to morality, humanity or natural justice".

NOTE

The overlapping jurisdictions result in some melding of the two court systems. This is reinforced by the appellate system described in the Campbell excerpt in section B3, which allows cases to be appealed from the customary court system to the national court system. Notable, too, is the fact that the Commissioner of Customary Courts has the review powers of a subordinate court. Moreover, cases involving penalties or costs beyond a certain level or amount from both court systems are automatically reviewed by the High Court. Recall that Mr. Justice Aguda said that this is particularly important in a legal system in which many of the court officers at the lower levels are not legally trained.

A major issue involved in assessing the effectiveness of Botswana's legal system is the question of how well the statutory courts can apply customary law. Another, is how individuals use the legal system to achieve personal goals. They suggest several rhetorical questions to consider as you read the rest of the Botswana materials in this volume.

QUESTIONS

1. Are statutory courts less accessible to litigants with modest means?

2. Are they more subject to evasion of justice by litigants employing legal technicalities?

3. In statutory courts, does the general absence of magistrates who speak Setswana put a Motswana litigant who doesn't speak English at a disadvantage—even when an interpreter is used?

4. Do customary courts inhibit modernization? Do they constrain individual innovative behavior in favor of routine conformity to tradition? For example, do they discourage the devolution of property in non-traditional ways? Are persons who wish to break with tradition likely to attempt to play the two kinds of law off against each other in some way?

5. Do customary courts sometimes charge a person with breaking a traditional as yet unwritten rule in violation of the constitutional provision that

litigants only be tried for violation of written offenses? If so, does this weaken the unity of the legal system?

6. What role do either the customary court system or the statutory court system allow for the customary law of the *non*-Tswana peoples of Botswana?

7. How can chiefs use their role as presidents of customary courts to maintain their position as persons of power?

8. Are there ways in which persons who are rivaling chiefs for power use the statutory courts and/or the customary courts as a tool for gaining that end?

4. Law in Botswana: Some Current Issues

NOTE

Because of its location next to the Republic of South Africa and its particular history, Botswana is very conscious of human rights. Its Constitution delineates human rights and their protection in great detail, and the nation is proud of its role as a leader in human rights in Southern Africa, indeed, in sub-Saharan Africa as a whole.

The precedence given imposed Western (Cape Colonial) law in the duality of the Botswana legal system subtly implies two classes of citizens, and two sets of human rights. This is so, notwithstanding the fact that the lingering duality in the system reflects the presence in the social fabric of two cultures. Because of Botswana's great concern with human rights, a major issue there is how to meld the indigenous customary law and imposed Cape Colonial law into one unified system. The Chief Justice's remarks at the opening of the criminal session of the High Court in 1981 (see page 100) detail some of the steps being taken to bring about that merger.

In moving toward merger, it is understood that altering or removing customary law too precipitously would further undermine the institution of the chieftaincy and weaken the social and political fabric in other ways. Thus, a critical question is whether early elimination of the status quo would be even more lethal to human rights than duality in the legal system. To be sure, in some quarters there also may be other objections to changing the status quo.

One of the factors reinforcing the goal of creating a completely unified legal system is the objective of maintaining a non-racial * ideology. Moving toward this goal encourages dismantling those aspects of the dual legal system which imply the appropriateness of separate judicial apparatuses for blacks and for others, even though that duality is rationalized in terms of culture or life style, rather than in terms of race. Striving to maintain non-racialism also means eliminating the automatic dominant role for expatriate judicial officials. And it means removing any remaining vestiges of separatism or racial preference that were imported over the years via South African judicial interpretations.

* Where Americans would use the term "multi-racial," the term "non-racial" is preferred in Botswana. In Southern Africa, "multi-racial" suggests the South African pattern of separate, "parallel" paths. "Non-racial" in Southern Africa suggests a society which is racially plural and in which the stated ideals rule out apartheid or other legal denial of political rights, particularly the right to vote for representation in a common legislative assembly, and other civil rights.

(GABORONE) BOTSWANA DAILY NEWS, FEBRUARY 5, 1980.

Workload in our courts continues to increase

Chief Justice Hayfron- Benjamin has expressed concern over the workload in Botswana courts, which he said, continue to grow phenomenally.

Performing the official opening of this year's High Court Criminal session in Lobatse on Friday, Justice Benjamin observed that the country's rapid economic development is giving rise to increased civil litigation and senior crime. But he noted that the situation would not get out of hand.

The Chief Justice, who said Botswana leads southern Africa in the field of civil liberties, pointed out that it would be a pity if the country's courts fail to reflect this leadership in their decisions.

He explained that the number of appeals from customary to magistrate courts show signs of increasing phenomena.

He stressed that it would be necessary to devise proceedures dealing with these appeals from the customary courts. He told his audience, which comprised cabinet ministers, heads of religious missions, diplomats and legal practitioners that. All proceedings in customary courts are in Setswana. But there is not a single magistrate who is conversant in the language."

The proceedings from the customary courts, he said, must therefore be translated before being heard in the magistrate courts.

He observed however, that this of course, places severe strains on the financial and human resources available.

The Chief Justice explained that the increase in crime and the piling up of affiliation cases have made it more difficult for magistrates to cope with their work.

He said that to deal with the problems of affiliation and appeals from the customary courts, "we propose in the coming year, to explore the posibility of appointing some Grade One magistrates, specially charged with the hearing of such cases."

All such magistrates should be Setswana-speaking. They would be at liberty to conduct their proceedings either in English or in Setswana, or both, he explained.

He said that he did not anticipate any difficulty in finding experienced and competent officers to discharge these duties

who can be recruited from the ranks of experienced clerks of court and other officers conversant with the Administration of Justice.

"They need not be lawyers," he said.

Chief Justice Hayfron-Benjamin spoke at length on the movement of staff of the High Court and the shortage of judicial facilities.

The question of exodus by senior civil servants featured prominently inside and, afterwards, outside the High Court after a short reply speech by Principal State Counsel Mr P.T.C. Skelemani.

He said that the staffing position in the Botswana's Attorney General's Chambers was not what it ought to be.

"We have lost a number of senior attorneys to the private sector," Mr Skelemani counted instances in which senior officers resigned from the Attorney General's Chambers, and complained of deterioration in the performance of the Chambers.

"We have some promising young men but we can't promise whether we shall be able to keep them," said Mr Skelemani.

He assured the High Court audience however that: "We shall not shirk our responsibility as officers of this court."

He pointed out that Botswana depends much on the police. They are trained to prosecute cases, but that should be the work of the Attorney General's Chambers.

Welcoming the Chief Justice's call for building up a judiciary staffed by Batswana, Mr Skelemani said that it is essential that people in the judiciary should understand the local language since it is easy to be misled by a translation.

The session which got underway yesterday in the High Court will hear 12 cases of murder, one of manslaughter and one of attempted murder.

It will also deal in a variety of other criminal cases which include stocktheft, rape, possession of Government trophy and illegal posession of diamonds.

Chief Justice Hayfron- Benjamin inspects Guard of Honour mounted by the BDF during the criminal session opening Friday

On a day-to-day basis the emphasis in Botswana is not on the end goals discussed above. Rather, the focus is on the steps involved in achieving merger or in improving the existing system. One of these steps is "localization" of the judiciary. Virtually all presiding court officials from the level of magistrates up are expatriates. No Motswana has even sat on the High Court. Absence of Batswana in the higher reaches of the judiciary is especially critical because it makes it difficult to develop statutory precedents deeply rooted in local practices and conditions. A recent development has been the appointment of High Court justices and justices of the Court of Appeal from other black African countries. This is encouraging because those justices have been more familiar with indigenous African life. And, notably, they—

and expatriate judges from other parts of the Commonwealth not normally represented on the Botswana higher bench—have made more use of non-South African precedents, sometimes citing English, and even American, law.

The Honorable D. N. Magang, a Motswana attorney who is also a member of Parliament, has raised some subtle and complex conceptual issues concerning customary law that must be resolved before the two legal systems can be fully integrated.* They include the question of whether there is a *common* customary law, i.e., customary law common to several Tswana (and other) tribes which is actually applied in customary courts, especially those in urban areas. If so, is *this* common law the common law that should be recognized as the National (common) law of Botswana rather than Cape Colonial law? Moreover, he asks, is the customary law (either common or localized) given appropriate definition and recognition in Botswana's statutes?

Other concerns and/or steps relating to developing a unified legal system that are current in Botswana include: changes in the process of appeal from customary to statutory courts, expanded places in the legal program of the University of Botswana and Swaziland, changes that would provide in-service legal training for existing Batswana court personnel, the development of a unified law of marriage, and plans for providing larger courts and additional magistrates in population centers.

The issues and proposals described above are matters that are being discussed or steps that are being taken to bring about melding of the two legal systems. In the meantime, Batswana, like we, are concerned with the *present* system and how it handles the four particular problems upon which we have chosen to focus these materials. They all are concerned with how just the outcomes are which are dispensed by that system. And many give thought to whether the duality of the legal system makes its handling of those four problems—and other problems—more complex and, possibly, less just.

* D. N. Magang, "Customary Law as Administered in Botswana." In (Proceedings of) The Third Judicial Conference Held at the High Court, Lobatse (Botswana) 28–29 January, 1981. Edited by Violet O'Dwyer and Bankie Forster, Gaborone (Botswana): The Government Printer, 1981, pp. 13–25.

Chapter 5

INTRODUCTORY NOTE ON CHINA AND THE
ROLE OF LAW IN CHINA *

A. LAW WITHOUT LAWYERS

NOTE

There are about half a million lawyers in the United States, or about one for every five hundred persons—quite an imposing figure! By contrast, the People's Republic of China (PRC) has less than ten thousand lawyers to service a population which is over four times our own. How does a large complex society manage to operate with virtually no lawyers? How are the functions which are performed by lawyers in the United States handled in China?

The consequences of not having a large cadre of legal specialists are important. On a very simple level, even if China wanted to adopt American legal theory and structure, the Chinese legal system would function very differently since it would be staffed by a few thousand instead of half a million specialists. Conversely, as China has only a few thousand legal specialists, it should not and would not think of constructing a complex legal system (such as exists in the United States) which requires the services of a very large number of professionally trained people.

With so few legal specialists, the Chinese legal system must, of necessity, be simple in structure, method, and content so that relatively untrained people or even members of the general public can play an active role in the legal process. But the emphasis on simplicity goes beyond this. The Chinese maintain that law ought to be simple: How is law to serve the masses if the masses cannot readily understand or easily use the law? This may be making a virtue of necessity, but I think it goes much deeper. The underlying principle is that law should be, and indeed must be, broadly based rather than the special province of a group of elite professionals. In that way, law becomes a tool by which the masses can carry out their wishes, rather than a set of rules for the use of the legal professional alone.

* This essay is based in part on Victor H. Li, Law Without Lawyers, A Comparative View of Law in China and the United States, Stanford: Stanford Alumni Association, 1977; and Victor H. Li, "Human Rights in the Chinese Context," in Ross Terrill, editor, The China Difference, New York: Harper & Row, 1979.

B. LONG STANDING ATTITUDES

NOTE

The PRC did not abruptly decide not to establish a complex legal system when it took over in 1949. The historical and cultural roots of the antipathy to formal law run very deep. For example, a lawyer in traditional China was often called a "litigation trickster" as "one who stirs up litigation"—a name hardly likely to uphold his social standing or to inspire bright young persons to join the profession. There were many complaints against lawyers for making a living through capitalizing on the disputes of others, complaints similar to the English common law attacks on inciting litigation. For example, an 1820 imperial edict declared:

> The multiplication of lawsuits among the people brings much harm to rural communities, and the machinations of the litigation tricksters are what produce all the inconsequential verbiage going helter-skelter into these accusations. These rascally fellows entrap people for the sake of profit. They fabricate empty words and heap up false charges. At their bidding, plaintiffs are induced to bring up stupid nonsense in their accusations whose empty falsity, when exposed at the trial, brings blame upon the plaintiffs themselves while the litigation tricksters stand to one side.
>
> The victims of these false accusations, once they have been dragged in, remain entrapped and their livelihood is gone. Even should they have the luck to be completely exonerated as a result of the trial, their families will by then have been ruined. No one knows how many lives have thus been damaged or brought to an end at the same time that the tricksters look on from the side and chirp their satisfaction. All these devilish doings certainly deserve our bitter detestation.

Is it any wonder that a legal profession did not develop in traditional Chinese society, or that contemporary efforts to establish a legal profession encountered great difficulties?

Along a similar line, the "rule of law" carried quite different connotations in the West and China. This concept has been one of the philosophic and political cornerstones of Western society. Yet in China, this term often was used in a critical or derisive way, at least until the end of the 19th century. In traditional Confucian terms, a ruler should govern by means of virtue rather than law. That is, through a painstaking process of socialization and education, the people first learn and then internalize the rules of proper behavior. Only when a person is an extreme recalcitrant or when the educational system has broken down would it be necessary to use the severe sanctions of law. If society is functioning harmoniously, law is something to be avoided—even feared. Thus, a ruler who governs by the "rule of law" is admitting the loss of virtue and the breakdown of the system of education. (I should note that other philosophical schools in traditional China, particularly the Legalists, did not view law in such an unfavorable light.)

Two quotations from Chinese and English sources highlight the difference concerning the rule of law. In the 6th century B.C., a Confucian scholar criticized the promulgation of an early criminal code:

> The ancient kings taught the people the principles of sincerity, urged them on by their own exemplary conduct, instructed them in what was most important, called for their services in a spirit of harmony, came before them in a spirit of reverence, met exigencies with vigor, and made their decisions with firmness. . . . In this way the people could be successfully dealt with, and misery and disorder be prevented from arising.

> When the people know what the exact laws are, they do not stand in awe of their superiors. They also come to have a contentious spirit and make their appeal to the literal words, hoping peradventure to be successful in their argument. They can no longer be managed.

The argument is that more laws do not make for a better and more harmonious society. On the contrary, the emphasis on law makes people more litigious and loophole-happy, and also diverts attention away from the more important work of moral education. Compare this view with a "Western" attitude toward law expressed by Sir Thomas More in Robert Bolt's play, A Man For All Seasons; a play in two acts, New York: Random House, 1962, p. 66.

> And when the last law was down, and the devil turned round on you— where would you hide, Roper, the laws all being flat? This country's planted thick with laws from coast to coast—man's laws, not God's—and if you cut them down—and you're just the man to do it—d'you really think you could stand upright in the winds that would blow then?

One aspect of de-emphasizing the role of law was the developing of different philosophical bases and vocabulary to explain how social order is, or should be, maintained.

Benjamin Schwartz, "On Attitudes Toward Law in China," in Milton Katz, editor, Government Under Law and the Individual, Washington, D.C.: American Council of Learned Societies, pp. 27–39, 1957.

No attempt will be made in this paper to account for all attitudes toward law which can be met in the millennial history of China. Our attention will rather be focused on what might be called the main line of Confucian development. While the attitudes discussed are typical they are by no means universal and do not even represent the views of all those in Chinese history who have called themselves Confucianist. The same holds true of our brief survey of the modern scene.

What might be called the typical Confucian attitude revolves about a basic dichotomy—the dichotomy between the concept of *li* and the concept of *fa*. The importance of this dichotomy can hardly be exaggerated. Not only does it have extremely ancient roots but it is linked with certain central events in Chinese history. This historic association lends the antithesis a resonance it would not have if it were merely based on a conceptual distinction derived in abstracto.

Li is associated with the great figure of Confucius himself while *fa* is associated with the harshly despotic Ch'in dynasty which united the Chinese world under the control of a centralized bureaucratic empire in the third century B.C.

Now we have available certain conventional English equivalents of these two terms. *Li* has been translated as "propriety" while *fa* has been translated as "law." On the basis of these translations, one might assume that any discussion of law in China would revolve about the concept of *fa*.

Unfortunately the actual situation is much more complex. The term *li* embraces a far richer range of meanings than anything encompassed by the pale word "propriety." On the other hand, Western words such as "law," "droit," and "Recht" are freighted with enormous accumulations of meanings. Finally, the word *fa* is probably much narrower in its scope of reference than many Western conceptions of the meaning of law. We thus find that while some meanings of the word *li* may overlap with some meanings of "law," the meaning of the word *fa* is hardly coextensive with all the meanings attributed to the word "law."

Thus, instead of attempting to find single-word definitions of these terms, it would perhaps be better to attempt to describe in as brief a compass as possible (with all the risks of error involved) some of the major associations with them.

In the background of the concept *li* there lurk certain assumptions which resemble some of the assumptions underlying Western conceptions of natural law. One is the assumption of the existence of an eternal "natural" order underlying both the human and the nonhuman world (*tao*). As far as human society is concerned, this *tao* is normative—it tells us what human society ought to be or what it "really" is in a Platonic sense. As in Western conceptions of natural law, we are constantly confronted with the problem of how actuality is related to the normative order. In the view of Confucius, his own period was marked by a tragic falling away of actuality from the *tao*. In the past—particularly during the early Chou dynasty—the *tao* had actually been realized in actuality. Thus in studying the institutions of the historic past one was, in effect, recovering the pattern of the *tao*.

So far, we are strongly reminded of some of the basic assumptions underlying concepts of natural law in the West. However, when we come to examine more closely the concrete vision of this "natural" order, we immediately note a marked difference of focus. The basic units of this order in the Confucian case are human beings enacting *certain fundamental social roles*. As in some modern schools of sociology, social role is the key term in the Confucian definition of social structure: the structure of society is basically a network of relations of persons enacting certain social roles. Social roles do not merely place individuals in certain social locations but also bear within themselves normative prescriptions of how people ought to act within these roles. The notion "father" does not refer to a social status but prescribes a certain pattern of right behavior. It is this, of course, which has led many to speak of the importance of personal relations in China. Actually, there is something very impersonal about these personal relations since they are always relations of persons acting according to norms prescribed by social roles. Later Confucianism reduces these relations to the "five relations"—relations between father and child, husband and wife, elder and younger brother, ruler and subject, friend and friend (the latter being the most "personal"). These categories are presumed to embrace all fundamental relationships. Actually the "ruler-subject" relationship involved a tremendous variety of patterns of behavior based on one's position in an elaborate hierarchy.

Now within this structure *li* refers to the rules of conduct involved in these basic relationships. They are the rules governing the behavior of the individual in his own social role and governing his behavior toward others in their social roles. Actually *li* has a wider range of meaning. The character is derived from the name of an ancient sacrificial vessel and many of the prescriptions of *li* involving sacrifices to ancestors and gods' festive rites, etc. belong to the category of religious ritual. This, indeed, may have been the original sense of the term. *Li* are thus rules of conduct governing the relations between men (in their proper social roles) and the gods and ancestors, as well as relations between men and men. However, leaving aside the much debated question of Confucius' religious attitude, there can be no doubt that the purely human aspect of *li* has become of central importance with him even though the religious rites continue to form an integral part of the whole order of *tao*.

Another basic aspect of *li* is its association with moral force rather than with the sanction of physical force. Confucian thought is marked by an extremely strong feeling for the antithesis between moral force or spiritual force and physical coercion. So strong is this feeling, that moral force is practically equated with the good while anything associated with the sanction of physical coercion is tainted with evil. Granet has gone so far as to maintain that moral force was regarded as a magical potency by the Chinese. A man in whom moral force has won the ascendancy will naturally live up to the ethical demands of his social role. He will submit to *li* without hesitancy. Furthermore, the moral force which the noble man manifests in his behavior and in his attitudes acts as a radiating force, as it were, bringing others into its field of radiation. Hence the tremendous emphasis on the power of example as well as on proper education. Furthermore, while the prevalence of *li* depends on the prevalence of this moral force, moral perfection of the individual can only manifest itself in outward behavior as *li*. There are, to be sure, many schools of thought within Confucianism concerning the actual relationship between moral perfection in the individual and *li*. Some maintain that *li* is merely a manifestation of the moral perfection of individuals. Others maintain that it is *li* itself which, through education, brings about the moral improvement of men. Others maintain that only the ancient sages possessed moral perfection innately, while mankind as a whole must acquire it through the training in *li*. In all cases, however, the moral force which works within men and the *li* which manifests itself in external conduct are inseparable.

Within the *ideal* Confucian order, the institution of government would play a peculiarly restricted role. The good ruler and his ministers would, on the one hand, provide the people with an example of proper behavior according to *li* (it should be noted that many of the duties of *li* are confined to the ruling classes), and on the other hand would educate the people in *li*. Within the ideal system, the ruling class becomes a sort of focal point of this moral force. Presumably the foundation of such a state would rest wholly on moral force rather than on physical coercion.

When we come to examine some of the concrete prescriptions which come under the heading of *li*, we find that many of them concern matters of proper ritual, etiquette, manners, gestures, and mien. There are points at which rules of *li* impinge upon matters which would come under the heading of civil or private law in the West—marriage, divorce, support of parents, burial responsibilities, disposition of property within the family, the status of concubines, etc. Taken as a whole, however, *li* as a body of rules, does not touch vast areas of experience which fall within the scope of Western law.

It is important to remember here that *li* is not a body of rules designed to take care of every circumstance. *Li* is an instrument for training character, and nourishing moral force. In a society where *li* prevails, unbridled self-interest is placed under effective control from within, as it were. Men may continue to have individual interests, and these interests are legitimate up to a point; but in a society where men are governed by *li*, conflicts of interest can be easily resolved. Both sides will be ready to make concessions, to yield (*jang*), and the necessity for litigation will be avoided. In such a society any highly explicit system of civil law would be unnecessary.

It is at this point, by the way, that the Confucian conception of *li* becomes linked to the Confucian attitude toward the whole realm of what we call "individual rights." Individuals have legitimate interests, to be sure, and in the good society these interests will be taken care of (in accordance with requirements of the individual's social status). To surround these interests with an aura of sanctity and to call them "rights," to elevate the defense of these individual interests to the plane of a moral virtue, to "insist on one's rights"—is to run entirely counter to the spirit of *li*. The proper predisposition with regard to one's interests is the predisposition to yield rather than the predisposition to insist. A man who has led a life conforming to *li* will know how to behave properly when his interests are involved.

These, it seems to me, are some of the main characteristics of *li* and the question remains—are we here dealing with a variety of law? According to some Western definitions of law, the roles of *li* would definitely fall under the category of law. Stammler maintains that law includes any rule of conduct considered to be inviolable, universal, and independent of the wishes of the individual, whether such rule is supported by political sanction or not. However, if *li* is law, it is law within a restricted framework. Presumably, in most Western conceptions of law the primary focus is on human behavior in various given circumstances. The subjects of law are only of interest to the extent that they are involved in the legal action. In *li* the primary focus is on the relations of social roles, and the rules of conduct are significant because they are concerned with these relations.

Now in discussing *li* so far we have been describing the ideal social order. Both Confucius and his followers were only too acutely aware that actuality falls short of the ideal. Confucianism recognizes that there are elements in human society impervious to the influence of *li*, and that there are whole periods when *li* cannot be made to prevail. There is even the notion that in periods of deep economic distress the masses cannot be led by *li*. The economic distress itself, of course, is generally attributed to the ruling class's failure to conform to the demands of *li*. In all areas where *li* cannot be made to apply, *fa* must be employed to maintain order. *Fa* is enacted law designed to keep order by the appeal to the fear of punishment. It is thus based directly on the sanction of force. So closely is *fa* associated with punishment, that the word has become a synonym of the word punishment. *Fa* thus represents the sanction of force in a very direct and literal sense and its first and primary meaning is penal law. Where *li* is ineffective in maintaining public order, *fa* must take over. Where the ruling class must place heavy reliance on *fa*, it is a symptom of its own inability to rule by *li*.

However, since Confucianism recognizes that there are always elements in human society which must be controlled by *fa*—that human reality almost inevitably embodies this element of defect—*fa* still occupies a legitimate, albeit regrettable, place in the general nature of things. It is recognized as a necessity but deprecated. "If the people be led by laws," states Confucius, "and uniformity sought to be given them by punishments, they will try to avoid punishments but have no sense of shame. If they be led by virtue and uniformity sought to be given them by *li*, they will have a sense of shame and, moreover, will become good." *Li* and *fa* produce as it were their own corresponding psychologies. Where government does not rely on *li*, *li* cannot exercise its educative effect—it cannot become a transmission belt for transmitting virtue to the people and the people will not be curbed by an inner moral force. *Fa* makes its appeal to the bare interest in avoiding pain. It works with a simple hedonistic pleasure-pain psychology. Not only does it lead men to think in terms of self-interest in avoiding punishment but makes them litigious—makes them skilled in the ways of manipulating laws to suit their own interests. In a society dominated by *fa*, the people as a whole will all develop the peculiar talents of the shyster lawyer and the sense of shame will suffer.

In one of the Confucian classics we find a fierce diatribe against a minister who has publicized a penal code (by having it engraved on bronze vessels). There is a double offense here—the heavy reliance on *fa* and its publicization. This act, it is contended, will inevitably lead to a litigious spirit on the part of the people. They will no longer look to their superiors for an example of moral behavior but "appeal to the letter of the text hoping that, by chance, they may succeed in their argumentation. . . . They will reject *li* and appeal to your text." Here we note that the psychology which underlies the litigious spirit has nothing to do with the psychology which underlies *li*. There is another significant point made in this passage which reflects an important facet of the whole Confucian attitude toward law. "The ancient kings," states our author, "deliberated on circumstances in deciding (concerning the punishment of crime)." The Confucian view that where men are guided by *li*, conflicts are easily resolved, has made it possible for Confucianists to develop an acute feeling for the uniqueness of every human situation—for the fact that "no two cases are alike" and a corresponding skepticism toward all attempts to subsume all possible circumstances under certain generalized legal categories. As a result, the judge—whom we may presume to be a man guided by *li*—will (within limits) simply think of the legal code as providing certain guidelines but in his judgment will rely very heavily on the unique features of the circumstances of the case. He may even base his judgment on some situation described in the classics rather than on the provisions of the code. Hence, as one Chinese author states, "it is the judgment and not the law which makes justice."

These, it seems to me, are some of the major characteristics of the Confucian concept of *fa*, as it developed in the centuries immediately following the Master's death. However, as we know, the Confucian gospel by no means found immediate acceptance in the stormy period which followed his death. It is interesting to note, however, that many of the basic antitheses established by Confucianism (which undoubtedly rested on a much older substratum of thought) furnish the frame of reference within which later thought operates. Thus in the fourth and third centuries B.C. we have the emergence of a group of political philosophers known as the "school of *fa*" or "legalists" in current Western literature. Their view of the nature of *fa* is strikingly similar to that of Confucius. *Fa* is penal law—directly based on the sanction by force. It presupposes that the people can be led only by an appeal to the pleasure-pain principle. However, not only do the legalists accept these definitions, but they frankly and boldly assert that social order can be maintained only by *fa*. Contemporary events led them to a radical disbelief in *li* and moral force as ordering principles of society.

However, their thought is not only characterized by a revaluation of *fa* but by what might be called its heavily statist orientation. Living in an environment where great powers were contending for domination of the Chinese world, they offered themselves to the rulers of this world as experts in the science of power. By relying on *fa*, the ruler would be able to establish a Draconian order within his borders. However, this was not the final end. By making the people a pliable instrument of his will, the ruler would be able to use them in increasing the economic, political, and military power potential of the state and thus make possible ultimate victory in the international struggles of this period of "contending states." Beyond their addiction to harsh penal law, the legalists thus became the advocates of what Max Weber would call the "rationalization" (within the limits of the period) of the social order from the point of view of enhancing the power of the state. They were advocates of the bureaucratic principle, of something like a conscript army, of sweeping economic reforms, etc. Thus, *fa* became with them not only penal law but all forms of state-initiated institutional change.

We know, of course, that the Ch'in dynasty, which finally united the Chinese world during the third century B.C. into a centralized bureaucratic empire, actually operated within the framework of a legalist philosophy. It not only established a harsh and detailed system of penal law but, by the very nature of bureaucratic government, brought about an enormous extension in what might be called administrative law. It also initiated all sorts of institutional changes by government enactment.

While the dynasty was short-lived, this historic experience strongly conditioned the whole subsequent orthodox Confucian attitude toward *fa chih* (which, ironically, must be translated as "rule of law"). Harsh despotism, heavy reliance on brute force, oppressive demands on the people by an interventionist state—all these are the orthodox associations with *fa chih*. Furthermore, all attempts to improve society by heavy reliance on institutional change initiated by state enactment has also been associated with *fa* as a result of this experience. Presumably, the common denominator between this meaning of *fa* and its meaning as "penal law" are the facts that (1) the sanction of force lies behind both, (2) they both try to reform men "externally" by using incentives of reward and fear, (3) in both, the reliance on *li* is neglected.

While the Ch'in dynasty disappeared, while Confucianism subsequently became the official state philosophy, the basic structure of the centralized bureaucratic state created by the Ch'in remained. To the extent that the Chinese state has had to rely on the machinery of compulsion and rules based on the sanction of force (and it has probably had to do so to the same extent as any other state) it has relied on a machinery whose basic skeletal structure was created by the Ch'in legalists.

Now, if we survey the immense period from the second century B.C. until the 1911 revolution, we find a considerable—albeit extremely slow—growth in the area of law. More and more detailed criminal codes make their appearance, culminating in the imposing Criminal Code of the late Ch'ing dynasty. There is a steady accumulation of rules governing government administration coinciding with the growing complexity of government. There is a slow evolution in the complexity of the specialized judicial organs of government, and we also have the emergence of certain recognized traditions of legal interpretation. Furthermore, while the official codes are thought of as criminal codes, they actually contain some categories which would fall under the heading of civil law in the West. Finally, we even find the emergence of a class of legal specialists (not lawyers). Almost invariably, however, such specialists occupy a lowly position in government both in rank and in prestige.

In spite of this modest growth of law, however, the Confucianized environment plays a decisive role both in shaping the direction of legal development and in inhibiting this development. We have what Professor Ch'ü T'ung-tsu calls the Confucianization of law. That is, matters of law which impinge on the area of *li* receive particular attention in this code; heinous crimes against the "five relations" receive particularly severe punishment so that the realm of *li* which is supposed to rest on the sanction of moral force comes to receive strong support from the criminal law itself. Furthermore, much of what can be called civil law in these codes involves matters which impinge closely on the realm of *li*—laws of inheritance, marriage, disposition of property, etc. While such laws appear in the law books, the general assumption is that respectable people will be able to settle such matters outside of court. In other civil matters local custom plays a much more important role than enacted law. While custom does not enjoy the high moral standing of *li*, it is superior to *fa*. It is not enacted; it does not rest on the sanction of political force; and it is generally permeated with the spirit of *li*. On the whole, however, the main effect of Confucianism has been to inhibit the growth of an all-inclusive legal system and of an elaborate system of legal interpretation. It has inhibited the emergence of a class of lawyers and has, in general, kept alive the unfavorable attitude toward the whole realm of *fa*.

* * *

All of this should lead us to a fresh look at some of our own unexamined assumptions concerning the "rule of law." The experience of Western Europe, particularly of the Anglo-Saxon West, has tended to establish an immediate mental association between reverence for the sanctity of law, freedom of the individual, and legal limits on the power of government. Yet even in the West it is well to remind ourselves that the growth of Roman law in the late Middle Ages coincided with the emergence of the absolute states. It is also extremely interesting to note that Max Weber—a man formed in a German rather than an Anglo-Saxon environment—tended to link the growth in the "rationality" of law in the modern world with the necessities of the absolutist bureaucratic state on the one hand and with capitalism on the other. It should be immediately added that Weber does not associate capitalism with the freedom of the individual but with the growing bureaucratization of human society.

It is undoubtedly true that a reverence for the sanctity of law is a necessary prerequisite for the emergence of a democratic state—that no such state is conceivable where such a reverence does not exist. It is probably also true that an absolute state which attempts to inculcate respect for legality within certain prescribed limits is not creating a very firm basis for such a respect. On the other hand, it is important to note that something akin to the old Chinese legalist conception of the role of the law has not only existed in various times and places, but has actually found concrete implementation.

When we turn to China, we find that there is very little in her past traditions of thought, historic experience, or even in her contemporary experience which would tend to establish a close association between the notion of "rule of law" and the notion of the freedom of the individual. There are those who optimistically maintain that if the present Communist regime is able to establish a respect for legality in the areas where legality concerns the state, there will be a growing clamor for the extension of legality to other areas. Actually one might also argue the very opposite case. At the present time, there is a close association between the emphasis on legality and the attempt to control every aspect of individual life. It is possible that a revulsion against this control might carry with it a reversion to early antinomian attitudes. At any rate, it would be extremely foolhardy to assume that, in China, the growing emphasis on the role of legality in the Communist sense must inevitably lead to the freedom of the individual under law. Certainly other factors must also intervene if this end is ever to be achieved.

NOTE

The cultural factors that led to deemphasizing law and lawyers were reinforced by the pre-Liberation experiences of the Communists themselves. It is interesting to note that virtually none of the major Chinese leaders had any training in law. The only exception was Dong Biwu, who at various times held the posts of chairman of the Political-Legal Affairs Committee, president of the Supreme Court, and at an advanced age became acting president of the country after the removal of Liu Shaochi during the Cultural Revolution. Dong studied law in Japan in 1916, but thereafter was engaged primarily in Party work rather than in legal work. By way of contrast, major legal figures held relatively little political power. For example, neither Shen Junru, the first president of the Supreme Court, nor Shi Liang, the minister of justice from 1954 to 1959, were Party members. This situation is a distinct contrast to the Soviet revolution where a number of the top leaders, such as Lenin, Krestinsky, and Krylenko, were lawyers, and where many others at every level of leadership were trained in law. For the early Soviet leadership, the use of legal structures and methods to solve problems was quite a natural thing to do.

Besides lacking formal legal training, the pre-Liberation Chinese leaders had only limited practical experience in law. Many of the early leaders were philosophers, teachers, and men of letters. After the onset of the Civil War in the late 1920s, military officers played an important role. In Kiangsi, Yenan, and other areas controlled by the Communists in the 1930s, efforts were made to establish a legal system and promulgate laws, particularly laws dealing with land reform and marriage. This system never developed beyond the fledgling stage, however, in part because the greater demands of military struggle with the Nationalists and with Japan diverted attention elsewhere, and in part because the relatively simple conditions in those areas did not require a large and sophisticated legal system.

C. LEGAL WORK IN CHINA: THE HANDLING OF DEVIANCY AS AN EXAMPLE

NOTE

The lack of an extensive formal legal system did not mean that "legal" problems did not arise in Chinese society. Instead, these problems were handled by processes and institutions which, to the Western eye, might not appear "legal." For example, as discussed in subsequent chapters, the clan or lineage had jurisdiction over "family law" matters, guilds settled commercial disputes, and local gentry members and village elders kept community affairs running smoothly. Thus, even though the courts may have been relatively inactive in traditional China, other means were found to resolve disputes, maintain order, and lay down rules of conduct.

Let me illustrate how an informal system of law functions—and contrast its mode of operation with that of a formal legal system—by focusing on the example of the control of deviancy. The following discussion deals with the PRC, but could also apply to traditional China.

Pictorially, the Western approach to the handling of deviancy resembles falling off the edge of a cliff. Long before a person commits a crime, such as an assault or a robbery, he would have manifested unhappiness or antisocial behavior in various minor ways—being sullen or aggressive, avoiding employment, or associating with undesirable persons. Such minor "deviations" from the desired norm are protected from official interference on the grounds of privacy, freedom, or individuality—several of our most important values. On a social level, friends and neighbors occasionally intervene, but the extent is limited by the same considerations of privacy and freedom. Moreover, if a person did not want such interference, the law would support his demand that others keep their distance. Thus, at the early stages of a problem, a person is given little help by the state, and may use the legal system to rebuff informal offers of assistance from others.

The situation does not basically change as a person's deviations grow more serious—becoming a bully or a neighborhood troublemaker—and he comes closer to the edge. At some point, he deviates too far and falls off the cliff—i.e., commits a crime. Then the formal legal system is invoked, and the full majesty of the criminal law descends upon him.

This process, or perhaps it is a dilemma, of having to leave a person alone until a crime is committed is worth dwelling on. Privacy and individuality are of clear value and importance, but they do not come without costs. By not giving help or not insisting that help be accepted at the early stages, we are unable to get at problems at a point when they still might be satisfactorily resolved. The line between freedom and alienation, or between respect for privacy and indifference to the circumstances of another, is often quite thin. Perhaps the high rate of recidivism in our prisons is related to this fact. After a person has gone through the criminal process and is returned to society, he is once more placed back in his original circumstances on top of the cliff. Without getting further assistance, he will almost inevitably wander to the edge and fall off again.

We also pay a price in not helping people at the early stages of their unhappiness, but rather waiting until a serious antisocial act such as a crime has been committed. It is far easier to act in a truly friendly and helpful manner toward someone thinking of dropping out of school than to be compassionate and conciliatory toward someone who has bashed in his neighbor's head.

One other point that should be noted is that the amount of deviancy that is tolerated—how wide the cliff is before one falls off the edge—is not a fixed thing. When society is feeling secure and confident, a great deal of leeway is given. During hard or threatening times, there is much less willingness to adhere to the idea that it is better that 99 guilty men go free than to have one innocent man be wrongly caught up in the meshes of the law. The internment of the Japanese-Americans in California during World War II is an extreme example. But there are many others—the May Day roundup of antiwar demonstrators in Washington, D.C. in 1968; enemies lists; illegal wiretaps and burglaries. And it is not just for illegal or immoral reasons that the amount of leeway is reduced. Some legitimate contemporary concerns about crime in the streets and efforts to limit restrictions on search and seizure by the police are examples.

In this regard, if hard and threatening times are sufficient justifications for not tolerating deviant behavior, then China would have some reason to tolerate hardly any kind of deviancy whatsoever. Internally, it has the vast task of economic development and political transformation. Externally, during the early years it faced the constant expression of threat from Taiwan and also fought a war in Korea with the world's major power. In the 1960s, it had to deal with the Vietnam War occurring on one border and a massive Soviet buildup on another border. Yet Chinese society, while disciplined, is far from wholly intolerant. And we can expect changes as China's perceptions of internal and external dangers decline.

Returning to the earlier image of the cliff, the top and the bottom of the cliff are two distinct worlds. The top is the province of the individual. Police and other legal officials generally are not present and sometimes are not permitted to enter. The rules of conduct are permissive, and activity usually takes place around one's home or place of work. At the bottom of the cliff, an entirely different process takes over. This world is populated by its own distinctive set of actors: police, prosecutors, judges, lawyers, and the like. Because much of the activity takes place in inconvenient or intimidating sites such as police stations and courthouses, people from the top of the cliff generally do not take part, or even are excluded from taking part, in what happens at the bottom.

In addition to such practical considerations, our legal theory supports the idea that these two worlds should be separate. Juries and sometimes judges and others who have personal knowledge about the defendant or the offense frequently are not allowed to participate in a case. Except for sentencing procedures, other actions and attitudes of the defendant not directly related to the offense in question generally are regarded as irrelevant. For example, a defendant's past criminal record usually cannot be introduced as evidence in a criminal trial. The partial exclusion of persons having personal knowledge of the defendant, and isolating the single event from other actions committed by the defendant, are thought to be important guarantees of impartiality in our criminal system.

The state, by virtue of its size and access to far superior human and material resources, possesses great power in dealing with a criminal case. The question then arises how the exercise of this power should be regulated so as to ensure the accused person is not simply overwhelmed by the state. Thus the fourth, fifth, and sixth amendments provide protection from unreasonable searches and seizures, and guarantee the right against self-incrimination and the right to a speedy and fair trial. An accused person also is provided access to legal counsel. This is especially important since in the American system a layman generally stands little chance against a trained prosecutor. Moreover, in theory the defense attorney is fully cognizant of the rights of the accused and has the freedom and incentive to make certain that these rights are implemented.

Such institutions and rules help to ensure at least a minimum level of fairness in the operation of our legal system. They also form the core of the standards used by Western commentators and international human rights documents for measuring the adequacy of the legal systems of other societies. When applied to the Chinese system, however, these standards do not fit very well.

As opposed to falling off the edge of a cliff, the Chinese approach to handling deviancy much more resembles a gradual slide to the bottom. As in the Western case, the first antisocial act is not a crime but some minor matter. However, as a person deviates a little from the general norm, he is not left alone. On the contrary, anyone who notices a sullen complainer or an aggressive bully is supposed to "help." The duty of one person to help another is as basic to the Chinese social system and philosophic beliefs as the concepts of privacy and individuality are to the Western.

In China, an intricate social fabric is made up of "small groups" of people who work or live together. These groups serve as a principal mechanism through which help is offered. At the early stages, help generally takes the form of discussion by the group about the root causes of a person's problem and possible solutions. Being immediate neighbors or co-workers with whom one deals constantly, group members obviously know a great deal about the individual and subject matter involved, and can exert considerable peer pressure.

If a person does not respond, but persists in antisocial conduct by becoming even more disagreeable and disruptive, the amount of help given is increased in both quantity and intensity. The Chinese sometimes describe the process by the term *shuofu*, "to persuade by talking." This may take the form of wide public discussion of the problem and lead to offering suggestions or criticisms that grow increasingly pointed. If the difficulties continue, additional persons become involved. Elected neighborhood leaders, factory officials, or the local policeman might be asked to join the discussion. Their presence not only increases the pressure on the person being criticized, but also provides some check on the actions of the group.

In carrying out these prolonged discussions, the local people work with the offender for a long time, trying to improve his conduct and gathering detailed information about his actions. As the policeman and others join in the attitudes of the group are conveyed to the officials and, indeed, help shape the official view. Even after the formal legal system takes over, legal officials come to the group members for additional information. In a real sense, these local people make the basic determinations of fact in the case. It is immediate neighbors and small group members rather than legal officials whom one must first convince of one's position. And what one's peers decide is unlikely to be overturned during later formal legal proceedings. Without drawing the analogy too far, this system has some resemblance to the early English jury which, until the end of the fifteenth century, was composed of witnesses who had personal knowledge of the case and could swear to the veracity of a party's claim rather than be mere impartial finders of fact.

Several other comments should be made about this gradual slide to the bottom. First, it takes quite a bit of doing to hit bottom. In some cases, a troublemaker might truly be convinced by the proffered advice and help; in other cases, it might be easier to conform to the socially desired norm than to continue to face criticism and pressure from close peers. Only the rare and extreme situation would require invoking the formal criminal process.

Second, the slide from the top to the bottom is basically a continuous process. Until fairly near the bottom, the principal actors are one's friends and peers, and the process is carried out in the familiar surroundings of one's place of residence or work. Even at the bottom, the legal officials have had considerable prior involvement with the community concerning the case; they also keep in close touch subsequently. The extensive participation of the public through the entire process is the essence of the "mass line" in legal work. With so many lay helpers, it is not surprising that the size of the legal establishment in China is relatively small. This approach requires a great deal of the public's time and labor, but these are assets China has in abundance.

Finally, with so many friends and neighbors extending "help"—whether one wants to be helped or not—there is little room for privacy in China. Group decisions and preferences also carry a great deal of weight relative to the individual. These are matters which might seem unpleasant or awkward to us, but we should consider whether they may be more "natural" to a person living in a Chinese milieu. For example, while the United States does not deny the importance of the larger group and community, the primary concern is the individual—whether in terms of legal status, personal fulfillment, or religious salvation. Consequently, the American system stresses individuality, privacy, diversity, and protection of the individual from undue outside interference. We begin with the premise that a person should have freedom of action, and then ask under what circumstances this freedom may be restricted.

The Chinese approach has historically been quite different. Chinese culture appreciates the importance of individuals but places greater emphasis on how a person functions within the context of a larger group. The Chinese language provides insights into both the historical past and the modes of thinking for the present. There is no simple Chinese term for "privacy." Pause on that point for a few moments. What would be other key attributes of a culture that lacks a term for privacy? How much importance might a contemporary Chinese attach to privacy, or, indeed, how would he think about such a concept? More relevant to our inquiry, how can universal standards be drawn when the Chinese lack a word for one of the West's most important values?

A related observation about the Chinese language is that the term for "self" often has carried a connotation of selfishness, and frequently was used in contrast with the term "public," which implied the "public good." This preference for the larger collective unit over the individual continues into the present day, although of course groups in the People's Republic are defined by loyalties other than kinship and hold to Communist rather than Confucian ideology.

Nor was there a clear sense of a concept of "rights" as the term is used in the West. On the contrary, the emphasis was on the idea of duty. Phrasing obligations in this matter affected the means of enforcement. The principal remedy was subjective, in the sense that a person was made to feel through social pressure that he must perform his duty. The general community was involved in showing disapproval through methods such as gossip or ostracism. There was far less emphasis on giving an aggrieved party a "right" that could be formally enforced in a court or elsewhere against the person failing to perform.

D. THE LI I–CHE WALL POSTER DEBATE

NOTE

Given this very different approach to the handling of deviancy and crime, how do we begin to measure the adequacy or fairness of the informal criminal process? This is an exceedingly difficult question to answer. To begin with, we lack adequate data about how Chinese society operates in actual practice. Perhaps even more importantly, we also lack adequate intellectual concepts or tools with which to evaluate such a drastically different approach to law. One of the tasks of this course is to try to develop some kinds of measures, however imperfect and incomplete.

At this point, it is much easier to describe how we should not measure the Chinese system. It is clear that most of the standards articulated in such Western documents as the International Covenant on Political and Civil Rights envisage a judicially supervised system of public trials that is not readily applicable to the Chinese setting. The important aspect of the Chinese legal process is the small group discussions, especially the stage where they move from ordinary conversations to more intense criticisms. The guarantee of a speedy and public trial focuses our attention on the wrong place, because most matters are resolved at the peer group level. Even where a person slides all the way to the bottom and the case is handled by the formal legal system, most of the decisions will have been made well before the defendant reaches the courtroom. Guarantees against self-incrimination also make little sense since at the beginning of the slide one could hardly refuse to engage in conversation with one's peers. The concept of right to counsel must be reshaped so that rather than referring to a defense attorney taking part in the formal legal process, it looks to whether there are mechanisms or procedures to ensure that an individual is not simply overwhelmed by the greater power and resources of the group.

How then do we try to evaluate the Chinese system? A number of Western observers have argued that the entire Chinese approach to the handling of deviancy should be rejected on the ground that the lack of formal institutionalized rules and processes, in and of itself, makes the risk of injustice and oppression by the group against one member intolerably high. At the other end of the spectrum, one might consider the Chinese approach to be the model of participatory democracy. Law indeed becomes everyone's business, and not just the exclusive province of legal specialists.

There has been no resolution of this debate in the West. Interestingly, the same issue was debated in a most spectacular fashion in China in 1974. Under the composite name of Li I-che, a group of "educated youths" in Canton wrote a hundred-yard-long wall poster that attacked the failure to implement socialist legality as well as the emergence of a "new class" of privileged officials.

The essay is phrased carefully and skillfully. The ostensible target of the authors is Lin Piao (Biao), the former minister of defense who attempted to assassinate Mao in 1971 and then died in a plane crash while trying to flee to the Soviet Union. The broader target, however, is the entire radical left group. These persons have since been discredited as the "gang of four," but in 1974 they were very influential at both the national and local levels.

The Li I-che essay was widely circulated all over China, although we do not know exactly how people outside of Canton managed to get copies. The essay was strongly criticized by various Party officials. (See the essay by the Propaganda Department of the Canton Communist Party writing under the name Hsuan Chi-wen, infra.) The authors were attacked as counterrevolutionaries and arrested. After the fall of the "gang of four" in 1976, however, they were released and praised for their perceptiveness and courage.

"The Case of Li I-che," 10 Chinese Law and Government, No. 3, pp. 42–43, 45–47, 49–51, 53–55, 57–58, Fall 1977.   (Notes omitted.)

* * *

In the summer of 1968, the rule of law under socialism "suddenly did not operate," and what operated in its stead was "political power is the power to suppress."   Across the length and breadth of the land, everywhere there were arrests, everywhere there was suppression and imprisonment of the innocent.   Where had socialist legality gone?   It was said that it was no longer of any use because it pertained to the old constitution and the new People's Congress was still pending.   It was a time of sheer lawlessness!

This was a rehearsal for socialist-fascism in our country, and Lin Piao was the rehearsal's chief director.

* * *

4. About the Situation Following the Criticize-Lin Campaign. The Lin Piao System reached its apex during the Great Proletarian Cultural Revolution, but this was only one side of the story.   What was more important was that it created its own reaction.   It created a new and rising social force encompassing people who, through the course of this great revolution and under the inspiration of Chairman Mao, have gradually come to understand Marxist-Leninism and the thought of Mao Tse-tung.   Following the downfall of Lin Piao, the popular upswing of aspirations for democracy has extended even further the mass base of these enlightened people.   Most of these people are victims of the Lin Piao System.   They hate the Lin Piao System from head to foot.   They demand the continuation of the revolution, the revolutionary great democracy of the people, and the reinstatement of socialist legality.

* * *

The downfall of Lin Piao did not mean the end of his system.   In the process of establishing the Lin Piao System, a force was created of an intelligentsia [*wen-jen*] who had obtained vested interests. These privileged people feared that the masses would rise up in an upsurge.   The tides to cleanse the Lin Piao System destroyed the basis of their vested interests.   Resorting to sophism and distorting the thought of Mao Tse-tung, they deliberately depicted the ultra-Right essence of the Lin Piao System as merely a "rightist tendency," or avoided mentioning the fact that when Lin Piao, the chief of the opportunist line, was in power, the policy implemented by him not only opposed that of Chairman Mao but also damaged the whole country. They used Lin Piao's shameful and reactionary remarks to cover up his shameful demagogy.   They stood on the opposite side of the people, who were demanding that the Lin Piao System be criticized. They smothered the boisterous criticize-Lin Piao mood.   They scolded the people and the masses for being "restorationists" and "reversing the tide," and upheld the flags of "antirestoration" and "antireverse the tide" as if they themselves were unshakable revolutionaries.

* * *

5. *Discussion on Going against the Tide.* The Tenth National Party Congress withdrew the principle of "unite and eliminate them" and "unite and struggle" against them that was stuffed into the "Ninth Party Congress" by Lin Piao and replaced it with the principle of going against the tide. This was a great achievement of the Tenth Party Congress.

However, now the situation is that because the slogan has become trendy, everyone shouts: go against the tide!

In August this year (1973), did a Chang T'ieh-sheng not come forth to "go against the tide"? The result was: First, his head was not chopped off; second, he was not jailed; and third, his wife did not divorce him. On the contrary, he has made his way up fast, and it is said that he has gone to a certain academic institution for advanced studies in the mystery and secrets of going against the tide. But in many cases, among many of those genuine revolutionaries who launched a fight against the Lin Piao System, the executed remain executed, and the imprisoned are still in jail. The dismissed officials are still dismissed. They do not have it so easy, do they?

People are not fools! They deeply understand the cause of their sufferings. The spearhead of their attack is directed toward the Lin Piao System. None of them expresses hatred of Chairman Mao's revolutionary line and policy. On the contrary, they hate Lin Piao and those who have benefited from his system, those who have distorted and hindered Chairman Mao's line and policy. They demand democracy, demand socialist legality, and revolutionary and personal rights that protect the popular masses. "What? You want democracy? You are reactionary! Because you are reactionary, you cannot have democracy." They argue forcefully and like to come up with a quotation from Chairman Mao's "On the People's Democratic Dictatorship."

But the word "reactionary" is not to be found emblazoned on the reactionaries' foreheads. "Give democracy only to the people" is very correct. However, when you were still shouting and screaming for the Lin Piao System, did you give a piece of democracy to the people who opposed this system? What they were given were only brutal struggles and imprisonment! "Don't give democracy to the reactionaries" is the way it ought to be. But remember that when the Lin Piao System was in full swing, when some hundred members of the Central Committee at Lushan sided with it, did democracy not serve the reactionaries? You need not give them democracy because they already had it, first they had the power and then they had the banner of revolution. But if you do not give democracy to the people, then they have no democracy, first, because they have no power, and second, because they sometimes cannot muster up the flag of revolution.

* * *

In his report, Comrade Wang Hung-wen called on the people to foster the "five-fearless" spirit when going against the tide. However, the present situation is that, without the approval of "VIPs" and the publicity of the Center's press and publications, no thought can form a current, let alone become a forceful tide. Now and before, China always has had some people who dared to speak out without fear of being executed. Lu Hsün naturally was one of them. But Lu Hsün still could manage to publish his articles through his Japanese friends. Today where can "five-fearless" people get their articles published? The spectre of the Great Proletarian Cultural Revolution often haunts them. Time and again they have thought of restoring the authority of the big-character poster. However, the Lin Piao System is oppressing them; the [dogma of] "loyalty" in the strict ritual formalities is restraining them; chains, iron bars, whips, and bullets are waiting for them.

Our country was born from a semifeudal, semicolonial society into socialism. The traditions formed by several thousands of years of feudal despotism stubbornly maintain their stronghold over thought, culture, education, law, and virtually every other sphere of the superstructure.

Did not the strong feudalism and patriarchism that were manifested by Liu Shao-ch'i, and by Lin Piao in particular, sufficiently prove that antifeudalism still remains one of the most important contents of our continuing revolution?

What is a more sacred pillar for defending the "rule of rites" of the Lin Piao System than the principle of "Down with whomever opposes Mao Tse-tung Thought"? In name, it is to uphold someone else; in fact, it is to establish oneself. If Lin Piao had been able to formally get up on the stage [of power], would it not then have been whoever opposes Lin Piao will be knocked down (which is just what he actually did)? Besides any VIP has only to declare himself to be the personification of Chairman Mao's revolutionary line, and then he will become unblemishably sacred forever. And that "handful" of revolutionary masses who dare to invade his dignity will definitely fail to be considered as falling under the protection of the law!

If we do not oppose this feudalistic principle of the "rule of rites" of "monarch-subject, father-son, know your place in the order of things," can we really implement the proletarian dictatorship's rule of law, "suppressing the enemies and protecting the people"?

This is an extremely big contradiction: On the one hand, the centralized leadership of the Party cannot be shaken; on the other hand, "the focus of the campaigns is to rectify the capitalist-roaders in the Party," at the same time that these capitalist-roaders are the concrete expressions of the centralized leadership in places and departments under their control.

Under the conditions of proletarian dictatorship, how can the people's rights, under the centralized leadership of the Party, be protected in the struggle against the capitalist-roaders and incorrect lines in the Party? This is a big topic facing the "Fourth National People's Congress."

Needless to say, the Party's leadership should carefully listen to the masses' opinions, and it would be similarly needless to note the people's rights to implement revolutionary supervision over all levels of the Party's leadership. It is even more unnecessary to say that rebelling against the capitalist-roaders is justified. Even though the masses' opinion might be incorrect or excessive, or even if they become discontented because of misunderstanding certain Party policies, is it justified to implement a policy of "suppress if persuasion fails and arrest if suppression fails"? Moreover, the fragrant flower and the poisonous weed, correct and incorrect, and revolutionary and counterrevolutionary, are not always easy to distinguish. It takes a long process and has to stand the test of time. Therefore, we should not be frightened by an open and honorable opposition as long as it observes discipline and plays no tricks and engages in no conspiracy.

The "Fourth National People's Congress" should enact regulations clearly in black and white which, aside from imposing a dictatorship over the elements involved in homicide, arson, vagrancy, robbery and burglary, and similar criminal offenses, as well as over those who instigate armed struggle and cliques who organize plots, will also protect all the democratic rights rightfully belonging to the masses.

b. Limitation of Special Privileges. Whether or not to recognize that there is emerging in China a privileged stratum which is similar to that in the Soviet Union (Liu Shao-ch'i and Lin Piao were no more than their political agents) is a basic theoretical problem of affirming or negating the Cultural Revolution.

First, it must be pointed out that the majority of our Party members are good or comparatively good. But this privileged stratum exists objectively. Its existence is based on the socio-economic conditions of our country and therefore is independent of the subjective will of the people.

What started the phenomenon of "today in society going in through the back door is the fashion"? Where did the practice of recklessly squandering the society's products and the unbelievable comforts enjoyed by the high levels come from? How did the matter-of-course right to possession of property, which is really a disguised form of inheritance from one generation to the next, arise? And on what does this political maneuver of the new bourgeoisie rely to take over this kind of possession and thereafter maintain it? Art and literature, education, "May 7 cadre schools," the policy of sending youths to settle in the countryside, abandoning the old and adopting the new, entering university, the cultivation of revolutionary successors, and so on and so forth—nearly every one of these realms known to people as "newborn things" can turn into grounds where special privileges work their miracles.

Could we not say that the mutation of the Soviet Union began with the high salaries paid to the high-level cadres in an attempt to emulate the bourgeois specialists? Even though, by tradition, our country accepts the idea that the old cadres, said to have shed a lot of blood for the revolution, will enjoy special care without much complaint from the men-in-the-street, can we overlook the corrupting effect it has on political authority and its influence on new social relationships? Can we close our eyes to the emerging and crystallizing new aristocracy, the new bourgeoisie?

* * *

d. Strengthening the Proletarian Dictatorship and Imposing Punishment on the Reactionaries. Have the democratic rights of the people not been written into our Constitution, Party Constitution, and Central Committee documents? Indeed they have. In addition, they have even stipulated the "protection of the people's democracy," "prohibition against taking revenge," and "strict opposition to giving credence to confessions extorted through compulsion." Unfortunately, in practice, these rights have often not been safeguarded. On the contrary, there has often been "permission" to impose fascist dictatorship on the revolutionary cadres and masses under which they have been killed or jailed, have had their cases fabricated, and have even been tortured with barbarian means on a large scale. The "strict prohibitions" have simply not been enforced!

The basic task of the Chinese people in the whole socialist historical stage is, under the guidance of the correct political line, to consolidate the proletarian dictatorship. Unfortunately, this revolutionary program of the proletarian dictatorship, when it has fallen into the hands of the reactionaries, has been transformed into a mockery of the revolutionary intention of the masses and has become the most harmful of lethal weapons in the hands of our irreconcilable enemies.

If no punishment is meted out to the popularly hated bandit clique of Chiang [Kai-shek], which is persisting in taking the counterrevolutionary road and changing the proletarian dictatorship to a fascist dictatorship with bloody suppression and massacring, then the socialist democracy and the legal system cannot be established and the proletarian dictatorship cannot be consolidated. We must suppress those who suppress the people. The "Fourth National People's Congress" should enact regulations clearly in black and white, punish the "mandarins" who have committed monstrous crimes, violate the law while knowing the law, violate the law while administering the law, fabricate false cases, use official influence to carry out personal revenge, privately cook up special cases, set up jails on their own, apply torture on a large scale, and treat human life as if it were coarse grass.

e. Implementing the Policy. Early in 1969 at the Ninth Party Congress it was already pointed out that "at present, the most important task is to make (the policies) 'down to earth.'" Now it is five years after the congress and three years after the collapse of Lin Piao. Why have so many important proletarian policies not yet been made "down to earth"?

At the same time, in the last few years policies have kept on changing, even to the point of having an order given in the morning and having it changed by evening. (It is a matter of ability to understand, but mainly it reflected the intensity of the struggle between the lines.) In addition, the local policies coming out one after another in all sorts of varieties have instilled chaotic thoughts in the people, even making them doubt the Party. We feel the "Fourth National People's Congress" should reaffirm those policies which the Party, in the historical stage of socialism, has proved correct through practice and should implement them for a long time to come, realizing them in an appropriate manner through the legal system. Policies and strategies are the life of the Party, and so those who have seriously damaged the Party policies should be strictly punished.

* * *

Husan Chi-wen, "Criticism of 'On Socialist Democracy and the Legal System,'" Chinese Law and Government, vol. 10, No. 3, Fall 1977, pp. 83–85, 103–108.

* * *

Arguments against the Imputation that Each Level of the Party and Government Leadership Is a "Privileged Stratum" and a "Clique of New Nobility". Li I-che, based on their analysis of "new class contradictions," arrived at this conclusion: "Now in China there has emerged a privileged stratum as in the Soviet Union." They also slandered each level of the Party and government leadership as having "completed a qualitative change from being 'the servants of the people' to being 'the masters of the people,'" also alleging that they are the "newborn bourgeois class," "the clique of new nobility."

Undoubtedly in this historical stage of socialism, among the ranks of our cadres certain people have the improper mentality of expecting special treatment and privileges and of being able to "go through the back door" and so forth. Certain of the weak-willed, because of the corrosive influence of the bourgeoisie, have "turned public into private," and there are even isolated cases of corruption and burglary, speculation and profiteering, and degeneration in personal qualities. There have even been people in power taking the capitalist road who have wormed their way into the Party and occupied leadership positions (for example, Liu Shao-ch'i and Lin Piao). These are reflections of the class struggle under conditions of the dictatorship of the proletariat. Chairman Mao, basing himself precisely on the reality of class struggle inside and outside the country and on the historical experience of the dictatorship of the proletariat, has raised the theory of the continued revolution under the dictatorship of the proletariat. Now, under Chairman Mao's guidance our Party is firmly taking a Marxist line, using Marxism to triumph over revisionism and using socialism to triumph over capitalism, so that our country advances victoriously along the socialist road. That is why no privileged stratum like the Soviet Union's has emerged in our country and why, even more so, there has been no degeneration into social-imperialism. The Li I-che [group] purposefully avoided these facts of decisive significance, but instead played around with despicable tricks. They took things which our Party opposes and struggles against—stuff like "going through the back door," "expecting special treatment" and "privileges," and so on—and forced them onto our Party's head, making it sound as if they are inherent in the leadership cadres of each level of the Party and especially the national leadership. Based on that, they tried in vain to arrive at the conclusion that our country has already formed a "privileged stratum." Is this not terribly absurd and laughable?

*　*　*

On Their Energetic Advocacy of Capitalist Freedom, Democracy, and Legal Systems; and Their Vain Attempts to assemble Freaks and Demons and to Incite the Masses to Reenact in China a "Hungarian Incident". Li I-che, under the cloak of "asking instructions in behalf of the people," trumpets a lot about "socialist democracy and the legal system" and has presented a pile of "requests" about this to our country of proletarian dictatorship. What kind of democracy are they really asking for? What kind of legal system? When condemning that renegade Kautsky's bourgeois "pure democracy," Lenin had pointedly remarked that when the question of "democracy" was opened up for debate, "Marxists never forget to pause to ask 'This democracy is for which class?'"

Regarding the sermon of Li I-che and their ilk, trumpeting about "freedom" and the "legal system," we should of course also not forget to sit back and ask: For which class are they asking freedom? For which class democracy? For which class this "system"?

Is it the democracy and rights of the proletariat or is it the "democracy and rights" which the bourgeoisie employs to attack the Party and socialism?

*　*　*

Should it be a legal system of the proletariat or a "legal system" to protect the reactionaries in attacking the Party and attacking socialism?

A legal system, like freedom and democracy, also has a distinct class nature. A socialist legal system reflects the people's democracy—that is, the dictatorship of the proletariat, which means exercising democracy for the people. Chairman Mao long ago clearly pointed out: "The people's state protects the people. Only when the people have such a state can they educate and remold themselves on a nationwide scale using democratic methods and, with everyone taking part, shake off the influence of domestic and foreign reactionaries." When talking of dictatorship, the case is very different. The dictatorship of the proletariat means "enforcing a dictatorship over the running dogs of imperialism, the landlord class, and the bureaucratic bourgeoisie, as well as over the representatives of those classes, the Kuomintang reactionaries and their accomplices." He also pointed out: "The first function [of this dictatorship] is to suppress the reactionary classes and elements and those exploiters in our country who resist the socialist revolution, to suppress those who try to wreck our socialist construction, or in other words, to resolve the internal contradictions between ourselves and the enemy. For instance, to arrest, try, and sentence certain counterrevolutionaries and to deprive landlords and bureaucratic capitalists of their right to vote and their freedom of speech for a specified period of time—all this comes within the scope of our dictatorship. To maintain public order and safeguard the interests of the people, it is likewise necessary to exercise dictatorship over embezzlers, swindlers, arsonists, murderers, criminal gangs, and other scoundrels who seriously disrupt public order."

However, what the Li I-che group said was: the Fourth National People's Congress should stipulate that the democratic rights of the broad masses of the people should be safeguarded, apart from the fact that a dictatorship must be enforced over criminal offenders such as murderers, arsonists, hoodlums, and embezzlers, and those who instigate violence and organize intrigues.

Worth noting is that among the targets on Li I-che's list over whom "dictatorship must be enforced," first, the landlord class has disappeared, the bureaucratic bourgeoisie has disappeared; the rich-peasant class, the bourgeoisie, rightists, and counterrevolutionaries have also all disappeared. Certainly this could not be accidental carelessness. Otherwise, how is it that in this big-character poster tossed out specially for expounding Li I-che's "system," which carries on so loudly about the "socialist" legal system, no one can find even a word mentioning that dictatorship must be enforced over the landlords, rich peasants, counterrevolutionaries, rightists, and bureaucratic bourgeoisie. Second, what has also vanished is that the proletariat must impose an all-around dictatorship over the bourgeoisie in the ideological sphere. It follows then that all feudalistic, bourgeois, revisionist reactionary ideologies, all anti-Party, antisocialist, anti-Marxist-Leninist, and all anti-Mao Tse-tung thought reactionary talk can run wild. Actually, all this has undergone painstaking "deliberation." From what can be seen from Li I-che's "system," people who subvert the proletarian dictatorship and attack Marxism-Leninism and the thought of Mao Tse-tung should be given "democracy" and "freedom" and should not be subjected to dictatorship. On the contrary, those people who carry out subversive activities and who spread reactionary rumors should be given the protection of the "legal system." Therein lies the essence of their so-called "socialist democracy and legal system."

* * *

The conclusion is very clear. Li I-che and his ilk have today once more raised the broken flag of bourgeois "democracy," "freedom," and the "legal system" precisely for their vain effort of assembling freaks and demons such as the landlords, rich peasants, counter-revolutionaries, bad elements, and rightists. Their effort is to stir up the masses and stage a new "Hungarian Incident" in our country, to subvert the dictatorship of the proletariat and restore capitalism. It turns out that the Li I-che group, which is waving the banner of a "frank and righteous opposition faction," is actually a reactionary faction brazenly taking up the cudgels.

E.   RECENT CHANGES

Victor H. Li, "The Drive to Legalization," in Anne Thurston and Jason Parker, editors, Humanistic and Social Science Research in China, Social Science Research Council, 1980. (Notes omitted.)

Since the fall of the Gang of Four in 1976, China has been moving sharply toward expanding the role of law. A new Constitution was promulgated in March, 1978 which, among other things, strengthened the courts and reestablished the procuracy. Thereafter, for the first time in nearly two decades, major articles were published stressing the importance of legal work. In October, 1978, Zhao Cangbi, Minister of Public Security and Vice-Director of the Political-Legal Commission of the Central Committee of the CCP, said that all original laws and statutes urgently needed to be revised. At that time, work was completed on 28 categories of the statutes, including a revised Marriage Law, a new law on protection of the environment, and regulations concerning the operation of the rural people's communes, the protection of forests, the strengthening of safety measures for industrial production, the encouraging and awarding of inventions, and the commendation and punishment of personnel of the state administrative organizations. In February, 1979, new Regulations Governing the Arrest and Detention of Persons Accused of Crimes was issued, with considerable publicity.

The second session of the Fifth National People's Congress promulgated seven new laws on July 1, 1979: the Organic Law of the Local People's Congresses and Local People's Governments; the Electoral Law for the National People's Congress and Local People's Congresses of all Levels; the Organic Law of People's Courts; the

Organic Law of People's Procuratorates; the Criminal Law; the Law of Criminal Procedure; and the Law on Joint Ventures. Moreover, work was progressing in a number of other areas, including civil law, civil procedure law, taxation, and enterprise law.

This is a formidable list indeed. After 20 years of not having legal materials from China to work with, there suddenly is a veritable flood of new legislation. These laws, together with efforts such as the expansion of legal training and the publication of new legal journals such as *Faxue yanjiu* and *Minju yu fazhi*, vividly demonstrate the desire of high level leaders to implement a formal system of law.

Nevertheless, an important question remains: to what extent will this legalization drive actually take root in Chinese society? We should remember that a similar effort was mounted in the mid-1950's and collapsed after the anti-rightist campaign. Some tentative steps to revive the legal system in the early 1960's were ended by the Cultural Revolution. In addition, the Nationalist attempt to establish a new Western-style legal system in the 1920's and 1930's also encountered considerable difficulties.

Most Western observers have tended to be fairly optimistic about the chances of success. I am more skeptical. I readily admit that I sometimes overstate my skepticism. I do so to balance the reports of Western lawyers and journalists who return from China quite aglow about the new drive to legalization.

It is clearly too early to state a definitive opinion about the future of law in China. My present feeling is that there is much more law on paper than in practice. Moreover, the current legalization drive must be slowed down considerably or face the possibility of failure. The promulgating of new laws and regulations is a major step forward in the legalization effort. But, as discussed below, much more must be done, perhaps more than China is able to accomplish at this point.

In order to implement the new legal system, several problems have to be resolved.

a. Personnel and Infrastructure. Who will staff the new legal system? In the United States, there are about 500,000 lawyers engaged in this work, not to mention accountants, policemen, probation officers, etc. It is clear that China will not need this number of legally trained persons, but it is equally clear that a substantial number will be required.

During the JCCC-CSCC visit, a number of Chinese legal scholars said that one million college trained (*juanye*) lawyers, over and above the ones now engaged in legal work, will eventually be needed—a formidable number.

The foundation for training more legal specialists is weak. For many practical purposes, systematic legal education nearly stopped after the anti-rightist campaign. The twenty-year training gap severely limits China's ability to staff new law schools and produce new teaching materials.

China has begun to expand legal training. Law departments operating at Beijing University, People's University, Hubei University in Wuhan, and Jilin University; new departments may be opened soon at Xiamen University, Nanjing University and Zhongshan University. In addition to these schools, there are political-legal institutes (*jengfa xueyuan*), which concentrate more on practical rather than theoretical training, operating in Beijing, Huadong (Shanghai), Xinan (Chongqing), Xibei (Xian), Zhongnan, and Hubei. There also are cadre training schools run by the central and provincial governments. All in all, in 1977 and 1978, over 40,000 political-legal cadres received further in-service training, probably in three-to-six-month programs. 5,600 students have enrolled in two-year intermediate level courses in law, and 1,100 in undergraduate or postgraduate courses. In 1979, an additional 1,740 undergraduates and over 100 postgraduates will enroll in universities, with 5,000 entering the intermediate level courses. These are impressive numbers for a training program just starting up after a twenty-year hiatus, but there is still a very long way to go before the target of a million new legal specialists can be reached.

In addition to increased personnel, China is developing other aspects of the legal infrastructure. An eight-year National Program for the Study of Law was adopted in 1978, calling for setting up research institutes on the history of China's legal system, international law, and other subjects. Studies also will be carried out concerning jurisprudence, constitutional law, civil and criminal law, economic law, and other subjects. A number of books, papers, dictionaries and reports will be published, both scholarly and popular. An International Law Society and a Legal History Society will soon be set up. The Ministry of Justice was reestablished to handle the administration of legal work. Various legal and drafting offices are being created in party and government organs.

b. Public Education. The reasons why law has been downplayed in the PRC for the last two decades are directly related to a deeply rooted cultural antipathy toward law. As part of the legalization drive, the thinking and work style of the public and of party and government officials at every level must be reoriented so that they will turn to the new legal institutions and processes to solve their problems.

A broad educational campaign is being conducted in China to teach the public about the new laws. Newspapers publish many articles explaining the new legal system. Lectures on law are given on the radio. Law schools are preparing materials of a popular nature for distribution. Law-related personnel attend lectures on law. Public trials and articles about trials also are used as educational tools. Several new pamphlets on law have been published.

Despite all this activity, I am not sure that enough is being done. Clearly, we must wait to see what the results of the campaign will be; at this point, my feeling is that it takes more than a series of lectures or articles, many of them quite dry and technical, explaining what the legal terms "offense" or "responsibility" mean to change deeply rooted cultural attitudes.

Also, some materials concerning law do capture public attention but may deliver unintended messages about the role of law. For example, the play Power and Law (Quan yu fa) is widely acclaimed in China. It deals with a corrupt party secretary who tries to intimidate a subordinate into not revealing his earlier illegal acts. Through the intervention of another party secretary, the subordinate eventually prevails, thus demonstrating that no official, however powerful, can be above the law. But there is a second message. When the subordinate needs help, she does not turn to legal institutions or processes—the rule of law—but rather to a good party official—still the rule of man. And when the party secretaries clash, the conflict is not resolved in a court of law but rather in a party committee meeting.

c. *Prospects for Changes in Civil and Economic Law.* Most of the legislation promulgated to date, and almost all the newspaper and journal articles on law, deal with criminal matters. This is understandable since the motive force behind the present legalization drive was the desire on the part of the victims of the Cultural Revolution to prevent future abuses of the criminal system.

But Chinese legal planners did not stop with criminal law. In a manner that is not entirely clear, they argue that the formulation of "rational rules" will make the economic system operate more efficiently, and hence will speed up the modernization program. In addition, the lack of an adequate dispute resolution mechanism also obstructs economic work. The recent establishment of an economic division in some people's courts alleviates the problem to some degree, but the jurisdiction of this division is limited, and public attitudes may be such that disputants may not turn to the courts for assistance. During the JCCC-CSCC visit, some Chinese scholars indicated that a Soviet-style *arbitrazh* system might be created to handle economic disputes.

Establishing a thorough system of civil and economic law will be a most difficult task. By comparison, creating a set of criminal and criminal procedure laws is relatively simple, since the institutions and methods for handling anti-social conduct are fairly well known, as are the protections an individual needs against possible arbitrary action by the state. Moreover, except for political offenses, the entire subject of deviancy can be relatively easily isolated from other aspects of social activity. To promulgate a tax law or a corporations law, however, will involve an enormous number of people and kinds of activity, and also will have far-reaching consequences in all of society.

The lack of adequate personnel and infrastructure may pose an obstacle to establishing an economic law system which cannot be surmounted for some time.

Conclusion. While there is a substantial effort to build legal institutions and promulgate new laws, I think that for a number of years, perhaps five or ten, the new legal system in China will exist more on paper than in practice. There are not enough trained persons to staff the legal system. Moreover, deeply rooted cultural biases against law are hard to change.

But the problem is more serious than merely incomplete implementation. I think the upper level leaders in China, possibly reflecting their own cultural and personal backgrounds, still feel uncertain about what law could and should be. Criminal law and civil rights remain politically sensitive subjects. The ending of Democracy Wall, the probable decision not to try the Gang of Four, and the annoyance shown to reactions to the trial of the dissident Wei Jingsheng are indications of this sensitivity. Civil law presents a different problem. The Chinese have great hopes that the forthcoming economic laws will considerably increase efficiency and productivity. They may be expecting more from law than law is able to contribute. And even if law can accomplish these desirable goals, the period of transition from traditional methods to the new legal system is likely to be quite confusing and will not increase economic efficiency.

The net result of the above uncertainties is that the new legal system—both criminal and civil—must prove its worth within a few years, or run the serious risk of losing political support.

*   *   *

My belief is that the cultural bias against law, the lack of personnel, and the sheer enormity of the task make it unlikely that the new legal system can produce visible and substantial results within a relatively short time. Consequently, there is a real possibility that the emphasis on law will decline after a couple of years. The decline can be reversed if the Chinese legal planners adopt a more gradual developmental strategy that lowers expectations and reduces need for resources, essentially following a para-legal "barefoot lawyers" route. So far, however, the signs are that these planners want to go full speed ahead.

I do not wish to suggest that for cultural or political reasons China cannot establish a Western style of law. Hong Kong and Japan, to cite just two examples, are Eastern cultures which have successfully adopted Western legal forms. But we must be careful not to let our own preferences for formal law—or perhaps it is our effort to find in Chinese society something familiar with which we can identify—color our belief that the new legal system can be readily established in China. The process of introducing a foreign approach to law requires much time and effort. And even then, the result may be more superficial than meets the eye.

Victor H. Li, Gang of Four Trial, Los Angeles Times, February 2, 1981, Part II, page 5.

One of the most dramatic and important political events in the history of the People's Republic of China has been played out in a Peking courtroom, as the Chinese for the first time subjected fallen politicians to the legal process.

The trial of the much-maligned Gang of Four and another "counterrevolutionary clique" of ex-generals represented a movement away from the Stalinist-style purges and mass tribunals of the Cultural Revolution toward greater reliance on regular legal institutions. As such, it was a noble and praiseworthy experiment.

But it was a schizophrenic proceeding, for the current leadership was using the trial for both legal and political ends. Unfortunately, those considerations often pulled in opposite directions, so that the trial ultimately turned out to be unsatisfactory from both political and legal points of view.

At the most visceral level, putting Jiang Qing, the widow of Mao Tse-tung, on trial vented widespread anger pent up since the Cultural Revolution of 1966–76. More than that, it theoretically gave the leadership a chance to explain to the Chinese people how such terrible abuses of power could have occurred for so long in a good Communist state.

The government of Deng Xiaoping and Zhao Ziyang naturally could not blame all the abuses on weaknesses in Communist doctrine or Chinese society, or even on an aging Mao whose judgment slipped in the last two decades of his life. Instead, the fault was identified as the evil, aberrant and power-hungry character of Jiang Qing and her supporters. Of course, in the process, the ultraleftist policies that they advocated also came under attack and the moderate policies of the current leadership seemed all the wiser by comparison.

The legal interests at stake in the trial were quite different. After the October 1976, fall of the Gang of Four, the new leaders—themselves victims of the Cultural Revolution, for the most part—were determined to prevent such abuses of power from recurring. They apparently concluded that some kind of rule of law was the answer, and began a major drive to establish formal legal institutions. This effort included the promulgation of a series of criminal codes, whose substance was familiar to Western lawyers and whose form resembled the inquisitorial trial model common through continental Europe. (Americans reading about the trial should not have expected Perry Mason style adversary proceedings; Chinese law follows the European, not the American, model.)

Trying the Gang of Four in a court of law was a key element in the legalization drive. The leadership, essentially, was telling the public that even the most critical national issues can be dealt with by legal means. The lesson was supposed to be that individuals and enterprises also ought to turn over their legal problems to the judicial system for resolution.

How well were these political and legal goals met? Not particularly well.

In any judicial system, a principal concern ought to be that defendants are tried for acts that were clearly criminal when they were committed. The lack of a codified criminal law in China before 1979 poses no particular problem: One does not need codes to know that fabricating evidence, torturing prisoners and planning the assassination of a head of state—among the charges against the defendants— are illegal. Only if defendants are accused of acts that were earlier perceived as something less heinous, deserving no more than political or social censure, do problems arise. And, in Peking, that sometimes was the case; the trial occasionally seemed to be a disguised attack by the victorious political faction on opponents already vanquished.

As long as the prosecution concentrated on incidents in which the defendants personally fabricated evidence or committed other common crimes, the proceeding could not be dismissed as a "political trial." Indeed, the prosecutors succeeded in identifying some clear criminal acts, ranging from personally ordered abuse of identified prisoners to plans for a massive armed rebellion in Shanghai, and linking them directly to the accused.

But, much of the time, the gang's criminal culpability was much less clear. The attacks that Jiang Qing and her colleagues mounted on other high-ranking leaders, their rivals for power 15 years ago, could be seen as part of a nasty political struggle, not crimes in and of themselves. The gang's 1974 campaign to bring down then-Premier Chou En-lai and Deng Xiaoping was also arguably a political, rather than a criminal, act. Moreover, the charge that the defendants persecuted 34,000 lower-level officials during the Cultural Revolution should have stood only if there were evidence that they knew or should have known of all the acts being committed, nationwide, by their subordinates—and there was no such proof.

Even if all the allegations had been supported, the trial would still have been troubling politically. Judging from the limited Chinese press coverage of the trial, which was closed to foreigners, Jiang Qing's accusers never fully dealt with her defense—that Mao authorized her to act in his name. The Communist Party-controlled press acknowledged, during the trial, that Mao was guilty of errors, but carefully differentiated his mistakes of judgment from the crimes of the defendants. Harsher judgments will probably be rendered against Mao in the future, but the party chiefs, inheritors of his mantle, are not ready to let anyone, certainly not his widow, force that subject. Similarly, the trial skirted the question of whether there is something inherently wrong in the Chinese system that allowed evil people to hold power for so long.

Whether the rule of law has been enhanced depends on how the Chinese public perceived the trial—and that is unknowable for now. The presence of the defense attorneys, the relatively quiet and dispassionate atmosphere and even Jiang Qing's outbursts probably contributed to an overall sense of fairness. At the same time, there seems no doubt that the defendants' guilt was determined in advance and that the verdict was reached not just by the presiding judges but also by key party officials.

To some extent, the trial was the last act of a morality play whose script had been written in advance and well rehearsed. Morality plays may have a certain purgative effect, but they do not provide the forum for the resolution of far-reaching social, legal and political problems.

NOTE

1. As you go through the materials in subsequent chapters which describe post-1976 legal developments, consider the extent to which Li I-che's position has been implemented.

2. Most of the materials in this chapter deal with criminal law. To what extent do the same considerations apply to civil law, especially the areas of economic regulation and interenterprise relations? In criminal law matters, the principal unit is the individual and the most important set of activities concerns interpersonal relationships on a fairly small scale. The methods of settling disputes can be slow and amorphous and depend in large measure on the close ties developed through the small group discussion process. In the economic sector, there is a greater need to deal with bureaucratic decision making and interenterprise relations and with activities that span long distances and large periods of time. While there are continuing relations among the economic managers, face-to-face dealings are much more limited. If a dispute arises, these persons cannot easily attempt to evolve a consensus the way a small group might. Moreover, at times it may be more important to terminate a disagreement so that production can continue rather than try to find out who actually was right or wrong. Thus, the need for efficiency in dealing with complex issues over long distances may require a very different approach to legal work in the economic sector.

From what we know of law in the United States, as well as from the Soviet experience, it would appear that the existence of clear, understandable, and known rules helps increase efficiency and reduce disputes and disruptions. Each party knows with considerable precision what are his obligations and also what are the consequences of his failure to perform. This kind of predictability of result helps reduce lawsuits, as well as the amount of effort needed to resolve a dispute.

From what little we know about the management of the economy in China, it does not appear such a system of rules developed in China—although I must stress that very little information is available on the subject. Is it possible to run a large complex economy without a formal and highly developed set of laws and legal institutions?

3. Chinese society has been undergoing drastic and rapid change. This condition is likely to last for some time. Might the United States and China hold different underlying assumptions concerning the relative roles of stability and change. Would you agree with the characterization that in the United States, and in the West in general, stability is regarded as the "normal" and preferred state. When necessary, some change is introduced to deal with new conditions that develop. The changes, however, tend to be gradual and smooth, producing at the end of the process a new stable state. Our approach to law reflects these attitudes. The great bulk of our laws and legal institutions have developed gradually over centuries. They not only define the status quo but support it as well. We regard as one of the fundamental virtues of our legal system the fact that it can provide both stability and hence predictability and yet allow change to take place in a controlled manner.

There is quite a different attitude toward stability and change in China. To oversimplify, traditional Chinese society was basically retrospective. Graham Peck in his book Two Kinds of Time uses an analogy to illustrate this: while a Westerner would face downstream to see where the river is going, a man in traditional China would look upstream and be concerned with where the river had come from. For many such people, the Golden Age had occurred several thousand years ago during the Chou dynasty. Somewhere along the line, man had fallen from that ideal state. The task of subsequent generations was to rediscover and then restore the Golden Age. Such a viewpoint would not be supportive of change, whether social or technological.

Contemporary China presents a completely different picture. Change and not stability is regarded as the normal state. In dialectical terms, originating from Hegelian and Marxist philosophy as well as from Taoist thought, every thing by definition has an opposite. These "contradictions" (or thesis and antithesis) are in constant interaction with each other, and their continual resolution produces a synthesis, which in turn continues to interact with its opposite to produce further change. In Chairman Mao's words: "The universality of absoluteness of contradiction has a twofold meaning. One is that contradiction exists in the process of development of all things, and the other is that in the process of development of each thing a movement of opposites exists from beginning to end."

In light of these attitudes, some apparently puzzling Chinese actions and statements become more understandable. For example, it should not be surprising that Western-style law, which supposes stability and restrains change, has not fared well in the People's Republic of China. That kind of law is too conservatizing in the philosophical sense of denying change as the normal and preferred state. In addition, while law can be used as a means of introducing new social or political programs, the cumbersome process of amending the law tends to inhibit the making of changes. Consequently, to formulate the practices of a particular moment into codes of law might imbue them with a greater sense of permanency than they ought to have. This problem is particularly serious in China where rapidly changing social and economic conditions require an equally rapid change in the rules to be applied.

Similarly, the Chinese penchant for debate and acceptance of a fairly high level of turmoil (by Western standards) in part reflects the belief that the process of development consists of the struggle of opposites and that the heightening of struggle will bring about more substantial change. Thus, the Chinese often say of the present international scene: "There is great disorder under the heavens; the situation is excellent." This is neither oriental mysticism nor praise of anarchy, but rather a statement that the increased disorder in the world will speed up the process of producing a new international order in which the two superpowers will not be able to continue their predominant roles.

Part II

INHERITANCE, SUCCESSION AND DESCENT

Chapter 6

INTRODUCTION TO INHERITANCE, SUCCESSION AND DESCENT

PROBLEM 1

An eminent person holding high office dies, leaving substantial wealth and numerous relatives. Who inherits the decedent's wealth? Who succeeds to the office? What happens to the decedent's status (e.g., social prominence, membership in an aristocracy, head of the family)? How does the law regulate these processes?

NOTE

Nothing so clearly illuminates the structure of a society as the patterns of distribution and redistribution from one generation to another of property, office and status. In some societies, at least in their idealized forms, the three are collapsed into a single category. Thus during high feudalism in England and Normandy one's tenure of land, office in governance of the realm and social position were acquired and transferred together. Throughout the West today the ideal is quite different; the object is to separate office from property and, for most purposes, to make inherited status irrelevant to either. One of the interesting questions in this problem concerns the extent to which this ideal is shared in other cultures and, where it is not, why a different ideal makes cultural sense to them and how that different ideal is expressed in their law.

Why does the law of inheritance, and the way that law is (or is not) put into practice, vary from one culture to another? That is a very big question which should be kept in mind while studying the materials in this problem. One obvious factor is received legal tradition. Thus the English common law, received in California, supplies the conceptual vocabulary, much of the substance and procedure, and the rich cultural history that give meaning to the California law. The tradition of Islamic law in Egypt and the tribal legal traditions in Botswana serve similar functions. Still, to say that legal systems differ because their legal traditions differ may seem merely to postpone the question. Why do the legal traditions differ? One important influence emphasized by Montesquieu in The Spirit of the Laws * is environment: the cli-

---

* Baron Charles de Montesquieu, De L'Espirit des Lois, originally published in France in 1748 and frequently published. An excellent 1766 English trans-mate, geography, resources, patterns of production and consumption, etc. The chain of relationships between environment, modes of subsistence, social structure, and the law, including the law of inheritance, is complex but, in the minds of most students of law and society, fundamental. For example, where the forms of inherited wealth vary from household goods (China) to livestock (Botswana), agricultural land (Egypt) and intangibles (California), does the law reflect such differences? Another influence is political/social/economic ideology: e.g., state socialism in contemporary China; a different version of socialism in Egypt; and so on. Can you think of other factors that would illuminate the sources of differences in the four systems of inheritance?

"All legal systems, primitive and civilized, assume the importance of the kinship group, and all support it as a medium of inheritance of property rights."* Professor Hoebel draws our attention to two centrally important variables: 1. How is the kinship group defined, for inheritance purposes, in each society; and 2. How is inheritance within that group allocated? As the materials on inheritance patterns in the four cultures show, there are substantial, sometimes startling, variations in the rules concerning who may inherit from whom. Such variations often make sense only in light of the kinship groups that have long constituted the basic components of these societies. Accordingly, one of the first inquiries in examining inheritance in any society is into the relations between kinship and inheritance. That question quickly suggests others: what are the relative positions of men and women in the scheme of inheritance? How is the surviving spouse (or spouses) treated? May children be disinherited? How significant is it that three of the four systems we examine (California is the exception) are, at least historically, patrilineal? That the rights of women appear to be increasing in all four systems? More generally in the different societies, how much control does one have over the distribution of one's property during life and at death? How much control does the law allow one to exert over what the people who inherit the property may do with it? To what extent is inheritance a form of social security for survivors of the deceased? Does the law of inheritance relate to other forms of social security? In short, an examination of the law of inheritance requires one to take a rather close look at large parts of the law of property and family law and to consider their relation to the system of social security in the culture under examination.

One way to think of inheritance is in terms that sharply distinguish living transactions from those transfers that occur at death. That seems to be the tendency in societies that are emphatically individualist; property belongs to a living person who may consume it, enjoy it, sell it, or give it away. When that person (the owner) dies, there is a disposal problem: who is to become the new owner of the deceased's property? A contrasting way of thinking about inheritance places more emphasis on the group—such as the family or household or clan in Botswana or China. During one's life he has authority to deal with property in which others have interests which must be respected. This power of management of property belonging to the group can be shared

lation by Thomas Nugent has been published in a number of editions. Montesquieu's discussion of the effects of climate and soil on the laws appears in books XIV–XVIII.

* E. Adamson Hoebel, The Law of Primitive Man: A Study in Comparative Legal Dynamics, Cambridge: Harvard University Press, 1954, p. 286.

with or transferred to other members of the group during life, a bit at a time, perhaps. At death the process begun earlier is completed, and the cycle begins again with the living. In such a society "inheritance" is not the same as it is in individualist systems. Death is merely the final point in a process that goes on during life. The social significance of the law of inheritance and the law governing it are bound to be different in such societies.

Where, as in some socialist nations, productive property is, at least in theory, owned by "all the people," so that the living are merely the temporary managers of it, a further variation on the meaning of inheritance appears. It still makes sense to speak of inheritance of the consumer goods in which private ownership is permitted, but for productive property a different set of ideas comes into play. One of the questions to consider as you study these materials is whether the law of inheritance in the People's Republic of China is more like that of, say, Botswana or that of California.

What is the significance of religious, economic or political ideology in the actual operation of the different inheritance systems? Are the dictates of Islam, or of state socialism, or of individualism dominant forces, or are they often (always?) in competition with other forces? To what extent does ideological principle become an obstacle that blocks, or requires elaborate fictions in order to achieve, contemporary social objectives? How are such fictions (e.g. in Egyptian law, but not only in Egypt) constructed and employed? What are their secondary consequences?

How would you characterize the respective importance of rules and process in the law of inheritance in the four systems? For example, would you say that property and office pass strictly according to rule in Botswana, or does it appear that the way they actually pass at death may be controlled by other factors? Where that is so, is there an apparent felt need to put the result into terms that conform to the applicable rule? Why should such a need be felt? Are matters different in China or in California? In rural Egypt?

It is always useful in studying legal materials to try to visualize the system in operation. In this problem you should continually ask yourself how the process actually works. Suppose George Zilch dies. Who determines that he is in fact dead? Who determines what property was his? Who decides who should get it? If there are disputes, who decides them? How is such a decision enforced if the losing disputant is reluctant to accept or comply with it?

You will recall the discussion of Max Weber in the section on What is Western about Western Law. Are Weber's categories useful in describing and distinguishing the inheritance schemes in the four cultures? Could any of the legal systems examined in this problem be described as formally or substantively irrational? To the extent that they are rational, what features of, say, the law of Egypt on who shall inherit could you classify as substantively or formally rational? How about the law of California?

When we in the West think about inheritance, we ordinarily think about the transfer of wealth, which is to say of rights, from the deceased to the living. To what extent does the law of inheritance in the other cultures deal with the transfer of obligations? What happens to the deceased's obligations on death? Are they passed on to or assumed by the heir?

One of the corollaries of the rise of the Western nation-state was the notion of a state monopoly on law-making. All law would be made by the state, and rival sources of law (the local jurisdictions, guilds, medieval corporations, religious authorities, etc.) were suppressed. The ideal was of a single national law applicable to all. Even within the West the extent to which this ideal has been realized in practice varies. Legal pluralism is, however, still widely resisted in the West. Is inheritance law in the other cultures examined here more pluralistic? Are there different traditional, tribal, sectional or other elements in competition with the official national law of inheritance in Egypt, China and Botswana? Is such legal pluralism bad, or is insistence on legal monism just a dogma of Western statism?

What kinds of changes in the law of inheritance have recently occurred or appear likely to occur in the four cultures? Are these changes progressive? What is the applicable standard of progress? Do such changes merely reflect adjustment of the legal system to accommodate social change, or are some kinds of legal changes causal, constituting a form of "social engineering through law?" What sorts of evidence are there to support the proposition that law can cause significant social change? That law can facilitate, even if it cannot cause, social change? That the best that law can do is get out of the way of social change?

You should try to make a systematic comparison of the inheritance systems in two of the four cultures, using the apparatus of comparison set out in the Introductory Note on Law at the front of this book. What are the differences in legal extension; in legal penetration; in legal institutions, actors and processes; in primary legal rules? Have you identified other variables that you think would be useful in comparing the four systems?

Finally, what conclusions can you draw from the process of comparison? If we assume that these four cultures are fairly representative of the world's variety (which they actually only incompletely represent), what generalizations about the law [of inheritance] can you draw from the materials in Problem I?

Chapter 7

INHERITANCE, SUCCESSION AND DESCENT
IN WESTERN LAW

A. INTRODUCTION

Lawrence M. Friedman, The Law of Succession in Social Perspective, in Halbach, Edward C. Death, Taxes and Family Property. St. Paul, Minn.: West Publishing Co., 1977, pp. 9, 23, 25.

Rules of inheritance and succession are, in a way, the genetic code of a society. They guarantee that the next generation will, more or less, have the same structure as the one that preceded it. In the long run, for example, there could be no upper class or aristocracy without rules about the inheritance of wealth and privilege, which permit the upper class or aristocracy to continue. And if rules permit free transfer of property and freedom of testation, a middle class society can be created and maintained. Rules favoring wives and children reinforce the nuclear family. Any radical change in the rules, if carried out, will radically change the society.

NOTE

This problem raises questions about the law of inheritance (of wealth), of succession (to office) and of descent (of status). In the West the first of these is obviously much the most important. The anti-feudal, anti-aristocratic, democratic character of the American Revolution (and its analogues throughout Europe and Latin America, see Robert Roswell Palmer, The Age of the Democratic Revolution: A Political History of Europe and America, 1760–1800, Princeton, New Jersey: Princeton University Press, 1959 and 1965) meant the elimination of privileged classes. All citizens were to be of one class. Office was to be allocated according to an open political process or by merit and could in no case be passed onto the incumbent's heir. (The contrast with pre-revolutionary law is striking. In the 18th Century Montesquieu, for example, inherited a judgeship, held it for several years, and then sold it.) Accordingly, a great deal of law governing the descent of class membership and hereditary succession to public office has disappeared from most Western legal systems. Hereditary royalty and hereditary lordships (including, for example, hereditary seats in the British House of Lords) survive in a few European nations, but the rest was swept away in the democratic revolution of the late 18th and 19th centuries. As a general rule what passes on death is property, at least so far as the law is concerned. Inherited property, in turn, can provide access to office in private governments (e.g. inherited stock can provide a seat on the board of directors of a corporation), but that is generally considered to be proper; it is public office that we think ought not to be directly or indirectly heritable. Wealth, particularly inherited wealth, is often related to social status, but not to legal status; "equal protection of the laws" forbids giving such social attributions legal significance. In fact, we know that wealth and social status do have significant legal consequences. Wealthy and influential people seldom go to jail. When they receive preferential legal treatment, however, we are critical; the legal system is not working properly.

Despite the egalitarian ideal there are numerous examples of ways in which inherited status has continued to have legal consequences in the West even after the 18th century revolutions. For example, racial and cultural identity are inherited. Until recently the inherited status of Black has had enormous legal consequences in the United States through laws directly or, particularly since the adoption of the 14th Amendment, indirectly discriminating against Black people. American Indians and Asians have had comparable problems. The treatment of Jews in much of Eastern and Western Europe (the Nazis and Fascists were only two prominent examples of this) is another case. The treatment of Armenians in Turkey is another. We now see clearly that the laws and the public officials that authorized such conduct were wrong, for a number of reasons. One of the reasons is our belief that in a democratic society inherited status should not have legal consequences.

Do we really mean that? Consider the following:

1. A child born abroad of U.S. citizens is a U.S. citizen. OK?

2. Members of some racial and cultural minorities are entitled to special benefits under a variety of governmental programs. OK?

3. Can you think of other ways in which inherited status has legal consequences in the United States?

A. Anton Friedrich, "The Economics of Inheritance," 1 Social Meaning of Legal Concepts 27, 33–37 (1948).

A social-economic appraisal of the institution of inheritance is concerned also with the effect of inheritance upon the distribution of wealth. An economy based upon private property will result in an unequal distribution of wealth and income. Differences in talent, energy, endurance, drive, personality, and also luck will result in unequal earnings and in windfall acquisitions. And this will happen even under the most favorable circumstances where, as nearly as possible, opportunities are equal to all.

So long as the individual family persists, opportunities cannot be wholly equalized although educational facilities available at general public expense may lessen the inequalities greatly. The children of the families with higher incomes will have superior advantages over the children of the very poor,—in part of a material sort such as training and social contacts, in part of a more subtle psychological kind. Attitudes and habits, ambition, determination, expectations, a sense of self-assurance are communicated in the milieu of family life.

Poverty, the sociologist informs us, is cumulative, forming a kind of culture which persists from one generation to another. The poverty of the parents forms the expectations of the children that they too will be poor and that there is little that can be done about it. But this is true also of the well-to-do and the successful. Success may be a habit which can be inherited quite apart from any disposition of material property.

Some measure of inequality may, therefore, be regarded as a natural consequence of a system of economics in which rewards are more or less proportionate to the importance of the individual and the work he does in the carrying on of economic activity. In a measure, also, recognizing the competitive inclinations of man, the expectations of earning more than others are inducements to individuals to excel in chosen occupations. Emulation, and the desire to be as good as or better than others, according to some observers of human behavior, are powerful components of the egoistic drives and are calculated to keep men in a state of feverish striving for the prizes of success.

Moreover, so long as the economy is dependent upon private savings to an appreciable extent for new capital, the conditions which facilitate accumulation have some measure of social justification. Inequality of income can offer a defense on grounds that the higher incomes are the major source of savings. The lower incomes are required wholly or primarily for the daily necessities of life. It is only when there is some excess that savings can accumulate in any considerable amount.

But this is true only within limits. If the inequality of income is greater than is necessary to inspire the superior to excel and the poor to emulate, then inequality loses its claims to social merit and becomes merely the expression of acquisitive license and unrestrained greed. If the inequality which is conducive to accumulation by the few imposes undue hardship upon the many, its beneficence may justly be questioned. . . .

The institution of inheritance is not the sole cause of inequality of wealth and opportunity. But the inheritance of property is of equal and perhaps even of greater importance than inherited abilities, environment, and opportunity in accounting for economic inequality. "Its influence," asserts F. W. Taussig, sometime Henry Lee Professor of Economics in Harvard University, "is enormous. It is this which explains the perpetuation of the incomes derived from capital, land, income-yielding property of all sorts, and so explains the great continuing gulf between the haves and have-nots. It serves also to strengthen all the lines of social stratification and reenforce the influences of custom and habit. Persons who inherit property also inherit opportunity. They have a better start, a more stimulating environment, a higher ambition. They are likely to secure higher incomes and preserve a higher standard of living by late marriages and a few offspring. The institution of inheritance promotes social stratification through its indirect effects not less than through its direct."

A hereditary-wealth class and the social stratification which it supports are sharply at variance with ideas of fair competition and equal opportunity. In competition on the athletic field, all contestants start from the same position, and if there are handicaps they are placed upon those who have superior ability. Competition for economic prizes works on opposite principles. Those who have inherited great wealth may win the coveted prizes without competing at all, and if they choose to compete they may extend their advantages even more and by inheritance bequeath them to their successors. In economic competition, the contestants are distributed over the course with the largest number farthest back. There are handicaps but they are placed not on the strong but on the weak.   .   .   .

In summary the social-economic interest in inheritance may be expressed as follows: (1) The institution of inheritance distributes wealth not in accord with productive performance and competence but according to family relationships and the interest and caprice of the testator. Wealth so distributed may in some cases, perhaps in many cases, and under some circumstances be generally at variance with the capital requirements of an expanding economy. (2) But in a society based on private property, the institution of inheritance may be the better, or if you will, the least bad alternative for disposing of property upon the death of the owners. (3) And the expectations of founding a family fortune and the right of bequest may offset, or outweigh, the disadvantages of inheritance by strengthening incentives for the accumulation of capital. (4) Yet the "continuing gulf between the haves and have-nots" not only violates the norms of social ethics but may exaggerate the divisive tendencies within society, thus leading to social discord and political instability, and, it should be added, may also weaken the incentives to produce on the part of the discontented many.

The relative importance which economists and social philosophers generally will attach to the above opposing considerations will depend upon their basic premises and ultimate values. Those who attach supreme importance to the ideal of economic and social equality will relegate the bearing of inheritance upon the formation of capital to a secondary position or will disregard it altogether. Those who regard private property as the more workable pattern of economic organization will stress the importance of inheritance as a factor in the accumulation of capital.

NOTE

For a statistical analysis of the impact of inheritance upon status in the United States, see John A. Brittain, The Inheritance of Economic Status, Washington, D.C.: The Brookings Institution, 1977; and John A. Brittain, Inheritance and the Inequality of Material Wealth, Washington, D.C.: The

Brookings Institution, 1978. Based upon IRS records and empirical data collected in the Cleveland area in the mid-60's, Brittain documents the effects of family status on the educational attainment, occupational status, income and residence quality of sons and daughters. His main finding is that one's economic status at birth and in maturity tends to be the same, that the degree of inequality of economic status among brothers is substantially less than among all males. Moreover, since women usually marry men with similar family backgrounds, parental influence on the economic status of daughters is as strong as that on sons. Brittain's findings also indicate that gifts and bequests, on the average, account for half or more of the net worth of very wealthy men and for most of the net worth of equally wealthy women, regardless of their age.

Edmond N. Cahn, "An Outline of Three Great Systems," 1 Social Meaning of Legal Concepts 1, 1–4 (1948).

. . . [A] Simplified summary (passing over all refinements and technicalities) of three great systems currently in operation, i.e., the Common Law, the Civil Law, and the Soviet system.

The State of New York will be taken as an example of the Common Law, the Republic of France as an example of the Civil Law, and the Russian Soviet Federative Socialist Republic as an example of the Soviet system.

For all practical purposes the rules of inheritance in New York, in France and in the Russian Republic are precisely the same whether the person dying be a man or a woman. As a matter of chivalry, however, in the following examples it will be assumed that the person dying is a male.

Let us assume that a man dies in the state of New York and leaves no Will. In that case if no widow survives him, all of his property will go to his children. If he leaves a widow and children, the widow receives one-third and the children share the other two-thirds. . . . .

We have been supposing that the man who died left no Will. If he chose to make a Will he could leave his property to anyone he might select without regard to family relationships. There are only two significant restrictions in New York law on the freedom to choose one's heirs. First, if a man leaves a widow and children, his Will must give the widow at least the income for her life of one-third of his estate. If he leaves a widow and no children, then his Will must give his widow at least the income of one-half of his estate. The second important restriction is that a man leaving a widow, child or parent surviving him, cannot leave more than half his estate to charity. But he can disinherit his children, his parents and all other members of his family, and leave the property to strangers. The only compulsory heir is the widow, and then only to the extent of enjoying certain income during her life.

Now, let us move across the ocean to France. The most important difference there arises out of the community property system. The basic idea of this system is that husband and wife enter into a partnership when they marry and that each becomes one-half owner of everything they acquire while they are married. (Under the Revenue Act of 1948, this has become the rationale of our own federal tax law.) So when a husband dies in France, his property is only one-half of the community property; the other half belongs to the other partner, his wife. Whether he leaves a Will or not, all that we can be concerned with is his one-half. Now, with certain minor variations, his property, that is, his one-half, will be distributed among the same people who would have taken it if he had died in New York, except that the widow is pushed down to the end of the line of inheritance. She comes in only just before escheat to the Republic of France. The theory is that she can afford to be at the end of the line because she has received one-half as partner.

In the law of inheritance we have a concept called "the laughing heir." The laughing heir is the expression used for a very distant relative who never even knew the man who died, never had to tolerate his idiosyncracies and never had to weep at his funeral. Under New York law the laughing heir is fully recognized because there is no limit to the degree of relationship that will entitle one to inherit. But in France, as in many other places, the laughing heir has been abolished. The French count the degrees of relationship and no relative who is more distant that six degrees will be considered as entitled to inherit. After six degrees comes the right of the widow, and if there be no widow, inheritance by the French Republic.

If a man makes a Will in France he can dispose, of course, only of his one-half of the community property. Even as to that one-half he cannot disinherit his children, or if he has no children, his parents. He is compelled to leave his children or his parents a specified fraction of what they would have received if he had made no Will. He can disinherit his widow, but again only as to his one-half.

Moving eastward to the Soviet legal system, we find a very interesting development during the past thirty years. The Communist Manifesto had stated that the abolition of inheritance would be one of the first steps in a communist revolution. Accordingly, in 1918 inheritance was abolished by the new Russian Government; in effect, the Government became everybody's sole heir. This state of affairs continued only five years. In 1923 inheritance was reinstated by law up to 10,000 rubles for each estate. In 1926 the 10,000 ruble limit was completedly cancelled.

The only persons, however, who were permitted to inherit were the husband or wife, children or grandchildren and any person actually dependent for support on the individual who died, and they would inherit in equal shares. The owner of property could make a Will directing how he wished his property divided within this limited class of heirs; he could not leave the property outside the class. He could disinherit any of these specified heirs except his children under the age of eighteen. He must leave his children under the age of eighteen three-fourths of what they would have received if he had made no Will. You can see that if there was little chance for a 'laughing heir' in France, there was no chance for one in the Russian Republic.

At the end of World War II the Russian Government stated that since so many possible heirs had been killed in the war, it was necessary to allow a second class of heirs wherever a man died leaving no one at all in the first class which I have just described. In other words, if a man leaves no widow or children or dependents, then his property goes to his parents, and if his parents also are dead, to his brothers and sisters. At this line the new second class of heirs stops, and if a man dies without a Will no one more distant than a brother or sister can inherit. But if he has no relatives in either the first class or the second class of heirs, he is now permitted to make a Will leaving his property to anyone he chooses. Thus he can leave it to a stranger, who could not possibly inherit if there had been no Will. That is the present system according to our latest information.

. . .

In this discussion I have omitted mention of one of the most important heirs of all: the tax collector. Estate taxes in the United States . . . run to very high figures. . . .

The French rates are likewise high and the Soviet inheritance tax used to run up to 90%. But in January, 1943 the Soviet inheritance tax was abolished. Now they impose only a filing fee when an estate is administered. This filing fee starts at a very low figure and goes up to only 10% on the largest estates. Some observers might say that this is a far cry from Marx and Engels' Communist Manifesto.

QUESTIONS

1. As Professor Cahn's brief survey indicates, all Western legal systems, including those in socialist nations, provide for the inheritance of property by relatives of the deceased. In the United States the power of testation and provision for intestate succession are so generally and thoroughly established that they seem part of the natural order of things. But suppose a state wished to abolish inheritance by making itself the sole heir of all decedents within its jurisdiction. Would such a statute violate some provision of the U.S. Constitution?

2. In fact, no U.S. state has tried or is likely soon to try to abolish the inheritance of property. However, if "the power to tax is the power to destroy," what are we to say of estate and inheritance taxes? The point has been raised in a number of cases challenging the constitutionality of such taxes. The following quotation is from the majority opinion of Mr. Jus-

tice McKenna in Magoun v. Illinois Trust and Savings Bank, 170 U.S. 283, 288–289, 18 S.Ct. 594, 596–597, 42 L.Ed. 1037 (1897):

. . . The right to take property by devise or descent is the creature of the law, and not a natural right—a privilege, and therefore the authority which confers it may impose conditions upon it. From these principles it is deduced that the States may tax the privilege, discriminate between relatives, and between these and strangers, and grant exemptions; and are not precluded from this power by the provisions of the respective state constitutions requiring uniformity and equality of taxation.

The second principle was given prominence in the arguments at bar. The appellee claimed that the power of the State could be exerted to the extent of making the State the heir to everybody, and the appellant asserted a natural right of children to inherit. Of the former proposition we are not required to express an opinion. Nor indeed of the latter, for appellant conceded that testamentary disposition and inheritance were subject to regulation.

3. How about equal protection of the laws? May the state constitutionally tax larger estates at higher rates? Consider the following quotation from the majority opinion by Mr. Justice White in Knowlton v. Moore, 178 U.S. 41, 109–110, 20 S.Ct. 747, 778–779, 44 L.Ed. 969 (1899):

. . . Lastly, it is urged that the progressive rate feature of the statute is so repugnant to fundamental principles of equality and justice that the law should be held to be void, even although it transgresses no express limitation in the Constitution. Without intimating any opinion as to the existence of a right in the courts to exercise the power which is thus invoked, it is apparent that the argument as to the enormity of the tax is without merit. . . . taxes imposed with reference to the ability of the person upon whom the burden is placed to bear the same have been levied from the foundation of the government. So, also, some authoritative thinkers, and a number of economic writers, contend that a progressive tax is more just and equal than a proportional one. In the absence of constitutional limitation, the question whether it is or is not is legislative and not judicial.

Thomas L. Shaffer, The Planning and Drafting of Wills and Trusts, Mineola, New York: Foundation Press, (2nd edition), 1979, pp. 118–120.

a. *The Tax System.* All of the states and the federal government have systems of death taxation. In the typical case, the systems reach far beyond what have been regarded in the common law as transfers at death; they reach beyond probate assets, too. They include joint-and-survivor property, employment benefits, life insurance, and inter-vivos trusts. Their reach does not depend on construction of wills, statutes or on common-law notions of transfer. Taxation turns on advertent (and novel) legislative language.

In the typical case, the system of taxation is designed to reach inter-vivos transactions, either by deeming them, for tax purposes, to be transfers at death, or by imposing a transfer tax on them at the time of the inter-vivos transaction. Both concepts are, in the federal system, comprehended by a unified tax on gratuitous transfers which covers virtually all forms of gift and inheritance.

This preliminary introduction to death taxes will consider only the federal system.

The original federal tax on gratuitous transfers was a tax on transfers at death, an estate tax. Its purpose was to raise money for World War I. After the war there was a movement to abolish it, which movement was compromised in Congress to provide instead an 80-percent credit for state death taxes. A state could, through its own system of death taxation, recover for itself four-fifths of what otherwise would have been paid by its dead citizen's estate to the federal government. In the 1930's the estate tax took on stronger revenue purposes—most of the funds diverted through the credit were taken back—and a social purpose as well. Reformers began to assert that inherited wealth should be redistributed and that death taxes were a means to that social end. In and after World War II, the tax was made to bear a heavier share of the federal revenue burden; it also became more sophisticated about the property interests it reached.

* * *

In 1976 the estate and gift taxes were re-codified into a single system, a unified tax on gratuitous transfers. The same tax is paid (theoretically) on a transfer from, say father to daughter, whether the transfer is made during the father's life or in the father's will or life-insurance policy. A running account is kept of all the gratuitous transfers Father makes—rather like the book St. Peter is said to keep in Heaven—and, at the end, when the last of Father's mortal coil is shuffled off, a final accounting is made to the government. This occurs at or after the time a final accounting is made to St. Peter. In the final accounting, gifts made during life are added to gifts made at death; a single system of progressive tax rates is applied to the total; credit is given for taxes paid during life; and the balance due is paid by the decedent's estate.

Neither the estate tax nor the gift tax was a significant source of income for the federal government; combined, they produced less than five per cent of the revenues of the country. There are no reliable studies on their effect as redistributors of wealth, but a guess is that they were not effective at that, either. The dominant opinion is that the income tax does more to divert wealth away from family accumulation than transfer taxes do. The estate tax probably had the incidental effect of encouraging dispositions to charity, such as the creation of public foundations by the nation's most wealthy families (Ford, Rockefeller, Getty).

Historically, the transfer taxes have had their greatest impact on the upper middle class. Inflation in the 30 years after World War II, though, caused the estate tax to reach into middle-middle class wealth and even into some modest family fortunes, particularly those in small business and in agriculture. By 1976, about ten percent of all estates were large enough to incur some federal estate tax; this figure was five percent in 1960. This broadened economic impact became a significant issue in the congressional and presidential elections in 1976.

The Tax Reform Act of 1976 raised the floor of the tax as it combined estate and gift taxes. The apparent purpose was to lift the burden of the tax from the middle-middle class, and to make up for lost revenue by raising the rates on the wealthy. For example, under the 1954 structure, a net estate of $60,000 or less paid no tax, and an estate of $200,000 paid $32,700. After the 1976 reform (i.e., by 1981) the estate of $200,000 is to pay $7,800, and a net estate of $175,000 or less is to pay no tax. On the other hand, under the 1976 rates, the tax on portions of estates over $1 million was raised from 39 to 41 percent, and the rate for the excess over $5 million was raised from 67 to 70 percent.

State death-tax systems are, typically, inheritance taxes rather than estate taxes. The difference is that inheritance taxes are imposed on the right to receive property, estate taxes on the right to give it. Inheritance taxes, for one practical difference, have two systems of variation on rates; estate taxes have only one rate structure. Inheritance-tax rates are lower for close relatives of the decedent. Both taxes have a progressive rate structure, in which larger estates pay a higher percentage than small estates.

Inheritance-tax rates have climbed in recent decades, even more than federal transfer-tax rates have, as state governments have cast about for sources of revenue; but the impact of state death taxes is still minor in comparison with the impact of the federal system. Here is an approximate comparison of impact, based on rates imposed as this edition was prepared:

	California	Virginia	Federal
$20,000 estate			
—to a minor child	240	150	0
—to a friend	2,470	950	0
—to a brother or sister	1,080	360	0
$10 million estate			
—to a minor child	1.4 million	482,900	6 million
—to a friend	2.4 million	1.5 million	6 million
—to a brother or sister	2 million	986,460	6 million
$200,000 estate			
—to a minor child	12,590	4,000	7,800
—to a friend	32,000	19,450	7,800
—to a brother or sister	23,270	12,460	7,800

The federal figures on the $10-million estate include the credit for state death taxes (§ 2011), so that, for example, the California-friend case would not result in a total tax of 8.5 million on a $10 million estate; some of the state death tax would be a credit against the federal estate tax.

NOTES

1. The federal estate tax was modified in 1981, substantially reducing the tax that would be payable on the $200,000 and $3 million estates.

2. Although the progressive feature is built into most income, gift and death taxes in the U.S.A., there is little agreement on the proper mix of revenue and redistributional objectives of such taxes. Nor are the various economic, social and political arguments advanced in favor of graduated tax rates entirely convincing. For a thorough discussion see Walter J. Blum and Harry Kalven, Jr. The Uneasy Case for Progressive Taxation, Chicago: University of Chicago Press, 1953.

B. INTESTATE SUCCESSION TO PROPERTY

CALIFORNIA PROBATE CODE

§ 200. Succession defined

Succession is the acquisition of title to the property of one who dies without disposing of it by will.

§ 201. Title of surviving spouse; portion subject to testamentary disposition or succession

Upon the death of either husband or wife, one-half of the community property belongs to the surviving spouse; the other half is subject to the testamentary disposition of the decedent, and in the absence thereof goes to the surviving spouse, subject to the provisions of sections 202 and 203 of this code.

§ 220. Succession controlled by contract and code

The separate property of a person who dies without disposing of it by will is succeeded to and must be distributed as hereinafter provided, subject to the limitation of any marriage or other contract,

. . ..

§ 221. Distribution to surviving spouse and issue

If the decedent leaves a surviving spouse, and only one child or the lawful issue of a deceased child, the estate goes one-half to the surviving spouse and one-half to the child or issue. If the decedent leaves a surviving spouse, and more than one child living or one child living and the lawful issue of one or more deceased children, the estate goes one-third to the surviving spouse and the remainder in equal shares to his children and to the lawful issue of any deceased child, by right of representation; but if there is no child of decedent living at his death, the remainder goes to all of his lineal descendants; and if all of the descendants are in the same degree of kindred to the decedent they share equally, otherwise they take by right of representation.

§ 222. Distribution to issue where no surviving spouse

If the decedent leaves no surviving spouse, but leaves issue, the whole estate goes to such issue; and if all of the descendants are in the same degree of kindred to the decedent they share equally, otherwise they take by right of representation.

§ 223. Distribution to surviving spouse and immediate family where no issue

If the decedent leaves a surviving spouse and no issue, the estate goes one-half to the surviving spouse and one-half to the decedent's parents in equal shares, or if either is dead to the survivor, or if both are dead to their issue and the issue of either of them, by right of representation.

§ 224. Distribution to surviving spouse where neither issue nor immediate family

If the decedent leaves a surviving spouse and neither issue, parent, brother, sister, nor descendant of a deceased brother or sister, the whole estate goes to the surviving spouse.

§ 225. Distribution to immediate family where neither issue nor spouse

If the decedent leaves neither issue nor spouse, the estate goes to his parents in equal shares, or if either is dead to the survivor, or if both are dead in equal shares to his brothers and sisters and to the descendants of deceased brothers and sisters by right of representation.

§ 226. Distribution to next of kin where no spouse, issue, nor immediate family

If the decedent leaves neither issue, spouse, parent, brother, sister, nor descendant of a deceased brother or sister, the estate goes to the next of kin in equal degree, excepting that, when there are two or more collateral kindred in equal degree, but claiming through different ancestors, those who claim through the nearest ancestor must be preferred to those claiming through an ancestor more remote.

§ 231. Grounds; charges and trusts; moneys held in trust for health and welfare, etc., benefits

(a) If a decedent, whether or not he was domiciled in this state, leaves no one to take his estate or any portion thereof by testate succession, and no one other than a government or governmental subdivision or agency to take his estate or a portion thereof by intestate succession, under the laws of this state or of any other jurisdiction, the same escheats at the time of his death in accordance with this article. . . .

§ 250. Right of representation defined; posthumous child

Inheritance or succession "by right of representation" takes place when the descendants of a deceased person take the same share or right in the estate of another that such deceased person would have taken as an heir if living. A posthumous child is considered as living at the death of the parent.

§ 251. Degree of kindred; determination

The degree of kindred is established by the number of generations, and each generation is called a degree.

§ 252. Lineal consanguinity; definition; division

Lineal consanguinity, or the direct line of consanguinity, is the relationship between persons one of whom is a descendant of the other. The direct line is divided into a direct line descending, which connects a person with those who descend from him, and a direct line ascending, which connects a person with those from whom he descends. In the direct line there are as many degrees as there are generations. . . .

§ 253. Collateral consanguinity; definition; computation of degrees

Collateral consanguinity is the relationship between people who spring from a common ancestor, but are not in a direct line. The degree is established by counting the generation from one relative up to the common ancestor and from the common ancestor to the other relative. In such computation the first relative is excluded, the other included, and the ancestor counted but once. Thus, brothers are related in the second degree, uncle and nephew in the third degree, cousins german in the fourth, and so on. (Stats.1931, c. 281, p. 598, § 253.)

§ 257. Adopted children; inheritance rights; restriction

An adopted child shall be deemed a descendant of one who has adopted him, the same as a natural child, for all purposes of succession by, from or through the adopting parent the same as a natural parent. An adopted child does not succeed to the estate of a natural parent when the relationship between them has been severed by adoption, nor does such natural parent succeed to the estate of such adopted child, nor does such adopted child succeed to the estate of a relative of the natural parent, nor does any relative of the natural parent succeed to the estate of an adopted child. . . .

QUESTIONS

1. Suppose D dies leaving a surviving spouse but no issue, parents, siblings or issue of siblings. Who gets how much of the estate?

2. Suppose D leaves a surviving spouse. D's children A and B predeceased her, but a third child, C, is still alive, as are A's child AC; B's children BC1, BC2 and BC3; and C's child CC. Who takes how much?

3. Suppose D, an only child, leaves no surviving spouse and no issue. D's parents are both dead. D's maternal grandfather had a sister DGS, now deceased, whose only living issue is her great-grandson X, whom D never knew. No other relatives of D can be found. Who takes how much under California law? Do you approve of such a result?

4. Of course D could have achieved a different distribution of her property in questions 1–3 if she had left a valid will. We will look more closely at wills in a moment, but first some information on testacy and intestacy in the United States.

C. TESTACY AND INTESTACY IN PRACTICE

NOTE

The figures set out below are derived from the following eight studies: (1) Edward H. Ward and John H. Beuscher, "The Inheritance Process in Wisconsin," 1950 Wisconsin Law Review 393, (Wisconsin Study); (2) Allison Dunham, "The Method, Process and Frequency of Wealth Transmission at Death," 30 University of Chicago Law Review 241 (1962) Chicago Study; (3) Olin Browder, Jr., Recent Patterns of Testate Succession in the United States and England, 67 Michigan Law Review 1303, 1306, 1320, (1969) (Michigan Study); (4) Sheldon J. Plager, "The Spouse's Nonbarrable Share: A Solution in Search of a Problem," 33 University of Chicago Law Review 681, (1965–66) (Plager Study); (5) Marvin B. Sussman, Judith N. Cates, and David T. Smith, The Family and Inheritance, New York: Russell Sage Foundation, 1970, pp. 122, 126–128 (Ohio Study); (6) Stein, Probate Administration Study: Some Emerging Conclusions, 9 Real Property, Probate and Trust Journal 596 (1974) (Minnesota Study); (7) John R. Price, The Transmission of Wealth at Death in a Community Property Jurisdiction, 50 Washington Law Review 277 (1975) (Washington Study); and (8) Note, Intestate Succession in New Jersey: Does it Conform to Population Expectations? 12 Columbia Journal of Law and Social Problems 253 (1976) (New Jersey Study).

The Wisconsin Study is based upon 415 proceedings in the County Court of Dane County, Wisconsin for decedents who died in 1929, 1934, 1939, 1941 and 1944. The Chicago Study is based upon 97 random chosen estates for which probate proceedings were initiated in 1953 and the estates of 73 decedents who died in 1957. The Michigan Study is based upon the 1963 probate court records of all probate proceedings in Washtenaw County, Michigan (which includes Ann Arbor and Ypsilanti). The Plager Study reveals the responses given by 84 attorneys who returned a questionnaire distributed to about 400 attorneys at a short course on estate planning in 1964. The Ohio Study covers 659 estates randomly selected from all estates closed in Cuyahoga County, Ohio (which includes Cleveland) from November 9, 1964 to August 8, 1965. The Minnesota Study is based upon all estates revealed by the 1969 probate court and inheritance department records in Dodge, Mille Lacs, Douglas and Hennepin counties. The Washington Study deals with the estates of 211 randomly selected adults who died in King County, Washington (which includes Seattle) in 1969. The New Jersey Study is based upon a sample of 100 randomly selected Morris County, New Jersey residents who died in Morristown during 1971.

TABLE 1. THE RATE OF TESTACY

	Year	No. of Estates	% Testate
WISCONSIN STUDY (p. 412)	1929	73	61.9
	1934	67	45.9
	1939	62	41.8
	1941	72	45.7
	1944	80	39.1
CHICAGO STUDY (p. 246)	1931–35	unavailable	44
	1936–40	"	46
	1941–45	"	43
	1946–50	"	43
	1953	97	60
	1957	73	55
MICHIGAN STUDY (p. 1306)	1963	346	54
OHIO STUDY (p. 64)	1964–65	659	69
WASHINGTON STUDY (p. 299)	1969	114	52
NEW JERSEY STUDY (p. 286)	1971	100	81

TABLE 2. TESTACY AND MARITAL STATUS

	Status	No. of Estates	% Testate
CHICAGO STUDY (p. 247; 1957 sample)	Married	239	54
	Widowed	152	59
	Divorced	18	50
	Never Married	72	54
OHIO STUDY (p. 70)	Married	383	69.5
	Widowed	202	72.3
	Divorced	14	57.1
	Never Married	37	56.8

TABLE 2. TESTACY AND MARITAL STATUS—Cont'd

	Status	No. of Estates	% Testate
WASHINGTON STUDY (pp. 290, 299)	Married	106	20.8
	Widowed	66	39.4
	Divorced	18	22.2
	Never Married	21	33.3
NEW JERSEY STUDY (p. 288)	Married	58	75.9
	Widowed	30	90.0
	Divorced	3	100.0
	Never Married	9	77.8

TABLE 3. TESTACY AND SIZE OF ESTATE

	Estate On Death	No. of Estates	% of All Estates	% Testate
WISCONSIN STUDY (pp. 401, 412; all years combined)	$0 or less	28	6.8	10.7
	$0–5000	160	38.6	35.6
	$5000–15,000	144	34.7	55.6
	$15,000–25,000	42	10.1	52.4
	$25,000–50,000	28	6.8	75.0
	$50,000–200,000	13	3.1	92.3
CHICAGO STUDY * (p. 250; 1950 data)	$0–5000	46	28.9	25
	$5000–10,000	22	13.8	56
	$10,000–25,000	47	29.6	63
	$25,000–100,000	34	21.4	
	$25,000–49,999			79
	$50,000–99,999			86
	Over $100,000	10	6.2	96
MICHIGAN STUDY (p. 1320)	$0–4999	34	18.2	Unavailable
	$5000–9999	30	16.0	"
	$10,000–24,999	49	26.2	"
	$25,000–49,999	26	13.9	"
	$50,000–99,999	22	11.8	"
	Over $100,000	26	13.9	"
MINNESOTA STUDY (p. 598)	$0–10,000	1018	39	Unavailable
	$10,000–20,000	593	22	"
	$20,000–30,000	304	12	"
	$30,000–60,000	307	12	"
	$60,000–100,000	151	6	"

* Table constructed on basis of figures and percentages in text.

TABLE 3.   TESTACY AND SIZE OF ESTATE—Cont'd

	Estate On Death	No. of Estates	% of All Estates	% Testate
MINNESOTA STUDY (p. 598)	$100,000–200,000	97	4	"
	Over $200,000	119	5	"
WASHINGTON STUDY (p. 306)	$0–4999	17	14.9	23.5
	$5000–9999	16	14.0	25.0
	$10,000–24,999	39	34.2	48.7
	$25,000–49,999	19	16.7	68.4
	$50,000–99,999	11	9.6	81.8
	$100,000 and over	12	10.5	83.3
OHIO STUDY (p. 173)	$0–1,999	85	12.9	Unavailable
	$2000–60,000	526	79.8	"
	Over $60,000	48	7.3	96

QUESTIONS

1. Although the samples are small and the Wisconsin data are contra, Table 1 appears to show a decline in the rate of intestacy over time. Can you think of any reasons why this might be the case?

2. Why should the rate of intestacy be lower among widowed decedents, as suggested by Table 2?

3. Why should the rate of intestacy decline so rapidly with the increase in size of the estate, as shown in Table 3? Taxes are one obvious consideration, increasing in importance with the size of the estate. By expert "estate planning," in which the will is a central device, the impact of estate and inheritance taxes can be reduced well below what would have to be paid according to the "statutory estate plan" embodied in the laws of intestate succession. What other considerations can you think of that would impel people of greater wealth to be more inclined to write wills?

4. The studies show that whenever a testator was survived by both a spouse and children there was a strong tendency to leave all of the property to the spouse and none to the children. If you were a California legislator and were confronted with this information, would you be inclined to suggest amendment of the provisions of the Probate Code dealing with intestate succession to property?

5. The following excerpt from the Ohio study describes the extent to which the heirs kept or "redistributed" the property they received from the decedent. Does this additional information affect your answer to question 4?

Marvin B. Sussman, Judith N. Cates and David T. Smith, The Family and Inheritance. New York: Russell Sage Foundation, 1970, pp. 122, 126–128.

Redistribution in the Testate Case. The number of testate cases in which the heirs redistributed the estate was small. From this, it may be inferred that the testator's disposition of the estate was satisfactory in most instances or that the heirs were unable to agree on a more satisfactory disposition.

Redistribution in the Intestate Case. There were 74 cases in which the spouse and lineal descendants or ascendants survived. In 60 of these cases (81 per cent), the distribution did not follow the normal pattern of a specific division between the surviving spouse and lineal kin. In 19 of the cases the estates were so small that the spouse received all the assets. In 38 cases, the spouse received all or more than the intestate share, most often because others who had claims to the estate signed over their shares. The remaining three cases deviated because of bankruptcy, out-of-state property, or remarriage.   .   .   .

The remarks of the children who had given up a share in their deceased parent's estate indicated that they made no searching analysis in reference to this decision. It was a matter-of-fact action; in their family it was the right and proper thing to do. "Why take the home away from an older parent who is still living? It is my mother's home." "Mother is more entitled to it than anyone else. She worked hard for that home." "The wife should be entitled to everything unless it's a second marriage." "Mother needs everything, she has many years ahead of her; she shouldn't have to be dependent on her children."

The parents who were the recipients of their children's generosity similarly took the action for granted for the most part. "My children wouldn't do that—not see that I have enough to live on." "The intestate pattern isn't fair. The wife should get it all. She should be able to do what she needs to do. My daughter is further ahead in her twelve years of marriage than we were much later." "If I get sick, I need the money; it is my security."

A less charitable explanation is that in depriving the surviving spouse of home and hearth, it may be necessary for the child to assume financial and social responsibility for the parent at a time not suitable for the child's family. Thus, in providing the optimum means for independence of the surviving parent, the children postpone the day when they will have to face the situation of providing for the final care of the aging parent.

The data on the large number of redistributions where a spouse and lineal kin survive indicate that the majority of people felt that the spouse should have sole rights of inheritance.   .   .   .

It should be remembered that children expect to inherit from their surviving parent; hence, they are not irrevocably renouncing their rights to the property.

D. FREEDOM OF TESTATION AND ITS LIMITS

Lawrence M. Friedman, "The Law of the Living, and the Law of the Dead: Property, Succession and Society," 1966 Wisconsin Law Review 340, 352, 353.

. . . Two practical principles of succession to property remain—succession through gift, and forced succession at death to heirs according to a fixed scheme of disposition. In fact our system is largely a combination of the two, with heavier emphasis on the method of gift. The principle of free testation is a part of the principle of gift. A person is free to give away his property, at death or before, to whomever he chooses. . . . These gifts may be made outright, or in trust; conditions may be attached to them more or less as the donor sees fit; they may be made randomly, as the spirit moves the donor, or according to some regular plan of giving. . . .

. . . The principle of *gift*, since it exalts the volition of the property holder, is consistent with free market economics. Just as a man can sell his property at any price he can get, so he can "sell" it at no price to a donee of his choice. Individuals as holders of private property may dispose of it as they see fit. The principle of gift can be called *economic*. Despite the paradox that a gift is not an economic transfer, the principle of gift is necessary to the economic system and is presupposed by it.

The principle of forced succession we might call *social*. Practically speaking, forced succession means succession within the family—to the wife, children, or other dependents. Forced succession imposes upon the testator the obligation to care for members of his family before satisfying any other desires and needs. In a sense, it converts private property at death to family property. The unit under the principle of gift is the individual; under the principle of forced succession it is the nuclear family, the basis of American kinship and social custom. As we shall see, the law of succession is deeply affected by tension between these two principles. . . .

1. The Surviving Spouse

Sheldon J. Plager, "The Spouse's Nonbarrable Share: A Solution in Search of A Problem," 33 University of Chicago Law Review 681 (1965–1966).

When a husband or wife wishes to leave his or her property to someone other than the surviving spouse, the state may feel compelled to intervene by requiring that the surviving spouse be permitted to share in the deceased's estate. The decision to accord the surviving spouse a share in the estate of the other regardless of the wishes of the decedent is attributable to a network of policy concerns which surround the protection of the family unit—the obligation of support, the presumed contribution of the survivor's family, and the state's interest in protection from the burden of indigents—as well as to policies favoring economy in transmission of property, equality of sexes, and fairness among beneficiaries. Giving effect to these concerns, however, frustrates such other policies as freedom of testamentary disposition, protection of creditors, and alienability of land, all of which militate against nonbarrable shares for the surviving spouse.

Faced with this conflict, the eight community property states and the civil law state of Louisiana protect the surviving spouse primarily by providing for a form of shared inter vivos ownership of marital property. Of the remaining forty-one states, only two leave the testator unfettered; thirty-nine states permit the surviving spouse to claim a share in the estate of the deceased spouse. . . .

. . . Although the specifics vary considerably, the thirty-nine states mentioned above have generally provided that the surviving spouse be entitled to a predetermined share, usually a third or a half, of the deceased's wealth. This portion is available regardless of the testator's wishes, regardless of the survivor's financial need, and regardless of how much or how little the survivor may have contributed to that wealth. . . .

An alternative is to provide a system of maintenance payments to the surviving spouse (and perhaps to other relatives) payable out of the decedent's estate. The amount of the payments would be keyed to the individual need of the survivor, the interests of persons who otherwise would be entitled to the deceased's property, the conduct of the survivor with relation to the deceased, the deceased's reasons for his dispositions, and the many other factors that might be relevant in a particular case. This is essentially the system established by the British Commonwealth decedent's family maintenance legislation.

a. Community Property

CALIFORNIA CIVIL CODE

§ 5107. Separate property of wife

All property of the wife, owned by her before marriage, and that acquired afterwards by gift, bequest, devise, or descent, with the rents, issues, and profits thereof, is her separate property. The wife may, without the consent of her husband, convey her separate property.

§ 5108. Separate property of husband

All property owned by the husband before marriage, and that acquired afterwards by gift, bequest, devise, or descent, with the rents, issues, and profits thereof, is his separate property. The husband may, without the consent of his wife, convey his separate property.

§ 5109. Separate property; damages paid by one spouse to other for personal injuries

All money or other property paid by or on behalf of a married person to his spouse in satisfaction of a judgment for damages for personal injuries to the spouse or pursuant to an agreement for the settlement or compromise of a claim for such damages is the separate property of the injured spouse.

§ 5110. Community property; presumption as to property acquired by wife

Except as provided in Sections 5107, 5108, and 5109 and subdivision (c) of Section 5122, all real property situated in this state and all personal property wherever situated acquired during the marriage by a married person while domiciled in this state, and property held in trust pursuant to Section 5113.5, is community property; . . . .

CALIFORNIA PROBATE CODE

§ 201. Survivor's Right to One-Half.

Upon the death of either husband or wife, one-half of the community property belongs to the surviving spouse; the other half is subject to the testamentary disposition of the decedent, and in the absence thereof goes to the surviving spouse, subject to the provisions of sections 202 and 203 of this code.

Estate of Murphy, 15 Cal.3d 907, 126 Cal.Rptr. 820, 544 P.2d 956 (1976).

WRIGHT, CHIEF JUSTICE.

John W. Murphy (Murphy) died on April 29, 1971, survived by his wife Royene, whom he had married in 1942. Murphy's will purported to place all of his and Royene's community property, as well as his own separate property, into two trusts in which Royene would have life interests plus a general testamentary power of appointment in the trust that included her community property interest. The will declared, however, that "[i]f my wife elects to take the rights given her by law, she shall nevertheless be entitled to the benefits given her by this Will with respect to all property remaining subject to it." Royene survived Murphy by only eight months. When she died on December 14, 1971, she had not exercised the power of appointment and had not declared any election to accept or reject Murphy's testamentary disposition of her community property interest. Although Murphy's will had by then been admitted to probate, there had been no judicial determination of her interest in his estate.

Thereafter Ruth L. Perry, executrix and sole legatee under Royene's will, filed a "Declination to Take Under Will by Executrix of Widow" in the Murphy estate proceeding. Murphy's executor thereupon filed a proceeding to determine interests in his estate (Prob. Code, § 1080), in which statements of claim were filed by Ruth Perry and by the legatees of the remainder interests in the trusts under Murphy's will—Willard Murphy, Murphy's son by a prior marriage, and Willard's two minor children (all hereafter referred to as "Murphy legatees"). After a court trial following waiver of a jury (Prob. Code, § 1081), the trial court awarded to Royene's executrix a half interest in all property of the probate estate which she claimed to be community.

Appealing from this judgment (Prob.Code, § 1240), the Murphy legatees make two basic contentions, each of which we conclude must be rejected for reasons to be explained. First, they assert that Royene's estate was bound by the provisions of Murphy's will disposing of her community property interest unless she affirmatively elected to take against the will and that the right of election was personal to her and could not be exercised after her death. To the contrary, her community property interest was beyond his power of testamentary disposition and could not be subjected to the will's provisions in the absence of her affirmative election to accept its benefits as hereinafter discussed. Second, the Murphy legatees contend that the property which the trial court found to be community was acquired with the income from two farms in Kansas and certain stock that were conceded to be Murphy's separate property. As we shall explain, the separate income was not traced as a source of the assets in question and the trial court properly concluded that Murphy's legatees had failed to overcome the presumption that assets acquired by purchase during the marriage are community property.

Survival of Widow's Right to Claim Community Property Interest Against Inconsistent Provisions in Husband's Will. Following antecedent Mexican law, the rule in California has always been that a wife is entitled to at least one-half of the community property on her husband's death and the husband's testamentary power over such property is limited to the remaining half. (Prob.Code, § 201); *Spreckels v. Spreckels*, 172 Cal. 775, 779, 158 P. 537, 539 (1916); *Estate of Buchanan*, Cal. 507 (1857). Accordingly, when a husband's will describes the property which it gives to the wife and others in general terms, e.g., "all my property," without affirmatively indicating any intention to deal with the wife's community property interest, the operation of the will upon community property is confined to the husband's interest and the surviving wife is entitled to receive both her half of the community property by operation of law and any interest in the deceased husband's share given her by the will. *Estate of Wolfe*, 48 Cal.2d 570, 574–575, 311 P.2d 476, 478–479 (1957); *Estate of Gilmore*, 81 Cal. 240, 22 P. 655 (1889).

However, if the will expressly requires the widow to elect between the provisions for her benefit and her community property rights (*Estate of Dunphy*, 147 Cal. 95, 103–104, 81 P. 315, 318 (1905); *Estate of Klingenberg*, 94 Cal.App.2d 240, 244, 210 P.2d 514, 517 (1949)) or if the testator purports to dispose of the wife's share of the community property and the will shows that to satisfy the wife's community property rights while giving effect to its provisions with respect to remaining property would thwart the testamentary intent (*Estate of Wolfe, supra*, 48 Cal.2d at p. 574, 311 P.2d 476; *Estate of Orwitz*, 219 Cal.App.2d 767, 769, 40 Cal.Rptr. 545, 547 (1964); *Estate of Roach*, 176 Cal.App.2d 547, 553, 1 Cal.Rptr. 454) the wife cannot take both her community property interest and the property given her by the will but must elect between them. Identical principles may require such an election by a surviving husband between his community property rights and the provisions for his benefit in the will of his deceased wife, whose testamentary power over community property is likewise applicable to only a one-half interest. (Prob.Code, § 201; *Estate of Johnson*, 178 Cal.App.2d 826, 3 Cal.Rptr. 408 (1960); Kahn & Gello, *The Widow's Election: A Return to Fundamentals* (1972) 24 Stan.L.Rev. 531, 532.)

. . . the Murphy legatees argue that the will's provisions controlled the disposition of Royene's community property interest unless she affirmatively elected to take against them and that her right to so elect was a personal right which could not be exercised by her representative after her death. This is indeed the usual rule of decision in American jurisdictions in which none of the acquisitions of resident married persons constitutes community property and the surviving spouse is given a right to elect between the testamentary gifts provided by the deceased spouse's will and a statutory share of the deceased spouse's estate. The purpose of the right of election in those jurisdictions is to assure the surviving spouse of personal enjoyment of a minimum share of the property formerly owned by the deceased spouse. (*Payne v. Newton*, 116 U.S.App.D.C. 319, 323 F.2d 621, 623 (1963); *Estate of Davis*, 129 Vt. 162, 166–167, 274 A.2d 491, 494–495 (1971); *Celenza's Estate*, 308 Pa. 186, 191–192, 162 A. 456, 457–458 (1932); *Estate of Dalton*, 60 Ill.2d 451, 328 N.E.2d 257 (1975); see Annot. 83 A.L.R.2d 1077, 1080.) This personal nature of the surviving spouse's right of election in those jurisdictions results from its being strictly construed as a limited exception to the deceased spouse's general testamentary power to control the disposition of his own property. (Cf. *Estate of Bunn*, 33 Cal.2d 897, 900, 206 P.2d 635, 637 (1949) (former statutory right to set aside charitable bequest strictly construed as personal to eligible relative); *Estate of Hughes*, 202 Cal.App.2d 12, 18, 20 Cal.Rptr. 475, 479 (1962) (same).)

In contrast, on the death of a married California resident the surviving spouse's half of the community property belongs to such survivor and is not subject to the decedent's testamentary disposition in the absence of an affirmative election to the contrary. The surviving spouse's interest is not a special exception to a decedent's right to dispose of his own property, provided out of solicitude for the survivor's personal comfort, but reflects a legal recognition of the survivor's right to absolute ownership of a share of the fruits of the marriage unless and until such right is voluntarily relinquished. . . .

Community Nature of Disputed Assets in Husband's Estate. The assets which the trial court found to be community property were a three-eighths interest in the family residence, real property used in the family business, shares in the corporation carrying on that business, savings accounts, stocks, bonds and an automobile. Although Murphy owned the family corporation shares at the date of marriage, the trial court found upon substantial evidence that the shares had "little if any significant value" at that date and that their added value at the time of Murphy's death was derived from advances of community assets to the corporation and from Murphy's personal services for which he was not adequately compensated by the corporation.   The other disputed assets were acquired by purchase during the marriage at times when adequate community funds were available for such acquisition. Murphy also had separate income during these times but there was no evidence from which that income could be directly traced to any of the assets in dispute.

"Property acquired by purchase during a marriage is presumed to be community property, and the burden is on the spouse asserting its separate character to overcome the presumption. (*Estate of Niccolls*, 164 Cal. 368, 129 P. 278; *Thomasset v. Thomasset*, 122 Cal.App.2d 116, 123, 264 P.2d 626.)" (*See v. See*, 64 Cal.2d 778, 783, 51 Cal.Rptr. 888, 891, 415 P.2d 776, 779 (1966).) The mere fact that Murphy received substantial separate income concurrently with the receipt of substantial community income does not dispel the presumption. Generally speaking there are two methods of carrying the burden of showing property purchased during the marriage to be separate: (1) direct tracing to a separate property source or (2) proof that at the time of purchase all community income was exhausted by family expenses. (*In re Marriage of Mix*, 14 Cal.3d 604, 611–612, 122 Cal.Rptr. 79, 81, 536 P.2d 479, 481 (1975); *See v. See*, supra, 64 Cal.2d at p. 783, 51 Cal.Rptr. at 891, 415 P.2d at 778.) In the present case there was no proof by either method requiring the trial court to find any of the disputed assets to be other than community property.

* * *

The judgment is affirmed.

NOTES AND QUESTIONS

1. H and W were married in 1970 in California where they have lived ever since. At the time of marriage W owned some General Motors stock. In 1971 W sold the stock for $10,000 and used the money to establish a catering business. She worked full time in the business and was very successful

at it. She was paid a salary out of the business which she regularly put in a joint checking account with H. Funds from this account were used for family and household expenses. In 1979 W sold the business for $500,000 and shortly thereafter she died, survived by H. W's will contains the following key provision "I leave all of my separate property to the Stanford Law School." How much of the $500,000 should the Law School get?

2. Observe the frequency with which the court's opinion refers to prior judicial decisions, statutes, and other forms of authority. We left the citations in this case so you could see an example of citation practice but will usually delete them in later cases, indicating the deletion by "[Citations]."

3. Why do courts cite prior decisions and other forms of authority? What other forms of authority are there? What makes them authoritative? For discussion of these and related questions, see John Henry Merryman, The Authority of Authority: What the California Supreme Court Cited in 1950, 6 Stanford Law Review 613 (1954); John Henry Merryman, Toward a Theory of Citations: An Empirical Study of the Citation Practice of the California Supreme Court in 1950, 1960 and 1970, 50 Southern California Law Review 381 (1977).

b. Common Law Property

In re Shupack's Will, 1 N.Y.2d 482, 154 N.Y.S.2d 441, 136 N.E.2d 513 (1956).

FULD, JUDGE.

Irving Shupack died in October of 1953, survived by his wife, a son and a daughter. His will, admitted to probate a month later, contained an absolute legacy of $2,500 to his wife and gave the residue of his estate to a trustee (also named as executor) "to be divided into three equal parts". One part was placed in trust for the benefit of his wife for life; upon her death, it was provided, the trust was to terminate and the principal was to be divided between the other trusts. The other two parts were placed in separate trusts for the benefit of the two children, each was to receive the income until his majority, and at that time the trusts were to end and each child was to receive the principal outright. The property left by the testator consisted primarily of six corporations which he wholly owned, two engaged in manufacturing, the other four in the real estate business, their gross assets totaling about $750,000.

We must decide two questions: first, whether the widow is entitled, under section 18 of the Decedent Estate Law, Consol.Laws, c. 13, to elect to take her intestate share of the estate and, second, whether the executor-trustee may exercise plenary managerial control over the property held by the real estate corporations. We answer both in the negative, and, since we agree with the Appellate Division's treatment and disposition of the second question, relating to the executor-trustee's control (see, also, dissenting opinion, 1 N.Y.2d 498–499, 154 N.Y.S.2d 453), we discuss only the first, the wife's right of election under the statute.

So far as it is pertinent, section 18 grants to a surviving spouse the right to elect to take his or her share of the estate as in intestacy, subject to the following limitation and condition:

"(d) Where the will contains an absolute legacy or devise, whether general or specific, to the surviving spouse, of or in excess of the sum of twenty-five hundred dollars and also a provision for a trust for his or her benefit for life of a principal equal to or more than the excess between said legacy or devise and his or her intestate share, no right of election whatever shall exist in the surviving spouse."

It is the widow's claim that she has a right of election because the trust in her favor is "inadequate" and "illusory." Her reasoning, briefly stated, is this. As a minority holder in closed corporations, she will be at the mercy of the holders of the majority of the stock for the declaration of dividends and for their amount. Her children, who will acquire the remaining stock upon attaining their majority, the boy in 1957, the girl in 1961, will be able to elect the directors who will decide whether to distribute or retain the corporate profits; and thus they, or any strangers to whom they might sell, will control the amount of her income. The Appellate Division, agreeing with the widow, reversed the decree of the surrogate and held that she was entitled "to elect to take against the will as in intestacy."

That decision rests upon an unwarranted expansion of section 18 and the legislative purpose underlying its enactment. We have more than once declared that the statute's purpose is to assure to a surviving husband or wife the right to claim his or her full intestate share, in spite of any will, "unless the instrument should provide substantial equivalents. A testamentary gift of an equal sum . . . or a gift in trust of such a sum for the use of the surviving spouse for life" constitutes such an equivalent.

By bequeathing to respondent the sum of $2,500 outright and also a life interest in a trust of one third of the residue of the estate, the testator provided her with the requisite equivalent for her intestate share and fully complied with the demands of the statute. The possibility which she fears, that her income may be impaired by hostile majority owners, results from the character of the property left by her husband rather than from any attempt to deprive her of her lawful share in the estate. It would have been far better for respondent if her husband had owned shares in General Motors, United States Steel or some other large publicly held corporation. But, the fact is, he owned only shares in such enterprises as Harjan Realty Corporation and American Hinge Corporation of Brooklyn. All that the testator owned, all he had to dispose of, was the stock in these personally held corporations.

While there is a danger that the widow will not receive an income from her trust proportionate to that received by her husband during his life, that consequence flows from the character of his property rather than from any failure on his part to comply with the provisions of law enacted for the benefit of the surviving spouse. If she were to take her intestate share, that is, a third of the stock outright, she would still have only a minority interest in each of these small corporations and the income would still be dependent upon decisions of directors selected by the majority stockholders. In such a case, she would, it is true, possess the right to sell her one third share, but this right is seriously impaired, if not effectively destroyed, by the practical difficulty attendant upon obtaining a fair-price buyer for a minority interest in a closely held corporation such as we have here.

* * *

This is not to say, though, that a testator, who dies possessed of both income producing and non-income producing property, may so divide his estate as to bequeath to his wife only the unproductive portion. When we are confronted with such a case, we shall deal with it. Nor does our decision mean, or even remotely suggest, that the widow would lack a remedy if the designated trustee were to prove faithless to the trust or were so to conduct and manage its affairs as to prejudice or discriminate against her interests. All we are not holding is that, where a testator has left to his spouse one third of all of his property, fairly and equitably divided, either outright or in trust in accordance with the provisions of the Decedent Estate Law, the fear or possibility of misconduct on the part of the trustee or of the corporate directors, managing the property, does not give rise to a right of election under section 18.

QUESTIONS

1. Shupack is about the surviving spouse's interest in property owned by the decedent at death. Can the surviving spouse's interests be diminished by giving away the property during life? Consider the following language from Newman v. Dore, 276 N.Y. 271, 9 N.E.2d 966 (1937):

    . . . In a few states where a wife has a similar contingent expectant interest or estate in the property of her husband, it has been held that her rights may not be defeated by any transfer made during life with intent to deprive the wife of property, which under the law would otherwise pass to her. . . .

    . . . In those states it is the intent to defeat the wife's contingent rights which creates the invalidity and it seems that an absolute transfer of all his property by a married man during his life, if made with other purpose and intent than to cut off an unloved wife, is valid even though its effect is to deprive the wife of any share in the property of her husband at his death. . . .

    . . . Motive or intent is an unsatisfactory test of the validity of a transfer of property. In most jurisdictions it has been rejected, sometimes for the reason that it would cast doubt upon the validity of all transfers made by a married man, outside of the regular course of business; sometimes because it is difficult to find a satisfactory logical foundation for it.

Intent may, at times, be relevant in determining whether an act is fraudulent, but there can be no fraud where no right of any person is invaded. "The great weight of authority is that the intent to defeat a claim which otherwise a wife might have is not enough to defeat the deed." . . .

2. Would you rather be a surviving spouse in a community property or a common law jurisdiction?

2. Children

Paul G. Haskell, Restraints upon the Disinheritance of Family Members, in Edward C. Halbach, Death, Taxes, and Family Property, St. Paul, Minnesota: West Publishing Company, 1977, pp. 105, 110.

Protection of Children. In the United States children are not protected from disinheritance, except in Louisiana which has a form of the Civil Law *legitime,* which is essentially a kind of forced share for children derived from that state's French legal tradition. It should be noted that in this country even minor children who are unprovided for in the decedent's will or otherwise, do not have any claim against the deceased parent's estate for support. The Uniform Probate Code makes no change in the law in this area.

It has been previously indicated that in Britain children, minor or of age, are protected from disinheritance if it can be shown that they are in need. Certain continental nations have a form of fixed forced share for children. Neither of these forms of protection has been accepted in this country, except in Louisiana.

Lawrence M. Friedman, "The Law of the Living, the Law of the Dead: Property, Succession and Society," 1966 Wisconsin Law Review, 362–363.

. . . Modern succession law, however, unmistakably prefers the nuclear family (and especially the wife) over more distant kin. To say that the law favors the nuclear family seems rather paradoxical at first glance, in view of the stubborn persistence of the right to disinherit children completely and without stating cause. In fact, however, disinheritance of children is both common and natural. The average man marries only once and his widow is the mother of his children. She succeeds to the husband's rights as guardian of the children and head of the family. Under these conditions, it is not "unnatural" to leave nothing to the children. The right to disinherit children survives in modern American law, whatever its antecedents, not only because of a bias in favor of freedom of testation, but because disinheritance is functional for the majority of testators. Indeed, one reason often given to convince people that they need to have a will is precisely that without one minor children share in the estate. An awkward, costly guardianship then has to be set up, and the wife's economic control of family property, even her position as head of the family, may be impaired. . . .

NOTES AND QUESTIONS

1. Despite the freedom to disinherit children there are two counter-influences in most state legal systems in the U.S.: (1) the rates of state inheritance taxes favor gifts to children; and (2) "pretermitted children" statutes protect children against the uninformed or incautious disinheriting testator. The applicable provision in California is Probate Code § 90:

   > When a testator omits to provide in his will for any of his children, or for the issue of any deceased child, whether born before or after the making of the will or before or after the death of the testator, and such child or issue are unprovided for by any settlement, and have not had an equal proportion of the testator's property bestowed on them by way of advancement, unless it appears from the will that such omission was intentional, such child or such issue succeeds to the same share in the estate of the testator as if he had died intestate.

   Statutes of this kind are the explanation for those provisions in wills by which a child is bequeathed a dollar or a shilling.

2. The contrast with forced inheritance of children in civil law nations (and in Louisiana and Puerto Rico) is striking. In Italy, for example, one half of the deceased's wealth (including any gifts made by decedent before death) passes to the child, if she leaves only one, and two-thirds, if she leaves more than one (Italian Civil Code, Art. 537).

3. The freedom to disinherit children is a treasured principle of American law, for which a variety of justifications has been given: (1) freedom of testation is a "natural right"; (2) testamentary freedom provides an incentive for the testator to work and save money to fuel the economy; (3) testamentary freedom is essential to the free alienability of property, which is necessary in our modern industrial economy; (4) members of a testator's family should not be entitled to an automatic share of the estate because they may be undeserving; (5) the elderly may be in a better position to secure attention if their families are not guaranteed benefits; (6) testamentary freedom allows a testator to transfer love, affection and identification along with his property; (7) freedom of testation offers the testator the gratifying prospect of achieving immortality through the "dead hand"; (8) restrictions on personal freedom should be avoided to the extent possible, and allowing testamentary freedom is one way to do so; (9) it breeds "rugged individualism in children" and is consistent with the spirit of "a land of pioneers." What do you think of the merits of these arguments? For a fuller discussion of the subject, see Marvin B. Sussman, Judith N. Cates, and David T. Smith, The Family and Inheritance, New York: Russell Sage Foundation, 1970, pp. 7–10; Paul G. Haskell, The Power of Disinheritance: Proposal for Reform, 52 Georgetown Law Journal 499 (1964); Louis S. Headley, Inheritance, A Basic Personal Freedom, 88 Trusts & Estates, 1949, p. 24.

4. Which is preferable, the common law power to disinherit children or the civil law scheme of forced inheritance?

5. Suppose T dies leaving no surviving spouse and a minor child. Two kinds of problems must be faced: who will care for the child (guardian of

the person) and who will administer the child's property (guardian of the property)? Although both may be (and usually are) performed by the same person, it is possible to separate and allocate these responsibilities to two people. Such guardian(s) may be nominated by the decedent (usually done in the will); if not, he will be chosen by the court. Even if the testator names a guardian of the person the court has the power to reject or remove him when this appears to be in the best interests of the child, but as a practical matter the testator's nomination is seldom questioned.

3. Controlling the Power of the Dead Hand

a. Gifts to Charity

NOTE

The earliest statutes of mortmain in England were directed against the Church and were promulgated in the interest of the King and the lords who, in a feudal property system, derived their chief income from the "incidents" of tenure of land. The profitable incidents, payable by the tenant to the lord, were: wardships (the right to administer the property of the minor heir of the tenant during minority); marriages (the right to arrange the marriage of the minor heir of the tenant); fines and reliefs (payments for the right to succeed to the tenancy inter vivos or at death) and forfeitures and escheats (the lord's right to take the tenant's lands for disloyalty, for commission of a felony, or on the tenant's death without heirs—an event sometimes engineered for this purpose by the lord). The problem with the Church was that it was never a minor, never married, never died, and never committed a felony. Accordingly, a string of mortmain statutes attempted, with varying success, to prevent or limit gifts to the Church and, later, to other charities and to corporations.

Lawrence M. Friedman, The Law of Succession in Social Perspective, in Edward C. Halbach, Death, Taxes and Family Property. St. Paul, Minn.: West Publishing Co., 1977, pp. 9, 23, 25.

. . . The fear of concentration of land and power in the church lasted well into modern times. Its continuing appeal was reflected in legal restrictions on testamentary gifts to charity. Fear of the churches was certainly one of the reasons why the charitable trust had such a difficult time in the United States—New York, for example, did not allow charitable trusts by will or otherwise; and a group of states—including New York—imposed a number of other restrictions on gifts to charity by will, if the will was executed less than 30 days before the testator died. One of the ideas behind this restriction was the notion that a man on his deathbed was all too likely to respond to the threats and promises of a clergyman, neglecting his own family in the process.

These fears have largely passed into history; and some of the minor "dead hand" statutes (California's for example) have been repealed. No state now refuses to allow the charitable trust, even if it is granted perpetual life. What stimulated New York to change its mind was the failure of the so-called Tilden Trust, in the early 1890's. A celebrated court case turned on the validity of a charitable trust, established under the will of Governor Samuel Tilden. The trust was successfully attacked by Tilden's heirs. Tilden's fortune, which he had meant to devote to public ends, passed instead to his heirs. This finally roused the New York legislature, and in 1893, the last legal impediments were removed.

Charities Again: Foundations. Since the 1940s, in another rather curious kind of reversal, policy debate has focused on the charitable foundations, their aims and methods, rather than on the fortunes held in private hands and left behind to the heirs. In the last generation, one hears little talk of increasing the estate tax, and even less talk about more radical means of ending the inheritance of estates. On the other hand, Congress has repeatedly investigated charitable foundations. The Reece Committee, in the 1950's, bitterly criticized many of the major foundations; according to the chief counsel, the committee found evidence of a "plot to penetrate the American foundations and to use their funds for Communist propaganda and Communist influence upon our society." This was a flagrant piece of hysteria, characteristic of the McCarthy period; but the feeling that the foundations were too liberal—or at best too free from any sort of public control—never vanished. The Ford Foundation, in 1968, handed out grants to some of Robert Kennedy's staff members. This struck many observers as further evidence that the foundations were far too political. This spark ignited another round of reform effort. In 1969, Congress imposed restrictions on charitable trusts and foundations, in the name of correcting "abuses." Most notably, for the first time, foundations were taxed; they had to pay a four percent "excise" tax, on investment income. Whether this law is the entering wedge of further taxation and regulation remains to be seen. The only safe prediction is that *some* sort of "dead hand" problem will continue to evoke public controversy. The precise form will change with changing times. . . .

b. The Dead Hand of the Testator

NOTE

The problem we confront here is how far the owner should be allowed to control the way his heirs dispose of his property after he is dead. To what extent can he dispose of his property (exercising his freedom of alienation) so as to tie the hands (restrict the freedom of alienation) of those to whom he leaves it, either by direct restraints on their powers to sell or give it away or by tying it up in a trust or chain of future interests? The desire of owners of property to control it after their deaths is amply demonstrated by the variety, ingenuity and occasional eccentricity of property dispositions that have come before the English and American courts during the life of the common law.

A large part of the most complicated and technical part of our law has grown out of this drama, in which the principal participants were people of property, lawyers, disappointed expectant heirs (and their lawyers) and judges.

Out of the centuries of ingenious drafting and litigation the common law has developed a series of rules designed to strike a balance between the property owner's desire to make detailed property provision for the future, the desire of future generations to deal as they wish with their property, and the social interest in keeping wealth available for all kinds of investment and consumption. There are three basic rules:

1. The rule against [direct] restraints on alienation. Thus, T cannot leave property to H and provide that H shall not have the power to sell it or give it away. The provision against alienation by H is void.

2. The rule against accumulations. Suppose the owner puts property in trust, directs that the property be invested and that the income also be accumulated and invested, rather than distributed. Out of fear that such accumulation, if unlimited, would eventually swallow up an enormous proportion of total wealth, which would be unavailable for risk investment or for consumption, courts developed the rule that the period of accumulation must be limited. Any provision for accumulation beyond that period is void.

3. The rule against perpetuities (the rule against remoteness of vesting). Suppose T leaves his property, directly or in trust, to A for life, and then to those children of A who survive him. It is obvious that until A dies we cannot know which of his living children will survive him. Nor, until nine months or so after his death, can we know if he will have further children who would fall into the class of "surviving children." In the law we call the gift to "those children of A who survive him" a "contingent" (as distinguished from "vested") interest. It takes little ingenuity to demonstrate that gifts of this kind could be used to tie up wealth forever: e.g. "to A for life, then to A's eldest surviving child for life, then to that child's eldest surviving child for life . . . etc."

The rule against perpetuities, developed entirely through the cases, states that no interest is valid unless all questions relating to (1) who will take, (2) whether any given person will take, and (3) when that person will take must be resolved no later than a period measured by lives in being at the creation of the gift plus 21 years and, where applicable, the period of gestation. Incidentally, there has been a tendency to use this period as the permissible limit of accumulation under the rule against accumulations. For further light on the rule against perpetuities see Lewis M. Simes, Public Policy and the Dead Hand, Ann Arbor, University of Michigan, 1955.

Estate of Ghiglia, 42 Cal.App.3d 433, 116 Cal.Rptr. 827 (1974).

FRANSON, ASSOCIATE JUSTICE.

Appellant, one of three surviving children of the testator, Frank P. Ghiglia, challenges the validity of a testamentary trust established for the benefit of appellant, his sister and their children (testator's grandchildren), on the ground that the gift to the grandchildren of a future interest in the trust estate, the possession of which is deferred until the youngest grandchild reaches age 35, is a class gift which includes any grandchild born after the testator's death, thus permitting the vesting of the interests of the class members beyond a life in being and 21 years in violation of the rule against perpetuities. We hold that, although the gift to the grandchildren violates the vesting rule, under the authority of Civil Code 715.5,[1] we should order the will reformed to require the vesting of the interests of all class members within the allowable period of time.

Frank P. Ghiglia died on January 1, 1972, a widower. He was survived by three grown children, Frank P. Ghiglia, Jr., Adeline Marguerite McClintock and Robert J. Ghiglia. Each child had two children. Frank P. Ghiglia, Jr. had two sons, Frank Joseph Ghiglia and George Frank Ghiglia. Adeline Marguerite McClintock had a son, John Arthur McClintock, and a daughter, Nancy Ann [McClintock] Berge. Robert J. Ghiglia had two sons, William Joseph Ghiglia and John Robert Ghiglia. At the time of the testator's death, the testator's daughter, Adeline, who was divorced, was about 53 years of age, the testator's son Robert, was about 51 years of age, and Robert's wife was about 45 years of age; all of the testator's grandchildren were adults.

Decedent left a will which was admitted to probate. The testator's oldest son, Frank, was named executor in the will. The will provides that Frank shall receive one-third of the estate outright after certain household furniture, automobiles and personal belongings are divided equally among Frank and the other two children, Adeline and Robert. The will then provides in the fourth clause as follows:

* * *

B) The remaining two-thirds, IN TRUST—to Frank P. Ghiglia and the Bank of America National Trust and Savings Association, for the uses and purposes hereinafter set forth.

* * *

E) The NET INCOME of THE TRUST ESTATE shall be distributed as follows:

1) One full share to my daughter Adeline Marguerite McClintock.

2) One full share to my son Robert J. Ghiglia.

3) The net income to my daughter Adeline Marguerite McClintock and my son Robert J. Ghiglia shall be distributed in

1. Civil Code section 715.5 provides: "No interest in real or personal property is either void or voidable as in violation of [the rule against perpetuities] if and to the extent that it can be reformed or construed within the limits of that [rule] to give effect to the general intent of the creator of the interest whenever that general intent can be ascertained. This section shall be liberally construed and applied to validate such interest to the fullest extent consistent with such ascertained intent."

convenient installments, not less frequently than quarterly during their lifetime.

F) Upon the death of my daughter Adeline Marguerite McClintock, the Trustees shall apportion her share of the net income and pay the same to my grandchildren Nancy Ann McClintock and John Arthur McClintock, equally.

G) Upon the death of my son Robert J. Ghiglia, the Trustees shall apportion his share of the net income and pay the same to my grandchildren William G. Ghiglia and John Ghiglia, equally.

Upon the death of each of my children, Adeline Marguerite McClintock and Robert J. Ghiglia, the trust shall terminate *provided, however, if any of my grandchildren have not attained the age of thirty-five (35) years, the two trusts shall continue until all of the grandchildren have attained the age of thirty-five (35) years. In other words, each trust shall continue in full force and effect, until all of my grandchildren reach the age of thirty-five (35) years.* Upon such termination the entire Trust Estate, shall be distributed to the persons for whom said estate is then held in trust, in proportion to the trusts then held for such persons and, if there shall be no such persons surviving, then said Trust Estate shall be distributed to my heirs, to be determined according to the laws of California relating to the succession of separate property in force at the date of such termination.

On March 12, 1973, Robert Ghiglia filed a petition to determine the interests under the will. The petition sets forth the fact that the three children were the decedent's heirs-at-law and alleges that the grandchildren's interests under the trust violated the rule against perpetuities. Following a hearing, the trial court upheld the validity of the trust by deciding that the testator's use of "grandchildren" in the will had reference only to the four children of Adeline and Robert alive at the testator's death and, therefore, the gift to them did not violate the vesting rule. Robert Ghiglia appeals from that decision.

Violation of the Vesting Rule. We commence our decision by reciting the general rules of law applicable to the questions before us. Civil Code section 715.2 codifies the common law rule against perpetuities; it provides that no interest in real or personal property is valid unless it must vest, if at all, not later than 21 years after some life in being at the creation of the interest. Civil Code section 715.6 sets forth an alternate period in gross; it provides that "No interest . . . which must vest, if at all, not later than 60 years after the creation of the interest violates Section 715.2 . . . ."

The determination as to whether a future interest vests within the time allowed is made as of the moment the instrument containing the limitation speaks; we are not permitted to wait and see what happens in order to determine its validity. Thus, the validity of an interest in a testamentary trust is determined at the time of the testator's death. Moreover, it is not the probability that a perpetuity may have been created that brings the rule into operation. If, at the time of the creation of the interest, there exists even a bare possibility that the interest involved may not vest within the prescribed period, the rule has been violated.

If the possession of a testamentary gift to a class is postponed to a future time, the class includes all persons coming within the description within the time to which possession is postponed. If the gift is not of a specific sum to each member or subgroup in the class, then the gift violates the vesting rule because the interest of each member cannot be finally ascertained until the membership is fixed.

In determining whether the testator intended the trust estate eventually to go to his four named grandchildren or to all of his possible grandchildren as a class, we must look to the language of the will and the surrounding circumstances and, inasmuch as a will speaks from the date of the testator's death, we also must consider the state of things then existing.

In the instant case, the testator's language is ambiguous. In subparagraph "F)" and "G)" of paragraph "Fourth" of the will, he provides that upon the death of the life beneficiaries of the trust (his daughter, Adeline, and his son, Robert), the trustee shall pay the net income to his four named grandchildren. Subparagraph "G)" then provides among other things that the trust shall continue "until *all of my grandchildren* have attained the age of thirty-five (35) years. In other words, *each trust* shall continue . . ., until *all of my grandchildren* reach the age of thirty-five (35) years. Upon such termination the entire trust estate shall be distributed to the persons for whom said estate is then held in trust . . .." (Emphasis added.)

The first question to be decided is whether the phrase "all of my grandchildren" was intended to include the testator's grandchildren by his oldest son, Frank. We think not, for Frank received his one-third of the estate free of the trust, and presumably the testator intended that Frank would support his children during their minority and that they would inherit his estate upon his death. That the testator had this in mind is borne out by the fact that upon the death of Adeline and Robert the income beneficiaries of the trust are only their respective children. Nor do we see any logical reason why the testator would use Frank's children, who are not named as beneficiaries of the trust, as measuring lives to determine when the trust corpus should be distributed to Adeline and Robert's children. Accordingly, we construe the phrase "all of my grandchildren" to exclude Frank's children.

The second question, admittedly more difficult to resolve, is whether the phrase "all of my grandchildren" used to describe the ultimate beneficiaries of the trust corpus was intended to include only the four grandchildren named as income beneficiaries, or whether it was intended to include any additional grandchild born after the testator's death. If we conclude that the gift of the trust corpus was not limited to the four grandchildren, then the gift was to a class and would include all persons coming within the class description before the time to which possession is postponed. . . .

. . . we conclude that a reasonable interpretation of the will before us, reading the particular language in the light of the entire testamentary scheme, is that the testator intended to make a gift of the trust corpus to all of his grandchildren, including any born after his death.

It is clear that the gift violates the rule against remoteness of vesting. Either Adeline or Robert, in the eyes of the law, possibly could have another child who might not reach age 35 within 21 years after their respective deaths. Moreover, the child could be born more than 25 years after the testator's death and would not reach age 35 within 60 years after the creation of the interest under the alternative period in gross provided by Civil Code section 715.6.

Can we sever the invalid portion from the valid portion, i.e., can we uphold the gift of the trust corpus to the four members of the class living at the testator's death and exclude only the gift to a future member born after his death? We think not, for, again, we find nothing in the will to suggest that had the testator foreseen the partial invalidity of his testamentary scheme that he nonetheless would have intended to exclude a member of the class in order to save the interests of the other members. The test of severability is "whether the two [parts] are so parts of a single plan or scheme or otherwise so dependent one upon the other, that by avoiding the invalid provisions and allowing the valid to stand there will result a disposition of the estate so different from what the testator contemplated or so unreasonable that it must be presumed that [he] would not have made the valid provisions if he had been aware of the invalidity of the others."

We hold the gift to the unborn members of the class inseparable from the gift to the living members of the class.

Reformation. Contrary to appellant's position, however, it does not follow that the trust should be declared void because the vesting of the grandchildren's interest exceeds the lawful period of perpetuity. The testator's general intent was to create a spendthrift trust under which his children, Adeline and Robert, would receive the income for their lives, but would not receive a fee interest in the corpus—only the grandchildren would receive such an interest after the death of Adeline and Robert. Appellant seeks to overthrow the dominant intention of the testator by having the trust declared entirely void for remoteness merely because the testator is unable to defer the vesting of the trust estate in his grandchildren as long as he wished.

Testamentary dispositions that are otherwise valid are not necessarily invalidated by illegal limitations. Moreover, Probate Code section 101 provides in part: "A will is to be construed according to the intention of the testator. Where his intention cannot have effect to its full extent, *it must have effect as far as possible.*" (Emphasis added.)

Of particular importance in the present case is Civil Code section 715.5. While we have been unable to find a California case applying this statute to uphold a testamentary disposition in violation of the rule against perpetuities, courts in other jurisdictions have taken such an approach. In Edgerly v. Barker, 66 N.H. 434, 31 A. 900, the testator left property in trust to be distributed among the children of his living son and daughter when the youngest reached age 40. In order to achieve the testator's primary intent and at the same time conform the trust to the limitation imposed by the rule against perpetuities, the court applied the *cy pres* doctrine and held that the grandchildren's interest would vest at 21 rather than 40. More recently, in Carter v. Berry, 243 Miss. 321, 140 So.2d 843, the court applied the doctrine of "equitable approximation" to make an invalid gift to the testator's children at age 25 distributable at age 21. This approach is in accord with English law where the severity of the common law rule has been mitigated by a statute providing, "[T]he disposition should be treated for all purposes as if, instead of being limited by reference to the age in fact specified, it had been limited by reference to the age nearest to that age which would, if specified instead, have prevented the disposition from being so void."

We recognize that the testator intended that the gift of the trust corpus to his grandchildren be delayed until the youngest was sufficiently mature to deal responsibly with his inheritance and that the testator believed that age 35 was a prudent age for this purpose. However, this does not mean that, if faced with the realization that by postponing the vesting in his grandchildren to age 35 he rendered the trust itself invalid, with the result that two-thirds of his estate would be taken outright by Adeline and Robert, he nonetheless would not have elected to set up a trust with the corpus vesting at the time the youngest grandchild reached age 21 rather than age 35. We believe that rather than forego his dominant testamentary plan of preserving two-thirds of his estate for Adeline and Robert's children, he would have intended to give his trust estate to their children within a permissible period of time.

Because it is the duty of the court to give effect to the testator's general intent to the fullest extent possible, we hold that the trial court must use its power as defined in Civil Code section 715.5 to reform the will so that distribution of the trust corpus will be made when the youngest grandchild reaches 21 with the result that all class interests must vest within the required time.

The order on the petition for determination of rights and distribution is reversed; the matter is remanded to the trial court with directions to reform the last will of Frank P. Ghiglia, Deceased, in accordance with this opinion.

GEO. A. BROWN, P. J., and GARGANO, J. concur.

QUESTIONS

1. What difference would it have made if the court in Estate of Ghiglia refused to apply Civil Code § 715.5?

2. This case provides an example of the unexpected ways in which the rule against perpetuities can trap the unwary, including experienced and knowledgeable lawyers. Here the court saved matters by applying Civil Code § 715.5, but at the common law and in most states today there is no equivalent of § 715.5. Even where something like it exists it would have been possible for the court to decide that changing 35 years to 21 years conflicts with "the general intent of the creator of the interest. . . ." Should a court have the power to make so substantial a change in the express provisions of a will?

3. Your answer to question two may be affected by your evaluation of the policies underlying the statutes establishing formal requirements in making wills, to which we now turn.

4. Formal Requirements

CALIFORNIA PROBATE CODE

§ 50. Wills; execution; attestation

Every will, other than a nuncupative will, must be in writing and every will, other than a holographic will and a nuncupative will, must be executed and attested as follows:

(1) **Subscription.** It must be subscribed at the end thereof by the testator himself, or some person in his presence and by his direction must subscribe his name thereto. A person who subscribes the testator's name, by his direction, should write his own name as a witness to the will, but a failure to do so will not affect the validity of the will.

(2) **Presence of witnesses.** The subscription must be made, or the testator must acknowledge it to have been made by him or by his authority, in the presence of both of the attesting witnesses, present at the same time.

(3) **Testator's declaration.** The testator, at the time of subscribing or acknowledging the instrument, must declare to the attesting witnesses that it is his will.

(4) **Attesting witnesses.** There must be at least two attesting witnesses, each of whom must sign the instrument as a witness, at the end of the will, at the testator's request and in his presence. The

witnesses should give their places of residence, but a failure to do so will not affect the validity of the will. (Stats.1931, c. 281, p. 589, § 50.) . . .

§ 53. Holographic will; form

A holographic will is one that is entirely written, dated and signed by the hand of the testator himself. It is subject to no other form, and need not be witnessed. No address, date or other matter written, printed or stamped upon the document, which is not incorporated in the provisions which are in the handwriting of the decedent, shall be considered as any part of the will. (Stats.1931, c. 281, p. 590, § 53.) . . .

§ 54. Nuncupative will; persons who may make; witnesses

A nuncupative will is not required to be in writing. It may be made by one who, at the time, is in actual military service in the field, or doing duty on shipboard at sea, and in either case in actual contemplation, fear, or peril of death, or by one who, at the time, is in expectation of immediate death from an injury received the same day. It must be proved by two witnesses who were present at the making thereof, one of whom was asked by the testator, at the time, to bear witness that such was his will, or to that effect. (Stats.1931, c. 281, p. 590, § 54.) . . .

§ 55. Nuncupative will; personal property disposable

A nuncupative will may dispose of personal property only, and the estate bequeathed must not exceed one thousand dollars in value. (Stats.1931, c. 281, p. 590, § 55.) . . .

Lawrence M. Friedman, "The Law of the Living, the Law of the Dead; Property, Succession and Society," 1966 Wisconsin Law Review 340, 353–354, 367–368, 371–372.

. . . All property not disposed of during a person's lifetime may be disposed of by a formal document called a will. This document must be in writing, and it must be witnessed by at least two witnesses. Most Southern and Western States recognize the so-called holographic will, which dispenses with witnesses, but which must be entirely written by the testator in his own hand. For estates of any size, however, the holographic will is no real alternative to a witnessed will. It is far too much trouble to write a long legal document in longhand. . . .

. . . Compliance with the will formalities is mandatory. A man who leaves behind a will which lacks a witness has died intestate; his purported will is a scrap of paper. In a state which recognizes the holographic will, the requirements for a proper handwritten document are equally stringent. A will in the testator's handwriting, but with two sentences typed on a typewriter, is invalid and has no legal effect.[37] . . .

. . . The formalities of executing a will are useful ones. They impress the testator with the solemnity of his acts; they ensure a standard written document, duly filed in court, recording the orderly disposition of goods and rights; they eliminate most of the danger of forgery and fraud; they encourage the use of middlemen (lawyers) who can help plan a rational, trouble-free disposition of assets. In general, formalities of execution, rule, and administration in the law of succession standardize and guide the process of transmitting billions of dollars of assets from generation to generation; they help make the process smooth, uniform, and efficient. . . .

. . . the standard rule is that a will cannot be judicially "reformed," even though an obvious mistake of fact or law was made in drawing it up. Suppose a man instructed his lawyer to write him a will leaving 10,000 dollars to his brother, George; the lawyer by mistake gave the money to brother Jim; the testator, in a hurry, failed to read the will carefully and signed it error and all. Courts are not supposed to entertain or act upon the evidence of the lawyer that George and not Jim was meant. The argument for this harsh rule goes as follows: the law insists that wills must be in writing, signed by the testator, and witnessed. If we let people testify that the testator meant Jim when he said George, we are transferring property, not through the vehicle of the will, but through the vehicle of oral testimony, and that is forbidden by the law. This, at any rate, is the accepted rule. It has been widely criticized as hypertechnical and even frivolous, but it has an inner core of sense. Correcting the mistake would, in fact, derogate from the standardized nature of the will as an economic document, by opening the will to inquiries outside of the "four corners" of the document, that is, outside of the text itself. This would make the will to that extent a less reliable document; it would make the probate process less uniform and efficient, clutter up the courts with inquiries as to the meaning of wills, and seriously interfere with the mass-market handling of estates. This in turn might impair the efficiency of transfer of property to succeeding generations. . . .

. . . "Our law," said Chief Justice Tilghman of Pennsylvania in 1821, "requires that wills should be in writing, and proved by two witnesses. But if the writing is to be contradicted by parol evidence, the object of the law will be defeated and all certainty destroyed"; the correction of scrivener's errors, through the scrivener's testimo-

---

37. In re Thorn's Estate, 183 Cal. 512, 192 Pac. 19 (1920). Thorn executed a holographic will. He left his "country place Cragthorn" to the California Academy of Sciences, together with the balance of his estate to "improve or care for Cragthorn Park." In two places the word "Cragthorn" was inserted with a rubber stamp. In every other respect the will was a perfect holograph. The court held that the will was invalid.

ny, "would open such a door for perjury and confusion, as would render wills of very little use." . . .

QUESTION

1. Do these considerations affect your answer to question 3, p. 178, supra? You might be helped in thinking about it by this additional information: the judicial attitude toward reformation of wills is a special application of the rule that oral evidence cannot be admitted to vary the terms of a written instrument.

E. PROBATE AND ADMINISTRATION

Bar Association of San Francisco. Probate Committee. How To Live—And Die—With California Probate. Long Beach, Houston: Gulf Publishing Co., 1970, pp. 143–146.

The Executor. What is involved in a California probate and administration? A California executor or administrator has important duties, some of which must be performed whether or not a living trust has been used by the decedent. Let's look at them.

When a Californian dies, the executor named in his will sees that burial instructions in the will or in a letter to the executor or funeral home are properly carried out even before the will is probated. He looks after unprotected properties such as securities, cash, jewelry, or perishable assets. He determines whether there is adequate insurance against loss. He confers with the heirs, finds out whether the widow has sufficient funds to meet household expenses and whether there are any other problems that need immediate attention. He helps with the proof of death for insurance purposes and generally prepares to collect the assets of the estate, which will be his responsibility when the will is probated.

Next, the executor must locate the will and have an attorney file it for probate. After ten days notice by publication in a newspaper and mailing to the heirs and beneficiaries, he obtains a certificate of authority (letters testamentary) to act as executor of the will. The executor now begins the task of finding out what the estate consists of. He must locate all bank accounts and transfer them to a proper account in the name of the estate, leaving money in savings accounts until the next interest date, if possible. He obtains custody of securities, which may or may not be transferred into his name as executor, depending on how long the estate will be in administration. He must assume authority over any business owned by the estate, and, if he does not know how to run it, he must find someone who does. He must locate and actually or symbolically take possession of all other assets of the estate.

If there is a safe deposit box in the name of the decedent by himself or with another person, the executor may not open it without a representative from the County Treasurer's office being present to inspect and list the contents. This is usually arranged by the attorney for the estate shortly after the executor has obtained his letters testamentary. (The decedent's safe deposit box may be opened immediately after his death, however, in order to obtain his will.)

It is necessary that he not let estate property get mixed with his own property, or with the property of any other person. If the decedent left a surviving widow, the executor must segregate the separate property of the decedent and the community property from the separate property of the widow. There may be problems with assets which are scattered in different states, or even in foreign countries. He must collect all the money owed the estate. He will have power to compromise, abandon, or sue for collection on an estate claim with court approval. He must arrange for publication of notice to the decedent's creditors to file or present their claims within four months of the first publication of the notice. If he and the court approve these claims, the executor pays them. If any are rejected, the creditor may bring a suit against the estate.

A detailed, sworn inventory of the estate assets must be made and they must be designated as community or separate property. This will be necessary for calculation of the state inheritance and federal estate tax use if the estate is of a size that will bring on these taxes. The court-appointed appraisers will determine the value of the property of the estate, but the executor must review these values to insure their fairness.

The executor must estimate how much cash is needed to pay funeral bills, medical bills, and current bills as well as taxes and administration expenses. He must provide for specific cash legacies that may be left by the will. If it is necessary to liquidate any assets to provide funds for payment of debts and cash gifts, then the executor must see to that also.

He must properly estimate, provide for, and pay the taxes that will be due for the portion of the year that had elapsed prior to the decedent's death. He must also take care of the estate's income taxes, since the estate is a separate income taxpayer from the decedent, and he must plan for and pay the estate tax. . . . He must prepare for and pay the California state inheritance tax. . . .

The executor must keep detailed records of all his operations in order to be sure everything is done properly. He must collect the income as it comes in and he should watch investments so that appropriate court action can be taken to protect estate values. If, for example, the price of a stock held by the estate goes down, it should be sold in favor of a more secure stock.

At the end of the period of administration he must distribute the estate in accordance with the will. He must determine the timing of distributions to beneficiaries for income tax purposes. If the will calls for the setting up of trusts, he must determine when and to what extent trusts are to be set up. If he handles this property, important tax savings can be made.

After distribution of the estate has been effected and all other disbursements are properly made, the period of his administration is over. He must, of course, depend on good legal advice in all these matters, but the responsibility is ultimately his. . . .

NOTES

1. While an "executor" is a person appointed by the deceased to carry out the terms of his will, an "administrator" is a person appointed by the court to manage the estate when the deceased dies intestate. When a will is made, but no executor is named, or the executor named therein dies or fails to petition or to qualify, or resigns, the court appoints an "administrator with the will annexed" to carry out the provisions of the will. Both executors and administrators are "personal representatives."

2. Many of the actions of the executor require approval by the court having probate jurisdiction. (In practice the court clerk does most of the work, which is purely routine, and the judge does not look closely at the papers he signs.) Each of these court actions requires payment of a fee by the estate. Unless the executor is also a lawyer and acts in both capacities the executor will have to hire a lawyer to handle the court proceedings. The lawyer's fees will be paid out of the estate. The executor, of course, is also entitled to fees from the estate, as is the inheritance tax appraiser and anyone else who renders services during the administration process.

3. Allegations of unjustified delay, expense and corruption in the probate and administration process are common, and a substantial popular literature has grown up that both feeds public apprehension and offers advice on how to avoid the process or limit its costs. (In this sense probate-administration costs and funeral costs are similar. Interestingly, empirical studies indicate that, although funerals don't take as long, they take a larger bite out of the estate than do probate and administration.) The extent of lay concern about probate may be indicated by the market for such books. The most famous of them, Norman F. Dacey's How to Avoid Probate, first published in 1965, has sold over a million copies. Here is a sample of his description of the problem.

Norman F. Dacey, How to Avoid Probate. New York: Crown Publishers, Inc., 1965, pp. 7–9.

In most areas of this country the probate procedure is a scandal, a form of tribute levied by the legal profession upon the estates of its victims, both living and dead.

The New York Herald-Tribune editorially denounced the probate system in that city where "clubhouse lawyers profit to the extent of $1,000,000 annually in fees, many taken, at a large percentage, from small guardianships where every dollar is needed".

This corrupt system has been a fixture in America for generations. New York's famous reform mayor, Fiorello La Guardia, called the probate court "the most expensive undertaking establishment in the world".

The magazine Trusts and Estates, a professional journal in the trust field, editorially condemned the corrupt practices in the probate field, observing that "the public respect for judges and members of the Bar is at stake".

An article in the Journal of the American Bar Association described the Connecticut probate system as "one of the most viciously corrupt systems ever distorted by the inventive minds of the greedy". An article in the Bridgeport Post called the probate system a "gravy train". . . .

Probably no area of the probate procedure is as openly scandalous as the appointment of paid appraisers. . . .

"The court-appointed appraiser is almost always a political henchman whose loyalty in getting votes to help re-elect the probate judge will be strengthened by his gratitude for the fees he will get. Instead of being disinterested and concerned with estimating the estate at the fairest possible figure, they place the highest values on the property with which they can get away in order to increase their own fees."

There have been countless instances where appraisers fees have been "kicked back" to the probate judge or to the clerk of the probate court or to the political party controlling the court in that jurisdiction, or to the lawyer handling the estate.

There are some exceptions to this practice of overvaluation. A documentary program recently shown on network television disclosed an instance where a probate judge, a court-appointed administrator, and two court-appointed appraisers conspired to inventory at $30,000 the real estate in a trust of which two children were the sole beneficiaries. They then formed a dummy corporation which bought the real estate from the administrator at that price—and promptly re-sold it for $240,000!

When you die, a probate judge will appoint two complete strangers to appraise your estate. The political boss of your town may have called the judge and said: "You remember old Joe Green, don't you, over in the 5th district? Joe's out of a job and has had a lot of hard luck lately. He needs a little help. Give him an appraisership." Two such "old Joe Greens" will be appointed as appraisers of your estate.

The executor whom you have appointed in your will, helpless before the legal mumbo-jumbo with which the probate process has been surrounded, will hire a lawyer to do the job. The lawyer will telephone a broker and obtain quotations on the stocks and bonds you've left. A friend of the lawyer in the real estate business will drive by your house and provide the lawyer with a rough estimate of its value. The lawyer will list these figures in an "appraisal". The two court-appointed "Joe Greens" will be called in and asked to sign their names at the bottom of the appraisal. Each will then be handed a check which will represent a chunk of your estate. Neither person did any work of any kind to earn the fee paid him. Perhaps your estate is small and it will be all that your widow and children can do to get by on what has been left to them. That is of no consequence. Before your family gets a penny, the probate racketeers will have exacted their legal tribute. . . .

So called "special guardianships" are another shocking aspect of the probate racket. These "special guardians", invariably lawyers, bleed the estates of minors of huge amounts annually. A probate court clerk in Chicago appointed 691 such guardians in a nine-month period. Forty percent of the guardianships went to four of his friends. One of them got 76 guardianships in that period—about two a week.

A trust officer reported: "The special guardian's fee seldom has any relationship to the value of the services rendered. In one case, a special guardian—a former city official—came in one Friday at noon. He said: 'Let's see these four securities the estate has. If you have those, I'll assume you have the rest and besides I want to make the first race at Jamaica.' At the most he was here twenty minutes and he asked for and got a special guardian's fee of $6,000." . . .

One lawyer to whom I protested the inequity of the probate system wanted to know what I was making a fuss about. "It's a dead man's money, isn't it?" he shrugged.

A common practice is for lawyers drawing wills to name themselves as trustees of the estates upon the testators' death. However expert they may be at the law, most lawyers simply are not competent enough at investing to assume such responsibility. However clumsy they may be at investment, though, the wills they draw provide them with a life annuity in the form of a trustee fee.

The practice of most lawyers tends to orbit around a specific bank. Every client who seeks to set up a bank trust will be directed to that particular bank by the lawyer drawing his will. A "gentleman's agreement" requires the bank to whom the executorship and trust are thus directed to reciprocate by hiring the lawyer who drew the will to probate the estate.

There are a lot of people to be paid off. The Connecticut League of Women Voters has pointed out that "the present system provides for a multitude of fees which are paid piecemeal at so many different stages that it tends to create a vested interest in complicated procedures". . . .

Under the conditions here described, it remains for each individual to search diligently for some way to avoid probate.

Estate of Albert Saxe, Surrogate's Court, New York County, New York, 1967. New York Law Journal, May 11, 1967, page 18, col. 1.

SILVERMAN, SURROGATE. The fee of the attorneys for the accounting trustees is fixed at the amount requested $1,500, plus disbursements of $130.95. The compensation of the special guardian, Joseph Cohen, is fixed at $200. The following statement in the special guardian's "Additional Affidavit of Services of Special Guardian" is of course entitled to no weight:

> "6. In addition to the foregoing, he [the special guardian] has as a public service prepared and filed the certificates of nomination for all of the Democratic candidates for Supreme Court in the First Judicial District for approximately ten years including Mr. Justice Silverman when he was nominated.

> "For all of which services he has never received compensation."

NOTES

1. The standard ways to avoid probate and administration are: (a) purchasing life insurance payable to your beneficiary (not to your estate); (b) placing your property in joint tenancy with right of survivorship in your joint tenant; (c) placing your property in a revocable trust during your life with instructions to the trustee to pay over to your beneficiary on your death; (d) the savings bank trust, which is a variation on (c); (e) giving your property away before you die. The trouble with each of these is that it too has disadvantages of one kind or another, incurs unanticipated costs in some situations, and occasionally produces surprising secondary consequences. Incidentally, none of these devices except (e) reduces estate or inheritance taxes, and (e) will, if the gift is substantial, make the donor liable for state and federal gift or succession taxes.

2. Probate reform in California has generally taken the form of complete removal of certain estates from the system. Probate Code Section 630 provides for summary disposition without administration where the decedent leaves no real property in California and the total value of his property in the state does not exceed $20,000, exclusive of any motor vehicle. The 1974 Legislature enacted the Community Property Set-Aside Law to allow the decedent's interest in community property to pass to the surviving spouse without administration of the decedent's estate.

3. A major effort at reform of the system of probate and administration is the Uniform Probate Code, approved by the National Conference of Commissioners on Uniform State Laws and by the American Bar Association in August, 1969. This Code was adopted by twelve states (not including California) as of 1978. Its principal effects are described in the Fratcher reading, below.

4. The argument might be (and frequently has been) made that the probate and administration process just described is no worse than other human institutions. It has its imperfections and is subject to abuse by unethical and criminal people, but—so the argument goes—it is necessary in order to pro-

tect the decedent, her property, her heirs and society from the even worse abuses that would occur without the protection provided by the system. The following excerpt should help you evaluate this argument.

William F. Fratcher, The English System: Simplified Probate in a Similar Context, in Edward C. Halbach, Death, Taxes and Family Property, St. Paul, Minnesota: West Publishing Co., 1977, pp. 152–153, 163–164.

In civilized societies, any system of wealth transmission incident to death is likely to involve all or most of the following processes: (1) determination of whether the decedent left an effective will; (2) appointment or confirmation of the universal successor, executor or administrator who is to conduct or manage the other processes; (3) identification and valuation of the property subject to the national estate or inheritance tax and determination of that tax; (4) identification and valuation of the property subject to the state or provincial estate or inheritance tax and determination of that tax; (5) identification and valuation of property burdened with community property rights, legitime, forced share or family allowance and determination of such rights, share or allowance; (6) identification and valuation of the property subject to claims of ordinary creditors and available for distribution to persons taking under the will or the statutes of descent and distribution; (7) collection of property and money in the possession of or owed by persons other than the universal successor, executor or administrator; (8) determination and payment of claims against the estate; (9) sale, lease, investment or encumbrance of estate property to dispose of perishables, secure income during administration, pay claims and facilitate distribution; (10) determination and execution of a plan of distribution in accordance with the will or the law governing intestate descent and distribution; (11) approval of the accounts and discharge of the universal successor, executor or administrator.

In the civil law countries, that is, virtually all civilized countries in which English is not a principal language and a few (e.g., Louisiana, Quebec, Rhodesia, Scotland and the Republic of South Africa) in which it is, all eleven processes may be carried out without judicial proceedings unless there is doubt or dispute as to legal rights or someone fails or refuses to perform his legal duties. Judicial proceedings are available in situations involving such controversy or nonperformance.

In most American states judicial proceedings are required for ten of the eleven processes, all except (3), the determination of the federal estate tax, even though there is no controversy or failure to perform legal duties. Moreover, judicial proceedings are commonly required in a court which is not an impartial tribunal because it is the state agency for collecting the inheritance tax and the court itself keeps a percentage of the tax. In states which have adopted Article III of the Uniform Probate Code and a few others all eleven processes except (1), proof of a will or intestacy, and (2), appointment and qualification of the executor or administrator, may be carried out without judicial proceedings in the absence of controversy or failure to perform legal duties. In most of these states (2) may be omitted and, in cases of intestacy, (1) also, if the intestate heirs are content to wait three or more years for clear title. At the end of the three years, however, a judicial proceeding is usually necessary to establish merchantable title in the intestate heirs. The Model Probate Code of 1946 was similar but the period was five years. Most states permit the omission of nearly all of the judicial proceedings in the case of very small estates. In all, judicial proceedings are available in situations of controversy or failure to perform legal duties.

England resembles the civil law countries in that the requirement of judicial proceedings is minimal in the absence of controversy or failure to perform legal duties. Even in small estates, however, persons claiming under a will cannot establish title without probate of the will and neither they nor intestate heirs can establish title without the qualification of an executor or administrator. Grants of probate and administration cannot be obtained without proceedings before a court official. In other words, processes (1) and (2) are required and are at least quasi-judicial. Judicial proceedings are available in situations involving controversy or failure to perform legal duties. . . . In civil law countries, wills are normally made in the presence and under the supervision of a notary public. In those countries a notary public is a lawyer with special training, whose office is quasi-judicial and charged with maintaining a registry of important papers. With these safeguards, there is no need for judicial proceedings for any of the processes listed at the beginning of this paper; the will has already been established before a public officer and deposited in his official files.

In England, as in the United States, wills may be executed anywhere without supervision by a lawyer or public officer. They are not usually delivered to a public office until after the death of the testator. This being so, determination of the existence or nonexistence of a will and of the identity of the person entitled to administer the estate must be made after death by someone. The English requirements for securing a grant of probate or administration from a registrar are geared to the essentials of protecting creditors and distributees. The fees charged by the registrar have been criticized but, apart from them, it is difficult to conceive of a scheme of administration of decedents' estates which would be simpler, faster or less expensive than that in use in England since 1926. . . .

Chapter 8

INHERITANCE, SUCCESSION AND DESCENT
IN EGYPTIAN LAW

James N. D. Anderson, "Recent Reforms in the Islamic Law of Inheritance," 14 Int'l & Comp.L.Q. 349, 1965:

> "There is no part of the sacred law . . . which is regarded with such pride by Muslims, or has been worked out by their jurists in such extravagant detail, such meticulous precision or such a spirit of religious devotion. There is even a famous dictum attributed to the Prophet that a knowledge of the shares allotted to the various heirs under this system is equivalent to half the sum total of human knowledge."

NOTE

In addition to exposing the students to Egyptian inheritance doctrine, these materials are designed to encourage speculation about the relationship between family structures, the economic and land tenure system, and inheritance law—a group of institutions which must harmonize with one another if society is to survive stably for several generations. Because these institutions are tending to diverge in modern Egypt, the materials are designed further to encourage thought about the problems of law reform and the particular characteristics of law reform when the law has a religious basis.

A. FAMILY STRUCTURE

Hani Fakhouri, Kafr el-Elow—An Egyptian Village in Transition, New York: Holt, Rinehart and Winston, 1972.

Family Structure in Kafr el-Elow. . . .

The smallest and least important family unit, from both an economic and social viewpoint, is the *bait* (nuclear family), consisting of a husband and wife and their unmarried offspring.

* * *

The nuclear family is usually part of, and subordinate to, a second and more complex family unit known as the *aila* (joint family), which consists of a husband and wife, their unmarried *and* married sons, their unmarried and divorced daughters, and any unmarried or divorced paternal aunts. At the head of the *aila* is the grandfather or, if he is deceased, the father. Traditionally, all members of a particu-

189

lar *aila* reside within the same *haush* (household), but each married son's nuclear family occupies a separate residential unit therein.
. . .

Upon the father's death, the *aila* is usually dissolved, the inheritance is divided among the sons, and each of the constituent nuclear families becomes the nucleus of a new *aila*. In other words, a constant cycle from nuclear to joint family and from joint family to nuclear families may be observed.

The *aila* is part of, and subordinate to, a still more complex family unit: *il aila il kabeera* (lineage). This third level of family extension may include five or more direct-line and collateral generations. Since the members of the *il aila il kabeera* do not reside in one household, as do the members of the *aila*, their relationships have greater social than economic significance. Each lineage has a head, referred to as *kabeer il aila* (the elder of the lineage), who speaks for the entire group, represents them at social events, and advises them on important matters.

The fourth level of family extension in Kafr el-Elow is the *hamula* (clan), which embraces all the lineages descended from a common ancestor. According to several elderly informants in Kafr el-Elow, until recently there were six clans in the village, varying in size and generational depth. There are many families in Kafr el-Elow, however, that have not been established in the village long enough to attain the generational depth required to form a *hamula*. The leader of a *hamula*, who is referred to as a *shaik* and whose position is usually hereditary, is expected to resolve disputes between members of his clan and to offer them hospitality when they visit his house.

Kinship Roles. In Kafr el-Elow, greater importance is placed upon paternal than upon maternal relatives, although they may both belong to the same lineage or *hamula* due to the prevalence of endogamous marriage in the village. If the maternal relatives are members of a different lineage or *hamula*, their subordinate position relative to the paternal relatives is even more conspicuous. This phenomenon is reflected in a proverb well known throughout the Arab Middle East—*il-khal imkhala wa-il-amm moowala*—the literal meaning of which is that after the father, the paternal uncle is the custodian of his nephews and nieces, rather than the maternal uncle. If a feud develops between paternal and maternal relatives, children are expected to identify with and support the former's cause. Nevertheless, children frequently have a strong attachment to their maternal uncles and aunts.

A married woman resides in her spouse's family home, where she plays a role subordinate to both her husband and mother-in-law.
. . . The man is unquestionably the head of the household and, as such, his authority is undisputed.

A wife with grown sons still plays a role subordinate to her husband, but she exercises considerable authority in rearing her children and in supervising the household activities of her sons' wives. Conflict frequently occurs if a mother-in-law shows partiality toward one or other of her sons' wives. The wife of a son who occupies a dominant position relative to his brothers by virtue of his superior education or greater financial contributions to the maintenance of the household, or the daughter-in-law who bears the largest number of sons, is very frequently the object of privileged treatment by a mother-in-law. . . .

In the village of Kafr el-Elow and throughout Arab countries, fathers guide and discipline their sons while mothers perform the same function for their daughters. Nevertheless, the fact that mothers frequently intervene to temper their husbands' disciplinary action against their sons and that fathers exercise a similarly protective influence with respect to their daughters helps to explain why boys tend to be closer emotionally to their mothers than to their fathers, and girls closer to their fathers than to their mothers, even though these feelings may not be overtly expressed.

In general, however, Arab children of both sexes feel deeply loved at home, in some cases are spoiled, not only by their parents, but also by grandparents, uncles, and aunts on both sides of the family. Paternal grandparents, in particular, tend to favor the children and to give them protection and refuge when their parents try to exercise discipline; it should be noted that their feelings are stronger for their son's male offspring than for either their sons' female offspring or their daughters' offspring (of both sexes). This phenomenon is expressed in the well-known Arabic proverb frequently recited to me by several grandfathers in the village of Kafr el-Elow: "Take care of your son's son and not of your daughter's son" (rabi ibn ibnak wa ibn bintak la). The rationale for this statement lies in the fact that the son's son not only perpetuates his father's family name, but is required to care for his paternal grandparents. That the daughter's son does not have a similar responsibility for his maternal grandparents reflects the greater strength of patrilineal than of matrilineal ties in the village.

Throughout his lifetime, a person is expected to accord courtesy and respect not only to his parents, but also to all older members of his hamula. In family gatherings he must play a subordinate role, socially and otherwise, to all older persons present, serving them food and giving them seats ahead of himself and all other younger members.

. . . Still another example of the importance of age is the fact that the oldest son often becomes temporary master of the household during his father's absence. Even when the father is at home, he frequently consults with his oldest son on various matters. The eldest son's prominent position in the family derives from the fact that he is the first sibling to help his father in the fields or to contribute his earnings from some other occupation to the family income. His younger siblings remain subordinate to him throughout his lifetime; it is his responsibility to care for them, even after his father's death. This behavior pattern reflects the traditional authoritarian character of interpersonal relations in rural areas of Arab countries. During the past few years, however, as the result of increasing educational opportunities, the main criterion determining one's status in the family has been shifting from age to education.

Daughters in Kafr el-Elow are expected to obey both their parents and their brothers. At the age of nine or ten, their mothers assign them certain household tasks such as cooking, cleaning, and caring for their younger brothers and sisters. After reaching the age of twelve, girls are not permitted to leave the house except to purchase necessities when no males are at home and can go instead. Walking through the village alone, they are expected to move swiftly and not to let their eyes wander. When accompanied by their fathers or brothers, they are supposed to walk ten to fifteen yards behind them so that strangers will find it difficult to learn their identity. Even in their homes, girls are not allowed to let themselves be seen by visiting strangers.

Harold Barclay, Study of an Egyptian Village Community, III Studies in Islam, 1966, pp. 143, 201, at 153–154.

* * *

Segmentation may result when a kinship group becomes so large and members so geographically dispersed that the expected social obligations which accompany membership in such a group can no longer effectively be performed, but this has so far not been a factor in Kaum segmentation. It is, further, a by-product of extreme endogamy and particularly of the preferred Arab marital arrangements of taking a father's brother's daughter as wife. A high incidence of such marriages occurring repeatedly means that in the course of several generations there appears within a lineage distinct constellations of closely interrelated kin which parallel agnatic segments of the lineage. At the same time the relationship between these segments is increasingly more distant and thus the link between them is weakened, provoking segmentation and the creation of separate lineages. Finally, segmentation is encouraged by internal quarrelling and disagreement coupled with the absence of a leadership that is able to prevent separation. Informants emphasized the role of strong and almost charismatic leadership in the preservation of the unity of a lineage and blamed segmentation on weak leadership. The early splintering of the Abū Bakr and Sa'īd lineages may be attributable to internal quarrelling and weak leadership.

NOTE

The author also suggests that the custom of marriage between a male and his paternal parallel cousin (father's brother's daughter) was so strong that the male had "priority" over this cousin. *Id.* at pp. 214–15.

QUESTIONS

1. Is the family pattern just described well adapted to nomadic herding life? to sedentary agricultural life?

2. Is the institution of polygamy consistent with the family pattern?

3. Do you expect this family pattern to survive for long in today's world? What will be the points of pressure?

B. INHERITANCE AND THE ISLAMIC REFORM

1. The Pre-Islamic Pattern

James N. D. Anderson, Law Reform in the Muslim World, London: University of London, The Athlone Press, 1976, pp. 147–148:

The system of agnatic succession, as this seems to have existed in pre-Islamic Arabia, was that a man's heirs were confined to males who were related to him through the male line. Priority between them was decided by three considerations: first, that descendants were given priority to ascendants, and ascendants to collaterals (and, among collaterals, descendants of the father to descendants of any more remote ancestor); secondly, that within each of these "orders" or classes the nearer in degree was preferred to the more remote; and thirdly, that where two claimants were equal in respect to both order and degree, then one related through both parents was preferred to one related only through his father. Thus a son, or even a son's son, was given priority over a father; a father, or even father's father, over a brother or nephew; and a brother of the full blood over a brother of the consanguine blood. In default of close relatives even the most distant agnatic cousins would inherit, for it was on a man's agnates that, in a tribal society, the primary responsibility to aid or avenge him lay. It is for this reason, indeed, that it is exceedingly likely that, originally, a father was given priority over a minor son, and that adult brothers were in all probability preferred to the father's father. But, however that may be, women had no right to inherit as such, although a dying man's request that part of his property should be given to a daughter, mother or wife would, no doubt, normally have been honoured by his agnatic heirs.

QUESTIONS

To understand the agnatic pattern, consider the following extended example (which will also be considered under Islamic doctrine):

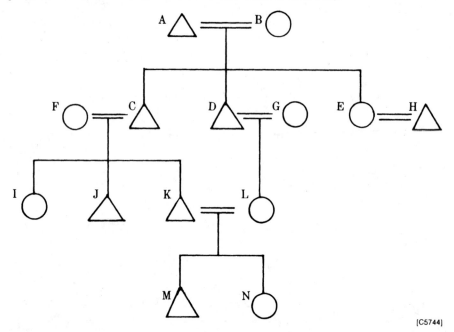

[C5744]

(△ stands for male, ○ for female, = stands for marriage, and the lines indicate descendents, A and B have two sons, C and D, and a daughter E, each of whom marries outside the immediate family. C and his wife F have two sons J and K and a daughter I. One of the sons, K, marries his paternal parallel cousin L, with issue M and N.)

1. Assume that the males die in a "natural" order, first A, then D, then C, then K. Assume further that sons share equally and that a son takes in preference to a son's son or to a brother. What happens to A's estate?

2. What if C dies before D?

3. Is this inheritance pattern suited to nomadic life? to sedentary agricultural life?

4. Under such a system, what maintenance responsibility must be assumed if all are to be cared for? How easy would it be to fulfill these responsibilities in such a system?

5. What interests are served by marrying a parallel paternal cousin under this agnatic pattern?

2. The Islamic Reforms Themselves

Noel Coulson, Succession in the Muslim Family, New York: Cambridge University Press, 1971, pp. 29–30.

The wife of Sa'd b. al-Rabi' came to the Prophet with her two daughters and said: "O Prophet, these are the daughters of Sa'd b. al-Rabi'. Their father died a martyr's death beside you in battle. But their uncle has taken Sa'd's estate and they cannot marry unless they have property." After this the verse of inheritance was revealed and the Prophet sent for the uncle and said to him: "Give the two daughters of Sa'd two-thirds of the estate, give their mother one-eighth and keep the remainder yourself." [1]

Sa'd's case embodies the essence of the changes introduced under Islam into the customary Arabian law of inheritance. In the tribal society of pre-Islamic Arabia the system of inheritance was designed to keep property within the individual tribe and maintain its strength as a fighting force. The tribe was patriarchal and patrilineal. Women occupied a subordinate and subjugated position within the group whose bond of allegiance was that of *'aṣabiyya*—descent through male links from a common ancestor. A woman who married into another tribe belonged henceforth, along with her children, to the tribe of the husband. The maternal or uterine relationship, therefore, lay outside the structure of tribal ties and responsibilities. In these circumstances the proper exploitation and preservation of the tribal patrimony meant, *inter alia*, the exclusion of females and non-agnate relatives from inheritance and the enjoyment of a monopoly of rights of succession by the male agnate relatives, or *'aṣaba*, of the deceased. Hence the initial appropriation of Sa'd's estate by his brother, as his nearest male agnate, to the exclusion of the wife and daughters.

Under Islam, however, the political and social scheme which had supported this customary system of succession was transformed. Politically, the bond of a common religious faith, with allegiance to the Prophet as the head of the community, transcended tribal ties and within the brotherhood of Muslims there was no place, in theory at any rate, for inter-tribal hostility or warfare. Socially, Islam emphasised the more immediate family tie existing between a husband, his wife and their children, and aimed at elevating the status of the female within this group. These changes are mirrored in the novel rules of succession introduced by Islam. Briefly, the Qur'ān establishes rights of inheritance between husband and wife and in favour of certain close female blood relatives—the mother, the daughter and the sisters—by prescribing fixed fractional parts (*farā'iḍ*) of the deceased's estate as their entitlement. Clearly, however, these rules in

---

1. This version of the Prophet's decision appears in *al-Mughni* of Ibn Qudāma, VI, 166.

themselves do not form a complete system of succession. In the Sunnî view they do not altogether abrogate but merely modify the customary system of succession by superimposing upon it a new class of legal heirs. The male agnates still inherit, but now after the satisfaction of the claims of those relatives nominated by the Qur'ān. Hence, in Sa'd's case, the brother inherited the residue after the Qur'anic heirs—the wife and the daughters—had taken their prescribed portions of one-eighth and two-thirds respectively.

Thus the Islamic law of inheritance rests basically upon the recognition of two distinct categories of legal heirs—the male agnates or 'aṣaba, the heirs of the tribal customary law, and the new Qur'anic heirs, who are called ahl al-farā'iḍ ("those entitled to prescribed portions"). Through the work of the early Muslim jurists these two distinct basic elements were gradually fused together into a cohesive system. But this process of amalgamation was not a simple one, and almost all the major complexities of the law stem from its dual basis and the attempt to harmonise the claims of these two categories of legal heirs.

The Koran, 4: 7 ff., 4: 176 (N.J. Dawood Trans. 4th ed., 1974) Harmondsworth, Middlesex: Penguin.

Men shall have a share in what their parents and kinsmen leave; and women shall have a share in what their parents and kinsmen leave: whether it be little or much, they are legally entitled to their share.

If relatives, orphans, or needy men are present at the division of an inheritance, give them, too, a share of it, and speak to them kind words.

Let those who are solicitous about the welfare of their young children after their own death take care not to wrong orphans. Let them fear Allah and speak for justice.

Those that devour the property of orphans unjustly, swallow fire into their bellies; they shall burn in the flames of Hell.

Allah has thus enjoined you concerning your children:

A male shall inherit twice as much as a female. If there be more than two girls, they shall have two-thirds of the inheritance; but if there be one only, she shall inherit the half. Parents shall inherit a sixth each, if the deceased have a child; but if he leave no children and his parents be his heirs, his mother shall have a third. If he have two brothers, his mother shall have a sixth after payment of his debts and any legacies he may have bequeathed.

You may wonder whether your parents or your children are more beneficial to you. But this is the law of Allah; He is wise and all-knowing.

You shall inherit the half of your wives' estate if they die childless. If they leave children, a quarter of their estate shall be yours after payment of their debts and any legacies they may have bequeathed.

Your wives shall inherit one quarter of your estate if you die childless. If you leave children, they shall inherit one-eighth, after payment of your debts and any legacies you may have bequeathed.

If a man or a woman leave neither children nor parents and have a brother or a sister, they shall each inherit one-sixth. If there be more, they shall equally share the third of the estate, after payment of debts and any legacies that may have been bequeathed, without prejudice to the rights of the heirs. That is a commandment from Allah. He is gracious and all-knowing.

*   *   *

They consult you. Say: 'Thus Allah instructs you regarding those that die childless. If a man die childless and he have a sister, she shall inherit the half of his estate. If a woman die childless, her brother shall be her sole heir. If a childless man have two sisters, they shall inherit two-thirds of his estate; but if he have both brothers and sisters, the share of each male shall be that of two females.'

Thus Allah makes plain to you His precepts so that you may not err. Allah has knowledge of all things.

NOTE

The Quran thus names nine heirs, each entitled to specific shares under specific conditions, most of whom are women and were not entitled to inherit under the tribal system. These nine "sharers" are the:

Widower (Husband)

Widow (Wife)

Father

Mother

Daughters

Full sisters

Consanguine sisters (by the same father)

Uterine brothers (by the same mother)

Uterine sisters (by the same mother)

Sunni jurists added to this list, by analogy:

True grandfather (the father's father, father's father's father, etc.—any male ancestor, how high soever, between whom and the deceased no female intervenors)

True grandmother (the mother's mother, mother's mother's mother, etc. and the mother of the father or of a true grandfather)

Son's daughter (including a son's son's daughter, son's son's son's daughter etc.)

The Quranic rules do not form a complete inheritance system—their incompleteness was suggested by Sa'd's case, quoted above, in which the Prophet said that Sa'd's brother was entitled to the residue after the Quranic heirs were satisfied. By analogy, then, the Quranic distributions were to be made and the remainder would be divided among male agnatic heirs according to the pre-Islamic tribal law. (There were various further categories, such as "distant kindred," also called "uterine kindred", who would take the residue if there were no male agnatic heirs).

This simple step of giving priority to the Quranic distribution did not, however, resolve all the problems left unsettled. There was still a problem of defining whether all Quranic heirs should take at the same time—for example, it did not seem appropriate for a grandfather to take while a father was still alive:

Abdur Rahim, The Principles of Muhammadan Jurisprudence, London: Luzac and Company, 1911, p. 350.

Then in order to regulate the number of relations who might inherit together the doctrine known as that of exclusion is applied. There are some persons, however, who are never totally excluded; the son, the father, the husband, the daughter, the mother and the wife. Exclusion may be sometimes partial. Exclusion is based on two principles: firstly, a person who is related to the deceased through another is excluded by the presence of the latter, for instance, the father excludes the grandfather, brother, and sisters and the son excludes the grandson, and this principle is extended among the residuaries so as to give preference to the proximity of degree, for example, a son excludes another son's son; secondly, the nearest in blood excludes the others, hence a relation of full blood always takes in preference to a relation by the father only, for instance, a brother excludes a consanguine brother or sister. To the first rule there is one exception, namely, that the mother does not exclude brothers and sisters from inheritance and the second rule is subject to the exception that uterine relations are not excluded on that ground. A person who is himself excluded may exclude others. It is also a general rule that when there is a male and a female heir of the same class and degree the latter will take only half of the former.

NOTE

With these new rules, it is now possible to chart the rights of the Quranic heirs, as shown in Table I.

Similar rules are needed to define the division of the residue, if any, among the residuaries. These are summarized in the following excerpt:

TABLE I. TABLE OF KORANIC HEIRS, CLASS I, SUNNITE (HANAFI) LAW

Heir	Share of One	Two or more Collectively	Entirely excluded by	Affected by	How affected
1 Husband — —	$\frac{1}{4}$		None — — —	Where no child or child of son h.l.s.*	Share increased to $\frac{1}{2}$.
2 Wife — —	$\frac{1}{8}$	$\frac{1}{8}$	None — — —	Where no child or child of son h.l.s.	Share increased to $\frac{1}{4}$.
3 Father — —	$\frac{1}{6}$		None — — —	Where no child or child of son h.l.s.	Made Agnatic Heir.
4 True Grandfather —	$\frac{1}{6}$		Father, nearer true grand-father.	Where no child or child of son h.l.s.	Made Agnatic Heir.
5 Mother — —	$\frac{1}{6}$		None — — —	Where (1) no child, (2) no child of son h.l.s., (3) *one* brother *or* sister, (4) husband or wife co-exist *with* father.	Share increased to $\frac{1}{3}$ of whole estate in cases (1) to (3); and $\frac{1}{3}$ of the *residue after* deducting husband or wife's share in case (4).
6 Grandmother h.h.s. (*Maternal*) —	$\frac{1}{6}$	$\frac{1}{6}$	Mother, nearer maternal or paternal grandmoth-er.	None.	
(*Paternal*) —			Mother, *nearer* maternal or paternal grandmoth-er, father, *nearer* true grandfather.	None.	
7 Daughter — —	$\frac{1}{2}$	$\frac{2}{3}$	None — — —	Existence of son — —	Made Agnatic Heir.
8 Son's Daughter —	$\frac{1}{2}$	$\frac{2}{3}$	Son, *more* than one daughter, higher son's son, *more* than one higher son's daughter.	Existence of (1) *only* one daughter, (2) *only* one higher son's daughter, (3) equal son's son.	Share reduced to $\frac{1}{6}$ in cases (1) and (2); made residuary in case (3).
9 Full Sister — —	$\frac{1}{2}$	$\frac{2}{3}$	Son, son h.l.s.,* father, true grandfather.	Existence of full brother	Made Agnatic Heir.
10 Consanguine Sister —	$\frac{1}{2}$	$\frac{2}{3}$	Son, son h.l.s., father, true grandfather, full broth-er, *more* than one full sister.	(1) Existence of *only* one full sister. (2) Existence of consan-guine brother.	(1) Share reduced to $\frac{1}{6}$; (2) Made Agnatic Heir.
11 Uterine Brother	$\frac{1}{6}$	$\frac{1}{3}$	Child, child of a son h.l.s., father, true grandfather.	None.	
12 Uterine Sister					

Note (1). In distributing the estate of a deceased Sunnite (Hanafi) Muslim we have first to see whether there exist any of the Koranic Heirs mentioned in Col. 1; then to see that they are not entirely excluded by the persons mentioned in Col. 3; then to assign to them the shares mentioned in Col. 2; unless their shares are affected by the persons mentioned in Col. 4; in which case, to assign to them the shares mentioned in Col. 5.

* h.l.s. = how low soever.

Asaf Fyzee, Outlines of Muhammadan Law, London: Oxford University Press, 3d ed. 1964, facing p. 396.

Asaf A. Fyzee, Outlines of Muhammadan Law, London: Oxford University Press, 3d ed. 1964, pp. 416–418.

Preference is given—

    A. first, to the *order*;

    B. next, to the *degree*; and

    C. lastly, to the *strength of the blood tie* (h).

    a. First—Order. A son and a father are both removed in the first degree from the propositus; but the son, as an Agnatic Heir, is superior, as he belongs to the order of descendants. The son, therefore, *qua* agnate excludes the father, who still has an independent Koranic share (*fard, farīda*) by which he gets 1/6.

The three 'orders' are: (i) Descendants; (ii) Ascendants; (iii) Collaterals. This shows the close kinship between the principles of the Hanafi law relating to '*aṣabāt*, and the ancient tribal law.

b. Next—Degree. This means that the Hanafi system does not recognize the right of representation; and also that the nearer in degree rigorously excludes the more remote. *P* dies leaving one son and the son of a predeceased son; the former takes everything, the latter nothing. On this point, the Hanafi (Sunnite) and the Ithnā 'Asharī (Shiite) schools are at one.

Similarly, in the line of ascendants, the father excludes the father's father, and a paternal uncle excludes a paternal uncle's son.
. . .

The second limb of the rule is the text of the *Sirājiyyah*: 'The nearest of blood must take.' *P* dies leaving Ali, a son, and Muhammad, the son of Husayn, a predeceased son.

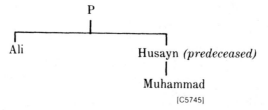

Ali excludes Muhammad, in all the schools. This is the direct negation of representation. . . .

c. Lastly—Strength of the Blood Tie. If the order and degree are equal, the full blood is to be preferred. A full brother excludes a consanguine brother; but the latter will exclude a full brother's son.

The foundation for the rule is a tradition of the Prophet quoted by the *Sirājiyyah*: 'Surely, kinsmen by the same father and mother shall inherit before kinsmen of the same father only.'

EXAMPLES

1. A man dies, survived by wife, one son, and one daughter:

    Wife takes Quranic share of 1/8, since there are children

    Daughter becomes an agnatic heir with son, but taking 1/2 as much.

    Hence, daughter receives 1/3 of residue: $1/3 \times 7/8 = 7/24$

    Son receives 2/3 of residue: $2/3 \times 7/8 = 7/12$

2. A woman dies, survived by husband and father:

    Husband takes 1/2 as Quranic heir in absence of child

    Father takes remainder of 1/2 (He would be the agnatic heir as well as a named sharer)

3. A woman dies, survived by father, father's father, mother, mother's mother, two daughters, and son's daughter.

Father takes 1/6 (Quranic heir)

Father's father (excluded by father)

Mother takes 1/6 (Quranic heir)

Mother's mother (excluded by mother)

Daughters 2/3 (1/3 each)

Son's daughter (excluded by daughters)

4. A man dies, survived by four widows and father

Four widows 1/4 (each taking 1/16)

Father 3/4 (as agnatic heir)

QUESTIONS

1. If a man dies survived by his wife, his mother, a son, a daughter and a full sister, to what share would each of the heirs be entitled?

2. Who are the intended beneficiaries of the Islamic reforms?

3. It is possible to trace through the inheritance pattern in the example on page 194 under Sunni law. Reasonable assumptions are that the parties die in the order A, B, D, G, C, F, K, and L, that E and H have children, that at the time of their death B has a uterine brother and no other living relative while F and G each have a living father, and that the estate consists of 1440 units. Under these assumptions, E takes 360 units, G's father takes 36 units, F's father 15 units, I takes 141 units, J takes 282 units, M takes 404 units, and N takes 202 units. How adaptable is this result to nomadic herding life? to sedentary agricultural life?

4. What does the example tell you about the role of marriage to one's paternal first cousin under this inheritance system?

5. Is a woman's inheritance position better or worse if she has children? What are the implications for family size and population planning?

6. Is Islamic inheritance law likely to be effective without religious backing?

NOTE

The rules presented so far are still not adequate to combine the Quranic and agnatic traditions. Some of the problems are quite technical. For example, see Asaf A. Fyzee, Outlines of Muhammadan Law, New York: Oxford University Press, 3d ed., 1964, pp. 408–410, for a discussion of what to do when the specified Quran shares add up to more than 1. You can also imagine the potential complications arising from paternal first cousin marriages, so that, for example, a decedent's husband is also her agnatic first cousin. The problem discussed in the following excerpt, however, should provide some insight into the way that Islamic lawyers handled legal argument—a way very different from the Western pattern.

Noel Coulson, Conflicts and Tensions in Islamic Jurisprudence, Chicago: University of Chicago Press, 1969, pp. 8–10, 12–19.

The particular problem of inheritance which I have chosen is the case of a Muslim woman who dies intestate and is survived by her husband, her mother, her paternal grandfather, her germane brother and two uterine brothers. How will her estate be apportioned among these surviving relatives?

* * *

. . . this problem, as with many problems discussed in the traditional textbooks of Islamic law, did not arise as an actual case but as a hypothetical one. It bears the name of Mālik's Rule, after the jurist who devised the case and solved it. I have perhaps said sufficient already to indicate that Islamic law in its developed form is a jurists', rather than a judges' law. It was expressed in textbooks as the doctrine of the jurists, not in law reports containing the decisions of the judiciary. It was a system where the academic lawyer controlled the practicing lawyer, where the chair was not only more comfortable but more influential than the bench. Consequently the problems which exercised the minds of the jurists were problems of pure law. Unhappily, perhaps, the speculation of the Muslim jurists lacks the color of particular factual situations and human circumstances, which, to the Western student of law at any rate, often demonstrate that truth is infinitely stranger than fiction.

* * *

The distribution of any estate under Islamic law must . . . depend upon the classification of the claimants either as Qur'ānic heirs or as residuaries. In our present case the husband, mother, and uterine brothers are Qur'ānic heirs, while the paternal grandfather and the germane brother are male agnate residuaries.

But this golden rule of distribution established by the Prophet's decision in Sa'd's Case is in fact, a secondary stage in the solution of a succession problem. It is clear that not every surviving relative of a deceased person, whether Qur'ānic heir or male agnate, can claim a share of the inheritance. The closeness or strength of relationship of one relative will put him in a superior position to other relatives. Rules of priority will serve to oust and exclude the weaker relationships so that the number of entitled claimants is reduced to manageable proportions. The primary task, therefore, is to determine which of the surviving relatives are entitled legal heirs. The rules of priority or exclusion which effect this owe very little to divine revelation— whether in the Qur'ān or the *sunna* of the Prophet—but derive almost entirely from the customary tribal law.

Roughly speaking, heirs fall into two groups with respect to priorities. A spouse, a child, or a parent is a primary heir and cannot be excluded from inheritance. More distant relatives are secondary heirs and may be excluded. But the overall cardinal principle is that only male agnates have the power to exclude other relatives from inheritance. The Qur'ānic heirs have no such power; they may be excluded themselves but can never exclude others. From this point of view they appear rather as supernumeraries. When they are not excluded from succession, they take their allotted portions and then leave the field to allow the real contest for succession to be fought out between the male agnates.

In our problem the husband and mother of the praepositus are primary heirs and cannot be excluded. On the other hand, no jurist doubted that the paternal grandfather, as an agnatic ascendant, was sufficiently superior to the maternal collaterals—the uterine brothers—to oust them from any right of succession. The only problem of priority, therefore, concerned the germane brother. Was he also to be excluded by the grandfather as an inferior agnate relative?

Juristic reasoning here started on the basis of the settled principle of customary law that the father of a deceased person ousts from succession the deceased's brother. From this some jurists derived the general principle that ascendants are a superior class of relatives to collaterals, and that therefore a grandfather, when he is the nearest surviving ascendant, takes the place of the father and, just as the latter would do, excludes the brother from succession. The majority view, however, laid emphasis not so much upon the class of relationship—ascendants or collaterals—but upon the degree of removal, from the praepositus, of the individual relatives concerned. Both the grandfather and the brother, it was argued, were at the second degree of removal from the praepositus, since there intervened between them and the praepositus the same common link, namely the father of the praepositus. And if class of relationship was to count as a secondary consideration, then it might be argued that it was the brother who had the stronger claim; for it was settled law that descendants as a class were superior to ascendants, so that it was the brother as the descendant of this common link (the praepositus' father), rather than the grandfather as the ascendant of it, who had the stronger tie with this common link and therefore, through it, with the praepositus himself. On these grounds the view prevailed that the grandfather did not exclude the germane brother but that both must rank on a parity as agnatic heirs.

Thus, from the Qur'ānic regulations and the Prophet's decision in Sa'd's Case, as supplemented by juristic reasoning based on the criteria of priority embedded in the customary law, emerges the systematic solution of the problem.

The uterine brothers are excluded by the grandfather. The husband takes his Qur'ānic portion of one-half and the mother her portion of one-sixth. The male agnates, the grandfather and the germane brother, stand on a parity and share the residue between them, each therefore receiving a share that amounts to one-sixth of the estate.

But now the inevitable discovery by the Muslim jurists, or at least of Mālik and his supporters, of the flaw in this solution. In the vein of hypothetical speculation to which Islamic jurisprudence is particularly prone, the question was put: "Suppose the grandfather had not survived the praepositus in this case? What then?" Then, in fact, the problem would have been identical with one which, it is recorded, some eight years after the death of the Prophet had confronted the then leader of the Muslim community, the Caliph Umar, and which acquired the celebrated title of "the Case of the Donkey" (al-himāriyya). Though this was not a holy or binding precedent, since Umar could claim nothing of the Prophet's contact with the Divinity, the decisions of the Prophet's companions, like Umar, always had a persuasive authority.

Faced with the task of distributing an estate between the deceased's husband, mother, uterine brothers, and germane brothers, Umar first decided that the golden rule of distribution as enunciated by the Prophet should be applied systematically—the Qur'ānic heirs should take their allotted portions and then the male agnates should take the residue. The result was most unfortunate as far as the germane brothers were concerned; for there was here no superior heir to exclude the uterine brothers, who, as Qur'ānic heirs, were entitled to a portion of one-third as a first charge upon the estate. And this, together with the husband's portion of one-half and the mother's of one-sixth, completely exhausted the estate, so that nothing remained for the germane brothers to take as residue. Now since the rights of the husband and mother, as primary heirs, could not be disputed, the case amounted to a straightforward competition for the remaining one-third between the germane and the uterine brothers—in other words a head-on clash between the old tribal heirs, the germanes, and the new heirs introduced by the Qur'ān, the uterines. And the germanes, despite their traditional preeminence as agnatic heirs, had been totally vanquished and forced to vacate the field empty-handed, chagrined no doubt by the reflection that a few years earlier they would have been the sole legal heirs in this case.

The germane brothers, however, proved to be persistent litigants. On appeal to Umar they contended that while they sought no advantage vis à vis the uterines from their agnatic tie through the father of the praepositus, at least they ought not to be penalized because of it and come off worse than the uterines. Did not the deceased, the uterine brothers, and themselves all have the same mother—this being the sole ground of the uterines' claim? Why then should not they, as germanes, be allowed to ignore their agnatic tie and, basing their claim on the fact that they had the same mother, at least stand on a parity with the uterines? Umar accepted the validity of this argument, reversed his original decision, and ordered that the third of the estate remaining after the claims of the husband and mother were satisfied should go in equal shares to both the uterine and the germane brothers. The name of this case, "the Case of the Donkey,"

is derived from the way in which the germane brothers expressed
their argument that they should be allowed to waive their agnatic tie
and, discounting their father, inherit because of their maternal connection. "O Commander of the faithful," the common version of the
case has them say, "suppose our father were a donkey of no account,
do we not still have the same mother as the deceased?"

Umar's decision in the Donkey Case was a controversial one, and
later jurisprudential debate upon it involved the whole question of the
role of human reason in the elaboration of Islamic law. One side
maintained that Umar's decision at first instance—the exclusion of
the germanes from succession, was the more systematically sound
and correct in principle. For them human reason was confined to the
regulation of new cases strictly by analogy with established rules of
divine origin. Here the relevant rule was the Prophet's decision in
Sa'd's Case—that after the Qur'ānic heirs had taken their portions
the male agnates succeeded to the residue. The germane brothers in
the Donkey Case were male agnates. And once a male agnate, always a male agnate. As a title to inherit it was a permanent quality
which could not be conveniently discarded in particular circumstances.

For the other side human reason was given freer rein. In particular cases strict analogy could occasion injustice, and it was then permissible to solve a problem on broad equitable considerations—this
necessarily rather vague and ill-defined process being given the label
of *istihsān*, or "equitable preference." For them Umar's final decision that the germanes should be allowed to inherit as uterines in
these particular circumstances was an acceptable equitable modification of the strict rule of analogy that they should always and only
inherit as male agnate residuaries.

Both sides, of course, were seeking justice in the individual case;
and it was axiomatic that justice was identical with the terms of the
religious law. The only question was what those terms were. It was
a division of opinion among the jurists of Islam concerning the relative significance of the letter and the spirit of an established rule
which seems not very far removed from the historical conflict in the
English legal system between the champions of the strict letter of the
common law and the advocates of equity.

To return now to our particular problem of succession: those jurists who accepted the principle underlying Umar's final decision in
the Donkey Case maintained that this precedent governed the present
case and therefore necessitated a revision of the systematic solution
that the grandfather and the germane brother should share equally
in the residue. If the grandfather were not present, they argued, the
germane brother would not inherit as an agnatic brother but as a
uterine brother. Why should this situation change simply because
the grandfather comes upon the scene? And if the status of the germane brother remains that of a uterine when the grandfather does

come upon the scene, then he must be excluded from succession, it being settled law that the grandfather excludes all uterines. In other words, why should the exclusion of the actual uterines by the grandfather not operate solely to his advantage? The germane brother did not exclude the uterines and would not inherit as an agnatic heir in the absence of the grandfather. Why, then, should he be allowed to do so simply because the grandfather is present, and to the latter's obvious detriment. Hence, the final solution of Mālik's Rule is to allow the grandfather to take the whole residue of one-third in these circumstances to the total exclusion of the germane brother.

My purpose here is simply to describe these juristic convolutions and not to criticize them. But the result is perhaps a little harsh on the hapless germane brothers. An equitable solution originally designed for their benefit is now systematically extended to their detriment. In the Donkey Case their father was deemed nonexistent, or at least asinine. Under Mālik's Rule their grandfather is now deemed nonexistent, or at least to have vanished temporarily, during an interim in which the brothers are deemed to have lost their agnatic tie. But the grandfather then reappears to exclude the brothers from inheritance and seize the whole residue of the estate. After this the germane brothers might well be in some confusion as to their precise status and identity.

QUESTIONS

1. How does the logical approach of the Islamic doctors differ from that of the American courts in dealing with similar uncertain questions, conflicts, and lacunae?

2. Do you agree with Professor Coulson's suggestion that the reason for the difference is that Islamic law is a scholar's law while ours is a judge's law? If not, to what do you attribute the difference? A different philosophy of the law (divine versus policy oriented)? The fact that the Quranic inheritance principles do not form a complete package? Something else?

a. Wills

Asaf Fyzee, Outlines of Muhammadan Law, London: Oxford University Press, 3d ed., 1964, pp. 349–350.

Testate Succession. The nucleus of the law of wills is, by common consent, to be found in a tradition of the Prophet, reported by Bukhārī:

> Sa'd ibn Abī Waqqās said: 'The Messenger of God used to visit me at Mecca, in the year of the Farewell pilgrimage, on account of (my) illness which had become very severe. So I said, "My illness has become very severe and I have much property and there is none to inherit from me but a daughter, shall I then bequeath two-thirds of my property as a charity?" He said, "No." I said, "Half?" He said, "No." Then he said: *"Bequeath one-third* and

one-third is much, for if thou leavest thy heirs free from want, it is better than that thou leavest them in want, begging of (other) people; and thou dost not spend anything seeking thereby the pleasure of Allah but thou art rewarded for it, even for that which thou puttest into the mouth of thy wife." '

Thus the policy of the Muhammadan law is to permit a man to give away the whole of his property by gift *inter vivos*, but to prevent him, except for one-third of his estate, from interfering by will with the course of the devolution of property according to the laws of inheritance. It is uncertain how the limit of one-third was fixed, but it has been suggested that Roman law may have influenced this decision. . . .

QUESTION

1. Would women be protected if the Prophet had given any other answer?

b. *Other Transfers and Maintenance Duties*

NOTE

There are many forms of transfer of wealth besides those made through succession or will. Islamic law recognizes great freedom to make gifts, so long as the gift is made immediately and is accepted by the recipient. Among the key exceptions are gifts made during a death-illness (which are valid only to the extent of one-third of the estate) and gifts made with an intention to defraud creditors. See Dinshah Mulla, Principles of Mahomedan Law, South Hackensack, New Jersey: Fred B. Rothman & Co., 17th ed., 1972, pp. 133–157.

As suggested by earlier questions, there are important care obligations.

Syed Ameer Ali, 2 Mohamadden Law, Lahore, Pakistan: The Punjab Religious Book Society, R. Kahn, 6th ed. 1965, pp. 384–385, 387–388.

MAINTENANCE OF RELATIVES

Pre-Islamic Customs. Among the pre-Islamic Arabs, no obligation existed on the part of either of the parents to maintain their children, nor was any relation bound to maintain another; on the contrary, we learn from history that, during that dark period of rapine, slaughter, and misery which immediately preceded the promulgation of the Islamic Laws in the Arabian peninsula, the birth of children imposed no obligations on the father. Female children, especially, were regarded as a misfortune, and were frequently buried alive to prevent their proving a burden to the tribe of their parents.

The Prophet's Rules. The Prophet of Islam strongly condemned this inhuman and unnatural practice, and declared the maintenance of children to be obligatory on the father; at the same time, he directed that where the parents were infirm and old and unable to support themselves, the children should provide for their support. He required the children to treat their fathers and mothers with respect and consideration; nor did he ever cease to repeat the words, which, according to MM. Perron and Sautayra, mark the great distinction between his legislation and all the ancient systems, that "a respectful and obedient child shall attain to heaven in the footsteps of its mother."

Primary Obligation on the Father. In consequence of these precepts, the Musulman Civil Law imposes on parents the duty of maintaining their children and of educating them properly. This obligation rests naturally upon the father; and the *Hedaya* declares in explicit terms that "the maintenance of minor children, rests on their father, and no person can be his associate or partner in furnishing it" (that is, share the responsibility with him).

In all cases concerning the maintenance of infant children consideration is chiefly to be paid to the interest of the children. So long as the father is able to maintain them, it is incumbent on him to do so, and debts incurred on their behalf by any person are recoverable from him. . . .

* * *

Principle. When a man is absent, but has left available property, the Judge may order maintenance out of the same for the following persons, *provided they are poor, viz.,* (*a*) the wife; (*b*) the male children, if young, or, if adult, unable to earn their own livelihood; (*c*) the female children whether young or adult (if unmarried); and (*d*) the parents.

A woman may compound with her husband for the maintenance of her minor children, but if such composition prove prejudicial to their interests, it would not be binding on the mother. In the same way, if a woman, on separating from her husband, were to agree to take charge of the children of the union and support them without requiring any assistance, and if she were to discover subsequently that she was unable to do so from poverty, the law would compel the husband to support his children, in spite of the stipulation entered into at the time of separation.

A husband is not liable for the support of the children of his wife by a former husband, unless he has expressly agreed to do so at the time of the marriage.

When children have means, they are bound to maintain their parents if in straitened circumstances, and it makes no difference in their liability whether the parents are Moslems or non-Moslems. Even should the parents be able to eke out a livelihood by manual labour, the children, if they have means, would not be absolved from the obligation of helping to maintain them.

QUESTIONS

1. How might gifts be used to circumvent the Quranic inheritance rules?

2. Should a legal system limit gifts in order to protect its inheritance law policies? Note that the U.S. system does so in order to protect the integrity of its death tax system, while European systems do so in order to protect their inheritance policies.

3. Are the maintenance obligations roughly those that are needed to make an agnatic system tolerable? Are they superfluous in the Islamic system?

c. *Eligibility to Inherit*

Syed Ameer Ali, 2 Mohamadden Law, Lahore, Pakistan: The Punjab Religious Book Society, R. Kahn, 6th ed. 1965, pp. 81–84.

Total Disqualification. Under the Musulman Law several causes debar a person from succeeding to the estate of the *propositus* notwithstanding that he may stand to the deceased in the relation of an inheriting kinsman.

The first is difference of faith technically called *kufr* (infidelity). *Kufr* means the *denial* of the unity of God (*wahdaniet*) and of Mohammed's Messengership (*risalat*), the two cardinal principles on which Islam is founded. Every person who acknowledges the Divine Unity and the Messengership of the Arabian Prophet is regarded as within the pale of Islam; nothing more is required. Those, however, who deny these cardinal principles are considered beyond the benefit of its rules. Accordingly, when a person dies leaving an heir who by birth or apostasy is a "denier", i.e., repudiates God's Unity and Mohammed's Ministry, such heir would be excluded from succession in preference to another who does accept those doctrines. Consequently, those who profess a different faith from Islam have no title to the inheritance of a deceased Musulman. So that if a Musulman die leaving behind him an heir who does not profess the Islamic faith, he is debarred from inheriting, even though he be nearest to the deceased. For example, if a man die leaving behind him a son who is a non-Moslem, and a grandson who is a Moslem, the son would be evicted from the succession, and the grandson would take the inheritance to the absolute exclusion of his father. . . .

Under the Sunni Law, a Moslem does not inherit from a non-Moslem, nor does a non-Moslem inherit from a Moslem. . . .

Difference of country involving difference of allegiance is also a bar to succession under the Sunni Law; but this is confined to non-Moslems only. *Moslems, among themselves, though owing different allegiance, succeed to each other.* The Musulman sovereigns, however, by special treaty regulations, have granted to the subjects of non-Mahommedan powers the privilege of acquiring property by inheritance in Mahommedan countries.

d. Inheritance of Status

NOTE

In general, due to Islam's fierce sense of the equality of all believers, there is no more inheritance of status than there is in California. Even the citizenship question posed in the California problem would have to be answered oppositely in traditional Islam, where the status of being a believer brought full civic rights in whatever Islamic area one happened to be, including the right to be a *qadi* or *mufti*. Louis Gardet, La Cite Musulmane, Vie Sociale et politique, Paris, Librairie Philosophique J. Vrin, 217, 4th ed., 1976. Today, of course, citizenship is a matter of nationality and is governed by laws comparable to those of other nations.

But, in addition to the likelihood, pointed out already, that an eldest son would inherit his father's leadership of a family and perhaps therefore the office of *umdah*, there are important inheritance-style issues associated with the office of Caliph or *iman*, an office now vacant. The formal issue at stake in the Shi'a—Sunni division was precisely whether the office should be hereditary, the Shi'ite position being that it should go to the descendants of Ali, (the Prophet's cousin, son-in-law, and companion), and the Sunni position that it should be filled by the consent of the learned men of Islam. Id. at 162–72, 196. Even the Sunni, however, agreed that a member of the Quraysh tribe, the Prophet's tribe, should be chosen if at all possible. Id. at 168–69. And, in practice, the Caliphate often became effectively hereditary.

Not surprisingly, the Shi'a have a completely different inheritance law, a single integrated system based on the Islamic reforms, contrasting with the Sunni effort to combine the Islamic and pre-Islamic concepts. The Shi'a system is much more oriented toward the nuclear family than toward the extended family as is the Sunni system. For details, see Noel Coulson, Succession in the Muslim Family, New York: Cambridge University Press, 1971, pp. 108–134.

e. Supporting Institutions

NOTE

Under *sharia* law, the duty of administering an estate lay on the State, acting through the *qadi*. The Islamic concept of administration, however, typically meant the distribution of the estate, often by the heirs themselves, rather than its administration as understood under modern law, for the estate never vested in the *qadi* and there was no equivalent of the modern executor or administrator. See Asaf A. Fyzee, Outlines of Muhammadan Law, New York: Oxford University Press, 3d ed., 1964, p. 368. Non-Muslim members of the Egyptian community would apply the law of their own religion, and there were some 14 sets of courts set up for the different religious groups. In case of conflict, e.g., different possible heirs of different religions, the case would go to the *qadi*.

The religious courts were abolished in 1956. At that time, there were 125 *qadi* courts, giving 200,000 judgments a year (including 30,000 against husbands for maintenance duties) for a community of 20 million Muslims. Under the abolition, responsibility for all issues was taken over to the regular courts. See Noel Coulson, A History of Islamic Law, Edinburgh, Scotland: Edinburgh University Press, 1964; Farhat Ziadeh, Lawyers, The Rule of Law and Liberalism in Modern Egypt, Stanford, California: Hoover Institutions Publications, 1968; Y. Linant de Bellefonds, La Suppression des Juridictions de Statut Personnel en Égypte, 8 Revue Internationale de Droit Comparé 412, 1956; Safran, The Abolition of the Shari'a Courts in Europe, 48 Muslim World 20, 1958.

Today, the procedure is very similar to that in the United States. At least for major estates, there is a formal judicial hearing to ensure that creditors are paid and to divide the assets. This proceeding may commonly be delayed until such time as the heirs wish a formal division. The court will prepare new land title documents, if necessary. In recognition of the sacred origins of the inheritance law, however, the Court formally "declares" the division rather than "adjudges" it. The *niyaba* has the responsibility to appear on behalf of minors in any inheritance proceeding.

QUESTIONS

1. What do the statistics on the *qadi* courts imply as to whether these courts were actually used by the average Muslim?

2. What are the implications of procedural integration for the future of the special laws maintained by the smaller communities? for the future of the *sharia* inheritance law?

C. EVADING THE QURANIC RULES

1. The Poor Person's Methods

NOTE

The Quranic rules discussed above clearly lead to the break-up of large estates, as actually happened in the 19th century. Such a result would be disastrous for a family holding a small piece of land. Historically, this problem has rarely been serious, for the small land holder or *fellah* has seldom been permitted to hold land for more than a generation or so. Egyptian history reveals a long series of land seizures and redistributions, usually for the benefit of new leaders, rarely for the benefit of the *fellah*. And during some eras, village lands were held in common and periodically redistributed (often on an annual basis) among the peasants. See Gabriel Baer, A History of Landownership in Modern Egypt 1800–1950, New York: Oxford University Press, 1962; Gabriel Baer, The Dissolution of the Egyptian Village Community, 6 Muslim World 56, 1959, pp. 56–66.

When land can actually be inherited, the small landowner has used two traditional techniques to evade the land fragmentation that would follow upon application of the *sharia*. The easiest is that of gift. As already suggested, a man could simply give his entire land to a suggested son. As long as he is not acting during a death-illness, the gift is a legally valid and effective way of transferring the property. This is not the only possible technique, however, as indicated by the following excerpts:

Hamed Ammar, Growing Up in An Egyptian Village: Silwa, Province of Aswan, Boston, Massachusetts: Routledge and Kegan Paul Ltd., 1954, pp. 23–24.

Whether to divide the land each attending to his share independently, or to keep it intact and farm it co-operatively, depends on the relationship between the heirs. Many factors are involved, such as the existence of half-siblings (brothers or sisters by the father only), where the possibility of division is very great, on the relations of wives and in-laws, on the father's treatment of his children while alive, and so forth. If the land as the symbol of family unity is tilled co-operatively, the married sisters then get their land produce according to their share as if they were renting it to their brothers. In cases of friction, the land is parcelled between the heirs, and boundaries are fixed; yet in the tax bill (wird) they are not divided and each has to pay his share of the tax, all being considered "heirs of so and so". This was originally a public demonstration of family unity. Lately, the separation of one's own land through official registration has been made an expensive task because of the fees required.

My informant, Mahmoud, told me that "in these days, more often than not, heirs insist on dividing the land, and this occasions the hottest disputes between brothers, sisters and relatives. Law-suits over land have sometimes cost people the land itself, when they had to mortgage more and more parts of their land to establish their rights over another part. No one 'yields a finger' in his share of his father's land; and above all, obstinacy and "the assertion of one's word" complicate the matter. Our life is mostly spent in setting my right and your right—hakki hakkak."

Harold Barclay, Study of an Egyptian Village Community, III Studies in Islam, 143, 201, 1966, pp. 147–48.

Broadly speaking, inheritance of wealth follows according to Islamic law. However, daughters are often prevailed upon to make a gift of their share of any landed property to their brothers. Thus, farm lands tend to remain in the hands of the same agnatic group and, in addition, a daughter acquires some insurance against the day when she might be divorced and thus put out of her husband's house. Because of her gift, a brother would feel more obliged to invite his sister to live with him.

QUESTIONS

1. Why doesn't the *fellah* follow the Quranic rules?
2. How effectively are the woman's interests protected under the actual practice? Note that the woman will normally marry into another family; if she is widowed or divorced, she will customarily return to her natal

family and be supported by her brother. How is your answer affected by the argument that the woman is freely entering a contract?

3. It is said that, toward the end of the '70s, women in the villages have become unwilling to enter the contract described in this section, and have insisted on division of the land. What reasons might explain this evolution? What effects might you expect on family structure? on land holdings? How would you respond if you were concerned about both the status of women and the fragmentation of land parcels, already often not large enough to support a family?

2. The Rich Person's Methods

Henry Cattan, The Law of Waqf, in Law in the Middle East, Mayid Khadduri and Herbert Liebesny, editors, Washington, D.C.: The Middle East Institute, 1955, pp. 203, 207–208.

Definition of Waqf. More than one thousand years ago, long before the birth of the doctrine of uses and trusts in English law, Islamic law recognized and developed a legal expedient under the name of waqf (plural, awqāf) which permitted an owner to settle his property to the use of beneficiaries in perpetuity, his intentions as to the devolution of the benefits, the determination of beneficiaries, and all other matters relating to the trust being observed and respected in the same manner as a legal enactment. The accepted definition of waqf according to the Hanafī school is "the detention of the corpus from the ownership of any person and the gift of its income or usufruct either presently or in the future, to some charitable purpose."

Property becomes waqf upon a declaration by its owner (the wāqif) permanently reserving its income for a specific purpose. Ownership is thereupon "arrested" or "detained": the wāqif ceases to be the owner of the property; it cannot be transferred or alienated by him, the administrator of the waqf, or the beneficiaries; and it does not devolve upon the owner's heirs. While waqf property must be dedicated to a charitable use, this purpose may be ultimate rather than immediate, as when the wāqif reserves the income to his children and their descendants in perpetuity, with a provision that upon the extinction of his descendants, the income shall be used for the relief of the poor or some other charitable object. . . .

* * *

The perpetuity of the waqf does not imply the perpetuity of its objects. It merely means that the appropriation of the income of the waqf to charity must be intended to be perpetual, even though the specific object of charity has not a character of permanency or perpetuity.

* * *

The effect of dedication of property as waqf is a relinquishment of ownership by the wāqif without any resultant acquisition of ownership by another person. Neither the wāqif nor his heirs after him have any proprietary interest in the corpus of the property. Moreover, the beneficiaries of a waqf have merely an interest in the usufruct, but none in the ownership of the waqf property.

* * *

The effect of inalienability is that property made waqf cannot be the subject of any sale, disposition, mortgage, gift, inheritance, attachment, or any alienation whatsoever. It can, as will be seen later, be leased because a lease implies the grant to the lessee of the right of user in consideration of a benefit without affecting ownership. There is, however, one exception to the general rule of inalienability. Waqf property may be exchanged for equivalent property; or it may be sold, subject to compulsory reinvestment of the price in another property, if the right of exchange or sale was originally reserved by the wāqif in the waqf instrument or, failing such reservation, if the original property falls into ruins or ceases to produce any benefit, so that the objects of the waqf cannot be fulfilled.

NOTE

In 1935, about one-seventh of Egypt's cultivated area was in *waqf*, for the benefit of about one-two-hundredth's of the population. The royal family received 515,000 to 1,000,000 Egyptian pounds of income annually from its *waqfs*. Louis Gardet, La Cite Musulmane, Vie Sociale et politique, Paris, Librairie Philosophique J. Vrin, 4th ed., 1976, p. 365.

QUESTIONS

1. How can the *waqf* be used to evade the Quranic rules?
2. Is the *waqf* approach likely to be more or less fair to women than the informal distribution arrangement previously described?
3. How does the *waqf* compare with a Western foundation?
4. How do the long-term social costs of the *waqf* system compare with those of the Western arrangements discussed under mortmain in the California problem?
5. Why would such an institution survive alongside the Quranic principles for so long?

D. TWENTIETH–CENTURY REFORMS

1. Inheritance Law

NOTE

Many of the traditional *sharia* inheritance provisions appear wholly unsuited to modern society. From an outsider's viewpoint, the central discrimination between men and women is a serious failure. This discrimination may not be so viewed from within the society, by men *or* by women, because the Quranic discrimination was clearly defined as a protection against a worse discrimination. This discrimination has not been reformed within Egypt and is unlikely to be reformed in the near future.

Other problems that are both more technical and more tractable arise from the fact that the traditional system provides relatively little protection for the nuclear family. One of the most basic difficulties is the prohibition against bequests to heirs, which means that a testator cannot augment the prescribed shares according to need. This scheme is particularly harsh in the case of the widow, who is limited to a mere one-fourth of her husband's estate (reduced to one-eighth if there are any children). There is no way the husband can supplement this amount in a will (although he could by earlier gift).

A second problem for the nuclear family derives from the traditional compromise between the Quranic heirs and distant agnates. If a man dies leaving a daughter and a distant agnate cousin, the estate will be divided equally between the two. While this no doubt made sense when the tribe was the basis of society, it may simply exasperate many contemporary urban Muslims who may not know these distant relatives at all well. This problem is even more pronounced in the case of the children of a predeceased daughter, who are excluded by any agnates, for they are not among the heirs explicitly mentioned in the Quran.

There are further problems of equity that may not have seemed important in an extended tribal life, but are likely to seem important now. The most pressing is that of orphaned grandchildren, who take nothing from their decedent grandfather in competition with their aunt or uncle. The result seems particularly unfair since it is the orphaned grandchildren that are most likely to need the money. A similar problem could arise under the principles of some of the schools according to which property went to a deceased's grandfather in competition with the deceased's brothers and sisters. When the grandfather then died, this very property would go to the first deceased's uncles and aunts rather than to his brothers and sisters.

Gradually, scholars throughout the Islamic world began to recognize these and other problems, and they began to search for ways to adapt the *sharia* to the requirements of the twentieth century. Since the *sharia* was regarded as immutable, however, the reformers had to accomplish their task without seeming to deviate from the tradition of strict adherence (*taqlid*) to the traditional law. To solve this problem, they eventually adopted four basic juristic methods of reform: (1) (mainly in the marriage area) simply removing certain cases from the jurisdiction of the *sharia* courts, a practice which had a long-standing precedent in the system of *mazalim* courts; (2) enacting legislation based not on a dominant opinion of any single school of jurisprudence, but rather on an eclectic choice of opinions from among the various schools and their many scholars, occasionally even combining two distinct views in a single provision (*takhayyur* and *talfiq*); (3) reinterpreting the original sources of law (*ijtihad*); and (4) promulgating administrative regulations that would add to, but not essentially contradict, the sacred law.

Leading the way among modern Islamic nations, Egypt enacted a series of laws dealing with family relations and inheritance between 1920 and 1952 which made use of all of the juristic methods of reform mentioned above. The most important laws regarding inheritance were Law No. 77 of 1943, which deals with intestate succession, and Law No. 71 of 1946, which deals with bequests. These laws in large part codified the well-known principles of the Hanafi law of inheritance (thus perhaps affecting the logic of future jurisprudence). Nevertheless, they also effected some changes in several of the most troublesome areas of the traditional law and represented the culmination of the movement calling for a new law to meet the needs of a changing Egyptian society. None, however, has even considered ending the fundamental discrimination of giving a man twice a woman's share. See James N. D. Anderson, Recent Developments in Shari'a Law IV, 41 Muslim World 186, 1951; James N. D. Anderson, Recent Developments in Shari'a Law VI, 42 Muslim World 33, 1952; James N. D. Anderson, Recent Developments in Shari'a Law VII, 42 Muslim World 124, 1952; Ibrahim Najjar, Formation et Évolution des Droits Successoraux au Proche-Orient, 31 Revue Internationale de Droit Comparé 804, 1979.

Article 37 of the Law of 1946 provides that a bequest in favor of an heir is valid and effective without regard to the consent of any other person. Such bequests may not, however, exceed one-third of the net estate. Article 30 of the Law of 1943 allows the spouse-relict to take the whole property when the deceased has left no Quranic, agnatic or uterine heirs, in contrast to the traditional scheme which excluded the widow from obtaining more than the Quranic share even if there were no other living relatives. It also gives benefits in certain cases to brothers and sisters excluded by grandparents. The problem of orphaned grandchildren excluded because of non-recognition of the doctrine of representation was solved in the 1946 law by a detailed system of obligatory bequests outlined as follows:

Tahir Mahmood, Family Law Reform in the Muslim World, South Hackensack, New Jersey: Fred B. Rothman & Co., 1972, pp. 58–59.

(i) If a person has grandchildren, male or female, whose link-parent died before or with such person, a bequest in their favour will be binding on such person. The amount of such bequest shall be equal to the share which the link-parent concerned would have inherited in case of his or her death just after the death of the propositus. It shall not, however, exceed the *bequeathable third* of the estate.

(ii) The grandchildren will not be entitled to an obligatory bequest if the grand-parent concerned has already made in their favour either a bequest or a gift *inter vivos* equivalent to what would otherwise be the amount of the obligatory bequest.

(iii) The principle shall be applicable, among the descendants of a predeceased daughter, to the first generation only, but among those of a predeceased son agnatic descendants how low soever will have its benefit.

(iv) While the entitlement to an obligatory bequest is being ascertained, each ascendant shall exclude his own descendants only.

(v) The share of each predecased descendant has to be divided among his or her heirs in accordance with the rule of "double shares for the males".

(vi) Where the propositus has already left a bequest in favour of an orphaned grandchild entitled otherwise to an obligatory bequest, if the optional bequest exceeds the amount of the obligatory bequest the excess will be governed by the general law of testamentary succession. On the contrary, if the amount of an optional bequest is less than that of the obligatory bequest, only the deficiency shall be made up.

(vii) In case of plurality of grandchildren, if an optional bequest has been made in favour of some of them only, the rest of them shall be given their due. The aggregate of the said optional bequest and what is given to the latter should not exceed the *bequeathable third* of the estate.

(viii) An obligatory bequest shall take precedence over an optional bequest. If necessary, the amount of an optional bequest shall be appropriated towards an obligatory bequest.

NOTE

In issuing the 1946 law, the government also issued a short explanatory memorandum, explaining its choice of non-Hanafi rules and divergent Hanafi opinions. The memorandum is reprinted in Majid Khadduri and Herbert Liebesny, editors, Law in the Middle East, Washington: Middle East Institute, 1955, pp. 185–186. In spite of all these careful efforts, opponents of reform were quick to note that the early scholars upon whom reliance was placed were often heretical scholars. Y. Linant de Bellefonds, Immutabilité du Droit Musulman et Réformes Législatives en Égypte, 7 Revue Internationale du Droit Comparé, 1955, pp. 5, 16. And in a general review of the personal status areas, a presidential committee, even in the Nasser era, could agree only on a draft less liberal than some already adopted in other Arab countries. Farhat Ziadeh, Lawyers, The Rule of Law and Liberalism in Modern Egypt, Stanford, California: Hoover Institutions Publications, 1968, p. 115. (The wife's rights in divorce proceedings, however, were liberalized in 1979; Decree Law No. 44 of 1979.)

When Egypt introduced a Social Security system in the 1970s, and drew up the schedule of what pensions to pay an insured person's survivors upon the insured's death, it did not, however, follow the *sharia* pattern. The only beneficiaries under the schedule are widows, widowers, parents, brothers, sisters, and children. The schedule makes no general distinction (like the two for one distinction of the *sharia*) between men and women in any context; the two take equal shares. There are, however, distinctions of a more specific form. Thus, sons take only if under age 21 (with certain exceptions going to disability, to being a student, or to just beginning to look for a job), while the analogous provision for daughters goes to whether or not the daughter is married. Similarly, a surviving husband receives a pension only if disabled; a test not applied to a surviving wife.   Law No. 179 for 1975; Promulgating the Social Insurance Law, Arts. 104–116; Schedule 3.

QUESTIONS

1. Of the various inheritance problems, which have been resolved?

2. Why is the body of inheritance law so hard to reform, particularly considering that it is so rarely followed?

3. Why do you think it was politically possible to make the Social Security system so different from the *sharia* pattern?

4. In light of the current Islamic revival, would you expect further reform in this area?

5. With or without the *sharia*, is there any body of inheritance law that Egypt could adopt that would respond to the combined pressures of the changing role of women, the possible shift to a nuclear family, and the increasing ratio of population to land?

2. *Waqf* Law

Gabriel Baer, A History of Landownership in Modern Egypt 1800–1950, New York: Oxford University Press, 1963, pp. 215–219.

The Reform of Waqf.   Discussion of the waqf question before the Military Revolution may be broken down into three basic approaches: preservation of the whole system without change; modification of its legal basis on the lines of the Waqf Law of 1946; [1] the abolition of *waqf ahlī* [family waqf; one whose current income is still received by private individuals].   No demand for the liquidation of *waqf khairī* [charitable waqf; one whose current income is actually going to charitable purposes] was made in Egypt; Mirrīt Ghālī expressed the view that it would be desirable to abolish waqf altogether, but he also felt that the time was not yet ripe to press for the abolition of *waqf khairī*, and that this question was subordinate to that of *waqf ahlī*. All those who expressed views on the question, whatever their opinions on waqf as such, were unanimously agreed that the system of private *nazirs* had to be reformed.   Indeed those who opposed reform of waqf as a whole were the most eager to put all the blame on the bad management and corruption of the *nāzirs* [trustees].   But none of them expressed the view that the state or some official agency should take over all *khairī* waqfs and do without the private *nāzirs*.   Furthermore nobody ever mentioned the royal waqfs, except for some eulogies in the Senate debate on the draft waqf law.

There were several important differences between the discussion of the land-distribution question and attitudes towards waqf.   First, the waqf problem was broached much earlier—in the 1920's.   Secondly, even before the Military Revolution of 1952, fundamental reforms were enacted in the Waqf Law of 1946.   However these two differ-

---

1. Described below in Ziadeh excerpt.

ences are the outcome of a third, which appears to us to be the principal one. Whereas all the parties represented in parliament were opposed to any reform in the distribution of land, supporters of each of the three basic approaches mentioned above could be found in almost every one of them.

Two of the most striking examples of conflicting views within a single party are furnished by the Liberal Constitutionalist Party and the Wafd. Among the founders of the former were three men, each of whom represented one of the three basic approaches: Muḥammad 'Alī 'Allūba; Shaikh Muḥammad Bakhīt, the former Mufti of Egypt, and Ibrāhīm al-Hilbāwī. 'Allūba Pasha, a former Minister of Waqfs, elaborately explained his arguments in two lectures given in 1926 and 1927 and which appeared in full in *L'Égypte Contemporaine*, and in his book *mabādi' fī-s-siyāsa al-miṣrīya* published in 1942. 'Allūba, also, submitted to the Egyptian parliament in 1927 a draft law including a rule that any *waqf ahlī* to be created in future must be a temporary one, for thirty years at most. In his lectures he denied the religious basis of waqf ahlī and tried to expose its economic and social disadvantages; and in *mabādi' fī-s-siyāsa* he suggested that legal heirs should not be excluded as beneficiaries; that *ahlī* waqfs founded before a certain date should be annulled; and that beneficiaries should be allowed to divide a property into separate waqfs according to the share of each in the income.

'Allūba's most outspoken opponent during the 1920's, was his fellow party member, Shaikh Muḥammad Bakhīt. In two lectures, delivered in reply to those of 'Allūba, he tried to refute the claim that the waqf had no religious basis and that it was economically harmful, and at the same time to establish its vital importance for the existence of charitable, educational, and health institutions and for the maintenance of noble families. Were it not for being waqf, he said, many properties would have fallen into the hands of foreign money-lenders.

* * *

In contrast to these divided opinions about waqf in the principal political parties there were two groups with a clear and unified policy. The first consisted of the royal family and its supporters, who opposed any change whatever. In 1943, when the draft provisions of the law for reform of the waqf system had become known, Prince 'Umar Ṭūsūn wrote an open letter to the Prime Minister strongly opposing it on the ground that it restricted the freedom of landowners to do what they liked with their property, and that its spirit was one of disregard for the property of the great families. In the Senate debate royalists such as Muḥammad Zakī al-Ibrāshī and Muḥammad Hilmī 'Īsā opposed some of the most important reforms and praised the usefulness of *waqf ahlī*.

The second group were the same intellectuals who stood for moderate land reform, the most prominent among them being once again Muḥammad Khaṭṭāb, Ibrāhīm Bayūmī Madkūr and Mirrit Ghāli. All three demanded the liquidation of existing *ahlī* waqfs and a ban on the establishment of new ones.

Apart from these two groups, however, there was no clear-cut relation between the position of individuals or organizations on the land reform and on waqf reform. Some of those who opposed any limitation of large landed property demanded the abolition of *waqf ahlī*—for example 'Alī Shamsī—but others only urged its reform, such as Muḥammad 'Alī 'Allūba. The Sa'dist Party, in August 1952, still opposed land reform, but demanded the abolition of *waqf ahlī*. In 1944, however, one of its most prominent leaders, Maḥmūd Ghālib, opposed most of the important provisions of the proposed Waqf Law. On the other hand the Muslim Brotherhood and the parties of the Left, who stood for the confiscation or limitation of existing estates, did not mention the waqf question at all, probably for different reasons.

A number of questions may be asked in connexion with the discussion of the waqf problem as described above. First, why did it start so much earlier than the controversy over the distribution of landed property? Secondly, why did it result in the 1946 law which reformed the waqf system, while before the Military Revolution no reform whatsoever was carried out in the distribution of landed property? Thirdly, how to explain the fact that parties opposing any reform in the distribution of landed property counted among their members advocates of quite extreme views on waqf, and that sworn enemies of land reform adopted radical demands in connexion with waqf?

At first glance the phenomenon may appear surprising, since the waqf was considered a religious institution, and one might suppose that to reform such an institution would be more difficult than to carry out reforms unconnected with matters of belief and religion. It should be noted, however, that even among the *'ulamā'* there was no uniform opinion on waqf, and many respected and influential *'ulamā'* disputed the religious element of *waqf ahlī* and even of *waqf khairī*. These views were part of the growing intellectual activity of the Muslim 'modernists' in Egypt, who attempted to prove that Islam in its original form was not incompatible with liberal, Western ideas, and that it is only later corruptions that have resulted in beliefs and practices which are harmful from the modern point of view. Many of the writings on waqf in the 1920's and 1930's correspond to this trend; their authors advance the thesis that waqf, or at least *waqf ahlī*, has no religious basis whatever, and can therefore be reformed according to modern requirements.

A fuller explanation must, however, be sought elsewhere. Whereas the demand to redistribute landed property was directed against the class of large proprietors whose influence in Egyptian society, parliamentary life, and political parties was predominant, within this class there were certainly a large number of deprived heirs, whose ancestors' property had been endowed as waqf, or beneficiaries of waqf property who suffered from limitations imposed by the *waqfiya* or by waqf law. The modification of the laws governing *waqf ahli* or even its liquidation would, therefore, have adversely affected only a part of the Egyptian ruling class, while the other part would have benefited. This also explains why the debate centred on *waqf ahli*. The abolition of *waqf khairi* would have harmed part of Egypt's "noble families", while no other part of the upper class would have benefited by it.

Farhat Ziadeh, Lawyers, The Rule of Law and Liberalism in Modern Egypt, Stanford, California: Hoover Institution Press, 1968, pp. 133–135.

In 1936 the Waqf Committee of the Chamber of Deputies returned to the attack and proposed legislation that would prohibit the constitution of any new family *waqf* and would limit the properties of charitable *waqfs*. This proposal was sidetracked, however, by the formation, on December 9, 1936, of a Personal Status Committee, composed of *ulema* and secular lawyers, to prepare a comprehensive code of personal status and such related matters as *waqfs*, inheritance, and testamentary dispositions. The results of the committee's labors were the Law of Inheritance (Law 77 for the year 1943), the Law of Testamentary Dispositions (Law 71 for the year 1946), and the Law of the Rules of Waqf (Law 48 for the year 1946). This last law incorporated some of the ideas previously advanced by 'Allūbah and his colleagues and provided, almost without precedent, that any future *waqf* (except a mosque or cemetery) would continue to be revocable by its founder, that any charitable *waqf* (except one in support of a mosque) might in the future be either permanent or temporary, and that family *waqfs* should henceforth last no more than sixty years or two generations after the death of the founder. Certain other reforms touching upon a variety of points which had given rise to complaint were carried out, although in most cases the reformers had to seek refuge in the opinion of some medieval jurist, or even a combination of opinions, that could be construed as agreeing with modern requirements.

Although the secular lawyers were not completely successful in their campaign to abolish family *waqfs*, they got most of the reforms they had been clamoring for, and the conservative elements could point out with pride that one of the main institutions of the *shari'ah* had been kept intact in form if not in content. With minor exceptions, there was general contentment with the compromise solution. Even the Lebanese followed the Egyptian example in the reform of their family *waqfs* in 1947. Nevertheless, the revolutionary government which came to power in Egypt in July, 1952, completely abolished family *waqfs* that autumn by Law 180. In the explanatory memorandum accompanying the law, dated September 14, 1952, the abolishment of family *waqfs* was tied to the earlier Agrarian Reform

Law, which had limited individual land holding to 200 *feddans* and provided for the distribution of land to peasants. Since many family *waqfs* consisted of extensive agricultural acreage, *waqfs* had to be abolished to make the agrarian reform more effective and to permit all types of land to be treated on an equivalent basis. The memorandum also advanced the economic arguments which had been leveled against family *waqfs* by two generations of lawyers. No attempt was made to justify the reform in terms of the *sharī'ah* or the opinion of any individual authority. The temperament of the new military regime was alien to the casuistic approach; all the memorandum said in this regard was that the freeing of the property opened up the field of dignified labor to the poor, which is "the highest form of righteousness and approach to God."

NOTE

The Ziadeh book also contains a detailed discussion of the early political background of *waqf* reform at pp. 127–33. In evaluating this reform it should be emphasized that there was some dispute about the solidity of the traditional basis of *waqf* law. See Joseph Chlala, La Suppression du "Wakf Ahli" en Égypte, 5 Revue Internationale de Droit Comparé 682 (1953).

Further, you should note that the 1952 Revolutionary Government actions were part of a combined program of *waqf* abolition, land reform, and creation of agricultural cooperatives. The land reform—which clearly required *waqf* reform—was carried out in several steps. The Agrarian Reform Law of 1952 limited land ownership to 200 *feddans* per person and the *waqf* reform of the same time abolished *waqf ahli*, allocating the property to the families holding it, not the ultimate charitable beneficiaries, and counting this allocated property against the ownership maximum. (One *feddan* equals 1.038 acres.) A 1958 amendment added a limit of 300 *feddans* to the land that a person and his dependents could hold, and a 1968 amendment lowered the individual limit to 100 *feddans*. These limits were further reduced to 50 *feddans* per person and 100 *feddans* per family in 1969.

Lands held in excess of these limits, as well as all *waqf* agricultural lands administered by the Ministry of Waqfs and all lands owned by foreigners, were taken over by the Ministry of Agrarian Reform for distribution, which leased or granted it to small farmers. Newly reclaimed desert land is being distributed to agricultural school graduates. The total amount of land distributed by the Ministry, including land which belonged to the monarchy, was about one million *feddans*. Not surprisingly, with the abolition of *waqf ahli*, essentially no new land has since been placed in *waqf*. By 1965, 94.5% of the landowners in Egypt owned less than 5 *feddans* each, and the total amount of land which they owned was 57.1% of all agricultural land. Those who owned up to 100 *feddans* constituted only .10% of the landowners, but they owned 6.5% of all agricultural land. Farhat J. Ziadeh, Law of Property in Egypt: Real Rights, 26 Am.J.Comp.L. pp. 239, 270, 1978. See generally Gabriel Saab, The Egyptian Agrarian Reform 1952–1962, Oxford: Oxford University Press, 1967.

But, for the government, the central goal may have been the creation of agricultural cooperatives, as a means of achieving some political control over the rural regions. These cooperatives were production-oriented, with the power to provide loans, to provide seeds and equipment and the like, to assist in choosing the farming techniques, and to sell the crops. Although voluntary in other areas until 1962, they were compulsory from the beginning in the areas where land was redistributed as a result of land reform. The cooperatives have not worked out well. At least early on, they have been said to be heavily under the control of the local bureaucracy, which in turn often maintains a close relationship with the families that had been large land owners. There is also said to be significant corruption. It is these institutions, however, which *infitah* has placed under question and which are more recently said to be empty shells. For background, generally on the pre-*infitah* pattern, see Bassam Tibi, Agrarreform und Genossenschaftswesen in einen Entwicklungland; Ägypten 5 Verfassung Und Recht in Übersee 57, 1972; Ottfried C. Kirsch, Agricultural Cooperatives as an Instrument of Agricultural Policy—Experience with Cooperative Promotion of Production in Egypt, 10 Verfassung Und Recht in Übersee 255, 1977; Raymond Baker, Egypt's Uncertain Revolution Under Nasser and Sadat 196–217, 1968.

QUESTIONS

1. How does the 1956 *waqf* reform differ from the rule on perpetuities in its intent and effect?

2. Could any but a revolutionary government have abolished the *waqf ahli*?

3. Why was the *waqf* law easier to reform than the inheritance law?

4. Would you see any value in reforming the *waqf khairi*?

5. What factors, other than the Socialist ideology of the period, might have motivated the coupling of the cooperatives with land reform?

Chapter 9

INHERITANCE AND FAMILY SUCCESSION
IN BOTSWANA

A. INTRODUCTION

NOTE

The aim of this chapter is to introduce the reader to some aspects of inheritance of property and succession to family headship among the Tswana of Botswana. The materials of the chapter have been selected to emphasize the following points:

Inheritance, as the transmission of property from one generation to another, is not something that occurs following death, but is a process that occurs over the lifetime of an individual and of the lifetime of the families of which he or she is a part. This is especially true among the Tswana, where devolution of property occurs over the lifetime of an individual and is closely linked to the development cycle of the family.

The chapter also explores how inheritance and succession to family headship are related to the predominately patrilineal nature of Tswana society and to its social and political structure, including family forms and marriage forms.

The case materials show that inheritance is not simply a "legal" matter of defining rights and responsibilities pertaining to the transmission of property and settling disputes about those rights. But devolution, including inheritance, is also a political process in that it is concerned with power and the management of resources—both human and material.

There is discussion of how patterns of devolution and guardianship are changing under contemporary conditions. "Conflict" of laws (i.e. conflict of the applicability of indigenous and imposed Western law) is laid bare in case material on the right to testation.

B. TSWANA TRADITIONAL INHERITANCE OF PROPERTY

1. Forms of the Family

Isaac Schapera, A Handbook of Tswana Law and Custom. Second edition. London: Oxford University Press, 1955, pp. 12–16, 18–19. Some footnotes omitted. Editor's interposed headings and summary in brackets. Footnote renumbered.

[*Overview of Residentially-based Groups.*] In addition to the territorial units formed by the districts and villages, the people of each

224

tribe are divided into several different groups all derived ultimately from the relationships established by blood and by marriage. The smallest of these groups is the *family*, consisting of a man, his wife or wives, and their unmarried children, own or adopted. One or more families make up a *household*, the group of people living in the same collection of huts. Several closely related households, living together in the same part of the village, make up the *family-group*. One or more family-groups, organized together into a well-defined local administrative unit of the tribe, make up the *ward*. . . .

Among the Kgatla and the Ngwato, finally, the wards are grouped together into the major divisions of the tribe here termed *sections*.

The two units most clearly defined in all the tribes are the household and the ward. The family, the family-group, and the kindred are less conspicuously demarcated. The family is merged in the household, and the family-group in the ward; . . . For convenience in exposition, we shall commence our description with the household, the smallest well-defined social unit in the tribe. . . .

[*The Household.*] Typically, the household consists of a man with his wife or wives and dependent children, together with any other relatives or unrelated dependants who may be attached to him. Its actual size and composition depend largely upon the rank, wealth, and age of the household-head. It may consist simply of husband and wife, with their dependent children, own or adopted; or of a widower with his second wife, and his children by one wife or both; or of a polygamist, with two or more wives, and his children by each. Often it may also contain unmarried dependants, such as the husband's younger brothers or sisters; or married dependants, such as sons, brothers, and possibly even sisters or daughters, with their respective spouses and children. Occasionally, too, there may be servants or other unrelated strangers living in the group.

Except in the case of polygamous households, the members of a household all live together in the same homestead or dwelling-enclosure (*lolwapa, lapa*). This consists of a number of huts and granaries, enclosed within a courtyard by a low rectangular wall of dried mud, a wooden palisade, or a reed fence. Chiefs and the wealthier . . . people nowadays * frequently have rectangular dwellings after the European style. . . .

. . . Each married couple in the household has its own hut, which it generally shares with its infant children. Young children of both sexes may share another hut, or live together with an older female relative, . . . while adolescent children or young unmarried people have separate huts according to their sex.

***

* [Editor's note: Throughout these materials keep in mind that Schapera's original fieldwork was done in the 1930's and continued until 1950. So his "nowadays" refers to a time period thirty to fifty years ago.]

[*The Polygynous* Household.*] It is seldom nowadays that the household is based upon a polygamous family. Probably even in the olden days most of the men had only one wife; and few commoners had more than two or, in exceptional instances, three. Large polygamous households, of four wives or more, were met with only among the Chiefs, their relatives, important headmen, and other prominent or wealthy people. Under modern conditions, polygamy is obviously declining. This is due in the main to the spread of Christianity. All mission societies operating in the Protectorate forbid their converts to have more than one wife, nor will they allow a woman belonging to the Church to become the wife of a polygamist. The Administration, by imposing additional taxation upon polygamists, has made it even more difficult for them to exist in large numbers, at least openly. Educational progress, and contact with Western civilization generally, have also contributed to the widespread abandonment of the practice. Accurate statistics are not available, but it is doubtful if at the present time more than five per cent of Tswana men have more than one wife, while the number with three or more is very small indeed. Nevertheless, polygamy is still a recognized institution and, except among the Ngwaketse, has nowhere been explicitly forbidden. . . .

The wives in a polygamous household are normally ranked in order of priority of marriage. The first wife married is the "great wife" (*mosadi o mogolo*). The next wife is spoken of simply as the "second wife" (*mosadi wa bobedi*); then comes the "third wife" (*mosadi wa boraro*); and so on.[1] Any junior wife, irrespective of her ranking, may also be spoken of as *mogadingwana* or *mosadi o mmôtlana* (the "small wife"), in contrast with the "great wife". . . .

[*The Seantlo.*] Any wife who had no sons of her own might . . . by arrangement with her husband and parents, formally bring in a *seantlo* (lit., "one who enters the hut") to bear a son in her "house". The husband could similarly take a *seantlo* for any wife

---

* "Polygamy" means "plural marriage" and it refers to both types of plural marriage: "polyandry" (one woman, several husbands), and "polygyny" (one man, several wives). Because polyandry is unknown in Africa, I use the exact term in referring to the form of plural marriage that is characteristic of Africa, which is polygyny. The layman is more likely to use the broader, less technical term, polygamy. Because Schapera wrote his book, A Handbook of Tswana Law and Custom for use not only by anthropologists, he used the term most familiar to his intended audience.

1. The only exceptions to this rule of ranking occur when a man, after marrying one or more wives, either marries the girl to whom he was first betrothed, as in cases of infant betrothal, or marries the daughter of his maternal uncle (*malome*). This new wife then takes precedence over the rest, and acquires the corresponding privileges, just as if she had been married first. Among the Ngwato, where infant betrothal was formerly practised on a large scale, the first wife married was known as *mmamoleta*, because she "waited for" (*go leta*) the great wife; and she ranked as the second wife in the household. The great wife when married was known as *mmadikgomo* (mother of cattle), because the cattle due to her parents as *bogadi* (bride-wealth) had to be given out before those for any other wife.

who had died without male issue. The *seantlo* was generally the younger sister or some other close relative of the woman concerned. She was socially identified with the latter, to whose "house" any children she might bear were regarded as belonging.

[*The "House".*] Each wife in a polygamous household has her own establishment or "house" (*ntlo, lolwapa*). By this is meant the social group comprising the wife herself, her children, and any other people directly attached to her. Each house is distinct from and independent of the rest, and has its own property in the form of cattle, fields, and household utensils, which are inherited within that house. An affiliated wife, however, is linked to the house of the wife to whom she is affiliated. Failing a direct heir by any senior wife, the eldest son of her affiliated wife succeeds to the property of her house, in preference to a son by the senior wife in another house. But every wife, whether senior or affiliated, generally has her own dwelling. The dwelling-enclosures of the various wives are as a rule built on to one another, but are not arranged in any specified order.
. . .

[*The Family-Group.*] Several different households, whose members are all closely related to one another, and which occupy the same part of the village or ward settlement, make up a family-group.
. . .

*   *   *

The family-group varies considerably in size and composition. Basically it consists of several families, whose menfolk are all descended in the male line from the same grandfather or great-grandfather. There may, however, also be a few married female relatives (aunts, sisters, or daughters of these men), with their husbands and children; possibly also one or more nephews (sisters' sons), who have come from their own fathers' homes to live permanently with their mothers' people; and in rare instances also one or more relatives (brothers or sisters) of a woman married into the group. Finally there may be one or more household servants or other unrelated strangers accepted into the group with their respective families. The family-group, therefore, is fundamentally, but not exclusively, a group of families closely united by blood or by marriage.

. . . The grandsons and great-grandsons of a man need not necessarily all live together. Some may have gone to live in other parts of the village, or even in other villages, generally with their wife's or mother's people. They are still connected by ties of kinship to their relatives remaining behind in the paternal home; but the latter are also specially linked together by ties of common residence. . . .

The family-group is the setting for the more important domestic events and activities of its constituent families. It deals as a unit with such purely domestic affairs as betrothal and marriage negotiations, the organization of feasts, and the division of an estate—matters regarded as concerning, not only one particular family, but the group as a whole. Its members co-operate in such major tasks as building and thatching huts, clearing new fields, weeding, and reaping; and they help one another with gifts of food, livestock, and other commodities. If big enough, the group may have its own little *kgotla*,* presided over by its hereditary elder (*mogolwane*), the senior male descendant of the common ancestor whose name it bears. This man, in conjunction with the other adult members of the group, arbitrates over any disputes occurring between any of its people; while, should any member be involved in a lawsuit with an outsider, he is assisted by the rest in the preliminary discussions and in the actual hearings at the tribal courts.

NOTE

[*Paternal Relatives.*] [Because the Tswana are a patrilineal society, it is to the patrilineal relatives that one has the firmest obligations and from whom, in turn, the greatest obligations are owed. Schapera points out that it is to the closest agnates, particularly those of the family group, that the mutual obligations are met most fully and conscientiously.

[Relationships with maternal relatives take on a different—and special—flavor.]

[*Maternal Relatives.*] *Ga etsho mogolo* is the place from which a man's mother comes, the home of her parents and brothers. Occasionally a man's maternal relatives will belong to his own family-group, for marriage within the group is not forbidden. More generally they belong to some other family-group and even to some other ward. In such cases children during their early years may be sent to live for a while with their mother's people; and they should always, even when grown-up, visit it frequently. A child is greatly honoured at its mother's home. *Setlogolo se segolo kwa gabo-mogolo*, says the proverb: "A uterine nephew is an important person at the home of his mother's people." He takes precedence there over his cousins at the eating of the firstfruits and in other ceremonies where precedence is involved; his word carries great weight in their family councils; and generally speaking he is treated there with utmost respect and has many privileges. Between him and his maternal uncle there exists a specially intimate relationship, reflected more particularly in exchanges of property and services, which plays a very important part in the whole social life of the people. A man should, if possible, marry the daughter of his maternal uncle; but whether he does so or not, he associates on terms of the greatest intimacy with her and her brothers. His maternal relatives, further, help him in all his domestic undertakings and troubles; and he can always, if necessary, find a welcome home among them.

[*In-Laws (Affines).*] *Bogwê*, the home of a man's wife, is likewise a place where he is greatly honoured. In some tribes (Ngwaketse,

* Kgotla = See chapter introducing
Botswana law and culture.

Rolong, Malete), the first few years of his married life are spent there. During this time he co-operates actively with his wife's people at work. After setting up his own home, he must still visit his parents-in-law frequently, help them at work, and make them occasional presents of food and other commodities. They reciprocate in the same way. A woman's lot at the home of her husband's parents (*bo-matsalè*) is, on the other hand, at first rather difficult, especially in those tribes where immediately after marriage she goes to live with him in his mother's homestead. Here she must be humble and respectful, work hard, and in general serve the whole household. But when her husband sets up his own household, and she becomes its mistress, she obtains much greater freedom. She should, however, spend much of her time with his people and assist them, as they assist her, in the various major domestic and agricultural tasks and undertakings.

NOTE

It is impossible to understand the nature of Tswana kinship unless one takes note of the fact, mentioned in the chapter introducing Botswana and its law, that the Tswana have preferential marriage with cousins. Unlike most African peoples who practice preferential marriage, the Tswana have parallel-cousin marriage with the father's brother's daughter (or a classificatory FBD *) as well as cross-cousin marriage (marriage with an actual or classificatory mother's brother's daughter or father's sister's daughter). This creates a situation in which relatives can be related to each other in multiple ways which, as we will see much later in this chapter, leads to more individualized kinship relations than are found in many African societies. Cousin marriage—especially parallel cousin marriage—also blurs the boundaries around patrilineal descent groups. But at the same time, it can reinforce group solidarity by keeping inheritances within the group. Schapera notes that cousin marriage was particularly common in the Ngwato royal family.

NOTE AND QUESTIONS

1. Q. N. Parsons (personal communication) notes that cousin marriage occurs much more frequently among Tswana nobles than among common-

---

* A classificatory relative is a person who falls into a kinship category as it is culturally (and, therefore arbitrarily) defined. Usually the classificatory (i.e., cultural) category is broader than one genealogical (i.e., actual biological) category. Thus, a classificatory category usually subsumes several genealogical categories. Thus, a classificatory father's brother's daughter is a relative who falls into the culturally-defined category of father's brother's daughter but who, genealogically, may fall into any of several categories vis-a-vis ego, such as father's father's brother's son's daugh-

ter. One consequence of the existence of classificatory relatives is that the rules for "preferential (often obligatory)" cousin marriage are not as confining as they seem at first blush. Thus, a man who is supposed to marry his father's brother's daughter is not limited to female cousins who fall into that one genealogical category. He may also consider female kinswomen who fall into the classificatory category of father's brother's daughter. This may involve several genealogical categories and, therefore, many dozen actual persons.

ers. The prominence given to cross-cousin marriage in Schapera's work reflects the fact that he focused so heavily on the noble class.

2. Is the composition of the Tswana household determined by agnatic kin ties? Is it a patrilineal extended family?

3. How widespread is polygyny in Botswana compared to Egypt?

4. In polygynous families, is there any possibility of ambiguity about which wife is the great wife?

5. What does the *seantlo* concept suggest about the importance of having a male heir?

6. Given the nature of Tswana housing arrangements, how aware are co-wives of events (e.g., inter vivos gifts of cattle from the husband-father) in other "houses?"

2.   Inheritance, Devolution, and the Family Cycle

NOTE

An orthodox, but artificial, view is to look at the transmission of property from one generation to another as "inheritance," the passing on of property at death. But, more realistically, it is clear that in all societies, the Tswana included, property is transferred between the generations at other times as well. The times for the intergenerational transmission of property are all connected with significant points in the cycle of a family's development:

John Comaroff and Simon Roberts, "A Chief's Decision and the Devolution of Property in a Tswana Chiefdom" in Politics in Leadership, edited by William A. Shack and Percy S. Cohen. Oxford: Clarendon Press, 1979, pp. 118–120. Some citations and footnotes omitted. Footnotes renumbered. Editor's insertions in brackets.

[In order to trace the process of devolution] . . . it is necessary to break into the development cycle at some point. The most convenient one, perhaps, is that at which a man has married and established a homestead separate from (but ideally adjacent to) that of his father. The latter probably still survives, and the newly created household will be a nuclear unit composed of the man himself, the wife he has lately married, and possibly some children born to them whilst the couple were living at the homestead of the man's father before the completion of his own. At this stage, the man is likely to have a small but identifiable herd of cattle and other stock. There is no need to examine the way in which this herd has been built up, as this will be implicit in the way in which the herd itself devolves. The initial phase of devolution is associated with a man's first marriage. Following this marriage, a portion of the herd and a tract of available arable land is identified and set aside for the benefit of the woman's house (i.e. the woman herself and the children born to her). The tract of land (*tshimo ya lapa*) is thereafter cultivated by the man and his wife and the produce is used to feed the members of the house. But, where a surplus is left over, any cattle or small stock acquired with this are credited to the house concerned. In the same way, the cattle (*dikgomo tsa lapa*) are used to provide milk for the children, draught oxen to plough the field and ultimately *bogadi* cattle for the sons of the house when they marry. Whatever the subsequent history of this and later marriages, these *dikgomo tsa lapa* continue to be identified with this house and the children born to it. If subsequent wives are taken, the cattle cannot be re-allocated to their houses. Separate allotments of land and cattle are made to each new house as it is formed, and the direction of devolution of further portions of the man's estate is thus determined.

The next step is associated with the birth of children. Among the Kgatla it is traditional for a man to earmark a cow under a custom known as *tshwaiso* for each son at the time of birth. The cow so earmarked, together with its issue, is then regarded as permanently allocated to that son. With good fortune the cow then multiplies and forms the nucleus of a herd for the son concerned. Even a man with few cattle will seek to *tshwaisa* a cow for each of his sons. Richer men may make bigger allocations by earmarking for each son all the calves born in the year of the child's birth; or, in the case of the very wealthy, all the beasts kept at a particular cattle-post. Where a *tshwaiso* beast dies without issue, it should be replaced. Ideally, a man should also *tshwaisa* a beast for each of his daughters, and this is typically done where there are enough cattle to make it possible.

Dispositions under this custom represent an important element in the over-all pattern of devolution and, in the case of some estates, a majority of the cattle devolve along this avenue. In any case, by the time a man's children are approaching maturity, the distribution of a considerable portion of the estate is already ordained.

The process continues as the children marry. When a daughter does so, her father should provide beasts known as *serotwana*. These cattle accompany her on marriage and form a contribution to the maintenance of the household which she and her husband establish. When she dies, the *serotwana* cattle devolve upon her children, preference being given to her daughters.[1]

On the daughter's marriage, *bogadi* * will also be presented for her, and the devolution of these cattle is fixed from this time. Traditionally, sons and daughters in a given house are 'linked' together in childhood by the father, and thereafter remain in a special relationship with one another. Among the responsibilities resting upon a man is that of looking after his 'linked' sister in later life, especially if she should be divorced and return to live among members of her own

1. Isaac Schapera, A Handbook of Tswana Law and Custom. London: Oxford University Press, 1938. S. A. Roberts, *The Kgatla Law of Succession to Property* (Gaborone: Government Printer, 1970). The *serotwana* practice seems a clear instance of dowry and, as such, deserves more attention from anthropologists than it has received. Some writers have gone so far as to deny that cases of dowry are encountered in Africa. . . .

* bogadi = bridewealth cattle.

descent group. In recognition of this obligation, the greater part of the *bogadi* presented for his daughter on marriage is transferred to her 'linked' brother, the idea being that he will use these beasts and their increase to maintain her if necessary. Of course, when the sons marry, *bogadi* cattle have to be found in respect of their wives.

As a man's sons mature, responsibility for managing his herd progressively falls upon them. Where they have their own posts, the father may give some beasts to each one to look after on his behalf. If the herd is large, each may also be given a cattle-post to oversee. Where care and skill are shown in their management, the father may actually transfer ownership of the beasts to the son concerned. Moreover, instructions to this effect are often conveyed well in advance of the father's death.

Later, before the father dies, he may inform his sons and some senior maternal kinsmen about the disposition of the residue of his estate. Typically, he will direct that this be divided among immature children, or children whose *tshwaiso* beasts have not prospered. The Tswana maxim, *lentswe la noswi ga le tlolwe* ('the voice of a dead man is not transgressed'), suggests that instructions given before death are taken very seriously by survivors.

Thus, by the time a married male household head dies, most—if not all—of his estate has been transferred to, earmarked for, or is in the process of devolving upon, the next generation. It is only in respect of unallocated cattle that the direction of devolution has still to be determined.

John Comaroff and Simon Roberts, Rules and Processes: The Cultural Logic of Dispute in an African Context. Chicago: The University of Chicago Press, 1981, p. 183. Footnote omitted.

In the light of contemporary usage in most Tswana chiefdoms, one further phase must be added to this description of the process of property distribution. According both to earlier accounts and to elderly living informants, the direct implications of divorce for the devolutionary cycle were insignificant in the past. When a woman was divorced, she returned to her own agnates to be looked after, and, irrespective of issues of fault, orders under which cattle from the husband's herd might be transferred to her were seldom made. Informants say that she would simply return with her *serotwana* animals and, perhaps, a further beast 'to carry her household goods.' As we saw in chapter 5, however, substantial awards are often made today in favor of divorced women. Indeed the socially accepted norms in most chiefdoms prescribe this unless the responsibility for conjugal breakdown can be laid solely at her door.

The beasts the wife is granted on divorce should eventually devolve upon the children of her marriage. If she is childless, however, the stated norms seem to vary. Among the Kgatla and the Rolong, it appears to be recognized that these beasts should devolve on members of her own descent group. In practice, even if the woman *has* children from the marriage, stock taken with her when she returns to her natal home are often lost to the husband's agnatic unit. Thus, the occasion of divorce has become a further stage in the devolutionary cycle at which property may effectively be transferred out of the segment.

QUESTIONS

1. What kinds of property are important enough to be a part of the Tswana devolution process?

2. From what you know so far, how equally are sons and daughters treated as far as inheritance is concerned?

3. From what you already know, in what ways is the custom of *tshwaiso* like an inter vivos trust in Western law? How is it significantly different?

4. What is the relationship between devolution and the family cycle in the United States? Are there particular points during the family cycle when property is most likely to pass to the next generation? Are these times as patterned as they are in Botswana?

5. Why do you think the Tswana ideal is for a man to pass along most of his cattle during his lifetime, or, at least to earmark it for passage during his lifetime?

6. In what ways does the Tswana system of property assignment help to insure that daughters who marry (usually into other agnatic groups) will be cared for?

SOME ADDITIONAL QUESTIONS

7. Is the custom of *serotwana* a subtle way of compensating for the agnatic emphasis of Tswana inheritance? If so, how does it do it, and how well does it do so?

8. Property passes out of an agnatic segment when a daughter-in-law is divorced. What marriage patterns keep property within the agnatic segment? Did you notice mention of such a marriage pattern earlier?

3. Guardianship

NOTE

Although the Tswana ideal is for a man to devolve most of his estate during his lifetime, there will be a residue at his death, even if he lives up to the ideal pattern of devolvement. Death also leaves the question of who will succeed as head of the family. Someone must be designated to care for the widow or—not often these days—widows and minor children. In the following excerpt, Schapera describes the Tswana normative pattern for transmission of any remaining property, for transmission of the deceased's family position and for guardianship. His account emphasizes the duties of kinpersons toward one another in the guardianship of widows and minor orphans.

Notice that these rules of traditional Tswana inheritance are complicated by the fact of polygyny. Polygyny is even less frequent now than it was when Schapera did his field work. But, apart from the emphasis on devolution during the life of the family head, the most distinctive aspect of Tswana traditional inheritance is the way it is affected by the structure of the polygynous family. The connection of polygyny and inheritance may be of more than historical and comparative interest, for there is a current movement in Botswana to make polygynous statutory marriages legal under certain circumstances (See Section C3).

Isaac Schapera, A Handbook of Tswana Law and Custom. Second edition. London: Oxford University Press, 1955, pp. 191–193. Headings inserted by editor are in brackets.

[*Successor and Guardian in a Monogamous Family.*] . . . When a man dies, his eldest son, if old enough, succeeds as head of the family. He becomes the guardian of his mother, brothers, and sisters, and takes over all his father's other duties and responsibilities, rights and privileges. His mother and the unmarried children must live with him, or wherever he directs, and as long as they recognize his authority he must suitably support and maintain them. They must in turn serve and obey him just as they did his late father. Failure on their part to do so, or to recognize his authority, would deprive them of any claim for maintenance or support. But as long as they behave dutifully towards him and render him the necessary services, they are entitled to maintenance out of his late father's estate. Should he neglect to provide adequately for them, they may appeal, through the usual channels, to the Chief, who, if their appeal is justified, will order him to set aside a certain number of cattle for their maintenance, and will appoint another son or near relative to act as their guardian.

[*Successor and Guardian in a Polygynous Family.*] In a polygamous family, the father is succeeded as head of the family by the eldest son of the great wife. The eldest son in each minor house takes charge of his own mother, brothers, and sisters, and of the property specifically assigned to that house or otherwise acquired by it. But in matters affecting the household at large he acknowledges the authority of the great heir, who is obliged to look after the general interests and matrimonial affairs of the minor houses in the same way as his father would have done.

If the children of a second wife are still minors, the youngest son of the great wife becomes the special guardian of their house, subject to the general supervision of his own eldest brother. This rule is observed also in the case of a widower who had married again after the death of his first wife. The eldest son by the first wife succeeds to the status of his father; the youngest son by the same wife becomes the special guardian of the second wife's children if they are all minors.

[*Successor and Guardian where the Children are Minors.*] If all the children, in either a monogamous or a polygamous family, are still minors, their late father's younger brother (usually the one linked with him) normally becomes the guardian. If there is no younger brother, the man next in order of seniority should take over the responsibilities of guardianship. In such cases, however, the relatives of [the] deceased often report to the Chief that there is no proper guardian. The Chief will then either approve of the next senior relative taking over the position or may ask the people concerned to nominate some other close male relative to look after the orphans and their property. There must always be a male guardian, even if the mother is still alive. The Chief himself acts as 'upper guardian' of all widows and orphans, and should see to it that they are properly cared for.

[*Duties of Guardian vis-a-vis Widow and Minor Children.*] The guardian was in former times expected to cohabit with the widow and so 'raise up seed' to his late brother. His other duties are to look after the cattle and other property of the estate; to feed and clothe the widow and her children; to help them plough their fields and to milk the cattle for them; to look after their welfare generally and, in consultation with the widow, to manage the matrimonial affairs of the children; and to render an account of his stewardship to the Chief should the latter desire it. He has the same authority over the widow and her children as if he were their husband and father, and he controls their use of the family property, in that they cannot dispose of it without first consulting him and unless he consents. He may plough with and inspan their oxen for his own purposes, and use the milk of the cows; and he can, if necessary, and after consultation with the widow, sell livestock from the estate to provide for the needs of his wards.

[*Remedies for Misconduct by a Guardian.*] But he cannot dispose of any of the property on his own behalf. Should he ill-treat or neglect the children, stint them in food and clothes, fail to plough or milk for them, appropriate their cattle, or otherwise fail in his duties, the other relatives have the right and the duty to intervene. Should he persist in his conduct, they must report him to the Chief, who, if it is found necessary, may then relieve him of his responsibilities and appoint another guardian, generally the man next in order of seniority. He may also be required to replace any cattle he has appropriated or otherwise disposed of for his own benefit. His responsibility ceases in any case when the eldest son comes of age. He must then hand over and satisfactorily account for his handling of the estate, failing which he can be sued and forced to restore whatever is missing.

[*The Widow's Rights.*] The widow, if she has any sons, has no power over the cattle of the estate. She has the right to be maintained and supported from these cattle, and to use the other house property, as long as she continues to live at the home of her late husband. Should she wish to dispose of any cattle on behalf of her children, she must do so through the male guardian, and she should also see that the latter does not squander the estate. If she refuses to stay at the husband's home, or if she marries again, she no longer is entitled to be supported from the estate. The children and the cattle remain with the male guardian. The younger children may go with their mother, in which case they must be supported by the guardian, but they can be reclaimed as soon as they are old enough. The widow is always entitled to return to her husband's home as long as her sons are there, and to be maintained by them; and they too, when old enough, have the right to take her back. If there are no sons, a widow, as long as she remains at her late husband's home, must be maintained from the cattle of his estate, over which she has considerable control, although she must always act through the male guardian. If she goes away, she loses the right to maintenance, but it is usual in such cases to give her some of the cattle from the estate to take with her as her own property.

QUESTIONS

1. What are the consequences for the Tswana inheritance system of the ranking of wives and sons?

2. Is a widow a jural minor no matter where she resides or does she have full jural status under some conditions?

3. How clear are the boundaries between the heir's use of the products and progeny of the cattle of an estate for his own purposes as opposed to using them for carrying out his responsibilities as guardian?

4. What hints does Schapera's account provide that guardians do not always carry out their duties vis-a-vis their wards equitably? What procedures exist to encourage them to do so? What checks exist to protect wards against losing the benefit of their inheritance? In particular, what checks does the inheritance system provide against a widow being mistreated by her guardian?

5. In spite of these checks and procedures, what kinds of tensions do you think develop between guardians and wards? How do these tensions work their way into the legal system?

SOME ADDITIONAL QUESTIONS

6. Why do secondary houses with minor children have a special guardian? Why is he from the house of the great wife?

7. In this patrilineal society, what are the responsibilities of matrilineal relatives to widows, semi-orphans, or orphans? Why do you think the responsibilities of matrilineal relatives differ in a patterned way from those of patrilineal relatives?

4. Content of the Estate, Patterns and Specific Duties of Heirship

NOTE

The preceding excerpt emphasized the guardianship responsibilities and obligations of kinpersons. The following excerpt reviews some of the same facts, but from a different perspective. Read it with a view to understanding the "how's" of guardianship, how the principle heir is supposed to carry out his stewardship—what property he receives and what he does with it, how he is supposed to administer the estate effectively to achieve the goals of guardianship. Note how inheritance varies with the kind of property and with status attributes of the deceased: gender and whether married monogamously or polygynously.

Keep in mind that Schapera is writing about the 1930's and 1940's. Also, be mindful of this paradox: If a man passes along most of his property before death in *tshwaiso* or other lifetime earmarkings, there should be little property left to be administered. So, why is there need for a major heir/administrator? What set of assumptions underlie the designation of such a person?

Isaac Schapera, A Handbook of Tswana Law and Custom. Second edition. London: Oxford University Press, 1955, pp. 230–234, 236–238. Headings inserted by editor are in brackets.

[*Pattern of Testation.*] Inheritance among the Tswana is governed by various traditional rules coming into force after the death of a person. Voluntary testamentation is not altogether unknown, in the sense that a man may inform his eldest son and some other men of his ward that after his death he wishes certain cattle or other property to be given to certain children or other relatives. His wishes are generally respected, for, as the proverb says, *Lentswe la moswi ga le tlolwe*, 'The word of a dead person is not transgressed.' But if in them he departs to any considerable extent from the ordinary rules of inheritance and deprives anybody of his due rights, the aggrieved person will appeal to the Chief to adjust the matter. Usually, however, a man wishing to make special provision for his younger children will do so during his lifetime under the *tshwaisô (setshwaêlô)* custom. Property thus donated does not form part of the estate to be dealt with afterwards by the customary rules of inheritance, but belongs absolutely to the child to whom it has been donated.

[*Pattern of Devolution.*] The manner in which property is inherited after the death of the owner depends both upon his marital condition and sex, and upon the nature of the property. The general rule regarding the latter is that sons inherit all cattle and other property specifically used by males; while daughters inherit the domestic utensils and other goods specifically used by females. Traditional variations occur, however, from tribe to tribe; and changes have also been brought about in some respects by recent modifications of the customary law. Fields and dwellings occupy a somewhat special posi-

tion, as they may be inherited by either sons or daughters, according
to their allocation.

ESTATE OF MARRIED MAN

[*Estate of a Man with Children.*] [Principal Heir: *mojaboswa.*]
When a married man dies, leaving a wife and children of both sexes,
his eldest son becomes the principal heir (*mojaboswa*), even if there
is an older daughter. If this son has been formally disowned by his
father, he cannot after the latter's death claim the estate. The rightful heir will be the oldest of the remaining sons. If the principal heir
is dead, his eldest son will succeed to his rights, taking precedence
over his father's younger brothers.

[*Distribution of Cattle to Brothers.*] The principal heir, in pure
Tswana law, inherits all cattle which at the death of his father had
not been allotted or donated to any special person. . . . He must,
however, out of them give each of his younger brothers one or more
cattle as *tatodi* (from *go latolêla*), a mark or token of regret and
condolence in respect of their late father's death. A similar beast
must be sent to the Chief's *kgotla* if deceased had been a man of
rank and standing. It is killed there immediately upon arrival and
eaten by the men who are present. The heir also inherits any cattle
specially allotted to his mother's house . . . . He was formerly entitled to them all, to the exclusion of his brothers and sisters. Nowadays, however, he is generally expected to provide out of them for his
brothers. The number of cattle he gives them depends mainly upon
his own wishes. He is not obliged to give them any definite number
or any specific proportion of the estate. Generally he keeps the majority for himself and distributes the rest in decreasing numbers according to the relative age of his brothers, the youngest getting the
least. If his brothers had already been given cattle of their own by
the father under the *tshwaisô* custom, their share of the general estate is almost always fairly small; but, if no such provision had been
made for them, they are entitled to a reasonable proportion. If dissatisfied with the share given to them by the heir, they can appeal to
their headman or to the Chief.

[*Distribution of Cattle to Sisters.*] Daughters formerly received
no cattle at all, nor did the widow. The heir was obliged to maintain
and support them while they were living with him. This is said still
to be the general rule in most tribes. Among the Ngwato, however,
Kgama introduced a law that daughters should also be given cattle.
If they marry during the lifetime of their father, he must give them
cattle as *ketêêtsô* (marriage portion). If they are unmarried, he may
give them *tshwaisô* cattle. In either case they have then no further
claim upon the estate. But, if no such provision has been made for
them, the heir when he succeeds must give them each cattle. Their
share, however, is always much smaller than that of their brothers,
for it is held that the bulk of a man's estate should remain with his

own people, whereas a daughter at marriage generally takes her property with her to her husband's home. . . .

[*Devolution of Fields and Household Effects.*] The eldest son also inherits the common household field . . . together with such uncleared land (*thitê*) as had not been specifically allotted to any other person. The house fields . . . remain in the hands of the widow and are not divided until after her death. The huts, with all their furniture and utensils, remain under her control in the same way. Wagons, ploughs, guns, horses, and similar male effects, together with any money left by deceased, all go to the principal heir, if not previously allotted to any house or person. He must out of this property make adequate provision for his brothers and sisters if this has not already been done by deceased. Clothes and similar personal effects generally go to deceased's maternal uncle, who is further entitled to a gun, a bull, and a heifer. His share of the estate is variously termed *setlhakô* (sandal), *diphatê* (mats), or *tatodi*. If the maternal uncle himself is dead, his successor receives it instead. He may keep it all for himself, but as a rule divides it among his own brothers and other relatives.

[*Estate of a Polygynist.*] The estate of a polygamist is divided along somewhat similar lines. All *kgotla* cattle, fields, wagons, money, horses, and other property which at the time of death had not been allotted or donated by deceased to any house or person are inherited by the eldest son of the great wife. This son also inherits the cattle and other male effects specifically allotted to the house of his mother. The eldest son in every other house similarly inherits the male property of that house. The principal heir to the whole estate has no claim to any house property but that of his own mother. But he is entitled to one beast from the estate of each minor house to indicate that he is now the head of the whole household in place of his father. . . .

[*Estate of a Remarried Widower.*] The same rules are followed with the estate of a widower who has remarried.

[*Estate of a Man with No Sons.*] [A monogamist.] When a married man dies, leaving a wife and daughters, but no sons, his estate was formerly looked after by the man who took his place as their guardian. This man was expected to maintain and support the widow and her daughters from the property under his care. It was also his duty, if the widow was of suitable age, to 'enter her hut' (*go tsêna mo tlung ya gagwê*) in order to beget a son. Such a son, being regarded as the legitimate child of the dead man, would then be the ultimate heir to the estate. Should the guardian fail to enter her hut, the care of the estate generally passed to the next of kin. Should all deceased's paternal relatives refuse 'to raise up seed' to him, the matter was reported to the Chief, who would then generally appoint one of the widow's own male relatives to look after the estate on her behalf.

Nowadays, in most tribes, the cattle and other property continue to belong to the daughters and their mother as long as she remains at her late husband's home. The husband's younger brother gets no share of it apart from a beast as *tatodi (tlhobosô)*, unless she chooses to give him something, but he must look after the cattle on her behalf. But, if she goes away, the estate falls to her husband's next of kin, who must provide for the daughters until they are married.

[*Polygynist with No Sons by One Wife.*] In a polygamous family, if there is no son by the great wife or her *seantlo*, the general heir to the household will normally be the eldest son of the second wife, unless arrangements are made to provide an heir for the great house by the custom of *go tsêna mo tlung*. Where the positions are reversed, and there is no son by the second wife, the heir to the property of her house will be the youngest son of the great wife.

Similar rules are followed with the estate of a widower who has remarried. If there are daughters by the first wife, but no son, the eldest son by the second wife inherits the whole estate, but he is nowadays expected to provide for his half-sisters out of the cattle allotted to their mother's house, unless they had previously received *tshwaisô* from their father. If there is no son by the second wife, the youngest son of the first wife inherits the property of the former's house, making similar provision for her daughters.

[*Estate of a Childless Man.*] Formerly, when a married man died, leaving no children, his wife received no share of his estate. It remained under the care of her late husband's younger brother or next male relative, who would take charge of her under the custom of *go tsêna mo tlung*. Any son this woman bore him would in due course inherit the property of her late husband. Nowadays the widow enjoys the use of the property as long as she lives at her husband's home, and on her death it passes to his younger brother. If, however, she marries again, or goes back to her own home, she must be given some cattle according to the wealth of the estate; but the bulk of the property belongs to the nearest male relative of the dead husband, along the lines previously described in connexion with the rules of succession. In the very unlikely event of there being no male heir at all to the deceased, his estate would fall to the Chief. . . .

ADMINISTRATION OF ESTATES

[*Timing of Division.*] The property of a dead man is usually not divided until some time after his death and often not until his widow is also dead. It all depends upon the relations between the surviving members of the family. If they get on well together, there is no haste over the division of the estate; but, if there is any dispute or ill-feeling, division may take place as soon as possible. Generally some time is also allowed to enable the cattle in the estate to increase sufficiently for each child to receive a reasonable number. In any case the estate is seldom divided while the principal heir is still a minor. It is looked after in the meantime by his guardian, in the manner previously described, and handed over to him when he comes of age. He may elect to divide it then, or prefer to wait until his younger brothers have also grown up.

[*Preliminaries to Division.*] He must, however, consult with his senior paternal relatives regarding the manner in which the estate is to be divided; and it is also the rule, especially where a big estate is involved, that the Chief should be informed and his consent obtained before the division is made. He may in such cases send along a couple of men to witness the division and report to him. Until the estate is thus divided, none of the property belonging to it should be disposed of by the heirs; but if any debts had been incurred by deceased they should first be paid before the final distribution takes place.

[*The Act of Division.*] [The initial division.] The division of cattle and other livestock generally takes place at the family cattlepost, where all the animals are brought together. The principal heir goes there with his brothers and sisters, with a few senior relatives as advisers and witnesses, and then proceeds to allocate the cattle, sheep, goats, and other property among those entitled to share in the estate. It is usual, but not essential, that every claimant to a share in the estate should be present at the division. If the minor heirs are not satisfied with their shares, as frequently happens, they have the right to appeal to their headman. If he is unable to make a satisfactory adjustment, he refers the matter to the Chief.

[*Handling Grievances About the Division.*] The Chief will first hear the complaint. He may then send a couple of reliable advisers of his own to make a fresh division. After doing so, they report to him at the *kgotla* regarding the property found in the estate, and the manner in which they had divided it. The heirs are then given an opportunity of raising any grievances they may have in connexion with the division. If no complaints are made, the winding-up of the estate is regarded as completed.

If there is still some dissatisfaction, the Chief orders all the cattle to be brought in to the *kgotla,* and himself divides them among the heirs. He may do this too without first sending messengers to undertake the division on his behalf. At this final division, the Chief may either uphold previous divisions, or may re-divide the cattle as he thinks fit, paying due regard to the claims of the eldest son. . . .

The house property and personal effects inherited by women are divided among themselves in the homestead, the eldest daughter and the senior female relatives presiding at the division. There is seldom any trouble over such a division, but, should there be, the matter would be referred as usual to the headman and possibly even to the Chief.

[*Other Chiefly Oversight.*] Even if no complaints are made to the Chief about the division of an estate, but reports are brought to him that the property is being wasted or neglected because it has not yet been properly divided, he may, after satisfying himself that the reports are true, send some men to divide the property among the heirs of the deceased owner. These messengers will first make an inventory of the estate and report to the Chief. He will then instruct them to go back and make a final division, or may go himself to do so.

QUESTIONS

1. Suppose a Tswana man dies leaving two wives. The first wife is the great wife. By the first wife he leaves two married sons and two married daughters. By the second wife he leaves an unmarried adult son, a married daughter, a minor son, and a minor daughter. During his lifetime he devolved cattle to each of his children via *tshwaiso* and, for the married daughters, via *serotwana*. The residue of his large estate consists of 120 cattle.

   Who will be the *mojaboswa?* How many cattle will he keep? How many will he give to each sibling? How many will go to each wife? Are there any other allocations that are mandatory? Any that are optional? When will the division take place? Why can't you answer all these questions?

2. Suppose a man's wife dies and he remarries. He takes some of the progeny of cattle that belonged to his first wife and gives them as *tshwaiso* to a son by the second wife. Is this permissible under Tswana law and custom?

3. In a polygynous family with two houses the first house has only daughters and the second house has sons and daughters. Who will be the *mojaboswa?* What does he inherit? Who else inherits and what do they inherit?

4. Let's return to the question asked rhetorically on page 237: If a man passes along most of his property during his lifetime, why is there a need for a major heir/administrator, a *mojaboswa?*

5. Can *tshwaiso* be used to evade the normal patterns of devolution? If so, what keeps the evasions from getting out of hand?

6. What evidence does Schapera's account give of change in the content of Tswana law of inheritance? What over-all pattern do you see in the changes that he saw in the middle of the Protectorate period?

7. What evidence is there that Tswana law has a principle of male ultimogeniture (inheritance by the youngest son) as well as male primogeniture (inheritance by the oldest son)? Are these two principles necessarily in conflict, or can they be reconciled?

8. What are the consequences of the fact that an estate often is not divided until long after the death of a male head of household?

9. Why must all of a deceased's living children be present for the division of an estate?

10. All of a deceased man's paternal relatives sometimes refuse to "raise up seed" to him. Why?

11. What evidence is there of bias toward males in the designation of the heir in the absence of a son in polygynous families? (e.g. in the case of a remarried widower with only daughters by his first wife, or, in a family with two houses where the second house has only daughters)?

SOME ADDITIONAL QUESTIONS

12. What does the traditional custom of *go tsena mo tlung* ("raising up seed") suggest concerning a disparity in ages between husbands and wives? What are the implications of this custom for inheritance distributions? For guardianship? For tensions between half-siblings?

13. Why does the household field go to the (male) heir while the house fields remain with the widow? What pattern of American devolution does this parallel?

14. How does Tswana inheritance law provide for children born after the death of their father?

5. Conflict Between Inter Vivos Provision for All Children and Inheritance by Primogeniture.

NOTE

Designating a *mojaboswa* as a principal heir recognizes the Tswana family (particularly the polygynous family) as a single corporate group. The principal heir succeeds to position as well as property. He becomes the new head of the family. As such, he acts not just as steward for his own "house," that of his mother and his full siblings, but for all the other houses as well. Implicit in this role is the view that the other members of the family are not (in the legal sense) competent to act on their own behalf. He, as the new head of the family is to be their protector and guardian.

But the interaction between the *mojaboswa* and the other members of the family does not always go according to the culturally-scripted ideal pattern. Consider the following case. What does it suggest about the possible effect on the different houses within an agnatic segment of the *mojaboswa's* carrying out of his role?

John Comaroff and Simon Roberts, Rules and Processes: The Cultural Logic of Dispute in an African Context. Chicago: The University of Chicago Press, 1981. Chapter V, pp. 181–183.

THE CASE OF RANKO'S CATTLE, RANKO'S GENEALOGY

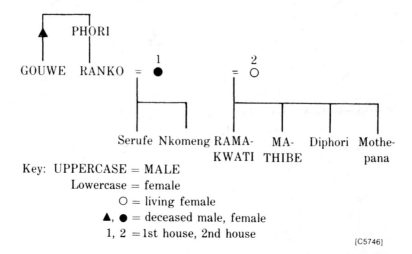

Key: UPPERCASE = MALE
Lowercase = female
○ = living female
▲, ● = deceased male, female
1, 2 = 1st house, 2nd house

[C5746]

Ranko's father, Phori, was born in Ramadiakobong ward but moved later to Morema ward and lived there for the rest of his life. Some say he was taken there as a child, while others suggest that he went as an adult, after his initiation and admission to an age-regiment. Whatever the actual circumstances, Phori established his marital household in Morema ward, where Ranko was born.

When Ranko himself entered a union, he built himself a homestead in Morema. Two girls, Serufe and Nkomeng, were born to this marriage. Following the death of his first wife, Ranko contracted a second union, which produced four more children who survived to become adults: two boys, Ramakwati and Mathibe, and two girls, Diphori and Mothepana. As is common when Kgatla males establish successive houses, relations between the children of the two wives were strained. While Ranko still lived, therefore, Ramakwati and Mathibe settled back in Ramadiakobong ward, where Ranko's father had once lived.

Following Ranko's death, the two girls of the first house complained to the Morema ward headman, Mothei, that Ramakwati was 'eating up' the cattle Ranko had left and that they had received no benefit. Serufe argued that the cattle should now be allocated so that she and her sister could be given some. Accordingly, Mothei, in his capacity as headman of the ward in which Ranko had lived, set aside a day on which Ranko's remaining stock would be distributed. He arranged for them to be collected together and informed the senior members of Ramadiakobong, where Ramakwati and his brother were living. Ramakwati and the Ramadiakobong men found these arrangements unacceptable. They replied that, since Ranko was truly a member of Ramadiakobong, it was up to them to organize the division. They did not, however, object in principle to the idea that the girls should have a share. In the face of these disagreements, the respective ward heads took the matter before the chief.

When the dispute came to be heard in the chief's *kgotla*, it was presented in the following manner:

GOUWE (Ramadiakobong ward headman and Ranko's FoBS): * I bring this matter before the chief. Ranko is not a member of Morema ward but of Ramadiakobong. Ranko died while living in Morema. Although he paid tax in Morema, the truth is that he is a member of Ramadiakobong. He is my uncle's [*rremogolo*] son. I am bringing this case [*tsheko*] as his father.

[After giving further information on the question of Ranko's tax, Gouwe continued:]

I was told by Ramakwati. He said I was wanted so that I could be there when Ranko's cattle were distributed. At that time the cattle had already been collected by members of the Morema ward. I replied that it was wrong to call me when the cattle were ready for distribution; they should have consulted me even before they were collected together.

Ramakwati told me that his sister had said they wanted to be given some cattle as well. He told me that he has said he was not against this but wanted to settle the father's debts first.

MOTHEI (headman of Morema): Ranko was my son. I am concerned with this matter as a headman. He pays tax to me and not to the Ramadiakobong ward. The source of the dispute is his estate [*boswa*]. Those who are quarreling are Ranko's children. They are quarreling over his estate. Ranko was married to two wives. There were two children born to the first wife, and both of them are girls. There were four children of the second wife, two of them boys and two girls. The children born to the second wife do not want to share the estate with those born to the first. The two boys are members of the Ramadiakobong ward, while the girls born to the first wife are members of Morema. I do not know who separated them. When the cattle were assembled there were found to be thirty in all. Linchwe divided them equally, so that each child received five beasts.

QUESTIONS

1. In the case of Ranko's cattle, in what different ways was tension between houses expressed?

2. In what way did Chief Linchwe's decision in this case differ from that which Tswana law would dictate? To what principle was he giving expression?

* Father's brother's son.

3. Linchwe's decision was innovative. What does that teach us about seeing the law as "dictating" outcomes?

6. Aberrant Timing in Devolution and Father-Son Tension as Friction Points in the Inheritance Process

John Comaroff and Simon Roberts, Rules and Processes: The Cultural Logic of Dispute in an African Context. Chicago: The University of Chicago Press, 1981. Chapter IV, pp. 190–191. Footnotes omitted.

The Case of Kgasane and Senwelo. Kgasane, of the Mosadimogolo *kgotla*, was a member of the Ntwane age-regiment [formed in 1892]. He is reputed to have built up a considerable herd of cattle as a youth, largely by selling arms during the Anglo-Boer War, but he entered a union for the first time only when he was already in his forties. This union produced a son, Senwelo (b. 1918), and later a daughter. While the two children were still young, their mother died, and Kgasane left Mosadimogolo to live with a second woman, Morekwe, on the western fringe of the village. Informants say that he neglected Senwelo and his sister, allowing their homestead to fall into ruins. Both were brought up primarily by maternal kinsmen.

Until the end of the Second World War, Senwelo spent most of his time away as a migrant laborer, finally settling down at Mochudi in about 1949. Soon thereafter, in response to complaints of neglect, Kgasane gave his eldest son a number of cattle to manage. The herd was composed of some of Kgasane's own stock, beasts that had been earmarked for Senwelo and others that had been set aside for Senwelo's mother's house. Under normal circumstances, Kgasane, who was over seventy by now, would have left these animals entirely under Senwelo's management and would also have transferred them to his ownership while he himself was still alive. The old man remained vigorous, however, and wished to retain overriding control of the herd. As a result, he repeatedly gave instructions concerning its husbandry. But Senwelo, who remained mindful of his father's early neglect and continued preference for the second house, ignored Kgasane's orders, even to the extent of selling beasts on his own initiative.

In 1958 Kgasane complained to the chief's *kgotla* that Senwelo was wasting his cattle. The latter admitted that he had disregarded his father, but he justified this on the grounds of paternal neglect and favoritism for the second house (a fact that was notorious at Mochudi). Reproved by the chief for allowing the homestead of his first wife to fall into ruins, Kgasane made no attempt to demand the cattle back. The matter ended with the chief carefully identifying, within the herd held by Senwelo, those animals that the son himself had acquired, those that were *tshwaiso* beasts, those that were house cattle, and those that still belonged to Kgasane. Of the last category, eight head were set aside as *bogadi* for Senwelo's mother, which was still outstanding. Senwelo was then warned to do nothing with the residue that might be contrary to his father's wishes.

It seems that Senwelo disregarded the chief's orders, for, in 1961, Kgasane returned to the *kgotla*, complaining again that Senwelo was selling his beasts without permission. By now, Kgasane was at least ninety; but he still had not transferred ownership of the animals he had given to Senwelo to manage. The chief repeated his warning to Senwelo to do as his father instructed and, specifically, to give him a beast that could be sold to maintain the homestead of the first house. Kgasane died a few years later without having made over to Senwelo the stock under his control. Senwelo has nonetheless retained these cattle and has not been challenged about this by members of the second house.

NOTE AND QUESTIONS

1. What is the age of majority under Tswana customary law? If the answer is not firm, what implications does this have for operation of the inheritance system?

2. In a polygynous society, older men often make new marriages late in life—with much younger women. What do you think the feelings of an adult Tswana son would be about his father making such a marriage? What considerations might shape his attitudes? How would his attitudes shape his father's inheritance arrangements or his attitudes toward those inheritance arrangements?

3. Young adult Tswana men whose fathers are married polygynously often press for early transmission of their inheritance. Why do you think they do so?

4. How can a Tswana father try to guard against filial mismanagement of cattle he has given his sons under *tshwaiso*? Against mismanagement of cattle obtained in devolution after death?

NOTE

Disputes like that between Kgasane and Senwelo are not uncommon among the Tswana. Schapera has constructed a generalized picture of how the Tswana handle such disputes between fathers and sons.

Isaac Schapera, A Handbook of Tswana Law and Custom. Second edition. London: Oxford University Press, 1955, pp. 183–184.

Disputes often arise between parents and children. A father may consistently favour one son by allocating him more cattle than the rest, or he may allow a second wife to use property belonging to the first; he may ill-treat or neglect his children, punishing them excessively or failing to provide them with clothes and other necessities; he may ignore the right of his eldest son to be actively consulted in family affairs; he may attempt to force his daughter into a marriage she does not like, or will refuse to let his son marry the girl the latter wants. The children, on the other hand, may deliberately and persistently disobey their parents, or abuse and dissipate the family property, selling cattle without permission or authority; they may refuse to work with their parents, or fail to support them in their old age, or in some other way openly commit a breach of duty.

If the matter cannot be settled within the household, it is dealt with at a general family gathering . . . . The injured child will complain to a senior paternal relative, or more frequently to his maternal uncle, who then calls the meeting; or the injured father may summon it. If no reconciliation can be effected here, the matter is referred to the headman of their ward, and if sufficiently serious may ultimately even come before the Chief. If it is shown that the parents do not treat their child properly, and that they are unable to live together harmoniously, they may be ordered to separate. The son may then build his own home in another part of the village, or go to live with some other relative, or, nowadays, go out to work among the Europeans. The father may also be ordered in case of a separation to give his son the share due to him of the family estate. The son will then be debarred from inheriting in future.

If the son is in the wrong, he will be severely reprimanded and ordered to obey his father. Sometimes he is also thrashed. The father may further be given the right, if the offence is sufficiently serious, to take back any property he may have given his son. This will not debar the latter from subsequently receiving a share of his father's estate, but he can no longer claim the cattle originally allocated to him. In extreme cases a father may completely disown his son. The son must be brought before the Chief at the *kgotla*. The father will there publicly declare that he no longer acknowledges the boy as his son. He will then be ordered to give the son whatever is due to him of the inheritance. Henceforth the latter has no further claim upon his father's estate, nor is the father liable for his misdeeds and debts. If the eldest son is disowned in this way, his next brother will become the main heir to the estate. But a father cannot disown a son without first taking him before the Chief at the *kgotla* and there publicly announcing his intention.

QUESTIONS

1. Under Tswana law and custom does a father have a right to disinherit a son?

2. How does the Tswana concept of "disownment" differ from disowning in the West, as you understand it? Is disownment a legal concept in the West?

NOTE

Schapera's generalized sketch of father-son disputes among the Tswana documents two aspects of Tswana procedure in conflict resolution that should be underscored. First, significant transactions or acts are carried out publically, before witnesses. An example is the inter vivos handing over of a portion of a father's estate. This has roots in earlier days when much of the population was non-literate. Should a dispute arise later, the testimony of witnesses is the equivalent of producing a notarized document. Public performance of transactions also serves the function of dramatizing them and, thus, underscoring to the parties their importance.

A second procedural principle is that a grievant always should start by going to a third person to help him or her to clarify the issues and his or her goals and, perhaps, to act as a mediator with the other party. A Tswana grievant does not go straightaway to court.

Even though most disputes about the timing of transmission of an inheritance center about delayed inheritance, Comaroff and Roberts report a striking case that apparently revolved around a father's attempt to give a son his entire inheritance early.

John Comaroff and Simon Roberts, "The Invocation of Norms in Dispute Settlement: The Tswana Case," in Social Anthropology and Law, edited by Ian Hamnett. London: Academic Press, 1977, pp. 100–101, 103–104.

THE CASE OF NAMAYAPELA, THE TROUBLESOME SON

This case is typical of those arising out of the transfer of property across the generations. Mooki was an ailing seventy year old member of the Manamakgothe ward in Mochudi, the Kgatla capital, and his mother had been a member of the lineage segment to which the ward headman, Molope belonged. Namayapela was one of the Mooki's younger sons

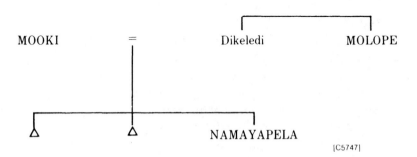

[C5747]

For several years there had been acute tension between him and his father. Because his other children were away as migrant labourers, Mooki feared that in the event of his death Namayapela would seize and waste their portions of his estate. Thus he had tried to arrange an *inter vivos* allocation to Namayapela. But the latter refused to accept it. So, Mooki complained and the case ultimately was heard at the kgotla of the chief in Mochudi.

MOOKI: I have come with a complaint. My son, Namayapela, gives me a lot of trouble. He has been troublesome for a long time. Recently I told my ward headman, Molope, that I intended to give Namayapela his portion of my estate. The point is to get rid of him, because I fear he would cheat my obedient children in the division of my estate if I did not give him his share now. However, he would not accept it.

I fear that Namayapela may kill me so that he can enjoy my cattle. That is why I want to give him what I think he is entitled to; then I may have nothing to do with him. I want to forestall his chances of doing what he likes when I am gone.

I went to see how the crops were doing after I had reported the case to Molope. When I returned, I went to join a bereaved family.

[That night Namayapela caused a row at his father's homestead. The news spread and Mooki was urged to stay where he was at the homestead of his bereaved friends. When he returned home the next morning, he and his son got into an argument and Namayapela assaulted his father. Namayapela, who had been called to the headman's kgotla because of his refusal to accept his inheritance, was then called there again because of the assault. The case eventually wound its way to the chief's kgotla for the present hearing.

Next in this hearing Mooki accused Namayapela of the assault, of selling cattle without permission, and of refusing his inheritance of cattle. Molope, the headman, accused him of refusing to come to his (the headman's) kgotla when called to answer to the latter charge. Dikeledi, Namayapela's mother, testified as to ways in which Namayapela had been disrespectful to his father and to her as well. She alleged that, during the row, Namayapela threatened suicide, but really wanted to kill his father. After his mother's testimony, Namayapela capitulated:]

NAMAYAPELA: I am willing to accept the cattle which my father, Mooki, wants to give me so that I may get away from him.

CHIEF: Namayapela, I have carefully heard the case between you and your father. Your father was very polite to you in discussing with you the fact that he wanted to give you your share. You refused to accept the cattle until you fought him.

You are not supposed to make life uncomfortable for your parents. If you are tired of living you are free to kill yourself rather than make life unbearable for them. You have decided to be rude to your parents. Rudeness, dishonesty and telling lies do not lead to eternal life. You must honour the word of the chief. Because of your rudeness you refused to respond to the summons by headman Molope, and did not appreciate the goodwill extended to you by your father. I find you guilty. For disobeying the summons by headman Molope I sentence you to five strokes. For refusing to accept the cattle I sentence you to four weeks imprisonment. The next week you must go with your father to the cattle-post so that he should give you your cattle.

NOTE AND QUESTIONS

1. Note the contrast between this case and The Case of Kgasane and Senwelo. In that case the father delayed devolution. In this case the father attempted to advance it.

2. What aim did each father have? Why did Kgasane attempt to delay devolution? And why did Mooki try to speed it up? Does this suggest any broad general conclusion about deviations from the normal timing of devolution?

3. In The Case of Namayapela, the Troublesome Son, what was Mooki really trying to achieve? In his attempt to mold what happened among his heirs after his death, was he like a Western father attempting to utilize the "dead hand" mechanism? Or, deep down, might he have wished to achieve something else?

7. Inheritance and Inheritance Disputes as a Means of Managing and Negotiating Kinship Relations

NOTE

We started Section 2 with the observation that inheritance is not simply the transmission of property at death, but that it is a process that extends over a lifetime, more so for the average Tswana man than for the average American man.

Now, let's tackle another myth. Inheritance is not just about "property." It is about relationships—especially kinship relationships. Tswana kinship bonds are measured by property relationships and, conversely, performance or denial of obligations vis-a-vis a property may be used to change or—even to deny kinship bonds and, ultimately, to terminate them:

John Comaroff and Simon Roberts, Rules and Processes: The Cultural Logic of Dispute in an African Context. Chicago: The University of Chicago Press, 1981. Chapter IV, pp. 199–200. Footnotes omitted. Editor's insertion in brackets.

[This] is exemplified by the relationship between filiation and devolution. The recognition of a father-son tie prescribes the mutual involvement of two men in the progressive transmission of movable assets from one generation to the next, with all the reciprocal obligations that this connotes. Conversely, a devolutionary transfer, the moment it is agreed to have been made, defines that particular relationship as a father-son tie. Thus, whatever the biological link between these men, the setting-aside of, say, *tshwaiso* beasts affirms its designation in paternal-filial terms, and, unless it is later disputed, this designation will continue to describe the bond. As a corollary of this, the absence of such transfers may express an attempt to repudiate filiation, again notwithstanding physical paternity. There are occasional exceptions, of course. However, once an individual acknowledges a youth as his child, and as long as he continues to do so, he is committed to the corresponding property relations. This means that a father who wishes to sever contact with a son to whom he has already allocated assets has these alternatives: he may try to recover the assets, or he will seek to transmit his *total* inheritance to this son in advance of the normal progress of the devolutionary cycle. As case 3 indicates, the latter act represents the unequivocal termination of the tie.

The accepted designation of a kinship bond, in summary, entails a commitment to a specific property relationship and vice versa; the two are perceived as reciprocal, as transformations of each other. . . . [A change in the property relationship between two people can be used to announce a desire to change the nature or quality of a kinship bond—or—to confirm such a change that already has taken place.]

NOTES AND QUESTIONS

1. In American society is the mutual commitment between a kinship bond and a property bond as permanent as it is in Tswana society?

FOR FURTHER THOUGHT

2. In what kinds of societies are disputes about relationships not likely to be cast directly in those terms (i.e., about relationships), but indirectly, as a dispute about property. Why is such a pattern of disputing characteristic of such societies?

3. Why are disputes about relationships more likely where the relationships involved are multiplex ones?

Where the validity of a kinship relationship is questioned, the ownership of the property which expresses that relationship may be questioned as in the following case in which the dispute was protracted:

(GABORONE) BOTSWANA DAILY NEWS, JANUARY 28, 1980

Inheritance dispute ends, rightful owner gets cattle

By Kwapeng Modikwe,

A sixteen-year-old dispute over the inheritance of cattle ended this week when 13 head of cattle were returned to a Mahalapye family and the would-be-inheritor jailed for four years.

Solomon Tlhalerwa was given a four year sentence by the Bakgatla Kgosi Linchwe Kgafela at Mahalapye Customary Court and ordered to return the cattle to the Tlhalerwa family.

The court decision ended a 16-year dispute involving four court cases.

The case was first heard in Serowe Customary Court in 1968 before the late Rasebolai Kgamane. At this hearing the court ruled that Solomon Tlhalerwa was not the rightful heir, because he was allegedly an adopted son.

Passing judgement, Mr Kgamane ruled that the rightful heirs to Chandzimula's cattle were his legitimate children.

An appeal against the findings of this court was heard by Magistrate A. Goodfellow in 1973 and the case was dismissed.

In his judgement, Magistrate Goodfellow quoted the anthropologist Isaac Schapera, who wrote in his "Handbook of Tswana Customs" that "an adopted son will not as a rule inherit from his foster father, even in the absence of a direct heir. The estate in such a case is claimed by the man's own near relatives".

Still not satisfied with the findings of the appeal court, Solomon Tlhalerwa took his case to the High Court where the former Chief Justice G. Dyke ruled that he should be given all those cattle bearing his brand mark a total of three.

Instead, the defendant allegedly took the entire herd of 53 cattle. The Tlhalerwu family appealed to the High Court and a new hearing was arranged.

At this latest hearing, which began last week, the defendant's claim was finally dismissed. The court ruled that he was not the rightful heir.

A will produced in court by the defendant was dismissed as a forgery. It was alleged to have been drawn up by Chandzimula's wife Thapelo.

The defendant claimed that he was present while the will was drawn up but he could not say who the other signatories were.

QUESTIONS

1. Under Tswana customary law, how does the conception of the adoptive parent/child relationship differ from that held in the West?

2. What was probably the reasoning behind former Chief Justice G. Dyke's ruling that Solomon Tlhalerwa be given those cattle bearing his brand mark? Why do you think Tlhalerwa was given a four-year jail sentence as well as being ordered to give up the cattle which he claimed?

C. CHANGES IN THE INHERITANCE OF PROPERTY

1. The Overall Pattern of Changes

NOTE

The pattern of traditional Tswana property inheritance described and discussed in Section B was that which prevailed during the period of the Protectorate. Even as Schapera was carrying out his fieldwork the change which always has characterized African societies—during the pre-colonial period and since—was proceeding apace. Simon Roberts, in several of his writings, has described and catalogued the changes that have occurred more recently in Tswana inheritance law. Among those developments are shifts in social conditions which are reducing the necessity for guardianship in Botswana:

Simon Roberts, Botswana I: Tswana Family Law, Restatement of African Law: 5, London: Sweet and Maxwell, 1972, pp. 318–319.

In the case of all the tribes investigated, traditional notions about domestic authority and the management of material resources co-exist uneasily with contemporary habits of life. Both men and women now absent themselves freely from the households in which they would previously have passed their entire lives. In the case of unmarried males, long periods may be spent away in the course of education or employment and during these periods they are beyond the control of their traditional guardians. When they return, they often bring with them resources which enable them to subsist without the guardian's material support. Similarly, it is increasingly common for unmarried women and women who have separated from their husbands to find employment and live on their own (together with any children born to them), often breaking off all connection with the households to which they would traditionally have belonged. At the same time, those people who would have been their guardians now find themselves engaged on their own account in the commercial exploitation of the herds and arable lands formerly managed on behalf of those subject to their guardianship. But despite these considerable changes in the conditions under which many Tswana tribesmen live, none of the courts investigated has made a general attempt to redefine the nature of guardianship, its duration, the extent of a guardian's control over property held by members of his household, or the limits of his liability for wrongs such persons may commit. The most that can be said is that there is a movement towards regarding a man as emancipated from guardianship once he has married and set up his own household, or when he has broken off all connection with the person who would traditionally have been his guardian. The position of women is even less certain. The courts are generally reluctant to recognize the practical reality of a woman's emancipation from guardianship even when she has broken off all ties with the household to which she would traditionally have belonged; although the Rolong, Ngwato and Tawana courts go some way towards an acceptance of this situation and its consequences. Only the Tawana courts have recognized that an emancipated woman may become, for the purposes of the law, the head of her own household and guardian of its members.

NOTE AND QUESTION

1. In negotiating their financial arrangements with their universities, American college students may declare themselves "financially independent." Suppose individual Batswana who are designated to receive bequests were to declare themselves as "competent and not needing a guardian's protection and oversight." How well do you think this would work?

2. There are other recent changes in Tswana inheritance law. Some of these changes are due to shifting practices within the customary law tradi-

tion. Others are due to increased utilization of options available under statutory law. Roberts in this next excerpt is writing about inheritance law among the Kgatla, but his analysis generally applies to the other Tswana tribal groupings in Botswana.

Simon Roberts, "Kgatla Law and Social Change" in Botswana Notes and Records, vol. 2, 1970, pp. 56–61. Sections have been renumbered by the editor.

. . . In the past the rules of inheritance did not have to provide for the *division* of a dead man's property, but simply for *the transfer of its management* to the person who succeeded him as the head of his immediate family. Today this is no longer the case; with progressive individualisation of interests in property, the rules are required to regulate the way in which his estate is *distributed* among a number of different individuals entitled to share it. . . .

I. The Response of the Law to Changing Conditions. The social conditions under which the traditional system could operate satisfactorily have long disappeared in the Kgatleng tribal territory. Today, interests in property like cattle have largely become individual, and the beneficiaries who formerly looked for support to the principal heir can no longer rely upon him to use the cattle for their benefit. In response to this situation, the rules of inheritance described [in earlier excerpts] have almost entirely given way to a system under which the property of a dead man is divided among the individual beneficiaries.

The necessary modification of the traditional rules to provide for the equitable distribution of a deceased person's property among his dependants has been brought about both by the introduction of deliberate changes by the tribal authorities and by the imaginative use of existing devices in the law by tribesmen themselves. It is worth discussing in some detail both these changes and the existing institutions through which change was indirectly brought about.

a. Express Alteration of the Customary Rules of Inheritance. The tribal authorities have from time to time expressly altered the rules of succession, either by a general announcement in *kgotla* or through a ruling in a particular case. The first of these changes were introduced by Chief Lentswe I (1875–1924). First, he ruled that the principal heir would in future be bound to distribute a reasonable number of the cattle forming the estate among his brothers, while continuing to retain the greatest number for himself. Secondly, he required that some beasts should be divided among the daughters. In neither instance were precise rules laid down, and the amount given to each child therefore depended upon the inclinations of the principal heir. Where younger children were dissatisfied it was always open to them to take their grievance to the Ward Headman and, if necessary, to the Chief's Court. In these courts it had become well established, even before the chieftaincy of Linchwe II, that all the male children of the deceased were entitled to a substantial, as opposed to a token, share of the herd when it was divided.

Development of the customary rules of inheritance along these lines is not peculiar to the Kgatla, and is noticeable in the case of almost all the main Tswana tribes. However, since the accession of Linchwe II, the Chief's Court at Mochudi has departed even further from the traditional rules. In the case of many estates which Chief Linchwe has been called upon to divide, he has adopted the principle of complete parity among beneficiaries, dividing cattle equally among them, irrespective of sex and traditional seniority. The first estate in which he adopted this method of division consisted of thirty-five beasts. The dead man left seven children; six sons (one already deceased, but represented by his own eldest son) and one daughter, and to each of these beneficiaries the Chief allotted five beasts. This procedure has been followed in numerous other cases. [cf. The Case of Ranko's Cattle on p. 244.]

The principle of equality has also been applied in dividing beasts between the different houses of a deceased polygynist, and between surviving widows, irrespective of seniority. This method of division is meeting with some disapproval among older and more traditionally minded members of the tribe, and it remains to be seen whether it will be persevered with while the Chief is absent.* In terms of abstract justice, the new system has much to commend it; but it does constitute a radical departure from tradition. It also takes for granted the complete breakdown of the traditional notions of family obligation, under which the principal heir was regarded as responsible for maintaining the family as a whole, and was accordingly given a large share of the family cattle with which to do so. It remains to be seen whether the Chief has moved too fast.

    b. The Use of Existing Legal Institutions to Modify the Traditional Rules. The simplest means available to an estate holder of ensuring the fair distribution of his property is to divide it during his lifetime. Many tribesmen have been using the *tshwaiso* custom . . . and a number of variations upon it for this purpose. Another means is through the institution of the will, forms of which have long been recognised by customary law.

    (i) The Tshwaiso Custom. . . . This form of disposition has the advantage from the point of view of the donor that he retains control of the beast and can thus prevent its premature or unfavourable sale. The law now appears to place no limitation upon the number of beasts which may be alienated in this way to a child of the donor, and the *tshwaiso* custom is thus a device through which an estate holder can effectively determine the devolution of his property. The device is widely used in practice, and in the case of some de-

* At the time Chief Linchwe II was Botswana's Ambassador to the United States.

ceased persons little is left to devolve according to the normal rules of inheritance. A variation of the *tshwaiso* custom is used in much the same way. Under this arrangement a father hands cattle into a dependant's care on the understanding that the father remains fully beneficially entitled to them. At a later stage the dependant is informed that he or she may retain the beasts when the father dies. This form of disposition differs from the *tshwaiso* in that cattle assigned to the potential beneficiary are severed immediately from the donor's herd, but not initially irrevocably alienated to the beneficiary. Once, however, the donor informs the beneficiary that the cattle concerned will belong to the latter when the former dies, the beasts are treated for all practical purposes as *tshwaiso* cattle and not part of the deceased's estate. An advantage of this variation from the point of view of the donor is that he retains effective control over the way in which the cattle are used as long as he wishes to do so, but is immediately relieved of the burden of their practical management. An estate holder may also dispose of his property among his dependants by way of outright gift (*kabelo*), but this means of securing a fair division of his property lacks all of the various advantages of the other two methods.

(ii) The Will. The Kgatla have long been familiar with the idea that a man should be able to give directions during his lifetime as to the disposal of his property after he dies, and there is a maxim: '*Lentswe la moswi ga le tlolwe*' (the word of a dead man is not transgressed). Traditionally such directions were given verbally, either at a family meeting arranged by the testator, or upon his deathbed. Today it is common for testamentary expressions to be in writing, either in the hand of the deceased himself, or that of some trusted friend or relation. Traditionally it seems that testamentary directions were not regarded as a means of disinheriting the principal heir, but of providing him with guidance as to the way in which he should use the property coming to him for the benefit of the family as a whole. Today, testamentary directions are certainly used as a means of altering the shares which particular beneficiaries, including the principal heir, would otherwise have been entitled to receive, although it remains an open question whether the courts will allow a testator to wholly disinherit the principal heir without good cause.

II. Outstanding Problems of Adaptation. It can be seen from the previous pages that the customary law of inheritance has undergone considerable changes over the last sixty years, and that it has in many respects accommodated itself to the situation under which the principal heir can no longer be relied upon to use the property he traditionally inherited for the general benefit of the family. How far does the law as it now stands provide a viable scheme of inheritance for present conditions? Potential difficulties arise from a number of sources.

Something will be said about each of these problems in the following pages.

a. The Administration of Estates.   Traditionally no formal procedure for the administration of a deceased's estate existed.   Nor was such a procedure necessary, as the principal heir simply assumed management of the deceased's herd and gave out the few beasts which had to be distributed by way of *tatodi*.   The herd remained under his management;   no division of it had to be made, and so no conflict of interest could arise, provided he made some semblance of using it for the benefit of the family as a whole.

Today, however, the situation is altered.   Now that the substantive rules as to the distribution of the estate have changed and the cattle have to be divided and distributed among a number of different heirs, there is need for better defined procedures to prevent the dissipation of the property.   The complaint that a principal heir has delayed dividing up an estate until he has eaten up much of its substance is very often heard at Mochudi today.   It is obviously in his personal advantage to delay division so that he can enjoy the use of the beasts to be given out for as long as possible, even if he ultimately intends to distribute the estate.   There is also a longstanding rule that an estate should not be dealt with while a widow of the deceased survives;   this now seems to provide no more than a convenient pretext for delay where the principal heir wishes to keep the estate for himself.   Obviously it is always open to the other beneficiaries to sue the principal heir if he delays division;   but they may well be reluctant to embark on litigation with the senior member of the family, and even if they do so, it may be several years before the matter gets up to the Chief's Court.   By this time the cattle have probably all been finished.

The introduction of new procedures for the administration of estates would inevitably involve government in the expenditure of time and money.   However, a considerable improvement upon the existing situation would be achieved with relatively little expenditure of money or labour if a system for registering estates could be introduced. Under such a system it would be incumbent on the principal heir, upon pain of a fine, to register the demise of a deceased and the details of the property, which he held at the time of his death within say, one month of the decease.   After the expiry of a further interval, possibly six months or a year, the principal heir might then have to register the division of the estate, recording the details of the distribution. Such a register could be maintained by the customary courts, the District Council or the District Commissioner, and be open to the public. It could probably be combined with existing schemes for the registration of deaths.   Divisions registered could be reviewed periodically by the registration authority, and it would always be open to an aggrieved person to bring complaints before the courts, as it is at present.   A procedure like the one outlined would force the principal heir to divide the estate promptly before it is eaten up, and secure publicity for the division.*

b. The Rules Governing Distribution. Leaving aside the controversial rules relating to division which have lately been introduced by Chief Linchwe II, the law governing the distribution of cattle forming part of an estate is in a very uncertain state. While the principle is clearly established that *all* the legitimate children of a deceased person are entitled to share his cattle, the precise proportion to which each is entitled remains very vague, and the principal heir still enjoys a wide discretion even in those cases where he effects division in conformity with the law. Unless the robustly simple solution adopted by Chief Linchwe catches on quickly, it may be necessary for government to assist in the process of adaption by laying down simple rules governing distribution.

The question of the will has also got to be considered in this context. The idea that a man may make a will during his lifetime directing the distribution of his estate after he is dead is well entrenched in Kgatla law, but the detailed provisions governing customary wills are still far from clear. First, some vagueness exists as to the necessary formalities which a testator must follow if a valid will is to be made, although it is clear that both written and oral declarations are permissible. Secondly, there is some doubt as to how far a customary will can be upheld where it departs radically from the normal rules of distribution on intestacy. In both respects legislation seems necessary to provide clarity.

c. The Devolution of New Forms of Property. One of the most difficult problems to be solved concerns types of property which were unknown when the customary rules of succession were formulated. Today, many tribesmen die leaving bank accounts, lorries, tractors and other forms of property unknown in the past. Rules simply do not exist to govern this kind of property, and in some respects they are very difficult to make.

Money, like cattle, is relatively easy to divide up even when it is found in small quantities, but it presents other problems. It is already common for tribesmen to die leaving sums of money in the Post Office, banks and similar institutions. While these institutions always take care to hand money lying in the name of a deceased person to the appropriate principal heir, there is little more they can do than this, and it is often complained that a deceased's eldest son has eaten up the institutional assets which came into his hands. This problem can only be solved within the larger one of administration of estates as a whole.

Modern moveable property creates problems of a different kind, largely on account of the fact that it seldom falls into convenient

---

* John Henry Merryman (personal communication) comments that this suggestion shows a common law bias in that it is a procedure followed in common law jurisdictions. Civil law jurisdictions solve the problem in a different manner.

units for division. A man dying recently in the Kgatleng tribal territory left, in addition to a considerable number of stock, one McCommick International tractor, one three-ton truck, one 1½ ton truck, three ploughs and one harrow, as well as two wives to quarrel over them. In some ways the sale of such articles, and the division of the proceeds, provides the only fair solution. But there are disadvantages in this, as the sale of agricultural machinery may leave the person inheriting the fields of the deceased unable to carry on their cultivation, at least on the scale the deceased had been able to achieve with mechanical aids. Customary law does not provide an answer to these problems, and government is left with a clean slate for introducing suitable rules to deal with them.

The case referred to in the last paragraph had other interesting aspects, because one of the wives asserted that the tractor belonged to her alone, and produced documents relating to its purchase to prove this. The Court was then obliged to grapple, possibly for the first time, with the problems associated with the possession of documents relating to title. These are difficult problems, of which even the common law tends to make heavy weather.

III. Conclusion. . . . Despite the law's present transitional state, the changes which have already taken place are impressive evidence of the flexibility claimed for customary law by some of its advocates. At the same time, the weaknesses noted in connexion with the administration of estates are part of a much wider problem which has repercussions throughout every branch of the law: the lack of a sound framework in which the law can be administered. Thus, while the substantive customary law can probably meet the demands made upon it by changing conditions, it can only do so if it is administered in an adequate system of courts.

QUESTIONS

1. What does Roberts see as the major problem areas in Tswana inheritance?

2. What distinctive, but traditional, use does a traditionally-oriented Mokgatla often make of the imported notion of a written testament?

3. In what ways are wills used to evade customary patterns of devolution?

4. Do you see any possible problems in instituting a pattern of registering estates and the process of distributing them? Would these problems be any different in a developing nation like Botswana than in the United States?

5. Roberts speaks of the problems that ensue when an estate consists partly of indivisible—sometimes movable—property. What could Botswana learn from practices pertaining to the division of property at divorce in community property states where the community property principle is less optional than it is in Botswana?

6. Inadequacies in Botswana's court system are alluded to. Can you speculate about what those inadequacies are?

2. Conflict of Customary and Statutory Law

a. Wills and Freedom of Testament

NOTE

In a country like Botswana where there is a base of traditional indigenous law and a surmounting layer of imposed law from a colonial period, a major problem is "conflict of laws," where the applicability to particular people or particular situations of the two kinds of law is uncertain. Where a person follows aspects of both tribal and modern life styles, should he or she be subject to customary law or statutory law? Is it proper for a person of tribal background and identification to use a statute based in imposed law to achieve a result that would be questionable under traditional law or contrary to traditional law or custom? In the preceding Roberts excerpt the latter question was raised concerning the use of wills. Such a use of a will is a critical issue in the following case, which dates from the end of the colonial period (1964):

Fraenkel and Makwati v. Sechele, 11 J. of African Law 51 (1967), Basutoland, Bechuanaland Protectorate and Swaziland Court of Appeal (1964), Headings interposed by editor in brackets.

MURRAY, A. J. A.: This matter comes to this court on appeal and cross appeal from a judgment of the High Court of the Bechuanaland Protectorate upon an application to it by the present Respondent for an order (the precise terms whereof will be set out later) restraining the first appellant from proceeding with the administration of the estate of the present respondent's deceased husband Kgari Sechele in terms of a last will executed on . . . October 26, 1946, by the deceased and a subsequent codicil * executed by him in favour of the second appellant on February 14, 1958.

The deceased, who died on September 19, 1962, was in his lifetime an African and the Paramount Chief of the Bakwena Tribe of Molepolole in the Protectorate. He and the present respondent, also an African and a member of that tribe, were married to one another at Molepolole on December 28, 1931, by a marriage officer duly appointed as such by law. In the said will the deceased appointed the first appellant and one Gower as his executors; the said Gower predeceased the testator. In the said will the deceased appointed such elder son as might be born of his marriage with the present respondent as his sole heir: in the event of such son predeceasing him, the present respondent was appointed his sole heiress. In fact there was no issue of the said marriage.

---

* A codicil is a supplement to a will containing an addition, explanation, modification, etc. of something in the will.

By his aforesaid codicil the deceased gave certain specified legacies to the second appellant who was an African woman, not of his
own tribe, with whom he had co-habited for some years at Molepolole.

[*Relief Requested of the High Court by the Plaintiff In the Original Case.*] [Issues agreed to.] It was common cause that as to
compliance with the formalities of the relevant statutes regarding the
execution of testamentary documents no objection could be taken to
either the will or the codicil referred to.

[*Respondent's Argument and Relief Sought.*] The present respondent's petition to the High Court was however based on the contention that according to the law of the Protectorate the succession to
the deceased's estate was governed by native law and the custom of
the Bakwena tribe: that such native law and custom did not sanction
the making of written testamentary dispositions: that the making of
testamentary bequests such as those to the second appellant in the
codicil mentioned was contrary to such native law and custom; and
finally that the first appellant was not entitled to administer the deceased's estate under the provisions of cap. 83 of the laws of Bechuanaland or to distribute the deceased's estate in accordance with the
terms of the said will and codicil in so far as those terms conflicted
with the laws and customs of the Bakwena tribe in view of the provisions of section 3(b) of the above cap. 83, in as much as he had not
applied under section 4(1) of cap. 77 to the appropriate Subordinate
Court for the necessary direction that the deceased's estate should
not be dealt with according to African law and custom. On the basis
of the above contention the present respondent sought an order restraining the first appellant from proceeding with the administration
of the deceased's estate under cap. 83 or at all, and from distributing
it in accordance with the said will and codicil until he had successfully
applied to the appropriate Subordinate Court under cap. 77. It was
further prayed that the High Court should direct that unless such
application was granted, the deceased's estate should be administered
in terms of the laws and customs of the Bakwena tribe.

[*Action of the High Court.*] The application to the High Court
came before the learned Chief Justice on two occasions, on each of
which a judgment was delivered.

A. In the first judgment, delivered on January 14, 1963, the
learned Chief Justice summarized his conclusions as follows:

For the reasons which I have endeavoured to state I hold:

1. As there is a dispute as to the validity of a will an application cannot effectively be made to the District Officer under s. 4(1)
of Chapter 77.

2. That the will of the deceased is a valid will under the laws
of the Bechuanaland Protectorate.

3. That Chapter 83 and Chapter 84 are inapplicable and the estate must be administered procedurally in accordance with Tswana Law and Custom.

It has to be decided whether the will of the deceased and the codicil are either of them wholly or partially in conflict with African law and custom and whether effect can be given to the wishes of the testator as expressed in the said will and codicil. Under the provisions of Rule 5(11) High Court Rules, I order that oral evidence such as the parties may desire to produce on the issues remaining outstanding may be heard on the 15th day of February, 1963. . . .

It will be necessary to consider at a later stage certain of the conclusions upon which such summary was based.

B. The second judgment which was delivered on July 8, 1963 commences as follows:

In my judgment of January 14, 1963, I held that it was competent for the late Chief Kgari Sechele to make a will and that the estate must be administered procedurally in accordance with native law and custom. I left open the question as to whether effect could be given to the wishes of the testator as expressed in his will and codicil. I have now heard evidence on the question and the matter has been fully argued by Counsel.

The learned Chief Justice thereafter dealt with the two questions argued. . . .

In the result an order was granted in the following terms:

1. That the will of the deceased Chief Kgari Sechele II dated October 26, 1946, and codicil thereto dated February 14, 1958, are valid at law to the extent that the said deceased had testamentary capacity to make the same.

2. That the appointment of the first Respondent as executor of the said will and codicil of the deceased testator is a valid appointment.

3. That the applicant, being the widow of the said deceased testator, is entitled to inherit the deceased's estate, under Tswana law and custom.

4. That the bequests contained in the said codicil of the deceased testator other than the bequest of household furniture contained within a certain house at Molepolole in the Bechuanaland Protectorate to the second respondent are not valid bequests.

5. That the first Respondent be restrained from distributing the estate of the deceased testator in accordance with the said will and codicil, and that the same be administered in accordance with Tswana law and custom.

6. That the costs of and incidental to this suit of the applicant and of the first and second respondents shall be paid and borne by the estate of the deceased testator.

[*Appeal from Decision of the High Court.*] Against such order appeal is now had, and a cross appeal has been noted against that portion of the judgment of the High Court sanctioning the first appellant's appointment as executor of the deceased's estate.

At this point, it is, I think, advisable to draw attention to an apparent change of view, in the later judgment, on one matter dealt with in the earlier judgment. In the earlier judgment (*vide* the quotation supra) it was held "(2) that the will of the deceased is a valid will under the laws of the Bechuanaland Protectorate". This decision had been preceded by the following statement in the same judgment:

Therefore one would expect to find a right in Africans to dispose of their property by will as a means of escaping from the rigid requirements of native law and custom. A right in an African to dispose of his property as he wishes is not an invasion of native laws or customs for he is free to follow native law and custom if he wishes to do so.

In his second judgment, however, the learned Chief Justice explained that the wording of this above-quoted finding was not happy; it was not intended to convey that the deceased's will affected a valid disposition of his property, but merely that under the laws of the Protectorate he possessed testamentary capacity. In consequence enquiry proceeded upon *viva voce* evidence to ascertain whether and if so with what limitations tribal custom sanctioned the making of wills. The effect of such evidence was found by the learned Chief Justice to be that though on occasion members of the tribe had made wills in form of law, such wills were recognized and enforced by the Bakwena tribe only in so far as they disposed of the deceased's possessions in accordance with certain principles of the customary law of that tribe governing the distribution of a deceased estate. As the codicillary bequests to the second appellant (with the exception of one of furniture) were not in accord with those principles, on the grounds:

(a) that she was only a concubine, not a wife either by law or by African custom, and

(b) that they were excessive.

they were held by the court below to be invalid.

[*Appellants' Arguments.*] Such decision is now attacked on appeal on the grounds that the testamentary capacity of the deceased and the validity in form and content of his will and codicil all fall to be determined in accordance with the law of the Bechuanaland Protectorate, with the consequences that the Tswana law and custom on these matters is irrelevant and that the evidence in regard thereto was wrongly admitted, and should be disregarded for the purposes of the present appeal.

[Content of Chapter 87 on Laws of Bechuanaland, 1959. (Wills Proclamation)]

The commencing statutory provision to be considered is section 4 of the Wills Proclamation, No. 19 of 1957 (Chapter 87 of the Bechuanaland Laws, 1959 Compilation, Vol. II, p. 1152), an enactment designed, *vide* its long title, "to amend and consolidate the law relating to the execution of wills". That section provides that every person of or over the age of sixteen years may make a will in the absence of proof of mental incapacity at the time of doing so. This Proclamation draws no distinction between Europeans and Africans . . . . According to the law of the Cape Colony entire freedom of testation, in so far as concerns the testator's choice of his beneficiary, has prevailed since the Cape Act No. 23 of 1874 and is recognized in the Protectorate by Chapter 86 of its Laws (1959 edition, p. 1148). Here too there is no differentiation between African and non-African.

* * *

[Content of Chapter 144 of Laws of Bechuanaland. (Marriage Proclamation)]

Counsel for the appellants referred this Court to certain statutory provisions which specifically contemplate the making of wills by Africans: these include the Native Courts Proclamation, No. 33 of 1943, and the African Courts Proclamation, No. 19 of 1961. But the clearest provision on this matter is to be found in section 19 of cap. 144, the Marriage Proclamation of 1917, which was being amended from time to time up to 1954. That section, which came into force in 1942 and which has not been relevantly amended since, would *prima facie* appear to be conclusive in appellants' favour, at any rate on the present appeal: it clearly provides in effect that if any African has married he may dispose of his property and "unless disposed of by will it shall devolve according to Tswana law and custom". As this section is in terms made "subject to the provisions of Chapter 77" it will be necessary now to consider this Chapter, which is relied upon by respondent in connection with the Marriage Proclamation, the Administration of Estates Proclamation of 1933 (cap. 83, section 3(b)), and the Death Duties Proclamation of 1941 (cap. 84, section 42).

The relevant section, No. 4(1) of cap. 77, reads as follows:

[Content of Chapter 77 of Laws of Bechuanaland (Dissolution of Property)]

> Where at the taking effect of this Proclamation a marriage subsists between African spouses having been duly solemnized by a marriage officer or according to the rites of the Christian religion if contracted before April 1, 1917, and if contracted on or after that date having been solemnized by a marriage officer appointed under Chapter 143, and where on the dissolution of such marriage by decree of a competent court or by the death of one of the spouses a question arises as to the disposal or devolution of any

property of either or both of the spouses such question shall be heard and determined in accordance with the law of the Bechuanaland Protectorate by the court of a District Officer having jurisdiction in ordinary civil cases if it shall appear to that court on application made to it that regard being had to the mode of life of the spouses during the subsistence of the marriage it would not be just and equitable that such property should be dealt with according to African law and custom.

The learned Chief Justice construed this section as capable of application to the present case despite the fact that the deceased's marriage had taken place in 1931, i.e., after the taking effect of cap. 77.

. . .

The language of the section, in its reference to "questions which arise as to disposal or devolution of any property of either or both of the spouses", would indicate that testamentary succession might also be a relevant factor in an enquiry as to whether it would not be just and equitable for the District Officer to deal with the property in accordance with the law of the Protectorate rather than it should be dealt with according to African law and custom.

[Content of Administration of Estates Proclamation No. 33]

As I see the position, it is anomalous that this protection should be accorded to married persons only, not to bachelors, spinsters or widowers; but the explanation presumably is that the Chapter was dealing primarily with the dissolution of marriage and not primarily with inheritance. The respondent contends that this section makes the only express legislative provision for an exception to the rule that questions relating to the inheritance of Africans are to be dealt with in accordance with African law and custom. The section obviously was not intended to constitute a definite pronouncement on the law of succession and I confess to some difficulty in seeing how it could ever be effective save in regard to the extremely limited class of cases to which it refers. Its only importance (if any) is due to its mention in later statutes now to be referred to.

[Content of Chapter 84 (Death Duties Proclamation)]

[*Respondents' Arguments.*] The respondent's case rests in the main on two statutory provisions. The first is section 3(b) of the Administration of Estates Proclamation, No. 33 of 1933, which provides that such Proclamation should not apply to the estates of deceased Africans, which shall continue to be administered according to the laws and customs of the tribe to which the deceased African belonged, except as otherwise provided in cap. 77. The second is section 42 of the Death Duties Proclamation, No. 58 of 1941 (cap. 84), to the effect that notwithstanding anything in that Proclamation contained, no duty should be charged, levied or collected upon or in connection with the estate of any African which is administered in accordance with African law and custom in terms of section 3(b) of Chapter 83. The respondent's contention is that unless a successful application is made under cap. 77 all questions as to an African's ability to make a will, or to what extent he may do so, and as to the validity of any particular will, are to be determined by African law and custom. This contention does not appear to be well founded. . . .

Whatever argument can be based by respondent on the terms of section 3(b) of Chapter 83, it seems to me that this section cannot over-ride the provision of section 19 of cap. 144, which, having first been enacted in 1942 by Proclamation No. 18 of 1942, must prevail over any previous legislation inconsistent therewith. I find great difficulty in appreciating why there should have been any reference to Chapter 77 in the other provisions mentioned above (*viz.* the administration of estates and the estate duty enactments). More particularly in regard to section 19 of Chapter 144 it seems to me that to subject the provisions of that section to anything contained in cap. 77 would create a repugnancy and render section 19 of cap. 144 nugatory. To qualify a substantive provision such as the last mentioned by applying cap. 77 would in fact amount to stating that where a will is made Tswana law need not be applied: but despite this definite provision Tswana law must be applied unless the District Officer has after enquiry under cap. 77 as to the equities directed that Tswana law must be applied. [sic] It appears to me that this would create an impossible situation and the only course is to construe section 19 in question as directly permitting any African to escape from the restrictions of tribal law by making a will in terms of the Wills Act. If there were any earlier statutory provision (and this court has been referred to none) which (either in specific terms or by subjecting them in all matters to tribal laws and custom) definitely debarred Africans from disposing of their property by will that provision has been changed by the general subsequent legislative terms of section 4 of the Wills Proclamation and the particular terms of section 19 of the Marriage Proclamation as from 1942.

* * *

If this conclusion is correct it follows that the evidence adduced *viva voce* as to Tswana law and custom regarding the testamentary capacity of the deceased and the validity of his codicillary bequests to the second appellant are irrelevant and that consequently the evidence so adduced was wrongly admitted and should be disregarded by this Court in deciding upon this appeal. On this basis it follows that no consideration should be given to any of such evidence, more particularly those portions (a) which restrict the deceased's power of testation to cases of compliance of his will with the terms of tribal requirements and (b) which were to the effect that all the codicillary gifts to the second appellant were ineffectual as being in conflict with tribal custom.

[*Decision of the Appeal Court.*] . . . in my view the judgment of the High Court was erroneous in holding (1) that though the deceased had testamentary capacity, such capacity was limited by the necessity that his will should be in compliance with Tswana tribal law and custom and (2) that the various codicillary bequests to the second appellant with the exception of the gift of household furniture specified in Clause 1(a) were totally invalid. It must be emphasized that this court expresses no opinion as to whether in fact the deceased had such personal rights in the property mentioned in the codicil as to entitle him effectively to dispose of the same: this is a matter for determination by the person who has to administer the deceased's estate.

It remains now to consider the question of the first appellant's appointment as executor, before the precise order of this court on the appeal and the cross-appeal can be framed. In its order the High Court declared (paragraph 2) the present first appellant's appointment as executor of the deceased's will and codicil to be valid, but (paragraph 5) that the first appellant should be restrained from distributing the estate in accordance with the said will and codicil, and that the same should be administered in terms of Tswana law and custom. The present appeal and cross-appeal deal with these portions of the order.

[*Appellants' Contention.*] The appellants contend that the restrictions on the first appellant's authority imposed by paragraph 5 above of the Order of the High Court should be removed: the respondent in her cross appeal contends that first appellant's appointment should be entirely set aside.

[Content of Chapter 83 of the Administration of Estates Proclamation]

[*Respondents' Cross-appeal.*] The cross-appeal is rested on the wording of section 3(b) of the Administration of Estates Proclamation of 1933, Chapter 83, to the effect that (save as to the provisions of Chapter 77) the estate of a deceased African must be administered according to the law and custom of his tribe, and that the Administration of Estates Proclamation is excluded from application. The section is not expressly confined to intestate estates. If a testate estate is in issue and if this section 3(b) is applicable, the liquidation and distribution of the estate, if tribal law applies, must be effected by a particular male relation of the deceased, and consequently non-members of the tribe, whether European or not, are debarred from executorships. It can hardly be contested that the carrying out of the will, without supervision by the Master, could in the case of estates of any value and wills of any complexity (and it is more than likely that with the natural emergence of the native population to higher educational social and economic level such estates will increase in number) be a matter of difficulty and might not give effect to the deceased's expressed intentions. The respondent however contends that the wording used had this necessary result, however unfortunate.

[*Appellants' Answer.*] On the other hand, the appellants' counsel contends that the position is really governed entirely by the provision above referred to made by section 19 of cap. 144. The present form of this section is as enacted in 1942 and as it is later in date than the Estates Proclamation of 1933 would if necessary prevail over the latter.

[*The Appellate Court's Reasoning.*] This in my view is the position even though the power to make wills existed long before 1917 and consequently section 19 of cap. 144, when it deals with wills, is substantially merely declaratory of the existing law except that it specifically directs the application of Tswana law in the event of a deceased not having disposed by will of his property. Now it seems to me that the recognition by section 19 of cap. 144 of the deceased's will as excluding the devolution of his property according to Tswana law and custom does not stop at mere recognition of the fact that an African can make a will, but that when the words "disposed of by will" are used the legislature meant to give full validity to the deceased's will. The deceased has in a properly executed will provided that his property should devolve on certain persons and if (as he would normally do and in this case did do) he provided who was to carry out his testamentary desires it appears that the section should be construed to validate not only the bequests but also the method prescribed by the deceased of carrying them into effect—*viz.* through a nominated executor who would be subject to the normal duties of an executor in law. It seems anomalous that the legislature should in testate estates have excluded the substantive provisions of tribal law as to devolution and yet have intended to leave untouched any machinery of administration which might possibly have been provided by such tribal administration. In the prevailing circumstances the appointment of an executor implies in my view the administration of the estate by the statutory machinery available for the purpose. To substitute a different form of administration would amount to the making of a different will for the testator and *pro tanto* to an interference with his freedom of testation.

[*The Decision.*] I have therefore come to the conclusion that on this aspect of the case as well the appeal succeeds, and the cross-appeal fails. The Order of this Court is as follows:

(1) The appeal is allowed.

(2) Paragraph 1 of the Order of the High Court dated July 17, 1963 is amended by the deletion of the concluding words "to the extent that the said deceased had testamentary capacity to make the same".

(3) Paragraphs 2 and 3 of that Order (the latter not being challenged on either appeal or cross-appeal) are affirmed.

(4) Paragraphs 4 and 5 of that Order are set aside and this Court declares that the bequests in the said codicil to the second

appellant are not invalidated by reason of their being in any way not sanctioned by Tswana law and custom.

(5) The costs of all parties both in the High Court and on hearing before this Court are by agreement directed to be paid and borne by the estate of the deceased.

ROPER, J. A.: I concur in this judgment.

QUESTIONS

1. What are the basic issues raised by this case which the courts had to address?

2. What would have been the distribution of Chief Sechele's property under customary law?

3. Why didn't the Chief change his will to make his wife his heir since he must have known that he was childless?

4. Is there any evidence for the assertion made in the case that making a statutory marriage means a commitment to a more or less total non-customary (or European) lifestyle?

5. Generally speaking, Botswana law holds that the property of Africans shall devolve according to African law and custom. But there are exceptions that allow for Africans' property to devolve according to statutory law. What are they? Do you think these exceptions operate consistently? How sure can an African citizen of Botswana be that his or her property will devolve according to statutory law and not customary law?

6. Why do African legislators and jurists push for express statutory provisions about matters such as how free the testamentary right is for a person of tribal background? What do the arguments in this case reveal about what happens in the absence of explicit statutory guidance?

7. In what way was the High Court's decision a hybrid (applying a set of rules from statutory and customary law to a single legal situation) while the Appeal Court's decision applied just one type of law? Which decision do you think produced the more equitable results? Why?

SOME ADDITIONAL QUESTIONS

8. What is the assumption that underlies Section Number 4(1) of cap. 77. Can it be construed as ethnocentric and/or subtly racist?

9. If one accepts the logic of the respondent, what ramifying legal consequences may flow from a person of tribal background marrying under statutory law?

b. Devolution of Property in Statutory Marriages

NOTE

The case of Fraenkel and Makwati v. Sechele, which was very well known in Botswana, pointed up the fact that it was uncertain whether customary law or statutory law would apply in the case of Africans who had married under statutory law. The source of this ambiguity is Chapter 29:06 of the Laws of Botswana [Dissolution of African Marriages (Disposal of Property)] [formerly Chapter 77 of the Laws of the Bechuanaland Protectorate]. Since *Fraenkel* the Parliament of Botswana has passed legislation designed to reduce the ambiguity.

Even though the law covering marital property has been changed in this way, it is interesting to note that the profile of cases published in Botswana Law Reports over the past several years shows that the transfer of property after death is less an area of conflict or uncertainty than the division of property at dissolution of marriage. However, the change in the law concerning the allocation of spousal property in marriage is likely to have some rub-off effect on freedom of testament.

Under the provisions of Chapter 29:03 of the Laws of Botswana [Married Women's Property], in statutory marriages between Africans, property shall be held and disposed of according to African customary law unless the parties take explicit, written steps to declare that they wish their property to be governed by statutory law.

Laws of Botswana, Chapter 29:03, Section 7.

Proprietary consequences of African marriages Cap. 29:06

7.   (1) Subject to the provisions of this section and of the Dissolution of African Marriages (Disposal of Property) Act, notwithstanding that the matrimonial domicile of a marriage between Africans (not being a marriage under any customary law) [is] in Botswana such marriage shall not affect the property of the spouses which shall be held, may be disposed of, and, unless disposed of by will, shall devolve according to customary law.

(2) Notwithstanding subsection (1), the spouses in a marriage between Africans may, where the matrimonial domicile is in Botswana, prior to the solemnization of the marriage or where such marriage was solemnized prior to 1st January, 1971, by instrument in writing, signed by each of them and in the presence of two persons, one of whom shall be an administrative officer or justice of the peace or a commissioner of oaths, who shall subscribe thereto as witnesses, express their intention to be exempt from the provisions of subsection (1).

(3) Such instrument shall be as nearly as possible in one of the forms set forth in the Second Schedule and shall specify whether the spouses wish to avail themselves of the provisions of this Act by excluding community of property and of profit and loss and the marital power or otherwise and if they do so avail themselves of such provisions then community of property and of profit and loss and the marital power shall be so excluded in accordance with the provisions of section 3(1); if they do not so avail themselves, the said instrument shall have the effect of an instrument executed under section 3.

. . .

SECOND SCHEDULE

(Section 7)

FORM A

We, the undersigned A. B. of _____ and C. D. of _____ do hereby solemnly express our wish to be:

  (a) that the proprietary consequences of our contemplated marriage should be regulated by the common law and not the customary law and in consequence we wish to be exempt from the provisions of section 7(1) of the Married Women's Property Act; and

  (b) to avail ourselves of the provisions of the said Act by excluding community of property and of profit and loss and the marital power.

Signed <u>A. B.</u>
<u>C. D.</u>

Witnesses: 1.

  Present: 2.

  N. B. One witness must be an administrative officer, a justice of the peace or a commissioner of oaths.

FORM B

We, the undersigned A. B. of _____ and C. D. of _____ do hereby solemnly express our wish to be

  (a) that the proprietary consequences of our contemplated marriage should be regulated by the common law and not the customary law and in consequence we wish to be exempt from the provisions of section 7(1) of the Married Women's Property Act, and

  (b) that we do not desire to avail ourselves of the provisions of the said Act as aforesaid.

Signed <u>A. B.</u>
<u>C. D.</u>

Witnesses: 1.

  Present: 2.

  N. B. One witness must be an administrative officer, a justice of the peace or a commissioner of oaths.

QUESTIONS

1. How does this recent law reduce the ambiguity that existed previously concerning the disposition of property of Africans married under the statutory law? In what way will this law probably increase freedom of testament for Africans married in this way?

2. Can this law be viewed as strengthening the role customary law or at least preserving it?

3. A Glance at the Future

NOTE

In January 1982 a proposal was made by a Parliamentary Committee in Botswana to the effect that plural marriages should be possible under statutory law in particular, specified circumstances:

Customary Marriage and Marriage Act Report

By Andrew Sesinyi

MAJOR CHANGES will creep into the marriage circles when a Bill is presented in the next session of Parliament, early this year implementing the recommendations of the report of the Law Reform Committee

The Parliamentary committee reported on the Customary Marriage and the Marriage Act, after widespread countrywide tours and extensive research.

The Report was accepted by the National Assembly last year and the process of implementation will start with the presentation of ammendment bills in the next session.

The Report recommends, among other things, that polygamy should be granted under special circumstances only. It had been observed by the public and the Committee that parallel marriages, i.e one under the Customary Law and the other under the Marriage Act must be eliminated. Under the Marriage Act all marriages are monogamous whilst under the Customary Law a marriage can be either monogamous or polygamous, depending on the wishes of the marrying parties.

"Therefore the Committee feels that there must be a provision to enable the parties to apply to a competent court for a waiver-/exemption to marry a second wife," the Report states.

The special circumstances recommended to apply under polygamous marriage are singled out as:

The couple have no children as a result of the first wife's infertility.

Provision has been made to give the first wife adequate property, i.e. not less than half of the property.

The first wife is provided with a separate and independent homestead

The first wife has freely and willingly agreed to the second marriage

Marriages under Muslim and other religious sects where polygamy is recognised, are also governed by the same special circumstances under the recommendations

Major changes also feature in the early stages of marriage

The Committee recommends that the Marriage Act should be ammended to provide that-

No marriage officer shall solemnise a marriage between those under 21 years without the consent of the respective parents

In the case of those over 21 years the marriage officer shall not solemnise the marriage unless he is satisfied that the respective parents of the marrying parties have been consulted

The requirements is what the Committee understands as "patlo."

Marriage procedures are generally to be tightened

The Committee recommends that the Marriage Act should be ammended to enable the Minister to appoint any Chief or Headman presiding over a Customary Court of Record to solemnise any marriage within the area of his jurisdiction Such marriage officers should issue the normal Marriage Certificate registered by the Registrar of Marriages

In this way, the committee believes, Batswana will have three marriage forums to chose from i e The ordinary man in the village will go to the Kgotla, the religiously inclined to the church and the urban types to the Magistrate/District Commissioner

In the event of divorce, the Committee recommends that the parties should have a choice of going to the highest Customary court in the District or to a Magistrate and that any appeal from such court should lie to the High Court, provided, however that the parties may apply direct to the High Court for the granting of their divorce

These recommendations will definitely draw a record crowd to Parliament when the Bill is presented between February and March this year
BOPA

QUESTIONS

1. What do you think the Law Report would have set out as the arguments for ending parallel marriages?

2. In the previous question would one of the arguments be that the proposed changes would be a step in the direction of unifying the legal system? If so, in what ways would the system be more unified?

3. Do you see any problems in implementing the recommendation, which holds that "provision has been made to give the first wife adequate property, i.e., not less than half of the property?" What about property that is acquired after the second marriage has taken place? How should it be held?

4. There also may be problems concerning inheritance in the proposed polygynous marriages. Again, still focusing on property acquired after the second marriage: how should it devolve after the death of the husband? Presumably, the first wife would be childless. Should this affect the pattern of devolution at all?

5. If the proposed changes are made, in fifty years' time what changes might one expect to see in the devolution of property from husband to wife in Botswana?

Chapter 10

SUCCESSION TO POLITICAL OFFICE
IN BOTSWANA

———

A. INTRODUCTION

NOTE

Suppose, in our hypothetical for Problem I, the man who dies intestate is a Tswana chief. We now know how his property would be disposed of. But what of the chieftaincy? How is succession determined? Given the centrality of chieftaincy, this is an important question.

Among the Tswana, succession to the office of "chief," like inheritance, is related to the predominately patrilineal nature of Tswana society and to its social and political structure, including family forms and marriage forms. Traditional succession to Tswana chieftaincy contrasts with succession to office in the West because the major criterion for eligibility is birth. Case materials, however, show that "appropriate" birth is not cut and dried but is a matter of negotiation: a dimension of law in action, as compared with law as a set of fixed rules. The cases also show that succession, again like inheritance, is not something that occurs after death, but is a continual process. This process is "political" even when it seems to involve matters that, on the face of it, pertain to kinship and marriage.

Finally, case material raises the issue of how, in the colonial and post-independence periods, the authority and concerns of the State influenced and even blocked succession to chieftaincy and accelerated a shift of the quest for political power to other arenas.

B. TSWANA SUCCESSION TO POLITICAL OFFICE

1. Introduction: Chiefly Succession Rooted in Marriage

NOTE

Eligibility for chieftaincy, traditionally, was by birth, by being the particular offspring of a particular marriage. But because marriage among the Tswana is rather negotiable, to understand Tswana succession to chieftaincy, we will need to examine the forms and formation of Tswana marriage more thoroughly than we did in the previous chapter. We will begin by looking at how anthropologists conceptualize marriage in general and then examine Tswana marriage in conceptual terms.

2. Conceptualizing Marriage

NOTE

Analytically and quite artificially, anthropologists conceptualize marriage in terms of the transfer of certain rights over a woman and her labor. Logically, however, marriage could be analyzed equally well in terms of rights acquired over men. There are five rights over a woman that a man may acquire in marriage: (1) exclusive (as defined by the culture) sexual rights over her, sometimes referred to as the conjugal right, (2) the right to her reproductive capacity, that is, the right to affiliate any children that she may bear exclusively with his kin group, (3) the right to determine her residence after marriage, (4) and the right to benefit from her labor. A few anthropologists have isolated a fifth right over a person, the jural right, the right to ultimate jural authority over a woman as measured by the right to claim compensation for her death and/or the right to avenge her death. Sometimes these rights are referred to as rights *in personam*, i.e., rights over the person.

3. Tswana Marriage

NOTE

With the rights in personam conceptual scheme as a frame of reference, let us turn to a descriptive analysis of the stages of Tswana marriage. A striking feature of these stages is that they involve a considerable amount of ambiguity.

John Comaroff and Simon Roberts, Rules and Processes: The Cultural Logic of Dispute in an African Context. Chicago: University of Chicago Press, 1981, pp. 133–137. Citations omitted. Footnotes omitted.

Classification of Unions. The Tswana classify heterosexual unions along a continuum delineated by duration and jural state. At one extreme are transient relationships in which couples merely cohabit intermittently over a short period, with neither party making any enduring commitment to the other. If the arrangement develops into an established liaison, it may be described by the term *bonyatsi*, which is usually translated as "concubinage." If the man and woman stay together more permanently but do not initiate any procedural formalities, they may be said to be "living together" (*ba dula mmogo*). Once official negotiations are set in motion, however, the union is on the way to becoming a "marriage" (*nyalo*). At the other pole of the continuum stand those relationships that have passed through all the various stages of the conjugal process.

Despite the apparent precision with which the continuum is ordered, everyday terminological usage does not distinguish clearly between the different forms of mating. Hence, for example, when a man speaks of his *mosadi* ("woman"), he may be referring to a partner of long standing or to a woman with whom he is having only a fleeting affair. Similarly, the term usually translated as "to marry" (*go nyala* [m.]; *go nyalwa* [f.]) may be loosely used to describe the creation of either an approved conjugal tie or a less formal liaison. The Tswana, of course, impute sharply contrasting social, material, and jural implications to these different kinds of bond, but in the context of everyday utterance such contrasts are latent rather than overt. It will become clear that the endemic ambiguity of these terms has a particular semantic value; their capacity to obscure distinctions is closely linked to the fact that, while the formal classification and definition of heterosexual unions are unequivocally shared, the status of many of them is open to negotiation for much of their existence. Moreover, the continuum itself will be seen to represent the range of possible constructions that an individual may seek to impose on a specific union. This characteristic of the continuum in turn is to be understood with reference to the process by which a legitimate union is ostensibly established.

The Formation of Unions. In common with patterns found in many African societies, a Tswana union is held to mature slowly, progressively attracting incidents as time passes. Traditionally, the first element of the process, at least as it is formally conceived, involved a spouse being selected for a man by his guardian and close kin, who undertook negotiations (*patlo*) in his name. (Today most men choose mates for themselves and later seek the approval of their close kin.) It is not agnatic *units* that participate in such negotiations, however, but those *individuals* who constitute the effective ego-centered kindreds of the respective parents. Typically, some of the paternal and maternal uncles of the couple are included among them. *Patlo* proceedings are concluded with the acceptance of a gift (*dilo tsa patlo; mokwele*) by the guardian of the woman, who thus expresses his agreement to the marriage.

The transfer of *dilo tsa patlo* is taken to signify the commitment of both partners and their kin to the union. It also entitles the couple formally to sleep together in the woman's homestead at night (*go ralala*), provided they are regarded as sufficiently mature by their guardians. In the past this stage might continue for several years, and it often developed gradually into uxorilocal residence. In fact, children were often born to the couple before the next phase of the process was initiated. Among the Kgatla this continues to be the case, albeit to a limited extent; in contrast, Rolong seldom observe *go ralala* formalities today. Furthermore, while cohabitation should not occur before the conclusion of the *patlo*, this seems to be complied with only rarely by modern Tswana.

The next phase of the marriage process should be the removal of the woman to a homestead prepared for her in the man's natal *kgotla*. It is said that, in the past, this was supposed to be preceded by further formal visits to the *kgotla* of her guardian, in the course of which representatives of the wife-takers would make ceremonial requests for a *segametse* ("drawer-of-water"). There has been a growing tendency, however—especially evident among the Rolong—for the conjugal home to be established with little formality or ceremonial.

Finally, bridewealth (*bogadi*) should be transferred to the woman's guardian at this juncture or some stage thereafter. It usually consists of two to six head of cattle, but it may also include small stock or cash. The mobilization of the animals is usually undertaken by the prospective husband himself, possibly with the aid of his father or his mother's brother. In theory, too, he may use some of the bridewealth received for his cattle-linked sister in making his own marriage payments, although this seldom occurs in practice; the unions of siblings, or the exchanges they involve, are, by and large, not carefully synchronized among the Tswana. Similarly, distribution patterns are straightforward: the woman's father will receive the stock and earmark them for her linked brother; if her father is dead, they will be integrated directly into her brother's herd, since these beasts should be used to look after her, particularly in the event that her own union is prematurely dissolved. Perhaps the most noteworthy feature of bridewealth arrangements in these chiefdoms is the widespread tendency to delay the exchange. Neither Kgatla nor Rolong insist that it be made either at, or soon after, the creation of a union. Both the amount and timing of *bogadi* are left entirely to the discretion of wife-takers. Not only are they nonnegotiable, but it is generally regarded as unseemly for the parties to allude even indirectly to such matters. And, as we saw earlier, many men delay the transfer at least until their children begin to marry (see below).

The final element in the establishment of a union, public recognition, is unlike the others in that it is not formally marked by a specific incident or event. In particular, there are no elaborate *rites de passage* to acknowledge the formation of a new bond. The transfer of bridewealth may occasion feasting, but this usually occurs late in the developmental cycle and serves, in reality, to define a union, qua marriage, as the *outcome* of a relationship over time (see below). It is also not infrequent for public opinion, where it is directly expressed at all, to be less than unanimous, for disagreements can and do arise out of competing interests in such a union. Nevertheless, it will become clear that Tswana courts, in deliberating upon a marital dispute, set great store by the way in which the relationship in question is regarded by kin and by local groupings. They appear to attach very limited weight to ceremonial formalities or exchanges in making their decisions.

The marriage process, then, contains a number of constituent elements: (1) the *patlo* negotiations; (2) the transfer of *dilo tsa patlo;* (3) *go ralala*, which permits nocturnal cohabitation but not coresidence; (4) uxorilocal residence and the birth of children, followed by the establishment of a permanent household in which the couple assume conventional conjugal roles; (5) the transfer of *bogadi;* and (6) public recognition. None of these elements, however, with the limited exception of the *transfer* of bridewealth, serves invariably or unambiguously to define or confer validity upon any particular union.

NOTE

The *normative* role of *bogadi* as it is seen by the Tswana is stated very succinctly in Schapera's major study of Tswana law. This passage parallels the main one to which Comaroff and Roberts refer in footnote 1 of the preceding excerpt. How can one reconcile Schapera's normative view with the more descriptive picture of actuality presented by Comaroff and Roberts?

Isaac Schapera, A Handbook of Tswana Law and Custom, London: Oxford University Press, 2d ed., 1955, p. 139. Footnote omitted.

But the main function of *bogadi* is to transfer the reproductive power of a woman from her own family into that of her husband. This fact is of considerable importance, for upon it rests the whole Tswana conception of legitimacy. Summarizing this briefly, it may be said that no form of cohabitation between a man and a woman is held to be a proper marriage unless it is accompanied by the transfer of, or understanding to transfer, *bogadi.* No man can claim, for any purpose, the children he has by any woman, until he and his family gave agreed to transfer, and under certain circumstances until they have actually transferred, *bogadi.* On the other hand, all children borne by a married woman, no matter who their actual father may be, are held to be the legal offspring of the man on whose behalf *bogadi* for that woman was given out. *"Bogadi"*, in the words of one informant, "is given out because the woman is coming *go agèla motse* (to raise up the village)." All the incidents flowing out of the *bogadi* transfer are directly derived from this conception.

QUESTIONS

1. Traditionally, what rights over a woman were transferred by conveyance of *dilo tsa patlo?*

2. Is transfer of *bogadi* necessary for a mate to acquire the right to determine a woman's residence? Is it necessary to acquire filiation of children born to a union?

3. In Tswana society when is a conjugal union a fully validated, "legal" union?

4. How do you think the apparent disagreement about whether particular incidents or transactions necessarily mark a proper Tswana marriage can be reconciled or explained?

FOR FURTHER THOUGHT

5. Why do you think the transfer of bridewealth is publicized and ritualized to some extent in almost all societies?

6. Is this transfer always ceremonialized among the Tswana? What are the consequences of the degree of ceremonialization there?

NOTE

Let us turn to Tswana cases to see with what certainty laws about marriage are applied to actual disputes. What does the following case suggest about the role of *bogadi* in defining a union as marriage? What does it imply about the function of the transfer of *bogadi* in determining the filiation of children:

John Comaroff and Simon Roberts, Rules and Processes: The Cultural Logic of Dispute in an African Context. Chicago: The University of Chicago Press, 1981, Chapter V, pp. 154–155. Footnotes omitted.

FIGURE 1. THE CASE OF TOLLO AND MOTLAKADIBE

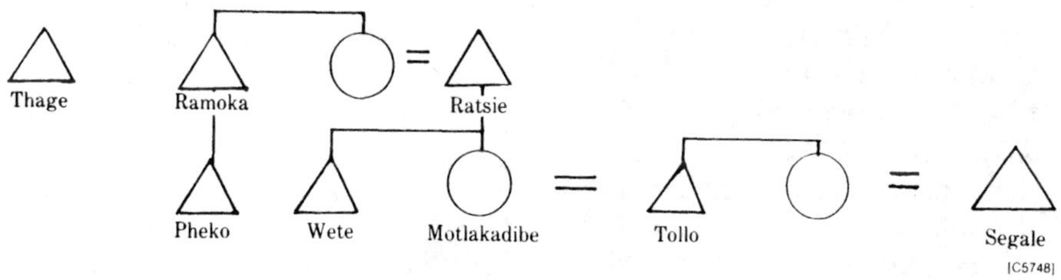

Motlakadibe is the eldest daughter of Ratsie, a Tebele immigrant who married a woman from Rampedi ward and settled there. Tollo, a member of the Morema ward, initiated *patlo* negotiations for her in 1942, while Motlakadibe was still at school. On his side, these negotiations were conducted by his ZH,* Segale, and, on Motlakadibe's, by a maternal uncle, Ramoka. Soon after, it was arranged for Tollo to "find his way into Motlakadibe's hut," and, before her education was finished, his kinsmen asked if she could accompany him when he went abroad to work. This was agreed to by her parents, and the couple spent approximately seven years in the Transvaal. No *bogadi* was presented for Motlakadibe. While they were away, they managed to buy some cattle and a plough. Five children were also born, and, when they returned, they settled down to manage the cattle and cultivate a field together among Tollo's kinsmen. They had not been back long when relations between them became strained. There were repeated quarrels, and Tollo accused Motlakadibe of having affairs with other men, particularly Setshwane Setshwane, whose home was in Moganetse ward, not far from Rampedi.

* sister's husband.

In the late 1950s Motlakadibe left Tollo and returned with the children to her father's homestead in Rampedi. By now, Ratsie was dead, and Motlakadibe and the children were given succor for most of the period 1959–60 by her maternal kinsmen and her younger brothers. Pheko, her MBS,* sold two beasts to provide food for her and her children, and her youngest brother, Wete, then working at the mines, sent at least R20 for their maintenance. All this time no word came from Morema *kgotla* about the breakdown of the union.

The dispute was eventually heard in the Morema *kgotla* toward the end of 1960, after Motlakadibe's kinsmen had themselves complained. When the matter was heard, Motlakadibe told of her marriage to Tollo and of his subsequent neglect. But Tollo responded by denying that they were married and claiming that Motlakadibe was just a concubine whom he had impregnated.

The headman dealt with the dispute as a case of impregnation and ordered Tollo to pay four head of cattle plus an additional R20 for the maintenance of the children. [This sum seems to have been related to the amount that Wete provided for the same purposes when Motlakadibe was back in the Rampedi ward during 1959–60.]

Motlakadibe's kinsmen then took the dispute to the chief's *kgotla*, complaining that the matter should be treated as a broken marriage and not as a simple case of impregnation. Before the chief, the dispute was introduced by Thage; one of Motlakadibe's maternal kinsmen. He told the *kgotla* of the original negotiations and how permission had been granted for Motlakadibe to accompany Tollo to work abroad. He then went on to describe how the couple had returned and started to cultivate a field together, and he said that he had been surprised to see Motlakadibe return alone with her children to Rampedi, without any word from the people of Morema. Finally, he mentioned how her kin at Rampedi had been obliged to maintain her and her children. Thereafter, Motlakadibe spoke of the property that she and Tollo had accumulated during their time together, objecting that Tollo had marked them with the brand of his ZH,** Segale. She ended her account by telling the court of her quarrels with Tollo; his neglect, she argued, had obliged her to return eventually to Rampedi.

Tollo attributed the souring of their relationship to Motlakadibe's affairs with other men. The final break had come when Motlakadibe had refused to sleep with him, ostensibly to force him to present *bogadi*. In this context, the defendant did not attempt to argue, as he had done in the Morema ward, that the dispute was simply one of impregnation. When pressed by the chief, he admitted that Motlakadibe was his wife.

In judgment the chief clearly accepted Motlakadibe's definition of the relationship. Since it had obviously broken down, they should now divorce. He ordered that the children be looked after by their

* mother's brother's son.   ** sister's husband.

mother and that Motlakadibe should retain the field to cultivate for them. The nine head of cattle that remained of the herd accumulated by the couple while they were abroad were to be divided: six were awarded to Motlakadibe, and three were left with Tollo.

QUESTIONS

1. Was *bogadi* transferred for Motlakadibe?

2. Is it clear from the judgment where the children were considered to be filiated as a result of the disposition of the case?

3. Why was this union held to be a marriage by the chief?

4. If the ultimate filiation of the children was with the mother's kin, was the total pattern of allocation of rights over the woman in this case consistent with proper marriage as the Tswana view it ideally?

ADDITIONAL QUESTIONS

5. Who assumed guardianship for a woman whose "husband" was neglecting her?

6. What does this case show about the relationship of Tswana to their maternal kinspersons?

NOTE

How consistent are Tswana dispute settlement agencies in defining the legal effect of transferring *bogadi*? Consider the following case:

John Comaroff and Simon Roberts, Rules and Processes: The Cultural Logic of Dispute in an African Context. Chicago: The University of Chicago Press, 1981, Chapter V, p. 160. (Footnotes omitted).

FIGURE 2. THE CASE OF RAMAJA AND MMAKGOTHA'S CHILDREN

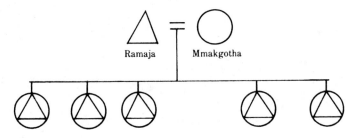

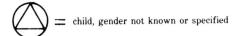 = child, gender not known or specified

[C5749]

Ramaja, a man from the Ramadiakobong ward, began negotiations to marry Mmakgotha, from Ramasilela, in about 1951. *Dilo tsa patlo* was presented, and not long afterward her parents allowed him to take her to Johannesburg, where he was working. In 1953 she returned to her parents to have her first child. Later she went back to Johannesburg for a while, but returned again to the Kgatleng, where she bore twins. In 1958, while still at home, she was made pregnant by a man from Tlokweng, and her relations with Ramaja seem to have deteriorated rapidly after that. She bore another child with the man from Tlokweng, and, in 1964, Ramaja brought her before the chief's *kgotla*, complaining of these births. Following the original negotiations, no further steps were taken, and no *bogadi* was presented.

Introducing his grievance at the chief's *kgotla*, Ramaja related how the negotiations had been completed and how her parents had allowed him to take her to Johannesburg. He then went on to say that he had been able to forgive her the first pregnancy by the man from Tlokweng but not the second. Mmakgotha confirmed what Ramaja said about the negotiations [*Ramaja o ne a mpatla sentle ka molao, a ba a gorosa dilo tsa patlo*]. She explained the birth of the children by the man from Tlokweng by saying that Ramaja had neglected her while she was at home. Other witnesses confirmed the negotiations, and Ramaja's relations told how they had taken corn to feed Mmakgotha while Ramaja was in Johannesburg (thus seeking to negate the charge of neglect). In answer to a question from the court, Ramaja explained that he had taken no action against the man from Tlokweng because he had "not yet presented *bogadi*" for Mmakgotha.

The chief placed the blame for the breakdown on Mmakgotha for bearing children with another man while she was Ramaja's wife. Ordering the couple to part, he directed that Ramaja's children should belong to his descent group and that those by the man from Tlokweng should go with Mmakgotha.

QUESTIONS

1. Was *bogadi* transferred for Mmakgotha?

2. What did the court determine as the filiation of the children?

3. In what way was the holding in this case inconsistent with that in The Case of Tollo and Motlakadibe?

4. What does this inconsistency suggest about the explicitness and clarity of Tswana norms about the transfer of rights in marriage?

NOTE

The Case of Tollo and Motlakadibe and The Case of Ramaja and Mmakgotha's children are just the tip of the iceberg. Consideration of a fuller range of Tswana disputes about marriage makes it still more clear that Tswana rules about the stages of marriage have many qualifications, exceptions, and most of all, ambiguities. These ambiguities characterize every step of the Tswana marriage process, but, as we have seen, the uncertainty that surrounds the application of norms about *bogadi* is a particularly apt case in point. What are the consequences of delayed transfer of *bogadi*? Think of this delay as creating an ambiguity. Does this ambiguity create any potential for negotiation or denial?

It is clear that, under customary law, the status of a Tswana union as marriage or as something else is negotiable. It is not simply a matter of whether certain formalities—especially formal exchanges—have taken place. The standing of the union depends on what characteristically spousely actions the couple have carried out vis-a-vis each other as well as what actions they have engaged in vis-a-vis their relatives and vis-a-vis other persons—including any lovers. "Public" recognition also is a factor taken into account. In assessing the import of all of these factors for the standing of the union, a version of the Reasonable Man (better Reasonable Person) concept comes into play.

4. Tswana Marriage and Tswana Politics

NOTE

Recent research on Tswana law by Comaroff and Roberts has focused particularly on marriage and politics. They have not studied marriage as an isolated institution, but in its field of interaction with political structures and political activities. This approach is influenced by contemporary social science thinking about decision-making, strategizing, and the kinds of costs and benefits of which actors take account in making decisions. Thus, Roberts and Comaroff's field research was informed by questions like the following: What kind of factors do Tswana men and women take account of when deciding whether to go through *patlo* negotiations, to simply cohabit, to press for the transfer of *bogadi*, or to seek divorce? When and in what way are political goals such as the need for political allies having political influence or the desire for political office one of the factors taken account of in making decisions about marriage? How do Tswana men and women use the legal norms about marriage—especially those about the definition of unions—to achieve their goals in marriage? If they see marriage as an instrument for achieving political goals, do they use legal norms about marriage—especially their ambiguity—to achieve those goals? In short, do Tswana use the conceptual repertoire of their law to help them achieve personal marital goals and political goals or, even, both at the same time? Does Tswana law lend itself to this? In this context, what are the consequences of the fact that many Tswana practice preferential cousin marriage, including parallel cousin marriage?

Consider the following biographical sketch of a Tswana notable which shows the relationship of the management of affinal (in-law) relations and politics:

John Comaroff and Simon Roberts, Rules and Processes: The Cultural Logic of Dispute in an African Context. Chicago: The Uni-

versity of Chicago Press, 1981, Chapter V, pp. 171–173. Footnote renumbered.

FIGURE 3. KABO'S CAREER

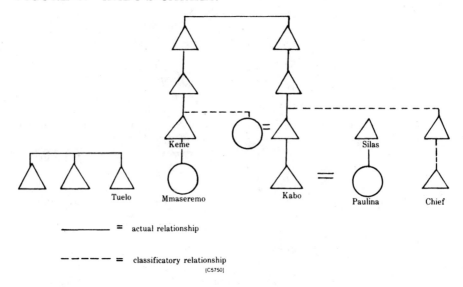

—————— = actual relationship

— — — — — = classificatory relationship
[C5750]

When he was in his early twenties, Kabo, a royal, entered a union with a commoner woman, Paulina, and they established a home at his cattle post. Informal *patlo* negotiations were initiated but, according to informants, were not completed. While it is not clear whether a promise of bridewealth was ever made, Paulina was certainly allocated a nearby field to cultivate. No children were born to the union, however. Kabo and Paulina's wealthy father, Silas, had always been on good terms, and, when the liaison was established, the two men arranged a cooperative farming enterprise. By the terms of this agreement, Silas used Kabo's land and some machinery he had recently inherited, and, providing the necessary labor and management, Silas shared the yield with the younger man.

Kabo had a partly derelict house in Kgosing, the chiefly ward, but he did not bring Paulina to live in it. At first he spent most of his time with her at the cattle post and visited the capital only intermittently. After three or four years, however, he began to participate more actively in the affairs of the chiefly *kgotla* and stayed for longer periods in Kgosing, where he rebuilt his homestead. Soon he began to take an interest in Mmaseremo, his FFFBSSD.* Although no formal negotiations took place on this occasion, either, the couple began to live together in Kabo's house, and three sons were born to the union in rapid succession.

Kabo gradually allowed the bond with Paulina to lapse. Both he and Silas admit to having discussed the matter, but little seems to

* Father's father's father's brother's son's son's daughter.

have been done about it. Kabo claims to have said that there had
been no marriage; and the question of formal divorce appears not to
have arisen, possibly because there were few assets, either material
or human, over which disagreement could occur. More important,
however, is the fact that Silas had little to gain from a dispute: he
was enjoying a substantial profit from the cooperative farming venture, which Kabo took care not to terminate for another two years.
Moreover, Paulina soon entered into another liaison and went to live
with her new partner at his village (outside the capital). Silas immediately took the opportunity to enter an agricultural contract with
him as well, so that the lapse of the prospective affinal tie with Kabo
involved no major material loss. Kabo also appears to have encouraged Paulina's new liaison. He, too, had benefited from his relationship with her, and its amicable termination meant that he could
now concentrate his marriage strategies in a new, and more appropriate, direction.

In establishing himself at the capital, Kabo became a trusted adviser of the chief, his classificatory FBS.* The father of Mmaseremo, Keme, a classificatory paternal *and* maternal uncle, was also a
powerful royal adviser, an influential public figure, and the head of a
large ward. Keme and Kabo became close allies; the former had no
personal ambitions with respect to the chiefship, but he persuaded
Kabo to think of himself as a future officeholder. Indeed, Keme's
behavior toward Kabo conformed largely to the indigenous normative
model of the MB–ZS ** relationship—in fact, it was in these terms
that the two men mutually labeled their bond. The union between
Kabo and Mmaseremo was successful for many years. Although no
patlo negotiations had taken place or *bogadi* been transferred, the
couple assumed the conventional conjugal roles of husband, wife, and
affine, and nobody questioned the status of their bond.

During the following eighteen years or so, Kabo gradually became one of the most powerful men in the chiefdom, and, when the
incumbent chief died, childless, a faction supporting his claim to office quickly asserted itself. It is impossible to recount the events
surrounding the succession, save to say that, in the process, relations
between Kabo and Mmaseremo became strained. Kabo had entered
a liaison with a younger (junior) royal, Tuelo, whose brothers had become his particularly close allies and were leading members of his
faction. Keme had disapproved of this alliance, fearing (he claimed)
that Kabo's reputation would suffer if it were commonly known that
he had recruited young and immature advisers. Kabo, in turn, suggested that Keme had become senile. (He certainly was very old by
now and was incapacitated for much of the time.) At first, Kabo
sought to maintain both sets of alliances, but, as Keme became more

* Father's brother's son.　　　　** Mother's brother—sister's son relationship.

critical of him, he decided that the support of Tuelo's agnates was of more consequence than that of the ailing elder.

Kabo wished to bring matters to a head; he therefore transferred bridewealth for Mmaseremo and then let it be known that he wanted to divorce her. The *bogadi* transfer was intended unequivocally to assert control over the three children, for, apart from the indigenously stressed desirability of a chief's having sons, the youths were fast approaching marriageable age. But Mmaseremo, advised by her father, confronted Kabo with the fact that she did not wish to be divorced. Keme himself then took matters further by spelling out to his son-in-law the dangers inherent in his strategy. The case would have to go to the local commissioner, since there was no chief in office and nobody else could or would hear it. The commissioner was unlikely to grant a divorce, for Mmaseremo's behavior had been impeccable and she would, moreover, publicly forgive Kabo's adultery. Under these conditions, he stood the risk of appearing either a fool or a miscreant if he pursued the case. In any event, his chances of becoming chief would suffer.

Kabo discussed this with several of his allies, including Tuelo's brothers. The consensus of the advice he received was to leave the matter in abeyance, at least until the succession was decided. About three months later, Kabo was designated as chief. At his installation, murmurings about the trouble between him and his affines were everywhere to be heard. Indeed, though her three sons were present, Mmaseremo did not appear in public that day.[1]

NOTE

Kabo's biography illustrates how marriage may be used to advance a career. Recall that Kabo was a royal. Do the structural situation and the actions remind you of the Tudors and the Stuarts? Notice how Kabo used the ambiguities of marriage to ease out of one union and into another. Note, too, how he utilized affines (in-laws) as political allies. Keme, because of earlier cousin marriages, was Kabo's classificatory father's brother and classificatory mother's brother, although he and Kabo emphasized the latter link. Kabo's claim to the chieftainship involved the mobilization of his various alliances—many of which were rooted in his own unions, as well as those of his forebears—into a faction or support group. But observe that Kabo's chances for the chieftainship were affected by the standing of his own marriage and that, accordingly, he postponed his plans for divorce. And, ironically, the formal standing of the marriage turned on his political goals and strategies, not events in the marriage itself. Marriage and politics were inextricably intertwined.

1. Because the period of fieldwork ended soon after the installation, we are unable to document subsequent events.

QUESTIONS

1. Was Kabo's union with Paulina a marriage? What paradigm for argument could Paulina and her father Silas use in asserting that it was? What paradigm for argument could Kabo use in his counter claim?

2. What about the union with Mmaseremo? Was it a marriage? What paradigms for argument could be used in claiming either that it was or was not?

3. Does this case suggest a possible generalization as to when in the cycle of marriage long-delayed *bogadi* may be transferred?

4. How did Kabo make use of the ambiguities surrounding the norms of Tswana marriage? How did these ambiguities help him to make use of marriage as a resource for constructing alliances?

5. How did Kabo use marriage as an "individuated" and "negotiable" resource?

6. Does this biographical sketch help you to understand the following statement by Comaroff and Roberts: "The exploitation of jural flexibility and the success of affinity are closely related: where an affinal alliance yields support, economic cooperation and, perhaps, control over the wife's property, the flexibility may never be utilized. But this will depend upon the actions of those involved in the relationship, as well as their previous social ties."

SOME ADDITIONAL QUESTIONS

7. If a Tswana man living in an informal union wants to claim the children of that union as members of his agnatic group what should he do?

8. Political strategy as delineated in this biographical sketch is very male-centered. Are women mere pawns in these processes?

9. How does Kabo's career demonstrate the advantages of examining marriage in the context of politics and economic strategy?

10. If one becomes chief on the basis of birth, how could Kabo's chances of being chief suffer if he divorced Mmaseremo?

NOTE

Now we turn to succession to the chieftaincy. This section we are concluding has shown us how marriage law permits a marked degree of negotiation and "management." Let us see what kinds of negotiation and management are involved in political succession.

5.   Empirical Evidence of "Anomalies" in Political Succession

John Comaroff and Simon Roberts, Rules and Processes: The Cultural Logic of Dispute in an African Context. Chicago: The Uni-

versity of Chicago Press, 1981, p. 36. Footnotes omitted. Editor's insertions are in brackets.

Tswana share a uniform repertoire of ranking rules associated with the devolution and incumbency of statuses throughout the hierarchy, [of residential and political groupings] from the household to the chiefship. In fact, if these rules are taken literally, the Tswana would seem to have a thoroughgoing ascriptive sociopolitical system, and they have usually been portrayed as such. However—and quite apart from the logical problems involved in conceiving of any political system in these terms,—the incidence of "anomalies" in the transmission of rank appears to be remarkably high. Thus, for example, the Tshidi royal genealogy, as it is presently formulated, suggests that 80 percent of all instances of chiefly succession fall into this category, and the rate is not significantly less for lower-order statuses. . . .

6. The Rule of Traditional Succession in Action

NOTE

The high percentage of "anomalies" in succession to office suggests that a re-examination of the operation of the rules of succession is in order. Comaroff did so in the research which is presented in the following material.

The events that occurred with respect to the chieftainship of the Tshidi between 1911 and 1919 show how the repertoire of rules about chieftainship, particularly about succession actually operate.

In the following excerpt the rules traditionally associated with accession to office are isolated and categorized by Comaroff. They are identified in the Comaroff excerpt by number and referred to by number in later sections of this excerpt.

John Comaroff, "Rules and Rulers: Political Processes in a Tswana Chiefdom," Man, Volume 13, No. 1, March 1978, pp. 3–4. Some footnotes omitted: other footnotes renumbered.

The primary rule is a straightforward formulation of the principle of primogeniture:

1. The eldest son of the principal wife of a chief (*kgosi*) is his rightful heir.[1]

The remaining rules appear to define this status, and to provide for situations in which an heir is lacking:

2. The principal wife of the son of a chief is selected for, and betrothed to him by his father or guardian and the chiefly advis-

1. The Tshidi, most of whom are at least nominal Christians, rarely practice polygamy any more. The rules are still stated as if they did, however, and many modern claims to office are made in terms of past events and arrangements. Hence I list them in the present tense.

ers when he is a young boy. She is the first woman to be betrothed to him.

There is no defined period in the young boy's life during which this should be done, but the arrangement should be made public. It is also significant that the heir's principal wife is not necessarily (indeed, is very rarely) the first woman he marries.[2]

    3. When a chief dies without an heir, a close surviving agnate must cohabit with his widow (*go tsena mo tlung*; lit., 'to enter the house') and raise sons on his behalf. Also, when a chief dies without having married, or having had sons by, a principal wife, this house must be entered (or created)—even if he had sons by other wives.

Although it is a younger brother who should 'enter the house', the rules do not specify that this must be a *full* brother. In fact, the identity of the genitor is secondary—a matter of preference only—and a wide range of agnates may actually undertake the task. Another point to note, since it is crucial in strategies of rule manipulation, is that there is no time limit upon the fulfilment of this prescription.

    4. If any of the chief's wives either die childless or prove to be barren, a substitute (*seantlo*) must be supplied without further transfer of bridewealth. Children of the *seantlo* are credited to the house of the barren woman.

    5. If an heir predeceases his father, right of accession passes through the dead man to his senior son. (If the deceased has no heir, rule 3 must be put into effect.)

    6. When a chief dies without having had sons and none have been raised in his name, right of accession passes to his younger full brother; if he has no full brother, it passes to his eldest brother of the second house, and so on. Order of proximity to office is defined by age within (and descent from)[3] ranked houses.

While rules 4 and 5 are straightforward, rule 6 appears to be residual, for it should only operate if the previous ones have not been applied. Subsequent prescriptions, however, demand that the next-in-line who is old enough may be required to act as regent when the heir is still a minor. This necessitates the constant ordering of proximity to office, and rule 6 apparently serves this end.

2. While the ranking of commoner wives tends to be correlated with marriage order, that of royal wives corresponds, in theory, to order of betrothal. However, the relative status of wives is often a matter of negotiation.

ways senior to his younger (or junior) brothers and their respective descendants. Lineal descent takes precedence over fraternal links, and age and genealogical seniority are not coterminous.

3. A prior corollary of rule 5, of course, is that the sons of a man are al-

7. A chief cannot be deposed.

The Tshidi often stress this: the office-holder may be scolded publicly or even punished. But, if he is a chief, he holds office until his death.

There are four additional prescriptions which I refer to collectively as 'regency rules'. The Tshidi themselves confirm that these belong to the accession set. In indigenous terms, they are simply an extension of the norms associated with the guardianship of a dead man's property, position and dependants [cf. the excerpt from Schapera on guardianship in the previous Chapter]:

8. When there is not an heir old enough to assume office, a regent (*motshwareledi*) must be designated. He must be the next-in-line in order of seniority who is also old enough to rule.

9. The regent enjoys all the rights and duties of office and may retain assets accruing to him while acting as incumbent.[4]

10. A regent must hand over to the heir when the tribe decides he is ready to rule.

11. If a regent exceeds his authority, neglects his duties or refuses to hand over when the tribe decides, he may be removed from office . . . .

QUESTIONS

1. What three ascriptive status attributes formed the basis of succession to chieftancy?

2. Do Tswana norms of succession recognize the doctrine of representation?

3. Under patrilineal succession who succeeds in the absence of sons?

4. A chief who marries polygynously would likely have as survivors sons who were half brothers. How was it determined which one of them would take precedence as heir?

5. Under what circumstances might there be ambiguity about which wife was the great wife?

6. Could a step-child succeed to the chieftancy?

NOTE

Comaroff goes on to discuss rules of incumbency:

John Comaroff, "Rules and Rulers: Political Processes in a Tswana Chiefdom," Man, Volume 13, No. 1, March 1978, pp. 4, 5.

These rules are not addressed to the *content* of the ruler's functions. Rather, they concern the *means* by which the affairs of the chiefdom are conducted. Tshidi place a high value upon consultation and participatory politics. Hence most formal statements regarding

4. Tshidi stress, in both word and action, that there is no observable difference between a chief and a regent while they are in office. All incumbents are referred to as kgosi ('chief'). The word for regent (*motshwareledi*) is only used (i) during an open debate over the relative status of two rivals for office; and (ii) when discussing the status of a former incumbent.

incumbency stress that the chief must seek, and heed, the advice of his subjects, whether it be proffered informally or in public. Deliberations concerning legislation and administration take place in three spheres—a close circle of advisers, a council (*lekgotla*) composed mainly of headmen, and the public assembly (*pitso*)—and he is responsible for encouraging free speech and the formulation of wise policy within each of them. In theory, any chiefly decision handed down in these contexts is binding. But, in practice, the ability to execute new policy depends largely upon the incumbent's legitimacy. Essentially, his success is assessed in terms of his material and governmental achievements, which the Tshidi subject to constant evaluation.

As this suggests, the Tshidi hold that legitimacy is a negotiable value. Indeed, this underpins their theory of incumbency and is systematically expressed in a model which describes the relationship between the performance of a ruler and his legitimate power. According to it, the rights of an incumbent are not immutably predetermined; rather, he and his subjects are constantly engaged in a transactional process in which the former discharges his duties and, in return, is delegated the authority to influence policy and people . . . the incumbency model represents a medium through which debate over chiefly performance and legitimacy may proceed.

These rules, then constitute the formal elements of the conceptual repertoire which underlies Tshidi political processes. In order to examine how this repertoire is expressed in competition surrounding the chiefship, I now describe the events which occurred in respect of this office between 1911 and 1919.

NOTE

Comaroff's account of events in the competition for the Tshidi chieftancy begins with the events of 1896. It provides background for the main events, those of 1911–1919, by identifying the two major factions in the succession competition, the Tau faction and the Tswana faction.

Figure 4, which represents the Tshidi royal genealogy as it is accepted today, identifies the major figures referred to in the account and shows their genealogical relationships. In following the account, most readers will wish to refer to figure 5, a simplified version of figure 4 which is incorporated on page 295.

John L. Comaroff, "Rules and Rulers: Political Processes in a Tswana Chiefdom," Man, Volume 13, No. 1, March 1978, pp. 5–9. Citations omitted.

a. Background. When Chief Montshiwa died in 1896, two rival factions had emerged around the chiefship. The core of the larger one, led by Lekoko, comprised many of the jural descendants of Tau. The other included several descendants of Tawana, headed by Joshua Molema. A third grouping, the boo Makgetla, also represented a ma-

FIGURE 4.

[Earliest Generation]
[Latest Generation]

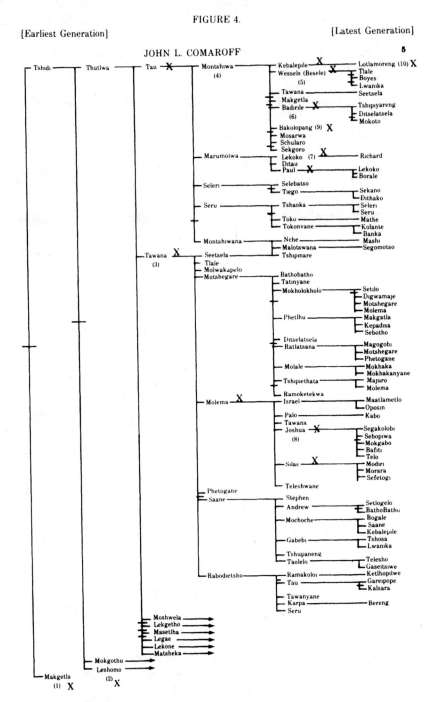

x = major figures in historical account and/or = incumbents

⟶ unlisted descendants

E division between houses

(1), (2) denotes incumbents and their sequence

[C6076]

jor political force. The descendants of a junior brother of Tshidi, they had frequently supplied the ruling line with wives. During this period they were aligned with the Tau faction, which contributed significantly to the hegemony it exercised over the chiefship.

Between 1896 and 1911, the Tshidi had two chiefs. Besele and Badirile. Badirile, in fact, had been backed by the Tawana faction which, for a brief spell, enjoyed a superordinate position of power. Early in his reign, however, it became clear that his incumbency was going to be a failure: he dispensed with his advisers, alienated tribal land and ran the Tshidi into debt. For reasons discussed elsewhere . . . the Tawana faction was nevertheless reluctant to see him deposed. The Tau grouping conspired in this, as they obtained public agreement for an arrangement whereby Lekoko, then the most influential man in the chiefdom, would act for the chief. The latter died shortly after.

FIGURE 5.

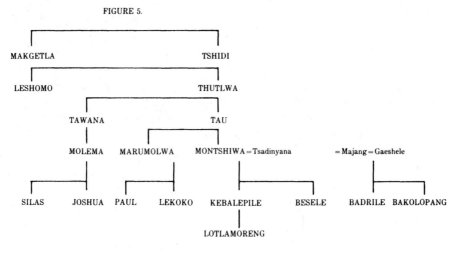

Names in capitals = Males
Names in lower case = Females

[C6048]

[Before showing how Lekoko, the leader of the Tau faction, acceded to the chiefship, Comaroff leads us on a flashback to how his two immediate predecessors, Besele and Badirile became successive chiefs. This exploration shows how different Tshidi rivals for office and their supporters use the same succession rules to justify competing claims to the chieftancy. Comaroff details many variations of this use of legal rules in later stages of the account. But this excerpt contains only some early events of the series of successions.]

The successive accessions of Besele and Badirile, who were sons of different wives of Montshiwa, had implied a transformation of the royal genealogy. When Besele was installed, he was generally viewed as the rightful heir of his father. His elder brother, Kebalepile, had died without having had sons and none had been raised in his name as yet. Rule 6 therefore applied, and Besele acceded as the new *chief* of the Tshidi—a status which was stressed at the installation. His mother, Tsadinyana, was popularly regarded as having been Montshiwa's principal wife. Thus the genealogy read as in fig. 6 [1]

FIGURE 6.

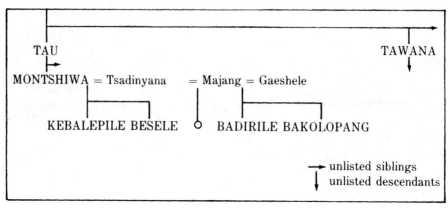

[C6049]

When Badirile acceded, however, it was also as chief; the Tawana faction argued successfully that Besele had merely been acting as a regent for him. Hence, in retrospect, the former chief was relegated to a relatively junior rank among Montshiwa's sons, and the genealogy came to read as in fig. 7:

FIGURE 7.

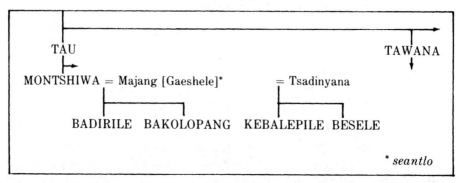

[C6050]

By this transformation, Majang was recognised as having been the principal wife of Chief Montshiwa, a view which her brothers (the sons of Tawana) and their descendants had long asserted.[2] She, however, had no sons of her own, so they had claimed that her BD *,

1. Figures 6 and 7 only include those children of Montshiwa mentioned in this account. For the greater genealogical context, see fig. 4. It should also be noted that Kebalepile had predeceased Montshiwa and, at this time, had no recognized descendants.

2. The fact that Majang had herself been a daughter of Tawana was one of the stated reasons why the Tawana faction had chosen her (jural) son as their candidate.

* Brother's daughter.

Gaeshele, was her *seantlo* and had borne the heir on her behalf. Badirile's accession had affirmed this status. The implication of his installation as chief, in terms of Tshidi prescriptive logic, was that he *had* to be his father's senior son (rule I). And this meant that his (jural) mother must have ranked first among Montshiwa's wives. The house of Tsadinyana and her sons, by extension of the same logic, was now relegated to a more junior rank.

[Exploring the successions of Besele and Badirile has introduced us to the fact that the nature of Tshidi marriage and marriage rules as well as rules about inheritance of status in the family and rules of succession to office make it possible for an identical genealogy and sets of rules to be used to obtain different outcomes. Now we return to the accession of Lekoko and an exposure to some subtler Tshidi strategizing.]

    b. The Accession of Lekoko (1911). Badirile died in 1911. By then, the Tawana faction was grooming his younger brother, Bakolopang, as a new candidate. But he was still too young to succeed, which explains why his followers had consented earlier to Lekoko's assumption of control on behalf of Badirile. This left Joshua and his supporters without a candidate at the time. Joshua and his younger brother, Silas, remained the outstanding figures within the faction. But the former was not himself a serious contender for the chiefship. Although rich and powerful,[2] he had a reputation for autocratic behaviour which made him an unpopular choice for the Tshidi at large. It seems that the long reigns of Montshiwa and Tawana before him had cut across the generations and had left the ruling group with few strong candidates of suitable age.

The leaders of the Tau faction, believing that the Tshidi would not accept another inexperienced or inept incumbent, suggested that Lekoko himself take office. Before, he had had good reason to avoid this, although it would not have been difficult for him to find a genealogical rationalisation. (Indeed, his daughter suggested two possible ones to me in 1969.) Lekoko's own strategy also had longer-term ends. He was apparently aware that, when he died, leadership of the faction would pass to his less forceful brother, Paul. For them to have any chance of preventing the designation of Bakolopang under the control of Joshua, it was necessary to start preparing their own future candidate. Lekoko chose a little-known member of Montshiwa's segment, Lotlamoreng. This man, who was not yet twenty, was a migrant labourer and is said to have had little interest in public affairs. The Tau faction leader, however, persuaded him of the scheme and brought him back to the capital.

At the meeting called to discuss Lekoko's accession, the latter declared his intentions: he would accept the nomination provided it was

2. It would not have been difficult for Joshua to formulate a genealogical legitimisation. Later, the descendants of Molema did try to argue several such claims in a series of bids to remove Lotlamoreng.

recognised that he was *not* the heir to the chiefship. Rather, the rightful person was Lotlamoreng, on whose behalf he would act as regent. The logic behind Lekoko's action had several aspects. First, his assertion of Lotlamoreng's seniority implied his own juniority; and, in terms of the rules, this meant that he *had* to be a regent. Second, he was conscious of the dissatisfaction among members of the Tawana faction over his accession. The declaration of regency, however, did something to alleviate this. For Lekoko's sponsoring of Lotlamoreng, who was younger than Bakolopang, gave the rival faction an implicit assurance that they would later have the opportunity to campaign for their own candidate. Had Lekoko been installed as chief, they might have feared the transfer of the office to Marumolwa segment, within which they had few friends. Of course, his designation as regent did not preclude this; but, while Lekoko was arguing Lotlamoreng's claim, the issue remained open. Thus the strategy transmuted potentially intransigent opposition into tacit, if grudging, support on the part of his opponents. Third, according to the regency prescriptions, Lekoko was entitled to all the resources of office (rule 9) and suffered no deprivation by not being a chief. He already enjoyed considerable power and his *de jure* status did not affect this; in this respect, the strategy had no political costs. Indeed, it demonstrates how politicians may also invoke the rules to prepare future campaigns and to limit opposition in the short-term.

Lekoko reigned successfully until his death four years later. As one indigenous source states: 'In patriotism and wisdom, he was a second edition of Montshiwa. His reign was brief but brilliant.' In order to avert factional conflict, Lekoko stressed the centrality of Joshua and Silas as advisers. He did not, however, fail to argue Lotlamoreng's claims, stating continually that the future chief was being trained and reiterating the genealogical justification for his designation. Joshua, on the other hand, kept Bakolopang's claim alive.

NOTE

In the article from which this excerpt is drawn, Comaroff carries the account forward to 1919, revealing further evidence of the principle of succession as a political process of which this segment of Tshidi history reveals only a portion. Interested readers should pursue the fascinating full account in the original source.

QUESTIONS

1. What difficulties would strict primogeniture or strict patrilineal succession (i.e. without genealogical management based on conflicting interpretations of the nature of various royal marriages and unions) pose for the successful operation of the chieftaincy?

2. Why is it important to revise genealogies after a change in the incumbency of a chief or regent?

3. In what ways does the ambiguity of marriage contribute to the possibility of genealogical revisionism that is an outcome of the Tswana succession process?

FOR FURTHER THOUGHT

4. Does ascriptive (i.e. agnatic, royal) status lead to political success or vice versa?

5. In fact, competition for the chieftancy is not limited to interregna but continues even when there is an incumbent. What mechanism allows for the removal of a chief without contravening rule 7? How is removal of a sitting chief rationalized?

6. Are there factors outside of the rules themselves that govern political success? What are they?

7. In what way is succession like devolution of property?

8. Does the material on Tswana succession help you to understand the conflict between the Tudors and Stuarts over the throne of England any better? Or vice versa?

7. A Contested Chieftainship: The Case of Sir Seretse Khama

NOTE

Sekgoma Khama, Chief of the Bamangwato, and son of Khama, the Great, died in 1925. His only son, Seretse Khama, was 4 years of age. Sekgoma's brother, Tshekedi Khama, Seretse's uncle, was selected as Regent and Seretse was designated as heir apparent. After Seretse's mother's death, Tshekedi acted as active guardian for Seretse. See Figure 8, following.)

Isaac Schapera, A Handbook of Tswana Law and Custom, London: Oxford University Press, 1955, 2d ed., p. 304. Some footnotes omitted. Footnotes renumbered.

FIGURE 8.

NGWATO LINE OF CHIEFS [1]

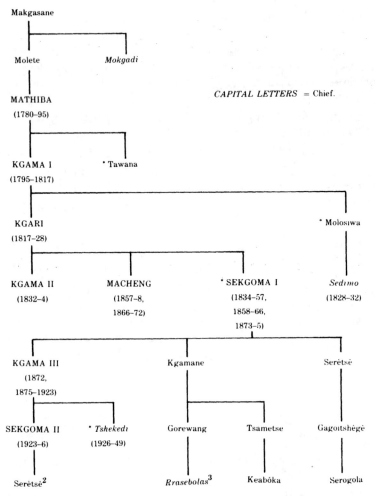

CAPITAL LETTERS = Chief.

1. [This genealogy is] . . . by no means complete. [It has] been specially adapted from much fuller records in order to illustrate primarily how the laws of succession to the chieftainship operated in practice in the various tribes. The names of true chiefs are printed in capitals (e.g., MOTSWASELE), the names of acting chiefs (regents holding office during the minority of an heir, or heads of groups temporarily separated from the main body) in italics (e.g., *Maleke*). An asterisk attached to a man's name (e.g. * *Tshosa*) implies that he was a half-brother of the man whose name is listed immediately before his. . . . .

2. Banished by the Administration, 1950.

3. Acting chief 1953-1964.

NOTE

In 1944 Seretse Khama was 23 and had completed his undergraduate education, having received his B.A. from Johannesburg's University of the Witwatersrand. His uncle and Ngwato headmen urged him to take his place as chief. But Seretse had other plans.

Eric Robins, White Queen in Africa, London: Robert Hale, 1967, pp. 37–38.

. . . The reluctant Seretse pleaded that he first wanted to go to England to qualify as a barrister. His wish prevailed, and, with the sanction of the tribe obtained through Tshekedi and other principal figures, he was admitted to Balliol College, Oxford, where he was a conscientious scholar and an above-average sportsman, being chosen to play rugby, a game which he had watched, studied and played in South Africa, for the college. He read law (at London's Inner Temple), economics and politics, and worked hard as a farmhand during vacations. Seretse wrote frequently and affectionately to "Father" back in Bechuanaland who, as time went on, put increasing pressure on "Sonny" to complete his studies and return home to be enthroned as ruler of the tribe.

In 1947, however, Seretse had met Ruth Williams, a honey-blonde with a trim figure who worked as a confidential clerk in the City of London to a Lloyd's underwriter. The couple fell deeply in love. Mixed unions were not unknown in Bechuana tribal histories. A white settler who died at Palapye left behind a yellow-skinned son who was brought up by the Bamangwato chief Kgari (killed in battle against the Shona tribesmen in 1826). The boy became huntsman to the chief's successor. And trader-explorer, J. H. Wilson, who claimed to have found Lake Ngami before Dr. Livingstone, married a daughter of Sechele, the Bechuana chief of Kolobeng, who was anxious to establish ties with Europeans and expand Christian influences as part of his mission to civilize his tribe.

But Tshekedi was shocked by his nephew's news; sorely wounded and angry that Seretse had kept his secret romance from him; fearful for the unity of the Bamangwato in the new, great crisis which threatened the entire structure of the tribe. Seretse was told by Tshekedi that he did not object to his fiancée as a white woman, but as one whose marriage to a sovereign head of the Bamangwato had not been endorsed by the tribe. Tshekedi foresaw a mixed marriage in a black tribal society, cheek by jowl with white racist South Africa, as catastrophic. So Seretse immediately came under pressure from his uncle to return to Serowe for consultations on his "mad idea" . . . Seretse remained adamant—and in England. Ruth and her relatives were overtly warned of the "ostracism and misery" awaiting her. She did not falter in the storm. She and Seretse steadfastly resisted all pressures from Africa and in England to postpone their marriage, grew more resolute and united as the efforts to separate them continued. .   .   .

NOTE

The couple were married in September, 1948. Seretse left his bride in London and returned to Serowe, the Ngwato capital, for a *gotla* on the question of the marriage.

John Redfern, Ruth and Seretse, London: Victor Gollancz, Ltd., 1955, pp. 46–48.

At the first *kgotla* of November, 1948, the Labour Government's White Paper stated, it was still thought that Seretse would give up his European wife, and there was an almost unanimous condemnation of the marriage.

"The tribe, with very few exceptions, resolved that all steps should be taken to prevent Seretse's wife from entering the Reserve." Two charges were made against Seretse: (1) he had married without the consent of the tribe; (2) he had married a white woman.

What the White Paper did not bring out is that Seretse was at a considerable disadvantage in this first confrontation. He had to go out from England. In Serowe and other parts of the Reserve the marriage had been discussed for several weeks. Naturally, the Regent's voice was not silent. Opinions had been formed while the younger man was still in Kensington.

Even at this stage some of the younger men were sympathetic towards him. But they were silenced. Tshekedi, still vested with the power of Chief, ruled that on this grave matter of the marriage only members of certain age-groups should be allowed to speak. The effect of this was to keep men under forty out of the discussion.

It was useless for Seretse to suggest that his grandfather had not sought consent for at least two of his marriages and that Tshekedi had managed without consent to one of his. The older men talked and talked, using the words that Tshekedi wanted to hear. Wagging his forefinger, one of the seniors warned, "If you marry this woman, the tribe will scatter and you will be chief over the bare poles in the marketplace!" "Scattering" is a sinister word in the tribal country. Many of those who listened must have been dismayed by the thought of rift and dispersal its use suggested.

The strong line Tshekedi took was responsible, I think, for the change in Seretse's favour shown at the second marriage *kgotla* in the following month. It was not decisive change, but it was significant.

The British Government's own comment was: "The subsequent meetings showed an increasing anxiety felt by the tribe that if Seretse were not allowed to return Tshekedi would become their permanent Chief, an event they were determined to avoid at all costs. Consequently, at the second meeting (December, 1948) there was stronger support for Seretse, although it was not decisively in his favour."

At this *kgotla* Tshekedi produced a little notebook, in which he recorded in two columns the speeches, according to whether they were for acceptance of Ruth or not. But his "tally" was afterwards questioned on the ground that he included as anti-Ruth some men who said that, although they disliked the marriage, they would not commit themselves until they had heard what the Government thought about it: the fence-sitters, in fact.

Anyway, at the December *kgotla*, although Seretse was still severely criticised over the marriage, the censures had lost some of their bite. The view was now coming out that the "offence" of the marriage was pardonable—especially if Tshekedi wanted the chieftainship. The *kgotla* finished abruptly without any final decision. The tribes seemed to think it would be a good idea for Seretse to return to London and resume his law studies while there was an interval for consideration by the Government and the people.

NOTE

Seretse went back to London. In June, 1949 he returned to Serowe for a third *kgotla* on the marriage and its impact on his elevation to the chieftancy.

John Redfern, Ruth and Seretse, London: Victor Gollancz, Ltd., 1955, pp. 49–50.

And now it is June, 1949, and the tribesmen are back in Serowe. This is the third *kgotla* and it goes on for five days, with several thousand men in attendance. Near the front sit a few of the white residents of the Bamangwato capital. Everyone feels that this is the crucial *kgotla*.

The Bamangwato argue it out. They rise when Tshekedi and Seretse arrive at the traditional meeting-place. Then they settle down on boxes or little stools, home-made in many cases. They lean forward, straining to catch the words that ring out, hour after hour, through the dusty air.

Once again the estranged men are side by side. Tshekedi bears himself with great confidence. Does he believe there is some way round: that the stubborn man at his elbow will be admonished for his impetuousness and then, ridding himself of this impossible wife, will return to his people, and things will be as they used to be?

Seretse sits easily. He makes no sign while Tshekedi buttonholes the respect for tradition which clothes all his listeners. He uses the tribe-father formula appropriate to a solemn occasion. Seretse becomes "Your-child-who-was-away-at-school." Then his voice rises as he comes to deal with "this white woman." He tells the people: "I will hand over the chieftainship to him, but if he brings his white wife here I will fight him to the end!" Again the note of personal power. Is the Regent (as he still is) making a big mistake?

Excitement mounts. Mr. Vivien Ellenberger, present on behalf of the Bechuanaland administration, stops his notetaking and rises to plead for calmness and dignity. "Let your decision be just and final," he counsels.

One relative of Seretse cries out: "Who can undo this marriage? We want Seretse! I accept the white wife!" Tshekedi retorts that his nephew has married an alien, and no chief can do that.

An old man of high standing in the tribe underlines this—picturesquely. "Seretse has broken the family waterpot!" he says, meaning that he has broken the tribe's tradition. Tempers are rising. Seretse is looking tired. "At this rate," he says, "we shall go on talking for years."

But they do go on talking until there is a surprise. Tshekedi asks seniors of the tribe who support him to come forward to the "platform." Nine respond and stand facing the audience. There is a buzz of voices and some of the tribesmen get into argument among themselves. An adjournment is announced.

As soon as the meeting resumes, Seretse makes a decision. Up on his feet, he says: "Now I should like to see which of the seniors are agreed that my wife and I should come." Seventeen of the "uncles" come forward for him. Seretse takes a long look at his people. Then he takes his opportunity. Gently, without a trace of excitement, he calls the meeting to order. Then he says that he will continue what Tshekedi began. He asks for all who are opposed to him over the marriage—"those against me and my wife"—to stand. Tshekedi makes no move, and here and there men pull off their hats and rise, their eyes swinging towards Seretse's. Pointing his arm, Seretse counts. He raps out the total: "Forty-three!"

Next, tasting success, he smiles slightly and says: "Now stand up those who want me and my wife!" It seems that nearly everyone is on his feet. And there is a shout of *"Pula!"* which in this context means something like "Hurrah!"

NOTE

In effect, the Ngwato had said that, to keep Seretse, they would accept Ruth. As Seretse himself put it, the tribe assembled in lekgotla could "forgive" a chief a transgression of Ngwato law and custom.

Tshekedi went into voluntary exile in Bakwena tribal territory, taking a significant group of elders with him. How was the British government in power, a Labor government to interpret the decision of the third kgotla?

John Redfern, Ruth and Seretse, London: Victor Gollancz, Ltd., 1955, pp. 52-53.

The Conservative *Daily Telegraph* in London, prepared in this instance to smooth the way for the Socialist ministers it generally attacked, suggested rather later: "The decision of the tribal assembly to accept Seretse is regarded as having been primarily an anti-Tshekedi move rather than a whole-hearted approbation of the younger man."

NOTE

Objection to the acceptance of Seretse as chief was conveyed to the Colonial Office in London by Southern Rhodesia and South Africa.

Tshekedi asked the British Government to call a judicial inquiry to make a determination as to Ruth's constitutional status. The inquiry was called by the High Commissioner of the Protectorate, Sir Evelyn Baring, in November, 1949. Its terms of reference were far different from those proposed by Tshekedi.*

It was to advise on whether the lekgotla held at Serowe for five days in June 1949 had been "properly convened and assembled" and its proceedings conducted "in accordance with Native Law and Custom." It also was to consider the question whether "having proper regard to the interests and well-being of the tribe, Seretse Khama is a fit and proper person to discharge the functions of a Chief."

The basis for the inquiry was the Native Administration Proclamation No. 32 of 1943 which stated that when a vacancy occurred in a chieftainship, the successor should be designated at a tribal meeting in the Chief's kgotla according to traditional law and custom. It also held that the person so designated could exercise the functions of the chieftainship, at their discretion, until he had been recognized by the High Commissioner and confirmed by the Secretary of State.

The findings of the inquiry were never published. But, apparently based on them, the British Labor government banned both Seretse and Tshekedi from entering Bamangwato territory. Seretse's ban was based on a subterfuge. He had been invited to London to discuss the future administration of the Bamangwato. While there, he was told that, if he would renounce his claim to the chieftaincy, he would be given a substantial annual allowance. He refused. Then, Mr. Patrick Gordon Walker, the Secretary of State for Commonwealth Relations, announced the ban and that Seretse's recognition would be withheld for five years.

---

* This brief account of the developments at the judicial inquiry is compiled from several sources. One of the most useful is: Seretse Khama and Botswana, by S. M. Gabatshwane. Kanye, Botswana: J. G. Mmusi and S. M. Gabatshwane, 1966.

Let us turn back to events at the judicial inquiry:

The discourse at the judicial inquiry, before which Seretse was a witness, of course, included the issues raised at the lekgotlas of the Fall of 1948 and the issue of the heirship should Seretse become chief.

[Speaking of Seretse's testimony before the commission of inquiry, Redfern writes that:]

John Redfern, Ruth and Seretse, London: Victor Gollancz, Ltd., 1955, pp. 90–91.

A good many of the Europeans had prophesied to me that he would make a mess of it when he gave evidence. Yes; he would be brash or off-hand, or touchy. These prophecies were all falsified by Seretse. When he faced the Inquiry there were sharp passages here and there, but the important things came out simply, almost casually. They were not the less effective.

Here is the line he followed in his evidence:

Yes, I married Ruth in England without the consent of the tribe. I have apologised to the tribe—not for marrying a white woman, but for marrying without consulting the people—and my apology has been accepted. I have told them that, as a Christian, I believe that husband and wife are one and there is no question of my putting my wife aside. Now nearly all the tribes-people want me as chief and my wife with me. If a son is born of our union, he may have the best claim to the chieftainship but if the tribe rejects him with the same enthusiasm as it has accepted me, he would be wise to follow Tshekedi's example and seek a home elsewhere.

That is, of course, a summary of Seretse's evidence. But the last sentence I have quoted verbatim. It was a clever sentence, for it chalked up at least four marks. In that sentence, he brought out (1) the status of his heir, (2) his standing with the people, (3) his uncle's "defeat", and (4) his uncle's choice of exile.

That night there was a good deal of comment over the sundowner drinks. This all sounded quite clever. Somehow, they had not calculated that Seretse was likely to be clever.

NOTE

Seretse's banishment was pronounced in February, 1950. In May Seretse and Ruth's first child was born in Lobatse, in southern Bechuanaland. Shortly thereafter, Seretse and Tshekedi began to reconcile.

Eric Robin, White Queen in Africa, London: Robert Hale, 1967, pp. 43–46.

. . . Seretse was given permission to go back for a brief period to see the golden-skinned baby and, with Tshekedi, to round up his inherited thousands of head of royal cattle. The two men, for sustained vindictiveness is not a characteristic of the African, came close together again in the face of momentous events which overshadowed their transient animosity towards each other. Tshekedi visited Seretse and Ruth in their home—his first meeting with her had been a casual one a short while before in a Lobatsi store—and gazed down tenderly at the "half-African" baby who had by then been named Jacqueline. The reconciliation, and Tshekedi's acceptance of Ruth, was growing.

At the strategical behest of his uncle, Seretse made it known before he returned to London in August of 1950 with Ruth and Jacqueline that he wished to be looked upon as "an ordinary citizen" among the Bamangwato, hoping that the British Government might allow him and Tshekedi to come back to Serowe to serve the tribe as private individuals. . . .

The following year Tshekedi went on another of his numerous "nuisance" trips to London. While there, he and Seretse agreed to press for permission to live with their people as commoners. The reunion was complete, and it was a gay first birthday party for Jacqueline in which Tshekedi joined wholeheartedly. Seretse and Tshekedi soon gained considerable public and Press support for their campaign, and in mid-1951 Seretse issued a statement to London newspapers and news agencies stating that, in order to prevent the Bamangwato situation deteriorating even further, he should be allowed to return to the tribe for a trial period.

After long and heated debates on the Bamangwato question in the House of Commons and the House of Lords, involving personalities like Churchill and Lord Salisbury and threatening the downfall of the British Government, riots broke out in Bechuanaland. Scores of people, including wildly screaming Bamangwato women, were arrested. Armed police reserves were rushed in from Southern Rhodesia to deal with mobs chanting Bamangwato war-cries. Rumours that Tshekedi was returning to claim the chieftainship led to attacks on some of his followers, but the ex-Regent, on his way back to Africa from London, declared without undue publicity that he would recognize Ruth as Queen Mother of the tribe. Everywhere among the Bamangwato, with families split, rootless and living in fear, the cry was for Seretse. For, like many other great men, Tshekedi had been vilified in his absence abroad by the jealous and the ambitious at the top of the tribe. As South Africa continued its claim to swallow up Bechuanaland, the chiefs of tribes other than the Bamangwato protested against the British Government's "dictatorship" in the issue of kingship and demanded that both Seretse and Tshekedi be given the freedom to rejoin their kinsmen.

The Tories came to power, with Churchill as Prime Minister, in 1951, and as a result Tshekedi's banishment decree was eased (later completely revoked on his undertaking that he would not take part in politics) with permission to look after his cattle on the Bamangwato lands "as a private person". In melancholy contrast to this benevolent gesture, it was announced a year later by the Secretary of State for Commonwealth Relations that Seretse would *never* be allowed to return to Serowe as chief. The order, it was stated, was "final and permanent".

The interim tribal leaders of the Bamangwato refused to co-operate with the Administration in Bechuanaland. Grave rioting again broke out in their midst in June 1951, and when the stone-hurling gangs were finally quelled after bloody clashes, three African policemen lay dead and many others, white and black, had been seriously injured. Seventy-five people, including members of the Serowe royal family, were arrested, and later sentenced to heavy terms of imprisonment.

The tribe, despite constant chafing by the Administration, steadfastly refused to nominate any other chief but Seretse.

During May 1953, the Labour Party, now the Opposition, urged—in a classic example of a political *volte face*—that Seretse be allowed to take the chieftainship. Tshekedi once more journeyed to London, three years later, and he and Seretse together handed the Secretary of State, Lord Home, a paper they had signed in which Seretse renounced for himself and his heirs all claim to the chieftainship. Tshekedi reaffirmed his earlier and similar renunciation. Both declarations had previously been made official by an Order in Council. The British Government now stated that Seretse and his family would be allowed to go back to Bechuanaland and the Bamangwato as private persons—after more than six years in exile—and that both he and Tshekedi could play their parts in the affairs of the tribe. It was further announced that the Bamangwato would in future be ruled by a tribal council, headed by a mild soldier-statesman Rasebolai Kgamane. * To this body Seretse and his uncle pledged allegiance. The free world, with the leading exception of South Africa, cheered!

On 10th October 1956, Seretse went back in triumph to his tribe. Large crowds were overjoyed, the women trilling shrill ululations and the men roaring the traditional welcome of "Pula". To them Seretse was the "Great Chief", and no action of the British Government far across the sea could rob him of this title or tarnish his lustre.

NOTE

In April, 1959, the British Government announced that a Legislative Council would be formed in the still Protectorate of Bechuanaland. Throughout British colonial Africa this was one of the first steps in moving formally toward independence. Tshekedi died in a London hospital in June with Seretse at his side.

* R. Kgamane was Seretse's second
cousin (see Figure 1).

We move now to 1962. In that and the following year "a series of tribal meetings were held throughout the Bamangwato territory to announce Rasebolai Kgamane's pending retirement as African Authority and to ascertain the views of the Bangwato on the succession issue." * Taking account of Seretse Khama's renunciation of the Chiefship, the Bamangwato ultimately decided that Tshekedi Khama's eldest son, Leapeetswe Khama, was the proper successor to Rasebolai Kgamane. But—the Ngwato held that they did not wish Seretse's children to be excluded from stepping into the chieftainship if, when they came of age, they wished to do so.

Eventually, these wishes of the tribe were written into an amendment of the Order-in-Council which provided that nothing in the order should prevent anyone named in it from being appointed to the office of African Authority. One purpose of the amendment was to retain the existing suspension of the Bamangwato Chieftaincy without abolishing the office. A second purpose was to enable Leapeetswe Khama to succeed Rasebolai Khama in office as African Authority, which he did in 1964.

Now, let us backtrack to 1961.

Lawrence Peter Frank, Khama and Jonathan: A Study of Authority and Leadership in Southern Africa, Ann Arbor, Michigan: University Microfilms, 1975, pp. 93, 95–96.

Seretse Khama's explicitly political career began in 1961, when he was elected to the multi-racial Legislative Council, which replaced the two, racially distinct councils that had existed previously. In 1962 . . . Khama and Quett Masire announced the formation of the Bechuanaland Democratic Party to oppose the Bechuanaland Peoples' Party, a Pan-Africanist group founded two years earlier. In contrast to the radical-sounding BPP, Seretse and the BDP were characterized as "moderate" and enjoyed the support of the administration and of some, but by no means all, traditional leaders. In 1962, Seretse was appointed to the senior unofficial post in the newly created Executive Council, the forerunner of a Cabinet, and since that time he has been the most prominent figure in Botswana politics. His appeal to many groups, both traditional and modern, has resulted in a politics of a . . . consensual nature. . . .

British support for Seretse and his party increased as the decade passed. As Seretse noted in 1966, "Since my return from exile, my relationship with the British Government has been very, very smooth."

Seretse Khama's dominant position in Botswana politics is not merely a function of British support, however. It is also in large measure a product of earlier British opposition, which made him the best known figure in the country and the personification of non-ra-

* S. M. Gabatshwane, Seretse Khama and Botswana, Kanye, Botswana: J. G.　Mmusi and S. M. Gabatshwane, 1966, p. 12.

cialism. And thirdly, his traditional status was of great political advantage, particularly in the pre-Independence period, when chiefs retained important powers. His widespread appeal was confirmed in the 1965 elections, when the BDP won 28 of the 31 directly-elected parliamentary seats. A new constitution provided for a bi-cameral legislature, the upper body being the House of Chiefs, which had only advisory powers and which caused great dissatisfaction among traditional leaders. The Independence Constitution also provided for a republican structure and for a President with full executive powers. In 1966, Seretse Khama became the first President of the Republic of Botswana.

NOTE

Sir Seretse and Lady Ruth Khama had four children, Jacqueline, born in 1950; Ian Seretse, born in 1953, who until recently was second in command of the Botswana Defense Force; and twins Tshekedi and Anthony, born in 1958.

In mid-1980 Sir Seretse Khama died after a few years of failing health. He was succeeded in the presidency by the Vice President of Botswana, Dr. Quett Masire.

QUESTIONS

1. Does traditional Tswana law allow for renunciation of chieftancy for one's self? What about for one's heirs? If it does, how often do you think either form of renunciation would be used as a strategy by those eligible for the chiefship?

2. What do you think some of the backstage strategies and paradigms of argument might have been in the discussions between the second and third lekgotlas? How might Tshekedi's and Seretse's followers marshall their strength?

3. What kind of issues do you think might have been discussed leading up to Rasebolai Kgamane's "retirement?"

4. Do you think one of Sir Seretse's sons succeeded to the chieftaincy? Were there any factors other than their mother's race and foreign birth that might have deterred them from accepting the position or the Ngwato from offering it to them? What factors would have disposed them to accept the position? Which son do you think would have been most likely to succeed to the chiefship?

5. Reflect on the difference between Ngwato beliefs concerning their chieftaincy and apparent British beliefs concerning their monarchy in the matter of marrying a consort of another race.

6. What does this case show about how the operation of Tswana customary law of succession has been affected by extraneous factors such as: colonial status, policies of surrounding white-ruled colonies or states, and national politics of Botswana as an independent nation state?

8. The restoration of the Ngwato Chieftainship

a. The Chieftainship Act of 1966

NOTE

During the period leading up to independence and in the period immediately afterwards, one of the central pieces of legislation passed was the Chieftainship Act of 1966, which effected one of several changes in the nature of local government in Botswana, by reducing the power of chiefs. The governmental structures that resulted are described in chapter 4, the introduction to Botswana.

The Act, which has been amended several times since 1966, formalizes and limits the role of the Chief. It reaffirms the traditional way of selecting a chief, but provides that the person designed becomes Chief by virtue of being recognized by the Government, specifically the President.

Chieftainship Act, Laws of Botswana, 1977. Chapter 41.01.

Part II. *Recognition and Removal of Chiefs.* . . .

3. There shall be an office of Chief (hereinafter referred to as the chieftainship) for each of the tribes.

4. (1) Subject to the provisions of this Part and of sections 23 and 26, no person shall hold or assume the chieftainship of any tribe or exercise or perform any of the powers or duties appertaining thereto unless he has been recognized as Chief of such tribe under this Act.

(2) Subject to the provisions of section 8, no person shall be recognized as Chief of any tribe unless he has been designated as the rightful successor thereto in accordance with section 5.

5. (1) Upon the occurrence of a vacancy in the chieftainship of the tribe, it shall be the duty of the tribe assembled in kgotla under the chairmanship of the senior member of the tribe to designate the rightful successor to the chieftainship according to customary law.

(2) Subject to the provisions of sections 6 and 8, the President shall by notice published in the Gazette, recognize the person so designated as Chief of such tribe.

6. (1) If the person so designated is below the age of 21, or, being of or above that age, is undergoing a full-time course of education approved for the purposes of this section by the President, such person shall not for the time being be recognized as Chief, and it shall be the duty of the tribe so assembled to designate a Regent of the tribe according to customary law.

NOTE

With the advice of a judicial commission which he appoints, the President has the power to determine any questions that arise concerning whether a person designated by his tribe as chief is a rightful successor. He also has the right to determine similar questions such as the date of termination of a regency, and so on. Where there is a vacancy in the Chieftainship of any tribe, he has the right to name a "Tribal Authority" to exercise and perform the duties of chief, pending the recognition or appointment of a Chief or Regent. The law does not require that the person so named be formally designated by the tribe.

The President also is given the power to suspend or depose any chief after: (1) informing him in writing of the charges against him and, (2) having an inquiry carried out and hearing any response the Chief wishes to make. Deposed chiefs may be banished from their tribal area by the President and no court has jurisdiction over matters relating to the recognition, appointment, suspension or deposition of a Chief. Jurisdiction over such matters is an exclusive presidential right, making the chiefs presidential appointees and giving the President complete authority over them.

The Chieftaincy Act is the backdrop against which the drama of the restoration of the Ngwato Chieftainship is played.

QUESTION

1. How does the relationship after independence of a chief to the President compare with the relationship of chief to the Crown (as represented by the High Commissioner) during the Protectorate?

b. *The Vacant Ngwato Chieftainship Held by Tribal Authorities*

NOTE *

Tshekedi Khama acted as Regent in the Ngwato Chieftainship until 1949. The then District Commissioner was appointed as Native Authority (the position styled Tribal Authority after independence) and served for three years.** In 1953, Rasebolai Kgamane, the third senior member of the tribe after Seretse and Tshekedi and cousin to them both, became Native Authority.*** (See Figure 9 on page 313.) Tshekedi Khama died in 1959, and Rasebolai Kgamane retired as Tribal Authority in 1964.

Leapeetswe Khama, Tshekedi's oldest son, was appointed Tribal Authority succeeding Rasebolai Kgamane in 1964 and he resigned in December 1973. Radiphofu Sekgoma served as Acting Tribal Authority for a few months and in April 1974 Sekgoma Khama, Leapeetswe's brother, became Tribal Authority, serving until April 1975.

Note that each of these men was a member of the Ngwato royal family. They served as Tribal Authority, not Chief or Regent, because the chieftainship was considered to be "vacant." They were appointed heads of tribe with

* Except where designated, this account is constructed from contemporary newspaper reports. See Figure 9 for a diagram of the genealogical relationships of the primary actors.

** Anthony Sillery, Botswana: A Short Political History. London, Methuen & Co., Ltd., 1974.

*** S. M. Gabatshwane, Seretse Khama and Botswana. Kanye, Botswana: J. G. Mmusi and S. M. Gabatshwane, 1966, p. 11.

consultation of the tribe to be sure. But they were not considered to be chief in the full sense of the word.

From the time that Tshekedi stepped down in 1949 until 1975 much had happened. Seretse had returned, led the country to independence, and accepted the Presidency. All the while, quietly bubbling on the cooking fire was the question of when the Chieftainship would be restored.

CAPITAL LETTERS = Chief.
T. A. = Tribal Authority

FIGURE 9.

NGWATO LINE OF CHIEFS * (CONTINUED **)

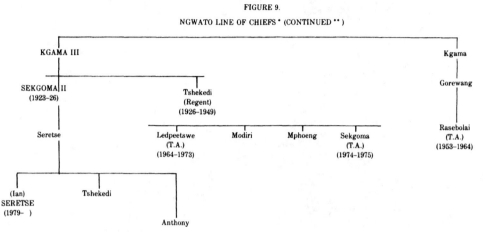

* Not shown: Radiphofu Sekgoma, Mokgacha Mokgadi.
** For earlier years of the royal line, see Figure 8

(C6087)

Ambivalent feelings about nominating a Tribal Authority rather than a Chief did not dampen Ngwato political processes very much. An account of the maneuvering for the nomination of one Tribal Authority during the long interregnum shows some of the flavor of the Tshidi succession process excerpted earlier in this chapter—and something of the mobilization of support we encountered in reviewing the struggle between Sir Seretse and his uncle, Tshekedi.

(GABORONE) BOTSWANA DAILY NEWS, APRIL 10, 1974

BOTSWANA DAILY NEWS

'THE MOST COMPETENT OF ALL MEN'

Sekgoma Khama nominated as Bamangwato Tribal Authority

From Action Ndaba

Sekgoma Khama, aged 33, was unanimously elected Bangwato Tribal Authority at a kgotla meeting in Serowe on Monday.

According to statistics from the tribal secretary Ronald Sebinanyane, 17 nominations from throughout the Central District,

among them Ministers Bakwena Kgari and K.P. Morake, were submitted for the position.

Seventeen villages nominated Sekgoma Khama and 11 nominated Lenyeletse Seretse, former Central District Council secretary, who recently resigned to take up politics.

Sekgoma Khama, aged 33

Speakers at the meeting referred to Sekgoma Khama, who did not personally attend the meeting, as "senatla sa dinatla," "the most competent of all men."

They accounted this for his having acted as tribal authority during his brother Leapetswe's overseas study leave. Others emphasised his birthright as one of the prime considerations for nomination.

Member of Parliament for Shoshong, G.S. Mosinyi dismissed the idea of considering birth right and pressed that a person should be nominated according to capability. He said that Sekgoma Khama's absence from the meeting was a disadvantage because people could have had his opinion and whether he accepted the offer.

The Deputy Tribal Authority, Molwa Sekgoma, stated that Sekgoma had been interviewed before and had not indicated he would decline the offer.

His brother Leapetswe Khama resigned two years ago due to poor health and for some time the post has been vacant. Among the more than 1000 people who attended the meeting were the Minister of Health, Labour and Home Affairs M.P.K. Nwako, A.C. Sikunyane and G.G. Sebeso, both Members of Parliament, and Permanent Secretary in the Ministry of Local Government and Lands B. Makoboie.

QUESTIONS

1. What seemed to be the interaction between the principle of accession by birth right and the principle of accession on the basis of competence in these deliberations?

2. What hints are there that the position of tribal authority is not divorced from national politics?

c. The Campaign for the Restoration of the Chieftainship

NOTE

Anxiety about the restoration of the Chieftainship began to climb after the death in 1973 of Rasebolai Kgamane, highly respected for filling the void after Tshekedi stepped down. By 1975 the discussion was out in the open.

Focus was on a series of important issues: First, should the Ngwato continue to be ruled by a Tribal Authority, or should the Chieftainship be restored? Put in the Tswana idiom of discourse, this question became: Should the head of the tribe be any Mongwato or a member of the royal family? Second, cross-cutting the first issue—however it was phrased—was the question of whether all Bamangwato should participate in the decision or whether, effectively, it should be made in Serowe, the tribal capital.

The scenario of maneuvering went as follows. At a February 1975 nomination meeting in Serowe of people from many towns those assembled voted to ask the District Officer to request that the Government abolish the title of Tribal Authority in favor of that of Paramount Chief. A few days later the Ministry of Local Government and Lands responded that the vacant post was that of Tribal Authority, not Chief. Almost immediately that decision was rejected by Ngwato district representatives. They invited Sir Seretse to come to Serowe to discuss the matter, not as Head of State, but as a member of the tribe. He did. In April, he appointed Mokgacha Mokgadi as Tribal Authority for a period during which the Ngwato were to deliberate and designate someone else to serve—as Chief. The Chieftainship was to be restored.

A series of nomination meetings were held in *lekgotlas* throughout the Ngwato area. Sir Seretse continually reiterated his view that the Chieftainship should be open to any Mongwato and that people from all over the Central District (the Ngwato area) should participate in the deliberations. In the end, the traditional pattern of succession was to prevail, with widespread participation of Bamangwato throughout the large tribal area.

Newspaper accounts of the series of nomination meetings do not recount all the deliberations, but they provide some sense of the issues and the arguments that were offered for various points of view.

(GABORONE) BOTSWANA DAILY NEWS, MAY 12, 1975

Tribal authority idea favoured

By Solomon Lotshe

The majority of people during a kgotla meeting at Sebina village praised the idea of a Bamangwato authority while others favoured the idea of a person being born a chief.

The meeting followed instructions by the President that people throughout Bamangwato district should consider people whom they wanted to become their chief (or tribal authority).

Those who favoured the idea of a

tribal authority said rapid developments have been achieved since the introduction of tribal authority. They further said that during the time of the chief, things were at a stand still.

They said that Mokgacha Mokgadi is a rightful person as tribal authority for Bamangwato.

Those who favoured a person being born a chief did not mentione any particular person who they wanted to become a chief

The meeting was attended by

people who came as far as from Maitengwe, Tutume and surrounding villages

The Subordinate Tribal Authority for Bokalaka district, M. Modie advised people to brand with a relevant brand certificate or bring evidence or witnesses to enable them to obtain permits for the selling of their beasts to speculators

Mr Modie   stressed that if a person fails to comply with the requirements will not be issued with a permit.

The first mention in newspaper accounts of Ian Khama, Sir Seretse and Lady Khama's oldest son, as the nominee was in September 1976. A month later, a large meeting in Serowe concluded that the nominee should be Ian Khama or one of the other "seven sons (of Sir Seretse and Tshekedi)." (See Figure 9.) In the national press, the tribe was reported as united that the designee should be a royal person.

Shortly after that Ian Khama was nominated. A year later, in November 1977, he was appointed Chief by Sir Seretse, the President, with the date of installation deferred for further deliberations by the tribe and for the Chief-

Designate to make a decision about how long to continue his duties as Brigadier in the Botswana Defence Force.

d. Associating the Chief-Designate With the Office

NOTE

Recall that legitimacy for a *kgosi* (chief) is not just a matter of fitting the
rules of succession, but of acceptance by his subjects and appropriate performance in office. The designation of Ian Khama as Chief presented an un-
spoken problem: How could a person who had the birthright to the Chieftainship, but who was not residing in the tribal area on a day-to-day basis and
not living the role of Ngwato nobleman, be perceived as a true chief and,
further, carry out the role of traditional leader? Some highly publicized activities centering on the young Chief-Designate seemed designed to answer that
question. One of them is reported below.

(GABORONE) BOTSWANA DAILY NEWS, APRIL 10, 1979

Brigadier Khama now head of 'Malwelamotse'

By Mishingo Mpaphadzi,

Brigadier Seretse Khama Ian Khama is now the leader of "Malwelamotse Regiment," Bamangwato's latest Mophato formed at   on Saturday at Serowe.

The regiment comprises about 500 youngmen from all over the Central District.

In line with tradition Mr Peto Sekgoma, the Brigadier's uncle instructed Malwelamotse to go and collect firewood from the bush and return before 8 o'clock in the morning. This was soon after he had named the regiment.

To the surprise of tribesmen, who had gathered at the Kgotla,
the new mophato returned 30 minutes before the stipulated time.

It is reported that Brigadier Khama gave members of his regiment a hard time while racing through the bush. He was dressed in military attire.

Among those who are in the regiment is Roy Blackbeard, the son of Serowe North Member of Parliament Mr Collin Blackbeard.

Giving a short talk after the arrival of the regiment Mr Sekgoma   applauded Malwelamotse's leader for the role he plays in the army which ensures the security of the country.

He said the ceremony was a step forward towards installing Brigadier Seretse as Chief of Bangwato next month.

Turning to the Mophato tradition, Mr Sekgoma said former regiments were originally created to cater for both military and public service.

He added, however, that since our society has changed dramatically, the Mophato tradition now only serves as a reminder of the 'good old days'.

Supporting him, Mr Radiphofu Sekgoma reiterated that Bamangwato have stayed for a long time without a chief, and that Brigadier Seretse is the only hope to revive their chieftainship.

QUESTION

1. What do you think are the manifest and latent functions of this ceremony? In what way does it contribute to the succession process?

e. The Installation of the Kgosi

NOTE

The installation of Kgosi Seretse on May 4, 1979 was a joyous celebration, viewed as the installation of the first proper Chief since the death of Sekgoma II. The Chieftainship had been restored.

(GABORONE) BOTSWANA DAILY NEWS, MAY 8, 1979

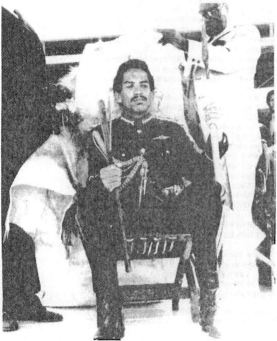

Kgosi Seretse of the Bangwato with home-made implements, symbol of traditional leadership

ABOVE: *A staunch tradtionalist at the installation ceremony*

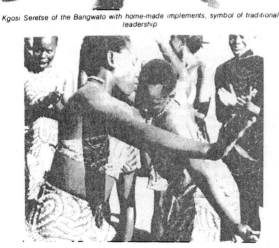

LEFT *Botswana's youth, who are regarded as the custodians of what some people refer to as our dying custom and tradition highlighted the Bangwato chief installation by their traditional dancing, singing and other performances.*

DYNASTY OF THE BANGWATO

'CO-OPERATE WITH NEW CHIEF''

Chapter in Bangwato old controversial chieftainship folds

STORY Andrew Sesinyi, Solomon Lotshe

PHOTOS Russ Molosiwa

A chapter of controversy in the Bangwato history was closed Saturday with the installation of Brigadier Seretse Khama Ian Khama as Kgosi ya Bangwato. The ceremony, held in Serowe, was attended by over 30 000 people.

The President Sir Seretse Khama, cabinet ministers and all diplomats in the country attended the ceremony, described by some village elders to be unprecedented since the installation of Kgosi Khama III more than a century ago.

President Khama officiated during the installation of his eldest son as Kgosi Seretse of the Bangwato, amidst continuous ululations from the sea of faces which witnessed the appointment of the long-called for traditional chief.

Controversy had plagued the Bangwato, who for a long time had looked at President Khama as their rightful chief. Bangwato had sent representations to the Government demanding the installation of a traditional chief in the place of a tribal authority.

The tight programme marking the occasion included football matches, traditional dancing, musical functions and feasting. Several cattle had been slaughtered for the occasion.

All the other tribes in the country sent their representatives to Serowe, and these were headed by their respective chiefs. Several speakers, including President Sir Seretse Khama, and Minister for Local Government and Lands L. Makgekgenene, expressed relief at the installation of the Bangwato Chief. They were hopeful that the Bangwato would now be pacified.

Serowe's two hotels and the one in Palapye about 40 kilometres away from Serowe, were reported fully booked by Thursday morning last week.

Most of Serowe residents offered accommodation to the thousands of guests who could not find places to stay in the three hotels.

The kgotla ceremony on Saturday beamed with life, and despite the pushing, jostling and screaming crowd as everyone fought to have a glimpse of the 26-year-old Bangwato kgosi, the programme ran smoothly.

Some babies were reported lost during the kgotla ceremony, apparently abandoned by their mothers in their bid to push through the crowd to the forefront.

President Khama told the Bangwato however, that Kgosi Seretse would remain in the Botswana Defence Force until the southern African war tension had subsided.

The night preceeding the installation seemed to be too long since people were impatiently waiting to witness the occasion, which pulled the largest number of people to Serowe in the history of the Bangwato.

During the installation, desperate people climbed on top of the Serowe Hill and Central District Council offices in order to see the ceremony.

It took about 10 minutes before President Khama could speak. Various appeals were made to the public to quieten down.

Information and Broadcasting Department teams public address system cables were sometimes cut off by the crowd which was pushing one another in an attempt to get a front seat.

Many speakers advised the chief to guard against bribery and that he is to cater for all irrespective of tribal differences. They called on the chief not to be harsh but be steady on his people. They said the chief's riches are his own people, but not his wealth.

Turning to the Bangwato, speakers called on them to co-operate and work closely with their traditional leader.

NOTE

Note the theme that President Sir Seretse Khama struck in remarks given at the installation of his son in the chieftaincy that he, Sir Seretse, never held:

(GABORONE) BOTSWANA DAILY NEWS, MAY 8, 1979

Batswana urged to refrain from tribalism

By Andrew Sesinyi

President Sir Seretse Khama on Saturday spoke strongly against tribalism and further warned that Botswana might be thrown into the chaos that exists in some African countries if Batswana continued practicing tribalism.

He also called on the chiefs to be more vigilant and remain impartial in their dealings with the various groups in their respective tribal areas.

President Khama said this at a Kgotla ceremony in Serowe marking the installation of his elder son, Brigadier Seretse Khama Ian Khama as Bangwato Kgosi.

Sir Seretse Khama told his audience that in Africa, tribalism has caused unrest and divisions among the people and quoted South Africa and Rhodesia as instances where he said black people were divided by tribalism even in issues relating to their liberation struggle.

Six million black people, are oppressed by a few thousand whites because the blacks are divided by tribalism, President Khama said.

He also quoted, as an instance, the South African bantustan policy which he said established pseudo-independent states like Bophuthatswana and the Transkei.

President Khama said South Africa's white minority regime had created and exploited the tribal differences among black people in establishing such bantustan states.

He further disclosed that he had observed some practices of tribalism in the administration of this country and called on Batswana to refrain from such practices as the country's peace and stability might be affected.

President Khama advised the new Bangwato Kgosi Seretse to work hard and consult his people; to adopt an open-mind attitude and accept criticism of his administration.

He further cautioned that if he felt Kgosi Seretse was inefficient he would not hesitate to remove him from office.

Sir Seretse Khama said Bangwato are made of different people from different tribal backgrounds and further called on Kgosi Seretse to be impartial in his administration.

"A chief must be a chief of the whole tribal group in the area and not just cater for those who are his blood relations," he said.

President Khama added: "Chieftainship is not arrogance." He said a leader of any group of people should be progressive.

Referring to party politics, President Khama said chiefs were not impeded from joining party politics but expressed that a chief would not be impartial if he ran the post of chief whilst affiliated to a particular political party.

He told Bangwato that he had no claim to the leadership of the tribe, and that he attended the ceremony to indicate his wish to instal Kgosi Seretse as the Bangwato Kgosi.

President Khama also stated that it was in Botswana's pursuit of democracy that Bangwato had been granted their wish....this being the installation of their traditional leader.

The President however told the audience that Kgosi Seretse would remain in the Botswana Defence Force until the political unrest in Southern Africa has subsided.

One of the speakers, Minister of Local Government and Lands Lemme Makgekgenene said: "At last, the wishes of the tribe have been fulfilled."

He continued: "It is a case of 'pelo tshweu boela mannong!"

Present at the ceremony were: Lady Khama, cabinet ministers, diplomats, top Government officials, and representatives from the various tribal groups in Botswana.

President Sir Seretse Khama.. "Chieftainship is not arrogance!"

SIR SERETSE KHAMA'S GRAVE. Sir Seretse Khama's grave, dedicated in
July 1981. Sir Seretse is buried on "Khama Hill," a rocky outcropping overlooking the Ngwato Paramount Chief's *kgotla* and the town of Serowe. Khama III
and other distinguished forebears of Sir Seretse also are buried in this royal cemetery.

QUESTIONS

1. What does Ian Khama's succession to the Chieftaincy show about the strength of Tswana customary law? About the strength of patrilineality? About stratification in contemporary Botswana?

2. What role do you think the media play in the succession process nowadays?

3. The possible succession of Sir Seretse Khama to the Ngwato Chieftainship was altered by the intrusion of Commonwealth concerns, especially fears of South Africa's reaction to his marriage. Are there any ways in which Ian Khama's succession may have been influenced by considerations other than tribal politics?

4. What does Sir Seretse's installation address suggest about the changing role of a chief? About new criteria for selection that might come into play in future successions?

Chapter 11

INHERITANCE AND SUCCESSION IN CHINESE LAW

A. INHERITANCE AND SUCCESSION IN TRADITIONAL CHINA

1. The Traditional Family

Maurice Freedman, "The Family in China, Past and Present," 34 Pacific Affairs, pp. 323, 326–327, (Winter 1961–62).

On the role of kinship in economic life we have no systematic and large body of information on which to rely, but we can make a general argument. If we start from the assumption that kinship relations and values predominate in the conduct of economic affairs, we must expect that enterprise will take the form of what is often called the family business. Now, of course, there is plenty of evidence to show that Chinese economic enterprise has tended strongly to be organized so that people associating their capital, or capital and labor, are related by kinship or affinity. But what is the real significance of this fact? Is it that the moral imperatives of kinship impel people to seek out kinsmen with whom to work? The answer is no. Given the nature of the capital market, given a legal system which offers little protection to business, given the tendency to rely on people with whom there is some preceding tie, we should expect that kinsmen would be associating with one another in economic activities. . . .

The experts have been insisting for the last twenty years that it is incorrect to say that the Chinese family in traditional circumstances was big. We need not, therefore, put much stress on the fact that average size of the family was five or six persons, but rather consider why it was that some families were very large and others very small, with many gradations between these extremes. Let us go back to the political point that the state looked to the family as the first unit of social control. The ideal family from this point of view was one in which large numbers of kinsmen and their wives were held under the control of a patriarch imbued with the Confucian values of propriety and order. Some families came close to this model, several generations living under one roof. They were powerful families. . . . By renting land and lending money they could exert influence over other people. They could afford to educate their sons and equip them for membership of the bureaucratic elite. . . . Such a family may be looked upon as a large politico-economic corporation with much power vested in its chief member. But this corporation could not grow indefinitely in membership, for with the death of its senior generation it split along the lines laid down by the constitution of the next generation, every son having a right to an individualized share of his father's estate on that man's death. However, despite the partition which took place every generation, high status families were able to remain large. The passing of the senior generation was likely to take place at a point when the men in the next generation were themselves old enough to have descendants sufficient for complex families of their own. . . .

At the other end of the social scale the family was, so to speak, scarcely Confucian. Poverty and powerlessness produced, instead of a strong patriarch, a weak father. He could rally no support from outside to dominate his sons. He had few resources to withhold from them. In fact, he might well have only one son growing to maturity. If, however, he had two or more sons reaching manhood, only one would be likely to stay with him, and perhaps even this one would leave him too. Demography, economics, and the power situation at this level of society ensured that families of simple structure were a constant feature of the landscape. . . .

2. The Family as a Religious Unit

NOTE

In addition to being an economic unit, the lineage or family also had an important religious function. A man's spiritual existence was linked to his ancestors before him and to his descendants to follow. Thus the begetting of sons was a religious as well as a social or economic act. Where a man did not have a son, the usual practice was to adopt a son of a brother (or at least someone having the same surname). If a man died without a son, posthumous adoption was practiced.

Chinese society was patrilineal. A woman generally left her natal family at the time of marriage and became a member of her husband's family, in both a physical and religious sense. In some instances, where the woman had no brothers, a man could take the surname of his wife and become the heir to her family line.

George Jamieson, "Chinese Family and Commercial Law," Hong Kong: Vetch and Lee, 1970, pp. 2–3, 17–19, 23 [originally published in Shanghai, 1921].

The foundation of Chinese society is the Family, and the religion is Ancestral Worship. Ancestral Worship is not a thing which the community as a whole can join in; it is private to each individual family, meaning by family all those who can trace through male descent to a common Ancestor, however numerous, and however remotely related. It is remarked by Sir Henry Maine (*Ancient Law*, p. 126) that archaic law "is full in all its provinces of the clearest indications that society in primitive times was not what it is assumed to be at present, a collection of individuals. In fact and in view of the men who composed it, it was an aggregation of families. The contrast may be most forcibly expressed by saying that the unit of an ancient society was the family, of a modern society the individual."

This observation is to a great extent a correct description of Chinese society to-day. The family is the unit. The Father or senior male ascendant has control over his sons, his grandsons and their wives as well as over hired servants and slaves. Municipal law does not greatly concern itself with what takes place within the domestic forum or family group; the head has certain discretionary powers, and unless these powers are grossly abused it will not interfere. In the Father is vested all the family property, and he alone can dispose of it. At his death his eldest son takes his place and the family goes on as before. It may continue so undivided for several generations and is still deemed a single unit. But the Father or Head is also the high priest. He alone is capable of conducting the ancestral worship, whether in the ancestral hall or at the tombs of the ancestors.

* * *

Excluding then all females, and their descendants, we have next to consider who among the kindred are entitled to succeed, and the order in which they are to be taken.

The first class is of course the sons and other direct descendants. Here there is no difficulty; the eldest son and his line born in lawful matrimony succeed as a matter of course by virtue of their birthright, and it does not seem that the father has any power of selecting other than the eldest. Failing sons by the principal wife, sons by concubines are entitled in order of their birth. This right of succession however gives no additional claim to the patrimony, which, as we shall presently see, is equally divided among all the sons, but only to the custody of the Ancestral Tablets and other insignia of the family existence. It also confers a general power of control over the younger brothers, especially in all family matters akin to that exercised by the Father.

The second class comprises all brothers' sons,—nephews, that is, of the person in want of a successor. The general rule to be observed in making a choice is that you must select from the generation immediately below you, beginning with those that are nearest and proceeding in order in the collateral line to those more remote.

* * *

The eldest son of the eldest brother must of course continue his own family line, as being the senior branch, and as he cannot, except under special circumstances, unite the two lines in his own person, he is not eligible. But the second, third, etc., son, who would otherwise found a new branch line of his own, is moved up to continue the already existing line of his uncle.

* * *

Should all these classes fail, the Code gives leave to appoint any of the kindred further removed still, and finally any one of the same family name. More than this, however, is not given. We nowhere find the right of free adoption independently of the claims of kin.

NOTE

While the eldest son succeeds as heir in the family line, with relatively few exceptions, office did not pass from father to son. Instead, public officials were recruited through an examination system.

Maurice Freedman, Lineage Organization in Southeastern China, London School of Economics Monographs on Social Anthropology, no. 18; 1958, pp. 56–59.

To enter the bureaucracy it was necessary either to qualify in state examinations, which was the "regular" mode of acquiring the status of a literatus, or to buy a literary title, which was the "irregular" mode. The status of literatus by itself was no guarantee of office, but the acquisition of the status was a necessary preliminary to office-holding.

* * *

The need to pass state examinations or acquire literary status by purchase imposed a brake on mobility. The examinations were technically open to all men other than those belonging to a few and small disfavoured categories (for example, the families of slaves, servants, prostitutes, and entertainers). At some periods in the history of the state examinations artisans and merchants and their immediate descendants were prevented from entering, but this restriction does not appear to have operated during the phase covered by Chang's study. Yet it was clearly difficult for the son of a peasant to compete on equal terms with the member of a "family" which had already established its position as an official-producing group. Candidates had to be guaranteed by literati; influence, favouritism, and other forms of advantage weighted the system against the humble candidate. More important still, the poor man could hardly afford to provide his son with the classical education on the basis of which he would need to be examined. Candidates were prepared for the examinations either by private tutors or in private schools. It is possible that where schools existed on a lineage or village basis, the sons of the peasantry, having access to them, might succeed in bringing themselves up to examination standards. . . . We may scarcely estimate the effective costs of a boy's education simply in terms of the expenses of his training; the sacrifice of his labour during the long years of study must have acted as a major disincentive to his father. Certainly, we have little reason to conclude that any large number of peasant lads raised themselves to high estate by means of the imperial examinations. It is, of course, even more obvious that entry into the stratum of the literati by means of payment was not likely to afford much opportunity to the poor.

* * *

It is clear, at any rate, that the greater part of the movement into the ranks of the literati from outside the gentry class must have taken place by means of money.

. . . [T]he building up of wealth to set social promotion going had to come from other kinds of economic activity: trade (which was not necessarily legal) and probably such less respectable applications of non-agricultural skill as military activities and banditry (from which soldiering was not always too clearly to be distinguished). Not that wealth was the unique means of rising into the ranks of the gentry; influence built up militarily or otherwise might ultimately promote individuals and their dependants through a system of patronage.

We are, then, faced by the paradox that the gap between the two great respectable orders of Chinese society, the gentry and the peasants, was probably bridgeable in the main only by one of the theoretically nonrespectable orders, the merchants. Trade was, in official theory, highly distasteful, but the contemptible business man could, in fact, travel the road to the higher respectable order through his sons, even if he chose not to buy literary status for himself. Despite the power which they might develop as men of commerce, both the ideals and economics of their society drew business men on to convert one type of capital into another: money went into land and sons into the examinations. By this process wealth could buy social status and political power; . . . .

3. Ownership and Management of Property

NOTE

In traditional China, property was owned not only by individuals, but also by larger social units such as the family or lineage. In the latter system, property is held in a corporate manner. The death of an individual member does not affect ownership.

a. Lineage or Clan Property

NOTE

The following item describes a pre-Communist village in southern China near the city of Canton.

C. K. Yang, A Chinese Village in Early Communist Tradition, Cambridge: Technology Press, Massachusetts Institute of Technology, 1959, pp. 41–43

Who owned how much land? First, it is necessary to recognize two types of land ownership, collective and private. The principal types of collectively owned land in this village were clan land, education land, and temple land. Clan land found in this village was largely confined to so-called sacrificial land, the income from which was used for sacrificial ceremonies to the ancestors, upkeep of the ancestral halls, and other activities connected with ancestor worship. The Wong clan, a poor clan, held only thirty mow of such land in this village. The clan land of the Lees was located in another county about eighty miles to the south, where the headquarters of the Lee clan were located, the clan in this village being only one of the branches. Every year the Lee clan of Nanching received over 10,000 catties of unhusked rice from the income of the headquarter's clan land. In addition, the subdivisions of the Lee clan did possess altogether about twenty mow of sacrificial land within Nanching.

Education land was also under the ownership and management of the clan, but it was set aside for educational purposes. In the imperial days, besides subsidizing the clan school, the income from this land also paid for the stipends of scholars who had passed the primary grade of civil service examinations and for travel subsidies for scholars to go to the provincial and national capitals to take higher examinations. In the Republican period it was used exclusively to support the village school. The Wong clan had somehow lost or sold its former education land. In the 1920's a wealthy merchant of the Lee clan contributed twenty mow of irrigated land for the support of a village school to educate the young of all clans within the village.

Temple land was owned by the temple, and the income from the land supported one priest and the temple. There was only one temple in this village, located immediately outside the northwestern corner of the village site. It had about ten mow of land under its ownership.

Altogether, there were about eighty mow of collectively owned land of various types, accounting for 6.2 per cent of the 1,200 mow of the village's cultivated land, leaving 93.8 per cent in the private ownership of individuals and families. This percentage of collectively owned land was low for a province where the clan and its economic functions were among the most highly developed in China. A village about two miles from Nanching had in 1948 about 70 per cent of its total cultivated area under clan ownership. Clan land averaged about 30 per cent of all the cultivated land in the whole Panyü County in which Nanching was located; and clan land was the leading form of collective land ownership in the province. The bulk of the Lee's clan land lay elsewhere, as pointed out. The Wongs formerly had large clan possessions, according to the elders, but different crises befalling the clan during the past century had led to the sale of most of the land to defray emergency expenses. This explained the relatively small percentage of collectively owned land in Nanching, a situation which affected the livelihood of the villagers substantially, particularly the Wongs, among whom there was a higher percentage of tenancy than among the Lees.

Collective ownership of land affected the livelihood of the peasants differently in different cases. Collective land, especially that in possession of the clan, tended to remain in collective ownership over a long period of time. The institutionalized value attached to such land was high; and selling the clan's land not only weakened the clan's financial resources but also caused a serious loss of clan prestige, since it was considered an offense against the ancestors' good reputation—only unworthy descendants would sell instead of adding to the property built up by their predecessors. The selling of collective land was therefore infrequent, though it did occur at times, especially by clans of declining economic and organizational strength such as the Wongs.

With the land remaining in possession of the clan, individual peasants could work on it only as tenants. The terms for renting collective land in this village were the same as for private land, with the land going to the highest bidder. The renter of collective land was thus subjected to all the normal disadvantages of tenancy, although he reaped certain indirect benefits in the form of clan services supported by such rent. But the terms of rent might be different in some cases, having a different impact on the peasants' life. In the neighboring village mentioned above, clan land, which accounted for 70 per cent of all the cultivated area, was rented to male clan members at nominal rates. In such a case collective ownership of land by the clan had the obvious effect of equalizing the right of clan members to use the land and preventing concentration of land ownership in private hands, a situation particularly beneficial to the poor peasants possessing insufficient or no land. A common complaint against clan ownership of land was corrupt management in the form of embezzlement of rents and favoritism in renting good land to well-placed members. While there was apparently some truth in such charges, a representative factual picture of clan land management has yet to be given.

b. *Family Property and the "Common Living" (t'ung-chü kung-ts'ai) System*

NOTE

Aside from property owned by the clan or lineage, families in most areas of China organize their households and manage their economic activities through the system of "common living." The following item describes the traditional manner in which "common living" operated. Other materials strongly suggest that these practices continue in contemporary China.

* * *

Shuzo Shiga, "Family Property and the Law of Inheritance in Traditional China," in David Buxbaum, editor, Chinese Family Law and Social Change in Historical and Comparative Perspective, Seattle and London: University of Washington Press, 1978, pp. 112–115.

The concept of *t'ung chü* contains three elements. The first of these, and the very core of the *t'ung chü* concept, is that the fruits of the labor of the several members go into a common account serving all of the members without exception. When all the members are farmers tilling the household soil, this expresses itself in joint cultivation of the land and joint reaping of the harvest. When some member of the family has a side income or when he lives apart and has a different occupation, it is his duty to place in the household account all clear profit accruing from these activities; that is, to hand it all over to the household accountant. The consumption of a part of the income as luxury for himself or for his wife and children, or the secret accumulation of one part of the income, is a violation of the rules, and close watch is kept by the head of the household and the other members of the family. This fact is pointed out in the writings of Olga Lang and Martin C. Yang and is brought out with particular clarity in the above-mentioned records of interviews in northern China. In the villages covered by the inquiry, cases in which the household was maintained on farm income alone were, if anything, rare. From every village a considerable number of men had gone elsewhere to earn their living, having fixed employment in metropolitan areas and other outside places and coming home only to celebrate the New Year. It was not unusual for some to spend the prime of their working lives away from home. Even in such cases they would leave their wives and children in the village in most instances and would send their earnings not to their wives but to their fathers, grandfathers, or brothers, in short to the person who remained in the ancestral home and managed accounts for the whole family

The second element of the *t'ung chü* concept is that the living expenses of all members are defrayed entirely from a common account. The household accountant remaining in the ancestral village pools all money sent in by persons who go out to do any but agricultural labor, using it all without distinction or discrimination to support the wives and children left behind in the village. All that is required is that a fair distribution be made on the assumption that expenses are expenses, without asking who earned how much. Especially important is fairness in the distribution of food, since collective cooking and eating constitute a central element of family life. The hearth, over which a portrait of the god of the hearth is installed, is the center and the symbol of the house. In order to divide the household, the hearth is invariably built separately, while rooms need not be, and usually are not, newly added. In the same way, clothing is also provided for jointly and distributed fairly. Those who go out to work have no choice but to be separate consumers, but all this means is that as a matter of convenience they are meeting their personal expenses, which in terms of their calculations are the expenses of their respective households, out of the money they earn at their place of work, money which likewise belongs entirely to their respective households. In theory they are not divorced from the relationship of the consumer community.

The third and last element is that surpluses left over from the joint account covering all living expenses of the type just mentioned are accumulated as common wealth for the good of all; that is, as household property. The favorite form of accumulating wealth, and the safest, was the acquisition of land. Land itself could then be a further source of income which, naturally enough, would be placed in a joint account. Then, when at some future date the household wealth was to be divided, it would be apportioned on a fixed scale determined by the status relationships of the several members of the family—the rule of thumb being equal division among brothers. There would be no stint in the share of a person who found himself unable to contribute anything to the household after leaving home or, even worse, who became a financial burden. Nor, as a rule, could a person who had made his fortune on the outside monopolize it.

*   *   *

In sum, *t'ung chü kung ts'ai* was a joint account relationship that covered all the aspects of consumption and the maintenance of wealth; the fruits of the labor of all the members and the profits accruing from commonly owned wealth were treated as income, and all the members' living expenses, of which funeral costs for the dead constituted an important part, were paid out of it. If there were a surplus, it would be saved as common wealth, while if there were a deficit, the wealth would be eaten into and life thus maintained. The expression "household property" *(chia ch'an)*, if it comes to that, was nothing other than a designation of wealth managed by such a joint account as has just been described. There is no feeling of landed property that should remain intact for generations in the expression "household property." Land did, to be sure, most commonly consti-tute the bulk of household property, but that very land could, depend-ing on the household income and expenditures, be bought and sold with comparative nonchalance. What this means, in other words, was that household property was, in essence, a fluid value that could be grasped quantitatively and that land was the safest accumulation device into which to convert it. Consequently, every time the joint account relationship itself was broken up, the land too could be par-celed up in any way whatever.

C. K. Yang, A Chinese Village in Early Communist Tradition, Cambridge: Technology Press, Massachusetts Institute of Technology, 1959, p. 91; and The Chinese Family in the Communist Revolution, Cambridge: Technology Press, MIT, 1959, p. 140.

Property ownership and management of income as a factor in the economic structure of the family was again based on sex and age differentiation. The right of property management belonged to the leader of the family's economic organization, the head of the household; when the head of the house died, it passed down the line of male inheritance. On this ground, the head of the house also dictated the disposal of income brought into the family by various members should they work outside; minor members in the status system, the young and the women, did not have complete control over the disposal of their own income.

Although management was dominated by the head of the household, family property was collectively owned, with other family members retaining their share. Under the collective principle family property was often legally registered in a form of corporate ownership known as *t'ang* (hall) under the direction and management of the head of the house and could not be disposed of without common consent of all the male members, each of whom held a share. A son might not have his share without the father's consent or until the death of the father. Female descendants had no claim on family property. A woman might own family property on the death of her husband, but she could not dispose of it without consent of the son if she had male children. As already pointed out, no divorced woman was permitted to take any part of the husband's family property into a new marriage or back to her own parents' family.

* * *

Farms were without exception family enterprises. The grocery store, the masonry shop, and the carpentry shop in the village were all family enterprises. Consequently, an individual's livelihood depended almost solely upon his membership in the family, particularly for minors and women. Even emigration of a mature son to the city would not entirely free him from economic control by the family as a unit of production, unless he severed all his family ties or became so successful in his urban adventure that he established another family unit of production in the city. The majority of emigrants eventually returned to the family fold in the village and resumed their place in the family.

The family unit of production was normally led by the male head of the family, either the father or a mature son, except in the case of widows with only young children. The head of the family decided on the means of employing the available family resources, decided what crops to plant in a certain year and with what investments, and commanded assistance from family members available for work.

* * *

The land, tools, house, and liquid capital were regarded as collectively owned by the family, but their disposal was generally decided upon by the male head of the family; in the case of a widow's family with minor children, the female head of the house would make the decision.

c. Partition and Inheritance

George Jamieson, Ta Ch'ing Lü Li [Code of Laws of the Ching Empire], in Chinese Family and Commercial Law, Hong Kong: Vetch and Lee, 1970, pp. 16–17.

SECTION 87

DIVISION OF FAMILY

Lü.

During the lifetime of grandparents or parents, the sons or grandsons are not allowed to set up separate establishments and register them as such, nor to divide the family property, under a penalty of one hundred blows, but the parents or grandparents must be the complainants. Also during the legal period of mourning for father or mother no division may take place, under a penalty of eighty blows; but in this case the nearest senior relations must be the complainants; and if the division has taken place in accordance with the last will of the father or mother, no action will lie.

Li.

1. The full penalty of the above law is incurred if the sons separate and divide the property, though they do not register themselves. If, however, the parents permit the division, there is no objection to its being done.

SECTION 88

DIVISION OF FAMILY PROPERTY

Lü.

If any of the junior members of a family living under the same roof appropriate without leave of the seniors any part of the family property, he shall be liable to punishment at the rate of twenty blows for every ten taels value so appropriated, and one degree more for every additional ten, not exceeding one hundred blows in all. If the elders living under the same roof, in dividing family property, divide it unfairly, they shall be liable to a similar punishment.

Li.

1. As regards children in general, hereditary official rank descends only to the eldest son and his descendants born in lawful wedlock, but all family property moveable or immoveable must be divided equally between all male children whether born of the principal wife or of a concubine or domestic slave. Also male children born of illicit intercourse shall be entitled to a half-share, or to an equal share in event of a successor having been adopted through default of other children. If no legal successor is in existence, then such illegitimate son shall be entitled to succeed and receive the whole patrimony.

2. In the event of a family becoming extinct for want of legal successors, the daughters shall be entitled to the property, and if there are no daughters the property shall be forfeited to Government.

NOTE

The lü of the Ching Code were statutory provisions formulated during the Tang dynasty (618 A.D.), or perhaps even earlier. The li were subsequent amendments. If the two conflicted, the later li prevailed. Why did the Chinese codifiers not merely amend the lü, removing the parts which were no longer desired?

George Jamieson, continued.

. . . Prior to division a deceased son's estate reverts to the common fund, after division it devolves on his sons or adopted successor according to the general law. No distinction is made between land and any other kind of property. To come within the scope of this general rule, however, it must be understood that the sons have, as a matter of fact, held together up to the time of a division. A partial dissolution often occurs when one son leaves the family for an official position or for purposes of a trade in a different part of the country. He is held to be "separately established," and his earnings would not fall into the common fund for distribution. Whether he would share or not would depend upon the arrangement at the time of his separation.

No special provision is made for the widow as such, but she is amply cared for. If she is also the mother of the family she can refuse to consent to a division of the estate, in which case she has the practical control of the whole inheritance, and if she is widow of a son dying before division, she is entitled to the custody and management of her husband's share in trust for her sons or the adopted successor.

In this particular, custom is all-powerful. On the death of a father the legal estate so to speak rests in the sons, but equity in the shape of custom forbids their dealing with it without the sanction of the mother. So long as the family estate was undivided, the sons would be tenants in common and would all be bound to join in a transfer of any portion, but even then, to give validity to the transaction, the mother must also be a party.

* * *

The father has no power to depart materially from the above scheme of distribution. Special circumstances may entitle him to allow one son a somewhat larger or smaller share, but generally speaking neither by will nor by gift *inter vivos* can he deprive any son of an equal or at least a substantial share. There is no such thing as disinheriting one son in favour of the others, much less any power to grant over to a stranger. It is said that in extreme cases, when a son is utterly incorrigible, the father may denounce him to the authorities, and solemnly expel him from the family in presence of the assembled kindred in the Ancestral Hall, but short of this extreme measure there is no means of cutting him off without his fair share.

It is unnecessary to say expressly, after the above general statement of the principles of succession, that the power of devising or bequeathing by *Will* does not exist. The term indeed is not unknown, but when used it relates exclusively to minor details regarding the mode of division, which the Father would have had power to arrange during his lifetime, or to moral exhortations and admonitions for the guidance of his children and posterity.

Shuzo Shiga, "Family Property and the Law of Inheritance in Traditional China," in David Buxbaum, editor, Chinese Family Law and Social Change in Historical and Comparative Perspective, Seattle and London: University of Washington Press, 1978, pp. 112–115.

Division of the Household Property. T'ung chü kung ts'ai is a relationship that comes into being of its own accord with no artificial prompting. The child at birth is automatically incorporated into the *t'ung chü kung ts'ai* relationship of the household into which it is born; the wife enters through marriage into a *t'ung chü kung ts'ai* relationship with her husband and, as a rule (in all cases, that is, except those of *chao hsü*; that is, matrilocal marriage), with his family. Yet, on the other hand, the *t'ung chü kung ts'ai* relationship is not one that is automatically dissolved. That is to say, the death of a member of the family—and this includes that of the father of the household—is no cause for the dissolution of a *kung ts'ai* relationship. Death means only that one person has left the common budget group; the relationship among the survivors remains just what it was. Also, even if one member of the family leaves the house in defiance of the wishes of the head of the household, the legal relationship of the common budget is not terminated by this mere fact. To sever the common budget relationship, a clear-cut legal act, that is, a division of the household's property, is needed. If the property is just left to lie, the *t'ung chü kung ts'ai* relationship will continue for several generations and may eventuate in an extended family embracing several hundreds of members.

* * *

However, in actual practice the brothers would usually, sooner or later, split up the household's property, and it was rare upon the deaths of all the brothers for the common budget relationship to survive among cousins. . . . [E]ven in households having virtually no wealth to distribute, "division of household property" has great significance in the sense that it severs the joint account relationship.

The precise point in time when division of the household's property takes place is not fixed and has no direct connection with the death of the father of the household. It may be provided for by the parents during their own lifetime, or it may be attended to some time after their deaths. However, whenever the deed is done, it must be done simultaneously for all the brothers, or, if the brothers are all dead, for all the cousins. It is not possible for them to achieve independence and then to split off one at a time. This applies even in cases in which there are brothers who are too young to be independent. At such times the parents, if they are alive, or, if not, one of the brothers, will take the youngsters in charge and rear them, managing their respective shares of the property in the role of guardian.

* * *

Division of household property did not mean an instant change in the way of life whereby the brothers and their respective wives and children would live in a cluster around the same courtyard. The legal relationship binding them would, however, change completely. Needless to say, the individual does not become independent as a result of a division of household property. The greater collectivity, consisting of parents and brothers, would break up into several smaller collectivities, each consisting of a brother, as head, and his wife and children. Also, within each smaller collectivity the "common living, common budget" relationship is maintained. "Common living, common budget" was for the Chinese an absolute truth decreed by Fate herself. The possibility of a family life rooted in any principle other than this one never even occurred to them.

* * *

Properties Not Belonging to Households. Under the family system just described, most property is preserved in the form of household property (*chia ch'an*). This is not to say, however, that there were no other forms for the preservation of property. There are cases in which the *tsu* owns property. This consists of property that is exempted at the time of division and maintained in common ownership, as well as property contributed by those members of the *tsu* who have been successful. It was managed as a sort of foundation by representatives of the *tsu*. On the other hand, there are cases in which the *fang*, or even an individual, may keep property. While there were cases of accumulation of private property in defiance of the law, it is not to be forgotten that there were also cases acknowledged within the system.

First, anything acquired, not as the fruits of labor, but in return for nothing at all, becomes the personal property of the acquisitor. An example of this that has realistically important significance is the wife's dowry, which remains the property of the couple and which is never pooled with the household property belonging to a larger group that includes the husband's parents and brothers. This was a cardinal rule, unchanged throughout the ages. Also, though it was the fruit of labor, there was in Yüan times legislation acknowledging the pay earned in civil or military service as private property. This was not, however, regarded as an unchanging, self-evident rule as it was in the case of the wife's dowry.

Second, the duty to bring the fruits of their labor into the household budget was something not strictly required of the women. Since the women's profession was housework, to the extent that they did not shirk it unwarrantedly, whatever side income they earned in their spare time was considered their own individually. There were even cases in large families in which women were paid by their household heads for lending a hand in the harvest. It was particularly easy for unmarried women to come by opportunities to work and save a bit.

NOTES AND QUESTIONS

1. D, a high government official, died and was survived by his wife, two married sons, a married daughter, and an unmarried sister. If these persons had maintained "common living," what share would each receive upon partition?

2. How would the distribution differ if the daughter was unmarried? What if D had had a concubine or secondary wife? See also the materials on bride price and dowry in IIID.

3. Must a partition occur upon the death of D? At what other points in time may a partition take place? What considerations contribute to the desire for a partition? See also the partition documents in IIB.

4. What if D had had no sons, but was survived by a daughter, a brother, and two nephews? By only a daughter? By only his father?

5. Under the facts of question 1, D made a will giving half of his property to his sister. What would have been the distribution of his estate?

B. INHERITANCE AND SUCCESSION IN THE REPUBLIC OF CHINA

NOTE

During the early part of the twentieth century, a vigorous debate took place on how to "modernize" Chinese society. In the family law area, some conservatives advocated restoring and strengthening the traditional family system. Other "modernists" argued for a drastic reform of the old system by establishing equality of men and women, ensuring freedom of marriage, loosening of parental controls over children, and secularizing the family in the eyes of the law. The latter group prevailed, and in the 1920s and 1930s, a series of laws were promulgated which were closely patterned on the continental European model.

During those years and for the next several decades, China was engaged almost continuously in a series of foreign and civil wars. Under such circumstances, it seems doubtful that these new laws were actually applied throughout the country. There were higher political and social priorities than reform of the legal system.

After going to Taiwan in 1949, a greater effort has been made to implement the Western-style legal codes, although many traditional practices continue extralegally.

1. The Civil Code of 1931

William S. H. Hung, Outlines of Modern Chinese Law, Shanghai(?) 1934, pp. 196–197, 201, 203–204, 207 (footnotes omitted).

With the abolishment of succession of duty of ancestral worship, want of lineal descendant no longer occupies any place of importance and recognition of women's rights is thereby facilitated. The present law has become much simpler in both its form and application. It deals chiefly with the class of persons who may be successors to a deceased's estate according to the order of sequence. It encourages the disposal by the testator of his property by will and also provides certain limitations in distribution of one's property.

* * *

The equal right of inheritance thus granted to woman has been the focus of continued dispute among jurists. Those who hold the dissenting views base their grounds on the fact that a son who receives the proportionate share generally has the burden of support in the family, whereas a daughter, receiving an equal share, is at liberty to carry it into her husband's family forming a part of her special property by marriage without any liability of family maintenance. Equal share of inheritance by woman is yet a new principle, which, in the eyes of men and as the facts show, means mere share of interest rather than share of burden, which does not make the meaning of the term *succession* complete in its technical sense. Little attention had perhaps been paid by the legislators to the accession of women's property rights upon marriage. According to the present view, a surviving wife may even carry away her share of inheritance upon remarriage. Marriage or re-marriage of a woman does not give effect to any restriction to her share of inheritance.

One's obligation arising out of succession does not confine its scope to deceased's debts before death, but extends to all the expenses incurred by the death of the deceased as well as the deceased's liability toward certain member of the family, who had been dependent on the support of the deceased. The provision made by the Civil Code with reference to liability for support of such member of the family is, according to its exact version in Chinese, as follows:—*The person who had been continually supported by the deceased during the latter's life-time shall, through the family council, be given such amount of estate as is appropriate to the extent of support received and other reasonable grounds.* The wording of this provision has been so wisely set as to embody the intended purpose of embracing in it the support of concubines, whose status cannot be expressly recognized but has to be taken care of in view of existence of the practice.

* * *

. . . In the Chinese law, however, a testator has no right to exercise his free will in distribution of his property beyond the limit of the special share of succession of the legatee, who is the lawful heir according to the order of succession. The protection of an heir's interest within the extent of his special share of succession may be considered as a force of inertia of the old practice of family succession.

Book V, Succession, of the Civil Code of the Republic of China, effective May 5, 1931.

Article 1138. Heirs to property other than the spouse come in the following order:

1. Lineal descendants by blood;

2. Parents;

3. Brothers and sisters;

4. Grandparents.

Article 1139. Among persons of the first order provided in the preceding article, the person nearest in degree of relationship comes first as heir.

Article 1140. Where an heir of the first order provided in Article 1138 has died or lost the right of inheritance before the opening of the succession, his lineal descendants shall inherit his successional portion in his place.

Article 1141. Where there are several heirs of the same order, they inherit in equal shares as per capita, unless it is otherwise provided by law.

Article 1142. The order of succession for an adopted child is the same as for a legitimate child.

The successional portion of an adopted child is one-half of that of a legitimate child, but, in case the adoptive parents have no lineal descendant by blood for their heir, his successional portion is the same as that of a legitimate child.

Article 1143. Where a person has no lineal descendants by blood, he may by will designate an heir to the whole or a part of his property, provided that the provisions concerning compulsory portions are not contravened.

Article 1144. Each spouse has the right to inherit the property of the other, and his or her successional portion is determined according to the following provisions:

1. Where the spouse inherits concurrently with heirs of the first order, as provided in Article 1138, his or her successional portion is equal to the other heirs;

2. Where the spouse inherits concurrently with heirs of the second or third order as provided in Article 1138, his or her successional portion is one-half of the inheritance;

3. Where the spouse inherits concurrently with heirs of the fourth order as provided in Article 1138, his or her successional portion is two-thirds of the inheritance;

4. Where there is no heir of any of the four orders provided in Article 1138, his or her successional portion is the whole of the inheritance.

Article 1164. The heirs may at any time demand the partition of the inheritance unless it is otherwise provided by law or agreed upon by contract.

Article 1165. Where the will of the deceased has determined, or asked a third person to determine, the method of partition of the inheritance, the method so determined shall be followed.

Where a will prohibits the partition of the deceased's property, the effect of such prohibition is limited to twenty years.

* * *

Article 1173. If one of the heirs has, before the opening of succession, received gifts in property from the deceased for the purpose of getting married, setting up a separate home, or carrying on trade, the value of such gifts shall be added to the property owned by the deceased at the time of the opening of the succession, thus constituting together the property of the succession. But this does not apply where the deceased has declared a contrary intention at the time of making the gifts.

The value of such gifts shall, at the time of the partition of inheritance form the successional portion of the heir in question.

The value of the gifts is determined at the time when such gifts were made.

CHAPTER III

WILLS

Title I. General Provisions

Article 1186. A person without disposing capacity may not make a will.

A person limited in disposing capacity may make a will without first obtaining the approval of his statutory agent. But a person who has not completed sixteen years of age may not make a will.

Article 1187. A testator may freely dispose of his property by a will, so long as he does not contravene the provisions in regard to Compulsory Portions.

Article 1188. The provisions of Article 1145 concerning the forfeiture of the right of inheritance apply to legatees *mutatis mutandis.*

Title II. Forms

Article 1189. A will shall be made in one of the following forms:
1. A holograph will;
2. A notarial will;
3. A secret will;
4. A "dictated" will;
5. An oral will.

Title VI. Compulsory Portions

Article 1223. The compulsory portion of an heir is determined as follows:

1. For a lineal descendant by blood, the compulsory portion is one half of his successional portion;

2. For a parent, the compulsory portion is one half of his successional portion;

3. For a spouse, the compulsory portion is one half of his successional portion;

4. For a brother or a sister, the compulsory portion is one-third of his or her successional portion;

5. For a grandparent, the compulsory portion is one-third of his successional portion.

QUESTIONS

1. D died and was survived by his wife, two married sons, a married daughter, a married daughter, and an unmarried sister. How would D's estate be divided under the Civil Code? How would the distribution differ if the daughter was unmarried? If D was also survived by his father?

2. What if D had been survived by a daughter, a brother, and two nephews? By only a daughter? By only his father?

3. Under the facts of question 1, D made a will giving half of his property to his sister. What would have been the distribution of his estate?

2. Documents on Partition in Taiwan

NOTE

At the time of partition, a formal document usually is drawn up describing in detail what property each person is to receive. The form of the document is a statement by the father "granting" the property to his heirs.

Myron Cohen, "Family Partition as Contractual Process in Taiwan: A Case Study from South Taiwan," in David Buxbaum, editor, Chinese Family Law and Social Change in Historical and Comparative Perspective, Seattle and London: University of Washington Press, 1978, pp. 200–201, 203–204.

DOCUMENT B

In compliance with our mother's command we four brothers shall equally divide among ourselves all property inherited from our ancestors and all present property so that each of us may carry on his livelihood, enhance the prestige of the family, and shed lustre upon our ancestors. The complete details of the distribution of the family estate are as follows:

1. The right to separate residence [obtained by Hsin-feng]: The old shop by the dike and the plot on which it stands, within its recognized boundaries, shall belong to Hsin-feng. The tobacco house itself shall be jointly used by the four brothers, who shall also share equally the right to plant tobacco; the two lower level rooms of the tobacco house as well as property rights to the land on which it stands belong to Te-feng.

2. The two rooms at the west end of our original house and the four rooms at the southern end of our house by the road plus their foundation land belong to Hsi-hung; the four rooms at the eastern end (of the original house), the bamboo pig-pen at the northern corner

of the road-side house and their foundation land belongs to Yüan-hung.

3. As compensation for construction expenses, the sum of NT$10,000 shall be removed from the common estate and given to Te-feng.

4. Hsi-hung, Te-feng, and Yüan-hung shall assume equal responsibility for full repayment of principal and interest of all our outstanding debts and taxes. Hsin-feng shall have nothing to do with these payments.

5. All four brothers shall assume full and joint responsibility for caring for their grandmother and mother, who are still living. They should pay for their living expenses, medical expenses, and for future funeral expenses. Moreover, the four brothers must take turns in making offerings to their ancestors.

6. Of our .73 *chia* plot of paddy land, .20 *chia* shall be given to Hsin-feng, and what remains shall be equally divided among Hsi-hung, Te-feng, and Yüan-hung; the .16 *chia* plot of paddy land shall be owned equally by Hsi-hung, Te-feng, and Yüan-hung. Also, cultivation rights to the .16 *chia* paddy land rented for 37.5 [per cent of the crop, the rate set by the Land Reform Laws] shall be given entirely to Hsin-feng.

7. Hsi-hung, Te-feng and Yüan-hung shall share equally cultivation rights to .6 *chia* of single-season public land at . . . which we rent, the .48 *chia* paddy field rented for 37.5 [per cent of the crop through Land Reform], and the .39 *chia* of redistributed land (through Land Reform).

8. From this day on, all four brothers shall take turns in descending order of birth in meeting the expenses of the annual celebration of their grandmother's and mother's birthdays.

In compliance with our mother's command, and with the assistance of a council convened by our agnatic kinsmen (*tsung-ch'in*) we brothers have arrived at the above terms of division. Four copies of the certificate of division have been made, and each of us shall keep one copy and forever abide by the terms agreed therein without dispute.

[July 17, 1958.]

DOCUMENT F

I, Yeh Ch'ing-feng, the executor of this testament of partition, live at . . . , and have four sons, who are, in descending order of birth, Ting-jen, Ta-jen, Hsing-jen, and Ch'ang-jen. Knowing that a large tree will naturally divide into many branches and realizing further that this very same principle is also applicable to human life, I conclude that future conflicts could be avoided if I invite, while I am still alive, some of our kinsmen to come here and distribute, equally and as agreed upon, all the movable and non-movable property which I bequeath [to my sons] forever. But after the final distribution, no one shall ever raise objections or cause any disturbances. It is for this purpose that I prepare this testament of partition; two copies have been drawn up to serve as proof for the future; one shall be kept by my eldest son Ting-jen, and the second by my three other sons, Ta-jen, Hsing-jen, and Ch'ang-jen. The details of the property division are as follows:

1. Plot A, .02 *chia*, paddy land, plot B, .265 *chia* paddy land, one share in the *Sheng-ting hui* [an association], and one share in the *Tien-hsüeh hui* [another association] shall forever belong to my eldest son Ting-jen.

2. Plot C, .395 *chia* paddy land, and plot D, .313 *chia* paddy land, shall be allotted to Ta-jen, Hsing-jen, Ch'ang-jen, and forever owned by them.

3. The .143 *chia* building ground and all buidings now located on plot E shall be set aside for the marriage expenses of Ting-jen, Hsing-jen, and Ch'ang-jen.

4. Plot F, .175 *chia* paddy land, and plot G, .19 *chia* paddy land, as well as all household effects, cattle, pigs, chickens, and so forth shall be used for paying up our present debt of approximately $1,000 and also for the living expenses and then the funeral of father, Yeh Ch'ing-feng.

5. Ting-jen, Ta-jen, Hsing-jen, and Ch'ang-jen shall share equally the interest [held by Yeh Ch'ing-feng] in the Yeh ancestral fields.

6. The land rented from Hsiao Yün-chin, comprising .88 *chia*, shall be allocated to Ting-jen for cultivation. He must pay the rent. Moreover, the security for this land, $210, and one share in the Trust Company, must be returned by Ting-jen to father, to pay for father's living expenses.

This testament of partition is hereby established.

[Nov. 1, 1939.]

QUESTIONS

1. How is the living pattern for each of the various families affected by the partition?

2. The first partition took place under the Republic of China government. Did the distributions agree with or contradict the provisions of the Civil Code?

3. The other partition occurred while Taiwan was under Japanese rule. Does the distribution of property in this case differ from the distribution pattern in the first case?

C.   INHERITANCE AND SUCCESSION IN THE PEOPLE'S REPUBLIC OF CHINA

NOTE

After the establishment of the People's Republic in 1949, a series of major steps were taken to implement the goals of the revolution. Land reform redistributed land to the poor; several years later, rural areas were organized into cooperatives and then communes. In the commercial and industrial sectors, private ownership of the means of production was gradually eliminated.

A Marriage Law was promulgated affirming sexual equality and freedom of marriage. A legal system was set up to enforce the new rules.

To what extent have these changes affected the rules and patterns of inheritance and succession? What property may be inherited? Who are the heirs? Does the "common living" system still operate? The following item gives a description of what the pattern of living is like in rural areas.

1.   Life in Rural Areas

Gordon Bennett, Huadong: The Story of a Chinese People's Commune, Boulder: Westview Press, 1978, pp. 15, 18–19, 110, 112–113.

. . . Today's communes are the lowest level of government administration. In that capacity, commune centers, usually in large market towns, have state personnel carrying out duties in banking, commerce, procurement of agricultural products, tax collections, and public security. At the same time, today's communes are the highest level of rural collective. . . . Commune-run enterprises earn as much as one-third of all rural income. Communes take advantage of their large size to build irrigation canals, drainage ditches, hydroelectric power stations, hospitals, small industries, schools, and other facilities for their membership.

*   *   *

Below the commune level are an average of fifteen "production brigades" (*shengchan da dui*), each with an average of 200 households or more, or about 1,000 people. . . .

*   *   *

. . . [B]rigade functions include: (1) helping teams make production plans and coordinating team production with the state economic plan, (2) supervising teams to insure fulfillment of plan targets, (3) guiding teams on the proper division of income between distribution to members and saving to develop production, (4) managing brigade water conservancy projects, and (5) providing services beyond the capacity of teams in such areas as militia, education, public health, and medium-sized agricultural machinery.

While today's production brigades give strong political leadership and support to their teams, they are not yet so autonomous in economic affairs. Few brigade-level enterprises earn very large profits; their role seems rather to be direct support of the teams. Common functions are tractor servicing, farm machine repair, electric power supply, animal husbandry, brick and tile making, and fish breeding. Ordinarily brigade enterprises earn less than one-sixth of all rural income.

*   *   *

Brigades average seven production teams (*shengchan dui*) each, and each team generally has about thirty households, or roughly 150 people. Most production teams bring together the residents of one small village, the age-old, basic-level community of rural China. Some are single surname villages, or lineages, where village ties may be reinforced by kinship bonds. Team leadership is not even a half-time responsibility, and team "headquarters" may be no more than the team leader's home. Teams are the basic level in the "three-level system of ownership." Each team owns the land, forest, and water resources within its area (other than those managed by the state), as well as its draft animals, small farm machinery, and farm implements. Teams are also the so-called basic accounting unit in rural China. This means that they organize their own production and distribution of income, handle their accounting, and are responsible for their own profits or losses. In other words, members of a team rise or fall together.

*   *   *

. . . Much larger than the average Huadong household of five, the Zhang family has thirteen members living together in three houses. Seven are income earners: the Zhangs' "labor power" in the production team is four, two are "workers" in other commune enterprises, and one attends to family sideline production.

Mr. Zhang Liyi	Team farmworker (labor power)
Mrs. Zhang (illiterate)	Manages family sidelines and family finances including salaries of working members
Son No. 1	Worker in coal mine (worker)
Daughter-in-law	Team farmworker (labor power)
Daughter No. 1	Sales girl in commune general store (worker)
Daughter No. 2	Team farmworker (labor power)
Daughter No. 3	Team farmworker (labor power)
Son No. 2	Senior middle school student
Daughter No. 4	Senior middle school student
Son No. 3	Primary school student
Daughter No. 5	Primary school student
Grandson No. 1	Preschooler
Grandson No. 2	Preschooler

The Zhangs built their house in 1962 for $150. They were able to use some materials from their old clay house. . . . The buildings are considered the Zhangs' private property and would remain with the family even if some members were to die or move away. The Zhangs are permitted to rent or sell, but this is rarely done.

Mrs. Zhang says that last year (1972) the four team workers together earned $490, most of it paid in kind with 3,100 kilograms of rice. The coal miner earned $222, and the salesgirl brought in $195. Another $150 came from the sale of four pigs to the commune purchasing station. A few more dollars were garnered from sales of vegetables on the free market. The total was about $1,100, roughly 15 percent of which (and about 25 percent of the cash part) was accounted for by the sale of pigs and vegetables. The Zhangs' private plot of 0.1 acre is located several hundred yards from the house. Mrs. Zhang works on it up to an hour a day. In addition to the small surplus of produce for market, the plot provides all vegetables consumed by the family and fodder for the pigs.

Mrs. Zhang, describing the family's expenditures, says that they live a quiet villager's life. They raise their own chickens, eggs, vegetables, and tobacco. The rice received from the team is more than they eat, and about 250 kilograms per year is set aside "against time of war or natural calamity." All they really need buy at the village store is fish at twenty cents per kilogram and pork at forty cents.

Documents of Chinese Communist Party Central Committee, September 1956–April 1969, Vol. I, Hong Kong: Union Research Institute, 1971, pp. 704–705, 710, 715–718.

REGULATIONS ON THE WORK OF THE RURAL PEOPLE'S COMMUNES (Revised Draft)

September 1962

20. Production teams are the basic accounting units in a people's commune. They carry on independent accounting, assume responsibility for their profits and losses, directly organize production of grains. Once established this system shall remain unchanged for at least thirty years.

21. All the land within the production teams belongs to the production teams. It is not allowed to rent, buy or sell the land owned by the production teams, including the private plots, private hills and residential land of commune members.

* * *

32. The production team should give rational remuneration to its members according to the quality and quantity of labor performed,

and egalitarianism should be avoided when labor is accounted for among these members.

* * *

When fixing the labor quota, it is necessary to fix a rational standard for work points, as dictated by the technical level required by different types of labor, the intensity of such labor, and the importance of such labor in the whole process of production.

* * *

When fixing and readjusting the labor quota and the standard of remuneration, the production team should pay attention not only to the quantity of farm work but also to quality of such work, and then such quota and standard must be discussed and approved at the general meeting of commune members.

* * *

Equal pay for equal work should be effected, irrespective of sex, age, cadres or commune members. The work points for each commune member should be entered into his work point book in time and a statement of work points of commune members should be published periodically.

* * *

39. The family sideline production of the commune members is a necessary ancillary part of the socialist economy. It comes under the collective ownership and all people's ownership economy and is their assistant. Under the premise that the collective economy is actively conducted, the development of collective economy is not affected and that the collective economy is guaranteed its absolute supreme position, the people's commune should permit and encourage its members to make use of their spare time or holiday for the development of family sideline production to increase social products, to increase the members' income, and to enliven the rural market.

40. Members of the people's commune may engage themselves in the following types of family sideline production:

(1) Tilling the private land allocated by the collective. The private land generally accounts for 5 to 7 per cent of the production team's total cultivated land. This is allocated to a commune member for his own use on a permanent basis. . . .

(2) Raising hogs, sheep, rabbits, chickens, ducks and geese or large animals. . . .

(4) Commune members may take up family or home handicraft industry such as knitting, sewing, embroidering, etc.

(5) They may take up subsidiary production such as herb collecting, fishing, hunting, silkworm raising, bee-raising, etc.

* * *

42. . . .

Protection should be given to all the means of subsistence of a commune member, including his house, furniture, clothing and bedding, bicycle, sewing machine, money deposited in the bank or credit society. These should always belong to the commune member and in no case can be infringed upon by any person.

The farming tools, work tools and other such means of production of a commune member shall be owned by him, and his draft animal shall always belong to him, and in no case can it be taken away from him.

* * *

45. The house of a commune member shall be owned by him forever.

A commune member has the right to sell or buy or rent his house. When he rents or sells his house, he may get a third party to assess for a reasonable rent or price to be reached, and an agreement or contract may be concluded between the buyer and the seller or between the lessee and lessor. . . .

NOTE

During the past year, the right of individuals to own property has been reaffirmed, together with the three-tier commune system.

Constitution of the People's Republic of China (1978), in Chinese Law and Government, volume 11, 1978, pp. 135–138.

Article 5. There are mainly two kinds of ownership of the means of production in the People's Republic of China at the present stage: socialist ownership by the whole people and socialist collective ownership by the working people.

The state allows non-agricultural individual labourers to engage in individual labour involving no exploitation of others, within the limits permitted by law and under unified arrangement and management by organizations at the basic level in cities and towns or in rural areas. At the same time, it guides these individual labourers step by step on to the road of socialist collectivization.

Article 7. The rural people's commune sector of the economy is a socialist sector collectively owned by the masses of working people. At present, it generally takes the form of three-level ownership, that is, ownership by the commune, the production brigade and the production team, with the production team as the basic accounting unit. A production brigade may become the basic accounting unit when its conditions are ripe.

Provided that the absolute predominance of the collective economy of the people's commune is ensured, commune members may farm small plots of land for personal needs, engage in limited household sideline production, and in pastoral areas they may also keep a limited number of livestock for personal needs.

Article 9. The state protects the right of citizens to own lawfully earned income, savings, houses and other means of livelihood.

QUESTIONS

1. What kind and how much property does a person own in rural China?

2. How does team-owned property differ from the traditional lineage or clan property?

3. The above materials deal almost entirely with rural areas—after all, China was a predominantly agricultural society; even today, 80–85% of the population are peasants. What differences would you expect to find in the patterns of property ownership and succession in urban areas? How might the present PRC rules change as the population becomes wealthier, more educated, and more mobile?

2. Inheritance and Wills

The Marriage Law of the People's Republic of China (1950), Appendix VII, M. J. Meijer, Marriage Law and Policy in the Chinese People's Republic, Hong Kong: Hong Kong University Press, 1971, pp. 300–302.

CHAPTER I

GENERAL PRINCIPLES

Article 1. The feudal marriage system which is based on arbitrary and compulsory arrangements and the superiority of man over woman and ignores the children's interests shall be abolished.

The New-Democratic marriage system, which is based on the free choice of partners, on monogamy, on equal rights for both sexes, and on the protection of the lawful interests of women and children, shall be put into effect.

Article 2. Bigamy, concubinage, child betrothal, interference with the re-marriage of widows, and the exaction of money or gifts in connection with marriages, shall be prohibited.

Article 10. Both husband and wife shall have equal rights in the possession and management of family property.

Article 12. Both husband and wife shall have the right to inherit each other's property.

Article 13. Parents have the duty to rear and to educate their children; the children have the duty to support and to assist their parents. Neither the parents nor the children shall maltreat or desert one another.

The foregoing provision also applies to foster-parents and foster-children. Infanticide by drowning and similar criminal acts are strictly prohibited.

Article 14. Parents and children shall have the right to inherit one another's property.

Article 15. Children born out of wedlock shall enjoy the same rights as children born in lawful wedlock. No person shall be allowed to harm them or discriminate against them. . . .

Article 17. Divorce shall be granted when husband and wife both desire it. In the event of either the husband or the wife alone insisting upon divorce, it may be granted only when mediation by the district people's government and the judicial organ has failed to bring about a reconciliation. . . .

Article 20. The blood ties between parents and children do not end with the divorce of the parents. No matter whether the father or the mother acts as guardian of the children, they still remain the children of both parties.

After divorce, both parents still have the duty to support and educate their children. . . .

Article 23. In case of divorce, the wife shall retain such property as belonged to her prior to her marriage. The disposal of other family properties shall be subject to agreement between the two parties. In cases where agreement cannot be reached, the people's court shall render a decision after taking into consideration the actual state of the family property, the interests of the wife and the child or children, and the principle of benefiting the development of production.

* * *

NOTE

The above legal provisions are not complete or entirely clear. In the early 1950s, Chinese legal officials attempted to clarify the rules on inheritance and wills by examining judicial practice.

Research Bureau of the Secretariat of the Standing Committee of the National People's Congress, Reference Material Relative to Problems of Inheritance in M. J. Meijer, Marriage Law and Policy in the Chinese People's Republic, Hong Kong: Hong Kong University Press, 1971, pp. 325–327, 329, 333–334, 336, 338–339.

* * *

1. Spouses. . . .

In confirming the rights of inheritance of the spouse and the order of heirs, the courts based themselves in most cases on Article 12 of the Marriage Law: "Both husband and wife shall have the right to inherit each other's property". In the majority of the cases they recognized the spouse as belonging to the first order of heirs. If the deceased had more than one wife, all wives had equal rights of inheritance and they would equally divide the estate. . . .

* * *

2. *Children.* . . .

In most cases married daughters were the ones who started the litigation. Some did so [immediately] after the death of the parent, some waited a long time before they laid claim to the inheritance. Their opponents were mostly nephews of the decedent.

The courts always protected the rights of inheritance of the children; even if the daughters had married, they were classified as heirs in the first category.

The Courts did not recognize the right of the son who had been adopted into another family to inherit the estate of his natural parents. . . . In another case where the relations between the child and its parents during their lifetime had been very bad, and it had been clearly announced that they had ceased to maintain the parent-child relationship, the court also rejected the right to inherit. . . .

3. *Adopted Children.* The adopted children as regards their family background (*shen-fen*) were mostly nephews of the decedent; those who had no consanguineous relationship with the decedent were very few. Some had been raised by the decedent from early youth, others had gone over into his family when they were already adult. All of those had the relationship of leading a life in common with the decedent, relations of mutual support, or quasi child-parent relationships.

* * *

In adjudicating such cases, the courts recognized that adopted children and natural children all had the same right of inheritance.

* * *

4. *Grandchildren, Maternal Grandchildren.* In cases where grandchildren claimed the inheritance of their grandparents the courts recognized their right to inherit by representation, and placed them in the first category of heirs.

* * *

7. *The Widow* [widowed daughter-in-law]. Those cases most frequently happened when a widowed daughter-in-law litigated about the inheritance of her parents-in-law; there was also a small number of cases in which the widow disputed the inheritance with the decedent's brothers. As regards their family circumstances some had children, others not. The courts in adjudicating these cases disregarded the fact whether they had children or not and in the majority of the cases decided that they possessed the right to inherit and placed them in the first category of heirs. . . .

B. *Special Problems in Connection with the Customs of the Masses*

When handling the above-mentioned cases on the right to inherit or the orders of heirs some could be explained by referring to the customs of the masses and only understood that way.

1. The Position of the Parents in the Order of Heirs. The courts took no account as to whether the parents had the capacity to work or not or the means to support themselves or not, but they unanimously recognized them as heirs of the first category; there was no instance of their being ranged in the second category. According to our understanding of the customs of the masses, matters are as follows: If the decedent had no spouse or children, the estate is inherited by the parents. If there are a spouse and children, the following differentiation is made: (a) if the decedent during his or her lifetime had been living apart from the parents, the estate is inherited by the spouse and the children—the parents cannot interfere and generally do not attempt to do so; (b) if the decedent during his or her lifetime had been living together with the parents and after his or her death the spouse is going to live apart from the parents, then the parents whether they have the capacity to work or not or whether they have the means to support themselves or not, inherit the estate together and in equal parts with the spouse and the children. If the parents in such a case were not allowed to inherit, it would not be in conformity with the people's customs.

* * *

Persons who have no capacity to work and who have been supported for a certain time by the decedent during his life time.

* * *

. . . [P]ersons who are unable to work and who have been supported by the decedent have been dependent on the fact that the decedent was alive, and if such a person is not allowed part of the estate, immediately the problem of his maintenance may arise. When we consult the provisions of the U.S.S.R. and Czech Codes, we find that such a person's rights to inherit are recognized, although there are differences as to the order in which he or she inherits. . . .

* * *

In our opinion it is not satisfactory that the parents should inherit in the same order as the wife and the children of the deceased, for not only do the daughters leave the house when they marry, and then in general do not live together with the parents any longer, but the sons when they marry and have children very often also leave the paternal house. Therefore the fact that the children and the wife of a decedent inherit his estate, does not affect the livelihood of the parents. If the parents are unable to work and need to be supported then of course the grandchildren bear the duty of supporting them. As we are also in favour of the rule that persons who have been supported for a certain period by the decedent during his lifetime should inherit in the first category of heirs, parents without capacity to work, who have been supported by the decedent during his lifetime naturally can avail themselves of this rule and obtain part of the estate. . . . Moreover we are of the opinion that so far as possible we should avoid the inheritance of estate by linear ascendants, because in that case, after the death of these persons, according to the rule that parents and children have the right to inherit, the estate could easily be dispersed and revert to collateral relatives, and as a result of these transfers the inheritance in a very short time would land on the brothers and sisters, uncles, aunts and cousins of the decedent who are his comparatively far removed relatives. . . .

* * *

1. *The Standard of Allotment.* Among the heirs of the same category equal distribution is the basic thesis. This has been adopted in the majority of the decisions at hand. But a suitable allotment based on the following considerations is made: the number of people concerned, the fact whether or not they have the capacity to work, their respective economic circumstances, the fact whether or not they have been living together with the decedent and whether or not they fulfilled duties of support and funeral rites towards the decedent. Therefore, when the economic circumstances of the heirs and their capacity to work are not greatly different, there is equal distribution; when there are great differences in this respect suitable adjustment must be made according to the court's discretion.

Some courts are of the opinion that a daughter's dowry must be deducted from her portion; others hold that any increase of the estate due to the contribution of one of the heirs must also be taken into consideration.

* * *

IV. WILLS

* * *

There are three different attitudes towards the system of wills: one is to abolish the system of wills altogether, the whole estate of the decedent being inherited according to law by the heirs established by the law; another system is of not only to recognize wills but also to recognize that the testator has an unlimited freedom to divide his estate as he wishes; the third attitude is to recognize the system of wills within strict limitations. In our opinion, under the present circumstances, it would be wrong to accord the testator the unlimited freedom to divide his estate as he wishes, for that would amount to the recognition of the sanctity of private property which cannot be invaded and to the absolute freedom of the owner to divide his property. This is obviously a capitalist line of thought which we cannot adopt. Yet the basic abolition of the system of wills also does not agree with the circumstances prevalent in our country, not only because in our country there is still a remnant of the capitalist class, but mainly because the majority of our working people under the socialist system will enjoy greater income from their labour, and if we do not accord to our citizens the freedom to divide the fruits of their labour, it may have an adverse effect on the incentive to work and on the development of production. Therefore the third attitude, i.e. recognition of the system of wills with the addition of necessary restrictions, is preferable. . . .

* * *

. . . A testator can institute an heir who inherits on an equal footing with the testator's own children. One can also by will design part of one's property to a certain heir "as capital to provide for his maintenance and to set up a family". It is also allowed to divide by will one's estate among one's heirs in a concrete way or according to a certain pattern. It is furthermore possible to designate an heir to receive the estate on condition that he undertakes a certain duty. However, when in the contents of the will there are provisions that clash with policy and law, such parts shall be invalid. . . .

* * *

. . . With regard to wills which deprive of their inheritance rights, persons who lack the capacity to work, they also should be subject to restrictions.

QUESTIONS

1. D died and was survived by his wife, two married sons, a married daughter, and an unmarried sister. How would D's estate have been divided? How would the distribution have differed if the daughter was unmarried? If D was also survived by his father?

2. What if D had been survived by a daughter, a brother, and two nephews? By only a daughter? By only his father?

3. Under the facts of question 1, D made a will giving half his property to his sister. What would have been the disposition of his estate?

4. In the Zhang family (Item C(1)(a)), if the father dies, what will happen to his property? If partition occurs, what will be the share of the surviving person?

5. What are the principal similarities and differences between the PRC rules and the ROC rules? Between the PRC rules and the traditional rules?

3. Other Forms of Distribution of Property

William L. Parish and Martin K. Whyte, Village and Family in Contemporary China, Chicago: University of Chicago Press, 1978, pp. 180–185.

Marriage Finance. . . .

. . . The Chinese Communists, we have noted, regard the payment of a bride price (at least a substantial one) as marriage by purchase; this is specifically prohibited in the 1950 marriage law. We

have also noted that the party feels that, besides the general mercenary connotations of "buying" a bride, the bride-price custom perpet-
uated class inequalities, by allowing the well-off to acquire the most
desirable brides, leaving poor males with the remainder, or unable to
marry at all. According to recent work by anthropologist Jack
Goody, however, true bride-price systems need not have all these implications. In fact, these systems predominate more in economically
unstratified than in stratified societies, particularly in West Africa,
with bride prices forming a sort of rotating fund. Bride prices are
constant from family to family, and a father uses the valuables taken
in when a daughter weds to marry off his son or, if there is no son, to
acquire an extra wife for himself. Some sons, particularly those with
no sisters, must delay marriage and some even have to leave their
home village in search of bridewealth. Polygyny and late marriage
are promoted, but over a number of generations the sex balance
among families is sufficient for no single class of families to gain
significant economic advantage over others. Dowry systems, in contrast, almost always imply economic inequality, with parents using
the dowry as a form of inheritance-in-advance to preserve their
daughters' social status as well as their own prestige. Parents try to
prevent their daughters from marrying males who do not bring a sufficient amount of inherited property to the marriage. Dowries stay
within a limited economic stratum rather than being distributed
among all segments of a community, and as a consequence dowries
act to perpetuate differential status and wealth. Thus pure bride
price, which appears to Western (and Chinese Communist) eyes as
more mercenary, is actually compatible with egalitarian systems;
while dowry, which to the same eyes appears more equal (allowing
women a share of family property), implies inequality and efforts to
preserve that inequality across generations.

The bearing of this argument on the Chinese case is problematic,
since traditionally Chinese peasants practiced a system that was part
bride price and part dowry, with many class and regional variants.
. . .

. . . For China as a whole peasants generally had male wedding expenses about 50 percent higher than female expenses, but for
those with very large farms female costs were about as high as male
wedding expenses. (This is as we should expect, given Goody's argument about the importance of dowries in preserving status differences.)

These generalizations do not exhaust the complications of the Chinese case. The major confusion arises because the valuables delivered by the groom's family in many cases did not serve as a true
bride price in Goody's terms. Instead they were an indirect dowry—
they were used to pay for a dowry, which returned with the bride on
the day of the wedding. Thus in some instances, instead of having a
surplus from the bride price with which to marry off their own sons,

a bride's parents would have to spend it all, and some of their own resources, to provide their daughter with a dowry. The groom's family, which looks like it is paying a substantial bride price, might receive most of that expenditure back with interest, in the form of extra dowry expenditures from the bride's family (although part or all of this was controlled by the bride and groom rather than by his parents). . . .

* * *

What has happened to marriage finance since 1949? From our interviews we can detect both persistence and change. First, in spite of the provisions of the marriage law, material considerations have not become incidental to marriage—far from it. We were told of only five cases of marriage which did not involve a bride price, and these were offered as unusual exceptions to local practice. In every village for which we have information, virtually all marriages involve a bride price (li-chin, or p'in-chin), although the amount varies. Bride prices are given even when a marriage is the result of free choice by the young couple. We asked informants whether local cadres, who are responsible for enforcing the prohibition on bride prices, themselves give a payment in marrying off their sons, and the usual response was that they had to if their sons were to find brides.

Does current practice involve a true bride price, though, or an indirect dowry? Are the funds used by the bride's family to furnish a substantial dowry for their daughter or to procure a bride for their son? On these points there is clear evidence of change. Dowries are now of negligible value in rural Kwangtung; they seem invariably to be much smaller than the cash and gifts delivered to the bride's family by the groom's family.

* * *

Our informants are emphatic that today, unlike in previous times, there is no negotiation over the items to be included in a dowry. The dowry will, in fact, include some items from the bride price—clothing items and perhaps jewelry. These may be supplemented by combs, mirrors, vacuum bottles, and similar gifts from the bride's family and friends. But the total value of the present dowry is quite small, and stocking it requires little or no extra expenditures by the bride's family. Items that in many areas used to be part of a dowry (such as furniture and bedding for the bridal room) are now the sole responsibility of the groom's family. His family buys these items directly, rather than delivering money with which the bride's family purchases them for inclusion in a dowry. Thus a man's family may have substantial other expenditures prior to the wedding in addition to the bride price and wedding feast (expenditures on the latter will be discussed in Chapter 13). In a few localities the groom's family is supposed to supply not only furniture for the bridal room but new housing for the couple, which may cost another 1,000 yuan or more.

Today only a small portion of the bride price goes to form part of the dowry, and thus could be considered an indirect dowry. Another portion, primarily the food items, is used for a separate wedding feast held in the bride's home (see Chapter 13). Most of the cash is saved and in many cases forms part of the bride price used to marry off a brother of the bride.

*   *   *

In sum, our information points to the emergence of something like a pure bride-price custom, with dowry and indirect dowry becoming much less important. Most of the wedding expenditures of a bride's family are met out of the bride price, and there is generally money left over to put toward a bride price to get a wife for the family's son. The groom's family, in comparison, has to view the transaction as more unilateral than used to be true, since what they expend does not return to them by way of a dowry.

*   *   *

NOTES AND QUESTIONS

1. The above study was done through interviewing refugees who left southern China, usually in the 1960s, and settled in Hong Kong. The extent to which bride prices are paid in other parts of the country is unclear.

2. Can you give any reasons why dowries were eliminated, but not bride prices?

3. How does the practice of paying large bride prices affect intra-family relations? Freedom of marriage?

4. The Succession to Status

M. K. Whyte, "Inequality and Stratification in China," 64 China Quarterly, pp. 684, 698–703, 706, 709, 1975.

Old Classes in the Chinese Countryside. At the time of the land reform campaign in rural China (roughly 1946–48 in the northern "early liberated areas" and 1950–53 in the rest of the country), detailed instructions were compiled for the grouping of families into class categories, based upon guidelines worked out by the Chinese Communist Party over the years from the time of Mao Tse-tung's first analysis in 1926. The most important divisions were:

1. Landlords—those who possessed land but did little or no labour, and lived off land rents, hired labour, and engaged in usury.

2. Rich peasants—those who possessed land and engaged in some labour, but also lived by renting excess land to others.

3. Middle peasants—those with more or less enough land for their own needs, who neither rented out land to others nor had to rent land from others to any significant extent.

4. Poor peasants—those who possessed little or no land, and lived primarily on land rented from others.

5. Hired peasants and other workers—those with little or no land, who lived by hiring their labour out to others.

At the time of the land reform classifications some elements of the rural population were also given the labels of "counter-revolutionary" or "bad element," indicating not their former economic position, but their pasts as members of the local Kuomintang political structure, landlords' henchmen, active opponents of the Chinese Communists, or simply bullies and bandits. The landlords and these counter-revolutionaries and bad elements were the official enemies of the period, and, in addition to having any excess land and wealth taken away, they were struggled against, subjected to "mass control" or penal sentencing, and in many cases beaten or killed. There were in addition some miscellaneous classifications used for those who did not fit neatly into any of the categories above: small land renters, small traders and pedlars, etc. The elements of the rural population besides landlords, counter-revolutionaries and bad elements were to have their property protected (including the rich peasants), and those with little or no land or houses were to receive shares from what had been merged in turn in 1958 into people's communes. In collectivization China's rulers continued to place great stress on the pre-1949 rural class designations, and Mao Tse-tung is on record as warning that co-operatives had to be formed in such a way that former poor peasants and lower-middle peasants (i.e. the less well-off portion of the former middle peasants, or former poor peasants who had improved their economic position somewhat after land reform) made up at least two thirds of the membership and dominated the positions of leadership in the co-operatives.

After collectivization had been completed, these class labels ceased to have any clear connection with prosperity or occupation, and their importance might have been expected to decline in time. Indeed, speeches by prominent Party leaders in 1956 did suggest that these class labels were losing their significance. Changes in the villages reflected this trend to some extend. Class enemies who remained in the village were generally subjected to "control," which meant that they were deprived of political rights, had special restrictions placed on their movements, had to report regularly on their "reform" to the local security defence cadres, were required to perform certain types of *corvée*, and so forth. But over the years some of these people were "uncapped." As a result of labouring well, refraining from disruptive activities and obeying the Party, they had some or all of these controls removed. This did not mean, however, that their class labels were changed from, say, landlord to middle peasant. Rather, the label was retained even after the "cap" was lost, and was in turn passed on to children and (paternal) grandchildren.[38]

A number of official policies in more recent years have tended to reinforce the importance of the land reform class labels. These are symbolized by the cryptic quotation taken from a 1962 statement by Mao Tse-tung: "Never forget the class struggle." This quotation symbolizes the official view that post-1949 gains have come about through struggle against hostile classes, and that this struggle must continue into the indefinite future. As a result, in a number of mass political campaigns in China the division between former enemy classes and friendly classes has been re-emphasized. Former class enemies have been repeatedly drawn out as targets for mass struggle meetings, if not for current crimes then as symbols of pre-1949 sufferings. There have also been repeated calls for vigilance against former class enemies who have worked their way into positions of local leadership and Party membership, or have tried to spread discord and dissatisfaction among the population. As a result, in some cases rehabilitated class enemies have been "re-capped," i.e. put under mass control once again or given more severe penalties.

As a result of such policies the class lines laid down over 20 years ago continue to have great importance in rural China, greater importance in some ways than the current economic status of the person or family. The bad class elements themselves are in many cases still under control, and in addition are discriminated against in various ways: e.g. are ineligible for welfare assistance if they need it, ineligible for coverage by a co-operative medical plan, unable to get loans from the credit co-operative, and so forth. Whether or not they are under control, the stigma passes on to a considerable extent to their children and grandchildren. While the younger generations are not subjected to mass control, they will be unlikely to be able to join the Youth League or Party, the basic militia, or be chosen for local cadre posts; they may, as mentioned, have difficulty getting into upper-middle schools and universities, they often find it hard to get married (particularly males), they may be given lower work points, for the same kind of work, than the offspring of poor and lower-middle peasants, and they may have difficulty getting access to loans and welfare assistance. In all of these aspects there seems to be much variation from village to village: in some places even bad elements under control are eligible for co-operative medical plans, while in other villages even uncapped elements and their offspring are excluded. In some villages exclusions may apply only to former landlord and rich peasant families, while in others they may extend to include former

---

38. This conclusion is based primarily on interviews that I conducted in Hong Kong during two research stays in 1968–69 and 1973–74. The labels of counter-revolutionary and bad element are not passed on in the same way from generation to generation, and offspring of these "elements" will have class labels determined by the economic status of their parents (or grandparents) at the time of land reform. If their elders are "uncapped" they will also revert to economically based labels.

upper-middle peasants. Discrimination in terms of holding cadre posts and joining the Youth League and Party seems to be quite general, while discrimination in work points is more unusual. It is therefore difficult to formulate a general rule, but it is clear that the stigma of class labels has important effects on the quality of life not only of former rural "bad classes," but also of their descendants.

All of this does not mean that the government advocates a theory of absolute class inheritance. Official policy stresses that the bad class status of people should be considered, but that they should be given opportunities to reform themselves and overcome the bad influence (the "class stamp") of their origins. In 1963 and 1964, during the Rural Socialist Education Campaign, directives were issued instructing rural officials not to treat the offspring of landlords and rich peasants just like their parents, but to remould them; and during the Cultural Revolution official documents rejected the slogans of "blood transmission of status" and "naturally red" under which some Red Guards were claiming that all offspring of good classes were revolutionary, and all offspring of bad classes were automatically bad. But in spite of such official qualifications, policies dealing with the future of the class struggle and the need to favour former workers and poor and lower-middle peasants seem to produce a situation in which the stigma of family origins is almost automatic.

* * *

New Classes in China. The class labels used in China, by focusing to a large extent on economic circumstances more than two decades ago, tend to divert attention from "new class" phenomena: the children of a commune Party secretary who rose from poor peasant status at the time of land reform can still claim poor peasant origins. But "new class" phenomena and their dangers are not ignored. To a considerable extent, political campaigns in China, particularly the Cultural Revolution, have been aimed at these new class dangers. The Chinese Revolution brought to positions of power and prominence new elites of many types. Once in high positions, there is considerable evidence that some of these new elites showed traditional concerns for preserving their comforts and privileges and passing these on to their offspring, in spite of the dangers these aspirations posed for the Spartan revolutionary universalism of the new government.

Over the years the Party has adopted a number of policies designed to limit the influence of such tendencies. The anti-elitist measures I touched upon earlier are designed not only to prevent the emergence of antagonisms among the "non-enemy" social strata, but also to check the desire of those on top to maintain and pass on their privileges. Rectification campaigns, staff simplification and "sending down" movements and mass recruitment drives periodically replace a portion of the existing elite and promote new faces from below, while chastening those who are kept on.

Entrance examinations can be argued to work in favour of children of the new elites, who, as in other societies, will grow up in an environment more conducive to examination performance than will other children. But new elite parents have more direct means of trying to secure a good future for their children. By using personal connections and official influence they may be able to subvert the policies described above, a procedure referred to as "going by the back door." The most publicized case involved a second year student at Nanking University. His father, an army official and veteran of the Long March, had used his personal contacts and influence to get his son out of his rural exile, first into the army and then into the university. The son, a Party member, subsequently began to feel guilty about "going by the back door," and applied to withdraw from the university and return to his rural post. His request was accepted and given nationwide publicity, and was followed by numerous other accounts of similar "back door" cases.

Policy Towards Descendants of Landlords and Rich Peasants. Beijing Review, Vol. 22, No. 4, January 26, 1979, p. 8.

Three peasants in northeast China's Heilongjiang Province, all descendants of former landlords or rich peasants, wrote a letter to *Heilongjiang Ribao* telling about their ups and downs before and after the smashing of the "gang of four." The letter was reprinted in *Renmin Ribao* with a commentary "Take a Correct Attitude Towards Descendants of Landlords and Rich Peasants."

In the days when Lin Biao and the "gang of four" held sway, the Party's policy of putting the stress on one's political stand rather than on class origin in judging a person was not implemented. The result was the sons and daughters of exploiters were treated on a par with the exploiters themselves. Descendants of former landlords and rich peasants, including those born after liberation, were discriminated against and deprived of the right to take part in political activities. They were barred from the Communist Party, the Communist Youth League, and senior middle schools and schools of higher learning. Thus isolated, these descendants felt that they were the depressed classes and there was no place for them in the new society.

Now they got a new lease on life. The Party's policy is now being correctly implemented. As long as they support socialism, they are no longer discriminated against. Greatly moved, the three peasants said in their letter: "Like parched sprouts revived by rainwater, we are now so happy."

The Party's policy towards descendants of former exploiters is very clear: "Class or family origin is taken into consideration, but it's not the sole, decisive factor. The emphasis is on a person's political stand." Therefore, these children should be united so long as they support socialism and draw a clear political demarcation line between themselves and their parents who were exploiters.

There is another factor which should not be neglected. Most of these people are grand-children or great grand-children of the land-lords or rich peasants. They were born after the founding of New China and their parents, generally speaking, are no longer exploiters. According to the Party's policy, they should not be classified as coming from families of exploiting classes, still less should they be looked upon as exploiting-class elements.

There is no denying the fact that the Party's policy cannot be put into practice in some places. Some cadres, who have been deeply influenced by the "like father, like son" theory spread by Lin Biao and the "gang of four," think that it is safer to be "Left" than to be Right. In their eyes, descendants of former landlords and rich peasants are inferior to ordinary peasants and to be harsh to them only demonstrates their firm "proletarian stand."

The *Renmin Ribao* commentary said: "This kind of thinking does not conform to Marxism-Leninism-Mao Zedong Thought. Since the sons and daughters of former landlords and rich peasants live on their own labour, it is quite obvious that they must not be equated with landlords and rich peasants who exploited other people. . . . It is better to have more people in building socialism. If we exclude these descendants, discriminate against them economically and politically, or push them over to the enemy's side, it will only benefit the enemy."

NOTES AND QUESTIONS

1. The importance of class labels in China has varied considerably over time. One rough pattern is that during "pragmatic" periods such as the mid-1950s, the early 1960s, and the present, a person's subjective class status—how one thinks and acts—is stressed, together with the ideas of equality of treatment before the law and of promotion on the basis of merit and performance. During radical periods such as the Great Leap Forward in the late 1950s and the Cultural Revolution of the mid-1960s, objective class background—who one's father and grandfather were—and class struggle were emphasized.

2. In addition to class background, a person also is designated as part of an agricultural or non-agricultural household. This designation strongly influences whether a young person would be assigned to urban or rural work. Interestingly, the label descends through one's mother. How does this method of descent affect marriage patterns, especially for urban youths sent to the countryside in the "rustification of youth" movement?

Part III

EMBEZZLEMENT BY PUBLIC OFFICIALS

Chapter 12

CRIMINAL JUSTICE SYSTEMS IN THE RADICALLY DIFFERENT CULTURES

PROBLEM II

A superintendent of a small rural county (or a paramount chief of a small chiefdom) collects funds for a county (chiefdom) celebration of a visit by the president of the country. The president will be visiting a small city just over the county (chiefdom) line. But he will stop in the county seat (chiefdom headquarters town) to greet local dignitaries and to partake of refreshments. The superintendent (chief) takes some of the funds and gives them to his son who uses them to open a small cafe in the county seat (headquarters town) which quickly becomes quite popular.

How is the matter handled? How do the various towns or settlements in the county (chiefdom) respond? Who, if anyone, is considered the culprit? The superintendent? The son? Both? The town that gains the cafe? Are informal social control steps taken first? If so, what are they? If a formal case is brought, before what forum is it aired? Who brings the complaint? How does it all come out? If formal restitution is made, who contributes to it and who shares in its distribution? Are there conditions under which the county's residents would "look the other way" and not pursue counteraction?

* * *

Problem II was chosen to show how law deals with anti-social behavior and how criminal law reflects a culture's values and primary legal rules. Nothing marks the distinctiveness of a legal system as much as its way of responding to criminal acts.

The chapters in this section focus on several questions about the criminal justice system. What is crime? Do all societies have different feelings about crimes than about other wrongs? Why do the conceptions of what is a crime vary from culture to culture? And in what ways do criminal justice systems and societal responses to crime also vary from one society to another? We also can ask: How much punishment (if any) to redress a crime is "enough?" Are there potential injustices and inequities in all criminal justice systems? If so, how do societies attempt to mitigate them?

A. WHAT IS CRIME?

1. Crimes vs. Other Kinds of Wrongs

An issue to consider first is whether certain kinds of behavior are considered not simply as incorrect or wrongful of another person but, somehow, contrary to society, as anti-social. Such a view is very basic in Western law which distinguishes between private wrongs and crimes, violations of law which are considered wrongs against the state and, therefore, are punished by the state.*

In the West the concept of a crime is not just a jural category, but a common sense one as well. Mr. or Ms. Doe think of a crime as a particularly outrageous kind of wrong. Is this view found in other cultures, too? If so, what kinds of wrongs are classed as crimes? Are there some laws the breaking of which universally is viewed as crime?

2. How Universal Is the Concept of Crime?

Legal anthropologist E. Adamson Hoebel surveyed the literature about law in the world's cultures to determine if there were any norms that universally were held to be so important that their infraction would be met by the application of legal sanctions by a person acting as society's "representative." ** He found that the following acts, as variously defined by each culture, are virtually universally treated as legal wrongs, sometimes as crimes:

1. homicide within the society under one or another set of conditions,

2. violation of the husband's right to exclusive sexual access to his wife,

3. breach of the recognition of the kinship group as the medium for the inheritance of property rights (a right of which we took note in Problem I),

4. violation of the right to hold some property as private goods, and

5. acts which abuse supernatural power or arouse supernatural forces in a way that jeopardizes the well being of the entire society.

Can you make a preliminary guess as to which two of these wrongs are categorized as crimes in most cultures in the world? Why are they considered to be crimes rather than some other category of wrong?

3. Cultural Variation in the Frequency and Definition of Crime

Just as each individual has a unique set of fingerprints, each culture shows a unique profile of characteristic legal wrongs and crimes. Thus, a culture may view one or more of the universally-recognized legal wrongs as particularly shameful. Islamic Egypt, for example, views adultery as a particularly serious wrong. Determine why as you read through the materials. In addition, each culture's profile of crimes will include some which are not univer-

---

* Western law recognizes several types of private wrongs: breach of contract; unjust enrichment; and torts which are various kinds of private injuries that do not grow out of breach of contract.

** E. Adamson Hoebel, The Law of Primitive Man: A Study in Comparative Legal Dynamics, Cambridge: Harvard University, 1954, pp. 285–287.

sal, but unique to that culture or to only some of the world's culture. Thus, Egypt sees public drunkenness as especially out of line, while Botswana reserves its strongest legal penalty for cattle rustling. China treats appropriating property from one's commune more severely than a U.S. firm normally treats "internal pilferage." If internal pilferage is not viewed as particularly serious, what crimes in the U.S. are viewed that way? Why? For that matter, how do you tell when a crime is viewed as particularly serious by a society?

As you read through the materials think about what factors determine which kinds of wrongs a culture is likely to view as crimes and which of those as serious crimes. Are they the same factors that shape a culture's law of inheritance and succession: habitat? social and cultural organization? economic, political, social, and religious ideology? values? history? a society's legal tradition? Is there a role for psychological factors? Also: focus this broad set of questions on a narrower issue: why is it that "embezzlement" which is considered as corruption in China is tolerated with varying degrees of acceptance in Botswana, Egypt and the U.S.? How can one explain the varying degrees of acceptance?

Societies vary not only in what they consider to be crime and in the profile of crimes but in the total amount of crime that characterizes them. An issue to keep in mind is why some societies have more crime than others.

B. THE EVOLUTION OF CRIMINAL LAW

Legal scholars consider the separation of criminal law from non-criminal (civil) law as an advance in the evolution of law. Why? Isn't there a clue in feelings that are engendered in the population at large by the commission of a crime? One reaction is outrage, which means that to leave correction and/or redress of a crime in the hands of the wronged party could result in excessive reaction and feud. Such a possibility exists much more strongly with crimes against the person than with crimes against property such as embezzlement, which is central to this problem's hypothetical.

The possibility of a vicious cycle of retaliation and counter-retaliation, it is speculated, led many societies to place the responsibility for the prosecution of crime in the hands of a neutral party, "the state," rather than in the victim's hands. As we noted earlier, this rationale is at the heart of Western "criminal law," although Western law often offers at least the possibility of both a criminal and a civil remedy. The rationale is found to a varying extent in each of the other legal systems as well. But, to what extent does the concept of retaliation by the wronged party remain a notion that explicitly or implicitly shapes the ideas and operation of the criminal justice system in each of the four cultures we are studying?

Societies have recognized that criminal law remedies alone are not always satisfactory to the wronged party. For example, a fine or imprisonment does not compensate the victim for his or her loss in burglary or embezzlement. Recognizing this, what legal systems allow a victim to file a supplemental civil action alongside the criminal one brought by the state? Is this good? Where this option is not available, what is the effect? The materials show that, in Botswana, the evidence in a trial may lead a presiding judge to change the complainant to the accused and to shift what is considered the appropriate remedy accordingly. This certainly shows that the sharp Western distinction between criminal law and civil law is not universal. Does it suggest that there are advantages to having a blurred distinction between criminal and civil law? If so, do they outweigh the disadvantages? Is this blurring a different evolutionary outcome than a hard and fast distinction between civil and criminal law? Is it a "better" outcome?

Correction and/or rehabilitation of criminals is a goal of Western criminal justice systems and, to varying degrees, of the other systems as well. Is this a feature of legal systems at each stage of development or is it somehow evolutionary, representing what the West sees as "progress?"

C. CRIMINAL LAW AND PROCEDURE

As with inheritance, in Problem I, it is important to visualize the criminal justice system in operation. To do so, one must raise questions such as: Who makes a complaint? What happens then? Who prosecutes? How is it determined what happened? How is it determined what the remedy or penalty should be? How is the remedy made to hold or "stick?" Now, we turn to some points to be kept in mind in seeking answers to these questions.

1. Prosecutorial Initiative

The up-from-the-feud rationale for criminal law underlies the concept of a representative of the state as the individual who prosecutes the alleged criminal, perhaps even making the initial complaint against the accused. How widespread is this pattern? At the small community level, Botswana law, as noted earlier, does not make a hard and fast procedural distinction between criminal law and civil law. Thus, an individual Tswana may bring direct court action against another individual who has committed a crime against him. The victim makes the complaint and prosecutes the case. In China, too, at the community level one community member may accuse another face to face in order to institute corrective action after a crime has been committed. In both cultures there seems to be confidence that the grievance tension between the parties will not necessarily increase or spread as a result of the face to face counteraction. Should grievance tension begin to spread, it is believed, other parties linked to both disputants by kinship and/or other mutual bonds would intervene because escalation of the dispute or spread of the grievance tension would be contrary to their interests.

What is it about the social structure of village-level Botswana and China that makes initial counteraction to crime by the victim himself or herself tolerable? However, under some conditions, in both Botswana and China accusations are made to a third party who files the complaint which formally activates the criminal justice system. What are those conditions? Why do they result in third-party activation of the complaint?

In Egypt, traditionally, a complaint against a person accused of a crime was brought by a victim. But, when some kinds of persons were accused or certain crimes were involved, the initiating complaint might be filed by a government official called the *ehl-i-'orf*. In these circumstances, what kind of persons were involved? What kind of crimes? The materials show that these exceptions reflect the religious values and early traditions of Islam. One can argue that they reflect an Islamic society's view of what kind of judicial inaction would be intolerable.   In the United States a person who has been wronged by a criminal act almost always complains to a third party, the police, who take the next steps in counteraction.   This is true even in civil action and in small claims court.   Why does our society so scrupulously avoid face-to-face accusations by the victim?

In sum, the principle of the third-party complainant or third party prosecutor characterizes criminal law.   But taking our four societies as a group, we can conclude that there are some important exceptions.   In some circumstances victims take the law into their own hands.   More precisely, they make face-to-face accusations against the accused.

2.   Abhorred Form of Injustice

Prosecution by the state pits the accused individual against a very strong adversary, the "state."   Inherent in this unequal contest is the possibility that the process will be unfair to the accused who has fewer resources to bring to bear in his or her defense than the state can use to sustain its prosecution.   Cultures differ greatly in the extent to which they see this inequality as a problem and, therefore, the extent to which they attempt in their criminal law system to redress the balance.   U.S. culture puts strong stress on individualism and is very fearful of a false conviction of the accused.   Thus, the criminal justice system has used a characteristic Western approach and highly elaborated defendant's "rights."   Egypt's Islamically-oriented law also is sensitive to the defendant's rights, but Botswana and China are more group-oriented and are more fearful of allowing unpunished or uncorrected trampling of society's rights by the accused.

Cultures differ, then, in their view of what kind of errant judicial outcome is most intolerable, or, put another way, cultures differ in what they perceive and define as "justice." *   Why?

It may be that a society's uneasiness about certain kinds of "wrong" judicial outcomes reflect culturally patterned anxieties or fears.   Thus, each society is likely to fear and to defend against a particular kind of procedural inequity.   Indeed, to the outsider, it may seem to overdefend against that particular abhorred outcome.

---

* Many legal scholars have attempted to conceptualize the differing notions of justice that characterize various societies. One of the most analytically penetrating is Herbert L. Packer's analysis of criminal law in American society, "Two Models of the Criminal Process," Univ. of Pennsylvania Law Review, vol. 113, 1964, pp. 1–68.   He notes that the U.S. criminal justice system is animated by two alternative models, the "crime control model" and "the due process model."   The former is oriented to a high degree of control of crime by predictable, highly efficient determination of factual guilt and conviction in a high percentage of cases in which a crime actually was committed. This model is oriented to society's rights. The due process model is more concerned with the manner in which convictions are obtained.   It is defendant-oriented and eschews obtaining convictions that violate the rights of the accused.   It is less concerned with factual guilt and elaborates a series of defenses based on due process that may avoid legal guilt even where the defendant is factually guilty. The models are informed by different, though complementary, concepts of justice.   (cf. also Herbert L. Packer, The Limits of the Criminal Sanction, Stanford: Stanford University Press, 1968.)

3. Placing, Timing, and Completeness of Investigation

Procedures in a society's criminal justice system reflect that society's view of what kind of judicial error is most intolerable, the matter just discussed. And these procedures also mirror a society's views of how dangerous or subject to misuse is the power of the police and of the prosecutorial arm of the state. Thus, criminal justice systems differ in how free a reign the police have in investigating an alleged crime, how much discretion the police and/or the prosecutor have about bringing a case to trial and in altering the charge, and the extent to which the "facts" of a case are developed before a jury as opposed to a judge.

In the two major legal traditions of the West, common law and civil law, the investigatory phase in a criminal law case comes early, not only before the trial, but before the indictment. This is because the Western defendant orientation makes both common law and civil law cultures reluctant to bring a person to trial unless it is established that there is a reasonable likelihood that a crime was committed.

There are also some differences between common law and civil law systems. Paradoxically, in civil law countries, and in Egypt which has adapted French criminal law procedures, the pre-trial investigation is more thorough than in common law countries. In common law countries pre-trial investigation is less complete. One reason for this is that the common law tradition holds that the full truth is less likely to be brought out by careful magistratorial investigation than by the examination and cross-examination of the adversarial approach. There the completeness and accuracy of the investigation rests more with the advocatory skill of the prosecutor and of the defendant's attorney than with the investigatory and examining role of the police, the prosecutor, and the presiding judge.* But is the adversary process really better at bringing out the truth? Legal scholars disagree as to whether the more thorough pre-trial investigation in civil law countries reflects less concern about police abuse of prosecutorial abuse as well as a different idea about how best to get at the truth.

At the local level in Botswana there is little fearfulness that presiding court officials will be unfair and investigation comes about largely at the trial rather than at the pre-trial phase. Investigation is via questioning by the parties themselves, by the presiding chief, and by other elders who assist him as "assessors." In the absence of large-scale legal extension and penetration, procedures can be simpler and more direct. A reduced defendant orientation also contributes to this outcome in Botswana.

4. Prosecutorial Discretion

A source of slippage and possible inequity in criminal justice systems is "police discretion" and "prosecutorial discretion." For the criminal justice system to be called into operation a complaint must be made, initially by the victim. Under what conditions do victims waive lodging a complaint? Does it have to do with the status of the accused? The relationship between the

---

* Using Packer's model of the criminal law process (see earlier footnote) the Civil Law criminal justice system is shaped more by the crime control model and the Common Law criminal justice system is shaped a bit more by the due process model.

accused and the victim? The victim is not the only one who may decline to prosecute. The investigating police official or judicial official with whom the complaint is lodged may also do so, say, because of lack of evidence. Or for other reasons. In Common Law countries the accused may engage in plea bargaining, usually, when the prosecutorial case has an imperfection, or, in order to obtain another goal like having an accused accomplice turn state's evidence against his or her colleagues.* Does prosecutorial discretion—used either by the victim or by a prosecuting official—operate equally to the advantage of all accused persons? Or, does it work primarily to the benefit of the wealthy and/or the highly placed? ** Why is China less lenient in applying prosecutorial discretion to the highly placed than to ordinary citizens?

D. GOALS OF CRIMINAL JUSTICE SYSTEMS

Criminal justice systems differ in their goals or functions. These include reinforcement of community norms and values, deterrence, retaliation or retribution, expiation of community and victim outrage, restoration and/or compensation to the victim, and rehabilitation of the accused. The U.S. and Egyptian criminal justice systems, of the four we are studying, seem most focused on retribution and this partially explains their concern with defendants' rights and abhorrence of false convictions to which we referred earlier. In these societies misplaced retribution is viewed as a particularly serious miscarriage of justice. Tswana criminal justice is concerned more with restoration of the victim and the accused to their prior positions. And the Chinese system is concerned not so much with restoring the victim as with rehabilitating the accused to resume a normal, useful role in society. Compared with the West, these Tswana and Chinese goals are in line with a focus on the victim's rights and society's rights and needs—and less on the rights of the accused. So, the legal systems we are studying vary strongly in terms of the criminal justice goals to which they give greatest emphasis.

The task of a criminal justice system is to react to legal wrongs by counteracting such breaches of norms and minimizing the tendency of the wrongdoer to enter a cycle of deviance. In a cycle of deviance a person becomes less and less susceptible to society's corrective attempts and more and more deviant. In the chapter introducing the Chinese legal system, this process is referred to metaphorically as "sliding down the mountain."

---

* Some comparative law schools have asserted that there is no prosecutorial discretion in the civil law criminal justice systems of France and Germany. But other observers [e.g., John H. Langbein and Lloyd L. Weinreb, "Continental Criminal Procedure: " 'Myth' and Reality." Yale Law Journal, vol. 87, 1978, pp. 1549–1569] who have looked at the actual operation of those criminal justice systems see the functional equivalent of prosecutorial discretion. Is it likely that automatic prosecution exists anywhere?

** The unequal impact of the application of prosecutorial discretion in the U.S. legal system is portrayed in Victoria Lynn Swigert and Ronald A. Farrell, Murder, Inequality and the Law: Differential Treatment in the Legal Process (Lexington, Mass. and Toronto: Lexington Books, 1976). See also the following symposium: Lawrence Edwin Abt and Irving R. Stuart, (eds.), Social Psychology and Discretionary Law. New York: Van Nostrand Reinhold Company, 1979, which contains papers on the role of discretion in many areas of legal process.

A criminal justice system's stated goals partly determine when in the deviance cycle it comes into play and the kinds of countermeasures that are attempted first. Thus, Chinese criminal justice, with its goal of rehabilitation, intervenes quite early and informally. As soon as a person commits a small breach it is likely that a co-worker, kinsman, neighbor, or co-party member will comment on the wrong and steer the offender to confession and a promise to do better rather than let him or her slide into additional wrongs. In China, most of the "law work" of counteracting breach seems to be done in this informal, immediate way. Little of it is left to the formal court system. These first responses to a deviant act are not viewed in the culture itself as "law" but more as what social scientists refer to as "informal social control."

Informal social control is contrasted with law which is the most formal mechanism of social control. Law is most formal when it involves courts as separate institutions with distinct, specialized personnel, and formal deliberate procedures. The separateness and deliberateness create the "formality," which sometimes is referred to as "institutionalization." In some societies informal social controls and the legal system are virtually identical, in other societies they overlap, and in still others, they are quite distinct.

We do not seem to know as much about early responses in the other three legal systems as we do about early response in China.* But, generally, in those systems what happens at this stage of reaction to breach in each of the four cultures? Who takes the first corrective, "shaping up" steps? What are they? If they work, do they forestall legal action? Under what circumstances? Finally, in the four cultures we are studying, what do we know about the relationship between informal social control systems and the formal criminal justice system? For example, in the U.S. why has the "due process" model of criminal law extended into so many institutions of our society?

In social control there are "grey areas" concerning, for example, wrongs which a society is unclear about classifying—or not classifying—as a crime. As we shall see, in many societies embezzlement (at least some embezzlement) falls in this area. Such actions seems particularly subject to informal controls. In studying legal systems it is important to observe what kind of actions fall into this grey area—and if falling there depends not only on the action but on the actor. We can also ask who may apply informal social controls and who may not. And who, if informal social controls do not work, may "kick the matter upstairs" to the formal social control process of the courts.

1. Goals and Outcomes

The goals of a legal system also influence what is viewed as acceptable outcomes. Is restitution or compensation of the victim sufficient or must a penalty also be imposed? Does the answer depend on the crime? For example, under what circumstances does an embezzler get away with restitution and the equivalent of a suspended sentence? When is it felt that a penalty of

* Two recent studies which have examined the actual workings of dispute settlement in various societies, including informal pre-court and non-court processes are: Laura Nader and Harry F. Todd, Jr., eds., The Disputing Process—Law in Ten Societies, New York: Columbia University Press, 1978, and Laura Nader, ed., No Access to Law: Alternatives to the American Judicial System, New York: Academic Press, 1980.

imprisonment also must be employed? Under what systems is an admission of guilt necessary even when the evidence makes confession unnecessary to reveal that guilt? Thus, why can an American convicted embezzler stand on her "not guilty" plea while a Chinese in similar circumstances be required to confess? Turning to a different goal, if restoring harmony between victim and the accused is the primary goal, does firmly and equivocally placing the blame on the accused jeopardize the outcome?

2. Goals and Penalties

The penalties characteristically utilized by a criminal justice system also reflect that system's goals. Penalties utilized widely in legal systems include death, corporal punishment, imprisonment, fines, payment of compensation, banishment, loss of rights (e.g., the right to vote, party membership) and loss of status. Why, in speaking of criminal law, are jurists prone to talk in terms of "penalties" rather than "remedies?" Does this suggest something about the psychological roots for the goals of criminal justice systems? Is this likely to be equally true of jurists in all four legal systems? Focusing more specifically: why is imprisonment used so much in the United States and so little in Botswana? Why do fines and compensation play so small a role in Chinese criminal justice?

E. PROOF AND EVIDENCE

How a criminal justice system achieves its desired outcomes depends largely on its conceptions of "proof" and "evidence." These, like many other aspects of the system, are rooted in a culture's values and primary legal rules. Consider how answers to these questions depend on a culture's values and primary legal rules: Is there an assumption of innocence until proven guilty? Where does the burden of proof lie, with the prosecutor or with the accused? For that matter, what constitutes "proof?" How much proof is needed? What constitutes "evidence?" How is evidence tested for validity? Is one witness enough? Are all categories of persons considered equally qualified ("competent" in lawyer's terms) to serve as witnesses? How are witnesses or their testimony assessed for truthfulness? Suppose witnesses offer contradictory testimony. How is the contradiction resolved? Are there forms of proof which are "irrational' in form if not in effect, such as oaths and ordeals? Questions such as these can be narrowed to focus on the particular cultures we are studying. For example, why under Islam does the testimony of two women equal that of one man? Why are lie detectors used in the United States but not in China?

F. INTENTION

In criminal cases there often is agreement on the facts. Thus, in the hypothetical of this problem it is likely that there is agreement that a government official and his son used community funds to open a cafe. The legal issue becomes less one of fact and more one of intentions. The accused claim that they were not acting for self-enrichment but to act for the community, to enable it to meet its obligations toward the head of state with appropriate dignity. Local cultural concepts about motivation and intention become the standard by which this assertion is assessed.* Would a reasonable person in that culture make use of community funds in this way without checking with some individuals in the community? Or is such autonomous action the normal thing for a person in that role in that culture? Is the individual profit the father and son would make viewed in that culture as a normal and appropriate emolument of office and kinship with an officeholder in that culture? Or, would it be viewed as corruption and nepotism? The answers to these two last questions would have some bearing on whether the motivation and intentions claimed by the accused are discarded. In sum, local cultural conceptions as they bear on intention, are very important in assessing evidence, in determining guilt, and in deciding on remedies and penalties.

G. SUMMARY

What can be said by way of summary? The profile of characteristic wrongs (especially crimes) that typify a society reflects its values, its forms of subsistence, ideologies, history, and—not least—the national character of its people.

Depending on a society's dominant values, a criminal justice system may emphasize informal social control processes and, thus, intervene very early in the deviance cycle, as in China where the emphasis is on social responsibility and rehabilitation. In the U.S. and other societies where the focus is more on individual rights and individual responsibility, the emphasis is on formal social control mechanisms and procedures, thus, on late intervention in the deviance cycle and on corrective measures that unintentionally may push the offender into the deviance cycle. A society's values about the correctability and rehabilitability of humankind also are significant in fixing the preferred point of intervention. The U.S. and China differ significantly on this point.

A society's values and the goal or goals of the criminal justice system together shape the form of the intervention via criminal law by molding such features as: the locus of the burden of proof, the nature and handling of evidence and proof, and the locus of investigatory initiative. Again, particularly important among the values that operate in this way to shape procedures are the opposed value set: individual rights vs. social responsibility. A negative value that is significant in this regard is what kind of judicial error is most abhorred in a culture, false conviction or uncorrected or unpunished crime. Avoiding that outcome also is a potent shaper of criminal justice procedures.

Goals of criminal justice and preferred outcomes are virtually synonymous. They are both connected directly to a culture's values and beliefs about how rectifiable people are. Thus, some societies place primary stress on retribution and punishment, while others put major emphasis on reconcili-

---

* The use of local cultural standards in the reasoning of the judicial process in a traditional African legal system is traced out well in Max Gluckman's works, The Judicial Process Among the Barotse of Northern Rhodesia, Manchester: Manchester University Press [Second enlarged edition, 1967] and The Ideas in Barotse Jurisprudence, New Haven: Yale University Press, 1965.

ation and rehabilitation. Moreover, a society's professed values may point in one direction while its actual behavior in this area points in another direction.

Some abuses are inherent in criminal justice processes. They include the possibility of the state overwhelming an innocent defendant, the society's and victims' rights being battered down by stout protection of defendants' rights by the state, and favoring of the powerful by features of the legal system such as prosecutorial discretion, the differential effect of time and costs,* and variable application of sanctions. Cultures can be characterized by which of those abuses are most common in their criminal justice system, by the ways in which they attempt to minimize them and, as noted already, which of these abuses they most fear or disvalue.

A note on which to end is whether one can measure the "goodness" of criminal justice systems. The rate of recidivism suggests itself as one measure of how well a criminal justice system works. The costs of a high rate of recidivism are obvious. And the benefits of a low rate are equally obvious. But, what are the costs of a low rate? Are they worth it? In China? In the U.S.? In Botswana and Egypt? If this is not a universally valid measure of the quality of a criminal justice system, what is? Or, is this not even the right question?

The substance of this summary/introduction can be recast as a series of questions that guide the task of comparing criminal justice systems. The questions follow. And the answers can be charted on the grid which follows the questions to provide a schematic profile of a criminal justice system.

H. SOME DIMENSIONS AND QUESTIONS FOR THE COMPARISON OF CRIMINAL JUSTICE SYSTEMS

1. *Goals/Functions.* What goals or functions receive the greatest relative emphasis? Common goals are: reinforcement of community norms and values, deterrence, retaliation or retribution, expiation of community and victim outrage, restoration and/or compensation to the victim, and rehabilitation of the accused. Which one or two receive the greatest emphasis in a society? Is there a difference between what is emphasized explicitly and what is emphasized implicitly?

2. *Philosophy and Rationale.* What are the major values that underlie the legal system? For example, what are the culture's views about the rectifiability of a wrong-doer? What is the relative emphasis on the rights of the accused as opposed to society's rights? What is the most abhorred judicial error, false conviction or uncorrected wrong-doing? Something else? How formal or explicit is the rationale? (Another way of putting this is which of Weber's types of legal reasoning is dominant?) Is there a distinction between criminal and civil law?

3. *Number of Crimes.* How extensive is the list of wrongs defined as crimes? Is the list short, limited to a few areas of conduct? Or is it long, ramifying through many realms of behavior?

* See "Introduction: The Disputing Process," in The Disputing Process— Law in Ten Societies, New York: Columbia University Press, 1978. (cf. Problem III in this volume on the non-monetary costs of contracts.)

4. *Most Serious Crimes.* What are the most serious crimes as measured by penalties? Why are these considered the most serious crimes? For example, is violence against people, property, or status and esteem most disvalued?

5. *Size of Total Case Load.* What is the size of the total case load? Of course, it is related to the number of wrongs defined as crimes (see #3 above). Is there an overload of the system or is there easy access and fairly quick resolution of cases?

6. *Number of Legal Specialists.* How numerous are recognized legal personnel and how separate are their legal roles from other social roles? Are there lawyers? How many? What about mediators and arbitrators? Other legal specialists such as police and jailers?

7. *Pervasiveness of Criminal Process Model.* Does the notion of "due process" that characterizes the culture's criminal justice model carry over to the response to wrongs that are not prosecuted in the formal criminal law process?

8. *Point of Application.* When in the deviance cycle does the formal criminal justice system come into play? Is it brought to bear early, after a relatively minor offense or is its use customarily postponed until later and/or after a serious offense?

9. *Equality of Application.* Does the criminal law apply equally to all? In principle? In practice? How strict is the standard of justice applied to the highly placed? If it is different, is it higher or lower?

10. *Locus of Complaint/Accusation.* Who makes the complaint and accusation of the accused after a crime has been committed? Is it done by the victim? Or is this task lodged with society in the form of some official representative as prosecutor?

11. *Prosecutorial Discretion.* Must the prosecutor prosecute whenever a complaint is lodged with him or her or may he or she exercise discretion? If so, how much? Is it used more for some categories of people than for others?

12. *Evidence/Proof.* What constitutes "evidence?" What is "proof?" Are there forms of proof which Weber calls "irrational" in form if not in effect, such as oaths and ordeals? How much reliance is there on cross-examination? How widely applicable are notions of "incompetence" as applied to witnesses?

13. *Preferred Outcomes.* What kinds of outcomes or settlements are preferred? Is restitution or compensation acceptable or must there be a penalty imposed? Is the admission of guilt mandatory? To what extent is reconciliation and a consensual solution stressed?

14. *Penalties.* If penalties are imposed, what are they? Common penalties include: death, corporal punishment, imprisonment, fines, banishment, loss of rights (e.g. the vote), and loss of status.

15. *Recidivism.* How successful is the criminal law system in minimizing further criminal actions by a convicted criminal?

A GRID FOR THE COMPARISON OF CRIMINAL JUSTICE SYSTEMS

EMPHASIZED FUNCTION	Retribution Expiation	Deterrence Reinforce norms	Restoration Rehabilitation
PHILOSOPHICAL BASIS	Explicit philosophy Focus on individual rights Humans as doubtfully correctable		Implicit philosophy Focus on society's rights Humans as certainly correctable
NUMBER OF CRIMES	High		Low
MOST SERIOUS CRIMES	Violence against people	Violence against property	Violence against status, esteem
SIZE OF CASE LOAD	High	Medium	Low
NUMBER, SPECIALIZATION OF LEGAL PERSONS	High	Medium	Low
PERVASIVENESS OF CRIMINAL PROCESS MODEL	High	Medium	Low
POINT OF APPLICATION	Late	Middle	Early
EQUALITY OF APPLICATION	Less to highly placed	Equally to the highly placed	More to the highly placed
LOCUS OF COMPLAINT/ ACCUSATION	Prosecutor/police		Victim
PROSECUTORIAL DISCRETION	High More for the highly placed		Low Less for the highly placed
EVIDENCE	"Hard" standards		"Soft" standards
PROOF	"Rational" forms	"Irrational" forms	Confession
PREFERRED OUTCOMES	Punishment	Restoration/ compensation	Rehabilitation
PENALTIES	Capital/Corporal punishment Fines		Imprisonment Loss of status/privileges
RECIDIVISM	High	Medium	Low

Chapter 13

EMBEZZLEMENT BY A PUBLIC OFFICIAL IN WESTERN LAW

A. INTRODUCTION

Jerome Hall, Theft, Law and Society, Indianapolis: The Bobbs-Merrill Company, Inc., 2d edition, 1952, pp. 36, 289–290, 299–300.

. . . Violation of public trust is probably one of the oldest notions in history, e.g. Aristotle refers to the embezzlement of funds by road commissioners and other officials. In England, the Articles of Edward I provided for the investigation of "overseers of works" who converted stone or timber which should have gone into public construction. In the *Mirror of Justices* similar offenses are expanded to include "those who receive more from their bailiwick than they answer for to the king." Apparently there was considerable embezzlement "by the highest officials . . . in the fourteenth century. . . ." An Elizabethan statute was directed against "persons who embezzled munitions of war . . . which had been entrusted to them." . . .

. . . The most distinctive facts regarding embezzlement are (1) the very high frequency of the offense and (2) its incidence in all strata of society. The discomforting likelihood, plainly indicated as one probes the data, is that if everyone was not sometime in his life an embezzler, at least a large percent of all types of person in every profession, vocation, social and economic status, has sometime committed embezzlement. . . .

Without idealizing past economic organizations, e.g. guilds and small enterprises, or overlooking the frequency of crimes of violence in earlier periods, one must recognize that embezzlement and other crimes against property not involving violence seem to have greatly increased in modern times. When economic units were small and their owners had a direct interest in the business, sole custody of the cash, and were in immediate contact with all the employees, dishonesty was apt to be discovered quickly and vigorously discouraged. These conditions stand in sharp contrast to contemporary commercial and industrial enterprise, e.g., enormous capital investments, corporate organizations directed by managers—with owners distant, disinterested, and scattered among thousands of unknown persons, indeed, with even the managers far removed from the daily conduct of

376

the employees. Even the symbols of traditional working relationships dissolve in the abstractions of huge corporate enterprise *vis a vis* solitary depersonalized wage earners. Under such conditions, loyalty to an employer becomes unreal and devitalized, while prevention tends more and more to depend on mechanical devices, checks, and audits emphasizing the tacit canon that no man is trustworthy.

NOTE

Embezzlement is sometimes spoken of as a "white collar" crime, but that may be a misuse of the term. The leading work, (Edwin H. Sutherland, White Collar Crime, New York: Holt, Rinehart and Winston, 1941 (reprinted 1961), p. 9) states: "White collar crime may be defined approximately as a crime committed by a person of respectability and high social status in the course of his occupation." Such people may indeed embezzle, but, as Professor Hall points out, so do others. The crime of embezzlement probably is not exclusively or predominantly "white collar." See Donald N. M. Horning, Blue-Collar Theft: Conceptions of Property, Attitudes toward Pilfering, and Group Norms in a Modern Industrial Plant, in Erwin O. Smigel and H. Lawrence Ross, Crimes Against Bureaucracy 46, New York: Van Nostrand Reinhold Co., 1970.

Much of the literature on embezzlement either focuses on the private sector or treats the social problem of embezzlement as though the identity of the victim were not important. From this point of view embezzlement by an employee of a private corporation or by a public official would be the same. In this connection consider the following excerpt.

Erwin O. Smigel, "Public Attitudes toward Stealing as Related to the Size of the Victim Organization," in Erwin O. Smigel and H. Lawrence Ross, Crimes Against Bureaucracy, 1970, pp. 3–5, 7, 10–12.

Bureaucracy as Victim. . . . The victims with which we are concerned are organizations—corporate or governmental—which are large, impersonal, and dominated by formal rules and regulations. Following Max Weber, we call these organizations *bureaucracies.* They are the concentration points in our society of great wealth and power and, as such, are the popular victims of many contemporary property crimes. . . .

. . . As victims, bureaucracies offer ambiguities to traditional conceptions of crime. The victim, usually an individual, is not, in the case of the bureaucracy.

However, bureaucratic procedures do involve people: officers, employees, suppliers, customers, and clients. The interest of many of these individuals in the welfare of the organization is minimal. In their relations with the bureaucracy a good portion of them encounter various inducements and opportunities to steal, to violate positions of trust, to commit some criminal act against the bureaucracy. We propose that the reasons they do so can be found in public attitudes toward bureaucracies and in the opportunity afforded by bureaucratic procedures.

The unpopularity of bureaucracies is a paradoxical fact in a society that depends on them for the provision of almost all goods and services. Among the reasons for this unpopularity are: the bureaucracy's impersonality in a society which still places a high value on personal relations; the conflict of interest between bureaucrats and the people they are expected to serve; and inefficiency in operation because of exaggerated emphasis on means (rules) instead of ends (goals) by workers in the bureaucracy.

In addition to being unpopular, bureaucracies are peculiarly vulnerable to types of criminal activity marked by low visibility. Thefts from bureaucracies often differ from conventional thefts in their subtlety. Unlike armed robbery, the theft of bureaucratic assets may involve an unobtrusive action, such as a shifting of numbers on a balance sheet, or falsification of reports and inventories. . . .

. . . Even the theft of physical goods, exemplified by shoplifting from a department store, can be carried out with a degree of unobtrusiveness that is very different from the types of crime envisaged by traditional criminology.

The low visibility of crimes against bureaucracies, combined with the unpopularity of the victims, leads to a failure of the public to stigmatize the perpetrators of these crimes. Even grand larceny may be quasi-legitimized as "chiseling," when the victim is a bureaucratic organization. The organization is denied access to an important source of protection afforded the personal victim: the sympathy and conscience of the general population.

This failure of the public to stigmatize crimes against bureaucracies leads, in turn, to another dilemma for the victims. Having apprehended a criminal, bureaucracies cannot routinely pass him on to official law enforcement agencies because the bureaucratic interest does not always coincide with a system of law enforcement based on the concept of a personal victim. The organization must retain a positive public image in order to avoid becoming an even more justifiable victim. Its interest, moreover, is in reimbursement more than retribution. Formal legal prosecution is also costly to the victim, in time and money. Consequently, bureaucratic organizations tend to develop their own systems of private dispositions, with remand to formal law enforcement being a sanction *in extremis*. . . .

. . . The size, wealth, and impersonality of big business and governments are attributes which make it seem excusable, according to many people, to steal from these victims. Theft appears to be easier to excuse when the victim has larger assets than the criminal, as exemplified by the Robin Hood myth. Congruent with this thesis is the tactic frequently used by bureaucracies: the attempt to "personalize" the loss. Witness this sign in a Midwestern motel: "If any towels are missing when you leave, the maid cleaning the room will be responsible for them." The notice attempts to deter theft by invoking sympathy for an individual rather than for the bureaucracy. Some bureaucratic organizations attempt to personalize the impersonal and to make the large corporation appear to be a family business.

Another reason why crimes against large organizations are more acceptable to the public than are other categories of crime may be that our system of ethics lacks rules which specifically apply to relationships between individuals and large organizations. All major historical religions originated in small communities, in which obligations concerned relatives, friends, and neighbors. From these static and personal communities a set of personal ethical norms developed; responsibility to great impersonal structures did not exist. Today, when large-scale organizations dominate our lives, men may be ethically unprepared to cope with the problem of the relationship between the individual and the corporation. . . .

. . . Our principal concern is with the thefts perpetrated mainly by individuals upon corporate, governmental, and other bureaucracies. The amounts stolen are enormous, especially so in comparison to the amounts stolen from personal victims. These acts generally fall squarely within traditional criminal law, and they are subject to ordinary criminal procedure.

QUESTIONS

1. Is the bureaucracy really the victim? Who ultimately pays the cost of embezzlement from General Motors, from Stanford University, or from the City of Palo Alto?

2. Observers generally state that embezzlements, even after discovery, rarely result in prosecution. Can you guess why? Consider the following readings.

Jerome Hall, Theft, Law and Society, Indianapolis: The Bobbs-Merrill Company, Inc., 2d ed., 1952, p. 304.

. . . Public attitudes have long condemned the conduct of thieves and "fences." These offenders' values are opposed to those of the community. There is no serious conflict among members of the community regarding the desirability of reducing the rate of larceny and criminal receiving by enforcement of the law.

In embezzlement we confront important differences. They result from the wholesale violations among all strata of the community, aggravated by a consensus of opinion regarding the values involved, i.e., the embezzlers recognize that they are violating their own values. More important is the fact that when detected, they are treated sympathetically by those in control. Thus, in sum, embezzlement is wrong; everybody, including most embezzlers, recognize that, and there is no basic challenge to the rightness of the prevailing standards. But, far from rigorous law-enforcement by the "dominant class" when its property interests are criminally appropriated, we encounter condonation and wholesale avoidance of legal coercion. In sharp contrast to what we find regarding *known apprehended* thieves and criminal receivers (against whom there is ample evidence for conviction), in the case of the embezzlers, there is such lack of law-enforcement as practically to nullify the legal controls. . . .

Gerald D. Robin, "The Corporate and Judicial Disposition of Employee Thieves," 1967 Wisconsin Law Review, pp. 685–689, 696–701.

. . . Three large, independent department store companies (hereinafter referred to as Companies A, B, and C) provided the source data. The population examined consisted of the confidential security records of all employees who stole from their firms and who were apprehended (1) from 1959 through 1962 in Company A, (2) from 1949 through 1963 in Company B, and (3) from 1956 through 1963 in Company C. The number of cases of such dishonest employees constituting the individual populations was 739, 584, and 358 in Companies A, B, and C respectively—a total of 1,681 dishonest employees. The largest single legal category of offenders consisted of embezzlers, and the trust violations involved both funds and property.

The present study offered an unusual opportunity to investigate empirically the role assumed by an organized private sector ("Big Business") in the treatment of offenders, to make some observations and inferences about the social factors that influence the sentencing behavior of judges, and to reflect upon the integration of private and official conceptions of justice and its implementation.

II. APPREHENSION OF EMPLOYEE THIEVES

The first and most important objective of the company when taking a dishonest employee into custody is obtaining his signed confession. Eighty-five percent of those apprehended signed a confession, while another three percent verbally admitted their guilt but refused to sign a statement to that effect. Only 12 percent flatly denied stealing, although many of these admitted "violations of store policy." Ninety-three percent of the trust violators in Company A confessed their guilt (90 percent signing a statement), compared with 87 percent in Company B (86 percent signing a statement) and only 78 percent in Company C (75 percent signing a statement).

The initial response of most offenders during interrogation was some form of denial: anger, shock, indignation, silence. However, as the questioning continued and the case against them developed, they ultimately "broke down" and confessed their thefts, often becoming repentant and pleading, "I realize what a terrible thing I have done and it will never happen again." Such promises of atonement are unwittingly prophetic because the company generally will not give an apprehended employee an opportunity to repeat his mistake. Many embezzlers are visibly affected by discovery and confrontation with the fact of their criminal behavior. They apparently are more concerned with concealing their conduct from "relevant" others, more concerned with potential social degradation, than with possible prosecution and imprisonment per se.

The company has three courses of action available for finally disposing of the offender: dismissal of the employee without criminal prosecution, dismissal and criminal prosecution, or retention. Prosecution was carried out for 288 of the 1,681 trust violators in Companies A, B, and C (17 percent). Eight dishonest employees were retained, two in Company B who had been recommended for employment by a very high official in the organization and who were therefore given a second chance, and six in Company C for reasons unknown to the researcher. No employee was prosecuted *and* retained.

The overall prosecution rate of 17 percent conceals important differences in attitude toward the disposition of thieving employees by Companies B and C on the one hand, and Company A on the other: 2 percent of Company B's 584 offenders and 8 percent of Company C's 358 offenders were prosecuted, compared with a surprisingly large prosecution rate of 34 percent for Company A. In addition, 32 unprosecuted Company A employees were turned over to military or juvenile authorities, thus raising to almost two-fifths (38 percent) the proportion of offenders in Company A against whom some official action was taken. Differences this large are not fortuitous but reflect basic policy differences over prosecution between Companies B and C on the one hand and Company A on the other.

Companies B and C were much more interested in terminating dishonest employee cases as quickly as possible, and they were more sympathetic toward employees who had violated their trust. They felt that prosecution generally served no useful purpose and wished to avoid any further publicity in an admittedly sensitive area. By contrast, Company A's position was that criminal behavior by its workers—biting the hand that feeds them—should result in observable, punitive consequences extending beyond loss of employment whenever possible.

The attitude of Company A toward prosecution is exceptional among department store organizations: Officials of six department store companies not part of the present study indicated in interviews that they prosecute 5 to 10 percent of their apprehended dishonest employees. Therefore, legal action against dishonest department store employees as an occupational group must be considered minimal, despite the unique attitude of Company A. For employee theft, as for white-collar crimes, the penal sanctions against criminal behavior have differential and selective implementation.

VI. JUDICIAL DISPOSITION OF COMPANY OFFENDERS

Two hundred and fifty-six of the 259 prosecuted trust violators in Companies A, B, and C were convicted, 249 (96 percent) pleading guilty. This near-perfect conviction record was a result of the companies' very careful selection of whom to prosecute and when. This care is further evidenced by Company A's declining to prosecute 172 violators who had admitted their dishonesty in signed statements; the company was not convinced that the evidence would sustain a conviction.

The offender was fined in 73 of the 256 cases. . . . The offender was both fined and ordered to make restitution in 27 percent of the cases. The offender's sentence was suspended in 55 percent of the 256 cases. Among those given any suspended sentence, the average length was 11 months, with two-thirds given less than 1 year and only 9 percent 3 years or more. Fifteen percent of the offenders were given a definite suspended sentence and ordered to make restitution only. The offender was put on probation in 46 percent of the 256 cases. . . .

    . . . Almost one-quarter were given a suspended sentence and placed on probation only; one-third were either given a suspended sentence or placed on probation only; and 30 percent were placed on probation and ordered to make restitution only.

The most significant and striking finding was that only 12 of the 256 convicted department store trust violators (less than 5 percent) were sentenced to and presumably served some time in prison. In 9 of these 12 cases the length of imprisonment was 6 months or less. The court avoided imposing punitive sentences in 95 percent of the cases. Moreover, the nonpunitive sentences imposed were not severe but were nominal, representing minimal judicial action. Two-thirds of those fined were fined 50 dollars or less, three-fifths of those receiving definite suspended sentences received them for 6 months or less, and two-thirds of those placed on probation were placed on it for one year or less (one-quarter for six months or less). Restitution, the most frequently imposed sentence, was in effect no more than a request by the court that the thief compensate the victim for his injury in direct proportion to that injury. . . . Why were the courts so lenient with the department store offenders? This condition cannot be attributed to the idiosyncratic sentimentality of one or two judges since the convicted offenders were sentenced in 90 cities throughout the United States. Hall is undoubtedly correct that courts desire to avoid punitive measures if restitution is made.

VII. THE PRIVATE ADMINISTRATION OF JUSTICE

Perhaps more than any other civil individual, an employer, or his corporate representative, is in a position where he must decide whether or not to report a known, apprehended offender to the law enforcement officials—a responsibility and power that has been largely ignored in the sociology of law. What effect does such discretion have upon the legal and moral order, upon the ethic of honesty that the law sustains, upon the offender and others like him? What are the implications of the ability of the employer to prosecute or release as many or as few trust violators as he chooses and to decide who will and will not be charged formally with a crime? . . . the department store companies in the present study have attempted to find their own solution to employee dishonesty, a solution giving their own interests priority. Their success is indicated by their ability to obtain complete or considerable recovery in a majority of cases without the aid of the court. It is arguable that the employer's power to prosecute often or infrequently and to select who shall be immune from contact with the law, is "the best one among practicable alternatives." Further, the practices and attitudes engendered by such a situation, and the consequences of these practices and attitudes, are "socially desirable." "[I]n effect, we have an enlightened private individualization of treatment which avoids the crudities of exposure and punishment and, in sum, is superior to official administration of the criminal law." Not prosecuting trust violators is humane in that the individual does not become a man with a "record." The offenders' punishment is discharge—no small loss for middle-class persons since they then find it more difficult to obtain new employment. At the same time, they are given another chance at respectability. Whether prosecuted trust violators make better adjustments to their future employment situations and whether they are in general more law-abiding as a result of such public exposure and conviction than those not prosecuted is, unfortunately, unknown. In a majority of cases, apprehension and interrogation by detectives or company officials, followed by accusation, admission of dishonesty, and dismissal, may be a highly effective deterrent to further criminal behavior while still providing the offender an opportunity to salvage his future and to learn from his past mistake. If minimal sanctions can accomplish the same objective as more severe ones, one may again ask what is to be gained by prosecution. . . .

NOTES AND QUESTIONS

1. One explanation for the relative infrequency of embezzlement prosecutions is the availability to the employer of a remedy outside the criminal process: The allegedly offending employee can be discharged or subjected to some lesser job-related discipline. This ability of the employer to impose sanctions outside the criminal process can, as the last reading suggests, be thought of as a system of "private criminal justice" in which the penalties are potentially quite severe (loss of job, of pension rights, of seniority, of a favorable employment record when seeking new employment). In such cases the employee seldom has substantive and procedural protection of the kind available to a defendant in the criminal process.

2. Where the private employee is protected by the union grievance process, the employer's freedom to impose sanctions is substantially reduced. The job security provisions of collective bargaining agreements display a tendency toward legalism—toward subjecting a relation formerly treated as "private" (the employment relation) to the requirements of a due process model that may include notice, a hearing, the right to representation, impartial third-party decision-making, and the right to an appeal. Is this a desirable development?

3. Suppose that the department store employees were unionized and that their contract contained strong "due process" job security provisions. Would you expect this to reduce or to increase the number of criminal prosecutions of allegedly embezzling employees?

4. Does the availability of a system of private justice make the public system unnecessary? If not, what is the actual relation between them? What should that relation be? In this connection, ask yourself why such a large number of employees in the Robin study signed written confessions?

5. How should the fact that the embezzler is a public official affect the decision whether or not to prosecute? One consideration is the special degree of job security of most public employees (other than those appointed to serve at the pleasure of the executive). The federal and state constitutions, legislation and judicial decisions relating to public employment (and to "due process of law") often leave the allegedly embezzling employee's superiors relatively little room for arbitrary administrative action. Cf. Gerald E. Frug, Does The Constitution Prevent the Discharge of Civil Service Employees? 124 University of Pennsylvania Law Review, p. 942, 1976. In the case of public officials, who are generally protected by specific statutory provisions governing tenure and removal from office, the opportunity for informal discharge is even more restricted.

6. Assume, however, that the embezzling public official can be removed from office. Should she also be prosecuted for the crime? Do the same considerations apply to the question whether to prosecute the embezzling official of a corporation? If not, what is special about the public official?

7. Suppose an embezzling employee fully reimburses the employer. As the readings indicate, this reduces the likelihood of criminal prosecution. Should it do so? Does it make any difference whether the employer is the government, rather than a private corporation?

8. Is embezzlement a typically bourgeois capitalist problem, or is it likely to occur with equal (perhaps even greater?) frequency in, for example, socialist societies? Consider the following.

John N. Hazard, "Soviet Socialism and Embezzlement," 26 Washington Law Review, pp. 301–302, 1951.

Socialism has been heralded as the cure for crime. To the Marxist the claim seems reasonable. He believes that crime springs from poverty coupled with despair. Reorganization of the economic and social structure of society under socialism is promised as the route to hope and wealth. In consequence, socialism should create conditions under which the citizen will have no need to steal and no desire to kill.

To examine the effect of the thesis upon the writings of Soviet authors and the policy of the Soviet leaders this paper will review what has happened to the crime of embezzlement over the years in the U.S.S.R. Embezzlement ought to be a type of crime which one could expect to find influenced at an early stage in the development of a socialist economy such as that claimed by the Soviet Constitution for the Soviet Union. Those convicted of embezzlement in capitalist countries have often explained their transgression in terms of need for money to meet unexpected sick bills or to speculate in the hope of gaining funds to meet a wife's claim for social distinction where money counts. Neither of these motives is on the list of those expected to be important to citizens living under conditions of socialism. What, then, has become of the crime of embezzlement in Soviet society?

The interest of Soviet legislators, courts, and authors in the crime of embezzlement has grown with the years. Recent decrees and court orders focus attention upon it. Authors link it with treason. Some of the highest penalties permitted by the criminal code apply to it. The constitution itself castigates it, by saying, "It is the duty of every citizen of the U.S.S.R. to safeguard and fortify public, socialist property as the sacred and inviolable foundation of the Soviet system, as the source of wealth and might of the country, as the source of the prosperity and culture of the working people. Persons committing offenses against public, socialist property are enemies of the people." In the Soviet lexicon there can be no greater condemnation. . . .

Jerome Hall, Theft, Law and Society, Indianapolis: The Bobbs-Merrill Company, Inc., 2d edition, 1952, pp. 301–303.

. . . Newspaper reports have long indicated that embezzlement is a serious problem in Russia. The doubts that may be raised regarding such reports are dissipated on reference to source materials. They reveal an interesting situation, highly significant for legal sociology.

Writing in 1933, N. Krylenko, after referring to various recent trials in Moscow, Leningrad, and other cities, states: "These were trials of embezzlers and marauders in the supply organizations and in the co-operative system . . . today it is impossible to find anywhere a single co-operative or government store free from pilferers, marauders, thieves, speculators, rascals, embezzlers etc. . . . In Moscow five death sentences were passed on people of just this type . . . in Leningrad there were two such sentences and the same number in Kharkov . . . What does this mean? It means that at present there is a channel through which the class enemy penetrates our midst . . . . He is aided by 'disinterested' assistants, who of course never put anything into their own pockets, or, well, just a trifle, don't you know! These include Communists, who hold jobs at vital nerve centers of trade, supply or the co-operative system and who 'disinterestedly' assist the thieves and connivers in misappropriating Soviet goods . . .". He then discussed the Decree of August 7, 1932 which imposed the capital penalty for theft of public property, with allowance for discretionary commutation to ten years' imprisonment and confiscation of property.

. . . It is quite clear, as Professor Hazard's study reveals, that embezzlement is frequent and widespread, and the available data do not suggest any political motivation, although the crime of embezzlement was for some years "the most common of all crimes committed by officials . . .". The cases are apparently ordinary crimes against property—the crucial difference being that Russian State-owned property is involved. Although statistics are not available, one learns from an instruction issued by the Office of the Prosecutor of the U.S.S.R. on May 5, 1936 "that he had much information on a large number of embezzlements and thefts from agencies of voluntary public organizations . . . . The circular says that in 1935 alone there were taken from *Osoviakhim* by embezzlement or theft 1,750,000 rubles. It criticizes the work of the prosecutors and declares that during 1935 there were 518 indictments for embezzlement or theft within the *Osoviakhim*, but that conviction of only thirty-nine persons resulted. It is noted that special growth of these offenses is found [in certain named republics and provinces]." In spite of the avowal, at least in the early periods, of theories of nonpunitive treatment of criminals, the sanction for embezzlement in Russia has sometimes been the capital penalty and, if it is not that now, it is certainly one of the most severely punished crimes. . . .

B. THE CRIMINAL PROCESS

NOTE

Assume that the decision has been made to prosecute the alleged embezzler. That means that the criminal process comes into play. What follows is a brief description of that process in the United States.

In reading this material, remember that the criminal processes in Botswana, China and Egypt are likely to be different (and, ocasionally, unexpectedly similar). Try to identify the central, characteristic features of the criminal process in the United States, so that you will have a basis for systematic comparison with the other cultures. In particular, try to identify the key actors (who are the people involved?), institutions (what public and private agencies provide the context of the process?), proceedings (what do these actors do in these contexts?) and values and objectives (what is the process trying to accomplish?). You should be sensitive to the possibility that a number of values and objectives are at play in the process and that they sometimes come into conflict with each other, so that some balance must be struck between them. For example, fairness to the accused and social defense against criminality may be mutually limiting ideas.

A Report by the President's Commission on Law Enforcement and Administration of Justice, The Challenge of Crime in a Free Society, Washington, D.C.; U.S. Government Printing Office, February 1967.

INTRODUCTION

America's System of Criminal Justice. The system of criminal justice America uses to deal with those crimes it cannot prevent and those criminals it cannot deter is not a monolithic, or even a consistent, system. It was not designed or built in one piece at one time. Its philosophic core is that a person may be punished by the Government if, and only if, it has been proved by an impartial and deliberate process that he has violated a specific law. Around that core layer upon layer of institutions and procedures, some carefully constructed and some improvised, some inspired by principle and some by expediency, have accumulated. Parts of the system—magistrates' courts, trial by jury, bail—are of great antiquity. Other parts—juvenile courts, probation and parole, professional policemen—are relatively new. The entire system represents an adaptation of the English common law to America's peculiar structure of government, which allows each local community to construct institutions that fill its special needs. Every village, town, county, city, and State has its own criminal justice system, and there is a Federal one as well. All of them operate somewhat alike. No two of them operate precisely alike.

Any criminal justice system is an apparatus society uses to enforce the standards of conduct necessary to protect individuals and the community. It operates by apprehending, prosecuting, convicting, and sentencing those members of the community who violate the basic rules of group existence. The action taken against lawbreakers is designed to serve three purposes beyond the immediately punitive one. It removes dangerous people from the community; it deters others from criminal behavior; and it gives society an opportunity to attempt to transform lawbreakers into law-abiding citizens. What most significantly distinguishes the system of one country from that of another is the extent and the form of the protections it offers individuals in the process of determining guilt and imposing punishment. Our system of justice deliberately sacrifices much in efficiency and even in effectiveness in order to preserve local autonomy and to protect the individual. Sometimes it may seem to sacrifice too much. For example, the American system was not designed with Cosa Nostra-type criminal organizations in mind, and it has been notably unsuccessful to date in preventing such organizations from preying on society.

A general view of The Criminal Justice System

This chart seeks to present a simple yet comprehensive view
of the movement of cases through the criminal justice system.
Procedures in individual jurisdictions may vary from the
pattern shown here. The differing weights of line indicate
the relative volumes of cases disposed of at various points
in the system, but this is only suggestive since no nationwide
data of this sort exists.

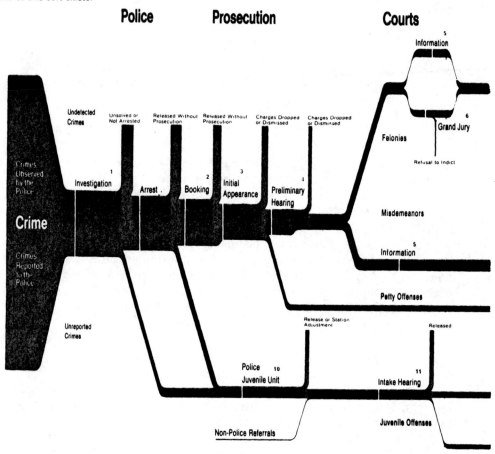

Police **Prosecution** **Courts**

1 May continue until trial.

2 Administrative record of arrest. First step at
which temporary release on bail may be
available.

3 Before magistrate, commissioner, or justice of
peace. Formal notice of charge, advice of
rights. Bail set. Summary trials for petty
offenses usually conducted here without
further processing.

4 Preliminary testing of evidence against
defendant. Charge may be reduced. No
separate preliminary hearing for misdemeanors
in some systems.

5 Charge filed by prosecutor on basis of
information submitted by police or citizens.
Alternative to grand jury indictment; often
used in felonies, almost always in
misdemeanors.

6 Reviews whether Government evidence
sufficient to justify trial. Some States have no
grand jury system; others seldom use it.

Corrections

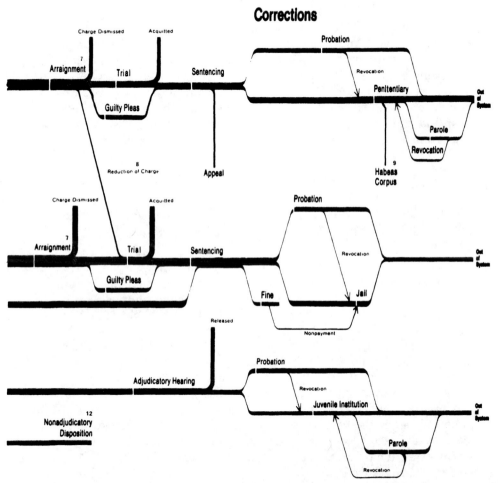

7   Appearance for plea; defendant elects trial by judge or jury (if available); counsel for indigent usually appointed here in felonies. Often not at all in other cases.

8   Charge may be reduced at any time prior to trial in return for plea of guilty or for other reasons.

9   Challenge on constitutional grounds to legality of detention. May be sought at any point in process.

10   Police often hold informal hearings, dismiss or adjust many cases without further processing.

11   Probation officer decides desirability of further court action.

12   Welfare agency, social services, counselling, medical care, etc., for cases where adjudicatory handling not needed.

The criminal justice system has three separateiy organized parts—the police, the courts, and corrections—and each has distinct tasks. However, these parts are by no means independent of each other. What each one does and how it does it has a direct effect on the work of the others. The courts must deal, and can only deal, with those whom the police arrest; the business of corrections is with those delivered to it by the courts. How successfully corrections reforms convicts determines whether they will once again become police business and influences the sentences the judges pass; police activities are subject to court scrutiny and are often determined by court decisions. And so reforming or reorganizing any part or procedure of the system changes other parts or procedures. Furthermore, the criminal process, the method by which the system deals with individual cases, is not a hodgepodge of random actions. It is rather a continuum—an orderly progression of events—some of which, like arrest and trial, are highly visible and some of which, though of great importance, occur out of public view. A study of the system must begin by examining it as a whole.

The chart on the following page sets forth in simplified form the process of criminal administration and shows the many decision points along its course. Since felonies, misdemeanors, petty offenses, and juvenile cases generally follow quite different paths, they are shown separately.

The popular, or even the lawbook, theory of everyday criminal process oversimplifies in some respects and overcomplicates in others what usually happens. That theory is that when an infraction of the law occurs, a policeman finds, if he can, the probable offender, arrests him and brings him promptly before a magistrate. If the offense is minor, the magistrate disposes of it forthwith; if it is serious, he holds the defendant for further action and admits him to bail. The case then is turned over to a prosecuting attorney who charges the defendant with a specific statutory crime. This charge is subject to review by a judge at a preliminary hearing of the evidence and in many places if the offense charged is a felony, by a grand jury that can dismiss the charge, or affirm it by delivering it to a judge in the form of an indictment. If the defendant pleads "not guilty" to the charge he comes to trial; the facts of his case are marshaled by prosecuting and defense attorneys and presented, under the supervision of a judge, through witnesses, to a jury. If the jury finds the defendant guilty, he is sentenced by the judge to a term in prison, where a systematic attempt to convert him into a law-abiding citizen is made, or to a term of probation, under which he is permitted to live in the community as long as he behaves himself.

Some cases do proceed much like that, especially those involving offenses that are generally considered "major": serious acts of violence or thefts of large amounts of property. However, not all major cases follow this course, and, in any event, the bulk of the daily business of the criminal justice system consists of offenses that are not major—of breaches of the peace, crimes of vice, petty thefts, assaults arising from domestic or street-corner or barroom disputes. These and most other cases are disposed of in much less formal and much less deliberate ways. . . .

What has evidently happened is that the transformation of America from a relatively relaxed rural society into a tumultuous urban one has presented the criminal justice system in the cities with a volume of cases too large to handle by traditional methods. One result of heavy caseloads is highly visible in city courts, which process many cases with excessive haste and many others with excessive slowness. In the interest both of effectiveness and of fairness to individuals, justice should be swift and certain; too often in city courts today it is, instead, hasty or faltering. Invisibly, the pressure of numbers has effected a series of adventitious changes in the criminal process. Informal shortcuts have been used. The decision making process has often become routinized. Throughout the system the importance of individual judgment and discretion, as distinguished from stated rules and procedures, has increased. In effect, much decision making is being done on an administrative rather than on a judicial basis. Thus, an examination of how the criminal justice system works and a consideration of the changes needed to make it more effective and fair must focus on the extent to which invisible, administrative procedures depart from visible, traditional ones, and on the desirability of that departure.

The Police. At the very beginning of the process—or, more properly, before the process begins at all—something happens that is scarcely discussed in lawbooks and is seldom recognized by the public: law enforcement policy is made by the policeman. For policemen cannot and do not arrest all the offenders they encounter. It is doubtful that they arrest most of them. A criminal code, in practice, is not a set of specific instructions to policemen, but a more or less rough map of the territory in which policemen work. How an individual policeman moves around that territory depends largely on his personal discretion.

That a policeman's duties compel him to exercise personal discretion many times every day is evident. Crime does not look the same on the street as it does in a legislative chamber. How much noise or profanity makes conduct "disorderly" within the meaning of the law? When must a quarrel be treated as a criminal assault: at the first threat or at the first shove or at the first blow, or after blood is drawn, or when a serious injury is inflicted? How suspicious must conduct be before there is "probable cause," the constitutional basis for an arrest? Every policeman, however complete or sketchy his education, is an interpreter of the law.

Every policeman, too, is an arbiter of social values, for he meets situation after situation in which invoking criminal sanctions is a questionable line of action. It is obvious that a boy throwing rocks at a school's windows is committing the statutory offense of vandalism, but it is often not at all obvious whether a policeman will better serve the interests of the community and of the boy by taking the boy home to his parents or by arresting him. . . . With juveniles especially, the police exercise great discretion.

Finally, the manner in which a policeman works is influenced by practical matters: the legal strength of the available evidence, the willingness of victims to press charges and of witnesses to testify, the temper of the community, the time and information at the policeman's disposal. Much is at stake in how the policeman exercises this discretion. If he judges conduct not suspicious enough to justify intervention, the chance to prevent a robbery, rape, or murder may be lost. If he overestimates the seriousness of a situation or his actions are controlled by panic or prejudice, he may hurt or kill someone unnecessarily. His actions may even touch off a riot.

The Magistrate. In direct contrast to the policeman, the magistrate before whom a suspect is first brought usually exercises less discretion than the law allows him. He is entitled to inquire into the facts of the case, into whether there are grounds for holding the accused. He seldom does. He seldom can. The more promptly an arrested suspect is brought into magistrate's court, the less likelihood there is that much information about the arrest other than the arresting officer's statement will be available to the magistrate. Moreover many magistrates, especially in big cities, have such congested calendars that it is almost impossible for them to subject any case but an extraordinary one to prolonged scrutiny.

In practice the most important things, by far, that a magistrate does are to set the amount of a defendant's bail and in some jurisdictions to appoint counsel. Too seldom does either action get the careful attention it deserves. In many cases the magistrate accepts a waiver of counsel without insuring that the suspect knows the significance of legal representation.

Bail is a device to free an untried defendant and at the same time make sure he appears for trial. That is the sole stated legal purpose in America. The Eighth Amendment to the Constitution declares that it must not be "excessive." Appellate courts have declared that not just the seriousness of the charge against the defendant, but the suspect's personal, family, and employment situation as they bear on the likelihood of his appearance, must be weighed before the amount of his bail is fixed. Yet more magistrates than not set bail according to standard rates, so and so many dollars for such and such an offense.

The persistence of money bail can best be explained not by its stated purpose but by the belief of police, prosecutors, and courts that the best way to keep a defendant from committing more crimes before trial is to set bail so high that he cannot obtain his release.

The Prosecutor. The key administrative officer in the processing of cases is the prosecutor. Theoretically the examination of the evidence against a defendant by a judge at a preliminary hearing, and its reexamination by a grand jury, are important parts of the process. Practically they seldom are because a prosecutor seldom has any difficulty in making a prima facie case against a defendant. In fact most defendants waive their rights to preliminary hearings and much more often than not grand juries indict precisely as prosecutors ask them to. The prosecutor wields almost undisputed sway over the pretrial progress of most cases. He decides whether to press a case or drop it. He determines the specific charge against a defendant. When the charge is reduced, as it is in as many as two-thirds of all cases in some cities, the prosecutor is usually the official who reduces it. . . .

When a prosecutor reduces a charge it is ordinarily because there has been "plea bargaining" between him and a defense attorney. The issue at stake is how much the prosecutor will reduce his original charge or how lenient a sentence he will recommend, in return for a plea of guilty. There is no way of judging how many bargains reflect the prosecutor's belief that a lesser charge or sentence is justified and how many result from the fact that there may be in the system at any one time ten times as many cases as there are prosecutors or judges or courtrooms to handle them, should every one come to trial. In form, a plea bargain can be anything from a series of careful conferences to a hurried consultation in a courthouse corridor. In content it can be anything from a conscientious exploration of the facts and dispositional alternatives available and appropriate to a defendant, to a perfunctory deal. If the interests of a defendant are to be properly protected while his fate is being thus invisibly determined, he obviously needs just as good legal representation as the kind he needs at a public trial. Whether or not plea bargaining is a fair and effective method of disposing of criminal cases depends heavily on whether or not defendants are provided early with competent and conscientious counsel.

Plea bargaining is not only an invisible procedure but, in some jurisdictions, a theoretically unsanctioned one. In order to satisfy the court record, a defendant, his attorney, and the prosecutor will at the time of sentencing often ritually state to a judge that no bargain has been made. Plea bargaining may be a useful procedure, especially in congested urban jurisdictions, but neither the dignity of the law, nor the quality of justice, nor the protection of society from dangerous criminals is enhanced by its being conducted covertly. . . .

An enormously consequential kind of decision is the sentencing decision of a judge. The law recognizes the importance of fitting sentences to individual defendants by giving judges, in most instances, considerable latitude. For example the recently adopted New York Penal Code, which will go into effect in autumn of 1967, empowers a judge to impose upon a man convicted of armed robbery any sentence between a 5-year term of probation and a 25-year term in prison. Even when a judge has presided over a trial during which the facts of a case have been carefully set forth and has been given a probation report that carefully discusses a defendant's character, background, and problems, he cannot find it easy to choose a sentence. In perhaps nine-tenths of all cases there is no trial; the defendants are self-confessedly guilty.

In the lower or misdemeanor courts, the courts that process most criminal cases, probation reports are a rarity. Under such circumstances judges have little to go on and many sentences are bound to be based on conjecture or intuition. When a sentence is part of a plea bargain, which an overworked judge ratifies perfunctorily, it may not even be his conjecture or intuition on which the sentence is based, but a prosecutor's or a defense counsel's. But perhaps the greatest lack judges suffer from when they pass sentence is not time or information, but correctional alternatives. Some lower courts do not have any probation officers, and in almost every court the caseloads of probation officers are so heavy that a sentence of probation means, in fact, releasing an offender into the community with almost no supervision. Few States have a sufficient variety of correctional institutions or treatment programs to inspire judges with the confidence that sentences will lead to rehabilitation.

The Task Force on the Administration of Justice, The President's Commission on Law Enforcement and Administration of Justice, Task Force Report: The Courts, Washington, D.C.: U.S. Government Printing Office, 1967, pp. 52–53, 65–66.

For two basic reasons representation by counsel is essential in our system of criminal justice. An individual forced to answer a criminal charge needs the assistance of a lawyer to protect his legal rights and to help him understand the nature and consequences of the proceedings against him. As the Attorney General's Committee on Poverty and the Administration of Federal Criminal Justice stated: "[A] situation in which persons are required to contest a serious accusation but are denied access to the tools of contest is offensive to fairness and equity."

The vital importance of counsel is obscured by asking simply whether a lawyer is needed to handle the trial of a criminal charge, for representation at trial is only a part of defense counsel's role. More often than not the defendant is lacking in education, intelligence, and capacity for insight. Standing alone he may be incapable . . . of developing facts which could either convince the prosecutor to dismiss the charge or favorably affect the prosecutor's decision in guilty plea negotiations or the judge's decision as to sentence. Without the support and perspective of counsel the defendant may have little understanding of what is happening to him or why.

The importance of counsel also proceeds from values transcending the interests of any individual defendant. Counsel is needed to maintain effective and efficient criminal justice. Ours is an adversary system of justice, which depends for its vitality upon vigorous and proper challenges to assertions of governmental authority and accusations of crime. Reliance upon the judge or prosecutor to protect the interests of defendants is an inadequate substitute for the advocacy of conscientious defense counsel. Limiting the right to counsel "gravely endangers judicial search for truth." . . .

It must be recognized, however, that the provision of counsel often will serve to delay the criminal process and complicate the finding of facts. Counsel will require that the courts deal deliberately with his client. He will make motions for discovery and suppression of evidence. Sometimes he will seek delay for tactical advantages, cast doubt on a truthful witness, or challenge legitimate proof. Many of the burdens counsel will impose are costs which must be borne for the sake of an effective adversary system. Although firmer controls on delay, clarification of the ethical standards governing the conduct of counsel, and insistence on strict adherence to these standards can minimize these burdens, they probably cannot be eliminated. Yet far higher costs would be paid and far greater sacrifices would be made in the quality of justice if the system were not built on the energetic participation of counsel for the accused. . . .

Judges. The quality of justice depends in large measure on the quality of judges. Good judges are essential for settling all types of legal controversies, whether the issue involves the custody of a child, the interpretation of a private business agreement or a will, or the power of the government to enforce a regulatory statute. But the demands which the criminal law makes on the judicial process are unique. For the criminal law contains rules of conduct essential to the maintenance of an orderly society and gives government the power to deprive an individual of his liberty or his life.

The trial judge is at the center of the criminal process, and he exerts a powerful influence on the stages of the process which precede and follow his formal participation. Many decisions of police, prosecutors, and defense counsel are determined by the trial judge's rulings, by his sentencing practices, and even by the speed with which he disposes of cases. His decisions on sentencing and probation revocation affect the policies and procedures of correctional agencies. And to a great degree the public's impression of justice is shaped by the trial judge's demeanor and the dignity he imparts to the proceedings in his courtroom.

Because appellate judges enunciate rules and principles to govern future cases, it is essential that they have both wisdom and a sensitivity to the practical problems of law enforcement. But the trial judge exerts a far greater influence on the quality of justice. For the principles of appellate decisions are viable only when they are applied to facts, and the trial judge supervises the fact-finding process. When he serves as trier of the fact on issues such as search and seizure and confessions, the trial judge has almost absolute power to assess the credibility of witnesses and to resolve conflicting testimony. A trial judge's decision to acquit even in the face of strong evidence of guilt may not be appealed, and it bars further prosecution. Through his attitude or expressions the trial judge may influence the jury's determination of factual issues in a way which will not be reflected in the record before an appellate court.

The power of the trial judge in sentencing is another example of his virtual autonomy. In most jurisdictions today the trial judge's sentence cannot be adjusted by an appellate court if it is within the statutory limits, no matter how harsh or arbitrary it appears to be. And even appellate review of sentences, proposed in chapter 2 as a useful procedure for correcting unjust sentences, would leave the trial judge with broad discretion in most sentencing decisions.

Although the great majority of defendants appear before the judge only to enter a guilty plea, which often is the result of negotiations with the prosecutor, his influence on these dispositions is nonetheless substantial. Much like the out-of-court settlement of a civil case, the informal disposition of a criminal charge is based largely upon the parties' expectations of what result would be reached if the case were brought to trial. In addition it is not uncommon for individual judges to regard certain offenses as too trivial to merit any substantial penalty or even to merit the court's time in hearing them. An experienced prosecutor is reluctant to antagonize the judge by bringing these cases to court despite the availability of sufficient evidence to convict the defendant.

A judge's attitude toward prosecutions for certain offenses also affects arrest practices of the police. In one large city, for example, it was noted that the number of arrests for prostitution and solicitation declined sharply during the months that a judge who routinely dismissed such cases was sitting in the misdemeanor division.

For most Americans the trial judge is the symbol of justice in our criminal courts. Few persons have witnessed an appellate argument; personal impressions are formed through appearing in a trial court as a juror, witness, or defendant. A public which has been taught to believe that judges are wise, fair, and dignified men who possess all the virtues traditionally associated with the judiciary will measure the judges whom they encounter.

Because the judge plays such a critical role in the criminal process, every effort must be made to ensure the highest quality judiciary. The first step is to employ selection procedures which will bring to the bench lawyers who are likely to be excellent judges. Although it is possible to identify such factors as professional incompetence, laziness, or intemperance which should disqualify a lawyer from becoming a judge, it is much more difficult to choose confidently the potentially superior judge from among a number of aspirants who appear generally qualified. And many of those who can become excellent judges come to the bench without certain skills or experience. Therefore it is important to provide training for judges, especially for those who are newly selected. Finally, there must be fair and expeditious procedures for disciplining or removing judges who are unwilling or unable to perform their duties properly.

Sentencing. The imposition of sanctions on convicted offenders is a principal vehicle for accomplishing the goals of the criminal law. The difficulty of the sentencing decision is due in part to the fact that criminal law enforcement has a number of varied and often conflicting goals: The rehabilitation of offenders, the isolation of offenders who pose a threat to community safety, the discouragement of potential offenders, the expression of the community's condemnation of the offender's conduct, and the reinforcement of the values of law abiding citizens.

Although in some cases these various goals may lead to the same result, in many other cases the judge must choose to enforce one goal while subordinating the others. Thus a person who violates the income tax or selective service laws may be sentenced to prison as an example to potential violators despite the fact that he presents no threat to the community's safety and is not apparently in need of correctional treatment. In another case a judge may properly impose a lenient sentence on a youthful offender who has committed a serious crime in order to maximize his chances for successful rehabilitation.

The burden of accommodating these values in each case falls primarily on the trial judge. Although his authority is limited by the statutory provisions which establish the range of sentencing alternatives, these statutes rarely provide any standards to guide the exercise of his discretion. Furthermore, his ability to impose an appropriate sentence is limited because knowledge about the deterrent or rehabilitative effect of any particular sentence is limited. And in many jurisdictions information about the offender's background, which is needed to predict the offender's potential for rehabilitation, is not furnished to the sentencing judge.

Statutory provisions affect sentencing decisions in individual cases in two primary ways. The statutes distribute sentencing authority among the legislature, the court, and the correctional agencies. They also determine the criteria used by the courts and correctional agencies to make the decisions delegated to them and place limits on their authority.

Within certain limits a lack of uniformity in sentences is justifiable. Indeed the reason for giving judges discretion in sentencing is to permit variations based on relevant differences in offenders. Unequal sentences for the same offense may also result from the fact that statutory definitions of crimes encompass a fairly broad range of conduct having varying degrees of seriousness. Finally, lack of uniformity may reflect geographic factors, such as differences in public apprehension of crime among communities in the same jurisdiction, or institutional considerations, such as the need to offer more lenient sentences to defendants who furnish information or testimony for the prosecution.

Unjustified disparity cannot be eliminated completely, if for no other reason than because reasonable men applying the same standards will not always reach precisely the same result. There are several steps, however, that may reduce the range in which individual differences among judges can affect the length and type of sentences. Enactment of criteria for sentencing together with educational programs to improve judicial sentencing proficiency would aid in the development of uniform sentencing policies. Furthermore, the removal of inconsistencies in severity of punishment among offenses and the elimination of severe mandatory sentences would tend to reduce the wide disparities caused by prosecutorial and judicial nullification.

The following sections consider two procedures, sentencing councils and appellate review of sentences, which are particularly helpful in reducing disparity.

Fines. Two unfortunate characteristics of sentencing practices in many lower courts are the routine imposition of fines on the great majority of misdemeanants and petty offenders and the routine imprisonment of offenders who default in paying fines. These practices result in unequal punishment of offenders and in the needless imprisonment of many persons because of their financial condition.

It is unlikely that all of the discriminatory consequences of fines will ever be eliminated. There will continue to be many instances in which offenders are deserving of punishment but the judges' realistic alternatives are limited to fines or jail. The fact that our society has not devised suitable alternative punishments gives rise to a vexing dilemma in the use of fines. For so long as jail is the routine alternative to a fine, those unable to pay will be punished more severely than those of greater means. Putting all offenders in jail is a wholly unacceptable alternative, as is relieving those unable to pay a fine of all penalties.

Probation. The Report of the Task Force on Corrections discusses the desirability of probation as an alternative to imprisonment. Its central advantages are that it facilitates the reintegration of the offender into the community, avoids the negative aspects of imprisonment, and reduces the financial burden on the State. Despite these important benefits many courts still view probation only in its historical context, that is, as "an act of grace and clemency to be granted in a proper case."

The statutory provisions authorizing the use of probation do little to dispel this image. Legislatures in almost all jurisdictions have restricted the courts' power to grant probation by limitations based on such factors as the type of offense, the length of prison sentence which could be imposed, and the offender's prior criminal record. Moreover, the criteria for granting probation to eligible offenders are often so highly abstract that they provide very limited guidance to the courts. In California, for example, the court is authorized to grant probation when it determines "that there are circumstances in mitigation of punishment prescribed by law, or that the ends of justice would be subserved."

Restrictions on the courts' power to grant probation have produced the same practice of avoidance by courts and prosecutors discussed in the context of mandatory prison terms. The absence of meaningful legislative standards for granting probation aggravates the problem of disparity of sentences because each judge is left virtually unrestrained in applying his own theories of probation to individual cases. And it may decrease the use of probation, because the court may be more reluctant to risk public criticism in the event of further criminality by a probationer when it is unable to justify its action at least in part by legislative direction.

NOTE

There is a great deal of variation among the states (and in the federal government) in the appointment, promotion, tenure, discipline and removal of judges. Appointment by the executive subject to legislative approval, with life tenure, prevails in some jurisdictions, popular election for limited terms in others. In between are hybrid systems of all conceivable, occasionally exotic, types. For a thorough description and discussion see: John Henry Merryman, Judicial Responsibility in the United States, 41 Rabels Zeitschrift, p. 332, 1977.

"A Report by the President's Commission on Law Enforcement and Administration of Justice," The Challenge of Crime in a Free Society, Washington, D.C.; U.S. Government Printing Office, February 1967.

Corrections. The correctional apparatus to which guilty defendants are delivered is in every respect the most isolated part of the criminal justice system. Much of it is physically isolated; its institutions usually have thick walls and locked doors, and often they are situated in rural areas, remote from the courts where the institutions' inmates were tried and from the communities where they lived. The correctional apparatus is isolated in the sense that its officials do not have everyday working relationships with officials from the system's other branches, like those that commonly exist between policemen and prosecutors, or prosecutors and judges. It is isolated in the sense that what it does with, to, or for the people under its supervision is seldom governed by any but the most broadly written statutes, and is almost never scrutinized by appellate courts. Finally, it is isolated from the public partly by its invisibility and physical remoteness; partly by the inherent lack of drama in most of its activities, but perhaps most importantly by the fact that the correctional apparatus is often used—or misused—by both the criminal justice system and the public as a rug under which disturbing problems and people can be swept.

The most striking fact about the correctional apparatus today is that, although the rehabilitation of criminals is presumably its major purpose, the custody of criminals is actually its major task. . . .

. . . Many jails have nothing but custodial and administrative personnel. Of course many jails are crowded with defendants who have not been able to furnish bail and who are not considered by the law to be appropriate objects of rehabilitation because it has not yet been determined that they are criminals who need it.

What this emphasis on custody means in practice is that the enormous potential of the correctional apparatus for making creative decisions about its treatment of convicts is largely unfulfilled. This is true not only of offenders in custody but of offenders on probation and parole. Most authorities agree that while probationers and parolees need varying degrees and kinds of supervision, an average of no more than 35 cases per officer is necessary for effective attention; 97 percent of all officers handling adults have larger caseloads than that. . . .

. . . Except for sentencing, no decision in the criminal process has more impact on the convicted offender than the parole decision, which determines how much of his maximum sentence a prisoner must serve. This again is an invisible administrative decision that is seldom open to attack or subject to review. It is made by parole board members who are often political appointees. Many are skilled and conscientious, but they generally are able to spend no more than a few minutes on a case. Parole decisions that are made in haste and on the basis of insufficient information, in the absence of parole machinery that can provide good supervision, are necessarily imperfect decisions. And since there is virtually no appeal from them, they can be made arbitrarily or discriminatorily. Just as carefully formulated and clearly stated law enforcement policies would help policemen, charge policies would help prosecutors and sentencing policies would help judges, so parole policies would help parole boards perform their delicate and important duties.

In sum, America's system of criminal justice is overcrowded and overworked, undermanned, underfinanced and very often misunderstood. It needs more information and more knowledge. It needs more technical resources. It needs more coordination among its many parts. It needs more public support. It needs the help of community programs and institutions in dealing with offenders and potential offenders. It needs, above all, the willingness to reexamine old ways of doing things, to reform itself, to experiment, to run risks, to dare. It needs vision. . . .

QUESTIONS

1. In recent years courts have taken a more aggressive interest in prison conditions and in the treatment of inmates than the foregoing excerpt suggests. For an excellent collection of the relevant cases and materials, see Sheldon Krantz, Cases and Materials on The Law of Corrections and Prisoners' Rights, St. Paul, Minn.: West, 1981, 2nd edition.

2. Do you agree with the authors that "the rehabilitation of criminals" is the major purpose of what they call "the correctional apparatus"?

3. More generally, what is (are) the purpose(s) of the criminal justice system? Why have one at all?

4. Could you design a realistic and coherent system of criminal justice that would be consistent with basic constitutional (and cultural) values and be preferable to the one described above? Give it a try, forcing yourself to think hard about the probable secondary (and tertiary) consequences of the reforms you propose.

C. THE LAW

CALIFORNIA PENAL CODE

§ 424. [Embezzlement and falsification of accounts by public officers: Misappropriating, lending or making profit out of "public moneys": Refusal or omission to pay over or transfer moneys: Punishment]

Each officer of this state, or of any county, city, town, or district of this state, and every other person charged with the receipt, safekeeping, transfer, or disbursement of public moneys, who either:

1. Without authority of law, appropriates the same, or any portion thereof, to his own use, or to the use of another; or,

2. Loans the same or any portion thereof; makes any profit out of, or uses the same for any purpose not authorized by law; or,

3. Knowingly keeps any false account, or makes any false entry or erasure in any account of or relating to the same; or,

4. Fraudulently alters, falsifies, conceals, destroys, or obliterates any such account; or,

5. Willfully refuses or omits to pay over, on demand, any public moneys in his hands, upon the presentation of a draft, order, or warrant drawn upon such moneys by competent authority; or,

6. Willfully omits to transfer the same, when such transfer is required by law; or,

7. Willfully omits or refuses to pay over to any officer or person authorized by law to receive the same, any money received by him under any duty imposed by law so to pay over the same;

Is punishable by imprisonment in the state prison for two, three or four years, and is disqualified from holding any office in this state.

As used in this section, "public moneys" includes the proceeds derived from the sale of bonds or other evidence of indebtedness authorized by the legislative body of any city, county, district, or public agency. . . .

§ 425. Officers neglecting to [keep and] pay over public moneys

Every officer charged with the receipt, safe-keeping, or disbursement of public moneys, who neglects or fails to keep and pay over the same in the manner prescribed by law, is guilty of a felony. . . .

§ 503. Definition

"EMBEZZLEMENT" DEFINED. Embezzlement is the fraudulent appropriation of property by a person to whom it has been intrusted. . . .

§ 504. Officers and deputies, etc., of state, political subdivisions, public or private corporations, societies, or association

Every officer of this State, or of any county, city, city and county, or other municipal corporation or subdivision thereof, and every deputy, clerk, or servant of any such officer, and every officer, director, trustee, clerk, servant, or agent of any association, society, or corporation (public or private), who fraudulently appropriates to any use or purpose not in the due and lawful execution of his trust, any property which he has in his possession or under his control by virtue of his trust, or secretes it with a fraudulent intent to appropriate it to such use or purpose, is guilty of embezzlement. . . .

§ 512. Defenses; mitigation of punishment; intent to restore property; time

The fact that the accused intended to restore the property embezzled, is no ground of defense or mitigation of punishment, if it has not been restored before an information has been laid before a magistrate, or an indictment found by a grand jury, charging the commission of the offense. . . .

§ 513. Defenses; mitigation of punishment; restoration of property or tender before indictment or information

Whenever, prior to an information laid before a magistrate, or an indictment found by a grand jury, charging the commission of embezzlement, the person accused voluntarily and actually restores or tenders restoration of the property alleged to have been embezzled, or any part thereof, such fact is not a ground of defense, but it authorizes the court to mitigate punishment, in its discretion. . . .

§ 514. Punishment; determination of value; defalcation of public funds; disfranchisement

Every person guilty of embezzlement is punishable in the manner prescribed for theft of property of the value or kind embezzled; and where the property embezzled is an evidence of debt or right of action, the sum due upon it or secured to be paid by it must be taken as its value; if the embezzlement or defalcation is of the public funds of the United States, or of this State, or of any county or municipality within this State, the offense is a felony, and is punishable by imprisonment in the state prison. . . .

. . . and the person so convicted is ineligible thereafter to any office of honor, trust, or profit in this State. . . .

NOTES AND QUESTIONS

1. The common law crime of larceny applied only to one who wrongfully took possession of someone else's property. It did not apply if possession were rightfully acquired (e.g. by a bailee, a clerk, or a servant) and the property subsequently misappropriated. That was embezzlement. This simple distinction placed an enormous strain on the notion of possession, leading to some interesting fictions (e.g. a distinction between "possession" and "custody") and some tortured reasoning. For a history of this aspect of embezzlement see Jerome Hall, Theft, Law and Society, Indianapolis: The Bobbs-Merrill Company, Inc., 2d edition, 1952, pp. 3–79.

2. If you would like to try your hand at applying the distinction, consider this case. Ashwell met Keogh in a public house one night, took him outside, and asked him for the loan of a shilling. Keogh consented, put his hand in his pocket and pulled out what he thought was a shilling and handed it to Ashwell, who took the coin without looking at it and put it into his pocket. Later that evening Ashwell was seen to obtain change for a sovereign at another public house. Keogh found when he got home that he had handed Ashwell a sovereign by mistake, and the next day he called on Ashwell (at 5:20 a. m.) who falsely denied having received the sovereign. Prosecution for larceny. Ashwell appeals his conviction, arguing that he did not commit larceny. What decision on appeal? Queen v. Ashwell, 16 Q.B.D. 190 (1885).

3. In the eighteenth century, Cesare Beccaria's Of Crimes and Punishments (1764) was an enormously influential book. Under its influence the death penalty was abolished in Tuscany and the maxims *nullum crimen sine lege* (no crime without a law) and *nulla poena sine lege* (no punishment without a law) became basic objectives of European criminal law reform. Although it now seems too obvious to call for comment, the principle that one should only be found guilty of a crime or subjected to punishment according to properly enacted (and published) laws in existence at the

time of the offense was not widely adopted in Western legal systems until the nineteenth century.

One effect of such reforms is to place great emphasis on the precise words of statutes. Do you understand why? In California, Penal Code §§ 424 and 504 (set out above) are both potentially applicable to embezzlement by a public official. The following cases illustrate the way the criminal process and these statutes work in California. In reading these cases you should be alert to two principal levels of significance: (1) What questions were raised by the parties and decided by the court? (2) What tacit propositions about the criminal process (actors, institutions, proceedings and values/objectives) underlie the reasoning of the court?

People v. Holtzendorff, 177 Cal.App.2d 788, 2 Cal.Rptr. 676 (1960).

* * *

BISHOP, J., PRO TEM. The People have appealed from the order granting defendant's motion to set aside the 52 count indictment that accused him of having committed as many felonies. . . .

* * *

We shall have occasion to note the evidence with greater particularity before we have finished, but for the moment it suffices to say that it introduces the defendant as the Executive Director, Secretary and Treasurer of the Housing Authority of the City of Los Angeles (the "Authority," for the purpose of future references). He became interested in a political campaign, in the early part of 1953, and undertook to help in the campaign. Some 19 of the Authority's employees were persuaded to assist in his efforts, and some typewriters were rented for their use. The compensation of the employees, while busy in the campaign, and the rental for the typewriters, were paid by checks drawn on the Authority's bank account.

The counts of the indictment fall into three groups. But for changes in names, amounts and dates, the odd numbered among the first 42 counts, to be hereafter referred to as the "odd numbered counts," read as does Count I: "The said Howard L. Holtzendorff is accused by the Grand Jury . . . of the crime of Embezzlement of Public Moneys in Violation of Section 424 Subdivision 2, Penal Code . . . committed . . . as follows:

"That on or about the 18th day of March, 1953 . . . Howard L. Holtzendorff, was an officer of the State of California, to wit, Executive Director, Secretary and Treasurer of the Housing Authority of the City of Los Angeles; that at said time and place, said defendant was charged with the receipt, safekeeping, transfer, and disbursement of public moneys of said Housing Authority of the City of Los Angeles; that at said time and place, said defendant was in receipt and in possession of $127.95 in public moneys of said Housing Authority of the City of Los Angeles; that at said time and place, said defendant did willfully, unlawfully and feloniously embezzle, and without authority of law, use said $127.95 in public moneys for a purpose not authorized by law, by making and issuing and causing to be made and issued, checks drawn on the payroll account of said Housing Authority of the City of Los Angeles, maintained at the Bank of America National Trust and Savings Association, payable to Audrey Aarhus, who was not entitled to receive said public moneys."

In the second group are the "even numbered" of the first 42 counts, of which the second count is typical:

"Count II

"For a further and separate cause of action, being a different statement of the same offense alleged in Count I, hereof, the said Howard L. Holtzendorff is accused . . . of the crime of Embezzlement of Public Moneys in Violation of Section 504, Penal Code . . . committed . . . as follows:

"That on or about the 18th day of March, 1953 . . . Howard L. Holtzendorff, was an officer and agent of a public corporation, to wit, the Housing Authority of the City of Los Angeles; that at said time and place said defendant had in his possession and under his control, by virtue of his trust as said officer and agent of said Housing Authority of the City of Los Angeles, $127.95 in public money, the property of said Housing Authority of the City of Los Angeles; that at said time and place, said defendant feloniously and fraudulently embezzled and appropriated said $127.95 in public moneys to a use and purpose not in the due and lawful execution of his trust as said officer and agent of said Housing Authority of the City of Los Angeles, by making and issuing and causing to be made and issued checks drawn on the payroll account of said Housing Authority of the City of Los Angeles, maintained at the Bank of America National Trust and Savings Association, payable to Audrey Aarhus, who was not entitled to receive said public moneys."

In the third group, the "last ten counts," charges are made of the falsification of public records, in violation of subdivision 3 of section 424.

Odd Numbered Counts

Our first question is this: Do the odd numbered counts charge the embezzlement of public moneys? Its answer depends upon the interpretation to be placed upon subdivisions 1 and 2 of section 424, Penal Code, read together with sections 503 and 504 of the same code.
. . . .

We approach the task of interpreting section 424 with these words in mind, taken from People v. Smith: " 'When language which is reasonably susceptible of two constructions is used in a penal law ordinarily that construction which is more favorable to the offender will be adopted.' " The defendant is entitled to the benefit of every reasonable doubt as to the true interpretation of words or the construction of language in a statute.

. . . Section 426, Penal Code, defines "public moneys" as those words are used throughout section 424, and the evidence in this case does not justify the conclusion that the moneys involved fall within the definition. "The phrase 'public moneys,'" section 426 declares, "as used in the two preceding sections, includes all bonds and evidence of indebtedness, and all moneys belonging to the State, or any city, county, town, or district therein, and all moneys, bonds, and evidence of indebtedness received or held by State, county, district, city, or town officers in their official capacity." As we shall see, the defendant was probably an officer, certainly an agent, of a public corporation, and the money that he appropriated was public money, as the words are used in section 800. But he was not an officer of the state or of any county, district, city or town, nor did the money here involved belong to the state or to any of the other state subdivisions listed in section 426. The public character of the Authority is not to be denied; it is abundantly certified in Housing Authority v. Dockweiler. But it is not to question the right of the Authority to condemn land for its purposes, to hold its property tax free, to be supported by public money, and to claim exemption from income and franchise taxes, to conclude that, a public agency though it is, it is not the State, nor a county, city, town or district. The Legislature, in adopting the definition it gave in section 426 for the use of the words in section 424, might have included moneys belonging to or officers of a public corporation, but it did not. The moneys and the officers of the Authority are not governed by section 424, Penal Code.

Last 10 Counts

There is a further consequence of this conclusion: there was no reasonable or probable cause for Counts 43–52 of the indictment. Each of these last 10 counts undertook to charge a violation of subdivision 3 of section 424, which, repeating its introductory paragraph, reads: "Each officer of this State, or of any county, city, town or district of this State, and every other person charged with the receipt, safekeeping, transfer, or disbursement of public moneys, who . . . 3. Knowingly keeps any false account, or makes any false entry or erasure in any account of or relative to the same . . ." is guilty of a felony. In each of the last 10 counts the defendant was said to have knowingly made false entries in and to have kept a false account "relating to the receipt, safekeeping, transfer and disbursement of public money owned by the Housing Authority of the City of Los Angeles." Each count goes on to specify that the false account was a payroll certificate showing a named employee to have been on vacation. As there is no other code section that makes the entry of a false entry or the keeping of a false account *re* public moneys a felony, and section 424 does not apply to an officer of the Authority, or to the money of the Authority, the evidence before the grand jury did not warrant any one of the last 10 counts of the indictment.

Even Numbered Counts, 2–42

The even numbered counts that pair with the odd numbered ones that we have considered, plainly charge violations of section 504, Penal Code, and so embezzlement. . . . With respect to these counts the questions we have to answer, are these: Was there evidence before the grand jury that found our indictment, that "would lead a man of ordinary caution or prudence to believe, and conscientiously entertain a strong suspicion," (to repeat the apt words from a quotation in Lorenson v. Superior Court) that: (a) the Housing Authority of the City of Los Angeles was a public corporation; (b) the defendant was either an officer or an agent of the Authority during the year 1953; (c) public moneys had been entrusted to the defendant as such officer or agent, which, in 1953, he had in his possession or under his control; and (d) the defendant fraudulently appropriated the sums to uses or purposes not in the due and lawful execution of his trust, by causing checks to be drawn on an account of the Authority in favor of persons not entitled to receive the proceeds? As already indicated, we find that there was such evidence as to each of the listed propositions.

QUESTIONS

1. "When language which is reasonably susceptible of two constructions is used in a penal law ordinarily that construction which is more favorable to the offender will be adopted." "The defendant is entitled to the benefit of every reasonable doubt as to the true interpretation of words or the construction of language in a statute." Why? Should a different rule of statutory interpretation guide the court in a civil (i.e. non-criminal) proceeding?

2. Notice that this was an appeal by the People. Do you understand why the defense of double jeopardy would not be raised by the defendant? Suppose the defendant had been acquitted below and the People appealed; would the defendant have the double jeopardy defense in that case?

3. Obviously there is no objection to an appeal by a convicted defendant. It appears that the right to an appeal after trial is a one way street running in the defendant's direction but not the People's. Ok?

4. In a civil proceeding a trial decision can of course be appealed by either party, even when one of them is the state (e.g. the state can appeal a decision against it in an action for breach of contract against a builder). Ok? Why should the rule be different in criminal cases?

People v. Qui Mei Lee, 48 Cal.App.3d 516, 122 Cal.Rptr. 43 (1975).

A jury convicted defendant of violation of subdivision 1 of section 424 of the Penal Code (misappropriation of public funds), and violation of subdivision (a) of section 19405 of the Revenue and Taxation Code (making a false state income tax return). She was acquitted of another tax charge contained in a third count. She was granted probation and appeals.

FACTS

Viewed in the light most favorable to the prosecution the evidence relevant to this appeal is as follows:

As Medical Director of San Joaquin County, Dr. Louis M. Barber was in charge of all county medical facilities. In such capacity, he was empowered to approve all invoices for medical and laboratory services provided to the county by private physicians and laboratories. Upon Barber's approval, those invoices were automatically paid by the county auditor. On behalf of the county's medical facilities, Barber also received state warrants and certain county warrants drawn upon the account of the local health district. These warrants represented payments to the county facilities for fulfillment of valid contracts to provide medical services to the local health district and the state. Upon their receipt, Barber was required to transfer such local health district and state payments to the accounts of the payee county facilities designated on the warrants.

Over a long period of time, however, Barber pursued a bizarre scheme. He forged and approved false invoices to the county for medical and related services ostensibly provided by private practitioners and laboratories. In payment of those invoices, the county auditor routinely issued warrants payable to the supposed providers of services. Barber also established a checking account for a bogus "Research Fund," into which he deposited the state and local health district payments.

Although Barber was not tried with defendant, defendant was prosecuted as an aider and abettor of Barber. Between 1968 and 1972, while employed as Barber's secretary, defendant rented post office boxes and an apartment in the names of the doctors and laboratories appearing on the fake invoices. Those addresses were used as mail drops for the receipt of county payments on the fraudulent invoices, as were other addresses, including Barber's office and defendant's home and post office box. The names of two physicians on the post office box applications were forged by the defendant. From the mail drops, she collected county warrants mailed there in payment of the forged invoices, and delivered the warrants to Barber. Some of the forged invoices were prepared on a typewriter found in defendant's home during a search by the police.

Upon Barber's instructions, defendant deposited the county warrants into various banks. She forged a bank signature card in opening one of those accounts, and opened other accounts in the names of the warrant payees. Barber forged the endorsements of the payees on most of the deposited warrants, and defendant's signature was affixed as a second endorsement. On occasion defendant deposited warrants by herself forging the payee's name. Checks drawn by Barber on the Research Fund also were deposited into those accounts. Defendant regularly wrote checks on one of the bank accounts (unknown to Barber, her personal account) to pay Barber's bills when he gave her lists of creditors for that purpose. She also cashed some of the warrants. Barber paid her $150 per month for those services, over and above her salary as a secretary.

II

CROSS–EXAMINATION OF CHARACTER WITNESS

Defendant next contends that the prosecutor engaged in prejudicial misconduct during his cross-examination of one of defendant's character witnesses, Dr. Eccleston. Dr. Eccleston testified on direct examination that defendant's reputation for truth and honesty in the community where she lived and worked was and is above reproach. He also in effect gave his personal opinion that defendant was and is honest. Upon cross-examination, the prosecutor interrogated the witness as follows:

"Q. Now, Dr. Eccleston, I'm going to ask you a series of questions and it's just about what you may have heard about the defendant. Okay?

"A. Uh-huh (yes).

"Q. All right. Have you heard that she forged a certain doctor's name on many county warrants?

"A. No.

"Q. Okay. Have you heard that she deposited checks in other doctor's names in her own accounts?

"A. I have read that in the paper.

"Q. Okay. Have you heard that she forged post office box applications and bank applications?

"A. Nothing of that nature.

"Q. Have you heard that she was receiving $150 a month for doing this which was not reported to the income tax authorities?

"A. I read something in the paper to that effect, but I don't even know the details as compared with the question.

"Q. Okay. Okay. Did you take into consideration then in your opinion as to her truth and honesty?

"A. Yes, I have.

"Q. Did you take into consideration, when I asked you whether or not you had heard about her forging certain names, is that correct?

"A. Well, only as I would say the reading in the paper. I don't even remember the details, as detailed by you in your question, except the question sounds familiar.

"Q. So you could not have taken that into consideration in forming your opinion, isn't that true, sir?

"A. No—what was that?

"Q. Well, I believe that you indicated that you had not heard that the defendant had forged a certain doctor, or a certain Dr. E. Patrick Quinn's name on many county warrants, is that correct?

"A. No, I'm not familiar with that.

"MR. BOSCOE [defense counsel]: Just a minute, doctor.

"THE COURT: Just a minute.

"MR. BOSCOE: At this time, for the purpose of the record, I assign all of those questions of counsel as reversible error and misconduct on his part, and he knows better than that. He is attributing—

"MR. VAN OSS [prosecutor]: Your Honor, I have a list of citations here I will give the Court.

"THE COURT: Let Mr. Boscoe finish.

"MR. BOSCOE: For the purpose of my record, he is asking this witness for specific items of misconduct. And he has no right to do that. All he has to do, he has an obligation only to cross-examine the witness on the question of what the reputation is in reference to the particular trait that is involved here, truth and honesty. [¶] Now he is asking questions in reference to the specific act, forging a name, unreported income tax, $150 a month, and fraudulently opening up mail boxes. That's all prejudicial error, to bring before the juror. And I will submit to Your Honor a case, and plenty of authority that that is misconduct on the part of the District Attorney. And I ask the Court now to admonish the jury to disregard those questions that have been asked of this witness."

For the reasons hereinafter set forth, we hold that the cross-examination was proper. Section 1102 of the Evidence Code allows a defendant in a criminal action to offer opinion evidence of his character or a trait of his character to prove his conduct in conformity with such character or trait of character. The defendant's reputation in that regard may similarly be offered. The character or character trait must, of course, be relevant to the offense charged.

The character witness may give his opinion or his knowledge of the defendant's reputation either (1) as of the time of and prior to the alleged offense, or (2) as was done here, as of the time of testifying. Section 1102 of the Evidence Code does not contain a time limitation. The time frame used on direct examination determines the extent of the cross-examination. If Dr. Eccleston had testified that as of the time of the alleged offenses (or even as of the time preceding his awareness thereof), defendant was honest or had a good reputation for honesty, any cross-examination regarding his having heard of the charged offense would exceed the scope of the direct examination and thus be improper. Such question could in no way test the credibility of the witness as to the subject matter of his direct testimony. Having testified that the defendant's reputation for honesty was good as of the time of or preceding the charged offense, whatever adverse comment he might have heard thereafter, including reports of the charged offense, could not possibly cast any doubt upon the integrity of such past opinion.

Quite another result obtains however, where, as here, the witness' testimony is delivered in the present tense. No one can seriously maintain that a character witness comes into a criminal trial unaware that the defendant is charged with a crime. Obviously he knows this. Obviously too, no person publicly charged with a crime such as misappropriation of public funds can have an unquestioned *present reputation* for honesty. Whatever his reputation might have been before the charge, after the charge it is at least dubious. Thus where the character witness nonetheless states under oath that such defendant's reputation for honesty is presently good, there is a strong suggestion (to say the least) that he is not a credible witness. And on cross-examination, such lack of credibility may be demonstrated by asking him whether he in fact has heard of the commission of the offense for which the defendant is on trial. Such a question is highly relevant, and therefore proper. Similarly, if the character witness gives his personal opinion that the defendant is presently honest, the same question on cross-examination is most relevant; for if he has heard of the offense charged, the validity of his opinion may be affected thereby.

Defense counsel can avoid the problem by limiting the scope of inquiry on direct examination. By initially directing questions of a character witness to the time of and reasonably prior to the alleged offense, defense counsel averts what is otherwise proper, and potentially damaging cross-examination. A further consequence of direct examination of a character witness directed to the time of the offense is that in rebuttal, the prosecution may only offer contrary character evidence as of such time. If the defendant offers character evidence directed to the time of trial, rebuttal evidence on the subject may be similarly directed.

In the instant case, because of the nature of the questioning on direct examination, the cross-examination was proper. Furthermore, even if "misconduct" (as that term is generally defined—had occurred, defendant could not have been prejudiced by the cross-examination of Dr. Eccleston. The asserted vice of asking a character witness whether he has heard of specific acts of misconduct by the defendant is that it brings before the jury, through an indirect type of hearsay, rumors of such misconduct. In the instant case, long before Dr. Eccleston was cross-examined as to whether he had heard of the acts mentioned by the prosecutor, the prosecutor had already placed evidence of all those acts before the jury as integral parts of the People's case. The jury could not have thought otherwise than that the questions put to Dr. Eccleston on cross-examination merely referred to the same misconduct which the prosecutor was attempting to prove. Indeed, apart from claiming that the $150 payments mentioned by the prosecutor were for reimbursement of automobile expenses, defendant had already admitted to the jury all the acts later cited during the Eccleston cross-examination.

III

PROSECUTOR'S ARGUMENT TO JURY

Defendant contends that the prosecutor's opening argument to the jury constituted prejudicial misconduct in that the prosecutor therein characterized the evidence as showing that Dr. Barber had "realized," in October 1970, that defendant "was tapping him for a little bit more than he wanted her to."

Even if the prosecutor's characterization of what Dr. Barber had "realized" was not a reasonable inference from the evidence, the point does not warrant reversal. It was a matter of minor significance. Furthermore, the record shows that no objection was made by defendant when the prosecutor made substantially the same assertion at four earlier times during his opening argument. Moreover, as previously mentioned, the jury was repeatedly instructed that counsel's statements were not evidence.

Whether Dr. Barber had "realized" that defendant "was tapping him" was collateral to the central issue concerning defendant's having profited financially from Barber's misappropriations—an issue which went not only to defendant's motive for aiding and abetting Barber but also to the substance of the tax charges against defendant. There was substantial evidence that defendant had indeed tapped Barber's illicitly acquired funds, at least during 1970. Consequently, the prosecutor's argument could not have been prejudicial.

The judgment is affirmed.

QUESTIONS

1. Why, in this appeal, should the evidence be "viewed in the light most favorable to the prosecution?" Note that the trial was before a jury, which convicted the defendant.

2. Defendant's counsel incautiously phrased a question to Dr. Eccleston, and the prosecutor took advantage of it on cross-examination. Is this sort of tactical game-playing an inevitable product of the adversary process?

3. Observe that the court says that even if the prosecutor's cross-examination and opening argument were improper they could not have

prejudiced the defendant. This distinction between harmless and reversible error is an important one. On what basis does the appellate court make such a distinction on appeal from a jury verdict (recall that the jury does not state the reasons for its verdict, indicate what evidence influenced it, etc.)?

People v. Battin, 77 Cal.App.3d 635, 143 Cal.Rptr. 731 (1978).

McDANIEL, ASSOCIATE JUSTICE.

The defendant was charged by indictment with theft (Pen.Code, §§ 484–487), misuse of public funds (Pen.Code, § 424, subd. (2)), and presentation of fraudulent claims to the county (Pen.Code, § 72). Trial was by jury. The jury returned verdicts of guilty on the misuse of public funds count, not guilty on the fraudulent claims count, and was hung on the theft count. The court later dismissed the theft count pursuant to the People's motion. Imposition of sentence was suspended, and defendant was given three years' informal probation on the condition that he serve six months in the county jail and pay a $3,500 fine plus penalty assessments. The court then suspended five of the six months of time to be served. Execution of the one month term was stayed pending this appeal. . . .

Defendant now comes before us seeking reversal of his conviction on many grounds.

FACTS

Defendant Robert Battin was elected Supervisor of the First District of Orange County in 1968, and was reelected to the same post in 1972. Early in 1974, while serving as supervisor, he decided to seek the Democratic Party's nomination for Lieutenant Governor of California.

During the months up to the time of the primary (February to June 1974), the defendant spent approximately 15–20 hours per week at his supervisorial office. He spent most of his remaining time at his Santa Ana law office. Because of his incumbency as a county supervisor, the county supplied defendant with four rooms of office space, a Xerox machine, regular typewriters, and a MAG card electric automatic typewriter, all to be used for his work as county supervisor. He was also given a staff of county-paid workers. One of the staffers was attorney Ted Moraitis who served as manager of the supervisorial office. Moraitis testified at trial that he had the job of "co-ordinating office activities and carrying out instructions . . . received from Mr. Battin . . . ."

After he decided to seek the nomination for Lieutenant Governor of California, defendant instructed Moraitis to have members of the supervisorial staff work on the campaign. Thereafter, from time to time throughout the months leading up to the June primary, the defendant would check on the staff's campaign activities or would question Moraitis about their progress. When asked, Moraitis would inform the defendant that the staff was performing campaign work during county working hours (approximately 8 a. m. to 5 p. m.). Just before the primary, the defendant informed the staff that the campaign was to take "priority." Throughout the campaign, the defendant paid no other people to work for his nomination, although he did receive some volunteer help from his girlfriend and her friends.

The atmosphere at the supervisor's office during this period was described at trial by Janet Turner: "There was a lot of secrecy in our office, hiding things from the other offices [that shared space on the defendant's floor], the campaign material being there, us working on county time doing mainly campaign work."

The county Xerox machine was located in an area common to other tenants of the building. Witness Turner described the procedures for Xeroxing off the defendant's campaign material: "When we were copying on the Xerox machine things that pertained to the campaign, we didn't leave the machine to go back to our desk or anything. We didn't want the other offices to see that material in the Xerox machine . . . I was told not to let any of the others see what I was doing." Finally, the campaign material which was stored in the supervisorial office was moved to the defendant's law office at his direction because "he didn't need the Grand Jury snooping around."

In the midst of all this activity, on May 8, 1974, Moraitis read a newspaper article stating that the use of county-paid staff for campaign work could be illegal. He discussed this with defendant, and they decided to remove all members of the supervisor's staff, except Moraitis and Dawn Papp, from the county payroll for the period May 13–28. For those two weeks, they were to be paid from the defendant's personal funds. Papp and Moraitis were kept on the county payroll because Moraitis felt that both were doing "substantially" county work (versus campaign work), yet both continued to perform campaign activities. Even after the remaining staff members returned to the county payroll after May 28, the defendant instructed them, as already noted, to give the campaign effort "priority." This effort continued until "thank you" letters were sent to the defendant's supporters after the June 4 primary. Those letters announced that the defendant would run for State Senator from the 37th Senate District.

* * *

Finally, we turn to the two arguments which defendant has emphasized most throughout his appeal. He contends that his conviction should be reversed because he was discriminatorily selected for prosecution and because a conflict of interest prevented the district attorney's office from properly performing its duties during the investigation and prosecution of the case. Both of these grounds were urged by defendant in his pretrial motion to dismiss the indictment. The trial court responded to the contentions by concluding that "[t]he action taken by the District Attorney constitutes in the Court's judgment reasonable law enforcement, and hence, the showing is inadequate to rebut the presumption that official duty has been properly and Constitutionally exercised." The court also found that there was no invidious discriminatory prosecution. Accordingly, the motion to dismiss the indictment was denied.

5. *Discriminatory Prosecution*

Discriminatory prosecution constitutes adequate grounds for reversing a conviction when the defendant proves: "(1) 'that he has been deliberately singled out for prosecution on the basis of some invidious criterion;' and (2) that 'the prosecution would not have been pursued except for the discriminatory design of the prosecuting authorities.' " The discrimination must be "intentional and purposeful." Further, defendant must carry the burden of proof that he has been deliberately singled out in order to overcome the presumption that "[prosecutorial] dut[ies have] been properly, and constitutionally exercised." With these rules in mind, we examine defendant's contentions and the evidence adduced at the hearing on the motion to dismiss the indictment.

Defendant attempted to portray himself as the innocent victim of District Attorney Hicks' deliberate scheme to "catch him" in some illegal activity. In this case, the activity was defendant's use of his staff for campaign work. He makes much of the fact that no other office holder has *ever* been prosecuted for such activity. He alleges that his prosecution was part of a systematic effort by the district attorney to prosecute members of a local political organization (of which defendant was a member) for a variety of crimes. He further alleges that those officials associated with the rival political group (of which Hicks is a member) committed similar acts, yet escaped prosecution at the hands of the district attorney. Finally, he contends that his prosecution was precipitated by personal animosity, which had been brought on by on eight-year long dispute between himself and Hicks.

As to his first claim, defendant is incorrect in stating that no other official has ever been prosecuted for using his staff in a political campaign. In People v. Sperl, which was mentioned before, the defendant was convicted for utilizing county marshals to make campaign telephone calls in behalf of the local incumbent. Also cited above was People v. Holtzendorff, in which a Housing Authority official was prosecuted for using nineteen staff members to work on the campaign of an office holder. Therefore, defendant's argument that his prosecution was discriminatory in that no one else has been charged for a similar act is groundless.

As to his allegation that District Attorney Hicks deliberately prosecuted members of one political group, while allowing those of the rival group to escape punishment for similar acts, the evidence presented at the hearing revealed that few members of the latter group were prosecuted, while several of the former were. However, evidence also indicated that investigations were conducted of members of *both* groups, *without discrimination*, whenever complaints were filed against them, and, for a variety of seemingly sound reasons (i.e., insufficient evidence to convict) many members of the latter group were never brought to trial. While it might have been possible for the trial court to believe that a systematic plan of discriminatory prosecution was in operation, the court's review of the evidence "fail[ed] to reveal . . . that the District Attorney embarked upon a systematic program of intentional and purposeful invidious discrimination." We are required to accept the trial court's finding because it is supported by substantial evidence. This position is further bolstered by the fact that we are unpersuaded that defendant has met the heavy burden of proof placed on anyone who attempts to use the defense of discriminatory prosecution.

Finally, defendant claims that the animosity between himself and Hicks brought about his prosecution. The evidence indicates that there was a certain amount of friction between the two. They were, indeed, members of rival political groups, and from 1968 to 1975, did occasionally clash over the policies of the district attorney's office. That friction seemed strongest in 1975, when one of the leaders of defendant's group came under investigation by the district attorney's office. In June of that year, defendant and a number of other supervisors voted to have 22 investigators transferred from the district attorney's office to the sheriff's department. This action alarmed the district attorney, who believed that defendant and other board members were controlled by the individual who was then under investigation. District Attorney Hicks believed that the transfer was a deliberate attempt to stymie the investigation of this individual. Thereafter, defendant and Hicks exchanged public insults and Hicks publicly announced his suspicions about defendant's motive in voting for the transfer. Our task here is to decide if the friction that existed between defendant and the district attorney brought about defendant's prosecution. This can best be accomplished by reviewing the evidence relative to how the prosecution began and how it proceeded.

In 1975, Michael Capizzi served as director of the "Special Operations" Division of the district attorney's office. One department in "Special Operations," called "Special Assignment," handled investigations of office holders. Capizzi testified at the hearing that "Special Assignment" investigations usually began with private citizen complaints or leads from various sources. Witness accounts of the offenses would then be taken and verified, and the "law" on the subject would be checked. Capizzi usually made the final decision to take a case to the grand jury. Hicks did not evaluate the "Special Assignment" cases, but he was kept informed of their progress.

The mid-1970's were busy times for the "Special Assignment" office. Many local officials, *on both sides of the political fence,* were being investigated and/or prosecuted for a variety of offenses. Among them were two members of the political group to which the district attorney belonged. Another investigation by that office was based on a complaint against the Orange County Assessor's Office. It resulted in the prosecution of 11 officials and employees for using county time to distribute election materials. Apparently, no one was safe from the vigilant eye of the "Special Assignment" office.

In early July 1975, Robert Dougherty contacted Hicks with the information about defendant. Hicks immediately turned the matter over to Capizzi, giving him no instructions relative to the case. Thereafter, the district attorney took no active role in the investigation or prosecution, except that he was informed of its progress and he was consulted once before the case was submitted to the grand jury. After hearing Ms. Papp's account, Capizzi reached a "preliminary analysis," if she was telling the truth, that the case was of sufficient magnitude to be brought before the grand jury. Capizzi then wrote to Jack Winkler of the Attorney General's Office to request the assistance of that office in the investigation and prosecution of the defendant. The Attorney General's Office sent three investigators to Orange County, but declined to assume the prosecution of the case because the district attorney's "past track record had been excellent in fairly and impartially investigating and prosecuting cases, and [the Attorney General's Office was] quite sure that [the district attorney's office] handled this one in the same fashion."

Before deciding to take the case to the grand jury, Capizzi discussed it with Hicks, two other members of the district attorney's staff, and investigators from the district attorney's and Attorney General's Offices.

At the hearing, Capizzi testified that he was aware of the differences between the defendant and Hicks, but that he was not at all influenced by this in his decision to bring the case before the grand jury. Hicks also testified, although he and defendant disagreed about policy and politics, that he had no personal animosity toward him.

The trial court found that no deliberate discrimination had taken place, and that the investigation and prosecution were proper. In our view, the above recited facts constitute substantial evidence to support the court's position. Therefore, we cannot agree with defendant that he was discriminatorily selected for prosecution.

Finally, defendant contends that the differences of opinion between himself and Hicks constituted a conflict of interest which tainted his prosecution. We have already discussed the presence of substantial evidence to the contrary. The investigation and prosecution proceeded as did most others in the "Special Assignment" office. There was no evidence that the district attorney "went after" the defendant in an effort to "get him" for some offense. In fact, Capizzi passed up three prior opportunities to prosecute defendant for trespassing and falsification of a letter. In addition, both Hicks and Capizzi denied being influenced by the confrontations between the district attorney and defendant. Such confrontations can be expected when one person or body holds the purse-strings of another. By no stretch of the imagination can we view the entanglements between Hicks and defendant here to be of the number or magnitude as those that existed in *Greer*. We therefore agree with the trial court that the prosecution was fair.

The judgment is affirmed.

QUESTIONS AND NOTES

1. How do you feel about prosecutorial discretion when the potential defendant is a publicly elected or politically appointed official? Suppose Battin had won the nomination and been elected Lieutenant Governor, is it less likely that he would have been prosecuted?

2. Europeans generally disapprove of prosecutorial discretion and plea-bargaining and believe that their own criminal process is free of them. Recent empirical research (which has been challenged) suggests that similar things do occur in Europe, although in different ways and, in all probability, on a smaller scale. See Abraham Goldstein and Martin Marcus, "The Myth of Judicial Supervision in Three 'Inquisitional Systems': France, Italy, and Germany," 87 Yale Law Journal, p. 240, 1977; John H. Langbein and Lloyd L. Weinreb, "Continental Criminal Procedure: 'Myth' and Reality," 87 Yale Law Journal, p. 1549, 1978; Abraham Goldstein and Martin Marcus, "Comment on Continental Criminal Procedure," 87 Yale Law Journal, p. 1570, 1978.

3. Some of Battin's arguments on appeal (omitted in this excerpt) were insubstantial, at best. Still, a good deal of expensive time and energy (of prosecutors, judges and their staffs) was spent in hearing and disposing of them. Would you favor limitation of defendants' rights to impose unnecessary costs on taxpayers in this way? How would you go about it, consistently with due concern for the protection of innocent defendants?

4. Persons convicted of violating § 424 or 504 are disqualified from holding public office and are also subject to fine and imprisonment. Might there be cases in which the primary purpose of the prosecution is to remove the official from office? Might that have been one purpose in the Battin case?

5. Battin's effective penalty was a fine of $3500 and one month in the county jail. He probably spent more than that, in money and time, on the appeal. Can you suggest why he decided to appeal?

6. Finally, what is your opinion of the penalty? Is it severe enough to meet the objectives of the criminal law? More generally, in the current debate over allegedly too-lenient sentencing (leaving to one side the capital pun-

ishment question, which raises special problems) where do you stand? Should penalties be more severe? Should they be fixed or indeterminate? Should judges have the power to suspend sentences?

Chapter 14

EMBEZZLEMENT BY A PUBLIC OFFICIAL
IN EGYPTIAN LAW

Raymond Baker, Egypt's Uncertain Revolution Under Nasser and Sadat, Cambridge: Harvard University Press, 1978, pp. 205–206.

* * *

Records of the corruption of the cooperatives by the more prosperous and influential peasants have appeared intermittently over the last decade. The most dramatic revelations came in the wake of the murder of Salah Hussein, an activist of the Arab Socialist Union in the village of Kamchiche (about fifty miles north of Cairo) on May 1, 1966, allegedly by members of the large landowning family that dominated the village. The government organized a Committee for the Liquidation of Feudalism, which launched an attack on "agrarian feudalists." The committee uncovered some startling evidence of abuses by the remaining large landowners. One family was revealed to have succeeded in retaining 2,320 feddans, while another was discovered to hold 1,200 feddans. As a result of the committee's activity, the capital and possessions of eighty-eight large landowners from seventeen provinces were sequestered; the landowners themselves were required to leave their villages and live in the cities. Twenty-five thousand feddans of illegally held land were uncovered, and by June of 1966, 239 village umdahs had been removed for their complicity with the large landowners.

A comprehensive survey of the problems of the cooperatives appeared in *al-Ahram al-Iqtisadi* of May 15, 1968. It was reported that through 1968 approximately three hundred boards of directors were dissolved by the Ministry of Agriculture for "causes ranging from misuse of influence and embezzlement to dealing on the black market."

Taking the province of al-Manufiyyah as a case study, the *al-Ahram al-Iqtisadi* report provided a detailed view of the nature of the corruption in the cooperatives:

The cooperative society of Mit Khalaf village, the report revealed, was turned into a family affair. One of its officials appointed five members of his immediate family to positions in the cooperative: three as watchmen, one as a mechanic, and a fifth as a cooperative treasurer.

In the cooperative society at Mit Mas'us one of the members of the board of directors had taken $1,570 from the cooperative fund without appropriate justification: he used the funds for investment in

420

trade. When asked to return it, he is reported to have delayed doing so for months.

Similarly, embezzlements were reported from the cooperative societies at Kafr al-Batanun ($415) and Mit Khaqan ($460).

On a much larger scale, an investigation at the office of the largest town in al-Manufiyyah showed that members of the board of directors had misappropriated about $11,500 for use in trade, the purchase of livestock, and other forms of business.

Other investigations established the fact that members of the boards of directors of some cooperative societies in the province sold insecticides on the black market, divided the profits among themselves, and then sprayed the peasants' fields with diluted insecticides.

These examples reveal the nature of the general trend: many members of the boards of directors gain possession of the profits of the cooperatives and use them in trade for their own benefit. The offense is compounded by the fact that by so doing they naturally deprive the peasants of the legitimate and intended use of those funds.

A. THE TRADITIONAL SYSTEMS

1. Background

NOTE

We know of at least two dispute settlement processes in the pre-Islamic (or *urf*) law tradition: the village council pattern and the pattern of retaliation (*qisas*) and its close relation, compensation (*diya*), a monetary amount paid to the victim (or his family) by the offender in lieu of retaliation.

The Fakhouri article describes a relatively contemporary council, but undoubtedly reflects traditional patterns of Egypt and possibly of the Bedouin. For additional data on the village structure, see James B. Mayfield, Rural Politics in Nasser's Egypt, a Quest for Legitimacy, Austin: University of Texas Press, 1971.

Hani Fakhouri, Kafr El-Elow—An Egyptian Village in Transition, New York: Holt, Rinehart and Winston, 1972, pp. 109–111.

THE SETTLEMENT OF DISPUTES

Urf Law (Customary Law)

* * *

According to *urf* law, each member of a clan is responsible for the welfare of all the other members, in return for which he receives assistance and protection from his clan. Vulnerability to death, physical harm or social penalties for violations of *urf* law also has a collective character in that any member of the aggressor clan may be killed in reprisal for the acts of a kinsman. However, the immediate kin of an injured person always have the option of accepting monetary compensation (*diyya*) through the tribal court in lieu of physical revenge, especially if the injury was inflicted unintentionally. . . .

The Tribal Court—*Majliss il-urfi*

Whenever a conflict arises, regardless of its type or cause, several elderly and prominent men in the village usually interfere to freeze hostilities by suggesting that the case be referred to the *majliss il-urfi* for settlement. The injured party then nominates three houses as potential sites for the hearing, one of which is to be chosen by the offender. If the offender refuses to accept any of the three, however, members of the *majliss* nominate several houses from which the two conflicting parties select one that is mutually acceptable.

After an agreement has been reached concerning the place for the hearing, the *majliss* determines the amount of the *rizka* or *sutra*. This is the money paid to the owner of the home agreed upon as the site for the hearing, the amount varying according to the nature of the case and the number of people invited to observe the proceedings and to serve as witnesses: usually, the heads of prominent families in the village and a few people from neighboring villages. Especially in cases of blood feud, the police commissioner or the governor of the *mouhafaza* may be invited to attend the *majliss il-urfi*. The *rizka* money is expected to cover all the expenses for food and entertainment incurred by the host, plus serve as compensation for his efforts at offering hospitality. Both parties in the conflict under investigation give *rizka* money to their host before the hearing takes place, but after the hearing the loser forfeits his contribution, while the winner receives a refund.

The number of members constituting the *majliss* for a particular case, as well as the mode of their selection, depends upon the nature of the conflict to be settled. Most commonly, both parties in the dispute select the members of the *majliss* by choosing an equal number from their two lists of nominees. The judges selected in this manner then meet to decide upon another judge whose role will become especially important if the original members reach a deadlock in attempting to settle a case. Objectivity is considered an essential attribute of all members of the *majliss*; indeed, their reputations are seriously impaired if they fail to maintain impartiality in every case. Unjust behavior is condemned by the Koran in the following verses:

> O believers, be you securers of justice, witnesses for God, even though it be against yourselves, or your parents and kinsmen, whether the man be rich or poor; God stands closest to either.

Then follow not caprice, so as to swerve; for if you twist or turn, God is aware of the things you do.　(Koran, 4:134–135)

On the date set for the hearing by the heads of the disputants' clans, both they and any other kin who may be involved in the case meet with members of the *majliss* and invited guests at the designated site.　After both the accused and the accuser swear on the Koran that they will not give false information to members of the *majliss*, their testimony is heard and members of the *majliss* interrogate them to clarify certain points.　Then the *majliss* adjourns to another room to arrive at a verdict; if the alleged offender is found guilty, a decision is made regarding the amount of money which he should pay the offended party.

Before publicly announcing its verdict, the *majliss* informs the heads of both disputants' clan of its decision in the case.　Moreover, if a fine is imposed, the amount announced publicly by the *majliss* is always larger than that which has been agreed upon privately, because guests at the hearing generally prevail upon the offended party's family to reduce the amount of money which they will demand from the offender's clan in honor of the governor of the *mouhafaza*, President Nasser, or some other person.　The *majliss* usually assigns a *kafeel* "co-signer" to each of the disputants to make certain that the verdict is executed, the persons performing this role are prominent residents of the village who have been nominated and selected by both parties in the case.　The verdict is usually executed without complications, but should any member of either disputant's family or clan challenge the *majliss'* decision, he would be publicly ostracized from his clan and no longer given support or protection in time of need.

At the conclusion of the hearing, the offender and the offended shake hands, kiss each other's heads, and swear on the Koran that they will forget what has happened.　Then the guests, members of the *majliss*, and the parties involved in the case all join together in eating a meal which their host has prepared.　According to Islamic belief, the judges constituting the *majliss*, and consequently playing the mediator role (*waseet*) in the solution of disputes, will be rewarded by Allah.　They also achieve high status and respect in the villages where they live for this part in restoring harmonious relationships between individuals and families.

QUESTIONS

1. What are the social prerequisites for systems of this character to be an effective means of enforcing behavioral standards?

2. Does the village system have advantages over more formal state-oriented systems?

3. What are the safeguards protecting the defendant?

4.   What is the likelihood that a village official will actually be prosecuted for corruption under this system?

2. The *Sharia* Reforms

NOTE

The *sharia* defined a new category of unalterable *hadd* punishments for specific crimes against God, but surrounded these punishments with new procedural safeguards. It also carried over the *qisas* and *diya* punishments and, in addition, defined a new category of more discretionary punishment, *tazir*. See Mahmood M. Mostafa, Principes De Droit Pénal Des Pays Arabes, Paris: Librairie Générale de Droit et de Jurisprudence, 1972, pp. 9–11.

The Koran, 24:2–14, (N.J. Dawood Trans., 4th ed.), Harmondsworth, Middlesex: Penguin, 1976.

*   *   *

The adulterer and the adulteress shall each be given a hundred lashes. Let no pity for them cause you to disobey Allah, if you truly believe in Allah and the Last Day; and let their punishment be witnessed by a number of believers.

The adulterer may marry only an adulteress or an idolatress; and the adulteress may marry only an adulterer or an idolater. True believers are forbidden such marriages.

Those that defame honourable women and cannot produce four witnesses shall be given eighty lashes. No testimony of theirs shall be admissible, for they are great transgressors—except those among them that afterwards repent and mend their ways. Allah is forgiving and merciful.

If a man accuses his wife but has no witnesses except himself, he shall swear four times by Allah that his charge is true, calling down upon himself the curse of Allah if he is lying. But if his wife swears four times by Allah that his charge is false and calls down His curse upon herself if it be true, she shall receive no punishment.

But for Allah's grace and mercy, His wisdom and forgiveness, this would never have been revealed to you.

Those who invented that slander were a number of your own people. Do not regard it as a misfortune, for it has proved an advantage. Each one of them shall be punished according to his crime. As for him who had the greater share in it, his punishment shall be terrible indeed.

When you heard it, why did the faithful, men and women, not think well of their own people, and say: "This is an evident falsehood"? Why did they not produce four witnesses? If they could not produce any witnesses, then they were surely lying in the sight of Allah.

But for Allah's grace and mercy towards you in this life and in the next, you would have been sternly punished for what you did. You carried with your tongues and uttered what your mouths did not know. You may have thought it a trifle, but in the sight of Allah it was a grave offence.

NOTE

This section was promulgated at a time when the Prophet's wife, Aisha, was accused of adultery.

Satya Sangar, Crime and Punishment in Mughal India, Delhi, India: Sterling Publishers, 1967, pp. 26, 28–30.

In Muslim law, punishments are divided into *Hadd, Qisās, Diya and Ta'zîr.*

HADD—Hadd signified boundary or limit, barrier or obstruction. In the *Qur'ān*, it is always found in plural, meaning the limits laid down by God, *i.e.*, the provision of the Law. *Hadd* is that punishment which has been exactly defined in the *Qur'ān* or the Hadîs by the Prophet. This is an unalterable punishment prescribed by canon law and is considered *haqq Allāh* or right of God.

Under this category were included the crimes of adultery, fornication and false accusation of adultery (*qazf*), apostasy, drinking of wine, theft and highway robbery.

QISĀS—Qisās means retaliation. It was of two kinds. *Qisās fi'l-nafs* or blood vengeance which is applied in cases of killing. The other is called as *Qisās fi-ma dun al-nafs* and applied to cases which do not prove fatal.

If a person committed a wilful murder or inflicted a wound which did not prove fatal, he was liable to *qisās* or retaliation. *Wali* or next-of-kin of the slain person, had the right to kill the offender under certain circumstances and under the supervision of the judge. The judge had to see that the slain person was not a descendant of the slayer and that the murderer was in full possession of his faculties and had reached the age of discretion. *Qisās* took place only if the next-of-kin demanded it. In case there are more than one claimant for the blood of the offender, all must be unanimous in their demand.

Although the punishment was fixed by the law, it could be remitted by the person offended or by the heirs of the murdered person.

DIYA—Diya means a sum extracted for any offence upon the person, in consideration for the claim of *Qisās*, or retaliation, not being insisted upon. *Diya* or *Aql* was compensation paid by one who had committed homicide or wounded another.

In case the legal conditions necessary to render the *qisās* possible were not present, or when the heirs of murdered person entered into a composition with the murdered for a certain sum, retaliation was remitted for *diya* or blood-money.

* * *

TA'ZĪR—Literally *ta'zir* means 'to censure or repel'. This punishment, intended to reform the culprit (*li'l-tashhir*), was not known to the Qur'ân and found its way into Muslim law at a comparatively later date. According to *fiqh*-books, *ta'zir* was inflicted for such offences which had no *hadd* punishment or *kaffārā* [atonement] prescribed for them, whether it was a question of disobedience of God or of crime against man.

The main object of this punishment being reformation, the degree of punishment varied with the social status of the accused. According to one writer, men were classified systematically for this purpose: "In the case of great men and notabilities it was a discreet warning uttered by a delegate of the *qāzi; fuqha* and such-like were called into his presence and admonished; merchants went to prison, and the common people received the lash."

While awarding punishment for this crime, the judge exercised his own discretion. It could be any thing from a public reprimand to whipping or banishment. In case of the divine law he could even remit the *ta'zir*, but not in case of crime against man.

Personal confession by the offender or the evidence by two witnesses could be sufficient ground for awarding the punishment.

QUESTIONS

1. When is retaliation (*qisas*) an effective form of criminal law? Is it adapted to the life of the Arabic Peninsula in Muhammed's time? Can you find similar systems in the contemporary West at either the domestic or the international levels? When do they work well?

2. American law scholars like to say that the criminal law serves four purposes: deterrence, retribution, prevention (as directly through incarceration), and rehabilitation. Are these categories adequate to describe the functions of *qisas* and *diya*, the components of Islamic criminal law that most directly reflect pre-existing law? If not, how would you supplement or modify them?

3. Are the categories adequate to describe the functions of *hadd*? Again, how might you supplement or modify them?

4. As noted above, in Islamic criminal law the personal claim of the victim against the criminal is closely associated with the social (or Divine) claim against the criminal. What can be said for or against making such a close association in criminal procedure?

5. As you may recall from the introductory chapter, the dominant Islamic philosophical position is that laws are the way they are because God arbitrarily made them that way. There is also a traditional philosophical position that causality amounts to no more than the regularities we happen to observe as God remakes the universe from instant to instant. Further,

the concept of predestination is strong for many Islamic philosophers. Does the *sharia's* criminal law appear to you to be consistent with these philosophical positions? Do you sense any similar problems in Western views of criminal responsibility?

3. Theft Offenses

The Koran, 5: 38–40 (N.J. Dawood Trans., 4th ed.), Hammond-sworth, Middlesex: Penguin, 1976.

* * *

As for the man or woman who is guilty of theft, cut off their hands to punish them for their crimes. That is the punishment enjoined by Allah. He is mighty and wise. But whoever repents and mends his ways after committing evil shall be pardoned by Allah. Allah is forgiving and merciful.

Do you not know that to Allah belongs the kingdom of the heavens and the earth? He punishes whom He will and forgives whom He pleases. Allah has power over all things.

Joseph Schacht, An Introduction to Islamic Law, London: Oxford University Press, 1964, pp. 179–180.

(*d*) Theft (*sarika*). *Sarika* occurs if a *mukallaf*, including a slave, takes by stealth something of the value of at least ten dirhams, in which he has neither the right of ownership (*milk*) nor *shubhat milk*, out of custody (*hirz*); this last consists either of keeping it in a properly secured place or of the presence of a custodian. The stipulation of *milk* or *shubhat milk* excludes everything that belongs to the class of things in which the absence of the ownership is possible, therefore everything that is found in Islamic territory without an owner such as wood, grass, fishes, birds, as long as the acquisition of ownership in it is not obvious, e.g. wood that has been fashioned into a door; assimilated to this are fruits which have not been harvested and easily perishable things such as meat. The same stipulation excludes things which cannot be objects of property, such as a free person, also wine and musical instruments; assimilated to this are things which on account of their holiness are not *in commercio*, such as copies of the Koran and also books on religious sciences. It finally excludes things of which the culprit is a part-owner, including public property, or to which he has a title, including the counter-value of a claim. The stipulation of stealth excludes open robbery (*nahb*) and snatching things unawares (*ikhtilās*, used of pickpockets, &c.). The stipulation of custody excludes theft from a near relative (*mahram*), from a house which the accused had been permitted to enter, and embezzlement (*khiyāna*). The stipulation of "taking" implies that the object must have been removed from the *hirz*; a thief who is caught red-handed within the *hirz*, e.g. within the house, is therefore not subject to *hadd* according to some, *hadd* does not even take place if the thief from inside the *hirz* hands the object to an accomplice outside. If there are several thieves, *hadd* takes place only if the value of the object, when divided by their number, at least equals ten dirhams. The punishment consists of cutting off the right hand and in the case of a second theft, the left foot; in the case of further thefts, and also if the other hand or other foot are not fully usable, the thief is merely imprisoned until he shows repentance. The *hadd* punishment excludes pecuniary liability; only if the stolen object is still in existence is it returnable to the owner.

QUESTIONS

1. Why might embezzlement not be considered as deserving *hadd* punishment? Does the distinction between embezzlement and other theft offenses seem likely to arise from the same sources as in the West?

2. Did the *sharia*'s system provide a complete and effective criminal law?

3. Could there be embezzlement in a Bedouin society? What could Islamic jurisprudes do as society changed?

4. Procedure

Uriel Heyd, Studies in Old Ottoman Criminal Law, London: Oxford University Press, 1973, pp. 244–246, 251–252, 257–258. Footnotes omitted.

6. Procedure. The procedure of an Ottoman criminal trial as reflected in the cadis' registers seems to have been quite simple and generally in conformity with the well-known rules of Muslim religious law.

First the plaintiff stated his case, and demanded that the defendant be interrogated, that the latter's statement or reply be recorded, and that punishment be meted out to him in accordance with the *sharī'a* or with the *sharī'a* and the *kānūn* (secular law). If the plaintiff was an official, he sometimes also asked for the fine due to him, while a private citizen requested retaliation, blood-money, damages, the return of the stolen property, or the like.

After the plaintiff had finished his statement the cadi asked the defendant to reply to the charge. If he admitted . . . his guilt of his own free will . . ., his confession was recorded in the cadi's register. In some cases the criminal explained his offence by saying "*seytāna uydum*", "I yielded to the devil".

The number of cases in which, according to the law-court registers, the defendant acknowledged his guilt is amazingly large. The reasons may have been a relatively high degree of truthfulness even among criminals, their reluctance to perjure themselves when required to take an oath (see below), their awe of the cadi as representing both religion and the Sultan, the fear of being subjected to torture, or a combination of several of these motives.

A defendant who later retracted his confession was, in the cadi's view (in accordance with the *shari'a* rule), not liable to the *hadd* penalties, such as the amputation of a thief's hand; but the secular authorities might sentence him to servitude on the galleys.

If the defendant denied the accusation, the plaintiff or prosecutor was asked by the cadi to produce legal evidence for his charge. In accordance with the requirements of the *shari'a*, the most important evidence was the testimony of witnesses.

In the trial of a Muslim, generally the testimony of two male Muslim witnesses was required. The testimony of a non-Muslim subject (*zimmī*) was, with certain exceptions, only accepted against another infidel, and that of a non-Muslim foreign resident only against another *müste'min* [non-Muslim foreign resident] not even against a *zimmī*.

Before accepting their testimony, the cadi had to establish that the witnesses were "of good character." Among the many people whose way of life made them, according to Ottoman *müftis* [legal advisers to the *qadis*) unfit for testifying in any lawsuit or trial were the tax-farmers and the men who co-operated, or made agreements, with the executive officers. Interestingly, Ebu 's-Su'ūd rules that an infidel who does not go to church (or synagogue) is not competent to testify. In the opinion of another *müftī*, the testimony of a peasant against a feudal lord is acceptable 'unless there is some other impediment.

According to another *fetvā*, the plaintiff may testify as witness only in cases where a "right of God" has been violated.

While the *shari'a* generally does not prescribe that witnesses must take the oath, several Ottoman *müftis* ruled that 'in our days' the cadis might administer it if they considered it necessary. (This is another example of a rule of the *siyāsa shar'iya* procedure for secular judges being adopted by the cadis.) Entries in the court registers show that cadis did in fact do so.

In the view of the *shari'a*, a Muslim is neither legally nor morally obliged to bear witness against a criminal who has violated a "right of God", for which he is liable to a *hadd* penalty. The Ottomans even regarded it as humane not to assist in such cases in the conviction of a fellow Muslim. It is for this reason that the Ottoman Criminal Code does not impose a fine on a person who fails to inform the cadi of a case of fornication, but does fine anyone who fails to do so in a case of theft: the former is only a "right of God", while the latter also violates a "right of man", since if a thief is not convicted the injured person may lose the chance of recovering the stolen article or obtaining compensation for it.

* * *

8. Exculpatory Oaths and "Compurgation". If the prosecutor or plaintiff could not produce witnesses to prove his allegation or if the witnesses' evidence did not meet the requirements of the *shari'a*, the cadi often acted in accordance with the *kānūn*: he inquired whether the defendant had a criminal record or called in the defendant's neighbours and asked them to testify to his character and conduct. In many cases the standing of a person in his community as reflected in such a testimony seems to have been a material factor in the decision reached.

When the defendant's guilt could not be proved and he had no criminal record or bad reputation, the cadi often asked him, on the demand of the plaintiff, to clear himself by swearing that he was innocent. This procedure is laid down in the Ottoman Criminal Code, but a later correction limits it, in accordance with the *shari'a*, to crimes that violate the "rights of men". Its application in cases, such as fornication, where a right of God is infringed and the *shari'a*, imposes a *hadd* penalty is forbidden.

When it occurred that a person was found killed at or near a village, the next of kin, if he was unable to prove anyone's guilt, sometimes demanded that fifty men chosen by him from among the villagers should swear that they had had nothing to do with the crime and did not know the murderer. This is the well-known *kasāma* procedure of the *shari'a*.

A Muslim took the oath on the Kur'ān, a Christian on the Gospels and a Jew on the Old Testament. According to a seventeenth-century European observer, the declarant first washed his hands and then swore with his left hand placed under the holy book and his right hand upon it.

After taking the oath (or if at the last moment the claimant absolved him from taking it), the defendant was usually acquitted and the plaintiff (but not, it seems, an official who had brought the action) was sentenced to a punishment for false accusation. . . .

However, the cadis' registers of the late fifteenth and the sixteenth centuries show that in an astonishingly large number of cases the defendants refused to take the oath although they thereby brought upon themselves conviction and punishment. The reasons for this may be partly the same as those which, as suggested above, led many accused persons to acknowledge their guilt from the beginning.

* * *

II. *APPEAL*

. . . According to the *shari'a*, the sentence, including the death sentence, of any cadi was final, and in general, unless it was contrary to the law, no appeal could be made against it. Consequently, no trial could be heard in an Ottoman cadi's court if the case had previously been examined and a sentence given except by special order of the Sultan. Even in that case the verdict was not subject to change provided that the sentence had been passed in accordance with the *shari'a*.

In practice, however, a revision of the sentence could be, and often was, made by the governors and by high officials in the capital. It goes without saying that their decisions were usually not based on strictly legalistic considerations.

Herbert Liebesny, The Law of the Near and Middle East, Albany: The State University of New York Press, 1975, p. 253.

The classical jurists of Islam accepted in principle the rule that the plaintiff had to prove his case through witnesses and that the defendant could clear himself through an oath. Many refinements and detailed provisions were worked out, however, and the various schools differ on some specifics. Generally, the Hanefite rules are stricter than those of the Malikites and Shafi'ites. As a rule, the defendant must take the oath if the plaintiff cannot prove his case. The oath has to be requested by the other party, but the defendant is ordered to swear by the *qadi*. The request by one party that the other take the oath is called tendering the oath. If the party to whom the oath is tendered does not want to take the oath, he can frequently retender it. In Islamic law, the Malekite and Shafi'ite schools permit retendering the oath, the Hanefite school does not. There are certain cases where the plaintiff rather than the defendant takes the oath. Thus the Shafi'ite and Malekite schools permit the plaintiff to take an oath in suits concerning property if he can produce only one witness.

It is a general characteristic of the decisive oath in practically all systems that, with few exceptions, it terminates the case and that even proven perjury does not constitute valid grounds for reopening it. This latter rule is due to the belief that a false oath will be punished by God, as expressly stated in Roman law as well as Islamic law.

NOTE

The oath mentioned in the above excerpts is a form of decisive oath, one that decides the case, contrasting sharply with the evidentiary oath taken by an American witness before testifying. This decisive oath is widely spread among Near Eastern and Roman legal systems, and still survives in French law. The historical relationships among these different decisive oath traditions are unknown.

The oath was not the only way to save the *qadi* from the burden of having to make a choice among conflicting testimony. There was also an extensive structure of presumptions. For example, if A wanted to prove that X was in good health at a certain time and B wanted to prove that X was sick at that time, A's evidence would be accepted in the absence of any other information, for a person is supposed to continue in good health. This use of presumptions supplemented an understanding of evidence that rejected the concept of falsehood; evidence could not be evidence unless true, and the court could not admit falsehood, so conflicting evidence could not be heard. See Abdur Rahim, The Principles of Muhammadan Jurisprudence, London: Luzac & Company, 1911, p. 350.

Noel Coulson, Conflicts and Tensions in Islamic Jurisprudence, Chicago: University of Chicago Press, 1969, p. 65.

* * *

The system was, I think, a conscious attempt by the jurists who formulated it to absolve the judge as far as possible from any direct responsibility for a miscarriage of the divine law. Because the testimony of the witnesses or the oath was decisive and binding upon the judge, and because it was merely the duty of the judge to apply the law to the facts as thereby established, it was as though the responsibility for a wrong conclusion as to the facts lay with the parties themselves. The fear of a miscarriage of the law was a very real one for the Muslim scholars and was the principal reason for their declared aversion to judicial office. An English Chancery judge, referring to the difficulties which confront the judge when he is attempting to construe the intention of a testator from the words in his will, is alleged to have said: "I shudder to think that in the hereafter I shall have to meet those testators whose wishes on earth have been frustrated by my judgments." There awaited the Muslim *qãdi* who misconstrued the religious law a much more serious situation in the world to come—namely, the wrath of the Lawgiver himself.

QUESTIONS

1. The Western analogue of the *sharia's* decisive oath and character investigation is cross-examination. Under what conditions is one or the other of these two approaches likely to be more effective?

2. In Western law, the concept of burden-of-proof is used in two ways. First, in the absence of any evidence, the party bearing the burden of proof loses. Second, in the presence of conflicting testimony, the party bearing the burden of proof loses unless the fact finder is convinced of that party's position "beyond a reasonable doubt" in a criminal case of "by a preponderance of the evidence" in a civil case. Are the presumptions of *sharia* law significantly different from the burden of proof concepts of the West? Why might the *sharia* have made the structure particularly elaborate?

3. Why might a society seek to remove the responsibility for fact-finding from its judges?

4. What are the risks associated with the decisive oath? Why might it survive?

5. How faithful is the *sharia* system to the approach defined by the Prophet in the Quran passage quoted at the beginning of this section?

6. Is the use of torture mentioned in the Heyd excerpt consistent with the *sharia*?

7. Assuming the *sharia* was actually followed, was it fair? What were the relative risks of an innocent defendant being found guilty and a guilty defendant found innocent?

B. PRACTICAL SUPPLEMENTATION OF THE SHARIA SYSTEM

NOTE

Not surprisingly, the *sharia* system was supplemented at both the official and unofficial levels.

Noel Coulson, Conflicts and Tensions in Islamic Jurisprudence, Chicago: University of Chicago Press, 1969, pp. 66–69.

It is essentially because of the idealistic scheme of procedure and evidence and the self-imposed limitations of the Shari'a as a practical system of law that there have existed in Islam since early medieval times jurisdictions other than that of the *qāḍi*'s court. The *qāḍis* had never formed an independent judiciary in the true sense of the term. Appointed by the political ruler and subject to dismissal by him, they exercised their judicial office as his delegates. And when, because of their allegiance to the idealistic Shari'a doctrine, their administration of justice proved defective, the ruler simply appointed other delegates.

This extra-Shari'a jurisdiction assumed a variety of forms. There was, for example, the summary jurisdiction in petty commercial affairs of the inspector of the market place; and of the chief of police in criminal cases. Another judicial officer was appointed solely to resolve cases which the *qāḍis* failed to resolve because they could come to no proper decision on the basis of the evidence offered. But the most important of these alternative jurisdictions was that of the official known as the "Master of Complaints," or *Ṣāḥib al-Maẓālim*. He came to have an extensive jurisdiction in those spheres where the speedy and effective administration of justice was of particular concern to the political authority—especially in criminal cases and in matters of land law. In a sense the various subordinate judicial officers I have mentioned may all be subsumed under the collective description of *Maẓālim* jurisdiction. The common feature of the various forms of *Maẓālim* jurisdiction was the latitude of discretion they enjoyed in matters of procedure and evidence. Their duty was simply to resolve litigation in the most effective way and on the basis of the best evidence available. While the *qāḍis* became identified as the servants of the Shari'a law, the *Maẓālim* officials were regarded essentially as the representatives of the political ruler's law. The distinction came dangerously close to a dichotomy between religious and secular jurisdiction, particularly as the usual seat of the *qāḍis* court was in, or close to, the mosque, while that of the *Maẓālim* officials would be within the official residence of government.

* * *

Ultimately, the rift that had come to exist between the ideal scheme of *Sharī'a* law as expounded by the jurists and the actual legal practice in Islam, was recognized and ratified by legal scholarship under the doctrine known as *siyāsa shar'iyya*, or "government in accordance with the precepts of divine law." Writers on constitutional law, from the eleventh century onwards, assert that while the Sharī'a doctrine embodies the ideal order of things for Islam, the overriding duty of the ruler is to protect the public interest; and in particular circumstances of time and place the public interest might necessitate deviations from the strict Sharī'a doctrine. Thus, states one writer: "Were we simply to subject each suspect to the oath and then free him, in spite of our knowledge of his habitual criminal activities, saying: 'We cannot convict him without two upright witnesses,' that would be contrary to *siyāsa shar'iyya*."

From this basis the doctrine of *siyāsa* proceeds to recognize the validity, on grounds of public policy, of the various forms of *Maẓālim* jurisdiction. In effect, the political ruler is recognized as the fount of all judicial authority, with the power to set such bounds as he sees fit to the jurisdiction of his various tribunals, including the Sharī'a courts. Certainly, in the contemplation of the constitutional lawyers, the Sharī'a doctrine remained the eternal ideal, and the alternative jurisdictions merely temporary deviations along the road to that ultimate aspiration. The doctrine of *siyāsa*, too, was based upon the assumption that the ruler was ideally qualified for his position—in terms of religious piety and knowledge of God's purposes for society. But the final submission of idealism to practical necessity comes with the doctrine of the constitutional lawyers that civil obedience is due even to the ruler who is in no sense qualified in this way. Public policy is often referred to, by Western judges seeking to safeguard the liberties of the individual, as "an unruly horse." The Muslim scholars had given this horse its head, and it had bolted. To the power of the ruler exercised on grounds of the public interest there were no constitutional limits. In the last analysis the extent to which Sharī'a law was applied through the jurisdiction of the *qāḍī's* court depended upon the de facto power and the conscience of the political authority.

QUESTIONS

1. Would you expect *mazalim* jurisdiction to provide the stringent safeguards for the defendant provided by the *sharia*?

2. As between *mazalim* jurisdiction and *sharia* jurisdiction, which would be more likely to become the normal way of maintaining order in the society?

3. Which would have more legitimacy for the believer? What are the implications for the believer's view of the role of the government? Consider in this connection the traditional view that the role of the government is to maintain and uphold the *sharia*. Also, consider the Ottoman example as a test of your answers to these questions.

4. Would the tension between the ideal role of the government and the practical actions of the government be debilitating or is it a tension with which the government official and the citizen could both live? What is the effect of similar tensions in the West, say in the enforcement of out-of-fashion laws or in efforts to avoid politically-unpopular judicial safeguards?

5. In any of the traditional systems, the *sharia*, *mazalim* jurisdiction, or the village council, do you sense an analogue to the Western concept of individual rights? See Noel Coulson, The State and the Individual in Islamic Law, 6 International and Comparative Law Quarterly, 1957, p. 49.

Bibliographic Note. For additional information on the traditional Islamic system, see, in addition to the sources excerpted above, Mahmood M. Mostafa, L'Évolution De La Procédure Pénale En Égypte, Paris: Presses Universitaires de France, 1973; Anwar Qadri, Islamic Jurisprudence in the Modern World, 2nd edition, 1973, pp. 285–300, (philosophy); Emile Tyan, Histoire de L'Organisation Judiciaire en Pays D'Islam, Leiden: E. J. Brill, 2nd edition, 1960, (procedure and court structure).

C. THE WESTERN CODE

1. The Adoption Process

NOTE

The Egyptian modernizers of the Nineteenth Century, responding to the short but very influential Napoleonic occupation and to the longer-term pressures of accommodation with Western ideas, some arriving directly and some filtered through the Ottoman authorities, moved with surprising rapidity to adopt a Western penal system. In 1830, Muhammed Ali promulgated a penal code governing village and agricultural life, following the *sharia* except in the punishment prescribed for theft. Seven years later he issued a code governing offenses committed by officials, particularly crimes of corruption. Around mid-century, there was a series of Ottoman Penal Codes, shifting in 1858 to a French basis. Egypt had resisted application of the earlier Ottoman Codes; this history was shaped primarily by power struggles between Constantinople (now Istanbul) and Cairo, but the Cairo desire for more severe punishments to control Bedouins in Egypt was also a running theme. Ismail decided in 1863 to supplement the 1858 Ottoman Code with special Egyptian provisions. The new draft was promulgated in 1875, with the expectation that it would be applied in the new Mixed Courts. When these courts were actually established, they proved to have little criminal jurisdiction so the new code remained a dead letter.

The decisive shift came in 1883 with the establishment (under the British) of a French style National Court system and the promulgation for these courts of a Penal Code and a Code of Criminal Procedure based on the Napoleonic codes with only minor changes to accommodate to the *sharia*. The *qadi* courts lost their criminal law jurisdiction and were confined to family law, *waqfs*, and inheritance.

The foreign character of these new laws is suggested by the fact that they were drafted in French and then translated into Arabic. Although the British had pressed somewhat for a British model, the depth of French cultural influence in Egypt, the fact that the Ottoman authorities were moving in a French direction, and the desire to use comparable procedures in the Mixed Courts and the National Courts led to choice of a French model. The Codes were revised in 1904, 1937, and 1950, and are still based firmly on the French model, with the most recent version even discarding certain earlier British adaptations. For more detail on this history, see James N. D. Anderson, Law Reform in Egypt: 1850–1950 in Peter Holt, Political and Social Change in Modern Egypt, New York: Oxford University Press, 1968, p. 109; and the chapter on Tanzimat in Egypt: The Penal Code, in Gabriel Baer, Studies in the Social History of Modern Egypt, Chicago: University of Chicago Press, 1969, p. 109.

J. Norman D. Anderson, Law Reform in the Muslim World, London: Athlone, 1976, pp. 14–16, 35–38.

* * *

In the early days, dating from about the middle of the last century, the impulse for reform came not from below but from above. It was not that ordinary Muslims, generally speaking, were dissatisfied with the law to which they were subject and began to demand its reform, but that these reforms were imposed on them by the Government. In the case of the Ottoman Empire, this was primarily in the interests of bureaucratic efficiency and military strength, in order to enable 'the sick man of Europe' to keep up with the challenge, and resist the encroachments, of the Western powers. But some of the Tanẓimāt reforms [18] were also designed to disarm European criticisms of those aspects of the Sharīʿa which were considered savage or crude, and thus to avert the danger of further interference. This is why the earliest reforms in the sphere of personal law were the introduction of a Commercial Code, a Penal Code,[19] a Code of Commercial Procedure and a Code of Maritime Commerce, for we have already seen that the rigid rules of the Sharīʿa had always been far

---

18. The Arabic word *tanẓim* basically means to organize or put in order; and Tanẓimāt was the term used of a whole succession of reforms in the Ottoman Empire starting in 1839.

19. There had, in fact, been a few rather half-hearted attempts, at a slightly earlier date, to introduce legislation on this subject whjch kept considerably closer to the Shariʿa; but these soon gave place to codes of frankly Western inspiration.

too restrictive either for the life of the markets or for the maintenance of criminal justice. . . .

* * *

The effect of these Ottoman reforms was to put the Sharī'a entirely on one side in regard to such matters as commercial and criminal
law and procedure, to substitute in its place codes of quite alien inspiration, and to establish a whole system of secular (*niẓāmiyya*)
courts, operating under modern rules of procedure and evidence, to
apply them.

* * *

Now at first sight, as has already been remarked, it might seem
the most radical expedient possible, in a Muslim country, virtually to
eliminate—from *any* sphere of life—a law regarded by all Muslims as
having divine authority. Such action might be natural enough, however hazardous, in the case of a colonial regime, but almost beyond
belief in the case of an independent Muslim government such as that
of the Ottoman Empire. However great the pressure for modernization and reform may have been, could not the necessary changes
have been effected, it may be asked, in some way less alien to Ottoman sentiment and less offensive to Muslim orthodoxy? But the fact
is that this was not, apparently, the way in which Muslims themselves thought in the middle of the last century. At that time it
seemed to them preferable to keep the Sharī'a intact and inviolable
(as the perfect law which had at one time, they believed, held absolute sway and which would no doubt come into its own again in the
golden age which would eventually dawn), even if this meant excluding vast sections of it from the hurly-burly of everyday life in favour
of legislation of wholly different origins—forced upon them, as they
felt, by the exigencies of the modern world—rather than to submit
the sacred law to any profane meddling with its immutable provisions. In other words it was better to keep it in its pristine purity, as
the eternal law which challenged the consciences of all Muslims, even
if this meant putting it (as it were) under a glass case, for reverent
contemplation rather than practical application. This seems, no
doubt, very strange to the Western mind; but it must again be remembered that, to a Muslim, it has always been a far more heinous
sin to deny or question the divine revelation than to fail to obey it.
So it seemed preferable to continue to pay lip-service to an inviolate
Sharī'a, as the only law of fundamental authority, and to excuse a
departure from much of it in practice by appealing to the doctrine of
necessity (*ḍarūra*), rather than to make any attempt to adapt that
law to the circumstances and needs of contemporary life.

* * *

But however easy it was, comparatively speaking, to introduce a
criminal code, and however possible it was, in commercial law, to
point to the innovations of modern life—and, indeed, to the age-old
customs of Muslim merchants—it remains true that a fundamental

change of attitude was inescapably inherent even in this stage of the reform movement. As we have seen, the orthodox position was that the Shari'a provided the blueprint to which society and all its members were bound always to attempt to approximate; that this blueprint had been divinely given and had an inherent authority of its own; and that the only scope for human legislation was in that intermediate category of behaviour left legally indifferent by the divine Lawgiver. It was God himself and his law which were sovereign, not the Government or people; and even a code of law such as the Majalla, the provisions of which were derived from the Shari'a, should not properly be promulgated by the authority of a human executive or legislature, for it was essentially inappropriate for man to determine or decree what parts of the divine law were to be enforced by the courts, and in what circumstances.

QUESTIONS

1. In the excerpt just quoted, Anderson suggests that the *tanzimat* may be viewed as an extension of *mazalim* jurisdiction; Baer, in contrast, makes no such suggestion. How did the adoption of Western criminal law differ from a simple contemporary exercise of the ruler's *mazalim* jurisdiction? What problems would be posed for the believer? For the government?

2. Is there significance in the fact that Ali's earliest penal legislation was in the areas of village-level official corruption?

2. Procedure

NOTE

The current Egyptian criminal law system is built on a French model, and thus raises, for the American student, all the difficulties of understanding continental criminal procedure. This section therefore begins with general background on the character of the French system. For additional information and for reflections on the contrast between the two radically different approaches to criminal fairness, see in addition to the sources excerpted here, Gerald Kock, The French Code of Criminal Procedure, South Hackensack, New Jersey: Fred Rothman & Company, 1964; Albert Sheehan, Criminal Procedure in Scotland and France, Edinburg: Her Majesty's Stationery Office, 1972; Mirjan Damaska, Evidentiary Barriers to Conviction and Two Models of Criminal Procedure: A Comparative Study, 121 University of Pennsylvania Law Review 506, 1973; and Structures of Authority and Comparative Criminal Procedure, 84 Yale Law Journal 480, 1975; Robert Vouin, The Protection of the Accused in French Criminal Procedure, 5 International and Comparative Law Quarterly 1, 157, 1956.

The Egyptian system itself, although very close to the French model, differs in important ways. Egypt has not accepted some of the post-Napoleonic French reforms such as the use of a jury in some cases. Moreover, the Egyptian lawyer will undoubtedly attach somewhat different meanings to concepts translated into Arabic than a French lawyer would attach to the French original. For sources, see Enid Hill, Mahkama! Studies in the Egyptian Legal System: Courts and Crimes, Law and Society, London: Ithaca Press, 1979; Mahmood M. Mostafa, L'Evolution de la Procédure Penal en Égypte, Paris: Presses Universitaires de France, 1973; and Principes de Droit Pénale des Pays Arabes, Paris: Librairie Générale de Droit et de Jurisprudence, 1972.

John Henry Merryman, The Civil Law Tradition, Stanford, California: Stanford University Press, 1969, pp. 134–138.

* * *

One of the commonest comparisons one hears made about criminal procedure in the two traditions is that the criminal procedure in the civil law tradition is "inquisitorial," while that in the common law tradition is "accusatorial." Although this generalization is inaccurate and misleading as applied to contemporary systems of criminal procedure, it has some validity when put into historical context. In a sense it can be said that the evolution of criminal procedure in the last two centuries in the civil law world has been away from the extremes and abuses of the inquisitorial system, and that the evolution in the common law world during the same period has been away from the abuses and excesses of the accusatorial system. The two systems, in other words, are converging from different directions toward roughly equivalent mixed systems of criminal procedure.

Let us first consider the accusatorial system, which is generally thought by anthropologists to be the first substitute an evolving society develops for private vengeance. In such a system the power to institute the action resides in the wronged person, who is the accuser. This same right of accusation is soon extended to his relatives, and as the conception of social solidarity and the need for group protection develops, the right of accusation extends to all members of the group. A presiding officer is selected to hear the evidence, decide, and sentence; he does not, however, have the power to institute the action or to determine the questions to be raised or the evidence to be introduced, and he has no inherent investigative powers. These matters are in the hands of the accuser and the accused. The criminal trial is a contest between the accuser and the accused, with the judge as a referee. Typically the proceeding takes place publicly and orally, and is not preceded by any official (i.e. judicial or police) investigation or preparation of evidence.

The inquisitorial system typically represents an additional step along the path of social evolution from the system of private vengeance. Its principle features include first, attenuation or elimination of the figure of the private accuser and appropriation of that role by public officials; and second, the conversion of the judge from an impartial referee into an active inquisitor who is free to seek evidence and to control the nature and objectives of the inquiry. In addition, the relative equality of the parties that is an attribute of the accusatorial system, in which two individuals contest before an impartial arbiter, has been drastically altered. Now the contest is between an individual (the accused) and the state. Historically, inquisitorial proceedings have tended to be secret and written rather than public and oral. The resulting imbalance of power, combined with the secrecy of the written procedure, creates the danger of an oppressive system, in which the rights of the accused can easily be abused. The most infamous analogue familiar to us in the common law world is the Star Chamber, which was basically an inquisitorial tribunal.

* * *

As a result of the work of Beccaria and others in the eighteenth century, public sentiment against the abuses of criminal procedure became very strong, and reform of criminal procedure became one of the principal objectives of the European revolutions.

The typical criminal proceeding in the civil law world can be thought of as divided into three basic parts: the investigative phase, the examining phase, and the trial. The investigative phase comes under the direction of the public prosecutor, who also participates actively in the examining phase, which is supervised by the examining judge. The examining phase is primarily written and is not public. The examining judge controls the nature and scope of this phase of the proceeding. He is expected to investigate the matter thoroughly and to prepare a complete written record, so that by the time the examining stage is complete, all the relevant evidence is in the record. If the examining judge concludes that a crime was committed and that the accused is the perpetrator, the case then goes to trial. If he decides that no crime was committed or that the crime was not committed by the accused, the matter does not go to trial.

In a very general way it can be said that the principal progress toward a more just and humane criminal proceeding in Europe in the last century and a half has come through reforms in the investigative and examining phases of the criminal proceeding. These reforms have been of two principal kinds. First, every effort has been made to develop a core of prosecuting attorneys who act impartially and objectively. In Italy, for example, prosecuting attorneys are now members of the judiciary, having a security of tenure and consequent freedom from influence similar to that enjoyed by judges. Second, a number of procedural safeguards have been developed to assist the accused in protecting his own interests during the examining phase. Principal among these is the right of the accused to representation by counsel throughout this phase of the proceeding. This does not mean that counsel for the accused has unrestricted freedom to cross-examine witnesses or to introduce evidence on behalf of his client. The examining phase is still conducted by a judge. Counsel for the accused can, however, participate in the proceedings in such a way as to protect his client's interests, calling certain matters to the attention of the court and advising his client on how he should respond as the proceeding unfolds.

As a consequence of the nature of the examining phase of the criminal proceeding, the trial itself is different in character from the common law trial. The evidence has already been taken and the record made, and this record is available to the accused and his counsel, as well as to the prosecution. The function of the trial is to present the case to the trial judge and jury, and to allow the prosecutor and the defendant's counsel to argue their cases. It is also, of course, a public event, which by its very publicity tends to limit the possibility of arbitrary governmental action.

George W. Pugh, "Administration of Criminal Justice in France: An Introductory Analysis," in 23 Louisiana Law Review, pp. 1, 22–27 (1962).

* * *

The French criminal trial (*audience*) is totally different from one in the United States. Of prime importance is the *dossier*, prepared in advance by the police at the *enquête préliminaire* (or first step of investigation), and, in many cases, also by the *juge d'instruction*. The *dossier* is at times lengthy indeed. As noted previously, the presiding judge has had access to it in advance of the trial, and in more serious cases, it is necessary for him to have studied it assiduously. Counsel for the prosecution, the defense, and the civil party (if there be one) have all also had access to it.

The trial itself is short compared to American trials. Interrogation of the witnesses is handled almost exclusively by the presiding judge. Counsel for the parties may request that the president ask certain questions, and this usually occurs from time to time during the trial. Questions thus suggested, however, are not numerous, and there is nothing in French criminal procedure akin to Anglo-American examination and cross-examination of witnesses by counsel. The extensive and painstakingly prepared *dossier* is the French means of clarifying the facts in advance of trial and pinpointing whatever contradictions remain.

What is necessary, and yet very difficult, for an American to understand is that, in the vast majority of French criminal proceedings, the defendant has already fully confessed several times, and does not contest the validity of his confessions. Of course, there are exceptions, but it seems to this writer, from observations and conversations, that generally by the time the trial arrives, it is quite apparent from defendant's confessions, thoroughly corroborated in the *dossier*, that he did in fact commit the act in question. Since, at the same time guilt or innocence is determined by the tribunal, sentence is also meted out, an extremely important consideration at the trial is determining what sentence should be given the defendant, if he should be found guilty. Naturally, this has great bearing as to the type of procedure employed, the evidence adduced, and the rules with respect thereto.

Because of the importance of the *dossier* and the role of the *juge d'instruction* in cases referred to him, it is noteworthy that this magistrate is charged with neutrality and obligated to develop for the *dossier* not merely facts favorable to the prosecution, but also those favorable to the defendant. It seems fair to state that in general this obligation is actually fulfilled. Since it is for the *juge d'instruction*, in cases referred to him, to decide whether an individual should be brought to trial, the standard employed by him in arriving at this decision is significant. Although the legislative texts are somewhat vague, it seems to this observer that the standard actually employed is much more defendant-oriented than that used for grand jury indictment. It appears that if the *juge d'instruction* is not reasonably convinced of guilt, subject to review by the accusatory chamber of the court of appeal at the request of the *procureur*, or the civil party, the defendant does not go to trial.

The presumption of innocence, although not expressly stated in the Code of Penal Procedure, is well recognized as a fundamental concept, and generally the burden of proof is clearly on the prosecution. However, in petty offenses and certain exceptional cases, a *procès verbal*, prepared by public officials outside of court, drawn in accordance with strict regulations, constitutes prima facie proof of guilt, rebuttable by evidence to the contrary.

At the trial, after the charge is read, the defendant is usually the first party examined by the presiding judge. As is the custom for witnesses, he stands. In serious cases, with painstaking care, the presiding judge, who has studied the *dossier*, interrogates the defendant, asking him to affirm or deny the truth of the statements contained therein, both his own and those of others. The judge attempts to bring out the pertinent circumstances, both favorable and unfavorable. Questions by counsel for the defendant and the civil party may be posed through the president of the court.

* * *

Persons other than the defendant usually give their testimony in narrative form, and are permitted to say whatever they feel is pertinent, uninterrupted by the objections of counsel that so often characterize American criminal proceedings. The judge, however, is in control. Broad and intricately developed rules of exclusion, such as the Anglo-American hearsay rule, rule against opinion testimony, etc., do not exist in French criminal proceedings. . . .

* * *

The judges are specifically prohibited from basing their decision on evidence other than that available at the trial. They may consider all matters within the *dossier* properly acquired, for it is felt that as trained professional magistrates, they can weigh the testimony and give it the value to which it is entitled. In arriving at their decision, the test to be employed is "inner conviction" (*intime conviction*).

The nature of this test is spelled out for lay jurors (sitting for the trial of *crimes* [felonies]), who are to be instructed by the president of the court before deliberation:

> "The law does not ask judges for an accounting as to the means by which they are convinced. It does not prescribe for them any special rules on which they shall make the fullness and sufficiency of the proof depend; it requires them to interrogate themselves in silence and reflection, and to seek to determine in the sincerity of their conscience what impression the proofs brought against the accused, and his defense, have made on their reason. The law only asks of them this single question, which encompasses the full measure of their duty: 'Have you an inner conviction?'"

Enid Hill, Mahkama! Studies in the Egyptian Legal System, London: Ithaca Press, 1979, pp. 26–33.

The *Niyaba*

The *niyaba* (or *al-niyaba al-ᶜamma*, which is its full title) is an institution taken directly from the French legal system. It is the *ministère public* or *parquet*, the so-called "standing magistry" who stand when they address the court, as opposed to the judges who remain seated. This obviously applies to the formal sessions of the criminal court when felonies are being tried and a representative of the *niyaba* presents the charges. In Egypt the representatives of the *niyaba* are to be found in many other kinds of court session, which are not so formal and where they do not stand.

There is no counterpart in the common law systems of England and the United States, although parallels are often noted. These officials of the magistry not only prepare and present the charges against an accused to the full session of the criminal court, but they have various functions in line with their prescribed duty to "protect the public interest" which, especially in Egypt, amounts to an almost unfettered authority to conduct investigations. Thus representatives of the *niyaba* are found at all levels of the court structure. They sit with the judges on the judicial bench or behind the judicial table. They have particular functions in personal status matters, which I have referred to and will discuss again. They notify persons living abroad and otherwise are charged to attempt to locate missing litigants or other persons. They have a special duty to be present in court when minors are involved or women are litigants without their husband's consent (ie without a "guardian" to protect their rights). Thus they figure prominently in suits concerning the guardianship of minor children and in divorce suits brought by women. They also have general investigative powers concerning public morals and welfare and a capacity to institute proceedings based upon their findings in such investigations. They are charged with supervising the finances of the courts, and with the inspection of prisons. In this latter function they would appear to be intended as a check on the police (that is, to make sure that people are not being incarcerated improperly), and on the general conditions within prisons. At the same time they work in co-operation with the police officials and the police force generally. There are certain police and quasi-police functionaries who are designated as *al-dabit al-qada'i* "judicial police" to whom the *niyaba* may issue instructions and over whom they are given authority and from whom they may ask assistance. It is upon these individuals that the *niyaba* personnel are dependent for any kind of coercive measures to bring in witnesses, arrest suspects, carry out search and seizure. The orders must come from the *niyaba* for such acts as entry and search of private residences.

The personnel of the *niyaba* are often translated as "attorney general", "district attorney", or "prosecuting attorney", but these are misappellations. The *niyaba* neither represents the government as a party litigant nor is its function, strictly speaking, to "prosecute" cases in the sense that prosecution is conceived of in America or England. The *niyaba* is the place where incidents are investigated, providing the background of evidence, and serving as a supporting organ which seeks to learn the "truth" and not to incriminate for the sake of having a case. They search for all evidence—of innocence as well as guilt. They have the authority to suspend investigations and "file" cases, as well as to recommend that a case be brought to trial. The individual who is given the task of preparing the charges for presentation to the criminal court may well be another individual than the one who was in charge of the investigation, indeed, he likely is, as all reports of investigations must be submitted to the superior officers of the *niyaba*, and then redistributed for preparation for trial. The *niyaba* is considered "indivisible".

Any of the personnel are interchangeable in the performance of the responsibilities which devolve upon the *niyaba*.

"The *niyaba* knows no barriers." This was our guiding principle, which required mutual co-operation between all members of the department and gave the *wakil al-niyaba* in Aswan the right to deal with the cases of his colleague in Alexandria in complete disregard of all considerations of time and place.

The *niyaba* is part of the Ministry of Justice, and its head official, the *na'ib al-ᶜamm*, is responsible to the Minister of Justice directly. It is both connected with and separate from the court hierarchy of judges. Its personnel assist the court in both prosecution of criminal cases and litigation of certain kinds of civil cases, and they have the "privilege of intervention" in court proceedings. The judges are, however, free to follow or to disregard their advice. The jurisdictional lines of each seem to be understood, although from the point of view of Anglo-American jurisprudence it does not seem all that clear. Comment by a French legal scholar on his own system seems equally relevant to Egypt:

> The judicial personnel of the parquet and the judges have constant contact and consider themselves part of a single corps, but at the same time each group has its own responsibilities, and often their points of view differ. It would never occur to a judge that the judicial personnel of the *ministère public* are there to spy on him or influence his judgements other than by proper legal arguments . . . .. It is clear that the independence of the judge is not affected.

However, I have heard of rivalry and jurisdictional disputes between the *niyaba* and the judicial police. The police, of course, come under the jurisdiction of a different ministry—that of the Interior. In this basic violation of all things dear to hierarchical bureaucracy is certainly potential for conflict, but custom seems to mitigate to some extent, as well as the respect and awe in which the *niyaba* is held. The *niyaba* is very careful to protect its reputation of incorruptibility.

The most celebrated activity of the *niyaba* in Egypt is its investigative responsibility. It has comprehensive and exclusive authority in regard to criminal cases. The law is very clear:

> *Al-niyaba al-ᶜamma*, and only it, has jurisdiction to raise criminal cases and investigate them.

Code of Criminal Procedure, Art. 1.

The investigations of the *niyaba* involve the interrogation of witnesses and the most visible functionary of this activity is the *wakil niyaba*. These gentlemen are the responsible official of that *niyaba* which is attached to each court organization and within a central *niyaba* constituted for special purposes. They are to be found representing the interests of the *niyaba* and the Ministry of Justice in the outposts of justice in the provinces. While "in co-operation" with the police, the investigation of a *wakil niyaba* are essentially independent and may go over exactly the same ground as that of the preliminary police investigation. It is the report by the *wakil niyaba*, however, which is important and which forms the written record of a case. The *wakil niyaba* calls witnesses and questions them, and may visit the scene of the crime. The person being interrogated has the right to have his lawyer present but the lawyer does not have the right to speak. The questioning of witnesses is usually done either in offices of the police *qism* or in the offices of the *wakil niyaba* which are located in the Ministry of Justice buildings, the courthouses. He may also question witnesses in other locations. Investigations by a *wakil niyaba* begins immediately after the crime is discovered, but may continue for weeks or even months thereafter and, if in a provincial outpost, may be transferred for further investigations to the central *niyaba* offices. Persons who have been involved in such interrogation proceedings indicate that a great deal of tension exists, and questioning may be sly and deliberately misleading, and at times accusatory. A *wakil niyaba* may develop a reputation of being a clever questioner. He may bring in other witnesses to confront a witness he is questioning. Otherwise the questioning sessions are done privately with only a *katib* present, relentlessly writing the Report. In a system where all cases, including criminal ones, are based heavily upon a written record, the Report is all-important, as Tewfik el Hakim relates:

> The point is that I always like to take pains with the compilation of the Report, and to see that it is well and logically arranged. The Report is the be-all-and-end-all in the eyes of higher authority. It is the only evidence testifying to the accuracy and skill of the *wakil al-niyaba*. Nobody worries, of course, about the mere apprehension of the criminal.

> The preamble was followed by a description of the assault, the clothes worn by the victim, and the place in which he was found. We saw no reason to be brief. I dictated to the clerk a detailed description . . ..

> The investigation wound its way through obscure paths, illuminated by no hope of reaching any tangible result. Nobody knew who the assailant might be. Nobody suspected anyone. The victim had no family in the village except an old sick mother whose sight had failed and who had lost the faculty of speech . . .. Nobody could suggest a reasonable or unreasonable motive for the assault . . ..

> I clasped my head in my hands, wondering what was to be done next in this case, and whom we could interrogate so as to bring our Report up to a minimum of twenty pages. For I have never forgotten what the *ra'is al-niyaba* said to me one day when he received a ten-page Report.

> "What's all this? A contravention or a misdemeanour?" *

> When I replied that it was a murder case, he shouted at me in astonishment:

> "A murder case investigated in ten pages! An assasination! The murder of a human being! All in ten pages?"

> When I replied that with those ten pages we had managed to get the murderer, he paid no attention whatever, and went on weighing the Report in his hand with careful accuracy.

> "Who would ever have believed that this Report could be a murder case?"

> I replied instantly: "Next time, God willing, we shall be more careful about the weight!"

---

* Contraventions, misdemeanors, and crimes are the steps in the French hierarchy of increasingly serious criminal offenses, comparable to our hierarchy of misdemeanors and felonies.

The more dramatic part of the work performed by the *wukala'
niyaba* is that of presenting the charges against the accused to the
criminal court. Different personality types obviously excel in one as
opposed to the other aspect of the work, as El Hakim also indicates,
together with something of what presentation of a case to a criminal
court involves:

> By nature I am fitted to be a hidden observer of people strutting
> across the stage of life—rather than to be a skilled actor flooded
> with limelight under the eyes of an audience. For such situations
> dazzle and unbalance me . . . ..
>
> I knew the heavy yellow envelope must contain criminal cases
> sent from head office to be studied and prepared for submission to
> the criminal court, which was to hold session that month in the
> capital of our province, I glanced at these cases and found them to
> contain hundreds of pages; . . . .. There was nothing which
> made me loathe the work of the *wakil al-niyaba* more than the
> task of making submission in cases of felony. My weak memory
> found it difficult to grasp all the details which went to make up a
> criminal charge so as to be able to set them out afterwards in due
> order and calm before three glowering judges of appeal, with
> counsel ready to pounce and an audience judging not according to
> the essence and core of the case, but according to skill of gesticu-
> lations and attitudes, the resonance of a voice in the court, facility
> in delivery, and violence in desk-thumping.

El Hakim notwithstanding, the position of *wakil niyaba* is a prestigious one. Those with the highest marks from the law faculties are
taken into the *niyaba*, maybe ten to twenty only from each law
faculty each year, I am told. From the ranks of the *niyaba* are chosen the judges, not exclusively, but primarily. The *niyaba* has a reputation for impartiality and uncorruptability. Any hint that there is
favoritism, or personal involvement with the parties to a case, may
cause another *wakil niyaba* to be put onto the case, or perhaps call
for the attention of the higher *niyaba* officials.

* * *

It should be emphasized that a *wakil niyaba* is, as his name indicates, an "agent". Of course, *niyaba* itself indicates agency or representation. This means that the *niyaba* personnel must follow the
recommendations of the written reports which they inherit or the directives of the *na'ib al-ᶜamm* or the Minister of Justice. To emphasize this, the *niyaba* personnel are specifically indicated to be "re-
movable" in contradistinction to the judges, who are appointed for
life. This distinction has very little significance, however, today in
Egypt as all government jobs are protected by law. What does have
significance, however, is that *niyaba* personnel are in direct hierarchical subordination through their chief, the *na'ib al-ᶜamm*, to the
Minister of Justice and from there to the Council of Ministers and the
President of the Republic.

The *niyaba* is thus representative of state interests at the same time that it is representative of the public interest. Being "defender of the public interest" and "protector of state interests" at the same time admits of a certain ambiguity, but only if they are seen as separable. For all practical purposes the "public interest" is what the state says it is. Powers of the *niyaba* are structured in Egypt in such a way that the *niyaba* (and therefore the state) has control over what cases are brought to trial and which ones are "filed", for good or not so good reasons. The point is, however, that once brought to trial, the opinion of the *niyaba* is not binding on the judges. Judges are quite free to disregard these recommendations if they wish. A representative of the *niyaba* is also supposed to be free to express his own opinion orally in a court, which custom I shall mention again.

Herbert Liebesny, The Law of the Near and Middle East, Albany: State University of New York Press, 1975, pp. 260–261.

If an offense allegedly has been committed, it is up to the public prosecutor (as representative of the *ministère public*) to decide whether there is a case. In cases of misdemeanors the public prosecutor may bring the case directly to the court, provided the police report contains enough information. If the case involves a major misdemeanor, the public prosecutor may at his discretion pass the case for preliminary investigation to an investigating magistrate (French: *juge d'instruction*). In felony cases a preliminary investigation by the *juge d'instruction* is mandatory, provided the public prosecutor believes that there is cause for further investigation of the allegations made. Investigating magistrates are attached to every summary tribunal and to every court of first instance. The investigating magistrate is in full control of and has sole responsibility for the investigation. The investigation is nonpublic, but the parties may demand copies of various documents and are informed of such acts of investigation as took place during their absence. In Egyptian law, as in the law of most Near and Middle Eastern and European countries, a party injured by the alleged offense, whether physically or financially, may join in the penal action as a so-called civil claimant. During the investigation, the accused, the victim, and, if there is such, the civil claimant may be represented by counsel. Counsel for the defendant may, however, speak only with the permission of the judge during the interrogation of the accused.

At the end of the preliminary investigation the investigating magistrate transmits the file to the public prosecutor. In case of a petty offense the accused is brought to trial in the summary court, and the same is the case, with a few exceptions for specific misdemeanors which are tried in the court of assizes, for misdemeanors (*délits*). If the investigating magistrate has come to the conclusion that the offense constitutes a felony, the accused is brought before the so-called *chambre des mises en accusations*. This body is part of every court of first instance and consists of three judges. The term may be translated as chamber for indictment, the body is somewhat comparable in function to a grand jury. The chamber makes its determination on the basis of the file which one of its members reports on and statements by the parties. The procedure is not public. The chamber can remand the case to the investigating magistrate, if it feels that further investigation is needed, can undertake such investigation itself, or, if it is satisfied that a felony has been committed, it sends the case for trial to the court of assizes. If the chamber believes that a misdemeanor only has been committed, it sends the case to the summary court. The chamber may also conclude that there is no punishable offense, in which case it can so find and the accused, if he was under arrest, is set free.

At the trial the indictment is read and then the prosecution and the civil party, if there is one, make their statements. The defendant is thereafter asked whether he pleads guilty or not guilty. If he pleads guilty, the court may pronounce judgment without hearing further evidence, if it is satisfied with the confession.

Mahmoud Mostafa, L'Évolution de la Procédure Penale en Égypte, Paris: Presses Universitaires de France, 1973, pp. 68–69 (footnote omitted).

In many places, the law has established a separation between the accusation function and the instruction [indictment] function, considering the contradiction between them. The fact of bringing the accusation really makes the Ministère public an adversary who cannot at the same time carry out the function of equitable instruction; French legislation rests on this basis.

In the first Egyptian legislation on penal procedure in 1885, the Code of Criminal Instruction applied this norm of separation. . . .

Later, it was decided to ignore this system of separation between accusation and instruction, leaving the task of instruction to the parquet as a general rule, while giving the authority to the judge in certain cases.

It is in this spirit that Decree-Law 353 was promulgated in 1952.[2]

2. The explanatory note to the draft of this decree law states that "experience has revealed that it is preferable . . . to give back to the Ministère public the authority for instruction with respect to crimes as well, . . . but the parquet can ask the president of the trial court to delegate a magistrate of the court to carry out instruction if, in the particular circumstances in matters of crimes or delicts, the Ministère public believes that there is value in using a judge for the instruction. . . . Among the important considerations supporting [this law] are the fact that the majority of modern European legislation no longer forbids integrating the powers of accusation and instruction, and thus the greater share of this legislation, including Italy, Germany, Poland, and Belgium, confers the task of preliminary instruction on the Ministère public. The regime of separation between accusation and instruction is today an object of criticism even in France, considering that the judge's activity is limited by a lack of contact with the agents of the judicial police. Moreover, experience reveals that evidence becomes dissipated and that there are gaps in instruction when witnesses are heard before several authorities. Finally, suppression of the regime simplifies procedure without attacking the course of justice."

. . . [Now] the Ministère public rarely asks for the delegation of a judge for instruction and neither the accused nor the civil party can compel the acceptance of their request for such a delegation; the regime of a judge of instruction in Egyptian law is thus a regime which exists simply in form and has practically no value.

NOTE

For more background on prosecution in Egypt, see Raoof Tbeid, Le role des organes de poursuite dans le procès pénal en Egypte; Mahmood Mostafa, Le role des organes de poursuite dans le procès pénal; and Ahmed Fathi Sourour, Le statut et le pouvoir discrétionnaire du Ministère public, in 34 Revue Internationale de Droit Pénal (Nos. 3 and 4) pp. 41, 52, 63, respectively, 1963.

QUESTIONS

1. What aspects of the civil law procedure just described appear likely to violate U.S. Constitutional norms?

2. Is the procedure fair? What issues are particularly sensitive?

3. As an advisor to the Egyptian government in the Nineteenth Century, which would you have recommended (leaving political considerations aside): the civil law model or the Anglo-American common law model? Why?

4. Would your recommendation be any different under today's military revolutionary government?

3.   Applying the Process to Official Embezzlement

John Waterbury, Corruption, Political Stability and Development: Comparative Evidence from Egypt and Morocco, 11 Gov't & Opposition 426 (1976) (Some footnotes omitted).

While it is very difficult to measure quantitatively the extent of corruption in any polity, it may well be that in an absolute sense it is more prevalent (although not necessarily more conspicuous) in "developing" economies and polities, than in societies with relatively high standards of living. This, if it is so, results from a concatenation of politico-economic factors which fosters the spread of corrupt practices in virtually all dealings between the citizenry and the state. In what follows, we shall consider three forms of corruption—endemic,

It is clear that this note has not succeeded in supporting the modification. In its reference to foreign legislation the note is in error; in reality the modification has been dictated by the government's desire to control the instruction of infractions attacking the power structure. In Egyptian law, there is a single Procureur Général who assesses and instructs himself or through his substitute in all the territory of the Republic and it is easy to influence him. Moreover, he may be dismissed, while it is not easy to influence judges who cannot be dismissed.

planned, and developmental—which, while analytically distinct, are not necessarily so legally or operationally.

* * *

Abstract definitions are easy to come by, and the following is close to representing a consensus of students of the phenomenon.[1]

> "Corruption is behavior which deviates from the formal duties of a public role (elective or appointive) because of private-regarding (personal, close family, private clique) wealth or status gains: or violates rules against the exercise of certain types of private-regarding influence."

Such a definition unfortunately gives us little guidance in identifying discrete manifestations of corrupt behaviour. It is generally possible to ascertain legally-defined corruption, but laws, especially in developing countries, tend to change rapidly. For example, Egyptian public servants are theoretically forbidden to engage in trade or commercial activity. A law of 1974 has laid it down that owning taxi cabs is not a trade or commercial activity, and a large number of bureaucrats who had apparently been violating their public trust suddenly found themselves not only tolerated but legitimized. Another recent example is provided by a court case against over fifty persons accused of violating the country's foreign exchange regulations and illegally transferring hard currency abroad. The case involved some public officials (a minister who was not accused may have lost his post because of his proximity to the affair) and dragged on in the courts for nearly three years. Finally in January 1975 the Criminal Court of Appeal dismissed the charges against most of the defendants in an obscure judgement which stated that changes in the regulations of the parallel money market, *subsequent to the arrest of the defendants*, had rendered the initial charges against them without foundation. Greater attention should perhaps be paid (and within the Marxist tradition it is paid) in studies of corruption to the "corrupt" creation and manipulation of the law itself to further private ends.

* * *

Endemic Corruption. Endemic corruption is the abuse of public office that occurs to varying degrees in any system. It may consist in buying one's way out of a traffic ticket, for the rich, or into a dispensary, for the poor. The more vital the service rendered by the administration, the more widespread will be this form of corruption. In developing countries gaining access to government services may

1. Joseph S. Nye, "Corruption and Political Development: A Cost-Benefit Analysis", American Political Science Review, LXI, N. 2 (June 1967), p. 416. Samuel Huntington has put it more parsimoniously: "Corruption is behavior of public officials which deviates from accepted norms in order to serve private ends." Political Order in Changing Societies, Yale University Press, 1968, p. 59. See also for important general discussions of corruption, James Scott, Comparative Political Corruption, Prentice-Hall, Englewood Cliffs, N.J., 1972, and Joseph La Palombara, Politics Within Nations, Prentice-Hall, Englewood Cliffs, N.J., 1974, pp. 402–419.

become a matter of survival. Three types of government action must be singled out for attention in this respect: welfare services, regulatory measures, and basic documentation. Egypt and Morocco, like most countries in the world, aspire to mass, universal welfare services for all citizens. Egypt, it must be said, has enunciated this ideal more forcefully and given it greater programmatic backing than Morocco. Education, public health, public housing, agricultural and small business credit, social security, health insurance, electricity, running water, irrigation systems, cooperative markets, make-work projects, all figure prominently among these services. In neither Egypt nor Morocco are government revenues sufficient to extend these services equally to all who claim them. Access to them may well entail abuse of public office for pecuniary or political advantage in the determination of who will get what, when.

In both countries limited welfare capability and its corrupt distribution is strongly and durably rooted in the low level of civil service salaries. Poorly-paid bureaucrats administer highly-valued programmes (occasionally even their budgets) and the temptation to levy a fee is seldom resisted. There may be some historical conditioning for the toleration of this phenomenon, for until the 20th century it was frequently the case in both Egypt and Morocco that several kinds of public officials did not receive salaries from the central government but rather sold their services for a fee or took a percentage of the taxes they were able to raise. However, too much should not be made of the notion of historical conditioning for many of the welfare activities in which these governments are engaged are without historical precedent.

Where the newer phenomenon may lead is well demonstrated in Egypt. It is common throughout the educational system, but above all at the secondary and university levels, for teachers and instructors to offer private tutoring to their students. The fee charged varies according to the level and the subject matter. In some faculties of medicine, private instruction may cost several hundred Egyptian pounds a year. In addition, passing and failing critical examinations has come increasingly to hinge on whether or not one takes the instructor's private course. The system works to compensate the teacher for his low salary, but also makes hay with Egyptian goals of free education at all levels, by reinforcing access according to income level.

* * *

In neither Egypt nor Morocco is corruption officially condoned; indeed it is resolutely denounced and condemned. But in both it is extremely widespread. Although there are marked differences in time sequence, both countries have come implicitly to accept and even encourage corruption.[4]

4. I have pursued this theme in detail elsewhere. See my "Endemic and Planned Corruption in a Monarchical Regime", World Politics, Vol. XXV, N. 4, July 1973, pp. 533–555.

Planned Corruption. . . . Corruption can and does serve many political ends. In other words, certain political actors may find it highly desirable to sustain a certain level of corruption within the system. This would seem to be the case as regards King Hassan II of Morocco; it has been the case as well with city-boss politicians, and those at higher levels of the federal government, in the United States. But in poor, developing countries "planned" corruption may become a particularly attractive political strategy in the face of acute disparities in income and resource distribution and nascent class cleavages.

* * *

The process is simple. The state in the developing countries holds a strong grip on the distribution of scarce resources. In theory, even if all the citizens cannot have equal access to these resources, distribution is determined by "objective" criteria of merit and competence. Endemic corruption undermines distribution on this basis, and systemic or planned corruption institutionalizes discriminatory distribution. Grants, favours, pardons and rewards replace the acquisition of desired goods according to legally-defined, objective need, merit, or rational qualification.

How could such a transformation of an administrative apparatus, designed in Weberian rational-legal terms, become desirable? From the point of view of the "boss", the head of state, or, in this instance, the king, there are at least three benefits that may be drawn from corruption. The first is that the chief planner, distributor and regulator of spoils guarantees his relevance to the system and, in the best of circumstances, his indispensability. To the extent that he is able to establish that the political game is about "spoils", then his role as chief dispenser becomes crucial.

The second major objective that planned corruption serves is that it undercuts within society, and especially within the public administration, the emergence of a meritocracy. Kings in particular, but many republican heads of state as well, are chosen for divine, emotional, or other purely "ascriptive" reasons including coercive self-imposition. If they wish to rule for a long time, they must beware of rationalization lest their own competence be called into question. The spoils game of discriminatory rewards focuses the attentions of the elite on access, pull, "piston", the right connections, and, of course, ostentatious loyalty and subservience to the chief dispenser of coveted goods. Moving to the top no longer counts on hard work, honesty, competence, training, achieving results—although these will not be excluded from consideration—but rather in accepting a game whose rules and unpredictable outcomes are determined by the "boss". Rewards do not derive from executing a programme, fulfilling one's ideological goals, or applying one's technical competence, but from winning material favours or avoiding disgrace.

Officials who become caught up in this game lose sight of the system as a whole. They are encouraged to focus on their narrow self-interests and are appropriately rewarded for doing so. They may be promoted, awarded an import license, a piece of state property, or, in general, the grant, but not the right, of exploiting their office to their personal advantage. The success of this strategy in Morocco was demonstrated throughout the 1960s. Its momentary failure due to the opposition of the senior officers corps became manifest only in 1971/2 when the king was forced to put on trial for corruption the cream of the elite he had nurtured during the 1960s.

The third objective served by planned corruption is the mitigation of class and social cleavages by the building of vertically-integrated clienteles, sustained by the distribution of spoils, cutting across class lines.

*   *   *

No one who knows the system can effectively challenge it, for knowledge generally is derived from participation in it and to expose the system is to expose oneself. Challenges can only come from those excluded from the spoils or from those willing to commit political suicide in the name of purifying the system.

It may seem natural for a monarch, a divine-right king, to pursue this sort of strategy in the name of his own survival, but we find the same strategy adopted under ostensibly different regimes, including the socialist republic of Egypt. Immediately one must pose a question of the consciousness or deliberateness with which heads of state articulate and formulate these "strategies" that have been confidently attributed to them. One cannot be sure that King Hassan has consciously worked out all the ramifications of the course that he is following, and even if he has he would deny it. The problem is all the more difficult with President Sadat (and was equally difficult with President Nasser) whose policies of planned corruption are so blatantly at odds with the official ideology and symbols of legitimacy of the regime.

Yet the facts seem to indicate that both Presidents Nasser and Sadat resorted to corruption as a means of political control. The constituencies they sought to keep in line are not, however, the same. To summarize, brutally, a very complex situation, Nasser's socialism was founded on the twin hopes of rapid economic development without any particular class having to make any very great sacrifice for it, and the "melting" of class differences in the absence of class conflict. To achieve such a formula would have been a momentous task for even the most gifted of politicians, which Nasser was not. He was essentially afraid of the free play of political and economic interests. Instead he contained them and closely monitored them through a complex series of parallel security, police, and intelligence networks, overlain with labyrinthine bureaucratic procedures into which all citizens were locked.[7] Had there been significant economic growth, Nasser's approach might have worked. But there was not, and as the objective conditions for social conflict were aggravated (occasionally spilling over into mass violence as in February 1968) more and more power slipped into the hands of the police and security apparatuses. Nasser's dilemma was then to find a device by which to keep the heads of these apparatuses—and senior army officers—in line. Allowing them to exploit their power for personal ends was *one* of the principal means adopted.

President Sadat is a politician and prefers to manipulate political and economic interests rather than suppress them. This approach has been at the heart of his economic and political liberalization measures since 1971. He has also significantly diminished the saliency of the police apparatuses within Egyptian politics. At the same time he too is faced with deteriorating economic conditions and growing popular discontent that can the more easily express itself in the freer atmosphere. For Sadat, allowing high-level and low-level corruption in combination with widespread black market activities has become a technique to domesticate strategic elites and to create intermediate "bought" clienteles between the regime and the impoverished masses.

Naturally, planned corruption necessitates playing at charades for what is tacitly condoned is legally condemned. The charade takes theatrical but generally empty forms.

. . . A "Where Did You Get It?" law has been on the books since 1969 in Egypt where no one can legally earn more than LE 10,000 per year from all sources. The "Where Did You Get It?" law has never been applied.

Obsolete, superfluous, or "retired" elite members may be kept on the public payroll at their former salary and perquisite levels. These may include ministerial salary, pension, state-owned villas and cars. Officials out of line with prevailing policy can be eased out and politically neutralized by keeping them on the dole. In Egypt there are allegedly 700 idle persons of ministerial rank. One ministry carries on its payroll 20 under-secretaries and deputy ministers who never go to work. The efficacy of planned corruption is, to some extent, a function of the size of the constituencies that are caught in its web. The smaller the strategic elites involved, the more economical and manageable the system. Similarly, smallness insures that coverage is comprehensive and that an internally-generated attack upon corruption becomes unlikely. In this sense Egypt, if it chose to do so, could try to do away with planned corruption far more easily than Morocco. The size of strategic groups "eligible" for inclusion in the Egyptian system is far greater than the resources available to absorb

7. See C. H. Moore, "Les syndicats professionels dans l'Egypte contemporaine: l'encadrement de la nouvelle classe moyenne", *Maghreb-Machrek*, Paris, July-August 1974, N. 64, pp. 24–34.

them. Thus the majority of the middle and upper middle classes draw scant advantages from planned corruption, and there are strong pressures all along the political spectrum to take decisive action against it.

Developmental Corruption. None of the three categories of corruption treated here are mutually exclusive, and the first two—endemic and planned—are inherent in and exacerbated by the process of economic development. Despite ostensibly radical differences in official ideologies, political structures, and symbols of legitimacy, many developing countries share a remarkable similarity in the kinds of economic challenges they face and the constitutional and procedural means they adopt in dealing with them.[12]

Egypt is a socialist republic based on the "alliance of working forces"—a formula for corporate representation—with strong emphasis upon public ownership of the means of production and centralized planning. Morocco is a monarchy with a multi-party system, lip service to parliamentary democracy, and an official credo of economic liberalism in which the private sector is to play an active role.

 . . . In both Egypt and Morocco, as we have seen in the previous section, the regimes have, for different reasons, been unwilling to impose the generalized austerity and forced savings formulae that a self-financed (in only a relative sense) development effort would require. The equal distribution of the burden would be particularly distasteful to the middle classes and elites, whether in public or private employ, whose consumerist proclivities would have to be curbed. Neither Morocco not Egypt has had the will to sweat their middle classes, largely for fear of undermining the regime itself. Failing that, a semblance of political stability has been bought through planned corruption. At the same time, while the upper strata are allowed to feather their nests at public expense, it becomes impossible to contain, still less to extirpate, endemic corruption which grows with the increased activities of the state itself and generally at its lower levels.

What one then finds is the prevalence of forms of corruption that relate directly to the role of the state in the developmental process. All of these forms are familiar and do not require lengthy description although a few examples will be presented here.

A parasitic symbiosis develops between the public and private sectors. The state is responsible for capital formation and investment, much of which are directed towards infrastructure projects—roads, ports, dams, schools, hospitals, housing—which in turn are contracted out to builders, fitters, electricians, plumbers, suppliers, etc. During the Egyptian first Five Year Plan (1960–1965) 40% of total public investment outlays went to private contractors, and this at a time when

12. This point has been nicely set forth by Galal Amin, "Income Distribution and Economic Development in the Arab World", *L'Egypte Contemporaine,* Vol. LXIV, N. 352, April 1973.

the regime was going through its most self-consciously socialist phase. Contracts can be, and frequently are awarded on a non-competitive basis with kickbacks, side deals and a whole series of quasi-legal commissions and handling fees that may raise the value of a project by 30 or 40%. Something of this kind is seemingly underway with regard to the reconstruction of the Canal Zone cities where estimated outlays in the coming decade will be on the order of LE 5 billion. The important point is that the private sector comes to depend upon the vast flow of publicly-disbursed funds for its survival, while public sector officials jockey for positions where they can control, and benefit from, the disbursement of these funds.[14]

* * *

The state becomes the major importer of goods and supplies needed in the development effort, and by controlling scarce hard currency it effectively controls imports of all kinds. This crucial aspect of the development process cannot, in my view, be overstressed. Countries like Egypt and Morocco have massive import requirements consisting in capital goods (factory equipment, machinery, vehicles, etc.), raw materials (supplies for industry, agricultural inputs, building materials), basic foodstuffs and clothing, and luxury goods. Even if the state is as fortunate as Morocco with substantial hard currency earnings through phosphates, tourism, and citrus fruit exports, it will nonetheless probably face chronic substantial deficits in its foreign currency budget. In the case of Egypt, despite its cotton, rice, onion and citrus exports, its deficit is staggering. The crux of the matter with regard to corruption is that the allocation by the state of hard currency to public and private users must be highly selective. Because the state can never import anything approaching what it would like to, those who do receive foreign currency win a prize that is fiercely contested. Import licences can be "bought" and paid for in cash, support, or reciprocal favours.

One of the most rewarding posts any top official can occupy is that of managing a large state contract or project which entails the importation of large amounts of goods. Commissions, or side payments, frequently deposited to foreign accounts, may tacitly accompany the contract. Indeed the phenomenon has manifested itself in large "brokerage fees" paid by Soviet state importers to Egyptian middle men for having arranged, for instance, shipments of citrus fruits. In an ironic way economic backwardness becomes big business. Egypt must now import about four million tons of grain (not to mention other foodstuffs) annually to meet its own production deficit.

14. A recent example from Egypt concerns Assiut University which contracted with a local labour supplier for 20,000 labourers to work on an experimental farm. The workers were to get 15 piastres a day (ca. US 30¢) but the labour supplier paid them only 10. The University Administration found out about this and annulled the contract. This is unusual and the recruiter must have failed to split his take—which amounted to LE 1,000 per day! On government-run land-reclamation projects equally lucrative deals have been successfully concluded.

At 1974 world prices this represents $700 or $800 millions worth of commodities and another $200 million in shipping charges. Small percentages on any of these transactions spell large, almost instant fortunes. Flowing from this are various kinds of "fixing", "fronting", or mediating operations between private or public foreign investors and interested state licensing and regulatory agencies, as well as the public or private recipients of the investments. Public officials may set up dummy public relations outfits, investment counselling agencies, law offices, and the like, run by non-public members of the family or old buddies who handle the business.

Import restrictions and the lack of basic foods have prompted Egypt and Morocco toward state efforts to regulate prices and to assure an equitable distribution of essential commodities. In both countries these policies have stimulated thriving black market practices. However, it should be kept in mind that black market operations connote corruption that is legally-defined. It is an illegal attempt to re-introduce market mechanisms of supply and demand into centrally-regulated pricing and distribution systems. People may not like high prices in the black market but that does not necessarily mean they consider them corrupt. On the other hand, if the state, or its agents, becomes a direct party to black market operations, then popular perceptions and legal definitions may coincide.

The Egyptian state has intervened far more deeply than the Moroccan in price fixing and the regulation of supply. For that reason black market corruption, as legally defined, is far more widespread in Egypt than in Morocco, although the latter does control prices of staples such as sugar, flour, kerosene, etc. The same symbiotic relationship existing at all economic levels between public and private sectors is replicated in black market operations. It would be tedious to pursue all the possible transactions in detail for they are legion. The few examples given here represent the tip of the iceberg. The state in Egypt sets the price at which basic crops—wheat, rice, cotton, sugar-cane—are purchased from the producers. These are generally below real market value, and wealthier producers are generally able to buy the privilege of marketing some part of their crop outside the state system. The reverse process involves agricultural inputs. The state is the sole supplier of fertilizers, pesticides, high-yield variety seeds, fuel, certain kinds of machinery, spare parts, pumps, and so on. None of these are ever in sufficient supply, and it is relatively simple for distributing agencies, such as agricultural co-ops, to allow quantities of these goods to slip into the hands of private distributors. Demand for these inputs is fairly inelastic and the peasantry must meet the black market price or sacrifice their crops. . . .

The building industry, which for the last twenty years has been the major outlet for domestic private investment, is subject to black market corruption at every step. First of all the private sector builds far more housing than the public but not enough even to begin to meet demand in the urban areas. At the same time the government has tried to control rents on unfurnished apartments, holding them at levels far below their actual market value. The result has been various forms of key money, rent "advances", or the direct sale of apartments in order to get round the laws.

The state controls the distribution of all building materials. Once a prospective builder has obtained a lot and presented plans approved by the city's engineers, he is put on a waiting list for the cement, steel reinforcing bars, window frames, glass, etc., that his plans require. The wait for any or all of the materials may be as much as three years. Few builders bother to wait. With a lot and approved plans they can apply for a low-interest loan from the real-estate bank. This will easily cover preparation of the site and purchase of some building materials on the black market. They can then advertise their as yet unbuilt apartments for sale, demanding half the price as immediate down payment. The down payments are generally sufficient to cover all the construction costs at black market prices and to leave enough left over for acquisition of more property and the start of a new building project. Further instalments or purchase price are pure profit. When the builder finally does take possession of his state-distributed building materials, he can sell them on the black market. This completes the cycle, and it is one that many public officials and private entrepreneurs seek to prolong.

One could go on with several other examples of black market and other forms of developmental corruption. However if the scope, prevalence and variety of the phenomena have been adequately highlighted in the preceding lines, it is probably best to conclude by a brief assessment of the effects of corruption upon the system as a whole. It may be overstating the case, but within the three manifestations of corruption discussed above—endemic, planned, and developmental—it is difficult to discern any positive aspects beyond the short-term survival of the regime and the consolidation of inequities in the distribution of goods in favour of certain strata of society. Corruption at lower levels of the bureaucracy may make the monotonous lives of poorly-paid bureaucrats more tolerable, but it leads to the discriminatory award of essential services to those who can pay most while reenforcing the resentment and suspicion on the part of the great mass of the poor citizenry towards the civil service and public authorities in general. This sort of gap can only have pernicious effects on the will of a national collectivity to work toward developmental goals.

* * *

Even if one agrees that corrupt practices do not deserve much tolerance, there may come a point in the lives of certain regimes where corrupt practices become so prevalent, that the regimes can no longer feasibly undertake their own house cleaning, even if they decide that it is in their interests to do so.   Egypt and Morocco are perilously close to that sort of paralysis.

EGYPTIAN PENAL CODE OF 1937

(Law No. 58)

Article 112.   Any tax collector [or] tax clerk . . . who embezzles or removes public or private goods . . . which he was holding in the course of his duties shall be condemned, in addition to the restitution of the embezzled goods, to an equal fine, and punished with detention.

Article 114.   Any public official whatsoever placed at the head of an administration [or] subordinate employee . . . who in the collection of fines, taxes, . . . indirect contributions or other taxes . . . arranges to be given beyond what he knows to be due, shall be punished as follows: officials placed at the head of an administration . . . by the penalty of detention; subordinate employees by imprisonment and dismissal.   The judge shall further pronounce the restitution of the sums improperly collected and a fine equal to the amount of this restitution.

Article 118.   Any public official who, in any way, passes to his own account the wealth of the state or facilitates an infraction of the same sort in favor of a third party will be punished by three to seven years of detention.

Article 341.   Anyone who embezzles, uses, or dissipates to the prejudice of the owners, any sums, [or] objects . . . which have been entrusted to him only by way of deposit, lease, . . . shall be punished by imprisonment to which there may be added a fine not exceeding L.E. 100.

NOTE

Detention takes place in a central prison while imprisonment is in a local one.   For details on the correctional system, see Mahmood M. Mostafa, Principes de Droit Pénal Des Pays Arabes, Paris: Librairie Générale de Droit et de Jurisprudence, 1972, pp. 175–179.

EGYPTIAN PENAL CODE, Art. 112

(as amended by Law 69 of Feb. 19, 1953)

Any civil servant or public official who embezzles cash, documents, chattels or anything else entrusted to him in the course of his duties, is liable to hard labor for a fixed period.   If the guilty person is a tax collector or official, or a trustee or accountant of public funds, who has embezzled the least part of what has been entrusted to him in his duties, he shall be liable to hard labor for life.

NOTE

The revolutionary government attempted to do more than tighten up the legal definitions and penalties for official corruption (the provision cited above was but one of a series of such changes in the penal code.) It also created a new enforcement system: the administrative *niyaba*, a special group of prosecutorial judges whose task is to investigate charges of administrative corruption. This force was created in 1954 by Law 480 of that year, and was initially attached to the Presidency. Over time, it was transferred first to Central Management and Organization, and then to the Ministry of Justice in 1958. Its jurisdiction has also been extended over time to include some public sector corporations.

The administrative *niyaba* prosecutes in the administrative court system; there is a graded structure of courts for junior and senior officials. This system, however, can deal only with administrative violations and can issue only administrative penalties. Thus, if an official is accused of issuing a building license that should not have been issued, and doing so in return for a bribe, the regular *niyaba* handles the case before the regular courts, because a criminal offense is charged. If, however, the only offense charged—or for which evidence is available—is the offense of issuing the building license in clear violation of the relevant policies and laws, then the issue goes to the administrative *niyaba*, which can impose sanctions such as suspension for a period, or, in the extreme case, dismissal.

QUESTIONS

1. Waterbury discusses three categories of corruption. Under which category does an embezzling *umdah* fall? What about the corrupt agricultural cooperative officials mentioned at the beginning of the Problem? Do you find his categories helpful? What categories might you suggest instead?

2. How does the temptation for embezzlement differ as between the U.S. and Egypt?

3. How likely is it that either the *umdah* or the corrupt agricultural cooperative official will actually be prosecuted?

4. Does the creation of an administrative *niyaba* make prosecution more or less likely? Would you advise creation of such a force?

5. Suppose a low-level and poorly-paid civil servant were brought to trial for corruption and you were the judge. What would you do?

6. As a villager hurt by the corruption, what would you do about it?

7. As a responsible minister in the Egyptian government, what would you do about corruption? Consider the various management actions that could be undertaken as well as the possible legal actions.

8. In response to corruption and embezzlement in the national agricultural cooperative union, this union was liquidated in late 1976. Several major financial functions were transferred from the local cooperatives to the

state Rural Development Bank at about the same time. See Ottfried C. Kirsch, Agricultural Cooperatives as an Instrument of Agricultural Policy—Experience with Cooperative Promotion of Production in Egypt, 10 Verfassung und Recht In Übersee 255, 262 (1977). Is this type of approach the only way to control embezzlement? Is it likely to be effective? What are the social costs?

9. How do the dilemmas surrounding the prevention of corruption in Egypt differ from those in the U.S.? In thinking about this problem, which poses the relatively obvious question whether corruption is strongly associated with specific economic policies, remember also that part of the reason the Ayatollah succeeded in overthrowing the Shah of Iran was the corruption associated with the Shah's regime. (Mubarak is believed to be quite interested in preventing corruption.)

Chapter 15

EMBEZZLEMENT BY A PUBLIC OFFICIAL
IN BOTSWANA

———

A. INTRODUCTION

1. A Hypothetical

NOTE

The Chief of a Tswana Chiefdom collects funds for a chiefdom celebration of a visit by the President of Botswana. The President will be enroute to another part of the country. But he and his wife will stop in the chiefdom capital to greet local dignitaries and to partake of refreshments. The Chief takes some of the funds, which were collected in name of the local District Council—of which he is a member—and gives them to his son, who uses them to open a small cafe in the capital. He says that the reception for the President will be held there, and that, afterwards, it can be a site for other community occasions.

2. Some Issues

NOTE

The hypothetical raises several issues which are explored in the materials: Is such a use of the funds considered wrong? Or, is the action interpreted in some other way? If this use of the funds is considered a wrong, what other similar wrongs take place? How widespread are such wrongs? What is the public attitude toward them?

Another set of issues also is embedded in the hypothetical: How do the status and roles of the Chief affect how the action is interpreted and the response to it? Is such an act treated differently when carried out by a Chief rather than an ordinary person? If a case is brought, who would institute suit? How similar or different would the procedures be from those in a Western court? From those in the other radically different cultures? How is the legal response to any charges that are brought affected by the presence of Western received law? By post-independence changes in the law?

463

3. Some Reported Cases of Embezzlement and Other Similar Wrongs

NOTE

Newspaper reports from Botswana indicate that, although embezzlement and similar wrongs are frowned upon there, they do occur.

(GABORONE) BOTSWANA DAILY NEWS, APRIL 8, 1974

JAILED 3 YEARS

Samuel Kgati, 27, who was senior clerk in the Bangwaketse Tribal Administration until late last year, has been sentenced to a total of 69 years jail for theft, the sentences to run concurrently over three years.

Kgati was found guilty in Kanye of 23 offences of misappropriating a total of R1 130 paid to the tribal administration as judiciary fines and compensation. He was jailed for 3 years on each count.

At the time he was sentenced, Kgati was already serving a one-year sentence for a similar offence of which he was convicted last year.

Magistrate B. Suttil also sent Mohibidu Lobatlamang, a court scribe with the tribal administration, to prison for six months for stealing R64,34. Lobatlamang was also serving a previous sentence for theft.

Assistant superintendent F.B. Lebala prosecuted.

(GABORONE) BOTSWANA DAILY NEWS, FEBRUARY 11, 1980

Traffic cop gets 45 months for five counts of theft

By Solomon Lotshe

Police Constable Tally Nathaniel Motswagole 26 of Traffic section was last week sentenced by the Francistown Magistrate court to 45 months' imprisonment on five counts of stealing by person imployed in the public service.

He pleaded not guilty to all five counts.

The court was told that the accussed stole the sum of P110 from differnt people which came to his possession by virtue of his employment but converted it to his own use.

He was sentenced to nine months' imprisonment on each count and the sentences are to run consecutively.

The court heard that during the coarse of last year the accused carried out traffic duties within Francistown and stopped a number of vehicles for inspection.

The court further heard that during inspection activities six motorists were charged for various traffic offences and issued with charge forms instead of official receipts.

The complainents paid the accused the money on the spot as he demanded which he later misappropriated. The court was also informed that the accused did not open any docket against any of the charged motorists.

charged motorists.

The accused in defence denied to have received any amount from any body.

In passing sentence chief magistrate, Mr G.L. Patel said the offences committed are serious and bear a maximum prison term of seven years.

The Magistrate further remarked that it would be sad if police men who are supposed to help and protect the public harass the people.

"I treat these offences with most seriousness," the Magistrate said.

The court he said has the duty to pass an appropriate deterrent sentence.

Assistant Superintendent N.M. Lekgaba prosecuted.

William Clifford, Introduction to African Criminology. Nairobi: Oxford University Press, 1974, pp. 138–140.

As *between* tribes in the rural areas, the fact that the concept of theft is frequently limited to the community or tribal society has given a certain amount of trouble. Jacqueline Costa confirms that to the people of certain pastoral tribes in French-speaking Africa, stock theft is less a wrongful act than an exploit bringing prestige to the perpetrator. "The word 'chorset' meaning theft, does not, of course, apply to the taking of cattle from foreign enemies. This makes it a real problem for the country in which such tribes live. . . ."

In the course of the study of juvenile delinquency in Zambia in 1964, tribal elders were closely questioned about the different types of wrongdoing and one gave the following interesting account of theft as it developed in this part of Africa:

> Theft has been regarded from the earliest times as a serious offence although there was very little to steal then as compared with today. It consisted mostly of food, groundnuts, maize, cassava, sugar cane or sweet potatoes. These might be stolen from the fields, gardens or granaries. Meat, fish, fowls, etc., might be stolen from houses. Usually a child's theft would be from his home where he might begin by helping himself to the relish in the pot without his mother's consent. If such misbehaviour is not checked at this stage it could get worse and extend beyond the family. With the coming of the Europeans, children were able to steal other things which were easily carried unseen such as money, soap, sugar, clothes and blankets.

It seems, therefore, that as village people have acquired more goods, and more valuable goods, of their own the temptations and opportunities to steal have increased. Moreover, the increasing problem of theft even in many of the rural areas of Africa today no doubt reflects the contact, especially via migrant labour, with urban standards, values and ways of life—with personal ownership and possession gradually reducing the significance of sharing and communal ownership within the tribe.

QUESTIONS

1. What are some of the factors that make theft less common in some traditional African communities than in modernizing African communities?

2. Clifford suggests that theft may be acceptable beyond the community's borders. Does "community" always mean tribe? Does the inclusiveness of "my people" vs. "your people" vary from society to society? If so, what are the implications for the extent of the applicability of the concept "theft?" For example, in contemporary American society where is the line between "theft" and "ripping off?"

B.　TSWANA DEFINITION OF CRIME

1.　The Concept of Theft in Africa

NOTE

Theft, broadly defined, is a likely candidate for a universally-valid list of "crimes." We will examine general African views and Tswana views concerning theft and use them as a vehicle for reviewing the broader question of whether the Tswana distinguish between crimes and torts, between criminal and civil law.

QUESTION

1.　What were notions of theft like in traditional, largely rural Africa?

William Clifford, Introduction to African Criminology. Nairobi: Oxford University Press, 1974, p. 139. Footnotes omitted.

.　.　. it appears that theft was a comparatively rare phenomenon in indigenous society. .　.　. [For example,] Vansina* provides a list of the cases heard by a *Chefferie* court from May 1952 to May 1953 which shows only 21 cases of theft in the year as against 246 other cases classed as criminal—including 74 assaults.

But theft was known, deplored and discouraged even within a tribal society, rare though its occurrence might be. There is a Nandi proverb that a "born thief" will respect nothing, not even hospitality (he will steal even from his host), and Lindblow observed that "even a cursory glance at what has been written about the judicial system of the Bantu people is sufficient to show that well nigh everywhere the punishment for theft is surprisingly severe". .　.　. Forde,** on the Southern Ibo, says that in the past the punishment for theft depended on circumstances. Petty theft by women or unimportant persons might be punished by shaming on the first occasion, the offender being tied up in public to be ridiculed and degraded. Persons guilty of persistent theft were liable to lose the protection of their close kin who connived at their abduction by the victim's lineage for the offender to be sold into slavery. .　.　.

* J. Vansina, "A Traditional Legal System: The Kuba," Kuba in African Law Adaptation and Development, editors, H. and L. Kuper, Berkeley: University of California, 1965.

** D. Forde, "Justice and Judgement among the Southern Ibo Under Colonial Rule, in African Law Adaptation and Development, editors, H. and L. Kuper, Berkeley: University of California, 1965.

2. Theft Among the Tswana

a. Conceptions During the Protectorate

NOTE

What were Tswana notions about theft as a kind of wrong as Schapera recorded them during the Protectorate? These conceptions emerge particularly sharply in Tswana treatment of cattle theft because cattle play such a critical role in Botswana society and culture.

In considering Tswana notions about theft it is useful to keep in mind a distinction between delicts and penal offenses. This is based on terminological usage of the British social anthropologist A. R. Radcliffe-Brown, employed by Schapera in analyzing his case material. A delict is a wrong and Radcliffe-Brown distinguished between public and private delicts as follows:

term	who initiates action	kind of sanction applied
public delict	the community or its representative	penal sanction
private delict	the injured party	restitutive sanction

In actual fact, many societies sometimes apply penal sanctions to private delicts in addition to applying restitutive sanctions. The distinction between "private delicts" and "public delicts" is roughly the distinction between "torts" and "crimes." We shall see, however, that—concerning delicts—societies draw the line between "public" and "private" in different places.

Isaac Schapera, A Handbook of Tswana Law and Custom. Second edition. London: Oxford University Press, 1955, pp. 271–273.

Theft, particularly of livestock, was formerly punished very severely. A thief found in the veld with stolen cattle in his possession was often killed on the spot, or very severely thrashed, or tortured by having his hands burned. Nowadays he must be brought to the *kgotla* for trial; and it is still not unusual for him to be severely thrashed by order of the Chief, particularly if he has no property of his own which can be taken from him. The general rule, however, in cases of theft is that the owner of the stolen property is entitled to receive twice the value of the article stolen. If the case comes to court, the thief may also be required to pay a special beast to its members. Where more than one man is involved in the theft and slaughter of an ox, the full penalty is exacted from each. But there must always be clear proof of the theft. . . .

Cattle may be stolen for ownership, slaughter, or sale. Should a man looking for a missing ox find it at another's cattlepost, and his claim to it be denied, he will sue the thief. The herdboys and other witnesses of both men will be called and asked, in the absence of the animal in question, to describe it minutely. If the details given by plaintiff and his witnesses are found to correspond with the markings and other peculiarities of the ox, it will be adjudged to him. The thief will also be required to give him another ox as *kgomo ya bogodu* (the ox of the theft). If the thief has done this sort of thing before, or if his demeanour during the progress of the case is found to be reprehensible, he will be made to pay an additional ox as a fine to the court. If unable to pay, he will be thrashed instead. Should it be found, however, that defendant had not really stolen the ox, but came across it in the veld and kept it, under the impression that it was his own missing animal, he is not punished in any way, but must restore the ox to its rightful owner. On the other hand, if he had refused to let the owner look in his kraal for the missing beast, this would be held as good evidence that he knew the beast to be stolen. The owner would then be entitled to the usual compensation, while the thief himself would be punished by the court.

Should the owner of a missing ox discover it in the possession of a man by whom it has been purchased, he will, after ascertaining how it came to be there, take action as usual against the man from whom it was purchased. The latter, if found guilty of the theft, must redeem the stolen ox from the purchaser, giving him one of his own instead. The ox is then restored to the original owner, who also obtains from the thief another ox as *kgomo ya bogodu*. The thief is further fined an ox by the court. Often he is thrashed as well, for this is regarded as a very serious offence, especially now that it is possible to sell cattle to the traders. . . .

When an ox has been stolen for slaughter, and the thief is found with the meat and skin in his possession, the standard penalty is the same. . . .

* * *

In regard to other forms of property, such as utensils, the stolen object is taken back, and the thief, if a young man, is thrashed. Older people are not usually thrashed, but must make twofold restitution. So, too, if clothing has been stolen it is taken back, and the thief must further pay the owner its equivalent in cash or kind.

QUESTIONS

1. Why do you think Tswana treated theft with an expectation of double restitution? And why was it expected that the convicted thief, under some circumstances, would hand over something to the court? What is the implication of assessing something beyond simple restitution?

2. In what way did Tswana customary treatment of theft take account of intention? How was intention ascertained?

b. *Frequency During the Protectorate and Later*

NOTE

We have examined conceptions of theft during the Protectorate; what was their frequency? Is this frequency changing? The answer is provided by an analysis of Tswana court records from the decade 1961–1970 compared with those from the early to mid-1930's.

In the material you are about to read, Schapera and Roberts (following Schapera in order to facilitate comparability) classify wrongs as "delicts" (private delicts) or "penal offenses" (public delicts).

Simon Roberts, "The Survival of the Traditional Tswana Courts in the National Legal System of Botswana," in the Journal of African Law, vol. 16, 1972, pp. 108, 110–111, 113, 116, 122, 126. Some headings omitted.

THE WORK LOAD OF THE CHIEF'S COURTS [A comparison of the 1960's material with Schapera's 1930's material . . .]

. . . indicates immediately that, with the exception of a single court, the case load of the courts he investigated has greatly increased. In a single year each of these courts now tries almost as many (and in some cases even more) disputes as came before it during the whole period of his research:

Chief's Court	Population of Tribal Territory in 1964 (to nearest 100)	Number of Disputes Recorded									
		1961	1962	1963	1964	1965	1966	1967	1968	1969	1970
Ngwato	201,000	381	475	734	662	621	533	446	489	457	453
Ngwaketse	71,300	82	116	164	98	139	114	142	120	130	162
Malete	13,900	112	118	78	67	102	98	128	109	116	108
Tlokwa	3,700	21	15	13	164	331	—	—	50	40	52
Kwena	73,100	78	103	170	151	106	146	129	131	—	—
Kgatla	32,100	46	80	144	113	88	93	61	76	107	148
Tawana	42,400	23	15	29	23	29	23	16	19	19	—
Rolong	10,700	—	—	—	—	—	—	—	—	—	—

Part of this increase must presumably be attributable to the considerable population growth which has taken place in the intervening period. But, although the number of disputes coming before a Chief's Court annually varies considerably from one tribal territory to another, there is no consistent correlation between the number of people in a tribal territory and the number of disputes coming before its Chief's Court.

NOTE

Figure 1 (on the next page) represents Schapera's 1943 data (from "The Work of the Tribal Courts in Bechuanaland Protectorate" in African Studies, vol. 2, p. 31). Figures 2 and 3 (also on the next page) present Roberts' 1960's data from the article from which this excerpt is extracted.

FIGURE 1. FREQUENCY OF TYPES OF DISPUTES (Mainly in the 1930's)

Schapera's Table I

(Schapera, 1943, 31)

	Ngwaketse 1910–16	Ngwaketse 1928–34	Ngwaketse 1936–40	Kgatla 1935–39	Kwena 1935–38	Ngwato 1937–38	Tawana 1935–39	TOTALS
DOMESTIC AND PERSONAL STATUS								
Marriage and Divorce	46	38	35	4	8	50	36	
Children: Legitimacy and Custody	9	4	1	2	1	1	4	
Parents: Rights and Duties	16	11	13	5	—	6	2	
Guardians: Rights and Duties	4	9	2	3	1	2	1	
Membership of Tribe or Ward	11	4	—	—	1	—	1	331
PROPERTY								
Ownership and Possession	30	25	2	12	13	15	44	
Inheritance	24	6	5	4	7	5	10	202
CONTRACTS								
Sale and Purchase	33	11	2	8	—	2	14	
Permissive Use	23	10	6	3	1	6	28	
Donation	7	—	—	1	1	2	2	
Services	34	25	3	8	—	5	25	260
DELICTS								
Defamation	8	12	7	1	—	2	2	
Insult	2	4	8	6	4	4	16	
Assault	36	19	14	31	24	21	24	
Seduction	8	11	4	4	3	6	6	
Adultery	4	5	2	—	—	5	19	
Damage to Property	26	11	4	8	11	8	16	
Theft	65	40	23	24	7	31	38	
Sorcery	26	28	6	2	3	15	5	
Rape	2	3	—	—	1	1	—	726
PENAL OFFENCES								
Political Misdemeanours	9	11	17	16	4	16	9	
Contempt of Court	14	14	27	31	6	—	5	
Statutory and Miscellaneous Offences	50	17	49	4	27	9	12	347
								1,866

FIGURE 2. FREQUENCY OF TYPES OF DISPUTES (1961–1970)

Kgatla: Chief's Court 1961–1970

[Roberts, 1972:122]

Type of Dispute	1961	1962	1963	1964	1965	1966	1967	1968	1969	1970	Total
DOMESTIC AND PERSONAL STATUS											
Marriage and Divorce	2	2	9	4	10	8	3	3	1	3	
Children: Legitimacy and Custody	—	1	—	1	—	—	—	—	—	—	
Parents: Rights and Duties	—	—	3	—	2	—	—	—	1	—	
Guardians: Rights and Duties	—	—	—	—	—	—	—	—	—	—	
Membership of Tribe or Ward	—	—	—	—	—	—	—	—	—	—	52
PROPERTY											
Ownership and Possession	3	4	20	13	8	6	3	9	14	17	
Inheritance	—	1	3	4	2	—	—	2	1	—	
Land	4	3	4	3	1	1	1	2	—	1	130
CONTRACTS											
Sale and Purchase	—	2	2	5	2	1	—	—	2	5	
Permissive Use	—	—	—	—	—	—	—	—	—	2	
Donation	—	—	—	—	—	—	—	—	—	—	
Services	1	4	2	2	—	2	1	2	4	4	
Debt	1	2	7	5	3	1	—	1	—	5	68
DELICTS											
Defamation and Insult	—	—	3	4	1	3	—	—	1	7	
Assault	8	21	21	16	12	15	14	13	31	35	
Seduction and Impregnation	1	3	4	4	3	2	5	2	1	8	
Adultery and Abduction	—	—	1	—	2	—	—	1	—	—	
Damage to, and Loss of, Property	1	2	3	1	2	5	3	3	2	3	
Theft	18	31	47	47	36	44	30	31	40	50	
Sorcery	—	—	—	—	—	—	—	—	—	—	
Rape	1	—	—	—	—	1	—	—	2	—	645
PENAL OFFENCES											
Political Misdemeanours	—	—	—	—	—	—	—	—	—	—	
Contempt of Court	—	—	—	—	2	—	—	2	—	2	
Statutory and Miscellaneous Matters	4	4	14	2	2	4	1	5	7	7	
Disobedience to Chief (Admin.)	2	—	1	2	—	—	—	—	—	—	61
TOTAL	46	80	144	113	88	93	61	76	107	148	956

FIGURE 3. FREQUENCY OF TYPES OF DISPUTES (1961–1970)

Kwena: Chief's Court 1961–1968

[Roberts, 1972:126]

Type of Dispute	1961	1962	1963	1964	1965	1966	1967	1968	1969	1970	Total
DOMESTIC AND PERSONAL STATUS											
Marriage and Divorce	—	4	3	1	—	1	—	2			
Children: Legitimacy and Custody ..	—	—	—	—	—	—	—	—			
Parents: Rights and Duties	—	—	—	—	—	—	—	—			
Guardians: Rights and Duties	—	—	—	—	—	—	—	—			
Membership of Tribe or Ward	—	—	—	—	—	—	—	—			11
PROPERTY											
Ownership and Possession	—	—	—	1	—	—	3	2			
Inheritance	—	—	—	—	—	—	—	—			
Land	—	1	—	—	—	—	—	—			7
CONTRACTS											
Sale and Purchase	—	—	—	—	—	—	—	—			
Permissive Use	—	—	—	—	—	—	—	—			
Donation	—	—	—	—	—	—	—	—			
Services	—	—	—	—	—	—	—	—			
Debt	—	—	—	—	—	—	—	1			1
DELICTS											
Defamation and Insult	1	1	2	—	—	1	—	1			
Assault	24	33	38	33	38	45	49	47			
Seduction and Impregnation	1	—	4	—	—	—	—	3			
Adultery and Abduction.............	—	—	—	—	—	—	—	—			
Damage to, and Loss of, Property ..	3	7	2	3	—	6	1	2			
Theft	30	35	97	82	49	63	50	50			
Sorcery	—	—	—	—	—	—	—	—			
Rape	1	2	—	—	—	—	—	—			804
PENAL OFFENCES											
Political Misdemeanours	—	—	—	—	—	—	—	—			
Contempt of Court	1	—	1	1	2	—	—	3			
Statutory and Miscellaneous Matters	12	15	13	23	9	23	21	18			
Disobedience to Chief (Admin.)	—	—	—	—	—	—	—	—			142
Missing	5	5	10	7	6	7	5	2			47
TOTAL	78	103	170	151	104	146	129	131			1,012

When Schapera analysed the business coming before the Chief's Courts of five Tswana tribes over varying periods between 1935 and 1940, he found that "the bulk of tribal litigation among the Tswana" was concerned with what he classified as delicts and penal offences; that delicts outnumbered the disputes in any other category; and that "thefts" and "assaults" constituted by far the largest sub-groups within the general category of delicts. Disputes concerning domestic and personal status, property, and contracts respectively, represented a much smaller part of the business of these courts. Expressed as percentages of all judicial business coming before these courts, delicts and penal offences made up 58% of the business, domestic, and personal status disputes 18%, property disputes 11%, and contracts 14%. Making a similar survey of the business undertaken by six Tswana Chief's Courts (four of which were among those covered by Schapera) over the period 1961–1970, I found that the general pattern noted by Schapera was confirmed, but that the detailed balance of the business had significantly changed. While the number of delictual disputes had everywhere greatly increased, the number of disputes concerning domestic and personal status, property, and contract, had shrunk, in many cases absolutely, and in all cases in proportion to the business of the court as a whole. . . . Delicts now account for 70% of all judicial business, compared with 39% for the period covered by his material; and when delicts and penal offences are combined, the total reaches 83% compared with his figure of 58%. At the same time, domestic, property and contract disputes have declined sharply from 18% to 5%, from 11% to 6%, and from 14% to 2% respectively. Admittedly, my results include materials from two courts not touched upon by Schapera. They also exclude figures for the Ngwato court where, to judge from the business of 1965 alone, the changes under consideration appear less marked.

In view of the considerable growth in delictual business which the contemporary records reveal, and the importance of this business in relation to that of the remaining categories, it is worth looking at the details of it more closely. Within this category thefts and assaults predominate, and taken together they now make up 63% of the business coming before the Chief's Courts, and this figure would be even higher if the deceptive Tawana figures were ignored. Of this total, assaults account for 28% and thefts for 35%. As in Schapera's time, thefts remain generally more numerous than assaults, although there are signs that this order is gradually being reversed in some courts.

. . . Although Schapera's system of classification has been followed some of his categories proved difficult to use in practice. . . .

I have [included] . . . under the category of theft only those cases in which it appears from the evidence that there has been a "dishonest taking". . . .

Both Schapera and Kuper * were unhappy with the description and composition of the two general categories of "Delicts" and "Penal Offences". [But] . . . there is some merit in classifying as penal offences only those matters which do not typically attract a compensatory claim by an individual in addition to an action by the state, even though in matters classified as delicts the penal aspect alone may sometimes be pursued.**

QUESTIONS

1. Roberts (and Kuper) followed Schapera's scheme for classifying wrongs in order for their studies and Schapera's to be comparable. Do you agree with Schapera's way of classifying wrongs?

2. Why do you think thefts and assaults, are classified as "delicts" under Schapera's (and the others') scheme, while our legal system would class them as "penal offenses?" (The answer may be clearer after you read Section C4.)

3. Speculate about why the relative frequency of thefts adjudicated in Tswana society increased during the thirty-five years covered by the research.

* Isaac Schapera, "The Work of the Tribal Courts in Bechuanaland Protectorate," in 2 African Studies 31 (1943); and Adam Kuper, "The Work of Customary Courts: Some Facts and Speculations," in 28 African Studies 37 (1969).

** The linkage between Tswana delicts and varying kinds of sanctions are described more fully in a Schapera excerpt in Section B4.

4. Theft and assault are relatively frequent offenses in Tswana society. In what kind of society do you think these offenses are likely to be significant in the profile of frequency of wrongs? What kinds of variables would one wish to take account of in seeking an answer to a question like this?

5. Does customary law make a distinction between crimes and torts?

3. Theft and the Botswana Penal Code

NOTE

Now, theft among the Tswana falls under the nation's penal code. Compare Schapera's description (in Section B2) of the treatment of theft under Tswana customary law with the following provisions from the penal code adopted for Botswana in 1964, two years before independence.

LAWS OF BOTSWANA, CHAPTER 08:01, PENAL CODE

Division V.   Offences Relating to Property

Theft

* * *

General Punishment for Theft

276.   Any person who steals anything capable of being stolen is guilty of the offence termed theft, and is liable, unless owing to the circumstances of the theft or the nature of the thing stolen some other punishment is provided, to imprisonment for three years.

Stealing Wills

277.   If the thing stolen is a testamentary instrument, whether the testator is living or dead, the offender is liable to imprisonment for ten years.

Stealing Postal Matter, etc.

278.   If the thing stolen is postal matter or any goods, money or valuable security contained in any postal matter, the offender is liable to imprisonment for ten years.

Stealing Stock

279.   If the thing stolen is any of the things following, that is to say, a horse, mare, gelding, ass, mule, bull, cow, ox, ram, ewe, wether, goat, pig, or ostrich, or the young thereof, the offender is liable to imprisonment for fourteen years.

Stealing from the Person: Stealing Goods in Transit, etc.

280. If a theft is committed under any of the circumstances following, that is to say—

(a) if the thing is stolen from the person of another;

(b) if the thing is stolen in a dwelling-house, and its value exceeds R10, or the offender at or immediately before or after the time of stealing uses or threatens to use violence to any person in the dwelling-house;

(c) if the thing is stolen from any kind of vessel or vehicle or place of deposit used for the conveyance or custody of goods in transit from one place to another;

(d) if the thing stolen is attached to or forms part of a railway;

(e) if the thing is stolen from a vessel which is in distress or wrecked or stranded;

(f) if the thing is stolen from a public office in which it is deposited or kept;

(g) if the offender, in order to commit the offence, opens any locked room, box, or other receptacle, by means of a key or other instrument,

the offender is liable to imprisonment for ten years.

Stealing by Persons in Public Service

281. If the offender is a person employed in the public service and the thing stolen is the property of the State or came into the possession of the offender by virtue of his employment, he is liable to imprisonment for seven years.

Stealing by Clerks and Servants

282. If the offender is a clerk or servant, and the thing stolen is the property of his employer, or came into the possession of the offender on account of his employer, he is liable to imprisonment for seven years.

Stealing by Directors or Officers of Companies

283. If the offender is a director or officer of a corporation or company, and the thing stolen is the property of the corporation or company, he is liable to imprisonment for seven years.

Stealing by Agents, etc.

284. If the thing stolen is any of the things following, that is to say—

(a) property which has been received by the offender with a power of attorney for the disposition thereof;

(b) property which has been entrusted to the offender either alone or jointly with any other person for him to retain in safe custody or to apply, pay, or deliver for any purpose or to any person the same or any part thereof or any proceeds thereof;

(c) property which has been received by the offender either alone or jointly with any other person for or on account of any other person;

(d) the whole or part of the proceeds of any valuable security which has been received by the offender with a direction that the proceeds thereof should be applied to any purpose or paid to any person specified in the direction;

(e) the whole or part of the proceeds arising from any disposition of any property which have been received by the offender by virtue of a power of attorney for such disposition, such power of attorney having been received by the offender with a direction that such proceeds should be applied to any purpose or paid to any person specified in the direction,

the offender is liable to imprisonment for seven years.

Stealing by Tenants or Lodgers

285. If the thing stolen is a fixture or goods let to the offender to be used by him with a house or lodging, and its value exceeds R10, he is liable to imprisonment for seven years.

Stealing after Previous Conviction

286. If the offender, before committing the theft, had been convicted of a theft punishable under any of sections 276 to 285, he is liable to imprisonment for seven years.

QUESTIONS

1. List the differences between the treatment of theft under Tswana customary law and under the Botswana Penal Code of 1964. Which are superficial and which indicate fundamental changes?

2. Note the variations in penalties in the Penal Code. What do they tell you about the degree of opprobrium attached to different types of theft? Or do you think the different penalties reflect the legislature's view of the differential in degree of deterrence that is needed?

3. Refer to the Problem II hypothetical. Assume that the Chief is "guilty." Which provisions of the Penal Code would apply? Which provisions would apply if the son were "guilty?"

NOTE

Review the Schapera excerpt at page 5 above. The practice described there of exacting from a thief restitution as well as a penalty to both the person wronged and to the court suggests to some Western observers the combining of civil and criminal suits in one trial. Some of these observers even go so far as to conclude that African customary law does not distinguish crimes from torts. But Schapera himself, in another place, asserts that the Tswana do have legal conceptions similar to the Western distinction between civil and criminal law.

Recall, once again, that Schapera is writing primarily about the 1930's and 1940's. The conceptual distinctions he recounts have remained more constant than some of the specific procedures.

Isaac Schapera, A Handbook of Tswana Law and Custom. Second edition. London: Oxford University Press, 1955, pp. 46–48, 50–51. Some footnotes omitted. Headings and other material inserted by the editor are bracketed.

CIVIL AND CRIMINAL LAW

[*Civil vs. Criminal Law.*] In practice, although not in theory, Tswana law is divided by the people themselves into two main classes. These may quite conveniently be termed "civil law" and "criminal law" respectively, although their categories are by no means identical with those of European systems of law. The civil law establishes *inter alia* the private rights of people in regard to personal status, property, and contracts; and provides for redress, if such rights are violated, by compelling restitution or compensation. The principal civil wrongs recognized in Tswana law include breaches of contract; seduction, adultery, and similar offences against family rights; trespass, damage, theft, and similar offences against property; defamation and other wrongs against reputation. The criminal law treats certain acts, not merely as injuries to individual persons, but as offences harmful to social life generally, and therefore deserving of punishment. The principal crimes thus recognized in Tswana law include all offences against the tribal authorities acting in their official capacity, and breach of the laws decreed by the Chief; homicide, grievous bodily assault, and similar offences against the person; sorcery, incest, and other "unnatural acts".

[*Merger: Civil and Criminal Law.*] It must be noted, however, that many civil injuries are on occasion also treated as crimes, the offender not only being forced to make amends to his victim, but suffering punishment as well. This applies particularly to cases of theft [as described above in the excerpt from Schapera in section B2]. . . . In the same way certain crimes, especially against bodily security, may on occasion also give rise to civil remedies. The man who assaults another is generally fined, the fine belonging to the Chief. But the general tendency in recent years has been to award part, if not all, of the fine as compensation to the victim; while for certain forms of assault there existed even in the olden days the right of retaliation. In cases such as these the offence is treated both as a wrong against some particular member of the tribe, who is therefore entitled to redress, and as an act harmful to society generally and therefore subject to punishment. In European systems of law the two aspects of such an offence are kept quite distinct and dealt with in separate proceedings. . . .

There is no such differentiation of procedure in Tswana law. The offence is tried in the course of a single action, and it is only in the verdict of the court that its dual nature is given explicit recognition. Nevertheless, the manner in which it is brought to trial is generally sufficient to show whether it must be regarded as primarily civil or criminal.

[*Civil Procedure.*] When a civil wrong is committed, the victim may, and indeed should, first attempt to obtain satisfaction by direct negotiation with the wrongdoer. Only if this fails will he sue him. The case must then as a rule first come before the local court, although it can afterwards be carried on appeal, or referred in case of difficulty, to the court of the Chief. The court will award the victim some form of redress, if his claim is upheld. He himself states what he wants, and the court may agree to award him this, or may vary the amount. It will at times go further, and also inflict punishment upon the wrongdoer, if his offence is regarded as sufficiently reprehensible. But unless the victim himself, or his representative, brings the matter to trial, the court has no jurisdiction.

[*Criminal Procedure.*] A criminal wrong, on the other hand, can never be settled out of court. It must be reported to the Chief or to some other competent tribal authority, who will then summon and prosecute the accused person in his court. The more serious crimes are always dealt with directly in the court of the Chief. Others may be dealt with and finally settled in the local or regimental courts. The accused, if found guilty, is punished. Where the punishment takes the form of a fine, this is paid, not to the victim of the wrong, but to the court, i.e. to the Chief (or some other authority) acting in his official capacity. The amount is fixed, not by the victim, as in the case of civil wrongs, but by the court. The court may also, if the nature of the case seems to warrant it, order the offender to make restitution or pay compensation to the victim.

REMEDIES AND PUNISHMENTS

[*Restitution and Compensation.*] Various remedies are available to the victim of a civil wrong. The two most frequent are restitution and compensation. Both can be obtained either through agreement between the parties concerned or through the verdicts of the courts. In restitution, the effect of the remedy is to cancel, so far as possible, the wrongful act. . . . In compensation, the victim receives damages for a wrong which cannot be undone, such as seduction, damage to property, and defamation.

[*Retaliation.*] Another remedy, more commonly exercised in former times than at present, is to "take the law into one's own hands" and forcibly exact what satisfaction one can.

[*Other Punishment.*] [During the Protectorate times about which Schapera is writing, other punishments included fines, thrashing, banishment, mutilation, and death. Now, of course, the penalties that all courts may mete out are fixed by statute. Courts, depending on their level and the terms of their establishment (warrant), may apply various of the traditional punishments except banishment and mutilation. Certain penalties are reserved to the High Court and the President may use banishment for certain offenses under the Chieftainship Act (much as the British did to Tshekedi Khama in the succession dispute described in Chapter 10.]

RESPONSIBILITY AND INTENT

[*Responsibility.*] In Tswana law the head of each family is responsible for all his dependants. His wife, unmarried children, and servants cannot as a rule take legal action against other people unless assisted and represented by him, nor can they be sued except through him. No contract entered into by them is valid unless approved of by him. He is further responsible for the payment of their debts, as well as of any fines imposed upon them or damages awarded against them. But where they commit an offence meriting punishment by thrashing, it is the actual offender who is punished, and not his guardian. The owner of livestock is similarly liable for any damage they do, provided it can be shown that he has failed to look after them properly. . . .

Formerly, if a man was himself unable to pay his debts, fines, or damages, his near relatives were expected, and could sometimes be forced, to come to his aid. Nowadays this principle of collective responsibility is no longer so generally observed . . . .

[*Intent.*] Every adult person is presumed to know the law, and to have intended the results following an act he has committed. Motive is not generally taken into consideration, although malicious prosecution of an innocent person may entitle the victim to damages for defamation. Allowance is, however, made for provocation, so that assault, and formerly even homicide, is in certain cases held to be justifiable and so is excused. Negligence, as a rule, involves liability for any resulting damage. Purely accidental wrongs are, on the other hand, almost invariably excused or far less heavily penalized. Less liability attaches to an unsuccessful attempt to do wrong than to one which has succeeded. The former, indeed, is not often brought to trial, for Tswana law in the main takes cognizance only of wrongs which have actually been perpetrated. So, too, the amount of damage actually inflicted is taken into consideration in assessing the amount of punishment or compensation . . . .

The character of a wrongdoer also plays an important part in determining the attitude adopted towards him. If he readily admits his offence, he may be dealt with lightly, and sometimes even excused altogether. But if he is insolent or obstreperous, even in the face of overwhelming evidence against him, he will be penalized more severely than usual. Similarly, an habitual offender is always more severely penalized than a first offender. . . .

QUESTIONS

1. Does it matter whether a society differentiates between civil and criminal wrongs by using separate terminology and distinct procedures? Or do

we expect such a dichotomy only because it fits our Western categories? Consider the dual system's effects on a victim's chances of receiving compensation.

2. Even in our own society is the jurist's classification of crime vs. tort the only distinction used? What of the folk classification of the "person in the street?" What does he or she define as a "crime?" With what does he or she compare it? Contrast it?

3. Why wasn't imprisonment a standard penalty in traditional Botswana?

4. What don't you know about Tswana thinking concerning crime? How is a crime distinguished from an immoral act? From a sin? For that matter, did the Tswana have that concept? Do they now?

NOTE

Now that you know more about Tswana conceptions of crime and criminal law, can you see why field workers who study Tswana law find it hard to categorize theft as the Tswana see it as either a "crime" or a "tort?" Note, that in contrast to American law, theft cases, until recently, always had to be brought by the victim. Why? John Comaroff has commented on this pattern:

Comaroff, Personal Communication, 1979.

". . . this reflects an indigenous theory of interpersonal relations: in a sense, 'crime' is the invasion and/or appropriation of one individual's personal space (his property, domestic domain, spiritual well-being, person [corporeal and incorporeal], productive capacities, etc.) by another individual's. It is not simply a contravention of an abstract normative order. The difference is very significant, especially in trying to understand when cases will go to the *kgotla* and when (legitimate) everyday interpersonal competition is transformed into a dispute case (*tseko*). This is a society in which the ideology of individualism and utilitarianism is highly developed and in which men are expected to compete; thus, the critical difference between legitimate rivalry and illegal activity is fundamental to an analysis of the concepts of crime and theft."

Keep Comaroff's comment in mind as you work through the rest of this chapter.

C. CHIEFLY STATUS AND CRIME: LEGITIMACY AND LEGALITY

1. Role of the Chief: Power, Wealth and Duty

NOTE

A second major issue raised by Problem II is whether one or more of: the perception of a wrong, the definition of a wrong, and the response to a wrong are affected by the status of the wrong-doer. Specifically, in Botswana would response to embezzlement by a chief be different than that to the same act committed by another person?

In order to answer the above question we need to examine the role of the chief. From Chapter 4, we know that his role has been central in Tswana society. Now, as we shall see, even though their formal powers have been diminished, they continue to be very important persons.

First, we will review the chief's role during the Protectorate as reported by Schapera—noting his duties and powers, the nature of his wealth and uses of it, and the type of checks and balances that applied to his powers. Then, we will take a more dynamic view, looking at how these powers and counterbalancing checks and balances were modified during the Protectorate. Finally, we examine the contemporary situation as reported by Gillett and Tordorff.

As you read through Section C1 look for indications of the extent to which there was a distinction between what was the chief's as opposed to what was the chiefdom's or the people's. What does a blurring of those distinctions imply concerning the potential for the possibility of misappropriation of funds or property—either deliberate or inadvertent? Also look for precedents and rationale for the role he takes on in the hypothetical of Problem II.

Schapera writes of the role of the chief before Independence, during the end of the Protectorate period.

Isaac Schapera, A Handbook of Tswana Law and Custom. London: Oxford University Press, 1955, pp. 62–72. Second edition. Some footnotes omitted. Headings interposed by editor are bracketed.

THE CHIEF'S PREROGATIVES AND WEALTH

[*Chief as Symbol.*] The Chief, as head of the tribe, occupies a position of unique privilege and authority. He is the symbol of tribal unity, the central figure round whom the tribal life revolves. He is at once ruler, judge, maker and guardian of the law, repository of wealth, dispenser of gifts, leader in war, priest and magician of the people. His exalted status is reflected in the ceremonial surrounding him and in the obligations of his tribesmen towards him. Although not rendered almost inaccessible to his people by an elaborate system of formal etiquette such as prevails in some other South African Bantu tribes, he is greatly honoured and respected, and always treated with a good deal of outward respect. It is a serious offence for any tribesman to use abusive language about him, or to speak or behave improperly towards him or in his presence. . . .

The Chief and his family normally take precedence in the tribe in matters of ritual, such as the firstfruits and initiation ceremonies; and he alone has the right to convene tribal meetings, arrange tribal ceremonies, and impose the supreme penalties of death or banishment. He has the first choice of a site for building his home, of arable lands, and of grazing for his cattle; and he is invariably the richest man in the tribe. All offences against him are generally punished far more severely than similar offences against ordinary tribesmen.

[*Chief's Coercive Authority.*] The Chief has the right in general to obedience from his subjects in all matters of public interest, and also in minor matters of more personal concern. He can send people where he likes and on any errand that he likes, and may also use their wagons and oxen, provided that the work involved is on behalf of the tribe. In particular he is entitled to free labour from the age-regiments for both public and private purposes . . .. Failure to comply with his orders is a penal offence, while disloyalty or revolt against his authority is one of the major crimes in Tswana society, punishable as a rule in former times by death and the confiscation of the culprit's property, and nowadays by banishment.

[*Chief's Tribute.*] The Chief is also entitled to the tribute known as *sehuba*. This consists primarily in the breast-portion (*sehuba*) of every big game animal, in one tusk of every elephant, and in the skins of every lion and leopard killed by his subjects, whether hunting alone, or in a regiment, or in a *letsholô* (tribal hunt). This tribute is compulsory, failure to deliver it being a penal offence. . . . Among the Kgatla, Tlôkwa, and Malete, he must further be given a cash payment, generally of £1, by every man who has been working abroad among the Europeans. This payment is also known as *sehuba* [1]. . . .

There is another tribute, formerly universal and still found among the Ngwaketse and Kwena, known as *dikgafèla*. This consists in a basketful of corn, which must be given to the Chief by every woman in times of good harvest. Its presentation is a ceremonial affair; and, from this corn, beer is brewed, which is drunk by all the people. Finally, in all the tribes there were (and in most of them still are) a number of large public fields . . . cultivated for the Chief by different portions of the tribe. The Chief provides the seed, and the people do all the work, from clearing the field to harvesting the produce, which must all be given to him.

[*Chief's Cattle.*] The Chief's most important source of wealth is cattle. As a rule he possesses by far the largest herds in the tribe. Most of them are the offspring of cattle originally looted in war. Such cattle were all brought to the Chief, who divided some among the successful raiders or among men who had otherwise distinguished themselves, but always kept a generous number for himself. The cattle he kept back are sometimes held to be his personal property, over which the tribe has no claim at all. But it is also maintained that they are tribal cattle, in the sense that the Chief merely holds them in trust for the tribe as a whole, and cannot use them recklessly for his own ends. . . .

1. Among the Malete and Tlôkwa, and probably also in other tribes, these forms of tribute were abolished in 1936, when Tribal Funds were established and financial provision made for the needs of the Chief.

Other cattle which accrue to the Chief, and which he is expected to use for tribal purposes as well as for his personal needs, are *matimela* (stray cattle). All such cattle must be brought to him; and, if after a time he is satisfied that their owners cannot be found, they belong to him. . . .

[*Later Sources of Wealth.*] In more recent times the Chief also had the disposal of the cash income accruing from the stand rents paid by traders and blacksmiths, from the annual premiums paid for mineral and woodcutting concessions in his territory, and from the annual commission paid by the Administration on the amount of hut-tax collected from his people. He could further, from time to time, impose a cash levy upon the tribe to finance some large public work; and he was not generally required to account for his handling of this money. Then, apart from the cash tribute already referred to, the Chief in some tribes was presented with large sums of money on his accession, similar in kind to the cattle formerly given. He could also raise a levy to pay the debts he had incurred, either personally, or on behalf of the tribe. The present policy, quite recently initiated by the Administration, is to divert the money and other revenue raised from rents, tax, fines, levies, and similar sources into a tribal fund kept apart from the Chief's personal income, and to pay him a salary based upon an estimate of their annual value. But in the past there was no such distinction between public and private revenue: it was all used and controlled by the Chief.

THE SERVANTS OF THE CHIEF

[*Malata, Former Serfs.*] Although the Chief has a right to the services of every member of the tribe, he also has a large number of servants directly attached to his household and performing its work. In one category are those known as *malata*, of whom the great majority, especially among the Ngwato, Tawana, and Kwena, are recruited from such servile communities as the Sarwa and Kgalagadi. . . .

[*Other Servants.*] The Chief has other servants (*batlhanka*), drawn from the ordinary members of the tribe. Among the Kgatla, and probably in most other tribes as well, a certain ward or certain family-groups were specially attached to the Chief's "house" as its servants. These retainers continue to work for him and his successors. They live at their own home, and have the same rights as other members of the tribe; but they also have special obligations towards the Chief. . . . The Chief in return lets them use his wagons, ploughs, and oxen for their own purposes; they can use the milk of the cattle they herd; he occasionally gives them cattle of their own, pays their tax, provides them with clothing, and may assist them with *bogadi*, blankets, and other objects when they marry.

["*Common Headmen*".] Among the Ngwato and Tawana there was another system of service as well. The Chief would entrust his share of the cattle looted in war and all other "tribal" cattle to commoners specially selected for their loyalty and bravery. . . . The cattle thus placed in the care of different "common headmen" belonged to the Chief himself, in his official capacity as head of the tribe, and were not specially allocated to any of his houses. . . .

The cattle entrusted in this way to common headmen were known as *kgamêlô* ("milk-pail") cattle, from the fact that it was one of the principal duties of the herdsman to milk them for the Chief's household and from time to time bring him thick milk (*madila*) in skin bags. . . .

. . . subject to various limitations, these men could use the cattle as their own property. In return they were expected to provide the Chief with meat and with milk, and to perform various domestic services for him. . . .

THE CHIEF'S DUTIES AND OBLIGATIONS

[*General Duties.*] The Chief's life is not merely one of immense privilege. He has many duties to perform for the tribe, duties which, if faithfully carried out, may impose an immense burden upon his time and energy. He must in the first place watch over the interests of his people and keep himself informed of tribal affairs generally.

* * *

It is his duty as trustee to treat his people well and justly, and to see that no harm or misfortune befalls them. He must give ear to all his subjects, irrespective of rank; and in particular he is required to attend regularly at his *kgotla* to listen to news, petitions, and statements of grievances from all parts of the tribe.

The wealth accumulated by the Chief he must utilize, not only for his own benefit, not only for the maintenance of his large household, but also on behalf of the tribe as a whole. One quality always required of him is generosity. He must provide liberal hospitality in beer and meat for people visiting him or assisting at his *kgotla*, or summoned to work or to fight for him. He rewards with gifts of cattle the services of his councillors, warriors, and retainers. Many of his cattle, as we have seen, are distributed for herding among his retainers, who live upon the milk, while in times of famine he must provide the people with corn from his granaries. The annual tribute of corn he receives he must use to make the beer given to the people at the harvest thanksgiving; every man bringing him the skin of a lion or leopard must be rewarded with the gift of a heifer, or nowadays with ammunition; the meat of the game killed at a tribal hunt he distributes among those taking part; the breast-portions (*dihuba*) of big game animals he cooks for the men at his *kgotla*, or sends to paupers or invalids. . . .

[*Executive Duties.*] The Chief is the executive head of the tribe. Nothing of any importance can be done without his knowledge and authority. But in administering tribal affairs he must always consult with his councils, both private and general, and it is one of his main duties to summon and preside over meetings of these councils as occasion arises. With them he must decide upon questions of peace and war, and see to the protection or relief of his people in case of war, famine, pestilence, or some other great calamity. He must see that the local divisions of the tribe are satisfactorily governed by their headmen, and take any action that may be necessary to ensure this. He must determine upon and organize any necessary public works, and see that they are carried out by the regiments or some other body; he must order and organize the formation at regular intervals of new regiments; he must order and organize the removal of the tribal head-quarters or the establishment of new villages as the necessity arises; he must control the distribution and use of residential, arable, and grazing land, and regulate agricultural, pastoral, hunting, trading, and other economic activities . . ..

. . . He is also the representative of the tribe to the outside world, and so must receive and entertain other Chiefs and their messengers, and be the spokesman of the tribe in all its external relations. . . .

[*Judicial Duties.*] [The Chief's judicial duties are described in Section D1.]

[*Military Duties.*] Formerly the Chief was also the head of the tribal army, and as such organized military expeditions, often accompanying them himself, performed the necessary war magic for the success of his troops, and disposed of the prisoners and loot.

[*Ceremonial Duties.*] The arrangements for all tribal ceremonies were in his hands, and could not be carried out save under his authority. . . .

* * *

In many of these ceremonies the Chief was the link between his people and the spirits which governed their welfare. His dead ancestors were held to afford supernatural protection and assistance to the people they had once ruled, and on all important or critical occasions he would sacrifice and pray to them on behalf of the tribe as a whole. The role he thus played as tribal priest—a role which only he, as ruling Chief, could fill—helps to explain the great reverence in which he was always held by his people. . . .

[*Changing Duties* (in the 1930's and 40's).] Under the influence of Western civilization, and especially of Christianity, this ritual aspect of the Chieftainship has considerably decayed, and with it one of the most powerful sanctions underlying the Chief's authority. . . .

In other respects, too, the functions of the Chief have changed. Under British rule his powers in regard to such matters as war, external policy, and certain aspects of jurisdiction have been taken away from him, and a right of appeal has been established from his verdicts.   On the other hand, he has become the local authority through whom the Administration issues its instructions and proclamations to the tribe; he is responsible for the proper collection of hut-tax, and he is expected to co-operate with the District Commissioners and other officials in all political, economic, social, and educational schemes and developments emanating from the Administration.   He must further deal with the missionaries, traders, labour recruiters, would-be concessionaires, and other Europeans coming into his country.   Changing economic conditions have necessitated the organization and execution of more extensive public works, such as boring for water, building dams, and erecting churches and schools, and have created new financial responsibilities in the form of handling the funds raised by tribal levies for these works.   The Chief's work in all these respects is perhaps more than he can now successfully cope with, even although he has his secretaries and official tax-collectors; but, owing to his pivotal position in the life of the tribe, nothing can be done without his active support and co-operation.

QUESTIONS

1.   What are the similarities in the role of chief and that of guardian which was described in Problem I?

2.   Consider the role of *batlhana* servants and the role of the common headmen.   How clear is the distinction between stewardship and appropriation?   Is the situation structurally similar to the one which led to the distinction between "possession" and "custody" made in common law and discussed in a note in Chapter 13?

3.   In the traditional relationships between Tswana political superior and subordinate, how pervasive is the merging of private pocket and privy purse?   In Botswana what values and ideology about traditional political relationships and roles support such blending?

4.   The economist Karl Polanyi distinguishes three types of exchange: barter, sale, and redistributive exchange.   In the latter, goods and services flow up to a central position or institution and then flow out to the community from that apical position in the form of goods and services.   How important was redistributive exchange in the traditional operation of the Tswana chieftaincy?   Is this type of exchange system likely to facilitate the development of sharp distinctions between private and public pockets at the apex?

2.   Role of the Chiefs: Checks and Balances

NOTE

Despite the chief's pre-eminence, his power was far from absolute.   He shared authority with his advisors, headmen, and his assembled tribesmen.

Isaac Schapera, A Handbook of Tswana Law and Custom. Second edition. London: Oxford University Press, 1955, pp. 84–85. Footnotes omitted. Headings inserted by the editor are bracketed.

LIMITATIONS UPON THE POWER OF THE CHIEF

[*Role of the Councils.*] The existence of the councils mentioned above greatly limits the Chief's actual exercise of his power. . . . Despite the fact that control over almost every aspect of tribal life is concentrated in his hands, and that in consequence his power is very considerable, he is very seldom absolute ruler and autocratic despot. In order to get anything done, he must first gain the co-operation of his advisers and headmen, who play an important part in restraining his more arbitrary impulses. Any attempt to act without them is not only regarded as unconstitutional, but will also generally fail. A good deal, of course, depends upon the personal character of the Chief. A forceful and energetic man, like Kgama, could succeed in dominating his subjects and ruling to all intents and purposes as a dictator. But the average Chief depends for much of his power upon the goodwill and support of the leading members of the tribe; and his behaviour is determined accordingly. Under an incompetent or irresponsible Chief their influence is more pronounced. Should he ignore them, factions will arise, with the result that the general welfare of the tribe inevitably suffers, ...

[*The Chief and the Law.*] Moreover, the Chief himself is not above the law. Should he commit an offence against one of his subjects, the victim can complain to the men at the *kgotla*, or to one of the Chief's near relatives, who will then privately report the matter to the Chief. The latter is expected to make amends for the wrong he has done. Should he not do so, it is said that among the Kgatla and Rolong he may be tried before his own court, his senior paternal uncle acting as judge. But this does not seem to be the general rule, and often enough, in practice, the victim has no real remedy except to leave the tribe and transfer his allegiance to another Chief. So, too, if the Chief appears to have sentenced a man harshly, the victim can get one of the Chief's brothers or uncles to intervene on his behalf. The Chief is normally expected to reduce the sentence and may even forgive him if adequate reasons are produced.

[*Response to Chiefly Misconduct.*] So great, however, is the reverence attached to the Chief by virtue of his birth and ritual position that the people will put up with much from him that would never be tolerated in one of lesser rank; and it is only under extreme provocation that drastic action will be taken against him. But if he persists in flagrantly misruling the tribe . . . then the leading headmen of the tribe come together and, after discussing the matter privately, warn him to amend his conduct. Should he fail to do so, they will withdraw their support and publicly attack him at tribal gatherings, or there may be a split in the tribe, leading to wholesale migration. If given sufficient provocation, the people may even begin to plot against the Chief. . . .

It is regarded as correct, when relations between a Chief and his people are very strained, for one of the parties to call in some neighbouring Chief to try and reconcile them. . . .

. . . Likewise, should a Chief feel unable to resist or take effective action against his opponents, he can flee to one of his neighbours. The latter will then intervene on his behalf. . . .

QUESTIONS

Now reflect on this section up to this point as a whole:

1. In the time of the Protectorate (the time period of the two Schapera excerpts) suppose a chief collected tribute for a tribal celebration, perhaps to honor a visiting chief from another tribe, what restrictions would there be on the use of those funds? Suppose he then gave part of the tribute to his son, now the headman of a large village, and the son used it: (a) to provide a feast for the entire village at his father's next visit; or (b) to enlarge his personal cattle herd. If the facts became known to the chief's senior advisors, what action would they take under (a)? Under (b)?

2. How would the public learn about the chief's action in Question No. 1? Was there any parallel in traditional Tswana society to the "watchdog" role of the news media and the opposition political party today? How was public opinion shaped and expressed in traditional Botswana?

3. Under the fact situation of (a) in Question 1, suppose the chief were accused of misapplication of funds or embezzlement, with what paradigm of argument do you think he would respond? What about under (b)?

4. If some of his constituents thought the chief were in the wrong, how likely is it that they would bring charges? Who would be likely to bring them? In what forum?

5. What evidence in Schapera's ethnography suggests that whether the use of the money is considered improper will depend on idiosyncratic circumstances?

NOTE

In thinking about Question 5, consider public response to identical behavior by a pair of chiefs:

John Comaroff, "Talking Politics: Oratory and Authority in a Tswana Chiefdom," in Political Language and Oratory in Traditional Societies, ed. Maurice Bloch. London: Academic Press, 1975, pp. 146–147.

Chief K, who wielded little effective power at the time (1969), agreed to alienate a piece of tribal land in exchange for another. The outcome of earlier meetings had made it clear that, "as is our custom", the incumbent should not conclude deals with outsiders before they were ratified by the *lekgotla* (council of headman; see below). When the chief's actions were discussed at a *lekgotla* meeting, he was criticised for ignoring this injunction and acting on his own initiative in the matter. Moreover, the deal was not seen to be a particularly favourable one for the Tshidi. In reply, Chief K claimed that it had been the ploughing season and many had been working at their fields outside the capital. Hence he could not have called the *lekgotla* together in time. Besides, the deal *had* benefited the tribe. He had discussed it with his advisers and had visited a number of *lekgotla* members in order to secure their agreement. This was not accepted by the majority, however. A spokesman for the strong opposition faction argued that a council "is not the same as the opinions of its members", and that the earlier decision could not simply be forgotten. Several speakers suggested that a public meeting should be called to discuss future land deals—although it seemed clear to all that the real issue was the chief's behaviour. At the public assembly, the opposition faction managed to obtain general support for the view that he had acted wrongly and had exceeded his rights. One of their number suggested that a committee be created to "help" him on future land questions. This was widely supported, along with the admonition that the incumbent must not take any decision without the agreement of the committee. Chief K, who was fully aware that this further reduced his already limited legitimate power, was forced to agree by the strength of public opinion.

. . . It should also be noted that Chief K's father, when he was at his most powerful, alienated a similar piece of land without a *lekgotla* decision. The Native Commissioner of the period wrote to the council of headmen before ratifying the agreement. In his letter, he asked whether a council decision was not required, and received a reply which accused him of insulting the chief. It continued: "He is the owner of the land of the Tshidi-Barolong and has the right to do this. Chief L knows our law. He knows to consult his advisers and always does so. We ask you not to question our rightful chief."

QUESTION

1. Why was Chief L able to alienate land without criticism while his son, as chief, was not able to do so? Can you construct an explanatory hypothesis utilizing legitimacy and legal leeway as variables?

NOTE

Perhaps the public response to Chief K's behavior reported in the Comaroff excerpt would surprise Schapera, who offered the following generalization in his discussion of the Tswana distinction between civil and criminal wrongs:

Isaac Schapera, A Handbook of Tswana Law and Custom. Second edition. London: Oxford University Press, 1955, pp. 51–52.

Another important factor is the relative status of the persons concerned in a case. The proverb says:

" 'We are not so much concerned with the person as with his fault'; and again: 'The law is blind, it even eats up its owner.' In theory, that is, there is no distinction between Chief and commoner, rich man and poor man. In practice this doctrine is qualified in several ways. Offences against a person senior to the wrongdoer in position or age are always regarded as more reprehensible than they would be if the positions were reversed; and the sentence of the court is determined accordingly. This is particularly so where the offence is committed against the Chief. Conversely, it is difficult, sometimes impossible, to obtain justice where the offender is the Chief himself or one of his senior relatives. . . ."

NOTE

But, then again, Schapera might not be surprised for he collected the following maxims among the Tswana.

Isaac Schapera, "Tswana Legal Maxims," in Africa, vol. 36, 1966, pp. 125–126. Footnotes omitted.

[There are many sayings] relating primarily to the judicial process itself; they state, as it were, rules of procedure rather than substance. In principle, we must note initially, Tswana courts should treat all men as equals: . . . "We look not at the person, but at the offence", or . . . "It is not the person who is disliked, but the . . . offence", i.e. judges must not allow personal prejudice to bias their decisions. Nor should they be influenced by a person's rank: . . .

"It is not 'Hunger that selects', it is 'Spears the killers of princes' ", i.e. whereas usually only poor people die of famine, everybody is subject to the penalties of the law (just as he is to the dangers of war); hence, if headmen or other notables do wrong they must be duly punished, nor should commoners be afraid to take action against them. Kgatla say, in this connexion, ... "A grasshopper will not bite itself": when a headman is accused of any fault, his people, instead of judging him themselves, take him to the chief, quoting the proverb to indicate that they do not feel able to deal adequately with their superior. The chief himself is not immune: . . . . "The law is blind, it even eats its owner", and again, ... "The law is a lion, it bites the great man too."

QUESTION

1. The above excerpts suggest that there is a contradiction between Tswana legal ideology concerning equality before the law and Tswana legal be-

havior. There is in the United States, too. How do we handle the contradiction in this country?

NOTE

In his paper, "Talking Politics: Oratory and Authority in a Tswana Chiefdom," excerpted above, Comaroff suggests that one of the ways in which Tswana exert pressure against an errant chief is by skillful utilization of two "codes" in public speeches before the *lekgotla*. One code exalts the chieftaincy and values attached to it and the other code, employed by the speaker later in the same address, evaluates the behavior of the chief as incumbent. The accepted, patterned use of the two codes makes it possible for a speaker to say, in effect: "I support and uphold the chieftaincy, but I find your behavior as incumbent chief not up to the ideals of the chieftaincy and, using this yardstick, I criticize you." Criticism cast in this form is acceptable and, as Comaroff notes, often effective in changing a chief's behavior or, ultimately, in bringing about his removal.

QUESTION

1. Can you see how Tswana use of the two codes ("formal" and "evaluative") as described above could help them to handle the contradiction between their ideology concerning equality before the law and actual legal behavior?

2. Note that besides being administrator and judge, a Tswana chief carried out many priestly or magical functions. Western monarchies still vest their royalty with many similar religious or ritual functions. What are some of the ritual and symbolic functions of the American presidency and judiciary (Examples: presidential inaugurations, 21-gun salutes, judicial robes, titles)? Does the existence of these roles have any bearing on the probability of a political figure's being accused of a wrong like misappropriation of funds?

3. The Chieftaincy in Transition

NOTE

Chief Kgama III (Khama the Great), chief of the Ngwato from 1872–1923, and grandfather of Sir Seretse Khama, the late President of Botswana, was the catalyst for far-reaching changes in the role of the Tswana chief. His conversion to Christianity effectively ended the priestly functions of the chief among the Ngwato and eliminated one source of his authority.

Kgama also abolished polygamy, thus depriving the chiefs of potential political allies from among the kindred of their wives. He gave away much of his livestock to the servants who tended the herds, and he stopped collecting much of the customary tribute due to chiefs, thus greatly reducing their wealth.

Introduction of the British Administration in 1885, when Botswana became Bechuanaland Protectorate, further altered the position of the chiefs.

Despite an agreement that the chiefs would continue to rule their people much as before, the British presence seriously undermined the chief's authority. As stated in the Schapera excerpt, they no longer had the right to wage war, enter into political agreements, or sit in judgment in homicide cases or in any action involving a European. Appeals from a chief's verdict could be taken to the British courts, and the chiefs were given administrative duties such as collecting taxes for the British.

However, when trouble developed with a tribe, as Schapera noted, the British Administration almost invariably supported the chief, making it possible for him to become much more autocratic and arbitrary than when indigenous checks and balances were not fettered in this way.

Simon Gillett, "The Survival of Chieftaincy in Botswana," in African Affairs, vol. 72, 1973, pp. 180–181. Footnotes omitted. Editor's note in brackets.

Under the Protectorate . . . the Tswana chiefs enjoyed almost unchallenged power; in theory they could be called to account either by the British Administration or by their own people. But in practice the former's loyalty to the convention that they intervened in tribal matters only through the chief meant that he could play off both sides against the middle. On the one hand tribesmen objecting to their chief's behaviour could be countered by threats to invoke the support of the Administration. On the other a district commissioner or even resident commissioner attempting to discipline a chief would find that in retaliation he was fomenting opposition to some other official proposal for whose success popular approval, and therefore the chief's encouragement, was crucial. In this situation the only way in which the British could prevent the chiefs from abusing their position was to transfer at least part of their powers to some other constitutional authority also acceptable to the tribes. It was this that the Native Administration Proclamation of 1934 was designed to achieve, but the opposition of Tshekedi of the Ngwato and Bathoeng of the Ngwaketse, the two most prominent chiefs, delayed its implementation for a decade. In their view, argued in the Protectorate Special Court, the agreement reached between Chamberlain and their fathers gave the British government no right to prescribe how they ruled their tribes. The government's position was that the Tswana could not develop either economically or politically without introducing some checks on the chiefs' powers.· Liberal as were the Administration's intentions, the chiefs' opposition cannot be dismissed as merely selfish and reactionary. It must be remembered that until as late as 1948 or even later it was always possible—however remotely—that Britain would hand over the Protectorate to the Union of South Africa. For the Tswana it was logical to view all whites as hand in glove and for them, as well as their chiefs, to regard any proposals to limit the chiefs' powers as a threat to their interests. In this situation even those Tswana sufficiently informed to imagine a world in which chiefly absolutism and privilege did not exist were reluctant to see any change in the *status quo* which, it seemed, might be only a step towards white domination on the familiar South African pattern.

[By the 1950's, however, young Tswana, educated abroad, began to develop a new vision.] Observing developments in west Africa, they were coming to realize that there were prospects of advance to some form of elective government both at the national and the district levels. As these hopes began to be realized from 1957 onwards it was the older chiefs, notably Bathoeng, who began to feel the bite of a wind of change which threatened to sweep away chiefly as well a white privilege and chiefs' as well as imperial rule. It was only at this late stage that the limits on the chiefs' power under colonial rule were first comprehensively defined, in the African Administration Proclamation of 1954. This was to be followed within three years by the first serious attempt to democratize these powers, the African Local Councils Proclamation of 1957.

However, the Local Councils Proclamation was an enabling act only gradually brought into force in each of the eight tribal territories and its impact was soon overtaken by constitutional changes at national level. These succeeded each other swiftly from 1961 and culminated in the first general election under universal adult suffrage in 1965 and the grant of independence in 1966. Because of these developments there was no time for the gradualist changes within the tribal system to have much discernible effect and the whole 80 years of British rule up to 1965 can therefore be regarded as a period of chiefly autocracy intensified and corrupted by British over-rule and only towards the very end marginally affected by British attempts to constitutionalize and temper its character. . . .

4. Chiefly Role Since Independence

Simon Gillett, "The Survival of Chieftaincy in Botswana," in African Affairs, vol. 72, 1973, pp. 181–182.

* * *

. . . all the chiefs have found the radical changes in their powers introduced since 1966 almost too much to accept willingly. Virtually every one of their former powers has been transferred to an elective or government-appointed body, to which they usually belong and on which they may play a major role, but which operates in accordance with regulations and by a system of majority decision that almost entirely eliminates the personal autocratic character of their rule in the colonial period. Thus an active chief may, for example as chairman of the District Council, still exercise powers he formerly enjoyed as chief, but he must carry the majority of elected members with him and if he is unable to do so or is merely inactive, the Council will carry on business without him and eventually ensure he is removed from office.

.   .   .   apart from the fact that chiefs must still in practice be selected from the royal family of the tribe, their appointment and removal from office are just as much at the government's discretion as those of the rest of the civil service.   Other legislation moreover has stripped them of their legislative and administrative powers.   The District Councils Law of 1966 has abolished—or transferred to the councils created by the law—their power to regulate the social and economic life of the tribe, including the right to levy regimental labour.   The Matimela Act of 1968 prescribes the manner in which District Councils and not chiefs collect and dispose of stray livestock, a vitally important matter in a country whose cattle are the staple of the economy; and the Tribal Land Acts of 1968–70 vest the powers of chiefs to grant and withdraw rights in land in Land Boards appointed by the Minister of Local Government and Lands and representatives of the District Councils.   Most important of all, the right to levy taxes, traditionally inherent in the chiefs and vested since 1943 in the Tribal Treasuries of which they were chairmen, was transferred by the Local Government Tax Law of 1966 to the District Councils.

Even in the sphere of Tswana customary law the chiefs and their subordinate headmen are now much more closely controlled than before independence, and this despite the fact that the government has continued the British policy of maintaining a dual system of customary and statute law.   To some extent this closer control is due to the greater readiness of tribesmen to appeal against the decisions of chiefs whose political powers have been so much diminished.   It is however also attributable to amendments to the Customary (African) Courts Proclamation [of] 1961 which, by prescribing definite procedural rules, have gone far to assimilate the practice of the chiefs' courts to those of the district commissioners and magistrates.   The result is that the chiefs' courts are no longer the barely formal venue for dispensing justice that they used to be and, although the chiefs themselves continue to hear occasional cases, the bulk of the work is now delegated to deputies, usually older men better fitted than the chiefs themselves by temperament and knowledge for the duties involved.

NOTE

   The Tswana chiefs have not passively yielded up their traditional authority under the post-independence statutory scheme.   Their present influence on tribal life, however, derives largely from the weight of tradition, the dignity attached to the royal family, and their relative wealth and personal influence. It is clear that many chiefs are striving to exercise political power within the new political forms (councils and boards) that have been established.

William Tordoff, "Local Administration in Botswana—Part I," Journal of Administration Overseas, vol. 12, 1973, pp. 179–180. Footnote renumbered.

We have already noted the negative attitude adopted by some traditional authorities towards the district councils. The fact seems to be that the great majority of people still pledge their loyalty to the Chief rather than to the council. This is another way of saying that, at the base of the political system in Botswana, legitimacy tends to adhere to traditional rather than to modern local government institutions. . . .

It is now evident that the transition from the pre-independence situation where local power lay with the tribal authorities to one where it has passed increasingly to modern-type local authorities, has been too abrupt either for the Chiefs to accept gracefully or for the people to understand fully. For the Government to abolish chieftainship outright would involve too great a political risk, given the strong attachment of the people to that institution. Political considerations, too—notably, the challenge to the ruling BDP made by the tradition-oriented Botswana National Front (BNF) [1]—have not encouraged the Government to resort to a device which, in not dissimilar circumstances, Ghana adopted between 1951 and 1959: that is, to provide for a substantial traditional representation on the rural local authorities. The Minister of Local Government and Lands already has the power to nominate members to a district (or town) council, and there is no legal provision which prevents him using that power to add more traditional members to the council. No action on these lines has been taken, or indeed can be expected; but other ways and means of closely associating the tribal administration with the district councils have still to be worked out.

QUESTIONS

1. Do you agree with Gillett's assessment of Tswana political organization under the Protectorate as characterized by "chiefly absolutism and privilege?" Why or why not?

2. Chiefs have been deprived of many of their traditional duties. And they also have lost many of their emoluments and "perks" of office. But, do you think Tswana expectations concerning chiefs' acting generously (as persons of still considerable personal prestige and influence) can have caught up with this changed picture of chiefs' rights and duties? If not, might this gap between expectations and reality provide a subtle pressure for embezzlement or misuse of funds? In fact, is the loss of emoluments and perquisites of office by itself a factor that would increase the likelihood of misappropriation of funds? If you predict an increase, how do

---

1. The effective control of the BNF has now passed from its radical-minded founders to the traditionalists, led by Mr. Bathoen Gaseitsewe, M.P., ex-Chief of the Bongwaketse.

you know that it would be real rather than a reflection of changing consciousness in the population at large about official malfeasance?

3. While you have your crystal ball out, what would you predict concerning the frequency with which contemporary chiefs' constituents would actually file charges about alleged misuse of funds? How would the frequency compare with the past? Why do you predict as you do?

4. Recall the hypothesis you developed concerning the relationship between legitimacy and legality. (See question on p. 489.) How does it fit the situation of chiefs in contemporary Botswana?

5. An option that some independent African governments have considered is abolishing chieftaincy. What effects might the disappearance of the Tswana chieftaincy have on tribal unity, national pride, and local government?

5. Political Corruption in Africa

NOTE

Outside observers of African political phenomena often comment on the visibility of apparent political corruption. However, the misuse of funds by a government official, while it may appear related to the crime of theft, often is viewed as something different.

Marshall B. Clinard and Daniel J. Abbott, Crime in Developing Countries. New York: John Wiley and Sons, 1973, pp. 51–54. Footnotes omitted.

. . . "corruption may be more prevalent in some cultures than in others, but in most cultures it seems to be most prevalent during the most intense phases of modernization". Myrdal concluded that if conditions in precolonial times were compared with those following independence "the usual view of both South Asian and Western observers is that corruption is more prevalent now than before independence and that, in particular, it has recently gained ground in the higher echelons of officials and politicians". . . .

Embezzlement and fraud among the élite in Africa is a widespread problem that saps the development potential of the newly independent states. . . .

Ministers receive from a promoter a gift of money or goods in appreciation of services they have rendered. In the local governments all the advisors want to be part of the public works committees, where side payments are frequent, while no one wants to be on education or health committees.

One writer stated that in Africa "venality pervades through and through the fabric of African states. After only a few years in office the top politicians have amassed fortunes worth a hundred times the sum of the salaries received."

Another pointed out that the most striking similarity between Nairobi and Kampala politics since independence has been the rise of extensive corruption, the violation of one's duty to the state as a citizen or public official. . . .

A lengthy account of current corruption in West Africa described payoffs as a way of life in Nigeria, Ghana, Ivory Coast, and Zaïre.

* * *

In developing countries corruption is seldom really regarded as a "crime," even though it is specified as a crime. Many developing countries, for example, have long had traditions of making "gifts" to persons in authority or to gain some personal advantage. Sometimes giving a gift fits accepted custom, but asking for it does not.

According to African traditions giving presents to public functionaries is not only accepted, it is also encouraged; and the public officer should not refuse such tokens of gratitude. If he solicits gifts, it will, of course, be bribery; but if it comes to him unexpectedly he cannot have a guilty conscience in accepting it. By African standards he will be even ill-mannered to refuse.

The extent of the corruption, however, generally grows out of the transition from a traditional to a rapidly modernizing industrial society in which village loyalties have not been replaced by loyalty to an emerging concept of a nation. Because many nations are new, the concept of national interest is weak, whereas loyalty to one's own relatives, friends, and fellow villagers or tribesmen remains strong.
. . .

An African who has reached the top is expected to provide jobs for hundreds of his clansmen, to give decent presents to a vast array of relatives as well as to the clan elders when he visits his village, to make contributions befitting his station to the association of people from his village who reside in the same town as he, to provide in his house food and lodging for kinsmen who come to the town seeking jobs and not finding them for months or even years, to help to pay for the education of the children of his poorer relatives, and last but not least to provide feasts and to defer the costs of sacrifices or funerals (including his own) apart from making donations to the church. As he cannot meet such extensive obligations out of his salary, he is compelled to squeeze bribes, embezzle public funds, take rake-offs and so on.

The transition from colonial rule to independence in many developing countries has brought changes that produce corruption. When foreign civil service employees have been forced to leave, their jobs have been filled largely by noncareer civil service employees who are still loyal to their families and clans and who have not yet developed national allegiance. López-Rey points out the importance of the lack among such government officials of the distinction between public administrative function and private interests. Another important factor is the low wages paid most officials, particularly at the lower and middle levels. In new states corruption is relatively easy to conceal because the official rules are neither clear nor enforced and it is difficult to distinguish between traditional gift giving and bribery.

QUESTIONS

1. What are the cultural roots of African political corruption?

2. Given these cultural roots, what special problems are posed for African legal systems when it comes to defining "theft," "embezzlement," "bribery," "misappropriation of funds," and similar "crimes?"

3. Are there any cultural roots supporting political corruption in the United States? If so, what are their legal implications?

6. Political Corruption in Botswana

NOTE

The apparent incidence of political corruption in Botswana is less than in most of Sub-Saharan Africa. For example, it is not included among the African countries cited in the Clinard and Abbott monograph. In contrast to much of West Africa, in everyday life in Botswana, one does not continually run into situations where he or she must proffer, "dash," a gratuity provided before or after the performance of a routine duty as well as after the performance of an optional duty. Expatriates stationed in Botswana who have served in other posts in Africa are emphatic in describing Botswana as virtually free of corruption. Indeed on some occasions Batswana themselves paint this picture of their country:

(GABORONE) BOTSWANA DAILY NEWS, MAY 1, 1979

No corruption in our civil service

Botswana is one of the few countries in the world where corruption in the civil service is virtually non-existent and where it is punished without any qualms when it is discovered.

This was said by the Minister of Education Mr K.P. Morake when delivering a farewell address at the completors" party held the the University College of Botswana last Friday night.

Mr Morake informed the completors that all of them will be employed, irrespective of their political affiliations and their family ties.

He reminded them that they have been on Government scholarships solely on the basis of merit and assured them that this does not happend in many countries. "This has been achieved by a few dedicated civil servants and you must build on this and I advise that this is where young peoples' idealism can be most fruitful" the Minister said.

He said corruption in the civil service is tantamount to signing a death warrant for a country because the hardest-hit will be the ordinary man in the street who always is in the majority.

Mr Morake further said that for a country that has to deal with world problems as well as its own development, the difficulties are simply compounded.

NOTE

On other occasions a different public stance is taken, and the fact that the position is headlined in the newspaper of record indicates concern.

(GABORONE) BOTSWANA DAILY NEWS, MARCH 13, 1981

Investigate, you will find corruption - MP

By Andrew Sesinyi

SHOCK-waves tippled through Parliament when the MP for Bobirwa (BDP) Mr W.G. Mosweu alleged that there was gross misuse of public funds in the newly formed Botswana Tele-communications Corporationa and that "an immediate" scrutiny of the Corporations' books should be carried out.

With disapproving grumbles from the Front Bench and a call for further details by the leader of the House and Vice President, Mr Lenyeletse Seretse on a Point of Order, Mr Mosweu firmly maintained his point: "Investigate and you will see the corruption."

He had earlier made a blanket statement accusing the Botswana telecommunications Corporation of corruption and abuse of Batswana staff, who he further alleged, were frustrated through being assigned to menial jobs and "denied their rights and privileges."

No amount of lobbying gestures from the floor dissuaded the soft-spoken MP from his submission that the Corporation's books must be investigated.

The Minister of Works and Communications, Mr Collin Blackbeard later said to Mr Mosweu: "Unless you can give me something definite, I cannot see myself doing anything about it."

Mr Mosweu was making his comment on the recurrent estimates for the Ministry of Works and Communications which seeks P31 670 230 for the 1981/82 financial year. These funds were approved.

Mr Mosweu's continued on slaught on the Corporation indicated that the Corporation "had failed to meet the expectations of the people of this country."

He said since its inception "there has been poor productivity" and senior members of the staff who he identified specifically as expatriates were in certain parts of the country not examplary enough, "coming late to work, or absenting themselves from work".

Referring to Botswana employees of the Corporation as "frustrated Africans" Mr Mosweu said it was binding on Goverment to make sure that qualified Batswana are not under-utilised.

"The morale of the local staff of Telecommunications is deteriorating since most of the African staff are being frustrated because they don't get privileges or rights they should get", said Mr Mosweu.

NOTE

So, even though corruption apparently is rarer in Botswana than in many developing countries, it is not unknown. In fact, cases are reported quite regularly in the Botswana Daily News.* However, publicly reported accusations of misappropriation of funds by chiefs are rare and convictions are rarer still. Much less rare are similar offenses by other public officials such as: revenue collectors; cashiers in various government agencies; civil, electrical, and sanitary engineers; district council employees, teachers and headmasters, court clerks, police officials, employees of the Central Transport Organization, and postal and telegraph employees. Answering a question in the National Assembly in 1975, the Minister of State Public Service said that 61 public officers were convicted of offenses involving dishonesty in the two year period between January 1, 1973 and December 31, 1974.** Of course, such a figure is difficult to interpret without much more data. How many public officers were accused and acquitted? How many offenses were unreported? How many are brought to trial but not publicized in the press?

Dishonesty evidently is not unknown in the private sector, either. Again, published newspaper accounts for the same time period reveal offenses such as misappropriation of property by store clerks, servants, store managers, accounts clerks, and a plant supervisor.

A significant number of cases—especially in the public sector—result in acquittals for lack of evidence or for other reasons, particularly when the charge is against a chief. Where the individual is found guilty, the amounts involved have been small compared to some cases reported from elsewhere in Africa, perhaps reflecting the pattern of national income in Botswana. Expatriates are among the convicted offenders in both the public and private sectors, although this is not usually specifically mentioned in published reports because of the nation's non-racial policy. It is striking that there are virtually no published cases of bribery. The most typical offense of this sort is misappropriation of property:

* All available copies of the Botswana Daily News for 1974–81 were reviewed for published reports of corruption.

** Botswana Daily News, March 7, 1975.

(GABORONE) BOTSWANA DAILY NEWS, AUGUST 22, 1980

Company chief gets 3 years

By Tarcisius Modongo

The Manager of Radiators Botswana in Francistown, Norman Albert Rundle aged 33 was on Tuesday sentenced to three years imprisonment for stealing P6,888,28 belonging to the company.

One year of the sentence was suspended for three years with effect from the date the accused is released from prison on condition that he does not commit the same offence in any way during the period of suspension.

The money was stolen between November 1979 and July this year. The accused has also been ordered to repay the amount.

In mitigation, the accused told the court that he realised late that he had been "stupid" in having taken the money adding that he would repay the amount.

Passing judgement, the Francistown Senior Magistrate, Mr P.T. W. Powell said stealing by servant was prevalent and this was a serious offence which carries a maximum penalty of seven years' imprisonment.

He said that persons who commit such offences must expect to be adequately punished for them.

Mr Powell said that the court assessed the judgement and took into consideration that the accused had pleaded guilty and had no previous convictions.

The court also bore in mind that the accused was a married man and he should however, have considered the possible consequences upon himself and his family before committing that offence.

(GABORONE) BOTSWANA DAILY NEWS, JUNE 22, 1979 *

SEKGOMA IS SENTENCED

TO TWO YEARS

By Andrew Sesinyi

The case of former Deputy Permanent Secretary in the Ministry of Agriculture, Mr Mokhutshwane Sekgoma, wrapped up Wednesday, with him being sentenced to two years imprisonment, 15 months of which were suspended for three years.

But Mr Sekgoma is to lodge an appeal after the 12-day Gaborone Magistrate Court session where he was acquitted on seven previous counts, six of these on Wednesday. The prosecution brought in 45 witnesses in the case which was described by Senior Magistrate R.F. Hunt as "Full of conflicting evidence."

Mr Sekgoma was convicted on a charge of obtaining money by false pretences. The court heard that Mr Sekgoma claimed the sum of P526 from Government on false establishment that he was using his own vehicle, whereas that was a Government vehicle.

A packed court listened to the magistrate singling out, analysing and dropping six counts on grounds of insufficient evidence.

Mr Sekgoma who is on P1 000 bail, is further obliged to repay Government the P526 he obtained by false pretences.

In passing sentence, Senior Magistrate Hunt said the offence was punishable by up to seven years' imprisonment. He said there was no question of Mr Sekgoma yielding to temptation on the count of obtaining money by false pretences.

Furthermore the magistrate said he was taking into account that Mr Sekgoma was a senior Government official who should have set examplary standards for his juniors. "Now he has set an example of dishonesty," he said.

The other considerations, the magistrate said, were that Mr Sekgoma was a first offender, the amount was only P526, and that he had lost his high rank in the Civil Service, plus his job.

In mitigation, the Defence Counsel Mr Jack Unterhallter said the court should "blend justice with mercy" considering that Mr Sekgoma was already suffering the effects of falling from high office. He added that the accused was a first offender, he is a citizen of Botswana, born here, and spent all his life here except travelling abroad on Government business.

"An element of suspension may play a part in what you think is an appropriate sentence," the Attorney Unterhallter applealed to the magistrate.

On the other hand, Litigation Consultant Mr D.D. Will felt the fact that Mr Sekgoma was a top Government official should make the sentence more severe.

* The appeal, heard before the High Court in November 1979 was lost.

BOTSWANA DAILY NEWS MARCH 4, 1981 NO.41 PAGE 3

CTO's surprise swoop nabs 15 Govt. drivers

By Andrew Sesinyi

WITH a dent on Government coffers at over half a million Pula money lost through misuse of or damage to Government vehicles the Central Transport Organisation (CTO) over the weekend nabbed 15 Government drivers in a two-hour swoop.

The Cabinet which has been informed of the results of the swoop, is reported "furious" over the misuse and waste of government vehicles and funds. One driver faces a prison sentence.

The CTO, very often the center-point of public, press and Parliamentary criticism, is out to clean up the misuse of Government transport in the face of an estimated P7,200 000, being the fuel budget for 1980/81.

Several drivers were found to be using Government vehicles for private purposes, and CTO's unprecedented raid poses the biggest talking point in government-drivers' circles.

It took only two hours, on Friday 4.00 p.m. till 6.00 p.m. to execute the suprise raid.

On Monday morning, the irate General Manager of CTO, Mr L.L. Mukokomani was striding the grounds, inspecting the 15 vehicles. Just as he was about to part with the Press, another culprit arrived in a five tonne Government truck.

The truck was carrying 100 packets of cement and was immediately declared overloaded. On top of this, there was furniture, as a cover-up, an apparent conveyance of property belonging to a retired civil servant. A large heavy tent covered the packets of cement plus the furniture, and it was only on close inspection that the cement bags were obvious.

In another misuse of the Government trucks, one expatriate civil servant was off to the reserves on private business.

According to CTO officials, his log-sheet was "not adequate," he was carrying his son without an indemnity permit, and had a rifle and ammunition.

Many drivers were off on a weekend, for private purposes, and several others were nabbed for transporting passengers without permission.

The latter situation, according to Mr Mukokomani, could involve Government in huge expenses in the event of accidents. Passengers carried in Government vehicles would under Third Party provisions be entitled to compensation from Government

One driver made a trip to Palapye and back to Gaborone without a log-sheet, and thus without permission from responsible authorities, and in another case, a driver authorised a Government vehicle himself.

In another incident, the passengers fled when CTO officials stopped the vehicle in which they were travelling

The CTO officials were unusually harsh in dealing with these case. Both driver and passengers were under all circumstances ordered out of the vehicles and left at the spot where the vehicles were confronted. Several drivers struggled to transport themselves back to their duty stations, where long "charge sheets" were awaiting them.

"It is a black week for us," said a down-hearted driver to the press.

Mr Mukokomani is giving the matter his most serious attention and he has circulated letters to all permanent secretaries, attorney general, auditor general, registrar of the High Court, all heads of government departments, all CTO out-stations, and all CTO fuel points, on the subject

"It is now the intention to prohibit the issue of fuel in drums, particularly on straight route like Lobatse-Gaborone, Mahalapye-Palapye Francistown Special requests for bulk fuel will be considered on application only from Heads of Departments and senior departmental officers in districts for inspection trips outside route Lobatse-Francistown."

The cost of providing fuel for the Botswana Government vehicles and Plant items has risen sharply in the financial year 1980/81. The fuel budget for the financial year 1978/79 was P2 600 000, and 1980/81 makes it minimal at P7 200 000

"This makes it obvious to everyone that vehicles must be used only for necessary trips," said the CTO General Manager.

Mr Mukokomani's criticism extends to directors of Government Departments who he charges "are allowing vehicles to be used on weekends and after duty hours when there is no good reason for it."

"Approximately 30 percent of Government vehicle accidents occur on weekends and after duty hours In most cases the officer was allowed to leave or return late on an official trip for his own convenience."

"Some departments allow vehicles at the end of the duty day to be parked at locations such as the Urban Police Station purely to provide a ride for employees to and from work. Vehicles will be parked at their place of duty unless the parking at another location is authorised by the Head of Department."

"Heads of Departments must also authorise trips always from the vehicles duty location during/after duty hours or weekend. Government vehicles commencing long trips late on Friday should have specific authority of the Head of Department "

"Any vehicle not so authorised when discovered by CTO inspectors will be grounded and the vehicle will not be returned to the department concerned until ample justification for the apparent unauthorised trip has been made," the stringent measure go again.

The vehicles affected were by Monday afternoon to be returned to the departments and the matter had been taken up with the respective authorities. **BOPA**

NOTE

Review the additional cases reported in Section A3 (page 464).

NOTE AND QUESTIONS

With the data available, it is not possible to say unequivocally that corruption in Botswana is high or low compared to that in other African or developing countries. It is reported in the press, sometimes prominently, and those reports suggest that it is disapproved of by judicial officials and by government officers in their official statements. This pattern raises many questions:

1. Keeping in mind the classification of corruption in developing countries outlined in the Waterbury excerpt in the chapter on embezzlement in Egypt, how would one classify the corruption that is found in Botswana? How do Waterbury's categories of endemic, planned, and developmental corruption apply?

2. How vigorous is the attempt to ferret out corruption in Botswana? Why do you answer as you do?

3. If, indeed, there is relatively little corruption in Botswana, why might this be the case?

4. Why do Batswana and expatriates, when asked about it, tend to deny the existence of the corruption that does occur in Botswana?

NOTE

From sessions with informants in Botswana, I conclude that a significant number of cases involving chiefs simply are not reported in the press. Most such cases apparently are "borderline," where the distinction between legitimate acquisition and misappropriation of property is hard to draw. Sample instances would be where a government bull breeding farm fails to prosper, has its public subsidy withdrawn and, subsequently, is acquired by the chief of the area in which it is located. Did he acquire it improperly? In another instance, a chief is being sued over the ownership of bore holes which the plaintiff alleges are public property and which the chief avers he, as chief, properly assigned himself in his capacity as a private citizen.

Another informant told me of a 1979 case, also unreported in the press, in which a chief was found guilty of illegally acquiring a matimela beast and sentenced to two years in prison. *Matimela*, stray cattle, are emotion-charged in contemporary Botswana. As noted in Section C1, the right to appropriate unclaimed stray cattle was a traditional perquisite of office of chiefs. In 1968 the Government passed the Matimela Act which gives ownership of unclaimed matimela to the districts. The Act (Chapter 36:06 of the Laws of Botswana) establishes procedures for each district to set up a matimela fund, into which monies acquired through the sale of matimela are funneled. The fund is used for public purposes. Matimela are handled by a government employee, the "matimela master," and procedures are laid out for attempting to find the owners of matimela, for owners to identify and claim their lost cattle, and for the sale of unclaimed matimela to individuals or to the Botswana Meat Commission.

Chiefs resent the loss of this lucrative "perk" of office and, it is reported, still sometimes claim matimela. When this occurs, they evidently are at least tacitly assisted in this tack by traditional, loyalist supporters. Some chiefs have been quick to point out shortcomings and improprieties in the operation of the Matimela Act, which has become a football in the struggle between chiefs—desiring to keep as much of their traditional power and authority as possible—and government and district officials who are trying to make the new local government apparatus effective:

(GABORONE) BOTSWANA DAILY NEWS, NOVEMBER 3, 1977

CORRUPT OFFICIALS MUST GET OUT!

Kgosi Linchwe II Kgafela of the Bakgatla has called for an immediate expulsion of "corrupt elements within the staff of the Kgatleng District council."

Kgosi Linchwe, who is chairman of that council, was speaking in an interview with the Daily News this week, on the continuing unsatisfactory report centring around the council's matimela stray cattle department.

He noted that there was corruption within that department which needs thorough investigation. Kgosi Linchwe referred to this week's case in which the assistant matimela master, Mochele Pheto, was sentenced by the Senior Magistate, Mr D. Hunt, to 18 months' imprisonment, 12 months of which was suspended for two years.

The accused was charged with stealing by person while employed in the public service. Particulars of the case were that during the month of August, he stole a matimela heifer.

Kgosi Linchwe also made another reference to matimela master Mr A.N. Mogomotsi, who together with four other herdboys, were ordered by the District Commissioner, Mr F.K. Kokorwe. to refund the susta-

nance fee of P56 to a certain Mr Mochele Linchwe.

The order was made at a meeting between the district commissioner and the complainant.

He also said he believed there was corruption in the matimela department.

Mr Kokorwe alleged that his previous attempts to stop this annoying state of affairs had failed.

Asked about his meeting with those parties, Mr Kokorwe said he noted that the sustanance fee, which was paid by Mr Linchwe, was unreasonable and unjustified.

According to his findings, the beast was collected by the herdboys at its grazing area to the matimela kraal. The district commissioner disclosed that he found, during the meeting, that the matimela registry was unsatisfactory.

He said it did not indicate the particular which led the beast being referrd to as a letimela. However, he went onto explain that under the circumstances which led to the collection of the beast to the matimela kraal, though the council could not be held responsible, it would refund Mr Linchwe and later surcharge the matimela master and herdboys.

(GABORONE) BOTSWANA DAILY NEWS, SEPTEMBER 16, 1980

Linchwe slams
the councillors

By Keofelakae Tolse

Bakgatla Kgosi Linchwe Kgafela II last week attacked the Kgatleng District Council for allegedly failing to interpret the Matimela Act correctly.

Kgosi Linchwe was addressing a well attended kgotla meeting in Mochudi last Friday. The meeting could have been held last week Monday but was postponed when he allegedly told his people to go and persuade the rest of the community to attend because the subject of the matimela "is a sensetive one." It was during that Friday's meeting that the community came in large numbers.

The Bakgatla Kgosi bitterly charged the district councillors for allegedly being "too weak" in their political assignments. Kgatleng councillors he said, have allowed themselves to be used as "tools" by council administrative officers. He singled out the Acting Council Secretary "as the man who misdirects the dicision of the council."

As tensions went high with the rest of the tribesmen except one councillor joining Kgosi Linchwe in his attack on the council, he told his people not to fear to claim their matimela from the council because the "Matimela Act was a straight forward instrument which does not oppress any body.

Kgosi Linchwe was reiterating a reply he was given by the Vice President and Minister of Local Government and Lands Mr Lenyeletse Seretse to his motion during the recent session of the House of Chiefs. Mr Seretse had told the house that the question of whether a letimela which has been in the council's custody for a period of over twelve months should or should not be handed over to the owner lies entirely with the council. He said the Matimela Act does not restrict any council from handing over an overdue letimela to the owner so long as the claimant has satisfied the council on his explaination. Mr Seretse had also made it clear that every discision of the council should be implemented by council secretaries whether they "like it or not."

During that last week meeting very strong and harsh words were used directed to some named council officials. However the District Commissioner Mr I. Zebe who also attended the meeting appealed to the Bakgatla to approach their parliamentarians if they wished an amendment to the Matimela Act.

QUESTIONS

1. What does the conduct of the *matimela* issue among the Kgatla reveal about the ways in which a *lekgotla* may be used to mobilize public opinion and political support?

2. Why would *matimela* become the issue over which a chief would focus his power struggle with district councillors?

3. The charge levied against the *matimela* master's staff is one of corruption. What does that suggest about how corruption is viewed in Botswana? Why fix that charge on one's opponents, rather than something else like "inefficiency," "wastefulness," or "incompetence?"

NOTE

Consider the following reported cases of chiefs, sub-chiefs, a head man, and a customary court official accused and acquitted of misappropriation of funds or other property. (Our review of newspaper accounts turned up no published case of a chief who had been *convicted* of such an offense.)

(GABORONE) BOTSWANA DAILY NEWS, FEBRUARY 19, 1974

Chief's representative in the clear at Ranaka

From Johannes Pilane

A joint plea by residents of Ranaka village in the Ngwaketse district that their chief's representative Kebalebile Telekelo be prosecuted for misappropriation of their funds has been vetoed.

The announcement was made at a kgotla meeting held there last week by the Acting Chief of Bangwaketse, Mookami Gaseitsiwe, who was asked last December to investigate the case. The allegedly misappropriated funds had been raised by the community at Ranaka some eight years ago.

He told the residents that his findings had revealed negligence and carelessness but not misappropriation of funds.

A number of people who attended the meeting criticised the decision and urged that disciplinary action be taken against Mr Telekelo. They demanded that he be removed immediately from his position as they "had lost all confidence in him."

The amount involved, reportedly some R355, was intended to be used to buy bulls in 1951. When the animals had not been produced by 1966, the tribe started making enquiries. Residents who attended this meeting felt that the chief's representative had been "tried in their absence," and suggested that they be given an appeal to higher authorities.

Villagers were so aggressive that the District Officer G.W. Matenge had to stand up and speak.

In his short talk Mr Matenge told the residents that the matter was dealt with departmentally and that Mr Telekelo had not appeared before any court. The matter had been investigated by the Bangwaketse Tribal Administration staff committee.

He said there was not enough evidence for Mr. Telekelo to be prosecuted for misappropriation of funds, adding that law cannot work on assumptions but on solid testimony. He then urged them to forget about the past squabbles and concentrate on developments.

(GABORONE) BOTSWANA DAILY NEWS, JUNE 10, 1976

Seepapitso acquitted

Chief Seepapitso IV of the Bangwaketse was last week acquitted and discharged in the Botswana High Court on two counts of theft.

In announcing the judgement Mr Justice Rowland Hill said that the two principal witnesess in the case against the chief were accomplices and were untruthful and it would therefore be unsafe to rely on their evidence.

Chief Seepapitso had been charged with stealing by person in the public service, namely the theft of two beasts acquired as court fines.

On an hour long judgement on the fourthday of the case Mr Justice Rowland Hill said according to the evidence of Simane Moisakamo (witness) he was an accomplice in the selling of one beast. He added that the court could only convict the accused with the evidence of an accomplice if that evidence is clear and straight forward.

Mr Hill also said that there was a possibility that the custom of a "mopako beast," which the Chief said he had used the beast for was still in practice.

He further said that the evidence given by the accused may be the truth and therefore he discharged him.

On count two Mr Hill described Mareko Abel Mosielele also a witness as a "self-confessed thief and a liar," he added "with regard to the false evidence given by Mareko the evidence of the accused cannot be dismissed."

He then found the accused not guilty and discharged him. Mr D.W. Campbell of Kurumane appeared for the defence and John Hoobs for the state.

The High Court was filled to capacity. Bathoen Gaseitsiwe Chief Sepapitso's father was also present. Chief Lenchwe II attended the first three days of the hearing.

(GABORONE) BOTSWANA DAILY NEWS, DECEMBER 2, 1976

CHIEF'S REP MAKABA RE-LEASED FROM BRIBE CASE

The Senior Chief's representative Makaba Makaba was recently discharged from a case of soliciting a bribe by the Bangwaketse Senior Customary Court.

Evidence had been led that he had accepted some liquor as a price for freeing a certain Magare Dikole from a charge of contempt of court when the latter had defied the customary court by failing to turn up for prosecution.

Dikole told the court that he gave Mr. Makaba some liquor which the latter shared with B.B. Nyenye, Chief Secretary in the Ngwaketse Tribal Administration "so that a contempt of court charge against me should be dropped".

Mr Nyenye on the other hand remembered drinking beer with Mr Makaba but argued that the whole matter had nothing to do with any court case whatsoever.

In his judgement, the presiding court president, Chief Seepapitso IV expressed sympathy with judicial officers "who are often accused of accepting bribes when in fact things were given to them under guise of friendship gestures or as expressions of good disposition existing among members of the society.

He held that judiciary office, like any other, did not have any rules dissociating staff from the rest of the members of the society. The Chief therefore discharged Makaba Makaba.

Court   President acquitted

By Jerry Masete

THE PELENG Customary Court President, Mr John Kgaboesele (71) was last Friday acquitted on three counts of suspected fraud by the Lobatse Senior Magistrate, Mr L. Chadwick.

According to the prosecution, the accused between December and January this year kept court fines amounting to over P60 instead of handing the money to Government revenue collectors. The fines were paid by three people.

In his defence, Mr Kgaboesele told the court that he retained the money not for private use but for kgotla cleaning and feeding the cleaners.

He said that no receipts were issued to those who paid the fines because it would have been impossible for him to get this money from government for that type of work.

Mr Kgaboesele explained to the court that the Peleng Customary Court does not have a vote from the Ministry of Local Government and Lands for kgotla cleaning. He said that it was logical and at his discretion to retain fines at his office or home in the interest of his community.

The State Prosecutor, Sub-Inspector Steve Baileng argued that public funds should at all times be kept in government coffers.

He said that government revenue officers were at Mr Kgaboesele's disposal and wondered why he decided to keep the money at his home. He said that was tantamount to stealing by person employed for the public.

Mr Baileng said that the accused should have applied for funds for kgotla cleaning or asked people to clean it vouluntarily instead of keeping public funds for the purpose unknown in government circles.

Summarising the case, the Magistrate, Mr Chadwick said that Mr Kgaboesele was not only a community leader but prominent and honest. He added that he proved before the court of law that he did not have fraudulent intention in keeping the money.

Mr Kgaboesele, as a court president had the welfare of the community at heart and also wanted them to live under healthy conditions, he said. He added that the state prosecutor failed to prove that the accused was wrong.

Mr Kgaboesele is now back at work.**BOPA**

(GABORONE) BOTSWANA DAILY NEWS, JUNE 2, 1981

NOJANE HEADMAN
ACQUITTED OF STEALING

By Johannes Pilane

THE HEADMAN of Nojane Village, Mr David Peter (42) who is also a member of House of Chiefs has been acquitted for stealing a heifer, by the Ghanzi Resident Magistrate Mr Gabriel Rwelengera at Nojane.

The prosecutor, Mr G.M. Europa told the court that the accused, last year at Nojane did steal one heifer belonging to Mr Joel Peter. The heifer is valued at P61.

The Court was told that sometime in 1976, the complainant found the accused in Gaborone and asked for financial assistance because he was in financial difficulties. The accused lent the complainant P110.

The contract was that if Mr Peter does not repay the money within a reasonable period, he will give the accused a beast, the court heard.

Four years elapsed before any kind of refund was made. The Headman then sent for a beast from the Joel Peter's cattle post and branded it with his brand.

When Joel Peter found one of his heifers branded with the Headman's brand, he reported the matter to the Police who laid a charge against the Headman.

The Senior Magistrate, Mr Gabriel Rwelengera said the action by the accused did not constitute such a grave crime, since it was not disputed that a loan of money between the two actually took place and the conditions made.

Mr Rwelengera however, ordered that the beast be returned to the original owner, Joel Peter and advised Headman David Peter to lay a Civil Suit against Joel Peter for refund of his money.

The Magistrate was on his familiarisation tour of his district of jurisdiction when he presided over the case. He is believed to be the first resident magistrate since independence. **BOPA**

QUESTIONS

1. In these five cases, what are the cultural roots of the accusations, the perception of wrong-doing? Similarly, what are the cultural roots for the paradigm of argument offered as a defense?

2. Why are chiefs, when they are accused of corruption, less likely to be convicted?

3. Why do you think the Botswana Daily News, which is government owned and operated, finds itself unable to cover all stories of chiefs accused and/or convicted of corruption?

D. "CRIMINAL" PROCEDURE

NOTE

As we noted in Problem I, Tswana legal proceedings are initiated by the person who has been wronged. Tswana begin the attempt to resolve a dispute by going informally to a third party who attempts negotiation, then mediation. Only if these fail does a matter go to the more formal forum of the headman's *kgotla*. A case of "theft" where informal settlement of this sort would be attempted first would be that described by Schapera in an earlier excerpt (page 513) where Y knowingly takes a beast from X's herd and X, at least initially, describes the animal as "lost." Schapera describes formal procedures under customary law as they existed late in the Protectorate period.

1. Formal Tswana Dispute Settlement Procedures in Customary Law

Isaac Schapera, "The Political Organization of the Ngwata of Bechuanaland Protectorate." in African Political Systems, edited by Meyer Fortes and Edward E. Evans Pritchard. London, 1940, pp. 63–64.

The judicial system is fundamentally the same for all courts. The victim of a civil wrong, such as breach of contract, seduction, adultery, trespass, damage to property, theft, or defamation, may either pass it over or, through the elder of his family-group, try to arrive at an agreed settlement with the offender. Failing this, he takes the matter to the court of defendant's ward-head. Crimes, such as offences against political authorities acting in their official capacity, breaches of the laws decreed by the chief, rape, assault, homicide, and sorcery, can never be compounded, but must always come to trial. All trials are heard in public, and any member of the tribe has the right to attend and take part in the proceedings, no matter in what court they are held. The parties concerned and their respective witnesses are heard in succession, listened to intently and uninterruptedly, and closely questioned by the people present. The judge then throws the matter open for general discussion, and the merits of the case are publicly argued by those wishing to do so. This is one of the principal functions of his personal advisers. Finally he sums up, in the light of the opinions thus expressed, and either pronounces his verdict or, if he feels that the case is too important or difficult, refers it to the court of his political superior. If either party is dissatisfied with the verdict, he can likewise appeal against it. The case is then heard again from the very beginning at the superior court, pending whose decision action is suspended. A case originating in a family-group may thus pass through three or four grades of intermediate court before ultimately reaching the chief.*

NOTE

Schapera reports that judgments were executed promptly, the losing party in a civil suit paying the damages or fine by delivering the required number of cattle to the headman or chief for distribution to the prevailing party and to

* For a fuller description of formal dispute settlement procedures in customary law see Schapera, A Handbook of Tswana Law and Custom. Second edition. London: Oxford University Press, 1955, pp. 279–300.

the court. If a thrashing was imposed, it was carried out immediately after the trial in the presence of the assembled *kgotla*.

The following abbreviated verbatim report of a 1934 ward court case illustrates how these procedures operated. The case is an assault and abuse suit in the Makgophuna ward court in the town of Mochudi, Kgatla Tribal Reserve, Botswana. It was written down in the vernacular by a Tswana observer.

Isaac Schapera, A Handbook of Tswana Law and Custom. Second edition. London: Oxford University Press. 1955, pp. 295–298.

I. RAMODIMO v. SEBELE (Kgatla)

Masilo (president of court): Recently when I came from the fields, Sebele said to me that he had fought with Ramodimo; they had fought on account of an ox. Sebele says that some time back an ox was taken by the Madikwe people [those living along the Marico River], because these cattle had eaten their corn; and the owner of the ox, being a woman, wanted all the people who had cattle in that kraal to collect corn to go and free that ox. This request was made to Ramodimo, who took no notice of it. Then this woman went to report her request to Sebele. Ramodimo did not like this, so he went to Sebele, and, not finding him, swore at him in his own *lapa*,* saying: "Sebele is a bastard (*ngwana wa dikgora*), how can he accept reports of this nature when I am about?" After I had been told all this by Sebele, one day I went to the Chief's office, going to fetch a permit for selling cattle. I met the Chief in the office, and he said to me: "Why are you here, and yet your people are in my *kgotla*?" I replied that I knew nothing about any case, the man concerned not having told me anything. Then the Chief said: "Come with me, and you just listen." When we got to the *kgotla*, the Chief asked Ramodimo whether he had reported himself to me. Ramodimo replied: "No, Chief." Then the Chief said to the parties: "Go back to your own *kgotla* and have the case there first." That is why we are here.

Ramogodi (one of the assessors): We hear, Masilo. We can ask the "owners of the case" [the people involved and their supporters], Modibedi, Ramoru, Habakuke [other assessors, and leading members of Ramodimo's family-group], there is the case.

Modibedi: It is so, sirs; we can hear from Ramodimo, as he is the plaintiff.

Ramodimo (stands up, which is not usual): It was in the evening when Sebele came to me and said to me: "I want you to-morrow." In the morning I went to his home. While I was there, his sister said to him: "Here is Ramodimo waiting for you." Sebele came to me and said: "Tell me, I heard that when I was away you came here to

* Courtyard, compound.

look for me." Sebele swore at me, and then his sister knocked me down with a *mogopô* (eating-bowl).

Masilo (president): I hear, Ramodimo. Sebele, stand and tell us what you have to say.

Sebele: Yes, sirs. We quarrelled about an ox with Ramodimo, an ox which had been taken by the Madikwe people. The owner of the ox reported herself to me, and Ramodimo did not like that; he said: "How can the matter be reported to a *ngwana wa marebana* (illegitimate child) when I am here, what does that mean?" He came to my home to look for me, but did not find me; I had gone to the cattle-post. He stood, I hear from my mother, in the middle of the *lapa* (courtyard), and swore and cursed, saying that I was a bastard. Then, when I came back, my mother told me Ramodimo was looking for me. Then I went to him and said: "I have come, as I heard you were looking for me." The next day he came to me; he sat on the *kgorwana* (entrance to the courtyard), and when I came to him he said: "I have come, as you wanted me." I said to him: "Don't say 'I have come', because I am waiting for you to tell me why you were here the other day, looking for me." He stood up, and said: "You are a bad MoKgalagadi, a bastard child, born in the prickly-pear thickets [lining some of the streets in Mochudi]; your mother conceives in the prickly-pear thickets." I left him, I went out of the homestead at the back, he followed me. When I was at the back, he followed me, and he continued to say *"ngwana wa dikgora"* (bastard). Then I kept quiet. Then my sister asked him, saying to him: "While you keep on saying Sebele is *ngwana wa marebana*, you, what are you?" Ramodimo replied: "I am the child of Mhere." Then my sister said to him: "You are also a bastard child." Then he smacked my sister on the mouth. My sister hit him with an eating-bowl, and the blood flowed out.

Masilo: Who were there?

Sebele: It was my mother, and some small girls, who are now at school.

(Masilo now sent one of the men to call Sebele's mother. She came to the *kgotla* and sat down. Nothing was said while she was away, apart from desultory conversation among the men. When she came:)

Masilo: Tell us about the fight that took place in your *lapa*.

Sebele's mother: The trouble is about an ox. At the Marico River [Madikwe], Mmatebekane [the woman whose ox had been taken] reported this to Sebele. Then Ramodimo came angrily to my home, looking for Sebele. He did not find him; and after Sebele came he went to Ramodimo to tell him, "I have come", Ramodimo came next day and sat at the gate, and said to Sebele: "I have come." Sebele said: "I am listening to you to tell me why you have been looking for me." Then Ramodimo swore at Sebele. Now as he kept on swearing at Sebele, calling him a bastard, the sister asked him why he was swearing at Sebele: "Are you not also a bastard?" Then they fought, and the girl knocked him with an eating-bowl.

Masilo: There is the case, *lekgotla*.

Habakuke (Ramodimo's senior): Just as Ramodimo has been saying, in the same way he told me, so also did Sebele.

Peo (a member of the *lekgotla*): We want to know if it is really true that Ramodimo did not swear at Sebele? Because, as far as we know, Sebele is not one who has ever interfered with anybody in the village; he is always a good man.

Ramodimo: I did not swear at him; he started.

Gaefete (a member of the *lekgotla*): No, sirs. I was in my *lapa*, I heard Ramodimo swearing in the *lapa* of Sebele's mother; it is he who started to swear at Sebele.

Ramoru (an assessor): Why did you go inside some one else's *lapa*?

Ramodimo: He had called me.

Makete (a member of the *lekgotla*): Sirs, this man Ramodimo is guilty; he must shave our beards, he must dust the little stones in our loinskins, he must be punished by thrashing. ["He must shave", &c., is when a man is fined, if he is junior to the person he has offended; "He must dust", &c., is done by the small boys at the cattle-post; they are made to clean the loinskins of their elders. The underlying idea is to make amends for an insult to a senior.]

Sekaku (a member of the *lekgotla*): I find Ramodimo guilty, I see him, he's fond of chieftainship, he interfered with Sebele.

Ramogodi (an assessor): I find Ramodimo guilty. A person never enters another's *lapa* to fight there. The word of our fathers says: "You don't follow a snake into its hole"; and he has also cursed an older person than he is.

(The *lekgotla* murmurs, everybody saying, "He is guilty, he has sworn at an elderly person [Sebele's mother], and he has sworn at Sebele too".)

Masilo: Ramogodi, the *lekgotla* finds Ramodimo guilty. Tell us what you do in such a case? [Ramogodi is senior to most of the others in regimental membership.] And you report the matter to Manamakgôtê [another name for the ward].

Ramogodi: If a person is knocked down like this, and he is the one who began by interfering with his assailant, we say: "*O a swêl-la*" [i.e. "He loses his case"]. I say he must *swêlla*.

Masilo: Habakuke [addressing Ramodimo's senior], I say you are guilty, your child has made a mistake, he went into some one else's *lapa*, and he has also sworn at people; and again you went to the Chief's *kgotla* without telling us, and also he has cursed at the old person Sebele's mother. I fine you a big ox.

Habakuke: Ramodimo, do you hear?

Ramodimo: I hear, but I don't agree, I appeal myself to the Chief's *kgotla*. I cannot be forced like this.

(All get up and break away, saying "Go, go".)

(Masilo goes to report his appeal to the Chief.)

QUESTIONS

1. Outline the procedural steps followed in the case above. To what extent do they parallel procedures used in American and European courts? How do they differ?

2. Is this a civil or a criminal case? Be sure to consider both the initiation of the case and the disposition of the case in reaching your conclusion.

3. Why is it customary to hear a case at the *kgotla* of the defendant?

4. In Ramodimo v. Sebele note that the Madikwe people seized an ox. What steps probably preceded that event? Why did they seize the ox? Have you ever heard of a similar act performed in conjunction with an American case and for a similar reason?

5. Who is Habakuke? (He is greeted by the senior assessor at the beginning of the hearing and addressed by him again at the end.) What does his role suggest concerning collective vs. individual responsibility in Tswana legal thinking?

NOTE

In this same case, note the assessors' use of the proverb, "Don't follow a snake into its hole." Schapera explicates its meaning:

Isaac Schapera, "Tswana Legal Maxims," in Africa, vol. 36, 1966, p. 126. Footnotes omitted.

. . . One doesn't invade a snake's hole, or *Noga gaelatellwe momosimeng*, "One doesn't pursue a snake into its hole", i.e. if you assault someone in his home (instead of taking him to court), you are punished more severely than usual, and if you yourself suffer injury there the court will give you no satisfaction. (*Ge otsenela noga momosimeng etlagoloma*, says one Kgatla version, "If you invade a snake's hole it will bite you.")

QUESTION

1. Proverbs are used quite regularly in traditional African courts. What functions are served by their use?

NOTE

Ramodimo seemed to go out of his way to insult and defame Sebele. Refer back to the Roberts excerpt in section B-5 to see how common this offense is among the Tswana. Schapera has pointed out that oral sorcery is a significant offense among the Tswana. It, too, involves what I would call "verbal aggression."

Isaac Schapera, "Oral Sorcery among the Natives of Bechuanaland," in Essays Presented to C.G. Seligman, edited by Edward E. Evans Pritchard, et al. London: Kegan Paul, Trench, Trubner and Co., 1934, pp. 296–298. Footnotes omitted.

[Schapera notes that the Tswana traditionally recognize *boloi ba dithlare*, "sorcery by medicine," performed by habitual or occasional sorcerers, persons who harm others through use of "medicines," material substances obtained from a professional magician/sorcerer. This is distinguished from] . . . *boloi ba molomo*, "bewitching with the mouth." Here the material element is entirely lacking. The potent factor is the feeling of malevolence, anger, or bitterness cherished against a person by someone else. The latter makes no use of *dithlare*, he utters no spells, he performs no special rites, nor does he have to observe any taboos or other special usages. All the normal ingredients of magic are lacking. The only thing necessary is for him to have a bitter heart against his enemy. As we shall see later, there is some difference of opinion as to whether this really constitutes *boloi* or not. But the name by which it is generally known seems to suggest that on the whole the BaKxatla are inclined to class it in the category of sorcery together with other forms of malevolent activity against the well-being of a person.

This particular variety of *boloi* may assume two different forms. In the one, known as *xo hutsa* "to curse", a person definitely threatens his enemy, or expresses the wish that some evil will befall him. For instance, when two men quarrel, the one who feels affronted may say to the other: *ke tla xo hutsa*, "I shall curse you," or *o tla ipônna*, "You will see for yourself (what will happen to you)," or *se ê nao*, "May it (misfortune) go with you," or he may even say outright, "I hope that you die, because I don't want to see you in this tribe." He is then said *xo bua maswe*, "to be speaking evilly." He remains cherishing in his heart a feeling of bitterness against his enemy. Then should the latter meet with any sort of misfortune, such as being gored by an ox, or being badly knocked about in a fight, or run over by a wagon, or falling ill, it is believed that he suffers this misfortune because of the curse put upon him. . . .

[In *xo hutsa*, it] . . . must be emphasized that there is no direct action on the part of the person who inflicts the curse. He merely tells you that he feels bitter against you, and that he wishes you harm, but he does nothing further. If he is not satisfied to let the matter rest there and wait for the realization of his threat, he may go to a magician and ask him to work against you, e.g. by *xo nêêla*, by sending an animal to injure you. But in this case he becomes a *moloi wa dithlare*, "a sorcerer of medicines," and is no longer *moloi wa molomo*, "a sorcerer of the mouth."

Analogous to *xo hutsa*, and known by the same name, is the action of a person who points his index finger at you. He need not utter any threat, but you know by his action that he is wishing you evil. In effect he is saying, *o tla ipônna*, "You will see for yourself." Then if any misfortune does overtake you, he will be held responsible.

I tried to discover what the reaction is against a person whose curse has brought misfortune upon another. No legal action can be taken, such as is permitted with *boloi ba dithlare*. The victim is fully aware, or the diviner will tell him, that his misfortune is due to the curse of his enemy, but the tribal court does not regard this as an actionable wrong. The only remedy is for the victim himself to use sorcery against his enemy, and this generally appears to be done. On the other hand, it is possible to avert the threatened evil by attempting to restore friendly relations before it is too late. If the breach is healed, and you are once more on good terms with your former enemy, his curse will no longer have effect. Among the other Chwana tribes there is a special ceremony of reconciliation performed in such cases, but in spite of careful inquiries I have so far been unable to find anything of the same sort among the BaKxatla. You try to conciliate your enemy with gifts or with fair words, but if he does not respond to your overtures nothing can prevent misfortune from falling upon you.

In the type of *boloi ba molomo* just described, the threat or hope is actually expressed that evil will befall the person with whom one has quarrelled. On the other hand, the person offended may merely brood over his grievance, without uttering any curse at all. But his attitude of mind is in itself sufficient to bring harm to his enemy. This is known as *kxaba* (sing.) or *dikxaba* (plur.). Willoughby, speaking of the BeChwana in general, summarizes *kxaba* as follows: "The anger of a living father, grandfather, uncle, or elder brother, as well as that of the dead, is thought to be physically injurious to its object; and immature members of the offender's household are more susceptible to its malign influence. If a child falls ill soon after a family quarrel, the diviner is apt to discover that the cause of the illness is the anger of the father's elders in family or clan. There is no cure for such illness till the anger of the offended elder has been assuaged, and he washes the child with 'medicine' and recites the formula over it: 'If it was I, let him heal!' "

"*Kxaba*," commented one of my informants, "is something incomprehensible. It can happen to anybody with relatives, for it is caused by the wish of a relative who is angry with you. . . ."

QUESTIONS

1. Does awareness of the existence of a belief structure concerning oral sorcery help you to see why Ramodimo's behavior was considered so offensive?

2. What is the operative distinction between the two forms of *boloi ba molomo* ("bewitching with the mouth"): (1) *xo hutsa* and (2) *kxaba*? Which of these two is likely to have the most potent effect as a mechanism of social control, i.e. as a means of inhibiting any negatively valued—even criminal—behavior? Why? What kind of psychological mechanism(s) do you suppose underlie the effectiveness of either type of *boloi ba molomo*? Does this question help you to see which form of *boloi* might be more powerful as a social control mechanism?

NOTE AND QUESTIONS

A dimension of the handling of Ramodimo v. Sebele that we have not examined yet is the treatment of evidence.

1. Sebele's sister, who played a key role in the incident, does not appear as a witness. The fact that she was struck by Ramodimo does not seem to be an issue in the case. Yet, Sebele's mother is called to testify and one of the charges against Ramodimo is that he cursed at her. What do these facts indicate about the admissibility or eligibility of women as witnesses in traditional Botswana? Of old people?

2. Ramodimo denied having insulted Sebele and his testimony was contradicted by Sebele, Sebele's mother, and Gaefete. How did the *kgotla* decide who was telling the truth?

3. What evidence was offered on motivation and intent? How did the *kgotla* make a decision on these dimensions of the case?

NOTE

Among African peoples the Tswana are unusual in not using supernatural means for obtaining and assessing evidence. The general picture in traditional Africa is described by Allott.

Antony N. Allott, "Evidence in African Customary Law," in Readings in African Law. Vol. I, edited by Eugene Cotran and Neville N. Rubin. New York: Africana Publishing Corp., 1970, pp. 87–88. Bracketed heading inserted by editor.

African law everywhere permits recourse to supernatural means of eliciting the facts or deciding a case. The principal means by which such recourse is made are: (i) oaths or conditional curses; (ii) ordeals; (iii) divination. Torture was also used in some tribes to extract the facts, or more usually a confession of guilt, from an accused (e.g. among the Haya of Tanganyika and the Barotse of Northern Rhodesia). The procedures by which these supernatural means of finding out the truth are brought into play vary widely. Such supernatural means naturally struck the European observer very forcibly; but it would be a mistake to think that these means were the usual mode of eliciting facts or deciding a dispute in African law. On the whole recourse to the supernatural was only made when natural methods of finding out the truth were insufficient: e.g. there were no witnesses (as in many witchcraft accusations), the witnesses fundamentally contradict each other, the members of the court do not agree among themselves as to the facts of the case and there is no means of resolving the division of opinion, and so on.

[*Oaths.*] Oaths may be either *guarantees of veracity* or a *means of decision*. The oath as a guarantee of veracity is an appeal to supernatural forces to support the story told by a witness; it lends weight to his evidence, and is an affirmation that he will speak the truth. It is generally taken by a witness (and may be used in the middle of his evidence), and is not conclusive of the issue. Often in form it is a conditional curse by which the witness imprecates on his own head supernatural consequences if he lies. . . . In other African tribes the oath as a guarantee of veracity is found; and here an interesting historical fact may be noted. Where the oath as means of decision was used, this is in some places changing its character, and becoming merely a guarantee of veracity. For example, among the Mende of Sierra Leone by the so-called "swear-procedure" the parties exchanged conditional curses which they invoked on their own heads, and these concluded the hearing. But now the "swear" is used as a guarantee of veracity only, both by the parties *and by the witnesses.*

The oath as a means of decision is commonly found in African law. The Mende example has already been mentioned. If a party refused to "swear", he lost his case. If both parties swear, then the decision is left to the supernatural. The court adopts the "swear-procedure" if the case of both parties seems reasonable and there is a lack of witnesses.

* * *

[*Ordeals.*] *Ordeals* are the doing or suffering by a party of something that is intrinsically dangerous, but which is harmless to the innocent and harmful only to the guilty. (Where the ordeal is undergone by proxy, e.g. by a cock in Ibo law, this is a form of divination.) Ordeals are practically confined to criminal cases, though they may also be used outside a court in some areas (e.g. to test a wife's virtue). They are often imposed by the court, though sometimes we find that they are voluntarily undergone by a party or imposed by his opponent. They are specially important in trials of serious offences such as witchcraft and in other cases where the true facts cannot be ascertained. Examples of ordeals found include, for the Kamba of Kenya, the hot knife ordeal,* the needle ordeal, the bead in the eye ordeal, the drinking of a poisonous mixture; these are very typical of other customary laws.

---

* The use of a hot knife ordeal to resolve a dispute among the Kpelle of Liberia is recorded in the ethnographic film, The Cows of Dolo Ken Paye (16 mm., 31 minutes) produced by James Lowell Gibbs, Jr., and Marvin Silverman. It is distributed by Phoenix Films, 468 Park Avenue, New York, N.Y., 10016 and is available from major film rental libraries.

[*Divination.*] *Divination* is the use of natural or preternatural occurrences as signs of guilt or innocence, by the doing of something not intrinsically harmful to a suspect. Often a professional diviner was employed (as among the Ashanti and the Ibo). Oracles (as among the Azande of the Sudan as described by Evans-Pritchard) are found. In some societies divination was either not used at all (cf. the Tswana of Bechuanaland as described by Schapera—they did not use ordeals either), or was not used in civil cases (the Barotse).

[(*Ashanti*) *"Oath-procedure"*.] Special forms of procedure are found in some tribes. Of these, one of the most remarkable is the Ashanti "oath-procedure" as described by Rattray. We are not here concerned with examining in detail the whole procedure; it suffices to say that it is a means (still employed in the Ghana local courts today) by which a case may be brought to a chief's court by using one of that chief's "oaths" in defence of his rights (the comparison with the ancient Roman *legis actio per sacramentum* has often been made). The effect is that the oath-taker becomes *prima facie* a criminal, since he has broken a tribal taboo by uttering a forbidden word or phrase, the "oath". He can escape liability if he can show that he justifiably invoked the oath in defence of his civil rights. The procedure in the chief's court in an oath case was in form criminal, though the substance of the case was civil.

QUESTIONS

1. Is the use of supernatural means for assessing the evidence indigenous superstition, or, is there an underlying rationale for their use that is understandable in Western terms, too? Are there recurring conditions under which the oath or the ordeal are used?

2. Compare the use of the oath in Sub-Saharan Africa with its use in North Africa in the Islamic courts of Egypt. Where does the Islamic use fit in Allott's classification?

3. Can you speculate about why the Tswana use neither the oath, nor the ordeal, nor divination in the legal context? Do they have other means of evoking the truth in the absence of witnesses?

NOTE

The threat of oral sorcery is not the only means for evoking truth in the absence of witnesses in a customary Tswana court, partly because this set of beliefs is not as strong as it used to be. John Comaroff (personal communication, 1979) observes that the Tswana believe that proper, skillful use of rhetorical questions will bring out the truth, even in the absence of witnesses. This, he argues, would be another reason why the Tswana do not resort to oaths, ordeals, or divination as a way of ascertaining the truth. The writing of Roberts on oaths and ordeals provides another hypothesis: that Tswana traditional political structures were powerful enough to enforce all decisions, right or wrong, without fear of constant dissension. He would argue that they do not have to pass this task along to a neutral mechanism such as an oath or ordeal (cf. John M. Roberts, Oaths, Autonomic Ordeals, and Power, 67 American Anthropologist, 1965, pp. 186–212.)

QUESTION

1. Now let's return to the hypothetical:

> You are a senior member of the tribal council of a Tswana chief. A clerk informs you that he has discovered alterations in the books of the tribal treasury indicating that the chief has withdrawn part of a special tax fund set aside to celebrate a visit by the president. You suspect that the chief has turned the money over to his son, who recently opened a popular cafe in the tribal capital. How do you proceed? What informal sanctions, customary procedures, or formal legal action might be taken? In what court could charges be brought and by whom? With what result?

E. CONFLICT BETWEEN CUSTOMARY AND EUROPEAN LAW

NOTE

In Problem I we confronted the problem of conflict between customary law and European law. Like other African nations, Botswana is presently engaged in unifying the disparate elements of its legal heritage. There, the problem is particularly difficult since, as noted in the chapter introducing Botswana, its general law represents a mixture of Roman-Dutch and British common law unique to several southern African states.

Thus, the Protectorate courts consisted of judges educated in British schools, applying a version of Roman law filtered through the Dutch courts and modified by English common law doctrines and precedent.

Consider the following case from the colonial period which shows how these elements were combined in practice. It also exemplifies another issue often raised by students of African legal systems: whether the greater procedural specialization or technicality of imposed law means that it more readily can be employed to circumvent equity.

The case was decided by the Privy Council in London, which was the court of last resort for all the British protectorates in southern Africa. This case originated in Basutoland (now Lesotho), where Roman-Dutch law also was imposed as the "received" law. Similar issues arise in contemporary cases heard in the High Court and Court of Appeal in Botswana.

High Comm'n Law Reports, 1954, pp. 38–47 [Editor's interposed headings in brackets.] Nkau Majara v. The Queen, (Criminal Appeal from Basutoland High Court.)

Present: Lord Goddard (The Lord Chief Justice of England).
   Lord Reid
   Mr. L. M. D. de Silva
   (Delivered by Mr. de Silva).

The term "accessory after the fact" as used in criminal law does not, under the law of South Africa—the Roman-Dutch common law— bear a meaning identical with that which it has under the English law. To constitute a person an accessory after the fact in South Africa it is sufficient to establish that assistance was given to the principal offender in circumstances from which it would appear that the giver "associated" himself with, in the broad sense of that word, the offence committed, and Roman-Dutch law makes no distinction for this purpose between giving assistance by remaining inactive and refraining from doing something, and giving assistance by doing something. The kind of impassivity, when it occurs after the commission of an offence by another, which has for its objective the giving of assistance to that other to escape, is under the law of South Africa punishable as the offence of being an accessory after the fact.

[*The Issue.*] Where, therefore, the appellant, a gazetted native headman in Basutoland, had, contrary to his duty as such headman under section 6(3) of the Native Administration Proclamation (Laws of Basutoland, 1949, c. 54), refrained from arresting the murderers on his arrival at the scene of a ritual murder, and thereby and by his subsequent conduct in failing to report the murder and to give prompt assistance to the police had assisted the murderers by giving them an opportunity to escape from justice, he had associated himself with the murder and was under the law of Basutoland which for this purpose was the same as that of South Africa, an accessory after the fact to the murder.

[*Citations Omitted.*] Further, the provision in section 14 of the Native Administration Proclamation, c. 54, which provided, *inter alia*, that a headman was liable to a fine if he wilfully neglected a duty imposed by the Proclamation, did not stand in the way of the conviction of the appellant, for the wilful neglect of the duty under the statute could occur without the objective of giving an offender an opportunity to escape, but where that latter element was present the graver offence of being an accessory after the fact had been committed.

[*Decision.*] Judgment of the High Court of Basutoland affirmed. APPEAL (No. 29 of 1953), by special leave, from a judgment of the High Court of Basutoland (February 9, 1953) whereby the appellant, a headman, was convicted of being an accessory after the fact to the murder of one Motetwa Memani and was sentenced to 12 years' hard labour.

[*Case before the High Court: The Facts.*] The appellant and 20 others were tried together by the High Court (Willan, C. J. sitting with assessors) on an indictment charging them with the murder. The case for the prosecution was that all the accused were members of a gang which on May 16, 1952, seized Motetwa Memani, took him into a hut, inflicted various injuries on him by a ritual process thereby killing him, and then threw his body over a cliff. Of the 20 other persons nine were acquitted and 11 were convicted of murder. The appellant was convicted of having been an accessory after the fact to the murder.

[*The High Court's Reasoning.*] The trial judge, giving the appellant the benefit of a doubt, found that "he was present immediately after the killing of the deceased and not before it". He then proceeded to convict the appellant of having been an accessory after the fact upon the following findings:

"First, that he is a gazetted headman of the area in which this murder took place. Secondly, that he was in a dominant position because he was a headman. Thirdly, that by virtue of section 6(3) of the Native Administration Proclamation (Cap. 54) there was a legal duty cast upon him to arrest any native he knew, or had information against, that such native had committed an offence for which an arrest could be made without a warrant. In this case accused No. 7 knew that murder had been committed in the hut by certain persons known to him. Fourthly, that he took no effective action afterwards when the body had been thrown over the cliff. In his own evidence he said he knew of the existence of this body at the foot of the cliff on Saturday, May 17, 1952, but he did nothing about it till the following Tuesday. Fifthly, as a headman he did not carry out the provisions of two circular instructions, Exhibits E and F, issued by the Paramount Chief of Basutoland regarding the immediate reporting of a ritual murder and the giving of prompt assistance to the police." . . .

[*Decision.*] Jan. 14, Lord Goddard, C.J. announced that their Lordships would humbly advise Her Majesty that the appeal should be dismissed, and that they would give their reasons later.

Cases referred to:

(1) R. v. Mlooi (1925) A.D. 131.

(2) R. v. Jongani (1937) A.D. 400.

(3) R. v. van Rensburg (1943) T.P.D. 436.

(4) R. v. Von Elling (1945) A.D. 234.

[*The Holding.*] March, 1954.

Mr. de Silva: This is an appeal by special leave from a judgment, dated the 9th February, 1953, of the High Court of Basutoland, whereby the appellant was convicted of being an accessory after the fact to the murder of one Motetwa Memani. . . .

[Mr. de Silva reviews the facts and the findings of the High Court including the five findings of fact stated by Willan, C. J. which were accepted by the appellant as a condition of the right to appeal.]

The sole question for determination by their Lordships is whether, accepting the said findings of fact, the appellant was rightly convicted of having been an accessory after the fact to the said murder.

Under section 2 of the General Law Proclamation (Cap. 26 Laws of Basutoland) the common law of Basutoland "shall as nearly as the circumstances of the country will permit, be the same as the law for the time being in force in the Colony or the Cape of Good Hope". The statute law consists of Acts passed by the Parliament of the Cape of Good Hope before the 29th May, 1884, and Proclamations made by the High Commissioner since that date.

It is not disputed that the determination of the question before their Lordships depends on the Roman Dutch Common Law which is the common law of the Cape of Good Hope and is also the common law in force in South Africa.

The view that the appellant was an accessory after the fact is founded on the fact that by refraining from performing his duties he gave the murderers assistance which in the ordinary course would, or might, have helped them to avoid being brought to justice. It has not been established that he gave assistance through any physical act.

It was conceded by counsel for the respondent that under the English Law the appellant could not be held guilty of being an accessory after the fact. It was suggested that under that law a necessary element of the offence of being an accessory after the fact was assistance to the principal offender by a physical act and not merely by omitting to do something. Counsel for respondent argued that the English Law made this distinction because assistance by omission, which under any system of law could but be logically regarded as reprehensible equally with assistance by commission, would in appropriate circumstances under the English Law constitute the offence of misprision of felony. He contended that the position was wholly different under the law of South Africa because, among other reasons, under the Roman Dutch Law there prevailing, an offence arising from assistance by omission could not be accorded a separate category.

It was argued for the appellant that the term "accessory after the fact" had to be given a meaning under the law of South Africa in no way different from that which it possesses under the English Law.

It is correctly stated by *Gardiner and Lansdown, 5th Edition,* in their treatise on South African Law and Procedure (page 120) that "the term 'accessory after the fact' is one derived from English Law and although quite unknown to Roman Dutch Law criminologists, has been adopted in South African practice". In support of this view it is sufficient to refer to the case of Rex v. Mlooi (1) at page 143, in which Solomon, J.A., referring to a set of circumstances, which, on the authority of *Moorman* and *Van der Linden,* he thought constituted an offence under the Roman Dutch Law, said:

"It does not appear that under the Roman Dutch Law any special name was given to this offence and it is convenient to adopt the English Law expression of 'accessory after the fact'. Its use is sanctioned not only by the practice of our Courts but also by the fact that it is to be found enshrined in our statute law."

It does not necessarily follow from the fact that the term "accessory after the fact" has been adopted from the English Law that it has the same meaning in the Law of South Africa as it has under the English Law. . . . In their Lordships' opinion an authoritative view of the true position is to be found in the following passage in the judgment of Innes, C. J. in the case of Rex v. Mlooi (1) referred to above:

He who intervenes to assist a criminal after the event may conveniently be called an accessory after the fact—not in the technical and restricted sense in which that term is used in English law, but in an extended sense applicable to crimes in general. So used, its meaning is well understood, and has received some degree of statutory recognition.

The statute law affords no assistance in the determination of the question before their Lordships because no South African Act or Basutoland Proclamation defines the term "accessory after the fact" for the purposes of the general criminal law although it occurs sometimes defined, sometimes undefined, in various statutes dealing with special subjects.

It appears to their Lordships from what has already been said that the term "accessory after the fact" does not, under the law of South Africa, bear a meaning identical with that which it has under the English Law.

No decision of the South African Courts was cited to their Lordships in which the question had been considered whether assistance to a principal offender given by omission is sufficient equally with assistance given by commission to render the giver an accessory after the fact. Nor have they been referred to the *dicta* of any of the Roman Dutch jurists bearing on the point. The *dicta* quoted in the judgments in the case of Rex v. Mlooi (supra) throw considerable light upon the elements which are necessary to constitute a person an accessory after the fact in South Africa. Those *dicta* and those judgments lead to this conclusion. To constitute a person an accessory after the fact in South Africa it is sufficient to establish that assistance was given to the principal offender in circumstances from which it would appear that the giver "associated" himself with, in the broad sense of that word, the offence committed. The *dicta* and the judgments do not concern themselves with the question whether assistance given by remaining inactive or refraining from doing something would render a person an offender equally with assistance given by doing something. In the absence of anything to the contrary in the Roman Dutch Law their Lordships would conclude that that law makes no distinction between the two ways of giving assistance. There is however not merely the absence of anything to the contrary but something which supports that conclusion.

It appears to their Lordships that the idea that a person was punishable, in appropriate circumstances, for refraining from action was prevalent in the Roman Dutch Law. For instance *Huber* in chapter 1, book VI, of his *Heedensdaegse Rechtsgeleertheyt* (translated by Percival Gane) dealing generally with crimes, says at section 10 "at times even refraining from action and mere impassivity makes a person liable to the ordinary penalty". . . . *Huber* deals with two kinds of "impassivity." In the one a person remains passive because although he has formed an intention to accomplish something prohibited, he does nothing and thereby he fails to accomplish it. In these circumstances he commits no offence. In the other by remaining passive and doing nothing a person accomplishes something prohibited, for instance by refraining from arresting an offender he accomplishes something prohibited, namely giving an offender assistance to escape. It is the latter form of "impassivity" which *Huber* styles "dangerous and detrimental" and which, according to what he has said earlier, is punishable as an offence.

From what has been said it appears to their Lordships that the latter kind of impassivity when it occurs after the commission of an offence by another and has for its objective the giving of assistance to that other to escape, is under the law of South Africa punishable as the offence of being an accessory after the fact. . . .

Their Lordships think one further point needs some comment. Statutory penal provision under which the appellant could have been punished is to be found in the Native Administration Proclamation (Laws of Basutoland, 1949, Cap. 54) section 14 which says:

A Chief, Sub-Chief or Headman shall be liable to a fine not exceeding fifty pounds upon conviction before a Subordinate Court of the First Class or before the Court of the Paramount Chief of any of the following acts or neglects:

(a) if he shall wilfully neglect to exercise the powers by this Proclamation conferred upon him for or in respect of the prevention of offences or the bringing of offenders to justice, or the seizure of property stolen or believed to have been stolen;

(b) if he shall wilfully, and without reasonable excuse, refuse or neglect to exercise any powers given or delegated to him under this Proclamation.

It has been suggested that the existence of this provision precludes the appellant from being punished as an accessory after the fact to the crime of murder. It sometimes happens that the elements which constitute a minor offence are present when a graver offence is committed. This is particularly true of minor offences created by statute. But whenever this happens no ground is furnished for not proceeding against the offender for the graver offence. . . . Their Lordships are of the opinion that the statutory penal provision referred to does not stand in the way of the conviction in this case.

It was not disputed that the appellant though charged with murder could under the law of Basutoland be convicted of having been an accessory after the fact to murder.

For the reasons which they have given their Lordships have humbly advised Her Majesty that the appeal be dismissed.

QUESTIONS

1. How does the development in Roman-Dutch law of the concept "accessory after the fact" show how South African law is a blend of two or, (considering the Roman roots of Roman-Dutch law) three legal traditions? Did you notice how Roman-Dutch law's borrowing from English law of the accessory-after-the-fact concept was not by statute, but by gradual usage? Note, too, that this usage borrowed the English law term, but not exact English law meaning. This is a good example of the complexity of the interaction between legal systems.

2. In this case, what did the existence of the two kinds of imposed law contribute to the effectiveness or efficiency of justice?

3. If, in this case, you think the appellant's lawyer was utilizing the dual roots of Roman-Dutch law as a technicality to circumvent proper justice, consider what implications the existence of such a possibility has for the measure of respect the average African (in this case a citizen of Lesotho) would have for European law?

NOTE

European law sees itself as superior to traditional or customary law. In fact under colonial rule there was always a phrase similar to that in the Bechuanaland African Courts Proclamation, which states that: " 'Customary law' means, in relation to any particular tribe or tribal community, the customary law of that tribe or community *in so far as it is not incompatible with the provisions of any written law or contrary to morality, humanity or natural justice* (emphasis supplied)." Compare the assessment of African law which is implicit—in fact, virtually explicit—in such a phrase with the assessment contained in the following excerpt.

Antony N. Allott, "The Future of African Law," in African Law: Adaptation and Development, edited by Hilda Kuper and Leo Kuper. Berkeley and Los Angeles: University of California Press, 1965, pp. 231–233.

Adjudication and Arbitration. It now seems to be taken for granted that African courts, and the African style of adjudication, are to disappear from Africa. "Improvement" of the African local, customary courts means in effect their disappearance through assimilation with the courts of European type. In the common-law countries, personnel, procedure, and jurisdiction are all to be progressively Anglicized. Although continual improvement in the lower courts is both vital and inevitable, the advantages that African courts and procedure may have had should not be overlooked. I summarize them briefly as follows:

(1) Justice was popular. The people could understand the machinery and the purposes of judicial arrangements, and the law applied by the courts. Often the people had control over the courts and those presiding over them, and in many places participated directly in judicial proceedings.

(2) Justice was local and speedy. The first point needs no development; the structure of African traditional judicatures reflected the needs of the local community rather than any desire for administrative efficiency or ease of supervision from the center. The argument that justice was speedy may seem to require justification, as the contrary has often been argued, especially by outsiders. It is true that traditional judicial proceedings in Africa can and could be long drawn out, especially by the wish to ensure that no person's opinion would go unregarded, or that no fact that might have a bearing on the successful conclusion of the case would be overlooked. But no one contemplating the history of modern land litigation in West Africa, with its interminable appeals dragging on from court to court, could argue that African justice was slow in comparison; modern Western-style justice is often slow precisely because it is not local or popular. Using the elaborate procedures of the English law of evidence, the courts require proof of facts that would have been well known without special proof to a traditional African tribunal.

(3) Justice was simple and flexible. There was no elaborate codes of procedure or evidence, though there were procedural and evidentiary rules, of course. A confrontation in detail of African and English ideas about evidence shows the advantage to lie in many respects with the African system. One healthy consequence of the desire to Africanize the legal system might be to devise an altogether different approach to the law of evidence, which, from the English side, is bogged down in technicalities dating back to the exigencies of a quite different, and now vanished, system of trial. Flexibility is to be observed, not only in the ease with which African courts avoided the procedural snags that often give English justice a bad name, but in what may be called the "arbitral approach to justice." In many African courts the judge would try, not merely to administer the law, but to find a solution to the dispute which would appear just to the parties and would put a stop to further litigation between them; if the law had to be stretched, or even to be ignored, in the process, this was justifiable if peace and harmony were restored. . . .

QUESTIONS

1. Would it be workable to maintain a court system and a body of law applicable only to members of a tribe and operating alongside a national court system? Thus some disputes and offenses that occur only in traditional relationships would be channeled into the customary courts, while those

covered by civil and criminal law would proceed through the national courts. Consider how certain institutions in western nations have maintained separate private courts and codes of law applicable only to their own members: the military services, some churches, perhaps some fraternal and professional organizations.

2. Are there fundamental differences between law handed down by oral tradition and law written in cases and statutes? How did legal systems function in western nations prior to the recording of judicial decisions and the drafting of statutes?

3. What are the effects of the introduction of lawyers into the legal process? Would you encourage the Tswana to permit parties to have representation by attorneys in customary courts?

Chapter 16

EMBEZZLEMENT BY A PUBLIC OFFICIAL
IN CHINESE LAW

A. THE HYPOTHETICAL PROBLEM IN
CHINESE CONTEXT

NOTE

Chang is head of a commune and also first secretary of the local Communist Party organization. He has been notified that a high government official, Deng Xiaoping, will be touring the area in the near future, and intends to stop at Chang's commune to greet local dignitaries and to partake of refreshments.

Chang withdraws ¥500 [about US$350, an amount approximately equal to Chang's annual salary] from the commune treasury to prepare a fitting welcome for Deng. ¥400 was spent to enlarge and refurbish the living room in Chang's house where the meeting with Deng will take place. Chang purchased the building materials from his close relatives, and also hired them to do the work. He paid 50% above the usual prices for the materials and labor because the project had to be completed in a very short time. The remaining ¥100 was used to purchase refreshments, again from Chang's relatives and at premium prices.

Do these actions constitute embezzlement or misuse of public funds? How will the matter be handled? If an offense has been committed, will Chang be formally charged with a crime and tried in a court, or will his conduct be evaluated and sanctions imposed through some other process? What would be an appropriate sanction?

Recall the administrative structure of Huadong commune described in Problem I. In addition, an overlapping Communist Party organization supervises, and takes part in, all aspects of commune work.

Gordon A. Bennett, Huadong: The Story of a Chinese People's Commune, Boulder, Colorado: Westview Press, 1978, pp. 41–44.

At the commune level, translation of central policies into action is the responsibility of a Party committee. This committee in turn directs the work of commune administrators under the day-to-day management of a hierarchy of revolutionary committees. . . .

. . .

The top level of the Party in the commune is the seven-member Standing Committee, which meets once a week. This leadership group is elected by and from among the twenty-one members of the Party Committee, which only meets about once every two months. All these individuals enjoy long tenure in office, even though they are elected every year or two by the commune Party congress. Generally speaking, Party members serving at this level are capable and respected people. The Huadong committeemen (and women) are returned to office again and again by the 450 delegates to the Party congress representing the 1,144 Party members in the whole commune. Some committee members develop specializations related to the economic life of the commune, such as in water conservancy, animal husbandry, or forestry. They may be sent to attend specialized courses, and after a while some of them come to be quite knowledgeable in their subject. Other Party committee members develop expertise in more strictly Party work, such as organization, membership and recruitment, propaganda and study, or women's affairs. They may attend training courses in a county or provincial Party school. Most of them hold positions in the commune administration (under the RC) and are responsible for day-to-day management of problems in their special area. As *Party* specialists, however, their job is to be concerned about broader matters of policy and political line.

Party structure in the commune parallels non-Party organization. The next level below the Party committee, the "Party branch," usually has between twenty and thirty members. Each branch meets about once a month and is responsible for Party work in its unit. Twenty branches are in production brigades, and twenty-two more are in commune administrative bureaus, enterprises, middle schools, the hospital, and the like. The basic level, called a "Party small group," exists wherever three or more Party members are found. Small groups meet once a week and afford the Party its most sensitive grass roots exposure. Many production teams have small groups along with shops, offices, clinics, primary schools, and pumping stations.

Roughly one Huadong Commune member in fifty-five (2 percent) belongs to the Party. The normal path to joining is for young men and women in the early teens to demonstrate a good attitude toward work and to stand out in political activities at school, thereby qualifying to join the Communist Youth League (generally in their late teens and early twenties). As Youth League members, if they show particular aptitude for ideological and political matters and take an active leadership role in League responsibilities, they may be recommended as probationary Party members. Should their progress continue as expected, they may be admitted as full members by their mid-twenties. An alternate path is first to join the People's Liberation Army. Political and technical training for soldiers is better than for civilians, and Party membership may be easier to attain there. Demobilized soldiers often return to their home village and expect to take an active role in local affairs.　.　.　.

*　*　*

B.　COMPLAINT AND INVESTIGATION

NOTE

The general community would have no difficulty learning about, or "discovering," Chang's actions. After all, a commune is a relatively small place where people know a great deal about each other's affairs. Note that such ease of discovery of possible crimes may not be present in other societies or apply to other kinds of offenses.

But who will bring a complaint against Chang? Is there a risk in accusing the leading local political and economic figure of committing a crime? If Chang ultimately prevails in this case, might he retaliate against his accuser? Conversely, even if outside authorities learn about Chang's actions, how could these authorities penetrate Chang's network of local relationship so that evidence and witnesses can be gathered?

"Poor Peasant Girl, T'ang Yu-lien, Bravely Struggles Against Theft of Collective Property," Chung-kuo ch'ing-nien pao (China youth news, Peking), Nov. 24, 1964, p. 1, in Jerome Cohen, The Criminal Process in the People's Republic of China, 1949–1963, an Introduction. Cambridge: Harvard University Press, 1968, pp. 168–169.

According to a *Hupeh Daily* report, T'ang Yu-lien, a nineteen-year-old peasant girl attached to production team No. 5 of Ch'ün-kuang production brigade of Shih-tzu-lu commune, Hsien-feng county, courageously exposed the theft of collective property by her uncle, T'ang Chiu-chiang, who was a deputy leader of the production team, and thereby protected the collective interests. For this, she has been praised by the vast masses of commune members and commended by the brigade Party branch and the [management] committee of the production team.

Well-to-do middle peasant T'ang Chiu-chiang was a man seriously affected by bourgeois ideology. Last winter, he pretended to be an active worker and was elected a deputy leader of the production team. He then obtained work in the brewery. After he got into the brewery, his behavior aroused the suspicion of the poor peasant girl T'ang Yu-lien who, working in a flour mill next to the brewery, discovered that T'ang Chiu-chiang drank wine three times a day during his meals, that after he returned from the market he would always bring back a piece of meat, and that some dubious characters often visited his house. When she went home, she told all this to her father, T'ang Yüan-hsiang, and put to him a string of questions: In the past one hundred catties [a catty is one and one-third pounds] of wine were produced in a year, but why were only seventy to eighty catties produced this year? Why did T'ang Chiu-chiang always have visitors? From what Yu-lien told him, T'ang Yüan-hsiang also became suspicious of T'ang Chiu-chiang's behavior . . . . He then asked Yu-lien to watch more closely T'ang Chiu-chiang's movements, and courageously struggle against his wrongful acts. Thereupon, T'ang Yu-lien paid more attention to T'ang Chiu-chiang's movements.

At noon one day, male commune members of the team went out carrying coal to make lime, while most of the female commune members were cutting grass on the slope. Only T'ang Yu-lien worked as usual at the grinder in the flour mill. Suddenly she was assailed by a strong smell of wine, and turning her head, she saw that T'ang Chiu-chiang was walking out of the brewery carrying two buckets. Yu-lien dashed into the brewery, where she found an enamel vessel hung on the wall, with drops of wine still dripping from it. Obviously, the vessel had been used for ladling wine. Her suspicion aroused, she wondered if her uncle had stolen wine from the collective. "Papa says that I am a poor peasant's daughter and should act like a poor peasant who must be honest even in small things and who must dare to expose and struggle against those who violate the collective interest." With this thought, she closely followed T'ang Chiu-chiang, determined to get to the bottom of the matter.

With the guilty conscience of a thief, T'ang Chiu-chiang knew that something was wrong when he saw his niece coming toward him. His face paled. When Yu-lien saw this, she knew what was going on. So she asked him directly: "What is inside your buckets?" T'ang Chiu-chiang muttered: "It is waste water from the brewery." "But waste water is turbid. How is it that the water in your buckets is so clear?" Knowing his trick had failed, T'ang Chiu-chiang changed the subject quickly and said: "Oh, the water had been boiled to heat the wine." Seeing that he was trying to deceive her, Yu-lien became indignant and asked him to put down the buckets for her to inspect the contents. It was wine, and good wine at that. Then Yu-lien criticized him angrily: "Uncle, you are a deputy leader. Why do you do such a thing?"

T'ang Chiu-chiang never expected that his niece would talk to him like this. At first, he tried to sweet talk her into covering up for him. When he found that this would not work, he opened his eyes wide and swore at her: "Whether or not there is wine in the bucket is none of your business." Then, he said threateningly: "If you dare spoil my reputation, I'll break your jaw and tear your mouth wide open." Yu-lien was not afraid. Taking a step forward, she grasped the bucket with one hand and caught hold of T'ang Chiu-chiang with the other. She said loudly: "If you dare to damage the collective, then I dare to mind your business. You have stolen wine and evaded taxes so I can mind your business." T'ang Chiu-chiang wanted to pour the wine into a well so as to destroy any evidence. But Yu-lien held the bucket until other commune members, attracted by the noise, came over, and T'ang Chiu-chiang dared not use violence.

Because in the past T'ang Chiu-chiang had committed the illegal act of obtaining unreasonably large profits and now he had also stolen collective property, the production brigade and the management committee of the production team dealt with him severely. They also commended T'ang Yu-lien for her exemplary act of honesty and for furthering justice. This gave great satisfaction to the vast masses of poor and lower-middle peasant commune members, many of whom expressed their determination to learn from T'ang Yu-lien.

QUESTION

Persons other than the niece must have noticed that the uncle drank wine with every meal and purchased a substantial amount of meat. Why did they not get suspicious?

Jerome A. Cohen, The Criminal Process in the People's Republic of China, 1949–1963, Cambridge: Harvard University Press, 1968, pp. 363–365. [An Interview with a Refugee in Hong Kong]

On his return from a meeting at the county seat in the spring of 1959 the chief of the security defense committee of a commune production brigade received a secret "tip" that the secretary of the brigades' Party branch and the brigade leader were the ringleaders of a group of important brigade cadres who had surreptitiously slaughtered oxen belonging to the brigade and sold the meat for their private profit. He immediately telephoned this report to the chief of the security section of the county public security bureau. Because this was obviously an important and delicate case, the section chief went with the bureau chief to report it to, and to seek instructions from, the secretary of the county Party committee.

The Party secretary determined that it was necessary to send a work group down to the brigade to investigate the matter. Among the group that was selected were four cadres from the bureau—a deputy bureau chief, who was appointed group leader, the chief of the security section, who was made a deputy leader, one of the secretaries of the security section, and an investigator. There were also a procurator, a judge, a representative of the Party organization bureau, a representative of the Party supervision commission, who was made a deputy leader, a representative of the Party agriculture department, two cadres from the office of the county Party committee, and a cadre from the women's federation. In order to avoid arousing the suspicions of the suspects and creating a situation in which the masses might become too frightened to cooperate with the investigation, this political-legal work group was designated as a "spring plowing work group of the county Party committee," a temporary Party organization the task of which was to lead and to supervise spring plowing.

After arriving at the brigade, the members of the investigating group dispersed among the various production teams, laboring with the peasants by day and taking part in meetings at night. In the course of conducting propaganda on the needs of production at these meetings, they gradually exhorted the team members to find out why there were insufficient oxen to take care of the plowing. At first the peasants, fearing the consequences of implicating their leaders, were reluctant to give any information about the matter, but in a few days the investigators began to earn their confidence, and conversations with individual peasants enabled them slowly to piece the facts together. After almost three weeks of investigation, the group was prepared to accuse the principal culprits—the branch secretary, the brigade leader, the leader of the brigade militia, the women's chairman, and two other cadres, all of whom were Party members. The accusations were made at a meeting of the brigade Party branch. The accused admitted having ordered the slaughter of the oxen but denied having done it for profit. They claimed that the oxen had been old, sick, and unfit for work and that the whole matter had been too insignificant for them to report to the commune.

After the meeting the investigators then undertook a series of intensive private, individual talks with the accused in an attempt to "mobilize" them to confess. Care was exercised not to frighten them about the consequences of their conduct, because the investigators did not want them to commit suicide, as often happened in such situations. Leniency was promised to those who made full confessions. After a few days of "mobilization," the women's chairman finally told the entire story. Having checked her confession, the group convened another meeting of the branch, at which the women's chairman gave all the details of the offense. When the other accused heard this, they too confessed.

Following this branch meeting there was a meeting of the members of the investigating group who were most knowledgeable about the disposition of such cases: the political-legal cadres and the representative of the Party supervision commission. The representative of the Party organization bureau, who normally would be present at such a meeting, did not attend, since he was deemed to be an inexperienced newcomer. The group discussed the case and prepared recommendations with respect to the sanctions to be given to each of the culprits, who included four non-Party members: a brigade accountant who had had custody of the proceeds of the sales and three peasants who had done the actual slaughtering of the oxen. The leader and deputy leaders of the group then returned to the county seat to submit the materials in the case to the public security bureau and to report orally to a meeting of the county Party secretary, the head of the county Party secretariat, and the bureau chief, the chief procurator, and the court president.

This five-man body approved the recommendations made by the investigation work group, which were as follows: the money that had been collected from the sale of the slaughtered oxen had to be surrendered to the brigade. The secretary of the Party branch, who was the instigator of the scheme, was to be expelled from the Party and arrested. It was understood that arrest meant criminal punishment, although no decision was yet made on the length of the sentence. The brigade leader was to be expelled from the Party and removed from his brigade position. Because it was clear that he had not taken the initiative in the plot but had followed the lead of the branch secretary, he was not to be arrested but was to be given ten days of detention for violation of the SAPA.* The leader of the brigade militia was to be expelled from the Party and removed from his brigade position, but he was to receive no punishment. Although her responsibility was deemed to be as great as the militia leader's and although her confession had not been spontaneous, the only sanction to be received by the women's chairman was a demerit on her Party record, because she had been the first to confess. The two other Party members had played minor roles and thus were to receive mere warnings from the Party. The accountant was to be removed from his position because he had improperly used it to safeguard the illegal proceeds. The peasants who had killed the oxen were only to receive criticism from their production teams in view of the fact that they had acted under orders. While they were not considered innocent, their responsibility was deemed to be greatly diminished.

Because the case was thought to have great educational significance, it was decided that, in addition to publicizing it in a bulletin to be circulated among all cadres in the county, disposition of the case should be announced at a forthcoming enlarged meeting of the important Party cadres of the county, commune, and brigade levels. Before the meeting took place the Party supervision commission was notified of the decisions with respect to those culprits who were Party members, and it prepared expulsion documents in the appropriate cases. Also, the commune Party secretary was informed about those who were to be removed from their brigade positions. The public security bureau's security section made out an application for an arrest warrant for the branch secretary and, after the application was approved by the bureau chief and by the procuracy, it made out the actual warrant. It also prepared a detention warrant for the brigade leader.

At the meeting the Party members who were involved in the incident were ordered to stand on the platform. They had all remained at large until that time and were ignorant of their fate. The secretary of the Party supervision commission briefly introduced the facts of the case and announced what Party sanction was meted out to

* Security Administration Punishment
Act, a misdemeanor law.

each of the members involved and the reasons underlying it. Then the deputy chief of the public security bureau, who had led the investigating team, briefly stated why the branch secretary had to be arrested, and he read aloud the arrest warrant, which charged the branch secretary with undermining production. At that point a people's policeman put handcuffs on the accused and led him away to the detention house. The chief of the bureau's security section then rose to state why the brigade leader had to receive detention. After he read off the detention warrant, a people's policeman led the brigade leader away, but without the use of handcuffs.

NOTES AND QUESTIONS

1. Could anyone in the brigade not have known that oxen, which are very valuable and needed for plowing, were missing? Might they also have known the identity of the culprits? After all, oxen slaughtering is a large and messy operation, not like the stealing of a chicken. Why had no complaints been lodged earlier? What social, economic, or political factors might discourage the making of complaints?

2. Why might the "tipster" have chosen to act secretly rather than directly confront the culprits as T'ang Yu-lien did? What steps could the state take to encourage more complainants to come forward?

3. Which persons and institutions made the decisions about how to dispose of the case? What is the significance of the recommendations made by the investigating group?

4. Note the amount of time and effort that went into the breaking of the oxen slaughtering ring. Could other quicker methods have been used?

5. The SAPA is a misdemeanor law which empowers the police to impose the sanction of detention up to 15 days. The brigade leader probably was sentenced to this type of detention.

6. Do you feel that the sanctions imposed were severe, just right, or lenient?

7. What was the role of the Communist Party in each of these cases? Are Party members who commit crimes treated differently than ordinary citizens?

The Party Constitution of 1977, Article 5, provided:

Article 5. When a Party member violates Party discipline, the Party organization concerned should give the member education and, on the merits of the case, may take any of the following disciplinary measures—a warning, a serious warning, removal from his or her post in the Party, being placed on probation within the Party, and expulsion from the Party.

* * *

Article 6. Any disciplinary measure taken against a Party member must be decided on by a general membership meeting of the Party branch to which the member belongs and should be submitted to the next higher Party committee for approval. Under special circumstances, a primary Party committee or a higher Party committee has the power to take disciplinary action against a Party member.

*   *   *

When a Party organization takes a decision on a disciplinary measure against a member, it must, barring special circumstances, notify the member that he or she should attend the meeting. If the member disagrees with the decision, he or she may ask for a review of the case and has the right to appeal to higher Party committees, up to and including the Central Committee.

NOTE

Throughout the Chinese literature on criminal law, there is great emphasis on the concepts of reform and education. Consider the following items, the first by a writer sympathetic to the regime, and the second by a critic.

As you go through the rest of the materials presented in this problem, consider the extent to which Chinese legal practice carries out the ideal of reform of wrongdoers.

Edgar Snow, The Other Side of the River, Red China Today. New York: Random House, 1962, p. 356.

For all criminals incarceration is the beginning of a long period of "education or re-education in the morals and purposes of socialist society." It is not enough that the sentence be served. The prisoner's jailer-teachers have failed unless he emerges a completely reformed man able "to distinguish between right and wrong" and ready to restart life with "the desire for unity." Is not this doctrine right out of old Calvinism—the supralapsarian conviction that Destiny (History) ordained the fall of man in order to create the opportunity for his redemption?

But the concept of law as an instrument of reform, education and ethical indoctrination is not wholly alien to traditional patterns of Chinese thought. Confucians generally believed that those who understood the difference between good and evil had the duty to teach others by positive example, as well as the duty to manage society, especially during periods of crisis. Mao's sense of ethical values churns the content of old teachings, but he also holds that man can be perfected by education. In this he is closer to Mencius, who believed that most men are inherently good, than he is to Han Fei-tzu, who believed that nine out of ten are bad, but even Han Fei-tzu agreed that man can be taught to be good—which is the underlying principle of thought reform.

In a casual conversation during my recent visit, Mao remarked (but without any reference to Confucian concepts), "Most men are good; only the minority is bad. Even bad men are not bad all the time and can be made better, just as good men can be made bad by negative example. The difficult thing is to discover what is good and how to teach it to others."

Mu Fu-sheng (pseud.), The Wilting of the Hundred Flowers: The Chinese Intelligentsia under Mao. New York: Praeger, 1963, pp. 180–182.

In China foreigners, and even natives who could not speak the particular local dialect, used to be overcharged in almost everything. When one considered the starvation level of income of the pedlars and the rickshaw men one would hardly call that a crime if one could afford it. This type of abuse was for obvious reasons difficult to deal with, but the Communists could eliminate it. A train pulled into Tsinan in Shantung one autumn morning with a woman ill on it. Her relative helped her to a rickshaw and went with her to a hospital. The fare asked was five dollars, but on arrival the relative thought the distance was too small for that amount. He paid the fare but took down the number of the rickshaw and later reported it to the police. Rickshaws in China are now organized into co-operatives with Party members to direct indoctrination or "education" in them. The police in this case agreed that the fare was exorbitant and telephoned the rickshaw co-operative. Since the cadre[s] there could be and probably were accused of not educating the rickshaw men properly, they got hold of the guilty man and sent him to the police station within minutes. There, after identification, he was simply asked to "confess any incorrect behaviour" that day. The man said he could not remember any. The police sergeant then took him to a bench at the other end of the room and asked him to sit down to think. After a few minutes he realised the futility of denial and came to the police sergeant to confess that he overcharged a man and a sick woman going to a hospital. Then he was given a long lecture on the correct behaviour in the socialist society, the importance of voluntary consideration for other members of the society, the meaning of labour and wages, and so on, and was asked if he understood now. The man said yes. The police sergeant then asked him some questions on the lesson by way of examination and the man did not answer entirely correctly. Off went the lecture from the beginning: the correct behaviour in the socialist society, the importance of voluntary consideration for other members of the society, till the man was "corrected". Only then was he asked to fix the correct fare himself, hand over the difference, apologise and leave.

Some edification probably does come from the long lectures used for correcting minor abuses, such as carving park benches, writing on walls and throwing paper in the street, but the main effect is likely to be the prolonged mental torment suffered, a combination of embarrassment and compunction, not so much for having done something wrong as for causing so much trouble to the ever-patient commissar or policeman. When rickshaw men violated traffic regulations the policemen used to strike them with their truncheon, but now one often sees in Chinese cities a man standing at the side of the street, rickshaw or bicycle in hand, facing with a sorry look the interminably lecturing policemen and a cluster of silent onlookers, the guilty man nodding once in a while to the questions: "We should all obey regulations voluntarily, shouldn't we?"—nod—"We need not wait till comrade policeman interferes, need we?"—shake—"What would happen if comrade policeman were not around? People might get hurt, might they not?"—nod. One can almost hear the victims speaking out of their eyes, "Please, give me three strokes with the truncheon and let me go."

C. DETERMINATION OF GUILT AND SANCTION

1. The Formal Legal System

NOTE

The Nationalist Chinese law reforms of the early 20th century established a set of legal institutions copied from continental Europe. After the Communists took over in 1949, China patterned many aspects of its governmental apparatus after the model of the Soviet Union. Not many changes had to be made in the structure of the legal system, however, since Soviet law was derived from continental Europe.

From 1949 until 1957, China slowly expanded the legal system, enacted a limited number of laws, and trained some lawyers. These developments were virtually halted by the antirightist campaign of 1957. For the next twenty years the role of law was downplayed, and legal work was characterized by a high degree of informality and mass participation. After the fall of the "gang of four" in 1976, however, the importance of law was again stressed, particularly with respect to the protection of individual rights.

Much of the present rhetoric on law resembles pre-1957 writings. The new legal structures and procedures, described in the following two items, also resemble the 1954–57 model.

Xing Zhong, Judicial Organs and Judicial Procedure in China, Beijing Review, January 12, 1979, pp. 30–32.

Readers have written to ask about China's present judicial organs, judicial procedure and penalties. The following is a sketch of basic facts by Xing Zhong, a jurist.—Ed.

I. JUDICIAL ORGANS

Organization. The judicial organs of China consist of people's courts, people's procuratorates and the public security departments.

People's courts are of four levels (see chart):

the Supreme People's Court of the People's Republic of China is the highest judicial organ in the country;

the higher people's courts of the provinces (or their equivalents—the autonomous regions and municipalities directly under the Central Government);

the intermediate people's courts of the prefectures, autonomous prefectures, cities directly under the provinces and municipalities directly under the Central Government;

the basic people's courts of the counties and autonomous counties (or their equivalents—cities and municipal districts).

There are also special people's courts (at present mainly military courts).

* * *

The people's procuratorates consist of the Supreme People's Procuratorate of the People's Republic of China, local people's procuratorates at various levels, special people's procuratorates (at present mainly military procuratorates).

* * *

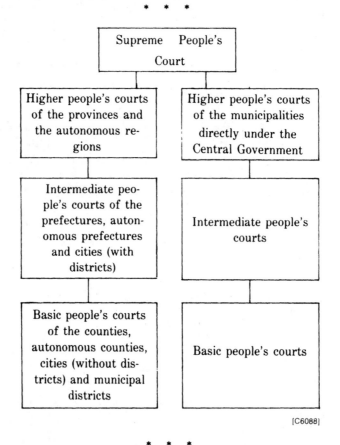

[C6088]

* * *

Local people's procuratorates at various levels consist of:

the people's procuratorates of the provinces, autonomous regions and municipalities directly under the Central Government;

the people's procuratorates of the autonomous prefectures and cities, and the branch people's procuratorates of the provinces, autonomous regions and municipalities under the Central Government set up when necessary;

the people's procuratorates of the counties (or their equivalents—cities and municipal districts).

The public security departments consist of the Ministry of Public Security of the People's Republic of China and the local public security bureaux at various levels.

* * *

II. JUDICIAL PROCEDURE

Criminal Procedure. There are generally five stages:

(1) The registry of a case: A case is registered when the public security department, the court, and the procuratorate, having examined the material denouncing a crime or presented by those who surrender themselves to the law, consider that a criminal act has been committed and that it is necessary to hold the accused to criminal responsibility.

(2) Investigation: The public security department conducts investigations, collects evidence and, should the case hold the accused to criminal responsibility, drafts a "memorandum of indictment." This memorandum, together with all relevant material, is then submitted to the procuratorate for examination.

(3) Indictment: The procuratorate examines the material submitted by the public security department and, on finding the facts of the crime clear and the evidence beyond doubt and sufficient for holding the accused to criminal responsibility, files an indictment against the defendant. The case is then held over for trial by the court.

(4) Trial: The trial proceeds in two stages—first instance and second instance. The first instance is generally administered by a collegiate bench of a judge and two people's assessors, and the case is heard in public. The court tries the case and gives its verdict in the presence of the parties concerned and the chief procurator (or a procurator).

The Constitution provides that the people's courts apply the system whereby representatives of the masses participate as people's assessors in administering justice. People's assessors are generally elected when people's deputies are elected at the basic level, and may also be invited by the court on a provisional basis. In court proceedings, the people's assessors have the same rights as the judge.

The second instance (or appellate instance) is conducted by a higher court which reviews the verdict of the court of the first instance if a party concerned appeals or the procuratorate protests against the verdict. The court of second instance hands down the final decision and is the court of last instance.

The law stipulates that if a party concerned contests the court's decision of first instance, he may file an appeal to the court at the next higher level within ten days after receipt of the written verdict. If the procuratorate finds the verdict improper, it also has the right to lodge a protest with the court at the next higher level.

(5) Execution of the judgment: After a judgment becomes legally effective, the court sends a notice of execution to the public security department, which shall carry it out.

Judicial Supervision. This is a special judicial procedure. The president of the court and the court and the procuratorate at a higher level have the right to rectify errors in a verdict in accordance with the proceedings governing judicial supervision, if they find the verdict of the court to be definitely in error, even after it has become legally effective (the same proceedings apply also to civil cases).

Peng Zhen, "Strengthen Legal System and Democracy," Beijing Review, July 6, 1979, pp. 33–34.

* * *

One. The relationship between the public security organs, procuratorates and people's courts is one of sharing out the work and cooperating with each other while checking each other under the leadership of the Party so as to defend the socialist legal system. As the draft law stipulates, the public security organ is responsible for investigation of crimes and detention of criminals; the procuratorate has the power of approving arrests and reviewing and prosecuting criminal cases. If the public security organ does not agree with a decision of the procuratorate, it may ask the procuratorate to reconsider the decision. The function of the people's court is to try cases. If the procuratorate disagrees with any court decision, it may lodge objection to that decision.

Two. The public security organ, the people's procuratorate and the people's court have the power of investigation, review, prosecution, the conduct of trials and the making of court decisions respectively according to law. The judicial organs should maintain necessary independence in their work. The draft stipulates that, in handling a case, the court, the procuratorate or the public, security organ must base itself on facts and take the law as its criterion.

Three. The accused not only can exercise his right to defend himself, but also has the right to entrust, according to his wish, his defence to lawyers, close relatives or guardians, or to defenders recommended by people's organizations or by his own unit. If a defendant does not nominate anyone to defend him, a people's court is duty bound to assign someone for the task. The responsibility of an advocate is to safeguard the legitimate rights and interests of the accused.

* * *

Five. The draft law stipulates that "evidence, investigation and study should be the basis of reaching a decision in any particular case, and that confessions by the accused should be viewed with caution." "It is strictly forbidden to extort confessions by torture and to collect evidence by threat, enticement, deceit and other illegal means." "The evidence can be established only after it has been verified." Statements by the accused alone without other corroborative evidence are insufficient to prove the accused guilty and liable to punishment. On the other hand, the accused can be proved guilty and subject to due punishment when the evidence is fully reliable even if no statements by the accused are forthcoming.

Independent Exercise of Functions and Powers. Explaining the draft organic laws of the people's courts and people's procuratorates, Peng Zhen reiterated that the people's courts administer justice independently, subject only to the law, and stressed that the people's procuratorates exercise functions and powers independently, subject to no interference from any administrative organ, organization or individual.

The draft organic law of the people's courts also supplements and revises in some measure the task of the courts, procedures for designating advocates and people's assessors, and procedures for making redress where people have been wrongly convicted, said Peng Zhen.

Referring to the organic law of the people's procuratorates, Peng Zhen said that the law stipulated: The nature of the procuratorate has been defined as that of a state organ which supervises the administration of justice. Its function and power lies in the safeguarding of the unity of the state legal system. People's procuratorates at various levels set up procuratorial committees to discuss and decide on major cases and other major matters according to the principle of democratic centralism.

In order to guarantee the unified judicial supervision by the procuratorates all over the country, Peng Zhen said, the relationship between a higher procuratorate and a lower procuratorate shall change from that of supervision to one of leadership. Local people's procuratorates are responsible to and report about their work to the people's congresses at their corresponding levels and their standing committees and, at the same time, accept the leadership of the people's procuratorates at higher levels.

The supervision of the procuratorate over the state organs and state working personnel, he said, is limited to cases where there have been violations of the criminal law and punishable by law.

NOTE

The following article describes a trial that took place before formal law came under attack in the antirightist campaign of late 1957. Contemporary trials generally follow the same format and procedure.

"Hearing of the Szu-ming-t'ang Medicated Liquor Store Case," Hsin-wen jin-pao (Daily News, Shanghai), June 4, 1957, in Jerome A. Cohen, The Criminal Process in the People's Republic of China, 1949–1963, an Introduction. Cambridge: Harvard University Press, 1968, pp. 445–448.

The case of Chiang Yeh-wei, former assistant manager of the Szu-ming-t'ang medicated liquor store who wounded manager Ch'en Chi with a knife, was heard yesterday at 1:45 P.M. at a session of the Huang-p'u district people's court in the city of Shanghai.

Chiang Yeh-wei's Statement. After Judge T'ao Yung-k'ang declared the court in session, Procurator Ch'eng Ch'en-han of the Huang-p'u district people's procuracy read aloud the bill of prosecution . . . . After the bill of prosecution was read, the judge asked defendant Chiang Yeh-wei: "You have heard the bill of prosecution. Do you have any views?" Chiang Yeh-wei said: "Yes. I took out the knife, but I did not stab him (referring to Ch'en Chi). I was only preparing [to defend myself], nothing else."

The judge then wanted Chiang Yeh-wei to relate the facts of his wounding Ch'en Chi on March 11. So Chiang Yeh-wei related the events. The judge asked: "Did your glasses fall off?"

Chiang Yeh-wei replied: "Yes, they fell off."

Question: "Do you know when Ch'en Chi's arm was wounded?"

Answer: "I do not know. At the time I did not notice it."

Question: "You did not stab him?"

Answer: "I did not."

Question: "At the time what did you suspect he was reaching for?"

Answer: "I suspected he was reaching for a gun."

Question: "What understanding [of your actions] do you have now?"

Answer: "I was wrong in taking out the knife and for this I can be dealt with in accordance with law. But the objective reason should be analyzed—was it to kill a person or to protect myself—and it should be studied in accordance with law."

People's assessor Ch'en Shao-chung then asked Chiang Yeh-wei: "You said that Ch'en Chi threatened you, saying that you were young and he was already over sixty years old and that if he fought you to the death, he would still be the winner [because he had lived a longer life than you]. When were these words spoken?"

Chiang answered: "In 1954, again in 1955, and again recently."

The judge asked the procurator whether he had any questions. The procurator asked Chiang: "When you went to the store did you have the knife?"

Answer: "Yes."

The procurator then asked: "When you went to attend the meeting were you also carrying it?"

Answer: "Yes, I used newspaper to wrap it up."

The judge asked Chiang Yeh-wei's defense lawyer, Li Kuo-chi, whether he had any questions.

The lawyer replied that he had, and he asked Chiang: "When you grabbed Ch'en Chi's hand, did he try to stop you?"

Answer: "He did not."

The lawyer then asked: "Did you stab and wound him with the knife?"

Answer: "I did not stab him."

* * *

So Ch'en Chi related the events: "When Chiang Yeh-wei returned to the store, I asked him: 'Where are you coming from?' Before a second sentence was spoken, he took out a knife. I blocked and ducked and then went outside and yelled for help."

The judge asked: "Did you reach into your clothes with your hand?"

Ch'en answered: "I do not clearly remember that."

Question: "Do you know when your arm was wounded?"

Answer: "I know." Then he said: "When I was at the public security sub-bureau and at the procuracy I requested that he should not be punished. But I requested that a judge determine who was right and who was wrong and that an explanation be published in the newspaper."

At that time, people's assessor Li Kuo-k'ang asked Ch'en Chi: "When Chiang Yeh-wei came in [the store] you only asked him one question?"

Ch'en Chi answered: "Only one. He took out a knife and stabbed at me, and I ducked down and ran outside."

Li then asked: "Is there a basis for your belief that Chiang Yeh-wei intended to stab you?"

Answer: "He said to me after the five-anti [movement] that he did not approve of my being his teacher. That was one inflammation [which rankled him]; second, there was the matter of salary; third, there was the question of the gun. There were these inflammations.

But to sum up, we have a teacher-apprentice relationship. I do not want him to be punished."

Chiang Yeh-wei's defense lawyer asked to talk with Ch'en Chi: "Is what you call inflammation, hatred?"

Ch'en Chi said: "There is no hatred between him and me."

The Statement of the Witness Hsü Chiang-ch'ing. The witness Hsü Chiang-ch'ing was summoned to come before the court. The judge wanted him to relate what he saw on March 11. Hsü said: "On the morning of March 11, I was the only person in the store. Ch'en Chi came at about ten, and at the time he did not have too nice an expression on his face. I was reading the paper. He sat down angrily. Not long after, Chiang Yeh-wei came in. Later, Chiang went to the rear. Ch'en Chi also went to the rear. When he came back, he took off his leather jacket and tied an apron around his waist. Not long after, Chiang Yeh-wei came back. Ch'en asked him: 'Where did you go?' Chiang said: 'I had business.' Chiang asked why he had not told him. In this way they began to struggle. When I raised my head to take a look, Chiang had a knife in his hand. I went up to them and grabbed Chiang's hand and pushed it down. I said that if there was something to be said he could say it but that he could not use a knife, and then some people came."

The judge asked: "Do you know when Ch'en Chi was wounded?"

Answer: "I do not know."

The defense lawyer asked Hsü: "Did Chiang Yeh-wei stab forward with the knife?"

Answer: "When I saw the knife, I pushed it away."

* * *

The Arguments. At this point, the judge announced: "The examination of this case has been completed. The arguments will begin." The procurator spoke first. He believed that from the investigation, from the questioning of the witnesses and the victim, and from the defendant's statement, it should first of all be determined as "a fact that the defendant had a knife in his hand on March 11 and that Ch'en Chi's arm was wounded by stabbing." He also said that "since the expert conclusion of the court-affiliated doctor was that the wound was a knife wound, the defendant, because he wounded the victim with a knife, should be held responsible for infliction of bodily injury. In our country, one's person is protected by law, and encroachment upon it is not permitted. To stab and wound with a knife is unlawful. Therefore, according to law the defendant should be given appropriate sanctions." The defense lawyer, Li Kuo-chi, then defended defendant Chiang Yeh-wei . . . .

The hearing went on until six P.M. The judge and the people's assessors then deliberated the case. After deliberation, the judge announced: "We believe that some of the facts need further study and analysis. Later, a time will be set to pronounce judgment."

NOTES AND QUESTIONS

1. The form of the trial in China is inquisitorial, with the judge and assessors taking the lead in questioning the parties and witnesses. This approach follows continental European procedure. Contrast it with the adversarial form of trial used in common law countries such as the United States. Note also that while there is a right to counsel in criminal trials, as discussed earlier, there are very few trained lawyers in China.

2. Compare the Chinese procurator and the American public prosecutor. Are their roles the same?

3. How does the Chinese assessor differ from the American jury?

4. Recall the manner in which guilt was found and sanctions determined in the cases presented in section B. Did the handling of those cases contradict the rules enunciated in section C? How might the contradictions be explained?

2. Implementation of the Formal Legal System

NOTE

The previous section described the formal structures and procedures established by law. But actually putting the system into operation proved to be much more difficult. A beginning effort was made in the mid-1950s to implement the formal legal system. This effort encountered serious resistance in the antirightist campaign of 1957.

As discussed in the following item, the failure to completely implement the formal legal system after 1957 was blamed in part on the political machinations and incorrect ultraleftist line of Lin Biao and the "gang of four." But charging these persons with subverting legal work can provide only a partial explanation for the sorry state to which law had fallen. They did not take over major portions of the national leadership until the Cultural Revolution in 1966, while the role of formal law had been downgraded since the antirightist campaign. The introductory essay on China gives some cultural and historical reasons for the failure of formal law to develop. The second item describes some of the political conflict within the legal bureaucracy in the 1950's.

"China's Socialist Legal System," Beijing Review, Jan. 12, 1979, pp. 25–28.

In the early years of the People's Republic, the Communist Party initiated several mass movements on a nationwide scale. Direct mass action rather than the force of law fuelled these tempestuous revolutionary movements. The aim then was to break down the old, reactionary social order, and in its place establish a new, revolutionary order.

* * *

New China's first Constitution was promulgated in 1954. In the same year, five organic laws—organic laws of the National People's

Congress, the State Council, the People's Courts, the People's Procuratorates and the local people's congresses and the local people's councils (i.e., local governments) were drafted and adopted. Of these, the Organic Law of the People's Courts set up the judicial system and procedures, which played an important role in protecting the people and striking at their enemy.

Somewhere about 1,100 major laws, decrees, codes and regulations were passed in the decade after 1954 when the Constitution was promulgated. These helped push China's socialist revolution and construction forward.

* * *

Of course, China's legal system was far from perfect. In his statements in 1956 and 1957, Comrade Dong Biwu singled out two shortcomings in the system. First, the laws were inadequate. Second, they were not always observed. There must be laws which people can go by, he declared, and, moreover, laws must be observed by all without exception. For this purpose, the judicial organs and system had to be strengthened.

* * *

A serious setback was delivered to the socialist legal system by Lin Biao and the "gang of four" just as efforts were being made to improve it. The socialist legal system stood in their way to usurping Party and state power, so right at the start of the Great Cultural Revolution in 1966, they began dismantling the public security departments and the procuratorial organs and charged that the socialist legal system was "a shackle" and "a straight-jacket" holding back the mass movements. China's judicial organs were suspended.

Abusing the power they had usurped, Lin Biao and the "gang of four" began cracking down on large numbers of revolutionary cadres and people. They let loose hoodlums and thugs to smash, grab and loot, to break into and ransack homes, illegally detain people, set up kangaroo courts and torture innocent people to extort confessions. In places and units they controlled there was no freedom of person because socialist social order was non-existent.

* * *

History always leaves behind something instructive. We have paid dearly, but we have learnt important lessons which we did not understand before. We have come to see that as a phenomenon of history Lin Biao and the "gang of four" had deep-rooted social and political causes on Chinese soil. Yet the inadequacy of our laws, the lack of a sound legal system and the absence of efficient enforcement agencies to protect socialist democracy gave them a chance. Moreover, under the cloak of "Leftists," they freely used the name of the Communist Party and the proletarian dictatorship to deceive many innocent people, particularly the young and inexperienced, and inveigle them into committing disastrous excesses. At first it did not occur to Party members and the people in general that they should exercise supervision over them. When they did, they could do nothing to check this power wielding minority because there were no judicial means on hand to bring them to book. The democratic means the Party and the people could employ were very much weakened, too gravely impaired to be of any use, so that cabal of political careerists and conspirators for a while had the field to themselves. This is a grim and bitter lesson which the people will never forget. They must take up the weapons of socialist democracy and the legal system, hold firm to them and use them.

Victor H. Li, Law Without Lawyers, A Comparative View of Law in China and the United States, Stanford: Stanford Alumni Association, 1977, pp. 22–26, 28, 30–31.

LEGAL REFORM AFTER LIBERATION [1949]

* * *

To staff the new legal system, the Communists retained a number of the legal specialists who had worked for the Nationalists, primarily because the Communists did not have within their own ranks people with the skill and knowledge to run a complex legal system. They also justified the use of former supporters of the Nationalists on the basis that, at that stage of the democratic revolution, all anti-imperialist and anti-feudal elements could join in building the New China so long as they were willing to reform their thinking along Communist lines over a period of time. And indeed, a large number of non-Communists had supported the Communist effort during the Anti-Japanese War and the Civil War.

* * *

The removal of some of the former Nationalist officials and the expansion of the size of the legal system after Liberation created many new legal positions. These were filled by a group of people I will call the "new cadres." This is an extremely interesting group since its members received their assignments not because of their legal skills but because of their ideological dependability or because of past services rendered. Indeed, most had no legal training or experience prior to their appointment, and some had virtually no formal education at all. Very few new cadres were appointed to law faculties, editorial boards of legal journals, or codification commissions. They filled most of the positions in the public security system and many of the positions in the judiciary, particularly at the trial court level.

* * *

The specialists were most influential during the early years after Liberation when the Chinese were trying to copy the Soviet model, since they were the only people who had the ability and know-how to carry out this work. They also appeared able to understand and to control this mysterious thing, "the law," and thus were able to over-whelm some of the less educated new cadres.

Through the efforts of the specialists, a number of laws were promulgated, law codification commissions were set up, judicial and police structures and rules of operation were established, law schools began to operate once again, and some legal books and periodicals were published. This process culminated in 1954 when a series of major laws was enacted, including the Chinese Constitution. . . .

* * *

. . . We do not hear much about the new cadres and their atti-tudes in the early years. This is due in part to the fact that legal writings—the principal source of information available to Western ob-servers—were controlled by the specialists and did not discuss the ideas of the new cadres except in a disparaging manner. Neverthe-less, by virtue of their sheer numbers and their political ties, these cadres strongly influenced the development of Chinese law during the early years.

The new cadres lacked legal skills and knowledge, but they did bring a fresh approach to law. Not having been brainwashed, if you will, by legal training, they did not automatically assume that China needed a modern legal system replete with codes and specialists. In-stead, they argued that law is *not* a mysterious thing. On the con-trary, it should be free of technicalities and easy for anyone to under-stand and use. Being so simple and straightforward, the legal system could operate without the services of specialists and even without a large legal bureaucracy.

* * *

The new cadres contended that better than the *rule of law* is a kind of *rule of man* wherein enlightened and conscientious officials would rule under the supervision of vigilant and concerned masses. So long as all people are knowledgeable about what is happening, make every effort to carry out their work properly, and are willing to speak up whenever any impropriety is seen regardless of who is the perpetrator or the victim, then society will operate smoothly and indi-viduals will be well protected. This view may be overly idealistic and naive. Nevertheless, its vision of utopia is very different from the utopia of the rule of law. The consequences of this difference are important. In a system emphasizing the rule of law, efforts to im-prove the human condition would be directed at the strengthening of law and the legal system. In the system emphasizing the rule of man, however, the new cadres stress the improvement of ideological and other kinds of education that produce citizens and officials who understand and appreciate the new social values and care about their correct implementation.

* * *

As might be expected, the specialists and the new cadres disagreed over many matters concerning law and legal work. The judiciary was one of the principal focal points for conflict since this organ contained large numbers of both types of personnel. The decline of the specialists' position by the late 1950s helps to explain the general downgrading of the role of the judiciary in the Chinese legal system.

* * *

Clashes between the two groups reached a second climax during the "hundred flowers" and antirightist campaigns of 1957. . . .

* * *

The complaints of the specialists covered the entire range of their differences with the new cadres. There were very few laws to go by, and not enough work was being done on the proposed legal codes. Even where there was a specific law, it often was ignored by the new cadres in order to allow local variation and flexibility. The new cadres also were criticized for failing to implement some provisions of the Constitution and for continuing to resist the use of legal procedure. Overall, the specialists seem to have felt that the new cadres, despite their lack of legal expertise, were stubbornly insisting on telling knowledgeable people what to do.

The quantity and vehemence of the ciriticism evoked during the hundred flowers period appears to have surprised and shocked the regime, and a crackdown, the antirightist campaign, began in August 1957. People who had voiced severe disagreement were themselves attacked, even though earlier that year they had been encouraged to speak out.

In the legal area, a broad counterattack against the specialists developed. Not only the specific critics but specialists in general came under fire. Even more important, in the course of attacking the specialists, the positions which they had advocated also were denounced. Thus, the things the specialists criticized now were praised and held up as good examples of the new people's system of justice. By the same token, the things favored by the specialists now were criticized as bourgeois and reactionary.

The majority of legal specialists were removed from legal work, and thereafter the legal bureaucracy was staffed largely by new cadres. The codification commissions stopped working, and no more was heard about the drafting of legal codes. Law schools continued to operate (except for a few years during the Cultural Revolution) but were reduced in size and shifted their emphasis from professional to political training.

NOTES AND QUESTIONS

1. Although the first item speaks of "1,100 major laws, decrees, codes and regulations" which have been promulgated, in fact the total quantity of this kind of material would hardly fill a small bookcase. If there are so

few "laws" in China, how does a person know what are the rules that purport to govern his life? How does an official know what kinds of action he should take?

2. What is the likelihood that the present leadership will be able to implement a new system of formal laws and legal institutions? What obstacles will they face? Who will staff the new system?

Peng Zhen, "Strengthen Legal System and Democracy," Beijing Review, July 6, 1979, p. 35.

Can the laws be enforced after their enactment? How is the principle of "doing things according to law, strictly enforcing the law and violations of the law must be investigated and dealt with" to be carried out? Peng Zhen made the following three points:

1. Extensive publicity and education concerning the laws must be given to the cadres and the masses. Putting the laws in the hands of the 900 million people, providing them with this instrument to see that the state organs and individuals act according to law, and to expose, report and struggle against any violations will make sure that the laws are carried out.

2. There must be special organizations set up and a powerful professional contingent built up to work on law enforcement.

3. Communist Party members and revolutionary cadres must play an exemplary role in observing and implementing the law. That every one is equal before the law is the watchword of the entire people, of all Communist Party members and all revolutionary cadres and is the ideological weapon against anyone seeking privileges.

All Party members and revolutionary cadres must set the lead in obeying the law in an exemplary way; there must be no exception made for them.

QUESTION

1. What concrete measures must be taken to carry out the above points?

3. Informal Legal Processes

NOTE

Historically, local social units such as the lineage (*tsu* or *zu*), rather than the formal legal system, handled much of the work of resolving disputes and maintaining order. In terms of the official governmental structure, a magistrate was appointed to govern a county-size area (*hsien* or *xian*). There was no idea of separation of powers; the magistrate was responsible for almost everything going on within his territory. He was assisted by a small personal staff, and by a larger group of local constabulary. Magistrates were usually transferred every three years, mainly to prevent the building of power bases by local officials. But the short tenure in each area also meant that a magistrate would have difficulty learning about local conditions and penetrating local social and other networks. For entertaining and fairly accurate reading about the life and work of magistrates, try reading the mystery novels concerning Judge Dee by Robert Van Gulik.

In reading the PRC materials, consider the extent to which local units continue to perform the same functions today.

Sybille Van der Sprenkel, Legal Institutions in Manchu China, London: Athlone Press, 1962, pp. 112, 114–115, 121–123.

The jurisdictional aspects of the *tsu*, the guild and the village have been examined in some detail, and it has been shown that, taken all together, they offered a substantial extension of the official legal machinery. It can be seen that in China offences were punished and disputes were formally adjudicated by the authority of the group most nearly concerned, and that this was done with the approval of the administration. The *tsu*, the guild and the village may be thought of as operating as subordinate tribunals of the official courts, and the norms they enforced as an extension or amplification of official codes which the official courts, if appealed to, would endorse. On this analysis, specialization took place—though with some blurring at the edges—at the lowest level: the *tsu* dealt with questions of inheritance, adoption and the ancestral cult, the guilds with the regulation of trades, and villages with land law and contracts of sale or tenancy.

Most of life for the majority of people in China fell within the scope of the *tsu*, village or guild organization. . . .

* * *

Below the formal or near-formal tribunals constituted by all the groups described, a great deal of informal mediation of disputes went on. This might be performed by the middleman responsible for negotiations out of which conflict had arisen, or by respected persons whose help was sought or, if neither of these succeeded in disposing of the quarrel, there were always people ready to gather to hear an argument and offer solutions. Such informal discussions sifted out the less difficult cases before they led to serious rupture, and reduced the need to appeal to official courts. That this was in accordance with official policy is confirmed by the K'ang-hsi Emperor's reply to criticism of the courts:

> . . . the good citizens, who may have difficulties among themselves, will settle them like brothers, *by referring them to the arbitration of some old man or the mayor of the commune.* As for those who are troublesome, obstinate and quarrelsome, let them be ruined in the law-courts—that is the justice that is due to them.

* * *

The village 'anti-litigation societies' set up by regulation as part of the community development planned in the nineteen-twenties seem to have been designed to give formal and permanent expression to something that had existed informally and contingently for centuries.

* * *

In practical matters such as adding to one's holding of land, being able to borrow in time of stress, or arranging favourable marriages, for example, to be a respected member of one's group was an important asset. Progress towards prosperity would be impossible unless one had the support of relatives, neighbours and fellow-traders. Nor could the successful afford to deprive themselves of this support lest they be attacked by enemies or 'bandits' with impunity. Not to stand well in the opinion of one's fellows would cause more certain discomfort than to incur the displeasure of an official in the *hsien* city. These considerations gave force to group judgments and sanctions, as well as to less formal mediation—and rendered them more effective supports of social norms than the official legal machinery would have been, if invoked.

* * *

A good deal has been said of the disincentive to going to law. There were, of course, magistrates who made a reputation for their handling of legal cases, and their arrival at a new post was no doubt greeted with a spate of plaints dealing with differences of long standing. However, in view of the difficulties and risks law cases involved, it can be understood that most magistrates did little to encourage litigants. It appears, however, that the wrong people were not always discouraged, and it may be well to consider how it was that law cases entered the *yamen* at all.

The complaint that cases involved great expenditure of time and money in travelling to court, and much expense in entertaining the *yamen* staff sent to pursue enquiries, occurs so often in connection with law courts (cf. Appendix 4, § 13) that one cannot avoid the inference that the courts must have appeared very differently according to whether one lived near the *hsien* city or in an outlying part of the *hsien*. In the more remote villages, the inhabitants of which would have been the people put to greatest trouble and expense by journeys to court, it would have been difficult to resist *yamen* runners' [constabulary] claims to hospitality or, so far from supervision, their other exactions. These considerations lead to the conclusion that residents of the *hsien* city and villages in its neighbourhood would have run less risk of loss by approaching the courts.

* * *

The courts were brought into action, of course, when cases of violence, kidnapping or arson occurred and could not be "hushed up", since these were open evidence of failure on the part of the administration and had to be redressed.

. . . being brought into court were mischief or malice on the part of those who had little to lose—either to damage an enemy or to pay off an old score. To involve someone in a lawsuit was a way of ruining him; when feelings ran high, it might be worth the trouble. This operated, of course, to confirm magistrates' harshness towards those who went to law, and made the individual more than ever dependent on his group for support in his defence. . . .

"How the Chuangtzup'ing (Kansu) Cooperative Carries out Experiment in Labor Custody [Rehabilitation Through Labor]," Kan-su jih-pao (Kansu Daily), July 20, 1958; translated in Survey of the Chinese Mainland Press, 1862:6–8 (September 26, 1958) in Jerome A. Cohen, The Criminal Process in the People's Republic of China, 1949–1963, an Introduction. Cambridge: Harvard University Press, 1968, pp. 251–254.

After the Chuangtzup'ing Agricultural Cooperative in Kaolan *hsien* [county] became a higher cooperative, it managed to increase its production year by year, and the enthusiasm of its members for labor became ever higher. But the cooperative cadres and members felt glum about the presence of several loafers in the cooperatives who had to be fed but did not work. These loafers refused to be led, cursed the cadres, and made trouble for fun. Loafer Yang Yu-wu, for example, contributed not a day of work after he joined the cooperative. He operated on his own in hog and goat trade and in speculative business. Yang Yuan-tung was another loafer. When his mother died in 1953, his neighbors and clansmen donated 90 catties of wheat for funeral expenses. But he stole 40 of the catties of wheat and spent the money recklessly. In the end his wife had to raise funeral expenses from other sources. He would take seven days of rest after he gave the cooperative one day of work. He frequently feigned sickness and claimed the "five guarantee" privilege from the cooperative. In 1956, he borrowed 20 [20 yuan] from the cooperative and 50 from the credit cooperative on the ground of hardship, and he never returned his loans. Because he did not work, his family of five had constantly to starve with him. Because of this his wife was frequently at odds with him and threatened divorce and [or?] separation. There was no tranquility in his family.

Although there were not many members of this kind in the cooperative, they had a very bad effect on the cooperative. The upright men were highly dissatisfied with them. They criticized the cadres by saying: "You know how to make the hard-working people work harder. But why do you not find some ways to deal with these loafers?" However, the cooperative cadres had . . . their difficulties. Those people committed small mistakes frequently but they never committed major mistakes. There was no good way to deal with them.

In August last year, the State Council promulgated its Decision on the question of labor custody [Decision of the State Council of the PRC Relating to Problems of Rehabilitation Through Labor]. The public security bureau of the *hsien* decided to make the Chuangtzup'ing Cooperative . . . an experimental point for carrying out labor custody [rehabilitation through labor]. At the beginning of the experiment, the leadership lined up the people for investigation on the one hand, and gave wide publicity to the spirit of the State Council's decision on the other. The *hsiang* [village] Party branch first called a conference for *hsiang* and cooperative cadres and Party and Young Communist League [Communist Youth League] activists. These people were organized to study the State Council's decision. After that, this decision was announced to the different production teams on blackboards. In the evenings, the masses were organized to study and discuss the decision item by item with the production team as the unit. After giving the matter wide publicity, the broad masses understood the merits of enforcing labor custody and voiced their support.

Following this, the different production teams organized the masses to agitate discussion according to the State Council's decision and in conjunction with the actual conditions of the people in the teams who did not work. According to the results of lining up people for probing and mass discussions carried out within the cooperative, there were 16 loafers, equivalent to 0.7 percent of the aggregate manpower in the cooperative, who had no proper employment. The Party branch made files out of concrete information on these 16 persons and discussed them at an enlarged meeting. After a consensus was reached, the approval of the *hsien* people's council was sought through the *hsiang* people's council. On October 7 last year, with the approval of the *hsien* people's council, labor custody was enforced in the cooperative.

Before labor custody was enforced, some preparatory work was done in the *hsiang* and the cooperative.

First, the people to be placed under labor custody and their family members were called to a conference in which the object of labor custody was explained to them. They were told that it was with the object of making useful men of them that they were placed under labor custody, that "labor custody" was not "reform through labor," and that the people placed under labor custody were paid according to their work like other cooperative members. They were told that they would be given a course of education on the glory of work so that they would make up their minds to work. At the same time, the Party branch also called on the masses to take pains in having these people transformed without discrimination or ridicule.

Next, some practical systems were drawn up. The people placed under labor custody are required to work together in day time and to spend two hours in the evening to record work hours and to study. They eat and sleep in their own homes. When they are unable to turn up for work or in meetings, they have to ask for leave of absence in advance. They have to meet to review their lives once a week, and are appraised quarterly. Subject to the approval of the *hsiang* people's council those who have completed their transformation may leave the labor custody team.

The cooperative specially drafted a Communist Party member, Comrade Wei Yu-ch'u, leader of the 4th production team, to head the labor custody team. Comrade Wei Yu-ch'u is firm in his stand and good at work. He knows production technique and is respected by the masses. The loafers also looked up to him with awe and respect. The cooperative got ready the land and tools for the loafers.

Thus prepared, collective labor custody was enforced. Because the Party branch took great pains to have the ideological and preparatory work well carried out, everything went well with the work. After the loafers were grouped together, they were divided into two sections, and two persons from among the people placed [under] labor custody were elected to head them. Comrade Wei Yu-ch'u, leader of the labor custody team, set . . . an example everywhere in production. His work was of good quality and his efficiency high. He showed concern for the people under labor custody in everything. At the beginning, because these people were not used to labor, knew no production techniques, and varied in physical strength, some difficulties were experienced in production. Comrade Wei Yu-ch'u did his very best to give every person the kind of farm work which he was physically capable of carrying out, and taught them techniques whenever necessary. In this way, these people gradually got used to their work and were able . . . slowly [to] master production technique.

In study, the people placed under labor custody were required to study chiefly the State Council's decision on labor custody and the system of the labor custody team during the first two weeks. Later, they were organized to study the regulations of the cooperative, important state events, and relevant policies and laws and decrees to enable them to remold their thinking. They met once every week to review their lives. Those who put up good performances were commended, and those who failed to abide by the system were criticized.

Wei Hung-yu was in a bad mood after he heard that his thinking had to be remolded. He quit work for two days without asking for leave of absence. Wang Yung-sheng talked nonsense while he worked. The team leader [promptly] called the whole team . . . to a conference, and organized the team members to discuss and criticize their mistaken thought. When these two persons found that other people were at variance with them, they bowed to admit their mistakes.

Apart from this, the cooperative constantly sent people to the families of those who had been placed under labor custody to find out their views and what progress the people in question had made in transformation. Because of this, the families involved were very satisfied.

After seven months of labor custody, these loafers have cultivated the working habit, and some are quite active in work. During the first 210 days, they each put in 209 days of work on the average. One of them, Yang Fu-k'o, put in as many as 301 working days [probably based upon an eight-hour workday].

By way of work and study, these people have witnessed changes not only in thinking and work style but also in financial standing because of their additional income. They have also improved their ties with their families. In the case of Yang Yuan-tung, for example, his wife [in the past] refused to have anything to do with him even when he was sick . . . . Because he works hard now and has straightened up his thought, his wife no longer quarrels with him and takes good care of him. She told the team leader: "Chairman Mao's policy is very good indeed, for he has saved the lives of our whole family. But for the labor custody, we would have nothing to eat." Chang San-hung who went through the process of labor custody said: "In the past, I worked only six days and earned five days of wages in eight months. I have now put in more than 200 working days in seven months. In the past, I did not work and was constantly sick with stomach ache. Having tempered myself in labor, I have cured my illness, and my stomach bothers me no longer." This method was also universally applauded by the masses.

NOTE

The decision mentioned in the above excerpt was promulgated on August 1, 1957—soon after the beginning of the antirightist campaign. An important additional fact is that the Decision was *repromulgated* by the State Council on November 29, 1979, several months after the promulgation of the new Criminal Code and Code of Criminal Procedure.

"Decision of the State Council of the PRC Relating to Problems of Rehabilitation Through Labor." Approved at the 78th meeting of the Standing Committee of the NPC, August 1, 1957; promulgated by the State Council, August 3, 1957, Chung-hua jen-min kung-ko-kuo fa-kuei hui-pien (Collection of laws and regulations of the People's Republic of China); volume 6, pp. 243–244, translated in Jerome Alan Cohen, The Criminal Process in the People's Republic of China, 1949–1963, Cambridge: Harvard University Press, 1968, pp. 249–250.

On the basis of the provisions of Article 100 of the Constitution of the People's Republic of China, the following Decision with respect to problems of rehabilitation through labor is made in order to reform into self-supporting new persons those persons with the capacity to labor who loaf, who violate law and discipline, or who do not engage in proper employment, and in order further to preserve public order and to benefit socialist construction:

1. The following kinds of persons shall be provided shelter and their rehabilitation through labor shall be carried out:

(1) Those who did not engage in proper employment, those who behave like hooligans, and those who, although they steal, swindle, or engage in other such acts, are not pursued for criminal responsibility, who violate security administration and whom repeated education fails to change;

(2) Those counterrevolutionaries and antisocialist reactionaries who, because their crimes are minor, are not pursued for criminal responsibility, who receive the sanction of expulsion from an organ, organization, enterprise, school, or other such unit and who are without a way of earning a livelihood;

(3) Those persons who have the capacity to labor but who for a long period refuse to labor or who destroy discipline and interfere with public order, and who [thus] receive the sanction of expulsion from an organ, organization, enterprise, school, or other such unit and who have no way of earning a livelihood;

(4) Those who do not obey work assignments or arrangements for getting them employment or for transferring them to other employment, or those who do not accept the admonition to engage in labor and production, who ceaselessly and unreasonably make trouble and interfere with public affairs and whom repeated education fails to change.

2. Rehabilitation through labor is a measure of a coercive nature for carrying out the education and reform of persons receiving it. It is also a method of arranging for their getting employment.

Persons who receive rehabilitation through labor shall be paid an appropriate salary in accordance with the results of their labor. Moreover, in the exercise of discretion a part of their salary may be deducted in order to provide for the maintenance expenses of their family members or to serve as a reserve fund that will enable them to have a family and an occupation.

During the period of rehabilitation through labor, persons who receive it must observe the discipline prescribed by organs of rehabilitation through labor. Those who violate this discipline shall receive administrative sanctions. Those who violate the law and commit crimes shall be dealt with in accordance with law.

As for the aspect of administering education, the guideline of combining labor and production with political education shall be adopted. Moreover, discipline and a system shall be prescribed for them to observe in order to help them establish [in their minds] the concepts of patriotic observance of law and of the glory of labor, learn labor and production skills, and cultivate the habit of loving labor, so that they become self-supporting laborers who participate in socialist construction.

3. If a person must be rehabilitated through labor, the application for rehabilitation through labor must be made by a civil affairs or a public security department; by the organ, organization, enterprise, school, or other such unit in which he is located; or by the head of his family or his guardian. The application shall be submitted to the people's council of the province, autonomous region, or city directly under the central authority, or to an organ that has been authorized by them, for approval.

4. If during the period of rehabilitation through labor a person who receives it behaves well and has the conditions for getting employment, he may, with the approval of the organ of rehabilitation through labor, separately [independently] get employment. If the unit, head of the family, or guardian that originally made the application for the person's rehabilitation through labor asks to take him back so that it can assume responsibility for disciplining him, the organ of rehabilitation through labor may also, giving consideration to the circumstances, approve the request.

5. Organs of rehabilitation through labor shall be established at the level of the province, autonomous region, and city directly under the central authority and shall be established [at lower levels] with the approval of the people's council of the province, autonomous region, or city directly under the central authority. Civil affairs departments and public security departments shall jointly be responsible for leading and administering the work of organs of rehabilitation through labor.

NOTES AND QUESTIONS

1. Consider all the antisocial acts which loafer Yang had committed over the years. How had he gotten away with it for so long?

2. Who decided that loafer Yang should be sent to labor custody? Who decided the form that labor custody should take for Yang? How flexible is labor custody? Could it be made much harsher or more lenient?

3. What if loafer Yang felt that the decision to place him in labor custody was wrong? How and to whom would he "appeal"? What would happen if Yang continues to loaf or refuses to work while under labor custody?

4. How do you think the 4th production team felt about losing the services of comrade Wei?

5. PRC writings frequently dwell on the importance of manual labor. There is a strong feeling that many problems, both ideological and physical, develop when a person despises or ceases to engage in manual labor.

6. What is your reaction to the extensive public involvement in loafer Yang's case? Does this practice reflect a belief that the community has some kind of collective responsibility for the behavior of its members?

There are some advantages to having the public play a large role in the process of handling social deviants, especially minor ones. The local community might make the best decision because it is familiar with Yang's circumstances; it also is particularly able to supervise his future conduct; members of the community might derive satisfaction from being able to take direct part in an important aspect of community life; local officials might feel more secure from possible future criticism over their handling of the case if "the broad masses" shared in the decision making; community based sanctioning costs the state relatively little in monetary terms since a large legal bureaucracy is not necessary. What are some other advantages?

But there also are disadvantages to "mass line" justice. How great is the danger of oppression of an individual by the social group to which he belongs? How is one to be protected against arbitrary action by the group? Does an informal system favor persons with good political or social ties? What are some other disadvantages?

Do you think that the advantages outweigh the disadvantages, or vice-versa? As you make this balance, be explicit about any philosophical or ideological assumptions you may be making.

7. What role did the police (or public security) play in this case? Recall that the police had authority under SAPA to impose minor sanctions such as detention up to 15 days. How does the authority of an American policeman compare?

8. It appears that the Rehabilitation through Labor decision, the Criminal Code, and the Code of Criminal Procedure are all currently in effect. How would a lower level legal officer, party official, or commune official decide whether to invoke the administrative process of rehabilitation through labor or the formal criminal process? Is there some way to reconcile the differences between the two processes?

D. THE LEGAL RULES

1. Definition of the Crime Before 1979

NOTE

In our hypothetical, Chang would defend himself by arguing that his actions were not improper. At the most, they reflected poor judgment or management, but could not be considered crimes.

Chang argues that the commune should treat Vice-Premier Deng with the highest degree of courtesy and hospitality. The people want to show their appreciation for what he has done for the country. More importantly, Deng visits only model communes. Many members of the press accompany him and report on local conditions. How can this commune be a model for the rest of the country to emulate if there was no suitable place to meet or food to eat?

Second, Chang asserts that the funds were not misused. His living room had been a convenient place to hold commune business meetings in the past, and now is an even better meeting place. The entire commune will benefit from the expenditure. Whatever Chang gains in having his living room enlarged and redecorated will be offset by the inconvenience of having many persons troop in and out of his house.

As for paying only his relatives, Chang claimed that he was related to a large number of people in the commune. He could hardly avoid dealing with his relatives. More to the point, Chang needed a great deal of work done well and in a hurry. The group he could best rely on to do the job was his relatives. Premium prices had to be paid because workers should receive extra compensation for difficult or rush jobs.

Finally, Chang states that his intentions in this case were good. He had also served the commune diligently for many years, and had greatly contributed to the commune's growth. Any error he may have committed here could be fully remedied through a series of commune-wide discussions or self-criticism sessions to air dissatisfactions about his management or leadership style.

Did Chang's actions constitute a crime?

Until the promulgation of the Criminal Law of the PRC on July 1, 1979, there were very few provisions directly applicable to this case.

The lectures in the third item come from a textbook used in criminal law courses in the 1950's. Its authoritativeness declined considerably after the antirightist campaign. With the recent revival of formal law, however, this work may again become an important legal document.

"Act of the PRC for Punishment of Corruption (1952)," in Jerome A. Cohen, The Criminal Process in the People's Republic of China, 1949–1963, an Introduction. Cambridge: Harvard University Press, 1968, pp. 308–310.

* * *

Article 2. All acts of embezzling, stealing, obtaining state property by fraud or by illegal speculation, extorting property of others by force, accepting bribes and other acts of unlawful profit-making that utilize public resources for private gain, [committed] by personnel of all state organs, enterprises, schools and their subordinate institutions, shall be considered crimes of corruption.

Article 3. Those who commit crimes of corruption shall be punished on an individual basis in accordance with the seriousness of the circumstances of their cases and in accordance with the following provisions:

* * *

(4) If the amount involved in an individual's corruption is less than [1,000] yuan of people's currency, he shall be sentenced to not more than one year of imprisonment, labor service, or control; or he may be exempted from criminal punishment and given the administrative sanction of expulsion, removal from office, demotion in office, demotion in grade, demerit, or warning.

Group corruption shall be punished on an individual basis according to the amount involved in each person's corruption and the circumstances of his case.

Property that has been obtained through corruption shall be recovered [from the guilty party]; when his crime is especially serious, a part or all of his property may also be confiscated.

*   *   *

Article 5. In any one of following situations, those who commit a crime of corruption may be given light punishment, reduced punishment, or suspension of sentence, or they may be exempted from criminal punishment and given administrative sanctions:

    (1) They take the initiative in confessing before they are discovered;

    (2) After having been discovered they thoroughly confess, sincerely repent, and also take the initiative in handing over as much of the property involved in their corruption as possible;

    (3) They establish their merit by denouncing others who have committed crimes [enumerated] in this Act;

    (4) They are relatively young in age or their past is pure, they committed a crime of corruption on [one] occasion, and they sincerely want to repent and reform.

"Security Administration Punishment Act" (1957) in Jerome A. Cohen, The Criminal Process in the People's Republic of China, 1949–1963, Cambridge: Harvard University Press, 1968, p. 217.

Article 11. A person who commits any one of the following acts damaging public property or property of citizens shall be punished by detention of not more than ten days, a fine of not more than twenty yuan, or a warning:

    (1) Stealing, swindling, or illegally appropriating small amounts of public property or the property of others;

    (2) Taking the lead in raising an uproar and carrying off small amounts of property of an agricultural producers' cooperative.

"Lectures on the Criminal Law of the People's Republic of China" in Jerome A. Cohen, The Criminal Process in the People's Republic of China, 1949–1963, Cambridge: Harvard University Press, 1968, pp. 328–333.

On the basis of our previous statements concerning the concept and class nature of the criminal law of our country, we may describe the concept of crime in the criminal law of our country as follows: *all acts which endanger the people's democratic system of our country, undermine the social order, or are socially dangerous and, according to law, should be subject to criminal punishment are crimes.*

Now let us analyze and explain this concept as follows:

First, a crime is a socially dangerous act. The social danger of an act is the most essential characteristic of a crime. A person's act is considered a crime because it is socially dangerous. An act not socially dangerous cannot be considered a crime.

In our country, whether or not an act is socially dangerous is determined by the will of the vast [number of] people of the entire country led by the worker class. To build a socialist society is the common desire of the vast [number of] people of our country. The people's democratic system of our country is a guarantee that our country can eliminate exploitation and poverty and can build a prosperous and happy socialist society through peaceful roads. But the smooth conduct of the undertaking of socialist construction is impossible without the safeguard of a good social order. Therefore, from the viewpoint of the interests of the vast [number of] people of the entire country, an act endangering the people's democratic system and undermining social order is a socially dangerous act.

By directly pointing out that from the standpoint of the concept of crime, the social danger of an act is the most essential characteristic of a crime, we have thus answered, from the standpoint of the class nature of crime, the question why certain acts are considered criminal.

Next, a crime is an act which, according to law, should be subject to criminal punishment. We say that social danger is the most essential characteristic of crime, but this certainly is not to say that all socially dangerous acts are crimes. Rather, only socially dangerous acts which, according to the viewpoint of the criminal law of our country, should be subject to criminal punishment, are crimes.

* * *

At the same time, what kind of socially dangerous act should be subject to criminal punishment is prescribed by the criminal law of our country. Only when a socially dangerous act is recognized by the criminal law can it be considered a criminal act. In our country, the social danger of an act and its unlawfulness are united. Therefore, a crime is an act which on the one hand is socially dangerous and at the same time is also a violation of criminal law. Here it must be pointed out that [the term] "violation of criminal law" cannot be understood only as violation of criminal legislation. Under circumstances in which the law is still not complete, relevant resolutions, decisions, orders, instructions, and policies of the Party and the government are also bases for determining whether or not a crime has been committed.

* * *

Since the degree of social danger is the criterion for differentiating crimes from other unlawful acts, the boundary between crime and noncrime is in substance a question of what determines the degree of social danger. We believe that it is mainly determined by the three intimately interrelated factors stated below:

First, the nature of the act itself: if the nature of the act committed by a person is itself serious, then the degree of social danger of this act is also great. A judgment as to what kind of act is a serious act can generally be made on the basis of peoples' social practice. In judicial practice, we regard as criminal acts counterrevolutionary acts which infringe the people's democratic system of our country, homicide which infringes the lives of others, robbery, rape, etc. The reason for there being no doubt about these acts is that the seriousness of these acts themselves is very obvious. It is just for this reason that the difficulty in the problem of demarcating the boundary between crime and noncrime does not occur in all general circumstances but only occurs in individual circumstances.

In judicial practice, demarcating the boundary between crime and noncrime is felt to be difficult mainly in situations in which the forms of the acts are the same but, because other factors are different, the degree of social danger is also different: for example, between crimes resulting from neglect of duty and administrative misconduct resulting from bureaucratism; between stealing property and taking advantage in a small way (such as picking some vegetables in another person's garden for one's own use); between backward words and deeds and counterrevolutionary provocation and incitement. The reason for feeling it difficult to demarcate these types of problems is mainly that too high an estimate of the significance of the form of the act is made in demarcating crime and noncrime, and the degree of social danger is ignored. The boundary between crime and noncrime is determined not only by the difference in the form of the acts but also by whether or not the results created by the acts are serious as well as by some factors involving the actor's subjective state. This situation frequently occurs: although the form of an act is the same as others, because other factors are different, some acts are crimes and some are not.

Second, the existence and amount of damage: the existence and amount of damage are also factors that determine the degree of social danger—for example, acts involving neglect of duty by state personnel; certain acts violating the rules of operation in a factory, mine, or enterprise; or minor acts of theft may be dealt with as if they were not crimes under circumstances in which there was no damage or the damage was very minor. Here, the boundary between crime and noncrime is determined by the existence and amount of damage.

In judicial practice, the question of whether or not stealing one yuan is a crime has arisen for some judges. Some people consider that since stealing is an act prohibited by law, any stealing is a crime and that the amount stolen certainly does not affect the establishment of a crime. This understanding is erroneous because it ignores the fact that a crime is not only a violation of law in form but must also be an act that in substance has a rather serious degree of social danger.

* * *

Third, factors involving the actor's subjective state: the degree of social danger is also determined by some factors involving the actor's subjective state, such as whether the actor acted intentionally or negligently or what his purpose was in committing a certain act. For example, intentional destruction of another's property is a criminal act, but negligent destruction of another person's property might not be dealt with as a crime. Here, intent or negligence becomes a factor for differentiating crime from noncrime. For another example, Article 12 of the Arrest and Detention Act of the People's Republic of China prescribes: "People's procuracies shall investigate officers responsible for unlawful arrest or detention of citizens. If this kind of unlawful act arose from malicious, retaliatory, corrupt, or other personal motives, they [these officers] shall be pursued for criminal responsibility." This provision clearly points out that the actor's purpose is a factor for differentiating crime from noncrime. In judicial practice, some backward words and deeds are sometimes erroneously dealt with as counterrevolutionary crimes mainly because a deep examination and study of the actor's purposes is ignored. For a counterrevolutionary crime to be established, the actor must have a subjectively counterrevolutionary purpose, and [one who is guilty only of] backward words and deeds certainly does not have such a purpose.

* * *

In circumstances in which there are already provisions of criminal law or where the criminal law has already been promulgated, what kind of socially dangerous acts should be subject to criminal punishment has already been comprehensively considered by the legislators and, from the point of view of the interests of the people of the entire country led by the worker class, written into provisions. Therefore, judicial workers only have to follow provisions of the criminal law to resolve the question of crime or noncrime; an act which meets the requirements prescribed by any provision of the criminal law of our country should be considered a criminal act. Any departure from the criminal law and arbitrary determination as to what are crimes and noncrimes are not permitted. Yet it is possible to have this situation: although an act that is committed by a given person in form conforms to the requirements prescribed by a certain provision of the criminal law of our country, on the basis of a consideration of the above-mentioned circumstances, its social danger in substance certainly, does not require the application of criminal punishment. Then, on the basis of the most essential characteristic of crime, that is, the concept that the social danger of the act must be fairly serious, this act ought not to be considered a crime. For example, a certain state employee on [one] occasion corruptly takes five yuan. Although in form this conforms to the provisions of the Act of the People's Republic of China for Punishment of Corruption, if the damage he planned to create or could possibly have created is only to that extent, then it might not be considered a criminal act.

QUESTIONS

1. If the Chang case occurred before 1979, based on the above materials, do you think Chang committed a crime of corruption? A SAPA offense? Some other crime or offense? To what extent does article 2 of the Act for the Punishment of Corruption help you decide whether Chang's acts constitute corruption?

2. Do you favor handling this case through the formal legal system or through informal legal process? Give explicit reasons for your choice.

3. What persons and institutions would decide the questions of guilt (and the appropriate sanction) if the formal legal system was used? If informal legal processes?

4. What would be an appropriate sanction to impose on Chang if he were found guilty of a crime or offense?

2. The Criminal Law of 1979

NOTE

At the 1979 meeting of the National People's Congress, seven laws were promulgated, the first such action in many years. These laws dealt with the organization of the local people's congresses, a criminal code and code of criminal procedure.

a. Substantive Rules of Law

Peng Zhen, Director of Commission for Legal Affairs of N.P.C. Standing Committee, at Second Session of Fifth N.P.C. on June 26, 1979, Explanation on Seven Laws, Beijing Review, July 13, 1979, pp. 8, 11–12.

Fellow Deputies,

Since the beginning of 1979, we have shifted the focus of the work of the whole nation to socialist modernization. In line with this historic change, we must conscientiously strengthen socialist democracy and the socialist legal system. Without a sound socialist legal system, a sound socialist democracy can hardly be realized. Comrade Hua Guofeng points out in his Report on the Work of the Government: ". . . Our country has a long feudal tradition and is relatively backward economically and culturally. . . ." Moreover, the pernicious influence of the gang of four has not yet been completely eliminated. In these circumstances, autocracy, bureaucracy, love of privileges, the patriarchal style of work, and petty-bourgeois individualism, liberalism and anarchism are apt to spread. Even now in some localities and units, the enthusiasm and initiative of the people are still held in check and their right of person and democratic and other rights are not always secure. All this shows that in order to give full play to socialist democracy, it is imperative to gradually perfect the socialist legal system so that in whatever they do the 900 million people will have rules and regulations to go by and bad characters and bad acts will be restrained and punished. Therefore, "people are craving for law," and the people of the whole country are eagerly demanding a sound legal system. As Comrade Ye Jianying states in his opening speech, "The people want to strengthen and improve China's socialist legal system. An improved legal system can effectively guarantee the people's democratic rights provided for by the Constitution and constantly develop stability and unity and a lively and vigorous political situation in the interest of socialist construction."

* * *

II. THE CRIMINAL LAW

Criminal law is one of the basic laws of the country. The present draft of the Criminal Law is prepared with Marxism-Leninism-Mao Zedong Thought as its guide and in the light of our concrete experience in exercising the people's democratic dictatorship led by the proletariat and based on the worker-peasant alliance, that is, the dictatorship of the proletariat. Its function is to "combat all counterrevolutionary and other criminal offences by inflicting penalties," and thereby protect the interests of the people and the state, consolidate and promote the lively political situation of stability and unity, and ensure the smooth advance of socialist modernization.

(1) One of the main purposes of the Criminal Law is to protect the public property of our socialist society and the legitimate personal property of its individual citizens. The draft provides that property owned by the whole people and property collectively owned by the working people shall be protected. At the same time, all legitimate private property shall be protected. This includes citizens' lawful income, savings, houses and other means of livelihood as well as such means of production as small plots of land for personal needs, livestock and trees lawfully owned or used by individuals or families.

(2) The draft Criminal Law explicitly provides that "the right of person, democratic rights and other rights of citizens shall be protected against unlawful infringement by any person or institution." It also provides that extortion of confessions through torture is strictly prohibited; that assembling crowds for "beating, smashing and looting" is strictly prohibited; that unlawful incarceration is strictly prohibited; and that frame-ups on false charges are strictly prohibited. Whoever fabricates facts to frame up another person (even a convict) shall be held criminally accountable in the light of the nature, serious-

ness and consequences of the false charges as well as with the criteria for imposing penalties. During the Cultural Revolution, the widespread practice of extortion of confessions through torture, the "beating, smashing and looting," and the unlawful incarceration and persecution on false charges perpetrated by Lin Biao and the gang of four led to extremely grave consequences with numerous cases of people being unjustly, falsely and wrongly charged or sentenced. Thus, the provisions in the Criminal Law declaring that these crimes shall be "strictly prohibited" accord with the wishes of the masses and are absolutely necessary.

* * *

(5) The Criminal Law should, on the one hand, fully protect the people in exercising their democratic rights, and on the other, help to effectively maintain public order, the order in production, work, education, scientific research, and the daily life of the people. Hence, the draft stipulates that "disturbance of public order by any person by any means shall be prohibited." We should definitely not give any counter-revolutionary, enemy agent, spy or other enemy of the people any freedom or right to endanger the people or sabotage the cause of socialism.

(6) The task of the Criminal Law is limited to dealing with criminal offences. Infractions which do not violate the Criminal Law should be dealt with under Party or administrative discipline or by civil law, government decrees, or laws governing economic affairs and must not be considered criminally liable. Therefore, such infractions are not enumerated in the Criminal Law.

Possibly Applicable Provisions of the 1979 Criminal Law

Article 1. The criminal law of the PRC takes Marxism-Leninism-Mao Zedong Thought as its guide and the Constitution as its basis and adheres to the principle of combining punishment with leniency. It is drawn up in the light of the actual situation and concrete experience gained by the people of all nationalities in our country in exercising the people's democratic dictatorship, that is, proletarian dictatorship led by the proletariat and based on the alliance of workers and peasants, and in carrying out socialist revolution and socialist construction.

Article 2. The task of the PRC's criminal law is to use punishment to combat all counterrevolutionary crimes and acts of criminal offenses, defend the dictatorship of the proletariat, protect socialist property of the whole people and of the collective and legitimate private property. This law is used to protect the personal rights, democratic rights and other rights of citizens, maintain public order and order in production, work, teaching, scientific research and the life of the people and insure the smooth progress of the socialist revolution and socialist construction.

* * *

Article 10. Any action which endangers state sovereignty and territorial integrity, jeopardizes the dictatorship of the proletariat, sabotages socialist revolution and socialist construction, disrupts public order, encroaches upon the property of the whole people, the collective or legitimate private property, infringes upon the personal rights, democratic rights and other rights of citizens or any other action which endangers society and is punishable according to law is an offence. However, if the offense is obviously a minor one and if its harm is negligible, it should not be considered a crime.

* * *

Article 151. Anyone who takes away a relatively large amount of public or private property by stealing, swindling or plundering will be sentenced to imprisonment for not more than 5 years, detention or surveillance.

* * *

Article 154. Anyone who extorts public or private property will be sentenced to imprisonment for not more than 3 years or to detention. In grave cases, the offender will be sentenced to imprisonment for not less than 3 and no more than 7 years.

* * *

Article 187. Any state functionary who inflicts heavy losses upon public property, the state or the people due to dereliction of duty will be sentenced to detention or imprisonment for not more than 5 years.

* * *

Article 79. Those who commit offenses not explicitly defined in the specifics of the criminal law may be convicted and sentenced according to the most approximate article in the criminal law. However, approval must be obtained from the Higher People's Court.

QUESTIONS

1. Does the new law change your definition of embezzlement or stealing?
2. Does the new law change your view about whether Chang has committed embezzlement or some other crime? Note the emphasis on protecting public property in the Peng Zhen article.

b. Sanctions

Article 28. Major punishments are as follows:
1. Surveillance;
2. Detention;
3. Fixed-term imprisonment;

4. Life imprisonments; and

5. Death penalty.

Article 29. Supplementary punishments are as follows:

1. Fines;

2. Deprivation of political rights; and

3. Confiscation of property

In certain cases only a supplementary punishment will be imposed.

* * *

Article 32. Light offenses that do not require punishment may be exempted from criminal sanctions. However, the offender may be reprimanded or ordered to mend his ways, apologize and pay compensation or be subjected to administrative disciplinary measures from the department in charge based on the seriousness of the offense.

Article 33. The period of surveillance is not to be less than 3 months and not more than 2 years. Surveillance must be ordered by the people's court and implemented by the public security organs.

Article 37. The period of detention is to be no less than 15 days and not more than 6 months.

Article 40. The period of fixed-term imprisonment is to be no less than 6 months and no more than 15 years.

Article 48. Imposition of fines should be based on the seriousness of the offense.

QUESTIONS

1. Do these provisions change your view about what is an appropriate sanction to impose on Chang if he is found guilty?

2. Under the new Criminal Law, is it still possible to handle Chang's case through informal legal process rather than the formal legal system? Can the sanction of rehabilitation be used?

3. The Issue of Discretion

NOTE

Every society struggles with the issue of how much discretion to grant to administrators of the legal system. Insistence upon strict adherence to rules of law leads to rigidity and may cause injustice in individual cases. On the other hand, giving too much leeway to administrators undercuts the concept that there are clear and known rules of law which govern the actions of individuals and officials.

Perhaps more than other societies, China has struggled with the issue of discretion. Earlier materials have discussed the concepts of stability and change in Chinese thinking, and also have described the new cadres' emphasis on the rule of man. In addition, in the 1950s, Chinese legal specialists realized that many provisions of law were incomplete, vague, or not fully defined. They also stressed that China was a large and diverse society where the attempt to impose a single uniform rule for the entire country is likely to produce unsatisfactory results. For example, the authors of Lectures favored the exercise of some flexibility and discretion in the handling of "concrete cases."

Lectures on the Criminal Law of the People's Republic of China in Jerome A. Cohen, The Criminal Process in the People's Republic of China, 1949–1963, Cambridge, Harvard University Press, 1968, p. 334.

It can be seen from this that in dealing with concrete problems we must start out from reality, act appropriately for the time and place, and correctly and thoroughly implement state policies, laws and decrees. Only by so doing can we achieve the goal of handling matters properly. This is just what Comrade Tung Pi-wu, President of the Supreme People's Court pointed out: to act appropriately for the time and place is a characteristic of our people's democratic legal system.

Here it should be pointed out that to act appropriately for the time and place certainly does not imply that an act which is uniformly prescribed as a crime by the criminal (law) legislation of our country can be considered a crime in district A and not a crime in district B (except in districts where national minority groups live together). When the criminal (law) legislation of our country defines certain acts as crimes, it does so uniformly throughout the country. But in dealing with concrete cases, that is, in determining the degree of social danger of a certain act, we must consider the complex circumstances of the act and the concrete circumstances of the time and place. Only in this way can we correctly use law and consolidate the people's democratic legal system.

NOTE

Luo Ruiqing, the Minister of Public Security who promulgated SAPA in 1958, went even further. In explaining how that law should be applied, he said that SAPA "cannot be executed in a mechanical and inflexible way. Naturally, it would be wrong to apply it uniformly and without inquiring into specific circumstances."

In view of such statements, how much leeway would a local official have in not applying the letter of the law?

Recent writings continue to discuss the issue of discretion, trying to find the proper balance between flexibility and strict adherence to rules of law. Do the following articles change your view on how Chang's case should be handled?

**"Supreme People's Court Vice-President Calls for Enforcing Law,"
Foreign Broadcast Information Service [FBIS:CHI], Sept. 5, 1979,
p. L4.**

It is essential to establish the facts of a crime and make a clear
distinction between guilt and innocence.

First, a clear distinction must be made between criminal actions
and ideological problems. An idea, however erroneous or even reactionary, does not constitute a crime if it is not put into action detrimental to society. Erroneous ideas must be corrected and reactionary ideas must be criticized, but this kind of criticism should be
conducted by reasoning things out and this is different from legal
sanction.

Second, there must be a clear distinction between a crime and a
mistake. Mistakes should be settled only through criticism and education or the enforcement of party or government discipline. A person who has committed a crime should not be given additional punishment for his mistakes.

Third, there must be a clear distinction between crimes and ordinary infractions of the law. Many cases of violation of the law do
not constitute criminal cases and therefore should be handled in accordance with party or government discipline or under civil, administrative or economic laws. It is essential to establish the true nature
of a crime and distinguish between counter-revolutionary and ordinary criminal cases.

**"Renmin Ribao Editorial Calls for Strengthening Public Order,"
[FBIS:CHI], February 4, 1980, p. L13.**

In order to strengthen social order, it is necessary to insist that
laws be observed, that their enforcement be strict, that lawbreakers
be dealt with and the criminals of all kinds be severely punished.
The primary problem at present is that some comrades are softheart-
ed, fail to strike hard blows at criminals and thus objectively abet the
bad elements' arrogance. The dissatisfaction of the masses of people
over this problem is completely understandable. We should never be
lenient with criminals and damage the dignity of the law. With regard to murderers, robbers, rapists, ringleaders of criminal gangs,
abetters and other criminals who seriously undermine social order,
they must be given stiff sentences according to the law and severely
punished without mercy. With regard to those who surrender themselves to the police or make a clean breast of their crimes and those
criminals who redeem themselves by informing against other offenders. They should be dealt with leniently according to the law. With
regard to those who commit minor offenses and do not need to be
sentenced, some should be reeducated through labor in accordance
with the "State Council's decision on reeducation through labor" and
the additional regulations of the State Council while the others should
be dealt with through other administrative disciplinary measures.
With regard to those who violated the maintenance of public security,

punishment should be in the form of a warning, fine or administrative detention, in accordance with "the PRC regulations on the maintenance of public security and punishment." Punishment represents in itself a compulsory educational measure. Our effort to deal strictly with criminals . . . themselves, but also at redeeming those who took a wrong step in life. Meanwhile, it will also help people to understand what constitutes a violation of the law and a criminal offense and what punishment one should get for breaking the law and committing a crime. This will contribute greatly to enhancing the people's observance of the law and discipline and will safeguard stability and unity.

**"Public Security Minister on Enforcement of Criminal Law,"
[FBIS:CHI], January 8, 1980, pp. L4–5.**

1. The Laws Must Be Observed. In handling all cases, public security organs must act in strict accordance with the Constitution and other laws. This is [a prerequisite] for strengthening the socialist legal system and for insuring that law enforcement is strict and that lawbreakers are dealt with.

* * *

2. Law Enforcement Must Be Strict. Public security work is done during the first stage of the judicial procedure and criminal cases. We must enforce the law strictly. [passage indistinct] We must apply the provisions of the law correctly to punish criminals and to insure that the innocent are not subjected to unjustified investigation. The law is not strictly enforced if the innocent are punished or if the guilty are not punished. The law is also not strictly enforced if one is punished more heavily than he deserves or if one is punished more lightly than he should be. All criminal offenders . . . must be severely punished according to the law. The masses also have the responsibility of requesting public security organs to deal with such criminal offenders according to the law. Since the law is very strict, its enforcement must be very strict. As a proverb says: "The law is strict, impartial and incorruptible." This means strict law enforcement. Only by strictly enforcing the law will we be able to handle cases impartially and not harm the innocent or leave criminals at large.

3. Lawbreakers Must Be Dealt With. All citizens are equal before the law. This is an extremely important principle of the socialist legal system. Our party's principles and the socialist state system require everyone to abide by the law. It is necessary for the ordinary working people to abide by the law, and it is even more necessary for Communist Party members and government functionaries, including the public security cadres and police, to do so. No one has the privilege to place himself above the law. No matter who commits them, all criminal offenses must be investigated and dealt with according to the law. Only by doing this will we be able to guard the supreme authority of the law.

Part IV

PRIVATE ORDERING

Chapter 17

INTRODUCTION TO PRIVATE ORDERING

PROBLEM III

A small food processor purchases agricultural produce from local farmers and sells finished products to a national distributor. After shopping around the processor contracted with a distant manufacturer for a new piece of equipment which would considerably increase production capacity. In anticipation of this increase, the processor arranged for the local farmers to grow and deliver more supplies, and also promised the national distributor larger quantities of finished products.

One component of the new machinery had to be imported. The government, in an effort to reduce a trade deficit, cancelled all import licenses. Consequently, the manufacturer was unable to deliver the new equipment. What obligations exist between the processor and (a) the manufacturer? (b) the local farmers? and (c) the national distributor?

* * *

This hypothetical problem describes "contracts" in different sets of circumstances. There are agreements between:

(1) the processor and the manufacturer—a one-time-only transaction between distant parties;

(2) the processor and the local farmers—a transaction between parties likely to have an on-going and face-to-face relationship;

(3) the processor and the national distributor—an on-going relationship between distant parties.

The following materials examine how these three types of contracts might be treated differently in terms of formalities, allocations of risks, and determinations of damages. The four societies studied present very different cultural and economic contexts for the operation of the contracts. For example, on religious grounds Islamic law proscribes certain kinds of contracts, including executory contracts promising some action in the future. State ownership of industrial and commercial property coupled with the desire to improve the marginal living of farmers may incline the Chinese system to protect the farmers and place the losses on units better able to afford it. Botswana's level of economic development may make parts of the hypothetical problem unrealistic. As you go through the materials, consider whether the same concept of "contract" can be applied in all four cultures.

A. THE ROLE OF CONTRACTS

NOTE

In the United States, very many of a person's activities are managed through contracts. For example, contracts are the means by which one rents an apartment, pays tuition in return for instruction, arranges employment, or fixes some of the terms for marriage or cohabitation. Many routine activities also involve contracts: buying groceries, ordering lunch, or going bowling.

At the same time, some of the most important aspects of one's life do not involve contracts. These include most relations and dealings within a family or with friends and neighbors, as well as matters concerning personal beliefs and values.

Two questions then arise about the nature of contracts. First, why are some activities handled through contracts, while others are not? Second, how does the pattern of using and not using contracts differ in various societies? This second question can also be raised by asking what we can learn about a society by analyzing its pattern of using and not using contracts.

An examination of some of the basic characteristics of contracts helps shed some light on these questions. Legal relations can be established through promissory as well as non-promissory means.

In Western legal systems, and probably in most others, this distinction is very important. It marks the difference between contract and tort (the distinction is sometimes very difficult to apply or to justify, but we need not deal with those problems here).

One way to talk about the difference is this: legal right-duty relations are created in two ways. One way is directly by law. Thus there is a rule of law imposing a duty of care on me when I drive and creating in you a correlative right that I not negligently harm you while I am driving. My duty and your right exist even though I have not made any promises or representations to you and do not even know of your existence. All drivers owe the same duty to all pedestrians. Other kinds of legal right-duty relations arise out of what European lawyers call "juridical acts" or "legal transactions" and Americans refer to as "private legal ordering."

Thus the duty of a seller to deliver specified goods to a buyer is the result of a legally binding promise made to the latter by the former. Of course the ultimate legal power behind the duty in such a case is still the law, which enforces promises of this kind. But until the promise is made there is nothing to enforce, and it is up to private individuals to decide whether to make such promises, whom to make them to, and what the terms of the promises shall be. Moreover, while the state plays a role in setting up rules and procedures for use of contracts, it generally does not directly intervene until requested by one of the parties. In this way, the area of contracts differs from the criminal law where the state directly intervenes to enforce certain norms of conduct. The subject of inheritance falls somewhere in between since the state prescribes rules on intestate succession and circumscribes the ability of a person to freely dispose of his estate through a will.

The category of private ordering includes contracts, wills, gifts, declarations of trust, acknowledgments of indebtedness and, in general, any such expression or representation that the law recognizes and enforces.

Second, contracts are legally enforceable. In the event of a contract breach, redress may be obtained through the intervention of some outside agency, often a governmental body. Thus, a contract is something more than an ordinary promise; the latter may create some moral obligation, but does not produce legal consequences.

Third, contracts usually deal with a fair exchange of more or less equal value between the parties; the architypical example is the purchase of goods at a fair market value. The contractual form fits less well for activities where no exchange is present, for example, in religious practices. Moreover, the idea of an exchange suggests that contracts generally deal with a single transaction or a series of similar transactions. In a multiplex situation, such as within a family or a close community or group of friends, where people have a wide variety of interactions going on simultaneously with each other, it often may be difficult to identify just what items are being "exchanged" in a particular transaction. Instead, much vaguer criteria such as filiality or neighborliness might be used to measure a person's standing and to determine the extent to which a favor or effort must be reciprocated.

In this regard, it should be noted that there is no intrinsic reason why a contract must involve an exchange. Enforceable contracts of gift are commonplace in civil law systems in the West. In China, "patriotic pacts" frequently are signed in which a person promises to undertake a certain activity—such as to limit the number of one's children or to work longer hours to help achieve the "four modernizations"—with attendant consequences for failing to keep the promise. Modern American contract law is moving away from the concept that a promise is enforceable when given in exchange for some value in return to a broader notion that a promise upon which another person has justifiably relied should be legally enforceable.

A fourth important characteristic is that a contract embodies a well-defined understanding of the obligations and expectations of each party. In addition, the understanding often is given publicity and more concrete form by bringing in witnesses, performing some ritual, or using a written document. The increased definitiveness of the terms contributes to more faithful execution of a contract, and facilitates enforcement by legal means should that prove necessary. At the same time, however, the process of trying to clarify and to provide outside verification involves transaction costs—asking witnesses to attend, hiring a lawyer to write the contract, hurting a friend's feelings by insisting on having a written contract, etc.—which may be considerable. Needless to say, actual resort to legal enforcement also involves substantive transaction costs.

Finally, we should note that the use of central economic planning affects the function of contracts. In one sense, the economic plan is an order by the state to subordinate production units to use certain materials to produce certain goods. "Contracts" are then signed by these units to implement the plan by specifying the terms of delivery, payment, condition of the goods, etc. The private ordering function of contracts is thus reduced, since many decisions about what to produce and possibly what prices to charge are fixed by the plan. Still, many other terms are arranged through contracts. Moreover, the process of planning itself involves a great deal of discussion and bargaining between the planning agency and each unit. In mixed planned-market economics, production units have more decision making power.

QUESTIONS

1. Why should a private individual be able to call on the power of the state to support her demand that the defendant perform his promise or pay damages for the failure to perform? In other words, why should the law enforce private ordering? Here are a few proposed justifications: (1) it is unethical not to keep a promise, and a civilized society should require ethical behavior; (2) promises induce reliance, and it seems fair to protect reliance; (3) promises are ordinarily made in return for something—there is some quid pro quo—and it would be unfair to allow a party to accept the benefit without requiring him to perform his part of the bargain. See Morris R. Cohen, The Basis of Contract, 46 Harvard Law Review 553, 571 ff. (1933).

2. The scope for and the importance of private legal ordering vary widely among societies. One kind of variation is summed up in Sir Henry Maine's famous statement: ". . . the movement of the progressive societies has hitherto been a movement from Status to Contract." Sir Henry Maine, Ancient Law, London: John Murray, 1897, 16th edition, p. 170. Would you say that a similar evolution has continued to take place in Western societies? Compare R. H. Graveson, The Movement from Status to Contract, 4 Modern Law Review 261, 1941; Morris R. Cohen, The Basis of Contract, 46 Harvard Law Review 553, 1933; Friedrich Kessler and Grant Gilmore, Contracts, 2d edition, Boston: Little Brown, 1970, pp. 1–15.

3. Another dimension of variation in the importance of private legal ordering can be observed by comparing the role of contract in the U.S.A. and in the U.S.S.R. Would you expect private legal ordering to have a greater or lesser role in the U.S.S.R.? Why?

4. The justifications stated in question 1 for the legal enforcement of private ordering are primarily ethical in nature. There is also a persuasive economic argument, in a capitalist society. Can you construct that argument? See Anthony T. Kronman and Richard A. Posner, editors, The Economics of Contract Law, Boston: Little Brown, 1979, pp. 1–7. Do you see the dependence of this argument on "private property"? The relation between "private property" and "freedom of contract"?

5. Can you think of other reasons why it is good social policy to enforce some kinds of private ordering?

B. THE USE AND NON–USE OF CONTRACTS

NOTE

The characteristics described in the introduction to this problem—private ordering, outside enforcement, fair exchange or justifiable reliance, and clarity—may not appear in every contract, but they do identify some basic factors that help explain when contracts are and are not used. The introduction also mentioned the unsuitability of contracts to govern matters such as acts of generosity or friendliness, or beliefs of a personal or religious nature. There are also many vague statements of hope or intent which are not meant to be strictly enforced, and hence would not be set into contractual form.

More broadly, in several circumstances, formal contracts are unlikely to be used. Thus, when the terms and obligations in a particular situation are fully understood by all parties, further clarification by a contract is not needed. The terms of most regular activities, including economic activities, within the family or close community are usually well known to all participants. In addition, for many status-related matters, such as filiality or vassalage, an educational and socializational process since childhood has imbued certain values and understandings in a person.

In addition, formal contracts are not likely to be used in routine activities where the transactional cost of creating a formal contract simply is not worth the benefits derived, given the minor nature of the activity or the low risk of breach. At this point, pause and consider: for which of your own activities that might be managed through the use of formal contracts would you decline using a contract on the grounds that no further clarity is needed or that the transactional cost is too high? Where contracts are used, for which ones would you not seek legal enforcement in the event of breach on the ground that the transactional cost is too high?

The following topography tries to suggest some generalizations about when contracts are used and not used, and why. Very many of a person's relationships, whether social or economic, are of a multiple and on-going nature. For example, a person expects to deal with a relative or a neighbor over many years and for many transactions, both simultaneous and sequential. Thus, one might have a regular exchange of labor services with one's neighbor, and be related by marriage to the neighbor, and have been friends with the neighbor since childhood, etc. The relationship between these two persons is not a set of discrete transactions, but rather a network of interrelated dealings. Moreover, the relationship is expected to last for some time.

This kind of multiple and on-going tie certainly describes relationships within a family, in a small close community, and with friends. Consequently, the description fits traditional societies very well. But it is most important to note that in a highly "modern" society such as the United States, a very large portion of one's dealings are still conducted within the context of multiple and on-going relationships. Many "traditional" elements remain: family, friends, some sense of community. Even in "modern" areas suich as corporate business or professional ties, as the Macaulay articles in the Western materials illustrate, one usually deals with the same persons for many matters over a long period of time. Perhaps in suggesting the idea of "movement from status to contract," Sir Henry Maine has focused too much of our attention on contract. Status still plays an important role; although contemporary American status is not—and should not—be defined by birth, one still functions within the context of status such as lessee, student, lawyer, consumer, or Oldsmobile dealer.

The contract form does not fit very well in a multiple and on-going setting (with the exception of the "insulating" contract discussed below). In such a setting, the parties are not so much concerned with a single transaction—which might be the subject of a particular contract—but rather with the entire network of relationships, present and future. Thus, if two people have ten simultaneous dealings with each other and one is going poorly, the parties will be more concerned with how the overall relationship will be affected rather than trying to push one's "rights" in the single case to their furthest limit.

The emphasis on the overall relationship has several major implications for the role of contracts. First, in trying to settle a dispute over a particular transaction, the range of what would be considered "relevant" would be very wide. It may encompass every part of the multiple and on-going relations; even if less than that, it would still be considerably broader than what Western law describes as "legally relevant."

Second, a major and sometimes the major concern is the restoration of some degree of harmony so that the overall relationship is not unduly damaged and that future relations can continue. In contrast, Western law—and definition of legal relevance—is aimed at resolving a single isolated dispute, and pays much less attention to the overall relationship. Moreover, the concern with the larger context may sometimes mean subordinating the interests of one person to the needs of the larger community so that the entire community can continue to function properly—an important factor in poor marginal communities. Obviously, this kind of concern comes into conflict with notions of individualism and individual rights.

The need to adjust disrupted relationships and to reestablish a basis for future harmonious dealings frequently makes adjudication by legal organs an unsuitable means of dispute resolution. Going to court often makes things worse by crystallizing antagonistic positions, exaggerating differences, and publicizing the dispute. An adjustment can more easily come about through informal methods such as the Kpelle moot or palaver, the Chinese methods of mediation, or the social and business pressures described by Macaulay.* In the last analysis, the principal means of getting someone to live up to obligations in a multiple on-going context are reliance on social pressure, denial of reciprocity to one who has failed to meet expected obligations, and stressing the self-interests and general interests served when everyone follows the rules of reciprocity.

The above discussion on the non-use of contracts is not meant to denigrate the role of that highly important social and economic instrument. Instead, the goal is to redress a likely imbalance in the view of a Western stu-

---

* Stewart Macaulay, "Non-Contractual Relations in Business: A Preliminary Study," 28 American Sociological Review 55, 1963.

dent (particularly a law student) which assigns too much weight to the role of contracts and the efficacy of legal enforcement.

In what circumstances, then, are contracts frequently used? Even in a multiple on-going relationship, one item may be of such great spiritual, personal, or economic importance that its being carried out outweighs the other elements in the relationship. Examples might include marriage, partitioning of family property and status, or a major economic transaction. In such situations, contracts might be used to clearly define rights and duties and to help ensure proper execution.

There are other circumstances where formal contracts would be used in a multiple on-going context. Where one aspect of the relationship is particularly sensitive, risky, or difficult, a contract can surround that aspect and insulate the rest of the relationship from possible disruptions caused by this aspect. Some examples are the Western contract of cohabitation and the contracts among Birwa neighbors. Similarly, where a new activity is being undertaken requiring new rules and allocations of risk, or where a matter is particularly complex, a contract can help provide needed clarity and assurance.

Finally, contracts play an important role when the parties do not have a multiple on-going relationship, and especially when they are engaged in a one-time-only transaction. In the absence of applicable social pressure, informal means of dispute settlement, and even mutual trust, a legally enforceable formal contract makes it possible for strangers to deal with each other. Thus, contracts are critically important in the process of extending one's dealings beyond one's family and immediate community.

QUESTIONS

1. The materials describe four basic characteristics of contracts: private ordering, legal enforcement, fair exchange or justifiable reliance, and clarity. In light of what you have read, how would you change or qualify this description? Do you need a different description for each culture, or will one fit all four?

2. Clearly, contracts play an important role in societies stressing individualism. Is the converse true: that the less the stress on individualism, the more constricted the role of contracts? How does the latter proposition apply in communistic China? tribal Botswana? How do you deal with Egypt in this line of analysis?

3. It is also clear that there is some relationship between the development of contract law and economic development. To what extent, if at all, does the lack of a thorough system of contract law affect economic growth in Botswana? Did Islamic beliefs about executory contracts and usury limit commerce?

Chapter 18

PRIVATE ORDERING IN THE WEST

A. THE FARMERS AND THE PROCESSOR

NOTE

The problem states that the processor "arranged for the local farmers to grow and deliver more supplies." Such arrangements could take a variety of forms (for example, the processor could have advanced money to the farmers for seed, fertilizer, clearing or leasing additional acreage, buying or leasing additional equipment, etc., thus financing their expanded production, perhaps taking in return notes payable by them out of the eventual proceeds of sale of their expanded production to the processor. The processor might in such a case have pledged the farmers' notes to the bank to secure its own credit with the bank). We will use a simpler case. Suppose that P, the president of the processor, appeared before a meeting of local farmers and told them: "We are increasing our plant capacity and will want a lot more tomatoes from you from now on." After the meeting one of the farmers, F, spoke with P, saying: "I could probably give you twice as many tomatoes next year," and P replied: "We will take all you can produce. You go ahead and grow the tomatoes, and we will be glad to have them." F increased his tomato planting and harvested a good crop, about double what he had sold the processor the preceding year, and offered it to the processor, who by then was in trouble because its new plant capacity was not ready. Is the processor legally bound to accept and pay for the crop or liable for damages for failure to do so? The following materials should help you deal with that question.

Mosekian v. Davis Canning Co., 229 Cal.App.2d 118, 40 Cal.Rptr. 157 (1964).

STONE, J. Defendant Davis Canning Company and its fruit buyer, defendant Adams, appeal from a judgment for damages resulting from a breach of an oral contract for the sale of plaintiff's peach crop. Defendants contend that Civil Code section 1724, subdivision (1), requiring a sale of goods for a consideration valued in excess of $500 to be in writing, bars plaintiff's recovery, and that defendants are not estopped from asserting this statute. The trial court found against defendants on both issues. Defendant Adams appeals from the judgment against him on the additional ground that he was acting as the agent of Davis Canning Company.

Summarizing the facts most favorably to the prevailing plaintiff, as we must, the following sequence of events gave rise to this case: Defendant Adams called at plaintiff's farm, identified himself as a buyer for defendant Davis Canning Company, and offered to buy plaintiff's peach crop. Plaintiff asked the price per ton, and Adams replied that since the price had not been set, the purchase would be on an "open contract." In the canning peach industry the cannery association sets a price each year when crop and market conditions are ascertained. Customarily canners contract to buy crops before maturity, agreeing to pay whatever price per ton the association thereafter sets; hence the term "open contract."

Plaintiff testified that Adams bought his crop "roadside" on such an open contract, and when he asked for confirmation Adams said he would bring a written contract for signature when the price was set. This Adams did not do. The peaches ripened, and plaintiff went looking for Adams. When he found him, at a neighbor's farm, he asked for picking boxes to "roadside" his fruit, which was dropping. Adams said he hadn't started taking fruit but that he would commence in a couple of days, at which time he would see plaintiff. Adams did not return, so again plaintiff went looking for him and when he found him advised that the fruit was ripening rapidly and falling on the ground. Adams replied, "Sell it to somebody else." Plaintiff, unable to dispose of his fruit at a cannery, sold it to a "dry yard." The trial court awarded plaintiff, as damages, the difference between the canning peach price and the dry yard price.

Defendants argue strenuously that conflicts between plaintiff's deposition and his testimony given in court cast grave doubts upon his version of the conversation with Adams. Since the court's finding that there was an oral contract rests largely upon plaintiff's courtroom version of the conversations, defendants argue that the evidence is not substantial. Nevertheless, it was for the trial court to resolve discrepancies within plaintiff's testimony, as well as the conflict between the testimony of Adams and that of plaintiff. The court accepted the testimony plaintiff gave at the trial, and it is not our prerogative to set aside this resolution of conflicting evidence.

We proceed to defendants' contention that the oral contract for the sale of a growing crop of peaches for a consideration in excess of $500 is within the purview of Civil Code section 1724, subdivision (1), which requires that: "A contract to sell or a sale of any goods or choses in action of the value of five hundred dollars or upwards shall not be enforceable by action unless the buyer shall accept part of the goods or choses in action so contracted to be sold, or sold and actually receive the same, or give something in earnest to bind the contract, or in part payment, or unless some note or memorandum in writing of the contract or sale be signed by the party to be charged or his agent in that behalf."

First, we note that when sold separately a crop of fruit growing upon trees is not considered to be a part of the real property insofar as pertains to Civil Code section 1624, subdivision 4, which requires the sale of an interest in real property to be in writing. This rule of law was established in a number of very early cases which are cited by plaintiff, and it was reaffirmed by the case principally relied upon by plaintiff, Vulicevich v. Skinner, often referred to as the landmark case on the question. The court in *Vulicevich* said: " 'Contracts for the sale of growing periodical crops—*fructus industriales*—are not within the statute of frauds, and therefore need not be made in writing. . . .' " This indiscriminate use of the term "statute of frauds" without reference to the particular statute or code section that the court was construing, apparently has given rise to uncertainty as to whether a contract for the sale of growing crops is within the provisions of Civil Code section 1724, subdivision (1), quoted above. Annotated codes appear to regard the language of *Vulicevich* as placing a contract for the sale of growing crops outside the purview of section 1724, subdivision (1), the so-called "sales act," and its counterpart, Civil Code section 1624a.

In our view such a broad interpretation of *Vulicevich* is not warranted because an analysis of the opinion reveals, first, that the requirements of Civil Code sections 1624a and 1724, subdivision (1), were complied with in that the buyer paid the seller $600 on account of the oral agreement to purchase the crop. Second, the court predicated its holding that the "statute of frauds" is not applicable to a contract for the sale of a growing crop, upon the cases of Marshall v. Ferguson, and Davis v. McFarlane, both of which were decided prior to the enactment of the Sales Act of 1874. Thus the sale of a growing crop in relation to a sale of goods was not an issue in either cited case. Third, the question presented in *Vulicevich* was whether growing crops are part of the realty upon which they are produced, not whether they are goods as that term is used in Civil Code sections 1624a and 1724, subdivision (1).

The sole statute of frauds question in *Vulicevich*, as defined by the opinion, is: "He makes the point that the crop of fruit growing upon the trees and vines *was real property*, and that the alleged contract of sale was void under the *statute of frauds*, as not being in writing, and that the court wrongfully charged the jury upon the matter." (P. 240.) (Italics added.)

The court answered the question it had thus posed, as follows: "We cannot concur with this view. 'Contracts for the sale of growing periodical crops—*fructus industriales*—are not within the *statute of frauds*, and therefore need not be made in writing. After some vacillation, this has become the settled doctrine.' "

The answer, standing alone, does not constitute the legal concept that emerges from *Vulicevich*, and quotation of the answer out of context, that is, without regard for the language of the opinion which precedes and delimits the answer, imputes to the case a broader scope than is justified. We conclude that in *Vulicevich* the court did not purport to pass upon the question whether a contract for the sale of a growing crop is within the purview of the Sales Act provisions of the various statutes falling within the broad language, "statute of frauds." It would be at least anomalous if *Vulicevich*, which determined that growing crops sold by contract are goods, *fructus industriales*, should be cited also as authority for the proposition that growing crops are not goods within the purview of Civil Code sections 1624a and 1724, subdivision (1).

Furthermore, we deem controlling the language used in Civil Code section 1796, subdivision (1), defining the term "goods" as applied to a sale of growing crops agreed to be severed before sale or under the contract of sale. Under the heading "Definitions" it is provided, in pertinent part: " 'Goods' include all chattels personal other than things in action and money. The term includes emblements, industrial growing crops, and things attached to or forming part of the land which are agreed to be severed before sale or under the contract of sale."

The foregoing definition is clear, and in the absence of any Supreme Court decision specifically forbidding its construction as an adjunct to Civil Code section 1724, subdivision (1), we hold that Civil Code section 1796, subdivision (1), is not abrogated by the broad language of *Vulicevich* taken out of context. Therefore, the trial court erred in finding that Civil Code sections 1724, subdivision (1), and 1624a are not applicable to the oral contract in this case.

A reversal does not follow, even though the provisions of Civil Code section 1724, subdivision (1), are applicable, since the trial court found defendants were estopped to invoke the statute. The doctrine of estoppel as applied to the statute of frauds is delineated in *Monarco v. Lo Greco*. Mr. Justice Traynor thus summarized circumstances under which the doctrine may be invoked: "It is contended, however, that an estoppel to plead the statute of frauds can only arise when there have been representations with respect to the requirements of the statute indicating that a writing is not necessary or will be executed or that the statute will not be relied upon as a defense. . . . however, where either an unconscionable injury or unjust enrichment would result from refusal to enforce the contract, the doctrine of estoppel has been applied whether or not plaintiff relied upon representations going to the requirements of the statute itself. . . . In reality it is not the representation that the contract will be put in writing or that the statute will not be invoked, but the promise that the contract will be performed that a party relies upon when he changes his position because of it."

Defendants argue that the evidence upon which the court based the finding of estoppel falls short of even the broad language of *Monarco*. The answer lies in whether there is acceptance of plaintiff's testimony which, standing alone, if believed, sufficiently supports the finding. The trial judge observed this 80-year-old man who is hard of hearing, and to the trial judge belonged the prerogative of believing or disbelieving his testimony, as well as all other evidence. The record reflects testimony of the plaintiff which supports the trial court's finding: "That the Plaintiff did in fact reasonably rely upon the agreements and representations of the Defendants described in Paragraphs (5) and (6) and was induced thereby to sell his growing crop of peaches to the Defendant Davis Canning Company, in June, 1960, and to hold said crop for the use and benefit of the Defendant Cannery and seek no other buyers therefor until after Defendants repudiated their contract of purchase about July 24, 1960, and by which date a portion of the crop had fallen due to overripening and a substantial part of the Plaintiff's peaches had become too ripe for sale to fresh fruit packers. . . ."

Plaintiff's change of position brings the case within the rationale of the *Monarco* case.

Well taken is defendants' third point on appeal, that the judgment against defendant Adams, the agent, is in error. Plaintiff argues that it was the burden of defendants to require him to elect between the agent and the principal, and that absent a demand both are liable. However, the cases cited by plaintiff on this question all concern an undisclosed agency. Here, at the outset, Adams was disclosed to be the agent of Davis Canning Company; plaintiff was never in doubt as to the identity of principal and agent. The judgment against Adams, personally, cannot stand.

The judgment against Davis Canning Company is affirmed; the judgment against Alvin B. Adams is reversed.

NOTES AND QUESTIONS

1. Civil Code § 1724(1) was repealed in 1963, when California adopted the Uniform Commercial Code (a major piece of law reform originally drafted and proposed for adoption by the American Law Institute and the National Conference of Commissioners on Uniform State Laws. It has been adopted, with occasional variations, in all the states). Commercial Code § 2201(1), which replaced it, reads as follows:

   § 2201. Formal Requirements; Statute of Frauds. (1) Except as otherwise provided in this section a contract for the sale of goods for the price of $500 or more is not enforceable by way of action or defense unless there is some writing sufficient to indicate that a contract for sale has been made between the parties and signed by the party against whom enforcement is sought or by his authorized agent or broker. A writing is not insufficient because it omits or incorrectly states a term agreed upon but the contract is not enforceable under this paragraph beyond the quantity of goods shown in such writing.

2. The Statute of Frauds requires evidence of some kinds of private ordering to be in writing. The full title of the original Statute of Frauds was

"An Act for the prevention of Frauds and Perjuryes" (29 Car. II, 1677). The direct derivation of UCC § 2–201(1) from Sec. 17 of the original is clear; the principal difference is that the amount in the original was "ten pounds Sterling" rather than $500. What sorts of "Frauds and Perjuryes" would occur in the absence of such a statute? Are there other reasons, besides prevention of fraud and perjury, why we might want to require some contracts to be in writing?

3. Observe that the court found that the contract fell within the terms of the Statute of Frauds. Why then was the canning company found liable to Mosekian for breach of the contract?

4. "Estoppel" is a notion that originated in the courts of equity that at one time existed as a separate jurisdiction, in addition to courts of law, in England and the U.S. The two have since merged into single sets of courts exercising both law and equity jurisdiction in all common law jurisdictions. Meanwhile the role of estoppel in the law of contract has greatly expanded.

5. The effect of estoppel is procedural; the party who is estopped is prevented from exerting a right or a defense granted to him by law. Thus the canning company in the principal case is estopped to plead the statute of frauds defense.

6. Would the processor be estopped to plead Commercial Code § 2201(1) in an action by F?

7. Does estoppel in such cases embody a judgment that the interest in preventing fraud is outweighed by the interest in fairness to the plaintiff? Or does it merely suggest that where the elements of estoppel exist the danger of fraud is reduced to an insignificant level?

8. One of the arguments the canning company might have made in Mosekian is that there was no contract (perhaps it did use that argument at the trial but decided not to raise it on appeal). Can you construct such an argument? Consider the following sections of the California Commercial Code:

§ 2204. **Formation in General.** (1) A contract for sale of goods may be made in any manner sufficient to show agreement, including conduct by both parties which recognizes the existence of such a contract.

    (2) An agreement sufficient to constitute a contract for sale may be found even though the moment of its making is undetermined.

    (3) Even though one or more terms are left open a contract for sale does not fail for indefiniteness if the parties have intended to make a contract and there is a reasonably certain basis for giving an appropriate remedy.

§ 2305. **Open Price Term.** (1) The parties if they so intend can conclude a contract for sale even though the price is not settled. In such a case the price is a reasonable price at the time for delivery if

    (a) Nothing is said as to price; or

    (b) The price is left to be agreed by the parties and they fail to agree; or

(c) The price is to be fixed in terms of some agreed market or other standard as set or recorded by a third person or agency and it is not so set or recorded.

(2) A price to be fixed by the seller or by the buyer means a price for him to fix in good faith.

(3) When a price left to be fixed otherwise than by agreement of the parties fails to be fixed through fault of one party the other may at his option treat the contract as canceled or himself fix a reasonable price.

(4) Where, however, the parties intend not to be bound unless the price be fixed or agreed and it is not fixed or agreed there is no contract. In such a case the buyer must return any goods already received or if unable so to do must pay their reasonable value at the time of delivery and the seller must return any portion of the price paid on account.

9. "Even though a manifestation of intention is intended to be understood as an offer, it cannot be accepted so as to form a contract unless the terms of the contract are reasonably certain. The terms of a contract are reasonably certain if they provide a basis for determining the existence of a breach and for giving an appropriate remedy . . ." Restatement (2d) § 33. This principle follows from the doctrine that there can be no contract without mutual assent (sometimes spoken of as "a meeting of the minds").

10. In an action by F against the processor, suppose the defendant pleads indefiniteness. How should the court decide? Why?

B. PROCESSOR v. MANUFACTURER

NOTE

We will assume that a legally enforcible contract was formed between the processor and the manufacturer—i.e. that both parties had legal capacity; that there was a "meeting of the minds" about terms; that there was adequate, legal consideration to support the mutual promises ("consideration" is a topic we would prefer not to go into here, particularly since it is not in question in this case); that there was nothing illegal or contrary to public policy about the deal; etc.

The manufacturer has failed to deliver the machine as promised. Unless this failure is excused he is liable to the processor for "damages." We will first examine the possibility of excuse and then the issue of damages.

Lloyd v. Murphy, 25 Cal.2d 48, 153 P.2d 47 (1944).

TRAYNOR, J. On August 4, 1941, plaintiffs leased to defendant for a five-year term beginning September 15, 1941, certain premises located at the corner of Almont Drive and Wilshire Boulevard in the city of Beverly Hills, Los Angeles County, "for the sole purpose of conducting thereon the business of displaying and selling new auto-

mobiles (including the servicing and repairing thereof and of selling
the petroleum products of a major oil company) and for no other purpose whatsoever without the written consent of the lessor" except
"to make an occasional sale of a used automobile." Defendant
agreed not to sublease or assign without plaintiffs' written consent.
On January 1, 1942, the federal government ordered that the sale of
new automobiles be discontinued. It modified this order on January
8, 1942, to permit sales to those engaged in military activities, and on
January 20, 1942, it established a system of priorities restricting sales
to persons having preferential ratings of A-1-j or higher. On March
10, 1942, defendant explained the effect of these restrictions on his
business to one of the plaintiffs authorized to act for the others, who
orally waived the restrictions in the lease as to use and subleasing
and offered to reduce the rent if defendant should be unable to operate profitably. Nevertheless defendant vacated the premises on
March 15, 1942, giving oral notice of repudiation of the lease to plaintiffs, which was followed by a written notice on March 24, 1942.
Plaintiffs affirmed in writing on March 26th their oral waiver and,
failing to persuade defendant to perform his obligations, they rented
the property to other tenants pursuant to their powers under the
lease in order to mitigate damages. On May 11, 1942, plaintiffs
brought this action praying for declaratory relief to determine their
rights under the lease, and for judgment for unpaid rent. Following
a trial on the merits, the court found that the leased premises were
located on one of the main traffic arteries of Los Angeles County;
that they were equipped with gasoline pumps and in general adapted
for the maintenance of an automobile service station; that they contained a one-story storeroom adapted to many commercial purposes;
that plaintiffs had waived the restrictions in the lease and granted
defendant the right to use the premises for any legitimate purpose
and to sublease to any responsible party; that defendant continues to
carry on the business of selling and servicing automobiles at two other places. Defendant testified that at one of these locations he sold
new automobiles exclusively and when asked if he were aware that
many new automobile dealers were continuing in business replied:
"Sure. It is just the location that I couldn't make a go, though, of
automobiles." Although there was no finding to that effect, defendant estimated in response to inquiry by his counsel, that 90 per cent
of his gross volume of business was new car sales and 10 per cent
gasoline sales. The trial court held that war conditions had not terminated defendant's obligations under the lease and gave judgment
for plaintiffs, declaring the lease as modified by plaintiffs' waiver to
be in full force and effect, and ordered defendant to pay the unpaid
rent with interest, less amounts received by plaintiffs from re-rent-
ing. Defendant brought this appeal, contending that the purpose for
which the premises were leased was frustrated by the restrictions
placed on the sale of new automobiles by the federal government,
thereby terminating his duties under the lease.

. . . Although the doctrine of frustration is akin to the doctrine of impossibility of performance. . . .

. . . since both have developed from the commercial necessity of excusing performance in cases of extreme hardship, frustration is not a form of impossibility even under the modern definition of that term, which includes not only cases of physical impossibility but also cases of extreme impracticability of performance. . . .

. . . Performance remains possible but the expected value of performance to the party seeking to be excused has been destroyed by a fortuitous event, which supervenes to cause an actual but not literal failure of consideration. . . .

. . . The question in cases involving frustration is whether the equities of the case, considered in the light of sound public policy, require placing the risk of a disruption or complete destruction of the contract equilibrium on defendant or plaintiff under the circumstances of a given case. . . .

. . . and the answer depends on whether an unanticipated circumstance, the risk of which should not be fairly thrown on the promisor, has made performance vitally different from what was reasonably to be expected. . . .

. . . The purpose of a contract is to place the risks of performance upon the promisor, and the relation of the parties, terms of the contract, and circumstances surrounding its formation must be examined to determine whether it can be fairly inferred that the risk of the event that has supervened to cause the alleged frustration was not reasonably foreseeable. If it was foreseeable there should have been provision for it in the contract, and the absence of such a provision gives rise to the inference that the risk was assumed.

The doctrine of frustration has been limited to cases of extreme hardship so that businessmen, who must make their arrangements in advance, can rely with certainty on their contracts. . . .

. . . The courts have required a promisor seeking to excuse himself from performance of his obligations to prove that the risk of the frustrating event was not reasonably foreseeable and that the value of counterperformance is totally or nearly totally destroyed, for frustration is no defense if it was foreseeable or controllable by the promisor, or if counterperformance remains valuable. . . .

Thus laws or other governmental acts that make performance unprofitable or more difficult or expensive do not excuse the duty to perform a contractual obligation. . . .

. . . It is settled that if parties have contracted with reference to a state of war or have contemplated the risks arising from it, they may not invoke the doctrine of frustration to escape their obligations. . . .

At the time the lease in the present case was executed the National Defense Act. . . .

. . . authorizing the President to allocate materials and mobilize industry for national defense, had been law for more than a year. The automotive industry was in the process of conversion to supply the needs of our growing mechanized army and to meet lend-lease commitments. Iceland and Greenland had been occupied by the army. Automobile sales were soaring because the public anticipated that production would soon be restricted. These facts were commonly known and it cannot be said that the risk of war and its consequences necessitating restriction of the production and sale of automobiles was so remote a contingency that its risk could not be foreseen by defendant, an experienced automobile dealer. Indeed, the conditions prevailing at the time the lease was executed, and the absence of any provision in the lease contracting against the effect of war, gives rise to the inference that the risk was assumed. Defendant has therefore failed to prove that the possibility of war and its consequences on the production and sale of new automobiles was an unanticipated circumstance wholly outside the contemplation of the parties.

Nor has defendant sustained the burden of proving that the value of the lease has been destroyed. The sale of automobiles was not made impossible or illegal but merely restricted and if governmental regulation does not entirely prohibit the business to be carried on in the leased premises but only limits or restricts it, thereby making it less profitable and more difficult to continue, the lease is not terminated or the lessee excused from further performance. . . .

. . . Defendant may use the premises for the purpose for which they were leased. New automobiles and gasoline continue to be sold. Indeed, defendant testified that he continued to sell new automobiles exclusively at another location in the same county.

Defendant contends that the lease is restrictive and that the government orders therefore destroyed its value and frustrated its purpose. Provisions that prohibit subleasing or other uses than those specified affect the value of a lease and are to be considered in determining whether its purpose has been frustrated or its value destroyed. . . .

. . . It must not be forgotten, however, that "The landlord has not covenanted that the tenant shall have the right to carry on the contemplated business or that the business to which the premises are by their nature or by the terms of the lease restricted shall be profitable enough to enable the tenant to pay the rent but has imposed a condition for his own benefit; and, certainly, unless and until he chooses to take advantage of it, the tenant is not deprived of the use of the premises." . . .

. . . In the present lease plaintiffs reserved the rights that defendant should not use the premises for other purposes than those specified in the lease or sublease without plaintiffs' written consent. Far from preventing other uses or subleasing they waived these rights, enabling defendant to use the premises for any legitimate purpose and to sublease them to any responsible tenant. This waiver is significant in view of the location of the premises on a main traffic artery in Los Angeles County and their adaptability for many commercial purposes. The value of these rights is attested by the fact that the premises were rented soon after defendants vacated them. It is therefore clear that the governmental restrictions on the sale of new cars have not destroyed the value of the lease. Furthermore, plaintiffs offered to lower the rent if defendant should be unable to operate profitably, and their conduct was at all times fair and cooperative.

The consequences of applying the doctrine of frustration to a leasehold involving less than a total or nearly total destruction of the value of the leased premises would be undesirable. Confusion would result from different decisions purporting to define "substantial" frustration. Litigation would be encouraged by the repudiation of leases when lessees found their businesses less profitable because of the regulations attendant upon a national emergency. Many leases have been affected in varying degrees by the widespread governmental regulations necessitated by war conditions.

The cases that defendant relies upon are consistent with the conclusion reached herein. In Industrial Development & Land Co. v. Goldschmidt, supra, the lease provided that the premises should not be used other than as a saloon. When national prohibition made the sale of alcoholic beverages illegal, the court excused the tenant from further performance on the theory of illegality or impossibility by a change in domestic law. The doctrine of frustration might have been applied, since the purpose for which the property was leased was totally destroyed and there was nothing to show that the value of the lease was not thereby totally destroyed. In the present case the purpose was not destroyed but only restricted, and plaintiffs proved that the lease was valuable to defendant. In Grace v. Croninger, supra, the lease was for the purpose of conducting a "saloon and cigar store and for no other purpose" with provision for subleasing a portion of the premises for bootblack purposes. The monthly rental was $650. It was clear that prohibition destroyed the main purpose of the lease, but since the premises could be used for bootblack and cigar store purposes, the lessee was not excused from his duty to pay the rent. In the present case new automobiles and gasoline may be sold under the lease as executed and any legitimate business may be conducted or the premises may be subleased under the lease as modified by plaintiff's waiver. . . .

. . . No case has been cited by defendant or disclosed by research in which an appellate court has excused a lessee from performance of his duty to pay rent when the purpose of the lease has not been totally destroyed or its accomplishment rendered extremely impracticable or where it has been shown that the lease remains valuable to the lessee.

The judgment is affirmed. . . .

NOTE

Lloyd v. Murphy was decided before California, in 1963, adopted the Uniform Commercial Code. California Commercial Code § 2615, which is identical to UCC § 2–615, provides as follows:

§ 2615. Excuse by Failure of Presupposed Conditions. Except so far as a seller may have assumed a greater obligation and subject to the preceding section on substituted performance:

(a) Delay in delivery or nondelivery in whole or in part by a seller who complies with paragraphs (b) and (c) is not a breach of his duty under a contract for sale if performance as agreed has been made impracticable by the occurrence of a contingency the nonoccurrence of which was a basic assumption on which the contract was made or by compliance in good faith with any applicable foreign or domestic governmental regulation or order whether or not it later proves to be invalid.

(b) Where the causes mentioned in paragraph (a) affect only a part of the seller's capacity to perform, he must allocate production and deliveries among his customers but may at his option include regular customers not then under contract as well as his own requirements for further manufacture. He may so allocate in any manner which is fair and reasonable.

(c) The seller must notify the buyer seasonably that there will be delay or nondelivery and, when allocation is required under paragraph (b), of the estimated quota thus made available for the buyer.

NOTES AND QUESTIONS

1. Would the manufacturer be excused from its obligation under either Lloyd v. Murphy or § 2615?

2. In an earlier and, some would say, more rigorous (others might say more primitive) time there was no frustration defense. Why should such a defense (and the impossibility defense) have been developed by the courts? Why not simply hold the manufacturer to its promise?

3. The previous question and some language in Lloyd v. Murphy should have made you think about the contract as a risk allocation mechanism. If the parties were indeed agreeing about the allocation of risk, why should it be concluded that this particular risk was allocated by them to the processor? Both the case and the statute seem to say that if the parties had contemplated the possibility that the part could not be imported, the risk would fall on the manufacturer, unless it was expressly assumed by the processer.

4. Isn't it more accurate to say that the parties failed to contemplate and provide for this eventuality? Accordingly it is up to the court to allocate the resulting loss. If so, why allocate it to the processor? What is the

allocating principle? Fault? Fairness? Productivity? Risk-spreading? A judgment that the processor was in a better position to protect itself?

5. Observe that Lloyd v. Murphy is a typically all-or-nothing decision. Under it the manufacturer is either totally excused or is fully liable to the processer. It is easy to justify such a stance where alleged fault is the basis of liability. But where neither party can be fairly said to be at fault, why not split the losses? In this connection consider the following "official comment" by the drafters of UCC § 2–615 (such "comments" are not part of the statute and do not carry its authority, but they were annexed to the proposed Code, indicating the drafters' intentions, and have some weight).

In situations in which neither sense nor justice is served by either answer when the issue is posed in flat terms of "excuse" or "no excuse," adjustment under the various provisions of this Article is necessary, especially the sections on good faith, on insecurity and assurance and on the reading of all provisions in the light of their purposes, and the general policy of this Act to use equitable principles in furtherance of commercial standards and good faith.

6. Adjustment according to "equitable principles" consistently with notions about "good faith" sounds fine, but how is the court to apply these notions to the facts of the concrete case? The party interested in "adjustment" (i.e. in paying less than full damages) will of course make its argument and the other party will, presumably, resist. Out of this dialectic process will emerge some considerations that the court may be persuaded should guide it in the case. Can you see how Official Comment 6, if it becomes law, places a premium on advocacy?

7. Which of these alternatives should take longer and consume more of the resources of the parties, their counsel, and the court:

> A. a determination that a party did not perform its promise and is liable for the resulting damage?

> B. a determination that a party did not perform its promise but may be excused by impossibility, frustration, or commercial impracticability and, if not excused, its liability may be equitably adjusted?

8. It is often said that the law should be clear and certain. Do you agree? Which of the alternatives in question 7 is more likely to provide clarity and certainty in the law?

9. It is also widely believed that the law should be just, fair, equitable. Which of the alternatives in question 7 should lead to greater justice, fairness, equity in specific cases?

10. Might economy, expedition and certainty, on one side, and sensitivity to the justice of the case, on the other, be mutually limiting values?

NOTE

Assume that the manufacturer is not excused and is, accordingly, liable to the processor. What is the extent of its liability? It should be clear that if the processor had made advance payments on the price of the machine to the manufacturer it should be able to recover them (with interest?). If the processor could buy an equivalent machine elsewhere, but at a higher price, it should recover the difference in cost. More interesting questions arise if we begin to examine less direct, but still arguably foreseeable, losses to the processor. The following materials introduce you to these questions, usually referred to as "consequential damages" questions.

Hadley v. Baxendale, 9 Exch. 341 (1854).

At the trial before Crompton, J., at the last Gloucester Assizes, it appeared that the plaintiffs carried on an extensive business as millers at Gloucester; and that, on the 11th of May, their mill was stopped by a breakage of the crank shaft by which the mill was worked. The steam-engine was manufactured by Messrs. Joyce & Co., the engineers, at Greenwich, and it became necessary to send the shaft as a pattern for a new one to Greenwich. The fracture was discovered on the 12th, and on the 13th the plaintiffs sent one of their servants to the office of the defendants, who are the well known carriers trading under the name of Pickford & Co., for the purpose of having the shaft carried to Greenwich. The plaintiffs' servant told the clerk that the mill was stopped, and that the shaft must be sent immediately; and in answer to the inquiry when the shaft would be taken, the answer was, that if it was sent up by twelve o'clock any day, it would be delivered at Greenwich on the following day. On the following day the shaft was taken by the defendants, before noon, for the purpose of being conveyed to Greenwich, and the sum of 2l. 4s. was paid for its carriage for the whole distance; at the same time the defendants' clerk was told that a special entry, if required, should be made to hasten its delivery. The delivery of the shaft at Greenwich was delayed by some neglect; and the consequence was, that the plaintiffs did not receive the new shaft for several days after they would otherwise have done, and the working of their mill was thereby delayed, and they thereby lost the profits they would otherwise have received.

[The plaintiffs claimed the profits they had lost. The defendants, who had paid £25 into court in satisfaction of the plaintiffs' claim, objected that these damages were too remote. The judge left the case generally to the jury, who found a verdict with £25 damages beyond the amount paid into court. The defendant obtained a rule nisi for a new trial.]

ALDERSON, B. We think that there ought to be a new trial in this case; but, in so doing, we deem it to be expedient and necessary to state explicitly the rule which the Judge, at the next trial, ought, in our opinion, to direct the jury to be governed by when they estimate the damages.

It is, indeed, of the last importance that we should do this; for, if the jury are left without any definite rule to guide them, it will, in

such cases as these, manifestly lead to the greatest injustice.
* * *

Now we think the proper rule in such a case as the present is this:
—Where two parties have made a contract which one of them has
broken, the damages which the other party ought to receive in respect of such breach of contract should be such as may fairly and
reasonably be considered either arising naturally, i.e., according to
the usual course of things, from such breach of contract itself, or
such as may reasonably be supposed to have been in the contemplation of both parties, at the time they made the contract, as the probable result of the breach of it. Now, if the special circumstances under which the contract was actually made were communicated by the
plaintiffs to the defendants, and thus known to both parties, the damages resulting from the breach of such a contract, which they would
reasonably contemplate, would be the amount of injury which would
ordinarily follow from a breach of contract under these special circumstances so known and communicated. But, on the other hand, if
these special circumstances were wholly unknown to the party breaking the contract, he, at the most, could only be supposed to have had
in his contemplation the amount of injury which would arise generally, and in the great multitude of cases not affected by any special
circumstances, from such a breach of contract. For, had the special
circumstances been known, the parties might have specially provided
for the breach of contract by special terms as to the damages in that
case; and of this advantage it would be very unjust to deprive them.
Now the above principles are those by which we think the jury ought
to be guided in estimating the damages arising out of any breach of
contract.   *   *   *   Now, in the present case, if we are to apply the
principles above laid down, we find that the only circumstances here
communicated by the plaintiffs to the defendants at the time the contract was made, were, that the article to be carried was the broken
shaft of a mill, and that the plaintiffs were the millers of that mill.
But how do these circumstances show reasonably that the profits of
the mill must be stopped by an unreasonable delay in the delivery of
the broken shaft by the carrier to the third person? Suppose the
plaintiffs had another shaft in their possession put up or putting up
at the time, and that they only wished to send back the broken shaft
to the engineer who made it; it is clear that this would be quite consistent with the above circumstances, and yet the unreasonable delay
in the delivery would have no effect upon the intermediate profits of
the mill. Or, again, suppose that, at the time of the delivery to the
carrier, the machinery of the mill had been in other respects defective, then, also, the same results would follow. Here it is true that
the shaft was actually sent back to serve as a model for a new one,
and that the want of a new one was the only cause of the stoppage of
the mill, and that the loss of profits really arose from not sending
down the new shaft in proper time, and that this arose from the delay
in delivering the broken one to serve as a model. But it is obvious

that, in the great multitude of cases of millers sending off broken shafts to third persons by a carrier under ordinary circumstances, such consequences would not, in all probability, have occurred; and these special circumstances were here never communicated by the plaintiffs to the defendants. It follows, therefore, that the loss of profits here cannot reasonably be considered such a consequence of the breach of contract as could have been fairly and reasonably contemplated by both the parties when they made this contract. For such loss would neither have flowed naturally from the breach of this contract in the great multitude of such cases occurring under ordinary circumstances, nor were the special circumstances, which, perhaps, would have made it a reasonable and natural consequence of such breach of contract, communicated to or known by the defendants. The Judge ought, therefore, to have told the jury that, upon the facts then before them, they ought not to take the loss of profits into consideration at all in estimating the damages. There must therefore be a new trial in this case.

Rule absolute.

CALIFORNIA COMMERCIAL CODE

§ 2713. Buyer's Damages for Non-Delivery or Repudiation. (1) Subject to the provisions of this division with respect to proof of market price (Section 2723), the measure of damages for nondelivery or repudiation by the seller is the difference between the market price at the time when the buyer learned of the breach and the contract price together with any incidental and consequential damages provided in this division (Section 2715), but less expenses saved in consequence of the seller's breach.

(2) Market price is to be determined as of the place for tender or, in cases of rejection after arrival or revocation of acceptance, as of the place of arrival.

§ 2715. Buyer's Incidental and Consequential Damages. (1) Incidental damages resulting from the seller's breach include expenses reasonably incurred in inspection, receipt, transportation and care and custody of goods rightfully rejected, any commercially reasonable charges, expenses or commissions in connection with effecting cover and any other reasonable expense incident to the delay or other breach.

(2) Consequential damages resulting from the seller's breach include

(a) Any loss resulting from general or particular requirements and needs of which the seller at the time of contracting had reason to know and which could not reasonably be prevented by cover or otherwise; and

(b) Injury to person or property proximately resulting from any breach of warranty.

NOTE

Sections 2713 and 2715 of the California Commercial Code enact without change §§ 2–713 and 2–715 of the Uniform Commercial Code. "Official Comments" 2 and 3 to § 2–715 read as follows:

2. Subsection (2) operates to allow the buyer, in an appropriate case, any consequential damages which are the result of the seller's breach. The "tacit agreement" test for the recovery of consequential damages is rejected. Although the older rule at common law which made the seller liable for all consequential damages of which he had "reason to know" in advance is followed, the liberality of that rule is modified by refusing to permit recovery unless the buyer could not reasonably have prevented the loss by cover or otherwise. Subparagraph (2) carries forward the provisions of the prior uniform statutory provision as to consequential damages resulting from breach of warranty, but modifies the rule by requiring first that the buyer attempt to minimize his damages in good faith, either by cover or otherwise.

3. In the absence of excuse under the section on merchant's excuse by failure of presupposed conditions, the seller is liable for consequential damages in all cases where he had reason to know of the buyer's general or particular requirements at the time of contracting. It is not necessary that there be a conscious acceptance of an insurer's liability on the seller's part, nor is his obligation for consequential damages limited to cases in which he fails to use due effort in good faith.

Particular needs of the buyer must generally be made known to the seller while general needs must rarely be made known to charge the seller with knowledge.

Any seller who does not wish to take the risk of consequential damages has available the section on contractual limitation of remedy.

NOTES AND QUESTIONS

1. Assume that the processor can show that its anticipated increase in production capacity, prevented by lack of the machinery in question, would have produced substantial additional net profits. Can it recover these lost profits from the manufacturer?

2. Suppose the processor feels obliged to accept and pay for the increased produce from the farmers but, since it lacks sufficient capacity to process the increase, must dispose of it at a loss. Can it recover the loss from the manufacturer?

3. Suppose that P, the president of the processor company, is removed by the directors in an effort to mollify irate farmers and the disaffected distributor. Should she be able to recover from the manufacturer for the loss of her job?

4. In general, is the line drawn by Hadley v. Baxendale, as modified by the Uniform Commercial Code, about right, or should it be moved? In which direction? Why?

C. PROCESSOR AND DISTRIBUTOR

NOTE

The processor is unable to perform its promise to deliver larger quantities of its finished products to the distributor, since it did not get the equipment it needed to expand production. Assuming that the promise created a binding legal obligation and that non-performance causes some loss to the distributor, it has a good cause of action for damages against the processor.

That is the way lawyers often think, but it is not necessarily the way business people think. The processor and the distributor may have a continuing business relationship that is valuable to them and that would be impaired by a lawsuit or the threat of a lawsuit, particularly where the "breach" by the processor involves no failure by it to conform to accepted business practices. There are many reasons why some potential plaintiffs do not sue some potential defendants, and the importance to the parties of a continuing business relationship is one of them. The following excerpt amplifies the point.

Stewart Macaulay, Non-Contractual Relations in Business: A Preliminary Study, 28 American Sociological Review, 55, pp. 61–67, (1963).

Exchanges are adjusted when the obligations of one or both parties are modified by agreement during the life of the relationship. For example, the buyer may be allowed to cancel all or part of the goods he has ordered because he no longer needs them; the seller may be paid more than the contract price by the buyer because of unusual changed circumstances. Dispute settlement involves determining whether or not a party has performed as agreed and, if he has not, doing something about it. For example, a court may have to interpret the meaning of a contract, determine what the alleged defaulting party has done and determine what, if any, remedy the aggrieved party is entitled to. Or one party may assert that the other is in default, refuse to proceed with performing the contract and refuse to deal ever again with the alleged defaulter. If the alleged defaulter, who in fact may not be in default, takes no action, the dispute is then "settled."

Business exchanges in non-speculative areas are usually adjusted without dispute. Under the law of contracts, if B orders 1,000 widgets from S at $1.00 each, B must take all 1,000 widgets or be in breach of contract and liable to pay S his expenses up to the time of the breach plus his lost anticipated profit. Yet all ten of the purchasing agents asked about cancellation of orders once placed indicated that they expected to be able to cancel orders freely subject to only an obligation to pay for the seller's major expenses such as scrapped steel. All 17 sales personnel asked reported that they often had to accept cancellations. One said, "You can't ask a man to eat paper [the firm's product] when he has no use for it." A lawyer with many large industrial clients said,

> Often businessmen do not feel they have "a contract"—rather they have "an order." They speak of "cancelling the order" rather than "breaching our contract." When I began practice I referred to order cancellations as breaches of contract, but my clients objected since they do not think of cancellation as wrong. Most clients, in heavy industry at least, believe that there is a right to cancel as part of the buyer-seller relationship. There is a widespread attitude that one can back out of any deal within some very vague limits. Lawyers are often surprised by this attitude.

Disputes are frequently settled without reference to the contract or potential or actual legal sanctions. There is a hesitancy to speak of legal rights or to threaten to sue in these negotiations. Even where the parties have a detailed and carefully planned agreement which indicates what is to happen if, say, the seller fails to deliver on time, often they will never refer to the agreement but will negotiate a solution when the problem arises apparently as if there had never been any original contract. One purchasing agent expressed a common business attitude when he said,

> if something comes up, you get the other man on the telephone and deal with the problem. You don't read legalistic contract clauses at each other if you ever want to do business again. One doesn't run to lawyers if he wants to stay in business because one must behave decently.

Or as one businessman put it, "You can settle any dispute if you keep the lawyers and accountants out of it. They just do not understand the give-and-take needed in business." All of the house counsel interviewed indicated that they are called into the dispute settlement process only after the businessmen have failed to settle matters in their own way. Two indicated that after being called in, house counsel at first will only advise the purchasing agent, sales manager or other official involved; not even the house counsel's letterhead is used on communications with the other side until all hope for a peaceful resolution is gone.

Law suits for breach of contract appear to be rare. Only five of the 12 purchasing agents had ever been involved in even a negotiation concerning a contract dispute where both sides were represented by lawyers; only two of ten sales managers had ever gone this far. None had been involved in a case that went through trial. A law firm with more than 40 lawyers and a large commercial practice handles in a year only about six trials concerned with contract problems. Less than 10 per cent of the time of this office is devoted to any type of work related to contracts disputes. Corporations big enough to do business in more than one state tend to sue and be sued in the federal courts. Yet only 2,779 out of 58,293 civil actions filed in the United States District Courts in fiscal year 1961 involved private contracts.

During the same period only 3,447 of the 61,138 civil cases filed in the principal trial courts of New York State involved private contracts. The same picture emerges from a review of appellate cases. Mentschikoff has suggested that commercial cases are not brought to the courts either in periods of business prosperity (because buyers unjustifiably reject goods only when prices drop and they can get similar goods elsewhere at less than the contract price) or in periods of deep depression (because people are unable to come to court or have insufficient assets to satisfy any judgment that might be obtained). Apparently, she adds, it is necessary to have "a kind of middle-sized depression" to bring large numbers of commercial cases to the courts. However, there is little evidence that in even "a kind of middle-sized depression" today's businessmen would use the courts to settle disputes.

At times, relatively contractual methods are used to make adjustments in ongoing transactions and to settle disputes. Demands of one side which are deemed unreasonable by the other occasionally are blocked by reference to the terms of the agreement between the parties. The legal position of the parties can influence negotiations even though legal rights or litigation are never mentioned in their discussions; it makes a difference if one is demanding what both concede to be a right or begging for a favor. Now and then a firm may threaten to turn matters over to its attorneys, threaten to sue, commence a suit or even litigate and carry an appeal to the highest court which will hear the matter. Thus, legal sanctions, while not an everyday affair, are not unknown in business.

One can conclude that while detailed planning and legal sanctions play a significant role in some exchanges between businesses, in many business exchanges their role is small.

TENTATIVE EXPLANATIONS

Two questions need to be answered: (A) How can business successfully operate exchange relationships with relatively so little attention to detailed planning or to legal sanctions, and (B) Why does business ever use contract in light of its success without it?

Why Are Relatively Non-contractual Practices so Common? In most situations contract is not needed. Often its functions are served by other devices. Most problems are avoided without resort to detailed planning or legal sanctions because usually there is little room for honest misunderstandings or good faith differences of opinion about the nature and quality of a seller's performance. Although the parties fail to cover all foreseeable contingencies, they will exercise care to see that both understand the primary obligation on each side. Either products are standardized with an accepted description or specifications are written calling for production to certain tolerances or results. Those who write and read specifications are experienced professionals who will know the customs of their industry and those of the industries with which they deal. Consequently, these customs can fill gaps in the express agreements of the parties. Finally, most products can be tested to see if they are what was ordered; typically in manufacturing industry we are not dealing with questions of taste or judgment where people can differ in good faith.

When defaults occur they are not likely to be disastrous because of techniques of risk avoidance or risk spreading. One can deal with firms of good reputation or he may be able to get some form of security to guarantee performance. One can insure against many breaches of contract where the risks justify the costs. Sellers set up reserves for bad debts on their books and can sell some of their accounts receivable. Buyers can place orders with two or more suppliers of the same item so that a default by one will not stop the buyer's assembly lines.

Moreover, contract and contract law are often thought unnecessary because there are many effective non-legal sanctions. Two norms are widely accepted. (1) Commitments are to be honored in almost all situations; one does not welsh on a deal. (2) One ought to produce a good product and stand behind it. Then, too, business units are organized to perform commitments, and internal sanctions will induce performance. For example, sales personnel must face angry customers when there has been a late or defective performance. The salesmen do not enjoy this and will put pressure on the production personnel responsible for the default. If the production personnel default too often, they will be fired. At all levels of the two business units personal relationships across the boundaries of the two organizations exert pressures for conformity to expectations. Salesmen often know purchasing agents well. The same two individuals occupying these roles may have dealt with each other from five to 25 years. Each has something to give the other. Salesmen have gossip about competitors, shortages and price increases to give purchasing agents who treat them well. Salesmen take purchasing agents to dinner, and they give purchasing agents Christmas gifts hoping to improve the chances of making a sale. The buyer's engineering staff may work with the seller's engineering staff to solve problems jointly. The seller's engineers may render great assistance, and the buyer's engineers may desire to return the favor by drafting specifications which only the seller can meet. The top executives of the two firms may know each other. They may sit together on government or trade committees. They may know each other socially and even belong to the same country club. The interrelationships may be more formal. Sellers may hold stock in corporations which are important customers; buyers may hold stock in important suppliers. Both buyer and seller may share common directors on their boards. They may share a common financial institution which has financed both units.

The final type of non-legal sanction is the most obvious. Both business units involved in the exchange desire to continue successfully in business and will avoid conduct which might interfere with attaining this goal. One is concerned with both the reaction of the other party in the particular exchange and with his own general business reputation. Obviously, the buyer gains sanctions insofar as the seller wants the particular exchange to be completed. Buyers can withhold part or all of their payments until sellers have performed to their satisfaction. If a seller has a great deal of money tied up in his performance which he must recover quickly, he will go a long way to please the buyer in order to be paid. Moreover, buyers who are dissatisfied may cancel and cause sellers to lose the cost of what they have done up to cancellation. Furthermore, sellers hope for repeat orders, and one gets few of these from unhappy customers. Some industrial buyers go so far as to formalize this sanction by issuing "report cards" rating the performance of each supplier. The supplier rating goes to the top management of the seller organization, and these men can apply internal sanctions to salesmen, production supervisors or product designers if there are too many "D's" or "F's" on the report card.

While it is generally assumed that the customer is always right, the seller may have some counterbalancing sanctions against the buyer. The seller may have obtained a large downpayment from the buyer which he will want to protect. The seller may have an exclusive process which the buyer needs. The seller may be one of the few firms which has the skill to make the item to the tolerances set by the buyer's engineers and within the time available. There are costs and delays involved in turning from a supplier one has dealt with in the past to a new supplier. Then, too, market conditions can change so that a buyer is faced with shortages of critical items. The most extreme example is the post World War II gray market conditions when sellers were rationing goods rather than selling them. Buyers must build up some reserve of good will with suppliers if they face the risk of such shortages and desire good treatment when they occur. Finally, there is reciprocity in buying and selling. A buyer cannot push a supplier too far if that supplier also buys significant quantities of the product made by the buyer.

Not only do the particular business units in a given exchange want to deal with each other again, they also want to deal with other business units in the future. And the way one behaves in a particular transaction, or a series of transactions, will color his general business reputation. Blacklisting can be formal or informal. Buyers who fail to pay their bills on time risk a bad report in credit rating services such as Dun and Bradstreet. Sellers who do not satisfy their customers become the subject of discussion in the gossip exchanged by purchasing agents and salesmen, at meetings of purchasing agents' associations and trade associations, or even at country clubs or social gatherings where members of top management meet.

The American male's habit of debating the merits of new cars carries over to industrial items. Obviously, a poor reputation does not help a firm make sales and may force it to offer great price discounts or added services to remain in business. Furthermore, the habits of unusually demanding buyers become known, and they tend to get no more than they can coerce out of suppliers who choose to deal with them. Thus often contract is not needed as there are alternatives.

Not only are contract and contract law not needed in many situations, their use may have, or may be thought to have, undesirable consequences. Detailed negotiated contracts can get in the way of creating good exchange relationships between business units. If one side insists on a detailed plan, there will be delay while letters are exchanged as the parties try to agree on what should happen if a remote and unlikely contingency occurs. In some cases they may not be able to agree at all on such matters and as a result a sale may be lost to the seller and the buyer may have to search elsewhere for an acceptable supplier. Many businessmen would react by thinking that had no one raised the series of remote and unlikely contingencies all this wasted effort could have been avoided.

Even where agreement can be reached at the negotiation stage, carefully planned arrangements may create undesirable exchange relationships between business units. Some businessmen object that in such a carefully worked out relationship one gets performance only to the letter of the contract. Such planning indicates a lack of trust and blunts the demands of friendship, turning a cooperative venture into an antagonistic horse trade. Yet the greater danger perceived by some businessmen is that one would have to perform his side of the bargain to its letter and thus lose what is called "flexibility." Businessmen may welcome a measure of vagueness in the obligations they assume so that they may negotiate matters in light of the actual circumstances.

Adjustment of exchange relationships and dispute settlement by litigation or the threat of it also has many costs. The gain anticipated from using this form of coercion often fails to outweigh these costs, which are both monetary and non-monetary. Threatening to turn matters over to an attorney may cost no more money than postage or a telephone call; yet few are so skilled in making such a threat that it will not cost some deterioration of the relationship between the firms. One businessman said that customers had better not rely on legal rights or threaten to bring a breach of contract law suit against him since he "would not be treated like a criminal" and would fight back with every means available. Clearly, actual litigation is even more costly than making threats. Lawyers demand substantial fees from larger business units. A firm's executives often will have to be transported and maintained in another city during the proceedings if, as often is the case, the trial must be held away from the home office. Top management does not travel by Greyhound and stay at the Y.M.C.A. Moreover, there will be the cost of diverting top management, engineers, and others in the organization from their normal activities. The firm may lose many days work from several key people. The non-monetary costs may be large too. A breach of contract law suit may settle a particular dispute, but such an action often results in a "divorce" ending the "marriage" between the two businesses, since a contract action is likely to carry charges with at least overtones of bad faith. Many executives, moreover, dislike the prospect of being cross-examined in public. Some executives may dislike losing control of a situation by turning the decision-making power over to lawyers. Finally, the law of contract damages may not provide an adequate remedy even if the firm wins the suit; one may get vindication but not much money.

Why Do Relatively Contractual Practices Ever Exist? Although contract is not needed and actually may have negative consequences, businessmen do make some carefully planned contracts, negotiate settlements influenced by their legal rights and commence and defend some breach of contract law suits or arbitration proceedings. In view of the findings and explanation presented to this point, one may ask why. Exchanges are carefully planned when it is thought that planning and a potential legal sanction will have more advantages than disadvantages. Such a judgment may be reached when contract planning serves the internal needs of an organization involved in a business exchange. For example, a fairly detailed contract can serve as a communication device within a large corporation. While the corporation's sales manager and house counsel may work out all the provisions with the customer, its production manager will have to make the product. He must be told what to do and how to handle at least the most obvious contingencies. Moreover, the sales manager may want to remove certain issues from future negotiation by his subordinates. If he puts the matter in the written contract, he may be able to keep his salesmen from making concessions to the customer without first consulting the sales manager. Then the sales manager may be aided in his battles with his firm's financial or engineering departments if the contract calls for certain practices which the sales manager advocates but which the other departments resist. Now the corporation is obligated to a customer to do what the sales manager wants to do; how can the financial or engineering departments insist on anything else?

Also one tends to find a judgment that the gains of contract outweigh the costs where there is a likelihood that significant problems will arise. One factor leading to this conclusion is complexity of the agreed performance over a long period. Another factor is whether or not the degree of injury in case of default is thought to be potentially great. This factor cuts two ways. First, a buyer may want to commit a seller to a detailed and legally binding contract, where the consequences of a default by the seller would seriously injure the buyer. For example, the airlines are subject to law suits from the survivors of passengers and to great adverse publicity as a result of crashes. One would expect the airlines to bargain for carefully defined and legally enforceable obligations on the part of the airframe manufacturers when they purchase aircraft. Second, a seller may want to limit his liability for a buyer's damages by a provision in their contract. For example, a manufacturer of air conditioning may deal with motels in the South and Southwest. If this equipment fails in the hot summer months, a motel may lose a great deal of business. The manufacturer may wish to avoid any liability for this type of injury to his customers and may want a contract with a clear disclaimer clause.

Similarly, one uses or threatens to use legal sanctions to settle disputes when other devices will not work and when the gains are thought to outweigh the costs. For example, perhaps the most common type of business contracts case fought all the way through to the appellate courts today is an action for an alleged wrongful termination of a dealer's franchise by a manufacturer. Since the franchise has been terminated, factors such as personal relationships and the desire for future business will have little effect; the cancellation of the franchise indicates they have already failed to maintain the relationship. Nor will a complaining dealer worry about creating a hostile relationship between himself and the manufacturer. Often the dealer has suffered a great financial loss both as to his investment in building and equipment and as to his anticipated future profits. A cancelled automobile dealer's lease on his showroom and shop will continue to run, and his tools for servicing, say, Plymouths cannot be used to service other makes of cars. Moreover, he will have no more new Plymouths to sell. Today there is some chance of winning a law suit for terminating a franchise in bad faith in many states and in the federal courts. Thus, often the dealer chooses to risk the cost of a lawyer's fee because of the chance that he may recover some compensation for his losses.

An "irrational" factor may exert some influence on the decision to use legal sanctions. The man who controls a firm may feel that he or his organization has been made to appear foolish or has been the victim of fraud or bad faith. The law suit may be seen as a vehicle "to get even" although the potential gains, as viewed by an objective observer, are outweighed by the potential costs.

The decision whether or not to use contract—whether the gain exceeds the costs—will be made by the person within the business unit with the power to make it, and it tends to make a difference who he is. People in a sales department oppose contract. Contractual negotiations are just one more hurdle in the way of a sale. Holding a customer to the letter of a contract is bad for "customer relations." Suing a customer who is not bankrupt and might order again is poor strategy. Purchasing agents and their buyers are less hostile to contracts but regard attention devoted to such matters as a waste of time. In contrast, the financial control department—the treasurer, controller or auditor—leans toward more contractual dealings. Contract is viewed by these people as an organizing tool to control operations in a large organization. It tends to define precisely and to minimize the risks to which the firm is exposed. Outside lawyers—those with many clients—may share this enthusiasm for a more contractual method of dealing. These lawyers are concerned with preventive law—avoiding any possible legal difficulty. They see many unstable and unsuccessful exchange transactions, and so they are aware of, and perhaps overly concerned with, all of the things which can go wrong. Moreover, their job of settling disputes with legal sanctions is much easier if their client has not been overly casual about transaction planning. The inside lawyer, or house counsel, is harder to classify. He is likely to have some sympathy with a more contractual method of dealing. He shares the outside lawyer's "craft urge" to see exchange transactions neat and tidy from a legal standpoint. Since he is more concerned with avoiding and settling disputes than selling goods, he is likely to be less willing to rely on a man's word as the sole sanction than is a salesman. Yet the house counsel is more a part of the organization and more aware of its goals and subject to its internal sanctions. If the potential risks are not too great, he may hesitate to suggest a more contractual procedure to the sales department. He must sell his services to the operating departments, and he must hoard what power he has, expending it on only what he sees as significant issues.

The power to decide that a more contractual method of creating relationships and settling disputes shall be used will be held by different people at different times in different organizations. In most firms the sales department and the purchasing department have a great deal of power to resist contractual procedures or to ignore them if they are formally adopted and to handle disputes their own way. Yet in larger organizations the treasurer and the controller have increasing power to demand both systems and compliance. Occasionally, the house counsel must arbitrate the conflicting positions of these departments; in giving "legal advice" he may make the business judgment necessary regarding the use of contract. At times he may ask for an opinion from an outside law firm to reinforce his own position with the outside firm's prestige.

Obviously, there are other significant variables which influence the degree that contract is used. One is the relative bargaining power or skill of the two business units. Even if the controller of a small supplier succeeds within the firm and creates a contractual system of dealing, there will be no contract if the firm's large customer prefers not to be bound to anything. Firms that supply General Motors deal as General Motors wants to do business, for the most part. Yet bargaining power is not size nor share of the market alone. Even a General Motors may need a particular supplier, at least temporarily. Furthermore, bargaining power may shift as an exchange relationship is first created and then continues. Even a giant firm can find itself bound to a small supplier once production of an essential item begins for there may not be time to turn to another supplier. Also, all of the factors discussed in this paper can be viewed as *components* of bargaining power—for example, the personal relationship between the presidents of the buyer and the seller firms may give a sales manager great power over a purchasing agent who has been instructed to give the seller "every consideration." Another variable relevant to the use of contract is the influence of third parties. The federal government, or a lender of money, may insist that a contract be made in a particular transaction or may influence the decision to assert one's legal rights under a contract.

Contract, then, often plays an important role in business, but other factors are significant. To understand the functions of contract the whole system of conducting exchanges must be explored fully. More types of business communities must be studied, contract litigation must be analyzed to see why the nonlegal sanctions fail to prevent the use of legal sanctions and all of the variables suggested in this paper must be classified more systematically.

NOTES AND QUESTIONS

1. Based on the Macaulay discussion, which would you expect to be more likely, that the farmers sue the processor or that the processor sues the manufacturer? Why?

2. Our legal system leaves decisions of this kind to the individual. The cause of action is treated as a form of private property, and its owner decides whether or not to sue or defend, how much to invest in suing or defending, what arguments to make, whether to accept a proposed settlement and drop the action, and so on. What do you think of this "private dispositive system?" Do you see its relationship to private legal ordering? Can you conceive of an alternative system?

3. What is the function of the judge in a private dispositive system? Should she intervene, where the plaintiff has failed to introduce a telling argument or the defendant has failed to claim a significant defense, and supply it?

4. One obvious set of limits on private litigation is the number and availability of courts, the size of judicial backlogs, and the cost of lawyers' services. Who decides how many courts and judges there are? What kinds of cases they have jurisdiction to hear? Who decides how many lawyers there are? How much they charge?

5. Where the cost of using the official system of civil justice is high enough, parties may choose to employ private systems of mediation, conciliation or, particularly, arbitration. Thus many contracts include arbitration clauses, which a) provide that any disputes under the contract shall be referred to arbitration; b) name or establish a procedure for selection of arbitrators (often three persons, of whom two are selected by the parties

and the third by the first two, but also frequently one person) and c) commit the parties to acceptance of the arbitration award. Should recourse to these private systems be deplored or encouraged? Why?

Chapter 19

PRIVATE ORDERING IN EGYPT

EGYPTIAN LAW OF CONTRACTS

NOTE

The Islamic nations were for many centuries among the leading trading nations of the world. The law used by pre-Islamic traders was apparently taken over into the *sharia* with only minor changes, and survived until the impetus of the West in the 19th century. In Egypt, it was then almost completely replaced by French law but is now facing the problem that any private ordering arrangements face under the pressure of bureaucratic regulation. Thus, the Egyptian contract problem presents the opportunity to examine the interplay of business practice and business law, a subtle interplay, for business interests help shape the law and business lawyers can also restructure transactions to meet the rules of almost any body of law.

A. THE ISLAMIC TRADITION

1. The Law

M. Hamid, Islamic Law of Contract or Contracts? 3 Journal of Islamic and Comparative Law, pp. 1–2, 3, 6, 7, (1969).

Islamic law knows neither a general theory of contract nor a definition of what a contract is. In the manuals of the classical jurists each contract received a separate and detailed examination.

* * *

The lack of a definition of contract is matched only by the corresponding lack of a general theory of contract. The Islamic jurists did not make any serious attempt to develop a general theory of contract. The nearest they have come to achieving that is by treating the contract sale as a prototype to which other contracts should conform. But in a regime where there are so many and varied contracts, a theory based on one contract is bound to have no more use than to provide premises for analogy. As would be expected, the exceptions easily overshadowed the theory.

The lack of a general theory of contract and the separate and individual treatment of each contract by the jurists may lead one to the conclusion that Islamic law, like Roman law, is one of contracts rather than contract. That is, in order to qualify as a contract, a transaction must fit in one of the recognized contracts. If this is true, it will logically follow that Islamic law does not recognize the principle of freedom of contract. The list of nominate contracts discussed by the jurists is closed and cannot be added to by the agreement of the parties. Those who believe that Islamic law has, to a greater or lesser extent, been influenced by Roman law, may take this superficial similitude in treatment of contracts as evidence to substantiate their claim.

It will, however, be suggested that this separate treatment of contracts is more of a reflection of the process by which Islamic law was developed than of any conscious desire to limit the sphere of contracts. It was, in particular, a necessary and inevitable by-product of the process of Islamicization—by which is meant the subjection of pre-Islamic institutions to the overriding norms of the Islamic religion—in which the jurists were engaged. This process was necessitated by the fact that Islam is regarded, not only as a religion, but as a way of life. All pre-Islamic institutions, therefore, had to be scrutinized to make sure that they conformed to the Islamic norms. The working of this process has been described by a learned writer in the following terms—"The starting-point was the review of local practice, legal and popular, in the light of the principles of conduct enshrined in the Qur'an. Institutions and activities were individually considered, then approved or rejected according to whether they measured up or fell short of these criteria." [2]

When applied to the sphere of contract law, the starting point must be the existing customary contracts of pre-Islamic Arabia. Most of what we now know as Islamic contracts were in existence in pre-Islamic Arabia. They represented the commercial and other customs and met the economic and other needs of that time. . . .

It is not here suggested that the form, incidents and contents of these contracts are necessarily the same as those of the corresponding Islamic contracts. Some or all of these aspects might have undergone some changes as a result of their subjection to the Islamic norms. But what is suggested here is that the subjection of the existing contracts to Islamic norms meant that each existing contract should be individually examined in order to erase any contradiction and to ensure conformity with Islamic norms. [11] The separate and detailed treatment accorded to each contract by the Islamic jurists is, therefore, consistent with and inherent in this process of Islamicization of contracts. Indeed, this is the only possible way in which these contracts could have been treated in view of the fact that some of the Islamic norms were general in nature and could affect not only each

2. Coulson: A history of Islamic law (Edinburgh University Press 1964) p. 38.

11. The term "Islamic norms" should not be taken to mean that there was a comprehensive set of rules derived from the Quran and Sunna which the jurists had merely to apply. In fact those two major sources offered nothing more than a few general principles. The bulk of the rules had to be worked out by the jurists themselves—through the legislative processes of consensus, analogy and preference.

contract but also different aspects of the same contract—for example, the subject matter, the price or the stipulations contained in the contract. Examples of such general norms are the blanket prohibition of usury *riba* and uncertainty *gharar* in contracts. Hardly any contract had been allowed to pass without being rigorously examined to ensure that it was not even slightly tainted with either. In their anxiety to achieve this, the economic viability of the contract may be sacrificed.

* * *

[These jurists have, however, created a] wide and useful exception in favour of economic necessity. It has already been seen that the jurists have treated some contracts as valid on the principle of preference, although by analogy, they ought to be invalid. The reason given for this departure is that the contract has been in customary use and there is need for it. This seems to be their way of saying that the strict application of Islamic norms would have rendered the contract invalid, but we are creating an exception because we acknowledge the economic necessity for the contract. In some of these contracts . . . the invalidity would have resulted from the application of the prohibition of uncertainty *gharar* in contracts.

. . . Moreover, the principle of economic necessity had, in fact, been used by later jurists to admit and give validity to contracts which came into existence at their time. The contract of sale with a right of pre-emption known as *bay 'al-wafa'* is one example. This contract probably came into existence in the fifth or sixth century after *hijrah*.[16] The prohibition of usury made it impossible to give a loan at an interest. Consequently those in need of money could not get loans, and those who had the money were reluctant to give for no consideration. There was thus a need for a contract to satisfy the economic interests of both borrower and lender, and, at the same time, to circumvent the prohibition of usury. *Bay 'al-wafa'* was the answer. The intending borrower sells his property to the lender on condition that he can have it back when he repays the price. In this way he gets a loan (the price) and the lender gets the use of the property as a consideration for the loan. When the jurists were called upon to give a ruling in this new contract, they were by no means in agreement. There were those who acknowledged the economic necessity for the contract and approved it as it is. Others were not so charitable in their approach. They argued that the contract in its present form amounts to a sale and a condition *bay' wa shart* which the Prophet prohibited. The contract was then interpreted as a mortgage and not as a sale with the consequence that the buyer (mortgagee) cannot have the use of the property as of right. The whole pur-

16. The author of Jami' al-Fisulayn (Bulaq 1300 A.H.) quotes al-Nusafi, a jurist who lived between 461–537 A.H., as saying "the sale that came into popular use *in our time* as a means of circumventing usury and is called bay 'al-wafa' . . ." vol. 1 p. 169; see also Radd al-Muhtar (Ottoman Press, Egypt 1326 A.H.) vol. 4. pp. 341–342.

pose of the contract has thereby been defeated. But the fact that many of the jurists treated the contract as valid on the grounds of economic necessity sufficiently makes the point.

It has been pointed out that some of the present Muslim jurists are of the opinion that the contracts of a loan at an interest and the contract of insurance are invalid. It must now be added that there are others who, while admitting that otherwise these contracts would be invalid, invoked the principle of economic necesssity to give validity, subject to certain limitations, to these contracts.

Joseph Schacht, An Introduction to Islamic Law, London: Oxford University Press, 1964, pp. 144–47, 153.

OBLIGATIONS IN GENERAL

1. Preliminaries. Unjustified enrichment and risk are both rejected on ethical grounds; this prohibition pervades the whole of the law, but shows its effects most clearly in the law of obligations.

* * *

3. Unjustified Enrichment (faḍl māl bilā 'iwaḍ). It is a general principle of Islamic law, based on a number of passages in the Koran, that unjustified enrichment, or "receiving a monetary advantage without giving a countervalue", is forbidden, and that he who receives it must give it to the poor as a charitable gift. This applies, for instance, to reletting a hired object for a greater sum, or to reselling a bought object, before payment has been made for it, for a higher price. Special cases are the giving and taking of interest, and other kinds of *ribā*, literally "increase", "excess". *Ribā* is defined as "a monetary advantage without a countervalue which has been stipulated in favour of one of the two contracting parties in an exchange of two monetary values". The prohibition applies to objects which can be measured or weighed and which, in addition, belong to the same species. Forbidden are both an excess in quantity and a delay in performance. If only one of these two conditions is realized (e.g. in an exchange of cloth of a certain kind for cloth of the same kind, which is not measured or weighed, or of wheat for barley, which do not belong to the same species), an excess in quantity is allowed, but a delay in performance remains forbidden. Similar rules apply to usufruct; therefore the hire of two objects, one for the other, is allowed only if they do not belong to the same species.

* * *

4. Risk (gharar, literally "hazard"). Starting from the Koranic prohibition of a certain game of hazard (*maysir*), Islamic law insists that there must be no doubt concerning the obligations undertaken by the parties to a contract. The object of the contract, in particular, must be determined (*ma'lūm*, "known"; opposite *majhūl*, "unknown"). This requirement is particularly strict as regards objects which can be measured or weighed, which are subject to the prohibition of *ribā*; no undetermined quantity (*juzāf*) is permissible here, not even if the price of a unit of weight or measure be stated. For the same reason it is forbidden to sell dates which are still unripe, to be delivered when they have ripened, because it is unknown whether they will ripen at all. The price, too, and the countervalue in general must be determined; the kind of coins in which payment is to be made must be mentioned; but it is permissible to sell for a countervalue which is present and is shown, even though it be not defined. Similar rules apply to the values exchanged in other contracts, e.g. the usufruct and the rent in a contract of lease. The same is true of any stipulated term, but a distinction is made according to the nature of the contract, and vague expressions which are rejected in the *salam* contract are admitted in the contract of suretyship. From this requirement and from the prohibition of *ribā* together derives the requirement in the case of goods which are subject to the rules concerning *ribā*, that possession must be taken and their weight or measure checked before they are resold. These rules are aimed at all kinds of gambling, one of the great passions of the ancient Arabs, and here, too, the old sources of Islamic law enable us to discern some of the aleatory transactions in which this passion found expression in the early Islamic period (the so-called *mulāmasa*, *munābadha*, and *ilkā' bil-ḥajar*). There are only two exceptions from the general prohibition of aleatory transactions: (1) in favour of prizes for the winner or winners of horse races, on account of their importance as a training for the holy war, and (2) for the winner or winners of competitions concerning knowledge of Islamic law.

* * *

A special kind of sale, although regarded as a separate kind of contract, is the *salam*, the ordering of goods to be delivered later for a price paid immediately. The term *ra's al-māl*, "capital", which is used to denote the price in this contract, shows the economic meaning of the transaction: the financing of the business of a small trader or artisan by his clients. The object of the *salam* is mostly fungible things, but it cannot be gold or silver. Because of its closeness to the subject of the prohibition of *ribā*, the contract of *salam* has been carefully worked out and is subject to numerous special rules. Its counterpart, delayed payment (*nasī'a*, the delay) for goods delivered immediately, is also possible, but this kind of sale plays a minor part in Islamic law. The name "sale on credit" (*bay' al-'ina*) is given *a potiori* to an evasion of the prohibition of *ribā* which is based on this transaction and is reprehensible; for instance, *A* (the creditor) sells to *B* (the debtor) some object for the sum of capital and interest, payable at some future date, and immediately afterwards buys the same object back for the capital payable at once. This amounts to an unsecured loan.

* * *

D. Hill and Abubakar Abbas, "Comparative Survey of the Islamic Law and the Common Law Relating to the Sale of Goods," 2 Journal of Islamic and Comparative Law 88, pp. 90, 91, 93–94 (1968).

Under Islamic law contracts for the sale of goods are divided into two classes. Firstly, there is the common contract of sale, which is equally applicable to other forms of property, called *Bai*, and secondly there is the *Sallam* contract, which is a contract providing for the future delivery of goods. No such distinction is found at Common Law, and the variations in the rules of Islamic law in relation to the *Sallam* contract will be dealt with as they arise in relation to the different aspects of the contract for the sale of goods.

In the case of a *Sallam* sale, although the essence of the contract is really an exchange of one commodity for another to be delivered at a later date, if it is to be related to the sale of goods as defined at Common law, instead of to the contract of barter, payment will be in the form of a monetary price, which must either be an immediate payment, or else within a period of three days, which may be provided for in the contract. The jurists are at variance as to whether this period can be extended though. The *Sallam* contract must be distinguished from *Mutuum*, or the loan for use of goods. In other words, if repayment is to be in the form of similar goods this would not be a *Sallam* contract.

* * *

Under Islamic law no article can be sold which is not capable of being separated from its immediate situation without causing injury to it. In other words it is not possible to effect a contract for the sale of part of a specified article. Neither can there be a valid contract where it is not possible to ascertain with certainty the existence of the subjectmatter or the correct quality of the goods. In other words anything can be sold providing it can be precisely ascertained. However, this does not mean that the subjectmatter of a contract cannot be for future goods as is possible at Common law. Under the latter a contract can be for the sale of "existing goods, owned or possessed by the seller, or goods to be manufactured or acquired by the seller after the making of the contract of sale," which are called "future" goods. A contract to sell future goods will be an "agreement to sell," as property cannot be immediately transferred. Under Islamic law, such a sale would take the form of a *Sallam* contract. Such a contract is valid in respect of any article or goods which can be subjected to a general description as to quality, for which the quantity can be ascertained, or which can be specifically defined.

* * *

Merely because goods are of a perishable nature does not prevent them being the subject of a *Sallam* sale, although there are certain restrictions in the case of fish and fleshmeat.

It is interesting to note that future goods which are to be manufactured, can be the subject of a *Sallam* sale. In other words although it is considered as a contract of workmanship, for this purpose the future goods are considered as capable of being the subject of a contract of sale, that is they are given a fictional existence. Likewise there is nothing to prevent a seller from supplying goods obtained from a third party as they will not be considered as ascertained until the buyer has approved them, and for this reason the seller under the *Sallam* can validly dispose of them to a third party before the buyer has approved of them.

However a *Sallam* contract can only be made in respect of future goods to be supplied by a manufacturer in respect of those goods which it is customary to bespeak. A *Sallam* is forbidden though in respect of produce of a certain place, as if an accident happens, delivery may become impracticable. Some jurists have considered such a sale to be lawful provided the quality of the goods has been defined.

* * *

P. Nicholas Kourides (Student Note), "The Influence of Islamic Law on Contemporary Middle Eastern Legal Systems: The Formation and Binding Force of Contracts," 9 Columbia Journal of Transnational Law 384, pp. 394–395 (1970).

III. THEORY OF CONTRACTS IN ISLAMIC LAW

The rules which bind Muslims to their obligations and covenants derive in the first instance from the *Quran* and the *sunnah*.

A. Pertinent References to the Principal Sources of Islamic Law

1. The Quran

(1) O ye who believe! Fulfil all obligations.

It is unanimously agreed that this classic verse is applicable to all obligations, contracts, and covenants undertaken between man and man and between man and God. Yusuf Ali notes that there are three kinds of obligations. First, there are divine obligations that arise out of a spiritual nature in our relationship with God. Because God has created us, made nature responsive to our needs, and sent us guidance through messengers and teachers, we are obliged to fulfill our spiritual covenant with Him. Second, in our mundane existence, we enter into mutual obligations with our fellow man in the form of promises, commercial and social contracts, and marriage contracts. We must be faithful in these relations. Third, there is a nebulous area of tacit obligations. We must remain true, loyal, righteous, and faithful in all our actions. It is man's obligation to morally uphold society's framework and be the host, the companion, and the helper of all men.

(2) . . . fulfil (every) engagement, for (every) engagement will be enquired into (on the Day of Reckoning).

These words are general and may be interpreted as applying to any human contract.

(3) But it is righteousness . . . to fulfil the contracts which ye have made; and to be firm and patient, in pain (or suffering) and adversity, and throughout all periods of panic. Such are the people of truth, the God-fearing.

The idea of righteousness and duty in one's obligations is a prevalent and recurrent theme.

(4) Fulfil the covenant of God when ye have entered into it, and break not your oaths after ye have confirmed them; indeed ye have made God your surety . . . and be not like a woman who breaks into untwisted strands the yarn which she has spun, after it has become strong. Nor take your oaths to practise deception between yourselves, lest one party should be more numerous than another . . . .

And take not your oaths, to practise deception between yourselves . . . ye may have to taste the evil (consequences) of having hindered (men) from the Path of God, and a mighty wrath descend on you.

Nor sell the covenant of God for a miserable price: for with God is (a prize) far better for you, if ye only knew.

Louis Gardet, La Cité Musulmane; Vie Sociale et Politique (4th Ed.), Paris: Librairie Philosophique J. Vrin (1976), p. 96.

. . . a fundamental principle in Islam: absolute necessity, as long as it lasts, dispenses with the application of the law.

[In footnote referenced to the above statement]:

A forbidden thing (*haram*) becomes permissible (*mubah*), licit, when there is necessity. The scriptural text (*nass*) on which the doctors generally rely is that of the Quran, 5, 3, where, following prescriptions governing clean and unclean meats, there is added: "Should anyone be constrained by famine to eat [what is forbidden], not intending to commit sin . . . certainly Allah is forgiving and merciful." By *qiyas* (reasoning by analogy), this dispensation stated in the Quran is extended to all cases of necessity. This is possible under the rules of traditional exegesis, because the text in question explicitly formulates the factual criterion, the motive (*illa*) for the dispensation, and the new juridical status that results, and this motive is precisely the state of necessity.

QUESTIONS

1. Why did traditional law reject the loan at interest? The insurance contract?

2. You will recall the general statement of the food processing problem. Under traditional Islamic law, which of the following contracts would have been valid? How could the transactions have been structured to make each valid?

   (a) The contract between the company and the manufacturer?

   (b) The contracts between the company and the local farmers?

   (c) The contract between the company and the national distributor?

3. Would the resulting arrangement be economically rational?

4. As best you can estimate on the basis of the rather limited information on Islamic impossibility doctrine given above, what would happen to each of the contracts of question 2 upon the government's denial of the import license? Where would the losses fall?

5. The *sharia's* aversion to risk/gambling (*gharar*) frequently avoids the impossibility problem by prohibiting entry into a category of contracts that would be impossible to perform. What conclusions might you draw about the medieval Islamic view of economic relations?

6. What sort of an economy can operate under the *sharia* restrictions? (Be careful with this question; even without the fictions about to be discussed, there is room for very substantial economic activity.)

2. The Real World

Abraham L. Udovitch, Partnership and Profit in Medieval Islam, Princeton, New Jersey: Princeton University Press, 1970, pp. 11, 63, 170–171, 175, 196–197.

The restrictions in the area of trade and exchange, as well as in other areas of life, placed certain aspects of practice on an inevitable collision course with legal theory. This situation gave rise to a special branch of legal writings, the *hiyal* (legal devices) literature, in which the lawyers attempted to narrow down the area in which actions would be in violation of the law by making them conform to the law formally while in reality circumventing it.

"They (*hiyal*) can be described in short as the use of legal means for achieving extra-legal ends—ends that could not be achieved directly with the means provided by the *shari'ah*, whether or not such ends might in themsleves be illegal. The 'legal devices' enabled persons who would otherwise have had to break the law, or under the pressure of circumstances would have had to act against its provisions, to arrive at the desired result while actually conforming to the letter of the law." Thus, for example, a number of devices were developed to circumvent the taking or giving of interest, and others to permit capital in the form of commodities to serve as investments in partnership and *commenda* contracts.

* * *

It is in connection with a specific prohibition that the efficacy of legal fictions (*ḥiyal*) can be observed. To paraphrase a proverb, Islamic law in this case provides the remedy together with the ailment; concurrent with the prohibition against goods as a valid form of partnership investment, the legal sources outline a method of its circumvention.

I said: "What is your opinion of two men wishing to form a partnership with their possessions, one of whom has merchandise worth five thousand dirhams and the other merchandise worth one thousand dirhams?" He said: "Partnership in goods is not permissible." I said: "What type of legal fiction can they employ which would make them partners in the merchandise they possess?" He said: "Let the owner of the merchandise worth five thousand dirhams purchase five-sixths of his colleague's merchandise with one-sixth of his own. If they do this, they will be partners in accordance with their shares in the investment; the one whose merchandise is worth one thousand dirhams becomes a one-sixth owner of the combined investment, and his colleague becomes an owner of five-sixths of it."

This passage is from Shaybānī's treatise specifically devoted to legal fictions. In later Ḥanafī literature, this particular method of circumvention is incorporated into the very body of the legal codes

. . . .

[*New Devices—The Commenda.*] In the medieval period, the partnership and *commenda* contracts were the two basic legal instruments for combining financial and human resources for the purposes of trade. This holds true for the medieval West as it does for the medieval Muslim world. In Islamic law and in Western commercial practice these two institutions were the chief methods for pooling capital and bringing together investors and managers. Having discussed partnership in preceding chapters, we will now focus our attention on the *commenda*.

The *commenda* is an arrangement in which an investor or group of investors entrusts capital or merchandise to an agent-manager, who is to trade with it and then return to the investor(s) the principal and a previously agreed-upon share of the profits. As a reward for his labor, the agent receives the remaining share of the profits. Any loss resulting from the exigencies of travel or from an unsuccessful business venture is borne exclusively by the investor(s); the agent is in no way liable for a loss of this nature, losing only his expended time and effort.[2]

2. This paragraph describes a unilateral *commenda*, the simplest, paradigmatic form of the contract, i.e., a *com-menda* in which the entire capital comes from the investor's side, and none from the agent. It is possible for the invest-

The *commenda* combined the advantages of a loan with those of a partnership; and while containing elements characteristic of both, it cannot be strictly classified in either category. In all Islamic legal writings, it is treated as a distinct and independent contract with a separate section or book (*kitāb*) devoted to it. As in partnership, profits and risks are shared by both parties, the investor risking capital, the agent his time and effort. However, in the *commenda* no social capital is formed, and the investor does not become directly or jointly liable with the agent in transactions with third parties; indeed, third parties need not ever be aware of the investor's existence. As in a loan, the *commenda* generally entailed no liability for the investor beyond the sum of money or quantity of commodities handed over to the agent; and in the event of its successful completion, the agent returned the capital plus a share of the profits (the latter, corresponding to the interest in an interest-bearing loan).

* * *

It appears very likely that the *commenda* was an institution indigenous to the Arabian peninsula which developed in the context of the pre-Islamic Arabian caravan trade. With the Arab conquests, it spread to the Near East, North Africa, and ultimately to Southern Europe. The *commenda* was the subject of lengthy and detailed discussion in the earliest Islamic legal compendia (late eighth century). Its legal treatment in these early treatises bears the hallmark of long experience with the *commenda* as an established commercial institution.

* * *

As in the case of partnership, the law justifies the licitness of the *commenda* contract on the religious grounds of traditional practice (*sunna*), the consensus of the community (*ijmā ʿ*) and, more interestingly, on the practical grounds of its economic function in society. After quoting a series of traditions describing the *commenda's* use in trade by the Prophet and his companions, Sarakhsī adds that it is also allowed:

> Because people have a need for this contract. For the owner of
> capital may not find his way to profitable trading activity, and the
> person who can find his way to such activity, may not have the

ing function to overlap and embrace the agent as well. In a bilateral *commenda*, part of the capital is furnished by the agent. (Re: these two types, cf. Lopez and Raymond, *Medieval Trade in the Mediterranean World*, p. 175.) The agent's contribution is, in a sense, not really part of the *commenda*, and is not governed by its rules, since the agent enjoys the total profit from his share. Its chief importance within the *commenda* is that the willingness of the investor to conclude the contract may be contingent on the agent's providing some capital as well. In view of the fact that the investor receives no direct financial benefit from imposing such a condition, the rationale behind it was probably less direct; e.g., the investor might calculate that a larger total sum in the venture would increase the opportunities of profitable trading activities, or he might feel that the agent's direct financial stake in the transactions would make him at once more cautious and more enterprising. Cf. below for a discussion of the problems involved in a bilateral *commenda*.

capital. And profit cannot be attained except by means of both of these, that is, capital and trading activity. By permitting this contract, the goal of both parties is attained.

* * *

. . . Suggested formulae for *commenda* contracts are given by Shaybānī in the *Aṣl*, and one is also found in Ṭaḥāwī's *Kitāb ash-shurūṭ aṣ-ṣaghīr*. A translation of Shāybanī's formulae follows:

If a man entrusts another with capital in the form of a *commenda* on the basis of half profit, and the agent wishes to draw up a document as proof against the investor containing the conditions of the *commenda*, and setting forth his portion of the profit, he (the notary) writes: This is a document in favor of *A* son of *B* drawn up on the part of *X* son of *Y* which says: "I have handed over to you such and such a number of dirhams of good weight in the form of a *commenda* on the condition that you use them to buy and sell for cash and credit in all categories of trade and in other related matters, and that you act in these matters according to your judgment. And whatsoever God, may He be exalted, grants, half of it is mine, and half of it is yours for your work. I have handed this money over to you and you have taken possession of it from me, and it amounts to such and such, in the month _____ of the year _____; it is in your possession according to what we have stated in this our document concerning this *commenda*." Witnessed _____.

And if the investor wishes to have a document drawn up as proof against the agent concerning the *commenda*, he (the notary) writes: This is a document in favor of *X* son of *Y* drawn up by *A* son of *B*, that says: "You have handed over to me such and such a number of dirhams of good weight as a *commenda* on the condition that I use them to buy and sell on cash and credit in all aspects of trade, and in other related matters, and that I act in all these matters according to my judgment. And whatsoever God, may He be exalted, grants, half is yours and half is mine for my work in it. You have handed over this money to me, and I have taken possession of it from you, and it amounts to such and such, in the month _____ of the year _____; and it is in my possession according to what we have stated in this our contract of this *commenda*." Witnessed _____.

Ann Elizabeth Mayer, Islamic Law and Banking in the Middle East Today, Middle East Executive Reports, p. 2, ff (October 1979).

What accounts for this sudden upsurge in Islamic banking after so many years when the Middle East seemed reconciled to banking practices along Western lines? In part this phenomenon can be traced to the growing influence of the oil rich states of the region, which are coincidentally ones where Muslim scholars tend to take a conservative approach when interpreting the requirements of the

Shari'a. In many other areas of the Middle East liberal interpretations of the verses of the Quran affecting banking have taken hold. Some prominent Muslim scholars have taken the position that the Quran's prohibition of *riba* (literally "excess") affects only exploitative or exorbitant interest charges. In the Arabian peninsula Muslim scholars have tended to stick to a traditional interpretation that the Quranic verses require the elimination of interest in any form whatsoever.

In the past this traditional interpretation has not always inhibited the charging of interest since the view was widely held that the legality of transactions in the Shari'a should be judged on the basis of form rather than substance. So, it used to be possible to circumvent the prohibition of interest simply by disguising interest charges as other, legitimate charges. For example, interest charges could be recouped if labelled "service charges," since the Shari'a allows one to charge for services rendered. However, this kind of formalistic thinking is no longer popular and is also disapproved of in the Hanbali school which prevails in much of Arabia, whence come many of today's most prominent advocates of Islamic banking. According to the theory of Islamic banking that seems to be gaining ground at the moment, all charges that are in substance interest charges are forbidden. (Genuine service charges remain, of course, licit.)

* * *

Profit and Loss Sharing

Despite the lack of consensus on the rules of Islamic banking, the new banks do share the view that fixed interest charges both on deposits and loans are forbidden. Any increment to capital must be "earned" in the sense that it is the result of the capital being put to work in some potentially productive way. Thus, one cannot collect interest at a fixed rate on a loan, but one is entitled to a return on loaned capital where it has been provided to an entrepreneur on the basis that the lender will receive a proportionate share in the profits of the enterprise. Because the loaned capital is productively employed and the lender is sharing in the risks of the enterprise, any profit that he makes is "earned." Of course, since he also bears the risk of losses, he may be unable under Shari'a principles to recover even his initial capital. Similarly, a bank depositor is not entitled to any fixed return on his deposit, but he may receive any return from investments for which he allows the bank to employ his deposit—although he also subjects himself to the risk of any losses incurred in such investments. Thus, arrangements akin to partnerships and profit sharing emerge as central features of the new Islamic banking operations.

Many of the new Islamic banking arrangements draw their inspiration from the medieval Islamic institution of the *mudaraba*, in which an investor supplied capital to an agent/manager in return for a share in the profits resulting from the investment. If losses were incurred, the agent/manager was under normal circumstances not liable to the investor, but he was entitled to a share in any profits on the grounds that he had earned them by his contribution of effort just as the investor had earned his by his contribution of risk capital. Today, a depositor may give an Islamic bank funds to invest or an Islamic bank may lend money to an entrepreneur using the *mudaraba* model for sharing profits.

Of course, the *mudaraba* model is ill-suited for the many situations where capital is borrowed or deposited for purposes other than investments in potentially profitable enterprises. Partnership and profit sharing arrangements hardly seem applicable to demand deposits, savings deposits, short term loans, consumer credit, and the like. In this connection the idealistic strain in the new theories of Islamic banking becomes manifest; it is assumed that bank depositors will be willing to place their funds in accounts that do not earn interest and that interest free loans will be made available as required. Because Islamic banking is in such an early stage of development, these assumptions have not yet been fully tested. Many of the new banks' customers have apparently been eager to put their funds in non-interest bearing deposits, but are these the pious few or are they representative of a large body of Muslims ready to eschew interest and deposit their capital in banks that promote the values of their religion?

There is a marked difference among the proponents of Islamic banking on the question of whether supplying interest free loans for unprofitable uses should be primarily a function of Islamic banks or of government agencies specially set up for that purpose. To some extent the banks can get compensation for extending credit where no return is possible using the Islamic profit sharing schemes by charging service fees and requiring that such loans be secured, and these practices are being resorted to in some cases.

* * *

NOTE

Note that *mudaraba* is the Arabic equivalent of the latin *commenda*. For an example of the theological controversy surrounding the *riba* issue, see Ziauddin Ahmad, The Qur'anic Theory of Riba, XX–XXII The Islamic Quarterly 3, (1978) and for information on other nation's approaches to developing an Islamic banking system, see M. Aftab, Profit-and-loss—a new Islamic concept, Far Eastern Economic Review, p. 100, March 27, 1981, and Salamat Ali, Crying Out for a Model, Far Eastern Economic Review, p. 82 (June 12, 1981). Historically, there may also have been reliance on a Christian and Jewish banking class. Louis Gardet, La Cité Musulmane; Vie Sociale et Politique (4th ed.), Paris: Librairie Philosophique J. Vrin, 1976, pp. 83, 219.

Egypt has not itself moved toward any of these new banking concepts. As noted in the introductory chapter, however, a few courts are interpreting the new 1980 constitutional amendment as incorporating the traditional *riba* principles and thereby making interest unconstitutional. Some Egyptian law firms are issuing qualified opinion letters to foreign lenders concerned about the legal status of interest payments.

QUESTIONS

1. Can you work out a way to use the *commenda* to structure the transaction between the farmer, the distributor, the company, and the machine importer? How might this structure affect the allocation of the loss?

2. What economic effects might you expect from a wider application of *sharia* principles to banking?

B. MODERNIZATION

1. The Economic and Legal Context of the First Civil Codes

Ahmed Abdel-Rahim Mustafa, The Breakdown of the Monopoly System in Egypt after 1840 in P. Holt, Political and Social Change in Modern Egypt, London: Oxford University Press, 1968, pp. 291–293, 301, 303–304.

The reign of Muḥammad ‘Alī marks the end of Egypt's isolation and its integration into the world economy. It witnessed the beginnings of the shift away from closed to open economy, and was characterized by the state's control of the greater part of economic activities.

Having destroyed the most formidable of his political opponents in 1811, the *vali* began to lay the foundations of a monopoly system, which in due time comprised all the economic activities of Egypt. He laid his hands on most of the lands of the country, and controlled both its commerce and industry. The lands were sequestrated and then given to the *vali*'s sons, relatives, and officers, by no law but his own pleasure . . ..

Commerce, according to that system, functioned in two principal ways: by the system of *appaltos* (farms), and by government monopoly. Trade was conducted in the manner most profitable to the *vali*. He issued *fermans* ordering the sale of his commodities to merchants with whom he chose to deal. He also tried to keep the prices high by all the means at his disposal. The result was that all commerce among the native traders came to end . . ..

Muḥammad ‘Alī drew large profits from these monopolies, which became, indeed, the keystone of his financial policy, and the means of equipping his army and navy, and paying for his military operations. As long as the monopoly system lasted, he was, practically speaking, the sole exporter of the country; and nineteen-twentieths of the export trade passed through his hands. But he had not the same control over imports as over exports, for an Imperial decree of 1820 came to remind him that by international convention with the Porte, foreign merchants had the right to introduce their goods for sale in all parts of the Ottoman dominions on a payment of an import duty of 3 per cent.

* * *

This monopolistic system, however, was developed at a time when free trade began to gain momentum in western Europe. Increased production in Britain had created a need for greater trading opportunities, and led the British government to examine trading conditions throughout the world with a view to revising existing treaties, and obtaining conditions more favourable to British trade.

The Porte had other reasons which induced it to adhere to the British inclination. The sultan intended to destroy Muḥammad ʿAlī's greatest source of revenue, thus undermining his ability to maintain an army which might threaten Ottoman sovereignty over Egypt and her possessions. The Porte offered customs concessions and exemptions to European states, having in view to lay impediments in the way of the *vali* and to weaken his relations with the great powers. In 1834, for example, it issued a *ferman* declaring the end of the government monopolies in Syria; and on 16 August 1838 the Anglo-Turkish Convention, or the Treaty of Balta Liman, was signed, aiming primarily at the destruction of the monopolistic practices in the Ottoman Empire. Its main stipulations were as follows:

   i. The free exchange of products;

   ii. British subjects were offered the status of the most favoured nation, and enjoyed all privileges conferred on the subjects of other countries;

   iii. The duties on imports were fixed at 3 per cent. with an additional 2 per cent. on retail; and additional taxes on imports were abrogated;

   iv. Export duties were fixed at 12 per cent., of which 3 per cent. were paid by foreign exporters.

* * *

Under ʿAbbās many changes took place, and affected Egyptian commerce and foreign relations. For many years, there had been a regulation, first promulgated by Muḥammad ʿAlī, that no contract for the purchase of produce from the *fallāḥīn* by payment in anticipation should be held valid; and with at least the tacit consent of the consuls-general that regulation was rigorously acted on. At first it was the subject of some complaint on the part of petty traders and agents, who were in the habit of visiting the provinces to buy up small parcels of produce which they subsequently disposed of in the markets of Cairo and Alexandria. In later times no such complaints were made, and it was generally represented that under the more easy rule of ʿAbbās, the law, though still existing, had been designedly left in abeyance. This, in some districts, was the case with the cognizance of the local governors; and there was also a system of evasion which was very generally and successfully adopted. The person who made advances to the *fallāḥīn* for produce which was not yet harvested, took from the cultivator, instead of a contract in the ordinary form, a money bond for a sum that included not only the cash which he had advanced, but such further sum as would, by his calculation, meet the market price of the article at the expected time of delivery. There was a verbal understanding between the parties; and when the *fallāḥ* delivered the produce, the merchant's agent acquitted the former of his money engagement. If the cultivator failed to deliver the produce, the local tribunal could be called on to enforce the money bond, in the amount of which a large profit had already been included. This appeared to be an irregular but safe proceeding; and it was found to be generally effectual for the protection of the parties who were willing to make advances for cultivators.

* * *

The *vali*'s attitude towards the Greeks [merchants] was connected with his general internal policy. The property inherited by the sons of Muḥammad ʻAlī and Ibrāhīm consisted of *chifliks*, that is the former property of the Mamluks, and of *ʻuhdas*. The *chifliks* were secured by *ferman*, and paid no tax to the government. ʻAbbās did not take them away directly; but as he was bent upon ruining their holders, he effected his purpose in the following manner. The governors of the provinces took care that the proprietor should not get money to carry on the cultivation; the *fallāḥīn* finding the land uncultivated, entered upon it, and cultivated it on their own account. By law they were required to pay the proprietor an amount equal to the land-tax; but the governors were instructed not to enforce the proprietor's demands and consequently he derived no income from it whatever, thus soon being driven to abandon it. Ibrāhīm left upwards of seventy villages held as *ʻuhdas* which were in great part, if not altogether, taken from his sons. The holder of the *ʻuhda* advanced capital, and carried on all such cultivation as sugar and cotton, which required considerable outlay. The wealthy shaykhs, or headmen, in the villages played an equally important part in the cultivation of their districts. They were rooted out in great measure; and the government, by reducing them to debt, was able to seize their considerable funds. In lands thus deprived of the services of the capitalists, while the state did nothing to fill the vacuum, the description of cultivation which gave the best return degenerated. Where the land was of inferior quality, the *vali* did not resume it, and the *fallāḥīn*, deprived of native capitalists, looked for assistance to the agents of the mercantile houses, who had customarily made advances on the security of the crops. The *vali*, who was most anxious to cut off this resource, revived a circular originally issued by Muḥammad ʻAlī prohibiting the sale of unripe crops. He in fact dreaded these agents, who could encourage the *fallāḥīn* not to deal with the agents of the government, and who could invoke the Capitulations in defending themselves against his harshness.

On his death, 'Abbās left the public finances charged with an internal debt which amounted to a hundred million francs, and the coffers of the state were completely empty.

NOTE

As you will recall from the introductory chapter, it was Egypt's bankruptcy that led to British intervention and indirectly to adoption of the French-style civil code in 1883 and the creation of the mixed tribunals, which applied their own, somewhat different, French-style civil code.

QUESTIONS

1. How was Egypt able to exist with Western penetration and a body of traditional law through much of the 19th century?

2. Did Ali's prohibition of the sale of unripe crops go beyond the requirements of the *sharia*?

3. Would you, as a poor Egyptian's lawyer (which may, admittedly, be a contradiction in terms) have argued for or against including the traditional uncertainty (*gharar*) doctrines in the 1883 Code? As a rich Egyptian's lawyer? As a Westerner's lawyer? In fact, the Code restated those doctrines prohibiting the sale of the fruit of a tree before the fruit has budded and of a crop that has not yet come up. Arts. 330 and 331. See Abd-el-Razzak Ah. El Sanhoury, Le Droit Musulman comme Elément de Refont du Code Civil Egyptien, Introduction A L'étude Du Droit Comparé, Recueil D'études en L'Honneur d'Edouard Lambert, vol. 2, Paris: Librairie de la Société Anonyme due Recueil Sirey, 1938, pp. 621, 626. The explanation is perhaps contained in the following excerpt.

Gabriel Baer, A History of Landownership in Modern Egypt, 1800–1950, London: Oxford University Press, 1962, pp. 34–35.

Another reason for the increase in loans and foreclosures was the legal sanction given to the acquisition of land by foreigners and the establishment of Mixed Courts in 1875, which brought about the introduction of mortgages as known in the West. Previously, as Ottoman Law did not recognize mortgages as we know them, the practice was to make a "conditional sale" to the lender (*vente à réméré, bai' bi-l-wafā'*). The "sale" is nullified as soon as the debt is redeemed, while in the meantime the creditor generally "leases" the land to his debtor. Occasionally another system was used, *rahn ḥiyāzī or bai' bi-l-istighlāl* (*antichrèse*, and in Egypt, *ghārūqa*), whereby a debtor landowner transferred part of his plot, and the right to cultivate it, as security on a loan until redemption.

Except in special cases Ottoman law did not provide for dispossession without an owner's permission. But the Mixed Courts empowered creditors (foreigners in the main) to foreclose on land belonging to indebted fellahs. To quote the Dufferin Report:

The Egyptian peasants maintain that in former days the creditor was not armed with the power of foreclosing and expropriating the debtor from his holding, nor under Mahommedan law could the case go against him by default; but in the same way as the introduction into India of British codes invested the creditor with new powers, so in Egypt the International Tribunals have, on the one hand, stimulated the fellah's borrowing instincts by constituting his holding a legal security, and on the other, they have armed the mortgagee with far too ready and extensive powers of selling up the encumbered owner.

Fellah indebtedness started to become a problem at the beginning of Ismā'īl's reign, in the early 1860's. The cotton boom led many fellahs to increase their crops on the basis of loans, principally from Greek and other Levantine traders, although West Europeans, for instance those who set up ginneries in the villages, also advanced credit. The end of the boom and the coincidental rise in taxes caused widespread bankruptcies among fellahs, and many sales of land.

4. Is it wise for the government to restrict a farmer's ability to mortgage his property? Do you think a 19th century Egyptian scholar would have analyzed this question the same way?

5. As a twentieth century Egyptian, how would you feel about the 1883 code?

2. The Drafting of the 1949 Civil Code

Farhat Ziadeh, Lawyers, The Rule of Law and Liberalism in Modern Egypt, Stanford: Hoover Institute Publications, 1968, pp. 135–146.

. . . The reform of the civil code evoked, surprisingly enough, almost as much discussion and heated debate as the reform of the *waqf* system. It might seem that this code, patterned after the French civil code and set forth in 1883, would have been so deeply entrenched in both theory and practice that when the time came for its reform there would be little likelihood of a move for its replacement by any completely new code, let alone one based on Islamic law. The civil law, unlike the law of personal status, was not even remotely connected with religion, so that no religious motives were involved; moreover, as early as 1926 Turkey had found its civil code based on Islamic law (the Majallah) to be unworkable and had replaced it by the Swiss code. Hence it is surprising that there would be a proposal at this date to base the economic life of the country upon medieval legal precepts innocent of any adjustment to modern needs. However, several circumstances combined to make this proposal into a serious challenge to those secular lawyers who wanted a code based partly on Islamic law, but with its major provisions derived from the previous code and other European models.

The very existence in Cairo of al-Azhar University, the guardian of Muslim learning, seemed to impose on Egypt the moral duty of championing Islamic matters. Some considered it futile for al-Azhar and the Egyptian University to continue to teach the *shari'ah* while it was being largely ignored in formulating the country's codes. Moreover, the detailed formulation of *shari'ah* rules by medieval jurists was, in nationalist views, a manifestation of the "Arab genius" which should be used in the rejuvenation of the entire Arab world and the unification of its laws. The current aura of national pride caused even the secular lawyers to sing the glory of the *shari'ah*. Following the early researches of Western orientalists in the *shari'ah*, many law students educated in French universities had written their theses on some aspect of Islamic law and invariably pointed out its excellence in comparison even with modern systems. The interest of these scholars persuaded the International Congress of Comparative Law in 1938 to declare the *shari'ah* as one of the independent sources for the study of comparative law. The Egyptian delegation at the Washington conference, held in April, 1945, to consider the constitution of the Permanent Court of International Justice, availed themselves of this opportunity to press for the appointment of a judge who represented the *shari'ah* (Islamic countries) at this court, a demand which resulted in the appointment of 'Abd al-Ḥamīd Badawi to that august office. Under these circumstances it seemed somewhat incongruous that the *shari'ah*, which was being respected abroad, should be ignored at home. An additional factor was that during the 1930s and 1940s, when the reform of the civil code was being actively pursued, the society known as the Muslim Brotherhood had gained strength among all segments of the population, including lawyers and judges. One of its fundamental tenets was that all laws should be derived from, or at least be consonant with, the Koran, and that it was useless to debate the reform of the civil code as long as this principle had not been agreed upon. In other words, the brotherhood wanted a code based on the *shari'ah*.

* * *

Al-Sanhūri proposed the appointment of a committee to codify the entire field of civil law, including personal status. Personal-status law was to be based on the *shari'ah* but to be so designed as to be suitable for non-Muslims as well. The other provisions of the code, those dealing with obligations, were to be derived from the jurisprudence of the Egyptian courts, from the modern codes of other countries, and from the *shari'ah*. By "jurisprudence of the Egyptian courts" al-Sanhūri meant those aspects of the law which had been neglected by the old code and which the courts had developed in their decisions, such as collective ownership, easements, third-party interests in contracts, and stipulations for penal damages. From the *shari'ah*, which he characterized as "one of the superior systems of law in the world," he proposed taking not only those provisions which had been adopted by the old code and the principles accepted by the courts as forming a part of the law, but also many new provisions relating both to general principles and to specifics. This interest in the *shari'ah* was not merely a reflection of the demands of conservative elements for basing the new code exclusively on the *shari'ah;* al-Sanhūri's own works demonstrate that it was, rather, a genuine effort to incorporate in the body of law as much as was feasible of a great heritage.

The utilization of the *shari'ah* as only a supplement to other sources was unacceptable to the traditional groups, particularly those trained in *shari'ah* law. It was barely two months after the publication of al-Sanhūri's article and one month after the appointment of the committee to revise the code that Shaykh Muḥammad Sulaymān, a judge in the supreme *shari'ah* court, called, in a public lecture delivered on March 31, 1936, for making the *shari'ah* the sole basis of the new civil code. This lecture must have had considerable impact in view of the wide circulation and comments in the press. Sulaymān, after a long introduction which endeavored to show that the *shari'ah* was suitable for application in modern times, lamented the fact that in the Ottoman Empire in the period of the Tánẓimát the Turks had adopted European laws and that in Egypt in 1883 the *shari'ah*, which had held sway for thirteen centuries, had been displaced by European codes.

* * *

It is indicative of the emotional appeal of the *shari'ah* as a "national" product that Sulaymān's first reason for advocating its restoration was not his religious belief, but what he called the "dictate of patriotism." He considered a nation to be distinguished from all other nations by its individual characteristics, chief among which is its jurisprudence.

* * *

The second reason Sulāyman gave was religion, language, and tradition, deference to which would require the reestablishment of the *shari'ah* in Egypt. Other significant arguments were the hope that the *shari'ah* would be a unifying force among the Middle Eastern states if they also adopted it as their basic legislation, the fact that the best legislation is one which people observe out of inner conviction, and the fact that the *shari'ah* was a jurisprudential treasure which would go to waste if it were not utilized.

The draft code, al-Sanhūri said, was derived from twenty civil codes representing countries in Europe, Asia, Africa, and the Americas; from the jurisprudence of the Egyptian courts; and from the *shari'ah*, along the lines he had suggested in his article on the subject. As it followed the *shari'ah*, he asserted, the draft code tended toward objectiveness, like the Germanic codes, instead of the subjectiveness characteristic of the codes of Latin countries.

. . . . Other general principles adapted from the *shari'ah* concerned the abuse of rights, the responsibility of young persons of imperfect understanding, the transfer of debt, and the principle of unforeseeable circumstances. In addition, many new individual rules were taken from the *shari'ah* to supplement the previous *shari'ah* provisions pertaining to leases of *waqfs* and agricultural lands, sale during death-sickness, fraud, option of inspection, easements, prescription, capacity, preemption, etc. Further, the principles of the *shari'ah* were made a general source of law in cases where no specific text of the code or usage was found applicable.

For three years the draft code was up for comment. In 1945 a five-man committee headed by al-Sanhūri studied all the comments and proposals, introduced some revisions, and prepared the draft for legislative action. When the parliament took it up, the new code faced its most serious challenge in a specially created Senate study committee. In March, 1948, while the draft code was under consideration by the committee, a group formed by Muḥammad Ṣādiq Fahmi, a counselor at the Court of Cassation, and consisting mostly of Azharite professors of the four orthodox schools, circulated among the members of the Senate a special issue of *al-Muḥāmāh* in which the draft code was bitterly attacked. The charges seem inconsistent. On one hand, it was maintained that the old code, which, with some exceptions, had been based on French law, was in need only of some modification here and there, and that it was only right and proper to preserve the "legal culture" already accruing to Egypt. On the other hand, it was maintained that should a complete recodification be allowed, such recodification should be based on the *shari'ah*. Perhaps the composition of the group—secular lawyers trained in the French legal tradition and professors of Islamic law at al-Azhar—was responsible for this inconsistency.

* * *

Faced with such opposition to the draft code, the Senate committee convened a general session on May 30, 1948, to which it invited judges and lawyers representing the Court of Cassation, the Cairo court of appeal, the mixed courts, the National Bar Association, and the Law School of Cairo University to give testimony. It is significant that none of the professors of the *shari'ah* from either al-Azhar or the Cairo Law School were present. The session, which lasted for a few days, revealed the ephemeral nature of the opposition in the face of the singlemindedness of al-Sanhūri, who was then Minister of Education, in pushing the draft to completion, and in the face of his truly phenomenal knowledge of both the *shari'ah* and comparative jurisprudence.

The question of utilization of the *shari'ah* in the draft code occupied a sizable part of the committee's time. Fahmi and his supporters among the Azharite *ulema* had insisted that the *shari'ah* alone should form the basis for any recodification. . . . M. M. al-Wakīl, pointed out that the neglect of the *shari'ah* would cause public indignation, and al-Sanhūri added that the *shari'ah* was preferable to the principles of equity and natural law as a reference because it was more precise. As for the position of Fahmi and his *ulema* supporters, al-Sanhūri reviewed the provisions that had been derived from the *shari'ah* and insisted that had it been possible to derive more, he would have gladly done so. . . .

After lengthy deliberation the committee approved the draft code with minor modifications. It is significant that one of the changes, approved unanimously, was the deletion of a provision for a *shari'ah* type of sale called *bay' bi-al-wafā'*, or sale with the right of redemption. The committee had found that this type of sale was a devious means of effecting a mortgage and had often resulted in divesting the vendor of his property for a very low price.

In the Senate chamber only one senator, 'Abd al-Wahhāb Tal'at, raised the question of whether the *shari'ah* had been sufficiently utilized in drawing up the code. Otherwise, the report of the special committee was enthusiastically received. On October 15, 1949, the day the mixed courts and the consular courts came to an end, the draft code became the Egyptian Civil Code.

EGYPTIAN CIVIL CODE: Art. 1:

* * *

Provisions of law govern all matters to which these provisions apply in letter or spirit. In the absence of a provision of law that is applicable, the judge will decide according to custom and in the absence of custom in accordance with the principles of Moslem law. In the absence of such principles, the judge will apply the principles of natural justice and the rules of equity.

NOTE

For additional information on the historical evolution leading to the 1949 Code, see Norman Anderson, Law Reform in the Muslim World, London: The Athlone Press, 1976, and Jean Marc Mousseron, La Réception au Proche-Orient du Droit Francais des Obligations, 20 Revue Internationale de Droit Comparé 37, 1968.

QUESTIONS

1. In what ways did the new Code reflect the intellectual "trend of the times"?

2. Did any of the reforms described in the above excerpts respond to specific prior abuses?

3. Would you expect Article 1 to be influential in preserving Islamic law?

3. The Relevant Content of the 1949 Civil Code

THE EGYPTIAN CIVIL CODE (executed 1948, in force 1949)
(selected articles)

Trans. by Perrott, Fanner & Sims Marshall

Object

Article 131. Things that may happen in the future may be the object of an obligation.

An agreement with regard to the succession of a living person is void, even if he consents to such an agreement, except in cases provided for by law.

Article 132. If the object of an obligation is something impossible in itself, the contract is void.

Article 133. When the object of an obligation is not certain as to its nature, it must at least be determinate as to its kind and quantity, as otherwise the contract is void.

The object of an obligation may, however, only be determinate as to kind, if the contract provides a method of ascertaining the quantity. If there is no agreement as to the degree of quality and the quality cannot be ascertained by usage or by any other circumstances, the debtor must supply an article of average quality.

Article 147. The contract makes the law of the parties. It can be revoked or altered only by mutual consent of the parties or for reasons provided for by the law.

When, however, as a result of exceptional and unpredictable events of a general character, the performance of the contractual obligation, without becoming impossible, becomes excessively onerous in such way as to threaten the debtor with exorbitant loss, the judge may, according to the circumstances, and after taking into consideration the interests of both parties, reduce to reasonable limits, the obligation that has become excessive. Any agreement to the contrary is void.

Article 148. A contract must be performed in accordance with its contents and in compliance with the requirements of good faith.

A contract binds the contracting party not only as regards its expressed conditions, but also as regards everything which, according to law, usage and equity, is deemed, in view of the nature of the obligation, to be a necessary sequel to the contract.

Article 159. When an obligation arising out of a bilateral contract is extinguished by reason of impossibility of performance, correlative obligations are also extinguished and the contract is rescinded.

Article 160. When a contract is rescinded, the parties are reinstated in their former position. If reinstatement is impossible, the Court may award damages.

Compensation in Lieu of Performance

Article 215. When specific performance by the debtor is impossible, he will be condemned to pay damages for non-performance of his obligation, unless he establishes that the impossibility of performance arose from a cause beyond his control. The same principle will apply, if the debtor is late in the performance of his obligation.

Article 216. The judge may reduce the amount of damages or may even refuse to allow damages if the creditor, by his own fault, has contributed to the cause of, or increased, the loss.

Article 217. The debtor may by agreement accept liability for unforeseen events and for cases of force majeure.

The debtor may by agreement be discharged from all liability for his failure to perform the contractual obligation, with the exception of liability arising from his fraud or gross negligence. The debtor may, nevertheless, stipulate that he shall not be liable for fraud or gross negligence committed by persons whom he employs for the performance of his obligation.

Article 221. The judge will fix the amount of damages, if it has not been fixed in the contract or by law. The amount of damages includes losses suffered by the creditor and profits of which he has been deprived, provided that they are the normal result of the failure to perform the obligation or of delay in such performance.

These losses shall be considered to be a normal result, if the creditor is not able to avoid them by making a reasonable effort.

When, however, the obligation rises from contract, a debtor who has not been guilty of fraud or gross negligence will not be held liable for damages greater than those which could have normally been foreseen at the time of entering into the contract.

Article 373. An obligation is extinguished if the debtor establishes that its performance has become impossible by reason of causes beyond his control.

Article 658. [Contracts for Services.] The contractor has no claim to an increase of price on the grounds of an increase in the price of raw materials, labour or any other item of expenditure, even if such increase is so great as to render the performance of the contract onerous.

When, however, as a result of exceptional events of a general character which could not be foreseen at the time the contract was concluded, the economic equilibrium between the respective obligations of the master and of the contractor breaks down, and the basis on which the financial estimates for the contract were computed has consequently disappeared, the judge may grant an increase of the price or order the cancellation of the contract.

NOTE

The first clause of Article 131 is a direct translation of French Civil Code Article 1130, which was clearly intended to authorize transactions such as the sale of crops not yet in existence. The new Egyptian Code has dropped all the prohibitions on such sales. It has also explicitly authorized such gambling contracts as those for insurance. The payment of interest is further contemplated in the Code.

In the U.S., there are two doctrines to meet the problems that arise when contract plans "go wrong." One is that of impossibility, typically claimed by the seller when performance has become absolutely impossible. (The only factory has burned down.) The other is that of frustration, sometimes claimed by the buyer when performance has become useless (his factory has burned down so he can't use the raw materials) and sometimes claimed by the seller (something has gone wrong, and he could possibly perform the contract, but it would be pointless because he would lose an unreasonably large sum).

These two doctrines are, roughly, reflected in contemporary French and Egyptian law as well. Corresponding to the impossibility concept is the *force majeure* concept (prevention by a "higher force") of French Code 1148 and Egyptian Code 159, 215, and 373. Corresponding to the frustration concept is the *imprévision* ("unforeseenness") concept, rejected in French general law but accepted in French administrative law and in Egyptian Code 147 and 658. For details of the French versions of these doctrines, see the articles on "Force Majeure" and "Imprévision" in Encyclopedia Dalloz, Repertoire de Droit Civil, Paris: Jurisprudence Générale Dalloz, 1972 and 1973, respectively.

P. Nicholas Kourides (Student Note), The Influence of Islamic Law on Contemporary Middle Eastern Legal Systems: The Formation and Binding Force of Contracts, 9 Columbia Journal of Transnational Law 384, pp. 421–425, (1970).

Following the example of the French courts, the Mixed Courts of Egypt had repeatedly rejected the doctrine of unforeseeable circumstances and held that an obligation is not extinguished except by reason of impossibility of performance. As long as performance was possible, the contract had to be performed, even if the performance was excessively onerous.

The Cairo National Court of Appeals followed the example of the Mixed Courts, but in one of its earlier decisions gave validity to the idea of unforeseeable circumstances. This case,[200] although immedi-

---

200. In this case the Department of the Border's guards entered into a contract with a private individual who undertook to provide a certain amount of corn in installments at a certain price. The department requested him to fulfill his contract and provide remaining installments. He refused on the ground that

ately reversed by the Court of Cassation, helped lay the foundation for Section 2 of Article 147. The Cairo National Court of Appeals held that although it is established that the contract is the law of the parties and must be respected as long as its performance has not become absolutely impossible as a result of *force majeure*, such performance is subject to considerations of justice and equity. Thus, if certain circumstances, unforeseeable at the time of concluding the contract, occur which would affect the rights and obligations of the parties by disturbing the balance of the contract in a grave manner and which would render performance onerous to a degree which the parties could not foresee under any circumstance, it becomes unjust to respect the contract fully. It becomes a matter of justice to help the debtor and to save him from destruction. This doctrine differs from the doctrine of *force majeure* which requires absolute impossibility of performance. This doctrine requires only circumstances which render performance excessively damaging to the debtor. The spirit which dictated the theories of unjust enrichment and abuse of right in the absence of a relevant statutory provision is the same spirit which dictates that full account be taken of the unforeseeable circumstances.

The Court of Cassation reversed this extraordinary decision. It held that a contractual obligation is not terminated by rescission except when performance becomes impossible as a result of circumstances amounting to *force majeure*. If the unforeseeable event does not render performance absolutely impossible but merely onerous to the debtor, his obligation is not extinguished. The Court expressed dissatisfaction with the Continental doctrine of *force majeure* and stated that the Islamic doctrine of unforeseeable circumstances was based on principles of justice and equity. Nevertheless, the Court could not apply the Islamic rule before the legislature had acted.

Professor Sanhuri saw the Court of Cassation's uneasiness with the old doctrine. He observed that the Court had rejected the doctrine of unforeseeable circumstances as a ground for extinguishing an obligation, but not as a ground for reducing an excessive obligation to reasonable limits. Since the Court of Cassation abided by the old code, it was powerless to recognize the doctrine of unforeseeable circumstances.

As late as 1947, the Court of Cassation again rejected the doctrine of unforeseeable circumstances. The Court declared that there was nothing in the civil code which would allow the judge to reduce obligations created by a contract, although Article 168 did authorize a judge in exceptional circumstances to grant a debtor one or more rea-

the price of this kind of corn had more than doubled after the government had abolished the ceiling price for sale commodities. 12 Majallat Al-Muhamah (Egyptian Bar Association Review) (in Arabic) 63, No. 41 (1931), cited in Sanhuri, supra note 197, at 636–638.

sonable delays in performance of an obligation provided there was no serious prejudice to the creditor.

Seeing the dissatisfaction with *force majeure* and the need for a doctrine of unforeseeable circumstances, Sanhuri and the Drafting Committee added Section 2 to Article 147 of the new Egyptian Civil Code. As discussed in the explanatory memorandum, however, this doctrine of unforeseeable circumstances may be invoked only under limited conditions. First, there must be an exceptional circumstance of a general character, such as an earthquake, a war, a sudden strike, or an epidemic. It should be noted that the preliminary draft required only exceptional or unpredicted events, but the Committee of Revision, motivated by the desire to restrict the application of the doctrine within reasonable limits in order to protect the binding force of contracts, added the phrase "of a general character." Therefore, cases where the exceptional events are related only to the debtor, such as his bankruptcy or the burning of his crops, may not be relied on to invoke the doctrine. Second, these exceptional events must be unpredictable; the flooding of the Nile or the spreading of the cotton worm would not suffice, since they are predictable events. Finally, such events should render the performance of the obligations onerous but not impossible. Here lies the difference between the "unforeseeable events" doctrine and the doctrine of *force majeure*. They both require that the events be unpredictable and beyond the control of the parties, but *force majeure* renders performance impossible, while exceptional events renders it only onerous. The results are also different. *Force majeure* extinguishes the obligation and the debtor is not liable for non-performance. The unforeseeable events doctrine does not terminate the obligation but merely reduces it to reasonable limits, and thus, in a more equitable formula, distributes the loss between debtor and creditor.

If the conditions of the doctrine of unforeseeable and exceptional events are fulfilled, the judge, according to the circumstances and after taking into consideration the interests of both parties, may reduce to reasonable limits an obligation that has become excessive. The judge enjoys a broad discretion in dealing with the situation. He may require the increase or decrease of either party's obligation, or stay the performance of the contract until the exceptional events terminate, if they are of a temporary nature. The judge is thus able to achieve an economic balance between the parties, but he may not, on his own, order the rescission of the contract.

The explanatory memorandum admits that an important source of Section 2 of Article 147 is the *principe de l'imprévision* recognized by the French Administrative Courts and Article 269 of the Polish Civil Code. The memorandum unequivocally states, however, that the decisive factor in recommending this view was the concept of necessity in Islamic law and the Islamic legal principle that a lease may be annulled for a sufficiently good reason. Both of these principles were long established in the Hanafi School and embodied in the *Majalla*. Sanhuri points out that Muslim jurists accepted the doctrine of unforeseeable circumstances in regard to leases. A lease is rescinded by excuse (*udhr*) according to the Hanafi School, for if the contract remained binding under the circumstances, the debtor would be bound to tolerate a prejudicial situation to which he did not intend to bind himself when he entered into the contract. Rescission in this case, in fact, is merely the refusal to bind oneself to prejudicial circumstances.

Abd-el-Razzak Ah. El Sanhoury, Le Droit Musulman comme Element de Refonte du Code Civil Egyptien, Introduction A L'Étude Du Droit Comparé, Recueil D'Études en L'Honneur d'Edouard Lambert, vol. 2, Paris: Librairie de la Société Anonyme du Recueil Sirey, 1938, pp. 621, 634–635.

The theory of *imprévision* is, however, very equitable and it is desirable for our legislation to adopt it in the new Civil Code. Moreover, it finds support in the "theory of necessity" of Islamic law. This latter theory has a very broad sweep; it has already received many applications, and it would easily serve as a vehicle for the theory of *imprévision*.

Besides, the theory of necessity has become one of the fundamental principles of Islamic law. As Professor Lambert noted to the Congress on Comparative Law held at The Hague in 1932, "it is the most categorical and general expression of an idea inchoate in the *rebus sic stantibus* concept of international public law, the *imprévision* theory of French administrative law, the English judicial development of the impossibility doctrine under the pressures of the economic aftermath of the war, and the chapter of American constitutional law governing emergencies."

Magdi Sobhy Khalil, Le Dirigisme Économique et Les Contrats, Étude De Droit Comparé, France-Egypte-URSS, Paris: Librairie Generale de Droit et de Jurisprudence, 1967, pp. 166–167, 350–352, 354–356, (footnotes omitted).

§ 262. This formulation becomes evident when the execution of the international contract depends on the grant of a license. This is the case for certain imports in France and in Egypt for all imports (without exception) and for certain exports.

§ 263. . . . A first hypothesis does not raise much difficulty. This is the case of the refusal of a license or the grant of a license modifying the contract's clauses, when the refusal or the modification arises through the enforcement of a control regime in force at the time of conclusion of the contract. In such a case, performance of the contract becomes impossible or very onerous. Can the "domestic" contractor invoke the doctrines of *force majeure* or *imprévision* to avoid or modify his obligation?

Majority opinion refuses the debtor such a defense. In effect, "unforeseeability," one of the three conditions necessary to the application of the doctrines of *force majeure* and *imprévision*, is lacking in this case. . . . The discretionary character of the control authority's power gives one who seeks a license foreknowledge that the license may be granted or denied. His duty of [reasonableness] obliges him to insert into the contract the clause necessary to protect himself from such a foreseeable refusal. It is his own fault if he neglects such a precaution; his contractual liability will be engaged.

§ 561. Certain older decisions of French courts have denied laws and regulations the character of unforeseeability. According to these decisions, legislative acts or regulations cannot be considered unforeseeable, because they are "in the constitutional domain of the legislative power."

These decisions have not been followed. Numerous are the decrees of both French and Egyptian tribunals which have recognized laws or regulations as having the character of unforeseeable events.

* * *

§ 563. And court decisions have formally condemned the opinion already mentioned, applying the theory of *imprévision* with respect to the Agrarian Reform law, which, at the time of conclusion of the contracts, could "not have been imagined" by the contractors.

§ 565. [Nevertheless, some legal changes may be foreseeable.] In a decision dated 26 April 1955, the Tribunal of Alexandria decided that since the sales tax regime had been in force since 1945, the extension of this regime to a new line of commerce (sale of fish), that had not previously been covered, had to be considered as a foreseeable event that would not permit application of the doctrine of *imprévision* to revise pending contracts.

Similarly, another decision of the same Tribunal held that Decree Law 18/1952 of 8 March 1952, closing the "Contract Exchange," did not constitute an unforeseeable event, given that everyone trading on this Exchange should know its regulations and, consequently, know of the right of the Minister of Finance to intervene to protect the national economic interest.

* * *

§ 570. One can recall with respect to Article 147, clause 2, of the Egyptian Civil Code, that it is constantly affirmed that the annual Nile flood is a foreseeable event, but an exceptional flood should be considered unforeseeable. (Citations to travaux préparatoires of the Code and to al-Sanhoury). An exceptional flood? In contract litigation, would it be defined by a Nilometer or rather by the importance of the harm that it caused one of the parties? Wouldn't a contract party be unable to invoke *imprévision*, even following an exceptional flood, if the losses caused to him were no more than those he undergoes annually by normal floods? Shouldn't the converse also be admitted: exceptional losses caused to a contractor by a normal flood should permit application of the doctrine of *imprévision*?

It is thus certain that at the heart of this theory, the predictability of the event must yield to the abnormality of the event's consequences. At least, it can be said that abnormality is enough to create a presumption of unforeseeability. As M. Voirin has written, the signs of unforeseeability are that performance of the contract has become particularly onerous, either because the contract has ceased to meet the social goal that was its *raison d'être* or, if this utility persists, that the contract's execution significantly shifts the balance of duties.

§ 571. Application of these ideas in the context of contractual upsets caused by the change of dirigiste legislation leads to the extension of the theory of *imprévision* to this domain just as it extends to other upsets caused, for example, by natural events. Certainly, in a general way, the constant modification of a tax or an exchange control regime in the past gives reason to foresee modifications in the future. Likewise, nationalization of certain industries or limitation of agricultural holdings encourages one to expect other nationalizations or other limitations in the future. It would, however, be incorrect to exclude the doctrine of *imprévision* on the basis of this abstract foreseeability of legislative change. It is rather the normal or abnormal character of the economic upset created by the change that should be decisive. One cannot lump together the oscillation of an existing tax with the creation of a new tax or restrictions on transactions in an exchange with the closure of the exchange. In the abstract, all these events may be foreseeable, but in the concrete, their repercussions for contracts are not all normal. . . .

§ 572. . . . the condition of unforeseeability appears as a restraint imposed on the judge's power to revise contracts, an artificial restraint demanded by the needs of business security and confidence. But it is significant that in the midst of constantly changing dirigiste legislation, these same considerations of business "confidence" argue in favor of admitting *imprévision*. Legislative instability inevitably provokes a "loss of confidence" in individuals that can cause them to become passive. To give them the possibility of revising contracts upset by legislative mobility is to alleviate their suspicions and, at the same time, support their economic vitality.

To this can be added a pragmatic consideration important to the general economic interest. "In revising a contract, the judge gives it force that had been believed lost." "To revise a contract is often to give it its only chance of being carried out," and, especially from a dirigiste viewpoint, "the economic interest of the nation is generally more closely associated with the performance of contracts than with their non-performance."

QUESTIONS

1. Of the three contracts discussed above in Question 2 on page 620, which are legal under the new Civil Code?

2. When the import license is denied, which contracts may be affected by the law of impossibility and which by that of *imprévision*? Which contracts are actually excused? What subquestions are important in answering this question, and what additional information might you like?

3. Where would you expect the loss to fall?

4. After this examination of several details of Egyptian contract law, how would you weigh the relative influence of French and Islamic doctrines in shaping the new Code? Is the result inevitable?

5. To what issues and problems is Khalil responding? Would al-Sanhoury have foreseen them?

C. THE CONTEMPORARY INTEGRATION OF CONTRACT LAW AND GOVERNMENT ECONOMIC ACTIVITY

NOTE

The preceding discussion raises the important problem of shaping private contract doctrine when governmental economic regulation upsets the parties' plans. But this problem reflects only one of the ways government influences economic activity; new kinds of problems arise when the government enters as an entrepreneur itself.

If the government, working as an entrepreneur, contracts with a private party, how will disputes be settled, and what happens if the government changes the rules in its own favor halfway through the contract? It seems hard to work out a way in which the government can be a fair decision-maker and legislator for situations in which it is an interested party. The government may also "contract" with itself—a government entrepreneur making an agreement with another branch of the government. How is this agreement to be enforced? If there is a frustration/impossibility problem in such a contract, (a situation which is essentially one of bureaucratic disagreement), how can it be resolved?

1. The New Entrepreneurial Institutions

NOTE

President Nasser created a new generation of government economic activities that raises these problems. At the rural level, there were the cooperatives described in the following excerpt. There were also the newly nationalized and newly created government businesses called "public sector enterprises." (As a vocabulary matter these were different from "public establishments," exemplified by a provincial government, and "public authorities," exemplified by an investment authority to arrange public investments in other activities.)

These systems are declining in importance in the face of *infitah*, and much new investment is private, especially under Law 43 of 1974, also excerpted below. This law sets up an elaborate framework by which new investment (not all foreign) can be submitted to an approval process that brings the investor many benefits.

Gabriel Saab, The Egyptian Agrarian Reform, 1952–1962, London: Oxford University Press, 1967, pp. 95–96, 98.

It has already been stated that in compliance with the system of supervised credit the only guarantee or collateral demanded by the co-operatives for loans in kind and in cash was an undertaking by their members to deliver their crops to the co-operative warehouses for sale. It was not easy to secure compliance with this undertaking, even though the crops marketed by the cooperatives often fetched far more than those obtained by direct sales by the beneficiaries and tenants. Many of the latter were reluctant to pay their debts and settle their accounts, as they seemed to consider that whatever they had received had been given by a government agency (i.e. the Agrarian Reform authorities of the co-operatives), and that as such there was no special reason to hurry up and repay.

. . . the cotton crop was therefore considered by the Agrarian Reform staff as the main guarantee for the loans made by the co-operatives and as the only tangible collateral for money due to them by their members. In consequence, picking of this crop was subject to the prior consent of the *mushrifs*, [supervisors] who never allowed the peasants to enter the cotton fields until a complete block of 30–50 feddans was fully ripe.

. . . According to the Agrarian Reform officials, a considerable amount of leakage in the delivery of the crop to the co-operative would have occurred if the peasants had been allowed to harvest their cotton in the customary manner; this would have given them the opportunity to take away part of their crops surreptitiously. Surreptitious picking would have been hardly noticeable and therefore difficult to prevent if the cotton were first picked when some of the bolls reached maturity and a second time when the remaining bolls ripened; it might easily have occurred at night between the two pickings and would have provided dishonest peasants with a unique occasion to move off the crop and avoid or delay settlement of their debts to the co-operatives.

* * *

When peasants showed signs of unwillingness to settle their accounts with their co-operatives, or if they repeatedly attempted to dispose of their crops secretly so as to avoid payments demanded of them, the Agrarian Reform Agronomists had the right to open judicial proceedings for the seizure of their crops.

**Law 43 of 1974 on Arab and Foreign Capital Investment and
Free Zones and its amendment 32 of 1977**

This Law shall be published in the Official Gazette and will receive the seal of the State and shall come into force from the date of its publication.

Signature of the President
19 June, 1974

CHAPTER ONE. INVESTMENT OF ARAB AND FOREIGN CAPITAL

Art. 1. The term "Project" in the application of the provision of this Law shall mean any activity included within any of the spheres therein specified and approved by the Board of Directors of the General Authority for Investment and Free Zones.

* * *

Art. 3. The investment of Arab and foreign capital in the Arab Republic of Egypt shall be for the purpose of realising the objectives of economic and social development within the framework of the State's general policy and national plan provided that the investment is made in projects in need of international expertise in the spheres of modern development or in projects requiring foreign capital. The projects, contained in the lists to be prepared by the Authority and approved by the Council of Ministers, shall be in the following fields:

1. Industrialization, mining, energy, tourism, transportation, and other fields.

* * *

4. Investment companies which aim at utilizing funds in the fields enumerated in this Law.

5. Investment banks and merchant banks and reinsurance companies whose activities shall be confined to transactions effected in free currencies.

6. Banks engaging in local currency transactions, so long as they are in the form of joint ventures in which local Egyptian capital holds at least 51%.

7. *Construction activities in regions outside the agricultural area and the perimeters of existing cities.*

8. *Construction contracting activities undertaken by Joint Stock Companies in which there is a 50% minimum Egyptian capital participation.*

9. *Technical consultant activities in the form of Joint Stock Companies in partnership with foreign international consultant firms provided that they are related to any project within the scope of activities mentioned herein . . . .. Spe-*

cial priority shall be given to those projects which are designed to generate exports, encourage tourism, or reduce the need to import basic commodities as well as to projects which require advanced technical expertise or which make use of patents or trade marks of worldwide reputation.

* * *

Art. 4. The capital invested in the Arab Republic of Egypt under the provision of this Law shall take the form of participation with public or private Egyptian capital in such fields and under such terms and conditions as are set forth in Articles 2 and 3 of the present law. By way of exception from the above:

* * *

Art. 7. Projects may not be nationalized or confiscated. The assets of such projects cannot be seized, blocked, confiscated or sequestrated except by judicial procedures.

Art. 8. Investment disputes in respect of the implementation of the provisions of this Law shall be settled in a manner to be agreed upon with the investor, or within the framework of the agreements in force between the Arab Republic of Egypt and the investor's home country, or within the framework of the Convention for the Settlement of Investment Disputes between the State and the nationals of other countries to which Egypt has adhered by virtue of Law No. 90 of 1971, where such Law applies.

Disputes may be settled through arbitration. An Arbitration Board shall be constituted, comprising a member on behalf of each disputing party and a third member acting as chairman to be jointly named by the said two members. Failing agreement on the nomination of the third member within thirty days of the appointment of the second member, the chairman shall be chosen, at the request of either party, by the Supreme Council of Judicial Bodies among counsellors of the judiciary in the Arab Republic of Egypt.

The Arbitration Board shall lay down its rules of procedure unrestricted by the rules contained in the Civil and Commercial Code of Procedures, save the rules which relate to the basic guarantees and principles of litigation. The Board shall see to it that the dispute is expediently resolved. Awards shall be rendered by majority vote and shall be final and binding on both parties and enforceable as any other final judgment.

The Arbitration Board shall decide on the costs of arbitration and shall determine who shall bear such costs.

* * *

Art. 9. Companies enjoying the provisions of this Law shall be deemed to belong to the private sector of the economy, irrespective of the legal nature of the indigenous capital participating therein. Legislation, regulations, and statutes applicable to the public sector of the economy and its employees shall not apply to said companies.

* * *

Art. 15. By way of exception from the provisions or the laws, regulations, and resolutions governing imports, enterprises enjoying the provisions of this Law shall be allowed to import, on condition of inspection but without a license, whether by themselves or through a third party, the production facilities, materials, machinery, equipment, spare parts, and transportation equipment required for the installation and operation of the project, that are compatible with the nature of their activities. Such operations shall be excepted from the procedure requiring submission to a committee for the purpose of selecting the best tender, but there shall be no obligation on the part of the Government to provide the foreign currency necessary for the importing operations beyond the bank accounts mentioned in the preceding Article.

Projects shall be authorized to export their products whether themselves or through an intermediary without a license, and without such projects having to be registered in the Registry of Exporters.

Art. 16. Without prejudice to more favourable tax exemptions provided for in any other law, projects shall be exempted from the tax on commercial and industrial profits and the taxes appendant thereto, likewise the profits distributed shall be exempted from the tax on the revenues from moveable capital and the taxes appandent thereto,

and, as the case may be, from the tax on commercial and industrial profits and the taxes appendant thereto, as well as from the general tax on income, relative to the taxable proportion of such profits as set forth in this provision,

such exemption to be for a period of five years from the first fiscal year following commencement of production or engagement in activities as the case may be. Such exemptions shall apply for the same period to the proceeds of the profits which are reinvested in the enterprise

and for special reserves that are debited to the distribution account after deduction of net profits and allocated to consolidate the company's financial position and undistributed profits earned during the exemption period and distributed after such period has elapsed.

The shares shall be exempted from the annual proportional stamp duty for five years following the date duties are legally due for the first time.

* * *

Art. 21. The party concerned may request the re-exportation or disposal of the invested capital after obtaining the approval of the Authority's Board of Directors, provided that five years shall have elapsed from the date of importation of the capital fixed in the registration certificate. (The Authority's Board of Directors may waive this condition if it is evident that the accepted project, for which funds have been transferred, cannot be implemented or continued for reasons beyond the control of the investor or for other exceptional circumstances to be considered by the Authority's Board of Directors in accordance with the following: [omitted])

* * *

CHAPTER THREE. GENERAL AUTHORITY FOR INVESTMENT AND FREE ZONES

Art. 25. *A General Authority whose Board of Directors shall be under the Chairmanship of the Minister of Economy and Economic Cooperation shall be created with the name "The General Authority for Invesment and Free Zones."* (herein referred to in this Law as "the Authority.")

Its principle offices shall be in the city of Cairo and it may maintain offices outside the Arab Republic of Egypt.

The Authority shall enjoy juridical personality, and shall have a Board of Directors to be constituted by Decree of the President of the Republic.

The Board of Directors shall be the prevailing authority in all matters of the Authority, shall discharge its duties, and lay down the general policy that shall be pursued. It may adopt any resolution deemed to be conducive to the achievement of the objectives for which the Authority was created.

By Decree of the President of the Republic, a Deputy Chairman of the Board of Directors of the Authority shall be appointed, who shall act as its Managing Director, and preside over the executive body of the Authority consisting of technical and administrative staff appointed in accordance with the organizational structure approved by the Board of Directors.

Art. 26. The Authority shall be competent to implement the provisions of this Law, more specifically, to perform the following:

1. Study the laws, regulations and resolutions in connection with Arab and foreign investment in the Arab Republic of Egypt and the Free Zones created therein, and submit such proposals as are deemed appropriate in this regard.

2. Prepare lists covering types of activities and projects in the participation of which Arab and foreign capital may be invited. . . .

3. Offer projects for investment by Arab and foreign capital and render advice in connection therewith, familiarize international capital markets and capital exporting countries with the approved lists. . . .

4. Review applications submitted by investors and present the outcome to the Authority's Board of Directors for action thereupon.

5. Register incoming capital. . . .

6. Approve remittance of net profits following examination of the documents which reflect the project's financial position . . . .

7. Facilitate procurement of permits necessary for executing Arab and foreign capital investment projects, including all necessary administrative permits, especially residence permits for businessmen experts, and foremen recruited overseas for working in projects enjoying the provisions of this Law.

8. *To approve projects established with Egyptian capital and owned by Egyptian nationals in accordance with paragraphs (2) and (3) of Article 6 of this Law.*

Executive regulations shall determine the rules and procedures under which the Authority shall perform its duties as described in this Law.

Art. 27. Applications for investment shall be submitted to the Authority. An application shall specify the amount of capital to be invested, the nature thereof and any other such particulars as shall be required to indicate the structure of the project covered by the application. The Board of Directors of the Authority shall have the authority to approve applications for investment submitted. Such approval shall lapse if the investor shall fail to take serious steps to carry out the project within six months of approval,

unless the Board shall grant renewed approval for such further period as it shall deem fit.

Art. 28. The Authority shall have a separate budget prepared according to the rules customary in commercial enterprises, unrestricted by the provisions governing the budgets of public authorities and public corporations.

Art. 29. The revenues of the Authority shall consist of the following:

1. Credits allocated by the state,

2. Revenues derived from its activities,

3. Charges for services rendered by the Authority.

It may receive such revenues in free foreign currency pursuant to the rules and regulations adopted by the Board of Directors.

4. Local or foreign loans when approved according to Law.

QUESTIONS

1. Keeping in mind both the concerns that the Saab article raises and the fact that the problems described in that article derive mainly from the

artificially low prices that Egypt maintains for agricultural production, what are the costs and benefits, from the farmers' and the public's viewpoints, if the food processor in our problem is a public enterprise?

2. Does Law 43 provide a better or a worse framework?

2. Dispute Settlement Procedures

NOTE

An enterprise like our food processing plant could take any of three legal forms: a public sector enterprise, a private enterprise under Law 43, or a plain private enterprise. During the 1960's only the first of these would have been likely, for reasons of investment confidence as much as of formal law; today, the latter two are much more likely.

Provisions for the legal settlement of disputes will be substantially different in the three cases. In general, although there is some confusion, disputes between a public sector corporation and a government agency will be handled by negotiation among the different components of the advice section of the Conseil d'Etat or by arbitration. Those between an individual and a public sector company will go either to a regular court or to an administrative court, depending on a complex body of case law. And those between an individual and a Law 43 or private sector company will go to a regular court. To add to the potential confusion, parties can always agree to arbitrate a controversy. Moreover, for an enterprise under Law 43, the dispute considered in our problem is technically impossible, for grant of the investment license brings an automatic right to import anything necessary.

Of the two new themes in this morass, one is arbitration, discussed in the first of the following excerpts. Arbitration is generally said to bring many pragmatic benefits of expertise, speed, and cheapness, although the last is said not to be the case in Egypt. The article also suggests a philosophical relationship between arbitration and socialism but overstates the role that arbitration plays in the Egyptian system. The second theme, developed in the second excerpt, is the development of special judicial arrangements for government contracts. In Egypt, this follows French administrative law; many nations have similar procedures and probably all have special procedures. For additional information, both on the role of the Conseil d'Etat, which ultimately supervises administrative law in Egypt and on administrative contracts generally, see Marcel Waline et Jean de Soto, Le Conseil d'Etat Égyptien, 65 Revue du Droit Public et de la Science Politique en France et a l'Etranger, p. 30 (1949); and George Langrod, Administrative Contracts, 4 American Journal of Comparative Law, p. 325 (1955).

Peter Feuerle, Economic Arbitration in Egypt: The Influence of a Soviet Legal Institution, 7 Journal of International Law and U.S. Foreign Economics, pp. 61, 64–67, 68–69, (1972).

* * *

Public arbitration, as it is officially called in Egypt, was introduced following a resolution of the Council of Ministers issued in October, 1965.[5] The arbitration system began its operation in March, 1966.[6] It has compulsory and exclusive jurisdiction over civil disputes involving public sector companies and governmental authorities as well as over certain disputes under administrative law, notably tax cases. (Administrative law disputes only amount to little over 1% of the entire case load.) If a dispute involves a private enterprise, the parties may voluntarily agree to submit their differences to arbitration. Labor disputes may be submitted either to arbitration or to the courts, but in practice they are not accepted by the arbitration officials since the fees are too low to interest the arbiters.

* * *

The organizational center of the Egyptian arbitration system is an Arbitration Bureau supervised by the Technical Counselor of the Minister of Justice. The Bureau consists of a staff of about ten persons and carries out clerical and general administrative tasks. The actual arbitration work lies in the hands of individual arbiters. These are judges of the ordinary and administrative courts who are chosen for listing by the Arbitration Bureau and in regular turn are called upon to handle particular cases. In practice an arbiter is assigned a group of cases, usually four to six, depending on their complexity; the arbiter may specify how many such groups he wishes to handle per year.[7] Cases are decided by the arbiter as president of the arbitration board together with two assessors, one named by each of the parties. If the litigants fail to nominate representatives, this is done for them by the head of the Arbitration Bureau.

Arbitration procedure is not bound by the code of civil procedure, although the basic principles of judicial action must be observed. Beyond this, there are few procedural prescriptions, so that the arbiters have a free hand and the proceedings are informal. An arbiter will, for example, try to negotiate a settlement first, using the telephone or other means of communication, and call for a formal hearing only after these first efforts have failed. The primary objective of arbitration proceedings is to reach a speedy conclusion of the dispute, which is supposed to be settled within three months. In reality, the decision of a case may take a few days to four months. Speedy settlement of arbitration disputes is guaranteed by an ingenious method of paying the arbiters. They receive £E. 200 taken from the fees after completion of each group of cases, a remuneration which compares favorably with the annual judges' salary of £E. 500–700.

Any kind of substantive settlement is permissible as long as it remains in agreement with the target figures for production and other

5. Decree of the Council of Ministers, January 10, 1966; Law No. 32, 1966.

6. Orders of the Minister of Justice No. 985 and 986 (1966).

7. This information as well as other details to be mentioned subsequently were made available to the author during a visit to Egypt in May, 1970, by Egyptian officials associated with the Ministries of Economics and Justice.

specifications issued by the government. There are no institutionalized mechanisms for supervising and guiding the arbiters in their
work, aside from the possibility of review—which, in view of the cumbersome procedure described above, will most certainly remain a rare
exception. It must be borne in mind, however, that after the 1969
purge of the Egyptian judiciary, which involved summary dismissal
and selective re-hiring, only those judges (and consequently, arbiters)
were retained in office whose loyalty to the government and devotion
to its policies was beyond doubt.

Practically speaking, arbitration is essential for the effective functioning of the Egyptian economy for the simple reason that it provides quick, authoritative solutions to economic disputes. The ordinary courts, which had handled public sector cases before the
arbitration was introduced, had a backlog of up to four years, which
made resort to them useless from a commercial point of view. Perhaps more significant is the fact that now all disputes arising within
the public sector, i.e., in the entire field of industry, finance, and
large-scale commerce, are settled by means of arbitration. Consequently Egyptian authorities are very much aware of the practical
significance of this new institution, and its performance to date has
been described as satisfactory.

* * *

There are ideological as well as logical reasons for the adaptation
of Soviet legal institutions. Since the USSR and its East European
allies are the primary advocates of central planning as the most effective method of achieving economic development, their institutions of
economic management possess a natural attractiveness for a country
trying to embark upon a similar course under the auspices of socialism (however vaguely defined this concept might be in the case of
Egypt). More important, in a centrally administered economy where
the agreements concluded by the public enterprises are theoretically,
at least, the final manifestations of the central plan, institutions
which guarantee the conformity of national plan and enterprise activities are necessary. When it comes to settling disputes, the institution
must combine technocratic expertise with responsiveness to central
direction and immunity from sectional interests. These problems are
known in the USSR as "localism" and "departmentalism." In terms
of internal organization, external subordination, and personnel, the
Soviet arbitration boards, and to an even greater extent the arbitration boards in some East European countries, have been established
so as to satisfy these requirements.

* * *

The basic reasons for the present differences between Soviet and
Egyptian arbitration are to be sought in the different methods of
managing the national economy. While the basic structural features
are the same, i.e., direction of the public sector according to a national plan by administrative means, Egypt is just beginning to approach

the stage where the plan is operatively rather than programmatically significant.[13]　As long as this is the case, dispute-settling remains a matter involving only the enterprises immediately concerned, rather than also involving the state as a directly interested party.　This situation is reflected in the official evaluation of Egyptian arbitration as satisfactory.　It seems that no attempts have been made to assess the influence of arbitration upon the execution of the national economic plan.　If arbitration's effectiveness in this area is not a matter of consideration, it is nearly impossible to arrive at a negative evaluation of its performance as long as cases are settled speedily.　Any authoritative settlement, even though disadvantageous to an enterprise, is acceptable to its director, since in contrast to their Soviet colleagues, Egyptian enterprise directors do not significantly depend for their income upon their enterprises' earnings.[14]　There is, significantly, never a problem in executing an arbitration award in Egypt.　Consequently, the Egyptian arbitration system as it now operates may cover up, perpetuate and perhaps even encourage severe inefficiencies in enterprise operations since there is no built-in mechanism for bringing such malfunctions to the attention of supervisory bodies.　This situation is bound to change as planning and economic administration are successfully developed into genuine instruments of control.　The foreign aid and technical and administrative expertise which Egypt receives from the communist states of Eastern Europe may well strengthen and accelerate this trend.　Such a development will necessitate a modification of Egyptian arbitration in the direction of its Soviet and East European models.

Administrative Contracts (French-language excerpt that does not give author's name, provided by Centre d'études et de documentation économique, juridique, et sociale, Cairo)

The rules governing administrative contracts are largely made by courts and are the work of the Conseil d'Etat . . .. These principles are in constant evolution to respond to the changing needs of the public services.

The theory of administrative contracts is also recent in Egypt, considering that administrative jurisdiction is still new there.　In fact, the various judicial, mixed, and national tribunals have applied the civil codes, instead of applying the rules of administrative law to ad-

---

13.　At the end of the first five-year plan (1960–1965), the only one to be implemented so far, the economy was in serious trouble.　The 1967 war and the continuing burden of defense have not contributed to efficient economic planning (cf. E. Kanovsky, The Economic Aftermath of the Six Day War, 22 Middle East Journal 131 (1968), so that the criticism voiced by this East German author

in 1965 remains valid: M. Engert, Planungsprobleme in der VAR, 10 Wissenschaftliche Zeitschrift der Hochschule fuer Oekonomie Berlin 209 (1965).

14.　An enterprise director's only penalty for not meeting his assigned targets would be no, or a lower, annual raise in salary, the amount of which might range from £E. 6 to £E. 60 per year.

ministrative contracts. When the Egyptian Conseil d'Etat was created in 1946, the provisions defining its jurisdiction were quite limiting and included nothing on administrative contracts. Article 5 of Law 9 of 1949, reorganizing the Conseil d'Etat, created administrative court jurisdiction over disputes relating to concession agreements, to provisions for public works, and to the administrative purchases of supplies by the State from others. The law restricted this grant of administrative jurisdiction by three conditions: the jurisdiction went to the three types of agreements only, it applied only to disputes between the administration and its co-contractor, and the jurisdiction was shared with the regular courts . . . .

The co-contractor or private party contracting with the government has three principal rights: to the specified price, to indemnity in particular cases, and to financial equilibrium in the contract . . . .

The courts have given the co-contractor the right to maintain the financial equilibrium of the contract in the face of the government's actions . . . . Thus, he will be . . . protected against the risks of those government acts called *fait du prince*, [loosely, acts of state] . . . . *Fait du prince* can be defined as any action by the government that increases costs for the co-contractor . . . Under the theory of *fait du prince*, the courts will give full indemnity for the costs arising from any administrative measure that upsets the equilibrium of the contract . . . .

In the situation in which the action increasing the contractor's costs is taken by a third public person, not by the administrative body involved in the contract . . . the French Conseil d'Etat has changed its position several times. In effect it has refused to apply the theory of *fait du prince* to general regulatory measures designed for economic management that affect the co-contractor. Instead, the Conseil applies the theory of *imprévision* in such situations. The Conseil's current tendency is to limit the application of the *fait du prince* theory to those acts taken by the contracting authority . . . . This tendency is unfavorable to the co-contractor . . . . *Imprévision* gives rise to indemnity only when the harm is ruinous, while *fait du prince* applies whenever the equilibrium of the contract is upset, even if only by a simple reduction of profit. Moreover, the remedy in *imprévision* is but partial . . ., while that in *fait du prince* is complete and covers all the harm done and profits lost.

NOTE

Infitah has had a significant effect on this elaborate structure. As an example of recent methods of conducting the type of operation described in our problem, the government has built a number of stills in Fayoum province for the distillation of geranium plants into a perfume base that is exported. The legal technique chosen is for the government to own the stills and let the local farmers use them for a fee. The farmer handles all growing issues and marketing of the extract on his own. Further information on the influence of *infitah* is available in Jeswald Salacuse, Back to Contract: Implications of Peace and Openness for Egypt's Legal System, 28 American Journal of Comp. Law, p. 315, (1980); and Jeswald Salacuse and Theodore Parnall, Foreign Investment and Economic Openness in Egypt: Legal Problems and Legislative Adjustments of the First Three Years, 12 International Lawyer, p. 759, (1978); and Jeswald Salacuse, Egypt's New Law on Foreign Investment: The Framework for Economic Openness, 9 International Lawyer, p. 647, (1975).

QUESTIONS

1. Why is the dispute settlement system so complex? Is the complexity avoidable?

2. Why, do you think, is there such a close tie between arbitration and socialism?

3. What are the likely differences in outcome depending on whether the dispute in the problem goes to a court or to arbitration? If to a court, what about the administrative versus regular court distinction?

4. How does the legal status of the plant (public enterprise, Law 43, or fully private) affect the outcome? Which status would you prefer if you were the force behind the plant? the farmer? the plant employees? (in fact, employees strongly want public enterprise status for the sake of employment stability).

5. Do the government's current systems conform with Islamic law?

6. As an advisor to the Minister of Justice, how much of the old contract doctrine would you suggest be resurrected as part of *infitah*? Why?

7. Do you sense important differences in the processes and politics of adoption of foreign law in the three examples here: the Civil Code of 1883, the Socialist law of the 1960's, and today's *infitah*?

8. Do you still believe Sir Henry Maine's statement about the movement from status to contract? What about possible paraphrases such as contract to bureaucracy? contract producing status? Is there any general trend implied by the character and spread of modern technological commerce?

Chapter 20

PRIVATE ORDERING IN BOTSWANA

———

A. INTRODUCTION

NOTE

The hypothetical of Problem III is one that is not generally applicable to the situation in Botswana. Contract cases brought there do not usually involve third parties and the domino-like chain of consequences of the hypothetical. In Botswana, a more typical hypothetical would be the one posed by Walker:

J. M. Walker, "Bamalete Contract Law," in Botswana Notes and Records, vol. 1, 1968, p. 71.

A man intending to sell soft drinks at an area-wide function orders and pays in advance for the drinks. He hires a man to build a stand for him. The seller fails to deliver . . . [and he is unable to sell any drinks.]

QUESTIONS

1. Is there a valid contract between the buyer of the soft drinks and the seller of the supply of soft drinks? Between the buyer of the soft drinks and the builder of the stand?

2. Under Tswana traditional law of contracts, should the buyer be able to recover his out-of-pocket expenses from the defaulting vendor? What about his lost potential profit?

3. Suppose, as a result of the buyer's failure to sell soft drinks on the day of the area-wide function, the Chief or the Chairman of the District Council cancels his right to sell drinks at the next area-wide function. Would the buyer be able to recover consequential damages for the loss of this expected income?

NOTE

Keep the Case of the Disappointed Soft Drink Vendor in mind as you read through the following materials on contract in Botswana. Although you can't answer the above questions now, you will be able to after you have worked through the rest of this chapter.

Here is another contract case from Botswana which involves statutory law.

Tswaing vs. Van Schalwyk, Botswana Law Reports pp. 149–155, 1980. Headings inserted by the editor are in brackets

[*The Plaintiff's Case.*] The Defendant in this case is a builder by occupation. On the 2nd November, 1978, property known as Lot 5368, Gaborone, Extension 2, registered in the name of the Plaintiff was transferred into the name of the Defendant which transfer was registered in terms of Deed of Transfer No. 283/78. The Plaintiff originally obtained a grant of the property from the State and was the registered owner thereof by virtue of Deed of State Grant No. 94/75 dated the 27th February, 1975. It is the Plaintiff's contention that the Defendant secured his signature to a Memorandum of Agreement and Power of Attorney to give transfer through—

(a) false representation

(b) a mistaken belief on the part of the Plaintiff

(c) Plaintiff's inability to read or write

and that the registration of the transfer on the 2nd November, 1978 was without his knowledge, and was effected wrongfully and illegally.

The Plaintiff states that he did not sell, donate or cede any of his rights to the property to the Defendant, and that he is still the legal owner of the property. The Plaintiff therefore claims—

(a) the release of the property from all encumbrances which might have been placed on it by the Defendant

(b) restitution of the property to Plaintiff by Defendant and

(c) registration of the property into the name of Plaintiff by Defendant.

He further claims the costs of the suit, and further and or alternative relief. The case of the Plaintiff as disclosed in his declaration is that he entered into a verbal agreement with the Defendant whereby the Defendant undertook to erect a building for the Plaintiff on the property. He does not remember the exact or precise date of this agreement, but the registrations took place personally between the parties with no intervention by any Attorney. The Plaintiff alleges that it was a term of the agreement that the building would be put up before the expiry of two years from the date of the State Grant No. 94/75. It was a further term of the agreement that the Defendant would hold the title deeds to the property as security for the cost of the building, which cost would be defrayed from the profits of a business to be run in the building, in which business the parties would be partners. The business which the Plaintiff intended to conduct from the premises was that of a butchery. In the event the parties did not enter into any partnership and no business was conducted from the premises. [sic] In breach of the terms of this oral agreement, the Defendant took more than 2 years in putting up the building, and furthermore secured the signature of the Plaintiff by representations which were false, in effecting the transfer of the property into his own name.

According to further particulars pleaded by the Plaintiff, the representations were made "during or about September, 1976 and July, 1978", and "were to the effect that the written agreement dated the 12th September, 1976 was a true memorandum of the oral agreement entered into between the parties and that it correctly reflected the terms thereof and that its purpose was to protect the rights of either party upon death. The representation which resulted in the signature of the agreement dated July, 1978 and the related transfer documents was to the effect that these documents and the agreement were to the same effect as the said oral agreement and that such were necessary, as the building was nearing completion." He further maintains that his inability to read and write resulted in his being unable to discern the meaning of the aforesaid written documents; he therefore formed a mistaken belief immediately the representations were communicated to him that they were true, and in this mistaken misbelief appended his signature to the aforesaid documents.

[*The Defendant's Case.*] The Defendant admits that he did not acquire the said property by way of donation* or cession** but pleads that the same was acquired by him in terms of an agreement of purchase and sale entered into between the parties. These agreements were in written form, and he exhibits them with his plea as Annexures "A" and "B". He denies that he entered into a verbal agreement with the Plaintiff "either in terms alleged or at all" and further denies that the transfer took place without the knowledge of the Plaintiff, or without just cause. He pleads that he is the registered owner of the property, and that the registration into his name was with the voluntary aid of the Plaintiff and by virtue of

(a) the Plaintiff's failure to pay the contract price of the building which had been constructed and

(b) the Defendant having exercised the option to purchase in terms of the written agreement entered in July, 1978, annexed to his pleadings as Annexure "B".

The Defendant denies all other allegations in Plaintiff's declaration with the significant exception of Plaintiff's averment*** that he the Plaintiff cannot read or write. The Defendant's answer to this averment is as follows:

"Defendant denies that Plaintiff's signature to Annexure "A" and "B" and to the Power of Attorney to give transfer were obtained

(a) by any false representation made by the Defendant

---

* by way of donation = as a gift.

** cession = ceded, as in a treaty.

*** averment = something alleged as true.

(b) by any mistaken belief on the part of the Plaintiff or

(c) by Plaintiff's inability to read or write and puts the Plaintiff to the proof thereof."

[*The Court's Analysis.*] It is a fundamental rule of pleading in all common law jurisdictions that a party must traverse* specifically each allegation of fact which he does not intend to admit. A pleading to an averment that a party's signature to an agreement was obtained because of his inability to read and write, which states that the other party denies that it was so obtained, does not necessarily mean that the party pleading denies the ability ** of the opposite party's illiteracy. Such a pleading can also mean that though it is admitted that the party cannot read or write, his signature was not obtained because of this disability. Such a pleading does not necessarily deny the averment of fact that the party cannot read or write. I must hold therefore that on the pleadings the Defendant has not specifically denied the averment, and he must be taken to have admitted that the Plaintiff cannot read or write. There is however, in practice, a difference between a person who though he cannot read or write, understands the language in which a document is written, and one who does not understand that language at all and cannot read or write it.

The legal position of such a party to a contract was stated by the Privy Council in the case of Kwamin vs Kufuor, Privy Council Appeal No. 94 of 1912 where Lord Kinnear, delivering the advice of the Committee said, "But then when a person of full age signs a contract in his own language, his signature raises a presumption of liability so strong that it requires very distinct and explicit averments indeed in order to subvert it. But there is no presumption that a native of Asbanti, who does not understand English and cannot read or write, has appreciated the meaning and effect of an English legal instrument because he is alleged to have set his mark to it by way of signature. That raises a question of fact, to be decided like other such questions upon evidence."

Subsequent cases have shown that in such cases the burden is on the party relying on the document to prove as a fact that the contents of the document were interpreted to the other party in a language that be understands, and that that party understood the meaning and effect of that document before appending his mark or signature to that document. The scope for the application of this rule in Botswana is limited by the fact that both English and Setswana are used extensively in commercial transactions. The document relied on by the Defendant herein, however, was made in the English Language only, and the Court would have applied this rule, if it was established to the Court's satisfaction, that the Plaintiff does not understand the English Language.

---

* traverse = deny formally.　　　　　　** ability (in this context) = power, having operative consequences.

The Plaintiff did not plead lack of understanding of the English Language. His original application to the Government for the land was in English, and the grant on which he relies was made in English. His discomfiture in the witness-box when under cross-examination on this point clearly indicates that he understands the English Language, and that he can even read it. I am satisfied that subject to any inherent invalidity in the documents themselves, the Plaintiff is bound by the documents he signed in connection with the transaction giving rise to these proceedings.

The question that arises for consideration therefore, is whether Exhibits "A" and "B" on which the Defendant places sole reliance are valid in law. The relevant provisions of Exhibit "B" for our purposes are:

PROVISION IN THE CASE OF NON-PAYMENT

In the event of the Owner failing to pay the contract price on due date the Contractor shall have the right and option exercisable forthwith to purchase the said property and all improvements thereon at that date for a purchase price of P38 000 (Thirty-Eight Thousand Pula) payable by set-off to the contract price aforesaid.

SECURITY

As security for the due payment of the contract price or in default as security for due compliance with the right of option referred to in paragraph 7 hereof, the Owner shall lodge with KIRBY, HELFER AND KHAMA, Attorneys for the parties, the following documents—

(i) The Title Deed of the Property;

(ii) Transfer documents duly signed in favour of the Contractor including but not limited to Power of Attorney to Pass Transfer which Power of Attorney shall be irrevocable;

(iii) Declaration of Seller.

> In the event of the owner paying the contract price aforesaid on due date then in that event the Title Deed and signed transfer documents shall be returned to the Owner by KIRBY, HELFER AND KHAMA.

Exhibit "A" is not dissimilar to Exhibit "B" and the same considerations apply to the two documents.

As long ago as 1762, Lord Nottingham L.C. summarised the whole attitude of equity towards such transaction when he said,

> "This Court, as a Court of Conscience is very jealous of persons taking securities for a loan and converting such securities into purchases and therefore I take it to be an established rule that a mortgage can never provide at the time of making a loan for any event or condition on which the equity of redemption shall be discharged, and the conveyance absolute, and there is great reason and justice in this rule, for necessitous men are not, truly speak-

ing, free men, but to answer a present exigency, will submit to any terms that the crafty may impose upon them."

Counsel for the Defendant has quite properly conceded that the agreement is equally illegal in Roman Dutch Law as constituting a *pactum commissorium.** [citation omitted] . . .

[*The Court's Findings.*] Exhibits "A" and "B" are therefore null and void and are of no effect. They cannot support the transfer of property from the Plaintiff to the name of the Defendant. The resulting position therefore, is that the relationships between the parties are the same as if the documents had not been executed. The fact that they are null and void does not give additional rights to the Plaintiff. The question therefore, is what were the rights of the parties immediately prior to the execution of Exhibits "A" and "B". The Plaintiff when giving his evidence explained in detail the business relationship between the Defendant and himself. He gave an account of previous transactions involving the building of a house on a speculative joint venture basis. The Plaintiff under the old transaction obtained a State Grant of land in Gaborone on which the Defendant built a dwelling house which was sold at a profit. The Plaintiff was paid the commission of that transaction by the Defendant who had financed the whole deal from the purchase of the land to the completion and sale of the house. The evidence suggests that a similar arrangement was entered into in this instance. Unfortunately none of the facts of the actual business relationship between the parties has been pleaded and the Plaintiff's learned Counsel insists that no judgment should be pronounced whether in his favour or not on matters which have not been pleaded. This Court therefore, should limit itself to the facts that have been pleaded in the declaration and the plea. The first claim by the Plaintiff as I have set out above is the release of the property from all encumbrances which might have been placed on it by the Defendant. The burden is of the Plaintiff to establish that the relations between the parties prior to the execution of "A" and "B" did not permit or empower the Defendant to place any encumbrances on the property. Far from discharging this burden, the Plaintiff himself has led evidence showing that the property was handed over to the Defendant subject to certain conditions. The conditions as pleaded were that the Defendant was to hold as security for costs of the building, the Title Deeds relating to the property and that the costs of the building were to be recouped out of the profits of a business to be run in the premises in which Plaintiff and Defendant would be partners.

The evidence adduced by the Plaintiff himself casts considerable doubt on the truth of these averments. It would seem to me that the true position and the real nature of the enterprise was that the De-

---

* pactum commissorium = an agreement for forfeiture in the event on non-payment of a mortgage. (Cf. An Introduction to Roman-Dutch Law [Fifth edition], by Robert Warden Lee. Oxford: Clarendon Press, 1953, p. 200.)

fendant would build on land acquired by the Plaintiff and pay the Plaintiff the commission for his efforts in the acquisition of the plot. I must therefore hold that the Plaintiff has failed to establish a case which would justify and instruct an order from this Court directing the release of the property from all encumbrances which might have been placed on it by the Defendant. I therefore dismiss the first claim on the declaration. The Plaintiff's second claim as set out in his declaration and as referred to above is one claiming an order for the restitution of the property to the Plaintiff by the Defendant.

As I have already said, the Plaintiff in his pleadings alleges that it was the understanding of the parties that the Defendant would hold the property as security until the costs of erecting the building had been recouped from the business to be carried on on the premises. The Plaintiff's own evidence shows that no such business was carried on. The Plaintiff can therefore succeed if he shows that the Defendant has otherwise recouped the costs of the building or that he the Plaintiff has tendered a sum covering these costs to the Defendant and the Defendant has unreasonably refused to accept it. The evidence in this case does not disclose that the execution of the property as security by the Defendant is anyway illegal or in breach of any contractual obligation. In the result I am of the view that the claim for restitution of the property is misconceived and I dismiss it. The Plaintiff's third claim is an order for the registration of the property into the name of the Plaintiff by the Defendant. In view of the Court's findings that both Exhibits "A" and "B" are null and void, the Plaintiff is clearly entitled to be placed in the same position that he would have been in if these documents had not been executed. The property was registered in the name of the Plaintiff immediately prior to the execution of these documents and the Plaintiff is entitled to an order that it be re-registered in his name and I so direct.

The Plaintiff has succeeded in one of his three claims and I am of the view that the justice of the case demands an order for one third of the costs of this suit in his favour. He has however, failed on two major claims and he will therefore bear two thirds of the costs of this action. I so direct.

NOTES AND QUESTIONS

This case raises the issue of the equity of a dual legal system where customary courts and statutory courts exist side by side with overlapping jurisdictions. It also raises the question of the degree to which law operates to the advantage of the more educated or more westernized party.

In *Tswaing* note how the Court cites both common law and Roman-Dutch law, both of the received law traditions which operate in Botswana.

1. Why is a pactum commissorium held to be an illegal contract?

2. Is an illiterate person making contracts in the modern, urban context likely to be at a disadvantage? What obvious steps could he or she take to

minimize their disadvantage in making contracts? What steps can a legal system itself take to minimize this kind of disadvantage?

As you read through the rest of the chapter, note how Tswana customary law tries to reduce the possibility of two parties to a contract having a different understanding as to what they agreed, and to resolve the disagreement should it occur.

3. Can the received law operate to protect the less educated, the less westernized, or more naive party? (Of course *whether* it always does so is another question.)

B. IS STATUS DOMINANT OVER CONTRACT?

NOTE

The hypothetical situation set out in the Walker excerpt on page 656 is one that could be found in contemporary Botswana. Common sense tells us that it falls under the rubric of contract. However, conventional wisdom about traditional societies is that relationships governed primarily by a contractual agreement are rare in those societies. Why? Recall the features of traditional society that we listed in the chapter introducing Botswana. And recall also the discussion of multiplex relationships in the chapters on inheritance and political succession in Botswana.

Nicholas Mahoney, "Contract and Neighbourly Exchange among the Birwa of Botswana," in Journal of African Law, vol. 21, 1977, p. 58.

. . . . For those, following Maine, who hold an evolutionary view of human society, contract is indeed something peculiar to the modern western world and is seen by them not just as something more developed in the West but as peculiarly characteristic of it, marking it off from earlier, and from contemporary but differently constituted, societies. But evolutionists and anti-evolutionists alike hold in common the view that contract is a specific means by which people can acquire rights and duties and that the incidence of contracts is not unrelated to the kind of social relationship which the contracting parties have. Perhaps the argument which has been put with most force is that contracts are unusual and inappropriate where people's relations with each other are multi-stranded and intense, where most transfers of property and services are made on the basis of people's social positions, and where obligation and generosity are held to be more important than rights.

NOTE

A well-known contemporary anthropologist has addressed herself to the same issue that concerned Maine. Although she wrote during the late colonial period, the gist of her argument is still applicable today.

Elizabeth Colson, "Native Cultural and Social Patterns in Contemporary Africa," in Africa Today, edited by Charles Grove Haines. Baltimore: The John Hopkins University Press, 1955, pp. 70–72, 79. Editor's insertions are in brackets.

Probably it is safe to say that over much of Africa, even today, life is conditioned by certain attitudes toward property and persons which are characteristic of a non-industrial stable society, in which opportunities and power depend upon status within social groups rather than upon control of investments; where, indeed, the safest form of investment, and often the only one, is still to be found in the building up of claims against persons. . . .

One can argue that this dependence upon personal relationships, institutionalized in various fashions, is the result of a long indigenous development within Africa. It is maintained by the hard facts of existence in present day Africa. The [Africans] are faced with the same problems that beset all people—security of life and property, provision for the nurture and maintenance of their children, assistance in sickness and old age, the mobilization of assistance for economic activities beyond the scope of the individual, and provisions for assistance to handle unforeseen accidents such as entanglement with the law, the necessity to meet a civil claim, or the payment of medical and funeral expenses. In the old days, over much of Africa, men depended for the safety of their lives and property, as they did for meeting their other needs, upon the obligation of kinsmen, or of other associates, to come to their assistance if the need arose. Men were therefore primarily concerned with associating themselves with those who had some diffuse obligation to assist and protect them, and the maintenance of these social ties was a matter which took precedence over other interests. The ambitious counted their wealth in terms of followers and used such wealth as came their way to increase the number of followers and to bind these more firmly to them. . . .

The introduction of a money economy, the opportunities for employment, and the development of capital resources have made it possible for the exceptional individual to provide for his own needs without reliance upon the assistance of others. But by and large, the new economic developments have not provided for the development of new institutions to meet the old needs, which are still present. The African continues to meet them in the same fashion, through a reliance upon personal obligations to him of those who stand to him in certain social relationships. What one of my colleagues has written of the Yao of Nyasaland applies generally to Africans in the rural areas everywhere.

. . . it should not be forgotten that the people are still bound most rigidly by their kinship obligations which they may not easily forego. If a man does neglect his duty to his kinsfolk they will soon criticize him and finally desert him. Their desertion means that he loses security socially and economically. He has no one to help him in infirmity, in illness and old age, and he cannot be assured of a proper burial. Furthermore, he will believe that he will be a target for his relatives' witchcraft. Men who become wealthy have done so usually by neglecting their kinship obligations and frequently by living too far away for kinsfolk to get at them. If they are accessible to their kinsfolk their obligations often prove too much and keep them down to a common economic level.[1]

* * *

. . . the [Africans] have been concerned to invest their capital, land, and cattle and their personal time in building up the system of mutual obligations incorporated in their social systems; and, in turn, in times of emergency they play upon this system to meet their needs. It is not surprising that they cling to this system and prefer to invest their wealth in maintaining it, for they have yet to develop the necessary legal mechanisms to ensure that direct contractual claims for the carrying out of specific obligations are enforced. As far as I know, under the various systems of native law still in force to govern relationships among Africans, there are few provisions which attach a penalty for the nonfulfillment of an executory contract. Those who attempt to provide for their needs on an impersonal contractual basis may therefore be left in the lurch. . . .

NOTE

As you read through the rest of this chapter, ask yourself how accurate is Maine's and Colson's assessment of the role of contract as a minor basis for providing goods and services in traditional societies? What was the role of contract in traditional Botswana? Did Colson's point about the nonenforceability of executory contracts apply to pre-independence Botswana? Does it apply now? How important is contract now in general in Botswana?

The next sections describe the kinds of contracts that were found in Tswana communities during the colonial period and regulated at that time by traditional law, the conceptual elements inherent in the Tswana model of contract, and remedies for breach of contract. Having described the traditional model of contract, we then review some ethnographic data, description of specialized contracts among a Tswanacized people, the Birwa, which forces us to look more critically at the broad question underlying Maine's work and the Colson excerpt that opened the chapter: Are relations governed by contract always to be contrasted with those governed by status? We conclude the chapter by examining the frequency with which contract disputes get to court in Botswana and by exploring the relationship between the traditional Tswana law of contract and modern law of contract.

1. J. C. Mitchell, "An Outline of the Social Structure of Malemia Area," The Nyasaland Journal, Vol. 4 (1951), 45–46.

C. PRIVATE ORDERING AMONG THE TSWANA

NOTE

1. Types of Contract

Tswana customary law recognizes several different kinds of situations that are governed by contracts. One of them is barter and sale.

a. Barter and Sale

Isaac Schapera, A Handbook of Tswana Law and Custom. Second edition. London: Oxford University Press, 1955, pp. 241–244. Editor's note: In reading this excerpt, recall that it describes the 1930's. Inserted headings in brackets.

[*Barter.*] Even before effective contact with the Europeans was established the exchange of goods (*thèkisô*, from *go rèka*, to buy) was a common practice among the Tswana. A man requiring metal goods, pots, baskets, wooden utensils, or similar objects which he did not himself make would procure them from an expert craftsman. He went directly to the latter, and either bought the object he wanted, if it was already available, or, as was frequently necessary, ordered it to be made. Such articles were also acquired by exchange, from other people possessing more than they needed at the moment. Livestock, too, were fairly often obtained in this way, while, in times of food shortage, grain was sought from more fortunate neighbours. There was no standardized medium of exchange. Grain, meat, cattle, small stock, fowls, hoes, and spears were all exchanged for one another and for other commodities. There were, however, certain stabilized relative values. . . .

A good deal of internal trade of this description still takes place, despite the existence of trading-stores (run by Europeans or Indians) in every village of any size. . . . [1930's]

[*Sale.*] Where the transaction is completed on the spot, the object sold and its purchase price both being handed over at the time, witnesses are not usually sought. But if only part payment is made, or something is bought on credit, the contract must be concluded before witnesses. Taking things on credit (*go tsaya molato*) is very common. . . .

. . . There is also a special form of contract known as *go tsaya mogwang* (to take an ear of corn), whereby a man needing corn, or meat, or some other foodstuff, will seek some from a neighbour, promising to repay it when he has reaped the corn growing in his field. In all these instances the receipt, on the one hand, of the purchase price or of the object bought, and the promise, on the other hand, to deliver the object or purchase price, complete the sale, and ownership passes.

* * *

[*Credit Sales.*] When anything is sold on credit, a time is usually specified for the delivery of the purchase price or object for which it has been exchanged. If no time is specified, it is customary to expect payment within a year. Should the time expire before payment has been made, the creditor will send word to the debtor that he is waiting for the settlement of the account. If nothing is done about it, he will wait for a while and then remind him again. If he still gets no satisfaction, he will report to the relatives or guardian of the debtor that he has been waiting in vain for payment, and that he now wants either payment or the return of his property. If this also does not help, he will then sue the debtor, first before the latter's headman, and then if necessary before the Chief. Should the debtor still refuse to pay, the Chief will order the creditor to go to the debtor's home, and take whatever he can find equivalent to the property owing to him. Any resistance on the part of the debtor will be punished by the Chief. The property thus seized, whether cattle, corn, or money, cannot be used by the creditor for his own purposes, but must be held as security for the payment of the debt. This practice is known as *go thukhutha*. It has occasionally led to charges of theft against the man seizing the property, but such charges are as a rule dismissed by the courts, unless it can be shown that he has disposed of the property.

If the debtor is unable to pay, his parents and relatives are expected to help him, and they will generally do so. But if they refuse, or are unable to help, he may be given some work to do for his creditor, such as helping him plough or cutting rafters for him. Should a man die owing some one else cattle or any other property, his heirs must pay the debt before sharing out his estate. Failing this, they can be brought to the *kgotla* and ordered to do so.

QUESTIONS

Here are some questions to consider on the basis of what you know so far. You will be able to answer them less speculatively after you have worked through sections C2 and C3.

1. In Tswana contracts involving barter and sale, must all of the terms of the contract be specified? Why not?

2. Under what conditions must the formation of a contract be witnessed? Why?

3. When is a Tswana contract complete? When the bargain has been struck? When the goods have been delivered? When they have been paid for? When?

4. What problems can arise because the buyer delays taking delivery of what he has purchased?

5. What do you think of the idea of seizing some of the property of a recalcitrant defaulting debtor in order to get him to settle the debt?

b. Some Other Types of Contract

NOTE

Other types of contracts that Schapera describes are those covering loans and leases (e.g., of wagons). And he shows how some transmission of property under the custom of Tshwaiso (see chapter on inheritance among the Tswana) can be interpreted as a contract in that receiving the property implies reciprocity at some point in the future. (Schapera, A Handbook of Tswana Law and Custom. Second edition. London: Oxford University Press, 1955, pp. 239–241, 244–246). Of particular interest and importance among the Tswana are contracts involving cattle herding and clientship and cattle:

c. Cattle Herding

Issac Schapera, A Handbook of Tswana Law and Custom, Second edition. London: Oxford University Press, 1955, pp. 253–254, 246–248. Bracketed headings added.

[*Cattle Herding I.*] The first contract to be considered under this heading is where a man agrees to let another's cattle run with his own. This is generally done when a man who is going away for some time leaves his cattle in the care of a friend or relative, or if he has purchased some cattle lets them remain with the seller until he requires them. Unless there is a special agreement to the contrary, the owner is not bound to make payment of any kind to the man looking after his cattle, although when reclaiming them he may if he wishes give him something to recompense him for his trouble. He may allow years to elapse before claiming them, but is then entitled to the original cattle and all their progeny. If any of the cattle have died or been lost, he cannot, however, claim compensation; but if they have been slaughtered or sold he can do so.

[*Cattle Herding II.*] This form of contract must be distinguished from another, equally common, where a man hires some one else to look after his cattle. The cattle in such cases remain at the owner's cattlepost, the herdsman going to live there. A special form of payment is agreed upon before the herding commences. It generally consists in a heifer, although sometimes the owner of the cattle will also undertake to supply the herdsman from time to time with food, blankets, and other necessities. The herdsman for his part is required to exercise every possible care over the cattle, being held responsible if through negligence any of them die or get lost. He may also be called upon to perform various other services for the owner, e.g. ploughing or digging a well for him.

d. Clientship and Cattle

Issac Schapera, A Handbook of Tswana Law and Custom, Second edition. London: Oxford University Press, 1955, pp. 246–248, 253–254, (continued).

MAFISA CATTLE. There is a special form of contract by which a man places one or more of his cattle into the keeping of another, who has the right to use them in various ways. Such cattle are known as *mafisa*. The herdsman takes sole charge of them for an indefinite period, which can be brought to an end at any time by either party. Should the herdsman die while the cattle are still in his keeping, his heir, if able to do so, may continue to look after them, but, if not, must send them back to the owner. *Mafisa* cattle, on the death of the owner, form part of his general estate, unless they had previously been set apart for any particular son. In the former case they will generally be sent for, and distributed among the heirs; in the latter, they may be allowed to remain with the herdsman.

Lending out cattle in this way is a very common practice. The herdsman, as will be shown in a moment, derives considerable benefit from the cattle thus entrusted to his care. The owner, on the other hand, has the task of herding his cattle greatly simplified. The practice serves also to insure against total loss from disease or some other agency which might annihilate a man's cattle should they all be concentrated in one kraal; and it is also a means of disguising the full extent of his riches, and so of escaping the jealousy and evil designs of less fortunate neighbours.

Mafisa cattle must be kept distinct from any cattle the herdsman himself may possess. He has the right, while the *mafisa* cattle are with him, to use their milk and to work with the oxen as if they were his own. He can plough his fields with them, inspan them to his wagon, and may even ride transport with them, using the proceeds for his own benefit. But he may not sell or slaughter them, use them in order to pay *bogadi*, or exchange them without the owner's authority. He may not lend them to other people, nor may he put his own earmark upon the calves they bear. The ownership of the cattle remains vested in the man by whom they are lent, and does not pass to the herdsman. They cannot, e.g., be seized for the payment of any debts or other liabilities the herdsman may have incurred. He has the right only to the use, and not to the disposal, of the cattle. No special fee is paid to him for looking after them; but it is customary, if they flourish under his care, to reward him with a heifer (termed in this connexion *kgomo ya madisa*), with any offspring it may subsequently have. He may occasionally be asked to help the owner of the cattle in ploughing and similar activities, but this is not an essential part of the *mafisa* contract, and must be specially agreed upon.

The herdsman is responsible for the welfare of the cattle while they are in his keeping. *Mogama-kgomo ya mafisa e re a e gama a be a lebile kgôrô go gopolêla mong wa yôna a tle a e tsaya*, goes the saying: 'The milker of a *mafisa* cow should, while he is milking it, look at the gateway (of the kraal), expecting the owner to come and take it', i.e., he must use it carefully, lest he forfeit the benefits he derives from it. The owner visits the cattleposts from time to time to see how his cattle are getting on, and the herdsman must account to him satisfactorily for their condition. The herdsman must exercise the same degree of diligence in looking after *mafisa* as he would in looking after his own cattle. Should any losses occur through death, straying, theft, or other causes, he must immediately report the loss to the owner and, in the case of dead beasts, produce the skin as well. Failing this, he will be held liable, and can be made to replace the lost animals. He is generally allowed to keep the meat of the dead animal, but if the owner is near by must produce it as well. He is further obliged to restore the cattle to their owner whenever required, and must then faithfully account for all their increase, which also belong to the owner.

The herdsman had formerly to obtain the consent of his whole family before he took over *mafisa*. If he was negligent, or stole or slaughtered any of the cattle, the family would be held responsible with him, for it was their duty to see that he looked after the cattle properly. They had therefore to make good any cattle lost through straying or other negligence. Nowadays, it is maintained, this system has deteriorated. *Mafisa* are taken by people without consulting their families or headmen, so that there is no one to keep them to their contract. If the herdsman kills any of the cattle, he can be made to pay; but, if he neglects them so that they stray or die of thirst, the only remedy the owner has in most cases is to resume the custody of those that remain.

KGAMÊLÔ CATTLE. Among the Ngwato and Tawana there was formerly a somewhat different system of contract governing the cattle entrusted to tribesmen by the Chief and other members of the royal family. From his 'tribal' and common household herds, i.e., those not specifically allocated to the houses of his wives or to his sons, the Chief would distribute cattle to be looked after for him by members of the tribe. Such cattle were sometimes entrusted to poor people, as a means of livelihood, but more generally to prominent commoners whose followers would help them to herd the cattle. It was regarded as a distinct honour, and also as a very profitable transaction, to be given cattle in this way by the Chief.

NOTE

In contrast to the *mafisa* relationship, holders of *kgamelo* could dispose of the chief's cattle as if they were his own. But, on the other hand, the chief could use for his own purposes all the cattle of the holder, including the holder's personal cattle. Schapera explains that: "The only way the *kgamelo* holder could free himself of his obligation was to return all the cattle in his possession at the time he wished to free himself." When the chief withdrew his *kgamelo* cattle, he could withdraw their increase and all the cattle owed by the *kgamelo* holder, ruining him. But Schapera notes: "The Chief as a rule withdrew his cattle when the holder proved disloyal or failed in his obligations, and this seldom happened. . . ." Nowadays, this form of contract no longer operates in Botswana.

NOTE AND QUESTION

1. What are the differences between the forms and functions of cattle herding, *mafisa*, and *kgamelo*? Think, for example, of the difference of the length of the contract and of goals to be achieved apart from obtaining cattle and cattle products or spreading risks concerning cattle. (Does the Colson excerpt help you to see *mafisa* and *kgamelo* through Tswana eyes?)

Now compare your thinking about *mafisa* with that expressed in the excerpt on pp. 676–677.

e. *Other Contracts for Service*

NOTE

Cattle herding was not the only type of service contract that existed among the Tswana.

Isaac Schapera, A Handbook of Tswana Law and Custom. Second edition. London: Oxford University Press, 1955, p. 250. Some footnotes omitted.

Service. Various forms of service contract exist among the Tswana. Reference has already been made in previous chapters to the special fees (*dikotlô*) claimable for the maintenance of children. The remaining forms of service contract may be grouped for convenience into: (a) domestic service; (b) care-taking or deposit, manifested chiefly in cattle-herding; (c) manual labour; and (d) the professional services rendered by magicians.

2. Viewing a Contract Conceptually

NOTE AND QUESTIONS

The previous section provided a wealth of descriptive material on types of contracts found among the Tswana. What analytical concepts have been employed to facilitate the observer's understanding of Tswana contract law?

As you read through the following material keep in mind the following questions. Are there some answers in the descriptions of contracts you have already read?

1. What notions of consent underlie Tswana notions of contract?

2. Who is competent or qualified to enter a contract?

3. Is a promise sufficient to make a contract, or must something be done or executed to make the contract valid?

4. Is some sort of ceremony necessary to validate a contract?

Isaac Schapera, "Contract in Tswana Law," in Ideas and Procedures in African Customary Law, edited by Max Gluckman. London: Oxford University Press, 1969, pp. 321–322. Editor's heading inserted.

a. Capacity to Contract; Consent

[*Women and Unmarried Children.*] In principle, women and unmarried children cannot make valid contracts without the consent of their male guardian (husband, father, etc.), who then also represents them at court in case of dispute; informants described instances (there are none in the records) of a father successfully reclaiming livestock or other goods disposed of without permission by a son. In practice, women nowadays engage independently in many kinds of transaction, and can also conduct their own cases at court; examples of such transactions found in the records include the sale of beer, hire of transport or a "doctor", loan of livestock, employment of a herdsman, and practice as a midwife.

[Editor's note: Nowadays women have much greater freedom to make contracts than they did in the 1930's and 1940's when Schapera carried out the bulk of his research.]

[*Men.*] On the other hand, even men occasionally need the consent of their near relatives before entering into agreements. This applies especially in regard to marriage: a betrothal, to be legally valid, requires the approval not only of the parents on both sides, but also of their siblings and other close kin (cf. Ngwaketse, 34/1934, in which the judge told a girl's father that he 'was wrong to join the children without the agreement of all their people, this is not marriage'). Informants said that in the old days a man also needed his kinsmen's approval before he could take cattle as *mafisa* (under agistment); * and that, even nowadays, a man should not give away or lend arable land without his neighbours' consent, which they can refuse if the prospective beneficiary has a bad reputation, say for being quarrelsome. I was given a few instances of the latter among the Ngwato; none appear in the records.

b. Promise vs. Execution

NOTE

In general in Sub-Saharan customary law a mere promise does not make a contract (Cf. the discussion of executory contracts in Islamic law.) The situation in another African country is typical of most of black Africa:

[* agistment = the feeding of other people's cattle on one's land for profit.]

Yash P. Ghai, "Customary Contracts and Transactions in Kenya," in Ideas and Procedures in African Customary Law, edited by Max Gluckman, London: Oxford University Press, 1969, p. 334.

There is no generalized concept of executory contract in customary law, which is to say that the mere exchange of promises by itself has no legal validity. . . .

NOTE

Traditional contract law in Botswana differs from that reported for Kenya and most other African countries in that:

Isaac Schapera, "Contract in Tswana Case Law," in Journal of African Law, volume 9, 1965, pp. 142–143.

A bare promise is sufficient to make an agreement legally binding.

1.   A (Lekwee) promised his wife B, when they got married, that he would not become a polygamist. He afterwards wanted to marry someone else. B (Goitumelang) thereupon complained at court that he was "putting her away" by breaking his promise, since she would not live with a co-wife. A said he wanted B to remain his wife, but he wanted to marry the other woman also. Asked by the judge if it was true he had promised not to marry polygamously, he replied, yes. Held: "In that case you must carry out your promise." (Goitumelang v. Lekwee, Ngwaketse, 74/1913.) [Schapera's citation form is explained on page 679.]

NOTE

We have already seen an instance of valid contract based solely on a promise in the discussion of bogadi as a critical element in defining a union as marriage in the chapter short on inheritance and succession among the Tswana. Here is that passage again:

Isaac Schapera, A Handbook of Tswana Law and Custom. Second edition. London: Oxford University Press, 1955, p. 139. Emphasis supplied and footnote omitted.

But the main function of *bogadi* is to transfer the reproductive power of a woman from her own family into that of her husband. This fact is of considerable importance, for upon it rests the whole Tswana conception of legitimacy. Summarizing this briefly, it may be said that no form of cohabitation between a man and a woman is held to be a proper marriage unless it is accompanied by the transfer of, or understanding to transfer, *bogadi*. No man can claim, for any purpose, the children he has by any woman, until he and his family have agreed to transfer, and under certain circumstances until they have actually transferred, *bogadi*. . . .

c. Ceremony

Isaac Shapera, "Contract in Tswana Law," in Ideas and Procedures in African Customary Law, edited by Max Gluckman, London: Oxford University Press, 1969, p. 320. Footnote omitted.

. . . all but the most trivial contracts (such as simple purchases paid for at once) are usually made in the presence of witnesses (*basupi*, from *supa*, show, point out). This is not essential to validate contracts, for the courts have upheld some to which there were no witnesses at all. It is done, rather, as an obvious and useful precaution in case of future dispute; the records show, for example, that a claim may be rejected owing to lack of corroborative evidence.

Normally, the parties first reach their agreement privately. They then call relatives or friends to listen while they repeat in detail its nature and terms. Alternatively, either or each of them will soon afterwards mention it to members of his family, and if livestock are involved he will in any case inform the herdboys. If the parties consider the agreement important enough, they may also go to the local *kgotla* (council-place) and describe it to the chief or village headman and all other men present; this ensures that its terms will be widely known and remembered. (The same procedure is occasionally followed by a man who wants to make a will.). . . .

QUESTIONS

One can ask other questions, rhetorical for the moment, about the conceptual dimension of Tswana contract law:

1. Does the seller imply a warranty?

2. If something happens to the item being sold or cared for before it is turned over to the buyer, is it the buyer or the owner who bears the risk involved?

d. Warranty and Risk

Antony N. Allott, Arnold L. Epstein and Max Gluckman, "Introduction" to Ideas and Procedures in African Customary Law, edited by Max Gluckman, London: Oxford University Press, 1969, pp. 75–76. Citations omitted.

[In this excerpt Gluckman summarizes the notions of warranty and risk found in several African societies including the Tswana. Note the varying conceptions about warranty and risk held in the traditional sector of African societies:]

(i) it was agreed that all African systems insist that where it is appropriate the transferor of goods must give warranty of title, and that a rightful owner can pursue goods and acquire them from an innocent acquirer;

(ii) Gluckman in the 1940s had found in Barotse law the rule that the seller gave an implied undertaking to deliver sound goods at a fair price (i.e. *caveat vendor* rather than *caveat emptor*) but in 1965 he was informed that for ten years the courts had changed the ruling to one by which buyers must test the goods and take responsibility for their condition. Schapera reported for the Tswana that goods must be delivered in sound condition at a fair price; but Ghai states that in Kenya there are few implied warranties and responsibility is with the buyer, though he cites no cases.

(iii) Ghai, Gluckman, and Schapera had found that risk remains with the seller until delivery, but increment is to the buyer; Ghai considers this is because "there is retarded development of the concept of negligence as affecting risk . . .".

Isaac Schapera, "Contract in Tswana Case Law," in Journal of African Law, Volume 9, 1965, p. 148.

In either sale or purchase on credit, ownership, but not risk, passes as soon as (but not until) something has been given in return for a promise to deliver or pay.

29. A's wife wanted to buy cattle with corn. Her brother B (Molefe) acted as her agent, and gave some of the corn to C in exchange for a heifer. The animal died while still in C's possession. Thereupon A (Manale), on behalf of his wife (B's sister), sued B. Held: B should give A a cow, and could then claim another from C (Manale Manale v. Molefe Nkwe, Ngatla, 19/1938.)

QUESTION

1. Does the prevalence of risks in a traditional, rather rural society have an impact on the degree of development of the concept of negligence as affecting risk?

NOTE

Walker combines the concept of bailment * with the criterion of whether the temporary transfer of property is for the benefit of the borrower or for

* bailment:

In thinking about risk, it is useful to bring to bear the notion of bailment: Bailment, a broad expression which describes the agreement, undertaking or relationship which is created by the delivery of personal property by the owner, i.e., the bailor, to someone who is not an owner of it, i.e., the bailee, for a specific purpose, which includes the return of the personal property to the person who delivered it, after the purpose is otherwise accomplished. In a bailment, dominion and control over the personal property usually pass to the bailee. The term is often used to describe, e.g., (1) The gratis loaning of an automobile for the borrower's use. (2) The commercial leasing of an automobile for a fee. (3) The delivery of an automobile to a repairman for the purpose of having it repaired. (4) The delivery of an automobile to a parking attendant for storage, when the keys are left with the attendant.

(from: Wesley Gilmer, Jr., Gilmer's Revision of Cochran's Law Lexicon. Fifth edition. Cincinnati, Ohio, W. H. Anderson. 1973, p. 38.)

the benefit of both the borrower and the lender to provide insight into permissive use loans and loans of *mafisa* cattle which were described in an earlier Schapera excerpt. He suggests that where the benefit lies is related to how rigorous is the view of what constitutes negligence.

J. M. Walker, "Bamalete Contract Law" in Botswana Notes and Records, volume 1, 1968, pp. 72–75.

Widely used among the Bamalete are agreements to temporarily transfer goods to another. Although these have been considered loan agreements by earlier writers on Tswana law, their resemblance is more to that of bailments in English law rather than loans. Interest is neither contemplated nor enforceable in customary law. Indeed, the majority of these agreements merely effect a temporary transfer of custody with the custodian expected to re-deliver the goods at some future date.

These loan agreements may be divided into two general sub-categories—permissive use loans for the sole benefit of the borrower and *mafisa* loans. The first type of loan arises when a lender lends certain property to a borrower to be used for a specific use by the latter. It is usually a short term arrangement lasting only until the specific function for which the property has been borrowed has been completed.

The *mafisa* loan differs from the permissive use loan in that it is for the mutual benefit of both the lender and the borrower. It is a loan of livestock, usually cattle, and is generally a long term transaction; rarely for less than a year and often for as long as ten or fifteen. . . .

* * *

The duration of the *mafisa* loan is not prescribed but is often intended to last for ten or fifteen years. Only in exceptional cases of hardship could the owner of the stock terminate his loan before a year was out. During all of this time the borrower of the stock has the full use of such stock short of slaughter or alienation. Thus, unlike the permissive use loan, the *mafisa* loan is for the mutual benefit of both parties to the agreement. . . .

The *mafisa* loan is formed in the same way as the permissive use loan and the requirements of formation are the same.

In return for the privilege of having full use of *mafisa* stock and its progeny short of slaughter or alienation, the borrower under the loan has certain obligations [which were spelled out in a previous Schapera excerpt.] The borrower . . . is expected to use the same degree of care respecting *mafisa* stock as he would use with his own beasts. In this connexion, it appears that because the loan is for the benefit of the lender as well as the borrower, there is a less burdensome duty of care upon the latter. For the lender to succeed in an action against the borrower for loss or damage, he would have to show a higher degree of negligence than in the case of the permissive use loan.

e. A "Standard" Contract

Isaac Schapera, "Contract in Tswana Law," in Ideas and Procedures in African Customary Law, Edited by Max Gluckman. London: Oxford University Press, 1969, pp. 323–324. Editor's inserted headings are in brackets.

[The contractual concepts which this section has laid out so far are incorporated in "standard" traditional Tswana contracts:]

[*Specific Conditions.*] [*Mandatory specification.*] . . . the parties must agree on the nature and amount of the payment due, including the sex and age of any animals involved in the transaction.

[*Optional specification.*] . . . They may also, but need not, agree on such other details as the time of payment or delivery of goods purchased, or when a loan should be repaid.

[*"Standard" or "Customary" Obligations—Optional or Implicit.*] In addition to such specific conditions, contracts of these kinds normally entail what may be called "standard" or "customary" obligations. These do not have to be stipulated whenever an agreement is made, but are generally taken for granted, and the courts in case of dispute will always assume that they apply. The following are examples of those featuring most prominently in the case records:

* * *

(c) In either sale or purchase on credit, ownership passes once something has been given in return for a promise to deliver or pay. But risk does not pass simultaneously; for example, if an animal purchased dies before having been taken away, the seller must give another in its place.

(d) If a cow or other female animal is bought and left for the time being with the seller, the purchaser when taking delivery (by going to fetch the animal) is entitled also to its offspring. The same rule applies to female stock one man may be holding for another under any other condition, say as *mafisa* (under agistment).

(e) A man looking after another's livestock must inform him promptly of losses due to death, straying, theft, etc., and must give him the hides of those that have died. Failing this, he can be held liable for the loss. He is also liable for losses or injury due to his own negligence (e.g. if he does not search for stray animals).

(f) The holder of *mafisa* cattle is entitled to a heifer as payment, either after a year or so, or when the owner takes back the cattle. But it can be withheld, or refused altogether, if he has not looked after the animals properly. Similarly, a man hired for some special task (such as building a hut, digging a well, or "doc-toring") is not entitled to payment until he has satisfactorily com-pleted that task.

(g) A gift of any kind, once made, is irrevocable (unless given to children or other dependents). . . .

(h) A debt must be paid on demand (or at the time agreed up-on), and is always due, no matter how long ago it was incurred. *Molato gaobole, gobola nama*, says the proverb, "A wrong [or debt] does not rot, [only] meat rots." . . .

NOTE

In section two we have examined five dimensions of contract which are conceptualized by Tswana and incorporated in their notions of a "standard" contract: (1) capacity to contract, (2) promise vs. execution, (3) ceremony, and (4) warranty and risk. We must look at the opposite side of the coin of contract—remedies for breach of contract.

3.   Remedies for Breach of Contract

NOTE

The settlement of contractual disputes is particularly important in tradi-tional societies where multiplex relations are significant:

J. M. Walker, "Bamalete Contract Law," in Botswana Notes and Records, Volume 1, 1968, p. 71.

. . . At the risk of over-simplification, it can be said that the primary function of tribal law is to ensure the perpetuation of tribal harmony through the speedy resolution of disputes. There is concern for justice to the individual, but in almost all cases it must yield to the greater interest of the tribe as a whole in preserving amicability between its members. This interest is not born solely of altruism but reflects a recognition that in a marginal economy very survival may depend upon sharing between friends and neighbours and upon the customary links between members which call for economic exchange. Any dispute, therefore, is thought to be of potential damage to the fabric of the tribe as a whole.

The notion of contract remedy in tribal law reflects this desire for amicable settlement. . . .

NOTE

What kinds of remedies for breach of contract are found in Tswana cus-tomary law? [In the following section many substantive portions of the ex-cerpt are drawn from Isaac Schapera, "Contract in Tswana Law," in Ideas and Procedures in African Customary Law, edited by Max Gluckman, London: Oxford University Press, 1969, and illustrative cases from Isaac Schapera,

"Contract in Tswana Case Law," in Journal of Africa Law, Volume 9, 1965. These two sources are identified in the following excerpts as Schapera 1969 and Schapera 1965, respectively. The case citation form employed by Schapera uses the following convention: the names of the litigants, followed by the name of the court, followed by the number of the case and the year in which it is heard. The latter two data are separated by a slash, and the number of the case refers to its ordinal sequence in the cases heard before that particular court in that year. Unless otherwise specified all the cases cited were heard at the Chief's Court (senior customary court) of the tribe named. Thus: Segaritse v. Kesupilwe, Ngawaketse 16/1912 is case #16 of 1912 of the Chief's Court, Ngawaketse.]

a. Suppose the Breach of Contract is Failure to Repay a Debt. What is the Remedy?

(a) If payment of a debt is refused or withheld, the debtor is ordered to pay; and if there was no excuse for his delay (e.g. if he had been approached several times in vain), he may have to pay more than was in fact originally due. In the old days, it may be added here, a man whose debtor would not pay had another remedy than going to court: he could "seize" (*thukhutha*) cattle or other property from the latter and hold it as security. This practice, though still found at times, is tending to be frowned upon by the tribal authorities, because of the many disputes to which it leads; among the Ngwaketse it was actually prohibited in 1898 by Chief Bathoen I, who decreed that any man "seizing" another's goods would not only have to return them, but would also forfeit what was due to himself. (Schapera 1969: 325.)

45. A (Sekgaritse) gave B (Kesupilwe) an ox to herd, and when he claimed it back was refused. Held: B must return the ox, "and pay another for his delay". (Sekgaritse v. Kesupilwe, Ngwaketse, 16/1912.) (Schapera 1965: 150–151.)

QUESTION

1. Do the assessments levied in this case seem to involve more than forced payment? What other dimension is present?

b. Sometimes the Breach of Contract Takes the Form of Non-performance of the Contracted Task. What is the Remedy Then?

NOTE

In many societies the remedy provided for non-performance is a court order that the neglected task be done, what is known as specific performance. In the customary law of Sub-Saharan societies specific performance is not common as a remedy for breach of contract.

The situation in Botswana traditional law concerning specific performance contrasts with that found elsewhere in Sub-Saharan Africa:

A defaulter may . . . be ordered to do work he has promised, or to finish a task he has abandoned or done badly; specific examples include digging a well, transporting goods, ploughing, and "doctoring". Occasionally this applies also to breach of promise to marry, the judge ordering that the marriage must take place. But if the defendant can show that performance was impossible he may be excused, as in cases where a herdsman could not search for stray stock because his employer had given him other work to do (Ngwaketse, 3/1928), or a man could not plough a field for someone else because it was waterlogged (Tawana, 233/1940). [Schapera 1969: 325–326.]

48. A (Maswe) lent B (Seiphetlho) an ox with which to plough, on condition that B then ploughed for him; he now complained that B refused to do so. Held: B "must carry out his agreement". (Maswe v. Seiphetlho, Ngwaketse, 28/1910). [Schapera 1965: 151.]

QUESTION

Is specific performance usually the appropriate remedy in breach of promise to marry? Why not?

Suppose there is non-performance in a situation where the contractor/buyer has made a partial payment for service or goods that were not provided?:

. . . if any payment has already been made, the court will usually order its refund, and thus cancel the contract. This applies also in cases of a girl's refusing to marry her fiancé: he is then entitled to recover the whole of his betrothal gifts. [Schapera 1969: 326.]

51. A (Mosweu) gave B (Openshaw, a European blacksmith) his wagon to repair, paying him an ox in advance. B took the wagon from Lehututu to Kanye (the tribal capital, 260 miles away), but instead of working on it "went to cut wood for sale". A sued for, and was awarded, the return of his ox, "because B had not yet repaired the wagon". (Mosweu v. Openshaw, Ngwaketse, 13/1910.) [Schapera 1965: 151.]

c. *In Many Societies a Remedy for Breach of Contract Where the Breach has Resulted in the Loss of Anticipated Profit or Benefit is Damages*

NOTE

In such circumstances in Botswana, how widespread are damages as a remedy? Walker describes the situation for one Tswana group, the Malete:

J. M. Walker, "Bamalete Contract Law," in Botswana Notes and Records, Volume 1, 1968, p. 75.

. . . the concept of fairness in Bamalete contract law differs markedly from that of most western legal systems. In the latter, fairness permits the entrepreneur to realize his bargained for profit as long as his conduct in respect of the contract is above reproach. This is not the case in Bamalete law.

The realization of profits, the Bamalete would argue, is not so praiseworthy a goal when measured against the economic hardship it would impose upon the compensating party who is living his life upon a slender margin of economic security. Nor is it a valuable end in itself when the net result of its attainment is to create disharmony among the families of the tribe. The integrity of the tribe could not withstand this divisive pressure; and the integrity of the tribe is essential to the survival of its members in a marginal economy.

It is with these thoughts in mind, then, that the Bamalete limit the remedy upon breach of contract to rectifying any imbalances in values due to exchanges between the parties while the contract was in force. Who can complain when matters are restored to their pre-contract condition?

NOTE

But Schapera, reporting research on customary contract law in five other Tswana groups finds remedies that differ pointedly from those described for the Malete:

A person who has suffered actual loss through breach of contract may be awarded special damages. Thus, when A did not plough a field for B at the time agreed upon, the court awarded B part of A's own crops (Tawana, 21/1937); and a man who borrowed and did not return another's bull for several years was ordered to give him the five calves that bull had sired on his own cows, "because the owner's cows had been without the services of their bull for a long time" (Kgatla, 22/1938). This applies also in cases where a girl is jilted by her fiancé, especially after she has borne him a child . . .. [Schapera 1969: 326.]

55. A (Molapisi) hired B (Diaramoka) to cut and bring him a supply of reeds (used for building huts). B did not deliver the reeds, and as A had to go and fetch them himself he sued B "for his expenses" (*ditshenyegelo*). Held: B must pay A 11s. 6d. or 23 bundles of reeds "for breaking his contract". (Molapisi v. Diaramoka, Tawana, 125/1938.) [Schapera 1965: 152.]

NOTE

Allott et al sum up concerning the Tswana employment of the concept of damages:

Anthony N. Allott, Arnold L. Epstein and Max Gluckman, "Introduction," in Ideas and Procedures in African Customary Law, edited by Max Gluckman, London: Oxford University Press, 1969, pp. 76–77.

Schapera cites cases where courts awarded what he calls "special damages," but [he does not use the phrase] with the technical meaning it has in English law . . . . The Tswana seem here, as elsewhere, to be exceptional for Africa in allowing for damages or loss flowing from breach of contract.

QUESTION

It is clear that a losing Tswana defendant in a contracts dispute may be assessed more than the amount at issue. Is this always "damages" in the sense of replacement of lost anticipated gain? (Review the earlier cases reported on pp. 673 and 679.) Do any of the "extra" assessments seem to play the role of a penalty?

d. Are There Any Special Remedies Available When a Person Breaching a Contract Seems to Act With Particularly Recalcitrant Intent?

If a case for breach of contract is due primarily to the defendant's obstinacy or other misconduct (e.g. if he has appealed from a lower court when he was clearly in the wrong, or if he told lies), the court, in addition to any other award, may inflict special punishment upon him, e.g. fine him 'for letting the matter come to court unnecessarily' (Kgatla, Mathubudukwane district court, 3/1936). Such penalties were imposed in 22 of the 310 cases. [Schapera 1969: 326.]

59. A (Ntiria) borrowed two oxen from B (Matlhoakgosi) for use in ploughing. They went astray, and he neither reported this to B nor looked for them; in court he tried to excuse himself by saying he thought B had already fetched them. Held: he must restore the animals (*i.e.*, their equivalent) to A, and also pay an ox as fine, "for letting the matter come to court unnecessarily". (Matlhoakgosi Tshukudu v. Ntiria Pule, Kgatla, Mathubudukwane district court, 3/1936.) [Schapera 1965: 153.]

NOTE

Traditional courts in Africa, in seeking remedies for breach of contract of one sort or another, also may take account of mitigating circumstances. Ghai in his Kenyan research noted the concepts of "mistake" and "duress" used in this way. "Hardship" and "unfairness" were used in this way in some of the Malete cases studied by Walker.

QUESTIONS

1. In cases cited by Schapera in the excerpts above, did you notice "excuses" and "impossibility of performance" cited as extenuating circumstances of which the court should take account in prescribing a remedy? Did the court do so?

2. Now that you have examined Tswana conceptions of contract, including remedies, return to the questions on page 656 concerning the would-be soft drink vendor.

D. IS IT REALLY STATUS VERSUS CONTRACT?

NOTE

Recall Mahoney's summing up early in this chapter of the conventional wisdom: that "contracts are unusual and inappropriate where people's relations with each other are multistranded and intense, where most transfers of property and services are made on the basis of people's social positions, and where obligation and generosity are held to be more important than rights."

Mahoney's own field research among the Birwa, a Tswana-cized Sotho group, has brought forth some empirical data which challenges that conventional "wisdom." The research focuses on production and economic and social relationships among groups of Birwa neighbors who form groups Mahoney identifies as "neighborhood sets." They have a mixture of status relationships and contractual relationships which bring into question the traditional Mainean view about status and contract that has been mentioned several times before.

1. Birwa Neighbors Have Multiplex Links

NOTE

Nicholas Mahoney's study of productive exchanges among the Birwa show that they are tied together in varied, overlapping ways.

Nicholas Mahoney, "Contract and Neighbourly Exchange Among the Birwa of Botswana," in Journal of African Law, volume 21, 1977, pp. 41–52. Some footnotes omitted. Editor's inserted notes and headings are in brackets.

[*The Birwa Settlement Pattern.*] In the Birwa region there are six villages where almost all of the Birwa maintain a permanent home. Bobonong, the largest of the six villages is the home village for more than two thirds of the region's total population and it was in and around this village that fieldwork was carried out. The village however is not the place in which production is undertaken; crops are

grown and livestock kept at settlements outside of the village.
. . .

* * *

[*Interdependency at the Settlements.*] In the course of their productive activities . . . all households are bound to enter into various kinds of transactions of labour and services with others. One
reason for inter-household productive exchanges is that households
vary with regard to their demographic composition and hence their
labour force, their control over basic productive assets, land and livestock, and hence their labour needs, and their ownership of ploughs,
draught animals and tractors. Arrangements have to be made to secure labour where it is needed or to hire or borrow ploughing implements. Inter-household exchanges are also necessary to meet the requirements of production. People living at settlements are often
separated from other members of their families and are away from
the home village and all the services available there. They therefore
have a whole range of welfare needs which can only be met by calling
upon neighbours. What is more, unpredictable crises can arise in the
course of routine production. When such emergencies arise it is
again necessary for householders to call upon neighbours for support.

* * *

Welfare needs are not the only ones which lead householders to
have recourse to neighbourly support. Particularly at livestock post
settlements neighbours often require each other to help out with
work problems specific to livestock keeping. Illness or the enforced
absence from work of the herdsman, perhaps because his wife has a
problem some distance away at the field settlement, has serious consequences in that animals, to a greater extent than crops, are at risk
if they are neglected. Some people have understandings with some
of their neighbours that they can be called upon to provide assistance, perhaps by sending a youth to help out for short periods.
. . .

[*Relations Among the Neighborhood Set: A Particular Pattern
of Reciprocity.*] * * *

Neighbourhood set relations are relations for solving problems of
a certain kind. The problems—sickness, straying cattle, etc.—can be
described as expected but unpredictable. The solutions to the problems are of a certain kind too: they are invaluable and may involve
much effort in emergencies but they are not of a kind to provide long-
term solutions. It is to the types of problems, the expected but unpredictable, that the diffuse, unspecific conceptualisation of
neighbourhood set relations can be attributed. The relations are fu-
ture-orientated but the precise nature of this future is unclear.
Therefore the relations between neighbourhood set members have to
be defined in terms of a general ethic of friendly, neighbourly, do-as-
you-would-be-done-by values—precise obligations or specified reci-

procity would be of little utility when neither the victim of misfortune nor its kind nor its extent can be foreseen. The diffuse, imprecise definition of the relations by set members is not a sign that the relations are less significant than others specified more precisely—the property rights of family members for example, but simply that they are relations of a qualitatively different type. . . . As Gouldner has observed, such relations combine both moral and self-interested, instrumental aspects: there is an expectation that those helped will later return help, that in the long term exchanges may balance, but above all there is a feeling that assistance *should* be rendered. Neighbourly relations among Birwa are of the general type discussed by Sansom for Southern Bantu peoples. Neighbourly support transactions involve "values that emerge directly out of the mode of production. . . . Acts of apparently unstinting giving are the premiums in social insurance, contributions to a fund of goodwill", without which secure productive activity would not be possible.

[The multiplex links that bind a Birwa neighborhood set are expressed in exchanges. These exchanges . . .] between neighbours at settlements outside of the village can be grouped into three broad categories. They are:

1. *Neighbourly assistance*, which may take a number of forms from the exchange of small gifts between friends to support in emergencies. Such assistance is freely given and sanctioned only by a diffusely defined morality.

2. *Reciprocal labour exchanges*, organized usually between women with neighbouring fields in order to accomplish the tasks of tending or harvesting crops, tasks which could be managed by the women working alone.*

3. *Contracts* made between neighbours, acquaintances or strangers for short- or long-term employment and for ploughing. The terms are formally agreed and said to be enforceable in law.

QUESTION

Is the neighborly assistance described in this excerpt "contractual"? Why or why not?

Among Birwa . . . the participants themselves, state, as is the case with so many neighbourly exchanges, that they co-operate only out of friendship. However the formal and overt emphasis on balanced reciprocity in the otherwise "friendly" transactions of members of work parties, and the open assessments of people's willingness to co-operate, make these groups an ideal setting for activating or confirming good neighbourly relations. What is more, attendance or non-attendance at such groups can be a means of making statements

---

* [Mahoney indicates that these reciprocal exchanges which take the form of work parties are a way of "assessing reputations and building trust among members of neighborhood sets, p. 52."]

about the current boundaries of a neighbourhood set; individuals are given the opportunity of choosing between one set and another. . . . work parties do not appear to provide a social means for meeting productive needs directly, but rather productive activity is used to cement relations which provide for social as well as other, more important, productive requirements.

2. Birwa Neighbor Contracts

NOTE

The section above states that Birwa neighborhood sets have three kinds of exchanges. Why do Birwa neighbors have contractual relationships alongside multiplex links and generalized reciprocity? To answer this question we first will look at a distinctive type of Birwa contract for services used in Birwa neighborhood sets.

Ploughing contracts are a good example of the contracts that are made . . . between kinpersons and neighbors for the hiring of labor and other specialized services because:

Nicholas Mahoney, "Contract and Neighbourly Exchange Among the Birwa of Botswana", in Journal of African Law, Volume 21, 1977, pp. 63–64. Some footnotes omitted. Headings inserted by the editor.

. . . they are the most common and embody the general features of the many different types.

[*Types of Ploughing Contracts.*] Ploughing contracts, all of which were formally defined and held to be legally enforceable, were of three main types. The first, "holding the plough" (*gotshwara mogoma*), was an exchange of labour for the use of ploughing equipment. The second was one in which both households contributed some labour and some equipment; and the third was the purchase of labour and the use of equipment for cash. The first usually involved the understanding that the contributor of labour was entitled to some crop at the end of the season, so that if his first sowing failed the owner of the plough should come a second time to plough and sow again. The other kinds of contract did not involve this understanding. The three basic types of agreement could be combined in a number of different ways in practice to give a range of actual contracts. In all, the definition of obligations and rights was made clear, and in all the transaction was restricted solely to ploughing and sowing.

It is necessary to distinguish between those more common ploughing contracts which do not involve the use of a tractor and those less common ones which do. Arrangements which make use of animal-drawn ploughs and human labour are constrained by the relative immobility of these factors. To be sure, all can be moved but this is regarded as extremely inconvenient, wasteful, and time-consuming at a stage in the season when timing is of the essence. The tractor on the other hand can move with its trailer loaded up with ploughs, planters, and fuel over large distances, and indeed does so in the course of the ploughing season. For the moment I am concerned only with contracts which *do not* involve tractors.

[*Neighbors' Ploughing Contracts vs. Other Neighborly Exchanges.*] The relative immobility of people, animals, and light ploughs means that people who wish to hire them have to look to close neighbours in order to do so. Those who want to be employed to carry out ploughing are similarly constrained to find customers close to their settlement. From observation of such ploughing transactions it is apparent that the neighbours involved are regularly fellow members of the same neighbourhood set. In order to understand why formal contracts are made for ploughing exchanges I want to compare the ploughing exchange with ordinary neighbourly exchanges in terms of people's perceptions of the costs incurred in each. Regular exchanges between neighbours, to recapitulate, involve mutual support in emergencies, participation in work groups, and frequent minor gifts and hospitality. What do these transactions cost the people involved and how do they perceive these costs? In short, the answer is that they cost and are held to cost very little. For example, if a person is called to assist another who is sick and thereby fails to weed his field for one day, the loss incurred is hardly measurable; furthermore there is the implicit understanding that one day the favour may well be returned and the balance redressed. When one person assists another in a neighbourly way their relative positions in terms of wealth are likely to remain unaltered. . . .

[*Critical Timing of Ploughing and Its Consequences.*] How does this compare with relations of ploughing which, after all, could supposedly be organized on the basis of neighbourly goodwill? The timing of ploughing is critical; a delay of only a few days after a period of suitable rainfall can significantly affect crop yields. This fact is clearly perceived by people, and there is the general belief that co-operation in ploughing because of the demands of critical timing cannot only be costly to one of the parties but also significantly affect the relative wealth of those involved. In the arrangement which involves an exchange of labour for the use of equipment it is generally understood that the owner of the equipment has the right to choose the days on which ploughing shall take place, and when he is satisfied with work in his own field will agree to move to the field of the labourer. Thus, whether the whole of the neighbourhood has experienced good rainfall or if the rains have been patchy, as they sometimes are, the owner of the equipment can always choose the optimum moment to plough his own field and therefore is more likely to produce the best crop. Not only is the labourer likely to get a worse crop, but because he has spent time helping the other his activity has directly contributed to the good yields that the equipment owner can expect. . . . Even in the arrangements in which labour

and services are contributed by both parties one necessarily has his
field ploughed first. . . .

* * *

QUESTION

Why are these exchanges related to ploughing regulated by contracts
while other neighborly exchanges are not? Are these ploughing exchanges
qualitatively different from the others?

3. An Hypothesis

**Nicholas Mahoney, "Contract and Neighborly Exchange Among
the Birwa of Botswana", in Journal of African Law, Volume 21,
1977, pp. 62–65. Emphasis supplied. Footnotes omitted.**

. . . It is my contention that among Birwa contracts are a feature of relations between close kin and neighbours, not because these
relations lack a "norm of reciprocity", nor because they are not multi-
stranded, but precisely *because* of their multi-stranded character.
My case is that contracts among close kin are made only in regard to
specific kinds of transactions and that the purpose of the contracting
parties is one of insulating that aspect of their relationship which is
characterized by freely given assistance and in which no one counts
the cost, from transactions which all hold to be potentially disruptive
and which are a regular cause of complaint and dispute. The circumstances of production in neighbourhood sets are such that generous
exchanges and potentially disruptive transactions have to be made between the same people. It is here that contracts can be effective.

In referring to contractual agreements, what is usually stressed is
the way in which people's obligations to one another are specified: A
is to render a specific service to B and B is to pay A a specified
amount in return. But the agreement can have another aspect: it
can define the *limits* of the parties' respective responsibilities. A is
to render a specific service to B and no more. It is this aspect of
contractual agreements which is used to prevent the conflicts arising
from certain kinds of transaction from affecting the already existent
multi-stranded relationship between the parties.

Contracts are made between neighbours because a multi-stranded
relationship characterized by a norm of generosity has to be combined with specific transactions which are regularly disruptive in
their effect.

I should make it clear from the outset that not all contracts
among Birwa are of this type. Many are made between relative
strangers with no other basis for their transaction. While such contracts have very much the same legal form as those made between
kin and neighbours, their sociological significance is quite different in

that they define minimum obligations rather than maximum responsibilities. . . .

[*How Does This Hypothesis Apply to the Ploughing Contracts Described Earlier?*] Each year the ploughing exchange which is perceived to be costly intrudes into a neighbourly relationship in which few costs are incurred and none counted. I would suggest that the differentiating and conflict-laden ploughing exchanges, exchanges which owe their character to the particular circumstances of ploughing in a particular environment with a particular technology, have somehow to be prevented from damaging the other relations which the parties to the transactions have. The problem is particularly acute, given that both neighbourly goodwill and support and the exchange of ploughing services are equally essential for the maintenance of productive activity. The contract can, in this light, be interpreted as a social (rather than a specifically economic, or legal) device to *contain* these disruptive exchanges by giving them a short-term specificity: the rights and duties and responsibilities of the parties last only for the duration of ploughing. Only for the duration of the contract, they give the partners clearly measurable rights and responsibilities. By means of this containment a problematic but necessary exchange is prevented from endangering the normal, long-term diffuse understandings which the partners hold. Thus through time the relations between neighbourhood set members can be seen to alternate between long-term diffuseness and short-term specificity, between neighbourly goodwill and complaint, between generalized reciprocity and contract.

Some tractor ploughing contracts resemble those already outlined; others, because of the mobility of the tractor, are something quite different. Contracts made between a tractor-owner and his neighbours, apart from the fact that the tractor-owner can enter into more of them than can an owner of an animal-drawn plough, are sociologically similar to those already discussed. The mobility of the tractor, however, facilitates the negotiation of ploughing contracts with many people outside the owner's neighbourhood.

. . . The exchange of money for ploughing services takes place in exactly the same way as it does in neighbourhood contracts, but the arrangement is different. Between unrelated parties the contract is a means of establishing a basis of interaction where none other exists; the contract reverts to defining minimum obligations and not maximum responsibilities.

QUESTIONS

1. How generalizable is Mahoney's hypothesis?

    a. Can you think of a situation in which two people in a close relationship (e.g. a married couple or roommates) made a contractual agreement about some area of their lives that was subject to tension in order to keep their life as a whole on even keel?

b.   Are there any other situations in our culture that are parallel to the Birwa ploughing context in that they combine continual diffuse obligations with equally important specific ones? For example, consider two mill workers, "puddlers," who work as partners in the mill and live in the same neighborhood in a "company town." Are they likely to have need of insulating contractual arrangements like those of the Birwa? Why or why not?

2. Given the situation that produces the Birwa containment contracts, are breaches of those contracts likely to be taken to court? Why or why not?

3. Why is it misleading for analysts of traditional legal systems to think of contracts as being "all of one piece"?

E. FREQUENCY OF CONTRACT CASES

NOTE

A contract often is defined as an agreement between two parties that is legally enforceable. How often are Tswana courts called upon to enforce contracts? Speaking of ploughing contracts among the Birwa, Mahoney observes: "Arrangements so made were said to be enforceable in law but in most cases both sides largely honoured their agreement, even if not always to the complete satisfaction of the other party, and recourse was rarely made to the chief's court." Nicholas Mahoney, "Contract and Neighbourly Exchange Among the Birwa of Botswana" in Journal of African Law, volume 21, 1977, p. 43.

Was the picture different in colonial times? Schapera presents the following table comparing the relative frequency of various types of civil disputes brought before Tswana and Southern Sotho courts in the 1930's. Figures are presented in percentages.

Type of Dispute	Tswana	S. Sotho
Domestic and Personal Status	40%	24%
Property	28	33
Contracts	25	25
Defamation and Insult	7	17

(Source: Isacc Schapera, "The Work of the Tribal Courts in the Bechuanaland Protectorate," in African Studies, vol. 2, 1943, p. 34.)

NOTE

Evidently, contract disputes were not a major part of the work load of Tswana courts during the colonial period.

Simon Roberts' more recent field research shows, if anything, even fewer cases involving disputes over contracts.

Simon Roberts, "The Survival of the Traditional Tswana Courts in the National Legal System of Botswana," in Journal of African Law, volume 16, 1972, pp. 114–115. Footnote omitted.

The most surprising feature of the contemporary Tswana figures is the decline in every case (except in the Ngwato Tribal Authority's Court and the Chief's Representative Court at Maun) in the incidence of contractual disputes. . . . It might have been reasonable to assume . . . that with increasing commercial activity in all the tribal territories (through stock sales and the availability of consumer goods) a much larger volume of contractual disputes would have been noticeable before the Tswana courts. But this is not the case. . . .*

QUESTIONS

1. If court enforcement is rarely resorted to to insure the carrying out of contractual obligations, why do you think such agreements are kept?

2. Do you think the need for enforcement of contracts would vary depending on whether the parties were in a temporary or permanent relationship?

3. When a contract is broken, might a Motswana forego his or her chance to seek a court settlement? Why or why not?

F. CUSTOMARY CONTRACTS AND THE MODERN LAW OF CONTRACT

NOTE

It is widely observed that contract law is one of the least well-developed areas of African customary law:

Anthony N. Allott, Arnold L. Epstein and Max Gluckman, "Introduction," to Ideas and Procedures in African Customary Law, edited by Max Gluckman, London: Oxford University Press, 1969, pp. 71–72. Footnotes omitted.

It is striking that the first twenty-two volumes of the series *Law in Africa,* from the well-known legal publishers Sweet and Maxwell of London, do not contain a treatise on the traditional law of contract. This is in despite of the fact that they concentrate only on two former British territories, Ghana and Nigeria, where, indeed, Africans were

---

* See also Simon Roberts' "The Survival of the Traditional Tswana Courts in the National Legal System of Botswana," in the Journal of African Law, volume 16, 1972, pp. 103–128.

more fully involved in new forms of production and business than Africans elsewhere. We can deduce two things from this situation:

(i) The traditional law of contract was not as well developed as were the laws of family relationships, succession and inheritance, the constitution, and property. Here we emphasize again that the major co-operation in producing and exchanging goods and services was between kinsfolk and in-laws, i.e. in transactions between persons already related by status. Transactions establishing legal relations between strangers, as legal transactors, lay on the periphery of these status relationships. The trading that went on was mostly petty, in standardized transactions of barter, sale, loan, pledge, service of men and animals, agistment, with a few formless transactions. Even in the proto-cities of West Africa, the considerable trade was mainly confined to small markets, or large markets with many petty traders, though there were extensive credit arrangements involved in the long-established trade by Muslims in these regions. These credit arrangements continue, e.g. in the kola-nut and cattle trading still carried on largely by Hausa linked in terms of creed, ethnic origin, and even kinship.

(ii) The traditional law of contract has not raised many causes of action in superior courts, since it has not been applied in the numerous activities created by new productive and commercial enterprises in Africa. These have come under the introduced law of contract.

[Editor's note: And there are very few cases of contract under introduced law either.]

NOTE

The relative absence of elaboration in African contractual law was no impediment to its functioning in the customary context. To the contrary, it probably was an asset. As Allott et al faintly imply, customary contract law was elaborated enough to do the job demanded of it. It fit the nature of production and exchange relationships. But its relatively unelaborated quality does seem to be a handicap in the modern situation.

There are few cases available showing contemporary statutory law of contracts in operation in Botswana. We have already reviewed Tswaing vs. Van Schalwyk in Section A. Now let us examine another one of those few:

FRANCISTOWN JOBBERS (PTY.) LTD. vs. INDUSTRIAL AND MINING SUPPLIES (PTY.) LTD., High Court, Edwards, J., 28th September, 1977. Botswana Law Reports, 1977, pp. 107–109.

* * *

This is an application for summary judgment under Order 22. The plaintiff sued for payment of P4 874,57, *mora* interest and costs. The capital was particularised as—

the balance of the agreed, alternatively a reasonable, cost of work done and materials supplied in connection therewith by the plaintiff for and on behalf of the defendant during the period June, 1976 to March, 1977.

* * *

The answering affidavit alleges that between May, 1976 and March, 1977 the defendant entered into several agreements with the plaintiff in terms of which the plaintiff was to carry out certain work and supply materials for the completion of the defendant's factory and warehouse building, the total contract price being P7 300,50 (paragraph 4). The plaintiff did not perform the work in accordance with the agreement (paragraph 5). It was an implied term that the work would be performed in an efficient, proper and workmanlike manner and that the materials used would be of first class quality (paragraph 6). In breach of this term, the work was not performed in the required manner and materials of inferior quality were used. By reason of this breach the value of the work actually performed was only P2 426,00. And, also by reason of the breach, the local authority had refused defendant a certificate of occupancy as the building was not in a habitable condition (paragraph 7). In verification, a copy of an architect's report was annexed (paragraph 8). The defendant has paid plaintiff P2 426,00 on account of the contract price, and is accordingly excused from making payment of any balance (paragraph 9).

This appears to be a perfectly *bona fide* defence. Lee & Honore, *South African Law of Obligation*, section 210, state—

> "Notwithstanding that by the terms of the contract the liability of one party is dependent upon entire performance by the other, if the first named party has taken the benefit of part performance, he may be held liable to compensate the other party to the extent of the benefit received, if in the circumstances it would be inequitable that he should be enriched without making compensation, but without prejudice to any claim he may have against the other party for breach of contract."

It is evident from the affidavit filed on behalf of the defendant that it contends that plaintiffs breach of contract is no matter of minor defects, but a very substantial breach. On that version the plaintiff is obviously not entitled to sue as upon a completed contract for the contract price subject to mere adjustments. He cannot sue either upon an express or an implied contract. The only claim he can prefer is one based on enrichment, and the basic measure of compensation for enrichment is that stated by Maasdorp A.J.A. in van Rensburg v. Straughan, 1914.

> The plaintiff is entitled to be reimbursed to the extent of his expenses provided they do not exceed the amount by which the defendant is enriched.

As pointed out by the learned judge, reference to the contract price is permissible for the purpose of ascertaining the extent of enrichment. The contract price may therefore have an evidential value. I do not see why the defendant should be obliged—as Mr. Sohn contended he was—to propound a calculation based on the contract price as part of his defence. The *onus* to prove enrichment does not rest on him but on the plaintiff. It seems to me unobjectionable for the defendant to say "the limit of any enrichment I may have gained in P2 426, and that amount I have paid you." Mr. Sohn appeared to be trying to transfer the *onus* when he said that the architect's report was irrelevant to the point the defendant was trying to establish, i.e. the value of the work done. It would, on the contrary, appear that the point the defendant was concerned to establish was the plaintiff's breach of contract to which the report is certainly relevant.

Mr. Sohn submitted that the relationship out of which the plaintiff's claim arises was one of buyer and seller, and sought support from Stassen v. Stofberg, 1973. In that case, however, it was held that the contract on which the plaintiff based his claim was undoubtedly one of sale. Here no contract of sale has been pleaded; the fact that the plaintiff relies on "work done and materials supplied in connection therewith" as the foundation for its claim does not import any contract of sale; what emerges from the papers is a constructional contract to which the supply of goods was incidental. For that reason Stassen v. Stofberg, even if it were otherwise relevant, would not assist the plaintiff. In the present case the defendant does not prefer a counterclaim and has no need to do so.

Apart from the foregoing, Mr. Kades is unquestionably right in contending that the plaintiff's claim is not one in respect of which the plaintiff is entitled to apply for summary judgment. The claim rests upon alternative bases: (a) agreement, and (b) reasonableness. In so far as the claim rests on reasonableness it is not one for a liquidated amount in money; the amount claimed as reasonable can only become ascertained and liquidated when the court has determined what is reasonable. In that respect it resembles a claim for damages. And obviously the fact that one of the alternative bases of the claim is agreement does not entitle the plaintiff to affirm that it is a claim for a liquidated amount in money. To do so would be like calling a piebald horse a bay merely because one of the colours of his coat was bay.

Since the applicant's claim as framed is not such a claim as is specified in Order 22 Rule 1, the application is dismissed with costs.

QUESTIONS

1. What are the issues in this case?

2. What body of Western law apparently is being applied here?

3. Would the issues have been different if the case had been brought under customary law? What about the procedures?

4. Does the case illustrate the claim that Western law of contract is more "elaborated" than Tswana customary contract law?

5. Does the degree of elaboration in the Western contract law applied in this case assist in its settlement? If the case had been brought under customary law, would the relative absence of elaboration of the concept of contract have proved to be an impediment? If so, how?

6. This case, unlike the general hypothetical this casebook has used for Problem 3, involves two parties, rather than three. Thus, it is simpler. Why do you think simpler (and fewer) contract cases are more characteristic of Botswana than of the other three nations whose legal systems we are studying?

NOTE

There is no material fully analyzing customary Tswana contract law in terms of its adequacy for the contemporary situation. However, it is clear from what you had read in the materials provided up to this point that Tswana customary law is more like Western contract law than most Sub-Saharan customary legal systems in that: it enforces executory contracts, it often allows for consequential damages, and it sometimes utilizes specific performance as a remedy.

QUESTION

1. What do these facts suggest about the capacity of Tswana customary contract law to adapt to changing conditions?

NOTE

Although Tswana customary law of contract has some of the features of Western contract law that makes it suitable for modern business and governmental operations, the customary law of contracts of many African nations lacks these features. Ghai's piece on contract law in Kenya lays out some of the reasons why much traditional African contract law there is not highly serviceable under modern conditions.

Yash P. Ghai, "Customary Contracts and Transactions in Kenya," in Ideas and Procedures in African Customary Law, edited by Max Gluckman. London: Oxford University Press, 1969, pp. 342–344, 338–339.

[Ghai speaks first of the limited number of remedies, especially of the fact that interest is not assessed on funds held up by contractual default. He goes on:]

Perhaps the greatest weakness of the customary law of contracts is in its provision of remedies. Specific performance in the sense of ordering the carrying out of the agreement is unusual, though orders requiring the transfer of cattle or produce are common. There is a certain lack of finality about transactions. People who come to court alleging a breach of contract by the other party merely claim to be put into the position they were in before they made the contract. Thus whether there was mistake, fraud, duress, or misrepresentation, the consequences are not much different. Nowadays when damages are being increasingly awarded in a monetary form, no consequential damages are given. Damages seem to be related as much to the benefit gained by the defendant as the loss suffered by the plaintiff. D entered into an agreement with P to hire P's sewing machine and to pay 25s. for it every month; no other terms were agreed upon. After the first month D terminated the contract and refused to pay for more than one month; he had the machine with him for nine months as P refused to accept it. D was ordered to pay the rental for only one month, but it is interesting to note that the court justified this result by remarking that if D had actually used the machine for a longer time, he would have had to pay for it. Another case is even more striking on this point. A borrowed some money from B at interest to start a business. The business failed and was closed down after two months. The money was not returned for several months. The court held that interest for only two months was payable.

[Partnerships, increasingly common in modernizing African Society also prove difficult for customary law to handle. (Cf. Tswaing vs. Van Schalkwyk excerpted in Section A).]

Commercial aspirations among the Africans are growing, and more and more of them are opening shops, replacing, to some extent, the Asian storekeepers. The shops are often partnerships. Disputes seem quite common, partly because these enterprises frequently do not succeed, due to lack of experience, and partly because the accounting system, etc., generally are non-existent. There is hardly any law to settle these disputes; the local African District Councils lay down some rules, but often there is total ignorance of these rules. The courts are trying to evolve rules to deal with these disputes. It now seems accepted that parties share in the profits in proportion to their capital contribution, and at the dissolution of the partnership, the assets are divided in a similar way. But the courts are not particularly suited for this task: there is little notion of binding precedents; and the cases are often most complicated and require skilled presentation. There is urgent need for some kind of legislation or guidance on this matter, if the governmental policy of Africanizing the economy is to succeed.

QUESTIONS

1. Even though Tswana customary contract law is more elaborated than that of many African countries, it does have difficulty in handling some situations that crop up nowadays. What do you think some of these situations might be? In what way would customary contract law seem inadequate to handle them?

2. What should a country like Botswana do to handle the contemporary legal problems involving contracts? Is simply adopting Western contract

law the ideal solution? What does current contract law in China and Egypt suggest about that route? Can you suggest any other alternative?

[The absence of consequential damages is a particularly vexing problem in Kenya's customary law and in Sub-Saharan Africa generally although, as we have seen, this is not a significant issue among most Tswana groups.]

In many of the modern type of contracts, like transport, loan, hire, consequential damages are not awarded. The instinct perhaps is right: I was frequently told in justification of this rule that it is difficult for the defendant to know the purposes for which the plaintiff wants the defendant's goods, or services, and so it was unfair to attach liability beyond knowable damages. Notions of ordinary, constructive, or imputed knowledge are not accepted, nor indeed actual knowledge if they lead to consequential damages.

Thus there is no great legal deterrent against committing breach of contract. Most contracts, other than the 'once and for all' transactions, are broken wherever any party feels like it.

It is unlikely that contracts would be abandoned so casually if customary law had the concept of consequential damages. If small-scale African efforts at commerce are to succeed, then it will be necessary to provide for consequential damages. Many African traders have had to give up their businesses because their customers did not pay for years and no interest was awarded; or their partners pulled out without notice and the courts allowed them to withdraw their capital.

[Absence of privity of contract * poses problems, too:]

There are several cases of agency . . . in which a person was asked to receive money on someone else's behalf, or to buy or sell for someone. It is interesting to note that in one sense the African contracts of agency display a mature rule of agency: the agent falls out once the transaction for which he was employed is complete. In one case A gave money to B to be given to X Company. B gave it to an official of the company, who probably absconded with it (this is not clear from the facts of the case). A brought an action against B for recovery of the money. His claim was dismissed, and the court held that he only had a claim against the company. The explanation of this rule is not the same as in the common law. It is more likely that the agent drops out not because he has completed what he was supposed to do, but because he no longer has the money. The ability of customary law to reach the person in possession of the goods in question is quite striking; the notion of privity of contract is only very rudimentary, and occasionally makes difficult the classification of a case as tort or contract.

* Privity of contract=notion that a contract includes only the direct parties to the contract. It cannot affect a person who has an indirect, derived interest in the contract.

Chapter 21

PRIVATE ORDERING IN CHINA

A. INTRODUCTORY NOTE

NOTE

There is very little information available on economic law in China. Chinese legal writers do not deal with this subject in part because it is often regarded as administration (rather than law) and consequently is handled principally through internal directives and documents. In addition, in the West, for a variety of reasons, scholars have concentrated on the study of the criminal system rather than civil law.

The initial efforts in the current legalization drive in China also dealt primarily with criminal law and procedure. There was some discussion of how "rational rules" and efficient means of dispute resolution would increase economic production, but except for laws related to joint ventures with foreign parties, very few civil laws have been promulgated. This is not surprising, since many of the advocates of increased emphasis on law were victims of the Cultural Revolution and are now trying to find means of ensuring that such abuses of individuals should not occur again.

Beginning in 1978, a major effort has been underway to stimulate economic growth through a series of new policies emphasizing decentralization, enterprise autonomy, and use of material incentives. These changes in turn have underscored the need to establish a better system of "private ordering"—commercial and contract law, dispute resolution mechanisms, etc.

At present, very few new economic laws have been promulgated. Consequently, the following materials describe the underlying transactions in considerable detail and then state a series of basic policies or principles concerning the determination of liability and damages. In many places, we are only able to ask the appropriate questions concerning how the three contract disputes will be resolved, but are not always able to provide the answers.

Earlier materials described the structure and organization of the rural sector. The following item discusses the industrial and commercial sectors.

Victor H. Li, Direct Investment and Economic Law in the People's Republic of China (1981, unpublished) (notes omitted).

State Enterprise System. The principal units of industrial and commercial organization in China are the 350,000 state-owned enterprises. Each is subordinate to a particular industrial (or commercial) bureau, the local arm of the national ministry in charge. That bureau in turn coordinates with a number of other agencies at the same horizontal level, such as with the economic commission on matters of current production, the bank branch on credit and financial matters, and the planning commission branch on future production. This horizontal and vertical organization is overlain by the network of CCP committees. The enterprise party committee is responsible to the local party committee, which also supervises and coordinates the work of other bureaus, commissions, and banks in line with directives from above.

* * *

The economic activity of state enterprises is generally prescribed by state plans. Eight kinds of targets are set: quantity of output, variety, quality, consumption of raw materials and fuel and power, labor productivity, costs, profit, and the utilization of working capital . . . .

The annual plan is the principal document directing the enterprise's ongoing activities:

> Known as the annual technological and financial production plan, it usually includes the following; the production plan—the major portion and nucleus of the plan of the whole enterprise—which determines the categories, quantity, and quality of products to be produced within the planning period; a plan covering technological readiness and research; a supplementary production plan; a plan covering workers' wages; a transportation plan; a plan covering material supplies; a cost plan; and a finance plan.

The annual plan is broken down into smaller units to guide day-to-day operations. Ideally each workshop or section or even individual worker has a monthly, ten-day, and daily plan that can be adjusted as circumstances change.

The plan is implemented in part by contracts signed between an enterprise and a department in charge, or more often between two enterprises. Contracts have been regarded as an integral part of the reform package, since they allow enterprises to set up their own system of private ordering of relations . . . .

The means to achieve the plan targets—capital, labor, and materials—are mainly allocated by the state. Until recently, fixed and working capital are usually provided interest-free by the state, and most material inputs are subject to planned allocation by the Materials Allocation Ministry. Enterprise products are bought by commercial departments at controlled prices. Enterprises remit all profits to the state, and also receive subsidies in case of losses.

Enterprise Autonomy. In July 1978, the Central Committee of the CCP issued the "30-Point Decision on Industry" that summarized the broad political tasks and economic policies for the current period. While it did not establish any of the specific reforms that would emerge later, the decision did open the way for substantial changes in enterprise management policy.

To provide incentive, enterprises that have fulfilled supply contracts and the eight economic and technical indexes

> may draw from their profits funds which will be mainly used to run collective welfare services in those enterprises. The proportion of profits drawn for use of funds of enterprises should be different in accordance with various trades and enterprises. Concrete stipulation should be made by the Ministry of Finance together with other relevant departments and units. (Article 9)

The retention of a portion of profits by enterprises was a radical departure from past practice. The Ministry of Finance struggled with the task of drafting regulations to implement this policy, while six enterprises in Sichuan were chosen as test sites.

The "Regulations for the Tentative System of Enterprise Funds in State Enterprises" . . . promulgated by the Ministry of Finance in December 1978 state that the funds to be retained are determined as a percentage of the annual enterprise payroll. Enterprises that fulfill contracts for goods and the four most important targets (output, variety, quality, and profit) retain 3% of the payroll, plus an additional 0.5% for each additional target fulfilled, to a maximum of 5%. Enterprises that produce at a planned loss could retain 3% of the payroll if all targets are achieved. Separate standards are to be drawn up for units in commerce, construction, foreign trade, etc. The enterprise funds are to be used primarily to support collective welfare facilities (dormitories, cafeterias, schools, health, etc.) and secondarily as a source of funds for production bonuses.

In addition, the departments (ministries) in charge of enterprises also are given incentive to increase productivity by being allowed to retain a percentage of the profit in excess of state plans of the enterprises under their jurisdiction. . . .

The five regulations [issued in July 1979 used a new] system of calculating the amount to be retained than was used for the enterprise fund. (Note that the enterprise fund remained in effect for those other enterprises experimenting with it.) The amount retained was set as a percentage of profits, not a percentage of payroll, so that overstaffing was no longer rewarded. After fulfilling state plans, enterprises could retain 5% of the planned profit and 20% of profits earned on production above the state plan. The decision-making power of enterprises also was expanded in the hope of spurring productivity. In Sichuan, where management reforms were previewed, enterprises received greater authority to organize above-plan production and marketing, and to discipline (but not fire) workers. Depreciation funds also were increased. To what degree these reforms were put into practice is, as always, problematical. For instance, more than a year after the reforms had been promulgated, not a single enterprise in Guangdong province had been able to get the share of foreign currency due it under the regulations. Moreover, the new profit retention system was not extended to all 350,000 units. . . .

In September 1980, the State Council approved a SEC "Report on the Experimental Expansion of Enterprise Self-Management and Opinions on Future Work" . . . that called for expanding the system of greater enterprise decision making powers to all state-owned industrial enterprises in 1981. The suggestion was repeated that provinces develop sites to test the system of taxing profits. Selected enterprises also could expand their power to market their own products, vary prices, share in foreign exchange earnings, and get more involved in questions of hiring workers and firing cadres. Note that these provisions follow the outlines of the Sichuan reforms of early 1979, and that the more radical changes—paying income taxes, self-marketing, and price adjustments—apply only to certain "selected companies."

B. CONTRACTS

NOTE

The concept of contract—in the sense of an exchange of agreed upon promises or goods—is well known in China. For many centuries, commerce flourished, and peasants engaged in complex transactions involving marketing arrangements, credits, and land tenure. As touched upon in Problem 1, contracts usually were enforced by organizations such as guilds or through social pressure, rather than by judicial or other governmental action.

Even before the current reforms, the PRC has stressed the importance of contracts in economic work. They help implement central planning by providing concrete details of what each party should do, and also by identifying problem areas which appear as breaches of contract.

Thomas Huang, "Reflections on Law and the Economy in The People's Republic of China," 14 Harvard International Law Journal, 261, 285–287 (1973) (notes omitted).

In a liberal-capitalist economy, the institution of contracts is the most important legal instrument for allocating resources, and its extensive use is itself an indication of a greater decentralization of economic decision making. Contrary to a mistaken notion, however, the institution of contracts also serves these functions in a revolutionary-socialist country such as China.

Between 1949 and 1954 three devices were used extensively in the PRC to induce production in the private industrial sector. Under a product processing (*chia-kung*) contract the state would pay a portion of the projected proceeds and would supply materials to the factories for processing according to specifications stipulated in the contract.

In this manner, the state at least partially controlled the private sector.

* * *

The most widely used contract in the public industrial sector has been the supply contract (*kung-ying ho-t'ung*) signed by state organs according to the distribution plan for the more important products such as steel and precision instruments.   There are three different types of supply contracts: (1) the general contract (*i-pan ho-t'ung*) concluded at the governmental level; (2) the concrete contract (*chu-t'i ho-t'ung*) which is negotiated at the local level between the supplier and purchaser based on the general contract and which is made under the supervision of the relevant governmental organ; and, if there is no general contract, the direct contract (*chih-chieh ho-t'ung*) between organs at the local level.   Usually there are "basic clauses" relating to the purpose of the contract, quantity, quality, price, penalties and other items prescribed by each ministry or department to be included into such supply contracts.

Contracts are also used in the allocational process in agriculture. Since collective ownership of cooperatives or communes does not amount to state ownership, the state uses contracts to influence production in the agricultural sector.   One of the most widely used contracts in the allocation of agricultural resources has been the advance purchase contract (*yü-kou ho-t'ung*) which was introduced in 1951.

The actual operation of the advance purchase contract can be illustrated by the purchase of cotton.   The state, acting through agents such as producers' cooperatives, concludes the advance contracts with cotton producers and furnishes the latter with the earnest and other supplies such as fertilizer.   Under such an arrangement the producers are able to obtain necessary capital and other assistance before proceeding with production and the state is able to control the amount of the cotton produced.   This arrangement is similar to the devices of ordering and advance purchase used in controlling the industrial sector.

As the state intensified its control over the agricultural sector, the united purchase and supply contract (*chieh-ho ho-t'ung*) was introduced.   Particularly after the initiation of the planned purchase of grain and oil in 1953 and wholesale purchase (*t'ung-kou*) of cotton in 1954, the use of the united contract has become extensive.   Under a united contract, the state supplies all the materials and assistance needed for production and later purchases a substantial portion of the major and sideline products from the cooperatives.

NOTE

The following item is from a textbook used in Chinese law schools in the 1950s. The legal principles are quite valid in the post-Cultural Revolution period, although there is at present greater stress on private ordering.

Basic Problems in the Civil Law of the PRC (Institute of Civil Law of the Central Political-Legal Cadres School, Peking, 1958).

GENERAL PRINCIPLES OF CONTRACTS

Section 1. General Concept of Contracts

A. Characteristics of Contracts. A contract is an agreement made between two parties in accordance with the requirements of the norms of law and in an attempt to create, alter, or extinguish certain civil juristic relations. From this definition, we can clearly see that a contract has the following characteristics:

(1) A contract is a juristic act of two parties, and is not an ex parte one.

(2) A contract is a lawful act done by the subjects of civil juristic relations, and is not a power activity of a state organ. This is the basic distinction between a contract and an administrative action. Some administrative actions may create, alter, or extinguish civil juristic relations. However, this is the power activity of the state organs which expresses the will of the people's democratic state, which is led by the worker class and based on the alliance of workers and peasants, and is not an agreement between parties.

B. The Role of Contracts in the National Economy. The system of contracts is mainly a legal system dealing with the distribution of products and the exchange of commodities. The relation of a contract always reflects the nature of relations in the distribution of certain social products and the exchange of commodities.

* * *

. . . Concretely speaking, the principal role of the contract system in the transitional period of our country is as follows:

(1) The contracts between socialist organizations should aim at the fulfillment of the national economic plan, and the system of contract should be used to combine the national economic plan with the system of economic accounting in enterprises. On this point, we may discuss the problem from two aspects:

(a) Contract is a method for systematizing the national economic plan and making it more precise. When the state plan for the distribution of goods is announced, the units concerned are required to conclude contracts in accordance with the plan. No such contract is allowed to be in conflict with the plan. On the other hand, the plan can only provide tasks for each enterprise, and it cannot provide details as to how each enterprise should complete its task. Therefore, when an enterprise concludes a contract, it must take into consideration its own conditions and determine the concrete contents of the contract.

* * *

(b) Contract is a system designed to organize socialist organizations for mutual supervision. Among socialist organizations, the parties to contracts are independent enterprises. Administratively, one enterprise may be subordinated to another, and the enterprises at a lower level have the duty to report their operation to the enterprises at a higher level. But, insofar as their relation in a contract is concerned, their legal status is equal. Through the contract relation, individual enterprises can be organized together for mutual supervision. If a party fails to perform his obligation, he is liable to pay the penalty or make compensation for damages. Thus, the violating party will not be able to complete his own financial plan, and consequently, he will receive criticism or administrative sanction from his superior authorities. On the other hand, if he wants to complete his plan, he must perform his contractual obligations. In the meantime, if one party violates the provisions of the contract, the other party can inform the superior authorities of the violating party of the conditions of non-performance so that the superior authorities can exercise their supervision and order the violating party to perform his obligations in accordance with the contract and to fulfill the plan for distribution of goods.

NOTE

A noteworthy feature of the Chinese effort to implement the contract system is that a push occurs each time there is a retrenchment away from "radical" policies. Thus, a spate of articles on the importance of contracts appears in 1961–62 after the Great Leap Forward, in 1970–71 after the Cultural Revolution, and at present. It seems—although Chinese writings are not explicit on this point—that during "radical" periods, many units were able to breach contracts with impunity by claiming that a previously agreed to arrangement should be altered in order to satisfy some new political or ideological goal. Requiring strict adherence to contractual obligations was an important means of re-establishing economic order.

The following item is a typical article re-emphasizing the contract system after a "radical" period. The next one reflects the major policy reforms concerning economic work in 1978.

"The Contract System Must be Correctly Applied," editorial, Ta-kung Pao (Peking), February 9, 1962; trans., U. S. Consulate General, Hong Kong, Survey of China Mainland Press, No. 2688, p. 7.

Commercial contracts, or transaction contracts, are no new things; they have been with us for a long time. Commercial contracts have achieved an unprecedented development in capitalist society, serve the bourgeoisie, and are tools with which capitalists exploit the workers and peasants and to edge out one another. In the socialist society, commercial contracts serve the worker-peasant alliance, being tools with which to protect the interests of the workers and peasants, to promote the exchange of commodities between urban and rural areas, to give impetus to mutual aid between urban and rural areas, and to advance industrial and farm production. In our country, the question is not one of whether or not we need the system of contracts, but one of how to master and apply it correctly. To implement the system of contracts gradually and realistically and apply it correctly to serve the socialist economy—this is an important task facing the workers in the economic field.

* * *

Initial experiences have shown that numerous advantages can be derived from correct implementation of the contract system. First, it is conducive to the strengthening of the planned character of the national economy.

. . . At the present stage, China's national economic plans consist of two parts, the economic plans under the system of ownership by the whole people and economic plans under the system of collective ownership. Between these two kinds of plans there must be intermediate "links" and "coordination". And one of the means to bring these about is the introduction of the contract system, which allows the planned character of the national economy to be further strengthened. Secondly, it is conducive to the arrangement of production and livelihood of the State, the collective and the individual. For the State can, through contracts signed with the peasants, understand the possibilities regarding the purchase of farm products on the one hand, and on the other understand what kind of commodities the peasants need and how much they need so as to arrange the production and supply work on a nation-wide basis. As for the production brigades and commune members, they can, through contracts signed with the State, similarly understand the needs of the State and the quantity of the means of production and subsistence they can obtain, and such a knowledge makes it easier for them to arrange their own production and livelihood. Thirdly, it is conducive to the development of a multiple economy in the countryside. . . . Fourthly, it is conducive to the investigation and study by the commercial departments, to increasing the accuracy of commercial planning and to the raising of the commercial management standards. Since contracts concern two sides, to make any contracts successful we must consult the masses and conduct mass work; in other words, the process of negotiating and signing contracts is a process of going deep into the masses to conduct investigation and study and propagating Party policies. The outcome of the investigation and study will be a clear understanding of what the masses can sell to the State, and how much and when. On this basis, the State purchasing plans will accordingly be drawn up, revised and finalized. Similarly, it will be possible to know what the masses need. . . . Commerce being the link between industry and agriculture, commercial departments must carry out investigation and study with thoroughness, master the laws governing production and marketing, and learn to do business. And having done so they will be able to promote the smooth development of industry and agriculture, advance the close cooperation between urban and rural areas, and further the consolidation of the worker-peasant alliance. In this respect, the introduction of the contract system can exert no small measure of effect.

. . . How can we correctly apply the contract system? First, we must strengthen Party leadership, do things in compliance with the Party and State policies, proceed from the fact that China has a population of 650 hundred million people in making unified arrangement and over-all planning and giving all-round consideration to all sides. This is particularly important. Contracts are entered into by the basic-level commercial units with the production teams or the commune members individually. Each contract represents a small part of the whole. Both parties to a contract may see their local interests very clearly but often fail to see the whole, or do not bother to think about it, or see the whole only after taking some time to think about it. For this reason, political and policy education must be conducted among the commercial workers, among the rural cadres, and among the broad masses of peasants with a view to enabling all of them to understand the truth about proceeding from the integral whole in making unified arrangements and over-all planning. . . .

Second, there must be ideological preparations. It is necessary to make not only commercial workers but also rural cadres and peasants understand correctly the meaning of the contract system. If this tool is to be properly used, it will not do not to recognize its significance and function.

Third, there must be material preparations. As far as the production teams and commune members are concerned, they must be made to arrange production properly, and be prepared to sell their products to the State. As for socialist commercial agencies, they must make full preparations for the supply of commodities to the peasants in consideration of the quantity of farm products to be purchased from the latter. With material preparations, it will be possible to fulfill the contracts and for both parties to safeguard the inviolability of the contract.

Fourth, the mass line must be followed. Since a contract binds both sides, one side cannot unilaterally impose rigid decisions on the other side. The process of signing the contract is thus also a process of democratic discussion and adequate consultation between the two parties. Only those contracts concluded with full agreement by the two parties can be truly effective.

Fifth, the system of contracts should be popularized after it has been subjected to serious experiment. We must properly coordinate the purchasing and marketing to be done by the peasants with the purchasing and marketing to be done by the State, and this is not easy to do. This involves a process of study and familiarization, for it cannot be achieved at one stroke. The system must be tried out first, then the experiences gained should be summed up and finally popularized. There is no other alternative for commercial workers, rural cadres and the peasants to get familiar with the contract system and apply it skillfully, and avoid taking "detours".

Sixth, once contracts are signed, they must be fulfilled by all means. After signing the contracts, the State and the peasants must earnestly organize production, purchasing and supply strictly in accordance with the provisions of the contracts.

Seventh, once the contracts are signed, regular examination and supervision must be conducted to insure their fulfillment.

Hu Ch'iao-mu, "Observe Economic Laws, Speed Up the Four Modernizations," Peking Review, Nov. 24, 1978, pp. 14–15, 17.

* * *

Promote the Contract System

We have adopted the contract system in many fields of economic work. This has proved fairly effective in practice, therefore it should be widely popularized. The system usually works like this: two enterprises sign a contract directly; they have considered economic interests quite carefully and placed rather detailed, practical obligations on each other; under it, conditions are worked out by both parties on a voluntary basis and each side can keep the other in check; generally, there are no arbitrary orders (the so-called "what-I-say-is-final contract" now in vogue is an abnormal thing born of chaotic economic management, which must be opposed by all means, but this is a different question), and when there are shortcomings, they can be easily surmounted without requiring examination and approval of the authorities at various levels.

The contract system may be applied between grass-roots enterprises, between producers, suppliers and marketers, between big corporations and specialized companies, between big corporations themselves, between specialized companies themselves, between local companies themselves and between various companies and grass-roots enterprises. This will help raise efficiency in economic work, ensure that economic activities are conducted in a planned way, and lessen the burden of the administrative organs at various levels.

Moreover, we are of the opinion that contracts may also be concluded between the state and enterprises (including both industrial and agricultural enterprises, enterprises owned by the whole people or collectively owned), between central and local authorities, between different localities, between localities of different levels and between an enterprise and its staff and workers. The contract system between the state and enterprises especially can play an important role in clearly defining the commitments of the two contracting parties, stimulating the initiative and enthusiasm of the enterprises and helping end chaos in the present economic management.

The practice of putting proletarian politics in command remains the prerequisite for the contract system to play its role fully and correctly although the co-ordination and guarantees of many other economic conditions are also required. But this does not mean that everything will be plain sailing and all problems can be solved automatically once the contract system is introduced. Still, the adoption of this system is conducive to strengthening the planning of the national economy and accelerating its development; it will promote specialization and co-operation in production and makes it possible to meet all kinds of economic and technical targets—first of all targets in respect to quality, variety and economical use of power, fuel and raw and other materials. It will also help bring the law of value into play, promote business accounting and raise labour productivity and the rate of profit on investment. The introduction of the system will also greatly help overcome bureaucracy, reduce waste, arouse the initiative of the masses, improve economic management and train managerial personnel. All these advantages are certain to accrue.

*　*　*

Developing Economic Legislation And Enforcement

The aforesaid contract system, the establishment of specialized companies, the strengthening of bank functions and other measures of the like, when put into practice, are bound to give rise to complicated, controversial issues. To seek prompt, impartial and correct settlement of these issues, it is necessary to strengthen economic legislation and enforcement and manifest in legal forms the interests of the state, enterprises, workers and staff members and consumers and the relations of the various interests, to be handled by judicial organs according to law. Without this, all these measures cannot easily become effective and things may go back to the old way of relying on purely administrative means.

We now have a contract system for ordering goods all right, but it is merely a matter of formality as many contracts are never fulfilled or not strictly fulfilled. When a fine is imposed, it is either included in costs or deducted from the profit made; the fine imposed does not directly affect the interests of the leaders or workers and staff members in the enterprise concerned. We have issued a good number of fine regulations and rules but, in most cases, they do not have a rigid legal form and therefore are not legally binding. To give them a legal form with clearly defined legal force, it is not only necessary to have genuine economic legislation widely publicized among the people throughout the country but also to have economic judicial organs that will deal with things conscientiously and strictly and mete out proper punishments to all enterprises and individuals for violating these laws.

Economic Contract Law effective July 1, 1982. An English translation can be found in JPRS 79807 6 Jan. 1982, China Report: Economic Affairs (No. 194). Abstracted from Xinhua 16 Dec. 1981.

Article 2. An economic contract is an agreement between legal persons for achieving a certain economic purpose and for defining each other's rights and obligations.

Article 3. Economic contracts, with the exception of those that are settled immediately, shall be in written form. Documents, telegrams and charts related to contract revisions agreed upon by the parties concerned through consultations are also component parts of a contract.

Article 6. An economic contract once drawn up according to the law has legal binding force. The parties concerned should fulfill all obligations stipulated in the contract. No one party is allowed to unilaterally alter or terminate the contract.

Article 12. An economic contract should contain the following major articles:

   1. Objective (referring to freight, service, projects, others);
   2. Quantity and quality;
   3. Prices or commission;
   4. Time limit, place and mode of fulfilling the contract;
   5. Responsibilities in case of violation of contract.

Other major articles of an economic contract comprise those articles that should be included as stipulated by the law or in keeping with the nature of economic contracts as well as those articles that any one of the parties concerned requests to be included in the contract.

Article 54. Individual businessmen and rural commune members should sign economic contracts with juridical persons with reference to this law.

QUESTIONS

1. Is it likely that the processor would have signed a formal written contract with the manufacturer? If so, how might this contract differ from the corresponding contract in the Western example? If there was no written contract, would Article 3 of the Economic Contract Law invalidate the arrangement?

2. Would the processor have signed a formal written contract with the distributor? with the farmers? If not, what kind of "agreement" was reached between these parties? Is such an "agreement" a contract as

defined by Basic Problems (item 1)? Would such an "agreement" be invalid under the Economic Contract Law?

3. Would an arrangement similar to Mosekian v. Davis Canning Co. (see Western materials) be enforceable in China?

4. Assume that the contracts being examined in this problem were entered into during the "radical gang of four" period. What reasons can the processor give to relieve itself of possible liability to the farmers or the distributor? Would these reasons be valid in a "pragmatic" period like the present?

5. How would putting the contract system into "legal form" as suggested by the author of item 4 help assure strict adherence to contracts? How does handling matters "according to law" differ from "relying on purely administrative means"?

NOTE

Central planning is still far from perfected in China. Frequently a unit must obtain supplies and market goods through extra-legal, though not necessarily illegal, means.

James Stepanik, "Supply Planning in China" (1978, unpublished manuscript) (notes omitted).

Ad hoc Procurement and Marketing Techniques

When supplies are inadequate to meet quotas, enterprises are often prompted to get materials through informal, direct contacts with other enterprises. People called "purchasing agents" (*cai gou yuan*) are employed to locate and procure scarce items by going around the country arranging barter deals. The practice is so widespread that in 1977 Peking and Shanghai ". . . had to receive approximately 50,000 to 60,000 people a day who were seeking supplies. All this put great pressure on the transport and service industries and caused considerable waste of state money." At the Talien Steel Works ". . . people came to press for delivery of goods and the reception room was crowded with people . . ." whenever production fell. The intense lobbying was apparently motivated by the fear that the Steel Works would renege upon its contracts. It is not surprising that municipal bureaus also send agents in search of materials if their subordinate enterprises are affected. Practices of this kind are condoned if barter deals that are struck observe a rate of exchange in conformity with the state's price structure, although some sources hint that all deals are illegal which involve ". . . state-controlled goods and materials." The authorities obviously prefer that commodity exchanges be conducted under state auspices, as at "material supply fairs" (*wu zhi diao ji hui*), which are convened by the government to facilitate swaps between enterprises or corporations so that surplus inventories may be traded for goods in short supply.

Another widespread practice, though one having opposite intentions, is to send sales people around the country in search of new markets for local manufactures. For example, in 1975, a team of textile wholesalers from Shanghai toured 20 provinces, cities and autonomous regions in order to negotiate deals with other wholesaling officials. They carried sample prints along, interviewed prospective customers, and upon their return they helped factories in Shanghai produce new designs for export. Although the state encourages these activities, salesmen are nevertheless reminded that ". . . they must not, for the sake of marketing more, go in for incorrect work style or be influenced by evil trends for that would be pounding against the state plan." Even peddlers (*huo lang dan*) are recruited to promote sales in rural areas, and stores have cut prices to get rid of excess stocks. But in such cases prices can be changed for certain goods only, and the changes must stay within specified boundaries. It is illegal for stores to arbitrarily change the grades of goods so that different prices may be affixed to them. Unfortunately little data was obtained on the ration coupon system, but it is known that local departments have discretion over policy.

* * *

Illegal trade by collective and private enterprises is apparently even more prevalant in rural areas than in cities. No source explicitly accuses these units of distributing food in cities in exchange for consumer goods, but circumstantial evidence nevertheless points to such a conclusion. Many peasants have been charged with organizing underground transport teams and stores, abandoning agriculture for trade, and in using fishing boats and tractors for private purposes. The authorities are particularly upset that a rapidly increasing share of China's farm vehicles are used on highways for commerce, and not on fields for farming. Ninety percent of China's farm vehicles were under the control of communes and production teams in 1978. Further confirmation that illegal urban-rural trade was practiced is found in reports urging commerce departments to wipe out speculators by increasing the level of legitimate commerce between town and countryside.

NOTE

The recent reforms have greatly increased the need for greater access to materials and markets by individual enterprises and also for loosening the structure of state-fixed prices. A number of efforts are being tried to deal with these problems.

Victor H. Li, Direct Investment and Economic Law. (Notes omitted).

The 1978 reforms attempted to add flexibility to the system of distribution. For one thing, in addition to requisitioning needed materials from allocation offices, goods also can be purchased directly from production units. A number of exchange fairs have cropped up where suppliers and buyers can seek each other out. The 1980 regulations on competition . . . set out some general rules:

> It is necessary to expand the avenues for commodity circulation and open the arena for competition. Enterprises, in principle, sell by themselves those products that they produce themselves, as well as new products produced on a trial basis. Among these products, those that are under state unified purchase, marketing and distribution but are in short supply should first of all be purchased by the state, but portions of some products may be allowed to be sold by the enterprises themselves . . . .. It is necessary to increase avenues for circulation, decrease intermediate links, and allow the enterprises to exercise various forms of management so that integration between the producing and marketing departments can be established and circulation of commodities can be expected. Sales organizations can be set up in different localities, cities and towns to run trade fairs, to sell commodities on a commission basis and to promote sales of products.

There also has been loosening of central control over allocation of means of production. Some means of production were redesignated "commodities," which meant they could be exchanged.

*   *   *

. . . The November 1980 Shanghai trade fair lasted nine days and did ¥42 million of business. One in Tianjin in March and April 1980 drew 10,000 people from 28 provinces, lasted 11 days and did ¥400 million in business, ¥200 million of it for Tianjin. Clearly this form of exchange is an important and growing part of the economic structure.

. . . [In addition,] in 1979, industrial departments established 16,000 retail departments of their own—bypassing the commerce system—which accounted for ¥10.3 billion worth of sales or 5.9% of the country's total retail sales.

QUESTIONS

1. Do the extra-legal means of obtaining supplies and arranging sales described above involve the use of contracts?

2. How are these "contracts" enforced? At what point do such extra-legal arrangements become illegal?

3. In view of the above materials and the discussion on patterns of dealings in the next section, what are some of the difficulties that might be encountered in trying to enforce Article 3 of the Economic Contract Law which requires written contracts?

C. PATTERNS OF DEALINGS

NOTE

On-going economic relationships—such as the purchase of supplies or the marketing of produce by a farmer—can be described in legal contractual terms. They can also be described in a more sociological manner as regular patterns of dealings in which the parties develop expectations, habits, customary practices, and reliances. Each individual transaction may be technically a contract, but this contract must be seen in the context of the larger set of on-going relationships. Thus, in the event that one particular transaction or contract is encountering difficulty, the parties would seek a solution that takes into account the desirability of preserving the overall relationship encompassing many transactions and continuing over a long time. Note that the same mode of analyzing behavior was employed in the discussion of deviancy in Problem 2.

We do not have detailed information about patterns of economic dealings at the local level in China. The following two items discuss some aspects of marketing of agricultural products in traditional and contemporary China that may help us think about the nature of the processor-farmer and processor-distributor contracts of the hypothetical problem.

G. William Skinner, "Marketing and Social Structure in Rural China," The Journal of Asian Studies, vol. 24, pp. 10–11, 30, 33, 394–397 (notes omitted).

Periodicity and Market Schedules

In Ch'ing China, as in most traditional agrarian societies, rural markets were normally periodic rather than continuous: they convened only every few days. This feature of traditional rural markets may be understood from several points of view.

On the side of the producer or trader, the periodicity of markets is related to the mobility of individual "firms." The itinerant peddlar, toting his wares from one market to the next with the aid of a carrying pole, is the archetype of the mobile firm in China. But equally characteristic of the traditional rural market are the wandering artisans and repairmen who carry their "workshop" about with them, and other itinerants purveying services of all kinds from letter-writing to fortune-telling. Why are these facilities mobile? In essence, because the total amount of demand encompassed by the marketing area of any single rural market is insufficient to provide a profit level which enables the enterpreneur to survive. By repositioning himself at periodic intervals, the entrepreneur can tap the demand of several marketing areas and thereby attain the survival threshold. From the point of view of the itinerant entrepreneur, periodicity in marketing has the virtue of concentrating the demand for his product at restricted localities on certain specific days. When a group of related markets operates on coordinated periodic (as opposed to daily) schedules, he can arrange to be in each town in the circuit on its market day.

* * *

From the point of view of the consumer, the periodicity of markets amounts to a device for reducing the distance he must travel to obtain the required goods and services. . . . In most parts of agricultural China, especially prior to the eighteenth century when the rural population was distributed relatively sparsely on the land, the number of households required to support a daily market would have meant marketing areas so large that villagers at the rim could not manage the trip to and from market in a single day. A market meeting only once in three or once in five days, however, could achieve a viable level of demand if only one-third or one-fifth as many villages fell within its dependent area.

* * *

Let us now look over the total complex of nested marketing systems and survey, first of all, the downward flow of merchandise. Exotic goods shipped to the central market town, and other goods produced in it, are distributed in part through the central market itself, in part by itinerants who circuit both intermediate and standard markets throughout the central marketing system, and in part to firms in the six intermediate market towns. Merchandise received by firms in each intermediate market town, together with other goods produced there, are similarly distributed: in part through the intermediate market itself, in part by itinerants who circuit standard markets within the intermediate marketing system, and in part to firms in the six standard market towns. The firms receiving goods in this downward flow consist, in the case of standard market towns, chiefly of small shops; in the case of intermediate market towns they include distributors who supply itinerants as well as dual wholesale-retail establishments; and in the case of central market towns they include most prominently wholesalers equipped with warehouses. Merchandise which is consumed by the peasantry or required by petty craftsmen flows down through the system to every market; consumer goods for the local élite and supplies for artisans moves no further down than the intermediate market; while consumer goods of interest chiefly to the bureaucratic élite, together with industrial supplies, normally go no further than the central market town itself.

The flow of goods upward through the marketing system begins when the peasant sells his product in the standard market, either to local consumers, to dealers based in the standard market who process and/or bulk the product, or directly to buyers who are visiting the standard market from higher-level market towns. Purchasing agents and buyers visit standard markets from central as well as intermediate market towns; they visit intermediate markets from local cities as well as central market towns. Whether the collecting firms are commercial houses or industries which process or consume the local products, these products are drawn up through the marketing system to ever higher-level centers.

* * *

The majority of standard marketing areas, then, are of a size which puts the most disadvantaged villager within easy walking distance of the town—3.4 to 6.1 kilometers. In the modal case . . . marketing areas are just over 50 square kilometers in size, market towns are less than eight kilometers apart, and maximum walking distance to the town is approximately 4.5 km. The average (mean) population of the standard marketing community is somewhat over 7,000.

It is clear, then, that even in the case of the typical community—1500 households in eighteen or so villages distributed over fifty square kilometers—we are not dealing with a cosy primary group structured through bonds of great intimacy or intensity. On the other hand, unused as most students of China are to thinking of marketing systems as communities and given the burden of the relevant literature, we are likely to be led far astray in this regard.

* * *

[T]he figures for [Kweichow and Szechwan] provinces suggest that the communes established in them in 1958 conform very closely to standard marketing communities. In the case of Kweichow, I have only the cited averages to go on, but for Szechwan there is much to confirm such a supposition. The province as defined in 1958 (less those *hsien* falling in non-agricultural China) had contained 4,586 townships as of 1948, when there was very nearly a one-to-one correspondence between market towns and township seats. A total of approximately 4,750 communes in 1958 is, therefore, strong presumptive evidence that the communes formed in that province were, for the most part, a direct continuation of pre-Communist townships. Informants from the Chengtu Plain report that continuity in lower-level administrative units was unbroken from republican times right through the initial communization of 1958. Even Szechwan, however, was unable to avoid entirely a certain minimum of commune consolidation near its major cities during the nationwide adjustment of 1959.

* * *

My interpretation of developments during the trying years, 1959–61, may be briefly stated. Intensified by the preoccupation with sheer survival, "local particularism" at first hampered, then frustrated, and finally defeated the efforts of Communist cadremen to organize collectivized units at a level above that of basic marketing systems. By the winter of 1960–61, Communist planners and cadremen alike had gained new respect for the enduring significance of natural social systems, and were seeking ways to use traditional solidarities for their own organizational ends.

* * *

In retrospect it can be seen that the subdivision of communes into units approximating standard marketing systems (or, in modernized areas, intermediate trading systems) was closely associated with the rehabilitation of periodic marketing which, while begun in late 1959, got into full swing only during the winter of 1960–61. Once a given market was back in operation, the town in which it was situated was, in the typical case, made the nucleus of a new, smaller commune.

G. William Skinner, "Vegetable Supply and Marketing in Chinese Cities," 76 China Quarterly, 733, 775, 779–780, 783–786 (1978).

* * *

There is great variation from one city to another in the organizational arrangements for getting vegetables from peri-urban communes to urban markets. One critical dimension of differentiation has to do with the precise definition of the two parties to an agreement or contract. On the production side, while it is true, as we shall see below in discussing planning, that all three levels within the commune—the commune itself, the brigade and the team—play a role in drawing up a seasonal or annual production plan, and while it is true that in some ultimate sense the accounting unit may everywhere be the production team, in practice either the team or the brigade may enter into contracts and agreements and assume primary responsibility for fulfilling them. Deliveries may be made by teams or by brigades, and sanctions may be applied at either level.

On the marketing side, while it is true that all deliveries of vegetables to the state for urban consumption count as procurement by the Municipal Vegetable Company, the actual party to an agreement or a contract with a producing unit may be a retail marketing cluster (which in effect means that cluster's leading market), a local management office of the vegetable company, or yet another agency of the company charged with assessing, wholesaling, redistribution and/or supervisory functions.

* * *

As in Sian, the contracting production unit in Canton is the team rather than brigade, and in fact for at least half of the vegetable production teams in Canton's peri-urban areas the system works just as in Sian. Each team is linked to and supplies only one particular leading market, and each market has contracts with a multitude of teams. A single large marketing cluster may have contracts with over 200 teams, although these would be heavily concentrated in the one or two nearest peri-urban communes. About one-sixth of the vegetable production teams have contracts not with marketing clusters but with one of the 13 suburban linking stations, in which case the team members bringing in a shipment log it first at the station and then proceed to the market designated, just as in Tsinan. The remaining third of the production teams are under contract with one or another of the seven wholesale depots. It will be recalled that Canton's local vegetable production is limited to eight communes within the municipality proper. The inner and outer zones together are, in a manner of speaking, only one commune wide to the south, west and northwest, but two communes wide to the north and east. In practice this means that four of the seven wholesale depots in the urban districts each deals largely with a single commune (e.g., the wholesale depot in Hai-chu District with Hsin-chiao Commune immediately across the Pearl River to the south).

Thus, Canton's system combines remarkable economy and simplicity with exemplary flexibility and differentiation. Despite the differentiation, transport costs are minimized. Each team has a lasting link with only one marketing unit. If its production is so specialized (say in aquatic vegetables in the case of a nearby team or in onions in the case of a distant team) that its harvest cannot be absorbed by a single marketing cluster, then its link is likely to be with the nearest wholesale depot. If its production is diversified or concentrated on basic vegetables, then it is likely to be linked to the nearest market or receiving centre. The distribution system, then, does nothing to inhibit specialization in accordance with the comparative advantage of different localities, and the advantages of differentiation are achieved with no appreciable increase in transport costs. As for a marketing cluster, it has the security of a diversified base in the nearest periurban sector (in the form of scores if not hundreds of teams producing solely for it) *and* access to wholesale depots for complementary and specialized items.

* * *

Planning and Pricing. In theory the planning of urban vegetable supply is jointly negotiated each year by two high-level municipal agencies: the Second Commercial Bureau and the Agricultural Production Bureau. Formal statements of the planning process indicated that necessary data on the demand side are collected through the marketing hierarchy culminating in the vegetable company, that necessary data on the supply side are collected through the production hierarchy culminating in the vegetable production unit of the Agricultural Production Bureau, and that the two sets of data (and discrepant perspectives and claims) are reconciled and mediated at the bureau level, where vegetables can be placed in the context of the other components of urban supply and other demands on agricultural resources. Near the end of our trip, however, I came to suspect that this picture was formalistic if not unreal, ...

In my view the critical level at which data inputs are integrated is not that of the bureaus but rather the level below it. In fact, the draft plan appears to be put together by the Municipal Vegetable

Company, which is able to dominate the planning process precisely because it collects and cumulates data not only on the demand side (from markets) but also on the supply side (from production teams and brigades). Production data and projections from vegetable teams and brigades, I argue, are aggregated and articulated and passed up to the vegetable company via its subordinate linking stations (recall the liaison men posted to particular brigades in Tsinan, Shanghai and Hangchow) and via its subordinate leading markets (recall the direct links between production and units and particular leading markets in Peking, Nanking, Sian and Canton). The managers of wholesale depots and receiving centres (which is to say, of linking stations with either or both of these functions) are concerned every day with matching supply and demand (and with mediating between production units and marketing units), and the managers of marketing clusters that have direct links with production units are strategically situated to command the facts and obtain authoritative projections not only from subordinate retail units but also from the teams or brigades that supply them. Thus, despite the variety of logistic arrangements, the vegetable company everywhere commands the data needed to make reasonable projections of both production and marketing needs—data it gathers from personnel who are themselves ever alert to the necessity of reconciling the two.

*   *   *

Whatever the precise nature of the plan, it is put into operation through detailed arrangements negotiated between the production unit and the particular linking station or market with which it deals. In Sian, teams enter into seasonal contracts with markets (usually for three of the five official seasons in the case of teams with continuous fields, and for only the autumn or winter season in the case of teams with only seasonal fields); elsewhere contracts may be annual or of indefinite duration. In Nanking, for instance, contracts are continued from one year to the next unless one side or the other initiates renegotiations. In still other municipalities, Tsinan for instance, formal contracts are dispensed with altogether, the disaggregated plan being specified for brigades through negotiations between the vegetable company's liaison man and brigade leaders and then allocated among component teams. One way or another teams have a clear understanding of what is expected of them during the coming agricultural year. These obligations are couched in terms of "five guarantees" made by the production unit to the state: total acreage, adequate variety, timing of delivery, quantity of total output and standards of quality. Nonetheless, teams and brigades are permitted considerable leeway in meeting these obligations; for instance, plantings by type of vegetable may depart from the specifications of the seasonal plan by as much as 10–15 per cent. Precise harvesting and delivery dates are continually being monitored—and negotiated, there being a leeway of at least a few days in most cases—by the marketing unit.

All prices are fixed by the vegetable company, whose stated objectives are to protect at once the interests of consumers (by maintaining a ceiling on retail prices), of producers (by keeping a floor on the purchase prices paid to teams and brigades), and of the state (by avoiding vegetable company deficits over the long haul). Prices are set for each grade (two to four in practice) of each variety and are adjusted in rough accordance with that variety's seasonal fluctuations. On Wiens's analysis, prevailing prices "reflect adjustments made incrementally over a 20-year period to earlier free-market prices" and accord rather closely with average supply and demand conditions. Grade-specific prices may be adjusted for a particular variety as many as 90 times in the course of an agricultural year, and Wiens finds it "surprising how closely socialist planning replicates the price fluctuations of the free market."

QUESTIONS

1. What inferences can be drawn from the above materials about the contractual relations and patterns of dealing between the processor and the farmers? How would the processor have "arranged" with the farmers to increase production? What would be the parties' expectations about how losses should be borne? If they had anticipated the possibility of the manufacturer's failure to deliver, how might they have assigned the burden for bearing losses?

2. What inferences can be drawn about relations between the processor and the distributor? Would the two parties have signed a formal contract?

3. What inferences can be drawn about relations between the processor and the manufacturer?

D. DISPUTE RESOLUTION

Dietrich Loeber, "Comparing Chinese Enterprise Administration and Settlement of Contract Disputes with Soviet Practices," 1 Review of Socialist Law, 7, 13–17 (1975) (notes omitted).

II. Settling Contract Disputes

In the Soviet Union a special institution has been created for the settlement of disputes between socialist organizations. It is called "*arbitrazh*". It may force a reluctant partner to conclude a contract; in cases of improper performance *arbitrazh* can order the payment of damages and fines.

Arbitrazh was created 50 years ago. The number of cases decided in this period reaches several millions. Over the years *arbitrazh* has developed a firm practice of handling disputes between economic organizations.

1. The Chinese Solution

China, strangely, has no *arbitrazh*. This is in contrast to North-Vietnam, North-Korea and Mongolia and the European socialist countries which have all created an *arbitrazh*-network based on the Soviet model. Only Yugoslavia and Hungary are exceptions; these two countries entrusted the courts with the settlement of economic disputes between enterprises. In Yugoslavia such disputes are handled by economic courts while Hungary established economic collegia within the system of ordinary courts.

Chinese courts do not usually handle disputes between economic organizations although, formally, they would be competent to do so.

a. Internal Organization of Contract Work. The techniques of such informal settlements have been ably described by Frank Münzel in a paper read at . . . [a] Conference in Berkeley in 1973. Each contracting enterprise is supposed to organize its work in such a way as to avoid disputes. Quality control and enforcing the rules on plan performance are important means of achieving this. The superior agency, moreover, checks whether and how its subordinates live up to their obligations. Much emphasis is placed on "cooperation" among enterprises. Teams from the producing units visit their customers. The teams discuss complaints, replace defective products and assist in making repairs. Münzel concludes that the "organizational aspect" of the contract relationship is "stressed more than the 'obligation' aspect".

If these devices for solving (contradictions) fail, administrative agencies and the Communist Party are called upon to settle contract disputes in China.

b. Administrative Agencies. No detailed statutes have been issued to establish the competence of administrative agencies in the resolution of disputes. An early regulation on contracts (1950) provides, with regard to disputes:

> if both parties are located within one large administrative region (in North-China—within one province or city), the other [aggrieved] party can apply to the Financial-Economic Committee performing direct guidance with the request to take the necessary measures. If the parties are not located within one large administrative region, province or city, the other party can apply to the Financial-Economic Committee of the State Administrative Council of the Central People's Government with the request to take the necessary measures.

The Rules of the Ministry of Heavy Industry (1956) stipulate:

> If . . . serious disputes occur before state arbitration organs have been established the parties may report to their superior for arrangement and decision.

A civil law textbook commented in 1958:

If the parties disagree concerning the terms of the draft contract, the case is submitted to the higher authorities in charge for arbitration and settlement, and the contract is then concluded on the basis of the decision of the higher authorities.

The administrative organ arbitrates contractual disputes. At present, there is no public arbitration organ in our country. Any dispute arising from a contract between socialist organizations, which the parties themselves cannot solve through negotiation, should be submitted to higher authorities for consultation and settlement . . . .

* * *

Other regulations provide for decisions by administrative authorities, but permit litigation in court as an appeal from such decision.

* * *

. . . The language of the rules varies: the activities are described as the "handling" (*ch'u-li*) of disputes, as a "decision" (*chieh-chüeh*) and as "arbitration" (*chung-ts'ai*). Jerome Cohen believes that disputes between Chinese enterprises "are often resolved through mediation processes". He defines mediation as a method "by which third persons seek to resolve a dispute without imposing a binding decision". It would be compatible with this notion, he writes, to "recommend the terms" of the settlement and to "mobilize such strong political, economic, social, and moral pressures upon one or both parties as to leave little option but that of 'voluntary' acquiescence."

　　c. Party Organs. Party organs may also act as guardians of the proper conclusion and performance of contracts. They play a role in enforcing contracts in addition to the superior agencies or in their place. The party intervenes, as a rule, informally and by using means typical of party work; these include persuasion, criticism and self-criticism, appeals and disciplinary measures.

The procedure for the resolution of disputes by administrative agencies and by the party has an internal character. It is probably not regulated by any strict rules. Many cases seem to be handled by using discretionary powers and on ad hoc basis. This readily explains why so little is known about the Chinese practice of dispute settlement. But even the few bits of information at our disposal are enough to attempt comparison.

2.　Legal Nature of the Chinese Solution

The Chinese solution, i.e. the absence of an *arbitrazh* procedure and the non-use of courts to ensure contract performance, is open to several legal interpretations:

　　(1) one could approach the subject from a civil law angle and maintain that inter-enterprise contracts in China are unenforce-

able obligations. According to such a view the handling of disputes by administrative agencies or party organs would lack a legal character; it would be considered as an activity falling into the sphere of internal administration or politics. Such interpretation, however, raises doubts. Chinese law, too, aims at ensuring the performance of contracts. If there is a difference, it is in the means, not in the aims. As long as contracts are, in fact, enforced, it does not matter too much by what means this is achieved. It might not be justifiable, therefore, to deny the obligatory character of contracts in China because (allegedly) non-legal means are used to enforce them.

(2) one could reverse the line of argument and claim that inter-enterprise contracts are enforceable in law, but that the relations called "contracts" are actually not of a civil law character. They are established under administrative law and are enforced by means of administrative law. Such interpretation would underestimate, however, the traces of civil law present in the relations between producer and buyer or between an economic organization providing services and its customer. The administrative law interpretation would be just as onesided as the civil law theory.

(3) the two extreme theories suggest a middle-of-the-road interpretation combining elements of both views. The impact of planning acts on the conclusion and performance of contracts results in a peculiar blend of civil and administrative law. The relative weight of civil and administrative law elements varies depending on the type of contract and the character of the contract partners. The enforcement of contracts may remain wholly in the realm of administrative law. Such an interpretation would make economic contracts a hybrid institution. This will seem strange to a lawyer trained in the common law or the civil law tradition. But it probably comes close to reality in China.

The combined theory is in harmony with the legal nature of economic contracts in a planned system of the Soviet type. The mixture of civil and administrative law elements has created a set of special contract rules different from the traditional contract law. There is no sharp dividing line between concluding and performing a contract on the one side and enforcing it on the other. This also applies in China. The use of administrative methods for enforcing contracts can be understood as an extension of the administrative elements already present in economic contracts.

QUESTIONS

1. What difference does it make in the dispute resolution process or in the outcome if contracts have a civil law, administrative, or hybrid character?

2. When Chinese officials are asked how interenterprise disputes are resolved, they generally reply that mutually agreeable settlements are arrived at through negotiations. They also say that there are extremely few cases where the disputants cannot reach some agreement. Is it possible that Chinese enterprises can resolve virtually all disputes without third party intervention? If so, this is a phenomenon a litigious society such as the United States should investigate carefully.

3. If third party intervention is frequently required, what form does this intervention take? Until very recently, courts did not handle such cases, and no administrative tribunals were known to exist. The following item is the most concrete example of a dispute resolution mechanism we know about.

Communique of the Central Committee of the Communist Party and the State Council Concerning the Strict Implementation of the Basic Construction Procedures and the Strict Implementation of Economic Contracts. Chung-hua jen-min kung-ho-kuo fa-kuei hui-pien (Collection of laws and regulations of the People's Republic of China), vol. 13, p. 62, December 10, 1962:

Article 2. All organs of the national economy must strictly implement their economic contracts; all production enterprises must produce in accordance with their contract demands, and guarantee the quality of their products and the time of delivery. Organs ordering goods must accept delivery and make payment in a timely manner, strictly implement the order contract, and not return goods. After today, if the ordered goods do not conform to production regulations or to the terms of the order contract, the organ ordering the goods may refuse to accept the goods, and the producing organ must repair the goods or deliver new goods; any loss suffered as a result shall be borne by the production enterprise. If, under special circumstances, the ordering organ must return the goods, or if the goods conform to production regulations and the terms of the contract, but the ordering organ does not accept the goods or make payment in a timely manner, any loss suffered as a result shall be borne by the ordering organ. Where disputes arise in the course of implementing a contract, the economic committees of each area shall arbitrate. The people's bank or construction bank of each area shall be responsible for carrying out the decisions of the economic committee, and shall charge the account (of the organ at fault).

NOTES AND QUESTIONS

1. The economic committee is a policy-making body organized on a territorial basis, cutting across functional or ministerial lines. For example, the major economic agencies and units in a city or province would be tied into the city or provincial economic committee.

2. What level economic committee would have jurisdiction over the processor-farmers dispute? Processor-distributor dispute? Processor-manufacturer dispute? How does the level of the economic committee affect its ability to handle dispute resolution work?

3. With the economic and legal reforms, renewed attention has been paid to the dispute resolution process.

"Economic Division Set Up in Court," Beijing Review, August 10, 1979, pp. 5–6.

A special division to handle economic disputes has been set up in the intermediate people's court in the city of Chongqing in southwest China's Sichuan Province. The court previously handled only criminal and civil suits.

The division is empowered to apply economic sanctions against those enterprises and organizations that violate the government's economic rules and regulations and to bring to justice those guilty of serious offences in economic affairs. This is aimed at safeguarding the socialist economic order and ensuring normal proceeding of economic activities and fulfilment of state economic plans.

At present, the economic division has jurisdiction only over major cases which cannot be handled by the authorities in charge through consultations and cases in which the parties involved refuse to accept mediation. These include:

(1) Cases involving heavy political or economic losses resulting from a breach of contract or failure to carry out the contracts conscientiously;

(2) Serious cases of deception or shoddy work causing heavy losses;

(3) Cases of failure to treat industrial wastes or neglect of operational safety, which seriously impair the health of workers or peasants and are harmful to public interests;

(4) Serious cases of neglect of duty that inflict heavy losses on products, commodities, equipment or other public property; and

(5) Cases of embezzlement of workers' wages or state funds or theft of equipment causing serious consequences.

In the past Chinese courts had no economic division. Cases of breach of contract or failure to carry out contracts causing losses to one party were generally solved through mediation by their superior organs. The defect with this method was that many economic disputes could not be solved after long wrangling. Now the intermediate courts of various provinces, municipalities and autonomous regions are beginning to set up an economic division. This has won the praise of the public.

"Draft Decision [by the Central Committee of the Communist Party, July 1978] Concerning Some Problems in Speeding Up the De-

velopment of Industry," (Part 2) **Issues and Studies, Vol. 15, January 1979, p. 76.**

All localities and all departments and units in charge must carefully reexamine the present relations of coordination in industry. Those which are reasonable should be made permanent; those which are unreasonable must be readjusted, those in need of rebuilding must be rebuilt as quickly as possible. Economic contracts must be signed by both parties which join the coordination program. Stable relations of coordination should be gradually developed towards the orientation of signing long-term contracts. Signed contracts must be strictly carried out. To violate the relations of coordination and the contracts is to disrupt the socialist planned economy. The party which has failed to fulfill the requirements in the contracts or which has arbitrarily broken off the relations of coordination must be held responsible and compensations must be made for losses. All disputes over the execution of economic contracts will be settled by arbitration of the economic committees at various levels.

QUESTIONS

1. Why have dispute resolution mechanisms become more important after the 1978 reforms?

2. How do you reconcile the reference to arbitration by economic committees in the last item with the establishment of economic divisions in the courts in the previous item?

Economic Contract Law effective July 1, 1982.

Article 48. When there are disputes over an economic contract, the interested parties should consult with each other on time to settle the disputes. When they fail to reach an agreement after consultations, any one of the parties concerned can request the organ governing contracts assigned by the state for mediation and arbitration. It may also directly bring a suit against the other side at the people's court.

Article 49. If an agreement has been reached after mediation, the parties concerned must implement such an agreement. If an adjudication is made in the course of arbitration, the organ governing contracts assigned by the state will work out a written judgment for arbitration. If one or both parties concerned are not satisfied with the arbitration, they may bring a suit at the people's court within 15 days after receiving the written judgment. If no suit is brought within the prescribed period, the adjudication is then legalized.

Article 50. The litigants of an economic contract must submit their request to the organ governing contracts for mediation or arbitration within 1 year from the date when it knows or should know that its rights have been infringed upon. No case will be handled if such request is submitted beyond the prescribed period.

QUESTION

1. In what ways does the Economic Contract Law change the dispute resolution process?

E. LIABILITY AND DAMAGES

NOTE

In addition to identifying the institutional framework for dispute resolution, we also have to determine what are the substantive rules concerning liability and extent of damages. For example, is a Hadley v. Baxendale approach used, or is there a tendency to let losses lie where they fall? Are state owned enterprises favored over collective enterprises? Is there a policy of favoring industry or agricultural producers? The following materials give some indication of the general policy trends.

Wu Chia-chun, Socialist Economic Accounting Brooks No Negation, in American Consulate General, Hong Kong: Survey of People's Republic of China Press, No. 6392–6396, August 1–5, 1977, pp. 152–153. (Peking Kuang-ming Jih-pao, July 18, 1977).

"Is Accounting of No Use" to Socialist Enterprises?

One of the fallacies of the "gang of four" is that "since everybody puts public interest to the fore, what is the use of accounting?" This is a most preposterous theory.

* * *

The socialist economy is for meeting the ever growing needs of the state and the people. It is more important for it to stress economic results and the economic use of working time than it has been in any society in the past. To stress economic results, it is imperative to practice economic accounting. Economic accounting is a form of expression of the law governing the economy of time under socialist conditions, and is also an important means for realizing increase of production and practice of economy. Only through the wholesale implementation of economic accounting can impetus be given to the development of production with greater, faster, better and more economical results.

Is it possible to think that under socialist conditions, it will do to keep books for the national economy as a whole, and that there is no need to keep accounts for each enterprise? Of course not. Socialist economy is planned economy and the whole national economy is a unified whole. However, the cells forming this whole are the enterprises. As independently operated socialist enterprises, they are allocated a given amount of capital by the state, and have the rights to make use of such funds for organizing their own production, supply, and marketing activities under the unified plan of the state. Between enterprises, economic transactions are carried out according to the principle of exchange of equal values. Their own income is used to make good their expenditures and to insure the surrender of profits to the state according to plan. An enterprise is required to hold itself responsible to the state for operational results, and the state is required to evaluate the operational activities of the enterprise according to plan. With a stringent accounting system, it is possible to thoroughly examine whether the business of an enterprise is profitable. Consequently, socialist economic accounting must be carried out with the enterprise as unit, and enterprise accounting is the base of accounting for the whole national economy. Only by making a success of enterprise economic accounting can the latent power be brought into full play, thus giving impetus to the development of the national economy as a whole. If, as advocated by the "gang of four," all enterprises do not seriously do a good job in economic accounting and even abolish economic accounting, then the socialist economy will be wrecked.

Hu Ch'iao-mu, "Observe Economic Laws, Speed Up The Four Modernizations," Peking Review, no. 47, pp. 18–20, November 24, 1978.

Narrowing the Price Scissors Between Industrial and Farm Products

In applying the law of value to the socialist economy, it is essential to see to it that there is exchange of equal values between industrial and farm products and that the price scissors between the two are eliminated. Already over 20 years ago Comrade Mao Tsetung gave the following explicit instruction: "In the exchange of industrial and agricultural products we follow a policy of narrowing the price scissors, a policy of exchanging equal or roughly equal values." Comrade Hua Kuo-feng said in his report to the Fifth National People's Congress: "The law of value must be consciously applied under the guidance of the unified state plan. We must study in earnest the price parities between industrial and agricultural products. . . . To promote production, we must appropriately raise the purchasing prices of agricultural products and, as costs are cut down, properly reduce the prices of manufactured goods, especially those produced to support agriculture."

* * *

It must be pointed out here that, in the last 20 years and more since the founding of the People's Republic, the purchasing price of farm produce has doubled while retail prices of industrial goods have risen only 28 per cent. The disparity between the two, though being gradually narrowed, is still fairly large at present. Besides, with the ever-growing use of industrial goods in farm production, this question has become increasingly acute. The rather large price scissors together with the rather slow pace in narrowing them naturally dampen the peasants' enthusiasm for developing production.

* * *

With the exception of the better areas, the income of the peasants, after a year's work, shows little or no increase at all in many places although production has gone up; in a few places, incomes have actually decreased with the increase in production. The reasons for this are manifold, but the existence of the price scissors is usually the major reason. If this situation remains unchanged, it will hinder rapid agricultural development, the movement to learn from Tachai in agriculture, the modernization of agriculture, and it will prevent us from getting the full advantages in carrying out rural policies; it is also at cross-purposes with consolidation of the worker-peasant alliance, with our bid to narrow the differences between industry and agriculture and between town and country, and with the policy of taking agriculture as the foundation.

Really Recognize Collective Ownership by the Peasants and the Right of Management By Production Teams

At the Second Chengchow Conference held in March 1959, Comrade Mao Tsetung pointedly criticized the mistake of taking away the peasants' and production teams' fruits of labour without compensation. In 1961 he personally presided over the drawing up of the Revised Draft for Regulations on the Work of the Rural People's Communes (known as the Sixty Points) which once more stressed the need to guarantee a production team's right to run its own affairs. According to the draft drawn up at that time, the production brigade was made the basic accounting unit *; later, when the production team was made the basic accounting unit, the latter's right to control its own affairs naturally had to be further expanded. However, due to interference and sabotage by Lin Piao and the "gang of four," this question has remained unsettled for more than ten years. This means that in quite a number of places, collective ownership by the peasants has not been protected and recognized in actual practice; there are many more places where it has not been fully protected or recognized. Where the communes are not run in a democratic way and where farming is not operated on a democratic basis, it means in actual fact non-recognition of the peasants' collective ownership, it also means in actual fact non-recognition of the socialist economic system and the socialist political system over an area peopled by 700 million peasants organized in collectives.

Why is it possible for some people to increase at random the burdens of the production teams in many parts of the country, . . . ?

---

* At present, in a rural people's commune a production team is generally the basic unit for cost accounting which is responsible for its own profits and losses and directly organizes production and the distribution of its gains. Ed.

. . . Why is it possible for certain leading bodies according to their own whim to order the peasants to uproot crops they have planted and grow other crops instead, without being responsible both legally and economically for the ensuing losses?

* * *

. . . They all point up the fact that in the minds of many a comrade, the peasants' collective ownership actually does not exist at all, that the right of the production teams, production brigades and the people's communes actually to control their own affairs does not exist at all, and that the various basic systems of the people's communes also do not exist at all. They show that the economic rights and interests of the communes, production brigades and production teams, and, indeed, the commune members' personal property and right of the person can be placed at the free disposal of the higher-up levels, of certain leader or leaders, including the individual cadres of a commune, a production brigade or a production team, and that the organs, meetings of commune members' delegates as well as general meetings of commune members at all levels of a commune can be ignored altogether.

The Party Central Committee headed by Comrade Hua Kuo-feng has now resolutely set right these mistakes and this fully reflects the wishes of the peasant masses. However, in order to solve this problem through and through, there must also be a stable system set up by the state in unequivocal terms in addition to Party policies. As stipulated in our Constitution, the state guarantees the consolidation and development of the socialist economy collectively owned by the masses of working people, that socialist public property is inviolable, that commune members may farm small plots of land for personal needs and engage in limited household sideline production. All this is very well, but this alone is not enough because people can still violate what has been stipulated without any misgivings. This tells us that, in order to really settle this matter, we need to enact special laws and set up special law courts and strictly punish according to law anyone who dares to break these laws.

With a view to protecting collective ownership by the people's commune, a contract system should be established to govern the economic relationship between the commune, the production brigade and the production team on the one hand, and the state (in matters not covered by law), all the enterprises, government organs and army units on the other; among communes, brigades and teams; between communes or brigades and teams; between communes, brigades or teams and the commune members. All contracts, moreover, should be approved in a democratic way according to a certain procedure. The commune, brigade, team and commune members have the right to reject any request not provided for in the contract and they have also the right to seek compensation for any lossses they suffer due to breach of contract. Only in this way can the collective ownership be really established. Only on this basis can the peasants feel that they are masters of their own destiny, masters of the production team, the production brigade and the commune, and masters of the state. Only then will they actively and boldly devote their energies into developing production and undertake the building of a modern, socialist countryside. This will not weaken but strengthen the Party's and the state's leadership over the peasants; it can not hinder but will ensure the transition of the basic accounting unit when conditions ripen.

* * *

"More Work, More Pay," Beijing Review, no. 16, April 20, 1979, p. 21.

Work Points

The remuneration system adopted by the brigade can be described as "fixed quotas and allocated work points according to the work done." This means that quotas and their corresponding number of work points to be given are announced for all farm work that can be so calculated. For instance, people harvesting wheat and planting autumn crops on the same plot of land will be given 3,000 work points to a hectare. If a ten-person group of a production team is assigned to this work and they have fulfilled their task satisfactorily, each member, provided every one of them has done the same amount of work, will be given 300 work points.

By the end of a year, if one has got 5,000 work points and the production team gives 0.8 yuan for every ten points, his income for the year will be 400 yuan. (Generally each able-bodied team member gets ten points per work day. In the case of particularly difficult jobs or jobs calling for more skill, he gets more work points, and vice versa.)

This encourages commune members to work hard and also helps get rid of the old practice of paying men more than women doing the same kind of work. Ideas of looking down upon women that persisted for several thousand years in Chinese feudal society are still evident today. Despite constant appeal for equal pay for equal work regardless of sex, in many places women still get less than men doing the same kind of work. It is ten work points a day for a man, but only eight for a woman.

* * *

After the fall of the "gang of four," the old system was gradually reintroduced, together with some additional measures for material awards. At the start of a new year, a production team would work out and make known its plan for the forthcoming year. How much it was going to produce, to sell, and its members were going to earn. Each production team member then gave the number of work days he or she will do in the year and the amount of manure he or she was going to hand in that year. (In rural China farmyard manure makes up more than one-half of the fertilizer used.) Overfulfilment is materially rewarded.

NOTE

Since 1978, a major effort has been mounted to increase the productivity of industrial and commercial enterprises, principally by employing material incentives to induce both management and workers to work harder and more efficiently. In the past, state-owned enterprises (including units such as processor, distributor, and manufacturer) turned over all their profits to the state; any losses were made up by the state. Salaries of employees were fixed by the state, with increases based almost exclusively on seniority.

As discussed in section A, under the 1978 reforms, enterprises were granted greater—though far from complete—autonomy in deciding what and how to produce, procuring materials, setting prices for finished products, giving bonuses to good workers, etc. As part of this program, enterprises were allowed to retain a fraction of their income which may be used for plant expansion, increased worker bonuses, etc. Enterprises operating at a loss did not receive these added benefits and sometimes had to make good the losses out of other funds. Thus, establishing fault, assigning liability, and obtaining compensation for breaches of contract took on new importance.

The next items give a general description of the reform of the industrial and commercial system. The following includes one of the basic policy documents defining the new system.

"Enterprise Management: Tentative Practice," Peking Review, no. 32, August 10, 1979, p. 5.

Since the beginning of this year, 100 enterprises in the metallurgical, machine-building, light and textile industries and communications and transport departments have been given greater power of decision than before with regard to production and management. Now these enterprises can do the following:

—Organize extra production, process raw materials from other units and sell products that are not purchased by the state commercial, supply and marketing or other departments, after state production quotas are met;

—Enlarge the proportion of the depreciation funds in relation to the fixed assets. This facilitates technical transformation and replacement of equipment;

—Draw enterprise funds in proportion to the total annual wages and the planned profit targets. In this way, there will be more money for collective welfare and more bonuses for the workers and staff members;

—Establish a system of checking on the work done and promotion of workers and staff members. This includes the improvement of the system of awards, the implementation of the principle of "to each according to his work," and the adoption of disciplinary measures and economic sanctions against workers and staff members who have neglected their duties; and

—Engage in business negotiations with foreign firms and sign contracts on exports.

For a long time in the past, China's enterprises had limited powers of their own. For instance, they were in charge of production but had to rely on other departments for supply of raw materials and sale of their products. All of their profits and most of their depreciation funds had to be turned in for unified allocation by the state. The enterprises had to apply for state investments if they wanted to rebuild or expand. Plans for technical innovation or any other initiatives had to be reported to the higher authorities for approval. Practice shows that all this hampered the development of the productive forces.

"Draft Decision [by the Central Committee of the Communist Party, July 1978] Concerning Some Problems in Speeding Up the Development of Industry," (Part 2) Issues and Studies, Vol. 15, January 1979, pp. 74, 87–89, 94–95.

* * *

IX. The Five Fixings in Enterprises and the Fund for Enterprises

We must do a good job in implementing the five fixings in enterprises and guarantee stable production conditions for enterprises.

The five fixings in enterprises are:

1. the fixing of the orientation as well as the scale of production;

2. the fixing of personnel and organs;

3. the fixing of consumption quotas and sources of supply of raw materials, semi-finished materials, fuel, power and instruments;

4. the fixing of assets and liquid capital;

5. the fixing of the relations of coordination.

This work must be jointly carried out in stages by relevant central departments, local departments and enterprises in the light of the institution of long-term plans and on the basis of the accomplishment of an overall balance and the suitable allocation of areas. The first and foremost thing is to fully implement the five fixings in large and medium-sized enterprises. This should be completed in two years or in a period slightly longer than two years. The contents of the five fixings, once decided on, will be fundamentally unchanged, but suitable readjustment will be made yearly according to the state plan. Necessary changes must be discussed and approved by the central and local departments in charge. Documents concerning the designs of new enterprises must include the contents of the five fixings, or else approval will not be granted.

Enterprises must guarantee the overall attainment of the eight economic and technical norms stipulated by the state and the fulfillment of all contracts concerning the supply of commodities. Those enterprises which have completely fulfilled or overfulfilled the state plan may draw from their profits funds which will be mainly used to run collective welfare services in those enterprises. The proportion of profits drawn for use as funds of enterprises should be different in accordance with various trades and enterprises. Concrete stipulations should be made by the Ministry of Finance together with other relevant departments and units. Enterprises which have not fulfilled the state plan must find out the reasons for their failures. If such failures are caused by subjective reasons, such as poor leadership and bureaucracy, the enterprises or relevant units in charge should be held responsible and their leading cadres must be removed.

XIX. Giving First Place to Quality, Variety and Specification of Commodities

All enterprises must continuously improve the quality of their products, strive to produce products of high efficiency, low consumption and enduring usage. Enterprises should enlarge in a planned way the range of various goods and their specifications, and be practically responsible for producing goods that meet the needs of consumers. Encouragement and support must be given to trial production and production of new products. Industrial enterprises must improve the quality of packing; they will be held responsible for any loss caused by poor packing. Communications enterprises must improve the delivery procedure of goods; they will be held responsible for all losses caused by loading and unloading. Undesirable actions which show irresponsibility to the state and the people such as the neglect of quality of products, production of large quantity of low-quality goods and profligate waste of state wealth should be opposed.

All products which are not up to standard in terms of quality, type and specifications and which do not meet the requirements of the contract will not be allowed to leave the factory. Such products will not be included in the calculation of the achievement index of the plan and the production value. The consumer units have the right to reject such products. As for products that have already left the factory, the factory will still be responsible for their repair, replacement, and even the payment of compensation for them. Replacement of the products that have been sold through business establishments will be carried out through business establishments. People who have caused serious losses must be held responsible and duly punished.

. . .

XX. Increasing Accumulation and Practicing Economy

All industrial and communications enterprises must go all out to carry out the state plan, fulfill and overfulfill the tasks of handing in profits and taxes stipulated by the state and accumulate more capital for the state. We must conscientiously and thoroughly implement the principle of building our country through diligence and thrift and put into practice a strict economic accounting system. We must severely criticize and resolutely correct the undesirable actions such as the neglecting of economic accounting and cost accounting, extravagance and waste, and raising or reducing prices arbitrarily. All enterprises must do a good job in setting up a permanent organization with a fixed number of personnel and in fixing labor quotas so as to raise labor productivity. Organizations of enterprises must be simplified. Non-productive personnel must be reduced and the number of people engaged in production must be increased. Those who should not be absent from production must return to their posts of production. Activities that should be conducted during spare time should not be held during production time. All are absolutely prohibited from doing jobs which were not originally listed in the plans. . . .

All enterprises must reduce non-productive expenditures and strive to lower costs of production. Expenditures other than costs should not be figured as costs. Enterprises which are losing money because of poor management must strive to completely counterbalance the loss in 1978. If they do not manage to counterbalance all losses in 1978, they will gain no more subsidies from financial departments and no more loans from the banks. As for the loss of enterprises caused by exterior influences, enterprises must actively adopt measures to change the unfavorable situation, and marked results should be obtained in this year. The amount of loss allowed by state policies must be reduced to the minimum. . . .

XXV. From Each According to His Ability, To Each According to His Work

In accordance with Chairman Mao's consistent teachings, we must integrate communist ideological education with current economic policies. Moral encouragement and material rewards must go hand in hand, with emphasis on the former. We must firmly put politics in command, teach staff and workers to cultivate the communist attitude towards labor of doing one's best to serve the people wholeheartedly without paying attention to rewards. With regard to distribution, we must adhere to the principles of "to each according to his work" and of "more pay for more work and less pay for less work." We are not only opposed to great differences between the highest and lowest wages, we are also opposed to equalitarianism. Necessary differences must be admitted. In this respect, we must adopt the following methods and measures:

1. Put into practice a normal wage adjustment system. All adjustments of wages must be approved by leadership organs after having been decided on by mass appraisals in accordance with the political performance of the staff and workers, their attitude

towards labor, and the level of their skills as well as their contributions.

2. Pay the staff and workers primarily on a time-rate basis. Payment on a piecework basis with limits may be applied to a few workers engaging in toilsome physical or manual labor.

3. Put into practice a wage system by which staff and workers are paid on a time-rate basis with additional bonuses.

4. Give pecuniary allowances for jobs requiring higher labor intensity or performed under worse working conditions.

5. Reduce the wage differences step by step in various areas so that wage-scales will correspond to the levels of commodity prices.

We must explain to the broad masses of people that we are still a developing socialist country and that our living conditions can only be gradually improved by increasing production and raising labor productivity. It is unrealistic and impossible to improve our living conditions without increasing production. We must constantly adhere to the excellent tradition of plain living and hard struggle and strive to push production forward.

QUESTIONS

1. Based on the above materials, must the processor purchase the farmers' extra production? If not, who should bear the loss? Would the result be different if the processor was a collective enterprise owned by a neighboring commune?

2. What, if anything, would the manufacturer be liable to the processor or others for?

3. What, if anything, would the processor be liable to the distributor for?

The Economic Contract Law deals in details with changing or cancelling contracts as well as with the question of liability and damages.

Article 27. An economic contract may be changed or canceled under one of the following conditions:

1. When both parties agree by mutual consultation, and when the change or cancellation does not harm state interests or affect state plans;

2. When the state plan on which the contract is based has been revised or canceled;

3. When one party of the contract can no longer fulfill the contract because the plant or enterprise has closed down, stopped production or been converted to other uses;

4. When a force majeure or factors other than a party's own fault which are beyond the control of the parties involved have made it impossible to fulfill the economic contract; and

5. When one party breaks the contract, and it has become impossible to fulfill the economic contract.

Article 32. If an economic contract cannot be fulfilled or can only be partially fulfilled because of the fault of one party, the party responsible for the fault must be charged with the responsibility of breaking the contract. If the fault is shared by both parties, they both must share the responsibility for breaking the contract according to the actual situation.

*   *   *

Article 33. If an economic contract cannot be fulfilled or can only be partially fulfilled because of the fault of a leading body at a higher level or the concerned unit in charge, then the leading body or the responsible unit should be charged with breaking the contract. The party breaking the contract must make a penalty payment for breaking the contract or pay damages to the other party in accordance with the proper stipulations, and the case will be handled by the leading body at a higher level or by the unit in charge which is responsible for the fault.

Article 34. If, because of force majeure, one party cannot fulfill an economic contract, it must promptly notify the other party of the reasons why the contract cannot be fulfilled, why its fulfillment must be delayed, or why the contract can only be partially fulfilled. If the party has obtained from the concerned unit in charge an approval on the postponement, partial fulfillment or total cancellation of the contract, the party may be partially or fully absolved from the responsibilities for breaking a contract.

Article 35. When one party breaks an economic contract, it must make a penalty payment to the other party for breaking a contract. However, if the losses caused to the other party exceed the amount of the penalty paid, the responsible party must also pay damages to make up for what the penalty payment has failed to cover. If the other party demands continuous fulfillment of the contract, the responsible party must comply.

Article 36. Penalty payments for breaking contracts and payments for damages are to be paid from an enterprise's portion of the profits it shares with the state and must never be included in the enterprise's production costs. For administrative units or institutions, these payments are to be paid out of the surplus from their unit budgets.

QUESTIONS

1. Based on the Economic Contract Law, must the processor purchase the farmers' extra production? If not, who should bear the loss? Would the result be different if the processor was a collective enterprise owned by neighboring commune?

2. What, if anything, would the manufacturer be liable to the processor or others for?

3. What, if anything, would the processor be liable to the distributor for?

Part V

POPULATION PLANNING

Chapter 22

INTRODUCTION TO POPULATION PLANNING

PROBLEM IV

The development of population planning technology creates a number of new issues for a society: should the government encourage or discourage the use of contraceptives, sterilization, or abortion? If so, how? Should their use be regulated in any manner? Should spouses or parents be consulted before use of any one of these technologies? Should the use of any of these technologies be compulsory? Should there be other supporting legal measures? Which of these questions are given legal answers? Do the legal decisions make any difference? How does the society reach a legal or administrative answer? To what extent is the debate cast in terms of rights or of any parallel legal concept?

*   *   *

Problem IV is the most value-laden of the problems presented in this book; one purpose of the topic is to show the interrelations between values and law and the limitations of law. On occasion, as in the Comstock laws described in the California material, values have decidedly shaped the law. In contrast, as in current Egypt, the state sometimes uses its authority to shape the preaching of those who contribute to the public's values. And the limitations of law appear starkly in this problem—exemplified in one fashion by the ineffectiveness of many population control efforts and the widespread disobedience of laws against abortion, and in another fashion by the Western rights theories that the law uses to limit itself.

The problem is also meant to illuminate the problems and mechanisms of legal change. It is easy to argue that legal change can be effective in a value-laden area only if it follows social change—a hypothesis that appears questionable if applied to China, but accurate if applied to the other societies. But the questions of the mechanism of change are more complex: why was "liberalization" a judicial matter in the West but a legislative or ministerial matter elsewhere?

These areas are probably the least well understood of any discussed in this book and the discussion is necessarily incomplete and imperfect; the reader is warned to approach this chapter with much greater skepticism than usual. Nevertheless, an effort at integration is likely to stimulate further, more critical thought. The issues are presented under three headings: the moral and social phenomena underlying attitudes toward population control technologies, the relation between the law and these underlying attitudes, and the processes of legal change.

A. UNDERLYING ATTITUDES

NOTE

Our view of sexual morality must derive from profound psychological roots, that probably differ from society to society. Although they may relate to views toward sexual pleasure itself, ranging from the frequently guilt-ridden views of the West to the allegedly more joyous views of Sunni Islam, they seem usually to relate more directly to the family. The traditional Western prohibition is framed against adultery, not against fornication; Freud wrote of Oedipus complexes; among the Tswana the birth of a child is important to the extended family, not just the parents. Precisely, what cultural rules are necessary to maintain a stable family structure obviously varies from culture to culture; all the societies discussed in this book, however, place some limitations on men's access to women, perhaps serving in part to ensure reasonably confident recognition of paternity. Such a concern could easily lead both to disapproval of promiscuity and to a carefully controlled life for women. (Concern about the identity of the father may be less important in some matrilineal societies not considered in this book.) Two of our societies, the Egyptian and the Tswana, also appear to place a high value on fertility itself. These values—along with others—are reflected in views toward population control technologies. All such technologies may be viewed as discouraging fertility, and perhaps as encouraging promiscuity as well.

But, to a remarkable extent, views toward population control technologies have also been shaped by completely different types of concerns. Both the Islamic and parts of the Western tradition question sterilization because they view it as a form of self-mutilation. Although the Catholic religious concern with contraception rests on an understanding about the purpose of the sexual act, the parallel concern with abortion (shared with Islam) rests more on a judgment that abortion is homicide. Yet, the homicide argument is rejected in some cultures; traditional Chinese culture restricted it to cases of battery that caused abortion, and parts of the Tswana culture may have accepted infanticide. The result is often a contradiction between moral views toward specific population control technologies and attitudes toward fertility. For some in the West, the goal of avoiding fertility appears good, possibly even morally required, while the means appear wrong. In contrast, for some in Islam, contraceptive means are acceptable and available, but the goal is rejected.

In addition, as suggested by the Youssef excerpt in the Egyptian material, attitudes toward fertility are themselves shaped by family structure: is one's vision of a happy life one of being surrounded by few or by numerous children? And this fundamental vision is modified by a host of factors that might be more manipulable. Are expectations placed upon women and men and rewards given to motherhood or fatherhood that, as in Islam or in Botswana, encourage fertility? Are there alternate careers available to women? What is the age of marriage? Is a child perceived as an economic burden as in China or California, or as an economic asset as in the Tswana? Are there child care arrangements, as in the extended family of Islam or the commune of China, that could ease parenthood? Are children important for care in one's old age, as in the extended families of Egypt, or do people look to other arrangments, as in the California nuclear families?

Clearly, these factors help explain why—formal laws and national programs notwithstanding—population control programs have been nearly irrelevant in Botswana and have generally failed in Egypt. Perhaps also the Chinese village, as reorganized by the revolutionary government, combines in some manner the extended family's benefits of care in old age and the nuclear family's economic incentives to favor the relative success of that nation's population control program.

The evolution of population control in California deserves special attention because here population growth began to fall long before there were any formal population control programs, and also long before formal changes in the laws on contraception or abortion. In both Europe and the United States, mortality fell early, so the concern that some children survive to one's old age did not long push toward a large family. In both areas, but starting later in the United States, social security systems became an alternate method of care in old age. In the United States case, although it is hard to be confident of the point, the entry of women into the labor force during World War II may have been especially important in changing the role of women. Undoubtedly, increased intersectional and rural to urban migration, associated with both the depression and the changed job market after the war, also helped break up the extended family and encourage the small nuclear family. There was also an intellectual evolution: the concept of equal protection, which had come to the fore in the 50's and 60's in the struggle against racial discrimination, became applied to sexual discrimination as well. In the midst of all these changes, new contraceptive technologies appeared, facilitating both population control and a change in sexual morality.

Little is known about the mechanisms of such profound social transformations. But it is clear that these social transformations are far more important to population control than are legal changes or planner's theories about the need for global population limitation. In the West, the fall in the birth rate substantially preceded the legal change. And in no society, save perhaps China, has the global population question been the concern of more than a few, typically upper class, individuals.

B. RELATION OF LAW TO THESE UNDERLYING ATTITUDES

NOTE

Historically, the state has rarely been as powerful as it is today and the family, or sometimes a religious institution, rather than the state, has often been both the enforcer of morality and the promulgator of moral principles. In Botswana, the family and the state were closely related, but in the West during the period of ecclesiastical courts, and perhaps in those Islamic societies that made a strict distinction between *qadi* and *mazalim* jurisdiction, it would be absurd even to think of a very strong relationship between the moral system and the state's legal system. Nor in China, where the law of the state—although almost coinciding with the moral law of the society—was considered inferior to moral law, would there be any question of seeking to restate morality in formal law.

More recently, however, as the official state became stronger, there have been pressures for the state to promulgate and possibly to enforce a dominant morality. This is clearest in the West, where the process can be observed in areas such as narcotics and gambling as well as in the sexual area. The legislators perhaps believe that the formal law ought to symbolize the moral aspirations of the society—these laws are often both hard to repeal and deliberately unenforced. For many legislators, there is perhaps also a sense of legitimate public interest, a view, for example, that the strength of the nation depends on the strength of the family, or a view, exemplified in Islam, that the state must help in purifying the community. In this area Islamic society, with its Judeo-Christian origins, is perhaps Western—all three religions have often been regarded as religions based on law. In high Islamic theory, the state gains its legitimacy from enforcing the *sharia*; there is perhaps something congenial to the Western mind about asking the state to promulgate moral codes.

In the West, this process peaked with the Comstock laws (and parallel European Codes) of the 19th century, seeking directly to use the criminal process to enforce a moral code. In addition to the broad motivations just described, there may also have been more parochial interests, such as the fear of the emerging medical community that uncontrolled abortion would undercut its economic position.

In the United States, the new legislation ultimately conflicted with a different tradition—that of religious freedom. The principle of religious freedom had emerged early in the West as one of the central aspects of freedom in a society of religious diversity. Although the principle was poorly honored in much of the 19th century, it gained strength in the 20th century, and, through Supreme Court interpretation, was transmuted into a separation of Church and State—a stronger principle that cast serious doubt on any legislation restating moral principles that are controversial in the society.

From there, the United States evolution was nearly foreordained. There might have been a popular majority favoring legislative relaxation of contraceptive legislation, but was probably none favoring similar relaxation in the abortion area. The pressure groups that took on both issues, however, following in the Western tradition, cast them as rights issues. The Supreme Court followed this lead and chose to avoid the religious freedom argument, even though religious factors explained the divisiveness of the issues. Instead, harking back to the one-time importance of the family as compared with the state, it defined a right of privacy for certain sexual areas in which the state would not be permitted to intrude. The court refused to take the further step of requiring the state to fund abortion and contraceptive services, a step that would have required an entirely different logic resting on either a global population concern or an extended equal protection argument.

Other Western societies faced the issue similarly, also using a "rights" type of approach; the key differences were whether or not a political majority was available for legislative change, and, in the case of Germany, the relevant court's view of the rights of the fetus as compared with those of the pregnant woman.

In the three other societies considered in this book, however, the evolution was radically different. In all three, a Western-style anti-abortion law had been imposed during the period of presumed Western superiority. In none of the societies (save perhaps China), however, was there an internal social transformation of the type that occurred in the West. The pressure for change was instead exogenous, coming from a planning perspective. Hence, the resolution of law and custom took place in a different manner. In Botswana, with relatively little planning pressure but a rather Westernized central legal system, the result has sometimes been a judicial evasion of Western norms, as suggested most clearly by the infanticide case. In Egypt, where the tie between Church and State is most strong, the Islamic distinction between contraception and abortion is maintained and reinforced by Western-style law; the Mosque is itself used to promulgate the planner's position that morality requires contraception. In China, the central government has succeeded in integrating a population control norm into a public morality that, in a Confucian manner, integrates custom and law.

Societies beyond those chosen for this book would show still further variations. Notable are India, where a Western rights concept has been argued against state-directed sterilization, and Iran, where the state has backed an exaggerated traditional morality in a reaction against what it views as a decadent Western morality.

C. THE PLANNER'S CONCERNS

NOTE

The concept of a global need to restrain population growth goes back to Malthus and immigration law changes after World War I, but gained important adherents in the West only in the period following World War II. In large part, the arguments of this movement can be accepted at face value. The spread of modern sanitation and medicine has radically decreased mortality. This leads to rapid population growth as the lifetime of today's population is increased and creates the potential for continued rapid growth as the probability of a child's surviving to reproductive age is also increased. If one projects any exponential growth curve, the results are eventually overwhelming; that eventuality comes rather soon with today's curves.

But something more than the face value may be relevant. It has long been possible to project exponential curves, but Malthus was not popular until recently. Part of the explanation is perhaps the economic success of the West and especially of the United States. For the first time in human history, a large group has been fortunate enough to think in terms of the quality of life. For the first time, also, relatively feasible contraceptive technologies are widely available, and there does seem to be a human desire to use and justify an available technology. There may also be intellectual reasons, such as a view of man that emphasizes the consumer—thinking of what the person requires rather than of what the person contributes.

The planning approach to population control often does emphasize the need for others to reduce their population growth rate. Few developed Western societies have population control plans for themselves. In large part, of course, this is because these societies have already stopped their rapid growth and also because many of them find such centralized planning uncongenial. But, in part, it also suggests a type of selfishness. Some of the early Western movements emphasized a need to reduce the fertility of the poor. The United States movement to control immigration arose at a time when those who sought to retain jobs for longer-term residents were beginning to challenge the political power of those who benefit from low wages. And the current pressure is largely one to get the Third World to reduce its growth rate. Population policy is inherently distribution policy.

During the 1960's, Western agencies, especially the U. S. Agency for International Development and the Ford Foundation, worked hard, and rather successfully, to persuade developing world planning ministries of the need to restrain population growth as part of their economic development program. Undoubtedly, there were cases in which the developing world planners were merely paying lip service to donors or interested in participating in a new bureaucracy. But the acceptance was often much more whole hearted. A rapid population growth makes the investment and educational requirements for economic development much greater. In most developing nations, population growth is accompanied by rural-urban migration, creating miserable housing conditions and possibly a source of political instability. And in a world of underemployment, an additional person may in fact consume more than he or she produces, so the problem of adequate food production becomes enormous. The planner's bias toward viewing people as aggregates of consumers is tragically verified. These factors tend to overcome the occasional counter-pressures such as the ability for Egypt and Botswana to gain foreign exchange remittances from their expatriate migrant workers in the Persian Gulf and South Africa.

The planners, therefore, introduced a population control program, but the program has usually failed. The failure goes back to the distinction between law and custom, and to the inherent limits of "change from above." Acceptance of the logical need for population planning creates only a ministerial constituency. The societies themselves have not evolved to self-limit their populations in the Western manner. Moreover, in a way reminiscent of the West's ability to distinguish between practice and law, legal change may be very difficult. Egypt has not considered modifying its abortion law, even though the law itself was imposed during 19th century Western domination and is clearly widely ignored. The law, of course, reflects Islamic principles. (India, in a similar situation, substantially legalized abortion, but only by building enormous legislative history emphasizing that the change was a health and medical matter, not a population control matter.) A more dramatic example, because more people might support the legal change, is that Egypt is still able to make only minor changes in the laws defining the status of women in marriage.

Thus, the planning ministries find themselves facing a traditional social structure that favors fertility and are unable to change the laws directly affecting that structure. The result, seen in a variety of societies, is that the population control program avoids the use of law. It becomes a combination of propaganda and of a network to dispense contraceptive devices (or, in some societies, abortion or sterilization as well). And all planners hope that economic progress will itself bring a slower growth rate.

It is clear that the law does not generally serve a mediation or communication function between the interested ministries and public practice in these highly moralistic areas as it often does in more technical economic areas. In the United States case, where there has been substantial public debate of the Supreme Court decisions, the political debate is not closed; if the debate has had any effect, it seems more likely to be that of ultimately conforming the law to the public's moral understanding. Practically no society has ever debated a legislative program that would radically reshape tax laws, medical laws, and marriage and family laws toward a goal of population control. Egypt is perhaps coming close with its effort to build new social security structures and encourage the employment of women; the indirectness of this approach does support the point that law has little direct effect on moral principles.

China is the special case. There are several possible explanations for the relative success of its particular combination of persuasion and easy availability of the technologies. One, which may be more important than we tend to think, is that the ministerial decision was a Chinese decision. When the government made its decision, it probably considered Western arguments, but was under no donor pressure corresponding to that of most developing nations. A second important difference is that China radically restructured its family life. Most of the restructuring took place as part of the fundamental economic reform following upon the revolution, but the reform evidently did produce a life style and incentive structure that were amenable to decreased fertility.

What is probably most significant, however, is China's combination of authoritarianism and a Confucian tradition. The Confucian tradition certainly paved the philosophical way for authoritarianism through its emphasis on the group rather than the individual and through its identification of morality with the highest form of law. The government, although very far away from the individual citizen, was able to take advantage of its authoritarianism and of its communications network to directly reshape public values. As China's move toward economic incentives suggests, even this approach, which is anathema in most societies, may face difficulties in shifting down to the one-child family.

Chapter 23

POPULATION CONTROL IN THE WEST

NOTE

Concern about the consequences of uncontrolled population growth is a common topic in the media, fuel for a large number of books and studies, an important item on the policy agenda of governments and international organizations, the rationale for a number of domestic and foreign aid programs, and the basis of a major, growing industry in manufacturing and marketing birth control substances and devices. The basic idea is a simple one: in a world of limited resources each individual's share and, in the case of exhaustible resources, the time remaining until exhaustion, are reduced by population growth. If there is only a given amount (of, say, open space or shoreline) to go around, less is available to each in a larger population. If the resource is exhaustible (e. g. oil) a larger population will exhaust it in a shorter time.

These propositions speak powerfully to people in all parts of the world, but the message varies from one society to another. In a poor nation, with a population living precariously on the edge of bare subsistence, the question is one of immediate urgency, of life and death. To those in a wealthy nation (e.g. Sweden, France, or the U. S.) the choices marginally affect the quality of their own lives and those of their descendants, lives that are (at present) comfortably cushioned against need. The disparity between the first and third worlds and the tensions such disparity causes in international relations can arguably be reduced by effective birth control programs in third world nations, and accordingly wealthy nations encourage and subsidize population control measures in poor nations. These efforts, however, raise complicated concerns about imperialism, exploitation (even, in extreme form, allegations of a kind of genocide). Despite these concerns, population control programs are in effect in much of the world through the efforts of private organizations (e.g. Planned Parenthood), international organizations (e.g. the United Nations) and national (and state) governments.

Contraception and abortion limit birth. Improved public health facilities, diet and medical care prolong life. The population is affected by both kinds of factors; one reduces population, the other increases it. A coldly "rational" planner, single-mindedly seeking to control population growth as quickly and effectively as possible, would attempt both to limit births and to shorten lives (at least, other people's lives). In fact, in all societies, including those most dedicated to population control, measures are consciously taken that increase life expectancy and hence reduce the effectiveness of birth control programs. Thus, even though the birth rate substantially declines (as, for example, in the U. S. A. since 1955) the population continues to grow. The inadmissibility of life control policies means that planned world population control is obtainable only through birth control and that offsetting life-extending and life-enriching programs limit its effect.

A. BACKGROUND

Note, Legal Analysis and Population Control: The Problem of Coercion, 84 Harvard Law Review 1856, pp. 1865–69, 1971.

It has become almost axiomatic that population growth in the United States will someday have to stop. At the current growth rate of just less than one percent per year, the population will double in seventy years, reaching approximately four-hundred million by about 2040. If this rate continued, the population would approach one billion by the end of the twenty-first century and mushroom thereafter.

Such doomsday projections are, of course, neither the sole nor the most persuasive argument for limiting population growth. More important justifications for a restrictive American population policy fall into three categories. First, the population growth of the United States is seen as part of the world population explosion. Although the contribution of the developing regions to total world population growth significantly exceeds that of the developed regions, because of vastly greater rates of production and consumption the United States and other developed nations can be viewed as at least equally culpable contributors to problems associated with the population explosion.

Second, along with per capita growth in disposable income and consumption, and insufficient regulation of waste disposal, population growth is seen as a major factor in the accelerating degradation of the American physical environment. However, the role that population growth alone plays in this process is a subject of some controversy, as are the relative priorities that should be assigned to finding and implementing solutions to the various causes of environmental problems.

Third, population growth is seen as an underlying cause of serious problems of the American social environment and as a stumbling block to their solution. A growing population is said to cause a serious strain on "social supplies—the capacity to educate youth, to provide privacy and living space, to maintain the processes of open, democratic government. . . ."

Such arguments have helped develop a consensus that the initial goal of American population policy should be to reduce the average number of children born to couples to a figure just large enough to insure that the population ultimately replaces itself each generation. Estimates of this "replacement fertility" vary from 2.1 to 2.5 children per couple.

However, immediate achievement of an average family size equaling replacement fertility would not mean immediate "zero population growth." If the average family size in the United States reached 2.1 in 1975, population would not stop growing until 2040. Meanwhile the population would have grown another thirty-five to forty percent, reaching a final figure of some 290 million. The time lag between attaining a replacement fertility level and reaching a zero growth rate results from the age distribution of the current population, which contains a greater proportion of women in reproductive ages and below than would be present in the eventual stationary population. Stated another way, because of the current age distribution, a built-in growth factor exists, which will gradually disappear as fewer children are born per couple and the average age of the population increases.

The goal of replacement fertility—an average of two-plus children per woman—is not merely an expedient compromise between accepting growth at the current rate and seeking zero growth immediately. Reaching zero growth immediately would require an average of just over one child per couple. And that average family size would, within a generation result in a badly skewed age distribution, marked by a serious shortage of young people, relative to current expectations. Labor markets would be badly jolted. Some public facilities, such as schools, universities, and athletic areas, would face such underutilization as to make their maintenance a serious economic liability. The traditional availability of mature sons and daughters to help their parents meet the trials of old age would be reduced. Government revenue expectations would have to be radically revised, as would, in turn, the entire pattern of government expenditures, thus affecting ingrained and socially justifiable reliance interests throughout the society.

Both the built-in "age distribution" momentum towards growth, and the enormous social problems that would result from trying to overcome that momentum while moving to attain immediate zero growth, can be seen as defining the boundaries within which the debate about population policy should take place.

NOTE

Here are some data from the U. S. Bureau of the Census, Statistical Abstract of the United States: Washington, D.C., U. S. Government Printing Office, 1980, 101st edition, pp. 58, 61.

FIGURE 2.1 VITAL STATISTICS

Birth and Death Rates: 1960 to 1979

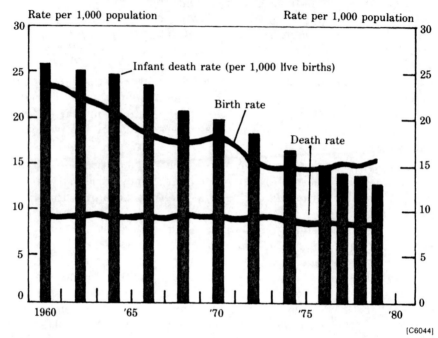

Rate per 1,000 population   Rate per 1,000 population

Infant death rate (per 1,000 live births)

Birth rate

Death rate

[C6044]

VITAL STATISTICS—FERTILITY RATE

No. 85. Live Births, Deaths, Marriages, and Divorces: 1910 to 1979

[Prior to 1960, excludes Alaska and Hawaii. Figures for deaths and death rates for 1910–1930 are for death-registration States only. Beginning 1970, excludes births to, and deaths of, nonresidents of the U.S. See Appendix III. See also Historical Statistics, Colonial Times to 1970, series B 1–5, B 142, B 167, B 214, and B 216]

YEAR	NUMBER (1,000)					RATE PER 1,000 POPULATION				
	Births[1]	Deaths		Mar-riages[3]	Di-vorces[4]	Births[1]	Deaths		Mar-riages[3]	Di-vorces[4]
		Total	In-fant[2]				Total	In-fant[2]		
1910	2,777	697	(NA)	948	83	30.1	14.7	(NA)	10.3	.9
1915	2,965	816	78	1,008	104	29.5	13.2	99.9	10.0	1.0
1920	2,950	1,118	130	1,274	171	27.7	13.0	85.8	12.0	1.6
1925	2,909	1,192	135	1,188	175	25.1	11.7	71.7	10.3	1.5
1930	2,618	1,327	142	1,127	196	21.3	11.3	64.6	9.2	1.6
1935	2,377	1,393	120	1,327	218	18.7	10.9	55.7	10.4	1.7
1940	2,559	1,417	111	1,596	264	19.4	10.8	47.0	12.1	2.0
1945	2,858	1,402	105	1,613	485	20.4	10.6	38.3	12.2	3.5
1950	3,632	1,452	104	1,667	385	24.1	9.6	29.2	11.1	2.6
1955	4,097	1,529	107	1,531	377	25.0	9.3	26.4	9.3	2.3
1960	4,258	1,712	111	1,523	393	23.7	9.5	26.0	8.5	2.2
1962	4,167	1,757	105	1,577	413	22.4	9.5	25.3	8.5	2.2
1963	4,098	1,814	103	1,654	428	21.7	9.6	25.2	8.8	2.3
1964	4,027	1,798	100	1,725	450	21.0	9.4	24.8	9.0	2.4
1965	3,760	1,828	93	1,800	479	19.4	9.4	24.7	9.3	2.5

YEAR	NUMBER (1,000)					RATE PER 1,000 POPULATION				
	Births[1]	Deaths		Mar-riages[3]	Di-vorces[4]	Births[1]	Deaths		Mar-riages[3]	Di-vorces[4]
		Total	In-fant[2]				Total	In-fant[2]		
1966	3,606	1,863	86	1,857	499	18.4	9.5	23.7	9.5	2.5
1967	3,521	1,851	79	1,927	523	17.8	9.4	22.4	9.7	2.6
1968	3,502	1,930	76	2,069	584	17.5	9.7	21.8	10.4	2.9
1969	3,600	1,922	75	2,145	639	17.8	9.5	20.7	10.6	3.2
1970	3,731	1,921	75	2,159	708	18.4	9.5	20.0	10.6	3.5
1971	3,556	1,928	68	2,190	773	17.2	9.3	19.1	10.6	3.7
1972	3,258	1,964	60	2,282	845	15.6	9.4	18.5	11.0	4.1
1973	3,137	1,973	56	2,284	915	14.9	9.4	17.7	10.9	4.4
1974	3,160	1,934	53	2,230	977	14.9	9.2	16.7	10.5	4.6
1975	3,144	1,893	51	2,153	1,036	14.8	8.8	16.1	10.1	4.9
1976	3,168	1,909	48	2,155	1,083	14.8	8.9	15.2	10.0	5.0
1977	3,327	1,900	47	2,178	1,091	15.4	8.8	14.1	10.1	5.0
1978	3,333	1,928	46	[5]2,282	1,130	15.3	8.8	13.8	[5]10.5	5.2
1979, prel......	3,473	1,906	45	[5]2,359	1,170	15.8	8.7	13.0	[5]10.7	5.3

NA Not available. [1]Through 1955, adjusted for underregistration. [2]Infants under 1 year, excluding fetal deaths; rates per 1,000 registered live births. [3]Includes estimates for some States through 1969 and also for 1976, and marriage licenses for some States for all years except 1973 and 1975. [4]Includes reported annulments and some estimated State figures for all years. [5]Includes 37,462 nonlicensed marriages registered in California for 1978 and 41,961 for 1979.

[C6089]

Roy D. Weinberg, Family Planning and the Law, Dobbs Ferry, New York: Oceana Publications, 1979, pp. 29–34.

Federal Law. Federal legislation respecting both contraception and abortion is embodied in the famous Comstock Act adopted in 1873. Literally, it prohibits the importation, mailing, and interstate transportation of birth control articles and literature. Many attempts at its modification have failed, but it has been largely nullified over the years by a series of federal decisions. Before examining these cases, it will be well to consider the actual provisions of the law. These, insofar as pertinent to our inquiry, appear in 18 U.S.C.A. 1461–1462 and 19 U.S.C.A. 1305. The first of these sections, 18 U.S.C.A. 1461, provides as follows:

"Every obscene, lewd, lascivious, indecent, filthy or vile article, matter, thing, device or substance; and

"Every article or thing designed, adapted, or intended for preventing conception or producing abortion, or for any indecent or immoral use; and

"Every article, instrument, substance, drug, medicine, or thing which is advertised or described in a manner calculated to lead another to use or apply it for preventing conception or producing abortion, or for any indecent or immoral purpose; and

"Every written or printed card, letter, circular, book, pamphlet, advertisement, or notice of any kind giving information directly or indirectly, where or how, or from whom, or by what means any of such mentioned matters, articles, or things may be obtained or made, or where or by whom any act or operation of any kind for the procuring or producing of abortion will be done or performed, or how or by what means conception may be prevented or abortion produced, whether sealed or unsealed; and

"Every description calculated to induce or incite a person to use or apply any such article, instrument, substance, drug, medicine or thing—

"Is declared to be nonmailable matter and shall not be conveyed in the mails or delivered from any post office or by any letter carrier.

"Whoever knowingly uses the mails for the mailing, carriage in the mails, or delivery of anything declared by this section to be nonmailable, or knowingly causes to be delivered by mail according to the direction thereon, or at the place at which it is directed to be delivered by the person to whom it is addressed, or knowingly takes any such thing from the mails for the purpose of circulating or disposing thereof, shall be fined not more than $5,000 or imprisoned not more than five years, or both, for the first such offense, and shall be fined not more than $10,000 or imprisoned not more than ten years, or both, for each such offense thereafter. . . ."

The importation and transport in interstate or foreign commerce of obscene matters, including contraceptives, is prohibited in 18 U.S.C.A. 1462 as follows:

"Whoever brings into the United States, or any place subject to the jurisdiction thereof, or knowingly uses any express company or other common carrier, for carriage in interstate or foreign commerce—

* * *

"(c) any drug, medicine, article, or thing designed, adapted, or intended for preventing conception, or producing abortion, or for any indecent or immoral use; or any written or printed card, letter, circular, book, pamphlet, advertisement, or notice of any kind giving information, directly or indirectly, where, how, of whom, or by what means any of such mentioned articles, matters, or things may be obtained or made; or

"Whoever knowingly takes from such express company or other common carrier any matter or thing the carriage of which is herein made unlawful—

"Shall be fined not more than $5,000 or imprisoned not more than five years, or both, for the first such offense and shall be fined not more than $10,000 or imprisoned not more than ten years, or both, for each such offense thereafter."

Prohibition of the importation of "immoral articles," including contraceptives, reappears in 19 U.S.C.A. 1305, together with the procedure prescribed for its enforcement. The text of this section, insofar as material to our study, is as follows:

"All persons are prohibited from importing into the United States from any foreign country . . .   any drug or medicine or any article whatever for the prevention of conception or for causing unlawful abortion . . ..

"Provided, That the drugs hereinbefore mentioned, when imported in bulk and not put up for any of the purposes hereinbefore specified, are excepted from the operation of this subdivision . . ..

"Upon the appearance of any such . . .   matter at any customs office, the same shall be seized and held by the collector to await the judgment of the district court as hereinafter provided; and no protest shall be taken to the United States Customs Court from the decision of the collector. Upon the seizure of such . . .   matter the collector shall transmit information thereof to the district attorney of the district in which is situated the office at which such seizure has taken place, who shall institute proceedings in the district court for the forfeiture, confiscation, and destruction of the . . .   matter seized. Upon adjudication that such . . .   matter thus seized is of the character the entry of which is by this section prohibited, it shall be ordered destroyed and shall be destroyed. Upon adjudication that such . . .   matter thus seized is not of the character the entry of which is by this section prohibited, it shall not be excluded from entry under the provisions of this section.

"In any such proceeding any party in interest may upon demand have the facts at issue determined by a jury and any party may have an appeal of the right to review as in the case of ordinary actions or suits."

Judicial Construction of the Comstock Act. The literal terms and apparent restrictive effect of the Comstock Act have, for most practical purposes, been abrogated by judicial construction in a series of landmark cases. In 1915, the medical profession was held to be exempt from the unqualified anti-abortion provisions of the Act in the case of Bours v. United States, 229 F. 960 (7th Cir.). In 1930, it was held in the case of Youngs Rubber Corp. v. C.I. Lee & Co., 45 F.2d 103 (2nd Cir.) that violation of the Comstock Act did not preclude an action under the Trademark Act, which barred actions only when trademarks were used in an unlawful business. In making this determination, the court declared:

"Taken literally, this language would seem to forbid the transportation by mail or common carrier of anything 'adapted' in the sense of being suitable or fitted, for preventing conception . . .   even though the article might also be capable of legitimate uses and the sender in good faith supposed that it should be used only legitimately. Such a construction would prevent mailing to or by a physician of any drug or mechanical device adapted for contraceptive or abortifacient uses, although the physician desired to use or prescribe it for proven medical purposes. The intention to prevent a proper medical use of drugs or other articles merely because they are capable of illegal uses is not lightly to be ascribed to Congress." Observing that the Act also forbade the mailing of obscene literature, the court noted that it had never been thought to bar from the mails medical writings sent to or by physicians for legitimate purposes.

The existence of an unlawful intent as a prerequisite to conviction under the Act was proclaimed in the case of Davis v. United States, 62 F.2d 473 (6th Cir. (1933)). In this action, in which the defendant was a wholesale druggist, the court said:

"If we are right in our view that . . . intent that the articles . . . shipped in interstate commerce were to be used for condemned purposes is a prerequisite to conviction, it follows that there was error in refusing to admit evidence offered by the appellants tending to show good faith and absence of unlawful intent."

Whatever the impact of these earlier decisions, the case which, in effect, dealt a death blow to the Comstock Act was that of United States v. One Package, 86 F.2d 737 (2nd Cir. (1936)). This landmark decision declared that the contraceptive provisions of the Tariff Act of 1930—similar to those of the Comstock Act—did not apply to physicians. The court concluded that the Comstock Act was not intended "to prevent the importation, sale or carriage by mail of things which might intelligently be employed by conscientious and competent physicians for the purpose of saving life or promoting the well-being of their patients."

Several subsequent holdings have fortified and extended this viewpoint. In United States v. Nicholas, 97 F.2d 510 (2nd Cir. (1938)), the mailing of matter describing contraceptives was held to be legal, but the addressee had the burden of proceeding with proof that he was entitled to receive it. Contraceptive books and pamphlets, said the court, are "lawful in the hands of those who would not abuse the information they contained. This excuses the magazines addressed as they were to their local editor; being lawful in the hands of physicians, scientists and the like, the claimant at bar was their most appropriate distributor."

In Consumer's Union v. Walker, 145 F.2d 33 (D.C.Cir. (1944)), the mailing of a report evaluating certain contraceptive material to members of the Consumer's Union, who had submitted statements that they were married and used prophylactic materials on the advice of physicians, was declared legal on the ground that the information therein "vitally concerned the lives and health of those to whom it was directed" and that "Congress did not intend to exclude from the mails properly prepared information intended for properly qualified people."

In 1960, a federal court held that an attempt to mail vending machines and prophylactics was not violative of the Comstock Act (United States v. H.L. Blake Co., 189 F.Supp. 930 (D.C.Ark.)). The court said that notations on the prophylactic packages specifying that they were sold only for prevention of disease indicated that there was no intent to supply them for the prevention of conception. The burden was on the government, as a prerequisite to conviction, to prove that the articles were mailed with a "specific intent" of being used for contraceptive purposes.

These cases make it clear that federal laws pertaining to contraceptive materials and information do not restrict their dissemination for lawful purposes related to the preservation of health and life. The sole surviving requirement of federal law would appear to be that such matter be made available only to married couples. The mere advocacy of contraception, of course, is protected by the Constitutional guarantee of free speech and press and should in no case be confused with the issue of dissemination of materials and information.

State Law. The enactment of the Comstock Act was followed by a series of so-called "obscenity" statutes on the state level. Legislation of this character was enacted in every state except New Mexico. Many of these laws mentioned contraceptives expressly but all were susceptible to a construction prohibiting their dissemination. Prior to the One Package decision, state as well as federal policy respecting contraception remained inflexible. Subsequent developments, however, have altered the situation radically on the state level as well.

NOTE

For a good discussion of the origins and the power of laws repressing birth control in the United States see David M. Kennedy, Birth Control in America: The Career of Margaret Sanger, New Haven: Yale University Press, 1970, particularly Chapter 8.

B. CONTRACEPTION AND THE CONSTITUTION

Griswold v. Connecticut, 381 U.S. 479, 480–486, 502–507, 527–531, 85 S.Ct. 1678, 1679–1682, 1691–1694, 1705–1707, 14 L.Ed.2d 510 (1965).

Mr. Justice DOUGLAS delivered the opinion of the Court.

Appellant Griswold is Executive Director of the Planned Parenthood League of Connecticut. Appellant Buxton is a licensed physician and a professor at the Yale Medical School who served as Medical Director for the League at its Center in New Haven—a center open and operating from November 1 to November 10, 1961, when appellants were arrested.

They gave information, instruction, and medical advice to *married persons* as to the means of preventing conception. They examined the wife and prescribed the best contraceptive device or material for her use. Fees were usually charged, although some couples were serviced free.

The statutes whose constitutionality is involved in this appeal are §§ 53–32 and 54–196 of the General Statutes of Connecticut (1958 rev.). The former provides:

> Any person who uses any drug, medicinal article or instrument for the purpose of preventing conception shall be fined not less than fifty dollars or imprisoned not less than sixty days nor more than one year or be both fined and imprisoned.

Section 54–196 provides:

> Any person who assists, abets, counsels, causes, hires or commands another to commit any offense may be prosecuted and punished as if he were the principal offender.

The appellants were found guilty as accessories and fined $100 each, against the claim that the accessory statute as so applied violated the Fourteenth Amendment. The Appellate Division of the Circuit Court affirmed. The Supreme Court of Errors affirmed that judgment.

Coming to the merits, we are met with a wide range of questions that implicate the Due Process Clause of the Fourteenth Amendment. Overtones of some arguments suggest that Lochner v. State of New York, 198 U.S. 45, 25 S.Ct. 539, 49 L.Ed. 937, should be our guide. But we decline that invitation. We do not sit as a super-legislature to determine the wisdom, need, and propriety of laws that touch economic problems, business affairs, or social conditions. This law, however, operates directly on an intimate relation of husband and wife and their physician's role in one aspect of that relation.

The association of people is not mentioned in the Constitution nor in the Bill of Rights. The right to educate a child in a school of the parents' choice—whether public or private or parochial—is also not mentioned. Nor is the right to study any particular subject or any foreign language. Yet the First Amendment has been construed to include certain of those rights.

By Pierce v. Society of Sisters, supra, the right to educate one's children as one chooses is made applicable to the States by the force of the First and Fourteenth Amendments. By Meyer v. State of Nebraska, supra, the same dignity is given the right to study the German language in a private school. In other words, the State may not, consistently with the spirit of the First Amendment, contract the spectrum of available knowledge. The right of freedom of speech and press includes not only the right to utter or to print, but the right to distribute, the right to receive, the right to read and freedom of inquiry, freedom of thought, and freedom to teach—indeed the freedom of the entire university community.

Without those peripheral rights the specific rights would be less secure. And so we reaffirm the principle of the Pierce and the Meyer cases.

In NAACP v. State of Alabama, 357 U.S. 449, 462, . . . we protected the "freedom to associate and privacy in one's associations," noting that freedom of association was a peripheral First Amendment right. Disclosure of membership lists of a constitutionally valid association, we held, was invalid "as entailing the likelihood of a substantial restraint upon the exercise by petitioner's members of their right to freedom of association." Ibid. In other words, the First Amendment has a penumbra where privacy is protected from governmental intrusion. In like context, we have protected forms of "association" that are not political in the customary sense but pertain to the social, legal, and economic benefit of the members. In Schware v. Board of Bar Examiners, 353 U.S. 232, we held it not permissible to bar a lawyer from practice, because he had once been a member of the Communist Party. The man's "association with that Party" was not shown to be "anything more than a political faith in a political party" and was not action of a kind proving bad moral character.

Those cases involved more than the "right of assembly"—a right that extends to all irrespective of their race or idealogy. The right of "association" is more than the right to attend a meeting; it includes the right to express one's attitudes or philosophies by membership in a group or by affiliation with it or by other lawful means. Association in that context is a form of expression of opinion; and while it is not expressly included in the First Amendment its existence is necessary in making the express guarantees fully meaningful.

The foregoing cases suggest that specific guarantees in the Bill of Rights have penumbras, formed by emanations from those guarantees that help give them life and substance. Various guarantees create zones of privacy. The right of association contained in the penumbra of the First Amendment is one, as we have seen. The Third Amendment in its prohibition against the quartering of soldiers "in any house" in time of peace without the consent of the owner is another facet of that privacy. The Fourth Amendment explicitly affirms the "right of the people to be secure in their persons, houses, papers, and effects, against unreasonable searches and seizures." The Fifth Amendment in its Self-Incrimination Clause enables the citizen to create a zone of privacy which government may not force him to surrender to his detriment. The Ninth Amendment provides: "The enumeration in the Constitution, of certain rights, shall not be construed to deny or disparage others retained by the people."

The Fourth and Fifth Amendments were described in Boyd v. United States, 116 U.S. 616, 630, as protected against all governmental invasions "of the sanctity of a man's home and the privacies of life." We recently referred in Mapp v. Ohio, 367 U.S. 643, 656, to the

Fourth Amendment as creating a "right to privacy, no less important than any other right carefully and particularly reserved to the people."

We have had many controversies over these penumbral rights of "privacy and repose."

These cases bear witness that the right of privacy which presses for recognition here is a legitimate one.

The present case, then, concerns a relationship lying within the zone of privacy created by several fundamental constitutional guarantees. And it concerns a law which, in forbidding the *use* of contraceptives rather than regulating their manufacture or sale, seeks to achieve its goals by means having a maximum destructive impact upon that relationship. Such a law cannot stand in light of the familiar principle, so often applied by this Court, that a "governmental purpose to control or prevent activities constitutionally subject to state regulation may not be achieved by means which sweep unnecessarily broadly and thereby invade the area of protected freedoms." Would we allow the police to search the sacred precincts of marital bedrooms for telltale signs of the use of contraceptives? The very idea is repulsive to the notions of privacy surrounding the marriage relationship.

We deal with the right of privacy older than the Bill of Rights—older than our political parties, older than our school system. Marriage is a coming together for better or for worse, hopefully enduring, and intimate to the degree of being sacred. It is an association that promotes a way of life, not causes; a harmony in living, not political faiths; a bilateral loyalty, not commercial or social projects. Yet it is an association for as noble a purpose as any involved in our prior decisions.

Reversed.

Mr. Justice STEWART, whom Mr. Justice BLACK joins, dissenting.

Since 1879 Connecticut has had on its books a law which forbids the use of contraceptives by anyone. I think this is an uncommonly silly law. As a practical matter, the law is obviously unenforceable, except in the oblique context of the present case. As a philosophical matter, I believe the use of contraceptives in the relationship of marriage should be left to personal and private choice, based upon each individual's moral, ethical, and religious beliefs. As a matter of social policy, I think professional counsel about methods of birth control should be available to all, so that each individual's choice can be meaningfully made. But we are not asked in this case to say whether we think this law is unwise, or even asinine. We are asked to hold that it violates the United States Constitution. And that I cannot do.

In the course of its opinion the Court refers to no less than six Amendments to the Constitution: the First, the Third, the Fourth, the Fifth, the Ninth, and the Fourteenth.

But the Court does not say which of these Amendments, if any, it thinks is infringed by this Connecticut law.

We *are* told that the Due Process Clause of the Fourteenth Amendment is not, as such, the "guide" in this case. With that much I agree. There is no claim that this law, duly enacted by the Connecticut Legislature, is unconstitutionally vague. There is no claim that the appellants were denied any of the elements of procedural due process at their trial, so as to make their convictions constitutionally invalid. And, as the Court says, the day has long passed since the Due Process Clause was regarded as a proper instrument for determining "the wisdom, need, and propriety" of state laws.

As to the First, Third, Fourth, and Fifth Amendments, I can find nothing in any of them to invalidate this Connecticut law, even assuming that all those Amendments are fully applicable against the States. It has not even been argued that this is a law "respecting an establishment of religion, or prohibiting the free exercise thereof." And surely, unless the solemn process of constitutional adjudication is to descend to the level of a play on words, there is not involved here any abridgment of "the freedom of speech, or of the press; or the right of the people peaceably to assemble, and to petition the Government for a redress of grievances." No soldier has been quartered in any house. There has been no search, and no seizure. Nobody has been compelled to be a witness against himself.

The Court also quotes the Ninth Amendment, and my Brother GOLDBERG's concurring opinion relies heavily upon it. But to say that the Ninth Amendment has anything to do with this case is to turn somersaults with history. The Ninth Amendment, like its companion the Tenth, which this Court held "states but a truism that all is retained which has not been surrendered," was framed by James Madison and adopted by the States simply to make clear that the adoption of the Bill of Rights did not alter the plan that the *Federal* Government was to be a government of express and limited powers, and that all rights and powers not delegated to it were retained by the people and the individual States. Until today no member of this Court has ever suggested that the Ninth Amendment meant anything else, and the idea that a federal court could ever use the Ninth Amendment to annul a law passed by the elected representatives of the people of the State of Connecticut would have caused James Madison no little wonder.

What provision of the Constitution, then, does make this state law invalid? The Court says it is the right of privacy "created by several fundamental constitutional guarantees." With all deference, I can find no such general right of privacy in the Bill of Rights, in any other part of the Constitution, or in any case ever before decided by this Court.

At the oral argument in this case we were told that the Connecticut law does not "conform to current community standards." But it is not the function of this Court to decide cases on the basis of community standards. We are here to decide cases "agreeably to the Constitution and laws of the United States." It is the essence of judicial duty to subordinate our own personal views, our own ideas of what legislation is wise and what is not. If, as I should surely hope, the law before us does not reflect the standards of the people of Connecticut, the people of Connecticut can freely exercise their true Ninth and Tenth Amendment rights to persuade their elected representatives to repeal it. That is the constitutional way to take this law off the books.

(The concurring opinions of Mr. Justice GOLDBERG, Mr. Justice HARLAN and Mr. Justice WHITE and the dissenting opinion of Mr. Justice BLACK are omitted. The decision was 5 to 4).

NOTES AND QUESTIONS

1. U. S. Bureau of the Census, Statistical Abstract of the United States, Washington, D.C.: U. S. Government Printing Office, 1980, 101st edition, p. 68.

No. 100. Contraceptive Use by Currently Married Women 15–44 Years Old, by Age, Race, and Method of Contraception: 1965 to 1976

[Data from 1965 and 1970 National Fertility Survey and 1973 and 1976 National Survey of Family Growth; see headnote, table 99]

RACE AND METHOD OF CONTRACEPTION	Total, 15–44 years old				15–24 yr. old		25–34 yr. old		35–44 yr. old	
	1965	1970	1973	1976	1970	1976	1970	1976	1970	1976
WHITE WOMEN										
Currently married (1,000)	22,382	23,220	24,249	24,795	5,595	5,412	9,578	10,993	8,047	8,390
Percent using contraception	64.9	65.7	70.5	[1]68.7	63.8	[1]69.8	69.0	[1]71.7	63.5	[1]64.4
Wife sterilized	4.1	4.9	8.2	[1]9.6	.4	[1]2.4	4.9	[1]10.7	8.2	[1]12.6
Husband sterilized	3.5	5.5	8.4	[1]9.7	.8	[1]1.1	5.4	[1]9.3	8.9	[1]15.9
Pill	15.6	22.4	25.1	22.6	37.6	43.9	23.7	23.4	10.2	7.9
Intra-uterine device	.7	4.8	6.6	6.3	5.3	6.3	6.6	7.5	2.3	4.8
Diaphragm	6.8	3.8	2.5	3.0	1.7	2.8	3.9	3.2	5.2	3.0
Condom	14.5	9.7	9.9	7.5	5.9	5.3	9.7	7.6	12.4	8.7
Foam	2.0	4.0	3.5	2.9	4.8	2.9	4.9	3.0	2.4	2.8
Rhythm	7.5	4.4	2.9	3.5	2.3	2.6	4.1	3.4	6.3	4.3
All other	10.2	6.2	3.4	3.6	5.0	2.5	5.8	3.6	7.6	4.4
BLACK WOMEN										
Currently married (1,000)	2,091	2,031	2,081	2,169	506	509	787	912	738	749
Percent using contraception	57.2	59.2	60.0	[1]58.5	60.5	[1]58.8	67.3	[1]62.7	49.4	[1]53.4
Wife sterilized	8.3	11.4	13.6	[1]10.9	1.0	[1]3.7	11.2	[1]9.2	18.7	[1]17.9
Husband sterilized	.3	.6	1.0	[1]1 7	–	[1].3	.7	[1].4	1.1	[1]4.3
Pill	12.4	22.1	26.3	22.2	35.9	35.8	26.4	26.6	8.1	7.7
Intra-uterine device	1.7	4.5	7.6	6.2	6.2	6.0	5.6	7.2	2.1	5.1
Diaphragm	2.9	3.1	1.2	1.8	1.5	.2	3.6	1.7	3.5	2.9
Condom	9.7	4.0	3.2	4.6	4.1	3.3	3.6	5.6	4.2	4.3
Foam	3.5	3.6	3.0	3.8	4.1	2.0	4.3	4.3	2.5	4.5
Rhythm	1.4	1.0	.8	1.4	.5	3.4	1.3	.4	1.1	1.4
All other	17.0	8.8	5.2	5.9	7.2	4.1	10.6	7.3	8.1	5.3

— Represents zero. [1] Due to changes in wording of the question on contraceptive intent of sterilization operations in the 1976 survey, estimates should be considered conservative.

Source: 1965–1970, Westoff, C. F. "Trends in Contraceptive Practice: 1965–1973." In Alan Guttmacher Institute, Family Planning Perspectives, vol. 8, No. 2, 1976; 1973 and 1976. U.S. National Center for Health Statistics, unpublished data.

2. Applying the reasoning in Griswold, how would you expect the U. S. Supreme Court to decide in a case challenging the constitutionality of a state statute that prohibited furnishing contraceptives to unmarried adults? In Eisenstadt v. Baird, 405 U.S. 438 (1972) such a provision was held unconstitutional.

3. How about a state statute making it a crime to sell or distribute contraceptives to minors under 16 years of age? In Carey v. Population Services International, 431 U.S. 678 (1977) this provision was held unconstitutional, relying on Griswold and Eisenstadt, among other authorities. In the same case additional provisions of the statute (1) prohibiting the distribution of contraceptives by anyone other than a licensed pharmacist and (2) forbidding anyone (including licenced pharmacists) to advertise or display contraceptives were held unconstitutional.

4. Why would statutes like the ones attacked in Griswold, Eisenstadt and Carey be enacted? Of the various reasons you can think of, which would seem to you to be constitutionally permissible, on the basis of the Griswold reasoning?

5. Except for a brief mention in Mr. Justice White's opinion, there is no reference to population control in Griswold (or, for that matter, in Eisenstadt or Carey). What then are these cases all about? Is population control irrelevant or is discussion of it artificially excluded by the structure of the judicial—constitutional process?

6. Although much of the population-control-through-contraception activity in the U. S. is the work of non-governmental organizations, governmental involvement is not insignificant. The federal "Family Planning Services and Population Research Act of 1970" appropriates money to be distributed by grants to the states and by contracts "to assist in the establishment and operation of voluntary family planning projects." 42 U.S. Code §§ 300 ff. In California an "office of Family Planning" has been established in the State Department of Health Services. Its principal function is to "make available to citizens . . . of childbearing age comprehensive medical knowledge, assistance and services relating to the planning of families." California Welfare and Institutions Code §§ 14500 ff. Adult and juvenile woman inmates of state correctional and detention facilities have the right to continue to use birth control measures while institutionalized, shall be furnished with information and education about the availability of family planning services, and shall be offered such services, including access to a licensed physician, at least 60 days prior to scheduled release. California Penal Code §§ 349, 4023.5; California Welfare and Institutions Code §§ 221, 1753.7. In each county the County Health Officer shall prepare "a list of family planning and birth control clinics" in the county. Copies of the list shall be furnished to all hospitals in the county and, on request, to all physicians and surgeons in sufficient numbers for voluntary distribution to patients. The list shall also be distributed by the County Clerk to all applicants for a marriage license. California Health and Safety Code §§ 463, 464; Government Code § 26808. Voluntary non-emergency sterilization is available under the Medi-Cal program (a state supported medical services system), subject to the condition of "informed consent" by the patient.

California Welfare and Institutions Code § 14191. The imposition of "special nonmedical qualifications" on someone seeking sterilization is prohibited. California Health and Safety Code §§ 1232, 1258, 1459, 32128.10.

C. ABORTION

Roy D. Weinberg, Family Planning and the Law, Dobbs Ferry, New York: Oceana Publications, 1979, pp. 1–2.

In legal terminology, "abortion" denotes an intentional interruption of pregnancy by removal of the embryo from the womb. Properly performed by a competent obstetrician in an accredited hospital where satisfactory pre-operative and post-operative procedures are observed, it is a comparatively safe operation. However, as a result of the severe legal restriction obtaining in all American jurisdictions, most women are driven to what are at least technically illegal abortions. Although the covert character of such surgical procedures renders reliable statistical estimates difficult, there seems little doubt that criminal abortions in this country approach a figure of close to 1,000,000 annually. It has been estimated that they exceed legal abortions by a ratio of 100 to 1 and that two-thirds of those aborted are married. Technically, of course, most "legal" abortions are actually illicit in the light of the strict terms of most statutes, which authorize abortion only when necessary to preserve the life of the mother. Modern medical advances have virtually eliminated the absolute necessity of abortion to save life in the cases of most maladies formerly recognized as imperative indications for invocation of this procedure.

Ordinarily, authorized abortions are performed during the first trimester of pregnancy when it is a safe and comparatively inexpensive procedure. Such surgery is known as dilation and curettage. The operation takes about 20 minutes and ordinarily entails hospitalization of one day. Later abortions usually involve hysterotomy, but newer procedures using concentrated oxytocin or intra-amniotic injection into the uterus of hypertonic solutions have also been employed in recent years. The latter procedures are unquestionably more hazardous than dilation and curettage (commonly known as D & C). Even a D & C of course, is not infallible and occasional complications, including death, are inevitable. Nevertheless, the overwhelming preponderance of illegal abortions, including attempts at self-abortion and the resort to quacks, is beyond doubt the source of most fatalities. Even wealthy women, who can command the services of skilled criminal abortionists, are exposed to greater hazards than those encountered in authorized hospital abortions because of the impossibility of ensuring adequate pre-operative and post-operative precautions under such circumstances.

Roe v. Wade, 410 U.S. 113, 93 S.Ct. 705, 35 L.Ed.2d 147 (1973).

Mr. Justice BLACKMUN delivered the opinion of the Court.

The Texas statutes that concern us here are Arts. 1191–1194 and 1196 of the State's Penal Code. These make it a crime to "procure an abortion," as therein defined, or to attempt one, except with respect to "an abortion procured or attempted by medical advice for the purpose of saving the life of the mother." Similar statutes are in existence in a majority of the States.

Jane Roe, a single woman who was residing in Dallas County, Texas, instituted this federal action in March 1970 against the District Attorney of the county. She sought a declaratory judgment that the Texas criminal abortion statutes were unconstitutional on their face, and an injunction restraining the defendant from enforcing the statutes.

Roe alleged that she was unmarried and pregnant; that she wished to terminate her pregnancy by an abortion "performed by a competent, licensed physician, under safe, clinical conditions"; that she was unable to get a "legal" abortion in Texas because her life did not appear to be threatened by the continuation of her pregnancy; and that she could not afford to travel to another jurisdiction in order to secure a legal abortion under safe conditions. She claimed that the Texas statutes were unconstitutionally vague and that they abridged her right of personal privacy, protected by the First, Fourth, Fifth, Ninth, and Fourteenth Amendments. By an amendment to her complaint Roe purported to sue "on behalf of herself and all other women" similarly situated.

The principal thrust of appellant's attack on the Texas statutes is that they improperly invade a right, said to be possessed by the pregnant woman, to choose to terminate her pregnancy. Appellant would discover this right in the concept of personal "liberty" embodied in the Fourteenth Amendment's Due Process Clause; or in personal, marital, familial, and sexual privacy said to be protected by the Bill of Rights or its penumbras, or among those rights reserved to the people by the Ninth Amendment. Before addressing this claim we feel it desirable briefly to survey, in several aspects, the history of abortion, for such insight as that history may afford us, and then to examine the state purposes and interests behind the criminal abortion laws.

It perhaps is not generally appreciated that the restrictive criminal abortion laws in effect in a majority of States today are of relatively recent vintage. Those laws, generally proscribing abortion or its attempt at any time during pregnancy except when necessary to preserve the pregnant woman's life, are not of ancient or even of common-law origin. Instead, they derive from statutory changes effected, for the most part, in the latter half of the 19th century.

1. Ancient Attitudes. These are not capable of precise determination. We are told that at the time of the Persian Empire abortifacients were known and that criminal abortions were severely punished.

We are also told, however, that abortion was practiced in Greek times as well as in the Roman Era, and that "it was resorted to without scruple." The Ephesian, Soranos, often described as the greatest of the ancient gynecologists, appears to have been generally opposed to Rome's prevailing free-abortion practices. He found it necessary to think first of the life of the mother, and he resorted to abortion when, upon this standard, he felt the procedure advisable. Greek and Roman law afforded little protection to the unborn. If abortion was prosecuted in some places, it seems to have been based on a concept of a violation of the father's right to his offspring. Ancient religion did not bar abortion.

2. The Hippocratic Oath. What then of the famous Oath that has stood so long as the ethical guide of the medical profession and that bears the name of the great Greek (460(?)–377(?) B.C.), who has been described as the Father of Medicine, the "wisest and the greatest practitioner of his art," and the "most important and most complete medical personality of antiquity," who dominated the medical schools of his time, and who typified the sum of the medical knowledge of the past? The Oath varies somewhat according to the particular translation, but in any translation the content is clear: "I will give no deadly medicine to anyone if asked, nor suggest any such counsel; and in like manner I will not give to a woman a pessary to produce abortion," or "I will neither give a deadly drug to anybody if asked for it, nor will I make a suggestion to this effect. Similarly, I will not give to a woman an abortive remedy."

Although the Oath is not mentioned in any of the principal briefs in this case or in Doe v. Bolton, it represents the apex of the development of strict ethical concepts in medicine, and its influence endures to this day. Why did not the authority of Hippocrates dissuade abortion practice in his time and that of Rome? The late Dr. Edelstein provides us with a theory: The Oath was not uncontested even in Hippocrates' day; only the Pythagorean school of philosophers frowned upon the related act of suicide. Most Greek thinkers, on the other hand, commended abortion, at least prior to viability. See Plato, Republic, V, 461; Aristotle, Politics, VII, 1335b 25. For the Pythagoreans, however, it was a matter of dogma. For them the embryo was animate from the moment of conception, and abortion meant destruction of a living being. The abortion clause of the Oath, therefore, "echoes Pythagorean doctrines," and "[i]n no other stratum of Greek opinion were such views held or proposed in the same spirit of uncompromising austerity."

Dr. Edelstein then concludes that the Oath originated in a group representing only a small segment of Greek opinion and that it certainly was not accepted by all ancient physicians. He points out that medical writings down to Galen (A.D. 130–200) "give evidence of the violation of almost every one of its injunctions." But with the end of antiquity a decided change took place. Resistance against suicide and against abortion became common. The Oath came to be popular. The emerging teachings of Christianity were in agreement with the Pythagorean ethic. The Oath "became the nucleus of all medical ethics" and "was applauded as the embodiment of truth." Thus, suggests Dr. Edelstein, it is "a Pythagorean manifesto and not the expression of an absolute standard of medical conduct."

This, it seems to us, is a satisfactory and acceptable explanation of the Hippocratic Oath's apparent rigidity. It enables us to understand, in historical context, a long-accepted and revered statement of medical ethics.

3. The Common Law. It is undisputed that at common law, abortion performed *before* "quickening"—the first recognizable movement of the fetus *in utero*, appearing usually from the 16th to the 18th week of pregnancy—was not an indictable offense. The absence of a common-law crime for pre-quickening abortion appears to have developed from a confluence of earlier philosophical, theological, and civil and canon law concepts of when life begins. These disciplines variously approached the question in terms of the point at which the embryo or fetus became "formed" or recognizably human, or in terms of when a "person" came into being, that is, infused with a "soul" or "animated." A loose concensus evolved in early English law that these events occurred at some point between conception and live birth. This was "mediate animation." Although Christian theology and the canon law came to fix the point of animation at 40 days for a male and 80 days for a female, a view that persisted until the 19th century, there was otherwise little agreement about the precise time of formation or animation. There was agreement, however, that prior to this point the fetus was to be regarded as part of the mother, and its destruction, therefore, was not homicide. Due to continued uncertainty about the precise time when animation occurred, to the lack of any empirical basis for the 40–80-day view, and perhaps to Aquinas' definition of movement as one of the two first principles of life, Bracton focused upon quickening as the critical point. The significance of quickening was echoed by later common-law scholars and found its way into the received common law in this country.

Whether abortion of a *quick* fetus was a felony at common law, or even a lesser crime, is still disputed. Bracton, writing early in the 13th century, thought it homicide. But the later and predominant view, following the great common-law scholars, has been that it was, at most, a lesser offense. In a frequently cited passage, Coke took the position that abortion of a woman "quick with childe" is "a great misprision, and no murder." Blackstone followed, saying that while abortion after quickening had once been considered manslaughter (though not murder), "modern law" took a less severe view. A recent review of the common-law precedents argues, however, that those precedents contradict Coke and that even post-quickening abortion was never established as a common-law crime.

This is of some importance because while most American courts ruled, in holding or dictum, that abortion of an unquickened fetus was not criminal under their received common law, others followed Coke in stating that abortion of a quick fetus was a "misprision," a term they translated to mean "misdemeanor." That their reliance on Coke on this aspect of the law was uncritical and, apparently in all the reported cases, dictum (due probably to the paucity of common-law prosecutions for post-quickening abortion), makes it now appear doubtful that abortion was ever firmly established as a common-law crime even with respect to the destruction of a quick fetus.

4. The English Statutory Law. England's first criminal abortion statute, Lord Ellenborough's Act, 43 Geo. 3, c. 58, came in 1803. It made abortion of a quick fetus, § 1, a capital crime, but in § 2 it provided lesser penalties for the felony of abortion before quickening, and thus preserved the "quickening" distinction. This contrast was continued in the general revision of 1828, 9 Geo. 4, c. 31, § 13. It disappeared, however, together with the death penalty, in 1837, 7 Will. 4 & 1 Vict., c. 85, § 6, and did not reappear in the Offenses Against the Person Act of 1861, 24 & 25 Vict., c. 100, § 59, that formed the core of English anti-abortion law until the liberalizing reforms of 1967. In 1929, the Infant Life (Preservation) Act, 19 & 20 Geo. 5, c. 34, came into being. Its emphasis was upon the destruction of "the life of a child capable of being born alive." It made a willful act performed with the necessary intent a felony. It contained a proviso that one was not to be found guilty of the offense "unless it is proved that the act which caused the death of the child was not done in good faith for the purpose only of preserving the life of the mother."

A seemingly notable development in the English law was the case of Rex v. Bourne, [1939] 1 K.B. 687. This case apparently answered in the affirmative the question whether an abortion necessary to preserve the life of the pregnant woman was excepted from the criminal penalties of the 1861 Act. In his instructions to the jury, Judge Macnaghten referred to the 1929 Act, and observed that that Act related to "the case where a child is killed by a willful act at the time when it is being delivered in the ordinary course of nature." Id., at 691. He concluded that the 1861 Act's use of the word "unlawfully," imported the same meaning expressed by the specific proviso in the 1929 Act, even though there was no mention of preserving the mother's life in the 1861 Act. He then construed the phrase "preserving the life of the mother" broadly, that is, "in a reasonable sense," to include a serious and permanent threat to the mother's *health,* and instructed the jury to acquit Dr. Bourne if it found he had acted in a good-faith belief that the abortion was necessary for this purpose. Id., at 693–694. The jury did acquit.

Recently, Parliament enacted a new abortion law. This is the Abortion Act of 1967, 15 & 16 Eliz. 2, c. 87. The Act permits a licensed physician to perform an abortion where two other licensed physicians agree (a) "that the continuance of the pregnancy would involve risk to the life of the pregnant woman, or of injury to the physical or mental health of the pregnant woman or any existing children of her family, greater than if the pregnancy were terminated," or (b) "that there is a substantial risk that if the child were born it would suffer from such physical or mental abnormalities as to be seriously handicapped." The Act also provides that, in making this determination, "account may be taken of the pregnant woman's actual or reasonably foreseeable environment." It also permits a physician, without the concurrence of others, to terminate a pregnancy where he is of the good-faith opinion that the abortion "is immediately necessary to save the life or to prevent grave permanent injury to the physical or mental health of the pregnant woman."

5. *The American Law.* In this country, the law in effect in all but a few States until mid-19th century was the pre-existing English common law. Connecticut, the first State to enact abortion legislation, adopted in 1821 that part of Lord Ellenborough's Act that related to a woman "quick with child." The death penalty was not imposed. Abortion before quickening was made a crime in that State only in 1860. In 1828, New York enacted legislation that, in two respects, was to serve as a model for early anti-abortion statutes. First, while barring destruction of an unquickened fetus as well as a quick fetus, it made the former only a misdemeanor, but the latter second-degree manslaughter. Second, it incorporated a concept of therapeutic abortion by providing that an abortion was excused if it "shall have been necessary to preserve the life of such mother, or shall have been advised by two physicians to be necessary for such purpose." By 1840, when Texas had received the common law, only eight American States had statutes dealing with abortion. It was not until after the War Between the States that legislation began generally to replace the common law. Most of these initial statutes dealt severely with abortion after quickening but were lenient with it before quickening. Most punished attempts equally with completed abortions. While many statutes included the exception for an abortion thought by one or more physicians to be necessary to save the mother's life, that provision soon disappeared and the typical law required that the procedure actually be necessary for that purpose.

Gradually, in the middle and late 19th century the quickening distinction disappeared from the statutory law of most States and the degree of the offense and the penalties were increased. By the end of the 1950's a large majority of the jurisdictions banned abortion, however, and whenever performed, unless done to save or preserve the life of the mother. The exceptions, Alabama and the District of Columbia, permitted abortion to preserve the mother's health. Three States permitted abortions that were not "unlawfully" performed or that were not "without lawful justification," leaving interpretation of those standards to the courts. In the past several years, however, a trend toward liberalization of abortion statutes has resulted in adoption, by about one-third of the States, of less stringent laws, most of them patterned after the ALI Model Penal Code.

It is thus apparent that at common law, at the time of the adoption of our Constitution, and throughout the major portion of the 19th century, abortion was viewed with less disfavor than under most American statutes currently in effect. Phrasing it another way, a woman enjoyed a substantially broader right to terminate a pregnancy than she does in most States today. At least with respect to the early stage of pregnancy, and very possibly without such a limitation, the opportunity to make this choice was present in this country well into the 19th century. Even later, the law continued for some time to treat less punitively an abortion procured in early pregnancy.

6. The Position of the American Medical Association. The anti-abortion mood prevalent in this country in the late 19th century was shared by the medical profession. Indeed, the attitude of the profession may have played a significant role in the enactment of stringent criminal abortion legislation during that period.

An AMA Committee on Criminal Abortion was appointed in May 1857. It presented its report, 12 Trans. of the Am.Med.Assn. 73–78 (1859), to the Twelfth Annual Meeting. That report observed that the Committee had been appointed to investigate criminal abortion "with a view to its general suppression." It deplored abortion and its frequency and it listed three causes of "this general demoralization":

> The first of these causes is a wide-spread popular ignorance of the true character of the crime—a belief, even among mothers themselves, that the foetus is not alive till after the period of quickening.

> The second of the agents alluded to is the fact that the profession themselves are frequently supposed careless of foetal life.
> .   .   .

> The third reason of the frightful extent of this crime is found in the grave defects of our laws, both common and statute, as regards the independent and actual existence of the child before birth, as a living being. These errors, which are sufficient in most instances to prevent conviction, are based, and only based, upon mistaken and exploded medical dogmas. With strange inconsistency, the law fully acknowledges the foetus in utero and its inherent rights, for civil purposes; while personally and as criminally affected, it fails to recognize it, and to its life as yet denies all protection. Id., at 75–76.

The Committee then offered, and the Association adopted, resolutions protesting "against such unwarrantable destruction of human life," calling upon state legislatures to revise their abortion laws, and requesting the cooperation of state medical societies "in pressing the subject." Id., at 28, 78.

In 1871 a long and vivid report was submitted by the Committee on Criminal Abortion. It ended with the observation, "We had to deal with human life. In a matter of less importance we could entertain no compromise. An honest judge on the bench would call things by their proper names. We could do no less." 22 Trans. of the Am. Med.Assn. 258 (1871). It proffered resolutions, adopted by the Association, id., at 38–39, recommending, among other things, that it "be unlawful and unprofessional for any physician to induce abortion or premature labor, without the concurrent opinion of at least one respectable consulting physician, and then always with a view to the safety of the child—if that be possible," and calling "the attention of the clergy of all denominations to the perverted views of morality entertained by a large class of females—aye, and men also, on this important question."

Except for periodic condemnation of the criminal abortionist, no further formal AMA action took place until 1967. In that year, the Committee on Human Reproduction urged the adoption of a stated policy of opposition to induced abortion, except when there is "documented medical evidence" of a threat to the health or life of the mother, or that the child "may be born with incapacitating physical deformity or mental deficiency," or that a pregnancy "resulting from legally established statutory or forcible rape or incest may constitute a threat to the mental or physical health of the patient," two other physicians "chosen because of their recognized professional competency have examined the patient and have concurred in writing," and the procedure "is performed in a hospital accredited by the Joint Commission on Accreditation of Hospitals." The providing of medical information by physicians to state legislatures in their consideration of legislation regarding therapeutic abortion was "to be considered consistent with the principles of ethics of the American Medical Association." This recommendation was adopted by the House of Delegates. Proceedings of the AMA House of Delegates 40–51 (June 1967).

In 1970, after the introduction of a variety of proposed resolutions, and of a report from its Board of Trustees, a reference committee noted "polarization of the medical profession on this controversial issue"; division among those who had testified; a difference of opinion among AMA councils and committees; "the remarkable shift in testimony" in six months, felt to be influenced "by the rapid changes in state laws and by the judicial decisions which tend to make abortion more freely available;" and a feeling "that this trend will continue." On June 25, 1970, the House of Delegates adopted preambles and most of the resolutions proposed by the reference committee. The preambles emphasized "the best interests of the patient," "sound clinical judgment," and "informed patient consent," in contrast to "mere acquiescence to the patient's demand," The resolutions asserted that abortion is a medical procedure that should be performed by a licensed physician in an accredited hospital only after consultation with two other physicians and in conformity with state law, and that no party to the procedure should be required to violate personally held moral principles. Proceedings of the AMA House of Delegates 220 (June 1970). The AMA Judicial Council rendered a complementary opinion.

7. The Position of the American Public Health Association. In October 1970, the Executive Board of the APHA adopted Standards for Abortion Services. These were five in number:

a. Rapid and simple abortion referral must be readily available through state and local public health departments, medical societies, or other non-profit organizations.

b. An important function of counseling should be to simplify and expedite the provision of abortion services; it should not delay the obtaining of these services.

c. Psychiatric consultation should not be mandatory. As in the case of other specialized medical services, psychiatric consultation should be sought for definite indications and not on a routine basis.

d. A wide range of individuals from appropriately trained, sympathetic volunteers to highly skilled physicians may qualify as abortion counselors.

e. Contraception and/or sterilization should be discussed with each abortion patient. Recommended Standards for Abortion Services, 61 Am.J.Pub.Health 396 (1971).

Among factors pertinent to life and health risks associated with abortion were three that are recognized as important:

a. the skill of the physician,

b. the environment in which the abortion is performed, and above all

c. the duration of pregnancy, as determined by uterine size and confirmed by menstrual history. Id., at 397.

It was said that "a well-equipped hospital" offers more protection "to cope with unforeseen difficulties than an office or clinic without such resources. . . . The factor of gestational age is of overriding importance." Thus, it was recommended that abortions in the second trimester and early abortions in the presence of existing medical complications be performed in hospitals as inpatient procedures. For pregnancies in the first trimester, abortion in the hospital with or without overnight stay "is probably the safest practice." An abortion in an extramural facility, however, is an acceptable alternative "provided arrangements exist in advance to admit patients promptly if unforeseen complications develop." Standards for an abortion facility were listed. It was said that at present abortions should be performed by physicians or osteopaths who are licensed to practice and who have "adequate training." Id. at 398.

8. *The Position of the American Bar Association.* At its meeting in February 1972 the ABA House of Delegates approved, with 17 opposing votes, the Uniform Abortion Act that had been drafted and approved the preceding August by the Conference of Commissioners on Uniform State Laws. 58 A.B.A.J. 380 (1972).

Three reasons have been advanced to explain historically the enactment of criminal abortion laws in the 19th century and to justify their continued existence.

It has been argued occasionally that these laws were the product of a Victorian social concern to discourage illicit sexual conduct. Texas, however, does not advance this justification in the present case, and it appears that no court or commentator has taken the argument seriously. The appellants and *amici* contend, moreover, that this is not a proper state purpose at all and suggest that, if it were, the Texas statutes are overbroad in protecting it since the law fails to distinguish between married and unwed mothers.

A second reason is concerned with abortion as a medical procedure. When most criminal abortion laws were first enacted, the procedure was a hazardous one for the woman. This was particularly true prior to the development of antisepsis. Antiseptic techniques, of course, were based on discoveries by Lister, Pasteur, and others first announced in 1867, but were not generally accepted and employed until about the turn of the century. Abortion mortality was high. Even after 1900, and perhaps until as late as the development of antibiotics in the 1940's, standard modern techniques such as dilation and curettage were not nearly so safe as they are today. Thus, it has been argued that a State's real concern in enacting a criminal abortion law was to protect the pregnant woman, that is, to restrain her from submitting to a procedure that placed her life in serious jeopardy.

Modern medical techniques have altered this situation. Appellants and various *amici* refer to medical data indicating that abortion in early pregnancy, that is, prior to the end of the first trimester, although not without its risk, is now relatively safe. Mortality rates for women undergoing early abortions, where the procedure is legal, appear to be as low as or lower than the rates for normal childbirth. Consequently, any interest of the State in protecting the woman from an inherently hazardous procedure, except when it would be equally dangerous for her to forgo it, has largely disappeared. Of course, important state interests in the areas of health and medical standards do remain. The State has a legitimate interest in seeing to it that abortion, like any other medical procedure, is performed under circumstances that insure maximum safety for the patient. This interest obviously extends at least to the performing physician and his staff, to the facilities involved, to the availability of after-care, and to adequate provision for any complication or emergency that might arise. The prevalence of high mortality rates at illegal "abortion mills" strengthens, rather than weakens, the State's interest in regulating the conditions under which abortions are performed. Moreover, the risk to the woman increases as her pregnancy continues. Thus, the State retains a definite interest in protecting the woman's own health and safety when an abortion is proposed at a late stage of pregnancy.

The third reason is the State's interest—some phrase it in terms of duty—in protecting prenatal life. Some of the argument for this justification rests on the theory that a new human life is present from the moment of conception. The State's interest and general obligation to protect life then extends, it is argued, to prenatal life. Only when the life of the pregnant mother herself is at stake, balanced against the life she carries within her, should the interest of the embryo or fetus not prevail. Logically, of course, a legitimate state interest in this area need not stand or fall on acceptance of the belief that life begins at conception or at some other point prior to live birth. In assessing the State's interest, recognition may be given to the less rigid claim that as long as at least *potential* life is involved, the State may assert interests beyond the protection of the pregnant woman alone.

Parties challenging state abortion laws have sharply disputed in some courts the contention that a purpose of these laws, when enacted, was to protect prenatal life. Pointing to the absence of legislative history to support the contention, they claim that most state laws were designed solely to protect the woman. Because medical advances have lessened this concern, at least with respect to abortion in early pregnancy, they argue that with respect to such abortions the laws can no longer be justified by any state interest. There is some scholarly support for this view of original purpose. The few state courts called upon to interpret their laws in the late 19th and early 20th centuries did focus on the State's interest in protecting the woman's health rather than in preserving the embryo and fetus. Proponents of this view point out that in many States, including Texas, by statute or judicial interpretation, the pregnant woman herself could not be prosecuted for self-abortion or for cooperating in an abortion performed upon her by another. They claim that adoption of the "quickening" distinction through received common law and state statutes tacitly recognizes the greater health hazards inherent in late abortion and impliedly repudiates the theory that life begins at conception.

It is with these interests, and the weight to be attached to them, that this case is concerned.

The Constitution does not explicitly mention any right of privacy. In a line of decisions, however, going back perhaps as far as Union Pacific R. Co. v. Botsford, 141 U.S. 250, 251, . . . (1891), the Court has recognized that a right of personal privacy, or a guarantee of certain areas or zones of privacy, does exist under the Constitution. In varying contexts, the Court or individual Justices have, indeed, found at least the roots of that right in the First Amendment, in the Fourth and Fifth Amendments, in the penumbras of the Bill of Rights, in the Ninth Amendment, or in the concept of liberty guaranteed by the first section of the Fourteenth Amendment. These decisions make it clear that only personal rights that can be deemed "fundamental" or "implicit in the concept of ordered liberty," are included in this guarantee of personal privacy. They also make it clear that the right has some extension to activities relating to marriage, procreation, and contraception.

This right of privacy, whether it be founded in the Fourteenth Amendment's concept of personal liberty and restrictions upon state action, as we feel it is, or, as the District Court determined, in the Ninth Amendment's reservation of rights to the people, is broad enough to encompass a woman's decision whether or not to terminate her pregnancy. The detriment that the State would impose upon the pregnant woman by denying this choice altogether is apparent. Specific and direct harm medically diagnosable even in early pregnancy may be involved. Maternity, or additional offspring, may force upon the woman a distressful life and future. Psychological harm may be imminent. Mental and physical health may be taxed by child care. There is also the distress, for all concerned, associated with the unwanted child, and there is the problem of bringing a child into a family already unable, psychologically and otherwise, to care for it. In other cases, as in this one, the additional difficulties and continuing stigma of unwed motherhood may be involved. All these are factors the woman and her responsible physician necessarily will consider in consultation.

On the basis of elements such as these, appellant and some *amici* argue that the woman's right is absolute and that she is entitled to terminate her pregnancy at whatever time, in whatever way, and for whatever reason she alone chooses. With this we do not agree. Appellant's arguments that Texas either has no valid interest at all in regulating the abortion decision, or no interest strong enough to support any limitation upon the woman's sole determination, are unpersuasive. The Court's decisions recognizing a right of privacy also acknowledge that some state regulation in areas protected by that right is appropriate. As noted above, a State may properly assert important interests in safeguarding health, in maintaining medical standards, and in protecting potential life. At some point in pregnancy, these respective interests become sufficiently compelling to sustain regulation of the factors that govern the abortion decision. The privacy right involved, therefore, cannot be said to be absolute. In fact, it is not clear to us that the claim asserted by some *amici* that one has an unlimited right to do with one's body as one pleases bears a close relationship to the right of privacy previously articulated in the Court's decisions. The Court has refused to recognize an unlimited right of this kind in the past.

We, therefore, conclude that the right of personal privacy includes the abortion decision, but that this right is not unqualified and must be considered against important state interests in regulation.

We note that those federal and state courts that have recently considered abortion law challenges have reached the same conclusion. A majority, in addition to the District Court in the present case, have held state laws unconstitutional, at least in part, because of vagueness or because of overbreadth and abridgment of rights.

Others have sustained state statutes.

Although the results are divided, most of these courts have agreed that the right of privacy, however based, is broad enough to cover the abortion decision; that the right, nonetheless, is not absolute and is subject to some limitations; and that at some point the state interests as to protection of health, medical standards, and prenatal life, become dominant. We agree with this approach.

Where certain "fundamental rights" are involved, the Court has held that regulation limiting these rights may be justified only by a "compelling state interest," and that legislative enactments must be narrowly drawn to express only the legitimate state interests at stake.

* * *

In the recent abortion cases, cited above, courts have recognized these principles. Those striking down state laws have generally scrutinized the State's interests in protecting health and potential life, and have concluded that neither interest justified broad limitations on the reasons for which a physician and his pregnant patient might decide that she should have an abortion in the early stages of pregnancy. Courts sustaining state laws have held that the State's determinations to protect health or prenatal life are dominant and constitutionally justifiable.

The District Court held that the appellee failed to meet his burden of demonstrating that the Texas statute's infringement upon Roe's rights was necessary to support a compelling state interest, and that, although the appellee presented "several compelling justifications for state presence in the area of abortions," the statutes outstripped these justifications and swept "far beyond any areas of compelling state interest." 314 F.Supp., at 1222–1223. Appellant and appellee both contest that holding. Appellant, as has been indicated, claims an absolute right that bars any state imposition of criminal penalties in the area. Appellee argues that the State's determination to recognize and protect prenatal life from and after conception constitutes a compelling state interest. As noted above, we do not agree fully with either formulation.

A. The appellee and certain *amici* argue that the fetus is a "person" within the language and meaning of the Fourteenth Amendment. In support of this, they outline at length and in detail the well-known facts of fetal development. If this suggestion of personhood is established, the appellant's case, of course, collapses, for the fetus' right to life would then be guaranteed specifically by the Amendment. The appellant conceded as much on reargument. On the other hand, the appellee conceded on reargument that no case could be cited that holds that a fetus is a person within the meaning of the Fourteenth Amendment.

The Constitution does not define "person" in so many words. Section 1 of the Fourteenth Amendment contains three references to "person." The first, in defining "citizens," speaks of "persons born or naturalized in the United States." The word also appears both in the Due Process Clause and in the Equal Protection Clause. "Person" is used in other places in the Constitution: in the listing of qualifications for Representatives and Senators, Art. I, § 2, cl. 2, and § 3, cl. 3; in the Apportionment Clause, Art. I, § 2, cl. 3; in the Migration and Importation provision, Art. I, § 9, cl. 1; in the Emolument Clause, Art. I, § 9, cl. 8; in the Electors provisions, Art. II, § 1, cl. 2, and the superseded cl. 3; in the provision outlining qualifications for the office of President, Art. II, § 1, cl. 5; in the Extradition provisions, Art. IV, § 2, cl. 2, and the superseded Fugitive Slave Clause 3; and in the Fifth, Twelfth, and Twenty-second Amendments, as well as in §§ 2 and 3 of the Fourteenth Amendment. But in nearly all these instances, the use of the word is such that it has application only postnatally. None indicates, with any assurance, that it has any possible prenatal application.

All this, together with our observation, supra, that throughout the major portion of the 19th century prevailing legal abortion practices were far freer than they are today, persuades us that the word "person," as used in the Fourteenth Amendment, does not include the unborn. This is in accord with the results reached in those few cases where the issue has been squarely presented.

. . . Indeed, our decision in United States v. Vuitch, 402 U.S. 62, 91 S.Ct. 1294, 28 L.Ed.2d 601 (1971), inferentially is to the same effect, for we there would not have indulged in statutory interpretation favorable to abortion in specified circumstances if the necessary consequence was the termination of life entitled to Fourteenth Amendment protection.

This conclusion, however, does not of itself fully answer the contentions raised by Texas, and we pass on to other considerations.

B. The pregnant woman cannot be isolated in her privacy. She carries an embryo and, later, a fetus, if one accepts the medical definitions of the developing young in the human uterus. See Dorland's Illustrated Medical Dictionary 478–479, 547 (24th ed. 1965). The situation therefore is inherently different from marital intimacy, or bedroom possession of obscene material, or marriage, or procreation, or education, with which *Eisenstadt* and *Griswold*, *Stanley*, *Loving*, *Skinner* and *Pierce* and *Meyer* were respectively concerned. As we have intimated above, it is reasonable and appropriate for a State to decide that at some point in time another interest, that of health of the mother or that of potential human life, becomes significantly involved. The woman's privacy is no longer sole and any right of privacy she possesses must be measured accordingly.

Texas urges that, apart from the Fourteenth Amendment, life begins at conception and is present throughout pregnancy, and that, therefore, the State has a compelling interest in protecting that life from and after conception. We need not resolve the difficult question of when life begins. When those trained in the respective disciplines of medicine, philosophy, and theology are unable to arrive at any consensus, the judiciary, at this point in the development of man's knowledge, is not in a position to speculate as to the answer.

It should be sufficient to note briefly the wide divergence of thinking on this most sensitive and difficult question. There has always been strong support for the view that life does not begin until live birth. This was the belief of the Stoics. It appears to be the predominant, though not the unanimous, attitude of the Jewish faith. It may be taken to represent also the position of a large segment of the Protestant community, insofar as that can be ascertained; organized groups that have taken a formal position on the abortion issue have generally regarded abortion as a matter for the conscience of the individual and her family. As we have noted, the common law found greater significance in quickening. Physicians and their scientific colleagues have regarded that event with less interest and have tended to focus either upon conception, upon live birth, or upon the interim point at which the fetus becomes "viable," that is, potentially able to live outside the mother's womb, albeit with artificial aid. Viability is usually placed at about seven months (28 weeks) but may occur earlier, even at 24 weeks. The Aristotelian theory of "mediate animation," that held sway throughout the Middle Ages and the Renaissance in Europe, continued to be official Roman Catholic dogma until the 19th century, despite opposition to this "ensoulment" theory from those in the Church who would recognize the existence of life from the moment of conception. The latter is now, of course, the official belief of the Catholic Church. As one brief *amicus* discloses, this is a view strongly held by many non-Catholics as well, and by many physicians. Substantial problems for precise definition of this view are posed, however, by new embryological data that purport to indicate that conception is a "process" over time, rather than an event, and by new medical techniques such as menstrual extraction, the "morning-after" pill, implantation of embryos, artificial insemination, and even artificial wombs.

In areas other than criminal abortion, the law has been reluctant to endorse any theory that life, as we recognize it, begins before live birth or to accord legal rights to the unborn except in narrowly defined situations and except when the rights are contingent upon live birth. For example, the traditional rule of tort law denied recovery for prenatal injuries even though the child was born alive. That rule has been changed in almost every jurisdiction. In most States, recovery is said to be permitted only if the fetus was viable, or at least quick, when the injuries were sustained, though few courts have squarely so held. In a recent development, generally opposed by the commentators, some States permit the parents of a stillborn child to maintain an action for wrongful death because of prenatal injuries. Such an action, however, would appear to be one to vindicate the parents' interest and is thus consistent with the view that the fetus, at most, represents only the potentiality of life. Similarly, unborn children have been recognized as acquiring rights or interests by way of inheritance or other devolution of property, and have been represented by guardians *ad litem*. Perfection of the interests involved, again, has generally been contingent upon live birth. In short, the unborn have never been recognized in the law as persons in the whole sense.

In view of all this, we do not agree that, by adopting one theory of life, Texas may override the rights of the pregnant woman that are at stake. We repeat, however, that the State does have an important and legitimate interest in preserving and protecting the health of the pregnant woman, whether she be a resident of the State or a nonresident who seeks medical consultation and treatment there, and that it has still *another* important and legitimate interest in protecting the potentiality of human life. These interests are separate and distinct. Each grows in substantiality as the woman approaches term and, at a point during pregnancy, each becomes "compelling."

With respect to the State's important and legitimate interest in the health of the mother, the "compelling" point, in the light of present medical knowledge, is at approximately the end of the first trimester. This is so because of the now-established medical fact, referred to above at 725, that until the end of the first trimester mortality in abortion may be less than mortality in normal childbirth. It follows that, from and after this point, a State may regulate the abortion procedure to the extent that the regulation reasonably relates to the preservation and protection of maternal health. Examples of permissible state regulation in this area are requirements as to the qualifications of the person who is to perform the abortion; as to the licensure of that person; as to the facility in which the procedure is to be performed, that is, whether it must be a hospital or may be a clinic or some other place of less-than-hospital status; as to the licensing of the facility; and the like.

This means, on the other hand, that, for the period of pregnancy prior to this "compelling" point, the attending physician, in consultation with his patient, is free to determine, without regulation by the State, that, in his medical judgment, the patient's pregnancy should be terminated. If that decision is reached, the judgment may be effectuated by an abortion free of interference by the State.

With respect to the State's important and legitimate interest in potential life, the "compelling" point is at viability. This is so because the fetus then presumably has the capability of meaningful life outside the mother's womb. State regulation protective of fetal life after viability thus has both logical and biological justifications. If the State is interested in protecting fetal life after viability, it may go so far as to proscribe abortion during that period, except when it is necessary to preserve the life or health of the mother.

Measured against these standards, Art. 1196 of the Texas Penal Code, in restricting legal abortions to those "procured or attempted by medical advice for the purpose of saving the life of the mother," sweeps too broadly. The statute makes no distinction between abortions performed early in pregnancy and those performed later, and it limits to a single reason, "saving" the mother's life, the legal justification for the procedure. The statute, therefore, cannot survive the constitutional attack made upon it here.

This conclusion makes it unnecessary for us to consider the additional challenge to the Texas statute asserted on grounds of vagueness.

To summarize and to repeat:

1. A state criminal abortion statute of the current Texas type, that excepts from criminality only a *life-saving* procedure on behalf of the mother, without regard to pregnancy stage and without recognition of the other interests involved, is violative of the Due Process Clause of the Fourteenth Amendment.

    (a) For the stage prior to approximately the end of the first trimester, the abortion decision and its effectuation must be left to the medical judgment of the pregnant woman's attending physician.

    (b) For the stage subsequent to approximately the end of the first trimester, the State, in promoting its interest in the health of the mother, may, if it chooses, regulate the abortion procedure in ways that are reasonably related to maternal health.

(c) For the stage subsequent to viability, the State in promoting its interest in the potentiality of human life may, if it chooses, regulate, and even proscribe, abortion except where it is necessary, in appropriate medical judgment, for the preservation of the life or health of the mother.

2. The State may define the term "physician," as it has been employed in the preceding paragraphs of this Part XI of this opinion, to mean only a physician currently licensed by the State, and may proscribe any abortion by a person who is not a physician as so defined.

In Doe v. Bolton, 410 U.S. 179, procedural requirements contained in one of the modern abortion statutes are considered. That opinion and this one, of course, are to be read together.

This holding, we feel, is consistent with the relative weights of the respective interests involved, with the lessons and examples of medical and legal history, with the lenity of the common law, and with the demands of the profound problems of the present day. The decision leaves the State free to place increasing restrictions on abortion as the period of pregnancy lengthens, so long as those restrictions are tailored to the recognized state interests. The decision vindicates the right of the physician to administer medical treatment according to his professional judgment up to the points where important state interests provide compelling justifications for intervention. Up to those points, the abortion decision in all its aspects is inherently, and primarily, a medical decision, and basic responsibility for it must rest with the physician. If an individual practitioner abuses the privilege of exercising proper medical judgment, the usual remedies, judicial and intra-professional, are available.

Our conclusion that Art. 1196 is unconstitutional means, of course, that the Texas abortion statutes, as a unit, must fall. The exception of Art. 1196 cannot be struck down separately, for then the State would be left with a statute proscribing all abortion procedures no matter how medically urgent the case.

(The concurring opinion of Mr. Justice STEWART and the dissenting opinion of Mr. Justice REHNQUIST are omitted.)

NOTES AND QUESTIONS

1. U. S. Bureau of the Census, Statistical Abstract of the United States, Washington, D.C.: U. S. Government Printing Office, 1980, 101st edition, pp. 69–70, sets out the following data on abortions.

No. 102. Legal Abortions, by Selected Characteristics: 1973 to 1978

[Number of abortions from surveys conducted by source; characteristics from the U.S. Center for Disease Control's (CDC) annual abortion surveillance summaries, with adjustments for
changes in States reporting data to the CDC each year]

CHARACTERIS-TIC	NUMBER (1,000)					PERCENT DISTRIBUTION					ABORTION RATIO [1]	
	1973	1975	1976	1977	1978	1973	1975	1976	1977	1978	1973	1978
Total legal abortions ...	744.6	1,034.2	1,179.3	1,320.3	1,409.6	100.0	100.0	100.0	100.0	100.0	193	294
Age of woman:												
Less than 15 years old	11.6	15.3	15.8	15.7	15.1	1.6	1.5	1.3	1.2	1.1	476	580
15–19 years old	232.4	324.9	362.7	397.7	418.8	31.2	31.4	30.8	30.1	29.7	280	432
20–24 years old	240.6	331.6	392.3	450.9	489.4	32.3	32.1	33.3	34.2	34.7	181	297
25–29 years old	129.6	188.9	220.5	247.4	266.0	17.4	18.2	18.7	18.7	18.8	128	205
30–34 years old	72.6	100.2	110.1	124.7	134.3	9.7	9.7	9.3	9.4	9.5	165	218
35–39 years old	41.0	52.7	56.7	61.9	65.3	5.5	5.1	4.8	4.7	4.7	246	338
40 years old and over	16.8	20.5	21.3	22.1	20.7	2.3	2.0	1.8	1.7	1.5	334	461
Race of woman:												
White	548.8	701.2	784.9	891.2	969.4	73.7	67.8	66.6	67.5	68.8	178	263
Black and other	195.8	333.0	394.4	429.1	440.2	26.3	32.2	33.4	32.5	31.2	252	399
Marital status of woman:												
Married	216.2	271.9	290.0	300.5	350.6	29.0	26.3	24.6	22.8	24.9	74	110
Unmarried	528.4	762.3	889.3	1,019.8	1,059.0	71.0	73.7	75.4	77.2	75.1	564	657
Number of living children:												
None	375.2	499.3	562.6	663.1	798.1	50.4	48.3	47.7	50.2	56.6	242	357
1	137.4	206.8	244.4	269.1	271.3	18.5	20.0	20.7	20.4	19.2	108	200
2	102.2	156.8	181.5	194.5	198.0	13.7	15.2	15.4	14.7	14.1	190	280
3	61.7	86.8	97.7	100.0	83.3	8.3	8.4	8.3	7.6	5.9	228	300
4 or more	68.2	84.4	93.1	93.6	58.9	9.1	8.1	7.9	7.1	4.2	196	275
Number of prior induced abortions:												
None	(NA)	822.1	911.3	969.4	994.5	(NA)	79.5	77.3	73.4	70.5	(NA)	(NA)
1	(NA)	170.4	213.2	268.6	315.5	(NA)	16.5	18.1	20.3	22.4	(NA)	(NA)
2	(NA)	30.4	40.4	55.4	71.9	(NA)	2.9	3.4	4.2	5.1	(NA)	(NA)
3	(NA)	11.3	14.3	27.0	27.7	(NA)	1.1	1.2	2.1	2.0	(NA)	(NA)
Weeks of gestation:												
Less than 9 weeks	284.3	480.6	559.9	659.7	707.8	38.2	46.5	47.4	50.0	50.2	(NA)	(NA)
9–10 weeks	221.6	290.4	333.8	362.2	388.4	29.7	28.1	28.3	27.4	27.6	(NA)	(NA)
11–12 weeks	130.6	151.1	171.3	180.0	187.7	17.5	14.6	14.5	13.6	13.3	(NA)	(NA)
13 weeks or more	108.2	112.1	114.4	118.5	125.7	14.6	10.8	9.8	9.0	8.9	(NA)	(NA)

NA Not available. [1] Number of abortions per 1,000 abortions and live births. Age of woman refers to age at time of abortion or birth.

Source: 1973–1977, Forrest, J. D., E. Sullivan, and C. Tietze, "Abortion in the United States, 1977–1978." In Alan Guttmacher Institute, New York, N.Y. Family Planning Perspectives, vol. 11, No. 6, 1979. 1978, Alan Guttmacher Institute, "Abortion in the United States, 1978–79," forthcoming report.

No. 103. Legal Abortions—Number, Rate per 1,000 Women 15–44 Years Old, and Abortion/Live Births, Ratio by State of Occurrence: 1973 to 1978

[Numbers of legal abortions are from two surveys of hospitals, clinics, and physicians identified as providers of abortion services, conducted by the Alan Guttmacher Institute. Abortion rates are computed per 1,000 women 15–44 years of age on **July 1** of specified year; abortion ratios are computed as the number of abortions per 1,000 live births from **July 1, 1973**, to **June 30, 1974**, from **July 1, 1975**, to **June 30, 1976**, from **July 1, 1977**, to **June 30, 1978**, and from **July 1, 1978** to **June 30, 1979**, respectively, by State of occurrence]

STATE	NUMBER OF ABORTIONS (1,000)				RATE PER 1,000 WOMEN				RATIO: ABORTIONS PER 1,000 LIVE BIRTHS			
	1973	1975	1977	1978	1973	1975	1977	1978	1973	1975	1977	1978
U.S	744.6	1,034.2	1,320.3	1,409.6	16.5	22.1	26.9	28.2	239	331	400	417
N. Eng	23.1	54.1	69.6	77.4	9.0	20.1	25.3	27.8	152	372	460	497
Maine	.7	2.0	3.3	5.2	3.5	9.5	13.9	20.9	47	136	218	335
NH	.6	1.8	3.5	4.0	3.5	10.8	18.8	20.9	52	178	273	311
Vt	1.5	2.2	2.4	3.3	15.4	22.1	22.5	30.2	233	350	363	464
Mass	12.4	33.3	39.3	42.6	10.0	25.7	29.7	31.7	173	488	568	596
R.I	1.1	3.3	4.2	4.6	5.8	16.0	21.2	22.9	96	298	357	379
Conn	6.8	11.4	16.8	17.8	10.0	16.1	24.2	25.4	188	328	474	484
Mid. Atl	252.9	250.6	293.3	300.2	31.3	29.7	35.6	36.3	536	532	617	630
N.Y	212.7	170.7	186.0	187.1	52.9	40.7	46.0	46.1	904	727	803	813
N.J	10.2	32.4	45.3	48.0	6.4	19.4	27.8	29.1	113	369	500	531
Pa	29.9	47.4	62.0	65.2	12.1	18.5	24.3	25.3	200	320	405	417
E. No. Cent	97.4	166.6	212.4	216.8	10.9	17.8	22.9	23.2	161	280	345	340
Ohio	17.3	44.6	60.3	57.1	7.3	17.9	25.0	23.5	109	290	384	345
Ind	1.8	7.7	10.4	15.3	1.5	6.3	8.7	12.8	21	94	126	179
Ill	32.8	60.3	71.9	70.3	13.4	23.6	28.5	27.6	199	363	420	399
Mich	37.5	42.7	53.6	56.6	18.7	20.3	25.4	26.5	272	330	392	407
Wis	8.2	11.3	16.2	17.5	8.6	11.4	15.8	16.9	129	176	236	248
W. No. Cent	29.6	51.4	62.5	63.8	8.6	14.3	16.9	17.0	127	208	234	235
Minn	7.3	12.8	17.2	17.6	8.8	14.7	19.4	19.5	137	229	281	277
Iowa	2.3	6.2	7.0	7.5	4.0	10.4	11.4	12.1	59	150	156	165
Mo	3.4	11.0	14.9	15.6	3.0	10.5	14.1	14.5	49	156	194	203
N. Dak	—	.9	1.9	2.2	—	7.1	12.9	14.7	—	80	157	180
S. Dak	1.6	1.6	1.4	1.4	12.5	11.5	9.5	9.2	153	138	119	115
Nebr	2.3	4.6	5.4	6.6	7.3	14.3	15.5	18.8	99	193	215	260
Kans	12.6	14.3	14.7	12.9	26.9	29.5	29.4	25.4	413	440	423	359
So. Atl	114.4	172.4	212.7	236.0	16.5	23.8	26.5	28.6	233	362	420	461
Del	2.1	2.4	3.0	3.5	16.0	17.4	21.5	24.2	255	280	346	389
Md	11.1	21.8	23.7	25.8	11.9	22.2	23.7	25.1	241	485	496	524
D.C	44.6	31.4	31.6	30.9	233.6	158.0	176.1	173.4	2,355	1,619	1,456	1,861
Va	8.4	20.3	28.2	30.4	7.8	18.0	23.0	24.2	124	303	400	420
W.Va	(Z)	.1	2.2	2.8	.1	.3	5.7	7.1	2	4	72	93
N.C	12.3	20.0	25.1	30.1	10.7	16.7	19.2	22.6	146	252	300	362
S.C	2.2	6.2	8.9	13.1	3.8	10.3	13.0	18.6	47	137	188	264
Ga	11.0	23.8	32.5	36.1	10.3	21.4	26.9	29.2	129	294	384	426
Fla	22.9	46.5	57.5	63.5	15.8	30.5	30.7	32.2	214	449	520	540
E. So. Cent	12.7	32.5	56.5	54.6	4.6	11.2	18.0	17.1	49	146	241	230
Ky	2.6	8.5	11.5	12.5	3.8	12.0	14.7	15.6	48	148	193	210
Tenn	5.3	17.6	30.5	23.0	6.1	19.2	31.2	23.1	79	269	445	320
Ala	4.6	6.0	11.8	15.1	6.2	7.7	13.9	17.6	78	105	197	247
Miss	.1	.3	2.8	4.0	.2	.6	5.2	7.4	3	7	59	89
W. So. Cent	19.1	65.9	99.0	112.9	4.4	14.6	20.1	22.3	53	179	256	277
Ark	1.1	2.6	3.6	5.2	2.9	6.3	7.5	10.4	35	78	108	147
La	—	5.3	14.6	13.3	—	6.2	16.4	14.7	—	78	196	171
Okla	.6	6.8	10.0	11.2	1.1	11.8	16.3	17.9	15	163	230	244
Tex	17.3	51.2	70.9	83.3	6.8	19.1	24.0	27.4	79	226	301	335
Mt	17.1	33.6	47.2	54.6	9.0	16.9	19.6	21.7	103	188	239	263
Mont	.5	1.5	2.3	3.1	3.1	9.9	13.4	17.2	39	124	177	233
Idaho	.4	1.1	1.7	1.8	2.5	7.0	9.0	9.0	26	67	93	92
Wyo	.2	.5	1.0	1.1	2.6	7.3	9.6	10.8	30	79	119	123
Colo	7.6	13.6	18.7	19.8	14.4	24.6	28.3	28.5	195	338	428	424
N. Mex	4.7	5.1	6.4	6.3	20.6	21.7	22.2	20.9	227	249	282	266
Ariz	2.8	6.7	9.7	13.4	6.9	15.8	17.5	22.9	78	170	226	313
Utah	.1	2.0	3.1	3.2	6.4	7.8	10.6	10.5	4	60	79	75
Nev	1.0	3.0	4.4	6.1	7.9	23.2	28.8	38.1	108	322	429	536
Pac	178.5	207.3	267.1	293.2	29.0	32.0	40.0	43.0	440	490	576	616
Wash	17.3	20.9	31.4	34.5	22.5	25.8	38.9	42.1	373	435	550	613
Oreg	11.4	13.3	15.1	14.5	24.5	27.0	28.8	26.8	356	381	388	347
Calif	143.9	165.6	209.9	234.5	30.8	33.6	41.7	45.7	485	523	612	668
Alaska	1.2	1.6	2.6	2.6	15.7	21.7	25.0	23.0	174	202	324	284
Hawaii	4.7	5.9	8.0	7.1	26.3	31.6	38.0	33.0	303	363	480	411

— Represents zero. Z Fewer than 50 legal abortions reported by providers.

Source: 1973 and 1975, derived from Sullivan, E., C. Tietze, and J. Dryfoos, "Legal Abortion in the United States, 1975–1976." 1977, Forrest, J. D., E. Sullivan, and C. Tietze, "Abortions in the United States, 1977–1978." 1978, Alan Guttmacher Institute, "Abortion in the United States, 1978–79," forthcoming report in Alan Guttmacher Institute, New York, N.Y., Family Planning Respectives, vol. 11, No. 6, 1978, earlier issues and forthcoming report.

2. The following chart is taken from Henshaw, Forrest, Sullivan and Tietze, Abortion Services in the United States, 1979 and 1980, 14 Family Planning Perspectives 5 (1982).

FIGURE 1.   RATES OF LEGAL ABORTION PER 1,000 WOMEN AGED
            15–44, VARIOUS COUNTRIES, 1980

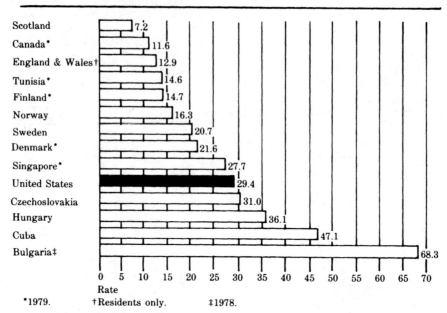

*1979.   †Residents only.   ‡1978.

Sources: C. Tietze, Induced Abortion: A World Review, The Population Council, New York, 1981; and data collected by C. Tietze from various sources.

[C6047]

3. In Doe v. Bolton, 410 U.S. 179, 93 S.Ct. 739, 35 L.Ed.2d 201 (1973), the court found unconstitutional those portions of a Georgia statute requiring 1) that any abortion be performed in a hospital accredited by the Joint Commission on Accreditation of Hospitals; 2) that the procedure be approved by the hospital staff abortion committee; 3) that the performing physician's judgment be confirmed by independent examinations of the patient by two other licensed physicians; and 4) that the patient be a Georgia resident.

4. A Missouri statute requires the prior written consent of the husband of a married woman seeking an abortion during the first 12 weeks of pregnancy. In the case of an unmarried woman under 18, the written consent of a parent (or a person in loco parentis) is required. These provisions were held unconstitutional in Planned Parenthood of Central Missouri v. Danforth, 428 U.S. 52, 96 S.Ct. 2831, 49 L.Ed.2d 788 (1976). In H. L. v. Matheson, 450 U.S. 398, 101 S.Ct. 1164, 1165, 67 L.Ed.2d 388 (1981), however, a Utah statute requiring a physician to "notify, if possible" the parents or guardian of a minor upon whom an abortion is to be performed was held constitutional.

5. What has happened to traditional attitudes toward the marital union and the family in the contraception and abortion decisions?

6. Observe that in many, if not most, states the legislatures would quickly and happily reenact contraception and abortion statutes like those found

unconstitutional in these decisions. In some states new legislation has been enacted that seeks to evade the effect of the court's decisions while limiting access to contraception and to abortion. Does this make you wonder about what the court is doing? If the majority want to control contraception and abortion, why should the court have the power to frustrate them?

7. The previous question should have forced you to think hard about constitutional interpretation. It is clear that, where the U. S. Constitution speaks, it controls over inconsistent legislative action. The difficulty is in determining when the constitution speaks and when it does not. In our legal system the courts have the last word; they are the final authorities on constitutional interpretation. Can you think of acceptable alternative systems? Would they work better?

Maher v. Roe, 432 U.S. 464, 97 S.Ct. 2376, 53 L.Ed.2d 484 (1976).

Mr. Justice POWELL delivered the opinion of the Court.

In Beal v. Doe, . . . we hold today that Title XIX of the Social Security Act does not require the funding of nontherapeutic abortions as a condition of participation in the joint federal-state Medicaid program established by that statute. In this case, as a result of our decision in *Beal*, we must decide whether the Constitution requires a participating State to pay for nontherapeutic abortions when it pays for childbirth.

I

A regulation of the Connecticut Welfare Department limits state Medicaid benefits for first trimester abortions to those that are "medically necessary," a term defined to include psychiatric necessity. Connecticut Welfare Department, Public Assistance Program Manual, Vol. 3, c. III, § 275 (1975). Connecticut enforces this limitation through a system of prior authorization from its Department of Social Services. In order to obtain authorization for a first trimester abortion, the hospital or clinic where the abortion is to be performed must submit, among other things, a certificate from the patient's attending physician stating that the abortion is medically necessary.

This attack on the validity of the Connecticut regulation was brought against appellant Maher, the Commissioner of Social Services, by appellees Poe and Roe, two indigent women who were unable to obtain a physician's certificate of medical necessity. In a complaint filed in the United States District Court for the District of Connecticut, they challenged the regulation both as inconsistent with the requirements of Title XIX of the Social Security Act, and as violative of their constitutional rights, including the Fourteenth Amendment's guarantees of due process and equal protection.

Although it found no independent constitutional right to a state-financed abortion, the District Court held that the Equal Protection Clause forbids the exclusion of nontherapeutic abortions from a state welfare program that generally subsidizes the medical expenses incident to pregnancy and childbirth. The court found implicit in Roe v. Wade, . . . the view that "abortion and childbirth, when stripped of the sensitive moral arguments surrounding the abortion controversy, are simply two alternative medical methods of dealing with pregnancy . . .." Relying also on Shapiro v. Thompson, and Memorial Hospital v. Maricopa County, the court held that the Connecticut program "weights the choice of the pregnant mother against choosing to exercise her constitutionally protected right" to a nontherapeutic abortion and "thus infringes upon a fundamental interest."

The court found no state interest to justify this infringement. The State's fiscal interest was held to be "wholly chimerical because abortion is the least expensive medical response to a pregnancy." . . . And any moral objection to abortion was deemed constitutionally irrelevant:

> The state may not justify its refusal to pay for one type of expense arising from pregnancy on the basis that it morally opposes such an expenditure of money. To sanction such a justification would be to permit discrimination against those seeking to exercise a constitutional right on the basis that the state simply does not approve of the exercise of that right.

The District Court enjoined the State from requiring the certificate of medical necessity for Medicaid-funded abortions. The court also struck down the related requirements of prior written request by the pregnant woman and prior authorization by the Department of Social Services, holding that the State could not impose any requirements on Medicaid payments for abortions that are not "equally applicable to medicaid payments for childbirth, if such conditions or requirements tend to discourage a woman from choosing an abortion or to delay the occurrence of an abortion that she has asked her physician to perform." Id., at 665. We noted probable jurisdiction to consider the constitutionality of the Connecticut regulation.

II

The Constitution imposes no obligation on the States to pay the pregnancy-related medical expenses of indigent women, or indeed to pay any of the medical expenses of indigents. But when a State decides to alleviate some of the hardships of poverty by providing medical care, the manner in which it dispenses benefits is subject to constitutional limitations. Appellees' claim is that Connecticut must accord equal treatment to both abortion and childbirth, and may not evidence a policy preference by funding only the medical expenses incident to childbirth. This challenge to the classifications established by the Connecticut regulation presents a question arising under the Equal Protection Clause of the Fourteenth Amendment. The basic framework of analysis of such a claim is well settled:

> We must decide, first, whether [state legislation] operates to the disadvantage of some suspect class or impinges upon a fundamen-

tal right explicitly or implicitly protected by the Constitution, thereby requiring strict judicial scrutiny. . . . If not, the [legislative] scheme must still be examined to determine whether it rationally furthers some legitimate, articulated state purpose and therefore does not constitute an invidious discrimination . . .."
Applying this analysis here, we think the District Court erred in holding that the Connecticut regulation violated the Equal Protection Clause of the Fourteenth Amendment.

A

This case involves no discrimination against a suspect class. An indigent woman desiring an abortion does not come within the limited category of disadvantaged classes so recognized by our cases. Nor does the fact that the impact of the regulation falls upon those who cannot pay lead to a different conclusion. In a sense, every denial of welfare to an indigent creates a wealth classification as compared to nonindigents who are able to pay for the desired goods or services. But this Court has never held that financial need alone identifies a suspect class for purposes of equal protection analysis. Accordingly, the central question in this case is whether the regulation "impinges upon a fundamental right explicitly or implicitly protected by the Constitution." The District Court read our decisions in Roe v. Wade, 410 U.S. 113, 93 S.Ct. 705, 35 L.Ed.2d 147 (1973), and the subsequent cases applying it, as establishing a fundamental right to abortion and therefore concluded that nothing less than a compelling state interest would justify Connecticut's different treatment of abortion and childbirth. We think the District Court misconceived the nature and scope of the fundamental right recognized in *Roe*.

B

At issue in *Roe* was the constitutionality of a Texas law making it a crime to procure or attempt to procure an abortion, except on medical advice for the purpose of saving the life of the mother. Drawing on a group of disparate cases restricting governmental intrusion, physical coercion, and criminal prohibition of certain activities, we concluded that the Fourteenth Amendment's concept of personal liberty affords constitutional protection against state interference with certain aspects of an individual's personal "privacy," including a woman's decision to terminate her pregnancy.

The Texas statute imposed severe criminal sanctions on the physicians and other medical personnel who performed abortions, thus drastically limiting the availability and safety of the desired service. As Mr. Justice Stewart observed, "it is difficult to imagine a more complete abridgment of a constitutional freedom . . .."

. . . We held that only a compelling state interest would justify such a sweeping restriction on a constitutionally protected interest, and we found no such state interest during the first trimester. Even when judged against this demanding standard, however, the State's dual interest in the health of the pregnant woman and the potential life of the fetus were deemed sufficient to justify substantial regulation of abortions in the second and third trimesters. "These interests are separate and distinct. Each grows in substantiality as the woman approaches term and, at a point during pregnancy, each becomes 'compelling.'"

In the second trimester, the State's interest in the health of the pregnant woman justifies state regulation reasonably related to that concern. At viability, usually in the third trimester, the State's interest in the potential life of the fetus justifies prohibition with criminal penalties, except where the life or health of the mother is threatened.

The Texas law in *Roe* was a stark example of impermissible interference with the pregnant woman's decision to terminate her pregnancy. In subsequent cases, we have invalidated other types of restrictions, different in form but similar in effect, on the woman's freedom of choice. Thus, in Planned Parenthood of Central Missouri v. Danforth, we held that Missouri's requirement of spousal consent was unconstitutional because it "granted [the husband] the right to prevent unilaterally, and for whatever reason, the effectuation of his wife's and her physician's decision to terminate her pregnancy." Missouri had interposed an *absolute obstacle* to a woman's decision that *Roe* held to be constitutionally protected from such interference." (Emphasis added.) Although a state-created obstacle need not be absolute to be impermissible, we have held that a requirement for a lawful abortion "is not unconstitutional unless it unduly burdens the right to seek an abortion." We recognized in *Bellotti* that "not all distinction between abortion and other procedures is forbidden" and that "[t]he constitutionality of such distinction will depend upon its degree and the justification for it." We therefore declined to rule on the constitutionality of a Massachusetts statute regulating a minor's access to an abortion until the state courts had had an opportunity to determine whether the statute authorized a parental veto over the minor's decision or the less burdensome requirement of parental consultation.

These cases recognize a constitutionally protected interest "in making certain kinds of important decisions" free from governmental compulsion. As *Whalen* makes clear, the right in Roe v. Wade can be understood only by considering both the woman's interest and the nature of the State's interference with it. *Roe* did not declare an unqualified "constitutional right to an abortion," as the District Court seemed to think. Rather, the right protects the woman from unduly burdensome interference with her freedom to decide whether to terminate her pregnancy. It implies no limitation on the authority of a State to make a value judgment favoring childbirth over abortion, and to implement that judgment by the allocation of public funds.

The Connecticut regulation before us is different in kind from the laws invalidated in our previous abortion decisions. The Connecticut regulation places no obstacles—absolute or otherwise—in the pregnant woman's path to an abortion. An indigent woman who desires an abortion suffers no disadvantage as a consequence of Connecticut's decision to fund childbirth; she continues as before to be dependent on private sources for the service she desires. The State may have made childbirth a more attractive alternative, thereby influencing the woman's decision, but it has imposed no restriction on access to abortions that was not already there. The indigency that may make it difficult—and in some cases, perhaps, impossible—for some women to have abortions is neither created nor in any way affected by the Connecticut regulation. We conclude that the Connecticut regulation does not impinge upon the fundamental right recognized in *Roe*.

Our conclusion signals no retreat from *Roe* or the cases applying it. There is a basic difference between direct state interference with a protected activity and state encouragement of an alternative activity consonant with legislative policy. Constitutional concerns are greatest when the State attempts to impose its will by force of law; the State's power to encourage actions deemed to be in the public interest is necessarily far broader.

This distinction is implicit in two cases cited in *Roe* in support of the pregnant woman's right under the Fourteenth Amendment. Meyer v. Nebraska, . . . involved a Nebraska law making it criminal to teach foreign languages to children who had not passed the eighth grade.

. . . Nebraska's imposition of a criminal sanction on the providers of desired services makes *Meyer* closely analogous to *Roe*. In sustaining the constitutional challenge brought by a teacher convicted under the law, the Court held that the teacher's "right thus to teach and the right of parents to engage him so to instruct their children" were "within the liberty of the Amendment." 262 U.S., at 400. In Pierce v. Society of Sisters, . . . the Court relied on *Meyer* to invalidate an Oregon criminal law requiring the parent or guardian of a child to send him to a public school, thus precluding the choice of a private school. Reasoning that the Fourteenth Amendment's concept of liberty "excludes any general power of the State to standardize its children by forcing them to accept instruction from public teachers only," the Court held that the law "unreasonably interfere[d] with the liberty of parents and guardians to direct the upbringing and education of children under their control."

Both cases invalidated substantial restrictions on constitutionally protected liberty interests: in *Meyer*, the parent's right to have his child taught a particular foreign language; in *Pierce*, the parent's right to choose private rather than public school education. But neither case denied to a State the policy choice of encouraging the preferred course of action. Indeed, in *Meyer*, the Court was careful to state that the power of the State "to prescribe a curriculum" that included English and excluded German in its free public schools "is not questioned." Similarly, *Pierce* casts no shadow over a State's power to favor public education by funding it—a policy choice pursued in some States for more than a century. Indeed, in Norwood v. Harrison, . . . we explicitly rejected the argument that *Pierce* established a "right of private or parochial schools to share with public schools in state largesse," noting that "[i]t is one thing to say that a State may not prohibit the maintenance of private schools and quite another to say that such schools must, as a matter of equal protection, receive state aid." Yet, were we to accept appellees' argument, an indigent parent could challenge the state policy of favoring public rather than private schools, or of preferring instruction in English rather than German, on grounds identical in principle to those advanced here. We think it abundantly clear that a State is not required to show a compelling interest for its policy choice to favor normal childbirth any more than a State must so justify its election to fund public but not private education.

The question remains whether Connecticut's regulation can be sustained under the less demanding test of rationality that applies in the absence of a suspect classification or the impingement of a fundamental right. This test requires that the distinction drawn between childbirth and nontherapeutic abortion by the regulation be "rationally related" to a "constitutionally permissible" purpose. . . . We hold that the Connecticut funding scheme satisfies this standard.

Roe itself explicitly acknowledged the State's strong interest in protecting the potential life of the fetus. That interest exists throughout the pregnancy, "grow[ing] in substantiality as the woman approaches term."

Because the pregnant woman carries a potential human being she "cannot be isolated in her privacy. . . . [Her] privacy is no longer sole and any right of privacy she possesses must be measured accordingly." The State unquestionably has a "strong and legitimate interest in encouraging normal childbirth," an interest honored over the centuries. Nor can there be any question that the Connecticut regulation rationally furthers that interest. The medical costs associated with childbirth are substantial, and have increased significantly in recent years. As recognized by the District Court in this case, such costs are significantly greater than those normally associated with elective abortions during the first trimester. The subsidizing of costs incident to childbirth is a rational means of encouraging childbirth.

We certainly are not unsympathetic to the plight of an indigent woman who desires an abortion, but "the Constitution does not provide judicial remedies for every social and economic ill." Our cases uniformly have accorded the States a wider latitude in choosing among competing demands for limited public funds. In Dandridge v.

Williams, despite recognition that laws and regulations allocating welfare funds involve "the most basic economic needs of impoverished human beings," we held that classifications survive equal protection challenge when a "reasonable basis" for the classification is shown. As the preceding discussion makes clear, the state interest in encouraging normal childbirth exceeds this minimal level.

The decision whether to expend state funds for nontherapeutic abortion is fraught with judgments of policy and value over which opinions are sharply divided. Our conclusion that the Connecticut regulation is constitutional is not based on a weighing of its wisdom or social desirability, for this Court does not strike down state laws "because they may be unwise, improvident, or out of harmony with a particular school of thought."

Indeed, when an issue involves policy choices as sensitive as those implicated by public funding of nontherapeutic abortions, the appropriate forum for their resolution in a democracy is the legislature. We should not forget that "legislatures are ultimate guardians of the liberties and welfare of the people in quite as great a degree as the courts."

In conclusion, we emphasize that our decision today does not proscribe government funding of nontherapeutic abortions. It is open to Congress to require provision of Medicaid benefits for such abortions as a condition of state participation in the Medicaid program. Also, under Title XIX as construed in Beal v. Doe, . . . Connecticut is free—through normal democratic processes—to decide that such benefits should be provided. We hold only that the Constitution does not require a judicially imposed resolution of these difficult issues.

III

The District Court also invalidated Connecticut's requirements of prior written request by the pregnant woman and prior authorization by the Department of Social Services. Our analysis above rejects the basic premise that prompted invalidation of these procedural requirements. It is not unreasonable for a State to insist upon a prior showing of medical necessity to insure that its money is being spent only for authorized purposes. The simple answer to the argument that similar requirements are not imposed for other medical procedures is that such procedures do not involve the termination of a potential human life. In Planned Parenthood of Central Missouri v. Danforth, we held that the woman's written consent to an abortion was not an impermissible burden under *Roe*. We think that decision is controlling on the similar issue here.

The judgment of the District Court is reversed, and the case is remanded for further proceedings consistent with this opinion.

Mr. Justice BRENNAN, with whom Mr. Justice MARSHALL and Mr. Justice BLACKMUN join, dissenting.

The District Court held:

When Connecticut refuses to fund elective abortions while funding therapeutic abortions and prenatal and postnatal care, it weights the choice of the pregnant mother against choosing to exercise her constitutionally protected right to an elective abortion. . . . Her choice is affected not simply by the absence of payment for the abortion, but by the availability of public funds for childbirth if she chooses not to have the abortion. When the state thus infringes upon a fundamental interest, it must assert a compelling state interest.

This Court reverses on the ground that "the District Court misconceived the nature and scope of the fundamental right recognized in *Roe* . . ." and therefore that Connecticut was not required to meet the "compelling interest" test to justify its discrimination against elective abortion but only "the less demanding test of rationality that applies in the absence of . . . the impingement of a fundamental right," . . .. This holding, the Court insists, "places no obstacles—absolute or otherwise—in the pregnant woman's path to an abortion"; she is still at liberty to finance the abortion from "private sources." . . . True, "the State may [by funding childbirth] have made childbirth a more attractive alternative, thereby influencing the woman's decision, but it has imposed no restriction on access to abortions that was not already there."

True, also, indigency "may make it difficult—and in some cases, perhaps impossible—for some women to have abortions," but that regrettable consequence "is neither created nor in any way affected by the Connecticut regulation."

But a distressing insensitivity to the plight of impoverished pregnant women is inherent in the Court's analysis. The stark reality for too many, not just "some," indigent pregnant women is that indigency makes access to competent licensed physicians not merely "difficult" but "impossible." As a practical matter, many indigent women will feel they have no choice but to carry their pregnancies to term because the State will pay for the associated medical services, even though they would have chosen to have abortions if the State had also provided funds for that procedure, or indeed if the State had provided funds for neither procedure. This disparity in funding by the State clearly operates to coerce indigent pregnant women to bear children they would not otherwise choose to have, and just as clearly, this coercion can only operate upon the poor, who are uniquely the victims of this form of financial pressure. Mr. Justice Frankfurter's words are apt:

To sanction such a ruthless consequence, inevitably resulting from a money hurdle erected by the State, would justify a latterday Anatole France to add one more item to his ironic comments on the "majestic equality" of the law. "The law, in its majestic equality, forbids the rich as well as the poor to sleep under bridges, to beg in the streets, and to steal bread" . . ..

None can take seriously the Court's assurance that its "conclusion signals no retreat from Roe [v. Wade] or the cases applying it," . . . That statement must occasion great surprise among the Courts of Appeals and District Courts that, relying upon Roe v. Wade and Doe v. Bolton, have held that States are constitutionally required to fund elective abortions if they fund pregnancies carried to term. Indeed, it cannot be gainsaid that today's decision seriously erodes the principles that *Roe* and *Doe* announced to guide the determination of what constitutes an unconstitutional infringement of the fundamental right of pregnant women to be free to decide whether to have an abortion.

The Court's premise is that only an equal protection claim is presented here. Claims of interference with enjoyment of fundamental rights have, however, occupied a rather protean position in our constitutional jurisprudence. Whether or not the Court's analysis may reasonably proceed under the Equal Protection Clause, the Court plainly errs in ignoring, as it does, the unanswerable argument of appellees, and the holding of the District Court, that the regulation unconstitutionally impinges upon their claim of privacy derived from the Due Process Clause.

Roe v. Wade and cases following it hold that an area of privacy invulnerable to the State's intrusion surrounds the decision of a pregnant woman whether or not to carry her pregnancy to term. The Connecticut scheme clearly infringes upon that area of privacy by bringing financial pressures on indigent women that force them to bear children they would not otherwise have. That is an obvious impairment of the fundamental right established by Roe v. Wade. Yet the Court concludes that "the Connecticut regulation does not impinge upon [that] fundamental right." . . . This conclusion is based on a perceived distinction, on the one hand, between the imposition of criminal penalties for the procurement of an abortion present in Roe v. Wade and Doe v. Bolton and the absolute prohibition present in Planned Parenthood of Central Missouri v. Danforth, . . . and, on the other, the assertedly lesser inhibition imposed by the Connecticut scheme.

*   *   *

The last time our Brother POWELL espoused the concept in an abortion case that "[t]here is a basic difference between direct state interference with a protected activity and state encouragement of an alternative activity consonant with legislative policy," . . . the Court refused to adopt it.

We have also rejected this approach in other abortion cases. Doe v. Bolton, the companion to Roe v. Wade, in addition to striking down the Georgia criminal prohibition against elective abortions, struck down the procedural requirements of certification of hospitals, of approval by a hospital committee, and of concurrence in the abortion decision by two doctors other than the woman's own doctor. None of these requirements operated as an absolute bar to elective abortions in the manner of the criminal prohibitions present in the other aspect of the case or in *Roe*, but this was not sufficient to save them from unconstitutionality. In *Planned Parenthood*, supra, we struck down a requirement for spousal consent to an elective abortion which the Court characterizes today simply as an "absolute obstacle" to a woman's obtaining an abortion. . . . But the obstacle was "absolute" only in the limited sense that a woman who was unable to persuade her spouse to agree to an elective abortion was prevented from obtaining one. Any woman whose husband agreed, or could be persuaded to agree, was free to obtain an abortion, and the State never imposed directly any prohibition of its own. This requirement was qualitatively different from the criminal statutes that the Court today says are comparable, but we nevertheless found it unconstitutional.

Most recently, also in a privacy case, the Court squarely reaffirmed that the right of privacy was fundamental, and that an infringement upon that right must be justified by a compelling state interest.

That case struck down in its entirety a New York law forbidding the sale of contraceptives to minors under 16 years old, limiting persons who could sell contraceptives to pharmacists, and forbidding advertisement and display of contraceptives. There was no New York law forbidding *use* of contraceptives by anyone, including minors under 16, and therefore no "absolute" prohibition against the exercise of the fundamental right. Nevertheless the statute was declared unconstitutional as a burden on the right to privacy. In words that apply fully to Connecticut's statute, and that could hardly be more explicit, *Carey* stated: " 'Compelling' is of course the key word; where a decision as fundamental as that whether to bear or beget a child is involved, regulations imposing a burden on it may be justified only by compelling state interests, and must be narrowly drawn to express only those interests." . . . *Carey* relied specifically upon *Roe*, *Doe*, and *Planned Parenthood*, and interpreted them in a way flatly inconsistent with the Court's interpretation today: "The significance of these cases is that they establish that the same test must be applied to state regulations that burden an individual's right to decide to prevent conception or terminate pregnancy by substantially limiting access to the means of effectuating that decision as is applied to state statutes that prohibit the decision entirely."

Finally, cases involving other fundamental rights also make clear that the Court's concept of what constitutes an impermissible infringement upon the fundamental right of a pregnant woman to choose to have an abortion makes new law. We have repeatedly found that infringements of fundamental rights are not limited to outright denials of those rights. First Amendment decisions have consistently held in a wide variety of contexts that the compelling-state-interest test is applicable not only to outright denials but also to restraints that make exercise of those rights more difficult. The compelling-state-interest test has been applied in voting cases, even where only relatively small infringements upon voting power, such as dilution of voting strength caused by malapportionment, have been involved.

Similarly, cases involving the right to travel have consistently held that statutes penalizing the fundamental right to travel must pass muster under the compelling-state-interest test, irrespective of whether the statutes actually deter travel. . . . And indigents asserting a fundamental right of access to the courts have been excused payment of entry costs without being required first to show that their indigency was an absolute bar to access.

Until today, I had not thought the nature of the fundamental right established in *Roe* was open to question, let alone susceptible of the interpretation advanced by the Court. The fact that the Connecticut scheme may not operate as an absoute bar preventing all indigent women from having abortions is not critical. What is critical is that the State has inhibited their fundamental right to make that choice free from state interference.

Nor does the manner in which Connecticut has burdened the right freely to choose to have an abortion save its Medicaid program. The Connecticut scheme cannot be distinguished from other grants and withholdings of financial benefits that we have held unconstitutionally burdened a fundamental right. Sherbert v. Verner, supra, struck down a South Carolina statute that denied unemployment compensation to a woman who for religious reasons could not work on Saturday, but that would have provided such compensation if her unemployment had stemmed from a number of other nonreligious causes. Even though there was no proof of indigency in that case, *Sherbert* held that "the pressure upon her to forgo [her religious] practice [was] unmistakable," . . . and therefore held that the effect was the same as a fine imposed for Saturday worship. Here, though the burden is upon the right to privacy derived from the Due Process Clause and not upon freedom of religion under the Free Exercise Clause of the First Amendment, the governing principle is the same, for Connecticut grants and withholds financial benefits in a manner that discourages significantly the exercise of a fundamental constitutional right. Indeed, the case for application of the principle actually is stronger than in *Verner* since appellees are all indigents and therefore even more vulnerable to the financial pressures imposed by the Connecticut regulation.

Bellotti v. Baird, . . . held, and the Court today agrees, *ante*, at 2382, that a state requirement is unconstitutional if it "unduly burdens the right to seek an abortion." Connecticut has "unduly" burdened the fundamental right of pregnant women to be free to choose to have an abortion because the State has advanced no compelling state interest to justify its interference in that choice.

Although appellant does not argue it as justification, the Court concludes that the State's interest "in protecting the potential life of the fetus" suffices, . . . Since only the first trimester of pregnancy is involved in this case, that justification is totally foreclosed if the Court is not overruling the holding of Roe v. Wade that "[w]ith respect to the State's important and legitimate interest in potential life, the 'compelling' point is at viability," occurring at about the end of the second trimester. . . . The appellant also argues a further justification not relied upon by the Court, namely, that the State needs "to control the amount of its limited public funds which will be allocated to its public welfare budget."

. . . The District Court correctly held, however, that the asserted interest was "wholly chimerical" because the "state's assertion that it saves money when it declines to pay the cost of a welfare mother's abortion is simply contrary to undisputed facts." . . .

Finally, the reasons that render the Connecticut regulation unconstitutional also render invalid, in my view, the requirement of a prior written certification by the woman's attending physician that the abortion is "medically necessary," and the requirement that the hospital submit a Request for Authorization of Professional Services including a "statement indicating the medical need for the abortion."

. . .

For the same reasons, I would also strike down the requirement for prior authorization of payment by the Connecticut Department of Social Services.

Mr. Justice MARSHALL, dissenting.

It is all too obvious that the governmental actions in these cases, ostensibly taken to "encourage" women to carry pregnancies to term, are in reality intended to impose a moral viewpoint that no State may constitutionally enforce. Since efforts to overturn those decisions have been unsuccessful, the opponents of abortion have attempted every imaginable means to circumvent the commands of the Constitution and impose their moral choices upon the rest of society. The present cases involve the most vicious attacks yet devised. The impact of the regulations here falls tragically upon those among us least able to help or defend themselves. As the Court well knows, these regulations inevitably will have the practical effect of preventing nearly all poor women from obtaining safe and legal abortions.

The enactments challenged here brutally coerce poor women to bear children whom society will scorn for every day of their lives. Many thousands of unwanted minority and mixed-race children now spend blighted lives in foster homes, orphanages, and "reform" schools. Many children of the poor, sadly, will attend second-rate segregated schools. And opposition remains strong against increasing Aid to Families with Dependent Children benefits for impoverished mothers and children, so that there is little chance for the children to grow up in a decent environment. I am appalled at the ethical bankruptcy of those who preach a "right to life" that means, under present social policies, a bare existence in utter misery for so many poor women and their children.

I

The Court's insensitivity to the human dimension of these decisions is particularly obvious in its cursory discussion of appellees' equal protection claims . . . .

That case points up once again the need for this Court to repudiate its outdated and intellectually disingenuous "two-tier" equal protection analysis.

As I have suggested before, this "model's two fixed modes of analysis, strict scrutiny and mere rationality, simply do not describe the inquiry the Court has undertaken—or should undertake—in equal protection cases." In the present case, in its evident desire to avoid strict scrutiny—or indeed any meaningful scrutiny—of the challenged legislation, which would almost surely result in its invalidation, . . . the Court pulls from thin air a distinction between laws that absolutely prevent exercise of the fundamental right to abortion and those that "merely" make its exercise difficult for some people.

. . . Mr. Justice BRENNAN demonstrates that our cases support no such distinction, . . . and I have argued above that the challenged regulations are little different from a total prohibition from the viewpoint of the poor. But the Court's legal legerdemain has produced the desired result: A fundamental right is no longer at stake and mere rationality becomes the appropriate mode of analysis. To no one's surprise, application of that test—combined with misreading of Roe v. Wade to generate a "strong" state interest in "potential life" during the first trimester of pregnancy, . . . —"leaves little doubt about the outcome; the challenged legislation is [as] always upheld." And once again, "relevant factors [are] misapplied or ignored," . . . while the Court "forego[es] all judicial protection against discriminatory legislation bearing upon" a right "vital to the flourishing of a free society" and a class "unfairly burdened by invidious discrimination unrelated to the individual worth of [its] members." . . .

As I have argued before, an equal protection analysis far more in keeping with the actions rather than the words of the Court, carefully weighs three factors—"the importance of the governmental benefits denied, the character of the class, and the asserted state interests," . . . Application of this standard would invalidate the challenged regulations.

The governmental benefits at issue here, while perhaps not representing large amounts of money for any individual, are nevertheless of absolutely vital importance in the lives of the recipients. The right of every woman to choose whether to bear a child is, as Roe v. Wade held, of fundamental importance. An unwanted child may be disruptive and destructive of the life of any woman, but the impact is felt most by those too poor to ameliorate those effects. If funds for an abortion are unavailable, a poor woman may feel that she is forced to obtain an illegal abortion that poses a serious threat to her health and even her life. . . . If she refuses to take this risk, and undergoes the pain and danger of state-financed pregnancy and childbirth, she may well give up all chance of escaping the cycle of poverty. Absent day-care facilities, she will be forced into full-time child care for years to come; she will be unable to work so that her family can break out of the welfare system or the lowest income brackets. If she already has children, another infant to feed and clothe may well stretch the budget past the breaking point. All chance to control the direction of her own life will have been lost.

I have already adverted to some of the characteristics of the class burdened by these regulations. While poverty alone does not entitle a class to claim government benefits, it is surely a relevant factor in the present inquiry. . . . Indeed, it was in the *San Antonio* case that Mr. Justice Powell for the Court stated a test for analyzing discrimination on the basis of wealth that would, if fairly applied here, strike down the regulations. The Court there held that a wealth-discrimination claim is made out by persons who share "two distinguishing characteristics: because of their impecunity they [are] completely unable to pay for some desired benefit, and as a consequence, they sustai[n] an absolute deprivation of a meaningful opportunity to enjoy that benefit." Id., at 20, 93 S.Ct., at 1290. Medicaid recipients are, almost by definition, "completely unable to pay for" abortions, and are thereby completely denied "a meaningful opportunity" to obtain them.

It is no less disturbing that the effect of the challenged regulations will fall with great disparity upon women of minority races. Nonwhite women now obtain abortions at nearly twice the rate of whites, and it appears that almost 40% of minority women—more than five times the proportion of whites—are dependent upon Medicaid for their health care. Even if this strongly disparate racial impact does not alone violate the Equal Protection Clause, "at some point a showing that state action has a devastating impact on the lives of minority racial groups must be relevant." . . .

Against the brutal effect that the challenged laws will have must be weighed the asserted state interest. The Court describes this as a "strong interest in protecting the potential life of the fetus."

. . . Yet in Doe v. Bolton, supra, the Court expressly held that any state interest during the first trimester of pregnancy, when 86%

of all abortions occur, CDC Surveillance 3, was wholly insufficient to justify state interference with the right to abortion.

If a State's interest in potential human life before the point of viability is insufficient to justify requiring several physicians' concurrence for an abortion, ibid., I cannot comprehend how it magically becomes adequate to allow the present infringement on rights of disfavored classes. If there is any state interest in potential life before the point of viability, it certainly does not outweigh the deprivation or serious discouragement of a vital constitutional right of especial importance to poor and minority women.

Thus, taking account of all relevant factors under the flexible standard of equal protection review, I would hold the Connecticut and Pennsylvania Medicaid regulations and the St. Louis public hospital policy violative of the Fourteenth Amendment.

II

When this Court decided Roe v. Wade and Doe v. Bolton, it properly embarked on a course of constitutional adjudication no less controversial than that begun by Brown v. Board of Education, . . . The abortion decisions are sound law and undoubtedly good policy. They have never been questioned by the Court, and we are told that today's cases "signa[l] no retreat from *Roe* or the cases applying it."

 . . . The logic of those cases inexorably requires invalidation of the present enactments. Yet I fear that the Court's decisions will be an invitation to public officials, already under extraordinary pressure from well-financed and carefully orchestrated lobbying campaigns, to approve more such restrictions. The effect will be to relegate millions of people to lives of poverty and despair. When elected leaders cower before public pressure, this Court, more than ever, must not shirk its duty to enforce the Constitution for the benefit of the poor and powerless.

[The concurring opinion of Chief Justice BURGER and the dissenting opinion of Mr. Justice BLACKMUN are omitted.]

NOTES AND QUESTIONS

1. " . . . the right of procreation without state interference has long been recognized as 'one of the basic civil rights of man . . . fundamental to the very existence and survival of the race'." This quotation appears in footnote 7 to the majority opinion in Maher. In footnote 11 to the same opinion the following appears: "In addition to the direct interest in protecting the fetus, a State may have legitimate demographic concerns about its rate of population growth. Such concerns are basic to the future of the State and in some circumstances could constitute a substantial reason for a departure from a position of neutrality between abor-

tion and childbirth." Are these two asides mutually consistent? Can you rationalize them?

2. Mr. Justice Brennan, in dissent, appears to argue that prohibiting something (e.g. abortion) and encouraging its alternative (e.g. by funding births but not abortions) amount to the same thing, so that if one is unconstitutional state action the other ought to be. How satisfactorily does the majority opinion deal with this argument? Does reference to some part of the Constitution help you to accept or reject the argument? If not, where does the authority for either the majority or dissenting view come from?

3. Suppose state law prevented Medicaid funding of both abortions and births. Would Mr. Justice Brennan and Mr. Justice Marshall both find this constitutionally acceptable?

4. In Harris v. McRae, 448 U.S. 297, 100 S.Ct. 2671, 65 L.Ed.2d 784 (1980), in a 5–4 opinion, the decision in Maher v. Roe was confirmed and extended to medically necessary abortions. That is, a state may constitutionally deny reimbursement for medically necessary abortions for indigent mothers, even though it funds other medical services.

5. As this series of cases, beginning with Griswold v. Connecticut and Roe v. Wade, illustrates, the answer to one novel legal question will often (always?) raise other novel legal questions. The following case exposes a whole new area of law that has grown up following the decriminalization of abortion (and of the distribution of birth control devices and advice).

D. IMPLICATIONS

Stills v. Gratton, 55 Cal.App.3d 698, 127 Cal.Rptr. 652 (1976).

WEINBERGER, Associate Justice.

In this action for medical malpractice filed by Hannah R. Stills and her minor son, Jessie Stills, against Doctors Richard Gratton and Allen F. Smoot, judgments of nonsuit were entered at the conclusion of plaintiffs' evidence in favor of the defendants and against the plaintiffs. This appeal is from the judgments so entered.

In late May or early June 1969 appellant Hannah Stills suspected that she was pregnant. She was unmarried, unemployed, and a part-time art student with a history of emotional problems which she described as "Depression and feelings of alienation." She was frightened at the prospect of having a child.

On June 10, 1969, on the recommendation of a friend, she visited Dr. Gratton, an obstetrics-gynecology specialist, who confirmed her pregnancy, and after discussing her emotional state, advised her that it might be in her best interest to have a therapeutic abortion. He informed her that it would be necessary for her, in order to qualify for such legal abortion under the provisions of Health and Safety Code section 25951, to obtain the approval of the hospital committee and to be examined by two psychiatrists with whom appointments were scheduled. On a return visit to Dr. Gratton on June 20th, Miss Stills was advised that arrangements had been made for a therapeutic abortion to be performed by him in Children's Hospital, San Francisco, on July 8, 1969. She entered the hospital the day before the surgery and was discharged on July 9th, going to her mother's apartment in San Francisco where she remained until July 25th when she moved to Los Angeles, as she had previously informed Dr. Gratton was her intention.

An expert witness called by appellants testified that standard procedure required that a specimen of the tissue removed from a patient be submitted for pathological study and report. The report in the instant case, dated July 10, 1969, indicated that upon gross examination (with the naked eye) the material removed from the patient's uterus revealed "placental tissue." However, microscopic examination showed no placental tissue and the final diagnosis by the pathologist was that the specimen was "desidua," meaning the inner lining of the uterus. This diagnosis, according to appellants' expert, indicates that the abortion had been unsuccessful.

Dr. Gratton conceded that the report, which he testified he received about July 20th, did not confirm that the fetus had been removed, but it was his opinion that since the gross examination revealed placental tissue the pathologist had simply failed to pick it up microscopically. He did not request any further studies because he believed the operation was a success.

There was also expert testimony that the 1969 standard of care for a doctor who had performed an abortion was to read the pathology report and to examine the patient after about two weeks "to make certain, as much as possible, that things have gone well, and the problem has been resolved."

Dr. Gratton testified that he normally required a return visit within two or three weeks but that in this case the patient had told him she was going directly to Los Angeles and had no forwarding address there. Miss Stills testified that she had no recollection of Dr. Gratton telling her that she should have a checkup following her abortion. Dr. Gratton testified that he did tell her that, under normal conditions, he would want to see her after about two to three weeks. He did not testify that he recommended that she arrange to see some other doctor in Los Angeles.

On or about August 8, 1969, Miss Stills went to a Dr. Wood in Los Angeles for a checkup and for birth control pills. She was told by him that he thought she was pregnant and a urine test confirmed this diagnosis. On the same day, appellant called Dr. Smoot, who had been her family doctor in San Francisco for several years. Upon learning that Miss Stills had seen a doctor in Los Angeles, that she had had an earlier abortion, and the result of the new pregnancy test, Dr. Smoot asked her who had performed the operation.

On being told the doctor's name he suggested that he call Dr. Gratton to try to find out what was going on. A day or so later, appellant called Dr. Smoot again. He told her that according to Dr. Gratton she had been completely aborted, explaining that the affirmative pregnancy test may be due to her "body chemistry" not having returned to normal. He then suggested that plaintiff take a regimen of birth control pills to regulate her menstrual period, and sent her a prescription for Enovid-E. The prescription was dated August 14, 1969, and was sent to her Los Angeles address. Appellant had it filled on August 19, 1969, and took the pills for 20 days as advised by Dr. Smoot. When her menstrual period did not begin within a few days after discontinuing the use of the Enovid-E, Miss Stills decided to return to San Francisco to see Dr. Smoot. She visited him in mid-September. He confirmed that she was pregnant and referred her to a Dr. Soldati for prenatal care. At this point, appellant believed that she was "too far along" to have a repeat abortion.

Dr. Soldati examined Miss Stills on September 30, 1969, and concluded she was 23 to 24 weeks pregnant. Abortion was no longer advisable because the legal deadline had passed, and because it was medically unsafe. He testified that on or about August 11, 1969, at 17 weeks, it would have been medically permissible to do a second abortion.

Doctors Gratton and Smoot agreed in essentials about their telephone conversation. After Dr. Smoot relayed what the patient had said, Dr. Gratton told him that decidual tissue was found by the pathologist, but that in his opinion the abortion was satisfactory. He told Dr. Smoot that if there was any question at all, plaintiff should be checked by him or Dr. Smoot or some other doctor. Dr. Smoot relayed to Miss Stills the opinion of Dr. Gratton that the abortion had been completed without mentioning the pathology report. He volunteered the possibility of "body chemistry" masking the fact that a former pregnancy had been terminated by an abortion.

With regard to the prescription of Enovid-E, Dr. Smoot testified that he prescribed it in order to bring on menstrual flow and that there is no reason to use the drug if a woman is pregnant. A drug called Gestest, if taken for a short time, for example, two a day for two days, would produce the same effect as Enovid-E, if the patient is not pregnant. If no menstruation occurs after the Gestest regimen, then further testing is called for. Dr. Smoot did not use Gestest because if the plaintiff was not pregnant, it would not protect her against conception. Dr. Gratton agreed that Enovid-E is not the "treatment of choice" if a woman is pregnant.

Under Dr. Soldati's care the appellant Hannah Stills gave birth on January 10, 1970, to plaintiff, Jessie Stills, who was described by his counsel in an opening statement as "a beautiful healthy baby boy . . . and there did not appear to be, and to this day [three and one-half years later] there does not appear to be, anything wrong with that little boy."

The issues raised by appellants are:

　　1.　Did the trial court err in granting a nonsuit in favor of the two respondent doctors?

　　2.　If appellants are successful in establishing liability, what is the proper measure of damages?

As regards the cause of action asserted by Hannah Stills, we conclude that the judgment of nonsuit must be reversed. The stringent rule by which a trial court's ruling on a motion for such judgment must be tested has already been stated. We must disregard conflicting evidence and give to plaintiffs' evidence all the value to which it is legally entitled, as well as indulge in every legitimate inference which may be drawn from the evidence.

What has been said regarding the cause of action asserted by Hannah Stills has no applicability to the alleged cause of action asserted on behalf of the minor plaintiff, Jessie Stills. This plaintiff's pleadings allege merely that he was born out of wedlock and that "various reasons" affect him to his detriment. The testimony disclosed that Jessie was and is a healthy, happy youngster who is a joy to his mother. His only damage, if any, caused by the respondents' conduct is in being born. As was stated in Zepeda v. Zepeda

　　.　.　.　"Recognition of the plaintiff's claim means creation of a new tort: a cause of action for wrongful life. The legal implications of such a tort are vast, the social impact could be staggering. If the new litigation were confined just to illegitimates it would be formidable." No court has yet recognized the tort and we are not persuaded that this court should be the first. The issue involved is more theological or philosophical than legal.

In Williams v. State　.　.　.　a child sued a mental institution for failing to provide protection to the mother from assault which resulted in his being born a bastard with a mentally deficient mother. The court rejected the argument that damages could be measured by comparing the plaintiff with a child born without the handicap of bastardy, stating, at page 908, that damages "would have to comprehend the infirmities inherent in claimant's situation as against the alternative of a void, if nonbirth and nonexistence may thus be expressed; and could not, without incursion into the metaphysical, be measured against the hypothesis of a child or imagined entity in some way identifiable with claimant but of normal and lawful parentage and possessed of normal or average advantages."　.　.　.

In tort, damages serve to compensate a plaintiff for injury caused by a defendant's conduct, and are awarded to the extent that a plaintiff can be restored to the position he would have occupied had the tort not occurred. "This Court cannot weigh the value of life with impairments against the nonexistence of life itself. By asserting that he should not have been born, the infant plaintiff makes it logically impossible for a court to measure his alleged damages because of the impossibility of making the comparison required by compensatory remedies."

In answer to respondents' contention that the fact of birth does not constitute a compensable injury, plaintiff Jessie Stills refers to Civil Code section 29, which states that "A child conceived, but not yet born, is to be deemed an existing person, so far as may be necessary for its interests in the event of its subsequent birth; . . . ." Nothing in this section obviates the requirement that to recover in tort a compensable injury must be alleged and proved. The motion for a nonsuit has been described as the modern equivalent of a demurrer to the evidence; it concedes that truth of the facts proved, but denies that they, as a matter of law, sustain the plaintiff's case.

It is concluded that the trial court's ruling on the motion for nonsuit on the fifth cause of action dealing with the alleged claim of Jessie Stills was correct, but the judgment entered in favor of respondent doctors against Hannah Stills, for the reasons set forth, must be reversed and the cause remanded for retrial on the issue of the malpractice, if any, of the respondents or either of them.

Both sides, anticipating the possibility that a retrial might be required, have briefed the question of what damages are recoverable in order to obtain a determination at this time to avoid repetitious appeals.

Some jurisdictions, for public policy reasons, deny damages when malpractice results in the birth of a healthy child. The reasoning, most recently expressed by the Wisconsin Supreme Court, assumes that the benefits of a child, as a matter of law, outweigh the burdens: "Every child's smile, every bond of love and affection, every reason for parental pride in a child's achievements, every contribution by the child to the welfare and well-being of the family and parents, is to remain with the mother and father. For the most part, these are intangible benefits, but they are nonetheless real." . . .

Certain courts have ruled in favor of granting the parents a cause of action, without discussion of the question of damages. Others have recognized the cause of action, but refused to apply the standard measure of tort damages. They limit the recovery permitted, using the same public policy reasons cited in Rieck v. Medical Protective Soc. For example, in Jacobs v. Theimer, . . . the court was faced with a demand for the cost of raising a child afflicted with defects resulting from rubella, who would have been aborted except for alleged negligence. The court allowed recovery for costs reasonably related to the child's physical defects but excluded expenses to be incurred in raising the child, following another Texas case, Terrell v. Garcia . . . in which the court said at page 128: "Who can place a price tag on a child's smile or the parental pride in a child's achievement? Even if we consider only the economic point of view, a child is some security for the parents' old age. Rather than attempt to value these intangible benefits, our courts have simply determined that public sentiment recognizes that these benefits to the parents outweigh their economic loss in rearing and educating a healthy, normal child."

Similarly, in Coleman v. Garrison, . . . parents of a healthy child born of a failed sterilization operation were limited to their actual expenses and anxieties attending the unexpected pregnancy.

A third group of cases recognizes the parents' cause of action and gives damages according to normal tort principles, without limitations based on public policy. For example, in Ziemba v. Sternberg . . . the court said that " 'the person responsible must respond for all damages resulting directly from and as a natural consequence of the wrongful act according to common experience and in the usual course of events, whether the damages could or could not have been foreseen by him.' "

In *Custodio*, the court dealt at some length with the problem presented here. The policy arguments against the parents' cause of action advanced by courts in other jurisdictions were analyzed, subjected to critical review, and finally rejected in favor of the concept that the usual damages recoverable under established tort principles should be recoverable upon a proper finding of malpractice in a case of this type.

In Troppi v. Scarf, . . . the court gave a lucid rebuttal to the various policy reasons used to deny a cause of action to the parents, or to limit their recovery, against the normal rules of tort damages. In that case, the defendant druggist negligently failed to provide the birth control drug prescribed for plaintiff mother. It resulted in the birth of an eighth child. The court concluded that there was no valid reason why the trier of fact should not be free to assess damages as it would in any other negligence case. . . . The court said that contrary to the idea that to allow damages would be against public policy, both state and federal governments encourage birth control.

Considering the argument that a child always confers an overriding benefit to the parents, the court applied the rule announced in the Restatement of Torts, section 920, page 616, as follows: "Where the defendant's tortious conduct has caused harm to the plaintiff or to his property and in so doing has conferred upon the plaintiff a special benefit to the interest which was harmed, the value of the benefit conferred is considered in mitigation of damages, where this is equitable."

The court in *Troppi* also considered the argument often raised: that parents of the unwanted child should either pay for the child's upbringing themselves or put the child out for adoption.

Many parents feel a moral sense of obligation to bring up as best they can a child unwanted at the time of conception. "A living child almost universally gives rise to emotional and spiritual bonds which few parents can bring themselves to break." No court can say as a matter of law that every mother, wed or unwed, is required to abort or place her child for adoption. . . .

In our opinion the holding in *Custodio* correctly states the law of this state and, along with similar cases such as *Troppi*, clearly demonstrates the weakness of the policy arguments which would limit full compensation recoverable for tort as provided in Civil Code section 3333. Accordingly, plaintiff Hannah Stills, in the event the triers of fact find in her favor on the liability issue, should be permitted to recover all the damages to which she is entitled under ordinary tort principles. Under those same principles the defendants may prove any offsets for benefits conferred and amounts chargeable to a plaintiff under her duty to mitigate damages.

The judgment of nonsuit as to the purported claim of plaintiff Jessie Stills, by and through his guardian ad litem, is affirmed. The judgment against Hannah Stills, individually, and in favor of the respondents Richard M. Gratton and Allen F. Smoot, is reversed and the matter is remanded to the trial court for proceedings in accord with the views herein expressed. Costs are awarded to appellant Hannah R. Stills.

NOTES AND QUESTIONS

1. Analogous problems arise in cases of pregnancy resulting from failed contraception. A leading case is Sherlock v. Stillwater Clinic, 260 N.W.2d 169 (Minn.1977) (child born as result of failed sterilization).

2. Do you understand why Jessie Stills was denied a cause of action in this case? Suppose that, instead of a "healthy, happy youngster," he was, because of a known genetic condition in the mother, seriously deformed at birth. Should that give him an action against Drs. Gratton and/or Smoot? Held yes, in Curlender v. Bio-Science Laboratories, 106 Cal. App.3d 811, 165 Cal.Rptr. 477 (2d Dist. 1980). The case also contains *dicta* to the effect that a defective child might have an action against parents who failed to prevent the birth of a probably (certainly?) defective fetus. Stills was treated by the court as a case in which the only injury alleged was illegitimacy, and the Curlender court agrees that illegitimacy is not legally damaging.

3. The Curlender opinion includes a review of the cases in other jurisdictions. See also Comment, Father and Mother Know Best: Defining the Liability of Physicians for Inadequate Genetic Counseling, 87 Yale Law Journal, p. 148, 1978.

4. One way to characterize the developments in the U. S., beginning with Griswold, is that the scope for freedom of choice about whether or not to have children has been significantly enlarged by the removal of substantial legal impediments to the free exercise of such choice. This should result in the birth of fewer unwanted children. The following excerpt

discusses this point and relates it to data on wanted children in the U. S. (NFS in the excerpt refers to the National Fertility Study).

Charles F. Westoff and Norman B. Ryder, The Contraceptive Revolution, Princeton: Princeton University Press, 1976.

Unwanted Fertility. Probably the best-known part of the NFS has been the estimation of the incidence of unwanted fertility in the United States. This subject has been of particular importance in population policy debates and thus has been subject to more criticism and methodological discussion than less controversial topics. The first estimates from the 1965 NFS were that, if American women had avoided all unwanted births in the 1961–65 period, well over four million births would have been averted; moreover, the cohort of 1921–30 would have experienced an average of 2.5 births rather than 3.0 births. The 1970 NFS produced estimates of a potential 2.65 million births averted in the 1966–70 period and a calculation that the elimination of unwanted fertility would have taken the cohort of 1926–35 almost two-thirds of the way down to replacement level fertility.

The population policy implications of this research can hardly be exaggerated. Only a few years ago there were voices calling for various radical measures to reduce U.S. fertility. The evidence that important and perhaps sufficient demographic change could be effected by facilitating the prevention of unwanted births—a nonradical, comparatively inexpensive and, for the most part, politically palatable "solution"—played a genuinely important role in the deliberations and ideological tone of the final report of the Commission on Population Growth and the American Future in 1972. It seems curious, if not ironic, that if unwanted fertility were nonexistent today, a scant three years later, U.S. period fertility would be considerably below replacement.

The measurement of unwanted fertility is a complex business at both the interview and the analytical stage, and we have almost certainly not yet said the final word on the subject. The meaning of the concept as communicated to the respondent, the problems of recall and *post factum* rationalization, the reliance on the wife's report only, the simplistic notion that a baby was either wanted or unwanted when our everyday impressions tell us that there is a large gray area of indifference or nonrational behavior—all of these and more remain unresolved difficulties.

The analytical difficulties were encountered in trying to determine the trend in unwanted fertility during the decade of the 1960's. The average number of unwanted births per women showed less decline across cohorts than we expected. The decline in the number wanted, however, implied an increase in the amount of time women were exposed to the risk of having an unwanted birth. Thus, when unwanted fertility was measured by relating the number of unwanted births to women-years of exposure to risk, a rather significant decline (more than a third) emerged across the decade.

The greatest declines in unwanted fertility rates were observed among blacks and among white Catholics. The race differential still existed as of 1966–70, with a rate twice as high among blacks, but signs of rapid convergence were evident. A similar and related convergence among educational categories is in process. The difference between Catholics and non-Catholics has virtually disappeared.

Fertility. The ultimate demographic objective of our interest in the subject of fertility control, on which we have concentrated so heavily in the 1970 NFS, is better understanding of differences and trends in fertility itself. Two socioeconomic characteristics have been singled out for special attention: education and income. Education has been shown consistently to affect fertility control and fertility, presumably through its exposure of individuals to different values, interests, and skills which play an important role in determining their routes through life. Over and above its connections with education, income has received special attention because of the provocative theoretical work produced by the "new home economics" school, in which income is viewed as constraining choice on the exercise of preference for children in competition with other consumer preferences.

The trend in fertility has been measured by two comparisons: the more or less completed fertility of women aged 35–44 in 1970 (the birth cohort of 1926–35, whose prime reproductive years spanned the baby boom and who produced the highest fertility in recent U.S. history) compared with an index of marital fertility analogous to the period total fertility rate for the years 1966–70, and then a comparison of this period rate with the same kind of rate calculated for the years 1961–65, derived from the 1965 NFS. The cohort fertility and the more recent period fertility have been partitioned into "wanted" and "unwanted" components (the 1961–65 rate was not so partitioned because of the problems of comparability between the 1965 NFS and the 1970 NFS in the measurement of unwanted fertility).

The following generalizations have emerged from our analyses:

1. Nearly all the excess of black over white marital fertility is due to the considerably higher unwanted fertility among blacks. Given the substantial reduction in the unwanted fertility rate among blacks, a rapidly increasing convergence of black and white marital fertility can be expected during the current decade.

2. Such a convergence was clearly evident during the 1960's in the trends of Catholic and non-Catholic fertility because of the greater decline among Catholic women. The differential remaining in the period fertility of 1966–70 (15 percent) is, unlike the white-black difference, due to differences in the number of children *wanted.* The source of this difference between Catholics and non-Catholics is suggested by the further finding that the number wanted among

Catholics, but not the number of unwanted births, varies directly and strongly with simple measures of religious commitment.

3. Probably the best single predictor of fertility uncovered in our study is age at marriage. The demographic importance of age at marriage for fertility has been widely advertised for developing societies in which little contraception is practiced, but its force has not been sufficiently appreciated in contracepting populations. The 1970 NFS data show a strong negative association of both wanted and unwanted fertility with age at marriage, holding constant the number of years married (thus eliminating the effects of simple duration of exposure to the risk of childbearing). The reason that age at marriage exerts such an influence on fertility is that it combines mutually reinforcing biological and sociological selective factors such as fecundability and education. Age at marriage is a variable that has not received adequate attention in fertility analysis, especially considering how infrequently one uncovers variables with such predictive power.

4. A strong negative association exists between education and both wanted and unwanted fertility. For both cohort and period rates, the two components make roughly equal contributions to the overall variance of fertility across educational categories. Among blacks, however, the association between unwanted fertility and education is the main determinant of the overall fertility-education relationship. The cohort and period rate comparison among Catholics reveals the transition from an older pattern of a nonlinear association of education and fertility to the emergence of a sharp linear negative association, due almost entirely to the variation by education in the number of children wanted. This transition is due to the sharp declines in fertility of the more educated Catholic women whom our earlier research had described as highly committed to Catholic doctrine; it was the young, college-educated Catholic women who were especially attracted to the pill.

Across the decade of the 1960's, there was some narrowing of the educational differential in fertility. With the greater reduction of unwanted fertility among the less educated and the increasing educational achievement of each new cohort, there is every reason to expect that educational differences will continue to diminish and probably disappear in a decade or two.

5. The 1970 NFS provides no support at all for the hypothesis that income bears a positive relation to fertility. One can object to the use of income as a measure incorporating all of the subtleties of level of aspirations and style of life, and one can raise very legitimate questions about our measure of current income in terms of its significance for fertility decisions long past. Nevertheless, we have isolated wanted fertility as the relevant component of the consumer choice model; we have examined the association within homogeneous educational categories which in theory eliminates confounding rising

"tastes" with rising income; we have also controlled for whether the woman is in the labor force; and finally, in a separate analysis, we have defined income in terms relative to the income of people of the same social stratum. None of these refinements succeeds in reversing the slight negative correlation that income has with the completed fertility of the 1926–35 cohort.

6. The analysis of the effects of women's employment on wanted fertility and on the timing of the first birth suffers from all of the typical complications of unraveling cause and effect. The findings are usually consistent with expectation but vary considerably across racial and religious subgroups. The hypothesis of competition between childbearing and nonfamilial roles is supported by the finding that sex-role traditionalism is positively correlated with wanted fertility among whites (although not among blacks).

7. The perception of the importance of population growth as a problem may play a substantial role in the number of children desired. Among young women (under 30) who already have one or two children, the average number of additional births intended is half as great among those concerned about population growth as it is among the unconcerned. This is at least an indication that the mass media have some effect, either in actually influencing attitudes toward fertility or, perhaps more likely, in providing a highly respectable rationale for a smaller family size preferred for other reasons.

8. An examination of the trend in unplanned fertility—that is, all pregnancies that occurred despite the couple's intentions to postpone or to terminate—yields a rather striking picture: *all* of the decline in marital fertility evidently resulted from the reduction in unplanned fertility. In other words, the entire decline in births within marriage across the decade of the 1960's can be attributed to the improvement in the control of fertility. Part of this improvement is due to the increased proportion of exposure time in which contraception has been used and part to the increased efficacy of contraception, reflecting both more successful (probably more regular) use and the use of more effective methods.

QUESTION

Suppose that it seemed urgently necessary, as a matter of national policy, to hasten the decline in the U.S. birth rate. The NFS conclusions, while phrased as generalizations drawn from survey data, suggest some possible strategies. What are they? Which would you favor? Why?

Chapter 24

POPULATION PLANNING IN EGYPT

NOTE

In the U.S., it can be argued, the increased use of contraception and abortion has had little to do with any population problem, nor has it derived from a change in law. It has very likely derived instead from an underlying social change in sexual ethics that was only subsequently reflected in law, modified under the pressure of institutional litigants.

In Egypt, in contrast, the government, viewing population growth as a major barrier to economic development, has taken the initiative to seek to encourage contraception. Thus, not only has the legal change occurred through different institutions, but the legal change has in large part preceded the social change.

These materials thus highlight the temporal and causal relationships between legal change and social change. The reader is warned, however, to be cautious in making any quick judgment: the apparent failure of the Egyptian program must be interpreted not only in the light of the U.S. history, but also in the light of the apparent success of the Chinese program, that was developed in a rather similar manner.

In addition to this central theme, these materials also explore several subsidiary themes. The concept of a "right" was important in the U.S. legal decisionmaking in the population control area. What are its analogues in Islam—or, perhaps better, how are the parallel concerns reflected? And the relationship between church and state is clearly an important aspect of population control law in both nations, but in significantly contrasting ways.

A. THE CHALLENGE

1. Population Statistics

Gerald Blake, Land of One-Third of All Arabs, Geographical Magazine, 46, September 1974, p. 699.

The bare facts of Egypt's population growth are remarkable, but by no means exceptional in the developing world. Until about 100 years ago the population had probably never exceeded 4,000,000, and in 1800 numbered only 2,500,000. By 1900 it had reached 10,000,000, increasing by mid-1974 to 37,600,000, representing just under one-third of the entire population of the Arab world, and second only to Nigeria among the countries of Africa. The annual increase in recent years has been about 2.8 per cent, but in 1973 it apparently fell to 2.1 per cent; if this rate is sustained, there could still be more than

807

70,000,000 people in Egypt by the end of the century. If it rises, the population could double in twenty-five years.

The chief cause of the accelerating rate of population growth has been the sharp decline in death-rates which were among the world's highest before World War II. The rural population in particular suffered appalling health, notably from water-borne diseases associated with the dense network of irrigation canals and ditches. Resistance to disease was low because of widespread undernourishment, poor housing, and inadequate sanitation. In recent years great progress has been made in providing medical facilities, piped water and electricity, and in the spread of education, all of which have helped reduce mortality, especially infant mortality. Birth-rates, however, have remained high, between forty-three and thirty-seven per 1000. Certain traditional economic and social motives for large families remain, and young marriages and high divorce rates are still common.

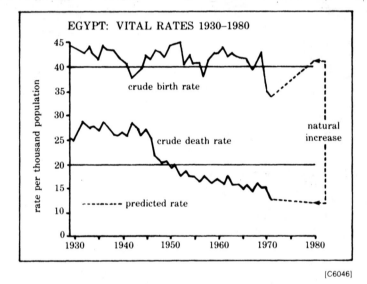

[C6046]

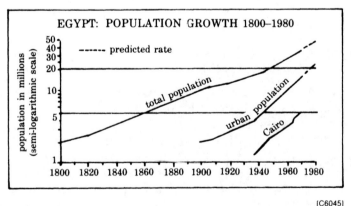

[C6045]

The implications of rapid population growth are well known. With 43 per cent of the population now under the age of fifteen in

Egypt, a high proportion are in the 'dependent' age group. An annual increment of about 800,000 people has led to heavy expenditure on imported food, and capital investment in new schools, hospitals and houses. But Egypt's problem is above all one of pressure on land. Although the area of Egypt exceeds 1,000,000 square kilometres, less than 4 per cent of the land supports more than 99 per cent of the people.

* * *

Both the cultivated area per capita, and the cropped area, which takes into account double and triple cropping made possible by perennial irrigation, are declining. A slightly less gloomy picture emerges if the rural population alone is considered, but by the end of the century, even allowing for migration to the towns, rural Egypt will have to absorb another 15,000,000 to 20,000,000 people.

* * *

In 1974 at least 45 per cent of the population of Egypt are urban dwellers, compared with only 25 per cent in 1937. There are now more than 100 towns with more than 20,000 inhabitants, including seventeen with more than 100,000 inhabitants. By far the most important urban centres are Cairo and Alexandria, the two largest cities in Africa, which together contain more than one-fifth of the total population and more than half of the urban population of Egypt. Cairo ranks about tenth in the world with an estimated 5,600,000 inhabitants in 1974, and Alexandria about thirty-fifth with 2,300,000 inhabitants. Greater Cairo region, with a population approaching 8,000,000 is one of the world's great conurbations.

NOTE

For more detailed statistics, see Abdel R. Omran, "The Population of Egypt, Past and Present," in Egypt: Population Problems and Prospects, Abdel R. Omran, ed., 1973; and RAPID (Resources for the Awareness of Population Impacts on Development), Egypt; The Effects of Population Factors on Social and Economic Development (undated AID contractor document).

2. The Sociological Background—Two Views

Abdel R. Omran, "The Fertility Profile," in Egypt: Population Problems and Prospects," Abdel R. Omran, ed. Chapel Hill: University of North Carolina Press, 1973, pp. 73, 101–102, 104, 108–109.

Rural Orientation of the Society. Preeminent among the high fertility determinants in Egypt is the pervasively rural orientation of society. Despite the rapid increase in the percentage of the population residing in urban areas, the dominant character of the society remains rural; this applies not only to the peasants and emergent industrial labor force but also to political leaders, intellectuals, the military elite, and the religious hierarchy. This rural orientation is unequivocally supportive of high fertility performance through all the mechanisms discussed below, including the agrarian economy, the value of children, the status of women, marriage customs, the high preference for male offspring, and the threat to family formation posed by high childhood mortality. The complex interactions of all these sociocultural factors—and not mere residence in an urban or rural community—shape family ideals and values and ultimately determine fertility performance.

* * *

The Value of Children. The traditional appreciation of children inherited by modern Egyptian society rests on strong religious and economic grounds. Probably no other religion places greater emphasis on the family or attaches greater value to children than does Islam. For centuries, the family has been the cornerstone of Egyptian society. In addition to the immense cultural and emotional satisfaction children have traditionally brought Egyptian parents, children in Egypt—as in most other agrarian societies—have been perceived as economic assets and perhaps even necessities. Particularly when cotton completely dominated Egypt's economic system, an additional child meant more of the cheap labor that was essential for cotton cultivation.

* * *

The economic burden of raising a child in a competitive society has become more pronounced in recent years with the realization, for example, that a child without vocational or university education will be lost in a society with shrinking opportunities for unskilled laborers. Because a large slice of a family's budget is needed to accommodate the health and educational needs of each child, fewer children per family greatly increase the likelihood that parental aspirations for their children will be fulfilled. Supportive of this new shift is the relative improvement in childhood survival.

Preference for Male Children and the Problem of Childhood Mortality. In Egypt there is an unmistakable preference for male offspring which is reflected, for example, in the inheritance system, which allocates male offspring double the share of the female. Much of the old tribal culture still permeates Egyptian society, attaching great value to the male as protector of family prestige, honor, and property. There is also great economic dependence on the male members of the family—whether father, brother, husband, or other relative.

Because of comparatively high childhood mortality, many families have felt the need to have a "surplus" of children in order to assure the survival of at least one male child. This inclination is reinforced by the regard for sons as "social security" for aged parents.

* * *

Education and Standards of Living. Considerable advances in educational and living standards as well as great strides toward the emancipation of women have been made since 1952. Several local and nationwide research projects have confirmed the almost universally strong relationship between education of both husband and wife, their socio-economic achievement, and their fertility behavior.

* * *

Marriage Practices. Marriage is considered a sacred institution in Egypt and is the goal of every boy and girl. It is also the only legitimate context for sexual gratification. Marriage is usually consummated at a relatively young age, sometimes in violation of the 1923 law which set the age of marriage at 18 for males and 16 for females. Among the numerous social advantages of early marriage in a traditional, predominantly rural-oriented society, the following deserve mention:

1. Early marriage is felt to preserve the girl's and the family's honor. Premarital relations are not accepted; virginity is revered and expected of every "good" girl. Hence, the earlier a girl marries, the lower is the risk of her exposure to situations in which she might lose her virginity. Even though Egyptian society is changing rapidly, the high value attached to virginity remains virtually unchallenged, and it is doubtful that the chastity norm will change in the near future.

2. It is felt that the earlier a girl is married the greater is the likelihood of her compatibility with the habits and tastes of her husband's family.

3. Because of the short life expectancy and excessive childhood mortality that prevailed until recently and because of the interest in heirs and in large families, early marriage provided the extended reproductive period needed to achieve large families.

4. Marriage is the norm in the society, and even today many Egyptians think it shameful for a woman to remain unwed.

5. Marriage and children are visible symbols of male virility and female fertility, both of which are highly valued in the society.

6. Marriage is a form of social security, especially for girls and their parents, for whom a major concern is to guarantee a secure life for their daughters.

7. The low literacy rate among women and the short time of "compulsory" education also make the female receptive to early marriage. In more recent years the increased educational opportunities available to women and their acceptance in employment have helped somewhat to postpone marriage. Education of men also affects marriage age. Sample surveys have found an increase in the age of marriage of the wife with an increase in husband's educational level. Expansion of the economy, greater job opportunities—even among the less educated—and rising social and economic aspirations have en-

couraged males to postpone marriage until they are economically secure.

Another feature of marriage in Egypt is polygamy. Although it is still legal (a man may have as many as four wives), polygamy is discouraged by the state. Its prevalence has declined considerably and is expected to decline further as the processes of modernization—urbanization and the education of women, for example—continue. The quantitative contribution of polygamy to fertility is hard to assess from census data; qualitatively, however, it represents another facet of the high fertility complex which has traditionally dominated Egyptian society.

Nadia Youssef, "The Status and Fertility Patterns of Muslim Women," in Women in the Muslim World, Lois Beck and Nikki Keddie, eds., Cambridge: Harvard University Press, 1980, pp. 69, 71, 76–79, 81, 84–87.

* * *

The two poignant observations of this study are, first, that all Muslim countries exhibit a very high fertility, despite pronounced diversities in ethnic background, economic infrastructure, and political ideology. Second, Muslim fertility levels on all variables are higher than those of non-Islamic countries currently at comparable levels of economic-industrial development.

* * *

From the outset it should be emphasized that the gap between the legally available options and rights and those that are accessible to Muslim women in actuality is very large. This is not only because of structural barriers, but because of prevailing cultural ideals that render many options in different life sectors totally unacceptable for women. Hence, Muslim society contains few explicit official and legal injunctions discriminating against women in public life. Even when these exist, they are of minimal importance when compared with censorship and control in the form of social stigmatization penalizing women who threaten to violate morality taboos.

* * *

Two interrelated considerations are of importance in understanding how kinship and family organization affect the status of women in Muslim society. One is the stipulation that a woman belongs to her agnatic group. This originally tribal concept has several structural ramifications. First, explicit provisions are made within the kinship unit for a male relative from the agnatic line to be economically, legally, and morally responsible for a kinswoman regardless of her marital status. The second consideration pertains to the criterion of familial pride and ratification of male identity in the Muslim community, which depend largely if not exclusively upon conformity to behavioral norms that are conceived as having to do with male "honor."

The honor is realized critically and importantly through the chaste and discreet sexual behavior of womenfolk in a particular man's life: premarital chastity of the daughter and sister, fidelity of the wife, and continence of the widowed and divorced daughter or sister. These are basic principles upon which a family's reputation and status in the community depend. Such principles of honor are at the highest level of cultural valuation and have a clear structural meaning. They reflect a solid corpus of cultural strictures that control behavior and act as effective checks on social relationships.

* * *

Honor alone, however, is not sufficient as a cultural ideal to implement control. For kinship sanctions to become fully effective, it becomes incumbent upon the kinship group to provide economic support for its women at all times. This is exactly what has happened up until now in most Muslim societies: the perpetuation of the status of women as economic dependents. Few women have felt the need to be self-sufficient through education or employment because of the availability of economic support. It is only when family responsibilities for the economic support of female relatives begin to be questioned that the present structure of control and the prerogative of male family members to impose restrictions on their women will become nebulous.

* * *

It is self-evident that a social system wherein men have continually to safeguard against a woman's sexual misconduct or suspicion thereof requires a strong machinery of social control geared to secure the segregation of the sexes and to guarantee nonexposure to viable alternatives to marriage. Thus, Muslim societies are characterized by numerous and highly effective institutional mechanisms that preclude contact with the opposite sex. To mention only a few: sex segregation in most public and private schools, rigid sex segregation at work, and informal separation of the sexes in most recreational and often familial activities.

Tight control through an early and parentally supervised/controlled marriage, as well as strict seclusion before that event, instill the idea that only one life exists for the woman. Motivation is channeled in the direction of marriage by creating desires for familial roles, by extolling the rewards accruing from the wife-mother status, and by severe community censure of spinsterhood. Alternatives to marriage are seen as compromising a girl's sex ethics and as potential threats to her eventual chances of marriage. The mere fact that a girl may be highly educated or employed will often jeopardize her chances of a good match. In the marriage market the working girl is still judged by many as loose, immoral, and, in certain cases, promiscuous, in contrast to those girls who are secluded in their homes and thereby considered paragons of virtue and chastity.

Given these circumstances, it is not surprising that very few young women continue their schooling beyond age fifteen, however late they may actually marry. It is also understandable why the number of single women employed outside the home is so minute. In Turkey, Syria, and Egypt, for example, among every one hundred single women only six, eight, and ten, respectively, are employed in income-earning activities in the industrial and service sectors. Among these, there are many from the ranks of the more highly educated segment. For example, 42 percent of all the single women employed in Egypt, and 35 percent of those employed in Syria, hold either professional or white collar jobs. Such women represent the urban elite minority who, because of their location in the stratification system, are spared much of the moral censure imposed on other social groups. It is important to realize, however, that the progressive attitude of this minority and their families does not imply a general acceptance of permanent legitimate alternatives to marriage. In Muslim society modernity is often a struggle to incorporate higher female education and occupational emancipation within the traditional boundaries that define roles in terms of marriage and motherhood, rather than an attempt to restructure relationships between the sexes in relation to society.

Societal mechanisms have succeeded well in channeling young girls into marriage by penalizing the single status. This is done in several ways. Whereas in other societies an unmarried girl who is educated or working enjoys emancipation from parental control, a more favorable position in the marriage market, and economic independence, in Muslim society she accrues none of these advantages. Her education, her employed status, and even her professional standing will not liberate her from traditional family restraints. The kind of freedom in decision-making that employed Western women know is practically unknown to employed unmarried women in the Muslim world. Working girls are expected to continue to live with their parents until marriage, to contribute their earnings to the family budget, to be restricted in their social life, and in many cases to be denied the right to choose when and whom to marry. Because activities involving the public are so easily linked with suspicions of promiscuous behavior, women who attend the university or go to work are likely to come under the continual scrutiny of their family in every move they make outside the home. It is precisely because of this strict control that marriage comes into perspective for the single woman as an avenue of greater freedom.

Yet Muslim girls are not legally compelled to seclude themselves prior to marriage; neither can they be legally forced into an early marriage. Such decisions often involve self-choices that could not have been sustained for long unless powerful mechanisms were operating in Muslim society to motivate the woman herself.

* * *

It is imperative to counteract the effective socialization young Muslim girls are subjected to, through educational and occupational enticements that would influence the desirability of marriage and motherhood, particularly at the young ages. However, any attempt to redefine the desirability of marriage will also have to recognize the parentally controlled marriage structure that prevails in most of the Muslim world. The gut issue here is how to release parents from the intensive compulsion to marry off their children, particularly at such young ages. Muslim parents as decision-makers have strong vested interests in their children's marriage—particularly the daughters' marriage since this constitutes an independent source of prestige and honor. Such a reward will not be relinquished easily unless it is replaced by an equally powerful and socially supported set of benefits and advantages. The kind of restructuring that is urgently needed requires manipulation of the social framework in such a way that "parents can indulge themselves by personally consuming the economic and social goods that their children may offer them, rather than pushing the offspring to devote their principal energies to a new generation."

Until now the social advantages derived from a daughter's early marriage have outweighed the possible economic benefits that could have accrued from her income-earning activities. With the advent of higher levels of economic development in the Muslim world, rising levels of expectations and aspirations may well create a situation where families will need to depend upon additional sources of income that a well-trained and employable unmarried daughter can provide.

* * *

The status and position of the married woman in Muslim social structure is most difficult to define. Traditionally, her inferior status has been underlined within the context of rigid systems of marital role allocation that uphold separate male and female worlds. The monopoly of suprafamilial activities is in the hands of the husband; wives are secluded and related to home care and children. This division of labor is supported by the age gap (typically 8–10 years) and the educational disparities between husband and wife.

There exist more critical aspects, related to the religio-legal prescriptions under which the Muslim wife functions, that provide grounds to argue for her subordinate position in the institutional structure. The principle of sex equality within the family and upon marriage is not provided by Islamic law, which governs Muslim family institutions in nearly all Islamic countries. In defending Islam against the accusation that it discriminates against women, apologists argue that Islamic law has always granted married women independent legal and property rights—a privilege only recently acquired by women in the Western world. We know well that such legal rights are often not implemented, for male family members appropriate their daughters'/sisters' property holdings on the grounds that these women will need economic support in case of divorce, separation, or widowhood. Even when a property right is protected, by itself it hardly outweighs the patriarchal arbitrariness of many of the legal codes regulating family behavior. By twentieth-century standards, the religio-legal sanctioning of polygamy; the husband's unilateral power in divorce, in custody over his children, and in enforcing the return of a rebellious wife; unequal female inheritance; and unequal weight to a woman's legal testimony can hardly be viewed as congruent with a married woman's equal position. Not all Muslims take advantage of these privileges. Nevertheless, their mere legal endorsement functions as a constant source of anxiety to many married women.

That Muslim women lack social and economic options outside marriage (which obviously constrains their behavior within marriage), often lack the freedom to marry the man of their choice, and are discriminated against by family and marriage laws mean that the Muslim wife occupies a subordinate status. However, within her domain—the women's world—the Muslim wife is given great respect and a considerable degree of real familial power. This is shown in her relationship with her husband, her strong influence over her children even when they are adults, and her special position within her parental home by virtue of her having attained the marriage and motherhood position. Women can draw on many sources of valuation for two reasons: one is that marriage and motherhood roles are greatly valued in the community and hence given very high status and respect, and two, that such high roles can be filled only by women.

* * *

Until recently, the Muslim wife has tended to accept her world. Outside of a highly educated and politicized minority, I have not found Muslim wives to perceive their status and role within the home and in relation to their husband as "subordinate," "oppressed," "inferior," or "powerless." Women's acceptance of their world reflects the combined effects of "false consciousness" and a highly effective socialization process. It may also indicate a volitional avoidance by the average wife of entering the mainstream of "modern life" at the risk of threatening the security and power she has accrued in her "own" world.

* * *

What inferences can be drawn from this discussion concerning fertility in Muslim society? As the situation is now, all seems to point to the maximization of natalist tendencies. Muslim women are fully cognizant of the need to attain marital position and motherhood for commanding respect and status in their own kin group and community. They are not about to deemphasize willingly the only role that now gives them a bargaining position in the social structure. Children represent much more than a form of social insurance against the threat of divorce or polygamy, for women derive status from motherhood even when divorced or rejected for a second wife. Offspring guarantee to the woman status and respect that extends far beyond her position in the conjugal home and reaches into the heart of her own family's and the community's valuation of her. Hence we may expect women to continue childbearing activities throughout their reproductive years—whether they are happy in their marriage or not. When Muslim countries report an average of seven live births per married woman and the extension of reproductive behavior to more advanced ages beyond thirty-five years, we should be able to appreciate the importance of maternal-related roles.

The highly educated Muslim wife is often ready to explore external sources of prestige and satisfaction, but not, however, to the exclusion of her maternal role. There is evidence that higher female education (particularly university) is accompanied by considerably reduced fertility and a relatively high proportion of employment in professional jobs.

The optimistic expectation of most demographers that an increased participation of married women in the work force will reduce reproduction within marriage has, however, to be approached with caution, as many Muslim working wives are able to escape the contradiction between the economic and familial role, which is a prerequisite for labor force participation to affect fertility. The availability of inexpensive domestic help and accessibility to baby-sitting provided by family members enable many working wives to combine the activities without much strain or guilt. Hence it is doubtful that the supply of female labor in Muslim countries is influenced by the number, spacing, and ages of children or that a substantial entry of married women into the work force will mean a reduction in fertility. Women who work have adjusted themselves to selecting occupations that allow some flexibility in work conditions: specifically, lower-class wives are mostly involved in cottage-type manufacturing, while upper-class wives choose careers in teaching, which enable them to plan childbirth during the three months' summer vacation.

NOTE

The traditional Egyptian pattern of women's rights in Egypt was probably one of the less discriminatory of the Islamic world, but change was late.

Gabriel Baer, "Social Change in Egypt: 1800–1914" in P. M. Holt, Political and Social Change in Modern Egypt, London: Oxford University Press, 1968, pp. 135–136.

* * *

Although the forerunners of a feminist movement had appeared as early as the end of the nineteenth century, their aims were as yet very modest and their influence on actual life was not felt until much later. At the beginning of the twentieth century male and female society were no less segregated from one another than at the beginning of the nineteenth. Urban women did not unveil or emerge from their seclusion before the First World War, while in some regions fellah women had not worn a veil even a century earlier. But where peasant women used to veil in the nineteenth century, they continued to do so in the twentieth (for instance, women of well-to-do fellah families in certain parts of Upper Egypt). The wife was supposed to be submissive, obedient, devoted, and respectful to her husband. He could easily divorce her, and urban husbands frequently used this right. According to authors who wrote at the end of the nineteenth and the beginning of the twentieth century, polygamy was relatively common not only among wealthy families but also among the lower classes. None of the legal reforms relating to the status of Muslim women had been introduced before the First World War.

* * *

NOTE

The following excerpt, prepared for an international symposium on Law and the Status of Women, and almost certainly intended to present a glowing picture, is revealing:

Attiat El-Kharboutly and Aziza Hussein, Law and the Status of Women in the Arab Republic of Egypt, 8 Columbia Human Rights Law Review, 1976, p. 35.

. . .   the spirit of Islam itself should be a source of inspiration for social change. It has inspired change in the past. For example, the Muslim women's rights to property and a legal status independent from that of her husband were both accorded to her more than 14 centuries ago.

III. Political and Civic Rights

The granting to women in 1956 of the right to vote and the opportunity to be elected to public office was their first recognition as full citizens. Now that the door to women's participation has been opened, women have been elected to the National Assembly. The eight newly elected women will most certainly be concerned with the status of the Egyptian woman in the family.

As a deterrent to polygamy, family identity cards are now required for the registration of a marriage contract. These cards indicate the marital status of the bridegroom and by this means plural marriage based upon deception is avoided.

The main argument still existing in favor of polygamy is that although many problems attend the practice, plural marriage is in many instances the lesser of two evils. For example, in the case of a wife's sterility, the alternative to polygamy is divorce and remarriage. Another argument in its favor is that it is in the best interest of the children of the former marriage. In any event, the percentage of plural marriages is relatively low, constituting three per cent of the total marriages in Egypt.

NOTE AND QUESTIONS

For additional information, see the other articles in L. Beck and N. Keddie, Women in the Muslim World (1978); E. Fernea and B. Bezirgan, Middle East Muslim Women Speak (1977); A. Khalifa, Status of Women in Relation to Fertility and Family Planning in Egypt, (National Center for Social and Criminological Research, Cairo, 1973).

1. Admitting that there is some overlap between Omran's and Youssef's arguments, what differences are there in the two analyses? Which analysis do you find more persuasive?

2. Under which of the two analyses will economic progress lead to significant slowing of the population growth rate? Under which analysis would the government find it easier to slow the population growth rate? Does the Youssef article suggest a dilemma that the traditional economic supports for women must be destroyed before birth control becomes attractive?

3. Both Omran and Youssef suggest that the family stucture encourages high fertility. What aspects of the inheritance law discussed in Problem 1 are especially relevant?

4. Would you expect a movement to arise in Egypt similar to that which brought the contraception and abortion issues to the U.S. Supreme Court? How about a women's rights movement?

5. After reading these materials, please outline the type of population control program you would choose if you had to define one for Egypt.

B. ISLAMIC DOCTRINES AND THE ROLE OF RELIGION

NOTE

With minor exceptions, the discussion has so far considered Islamic doctrines only as they affect the population issue indirectly through family structure. There is also a more direct, although limited, effect derived from the *sharia's* permission and prohibition of specific population control techniques. Because these restrictions are viewed as coming from God rather than the state, they become limitations upon what the government can do, and almost amount to "rights" comparable to those found in Western privacy law.

1. Traditional *Sharia* Views and Their Evolution

Ahmad El-Sharabassy (Al Azhar), Islam and Family Planning, 1965, Sayed Ismail, translator, Cairo: The Egyptian Family Planning Association, 1969, pp. 114–115, 135–140, 143–146, 149–150.

RÉSUMÉ

We may now conclude our discussion with a résumé centralised on the following points:

(1) The family is the basis of society in Islam. It issues from the sacred bond of marriage. Islam therefore encourages marriage and the formation of a family.

(2) Children are held in high esteem and veneration. They are acknowledged as a great bounty from God. To bring them up soundly certain responsibilities and obligations must be undertaken by the parents. If this is not possible they would turn into misfortune and evil. It is the duty of the married couple to avail themselves to shoulder these responsibilities.

(3) Islam does not forbid married couples from temporary birth control; providing the methods used are legal and the circumstances that prompt it are valid and legitimate. Birth control must be practised by mutual consent and it must not be injurious to either party.

(4) Family planning is not a public law. It is neither a permanent ordinance nor a system to be applied by the whole community. It is subjected to various individual conditions and circumstances. In duress and under pressure each person may adopt it according to his requirements. It can be adopted when required and dispensed with when the necessity is removed.

(5) The necessities that urge the practice of birth control are varied. Some are social, others economical and some are purely for health reasons. Without any legitimate reason, birth control is forbidden.

(6) There exists a clear distinction between birth control and induced abortion. While under pressure of necessities the former is legitimate the latter is forbidden by concensus of opinion if signs of life are apparent in the foetus. There is however one reservation. If the harms of abortion are lesser than the harms of not aborting then it is permitted.

(7) Birth control is not the only solution to the population problem nor is it the only alternative to raise the standards of living. In fact there are other means as mentioned in the National Charter. These include raising production by developing the industrial, agricultural and manufacturing sectors, etc.

Sheikh Mahmoud Shaltout's Statement. In his book "Al-Fatwa" the late Sheikh Mahmoud Shaltout, former Rector of Azhar, discussed the question of birth control. Writing under the heading, "Progeny: Restricted or Planned", he went on to say:

Birth control, as a statute law, binding the nation to stop producing children at a specific limit, without due consideration of the prevailing differences among individuals, is something no person desires, let alone a nation that wants to exist. Such a concept is unnatural. It is rejected by nature itself which is in continuous progress. It is also rejected by the Wisdom of God.

Commenting on this, the Sheikh goes on to say that he did not believe that such were the intentions of those who advocated birth control. Elaborating on the point he added:

Birth control in the sense of planning and regulating births for women who conceive quickly, who have hereditary illnesses and such sporadic cases that cannot bear the responsibilities of children are all individual cases. It is in the same with cases that do not get the support of their well to do people. All these cases, in reality, are singular cases and may be termed as treatment cases. They are under treatment. Their sicknesses are being cured so that a healthy generation may issue.

Birth control in this case is not unnatural. It is not disliked by the conscience of the nation and is not prohibited by religion.

When religion demands a strong and healthy progeny, it is virtually safeguarding the progeny from unhealthy breeding. It also works hard to wave off any harms that beset mankind. In this respect religion has a rule:

Detrimental matters must be warded off,

This must be done to the utmost of our ability.

The theologians have therefore permitted the parents to practise temporary or permanent birth control. They are granted this permission if either of them suffers from hereditary illnesses which could easily pass unto the children and grand children.

To practise in such specific circumstances with a view of stopping its ill effects from spreading on a wide scale, is permitted by religion. At the same time it is not making it a general rule for the whole nation. The provision is specific and the cases involved are limited.

OPINION OF SHEIKH ABDUL MAJID SALEEM

Below we present the original version of the verdict issued by His Eminence Sheikh Abdul Majid Saleem, Grand Mufti of Egypt, on the 12th Thil ada, 1355 (25/1/1937). The text runs as follows:

Question. A person asked: What is your excellency's verdict on the following matter?

A married man is bestowed with a child. He is afraid that he will be put into an embarassing situation if he produces many children. He will not be able to look after them and give them the necessary education and upbringing. He is also afraid that it impairs his health and thus disable him from shouldering his responsibilities. Or that he may ruin his wife's health if she continued getting pregnant and bearing children without adequate periods of respite between each pregnancy, a period that would restore her strength and give her further vitality. In such a situation, is the husband allowed to make use of any of the methods prescribed by the physicians to avoid plenty of children?

Could they, for instance, extend the period between conception, to allow the mother to rest and save the child from social, financial and health mishaps?

Answer. We have read this query. We wish to advise that according to the opinions of the Hanafi Ulamas it is permissible to use some of the methods prescribed for birth control in the circumstances mentioned, for instance, emitting the semen away from the woman's genital passage or by using anything that would effectively seal the womb from allowing the male fluid to enter.

Originally, according to them, it was not allowed to deposit the semen away from the woman's genital passage without her consent, as it was not allowed for the women to seal her womb without her husband's permission. But later Ulamas, in view of the changing circumstances, allowed the husband the privilege, irrespective of the wife's consent, if he feared that the children would turn out to be a moral risk. The author of "Al Mughni" said:

One should consider such excuses as legitimate grounds for waiving of the wife's consent.

In the light of the above, a man travelling on a very long journey with the fear about his children and their future, may consider it a valid excuse. Deducing from the above the Ulamas of later times gave their ruling. They said it is permissible for a woman to seal her womb without her husband's consent if she has a valid excuse.

In summary we may conclude that it is permissible for both the husband and the wife, by mutual consent, to practise birth control. And in the opinion of the later Ulamas of the Hanafi sect, it is permissible to practise it, irrespective of the consent, providing there is a legitimate excuse.

It remains to be said whether abortion is permissible after conception has taken place and before life is instilled in it? The Hanafi Ulama are not agreed on this point. Generally speaking it appears that they disapprove of this and do not permit it without any legitimate excuse. We may consider the stoppage of the breast-milk of a mother who has a child, after a subsequent pregnancy a valid excuse, especially if the father cannot get any wet nurse to feed the child and fears for the child's life. As for abortion after life is instilled in the child, it is obvious that it is not permissible.

SHEIKH HASSAN MAMOON'S STATEMENT

The Grand Sheikh al Azhar, Hassan Mamoon, on the 22nd August 1964, issued a statement in the daily newspaper "Akhbar al Youm" in which he discussed "Birth Control and Islam". Therein he said:

The Islamic view on this subject is unambiguous and clear. Perhaps it is the following question that disturbs your mind:

What are the traditions of Islam in this respect? At times it invites one to marry and increase the progeny, urges the youth who can bear responsibility to marriage and invites one to marry a fertile woman who can shower plenty of love. These and many other things have forced some to think that Islam has no other opinion besides this. Of course we may be able to treat the subject from another angle which is basic and fundamental in most cases when we desire to make religious laws. And that is the decisive wisdom upon which the rules and religious laws are based and which it tries to establish. In respect to the subject we are dealing with, it was the demand of wisdom at that time to call for marriage, plenty of children and encouragement.

The Muslim society at that time was a foreign body in the pre-Islamic polytheist society. It was scanty in number, weak in influence and powerless amidst the rebellious majority which boasted of its wealth and influence. During such circumstances it was imperative upon the Muslims to increase and multiply their numbers. Not only was this essential for the defence of their new message but also against the enemy who outnumbered them heavily and constantly challenged the pure religion of God. The circumstances, as we observe them, now, have radically changed.

Our population throughout the world is now menacingly threatening the standard of living that is essentially necessary for mankind. It has reached extreme proportions. So much so that it has forced the intellectuals of every country to adopt birth control to ensure that their resources do not fail to meet the demands of their inhabitants.

Islam, the natural religion, has never opposed the benefit and advantages of mankind. On the contrary it has always vied to establish and achieve them, providing they were not against the commands of God. I, personally, do not see any objection to birth control, if,

1. it is essential.

2. enacted by the mutual good will of the people.

3. its methods are congenital and valid.

OPINION OF FATWA COMMITTEE, GAZA, PALESTINE

The Fatwa Committee of Gaza, Palestine received a query regarding birth control. The Committee replied to this query. It was published in the "Nur al Yaqeen" magazine of Ramadan 1384 Higry. Here is the text:

Religion has invited mankind to marry. The reason it gave was for purposes of pro-creation. The human progeny is created to worship the Almighty, fill the earth, and exploit its treasures, to defend land and spread virtues.

God has assured mankind of his provisions and sustenance. He has created all kinds of food and sustenance in proper measure. In the Quran we read this fact:

And bestowed blessing on

The earth, and measured therein all things

To give them nourishment in due proportion.

Surah 41—Verse 10.

In another verse we read:

And in heaven is your sustenance (also)

That which ye are promised.

Then by the Lord of heaven and earth

This is the very truth

As much as the fact

That ye can speak intelligently to each other.

Surah 51—Verses 22, 23.

In another verse we read:

There is no moving creature on the earth

But its sustenance depends on Allah:

He knoweth the time and place

Of its definite abode and its

Temporary deposit:

All is in a clear record book.

Surah 11—Verse 6.

It is for this reason that Islam waged a war against the corrupt practice of child killing and infanticide. It was the custom of the pre-Islam Arabs to bury their female children alive for fear of poverty and social disgrace. Allah warns in the Quran:

Kill not your children for fear of want:

We shall provide sustenance for them

As well as for you.

Surah 17—Verse 31.

In another verse there is a little change:

We shall provide sustenance for you

As well as for them.

Surah 6—Verse 151.

*　*　*

It surprises us to see those among us who can really afford having children, are sophisticated and cultured but are the very people who practise birth control. While those who cannot afford it and are in no position to look after their children are the very people who do not practise it. The people who are granted the permission to practise birth control do not make use of their privilege. We see the poor person producing too many children and for this reason practises polygamy. His only object is to produce a bevy of children. He is the least bothered whether the children are fit or unfit, healthy or sick. It does not worry him if his children become the cause of widespread evil on earth.

There is nothing in the world as good as religion. It has come to elevate mankind and shower it with joy, happiness and prosperity. How nice it would be if we may understand and comprehend this factor and strive to follow such a noble lead.

In conclusion I submit to God and place my trust in Him. He is the Giver of power. Salutation to the Prophet PBUH [Praise Be Unto Him], his family and his companions.

QUESTIONS

1. Several such statements distinguish sterilization from contraception. What concerns might have motivated the scholars to make this distinction?

2. Several of the theological statements carefully consider the consent of the spouse to the practice of contraception. What concerns might have motivated these scholars? How do they differ from the concerns at issue in the U.S. Supreme Court cases on spousal and parental consent?

3. The statements make a rather surprising distinction between the individual practice of contraception and a national program to encourage population control. Does this distinction appear founded in the theological sources? What concerns might it reflect? How close are those concerns to "rights" concerns?

4. How much does the formal Islamic doctrine restrict the shape of a population control program in Egypt? What about the apparent mood and tone of the religion, as opposed to its formal teachings?

5. In the face of these sensitivities, would it be better to title a program a "population control program" or a "family planning program?" What is the difference between the two emphases?

6. How important do you expect these Fatwas to be to an upper-class urban Egyptian? to a villager?

2. Abortion

Ahmad El-Sharabassy (Al-Azhar), Islam and Family Planning, 1965, Sayed Ismail, translator, Cairo: The Egyptian Family Planning Association, 1969, pp. 106–108, 109.

The Difference Between Family Planning and Abortion. At this point it is of paramount importance for us to acquaint ourselves with the basic differences between family planning, which is avoiding conception and is not a crime against the soul, and abortion which constitutes an attack on a living foetus especially after it is instilled with life. To avoid conception before the sperm meets the ovum by any unharmful, valid means is not a crime and cannot be equated with murder. The excellent exposition of Imam Ghazali, on this point is sufficient. Speaking of coitus interruptus he writes:

This is not similar to abortion or infanticide which is a crime against a being in its various stages. The first stage of being is when the sperm meets the ovum and is ready to accept life. To injure it at this stage is a crime and as the foetus begins to develop the crime becomes worse. When it becomes a clot and then a lump the crime would be much more severe. Eventually when the foetus is instilled with life the crime reaches its peak. After it is born the crime of killing it would be at its highest.[1]

In this respect the late Sheikh Shaltout, Head of Al-Azhar, has the following remarks to add:

As for abortion our theologians have dealt with the subject at length and are unanimously agreed that to perform the abortion after the soul is instilled in it, which according to them is usually after four months is a heinous crime. It is forbidden. A Muslim is not allowed to perform abortion in such a case. It would be a crime against a living soul which is complete in its flesh and form. They maintain that blood money would be necessary if the child is aborted alive and a smaller sum of money would be necessary if the child is dead. The theologians also maintain that if the continued existence of the child endangers the mother's life and her existence, then the Islamic Laws, in view of its flexibility, especially when there is no alternative between two evils but to choose one, regards abortion as lawful. The lesser evil is accommodated and abortion is permitted. The mother cannot be sacrificed for the child. She is the original source and her life is already in existence, she enjoys a place in society and has responsibilities and duties. Above all she is the pillar of the family.

It cannot be logical to sacrifice the mother of the child whose future is unknown; and who has no rights or obligations. And as for abortion in the early stages before life is put into the foetus, (before four full months), the theologians have varying opinions.

1. "Ihya al Uloom al Din" Vol. 4 page 47.

In view of the fact that there is no life in it, some theologians say that it is permissible. They do not believe that it constitutes a crime; others view it differently. They say it is prohibited and unlawful. Although there is no life in it there does exist some sort of growth and development in it.

Imam Ghazali has discussed this question. He has made a differentiation between abortion and birth control. Sheikh Shaltout has quoted Imam Ghazali's view and said:

Imam Ghazali has a novel explanation at this point. He likens the meeting of the male sperm with the female ovum, to the "acceptance and confirmation" procedures of a legal contract. Whoever offers a commodity for sale and before the other party confirms, withdraws from the contract, is not considered committing a breach of contract.

Once the acceptance is confirmed, the contract becomes binding and valid. Withdrawal thereafter would be considered a breach of contract. He believes it is the same with birth control. Once the sperm meets the ovum, abortion would be a crime.

We believe that Imam Ghazali's views and those who follow him in outlawing abortion after conception has taken place are consistent with the views of the physicians. The difference is minor and trivial. The difference is in expression. They believe that the spermatozoons are living cells that swim and struggle to reach the ovum. Once any single sperm has succeeded in making its way to the ovum the others are rejected. The theologians have accordingly made laws and ordinances corresponding with this life and its consequences. For instance any person who breaks an egg is demanded to pay liability since according to them it contains life and is the origin of the creature.[1]

As for life that comes to the child after four months it is the life that is felt and in motion. The mother begins to feel the movement of the baby and it becomes obvious and apparent. This is expressed in the traditions as the time when the spirit is blown into the child.

Perhaps the life that has been rejected by some theologians before the spirit is blown into it, is this obvious and apparent one. They do not, however, dispute that the foetus is a living organism and that this life-factor makes it possible for the foetus to absorb nourishment from the mother.

It is possible for us now to understand the reason for the differences of opinion on this point. It all results from insufficient information about the various stages through which the foetus passes. Some theologians were not fully informed of this. It could be said that the law of prohibition varies according to seriousness of the

1. The author did not discuss the state where the ovum is fertilized but not yet "implanted". The woman is not considered clinically or biologically pregnant till after implantation; hence there is no abortion if pregnancy has not taken place yet. Medical reviser.

case. Abortion before the four months is not like abortion after the four months period. The latter is serious since the development of the child is complete and there is movement.

We may now summarise the whole question. It is agreed by both groups that abortion is prohibited and forbidden. It is prohibited at all stages during pregnancy. At the same time there is proper evaluation of circumstances and emergencies. Each case will be treated according to its necessity and circumstances. In this way both the views of medicine and theology mutually harmonise.

EGYPTIAN PENAL CODE; Law No. 58 of 1937

Article 260. Whoever, by blows or other violence, willfully procures the abortion of a pregnant woman will be punished by a term at forced labor.

Article 261. Whoever, by the administration of medicine, the use or the indication of specific methods for the purpose, procures the abortion of a pregnant woman will, whether or not she has consented, be punished by imprisonment.

Article 262. The woman who has consented to take the medicines knowingly or to employ or permit employment of the indicated means, and who has in fact aborted, will be punished with the same penalty.

Article 263. If the guilty person is a doctor, surgeon, pharmacist or midwife, he will be condemned to a term at forced labor.

Article 264. Attempted abortion is not punishable.

Abdel R. Omran, "Prospects for Accelerating the Transition in Egypt," in Egypt: Population Problems and Prospects, Abdel R. Omran, ed. Chapel Hill: University of North Carolina Press, 1973, pp. 430–432.

* * *

The Rising Wave of Abortion in Egypt. Unfortunately, very little information is available on the epidemiology of abortion in Egypt. Fertility surveys give figures that are unbelievably low (7 percent in Kamel, Hanna, Wahdan, and Kamel's study, for example). Such low figures are probably a reflection of the inadequacy of the research tools and/or the unwillingness of women—especially those of traditional orientation—to admit having had an induced abortion.

There are indications from hospital statistics, however, that abortion is becoming an increasing burden on medical services. The ratios from the records of the three major university hospitals given below indicate that abortion is responsible for a high proportion of obstetric admissions.

	Deliveries	Abortions	Abortions per 100 deliveries
Alexandria (1965)	4,437	2,569	57.9
Ain Shams (1967)	3,708	1,840	49.6
Cairo (average of 1959 and 1969)	5,377	3,676	68.4

Kamal, Ghoneim, Talaat, Abdallah, Eid, and el-Hamamsy's study of hospitalized abortion in Cairo also gives some interesting details. The authors compared four groups of patients, and their data yielded the following abortion rate per 100 pregnancies (recalculated from data in Table 1 of their chapter):

	Pregnancies	Total abortions	Abortions per 100 pregnancies
Abortion group	2,104	472	22.4
Delivery group	1,356	168	12.4
Family planning clinic group	3,695	619	16.8
Private patients	1,247	254	20.4

In their original paper the authors used various criteria to conclude that some 35 percent of these abortions had been induced. They found that the family planning clinic patients admitted relatively more induced abortions (32.95 percent) than the other groups. The authors also calculated that induced abortion was responsible for 50 percent of the hospital's expenditures on maternity services.

Professor Foda and his colleagues, also at Cairo University, conducted a study of four groups of women and found that the average incidence of abortion was 19.7 per 100 pregnancies, ranging from 13.1 percent in the rural, 14.3 percent in the urban, and 21.4 percent in the hospital to 32.2 percent in the private group. The ratios of abortions per 100 live births were 66, 92, 103, and 101, respectively, with an average of 97. In all but the private groups, the incidence of abortion was highest in the low income groups while the reverse was noted for the private patients. Of interest also was the observation that 34.7 percent of all women studied practiced some form of contraception and that the percentage of women using contraceptives increased in proportion to the number of living children.

* * *

Further, if the restrictive legal code in Egypt continues to treat abortion as a criminal act *or* if the moral/ethical code of trained physicians continues to push women with unwanted pregnancies into the squalor of shanties and the hands of butchers, the anticipated result must not only include unnecessary maternal mortality and morbidity, but a deluge of complicated, septic abortion cases requiring extensive medical care and services.

Too often, physicians in Egypt and the many other countries where legal and moral taboos against abortion persist find themselves in the incongruous position of unconditionally rejecting the idea of pregnancy intervention—until faced with an incomplete or septic abortion by which time extensive damage has already been done to the mother and astronomical fiscal and human resources are required to save one life and to prevent another. Furthermore, because the treatment of septic cases is often far removed from contraceptive counseling and services, the women who somehow manage to survive this trauma are high-risk candidates for relapse. Clearly, the concerted practice of preventive medicine—with regard to unwanted pregnancies and abortions—is an urgent matter in Egypt and the many other countries with similar demographic and public health problems.

Demographic history bears witness to the fact that no country has achieved an accelerated transition within a few decades without the assistance of induced abortion. In Japan, for instance, the birth rate dropped from 34 per thousand in 1947 to 17 per thousand in 1957, a reduction of 50 percent in ten years. According to Koya, this reduction was 80 percent due to induced abortion and only 20 percent to contraception.

QUESTIONS

1. Is the abortion statute more or less severe than Islamic law? Is it likely to have derived from Islamic sources or from European sources?

2. How likely is it to be changed? Are Omran's arguments likely to be persuasive in Egypt?

C. THE GOVERNMENT'S RESPONSE

1. Background and Evaluation of the Program Through 1973

NOTE

Egypt developed an interest in population control relatively early; domestic family planning movements existed even before World War II. However, it was not until the 1960's that this interest led to a significant government program. The history and the 1960's era program are summarized in the following excerpt. For additional data on this early program, see Haifa Shanawany, "Stages in the Development of Population Control Policy," and Abdel Omran and Malek el-Nomrossey, "The Family Planning Effort in Egypt: A Descriptive Sketch," both in Egypt: Population Problems and Prospects, Abdel Omran, ed. Chapel Hill: University of North Carolina Press, 1973, pp. 219 and 189.

USAID/Egypt, Multi-year Population Strategy; Arab Republic of Egypt, March 1978, pp. 12–17, 21–24.

II. Assessment of Current Population Efforts

A. Public and Privately Financed Programs

1. The Egyptian Government's Program—Background. The Egyptian Government initiated the National Family Planning Program officially in February 1966. Program beginnings actually go back to the 1930's when family planning services first began to be offered by a few private physicians. In 1939 the Ministry of Social Affairs was organized and, as a part of its initial functions, was charged with studying the country's population problem. Because of World War II and subsequent developments, little movement on the family planning front took place until the end of 1953. At that time, upon the initiative of the Minister of Social Affairs, a National Population Commission was formed. In 1955 the Commission established 18 Family Planning Clinics to be run on an experimental basis. Ultimately the Commission became the Egyptian Family Planning Association.

The first high-level statement on the country's population problem was made in May 1962 when President Nasser proposed a National Charter (constitution) which explicitly referred to family planning. Subsequently a Population Studies and Family Planning Division was established in the Ministry of Social Affairs in 1964 and family planning work activities were undertaken in Government housing units in 1965. In 1965 the Ministry of Health (MOH) established an advisory post for family planning and introduced family planning in approximately 40 MOH clinics. In late 1965 the Government moved to coordinate the several family planning initiatives with the establishment of a Supreme Council for Family Planning headed by the Prime Minister, including various ministries, the Director of the Central Organization for Mobilization and Statistics, and the Chairman of the Executive Board for Family Planning as members. Early in 1966 the first national family planning program under the overview of the Executive Board for Family Planning of the Supreme Council was launched. In 1973, reflecting a change in the philosophy of the program, the designation of the Supreme Council was changed to the Supreme Council for Population and Family Planning.

In terms of policy orientation the Government population program has gone through various phases.

a. Traditional family planning approach. From 1965 through 1973 major focus was on the provision of clinic-based family planning service delivery additive to other health services, but delivered through the same infrastructure. The Family Planning Board viewed itself as the agency responsible for providing program leadership, direction, monitoring and supervision of service delivery. From 1971 to 1973 there was increased integration with other health services.

b. Population growth reduction. From 1973 to 1975 first steps were undertaken toward a population growth reduction policy. The Supreme Council changed its designation from the Supreme Council for Family Planning to the Supreme Council for Population and Family Planning, and the Board became the Population and Family Planning Board (PFPB). At the same time the PFPB's role was changed from that of overall administration to planning and coordination. The PFPB plan for 1973–1982 reflected a change in emphasis to focus on population growth reduction through socio-economic development and promotion of population redistribution rather than on service delivery. The plan also annunciated for the first time a statement of demographic goals.

c. Integrated developmental approach to population problems. Since 1975 population growth reduction has been the major objective of the program. The population problem, which heretofore had been defined primarily in terms of growth rate, is now defined in terms of three major interrelated aspects: growth, distribution, and characteristics (e.g., education level, sanitation, status of women, etc.).

2. The Egyptian Government's Program—Organization. Population policy is the responsibility of the Supreme Council for Population and Family Planning. The Population and Family Planning Board is the secretariat of the Supreme Council and is responsible for policy coordination, monitoring and evaluation of the activities of the ministries and organizations involved in implementing policy.

*   *   *

The Ministry of Health is responsible for implementing family planning services. The Minister of Health chairs a Ministry of Health Committee for Family Planning Services which coordinates family planning service implementation with other ministries, organizations and agencies. Within the Ministry of Health the Department of Family Planning is responsible for family planning operations, and provides guidance to the Governorate Health Services, which have administrative responsibility for services delivery. The Director General of the MOH Department of Family Planning has been designated Project Director for the USAID bilateral Family Planning Project.

In terms of implementation, the family planning program originally operated under the overview of the executive board of the Supreme Council for Family Planning. At the governorate level the Council established family planning committees headed by the governors with directors of the various governorate departments as members. In addition, branch executive boards (bureaus) were established in the governorate to supervise actual implementation of the program. Administrative and supervisory branch personnel were recruited largely from among the Ministry of Health and department staff to serve in part on an overtime basis and are in theory remunerated for this work at a rate equivalent to about 30 percent of their base pay.

In 1966, in the interest of controlling expenditures and not duplicating infrastructure, the Government decided to utilize existing Ministry of Health facilities and personnel for family planning activities. Actual government-provided family planning services are provided by the staff members of the involved health communities. Services are provided through health units in rural areas, certain units in urban areas as well as volunteer centers registered by the Minister of Social Affairs. The organization of this network has remained much the same since 1966 and now includes approximately 3,500 units, including 2,800 Government health service centers, 263 hospitals, and 446 voluntary clinics. About two-thirds of these are in rural areas. In addition, contraceptives are made available in over 2,000 pharmacies, primarily in urban areas.

The primary contraceptive method initially used was the oral pill. The IUD, which required a physician trained in the proper method of insertion, was available only at a limited number of urban clinics. Since the provision of family planning service delivery was thought to be beyond the capacity of the clinic staffs during regular clinic hours, it was decided that all such services would be offered only on a part-time basis, for a limited time (two hours), three afternoons a week in participating communities.

As no budgetary funds were available for services, consequently provision was made for incentive pay for the staff involved by earmarking the proceeds realized from sale of pills. Payment from this earmarked fund was made to the staff on a pro-rated basis, 50 percent to the physician, 25 percent to the social worker, with the remaining 25 percent being divided among the other health unit staff members. We understand the subject of incentives is under active review by the GOE [Government of Egypt].

Normally the staff of the health units in the rural areas is comprised of one general practitioner, a midwife, three assistant midwives, an assistant nurse, a sanitary and a laboratory technician, and supplemented by a social worker seconded from the Ministry of Social Affairs. Charges for contraceptives were set initially at 10 piasters per pill cycle but more recently have been reduced to 5 piasters. No charge is to be made for the IUD but the clinic is paid by the Population and Family Planning Board (PFPB) on the basis of L.E. 1 per reported insertion. Funds paid by the PFPB to each clinic for the IUD insertions also go into a general fund earmarked for pill sales and are utilized to pay clinic staff.

[The document goes on to explain that the Egyptian population program has received substantial external assistance since the mid-1960's from United Nations Fund for Population Activities, United Nations Children's Fund, World Bank/International Development Association, CARE, Ford Foundation, and International Planned Parenthood Association (IPPF).]

B. Assessment of Program Effectiveness

1. Overview. We believe it useful to start this assessment of Egypt's population program from the perspective of the Government. This is perhaps summarized by the following statement which was prepared by the Ministry of Health as a presentation to IBRD in December 1977.

> The preceding historical overview leaves no doubt as to serious government interest in the country's demographic problem. There is a declared policy, a prestigious council, a coordinating board, with 438 employees including representatives at the governorate level, and a sizeable running budget obtained from the government as well as from foreign sources. Cultural and religious attitudes are generally favorable toward the idea of family planning. The network of over 2,800 government health service centers, 446 voluntary (semi-governmental, EFPA) clinics, and over 2,000 pharmacies, is far more extensive than that found in many developing countries. The supply of medical and paramedical personnel is reasonably good. Add to this the fact that high density population living in a compressed habitable area greatly eases problems of service delivery and supervision, and the end result is a pill-oriented program which has reached some 15% of the married population in the fertile age group. Nevertheless, there are still numerous constraints which presently hinder efforts at greater optimization of program efforts.

From the preliminary results of the 1976 national census, from data from a sample survey administered in Beni Sueif Governorate, Upper Egypt, showing the impact of family planning on fertility, and from preliminary reports published recently by CAPMAS of the National Fertility Survey 1974–1975 (NFS), the following inferences have been made in relation to the size and characteristics of family planning practices in Egypt:

The distribution of women who had ever used contraceptives by the onset of use shows that less than one-half percent of the women practicing contraception started to practice right after marriage, about 17 percent started after the first child, and about 14 percent started after the second child. A further third of the women using contraceptives started to use them only after having five or more children. However, preliminary results of the NFS show a new trend of birth control practice during early years of marriage.

The 1975 data show that on a national level 60 percent of non-contracepting women want to have children at a rate of about 4.5 children. For women who ever used contraceptives the main reasons for use were as follows: 34.5 percent said they had enough children; approximately 30 percent said they were busy taking care of their present children; and 23 percent cited economic reasons.

Regarding current users (all methods), the NFS data found that 40 percent of the urban women and 16 percent of the rural women interviewed said they were using some means of contraception. Of the main methods used, 77 percent of the urban and 75 percent of the rural women were using oral contraceptives. An additional 8.5 percent urban and 9.7 percent rural women were using an IUD. Education of the respondent also had a marked relationship on the percent of current users. Those with no schooling practiced contraception at a level of 20 percent and those with schooling at 50 percent, for a national average of 26 percent.

The national data relate closely to the data from the Beni Sueif study which indicated that educated women in Beni Sueif practiced contraception at a level of 50 percent and this percentage dropped markedly to 17 percent among illiterates.

* * *

As the above suggests, despite an extensive delivery network and a variety of other favorable factors, Egypt's population efforts have met with only limited success. In fact, after an initial decline, population growth in Egypt appears to be on the increase. While the average annual growth rate declined slightly between the sample census of 1966 and 1976 (2.54% to 2.31%), sample surveys by the PFPB indicate that the rate of natural increase had risen to 2.64% in 1975 with a birth rate of 39.41 and a death rate of 12.97 per 1,000. Although the urban birth rate continued to decline slightly, the rural rate had gone back up to the pre-program rate of 43.78. With the probable continued decline in mortality, a continued upward trend in growth might well take place unless some major change in the situation takes over.

Raymond Baker, Egypt's Uncertain Revolution Under Nasser and Sadat. Cambridge: Harvard University Press, 1978, pp. 77–79.

* * *

Birth control as a developmental problem simply did not lend itself to the kind of engineering solution possible through the new administrative instruments. Effective population planning required alteration, through persuasion and coercion, of mass attitudes, values, and practices. The regime had neither the necessary ideological impetus nor the cadres even to contemplate such a massive undertaking. Instead, Egypt's leaders viewed the population question as primarily a technical issue, linked to the broader problem of economic development. In the early years of the regime it was felt that the drive to industrialize would itself solve the population problem: an industrialized Egypt would provide, if necessary, for a larger number of Egyptians; and a birth control mentality would be an inevitable by-product of life in an industrialized society.

Consequently, population planning was viewed as a low-priority, low-budget medical problem. Responsibility for the program was lodged not in a separate ministry but rather in a prestigious but largely symbolic and inoperative interministerial body, the Supreme Council for Family Planning. Created in 1965, the council was to bring together a group of officials of ministerial rank including the prime minister and the ministers of public health, higher education, national guidance (now information), planning, religious affairs, social affairs, the head of the central agency for mobilization and statistics, and the ministers of state for prime minister's affairs and local administration. However impressive the titles, the supreme council accomplished little. Initially charged to meet fortnightly, this body of overworked ministers rarely met as a group. In addition, the rapid turnover at the ministerial level typical of Egypt served to undermine its organizational coherence.

The problem of ministerial rivalries has been even more debilitating than these top-level impediments to the birth control effort. Since the population question was initially viewed primarily in its technical (medical) dimension, basic responsibility for the program went to the Ministry of Health, where it was consistently challenged over the years by the Ministry of Social Affairs. Typical of the infighting was a 1973 claim by the minister of social affairs to supervision of the program. Family planning, the minister argued, is fundamentally a social rather than a medical problem and it was originally studied by the Ministry of Social Affairs. Intolerable, according to the minister, were the efforts of the Ministry of Health to "monopolize the project." Little wonder that the press has spoken of the family planning project as an "open battlefield for a power struggle" between the two ministries.

Rivalries at the center had devastating results in the field, where personnel were frequently caught in the crossfire. Increasingly, accounts of such clashes found their way into the Egyptian press. *Al-Ahram* in April 1973 reported on one such typical incident at a family planning center in Lower Egypt. An inspector from the Ministry of Health was annoyed with a doctor who refused him inventory information that the doctor had already given to the Ministry of Social Affairs. The health department officials retaliated by submitting a report to the provincial governor accusing the doctor in question of smuggling birth control devices to Lebanon! The overlap between the two ministries has also resulted in wasteful duplication. In one area two family planning centers operated within 90 meters of one another—one administered by the Ministry of Health, the other by the Ministry of Social Affairs. When the duplication was brought to the attention of the central authorities, "both Social Affairs and Health dug in their heels with regard to their centers and, in order to resolve the dispute, the governor decided that each center should operate three days a week. However, the rivalry was the same and the dispute continued."

The difficulties flowing from the competition of the two central ministries were further compounded by the more traditional inefficiencies of each individual ministry. Officials in the Ministry of Health, for example, were wary of involvement in the population program, since its ostensibly interministerial character did place it somewhat outside the regular patterns for career advancement. Fearing that their professional rise through the grades would be adversely affected, the health ministry bureaucrats connived to transfer out of the program. Attempts to stimulate commitment led with inexorable bureaucratic logic to further corruption. Dr. Khalil Mazhar, professor of gynecology at Cairo University and first chairman of the executive board of the Supreme Council for Family Planning, initiated a system of incentives for medical workers engaged in population control activities. Proceeds from the sale of birth control pills and a special payment for the insertion of each intrauterine device (IUD) were divided among the clinic staff, with 40 percent going to the doctor, 25 percent to the social worker, 25 percent to the midwife and/or nurse, and 10 percent to the janitor.

Abuses soon appeared. After 1967, when Dr. Mazhar left the program, incentive payments were no longer made on the spot as originally planned, but had to be cleared at the center. This procedural change greatly expanded the paperwork for medical personnel. But the bureaucratic logic—and interest—behind the measure was clear: the change was advocated forcefully by the Ministry of Finance, which now took 10 piasters in tax on every 40 paid to the doctors!

Even more disruptive than the problems of increased red tape have been the corrupt practices evolved to maximize health workers' "profits" on the incentive program. Patients have been forced to buy pills while obtaining other medical services at clinics; government-issued birth control devices have been resold to pharmacies for a profit; there have also been reports of large quantities of pills reaching the Lebanese market, where their resale value is even higher. The populace generally has also sought to play the incentive system to advantage. When the program was first set up, new users as well as those who recruited them were rewarded financially. Before long, roving teams of recruiters and users were making the rounds of area clinics, putting in IUDs and taking them out—all the while enjoying the multiple monetary rewards of their exemplary civic virtue. Exposés have often revealed that clinic staffs actively connived in the whole process.

NOTE

For a more restrained critique, see Abdel Omran, "A Brief Critique for the Egyptian National Family Planning Program" in Abdel Omran, Egypt; Population Problems and Prospects, 1973. For a more recent review, see Saad

Gadalla, Is There Hope? Fertility and Family Planning in a Rural Egyptian Community, Cairo: American University in Cairo Press, 1978.

QUESTIONS

1. As between the Omran and the Youssef analysis, which one evidently served as the basis for government policy?

2. Could the government have chosen otherwise?

3. Why was the pill chosen as the technique to emphasize?

4. Why was the decision taken as a technical one with little legal logic like that of the U.S. Supreme Court?

5. Why did the program fail: Religion? Special personal sensitivities? Bureaucratic design? Something more fundamental?

2. The Contemporary Program and AID's Reaction

Excerpt from The Supreme Council for Population and Family Planning, National Strategy Framework of Population, Human Resource Development, and the Family Planning Program, (December 1980) pp. 1, 3–6, 8–9, 11–13, 15–17.

I. The Population Problem

The relationship between population problems and the state and process of development is now well-established. In a less developed country a high rate of population growth, maldistribution and adverse population characteristics place severe strains on the society's attempt to develop. Concomitantly, population trends are determined by the country's development performance. Population problems must, therefore, be tackled within the framework of overall national development plans. Egypt's population problem encompasses three interrelated dimensions: high growth rate, unbalanced spatial distribution and unfavorable population characteristics particularly in terms of health, education and the status of women.

* * *

II. National Policies

B. National Policy on Population and Family Planning

1. Objectives. Within the overall development policy of the country, the National Population and Family Planning Policy aims at the attainment of the following interrelated objectives:

a. An optimum population growth rate. This is to be achieved through lower birth rates, reduction of infant mortality and greater attention to the recent trends of emigration:

— Lower birth rates are to be operationalized by the reduction of the crude birth rate by about twenty points by the year 2000 through raising the level of overall contraceptive practice among married women in reproductive age;

— Infant mortality is to be further reduced through upgrading the efforts in the areas of health and sanitation;

— Recent trends in emigration need to be thoroughly studied in order to facilitate the development of a comprehensive strategy.

b. A better population distribution to be attained through:

— Slowing the trend of rural to urban migration in response to integrated development of the rural areas;

— The development of Egyptian deserts and the creation of new settlements.

c. Improved population characteristics particularly in the areas of health, education and the status of women to be attained through promotion of continued and renewed efforts by various ministries and agencies.

2. Policy Directions. The first national population policy declared in 1965, centered on one aspect of the population problem, viz., growth, and aimed at fertility reduction. A family planning program was developed as the instrument of this policy. It adopted a medical orientation, conforming with family planning programs in existence at that time.

Subsequently, the national population policy went through two successive stages of development. The second phase of the policy which was fully developed in 1973 can be called "The Socioeconomic Approach to Fertility Reduction". While fertility reduction was still the primary concern, the policy recognized the role of socioeconomic variables in relation to fertility and identified nine factors as critical fertility influencers which have to be manipulated simultaneously. These are: the socioeconomic standard of the family, education, the status of women (stressing participation of women in the waged labor force outside the agricultural and domestic fields), mechanization of agriculture, industrialization (with emphasis on agro-industries), infant mortality (with improvement of nutrition and sanitation as basic elements), social security, information and communication, and family planning delivery services.

The third and present population policy phase which started in 1975 may be called the "Development Approach to the Population Problem". It is an elaboration on the previous phase and has developed on the basis of a greater realization of the magnitude and implications of population growth, the limits within which it can be reduced, and a better understanding of both population dynamics and the interrelationships between population and the socioeconomic environment. This phase differs from previous policy phases in defining the population problem in its entirety, in terms of growth, distribution and characteristics.

The policy relates population activities to the three hierarchical levels of the country's administration, the central, governorate and

community levels.   The policy takes the community as its platform
for action and programs are designed to transfer the responsibility
for implementing population and family planning policy to the local
administration and community.   In this respect, efforts capitalize on
the recent law decentralizing the government's responsibilities.

* * *

III. Program Strategy Framework

This program strategy is basically in relation to population growth
and more specifically to fertility reduction.   With regards to population distribution and characteristics, intensive studies and research
are needed in order to further develop distribution and characteristics
strategies.   The national population and family planning program encompasses three interrelated programmatic areas primarily directed
towards achieving the policy objective of reducing the birth rate by
twenty points by the year 2000 through raising the prevalence rate of
contraceptive practice.

The three programmatic areas are:

A.   Upgrading family planning services integated into relevant health and social activities.

B.   Institution of community based socio-economic programs
of development conducive to family planning practice.

C.   Strengthening educational, population education and IEC
programs which aim at fertility behavior change, institution of the
small family norms, and widespread contraceptive practice.

A.   Family Planning Services

This program area aims at attaining the policy goal of increased
prevalence rate through efficient delivery of health and social care
related to family planning practice.   As an immediate goal it seeks to
capture the potential population desiring and willing to practice family planning.   It has two major components: health/social and family
planning services and contraceptive availability.   In addition, achievements in this program area will contribute to improved population
characteristics, particularly in terms of health and the status of
women.

B.   Community Based Population Oriented Socio-Economic Development Programs

Whereas family planning programs are largely responsive to behavioral changes, community based population oriented socio-economic programs aim at inducing or even precipitating behaviorial changes
consistent with the small family norms and family planning practice.
These programs are distinguished from general developmental activities in a number of ways: (i) they are population oriented, meaning
that they are selective in promoting a number of factors identified as
being strong influencers of population trends; (ii) the social and economic activities they promote are ultimately measured in terms of

population objectives; (iii) they are community based meaning that they seek popular participation in target setting, activity design and management of such activities; (iv) they are not alternatives to family planning programs but rather include health/family planning services as one of their main components.

Projects within this program area aim to contribute to fertility reduction through a number of interrelated projects simultaneously attempting to: raise the quality of health/social/family planning services, improve the status of women through functional literacy programs and greater participation in waged economic activities, promote small scale and cottage industry, improve sanitation, promote mechanization of agriculture, facilitate access to urban areas, institute cultural activities, and promote information and communication through community institutions such as mosques and youth clubs, and through community outreach workers. At the same time, the activities are designed to contribute to the improvement of population characteristics and to a better spatial distribution by making the rural village a more suitable place in which to live.

* * *

Priority will be given to projects aiming to:

— Strengthen ongoing projects.

— Expansion to nation wide coverage, including extension on a pilot scale to satellite villages and hamlets and to desert and coastal communities.

— Strengthen the components related to sanitation, upgrading the status of women, and literacy, especially women's literacy.

— A greater coordination of inputs provided by various ministries and agencies.

C. Education, Population Education and IEC Programs

1. *Education.*

* * *

3. *Information, Education and Communication (IEC).* IEC activities aim at creating and maintaining public awareness of the ill effects of rapid population growth on both national development efforts and family well-being, motivating individuals to adopt the small family norm, informing and educating the target population on contraception, overcoming adverse social reactions and misinformation, and maintaining a dynamic momentum for leadership and program personnel.

IEC programs endeavor to: reinforce the role of mass media (television, press and radio) at the national level in conjunction with the institution of regional television and broadcasting facilities; involve the active participation of various institutions such as the Ministries of Social Affairs, Culture and Information, the Supreme Council for Youth, Labour Force, Agriculture, Wakfs (Religious Affairs), reinforce the role of voluntary organizations in IEC programs, give greater emphasis in community based programs to the role of community outreach workers in home visiting; develop local community IEC programs with indigenous efforts; and experiment with action research communication programs.

Priority will be given to projects which aim to:

— Sustain and upgrade mass media IEC activities and promote their geographical diversification.

— Promote face to face and group communication as a main responsibility of community and voluntary institutions coordinated with the upgrading of training programs for IEC personnel with special emphasis on the training of community leaders and outreach workers in face to face communication.

— Create greater interaction among face to face, group and mass communication.

— Involve the active participation of the Ministry of Culture and Information.

— Promote workers education in the industrial sector.

— Promote IEC in youth programs.

— Promote the active participation of the Ministry of Wakfs (Religious Affairs).

— Involve the active participation of the Ministry of Agriculture.

— Reinforce the role of voluntary organizations in IEC activities.

— Experiment with action research communication programs.

— Promote research on IEC.

IV. Support Activities

Social Development. While aiming to preserve the genuine cultural norms of the Egyptian society, the National Development Strategy and the Population Policy aim to induce social change and social mobility conducive to influencing population parameters.

In this respect the program strategy gives priority to projects aiming to:

— Expand coverage of social securities.

— Promote women's participation in all aspects of political, social and economic activities.

— Promote programs to meet children's needs.

— Increase the role of youth as change agents.

Excerpt from USAID/EGYPT, Multi-year Population Strategy; Arab Republic of Egypt, March 1978, pp. 60-61, 63.

IV. Implications for U.S. Population Assistance

A. The Present Program

Although the United States since 1971 has provided family planning assistance to Egypt through support of international organizations and contractors, the first bilateral project agreement was signed in September 1977. . . . The project developed from a request from the Egyptian Government and was spurred by our recognition that population pressures impact on nearly all aspects of the economy, particularly development activities; hence support of a fertility reduction program was in full accord with U.S. Government policy.

Because of the lack of clearly defined Egyptian priorities, staff limitations and the press of time, project design did not undergo as rigorous analysis as might otherwise be desirable. What emerged was consciously designed as a target of opportunity approach which would permit flexibility as Egyptian priorities developed more fully, as activities were evaluated, and as our experience grew. . . .

Under the project, the Government of Egypt will be assisted to strengthen its family planning delivery system in order more effectively to deliver services to increasing numbers of Egyptians by financing technical assistance, training, engineering and construction services, commodities, and operational support (a) to increase the supply of contraceptives available in Egypt; (b) to support family planning staffing and operations of the Ministry of Health; (c) to extend the integrated social service delivery system, which is presently operating in 38 villages in the Menoufia Governorate, to all of the villages in that Governorate; (d) to improve the family planning training of medical school graduates, paramedical personnel, nurses, and social workers by developing and implementing short-term training courses, renovating the Al Galaa Maternity Hospital, developing a rural field training site integrated with the Higher Institute of Public Health, and long- and short-term participant training; and (e) to develop and carry out small-scale innovative activities involving transfers of family planning technology. . . .

B. Recommendations

We recognize that the target of opportunity approach outlined above is not the program to which we should ultimately aspire. We believe, however, that this is the best course of action for the U.S. to pursue under present circumstances in Egypt. At this time, we are reasonably sure what efforts have not succeeded in reducing fertility and why. What we do not know is what initiatives actually "work" and how effectively they do. We anticipate it will take three to five years to permit these initial activities to be implemented and evaluated, to ascertain governmental commitment, and to develop a consensus as to the specific actions which will be most effective in reducing fertility. In the meanwhile, we believe that this targeted approach will, in the short-term, have a positive effect on fertility reduction while permitting considerable flexibility for the U.S. to respond to GOE program innovations as they develop. In the medium-term, which we estimate will be five to fifteen years hence, we hope that it will be possible to shift to specifically tailored family planning activities which are themselves fully integrated within a coordinated social and economic development program targeted to effective fertility reduction.

1. *Continuing Efforts.* Therefore we recommend that for the short-term, that is, for the next three to five years, that as an integral part of our developmental assistance, we continue the approach outlined above. Our focus must be on assisting delivery of family planning services, primarily through the health sector, public and private. While family planning services delivery must be the cutting edge of U.S. population assistance, population-related activities in other (non-health) sectors can and should be encouraged wherever possible as timing is appropriate and funding available.

THE EGYPTIAN GAZETTE, MONDAY, FEBRUARY 2, 1981

Farmers accept birth control

PEOPLE in rural areas have become convinced of the importance of family planning as the only way to overcome the population explosion which threatens any development activities, according to a field study the State Information Service lately conducted.

"Most astonishing," said an official, "is that out of a sample of 2000 families, 87 per cent in the rural areas favoured the idea of family planning while the rate of supporters in Cairo and Alexandria did not exceed 80 per cent."

The results of the study are to be discussed at the International Conference on Population which opens tomorrow in Cairo under the auspices of Mrs. Jihan el-Sadat. Delegations of 14 countries will take part in the first conference of its kind to concentrate on the best ways to minimise the possibilities of population explosion.

"It was also the first time in Egypt that people have to accept the idea of small families with no more than four children," said the official "while a decade earlier people were quite satisfied with the wish to have a number of children ranging between 5 and 6."

This result proves that the Egyptian families, especially those living in rural areas, have changed to the better as regards their attitude towards the family planning call.

Answers to questions posed have reflected that change. "Our questions generally dealt with economic social and religious considerations. The answers were really stunning" said one of the researchers.

INCOME

Eighty seven per cent of people in the rural areas said that their children would not bring income to the family as much as the amounts of money to be spent on their breeding, which means a drastic change on the rural family's view about the children as a source of income.

"What has brought about such change?," a researcher asked. "The answer, of course," he continued "can be derived from a consideration of the new variables currently affecting life in the rural areas".

Such variables include: the higher wages now available for boys working in fields which makes a fewer number of boys win the large amounts a large number used to win in the past; the mechanisation of agricultural activities, which renders large numbers of boys useless; and the expansion of social insurance services which makes dependence on children in old age unnecessary — GSS

[C6822]

QUESTIONS

1. Which aspects of the Egyptian program seem most likely to you to be helpful?

2. As an Egyptian Minister of, say, Agriculture, how would you feel about the new program? Is your attitude dependent on the presence of foreign donors?

3. How does the Supreme Council for Population and Family Planning now differ from the central economic planning organization? Are overlaps in responsibility likely to create problems? What about decision-making on specific issues such as whether to encourage mechanization in agriculture, favored for population-control reasons in order to reduce the incentives to have children to help in the labor, questioned by some agriculturalists on the grounds that the fodder crops needed for the animals are also the nitrogen-fixing crops that replenish the soil?

4. Why do you think AID is still urging a device-distribution style approach?

5. Which approach do you prefer? Even if you prefer the Egyptian approach, might AID still be right in concentrating its funds on device procurement and distribution?

6. Are you persuaded by the newspaper clipping? What does it tell you about strategies?

3. Other Legal and Sociological Approaches

Nadia Youssef, "The Status and Fertility Patterns of Muslim Women," in Lois Beck and Nikki Keedie, eds. Cambridge: Harvard University Press, 1980, pp. 69, 95–96

* * *

As children in Muslim society become more difficult and more expensive to raise, a reduction in the male demand for children will occur. This is, of course, the very cornerstone of the demographic transition that has occurred in so many countries of the world. References abound in the literature as to the immediate effect this phase of the transition has had upon the fertility levels. Not much systematic research has been done, however, on the effects of a decline in the value of children upon role-related behavior and concepts of self-identity among women.

With respect to the Muslim female, the structural ramifications of a reduction in the value attached to children, and consequent lower appreciation of the only role and function from which she derived status for so long, could be severe. The danger lies in the particular mechanisms of adjustment that will be made available to women during the transition represented by a loss in the value of roles which only women can fulfill, to a restructured and redefined situation that supports and honors women's status in terms of their accomplishments in areas from which men derive their authority and prestige.

In some Islamic societies there have been structural "facilitators" to allow for the restructuring of women's role options. The beginnings of female modernism in the Muslim world cannot be traced to a feminist movement; rather it is symbiotically related to intrinsic tensions generated by rapid economic change, on the one hand, and political conditions accompanying a postcolonial era, on the other. Granted that the official stance in Muslim society toward the full participation of women in political life has been less than wholehearted, still political leaders have recently vocalized the need to mobilize womanpower for social and economic development goals. Whether official action thus far on issues relating to the status and roles of women has been primarily symbolic, statements supporting greater equality of women, the enfranchisement of women, and even in certain cases (Egypt and Iran) the appointment of women to cabinet office, have all provided a form of legitimation to any future strides women may make in the direction of greater participation in social, economic, and political activities.

But can woman's desire for greater participation in such extrafamilial activities be guaranteed? Does Islamic society provide fertile ground for the birth and growth of a feminist movement in which women would be organized to protest and rebel against their secluded position? What realistic prospects exist for a challenge to the deeply entrenched cultural ideal related to the criterion of family honor in the Muslim community, which has thus far legitimated the exclusion and seclusion of women from participation in public life? Answers to such motivational and structural issues would seem to be more important in predicting future influences upon the status of women than are those related to the attitudes of the government and the Muslim clergy.

I do not foresee in the immediate future the growth of a multiclass feminist movement in the Muslim world. The very women who could provide the leadership for a feminist movement, those with education and high social standing, generally are little inclined to do so since they suffer the fewest disabilities at present.

Rather, I would tend to locate the most crucial determinant for the continuing demise of the traditionally subordinate position of the Muslim woman in the economic constraints currently emerging in Islamic countries that are intrinsic to the process of economic modernization itself. Such constraints will increasingly challenge the control exercised by male members of the kinship group over their womenfolk and will lower the valuation of maternal related roles.

* * *

T. Paul Schultz, "Fertility Patterns and Their Determinants in the Arab Middle East," in Economic Development and Population Growth in the Middle East, Charles Cooper and Sidney Alexander, eds. New York: American Elsevier Publishing Company, 1972, pp. 400, 443–445.

* * *

It is tempting to believe that the public sector could effectively hasten the reduction in desired and actual fertility by selective policy measures. To this end, programs would promote child health, education, and interests within the family, and assist women to acquire and employ marketable skills in the paid labor force. But at the moment, the determinants of family decisionmaking and their bearing on reproductive behavior are not understood well enough to interpret them confidently. As working hypotheses, however, these inferences might help guide the more extensive micro-empirical research and multivariate analysis clearly needed in this field. At the moment, though, little is being done in the Middle East either to disseminate modern means of birth control or to discover how development policies should be structured to help more parents seek fewer children.

Among the countries of the Middle East only the government of the United Arab Republic has specifically responded to the population problem with a national family planning program. From a small-scale operation that expanded gradually from 24 clinics in 1958 to 38 in 1964, family planning activity has grown rapidly if unevenly since President Nasser's address to the National Assembly on March 26, 1964. By May 1968, 2,632 rural and urban combined service centers were supplied with pills (oral steroids) and 470 provided for the insertions of intrauterine devices, allocating 3 afternoons a week to free family planning services. By May 1968, domestic production of pills could have provided pregnancy protection for about 8 percent of Egyptian women of childbearing age, while another 2 percent may have been protected by intrauterine devices.

Though an important start has been made toward reducing the number of unwanted births, the family planning program in the United Arab Republic has also had its problems. By relying only on the provision of services through health centers rather than mobilizing field workers to personally contact, inform, and motivate all members of the population, the program is likely to reach only the already motivated, educated, and upper social and economic groups.

The second element of a population policy—influencing family size goals—has not, to my knowledge, received systematic attention in any country of the Arab Middle East. Obvious candidates for change are policies bearing on the status of women. Islamic and civil law are one in most countries of the Arab Middle East. In practice, however, the legal and religiously derived rights of women to inheritance and common property are often abrogated. Because welfare schemes and institutions are widely adopted by low-income countries directly from industrialized high-income countries, such anachronisms as child allowances and maternity benefits are written into labor codes. For example, the U.A.R. labor code shelters parents from the real costs of maternity and provides employers with strong incentives to avoid hiring women. If the population policy is judged important, precisely the opposite goals should be stressed when the government intervenes in the labor market.

Extending primary and secondary schooling to rural and urban segments of the population, particularly women, should be viewed not only as a cultural advance and an economic investment, but also as a contribution to mitigating the population problem. Assigning greater priority to achieving universal basic education than to expanding further higher education might then appear a sound development strategy. At the minimum, the interactions between educational and population policies should be emphasized more frequently and explicitly in development planning.

Finally, child and maternal health care could be expanded in conjunction with the provision of family planning services and supplies through the existing network of rural and urban combined service centers in the United Arab Republic and similar institutions elsewhere. Low-cost tetanus innoculations, nutritional supplements for pregnant women, and protein additives for young children could drastically cut death rates. Such a program would require a new ordering of policy priorities and bold and resourceful leadership, as well as probably some outside financial assistance. But by its impact on child mortality and maternal health, it could establish the preconditions for increased demand for birth control in the 1970s, a subsequent fall in birth and population growth rates, and accelerated development prospects in the 1970s and 1980s.

Haifa Shanawany, "Stages in the Development of a Population Control Policy," in Egypt: Population Problems and Prospects, Abdel R. Omran, ed. Chapel Hill: University of North Carolina Press, 1973, pp. 189, 212–213.

Other measures "beyond family planning" that have been contemplated are changes in the Personal Statute Law which is based mainly on the Islamic law, *Shareia*. The minimum age of marriage, as set by an Egyptian law of 1923, is 16 years for girls and 18 for boys; proposals at the National Assembly sessions in April-May 1970 to raise the age of marriage for girls to 20 were defeated. Dr. Khalil Mazhar, chairman of the Executive Organization for Family Planning, contended that such a change would have minimal effects on the birth rates and would simply result in unregistered marriages or behavioral deviance. It was also argued that education, particularly in rural areas, would curb early marriages and that the solution lay in convincing people to marry later rather than trying to force them to do so through legislation. Other modifications in the law aimed at restricting easy divorce and prohibiting polygamy have been under study for many years, but the relation of these to alleviation of the population problem seemed negligible to members of the National Assembly.

QUESTIONS

1. What other legal approaches might you consider in the Egyptian context? tax reforms? social security? family law or inheritance law reform? educational reform?

2. Which components of this package are likely to be politically or economically feasible? Note that there is in fact an effort to extend social security to the agricultural community and also consideration of whether various subsidy programs should stop for children after the second.

3. Is it possible that the family structure issues are completely beyond the government's control?

4. Are compulsory population control laws an option in Egypt?

5. What do you expect to be the population control impact of the fact that one-tenth of the labor force is working abroad, usually without families?

6. The official infant mortality rate is about 60 per 1000. This estimate is probably too low by a factor of about two to four. One of the major AID programs is to distribute antidehydration technologies that will help control infant diarrhea and thus lower this rate. What effect do you expect this program, if successful, to have on the population question?

4. The Government's Use of Religious Authority

NOTE

You have already noticed that al Azhar, which is in many respects subject to the control of the government, has been relatively cooperative with the government in issuing *fatwas* that provide at least general support for the population control program. In addition, certain of the regular Friday sermons in the mosques, some of which are televised, are conducted on topics specified by the government, sometimes including population control. The following excerpt helps explain this relationship between church and state:

Bruce M. Borthwick, Religion and Politics in Israel and Egypt. 33 Middle East Journal 145, 156–158 (1979).

Beginning in 1961, the government imposed a reform on al-Azhar, the last stronghold of the conservative *'ulamā'*. By law, it was attached to the Presidency of the Republic, and a Minister of al-Azhar Affairs was appointed by the President. Its various departments were placed under the leadership of men from outside the ranks of the *'ulamā'*, its curriculum was reformed, and four modern secular faculties (Medicine, Engineering, Agriculture, Commerce) were added. A girls college was established with its own branch of studies. Simultaneously, a withering attack was leveled against the *'ulamā'* through the media; they were charged with being old fashioned, obstructionist, obscurantist and of forming a "priestly" caste. They were also charged with being unable to deal with modern times, and this, the government said, was turning people away from Islam.

Under a law promulgated in 1960 but not implemented until after 1973, the Ministry of *Awqāf* was directed to take charge of all mosques in the country. It already had about 4000 "public" mosques under its administration, but there were at least 15,000 "private" mosques and thousands of prayer rooms (*zāwiyahs*) not under its jurisdiction. The rationale behind this law was explained in a clarifying memorandum:

> It has been observed that many mosques were not subject to the supervision of the Ministry of Waqfs, and that the affairs of these mosques are left up to chance. Since the continuation of this situation may lessen the value of religious guidance and weaken confidence in the mission of mosques—especially since what is said in the pulpits of the mosques is said in the name of God—circumstances make it necessary to lay down a statute for the supervision of these mosques, in such a way as to assure the achievement of the lofty goals of general religious instruction, the correct orientation of the rising generation, and its protection from all alien thought.

Or as a Parliamentary Report said: "the Ministry was to take charge of the administration of the mosques . . . and of guiding the leaders in such a way that they (the mosques) would fulfill their religious mission in the proper way."

* * *

Attending the Friday worship service is a common practice of the government leaders. On a few occasions of national crisis, Nāṣir himself even ascended the pulpit and delivered the sermon. Every week, a government ministry in Cairo prepares a model sermon and then distributes it to the preachers throughout the country who either read it or put its contents and meaning into their own words. In them, government policies are espoused and backed up with quotations from the Qur'ān and the *Sunnah*. The government solicits from the *'ulamā'* formal legal opinions (*fatwās*) on a wide range of subjects, including birth control, land reform, nationalization, scientific research, foreign policy and social affairs. . . .

Iliya Harik, The Political Mobilization of Peasants: A Study of an Egyptian Community. Bloomington: Indiana University Press, 1974, pp. 180–181.

In 1967, there were five *imams* in Shubra, four of whom were graduates of al Azhar University in Cairo; the fifth received his education in a provincial religious institution. *Imams* are paid officials of the state, and Nasser put them on a pay scale almost equal to that of other civil servants of the same grades. All but one resided in Shubra, although only two of them were natives of the village. Four of the five *imams* were in their early thirties, and the fifth was in his sixties.

The Azharite *imams* of Shubra share, to a great extent, a common attitude toward the regime and its rural policies. With some individual differences, they all subscribe to Arab socialism. The three *imams* who are not native to Shubra, however, are less active in the political life of the village.

Hadi Hammal, one of the most active *imams*, is typical of the generation of *imams* in Shubra who came of age under the Revolution.

* * *

Back in the village, Shaykh Hammal became active in the ASU and was one of the first persons chosen to attend Shubra's socialist institute. After completing the course, he was chosen to teach at the institute, where socialist ideas, achievements of the Revolution, and the Revolution's version of the modern history of Egypt were the subjects of his course. He did not refrain from drawing on the teachings of the Revolution in the sermons that he gave in the mosque, pointing to the Islamic character of socialist ideas and the regime's policies.

Shaykh Hammal's approach to family planning and savings illustrates the position of the socialist *imams* on these issues. In supporting family planning, the *imams* were in part acting in response to their own sense of urgency about the population explosion in Egypt but were also encouraged by officials of the Ministry of Awqaf and Religious Affairs to discuss the subject. They were quick to find religious justification for the policy of family planning, following in that path the leaders of the religious establishment. Shaykh Hammal was able to unearth from religious books some traditions of the Prophet that suggested the Prophet's consent to limiting the number of children in a family. Not only did he preach on the subject himself, but he also opened the mosque to the physician and the mayor to lecture on the same topic, a step not quite in accordance with mosque regulations. However, much of the political activities of the ASU in Shubra waived administrative regulations when, in the leaders' judgments, national interest called for that.

Shaykh Hammal followed the same practice with regard to the savings policy, an issue that differed from family planning in two ways: first, he was not required to provide religious justification for this policy, but acted out of his own interest as a leader in the ASU; second, it was not as easy to find a religious justification for savings as it was for family planning. In principle, the interest on savings and loans is clearly prohibited in Islam, and, despite the writings of Shaykh Mahmud Shaltut, a former rector of al Azhar University, in support of interest and banking, there was no noticeable conversion among religious authorities in Egypt to accept his point of view. At any rate, Shaykh Hammal found in the writings of Shaykh Shaltut the authority that he needed to advocate savings in his Friday sermon.

QUESTIONS

1. Is the government's use of Islamic institutions to propagandize for population control likely to be effective in the short run?

2. What about the long run? Suppose, for example, that there were a reemergence of a view that the government has the duty to uphold traditional standards of sexual morality?

3. What are the costs and benefits of this close relationship between the state and the church for the state? for the church? In thinking about this question, remember that Egypt has a sizable Christian minority (about 15%), and fairly substantial freedom to practice religions other than Islam. Remember also the impact on a society of having organizations outside the government suggesting moral standards.

4. Is the relation between church and state found in contemporary Egypt consistent with *sharia* traditions?

5. How do you evaluate the role that Ms. Sadat has played in the population control area in Egypt? In thinking about this question, you might want to consider the popular reaction to the Western ideas expressed by the Shah and his family in Iran.

6. Egypt faced the population control issue bureaucratically rather than legislatively or judicially. Do you think this difference made any difference in the effectiveness of the program? in the timing of the decisions?

7. If you were a minister with responsibility for the population control issue, what would you do now?

Chapter 25

POPULATION PLANNING IN BOTSWANA

A. A TSWANA POET'S VIEW

NOTE

The dominant Botswana view of the issues that surround the matter of family planning, population control, and abortion are expressed clearly, yet lyrically, in a pair of poems by a Tswana poet:

From *Marang* (Journal of the Writers' Workshop, University of Botswana), Number 3, 1980–81, pp. 1 and 2.

(For those who die before they begin to live)

ABORTION

by Onalenna Doo Selolwane

   . . .   is decay
Eating away at the tender roots
Of a defenseless foetus
     Clinging faithfully
To a treacherous womb.
Her delicate foetal tentacles
     untimely ripped
As dark ugly death
     snuffs life from hope.
The seat of origin
     denied
       crumbles
Shedding thick reluctant clods
Of deathly polluted blood,
Hope deterred.

(A Poem in dedication to life)

THE BEGINNING

by Onalenna Doo Selolwane

. . .   is seed
    pregnant with life
Quickened:
    Reaching out tentatively;
Delicately landing
    On the rich bed of promise:
The origin of future possibilities.

The womb in expectation
    Thickens with fertile blood:
Giving hope to life
And life to hope.

The foetus clings trustingly
Pulse beating slowly
    Faintly at first
Then gaining momentum with new confidence
    In renewed hope.
The promise of new life.

B. THE DEMOGRAPHIC PROFILE OF AFRICA

NOTE

As background to the relationship between law and population control in Botswana it is helpful to examine demographic trends in Sub-Saharan Africa as a whole.

Sub-Saharan Africa, comparatively speaking, is an area of low population density.

R. K. Som, "Some demographic indicators for Africa," in The Population of Tropical Africa, editors, John C. Caldwell and Chukuka Okonjo, New York: Columbia University Press, 1968, p. 190. Footnote omitted.

Density of Population. There were, in 1964, about ten persons per square kilometre of total area of Africa as compared to the world average of 23. This is the level of Northern and Latin America and of the USSR, and higher only than that in Oceania.

However, there are great variations in the density of population between the different sub-regions, between individual countries, and between different localities within each country. The data for the African countries and sub-regions show that of the African sub-regions, the highest density is recorded in the West (16) and the East (14), and the lowest in the Central (5) and the South (7). However, even the highest density of population in Western Africa is exceeded by all the sub-regions of Europe and Asia, except for South-west Asia, which has a density of 14, and by Middle America, the Caribbean, and Polynesia and Micronesia, among the other regions of the world.

Among the individual countries in Africa, excluding the small islands and possessions, the density ranges from one or less in Libya, Mauritania, South West Africa [Namibia], and Bechuanaland (Botswana), to 89 in Burundi and 116 in Rwanda. . . .

[Editor's Note: The 1979 density per square kilometer in Africa was 15. Source: United Nations Demographic Yearbook, 1979, New York: United Nations (Dept. of International Economic and Social Affairs, Statistical Office), 1979, p. 157.]

It is clear that except for a few areas (for example, most of the Nile river area, some areas in the equatorial highlands, parts of Western Africa, and the small islands), there does not seem to be much pressure of population on land in Africa as measured by the density of population in relation to the total land area.

As Africa is still mainly agricultural, two more useful measures of the pressure of population on land are the densities of the total population and of the rural population per square kilometre of arable land. For Africa, this density was 114, as compared with the world average of 212 in 1960 . . .). This is higher than those in Oceania, USSR and Northern America, but half that in Latin America (206) and one-third that in Asia (377). Defining the rural population as those living in places of less than 20,000 persons, the density of rural population per square kilometre of arable land was 99 in Africa, as compared with the world average of 160. This is again higher than the figures for Oceania, USSR and Northern America, but much lower than those in Latin America (140) and Asia (313).

NOTE

Sub-Saharan Africa is also an area of high fertility and declining mortality.

R. K. Som, "Some demographic indicators for Africa," in The Population of Tropical Africa, John C. Caldwell and Chukuka Okonjo, editors, New York: Columbia University Press, 1968, pp. 192, 195. Footnote omitted.

Fertility and Mortality. Registration of vital events is either non-existent or defective over most parts of Africa, and although attempts are being made to achieve complete civil registration, substitute measures have to be relied upon for quite some time to come. . . .

Fertility. The three measures of fertility considered are: (Crude) Birth Rate, General Fertility Rate, and the Gross Reproduction Rate. The Birth Rate is computed per 1,000 population and the Fertility Rate per 1,000 female population aged 15–49 years. The Gross Reproduction Rate is defined as the number of daughters that would be born to a generation of women having, at each age in the potential child-bearing period of their lives, the age-specific female birth rates observed for a given population at a given time, on the assumption that none of the women die before reaching the limit of their potentially fertile years. . . .

For Africa as a whole, the average birth rate is estimated at 46 per 1,000 and the gross reproduction rate at 3.1 around 1960. Africa had the highest birth rate amongst the world regions; the rates in the other regions range from 24 in Northern America and the USSR to 43 in South Asia, the world average being 34 per 1,000 . . . ..

[Editor's Note: In 1979, the average birth rate for Africa remains at 46 per 1,000. Source: U.N. Demographic Yearbook, 1979.]

Mortality. The three measures of mortality considered are: (Crude) Death Rate, Infant Mortality Rate, and the Expectation of life at birth. The Death Rate is computed per 1,000 population and the Infant Mortality Rate per 1,000 live births. Expectation of life is the average number of years of life remaining at birth. . . .

For Africa as a whole, the average death rate is estimated at 23 per 1,000 and the life expectancy at birth 41 around 1960. As with the birth rate, the death rate in Africa is estimated to be highest amongst the world regions. The rates for the other regions range from 7 in the USSR to 20 in South Asia, the world average being 16

. . . ..

[Editor's Note: In 1979 the average death rate for Africa as a whole was 19 per 1,000. Source: U.N. Demographic Yearbook, 1979.]

NOTE

Because of high fertility and declining mortality the projected population increase for Sub-Saharan Africa is prodigious.

R. K. Som, "Some demographic indicators for Africa," in The Population of Tropical Africa, John C. Caldwell and Chukuka Okonjo, editors, New York: Columbia University Press, 1968, p. 197. Table and footnotes omitted.

Estimates of population in the different world regions have been computed by the United Nations.

For 1958–63, the average annual per cent rate of population increase in Africa, 2.3 per cent, was lower only than that in Latin America with 2.7 per cent. For 1960–63, the rate of growth of population in Africa is estimated at 2.5 per cent per year, lower again only than that of Latin America, which had 2.8 per cent. However, the population estimates made by the United Nations indicate that in about two decades Africa may have the highest rate of population growth of the world regions.

[Editor's Note: For 1979, the annual rate of population increase for Africa as a whole was 2.7%. Source: U.N. Demographic Yearbook, p. 157.]

Next to Latin America, Africa has the highest rate of growth of population. However, in contrast to densely populated developing regions at a relatively advanced stage of development, most of Africa is sparsely populated and still at an early stage of development. There is also the prospect of further acceleration of the rate of growth of population in the near future.

It is clear that possibly sooner than can now be anticipated the African countries will have to make population trends the subject of a deliberate and comprehensive policy in their planning for economic and social development, and not merely an item to be taken into account in their planning: some other countries of the world are now taking this view.

C. THE DEMOGRAPHIC PROFILE OF BOTSWANA

John C. Kabagambe, "Demographic Trends and Family Planning in Africa," in Africa Link. July 1979, p. 9.

[NOTE: CBR = Crude Birth Rate;   CDR = Crude Death Rate;   IMR = Infant Mortality Rate. These terms are defined in the excerpts in Section B.

TABLE I. SELECTED DEMOGRAPHIC CHARACTERISTICS FOR 18 COUNTRIES IN THE AFRICA REGION OF IPPF

Country	1965–1970					1970–1975				
	CBR	CDR	Rate of Increase	IMR	Life Expectancy	CBR	CDR	Rate of Increase	IMR	Life Expectancy
Benin	50.9	25.5	2.54	109.6	38.5	49.9	23.0	2.69	109.6	40 +
Botswana	44.2	22.6	2.16	—	41.0	45.6	23.0	2.26	—	43 +
Ethiopia	45.6	25.0	2.06	84.2	38.5	49.4	25.8	2.36	84.2	37 +
Gambia	42.5	23.1	1.94	—	41.0	43 3	24.1	1.92	—	39 +
Ghana	46.6	17.8	2.88	156	46.0	48.8	21.9	2.69	156	42 +
Kenya	47.8	17.5	3.03	—	47.5	48.7	16.0	3.27	—	45 +
Lesotho	38.8	21.0	1.78	181	43.5	39.0	19.7	1.93	181	44 +
Liberia	48–52	16.20	3.2	140–145	—	49.8	21.0	2.88	159.2	54 +
Madagascar	46	25	2.1	102	33	—	—	—	—	—
Mali	49.8	26.6	2.32	120	37.2	50.1	25.9	2.42	120	37 +
Mauritius	26.7	7.8	1.89	57	60 +	25.1	8.1	1.70	46.6	60 +
Nigeria	49.6	24.9	2.47	—	36 +	49.3	22.7	2.66	—	35 +
Sierra Leone	44.8	22.7	2.21	—	41	44.7	20.7	2.40	—	43 +
Tanzania	47	22	2.5	160–165	40–41	—	—	—	—	—
Togo	50.9	25.5	2.54	127	34 +	50.6	23.3	2.73	127	35 +
Uganda	43.2	17.6	2.56	160	47.5	45.2	15.9	2.93	160	50 +
Zaire	44.4	22.7	2.17	104	34 +	45.2	20.5	2.47	104	43 +
Zambia	49.8	20.7	2 91	259	43.5	51.5	20.3	3.12	259	43 +

Source· UN Demographic Year Books 1970 and 1975

[C6077]

[Editor's Note: The estimated birth rate (1975–1980) for Botswana was 50.9 and estimated death rate was 17.4, showing a rate of natural increase that has gone up since 1970–75.*

* Source: Population and Vital Statistics Report: Data Available as of 1 July 1981. New York: United Nations, 1981, p. 5.]

TABLE II. RELATIVE CHANGES IN THE CRUDE BIRTH AND
DEATH RATES FOR 16 OF THE 18 COUNTRIES

Country	1965–1970		1970–1975		Relative Change	
	CBR	CDR	CBR	CDR	CBR	CDR
Benin	50.9	25.5	49.9	23.0	− 1.9	− 9 8
Botswana	44.2	22.6	45.6	23.0	+ 3.1	+ 1 7
Ethiopia	45.6	25.0	69 4	25.8	+ 8.3	+ 3.2
Gambia	42.5	23.1	43.3	24.1	+ 1.8	+ 4.3
Ghana	46.6	17.8	48.8	21.9	+ 4.7	+ 2.3
Kenya	47.8	17.5	48 7	16.0	+ 1.8	− 8.5
Lesotho	38.8	21.0	39.0	19.7	+ 0.5	− 6.1
Liberia	48	16.0	49.8	21.0	+ 3.7	+ 3.1
Mali	49.8	26.6	50.1	25.9	+ 0.6	− 2.6
Mauritius	26.7	7.8	25 1	8.1	− 5.9	+ 3.8
Nigeria	49.6	24.9	49.3	22.7	− 0.6	− 8.8
Sierra Leone	44.8	22 7	44 7	20 7	− 0.2	− 8.8
Togo	50.9	25.5	50.6	23.3	− 0.5	− 8.6
Uganda	43.2	17.6	45.2	15.9	+ 4.6	− 9.6
Zaire	44.4	22.7	45.2	20 5	+ 1.8	− 9.6
Zambia	49.8	20.7	51.5	20.3	+ 3.4	− 1.9

[C6078]

Source. Derived from table I.

QUESTION

1. What do the data in these two tables suggest about Botswana's future population profile?

Allan Osborne, "Rural Development in Botswana: a Qualitative View," in Journal of Southern African Studies, vol. 2, 1976, pp. 204–205. Footnotes omitted.

The population of Botswana in 1971 was 630,379 persons, representing a natural annual growth rate of 3.08 per cent between 1964 and 1971. Carried forward this means that the population will almost double in the next 20 years. [There is] a projected population of $1\frac{1}{8}$ million by 1990 . . . .

M. D. Crone, "Aspects of the 1971 Census of Botswana," in Botswana Notes and Records, vol. 4, 1972, pp. 32–33.

The reported population of Botswana, compared with 1964, was:

Year	De facto	Absent less than one year	Absent more than one year	Nomads *	Total or de jure
1964	500,238	28,727	6,405	14,050	549,510
1971	574,094	24,012	21,723	10,550	630,379

* estimate for those not otherwise enumerated.

. . . Census results prior to 1964 are defective in varying degrees, but the comparative figures are given for the sake of completeness:

1911	123,350
1921	152,983
1936	265,756
1946	296,310
1956	309,175

The 1956 figure was derived from a defective sample survey based on the tax registers. The 1964 Census is thought to be comparable in accuracy to the 1971 Census and it can be seen that there has been an apparent increase in the population of 80,869 during the seven years and four months between the two, which gives an apparent rate of growth of 1.8% per annum. The present rate of growth, derived from the data on fertility and mortality which is being analyzed by Dr. J. G. C. Blacker, ECA Regional Adviser in Demographic Statistics, is 3% per annum.

[Editor's Note: The 1981 census of Botswana yielded a (rounded) population figure of 940,000. Source: Embassy of the Republic of Botswana, Washington, D.C.]

QUESTIONS

1. Does the demographic profile for Botswana suggest the need for population control? Why or why not?

2. How pressing does the need for population control seem when you consider what you learned in the chapter introducing Botswana about the distribution of the population and of water?

D. SOCIO–CULTURAL FACTORS AND POPULATION GROWTH IN BOTSWANA

1. An Overview of Pro-Natalist and Anti-Natalist Forces in Sub-Saharan Africa

F. Olu Okediji, "Socio-Legal Considerations and Family Planning Programmes in Africa," in Africa Link, January, 1975, p. 7.

The question which ought to be raised at this point is as follows: "What factors account for pro-natalism in most African countries?" These factors can be classified into four categories: (1) the nature of the socio-economic organisation of most African countries; (2) the prevalence of high mortality rate, especially high infant mortality rate; (3) the existence of sizeable areas of subfertility/infertility and (4) the character of Moslem cultures.

* * *

What factors account for these pathological conditions of infertility and subfertility in some areas of Africa? [. . . They include:]

(1) demographic factors such as age at marriage, patterns of marriage including types of marriage, incidence of divorce and marital instability; (2) socio-cultural factors which include traditional practices in regard to dowry, pregnancy and delivery which have been identified or suspected as plausible channels through which the phenomenon of infertility or subfertility manifests itself; and medical and pathological factors.

It is somewhat obvious that in those areas where infertility and subfertility are prevalent, pronatalist attitudes will also be prevalent.

NOTE

Many demographers, writing about African population patterns, posit a kind of calculus in which African populations, faced with multiply-determined sub-fertility, infertility, and high mortality rates, compensate for these anti-natal factors by having more children. In other words, anti-natal factors are balanced by deliberate pro-natal practices. Following similar assumptions about making choices, many analysts have noted that Africans often opt to have many children because of the utility in their lives of their children, particularly children's labor.

Anthropologist Meyer Fortes offers an extended comment on some of the socio-cultural features of African society that impinge on family size. He explicates the strength and centrality of values concerning fertility, child bearing, and parenthood. His empirical focus is West Africa but his analysis is equally applicable to Botswana.

Meyer Fortes, "Parenthood, Marriage and Fertility in West Africa," in Journal of Development Studies, vol. 14, 1978, pp. 125–126. Footnotes and citations omitted.

In contrast to the traditional European emphasis on *marriage* as the nodal relationship in family structure, in Africa the critical feature is *parenthood*. As is well known there are some societies in which, before the advent of western cultural influence, the necessary connection between sexual intercourse and procreation was either unknown or at least unacknowledged, ... But there is nowhere in Africa where the connection has not always been fully understood. . . .

. . . fertility, that is the mobilisation of capacity to produce offspring, is in a different category. It was traditionally and still is valued above all other human endowments, in all strata and among all types of African society. And it is valued primarily as the indispensable condition for the achievement of parenthood. The personal misery, often accompanied by social stigmatisation, of childlessness is a recurrent theme in studies of African family systems.

I do not think it will be possible to understand West African attitudes about family planning unless one understands the significance of parenthood for the individual and the kin group in West Africa. At this point it is enough to say that the achievement of parenthood is regarded as a *sine qua non* for the attainment of the full development as a complete person to which all aspire. Indeed as I was often told by both my Tallensi and my Ashanti friends, a person does not feel he has fulfilled his destiny until he or she not only becomes a parent but has grandchildren. But parenthood is much more than a special form of individual fulfilment. In West Africa it is also a fulfilment of fundamental kinship, religious and political obligations, and represents a committment by parents to transmit the cultural heritage of the community. . . . It is a reflection of the crucial importance of the recognition of ancestry in West African social organisation. For ancestry, as juridically rather than biologically defined, is the primary criterion in most West African societies for the allocation of economic, political, and religious status. That is why grandchildren are specially valued, since they give better assurance of the prospects of continuing a descent line and in many traditional West African societies, in consequence, of perpetuating the ancestral cult, than does a filial generation by itself, subject as it may be to the hazards of mortality . . . .

*   *   *

What, then, must not be overlooked, in considering the values attached to fertility in West African social systems, is that the child whose birth confers parenthood is born not only to its parents and into its family but also into a lineage, a clan, a community, to all of which its survival, at the limit to reproductive age, is of critical economic, juridical and religious interest.

NOTE

Next, Fortes considers the validity of the interpretation that Africans desired to have a large number of children as "insurance."

Meyer Fortes, "Parenthood, Marriage and Fertility in West Africa," in Journal of Development Studies, volume 14, 1978, pp. 139–142. Footnotes omitted. Headings inserted by the editor are in brackets.

[*Rational, Prudential Explanations.*] Why we must ask, in most West African societies, is the maximum number of children a couple can produce in their lifetime so ardently desired rather than just the minimum of two needed to complete the family? Explanations generally offered by the outside observer are couched in the rational, economic, or prudential terms cited earlier. Thus it is argued that in a subsistence economy not only is marriage, especially polygynous marriage entered into in order to build up a labour force but that children are bred with the same end in view as well as with the insurance motives previously referred to. . . .

. . . There is need for closer analysis, from both a sociological and an economic point of view and in the context of the theory of the Developmental Cycle, of the objective data as opposed to informants' statements of their motives. It is arguable, for instance, that small families have the advantage that parental investment can be much greater *per capita* than in large families and that the consequent greater benefit to the children individually would be more of a guarantee of their insurance value to the parents. . . . But what about the ideal that maximum is optimum for number of off-spring? . . .

In questioning the rationalistic explanations that have been offered for this aspiration. I want to add here that it stands for a deeply felt commitment to maximum fertility—and be it remembered that this applies equally to men and women. A more persuasive hypothesis, which however also fails to convince me, is that the experience of high infantile mortality rates makes parents and their kin anxious to ensure that some offspring survive to inherit property, succeed to office and rank, and above all to perpetuate their descent line and, where ancestor worship is practised to maintain the religious cult.

To my mind this emphasis on the purely numerical implications of maximum fertility aspirations can be misleading. As I said earlier I do not altogether discount prudential motives; but as I also argued most people are, I am convinced, well aware that offspring impose responsibility and burdens economically, socially and to no small extent emotionally and morally in view of the constant hazards of sickness and death in the early years; and the returns to be hoped for from them are far from predictable.

[*Explanations Centered on Sense of Parenthood.*] What the rationalistic explanations neglect is, firstly, certainly pan-human proclivities, and secondly the specific cultural values associated with parenthood and progeny in West Africa. In the first place I would argue that there is a pan-human proclivity, an urge and need for men and women to seek to perpetuate themselves in progeny. One can think of it as a desire to perpetuate one's own existence or to replicate oneself or to satisfy a built-in nurturing drive. The very widespread cross-racial and cross-cultural dread of sterility and the ever-increasing resort to fertility drugs and to artificial insemination, testify to this.

In the West African situation the cultural evidence suggests additional considerations. There is first of all the principle I have previously stressed that no one is a complete person until he or she marries and achieves personhood. Indeed in some areas a man or woman who never succeeds in getting married is not regarded as fully adult and will not therefore at death be buried with the full adult mortuary ritual . . . .. Nor are these practices confined to the more traditional rural areas. More drastically, married people who died childless by reason of infertility would formerly have been buried in a peculiarly ignominious way in the communities I have listed and especially in Ashanti . . . . Secondly, there is the deeply ingrained ideal that normal men and women should continue to beget and bear children throughout their fecund years. And I want to emphasise in particular what this means for men. Everywhere in West Africa the achievement of parenthood is, for a man, evidence of what is pre-eminently significant for him, his virility and potency—even among the urban elite. . . .

But next to achieved parenthood there is also the wish and the need to demonstrate continued virility, potency and fecundity; and a numerous progeny is the best evidence there can be for this—which, incidentally, is also a motive for polygyny. Masculinity is equated with virility, so a man who ceases to beget children is deemed to have passed the zenith of manhood and to be on the way towards otiose eldership. In Ashanti, and I suspect elsewhere in West Africa, impotence or sterility was and remains an insuperable bar to holding high office . . . and by contrast the birth of many children, especially of sons, often helped to keep a chief in office against opposition. Similarly for women, it is their fertility that is considered to be uniquely distinctive of womanhood. A woman becomes a woman when she becomes able to bear children and continued childbearing is irrefutable evidence of continued femininity. At the menopause, a woman becomes a kind of honorary male, as is recognised in some traditional settings by her being allowed to act as a male in ritual situations.

. . . Thus large families are not only sources of prestige but also of self-esteem for both men and women thus fulfilling fundamental human propensities.

What I am suggesting, then, is that it is cultural values of this sort, with their deep psychological resonance, that are powerful, if not the most powerful motives for the desire to have large families that is common in West Africa.

QUESTIONS

1. What are some of the deep-lying values of Sub-Saharan societies which support a pro-natalist stance? How do they differ from the pro-natalist values of the West?

2. What does Fortes' argument suggest about the strength of pro-natalist values in Sub-Saharan Africa? About the difficulty of instituting population planning at the family level?

2. Socio-cultural Factors in Botswana Which Affect Population Size and Growth

NOTE

As pointed out in the Okediji excerpt, in any society there are a host of socio-cultural factors which affect population growth and size. We now examine a list of such relatively specific factors which operate in Botswana. The materials focus on the late colonial period when traditional modes were more widespread than they are now. These modes shape the behavior of rural people more than urban folk and of the elderly more than the middle aged and the young.

a. Traditional Beliefs About Conception

NOTE

Traditional Tswana beliefs about conception are not compatible with reliable spacing of births or with reliable contraception.

Isaac Schapera, "Some Kgatla Theories of Procreation," in Social System and Tradition in Southern Africa: Essays in Honour of Eileen Krige, edited by John Argyle and Eleanor Preston-Whyte. Cape Town: Oxford University Press, 1978, pp. 166–167.

Adults believe that children are produced by copulation, from a mixture of the man's semen (*marere*) with the blood inside the woman's womb (menstrual blood, *mosese*). The semen goes into the womb (*tsala*) and rests there until, after the fourth time or so of intercourse, it is sufficient in quantity. Then a mixture takes place. This mixture is not formed at the first coition, but after several; and when it has occurred, the woman ceases to menstruate. . . . She dates her pregnancy from the cessation of her menses, and starts counting the new moons; and when eight months have passed, she knows that she will bear her child in the ninth. . . .

According to some informants a single act of coitus was enough to cause pregnancy, 'if there is nothing wrong with husband and wife' (Natale) or 'if their bloods agree' (Lesaane, Tsholofelo). But most of them said, like SEGOGWANE, that repeated coition was necessary, say 'for at least three successive nights' (Sofonia) or 'for three or four nights running' (Rapedi), in order that enough semen could accumulate in the womb.

NOTE

In the following excerpt note the parallels to the sentiments Fortes reports for West Africa.

Isaac Schapera, Married Life in an African Tribe. New York: Sheridan House, 1941, pp. 213–214.

The Kgatla would readily agree with the Anglican Prayer Book that marriage is "ordained for the procreation of children." To them it is inconceivable that a married couple should for economic or personal reasons deliberately seek to restrict the number of its offspring, or even refrain from having any at all. They insist rather that a wife should bear her husband as many children as she can, provided only that she does not become pregnant until she has weaned the child already at her breast. A woman with a large family is honoured as highly as she would be in any modern Fascist state, while a childless wife is an object of pity, often tempered with scorn.

With the birth of their first child, married people acquire a new dignity. The husband has proved his manhood and become the founder of a line that will perpetuate his name and memory; the wife has fulfilled her supreme destiny, and freed herself from the most humiliating reproach that can be made against a married woman. To their respective relatives, too, the birth is a matter for rejoicing and congratulation. The husband's people are pleased that the woman they "sought" for him, and for whom they gave or will give *bogadi*, has rewarded their choice by helping "to build up their village"; her own people are happy that she has saved them from shame, and that her married life will henceforth be more securely founded. The enhanced status of the couple is reflected in change of name. They now become generally known by the child's name, preceded by the affix *rra* (father) or *mma* (mother), as the case may be. . . .

. . . As more children are born, the parents gain in prestige. Children mean additional help in labour, and increased self-sufficiency in production; they ensure that their parents will have security in old age; when they marry they extend the range of people with whom their family is allied, and so consolidate its standing in the tribe. "The cunning of the *phala* antelope comes from its young," says the proverb, i.e. a person with children cannot be lightly molested, for he is always sure of protection and support.

b. Boy-Girl Relations During Traditional Childhood and Adolescence

Isaac Schapera, "Some Kgatla Theories of Procreation," in Social System and Tradition in Southern Africa: Essays in Honour of Eileen Krige, edited by John Argyle and Eleanor Preston-Whyte. Cape Town: Oxford University Press, 1978, p. 170.

It was likewise held that a girl cannot conceive until she has started to menstruate. This explains the tolerance shown by some adults for the sexual play of children, which often included attempts at copulation.

But when a girl's breasts began to swell, and especially when she menstruated for the first time, she was generally warned about the dangers of sexual intercourse.

c. Traditional Attitudes About Pre-marital Sex

NOTE

The stated ideals were quite strict:

Isaac Schapera, A Handbook of Tswana Law and Custom. Second edition. London: Oxford University Press, 1955, p. 171.

In the olden days an unmarried girl who became pregnant was the object of universal scorn and suffered numerous public humiliations. Her child was often enough killed at birth, or if allowed to live always laboured under a pronounced social stigma. Nowadays, with the increasing frequency of premarital pregnancies, the girl is no longer so harshly treated. But she is said to have been 'spoiled' (*o senyegile*), and she is seldom regarded with approval as a possible wife. An illegitimate child is also no longer killed, and is allowed to take a full part in the normal tribal life. But it is often insulted and taunted, and is universally termed *ngwana wa dikgora* (a child whose father crept in through 'the fence', i.e. surreptitiously and with no legal right).

[Recall that the bulk of the research upon which this passage is based was conducted in the 1930's and 1940's.]

[In the 1920's the "scorn and public humiliation" that was directed at a woman who became pregnant before marriage was quite strong:]

Isaac Schapera, "Premarital Pregnancy and Native Opinion: A Note on Social Change," in Africa, vol. 6, 1933, pp. 65–67, 71–72.

My informants . . . were able to describe to me, rather sketchily it is true, what happened to an unmarried girl who had conceived. But they all emphasized that such cases were very infrequent. It was regarded as a profound disgrace by her family if an unmarried girl became pregnant, and every effort was made to conceal the fact. If the matter ever became general knowledge, the unfortunate girl was subjected to every possible humiliation. She was stripped of all her decorations and no longer allowed to wear them; she might not cut her hair, but had to wear it long as a sign of disgrace; she was not allowed to mix with the other girls, lest she pollute them as well; she might not wash her head, nor smear her face and body with the usual ointment of fat; and if she had not yet been initiated she was not sent to the *bojale* (girls' initiation school) with the rest of her coevals, but was separately treated. It was even said that attempts would be made to bewitch her, so that she might die together with the child in her womb. She was called by all sorts of opprobrious names, such as *seaka* (whore), and above all she was publicly mocked by the other girls and women, who would gather at night round her *lapa* (household enclosure) and sing obscene songs reviling her and her people. In these songs the women allowed themselves every freedom of speech. . . .

All night long they would sing in this strain, and nobody would check them. If the pregnant girl, maddened by their mockery, rushed out of her hut to swear back at them, they listened quietly without interfering; but as soon as she had finished they would renew their singing with additional emphasis. Even if the chief himself tried to intervene, they would revile him in their songs as well, for they feared no one at this time. They kept on in this way until the girl was delivered of her baby, and by then the whole tribe would have become aware of her disgrace. Their mockery is said to have been the most powerful sanction against premarital pregnancy, for it was the one thing which the girls feared above all else.

NOTE

But, even in the 1920's attitudes about post-pubertal sexual relations varied:

Isaac Schapera, "Premarital Pregnancy and Native Opinion: A Note on Social Change," in Africa, vol. 6, 1933, pp. 71–72.

In their attitude towards concubinage in general the BaKxatla vary a great deal. Some of my older informants, who were pillars of the Church, condemned the practice as indecent and shameful, but admitted that it had become very widespread and generally tolerated, and spoke sadly of moral degeneration. Others not only regarded it lightly, but even defended it. . . .

The younger men, naturally enough, tended to approve of it, and cheerfully boasted of their *dinyatsi*. On the whole, it may be said that concubinage is now an accepted practice, although it is not officially admitted in Kxatla law, especially in the case of unmarried people.

The same variation is found in the care exercised by the people over the chastity of their daughters. Some parents encourage their daughters to receive male visitors, and give them every facility for being alone with the boys. The mothers will even teach their girls what love medicines to use in order to attract the young men to remain with them. Sometimes they act in this way because they are pleased that their daughters prove more attractive than those of other women. Sometimes they hope that one of the boys will ultimately marry the girl. Some are even more mercenary still, and, in effect, prostitute their daughters so as to be able to claim the fine of cattle which must be paid if she becomes pregnant. A few of them also believe that, if their daughter is still a virgin at marriage, she will hurt the back and thighs of her husband when he has intercourse with her, and are therefore willing to see her deflowered beforehand. . . .

* * *

Other parents, said to be in a minority nowadays, are more strict about the morals of their daughters. They discourage male visitors, and, if possible, never allow them to be alone in her hut with the girl. There is no legal redress for seduction when it is not followed by pregnancy, and the tribal courts will refuse to judge a case of this nature. . . .

NOTE

Since Schapera's last field research Tswana attitudes about unmarried mothers have relaxed still more, stimulated by the fact that, in many areas, women outnumber men. (In the 1971 census the ratio of men to women in the country as a whole was 84:100.)

(GABORONE) BOTSWANA DAILY NEWS, July 25, 1975, p. 3

Unmarried fathers not paying full maintenance

Three-quarters of the babies registered at Serowe between January 1973 and December 1974 were illegitimate, according to local registrar N.B. Ntesang.

Over that period altogether 5796 babies were registered in Serowe and nearby 598 of them to married mothers.

Mr Ntesang said that in many cases, the fathers paid maintenance for the illegitimate child only for a month or two and then they disappeared leaving the mother and child without any support.

Hundreds of unmarried mothers come to the registrar's office hoping for hlep but have to return home empty-handed, he reported.

A spokesman for the District Commissioner said that the figures represented an increase in the number of illegitimate children registered in Serowe and area. He attributed this partly to the increase in social gatherings from which old people — who traditionally exercise discipline on the younger ones — are absent.

Contraceptive measures are not popular among they young couples, the spokesman added.

NOTE

After independence, in 1970, the Botswana Parliament passed a law, entitled the Affiliation Proceedings Act (Laws of Botswana, Chapter 28:02), which serves to provide better for the welfare of an illegitimate child. Under the Act, a subordinate court of the first class may make a determination of the paternity of an illegitimate child and issue orders for the maintenance of such a child. The orders provide for periodic payments to the mother or guardian of the child for the child's maintenance. Payments usually are mandated up to the age of 16. Additional payments may be required for the child's education from the age of 16 as far as age 21, if he or she is pursuing further education at that point. A stiff penalty is provided for misappropriation of the funds by the mother or guardian. Note that the act provides for the payments to be made to the mother (or the guardian of the child), not to the guardian of the mother. And the payments are for the maintenance of the child, not the mother.

The existence of the Act has lessened the pressure against pre-marital sex because it mitigates one of the consequences which, formerly, sometimes acted as a deterrent, fear of pregnancy. In 1982, the Magistrate's Court in Gaborone reported "at least fifteen cases a week" of affiliation hearings. Cases of abortion, correspondingly, are not unknown, but much more rare. The ease of access to affiliation hearings (no court fees are charged) seems to add to the tendency to eschew marriage and to the high incidence of illegitimacy.

More permissive attitudes toward illegitimacy have led to one other, more recent, attempt to change the law so as to provide for the welfare of a woman who becomes pregnant out of wedlock and for her child:

(GABORONE) BOTSWANA DAILY NEWS, OCTOBER 8, 1979

Seduction fine now up to P720

The Bakgatla Paramount Chief Linchwe II has announced a big increase in the Customary Law Seduction fine. Addressing a well attended Kgotla Meeting in Mochudi Chief Linchwe said the P180 seduction fine had been increased to P720 per case.

He however said the four herd of cattle fine still stands as it is. The increase comes as a result of the growing rate of seduction cases in the district as well as to match with the value of the four head of cattle fine.

Earlier, before the announcement was made in the Kgotla, the Kgosi had given the tribe the chance to discuss what he described as the anomalies within the Bakgatla Customary Law Seduction fine, according to sources.

The tribe felt that the present P180 fine per case was not enough and equivalent to the value of four head of cattle.

It was unamimously felt that the law does not equally favour the two parties. The men choose to either pay with four head of cattle or P180 but usually jump to cash, which is too little to maintain both the baby and the mother in this day of high cost of living.

The new change would be effective this month of October. The Kgosi reminded defaulters to settle out-standing fines before the new increase is implemented. According to the Tribal Office, there is a lot of out-standing seduction case fines in the case record.

Some people returned home happy about the increase after the meeting. Many felt this would encourage marriage, while a few complained that it would encourage pregnancy on the part of girls and promote the idea of abortion on the boys' part.

The number of illigimate babies born since January this year was estimated at 311, in the Kgatleng District alone.

d. Decline of Initiation Rites

NOTE

Even by the 1930's the traditional regimental structure of the Tswana had begun to die out. In traditional times the formation of a male regiment was preceded by circumcision ceremonies and a man who had not been circumcised could not marry and, according to Schapera, was "regarded with contempt by the women." The formation of the parallel women's regiments also was proceeded by puberty ceremonies.

These men's and women's regiments played an important role in regulating sexual behavior of young unmarried adults:

Isaac Schapera, "Premarital Pregnancy and Native Opinion: A Note on Social Change," in Africa, Volume 6, 1933, pp. 64–65. Footnote deleted.

. . . Circumcision, with its associated rites and taboos, has been completely abandoned, nor is the secrecy, which was so marked an element of the old ceremonies, any longer maintained. It is not even compulsory nowadays for a boy to pass through the initiation rites before he is accepted into a regiment. These modifications of the old initiation system have inevitably affected the marriage regulations, and also the whole aspect of premarital sexual life.

Marriage in the olden days was permitted only to those who had been admitted into a *mophato*,* i.e., to those who had been through the initiation ceremonies. The girls were generally married soon after they came out of the initiation "school." The boys, however, were expected to marry, not into the *mophato* of girls roughly contemporaneous with themselves, but into the one formed after that. This meant, in effect, that they had to wait anywhere from four to seven years after initiation before they could marry. Even then not all of them would be successful in obtaining wives immediately, for, owing to the practice of polygamy, many of the newly-initiated girls would become the junior wives of elderly or middle-aged men. It was an accepted practice, however, that such boys should be allowed secret access to the younger wives of their male relatives in the same *kxoro* (lineage group). . . .

These privileges were allowed only to boys who had been admitted into their *mophato*, and the women are said to have thought it shameful to sleep with anybody who was not circumcised. Before they had been initiated the young people of both sexes were expected to live chastely. . . . The boys were sent out to the cattle-posts away from the villages, and were kept there as long as possible, sometimes even after they had been initiated   . . . But in spite of this sexual segregation at adolescence, and although my informants maintained that premarital sexual intercourse in the olden days was an "unheard-of thing," it is obvious . . . that chastity was not universally observed.

e. Age of Marriage

Isaac Schapera, "An Anthropologist's Approach to Population Growth: Studies in the Bechuanaland Protectorate," in The Numbers of Man and Animals, edited by J. B. Cragg and N. W. Pirie. London: Oliver and Boyd, 1955, p. 28.

The continued absence abroad of so many bachelors, and the decay of polygyny, have also contibuted to a general rise in the age of marriage. In the old days, most people married soon after they had been ceremonially initiated into the status of adult, when about 16 to 20 years old. Today the usual age of marriage varies from 21 to 25 for women, and 25 to 30 for men.

---

*   *mophato* = regiment.

f. Traditional Birth Control Methods and Inauguration of Modern Ones

Isaac Schapera, "Some Kgatla Theories of Procreation," in Social System and Tradition in Southern Africa: Essays in Honour of Eileen Krige, edited by John Argyle and Eleanor Preston-Whyte. Cape Town: Oxford University Press, 1978, pp. 179–181.

The interval between one birth and another was usually longer than is physically possible. An important reason was the rule that a woman should not become pregnant again before having weaned a sucking child. This she seldom did until it was able to walk steadily, at the age of about two or three years. Should she conceive sooner, it was said, the child at her breast would suffer. . . .

. . . in general, most children were born two or three years after their immediate predecessors.

A husband's often lengthy absence at work abroad must have helped to bring this about, assuming of course that his wife remained chaste while he was away. But a much more widespread, and older, cause was that the Kgatla knew and practised various methods of contraception.

The most common was coitus interruptus. . . .   It was widely practised not only by married people, especially while the wife was suckling a child, but also by unmarried lovers. The necessary action had to be taken by the man; an unmarried girl, for instance, would sometimes yield to his advances only if he promised to do so.

Should the man nevertheless ejaculate into her, the woman could try other expedients. According to male informants, 'immediately after copulation she goes outside and pisses to get rid of the semen' (SEIKANELO), or 'she turns on her belly after sleeping with the man, then his blood flows out and she cannot become pregnant' (Natale). . . .

* * *

Another practice, described by two unmarried youths only, was the use of medicines. . . .

Another traditional custom with implications for birth control, one still practiced today, is prolonged absence at the cattle posts by men. Like labor migration (see below) it can stretch the interval between births.

The methods so far described were all traditional, and some were said to be taught to children by their parents or other elderly relatives. In about 1930 youths who had either worked abroad or been to school there also began to use condoms (which they called by the English name 'French letters'). These they obtained in the towns, or from local traders (one of whom first stocked them in 1932). They regarded this method as more reliable than coitus interruptus, but

. . . girls apparently disliked it. I did not hear of its being used by married people.

NOTE

As we will see in Section F2, Tswana continue to be ambivalent about condoms as a contraceptive device.

g. Attitudes About Abortion and Infanticide

Isaac Schapera, A Handbook of Tswana Law and Custom, London: Oxford University Press, 1955, pp. 262–263. Headings inserted by the editor are in brackets.

[*Abortion.*] Procuring abortion (*go ntsha mpa*, to take out the foetus) is practised fairly extensively, especially by young unmarried women. Sometimes the girl's lover persuades her to do so, fearing that he will have to pay damages to her father, and possibly also lose his position if he is a teacher or holds some other responsible post; sometimes it is her mother who persuades her, anxious that she should make a good match; while sometimes the girl herself will resort to abortion for the same reason. The most common abortifacients nowadays are ordinary writing-ink, sometimes mixed with the pulverized heads of matches, or a strong solution of washing-blue, or of potassium permanganate crystals, all of which can be easily obtained from the trading stores. Various Native preparations are also used, some of which are fairly commonly known, while others are obtained from the magicians (*dingaka*). Abortion is generally suspected when a girl who was known to be pregnant suddenly recovers her normal physical appearance, without anybody knowing when and where she had given birth. Or, when a foetus is found lying about, all the unmarried women of the vicinity are called and examined . . . .

. . . The one whose breasts are found to contain milk will be regarded as guilty.

As a rule very few cases of abortion come to general notice, partly through pity for the girl, partly for fear of the trouble that would ensue. It is usually only when publicity cannot be avoided that the matter is reported to the Chief. The headman of a ward has no power to deal with such cases, although he should first inquire into them to ascertain the facts. Among the Ngwato the usual procedure in recent times has been for the Chief to report the girl to the District Commissioner. The local Medical Officer will then be asked to examine her, and if the accusation is found to be true the girl will be tried in the District Commissioner's court. Among the Kgatla, in the few cases that did come before the Chief in Lentswe's time, the usual punishment was to thrash the girl fairly severely, and also her lover, if he was known. The foetus of the aborted child was also dug up and, after being doctored, buried in a pot inside the girl's hut, while the girl herself was smeared all over the body with a solution of *mogaga** and other medicines.

(GABORONE) BOTSWANA DAILY NEWS, SEPTEMBER 19, 1974, p. 2

Baby's corpse

discovered:

girl is held

An 18-year-old girl is receiving treatment at the Lobatse Athlone Hospital under police care after a dead child was discovered by the police on September 13.

Police believe that the girl aborted the infant, wrapped it in a rag and placed it behind a hut, where it was found by police later, in Maipei Location.

The police reported that this was the first case of its nature they had dealt with this year.

The medical condition of the young mother is "satisfactory."

[A contemporary case of abortion is reported in Section F3 below.]

Isaac Schapera, A Handbook of Tswana Law and Custom, London: Oxford University Press, 1955, pp. 261–262.

[*Infanticide.*] Infanticide was in the olden days generally practised in regard to children born feet first, or cutting their upper teeth first, and sometimes also in regard to twins. Such children were regarded as evil omens (*ditlhodi*), which had to be put out of the way as soon as possible lest they bring disaster upon their parents. In such cases no action was taken against the parents. But any other form of infanticide could, at the discretion of the court, be treated as murder.

The killing of an illegitimate child by its mother was regarded more leniently. If the corpse of an infant were found in the open, the fact had to be reported to the Chief, who would cause all the unmarried women of the village to gather in his homestead, where their breasts would be tested for milk by the old women.

. . . The actual culprit was then smeared all over her body with a mixture of medicines, principally the juice of the *mogaga* bulb, which caused an intense smarting pain. This treatment, which was regarded as sufficient expiation for the crime, was associated with the beliefs concerning rain. It was held that as long as the women

* See next page

was not purified her body would be "hot", and would therefore keep off the rain. The place where the corpse had been found was also said to be "hot", causing the land to dry up and the sun to be strong, so that the rain would not fall. It was accordingly sprinkled by the rainmakers with a similar mixture of medicines, so as to become "cool", while the corpse itself was buried in the shade of a hut.

Cases of infanticide are still met with occasionally. In theory they should be handed over to the European authorities for judgement, and this is sometimes done. But it is said that often enough, when such a case is reported to a headman, he will not send it to the Chief, but will order his informants to keep the matter dark, as it will otherwise lead to too much trouble. Among the Kgatla, during the time of Chief Lentswe, when such cases came before him he would order the girl to be beaten very severely, after which her body would be smeared with *mogaga* as described above.

(GABORONE) BOTSWANA DAILY NEWS, JUNE 6, 1974, p. 7

Child murderers will be hanged

From Olerile Makata

Two women both from Shakawe in the North West District have each been given a death sentence by the Chief Justice T.A. Aguda in a High Court session held in Maun recently.

They were both found guilty of murdering an infant. The court was told that the two women killed a baby after it had been born to one of them, whose husband was working in the mines in South Africa.

The child was conceived during the absence of her husband. The second woman who helped in the killing of the child was said to be a relative of the man who seduced the mother.

According to the court findings, both women had their malicious intention "well organised."

In answering a question why she killed her child, the mother replied: "I killed my child because I conceived during the absence of my husband. I was afraid that he would kill me when he heard of it. I wanted to hide the secret from him."

[Another recent infanticide case is reported on page 899 below.]

h. Forms of Marriage and Partnership

NOTE

Recall that, as noted in the chapter introducing the culture and legal systems of Botswana and in the chapters on inheritance and succession in Botswana, the Tswana had several forms of marriage which are very seldom found nowadays. They included polygyny and forms of secondary marriage, the sororate and the levirate (specifically, practices such as the taking of a *seantlo* and the "raising up of seed" for a man who died without a son.) Another form of partnership already referred to in this section was the taking of concubines. Contrary to the conventional wisdom, polygynous unions have been shown to be less fertile than monogamous ones, but this is of little di-

rect import in Botswana today since polygyny is so rare. Of more consequence is the continuation of attitudes originally linked with polygyny (e.g.,
continual siring of children as a way of proving virility as described in the
excerpt by Fortes).

i.　Labor Migration

NOTE

The connection between labor migration and the effectiveness of the use
of lactation as a device for the spacing of children already has been mentioned. However, to assess properly the impact on fertility of labor migration
one must take account of its interaction with other factors.

**Isaac Schapera, "An Anthropologist's Approach to Population
Growth: Studies in the Bechuanaland Protectorate," in The Numbers of Man and Animals, editors J. B. Capp and N. W. Pirie,
London: Oliver and Boyd, 1955, p. 28.**

To some extent, therefore, the adverse effects of migrant labor
upon legitimate child-bearing have been counterbalanced by what
seems to be a marked increase in the number of children borne by
unfaithful wives and unmarried girls. But even if we allow for this,
there is no reason to doubt the validity of the local argument that
owing to the prolonged absence of men at labor centers and the decay
of polygyny, with the associated rise in the general age of marriage,
fewer children than before are being born.

NOTE

Labor migration also is associated with a higher rate of venereal disease
which in turn affects fertility levels.

j.　Changing Forms of the Family

NOTE

Extended families are breaking up—with implications for the stability of
the marriages of their younger adult members and, undoubtedly, for the fertility of those persons.

**B. C. Thema, "The Changing Pattern of Tswana Social and Family
Relations," in Botswana Notes and Records, vol. 4, 1972, p. 41.**

. . . In many instances extended families are being broken up
by the necessity to take up employment far from family settlements
and by and large there is a growing feeling of individuality, and the
extended family is gradually narrowing, mostly as a result of the
costliness of living. The combined effect of these factors is that
more often than not marriages are contracted without the involve-

ment of the immediate parents, let alone of such members of the extended family as maternal uncles and paternal aunts.

. . . the involvement of the families in the marriage of their children lent stability to the union. If the parents did not restrain the waywardness of their married children they were held responsible should the marriage finally break up. . . . Admittedly many marriages are still essentially family unions, but Tswana marriage is becoming more and more of a contract between two individuals, with the resultant disappearance of the restraining and steadying influence of the older members of the families, especially now that employment in wage-earning occupations compel members of many families to live apart.

NOTE

It is probable that these more independent marriages are both rockier and less fertile over a long period of time than marriages where the extended family was more involved.

k. *Reduction of Traditional Forms of Welfare*

NOTE

Break up of extended families also has eroded traditional forms of welfare which may lead some couples to have fewer children and others to have even more.

l. *Child Mortality*

NOTE

The level of child mortality is a factor which influences couples' decision as to child bearing.

Isaac Schapera, "An Anthropologist's Approach to Population Growth: Studies in the Bechuanaland Protectorate," in The Numbers of Man and Animals, editors, J. B. Capp and N. W. Pirie, London: Oliver and Boyd, 1955, p. 29.

. . . information gathered from 695 women, who collectively had borne 2,146 children, shows that of every 1,000 children born alive 62 die while their mother is still secluded (i.e., within about two months of birth), another 81 before being weaned, and still another 116 in later childhood; altogether, that is, 259 fail to reach the age of puberty. The anthropologist can point to defective childrearing practices, to malnutrition, and to the high incidence of venereal disease (another product of labor migration), as among the contributory factors; but the investigation and interpretation of child mortality should be undertaken by medical officers and others better qualified than he is in matters of this kind.

NOTE

As noted in the Fortes excerpt at the beginning of this Section, high child mortality often leads parents to compensate by having more children so that a few will survive.

From the point of view of "development" strategy, the need for population control in Botswana is very strong. The rate of population increase in Botswana is very high, the population is very young and, therefore, dependent. The amount of arable land and dependable water is strictly limited. So, the present carrying capacity of the land under existing means of subsistence is being reached. And a large part of the gross national product is needed just to provide services at the existing level for the increase in the population. Significant economic growth is almost precluded.

Paradoxically, Tswana culture shows both pro-natalist and anti-natalist values, beliefs, and practices. The discreet practice of abortion and infanticide are strikingly anti-natalist practices. Less striking and more constant anti-natalist practices are labor migration and long sojourns at the cattle posts.

Since the turn of the century the balance between pro-natalist and anti-natalist factors has shifted more and more to the pro-natalist side. Migratory labor in the mines created an unbalanced sex ratio because the mines took their toll in deaths and reduced longevity for men. The activity of the missions and Western education exacerbated the effects of the uneven sex ratio. Traditional polygynous marriages could absorb "extra" women, including the larger number of women culturally deemed of marriageable age even under balanced sex ratios. But the missions undermined the practice of polygyny, removing that solution for the "problem" surplus of women.

The ever-widening surplus of women put more and more pressure on the sanctions against having children out of wedlock. Given the high value placed on fecundity and parenthood, it is better to be an unmarried mother than to remain a childless woman. The stigma of illegitimacy and out-of-wedlock pregnancies was weakened on other fronts, too: by the dropping of derisive serenading of women who became pregnant out of wedlock, by decline of initiation rites and weakening of the regiments, and by the undermining—and even outlawing in some chiefdoms—of *bogadi*.

In sum, the pro-natal trends and forces have become stronger and stronger in Botswana since 1900. Infanticide as an anti-natal practice is still frowned upon, although the application of sanctions may be tempered by recognition of mitigating circumstances. Abortion is more common than in the past, but also disapproved. More positive anti-natal trends such as limiting family size in order to be able to provide more fully for children's education and other needs have not yet become very strong. The social forces that fuel the move to family planning in more developed countries are barely gaining strength in Botswana.

It is against this background that the International Planned Parenthood Federation began to work in Botswana in 1969. We turn now to an examination of national planning and strategies and planning for population control in Botswana. But, first, consider the following questions.

QUESTIONS

1. Assume a rural Tswana hamlet in which most of the traditional factors described in this section still hold sway. Assess each factor to determine the degree to which its net impact is pro-natalist or anti-natalist. Indicate why you think its net effect is as you calculate it to be.

2. Referring back to the materials on Tswana and Problem 2, what do you think is the effect of the patterns of inheritance and succession on natalism? Be specific in tracing out your answer.

3. Which of the socio-cultural factors detailed here are amenable to change? through law? by other means? (What other means do you have in mind?)

4. Are there any factors which affect natalism which you believe were omitted?

E. NATIONAL PLANNING AND STRATEGIES FOR POPULATION CONTROL

NOTE

We have examined some of the socio-cultural factors that affect natality in Botswana. Before we turn to the Botswana government's policy concerning family planning, let us look, first, at some general issues pertaining to population planning in Africa and, then, at the pattern of population planning activities throughout Sub-Saharan Africa.

1. General Issues in African Population Planning

NOTE

The economic and developmental implications of burgeoning African populations are traced in the following excerpt.

William A. Hance, Population, Migration, and Urbanization in Africa: New York: Columbia University Press, 1970, pp. 429–430.

One additional subject which requires discussion is the relation of population growth to economic development. Economic theory now holds that a high rate of population growth is itself an obstacle to advance, and this applies not only to those regions which are affected by pressure of population. This is so because the capital needs of the increasing population are likely to absorb a substantial fraction of investment capital thus reducing the amount available for "progressive" investment; it may be roughly estimated that it takes 3 to 4 percent of new investments to provide the additional population with essentially the same standards as the existing population.[102] Most

102. See, for example, Joseph J. Spengler, "Population and Economic Growth," in Freedman, ed., Population: The Vital Revolution, p. 67.

African countries are simply not investing enough and would have great difficulty in investing enough to achieve desired rates of economic growth.

To illustrate the differences under varying rates of population growth, if one assumes a population increase of 3 percent and an increase in the national income of 5 percent, then there would be a 2 percent annual improvement in national per-capita incomes, requiring about 35 years to double per-capita incomes. If the population increase could be reduced to 1 percent per annum and the same 5 percent increase in national income were maintained then per capita incomes would more than quadruple in the same period.[103] Several studies have revealed that investment in reducing fertility can provide greater gains than any alternative investment, though it is obvious that investment in population control complements and does not replace expenditures on economic development.

Reduced birth rates affect the rate of growth of per-capita income in three obvious ways: the resulting lower population shares the national income, the lower number of children reduces the burden of dependency permitting the diversion of capital to promote faster growth of total income, and a long-term reduction in the labor force, an advantage in those countries with surplus labor or problems of unemployment and underemployment.[104] Zaidan proposed that additional benefits could be better nutrition, health, and education which would affect positively the quality of the labor force.

These considerations, it should be noted, apply to any country, but the higher rates of population growth in underdeveloped countries mean that a considerably higher proportion of their GNPs has to be invested in order to keep per-capita incomes at a constant level, they have less capacity to invest, and the need to increase incomes is very considerably more urgent. The youthfulness of most African populations, reflecting the continuing high birth rates coupled with recent sharp declines in the death rates, mean that dependency rates are unusually high. About half of the population of the continent is in the dependent age group, compared to about 30 percent in the United States. Furthermore, the ratio of dependents to supporters may be expected to increase in the next decade or so. The high dependency rates call in particular for high investment in education and the larger numbers entering school at the lower level may make it far more difficult to finance higher and professional education, whose products are most needed for effective development.

103. See A. J. Coale, "Population and Economic Development," in Hauser, ed., The Population Dilemma; Simon Kuznets, "Population and Economic Growth," Proceedings of the American Philosophical Society, VIII, No. 3 (June, 1967), 170–93.

104. George C. Zaidan, "Population Growth and Economic Development," Finance and Development, VI, No. 1 (March, 1969), 4.

It is no wonder that Spengler finds that an increase in population and population densities is a source of net economic advantage in but a few countries,[105] or that Kamarck concludes that "it is no exaggeration to say that the policy on population adopted by an African nation may well prove to be the most decisive factor in deciding what kind of an economic future lies ahead for it." [106]

QUESTION

One recent estimate places Botswana's rate of population growth at 3.15% per year. What implications does that have for real economic growth in Botswana?

Since, as Hance notes, the consequences of lowering birth rates in African countries are so far-reaching, the nature and scope of population planning efforts on that continent are critical. The next excerpt notes some of the difficulties encountered in early population planning activities in Africa and discusses the definition of "family planning" and what constitutes acceptable "government policy" regarding family planning.

Dr. F. T. Sai and others, Rapporteur's Report from International Planned Parenthood Federation Regional Conference on Family Welfare and Development in Africa, held at the University of Ibadan, Nigeria, 1976. In Africa Link, vol. 3, #4, July-October 1976, Supplement, pp. II–III.

Population and Family Planning in Africa. Organised family planning activities are of rather recent introduction to Africa. Unfortunately their origins, methods of introduction and the persons advocating them were in many instances so insensitive to local sensibilities as to lead to great resistances if not outright rejection.

The advocacy of family planning as synonymous with or contributing to population control, considered by the advocates as a basic requirement for economic development, was almost universally rejected in Black Africa. In some areas these were viewed as thinly veiled efforts at genocide, or at best an unrealistic approach to the real issues of development. Often the earlier advocates did not recognise many traditional practices as being family planning practices. The tradition of spacing children at intervals of about 3 years through prolonged breast feeding, abstinence, geographic separation, the use of charms and herbs (effective or not) had been ingrained in many cultures for generations. Organised family planning would possibly have had easier acceptance if it had been introduced as a substitution of some of these traditional methods which had become difficult or impossible of practice with modern technology and scientific information. The IPPF entered the African scene in the mid-sixties and it has been trying ever since to help correct the wrong impressions cre-

105. Spengler, "Population and Economic Growth," p. 67.

106. Kamarck, The Economics of African Development, p. 27.

ated. It is the hope that this conference will help the movement further along its being understood by the peoples of Africa. . . .

The overall growth rate of the population (about 2.5 percent per annum) means a likely doubling in one generation. The loads that such a large infusion of new children place on education, health and other welfare services need to be recognised. This conference has rightly refused to accept that population is itself the root cause of Africa's development problems; but it has also agreed that in many situations such rapid growth rates can stultify the best efforts of governments and peoples towards the attainment of legitimate developmental objectives. . . .

. . . the general concensus is that those countries that consider their growth rates inimical to their development efforts have a right to pursue programmes aimed at decelerating the rates of growth.

Mauritius, Kenya and Ghana were mentioned as countries with expressed demographic objectives in their population policies. It would perhaps be best to talk of planned population growth rather than population control when talking of population activities in Africa at the present time.

There was complete unanimity about the definition and reasons for family planning. Family Planning encompasses a group of activities which ensure that individuals and couples have children when they are socially and physiologically best equipped to have them; that they are enabled to space them satisfactorily and that they stop when they have had the number they desire; these activities should include education in human sexuality, marriage guidance or counselling, and the investigation and treatment of infertility and subfertility. Family planning is endorsed as a basic right of individuals and couples, it is necessary both for the welfare of families and communities.

There was no agreement on what should constitute a population policy, nor indeed on the actual necessity for governments to express such policies overtly. What the governments do or permit voluntary and other agencies to undertake in the field of population and family planning must be considered as, at least, of the same importance as the promulgation of an official policy. Against this attitude must be presented the well-known situation in many parts of Africa that the press, the media, the health education and community development services—all of which may have vital roles to play in family planning—are in the hands of government or under some kind of government control. Therefore a clear statement of government support of family planning activities even without a written policy, is often necessary to ensure the mobilisation of these vast resources for programmes. The size of the needs in almost all countries is such that Governments must be involved if much progress can be achieved.

QUESTIONS

1. Why did the IPPF conference prefer the term "planned population growth" to the term "population control?"

2. Why did the conference declare the necessity for governmental support of family planning activities and, yet, settle for as little as government support "even without a written policy?"

NOTE

This section of the IPPF Conference Report lays out some particular activities aimed at improving "family welfare," including family planning.

T. Sai and others, Rapporteur's Report from International Planned Parenthood Federation Regional Conference on Family Welfare and Development in Africa, held at the University of Ibadan, Nigeria, 1976. In Africa Link, vol. 3, #4, July-October 1976, Supplement, pp. III–IV.

Family Welfare. One cannot discuss family welfare without attempting a definition of family. A 1969 UN Declaration on the family states:

> The Family is the basic unit of Society, and the natural environment for the growth and well-being of all its members particularly *children* and *youth* and should be assisted and protected so that it may fully assume its responsibility within the community.

The simplest and most fundamental family unit is that of mother and child. Socially a father may or may not be considered part of this unit. In most African societies today two types of family co-exist:

(1) The nuclear (mostly urban);

(2) The extended (mostly rural but also found in urban areas).

These patterns of family structure are undergoing tremendous changes and with these come changes in the roles of various family members and the place of children with the family. Children are loved and welcomed, and, except for issues of taboo marriages, even those born outside wedlock (traditional or modern) are not treated with scorn but are integrated into the homes.

Barrenness is a disaster for the affected individual in many cultures; and whereas the traditional extended family might mitigate its effects on the individual the same cannot be said of the nuclear family. Children are not only loved, they are a means of security, an insurance for old age, and carry responsibility for giving their parents a decent burial. The ensurance of family health and welfare is therefore considered a necessary adjunct to a good family planning programme.

Family welfare was defined as improving the quality of life of the family unit, and should not be equated with family planning—the latter, family planning, is a component of the former, family welfare.

The following are some of the activities considered important in ensuring comprehensive family welfare development:

1. Preparation for parenthood.

2. Antenatal care; supervised delivery; postnatal care.

3. Ensurance of adequate child nurture, growth and healthy development through immunisation, nutrition and immediate primary health care.

4. Family spacing information and services.

5. Marital counselling—adoption services.

6. Sexuality education.

7. Support by community in difficulties.

8. Ensurance of education and socialisation of the [sic]

9. Treatment of infertility and subfertility.

10. Ensurance of employment for members to enable them to contribute.

The family whose welfare we seek to improve and develop can best be helped by FPAs* in the following ways:

1. Make inputs in MCH ** services in their countries;

2. Provide information and clinical services for family spacing;

3. Help in the treatment of infertility, sub-fertility, and hyperfertility, and in providing services for the termination of the early unwanted pregnancies where the country so permits.

In areas of Africa where the law of the land does not permit termination of pregnancy, or surgical treatment of hyperfertility, FPAs should, in association with other organisations, where acceptable, initiate actions for changes in the law which may be deemed necessary.

4. Collaborate with various youth and other societies, Government and voluntary organisations, schools, and cultural organisations in the dissemination of information about:

Sex education;

Education as a preparation for parenthood;

Marital counselling.

QUESTION

1. What factors do you think a Botswana FPA should take account of in deciding which of the suggested activities to carry out first?

* FPA = Family Planning Agency.   ** MCH = Maternal and Child Health.

QUESTIONS

1. Why does the IPPF place planned parenthood under the broader rubric of "family welfare?"

2. Is the IPPF view of family welfare really very comprehensive? Why do you answer as you do?

3. Isn't it striking that references to law and legislation in this section of the report refer only to laws relating to "termination of pregnancy or surgical treatment of hyperfertility?" If you were advisor to an FPA (Family Planning Agency) in Africa what other areas of legislation would you suggest they lobby for or against?

NOTE

In the following excerpt you can test out the accuracy and completeness of your advice in response to question 3.

Dr. F. T. Sai and others, Rapporteur's Report from International Planned Parenthood Federation Regional Conference on Family Welfare and Development in Africa, held at the University of Ibadan, Nigeria, 1976. In Africa Link, vol. 3, #4, July-October 1976, supplement p. V.

Law and Planned Parenthood. The Conference was reminded that law is a tool used by society to establish, define and enforce certain norms and standards. In certain areas especially those of human relations, including family welfare, the law is a rather crude instrument.

"Too frequently there is attributed to law and its agents a magical power—power to do what is far beyond its means. While the law may claim to establish relationships (for example in marriage law) it can in fact do little more than give them recognition and provide an opportunity for them to develop. The law, so far as specific individual relationships are concerned, is a relatively crude instrument".

It would be a mistake when dealing with law and planned parenthood to dwell exclusively on those that affect family planning practices directly, such as laws of contraception, abortion and sterilisation. Important though these are, there are many others which have far reaching influences on fertility behaviour and family welfare. These would include tax laws, e.g. child relief provisions, inheritance taxes or estate duty; welfare legislation, e.g. maternity provisions, old age pensions, employment laws, child and female labour regulations, housing legislation and education laws, family law, and personal status, e.g. polygamy and the extended family systems, penal laws, etc.

In many parts of Africa the new laws sit very uneasily with old traditions and customary usages. Many instances exist of conflict between the "imported laws" and the customary ones. There is no doubt that legal reforms and new enactments are needed in many countries to foster the aims and objectives of family welfare. It is however true that in many instances lack of knowledge of the law or wrongful interpretation of its provisions have unnecessarily hampered action. The Regional Council through its Law Panel may work out an action plan to get facilitative laws which encourage and assist the performance of family welfare activities. . . .

Law can be a tool for social change, but if it does not harmonise with the society's needs and aspirations it may fall into disuse or disrepute and be worse than no law at all.

QUESTION

1. How well did you do as an advisor?

2. Abortion Law in Commonwealth Africa

NOTE

One of the factors affecting the kind and amount of population planning in African countries is laws about abortion. Botswana is a commonwealth country, and commonwealth countries vary rather widely in their laws concerning abortion. Botswana is one of the more conservative commonwealth nations on this issue.

Rebecca J. Cook, "Abortion Law in Commonwealth Africa," in Africa Link, vol. 3, Number 2, October 1975, p. 10.

Introduction. Law is nothing but a tool—a tool used by a society to establish, define or enforce certain norms or standards. We often lose sight of the fact that this tool should only be used to promote the well being of individuals and communities. It made medical sense over a hundred years ago, when surgery was in its infancy to use this tool to prohibit abortion in order to promote the physical well being of the woman. And this is just what the British did in 1861 when they passed the Offences Against the Person Act which made it a criminal offence for any person, unlawfully, to procure a miscarriage or attempt to procure a miscarriage. This 1861 Statute makes no exemptions from criminal liability even if the abortion is necessary to save the life of the woman. Then in 1929 the British enacted the Infant Life (Preservation) Law creating the new offence of Child Destruction. This 1929 Act made one exception to this new offence—to permit medical termination of pregnancy if it is done for the purpose of saving the life of the woman provided it is done during the first 28 weeks of pregnancy. This 28 week gestation limitation set in 1929 is the one that remains in force today. Nine years later, in 1938, a London obstetrician, Dr. Bourne, openly and knowingly challenged the 1861 law with an eye to liberalise the Abortion Act. His challenge successfully extended the grounds for the purposes of preserving the physical and mental health of the woman.

Commonwealth Africa. At the time of colonisation, the majority of 13 Commonwealth African countries usually inherited English law into their legal systems by a process called "General Reception". This "General Reception" of the law means that the inheritance of the English Offences Against Person Act of 1861 and the Infant Life (Preservation) Act of 1929 were embodied, as such, into 13 legal systems of Commonwealth Africa. Commonwealth Africa, then, has basically three different kinds of laws based on the development of the English Abortion Law.

1. At least eight countries have restrictive laws identical to the 1861/1929 laws permitting abortion only to save the life of the woman. (Botswana, Gambia, Lesotho, Malawi, Mauritius, Sierra Leone, Swaziland, Tanzania).

2. The next category are those countries (Ghana, Kenya, Uganda) which permit abortion for reasons of physical and mental health along the lines of the Bourne case. Some other countries might recognise the Bourne case but in the absence of any court cases to test this recognition, or in the absence of any clarification on the part of the legal authorities, it is hard to determine whether or not these grounds would be respected. As a result of this vagueness in the law doctors in some countries are hesitant to perform abortions for health reasons. To avoid this vagueness, Ghana and Kenya have amended their laws since independence to permit abortion for reasons of physical and mental health. In essence they have codified the grounds for abortion as set forth in the Bourne case.

3. The third and final category of Commonwealth countries are those that permit abortion along extended grounds. Zambia is the only country with a far reaching abortion law. Zambia reformed its laws in 1972 to permit abortion along the lines of British Act of 1967 thus permitting the termination of pregnancy to save the life of the woman, for reasons of physical and mental health, fetal deformity and socio-economic conditions provided three medical practitioners are of this opinion. The abortion must be done in one of Zambia's 79 hospitals. The law leaves the gestation limitation to the discretion of the doctor.

In considering the three general categories of abortion in Commonwealth Africa, it is important to keep in mind that the practice of abortion can vary widely with what the actual law permits, in other words, the difference between law and practice. Another important fact to consider is the custom on abortion. Oftentimes, statutory laws can be reformed but if the customs and attitudes are against abortion it could be difficult to implement the law. Likewise the converse holds true where customs, and practice facilitate the availability of abortion while the law inhibits it. One way of determining the difference between law and practice is to investigate to what extent the legal authorities implement the law by prosecutions.

Generally police do not tend to move to prosecute under obsolete or controversial legislation that is obviously out of accord with public opinion. Police do not normally proceed against a woman who commits an abortion on herself but only charge the backstreet abortionist. It would be difficult to persuade a jury to convict a woman for what many would consider an imaginary crime. This practice which amounts to the virtual repeal of the 1861 statute might not be respected in certain Commonwealth African countries. An investigation on the number of prosecutions brought by the legal authorities to determine to what extent the authorities use their discretion in prosecuting abortion crimes would be a useful way of determining the difference between law and practice.

QUESTIONS

1. Why do you think Botswana falls as it does on the spectrum of positions concerning the law of abortion?

2. On the basis of the material you read in Section D2, can you make any guess as to the fit between law and practice concerning abortion in Botswana?

3. Abortion Law in Botswana

BOTSWANA PENAL CODE, Laws of Botswana,
Vol. II, Chapter 08:01 (1974)

[*Abortion.*]

160. Any person who, with intent to procure a miscarriage of a woman, whether she is or is not with child, unlawfully administers to her or causes her to take any poison or other noxious thing, or uses any force of any kind, or uses any other means whatever, is guilty of an offence and is liable to imprisonment for seven years.

161. Any woman who, being with child, with intent to procure her own miscarriage, unlawfully administers to herself any poison or other noxious thing, or uses any force of any kind, or uses any other means whatever, or permits any such thing, or means to be administered or used to her, is guilty of an offence and is liable to imprisonment for three years.

162. Any person who unlawfully supplies to or procures for any person any thing whatever, knowing that it is intended to be unlawfully used to procure the miscarriage of a woman, whether she is or is not with child, is guilty of an offence and is liable to imprisonment for three years.

229. Any person who, when a woman is about to be delivered of a child, prevents the child from being born alive by any act or omission of such a nature that, if the child had been born alive and had then died, he would be deemed to have unlawfully killed the child, is guilty of an offence and is liable to imprisonment for life.

241. A person is not criminally responsible for performing in good faith and with reasonable care and skill a surgical operation upon any person for his benefit, or upon an unborn child for the preservation of the mother's life, if the performance of the operation is reasonable, having regard to the patient's state at the time, and to all the circumstances of the case.

[*Infanticide.*]

213. Where a woman by any wilful act or omission causes the death of her child being a child under the age of twelve months, but at the time of the act or omission the balance of her mind was disturbed by reason of her not having fully recovered from the effect of giving birth to the child or by reason of the effect of lactation consequent upon the birth of the child, then, notwithstanding that the circumstances were such that but for this section the offence would have amounted to murder, she shall be guilty of an offence, to wit of infanticide, and may for such offence be dealt with and punished as if she had been guilty of the offence of manslaughter of the child.

[*Beginning of Life: When a Newborn Is Capable of Being Killed.*]

215. A child becomes a person capable of being killed when it has completely proceeded in a living state from the body of its mother, whether it has breathed or not, and whether it has an independent circulation or not, and whether the navel-string is severed or not.

[*Concealing a Birth.*]

228. Any person who, when a woman is delivered of a child, endeavours, by any secret disposition of the dead body of the child, to conceal the birth, whether the child died before, at, or after its birth is guilty of an offence.

QUESTION

1. Which section of the Penal Code allows abortion to save the life of the mother?

F. FAMILY PLANNING IN BOTSWANA

1. The Botswana Government's Policy Re Family Planning

NOTE

The following excerpt contains a statement of the official policy position of the Government of Botswana as it appears in a National Development (Five Year) Plan for 1973–1978.* Note that the frame of reference and tone are hardly anti-natalist and not at all coercive.

University of Botswana, Lesotho, and Swaziland, World Population Year Conference, May 22–26, 1974, Report (mimeographed). Gaborone, Botswana: Department of Statistics, University of Botswana, Lesotho, and Swaziland (portion excerpted not paginated).

At Botswana's stage of development economic growth is in no way assisted by the rapidly rising population. Living standards are reduced in proportion to the growth in population. Although Botswana is a large country in terms of area, it is not at present underpopulated in terms of current resource endowment.

Over the past ten years lack of economic opportunity forced over 40,000 Batswana to emigrate permanently. If this had not occurred, the population pressure on resources (such as schools, medical facilities, etc.) would have been even greater than it is. Emigration on the same scale may not take place in future. A conscious and planned effort must therefore be made to stabilize the growth of the population.

Before the introduction of modern medical practices, a high birth rate was necessary to offset heavy infant mortality and to prevent an absolute decline in the total population. This situation no longer exists. Better medical care and the eradication or control of diseases, such as malaria and smallpox, have greatly reduced mortality rates in Botswana. A relatively rapid rate of population increase, if sustained over a number of years, could seriously reduce and retard the general impact of economic development on the lives of Batswana.

It is not the intention of the Botswana Government to interfere with the lives of Batswana or to achieve its objectives through coercion. The country is faced with a serious problem, however, and it is the concern of the Government to create a better understanding of the issues involved and the choices which exist. A strong nation is one where the individual citizen is healthy and properly educated. Botswana cannot build such a nation if the development effort is continuously undermined by the sheer increase in numbers for whom basic services must be provided. If the health and welfare of mothers

---

* Ministry of Finance and Development Planning, National Development Plan 1973–78, Part I: Policies and Objectives, Gaborone, Botswana: Government Print, 1973, p. 40.

and children are to be adequately cared for, if women are to participate more effectively in the economic activities of the family, as well as the development activities of the community and the nation, it is essential that the children in a family are well spaced.

To improve the health of the nation a country-wide network of health posts and clinics will be established at which not only medical care but also family planning advice will be available to those who seek it voluntarily.

QUESTION

Although this policy statement is not strongly anti-natalist, it does contain a rationale for utilization of family planning by the nation and by individual families. What is that rationale?

NOTE

The health aims of the National Development Plan give very high priority to bringing more and more health care facilities to the widely scattered, largely rural population of Botswana. They also involve a particular structure of health care facilities and health care staff. For 1978, the Plan called for the following:

(Botswana) National Development Plan 1973–78, Part I: Policies and Objectives, 287. Emphasis supplied.

* * *

11 hospitals, each with laboratory facilities, an operating theatre, and a minimum of one resident doctor;

8 health centres, each run by an experienced public health nurse (a health centre is defined as having between one and 30 beds for curative medicine, as well as ancillary facilities);

90 clinics (a clinic is a permanently staffed building with one observation bed, up to six beds for maternity care, and no beds for curative care). There will be a steady upgrading during the Plan period from three-roomed clinics staffed by a single enrolled nurse/midwife to clinics with a maternity unit, staffed by a staff nurse/midwife and an enrolled nurse/midwife; and

178 health posts (a health post is a two-roomed building, visited regularly by staff nurse/midwives or medical officers on tour).

14.12 A programme will therefore be embarked upon to construct the necessary health centres, clinics and health posts that will be required to provide an effective service in 1978. It will entail the construction of an additional 62 clinics and 156 health posts. In the initial stage those buildings are identical—the difference between them lies in the permanent staffing of a clinic by a nurse whereas a health post has no resident staff.

[Note especially the role of the family welfare educator.]

14.13 Those units, together with the hospitals, will be the foci of curative medicine in Botswana. However, curative medicine will not radically improve the welfare of the community. That will be achieved only through a gradual process of education of the population in the techniques of simple *preventive* medicine. To disseminate such education, a cadre of 250 family welfare educators will be trained, and one posted to each village. Over the past two years the Government has experimented with such a cadre. A woman is selected from within a village, and given a training of 10 weeks in the rudiments of personal and public health, nutrition, health education, child care and *family planning*. She is also taught how to recognise and treat a few simple diseases, such as scabies, how to identify and cope with malnutrition in children, and how to follow up tuberculosis patients and their contacts. Such a worker, called a family welfare educator, requires frequent encouragement, supervision and additional in-service training.

QUESTIONS

1. What do you think is effective about the family welfare educator idea? What might be ineffective or incomplete about it?

2. How do you think family welfare educators actually spend their time? What proportion of it actually gets spent on introducing family planning concepts and methods?

3. What other parts of the National Development Plan would you like to see in order to assess the effectiveness of the over-all population control program in Botswana?

2. National Family Planning Policy in Action

NOTE

Because of the depth of pro-natalist sentiment and its concentration in the older, hence more powerful, segment of the population, Botswana national policy on population does not espouse population control. But it does allow for family planning. The government has no policy concerning specific ideal family size. Nor does it have an explicit policy of limiting family size. Rather, the emphasis is on encouraging each family to provide the optimum life for its children.

Because of this emphasis, such education and training for family planning that does take place occurs under the aegis of the Department of Health. It falls under their rubric of Maternal and Child Health (MCH) or Maternal and Child Health and Family Planning (MCH/FP). The focus in family planning efforts is on spacing of children as a measure for enhancing the health of mothers and children. As we have noted, there is a cultural tradition of spacing births via lengthy lactation and a post-partum sex taboo. The emphasis on spacing which characterizes family planning programs builds on these cultural roots. Relevant specific features of health and family planning services are summarized in the following excerpt from a field study of women who had attended MCH/FP units.

Betsy Stephens, Family Planning Follow-Up Study, Gaborone, Botswana: National Institute for Research in Development and African Studies, University of Botswana, Documentation Unit, Discussion Paper Number Five, July 1977, p. 3. Footnotes omitted. (Mimeographed)

1.3.2   Health Services.   In accord with the official policy of accelerated rural development, health facilities in the rural areas are being improved and expanded rapidly. More than three-fourths of the population has a residence within 15 kilometres of a stationary or regularly visited mobile health post.

Primary care is provided almost entirely by nurses with two to four years of basic training, plus a specialized short course in maternal and child health, and family planning. They are supervised by doctors and public health nurses, and assisted by family welfare educators with primary responsibility for health promotion. The family welfare educators are predominantly women, chosen from the village in which they work. They receive three months pre-service instruction and attend annual in-service courses. Most are supervised directly by nurses, but some serve relatively independently in rural health posts which are visited by mobile health teams.

1.3.3.   The Family Planning Program.   The family planning program began in 1969 under the auspices of the International Planned Parenthood Federation. From its inception, the program has had official Government support and has been administered by the Ministry of Health. The policy is that every woman should have the option of controlling her own fertility. The primary concern of the Ministry is the health and welfare of the woman, and the family. As such, family planning is a component of the integrated health service.
. . .

Family planning is currently available at all national health service units throughout the country, and virtually unavailable elsewhere. A few private doctors dispense birth control and commercial distribution of non-clinical methods is planned. Ministry of Health facilities charge clients a small fee (40 t=$.48) once a year for which they are entitled to unlimited service.

All common methods are available and most clinics are usually well stocked. Pill users are given Norinyl 28 or 21 day cycles, with Anovular used as a backup drug. The Lippes loop is used for IUD acceptors. Depo-provera is generally recommended only to older or multiparous women. Foam tablets are offered primarily as a stop gap measure.

NOTE

The law is moot on the question of the legality of contraception. Health workers who provide instruction in family planning do not deplore the silence of the law on this point because it extends to ancillary issues such as whether a married woman using contraceptives needs her husband's permission to do so. This is a salient issue because of Botswana men's attitudes about contraception:

Stephens, Betsy, pp. 52–53, Male disapproval of family planning for female partners was a factor in terminal defaulting,* and the reason for some unwanted pregnancy among defaulters.** In most cases males felt that female practice of family planning was a license for "promiscuity." In a few instances men feared that female use of family planning would reduce sexual pleasure.

NOTE

In the absence of a specific legal requirement re spousal permission, the provision of contraceptive information to a woman is considered to be a matter between her and her physician or health care deliverer:

Stephens, Betsy, p. 53, Programme policy is to provide family planning on demand to all females of reproductive age, and it is a confidential matter between staff and client. Thus women are legally free to accept without their husband's consent. And only one-third of new acceptors said the partner knew of their use of family planning. However, in practice many women are not free [to use family planning without spousal permission.]

NOTE

In Botswana public attitudes are accepting of the concept of protecting maternal health but, at best, are ambivalent concerning contraceptives themselves, especially male contraceptives. An experimental program to distribute condoms not just in health facilities but more widely in test communities failed because people did not want to see them displayed publically. (Indeed, in contrast to many Western countries, condoms are not in sight but out of reach behind the counter in pharmacies, since they are available only through the health facilities.) Certain community leaders threatened to lead a mass vote against the party in power if the experimental program were not terminated. Similarly, a public information campaign that emphasized the dual effect of using condoms (family spacing and disease control) met strong resistance. One cause for these attitudes is the belief of some males, noted

---

* Terminal defaulters were those who were in default (i.e. not receiving services) at the end of the study.

** "Defaulters" were family planning clients ("acceptors") who, sometime during the ten-month long study, stopped coming to the health center to receive family planning services.

earlier, that contraceptives promote promiscuity. Another is basic, strong pro-natal values.

Younger people in Botswana have expressed interest in sex education in the schools. But a program of this nature has not yet met approval.

Not surprisingly, in Botswana the churches and mission hospitals vary in their attitudes about family planning though they have a basic pro-natalist stance. For example, Catholic hospitals do not perform tubal ligations and Seventh Day Adventist hospitals do not give contraceptives to unmarried mothers.

Recently, some health officials have sought to have a law promulgated that would allow abortion when a method of contraception (e.g., an intrauterine device) can be proven to have been used and failed. However, as of the summer of 1981 this concept had not even been drafted into legislative form as a proposed bill.

Stephens' recent field study, excerpted above, reveals some additional problems involved in operating the Government's family planning program. The research focused particularly on the reasons why some acceptors dropped out for a period of time or permanently. The study also developed recommendations for improving services. One reason given for skipping or dropping family planning services, disapproval by male family members, was mentioned earlier. Other reasons uncovered were: distance from a health center, mobility, misinformation about family planning, undesired side effects, a delay between the time of deciding to use family planning and actually practicing it, and a decision to become pregnant.

Stephens, Betsy, pp. 40, 52, 53, 56. Headings inserted by the editor.

[*Distance from a Health Center and Mobility.*] Clients closer to the clinic were more likely to revisit, and many delayed visits were attributed to distance. It is evident that the largest single problem affecting follow-up utilization of services relates to client distance from the clinic. This is probably the major problem which Botswana faces in the delivery of all health services. It is a combined issue of widespread population settlements, poor communication, and the extraordinary amount of mobility which is so characteristic.

Gradually, as delivery points are increased, especially as the family welfare educator program expands, there will be greater accessibility. However, this must be supplemented with increased capability for loop insertion, and greater responsibility among family welfare educators for the distibution of family planning methods. Furthermore, clinic hours should be more flexible to provide accessibility to women who have regular working hours. (Surprisingly, we found women even in very rural areas who had civil service or other modern sector jobs, and were unable to get to the clinic.)

Family planning pill users should routinely be asked whether they need an extra supply because of anticipated difficulties in returning to the clinic on time. Alternatively commercial distribution may provide a more accessible source for some. The Ministry of Health should also think of other forms of distribution by rural and urban extension workers in other ministries, by women's clubs, and maybe through traditional healers.

[*Misinformation About Family Planning.*] Adverse and inaccurate stories about family planning circulate (i.e., pills accumulate in the stomach, the loop is carried in the hands of newborn babies). There are misconceptions about family planning among staff and clients.

[*Undesired Side Effects.*] Side effects result in a significant proportion of drop out. In part, this is because new acceptors are not adequately prepared by clinic staff to anticipate the nature and the duration of side effects. Also, they must understand at the outset that, rather than default when they cannot endure side effects, other methods are available. In particular, the cap, foam, and condoms should be offered more frequently. (Even though the cap is a poor choice of method in households where there is no running water, it is an ideal method for some, especially in the urban areas). . . .

Continual use is higher among loop users than either pill or injection acceptors. This is to be expected, especially in a society like Botswana which has a large rural population, and a very high rate of mobility. However, the experience of side effects was greater among loop users, and loop acceptors were more likely to change method than the others. Therefore, while in many ways it is a preferable method for Botswana, it should be used with caution. Clinic staff must prepare acceptors for the possible experience of side effects, and the program must have accessible facilities for servicing loop users. Otherwise, users who have a bad experience with IUD will spread disparaging stories in the community, and there will be a backlash against the method.

[*MCH/FP Recommended Delay Between FP Acceptance and Practice.*] A large number of acceptors were delayed at the outset because they were told that both start-up of pill use and IUD insertion should occur during menses. Many of those clients never started because either they became pregnant or lost interest. Preferably, clients should be given the method of choice at the time of acceptance. However, the advantages of immediacy have to be weighed against technical disadvantages. In cases where the method of choice cannot be used immediately, clients should be encouraged to use another suitable method in the interim.

Only 14% of all parous acceptors made their first family planning visit to the clinic within 6 months of the most recent birth. Family planning education during ante-natal and under five clinics should stress early use of family planning after childbirth.

All women delivering in maternity units should be offered family planning. Acceptors should commence before leaving the clinic. (IUD insertion in the immediate post partum period results in high expulsion rates, but also high rates of return for re-insertion. Total use rates are higher than in programs where acceptors are instructed to delay insertion for six weeks after delivery.)

Certainly the delays in start-up of new family planning acceptors are unwarranted, and it is well known that lactation is not a secure substitute for scientific methods of birth control. Furthermore, any delay is likely to reduce motivation in new acceptors. Therefore, clinic staff must offer immediate service (and preferably the method preferred) to all family planning clients. If there are well defined contra-indications for the method of choice, clients should be encouraged to accept another method temporarily.

In situations where a client is interested in loop insertion, or pills, or any method, they should be serviced immediately—even if it is not the established clinic time for family planning. In cases where a client accepts pills during a home visit, the family welfare educator should give her a cycle straight away, pending a medical check by the nurse. If, during a home visit, the client indicates a preference for the IUD, or injection, she should be given another method immediately and encouraged to attend the clinic as soon as possible. Gradually, family welfare educators could be trained to take greater responsibility of pill and injection users, and perhaps could be trained for IUD insertion.

QUESTIONS

1. What are the major issues in the population planning movement in Botswana? How do they differ from those in the other three countries whose legal systems we are studying? Why does the population planning movement in Botswana have those particular concerns?

2. In what ways does the Botswana population planning movement try to build on traditional cultural beliefs and practices about sex and reproduction?

3. Botswana law is moot concerning contraception itself. Why do you think this situation has been allowed to go unremedied?

4. Why is male resistance to family planning so strong in Botswana? Do you think it could be rooted partially in the patrilineal system of descent? Could the fact that Tswana males tend to associate contraception with female promiscuity have something to do with their sexual experience (or enforced lack of it) while they are working as migrants in the mines in the Republic of South Africa?

5. What implications do the geographical spread of Botswana's population and the seasonal pattern of movements of people have for the population planning movement?

6. For Botswana's situation, what are the pros and cons for the general use of each of the major methods of contraception? What method or methods do you think should be most emphasized? Why?

7. How could the role in family planning of the family welfare educators be improved?

8. Refer back to the IPPF Conference's list of suggested activities for FPA's and MCH/FP units. Are there any that have been relatively neglected by the Botswana population planning movement? Do you think this is simply a matter of oversight?

3. A Case of Abortion

NOTE

The Stephens research excerpted at several places in Section F2 reveals several ways in which the practice of family planning in Botswana may be imperfect. A woman may be unaware of modern technology of family planning: she may not have steady access to a MCH/FP center: she may have a break in her attendance at the center and, thus, be unprotected for a period of time: she may use her chosen contraceptive method improperly; or she may be dissuaded from continuing to use family planning. For any or all of these reasons she may become pregnant and, yet, not wish to bear the child. Methods of abortion are a part of traditional knowledge in Botswana and abortion was and is practiced discreetly under certain circumstances.

Abortion as a public health problem is exacerbated by the fact that, legally, it is available only to save the life of the mother. There have been no test cases to probe how far "saving the life of the mother" can be extended to embrace "preserving the health (including mental health)" of the mother.

The record of the following recent case was made available through the courtesy of Gaborone Chief Magistrate, Mr. G. L. Patel:

CHARGE

Person(s) Charged:

NAME: Boitumelo Ncube, Female aged 22 years.
ADDRESS: Mmopane Village
OCCUPATION: Unemployed.

SINGLE COUNT

STATEMENT OF OFFENSE

Attempt to procure abortion contrary to Section 161 of the Penal
Code Cap 08:01

PARTICULARS OF OFFENSE

Boitumelo Ncube on the 14th day of December, 1980 at Ramankhung Lands in the Kweneng Administrative District, being with a child, with the intent to procure her own miscarriage, used any other means by inserting a piece of plastic device through her vagina into the womb.

STATION: C.P.S. Gaborone
DATE: 24th December 1980   P. S. MATHUMO, INSPECTOR
    Public Prosecutor

FACTS OF CASE

THE STATE VS.: BOITUMELO NCUBE

The accused is unemployed. She stays at Ramankhung Lands in the Kweneng District. On the 14th day of December, 1980, at Ramankhung Lands in the Kweneng Administrative District, being a woman with a child, with the intent to procure her own miscarriage, inserted a plastic device through her vagina into the womb. After miscarriage she dug a hole and hid the foetus therein. She had been pregnant for twelve weeks. After miscarriage, she noticed that she was bleeding too much which could lead to her death. She went to Princess Marina Hospital [in Gaborone] with the piece of plastic device still stuck into her vagina onto the womb. This was then on the 15th December, 1980 on which day the doctor at Princess Marina Hospital examined her and discovered that she had miscarried [sic] and that she still had the piece of plastic device still stuck partly in her uterus and vagina. The same doctor phoned the police at Central [Station] who attended and interviewed her. She admitted having miscarried and was accordingly warned for a charge as now charged. The medical report was completed by the doctor and it is produced as an exhibit P. 1 in court. The piece of plastic device which the police took possession of is also produced as an exhibit [P.2] in court.

STATION: C.P.S. Gaborone
DATE: 23rd December, 1980   P. S. MATHUMO, INSP.
    PUBLIC PROSECUTOR

DATE: 24th December, 1980   CRIMINAL CASE NO. G951/80

THE STATE VERSUS BOITUMELO NCUBE

BEFORE:	MR. G. L. PATEL CHIEF MAGISTRATE INSP. MATHUMO, PROSECUTOR MR. MOTLHALE, INTERPRETER
COURT:	Charge is read over and explained to the accuse in [her] own language and [she] is required to plead thereto.
PLEA:	I understand the charge. I plead guilty.
COURT:	Facts are read as per appendix 'A' and they are fully explained to the accused in Setswana. Medical Report is marked Ex. P1 and Plastic stick as Exh. P.2.
ACCUSED:	I heard the facts. They are all correct.

COURT: Entered as a plea of guilty. The accused is found guilty
                  as charged and is convicted of attempt to procure abor-
                  tion C/S 161 of the Penal Code.

G. L. PATEL
CHIEF MAGISTRATE

P[ublic].   No previous convictions. These are very prevalent of-
P[rosecutor].   fenses. Young girl on taking pregnancies very lightly.
                  Public treats this very lightly. For these young girls to
                  walk away from court would in a way encourage them
                  into these activities.

IN MITIGATION: (Accused) My husband is in South Africa in the mines.
                  I fell in love with someone who caused pregnancy which
                  he then denied. I was forced in these circumstances in-
                  to this act.

SENTENCE:

Accused has pleaded guilty and is a first offender. I have considered
all facts of the case and all that has been in mitigation. I agree with
the prosecutor that to pass a type of sentence which will allow these
girls to walk out of court would be encouraging those who would be
enticed to commit these types of offenses.

I sentence the accused to twelve months imprisonment but eight
months imprisonment of this is suspended for three years on the condition that she does not commit a like offense during the said period.
Rights of appeal explained. 14 days.

G. L. PATEL
CHIEF MAGISTRATE 27.12.80

QUESTIONS

1. Why do you think the defendant pleaded guilty?

2. Was the defendant represented by counsel? If not, why not?

3. Is the completeness of the record such that you can be sure of your an-
    swer to question two?

4. Why did the Chief Magistrate impose the sentence that he did? Was his
    sentence at all in line with what would have been handed down in a cus-
    tomary court?

4. A Case of Infanticide

**Botswana Law Reports, 1974 (2), pp. 21–28. State vs Collet
Mothibi.**

ROONEY, J.

The accused has pleaded not guilty to the murder on the 18th October, 1973, of her newly born infant child. At the time the accused
was in her 19th year. She comes from Tshane village in the Kgala-

gadi District but she was working as a domestic servant at Selebi-Pikwe. She gave birth to the deceased baby on the 18th October after a pregnancy which had lasted about 36 weeks, whereas the normal period of gestation is 40 weeks.

Three witnesses were called for the prosecution and the accused gave evidence. As a result, the Court has before it the following issues:

(1) Was the deceased born alive?

(2) If the answer to (1) is in the affirmative did the accused cause the death of the deceased?

(3) If the answer to (2) is in the affirmative is the accused guilty of murder, infanticide or any other offence?

The evidence adduced at the trial can be summarised as follows:

On the afternoon of the day in question two girls Rebecca Dikabota (PW1) and Polina Moana (PW2) were walking in the bush near Selebi-Pikwe. They passed some distance from a woman who appeared to them to be bending down and digging in the vicinity of an anthill. Shortly afterwards they passed near to the woman again. Rebecca said that the woman called to her asking for the loan of an axe saying that she wanted to cut wood. Neither Rebecca nor her companion were carrying an axe at the time.

It is not disputed that the woman was the accused. As Rebecca approached her she noted something that looked like blood on her legs and clothes. Rebecca questioned the accused about her condition. When the latter replied that she was menstruating, Rebecca remarked that her condition suggested that she had had a miscarriage. The accused then replied "Yes, I was pregnant but I have miscarried."

Rebecca asked to view the child. Rebecca said that she heard a noise like a soft short crying note. She gave an imitation of it to the Court. I cannot judge the accuracy of her performance, but the witness emitted something akin to a soft crying note.

Near the accused Rebecca saw the face of a child half buried in a hole. According to Rebecca, the accused pushed the child further into the hole while it was still making the noises which she described. The accused complained that they wanted to get her into trouble. The hole was at the base of an anthill and appeared to have been dug out. Rebecca then called out to Polina, who was standing some distance away, "See how beautiful the child is." Polina, who was carrying a baby herself, ran off. On seeing the child Rebecca asked the accused to hand it over. The accused refused to do so. Rebecca offered to take the accused to her people but she replied that she had just come to Selebi-Pikwe. When Rebecca tried to touch the child the accused pushed her away and said "You want to put me in trouble." The accused used a stone to push the baby further into the hole, striking the child on the head with it. The child then stopped making noise. Rebecca in evidence said that the accused hit the child twice on the head with the stone. She identified to the Court a heavy stone which she said was used by the accused. It was admitted by the defence that this stone was shown by Rebecca to a Police Officer investigating the occurrence.

In cross-examination, Rebecca admitted that even if the accused had not asked for an axe she would have passed close to where she was. She was questioned closely as to what she had seen of the baby. She said that it was covered with oil and some plastic material and that she considered that the child was alive, as it moved.

The accused was a stranger to her. Rebecca said that Polina saw the child before she ran away. She insisted that she saw the accused actually hitting the child with a stone. She and Polina arranged for the matter to be reported to the Police. According to Rebecca, the accused told her that she had no relatives, but she refused to agree to be taken to the hospital.

In her evidence Polina said that she did not come closer than about 50 metres from where the accused was standing. She heard Rebecca invite her to see the "beautiful child". She did not go nearer. She saw the accused taking hard soil from the anthill and throwing it into a hole. Polina confirmed that the accused asked if they had an axe. The accused mentioned that she wanted to collect firewood. Rebecca told Polina about the child being in the hole. This made the latter afraid, as she was carrying a baby on her back. Polina agreed that Rebecca was not correct when she said in evidence that she came up and inspected the child before running away.

Although in examination in chief this witness said that she did not hear anything, in cross-examination she talked about hearing a soft crying noise coming from a hole. She described this as loud. She did not speak with the accused at all, but she noticed the blood on her.

The final State witness was Dr. Karen Maria Jakobsen, a Government medical officer stationed at Selebi-Pikwe. On the 19th October she performed a post-mortem examination on the body of the dead infant. The body was that of a prematurely born female. The witness estimated the duration of pregnancy as 36 weeks. There were no indications of deformity, there were two wounds on each side of the head. The skull bone was separated by half a centimetre, the two sides being fractured "at the corners" and brain tissue was visible. The doctor was of the opinion that the wounds which she described could have been inflicted with the heavy stone exhibited, if not much force had been used.

Dr. Jakobsen dissected the lung. Portions placed in water floated. This is known as the hydrostatic test and it indicates the presence of air in the lung. It was suggested to Dr. Jakobsen that the correct procedure in performing the hydrostatic test was to dry the pieces of lung with a towel before immersion in water. She replied, that she did not say that the child's lungs had been completely expanded by breathing to the extent that every portion of lung tissue would necessarily have floated if dried before immersion. She said that she was satisfied that the lung had floated in water and that it could be deduced from the presence of air that the child had breathed and was therefore alive at or after birth. She discounted the possibility that putrefaction of the lungs had already set in and could have accounted for the presence of a gas in the lung tissue which was lighter than water.

Dr. Jakobsen was unable to say if the head wounds had been inflicted upon the baby before or after death and it follows that she is uncertain as to the exact cause of death. However, she was satisfied that if the injuries to the head had been sustained by the infant while it was alive they would inevitably have been fatal.

Dr. Jakobsen saw the accused when the police brought her to the hospital on the afternoon of the 18th October. She was shivering from cold, exhaustion and loss of blood. The doctor did not speak to the accused much on account of her condition. The accused answered such questions as were put to her and carried out instructions. The physical condition of the accused was such, that the doctor was satisfied that she had had a difficult time in giving birth notwithstanding a quick delivery. She suffered much loss of blood.

It was put to Dr. Jakobsen, by Mr. Ackerman that if the accused had unexpectedly given birth to a premature child in the bush without assistance she could have been affected by the event to the extent that the balance of her mind was temporarily disturbed and Dr. Jakobsen agreed that this was very likely.

It was admitted that on the 27th October, 1973, the accused made a voluntary statement to Sergeant Seboletswe of the Botswana Police, which statement was admitted in evidence by consent. In this statement the accused said that while shopping for her employer on the afternoon of the 18th October she felt as if liquid was flowing from her and that she went into the bush thinking that she would pass urine. She sat under a tree near an anthill and gave birth to a child. The statement continues, I quote:

. . . I noticed that the baby was not alive, because I did not see it breathing, as I saw that she was not breathing, and not alive, I decided to bury her. I saw a hole on an anthill and I put the baby in that hole, and started to cover it with soil and some stones. While I was still doing that, the covering, certain two ladies came and one of them approached me and asked me what the blood she saw on my thighs and on the ground where I sat was for, I told her that I got a miscarriage. She asked me where the baby was, and I told her that the baby was dead and I had covered it on the anthill with soil.

I showed that lady the baby, she asked me to give her that baby but refused saying how can I give you a dead baby. Then that lady ran away saying a person has killed a baby, with a stone, she was seeing a wound on baby's head which was caused by a stone which fell on its head, while I was covering the baby . . ..

In her evidence to the Court the accused described in the same terms as in her statement, how it came about that she gave birth to the child. After the baby had emerged she said "I looked at the child and I found that it was lying still." She did not cut the navel cord as she had nothing to cut it with. When she saw that the baby was not moving she left it in a sort of ditch and went to report to her employer.

She described meeting the two women Rebecca and Polina. She said that she told them that she had had a miscarriage. She agreed that they asked her to show them the child. The women told her that they had been to the bush collecting wood and the accused asked them why they had no axe with them. The witnesses went away accusing her of having killed the baby. The accused maintained that she never heard the child make any crying noise. She said that she was a bit absent minded at the time and that she has not been normal since or before. She said that she did not wake up until she came to Mmadinare Hospital. She was not in her proper senses. She did not know that the child had any injuries. The child was not due to be born until November and she had arranged to go to Tshane to the home of her parents for her confinement. The accused said that she did not think she killed the child but, that even if she did, she was not in her proper senses at the time.

Cross-examined the accused said that when she was asked by the two girls to hand over the newly born baby she told them "I cannot give you a dead child." She explains her action in covering the baby, before reporting to her employer, as an effort to protect it. She had every intention of bringing her employer back to show her the child. But she was not able to give this Court a satisfactory explanation as to why she did not go to her employer with the dead baby and tell her what had happened, instead of burying the child. This was not her first born child. She had had another who had died a few weeks after it was born.

The accused denied that she had hurt the child saying that she merely covered it with stones and did not know whether this action had injured the baby in any way. She said that it was possible that the injuries were caused by the rough stones. She agreed in answer to questions put to her by one of the assessors that she felt pains when she was shopping in town. There can be no doubt that she was well aware that these were labour pains.

Section 210 of the Penal Code reads as follows:

210. A child becomes a person capable of being killed when it has completely proceeded in a living state from the body of its mother, whether it has breathed or not, and whether it had an independent circulation or not, and whether the navel-string is severed or not.

Rebecca (PW1) is a stranger to the accused and can have no possible motive in fabricating evidence against her. She told the Court quite clearly that she heard the baby make soft noises, and that she even saw it to be alive. She tried to recover the baby from the accused without success. She called out to her friend Polina and asked her to come and see the beautiful child. Rebecca may well be mistaken, when she says that Polina responded to her invitation and did in fact see the child before she ran away, but I do not think that she can possibly be mistaken when she says that she heard faint crying noises. Her evidence that the child was alive is corroborated by the result of the experiment performed by Dr. Jakobsen which revealed that the lungs had received air.

The accused in her statement to Sergeant Seboletswe said that the baby was not alive after its birth. In her evidence in Court she was evasive on this point. True, she said she did not notice the child move or did not hear it make any sound, but she introduced an element of doubt and confusion into her testimony with the suggestion that her recollection was not clear. I have no difficulty whatsoever in reaching the conclusion that the deceased baby was born alive and was a person capable of being killed within the definition of the Penal Code quoted above.

The baby was born alive. How and why then did it die so soon afterwards? Although premature the child was not deformed. Its body was injured and such injuries if inflicted upon it when alive would have been fatal.

Rebecca says that she saw the accused pushing the live child into the anthill and actually hitting it with the stone. The accused refused assistance offered, saying that the child was dead. Rebecca may be mistaken in her identification of the stone, which she says that the accused used to hit the child. If the exhibited stone was used to push the child further into the hole it could have caused the injuries described. On this point the evidence of the accused is of little assistance. She does admit however, that she covered the child with rough stones.

Having heard all the evidence I am satisfied beyond all reasonable doubt that the accused caused the death of her child when she attempted to bury it in the anthill under soil and stones. The accused told Rebecca that the baby was dead. She knew that this was not so. She must have known that the act of burying the child was likely to cause its death. She may have been indifferent to the consequences of her action. She accused Rebecca and Polina of trying to get her into trouble. The only trouble which she then faced arose out of her responsibility in the matter of the death of her child. The circumstances set out above prove the existence of malice aforethought as defined by Section 204(b) of the Penal Code. The circumstances therefore are such that the action of the accused in this matter amounts to murder, and unless she comes within Section 208 of the Penal Code, she must be found guilty of murder.

Section 208 of the Penal Code reads as follows:

208. Where a woman by any wilful act or omission causes the death of her child being a child under the age of twelve months, but at the time of the act or omission the balance of her mind was disturbed by reason of her not having fully recovered from the effect of giving birth to the child or by reason of the effect of lactation consequent upon the birth of the child, then, notwithstanding that the circumstances were such that but for this section the offence would have amounted to murder, she shall be guilty of an offence, to wit of infanticide, and may for such offence be dealt with and punished as if she had been guilty of the offence of manslaughter of the child.

The offence of infanticide is a statutory creation which did not spring from the law of England but was created by the Statute to deal with a particular problem. This statutory offence has now found its way into the Penal Codes of several former British possessions.

Infanticide as a separate offence does not exist under the criminal law of South Africa except in the province of Natal, however Section 330 of the Criminal Procedure Act of South Africa provides that a woman who is convicted of the murder of her "newly born child" need not, even in the absence of extenuating circumstances, be sentenced to death. In Natal the position is governed by Act No. 10 of 1910 which makes the unlawful killing of any child within one week of its birth a crime under the name of infanticide punishable by a maximum of 5 years imprisonment. In Swaziland a proviso to Section 296 of the Criminal Law and Procedure Act No. 67 of 1938 appears to establish infanticide as a defence to a murder charge, leading to a conviction for culpable homicide only if at the time of the commission of the act which caused the death of the child the balance of the mind of its mother was disturbed for the same reasons as are set out in Section 208 of our Penal Code. The same position obtained in this country prior to the enactment of the Penal Code in 1964.

I mention the laws of other countries because it seems that there is little unanimity among legislators as to the proper approach to the particular problem of infanticide.

All that the Section 208 requires for it to become operative is that at the time of the act or omission the balance of the accused's mind was disturbed. This is something far less than insanity as defined by Section 13 of the Penal Code. There is no onus upon an accused to show the existence of any disease affecting the mind. We are concerned here with a wilful act or omission which in other circumstances would amount to murder. In Mr. Collingwood's book on "The Criminal Law of East and Central Africa" at page 188 reference is made to the case of Namayaja vs. R. 20 EACA 204. The learned author says that the Court of Appeals for Eastern Africa expressed the view that in cases of infanticide the standard of proof required to show a disturbance of the balance of the mind is not as high as in the case of a defence resting on insanity. This may mean no more than that the accused has the evidential burden of adducing some evidence in support of a finding of infanticide. The actual report of Namayaja vs R is not available to me but accepting that Mr. Collingwood's interpretation is correct the principle he enunciates appears to me to be reasonable.

In a Judgment dated December 13th, 1973, in Review Case No. 301 of 1973 the State vs Kabiso Tachabana I held, following R. v. Soanes, 1948 1 AER 289, that a woman should not be charged with infanticide and a Court should not convict on a plea of guilty, to such a charge unless it is satisfied that there is some evidence available to support the contention that the balance of the accused's mind was disturbed.

Turning now to the present case I may say that I was not impressed with the accused's evidence to the effect that she was confused at the time and could not remember events properly. She makes no mention of such confusion in her statement to Sergeant Seboletswe when she made the case that the baby was not born alive. On the other hand, a finding of amnesia or confusion is not necessary. I find two aspects of the accused's behaviour altogether strange. Why did she ask for an axe? I am satisfied that she did so although she now denies it. Placed in a position of some peril by the unexpected arrival of the two witnesses, she ignored every precaution and proceeded to bury the infant under the very eyes of Rebecca.

Dr. Jakobsen agrees that the sudden termination of her pregnancy accompanied as it was by heavy bleeding would be most likely to have affected her mental inbalance. Standing along the doctor's evidence is mere speculation. However, if it is considered in the light of the strange behaviour of the accused there appears to me to be some substance in this theory. What it amounts to is this, would the accused have inevitably killed her child if it had been born in other circumstances? Had she formed a settled intention of doing away with an unwanted child? I do not know the answer to these questions, but I do know that it is possible that the accused acted wilfully but impulsively, whilst she had not yet recovered from the effects of child birth. On the balance of probabilities I find that she lost the balance of her mind for a temporary period. My assessors accept this finding. Consequently, I find the accused not guilty of murder but guilty of infanticide contrary to Section 208 of the Penal Code. (Counsel address the Court on Sentence).

SENTENCE

The accused has been convicted of the wilful and unlawful killing of a child, who was permitted life only for a few minutes. It should be borne in mind that it is an essential element of the offence of infanticide that the crime was intended. A person convicted of this offence is liable to imprisonment for life.

The law protects the sanctity of human life, irrespective of the age of any living person. To kill a child but a few minutes old is no less a matter in the eyes of the law than to kill an adult. I am aware that during past years, a number of cases of this nature have been brought before the Subordinate Courts. There has been a tendency on the part of some magistrates to deal leniently with offenders.

My assessors assure me that many cases involving the death of children go undetected. For this reason, we have resolved upon a sentence which shall bring home to the accused the enormity of her offence and may underline that in future people who are found guilty of child murder (because that is all it is in plain language) should not expect to receive sympathy from this Court.

Bearing in mind that the accused has been in custody since last October, she is now sentenced to 4 years imprisonment of which sentence one year is suspended for a period of 3 years on condition that the accused is not, during the period of suspension, convicted of the offence of infanticide, of the offence of concealment of birth or of any other offence which involves a breach of duty towards a child.

QUESTIONS

1. A significant issue in this case is how much continuity there is between treatment of cases of infanticide under customary law during the colonial period and now, under statutory law. Several specific questions suggest themselves:

    a. In handing down the sentence Mr. Justice Rooney makes explicit use of judicial discretion. Was such discretion exercised by chiefs and magistrates handling infanticide cases in the colonial period?

    b. The decision in this case turns on the issue of the mental "balance" of the mother immediately after birth? Is there any indication that the mother's post-partum mental state was a dimension to be taken account of in the handling of infanticide cases in chiefs' courts or other courts during the colonial period?

    c. How much continuity is there in the degree of leniency the judge showed in this case? To what extent is the severity of the sentence in harmony with traditional attitudes about infanticide? In harmony with the decisions of contemporary magistrates? Is Mr. Justice Rooney "leading the law" here? If he is, what are the probable long-run consequences?

    d. Exerting deterrence against infanticide was an issue in earlier times and now. The excerpt from Schapera on infanticide during the colonial period describes means of exposing mothers who had committed infanticide. One such mechanism linked ecology and supernatural beliefs to the need to ferret out those mothers. What was the mechanism and what was the rationale that connected these elements? Why would the linking of the elements have made the mechanism all the more compelling in its effect? How did its potential effectiveness compare with that of Mr. Justice Rooney's deterrent efforts?

2. This case also reveals some interesting aspects of procedure in a Tswana court. Consider the following questions:

   a. Max Gluckman, the anthropologist, in analyzing the law of Bartose of Zambia, observed that they used the standard of "conduct of 'the Reasonable Man' " in assessing the significance of testimony. What evidence do you see of the use of this concept during this trial? Is this a concept found only in African courts?

   b. What was the role of the assessors in this case? How do they contribute to the validity and/or effectiveness of the outcome?

NOTE

Now that you know more about the law concerning family planning in Botswana and Botswana social institutions related to family planning you may find that you can approach the poems in Section A with more insight.

Chapter 26

POPULATION PLANNING IN CHINA

A. CHINA AND MALTHUS

Mao Tse-tung, "The Bankruptcy of the Idealist Conception of History," in Selected Works of Mao Tse-tung, Peking: Foreign Languages Press, 1967, volume IV, pp. 451–454.

The Chinese should thank [Dean] Acheson also because he has fabricated wild tales about modern Chinese history; and his conception of history is precisely that shared by a section of the Chinese intellectuals, namely, the bourgeois idealist conception of history. Hence, a refutation of Acheson may benefit many Chinese by widening their horizon. The benefit may be even greater to those whose conception is the same, or in certain respects the same, as Acheson's.

What are Acheson's wild fabrications about modern Chinese history? First of all, he tries to explain the occurrence of the Chinese revolution in terms of economic and ideological conditions in China. Here he has recounted many myths.

Acheson says:

> The population in China during the eighteenth and nineteenth centuries doubled, thereby creating an unbearable pressure upon the land. The first problem which every Chinese Government has had to face is that of feeding this population. So far none has succeeded. The Kuomintang attempted to solve it by putting many land-reform laws on the statute books. Some of these laws have failed, others have been ignored. In no small measure, the predicament in which the National Government finds itself today is due to its failure to provide China with enough to eat. A large part of the Chinese Communists' propaganda consists of promises that they will solve the land problem.

To those Chinese who do not reason clearly the above sounds plausible. Too many mouths, too little food, hence revolution. The Kuomintang has failed to solve this problem and it is unlikely that the Communist Party will be able to solve it either. "So far none has succeeded."

Do revolutions arise from over-population? There have been many revolutions, ancient and modern, in China and abroad; were they all due to over-population? Were China's many revolutions in

909

the past few thousand years also due to over-population? Was the American Revolution against Britain 174 years ago also due to over-population? Acheson's knowledge of history is nil. He has not even read the American Declaration of Independence. Washington, Jefferson and others made the revolution against Britain because of British oppression and exploitation of the Americans, and not because of any over-population in America. Each time the Chinese people overthrew a feudal dynasty it was because of the oppression and exploitation of the people by that feudal dynasty, and not because of any over-population.

It is a very good thing that China has a big population. Even if China's population multiplies many times, she is fully capable of finding a solution; the solution is production. The absurd argument of Western bourgeois economists like Malthus that increases in food cannot keep pace with increases in population was not only thoroughly refuted in theory by Marxists long ago, but has also been completely exploded by the realities in the Soviet Union and the Liberated Areas of China after their revolutions. Basing itself on the truth that revolution plus production can solve the problem of feeding the population, the Central Committee of the Communist Party of China has issued orders to Party organizations and the People's Liberation Army throughout the country not to dismiss but to retain all former Kuomintang personnel, provided they can make themselves useful and are not confirmed reactionaries or notorious scoundrels. Where things are very difficult, food and housing will be shared. Those who have been dismissed and have no means of support will be reinstated and provided with a living. According to the same principle, we shall maintain all Kuomintang soldiers who have revolted and come over to us or been captured. All reactionaries, except the major culprits, will be given a chance to earn their living, provided they show repentance.

Of all things in the world, people are the most precious. Under the leadership of the Communist Party, as long as there are people, every kind of miracle can be performed. We are refuters of Acheson's counter-revolutionary theory. We believe that revolution can change everything, and that before long there will arise a new China with a big population and a great wealth of products, where life will be abundant and culture will flourish. All pessimistic views are utterly groundless.

NOTE

Despite these optimistic words, food production has been an important concern in China since 1949. While there is considerable disagreement over the precise figures, it appears that grain production has increased an average of slightly more than 2% a year, but population also has increased at almost the same rate. (The grain figure is somewhat misleading since it does not take into account the increase in consumption of non-grain foods—beans and vegetables, fish, meat, etc.—or the replacing of "coarse" grains such as sorghum by rice and wheat.) While the population appears well-fed, Chinese agriculture operates on a very thin margin. A major goal of the current modernization drive is to increase agricultural production by 4–5% annually, a formidable task.

Balancing Population and Food, Population and Family Planning in the People's Republic of China (The Victor-Bostrom Fund Committee and the Population Crisis Committee, 1971).

Between 1948 and 1970—the span of a generation—the population of mainland China has risen from 530 million to 800 million, according to various estimates. The "normal" annual growth would have been 2.2 percent had it not been for famine in 1959–62, in part natural and in part resulting from the collapse of the Great Leap Forward. During these famine years birth rates dropped and death rates rose, so that the actual average annual growth was 1.9 percent.

*   *   *

Peking reported grain outputs of 154.4 million tons in 1952 and 200 million tons in 1965, while U.S. estimates based on Chinese data project output at 225 million tons in 1970. The average annual 1952–70 growth in grain output is just over 2 percent, but, adding grain imports, the annual growth in the grain supply is about 2.2 percent. The expansion in the grain supply has therefore just about kept pace with population growth so far.

*   *   *

Farm experts have rated Chinese agriculture as perhaps the most "advanced" of pre-modern farm systems in the industry of its peasants and the intensity of land use. The Chinese peasant in seeking high yields tends his crops with the care of a gardener, and sustains the fertility of his fields with sophisticated crop rotations and much effort in returning organic materials. At the same time, the Chinese peasant, investing more labor hours in farming for no more of a return than his counterpart in many other societies, has the world's lowest labor-hour productivity.

About 11 percent of the land is cropped, almost all in the habitable eastern third of the nation. *The long history of population pressures and the nature of Chinese farming suggest that nearly all the land that can be cropped is in production.*

China's agriculture in 1971 is relatively vulnerable. Annual growth in farm output, which averaged 4.5 percent during 1953–57, has dropped to 1.25 percent during 1957–70. To bolster food supplies, China has imported five million tons of grain annually in the decade of the 1960s, and in the same period, has shifted a significant amount of land to grain from non-grain crops and oilseeds. The urban population supported by agriculture, which arose from 11 percent of the total in 1950 to 15 percent in 1957 and to an unsupportable 19 percent in 1960, has now shrunk to 12–13 percent.

| | | Year-end | | Per Capita |
Year	Crop Weather	Population (millions)	Grain Output (million tons)	Grain Output (kilogram)
1952	Good	575	154.4	269
1953	Average	588	156.9	267
1954	Poor	602	160.5	267
1955	Good	615	174.8	284
1956	Poor	630	182.5	290
1957	Average	645	185.0	287
1958	Good	659	(200) *	(303) *
1959	Average	669	(165) *	(247) *
1960	Poor	676	150	222
1961	Poor	680	162	238
1962	Good	687	174	253
1963	Average	697	183	263
1964	Good	712	200	281
1965	Average	728	200	275
1966	Average	742	206	278
1967	Good	757	218	288
1968	Average	776	210	271
1969	Average	795	212	267
1970	Good	815	225	276

Food and Population Trends

* Estimates for "Great Leap" claims.
Source: U.S. Department of State.

Again, imports of food and fertilizer were negligible in the 1950s, but in the 1960s have accounted for a substantial part of annual imports. Wheat imports have remained relatively stable at between 4 and 6 million tons annually, while fertilizer imports have increased steadily over the decade. By 1970 China imported over 8 million tons of fertilizer, accounting for 20 percent of world fertilizer imports. In other words, China, self-sufficient in the 1950s, had by 1970 become dependent on imports—of grain directly and of fertilizer indirectly—for 10–11 percent of its grain supply.

Population projections for the 1970s indicate that China must increase its grain output by 50–60 million tons over the decade merely to maintain present per capita levels. Such an increase would require between 20 and 30 million tons of chemical fertilizer. More importantly, the increase would require major modernization efforts in various farm areas, including improved marketing facilities, transport, research, extension, and cropping systems. Current policies clearly focus on the rural sector. There is promise of expanded rural education and some possibility of permitting migration to the cities, as well as of the development of rural industry and the introduction of urban amenities in the countryside.

NOTE

In order to foster economic development by limiting population size, while at the same time upholding the belief that "[o]f all things in the world, people are the most precious," China carried out a program of "planned births." Note that, as in Egypt, the term "birth control" is avoided: it carried a possible connotation of coercion, and also is associated with a Western effort to reduce population growth in developing countries.

"Chinese Observer on Population Question," Peking Review, no. 49, December 7, 1973, p. 10.

China pursues a policy of developing its national economy in a planned way, including the policy of planned population growth. We do not approve of anarchy either in material production or in human reproduction.

Man should control himself as well as nature. In order to realize planned population growth, what we are doing is, on the basis of energetically developing production and improving the people's living standards, to develop medical and health services throughout the rural and urban areas and strengthen our work in maternity and childcare, so as to reduce the mortality rate on the one hand and regulate the birth rate by birth planning on the other.

What we mean by birth planning is not just practising birth control, but taking different measures in the light of different circumstances. In densely populated areas where the birth rate is high, marriage at later age and birth control are advocated. However, active medical treatment is provided for those suffering from sterility. In the national minority areas and other sparsely populated areas, appropriate measures are taken to facilitate population growth and promote production. However, proper guidance and assistance are also made available to those who have too many children and desire birth control. All those who voluntarily ask for birth control are provided by the state with contraceptive drugs and relevant medical service free of charge.

"China's Position on the Population Problems Expounded," Speech by China's Observer at the Special Session of the Population Commission of the United Nations, Peking Review, no. 12, March 22, 1974, pp. 8–9.

At present, many countries have population problems, such as unemployment, starvation, high morbidity and mortality. All these problems should be examined in the context of the given political-economic conditions, instead of by an abstract approach separated from those conditions. What is the root cause of the population problems existing in many countries today? Some people attribute them to the quick and excessive growth of the population. According to them, big population is the cause for slow economic development, inadequate resources, pollution of the environment and a miserable life in the families of the developing countries. . . . They maintain that the excessively large population of the developing countries in Asia, Africa and Latin America is the 'root cause of all problems' in the world."

Fundamental Cause of "Population" Problems. Hsu Li-chang continued: "In our view, such assertions are entirely wrong for they are totally inconsistent with the actual fact. The fundamental reason why there are poverty and 'population' problems in some developing countries is the hegemonism, aggression and plunder perpetrated by imperialism, colonialism and neo-colonialism, especially the two superpowers."

The Chinese observer pointed out: Poor countries are not poor from the very beginning, nor is a large population the cause of their poverty. They are poor because of brutal plunder and exploitation. At present, population densities in most of the developing countries are lower than the developed countries. How can it be said that their population is too large?

We maintain that of all things in the world, people are the most precious. Once the people take their destiny into their own hands, they will be able to perform any miracles. Take China for example. Under the leadership of Chairman Mao Tsetung and the Communist Party of China, the Chinese people have overthrown the rule of imperialism and its lackeys, become the masters of the country and are building socialism independently and through self-reliance. Over the past two decades and more, although China's population has grown from around 500 million to more than 700 million, our economy has developed faster and not slower; our resources have become richer and not poorer; our environment is gradually improved and not worsened and our people's living standard has been raised step by step and not lowered. With the emancipation of the people, man and woman are equal. They help and love each other, work together and strive to build a new society. This historical fact has fully borne out the truth that the question of feeding the people can be solved through revolution plus production. The view that a large population is the "root cause of all problems" is wholly untenable.

* * *

"It is China's consistent position to combat imperialism, colonialism, neo-colonialism and superpower hegemonism, and support the developing countries in their struggle to safeguard national independence, develop independent national economy and improve and raise the living standard and cultural level of the people step by step. It is also the common demand of the Asian, African and Latin American developing countries and the earnest desire of the broad masses of the people of the world," he said. "We are of the opinion that this session and the forthcoming World Population Conference should give full expression to this just demand of the developing countries which constitute two-thirds of the world population. At the same time, full expression should also be given to the just demands of the vast majority of the people in the developed countries for winning and protecting their right to work, improving their living conditions and ultimately eliminating the root cause of unemployment," he added.

Future of Mankind Is Infinitely Bright. Hsu Li-chang pointed out that some people, basing themselves solely on demographic forecasts, had painted a black and depressing picture of the future of mankind. More than a hundred years ago, when the world population was less than 1,000 million, Malthus raised a hue and cry about "overpopulation" and the impossibility for the growth of production ever to catch up with that of population. Today, more than a hundred years later, the world population has more than trebled, but there has been even greater growth of the material wealth of society, thanks to the efforts of the broad masses of the people in surmounting numerous obstacles. In the short span of the 20-odd years since her founding, the People's Republic of China has increased her industrial and agricultural production several times, her rate of production growth exceeding that of her population increase. "History is progressing, and mankind is advancing. We are fully confident that the future of mankind is infinitely bright," he said.

"Population Growth and Modernization," Beijing Review, June 1, 1979, p. 5.

In old China, population growth was in an anarchic state. Mortality rate was as high as birth rate, and natural growth was low. Since the founding of New China in 1949, the people's living standard and public health work have improved, and the mortality rate has dropped from 28 per thousand in pre-liberation days to 6 or 7 per thousand at present. There was a rapid increase in population in the 50s and 60s resulting from lack of family planning. This was why the rate of growth remained at 20 per thousand for quite a long time.

On May 15, *Renmin Ribao* published a signed article entitled "Population Growth Must Be Controlled." Among other things it said:

—The present labour force in China is almost equal to the total in the first and second worlds. A big population is an asset in construction, but it does not follow that the greater the labour force, the more advantageous it is.

—Compared with 30 years ago, China's farmland per capita has dropped by half. Arable land for each agricultural labourer is even less than in Japan.

—Now approximately 10 million people will reach the age to join the country's labour force every year and arrangements have to be made for them to work or continue their studies. Without an adequate amount of means of production available, the increase in labour force will mean a drop instead of a rise in labour productivity.

—As China now has a bigger population than in the past and the number of women of child-bearing age is also greater, more children will be born every year in the future unless population growth is brought under control. Moreover, the newborns from now on will be dependants till the end of this century; they will consume large quantities of social wealth, thereby affecting the accumulation of funds for construction.

—Funds for popularizing education will have to be increased in the wake of population growth, while the money used for bringing up specialists will be decreased accordingly.

—Under socialism, the people's material and cultural well-being should be gradually improved on the basis of increased production. Quick population growth inevitably produces unfavourable results.

The article said in conclusion that while developing production at high speed, it is necessary to bring population growth under control so as to accomplish socialist modernization at an early date.

B. THE PLANNED BIRTHS PROGRAM

Bernard Berelson, "An Evaluation of the Effects of Population Control Program," 5 Studies in Family Planning, pp. 2, 4, 1974.

How, in theory, can India cut its birth rate in half?—get a major proportion of the labor force into industry and thus sharply raise the standard of living and promote urbanization, give every Indian including the girls at least 6–8 years of schooling, forbid child labor, cut infant mortality to below 25, raise the female age at marriage to 25 or so, establish the nuclear family with separate residence, get 35–40% of the women of reproductive age into the labor force, set up a functioning system of social security . . . . The point is less that such measures are uncertain of success, than that they cannot be achieved: the policies are reasonably clear, their early implementation is impossible.

NOTE

The above measures suggested by Berelson for India closely resemble China's approach to planned births. As might be expected, the Chinese effort has not been entirely consistent or easy to carry out over the past thirty years. The cultural tradition of wanting many children, particularly sons, is deeply engrained. In the past, filial piety required a person to produce sons to carry on the family line. On the economic side, a person had to rely on one's sons for support in old age. (Recall that daughters generally married out of the family.)

Examine China's approaches to carrying out planned births in light of the above considerations. Compare these methods to methods used to affect behavior on other matters such as control of deviancy or implementation of contracts.

Pi-chao Chen, with Ann Elizabeth Miller, "Lessons from the Chinese Experience: China's Planned Birth Program and Its Transferability," 6 Studies in Family Planning, pp. 354, 356–358, 1975.

Population Policy. Since 1949, China's population planning policy has evolved through several stages; its fluctuations seem to have been caused more by economic and political dynamics than by attitudes toward birth control. When the Communists came to power in 1949, their leaders were confident they could solve China's "population problem"—if one existed. In the summer of 1953, the government initiated the first nationwide enumeration. Soon after the results became known in late 1954, the government drifted toward an antinatalist position and announced in mid-1956 that it favored birth limitation. Since then, China's leaders have supported antinatal programs and policies, increased services as new methods of contraception were developed, and concentrated on changing social attitudes that hindered birth limitation. Twice programs have fallen into abeyance during periods of economic difficulties and political turmoil: first, during the Great Leap Forward, when collectivization and communization were succeeded by serious droughts and food problems; second, during the Cultural Revolution, when political upheaval disrupted the party and state bureaucracy resulting in de facto suspension of many programs, including birth planning. The programs have been resumed, expanded, and intensified since the early 1970s.

China's current policy indicates an unequivocal commitment to the planning of births. A 1971 State Council Directive (No. 51) set the tone for the 1970s:

> Planned birth is an important matter which Chairman Mao has advocated for many years, and demands serious attention by the leading comrades at the various [administrative] levels. Except for thinly populated national minority and certain other areas, the leading comrades at each level must strengthen leadership and conduct penetrating propaganda and education so that late marriage and planning of birth becomes voluntary behavior on the part of the broad masses in cities and the countryside, and [comrades must] strive hard to accomplish outstanding results during the Fourth Five-Year-Plan period (1971–1975).

In typical Chinese Communist administrative style, the directive does not establish targets to be achieved; rather it urges leaders to achieve "outstanding results." Interviews with numerous cadres in charge of planned birth work at various levels, however, gave the distinct impression that, with few exceptions, provincial administrations have set targets: reduction of the natural increase rate to 10 per thousand in cities and 15 per thousand in the countryside by 1975. These cadres seemed confident that the goals for urban areas will be realized but were less sure about rural areas, where cultural and economic conditions are not as favorable.

Since 1971, the planned birth program has aimed to accomplish the following goals:

1. Late marriage: late twenties in urban areas (age 28 for men, age 25 for women); early to mid-twenties in rural areas (age 25 for men, age 23 for women).

2. Childbirth spacing: four-to-five-year intervals after the first child.

3. Inculcation of small-family norms: two children in urban areas and three in rural areas—regardless of sex (that is, the number of sons).

Actual implementation of the program takes place at the county and lower administrative levels; the central government establishes policy, handles publicity, and coordinates sharing of information and diffusion of successful strategies. . . .

Planned Birth Educational and Motivational Work. Planned birth subcommittees conduct local educational and motivational work by several means. They organize "political evening schools," film and slide shows, radio broadcasts, and variety shows. They also arrange for medical personnel to explain contraceptive methods at local meetings.

Motivational work is also carried into homes; women who work as "women's work" cadres, barefoot doctors, and committee members or voluntary activists visit homes to deliver contraceptives, motivate women to plan births, and speak to members of the family who favor excess childbearing. They also make sure those who wish to practice contraception receive the supplies or services they prefer.

* * *

Primarily, however, the planned birth subcommittees use the institutionalized small groups to full advantage. Virtually everyone above school age in contemporary China belongs to some small group of 10–20 persons. Such groups are organized in schools and factories; housewives, retired workers, and others who are not affiliated with an institution are organized into groups in their neighborhoods. Peasants meet in their production teams, which may also be regarded as small groups for all practical purposes. When the need arises, the small groups join to form larger meetings, comprising all or part of the members of a given unit. Urban groups meet regularly, and rural groups meet according to the farming season. At such meetings, they study and discuss ideology, latest policies and current events, as well as deal with the unit's business (production). Planned birth is also an item on the agenda in all groups of adults of reproductive age. Using criticism and self-criticism, these groups exert peer pressure to arouse positive attitudes toward government policies. Thus, no additional organizational efforts are needed to deliver the planned birth message to the people.

The government asserts that birth planning is important for many reasons. The official arguments used in educational and motivational campaigns are that birth planning is needed to:

1. Reduce the burdens of childbearing and household chores and allow more time to study Marxism-Leninism and Mao's teachings, as well as to acquire and improve job-related skills and knowledge;

2. Release the energy of the young and masses for production, construction, and defense, rather than diverting all their efforts into building families;

3. Regulate population growth to facilitate national development, raise living standards, and continue the socialist revolution;

4. Protect the health of women and children and achieve better health and prosperity for the nation;

5. Insure and improve the welfare and quality of the next generation by permitting better education, health care, and upbringing of the young: parents can provide better care for fewer children, while the state can provide better education, health care, and employment for fewer youths.

In motivational work, workers are urged to use examples and idioms meaningful to the people. They use local cases and statistics to illustrate their arguments. A common tactic is to point to "preliberation" (pre-1949) living and health conditions and contrast them with the present ones to show that under socialism it is no longer necessary to have many children in order to ensure the survival of a few and have security in old age.

Health System and Delivery of Planned Birth Services. Planned birth services are completely integrated into the health delivery system . . . Just as each administrative level has a planned birth subcommittee, so it also has a corresponding medical unit that is responsible for the service aspects of birth planning.

* * *

Commune health stations have college-trained medical doctors, traditional doctors, and *feldshers* (physician-assistants with vocational medical middle school training), who concentrate on outpatient care. Larger communes have comprehensive health care centers with college-trained doctors, traditional doctors, nurses, laboratory technicians, dispensers, and other aides. Such health centers are equipped for a limited range of inpatient care and abdominal surgery. Their staffs work full-time and are salaried.

* * *

Each level in the health system provides planned birth services commensurate with its facilities and personnel competence. Health aides and midwives distribute pills and conventional contraceptives. Barefoot doctors supervise the use of pills, and some (for example, those serving in remote villages far away from urban centers) are trained for IUD insertion and induced abortion. Commune health stations or centers perform abortions and sterilizations and sometimes send mobile teams into remote areas. Virtually all hospitals have birth planning clinics.

There are two other important features of this program: (1) the use of unpaid nonprofessionals for nonclinical work; and (2) the simplification of techniques so that they may be performed inexpensively at the lowest possible level in the health system. Housewives, women's work cadres, and activists carry out motivational and educational work; they keep records of such information as contraceptive use, family size, and children's ages, and help organize access to services. They also arrange for transportation to distant clinics and help in homes when women are away for IUD insertions, abortions, or tubal ligations. Simplification of methods has included developing abortion by vacuum aspiration using an alcohol bottle or pump (designed for areas without sophisticated equipment or electricity); simple pregnancy tests that can be done by a barefoot doctor; and three types of pills, one of which is a lower dose needing less supervision.

* * *

Since 1970–1971, all planned birth services have been provided free; provincial and county governments appropriate budgets for this purpose. In the case of clinical planned birth methods, a person receives services free and the state reimburses the hospital (5 yuan for each tubal ligation and 3 yuan for each vasectomy). If expenditure exceeds appropriation, supplementary funds are appropriated, since planned birth is a high priority policy. Thus, the health system is maintained by local areas, but planned birth costs are provided for by the state.

* * *

NOTE

Two of the characteristics of China's program of planned births, illustrated in the next several items, are an extraordinarily meticulous and thorough infrastructure to support the program, and a major effort to link reduction in number of children to improved educational and economic opportunities for women.

Frederick S. Jaffe and Deborah Oakley, "Observations on Birth Planning in China, 1977," Family Planning Perspectives, vol. 10, no. 2, March/April 1978, pp. 101, 104–105.

Birth Planning Reporting Form. Another insight into the birth planning program's scope may be gained from the reporting form which is used by the Soochow Municipality family planning office to obtain quarterly information on program progress from factory and neighborhood clinics, communes, production brigades and teams, and other administrative units. The form, which was obtained from the family planning workers at Chang-Ching commune, is translated in Figure 1. It enumerates the number of members of each unit who are married women of reproductive age and

- are fecund
- use each contraceptive method
- do not use fertility control, and why (newly married, pregnant, lactating or separated or object philosophically)
- are not exposed to the risk of pregnancy because they are widowed, divorced or menopausal or have not become pregnant in three years without using contraception.

* * *

The form includes several standardized evaluation measures: the *rate of family planning* (column 15), expressed as the total number of contraceptors divided by the total number of fecund married women; the *planned birthrate* (column 36), expressed as the total number of first and second births meeting the program's age-at-marriage and spacing criteria, divided by total births; and the *late marriage rate* (columns 43 and 46), expressed as the total number of newly married men and women who meet the program's age criteria, divided by the total number who marry.

The form reflects a considerable effort in Soochow to obtain comparable information from all reporting units—indeed, more information on the status of reproduction, marriage and fertility control is assembled for that entire community than for communities in most nations, including the United States. It seems unlikely that the Chinese would attempt to collect such information unless it were to be used for evaluation purposes.

FIGURE 1. QUARTERLY REPORT FORM ON LEVEL OF FAMILY PLANNING WORK IN SOOCHOW MUNICIPALITY, 1977 (column headings)

Unit	Workers and staff			Married women of childbearing age		
	Total (1)	Male (2)	Female (3)	Total (4)	Fecund (5)	Nonfecund * (6)

Fecund couples †

Adopt contraceptive measures

Sterilization		IUD (9)	Pill (10)	Instrument (condom) (11)	Injection (12)	Other (13)	Total (14)	Rate of family planning (15) (14 ÷ 5)
Male (7)	Female (8)							

Fecund couples (continued) †

Do not adopt family planning

Newly married ‡ (16)	Pregnant (17)	Lactating (18)	Separated (19)	Those who reject this ideology (20)	Blank (21)	Total (22)

Nonfecund couples

Lost spouse (23)	Divorced (24)	Menopause (25)	Not pregnant after 3 yrs. of marriage without contraception (26)	Other (27)	Blank (28)	Total (29)

Births								No. of abortions	
Total (30)	1st births		2nd births		≥ 3rd births (35)	% of births planned (36) $\left(\dfrac{31+33}{30}\right)$		To married women (37)	To unmarried women (38)
	Meet late marriage criterion § (31)	Do not meet late marriage criterion § (32)	Meet spacing criterion ** (33)	Do not meet spacing criterion ** (34)					

Unmarried youths		No. of late marriages §							No. of deaths (47)
Male (39)	Female (40)	Males newly married			Females newly married				
		Total (41)	No. meeting late marriage criterion (42)	% meeting late marriage criterion (43) (42 ÷ 41)	Total (44)	No. meeting late marriage criterion (45)	% meeting late marriage criterion (46) (45 ÷ 44)		

* Excluding those sterilized for contraceptive reasons.

† The number of married, fecund women of childbearing age refers to those under 49, minus those who are widowed, get divorced, stop menstruating or are nonfecund (i.e., after having been married three years and not using contraception, the woman has not gotten pregnant).

‡ The number of newly married does not include those who have been divorced and are remarrying or widows or widowers.

§ Countryside: males at 25 years or older; females, 23 years or older; city: males, 26 or older; females, 24 or older.

** The criterion on spacing between the first and second child is four years. Births beyond the second do not meet the criterion.

Note: The form is to be signed by the leading member of the unit, as well as the person who fills it out. Copies of the original Chinese form are available in D. Oakley, Journal of a Trip to China, 1977 (mimeo).

"Family Planning in Jutung County," Peking Review, April 7, 1978, p. 19; April 14, 1978, pp. 26–27; April 21, 1978, pp. 23–25.

*   *   *

Family planning also helps liberate women from onerous household chores to enable them to take a direct part in socialist construction. This is conducive to women's liberation, and to socialist construction.

Family planning also improves women's health and has proved to be a boon to their children's upbringing and education.

When 20-year-old Shan Yung-li of the Hsinyao Commune came back home upon her graduation from senior middle school, she became an agro-technician in the production team she belonged to. Some young men were taken up with her but she preferred to acquire more knowledge when young and marry at an older age as the state had called on the young people to. Now the production team Shan worked in was a large cotton-producer, where ladybirds were needed to bring the cotton aphis under control. But they had to be brought in from the south every spring because of the cold winter there. So the local agricultural institute suggested that Shan should find out a way for these bugs to live in the locality through the winter. Night and day Shan spent her time in the laboratory breeding these bugs and finally found the way. She made rapid progress in her studies and came to the fore in productive labour. In 1975 she was admitted into the Chinese Communist Party and became the deputy secretary of the production brigade Party branch. Now 27 she will soon get married.

I also knew a Liu Mei-ying of the Chanan Commune who got married at 19 and gave birth to a daughter the following year. When the commune called on its married members to practise planned parenthood in 1970, she decided that she would not have her second child until her first one was nine. Her mother-in-law, who wished to have a grandson at an earlier date, at first wasn't happy about the idea. It was Liu Mei-ying who patiently persuaded the old lady to her point of view. This year the second son of the family also got married and planned to have a child next year. The mother-in-law again urged Liu Mei-ying to have her next baby in the same year so that she could help bring them up together. Liu Mei-ying again persuaded her mother-in-law to give up the idea.

Family planning in Jutung County did not come easily.

Breaking Down Old Ideas. Although family planning is conducive to the planned development of the socialist economy and to women's health and their children's upbringing, not many people could appreciate all these at the first onset. Many people, bound by old ideas, preferred boys to girls, thinking that only the former could carry on the family line. They may already have several daughters but still wished to have a son and this was one main reason why there were so many children in a family.

In introducing family planning, there must be a rupture with traditional ideas, involving a large amount of work in publicity accompanied by effective measures.

Accordingly, cadres from the county Party committee down consider this a matter of first importance, put it on the order of the day and check up work in this field as they do in other fields. The success or failure in the work of family planning is also considered as one of the essential factors in commending advanced individuals and collectives.

* * *

Living With Wife's Family. In China's countryside there is still the old idea that daughters are "tipped out" like used water—of no more use to the family once they are married. Only sons are expected to support the parents in their old age and only sons can inherit property. The property of those without a son then goes to a nephew of the same clan. Married men going to live with their parents-in-law in the old days were targets of ridicule and discrimination and were frequently driven away over the issue of inheriting property. This view is still alive with many people so that couples already with several daughters still want a son.

Jutung County constantly propagates the idea that daughters too should support their parents in their old age and encourages men to marry girls with no brothers and to go and live with their in-laws. There is a regulation made by the county that husbands moving in to live with their parents-in-law must be considered native members of that community and must not be discriminated against.

I called in on one family in the Chapei People's Commune which had only a daughter in each four generations. All four sons-in-law lived with the wife's family. Chi Fang-chen, the fourth generation, has only a daughter (in primary school) but she is not keen on having another child—son or daugher—yet. Altogether there are seven in her family, a great grandmother, grandmother, mother, father, husband and daughter . . . .

* * *

With only one child, Chi Fang-chen has plenty of time and energy for work and study. She was admitted into the Communist Party in 1975 and she is chairman of brigade women's federation, vice-chairman of the commune women's federation and a standing committee member of the county women's federation. With two male labourers, the family leads a happy life. They have a brick-and-tile house of eight rooms, adequate furniture, a bicycle, a sewing machine and wristwatches. Before liberation her family had lived in a damp straw hut. Now life is much better. With four sons-in-law living under one roof the Chi family shows that it makes no difference today whether a family has sons or daughters.

Men and Women Get Equal Pay for Equal Work. This is state policy, but because of the feudal idea that men are superior, women inferior, the policy is still not fully implemented in some rural areas where men and women doing the same job get different pay. In Jutung County, the policy on the whole has been well carried out. More work points are given for more work and better work done regardless of sex. This has greatly stimulated women's initiative. Women in this county today do most of field management work as well as a part of the heavy physical labour; they are paid the same as men.

Good Care Taken of Elderly Childless Couples. Parents raise children who in turn support their parents when they are old. This tradition is still very much so in New China, so the idea of "bringing up sons against old age" still persists. The rural people's communes in Jutung take good care of the old people who have no children and are unable to work any more. They are provided with food, clothing, housing and medical care, a standard of living not lower than that of an average peasant in the locality, by the communes. Cadres and commune members often help them with chores about their house. Hence the peasants see that only the socialist system is the basic guarantee for a happy, care-free old age.

* * *

What Family Planning Accomplished. Family planning in Jutung County has proved beneficial in many aspects.

In the past, women with five or six children were burdened with onerous household chores and reduced to mere drudges.

Now, with only two children and an extended interval between births and with nurseries and kindergartens to lighten the family's burden of looking after them, a woman spends less time looking after babies and more time for work, study and social activities.

Farming needs a lot of manpower. Prior to 1965, the turn-out rate of able-bodied women participating in labour was 75 per cent because of too many children and onerous household chores. Since family planning was introduced in 1970, women in the county have fewer children and many more are able to take part in collective production. The turn-out rate in 1976 was 96 per cent—the 4 per cent represented monthly, nursing, pregnancy and confinement leave.

Women take part in sowing, field management and harvesting together with men. They do up to 90 per cent of the work in cotton fields. The men are engaged mainly in levelling the land, digging canals and shoulder-pole work. In the old days no woman in fishing communes went out to sea to fish, but today women accompany the men out at sea for two to three months at a stretch. Those who stay home fish along the coast.

As a result of participation in revolution and production as well as study of politics and culture, women enhance their political consciousness and abilities. Many have become agro-technicians, tractor or truck drivers, barefoot doctors and workers. And there are more and more women cadres and teachers in the county.

Having children later, less children and extending the interval between births are a boon to women's health and their babies. Fewer babies mean better care and better babies. Children can now all go to school; usually they can finish junior middle school.

NOTE

An ideal or idealized planned births program might operate in the following manner.

Victor H. Li, Law Without Lawyers, A Comparative View of Law in China and the United States, Stanford: Stanford Alumni Association, 1977, pp. 48–53.

A compaign to convince the public to practice family planning might occur in the following manner. Newspapers and magazines would publish a series of articles that would present the arguments in favor of smaller family size and smaller national population. Radio and television also would broadcast supporting programs.

One set of articles might discuss broad policy issues. Family planning is a private matter in that it concerns one of the most important aspects of one's private life, but it is also a public matter since the size and rate of growth of a society's population are major factors affecting that society's ability to meet its economic, social, and political needs. . . .

* * *

A second category of articles would discuss the advantages of having fewer children from the point of view of the family. These arguments are quite similar to the arguments made by the Planned Parenthood Association in the United States. Having a large number of children strains the economic capacity of a family and makes it more difficult to meet adequately the needs of each child. The health of the parents, particularly the mother, might be adversely affected. The ability of the parents, again particularly the mother, to develop their own career and personal interests also would suffer.

Moreover, changes in social and political conditions during the quarter century since Liberation have brought about a completely new situation with respect to the question of having children. First of all, the old superstition of wanting sons rather than daughters has been exposed. Parents now value daughters as much as sons, and consequently need not bear many children in order to have the desired number of sons. Second, the vast improvement in health care means that it is not necessary to have a large number of children born in order to ensure that a few survive. Finally, in the past the only source of support in one's old age was one's children. Since only about one child in three grew up to adulthood and since daughters generally moved away after marriage and no longer contributed economically to their natal family, one would need six children, statistically, to ensure that one son would support the parents in old age.

. . .

A third set of articles would discuss the particular methods of contraception and other means of limiting population growth. The present Chinese planned birth program urges that couples marry late, with the combined age of the husband and wife totaling about 50. Young people should not develop an interest in sexual matters too early. The articles would explain to the young people that during their teens and early twenties they should devote all their energies to the development of themselves and of China generally rather than think about getting married and raising a family. . . .

* * *

For married couples, the articles would describe the available contraceptive methods. These descriptions often are quite technical and detailed so that the reader would understand the scientific basis for each method. The pill and the IUD are the favored methods of contraception, with other methods also being used. Where the resources are available, abortion is sometimes used in the event of contraceptive failure. A spacing of four to five years is encouraged between children. After the second child, the parents are urged to consider sterilization.

One other group of articles might be anecdotes in which various families or communities would describe their planned birth programs and how this effort has improved their lives. Other articles might ask questions or raise doubts about the program, so that they could be answered and dispelled. For example, a newspaper might publish a "letter from a reader" that asks whether it would be dangerous or uncomfortable to wear an IUD while engaged in manual labor—a question that may concern many peasant women. The newspaper could then give the proper assurances, perhaps supported by scientific explanations and expert testimony.

Action By the Small Group. As these articles appear, the small group would read and discuss them as a part of the regular study process. Many hours would be spent going through the rationale and methods of the planned birth program. The local barefoot doctor or some other person with particular knowledge in this area would play an especially important role in the discussions. Members of the small group would be encouraged to express any uncertainties they might have. Such expressions are important because unless a person's doubts are aired and dispelled, he would not become truly convinced and consequently may not fully comply with the program.

Since ideas in the abstract take on real meaning only when applied to concrete situations, the discussions should be phrased in terms of how the planned birth program would affect the lives of the participants in the small group. How many children do each of us have, and how many more should we want? Is youngster Chen too young to think about getting married? Should he spend more time on his school work and less time with Ms. Chang? Why does Old Man Wang have such a male chauvinist attitude? He knows that a vasectomy is a simple operation and yet wants his wife to get a tubal ligation instead.

At the beginning of the small group discussions, the main task is explaining the program and its rationale to the public. As the discussions continue, the members of the group begin to understand and then to agree with the program. The next step comes about quite naturally. Having agreed with the program and having discussed it in terms of how it might apply to their own lives, the group members begin to translate the discussions into action. Various members of the group would undertake to use one or another method of contraception, youngster Chen would devote more attention to his school work, and so forth. In some instances, the group itself may take action. A number of reports coming out of China recently say that some groups agree to a birth limit for the entire group, and then allocate "quotas" to individual members of the group.

In addition to actions taken by the group and its members, the larger social system is also mobilized. Pharmaceutical factories must produce the necessary pills, and a system of distribution must be established. (Almost all contraceptives, incidentally, are provided free of charge, but only to married couples.) Hospitals and clinics have to be prepared to insert IUDs and perform sterilizations. A great deal of similar work must be done to make sure that social resources are ready to support the planned birth decisions made by groups and individuals.

Viewing this process in terms of shaping conduct and controlling deviancy, in the ideal case people would find the argument in favor of planned birth so sensible and compelling that they would be convinced of its value. For these people, compliance is no problem. Some others may not be convinced, but find it increasingly difficult and counterproductive to continue to resist peer pressure—to be the target of "persuading by speaking"—day after day and week after week. They might decide it is better to conform their conduct to the peer group norm even though they are not fully convinced in their minds. This obviously is not as desirable a result as the first case but would still produce approximate compliance. Finally, there may be some who disagree strongly with the program and will not comply. These "deviants" would continue to be subjected to peer pressure and begin the slide to the bottom of the cliff.

The Persuasion Process. In looking at this discussion-persuasion process as a whole, a number of points should be stressed. First, great emphasis is placed on positive incentives rather than on just criticism or negative incentives. If Old Man Wang says at some point that he has seen the light and would undergo a vasectomy, the group should loudly and publicly congratulate him. Perhaps his name might be posted on the village bulletin board as a model progressive person. These expressions of support are strongly reassuring and reinforcing. In addition, it would be rather awkward for Old Man Wang later to think about changing his mind. . . .

Third, in order for the system as described above to work, it is vital that in most cases (although perhaps not necessarily all cases) the majority of people, after sufficient study and discussion, in fact find the proposed rules or norms to be sensible and compelling. Peer group pressure would not work very well if many members of the group felt that the program was wrong or frivolous. On occasion the government authorities would be able to force through a program without truly convincing a majority of people, but such an action is likely to create problems concerning compliance and lax group self-enforcement. If programs are frequently forced through without adequate education and persuasion, the entire concept of local decision making and mass line politics would be undercut, which would in time produce passivity and cynicism. Thus, reliance upon a general system of self-education and self-enforcement in turn limits the ability of governmental authorities to bypass this system for specific matters.

Pi-chao Chen, with Ann Elizabeth Miller, "Lessons from the Chinese Experience: China's Planned Birth Program and Its Transferability, 6 Studies in Family Planning, p. 375, 1975.

Group Planning of Births. The latest tactic in birth planning is to "let the masses draw up their birth plans and follow them through." Taking advantage of all the infrastructures described above, suggested targets are transmitted down through the organizational networks, and the local small groups are urged to draw up their own birth plans accordingly. Thus, local people decide how to meet targets, take responsibility for lowering fertility, and exert peer pressure to comply. Only they understand the local and personal factors that must be taken into account; and since they must also do the planning for production, income distribution, reinvestment, and social welfare, they learn the relationships between child rearing and costs to the local community.

For example, the ward or commune leadership suggests that the crude birth rate be brought down a few points from that of the previous year, say from 25 per thousand to 22 per thousand; this target (not binding at lower levels) is passed down through administrative channels. The eligible couples meet in their production team, residents' group, or factory to plan how to meet such targets. Taking into account their population size, they calculate the number of births that would yield the proposed birth rate and then proceed to "allocate" the births among themselves—deciding who among them should have a child in the coming year. Priority is given first to newly married couples, who are free to bear a first child without delay (in some areas, they may not even receive birth control education until after the first child); second to couples with only one or two children; and third to couples whose youngest child is closest to age five. These priorities are based on the assumptions that young people do not marry until they reach the recommended ages and that each couple is spacing births at intervals of four to five years and will have a complete family size of two or three children regardless of sex. Couples thus designated to have children refrain from practicing contraception while the others practice contraception. Obviously, adjustments have to be made for failure to conceive within the planned year, for unplanned pregnancies due to contraceptive failure, and for situations where the husband works away from home; such adjustments are made by mutual agreement at group meetings. Birth plans are generally made in the winter, but adjustments are made throughout the year.

This system of birth planning was apparently first developed in Shanghai in 1971–1972 and has spread rapidly to other cities (Han Suyin, 1973a, 1973b); the extent of its spread through rural areas is not known, although it has been introduced into such remote provinces as Shensi in the northwest and Kweichow in the southwest.

NOTES AND QUESTIONS

1. Judging from the above materials, to what extent has China solved the problems of providing support in one's old age and of achieving equality for women? What is the difference in the industrial and agricultural sectors?

2. At least in theory, and also to some degree in practice, contraceptives are not available to unmarried youths. At the same time, there does not appear to be a high incidence of illegitimacy or of abortions performed on unmarried women. (But note that the chart on p. 922 contains an entry for abortions to unmarried women). How do you explain this phenomenon? Is it possible that unmarried youths do not engage in sexual intercourse? These questions need to be addressed—and not merely smiled at as curiosities.

3. Note that the late marriage at 25 plus a five-year spacing between children, possibly followed by sterilization, reduces by about half the reproductive years for a woman. The late marriage age limits are goals rather than hard and fast rules. What would happen if a 20 year old couple wants to marry?

4. How important is the infrastructure of paramedics, neighborhood clinics, and other local support mechanisms? Could these be replaced by some other persons or institutions?

5. How does the effort to implement birth planning programs compare with the system of controlling anti-social conduct described in the Introduction and in Problem II?

6. Group birth planning exerts greater peer pressure on the couple. Is there an economic reason as well for the state to favor this method?

C. CONTINUING PROBLEMS OF IMPLEMENTATION

NOTE

Although the planned births program has ben highly successful, China still is encountering quite a bit of resistance in its effort to reduce family size. The following recent items illustrate some of the difficulties. These items should be read in the proper context: despite the difficulties, China has reduced its growth rate from over 20 per 1000 a decade or two ago to a present rate of approximately 12 per 1000.

Two Letters from Readers and an Investigation Report by Renmin Ribao Reporters: "Why Is It Difficult to Carry Out Birth Control Work in Wenzhou?" Foreign Broadcast Information Service: CHI, April 23, 1980, pp. 01–03.

First Letter From All Cadres Responsible For Birth Control Work in the Dongcheng Area of Wenzhou Municipality, Zhejiang.

The main question in birth control work in Wenzhou Municipality, Zhejiang, is: Some leading cadres go so far as to refuse to practice birth control instead of supporting this work.

The wife of comrade Lin Xianren, a member of the Standing Committee of the party municipal committee, gave birth to a third child last March. Up to now, they have refused to practice birth control. Lin's wife is a school teacher. She scolded the cadres who called on her to persuade her to practice birth control.

Wang Danwen, a member of the provincial revolutionary committee and deputy director of the municipal posts and telecommunications bureau, was pregnant with her third child, but did not break the news until she was 8 and a half months pregnant. This caused great difficulty for the birth control work carried out by the posts and telecommunications bureau.

* * *

We have reported these cases many times to the municipal committee leadership, but the cases remain unsettled. In Wenzhou Municipality at present, many young people get married too early and many young women are married and pregnant too early or are pregnant before they are married. The masses say: "When those above behave unworthily, those below will do the same." "The party's policy is correct, but is not applied to all people alike." The secretary of the CYL committee of the No. 2 hat factory was pregnant with her third child. We tried to persuade her many times to have an abortion, but to no avail. Although we asked the second bureau of light industry to adopt relevant measures, its leader said publicly: "When the wife of a member of the Standing Committee of party municipal committee was pregnant with her third child, the party municipal committee did not take any action. When it takes action on this case, we shall act likewise."

To achieve the four modernizations, it is imperative to perseveringly practice birth control. How shall we proceed with our work when some leading cadres act this way?

Second Letter From the Wenzhou Municipal Birth Control Office. After the letter from the cadres responsible for birth control work in the Dongcheng area of our municipality was referred to us, the following actions were taken under the pressure of the provincial investigation group and public opinion:

1. Comrade Li[n] Xianren made a self-criticism at a municipal meeting of grassroots level cadres and underwent . . . (vasoligation) that afternoon.

2. Comrade Wang Guihua underwent vasoligation. However, he has had ideological relapses recently because the leadership of his unit sympathizes with him.

Investigation Report by RENMIN RIBAO Reporters. In the province, Wenzhou Prefecture lags behind in carrying out birth control work. Last year, the province's population growth was 11.07 per 1,000 while that of Wenzhou Prefecture was 18.39 per 1,000.

The fundamental reason birth control work in Wenzhou lags behind is that some cadres do not practice family planning and urge their sons and daughters to marry too early. According to an investigation, 496 of the 728 cadres, or 68.1 percent, in 6 areas in Ruian County have 3 or more children. Two of them have 8 children, 10 have 7, 53 have 6, 101 have 5, 164 have 4 and 166 have 3. The wife of a deputy secretary of a commune in Taishun County gave birth to her 11th child last year. The wife of a section chief of the Leqing county bank had a seventh child last year. Yet, this section chief told the comrades of the county office responsible for birth control work: "Each of my children is prettier than the last. The more children my wife bears, the younger she looks." Comrade Wang Danwen, a member of the provincial revolutionary committee, deputy director of the municipal posts and telecommunications bureau and a member of the leading group responsible for birth control work in this bureau, did not make a self-criticism after she had given birth to her third child. On the contrary, she tried to shirk responsibility by all possible means and went so far as to deride and hit at the cadres who practiced birth control. The provincial investigation group conducted a special investigation into this case but left it unsettled. The masses said: "The deputy chief is allowed to have a third child. We better follow this example and hurry up and have another child." Because the leading cadres go against the policy and the offenses are not handled seriously, birth control work cannot be carried out well. . . .

Guizhou Provincial CCP Issues Circular on Disciplinary Action Against Two Leading Cadres at Prefectural and County Levels for Failure to Practice Birth Control, Foreign Broadcast Information Service: CHI, September 19, 1979, p. Q1.

The Guizhou provincial party committee recently issued a province-wide circular concerning comrades Zeng Yixiang and Pan Delin, who made the mistake of refusing to practice birth control. The circular demanded that party committees at all levels carry out planned parenthood work just as efficiently as they carry out economic construction. Those who refuse to practice birth control should be severely punished in accordance with the regulations concerned.

* * *

Pan Delin is deputy chief of the organizational department of the Anshun prefectural party committee. When his wife was pregnant with her third child, responsible comrades of the prefectural party committee advised her to have an abortion. However, Comrade Pan Delin turned a deaf ear to the advice and his third child was born last June. His behavior had an adverse effect on the masses. The Anshun prefectural party committee decided that in accordance with "Provisional Measures of Planned Parenthood in Guizhou Province," 5 percent of the salaries of both Pan Delin and his wife would be deducted starting in July. Additionally, they were ordered to write self-criticisms for the party organization.

Guizhou Officials Punished for Birth Control Failures, Foreign Broadcast Information Service: CHI, June 27, 1980, p. Q1.

Beijing, June 25 (KYODO)—More than 100 party and municipal officials in a Guizhou Province city underwent [sterilization] to take the blame for their laxity in enforcing birth control. According to the Guizhou Daily dated June 22 reaching here Wednesday, party officials at Zhijin City who were supposed to see that couples were not to have more than one child failed to enforce this limit and consequently the rate of natural population increase in the area had become the highest in the province.

When the provincial government criticized the officials, they hastily conducted self-criticism and more than 100 of them underwent vasectomy or tubal ligation in May, the paper said. The mass sterilization prompted more than 1,700 married people to undergo similar surgery in a span of only 40 days, according to the GUIZHOU DAILY.

The strict birth control measures enforced by the Chinese Government have caused some resentment among the farmers. Recently, a group of farmers attacked a party official who tried to force a pregnant woman to undergo abortion, seriously injuring him. A man divorced his wife because she chose abortion against his wish.

Shaanxi Court Sentences Swindler, Foreign Broadcast Information Service: CHI, December 3, 1979, p. T4.

The Qishan County People's Court sentenced a swindler (Lin Yigui), to 2 years' imprisonment on charges of undermining family planning by illegally removing the intrauterine device from women and taking their money. (Lin Yigui) had been a doctor of a production brigade medical station and a commune health center before he was dismissed for embezzling public funds. But he continued to practice medicine illegally. Between the spring of 1976 and August 1978, he illegally removed the loop for 26 women in Qishan and Baoyi counties. As a result, 21 of these women became pregnant again. He made a lot of money in performing the illegal operations.

D. THE CURRENT CAMPAIGN FOR ONE CHILD FAMILIES

NOTE

China is pressing harder than ever to control population growth. The current campaign encourages one-child families. In addition, material incentives and disincentives are being used in a direct way.

In February 1980, Chinese demographers projected population size assuming a certain number of children per woman of childbearing age.

Carl Djerassi, The Politics of Contraception, The View from Beijing, 303 New England Journal of Medicine 334, 335 (1980).

TABLE 1. PREDICTED CHINESE POPULATION ACCORDING TO NUMBER OF CHILDREN PER WOMAN OF CHILDBEARING AGE FROM 1980 ONWARD

Number of Children	Yr. 2000	Yr. 2027	Yr. 2050	Yr. 2080
	Population in Millions			
3	1414		2923	4260 *
2	1217		1529 *	1472
1.5	1125	1172 *		777
1	1054 *†	960	613 ‡	370

* Peak population.	† In 2004.	‡ In 2060.

At present, every Chinese woman of childbearing age bears an average of 2.3 children. If this trend continues, the population will reach 1.282 billion by the year 2000 and 2.119 billion by 2080.

Renmin Ribao editorial: It is Imperative to Control Population Growth in a Planned Way, Foreign Broadcast Information Service: CHI, February 15, 1980, pp. L13–15.

In 1949 the population of our country was over 540 million people. In 1978 the population increased to more than 970 million people (including Taiwan province). Within 30 years the population increased by more than 420 million people and the natural growth rate was on average as high as 20 per 1,000. Rapid population growth affects the accumulation of construction funds and obstructs the rise of scientific and cultural levels. It also adversely affects improving the people's living conditions. If we fail to make great efforts to control our population growth during the 20 years left in this century, it will be very difficult to reach our goal of four modernizations. The composition of the present population of our country reveals that in the coming 20 years it will remain impossible to reduce our population growth rate to zero. We can only control the birth rate and gradually reduce the natural growth rate, so that by the year 2000 our natural population growth rate will be reduced to zero, that is, our population will not longer increase and is stabilized at about 1.2 billion people. This is a strategic task which we set in accordance with the actual conditions of our country and which we must fulfill. To insure the fulfillment of this strategic task, the current pressing matter is to shift the focus of family planning to advocating one child for each couple. Our population base is large and the proportion of women with more than one pregnancy was high in past years. As a result, the birth rate has remained high for a long period of time. At present, young people under the age of 21 constitute 50 percent of our total population. Before the end of this century, an average of 20 million of them will get married and bear children each year. In coming years those born in 1963, 1964 and the late 1960's, which were peak birth years, will get married and bear children. The birth peak will appear again. Therefore, from now on we must spare no efforts to advocate one child for each couple. This is the best method for reducing the birth rate and mitigating the birth peak tendency and will guarantee zero population growth in the year 2000.

* * *

According to preliminary statistics from the departments concerned, approximately 5 million married couples of child-bearing age throughout the country have voluntarily applied for and received certificates for having one child only, representing some 29 percent of the married couples of child-bearing age who already have one child. Recently, the family planning leading group of the State Council, the All-China Federation of Trade Unions, the All-China Women's Federation, the CYL Central Committee and the family planning leading group of Beijing Municipality called a joint symposium to discuss the new nature of marriage, family and family planning. The speeches delivered at the symposium by the advanced representatives of family planning eloquently show that the broad masses of the people have indeed fully understood the close relationship between childbirth, the realization of the four modernizations and happy life for many generations to come. As long as we truthfully explain the situation to the masses and help them to understand the importance of family planning, more people will happily accept the principle of single child families.

In order to reduce further the birthrate on the basis of our current foundation, the volume of work will definitely be greater than in the past and there will also be more hardships. Therefore, it is necessary for the party committees and people's governments at various levels to strengthen their leadership and to include work regarding family planning and population growth control as a major agenda item. Each and every mass organization should also grasp this task strenuously. The administrative departments of propaganda, education and health are responsible for using various methods to vigorously publicize the relations between family planning and the realization of the four modernizations, to publicize our country's goal and measures to control population growth, to continuously eliminate the decadent concept that more sons will bring greater fortune and that men are more important than women, and to publicize the benefits of having only one child. We hope that by proceeding from the overall needs of achieving the four modernizations, each married couple of child-bearing age would consider having only one child as a great honor. Eight hundred million of our people live in the rural areas. Stress in family planning must be placed on the rural areas. Efforts should be made to continuously publicize and implement the family planning regulations and measures laid down by each province, municipality and autonomous region.

In dealing with the obstacles arising from force of habit, we should not adopt simple administrative means and coercive measures. We should provide positive guidance by means of combining thorough ideological work with typical cases. Meanwhile, further efforts should be made to popularize the scientific knowledge on birth control, promote all kinds of birth control methods, research as well as produce contraceptives which are highly effective, safe, simple and economic, and insure the supply of contraceptives. Furthermore, it is also necessary to train and evaluate personnel who conduct birth control operations in order to further improve their quality. In order to encourage more people to have only one child, attention should be paid to improving maternity and child care services and to do an even better job in providing proper care for women during the period of pregnancy and delivery. In order to look after infants in both body and mind, it is necessary to do a good job in running child care centers so that every child is in good health and the parents with one child have nothing to worry about. With regard to childless old people, social security should be further improved so as to provide them with "proper care during old age."

In promoting family planning among the minority nationalities, a different approach should be taken to facilitate their development. Different areas and national minority areas should be handled differently and under no circumstances should we seek "uniformity in everything."

Pi-Chao Chen and Adrienne Kols, Population and Birth Planning in the People's Republic of China, Population Reports, Jan.-Feb. 1982, pp. J577, J600–601, J603–606.

The One-Child Policy. In 1978 Vice-Premier Chen Muhua provided a statistical rationale for the one-child campaign. Noting that, in 1978, 30 percent of all births were third or higher parity, she concluded that eliminating only these births would reduce the natural increase rate from 12 to 7 per 1,000, short of the proposed target of 5 per 1,000 (115). If the target was to be reached, some couples would have to have only a single child. At that time, the national goal established was that 80 percent of all couples in the cities and 50 percent in the rural areas should have only one child, excluding, of course, those who already had more (342). Since then birth planning rhetoric has cited higher goals. In a February 1980 speech Chen Muhua stated:

> We will try to attain the goal that 95 percent of married couples in the cities and 90 percent in the countryside will have only one child in due course, so that the total population of China will be controlled at about 1.2 billion by the end of this century. (170, 176)

Some Chinese leaders opposed vigorous pursuit of the one-child policy. During the National People's Congress held in the summer of 1980, delegates were divided over the issue (64). Two factions led the opposition. Rural delegates argued that the one-child policy jeopardized old-age security—parents could not rely on a single child for support in later years, especially if that child was a girl. At the same time, army officers feared a dearth of young male recruits, which would cripple China's ability to resist a Soviet threat (91). Military leaders argued that families would be reluctant to allow only sons to serve in the army—especially if they were only children, too (77). Because of a lack of consensus among the leadership, the National People's Congress did not pass a proposed law instituting incentives and disincentives, and instead the CCP Central Committee compromised by issuing an open letter to all Party and Communist Youth League members endorsing the one-child campaign. In the letter the Party elite called on all Party and Communist Youth League members, especially the cadres, to "take the lead" in responding to the new policy, offer a good example to the rest of the nation, and "actively, conscientiously, and patiently publicize the call among the broad masses" (174).

The call for a one-child family is a compromise between the government's desire to reach zero population growth and Chinese social realities. To reduce the natural increase rate to zero in a decade or two would mean that many people could not have any children. China's leaders have recognized the impossibility of such a plan, since universal marriage and reproduction is culturally mandated and economically important to individual households. The goal of a one-child family is a calculated risk: the government believes that it is the most extreme reduction in fertility tolerable to the people. While the one-child family is possible, having no children at all would be "impractical and infeasible" (414).

*   *   *

A survey concerning the one-child program, conducted in 1979 in an 8-block area of Hefei city, Anhui province, revealed some problems in the implementation of economic rewards (80). Great disparities existed among the incentives offered by various employing units and were a source of considerable dissatisfaction among the people. Poor units might offer "a couple of towels, a thermos bottle, some toys, a washing basin, or nothing at all," while more profitable enterprises paid substantial money bonuses and supplied free health care and schooling to the only children. The better housing promised to certificate holders had not materialized at all. Some units ignored the housing priority assigned to the certificate holders, while in other areas the buildings themselves were nonexistent. Also, many benefits lose their value when the majority signs up for the one-child certificates. For example, priority in health care or jobs means little when it is shared with 70 percent of all couples. Perhaps because the economic rewards of the one-child certificate had proved illusory, the survey reported that

> families with financial difficulties [were] most likely to refrain from applying for [the] certificate or to waver in thought after receiving certificates. (80)

Poor families most concerned with economic issues were not convinced that the one-child pledge would improve their standard of living.

Economic incentives complement but do not replace persuasion and educational work. The themes used in the one-child campaign are different, however, from birth planning themes used earlier. Appeals cite national concerns rather than personal and familial goals. Editorials urging birth planning now describe it as a "strategic task" important for "the development of our national economy," "the Chinese nation's prosperity," "the speed and future of the four modernizations," and the "health and happiness of generations to come" (174, 226). Chen Muhua, announcing the one-child campaign in 1979, explicitly stated that the interests of individuals must "voluntarily be subordinated" to the interests of the state (115).

In order to overcome the traditional Chinese desire for a son to provide support in old age, the government has designed additional incentives for the one-daughter family. In old China a daughter was a transitory asset because she went to live with her husband's family after marriage and never contributed to the welfare of her own parents when they grew old (417). Hence the saying, "a daughter who has been given away in marriage is like spilt water" (241). Chinese parents are less likely to stop at one child if the first is a girl. The 1979 survey in Hefei city found that the reason most often cited for not applying for the one-child certificate was the desire for a boy (80). To try to solve this problem, officials are now encouraging young men to move in with their in-laws when they marry an only daughter. (This strategy has worked in a few cases, but the traditional pattern of living with the husband's parents still prevails.) Also, daughters are now legally responsible for their parents' welfare in the same way as sons. A daughter as well as a son may now take over the father's job when he retires, and job preference in general is given to children from one-child families and to girls who have no brothers (13, 65). According to a recent law in Guangdong province, property can be distributed to daughters as well as to sons; the brigade or commune must supply building materials to the father of an only daughter when he wishes to build a house; and there are special celebrations each time a man settles with his wife's family (2).

Penalties. Just as the state rewards one-child families for restricting their fertility, it penalizes those who do not comply with government policy. There is wide provincial and local variation in the penalties, but these are among the most common: Parents who break their pledge by having a second child are required to return all the stipends or work points they have received. If any couple has a third child, their monthly wages are reduced by 10 percent or more, and they must remain in housing meant for a 2-child family. Families with more than two children do not receive subsidies when they are in financial difficulties, and they are charged for the pregnant mother's medical care and the extra child's grain ration (292). The child cannot enroll in any cooperative medical care scheme and receives no preference in school and job assignments (248). Regulations in Guangzhou make those who violate birth planning norms ineligible for three years for job promotions, wage increases, production awards, and participation in worker competitions (4). Multiple births are an exception to these rules. Also, if an only child dies, the parents may have another without penalty.

In some areas, such as Shanghai, where the one-child campaign is intensely promoted, the government now penalizes second as well as third and higher births. Municipal regulations permit parents to have a second child without penalty only if the first child has a disabling disease, is the child of an earlier marriage, or was adopted because of the woman's presumed sterility (228, 235).

The incentives and disincentives of the one-child campaign have to some extent reversed China's welfare policy. Before 1978 official regulations governing the distribution of housing, welfare subsidies, grain rations, and private farming plots favored large families. The pronatalist effect of the earlier regulations has therefore been reversed.

The penalty systems are indicative of China's new, more urgent attitude toward birth planning. The resolve expressed by birth planning rhetoric has hardened, as illustrated in this 1981 provincial policy statement:

> We must continue to commend and reward couples who have only one child, strictly control the birth of a second child and resolutely put a stop to the birth of third. We must mobilize couples of child-bearing age to implement effective contraceptive measures, fine those who violate planned parenthood, and punish those who sabotage it. (184)

Reports from Sichuan province state that many people have been treated as criminals for activities harmful to birth planning (43). Complaints in the local media describe women who are forced to accept contraception or abortion (192, 210), and there are even reports of the abandonment or drowning of female babies (17, 150, 411). A recent, revealing circular issued by the Ministry of Justice announces sanctions against "people who sabotage birth control plans by removing women's intrauterine contraceptive devices" (208). Evidently women who submit reluctantly to IUD insertion are paying to have the devices removed with homemade wire hooks, since most Chinese IUDs lack strings (104, 173). In one district of Guizhou province, more than 6,700 women (over 30 percent of those fitted with IUDs) reportedly had their IUDs illegally removed (422).

National policy statements continue to reject coercion, however. In his 1980 speech at the Third Session of the Fifth National People's Congress in Beijing, Chairman Hua Guofeng deplored the use of compulsion and arbitrary orders and described them as local aberrations in violation of national policy (261).

* * *

Difficulties of the One-Child Goal. Despite achievements to date, there are serious problems inherent in the goal of a one-child family. Until China builds an adequate social security system in the countryside, it will be difficult to sustain a one-child rate of more than 50 percent over a long period of time. Peasants' preference for a son is not a curse of Confucian heritage but a rational calculation. In China today, as in the past, the average person looks to a son for support in old age (416). There is an adequate old-age pension system only for those employed in the state-owned, urban-industrial sector, and these workers constitute at most 10 percent of the total population. In rural areas the agricultural collective's "five guarantees"—food, shelter, clothing, medical care, and burial—provide only limited aid and are no substitute for the physical and psychological support provided by one's own child. Couples living with the bride's parents if her parents have no male child is not a solution. If an only son marries an only daughter, the couple can live with and take care of only one of the two sets of parents. At the same time, they must financially support both sets of parents, straining their resources relative to those who have only one set of parents to support. Therefore, it makes sense for parents to have a minimum of two children, regardless of sex. Presumably, even if the average peasant couple did stop at one child if the first was a boy, they would have a second child if the first was girl. Given an almost even number of each sex at birth, in the long run no more than 50 percent of all couples are likely to have only one child.

The State Birth Planning Commission seems to be in agreement with this assessment. A recent Japanese delegation to China quoted Wan Soudao, a member of the Commission and the President of the Birth Planning Association of the PRC, as saying, "Our current program is aimed at reducing the average number of children per married couple to 1.5 on a step-by-step basis" (265). Assuming that all third and higher parity births are eliminated, a total fertility rate of 1.5 implies a 50 percent first-birth ratio. This suggests that Chinese leaders will be satisfied with something less than their expressed goal of nearly 100 percent one-child families.

Another problem with the implementation of the one-child campaign is financing. Where will the rewards come from? So far payments have been made by urban employing units and rural production teams. In the case of the production team, this means in practice that one-child families benefit at the expense of the rest. Poor production teams may lack funds to bestow rewards on a few without endangering the standard of living of the others. In the city some factories and businesses are unprofitable and find it difficult to pay wages; they cannot afford extra benefits, unrelated to productivity, for one-child families (80). Some rural officials have pointed out that one-child rewards cost the community less than the expenses of a second child (292), but payments of 60 yuan (about $36 US) or more a year to one-child families for 14 years are a major financial burden in an economy with a per capita GNP of only $250. In an October 1979 meeting several vice-premiers endorsed the idea of having the national government set aside funds to finance economic incentive schemes (290). Since that date, various provincial leaders and researchers have argued that national appropriations for national one-child incentives are indispensable and have recommended a change of government policy (9, 80). No final decision has yet been announced.

NOTE

In the current planned birth campaign, China has relied on a new means of communicating the desired norms of conduct to the population and the bureaucracy: the use of law and legal rules. The following item, prepared by Pi-chao Chen, is illustrative of similar regulations passed by many provinces and municipalities.

Guangdong Province Planned Birth Ordinance (Excerpts) (1981).

Section I.

Article 1. Planned birth is one of the most important strategic tasks of the socialist cause. It has a direct bearing on the development of the national economy, the expediting of the process of modern construction and the health and prosperity of the whole nation. In order quickly to put population growth in our province under control, in accordance with Article 53 of the Constitution of the People's Republic of China which states "the state advocates and carries out planned birth," and taking into account the practical conditions of our province, the Guangdong Province Planned Birth Ordinance is established.

Article 2. Planned birth is carried out mainly through ideological education, supplemented with necessary economic and administrative measures.

Section II. Marriage and Birth

Article 3. The demand of practicing planned birth is "late marriage, late procreation, and fewer births," with the stress on fewer births. Late marriageable age should be: for females, 23 years and over; for males, 25 years and over (rural) and 26 years and over (urban). Late procreation refers to women who give birth at age 25 and over. Fewer births mean that each couple bears only one child. For second-parity births arranged by population planning, the birth interval must be over four years. Remarried couples where both parties already have a child, or either of the parties has two children, may not be allowed to procreate any more. People with hereditary disease(s) that bear significant effects on the normal growth of the descendant's physiology and psychology shall not be allowed to procreate.

Article 4. Before getting married, youths of both sexes must study the Ordinance, receive education on birth control within their own work units, and obtain papers and go through the process of marriage registration at the Registration Office. For those marriage registration applicants who fail to conform to the rules of late marriageable ages, education must be given and discussion must be carried out so that they conscientiously practice late marriage.

Institutions of higher learning, polytechnical schools, and schools for technicians recruit only unmarried youths as students. During the schooling period, students are not allowed to marry and procreate. Offenders, irrespective of sex, must be ordered to quit school.

Vacancies for apprenticeships and trainees can be filled only by unmarried youths. While serving apprenticeships, those who marry in violation of the rule of late marriage must be ordered to quit.

Article 5. All administrative districts, cities, and counties must work out a population plan. The administrative district or rural people's commune examines and approves the names of women selected for procreation. Priorities for having first babies must be given to women who marry very late, and birth quota arrangements must be made for individual women by their units of work. For women who are without a birth quota, the government guides them to adopt birth control measures appropriate to their individual cases. No one is allowed to interfere and tyrannize.

Article 6. Han people in autonomous areas must obey the Ordinance. The minority nationals are encouraged to plan births, but no controlling quotas will be imposed on them. Mother and child health work must be well accomplished, and knowledge of birth control must be spread. Guidance and assistance must be given to those who demand birth control.

Section III.

Article 7. All those who have only one child and have taken effective measures to ensure they do not procreate again will be commended and given awards as follows:

  i. Through application by couples of childbearing age and verification by their work units, Only Child Preferential Certification may be issued by the people's commune or district or organs and enterprise units equivalent to or higher than county level. There are two types of preferential measures which may be chosen [by the couple]. A choice once made shall not be changed thereafter.

  1. The only child will not pay nursery and kindergarten fees up to age seven, school fees from primary to high school, and will enjoy free medical service until 14 years old.

  2. The only child of a cadre, worker, or urban unemployed person will have a monthly allowance of five *yuan* until 14 years old. The only child of a rural commune member will be awarded monthly work points equivalent to six work days by the production team until 14 years old. Each unit may arrange a suitable lump sum award in accordance with its own financial condition. . . .

* * *

  ii. The only child's grain ration should be the same as the per capita average of the basic accounting unit in rural areas; the child is entitled to have a double quota of private plots. In urban areas, only-child families have priority in living-quarters allotment and shall enjoy the same amount of space as two-children families; fuels and nonstaple food should be supplied to them in the amount of the two-child family's ration.

iii. Only-child mothers are entitled to three months' [paid] maternity leave.

iv. Rural parents of an only child have priority in assignments of industrial and sideline jobs. For housing construction, the production team should give them precedence in providing foundations for building and allowances for construction materials and labor. Their only son or daughter should be preferentially recruited in industrial employment and army enlistment.

Couples who have enjoyed the above benefits and yet procreated a second child shall reimburse all the expenses to their work units.

Article 8. In cases of cadres, staff, and workers, couples who procreate only one child shall be paid, upon old-age retirement, 5% more than the normal pension on the basis defined by the Retirement Ordinance; but no additional payment shall be made if 100% pension is paid. In the rural commune, members who lose their ability to work because of old age shall be given a monthly allowance of work points equivalent to five work days.

Article 9. Cadres, staff, and workers who are childless for their entire life shall, upon retirement, enjoy a 100% pension. Rural commune members who lose their ability to work shall be given an allowance as "five-guaranteed families." . . . The state and the collectives should guarantee them a life somewhat better than the average living standard of the local commune members.

Article 10. Conscientious practitioners of late marriage must be commended. Conscientious practitioners of late procreation after late marriage shall be appropriately rewarded for each year of postponement. The expenses shall be covered as defied in the fifth paragraph of Article 7.

*   *   *

Article 13. Change the old custom of regarding men as superior to women. Develop new wedding customs. Enthusiastically encourage male commune members to move to production teams where the sonless bridal families reside and marry there. Sonless old couples may move to production teams where their daughters are married and live with them. They share the same political and economic rights as well as obligations as the other commune members. No one is allowed to obstruct, put up obstacles, or discriminate. The sons-in-law who are responsible for the support of their wives' parents and the parents-in-law shall be recognized as directly-related members of the family. Daughters of rural sonless couples who are married to urban cadres, staff, or workers, and their children as well, are permitted to keep their household registration at the original production teams and enjoy the same treatment aforementioned.

Daughters and sons-in-law of [single child] workers who retire, resign, or are discharged have the right to fill the vacancies. Parents of sonless families enjoy the treatment of labor medical insurance for their daughters' or sons-in-law' directly related family members.

Section IV. Limitations and Punishments

Article 14. Couples of reproductive age who refuse to practice planned birth shall have excessive birth charges imposed on them:

    i. Anyone who procreates a third- and higher-parity child (including fostering or adoption from others), beginning from the fourth month of pregnancy up to the child's 14th birthday, shall have excessive birth charges imposed on them.

    ii. Women whose birth interval between the first and second child is less than four years shall have excessive birth charges imposed, beginning from the fourth month of pregnancy to the time when the first child is four years old.

    iii. Births outside marriage are illegal acts. Illegal procreators shall have excessive birth charges imposed beginning from the fourth month of pregnancy up to the ninth month after a marriage license has been obtained.

Methods of collection: Ten percent of monthly wages for each of both parties of cadres, staff, or workers shall be deducted by their work units. For commune members, 10% of work points earned for each of both parties (calculated on the basis of annual average earnings of work points per labor force as the specific basic accounting unit) shall be deducted.

* * *

For births in excess of three, starting from the fourth birth, 5% additional excessive birth charges shall be imposed for every additional birth.

* * *

Article 18. All medical services for nonplanned pregnancy, including antenatal examination, child delivery, and hospitalization, shall be at the parents' expense. Mothers with unplanned births shall not be entitled to the benefit of maternity leave with full pay or work point allowances. The third- and higher-parity children shall not enjoy overall medical treatment or cooperative medicine for directly related family dependents.

Article 19. The amount of grain for factories and workshops belonging to the commune or production brigade that depends on state supply must be fixed according to population growth quota assigned by the state. No increase shall be made to unplanned population growth, nor shall the fixed amount be decreased for fewer births.

Article 20. The criterion for urban living quarters allotment is confined to two children per couple. The allotment of building foundation in the rural areas is confined in the same manner. No addition shall be given to accommodate any excessive birth(s).

Article 21. Planned birth work of all departments (units) must be taken as one of the important criteria in appraising performance through comparisons for advanced groups. A deduction of 2% from profits will be made for enterprise units that exceed the assigned planned birth quota.

Article 22. People who refuse to practice planned birth and women who illegally remove their IUDs must be criticized and educated. For those who, after education, refuse to mend their ways, disciplinary measures must be executed. Persons who exploit their office, practice favoritism and embezzlement, spread rumors, retaliate against and accuse planned birth personnel and activists must be seriously dealt with. Those saboteurs having serious ill effects shall be punished by the law.

Section V.

Article 23. Leaves of absence [with pay] listed below are given to those who have undergone birth control operations with a doctor's certification:

i. Three days' leave starting from the date of operation is given to women who have had an IUD inserted. Workers engaged in heavy physical labor are exempted from such labor for a week after the operation.

ii. Rest on the day when an IUD is removed.

iii. Seven days' rest for vasoligation cases.

iv. Three weeks' rest for simple tubal ligation.

v. Two weeks' rest for induced abortion. Women who have induced abortion and an IUD insertion on the same occasion shall be granted a rest of 17 days. Those who have induced abortion and tubal ligation on the same occasion shall be given 35 days for rest.

Cases of midperiod termination of pregnancy will have a rest of 30 days. Cases of this termination with tubal ligation on the same occasion shall be given 51 days for rest.

vii. Cases of tubal ligation after child delivery will have 21 more days of rest in addition to the normal maternity leave.

Special cases that demand more rest days than listed above should be decided at the doctor's discretion.

* * *

Article 25. Sterilized couples with only one child shall be given anastomosis free of charge upon application if their only child dies or becomes seriously disabled after the couple's sterilization and if the facts of the case are certified by their work units. . . .

QUESTIONS

1. What obstacles do you think the PRC was encountering that led to the introduction of material incentives and disincentives to the planned births program? Will these material factors overcome the perceived obstacles?

2. What new obstacles or problems will the one-child family program encounter?

3. Why did the Chinese choose to use legal forms to define its planned births program? How does making planned births a legal matter help—or hinder—the effective implementation of the program?

Beijing Couple Suffers Economic Sanctions for Fourth Child, Foreign Broadcast Information Service: CHI, April 21, 1980, p. R1.

(Zhou You), section chief of the machine parts department of the Beijing No. 3 Ball-Bearing Factory and (Ding Chunxiu), a cadre of the education section of the Beijing Steel Plate Factory are married and both are party members. However, they ignored the calls and regulations on planned parenthood and had their fourth child in January this year. Thus, they have suffered economic sanctions.

According to the Beijing Municipality's temporary regulation on planned parenthood and other relevant documents, the Beijing Municipal No. 3 Ball-Bearing Factory and the Beijing Steel Plate Factory have dealt with them in the following ways: They are charged a 15 percent excess child fee from the period of pregnancy till the child reaches 14; the salary of the husband has 9.21 yuan deducted monthly and that of the wife 8.4 yuan; they had to pay for the consultation fees during pregnancy, hospital and delivery charges themselves and were not entitled to maternity allowances; the wife received no salary at all during her maternity leave; the husband will not receive bonuses for 1 year and the wife for 3 years; and they must return the year end bonus of 1979 which had already been distributed. The above items amount to over 3,000 yuan.

Guizhou Couple "Punished" for Having Third Child, Foreign Broadcast Information Service: CHI, March 25, 1980, p. Q1.

Beijing, March 24 KYODO—A Chinese couple in Guizhou Province have been subjected to severe disciplinary steps for having a third child in defiance of the state guideline for controlling population growth. According to the GUIZHOU DAILY, reaching Beijing Sunday, the wife, Wen Jifang, who had been deputy chief of a county people's court in the province, was stripped of the court post as a disciplinary measure. The husband, Lu Yutang, deputy chief of the public prosecutor's office in the same county, was ordered to receive sterilization surgery.

In addition to the punishment, the county Communist Party committee harshly reprimanded the couple for having ignored the party's urging that an abortion be carried out, the paper said. Both the husband and wife had their salaries cut, it said. The couple had two girls before the wife gave birth to a son last November despite the local party leadership's repeated persuasion for an abortion, the local paper said. The couple had the strong hope to have a boy, it said. The paper blasted the couple for failing to discard the "old thinking" setting a higher value on males.

The local authorities' action against the couple received strong support among the general public in the province, the paper said. China is imposing strict control on population growth with the goal of zero growth by the end of this century. It failed to achieve last year's target which was a growth rate of less than one per cent.

China set a severer goal this year of allowing only one child for 95 per cent of the total couples living in urban areas and for 90 per cent of the couples in provincial areas. Couples who are Communist Party members are liable to harsher disciplinary action in case of "excessive" childbirth.

E. STERILIZATION AND ABORTION

NOTE

Sterilization is becoming an increasingly popular method of contraception in China. Both tubal ligations and vasectomies are performed, often after the birth of the second child. The official program favors vasectomies because of their low cost and simplicity, but there still appears to be uncertainty on the part of some men about undergoing this operation.

Abortion also is widely practiced in China today, both for therapeutic reasons and in cases of contraceptive failure. Indeed, the principal limitation on abortion, aside from the wishes of the parents to have the child, is the shortage of medical facilities rather than some religious, legal, or cultural prohibition.

Under traditional Chinese law, a person who causes an abortion by attacking a pregnant woman was punished under the law of assault; note that the object of this law is to protect the mother, not the fetus. Similarly, if a woman dies in the course of aborting an illegitimately conceived fetus, the adulterous partner is punished for risking the woman's life in an attempt to conceal the adultery.

Other than examples such as the above, traditional Chinese law was generally silent about abortion. It may be that since parents had very great authority over a child, they also were thought to have great control over a fetus.

In the early part of the twentieth century, Chinese law was thoroughly revised. The new legal rules on abortion reflected Western ideas about morality and health. Abortion was prohibited with certain exceptions, principally when the life of the mother was endangered. As in other areas, it appears that these new rules were not thoroughly implemented.

QUESTIONS

1. Why is it that issues concerning abortion are handled through legal channels in the West, but political or administrative channels in China? Beyond the simple response that China's legal system is not well developed,
   what other explanations can you give?

*

INDEX

(References are normally to the beginning page of cases or other materials which bear upon the topic indexed. On occasion, references have also been made to items deserving of special attention which are found within the text of a case, a note, etc.)

†